THE OFFICIAL GUIDE TO
AMERICAN HISTORIC INNS

Rated "Outstanding" by Morgan F
Winner of Benjamin Franklin Aw
Best Travel Guide
Winner of Travel Publishing New
Best Travel Reference
Winner of Benjamin Franklin Award
Best Directory

Comments from print media:

"... helps you find the very best hideaways (many of the book's listings appear in the National Register of Historic Places)." — **Country Living**

"I love your book!" — **Lydia Moss, Travel Editor, McCall's**

"Delightful, succinct, detailed and well-organized. Easy to follow style . . ." — **Don Wudtke, Los Angeles Times**

"This is one of the best guidebooks of its kind. It's easy to use, accurate and the thumbnail sketches give the readers enough description to choose among the more than 1,000 properties detailed . . ." — **Dallas Morning News**

". . . thoughtfully organized and look-ups are hassle-free . . . well-researched and accurate . . . put together by people who know the field. There is no other publication available that covers this particular segment of the bed & breakfast industry - a segment that has been gaining popularity among travelers by leaps and bounds. The information included is valuable and well thought out." — **Morgan Directory Reviews**

"This guide has become the favorite choice of travelers and specializes only in professionally operated inns and B&Bs rather than homestays (lodgings in spare bedrooms)." — **Laguna Magazine**

"This is the best bed & breakfast book out. It outshines them all!" — **Maggie Balitas, Rodale Book Clubs**

Comments from innkeepers:

"Your book is wonderful. I have been reading it as one does a novel." — Olallieberry Inn, Cambria, Calif.

"We want to tell you how much we love your book. We have it out for guests to use. They love it, each featured inn stands out so well. Thank you for the privilege of being in your book." — Fairhaven Inn, Bath, Maine.

"What a wonderful book! We love it and have been very pleased with the guests who have made reservations using your book." — Vermont innkeeper

"We have had fantastic response. Thanks!" — Liberty Rose Colonial B&B, Williamsburg, Va.

"American Historic Inns is wonderful! We are proud and delighted to be included. Thank you for creating such a special guidebook." — The Heirloom, Ione, Calif.

"Thanks so much for all your hard work. We receive the largest number of guidebook referrals from The Official Guide to American Historic Inns." — Saddle Rock Ranch, Sedona, Ariz.

"Your book has been invaluable to us." — Ellis River House, Jackson, N.H.

"Your guide has high praises from guests who use it." — The Inn on South Street, Kennebunkport, Maine.

"Thank you for all the time and work you put into this guidebook. We have had many guests find our inn because of you." — Kaleidoscope Inn, Nipomo, Calif.

In loving memory of my brother, Douglas Edwards, who helped make our first book possible and whose unique charm, one-of-a-kind adventures and wild stories will always be cherished.

THE OFFICIAL GUIDE
— TO —
AMERICAN
HISTORIC
I N N S

BED & BREAKFASTS AND COUNTRY INNS
SIXTH EDITION

BY DEBORAH EDWARDS SAKACH

Published By

AMERICAN HISTORIC INNS INCORPORATED

PO Box 669
Dana Point
California
92629-0669
ahii@ix.netcom.com
http://homearts.com/inns

The Official Guide to American Historic Inns — Bed & Breakfasts and Country Inns

Every effort has been made to produce a dependable reference guide based on information gathered from innkeepers. American Historic Inns, Inc. makes no representations or warranties with respect to the establishments listed herein and specifically disclaims any warranties of fitness for any particular purpose. We recommend that you contact each inn and B&B to verify information prior to making reservations. Although every attempt was made to be as accurate as possible, American Historic Inns, Inc. does not make any representation that this book is free from error. Information included in this publication has been checked for accuracy prior to publication. Since changes do occur, American Historic Inns, Inc. cannot be responsible for any variations from the information printed.

FRONT COVER (FROM TOP LEFT):

Liberty Rose Colonial B&B, Williamsburg, Va.
Photo by Bruce W. Muncy

Seven Gables Inn, Pacific Grove, Calif.
Photo by American Historic Inns, Inc.

Two Meeting Street Inn, Charleston, S.C.
Photo by American Historic Inns, Inc.

Chalet Suzanne, Lake Wales, Fla.
Photo by Dave Woods

BACK COVER:

Scofield House B&B, Sturgeon Bay, Wis.
Joshua Wilton House, Harrisonburg, Va.
Great Oak Manor, Chestertown, Md.
Photo by American Historic Inns, Inc.

Grand Victorian B&B Inn, Bellaire, Mich.
Photo by Don Rutt

Le Grande Maison, Broussard, La.
Photo by Allen Breaux

COVER DESIGN:
David Sakach

OPERATIONS MANAGER:
Sandy Imre

DATABASE ASSISTANTS:
Ami Gerbac, Julie Mayer, Joyce Roll

ASSISTANT EDITORS:
Tiffany Crosswy, Alex Murashko, Carol O'Connell,
Lucy Poshek, Joshua Prizer, Stephen Sakach

PROGRAMMING AND CARTOGRAPHY:
Tim Sakach

DIGITAL SCANNING:
Jennifer Kim, James Lin, Andrew Lithgoe

Publisher's Cataloging in Publication Data

Sakach, Deborah Edwards
American Historic Inns, Inc.
The Official Guide to American Historic Inns

1. Bed & Breakfast Accommodations - United States, Directories, Guide Books.
2. Travel - Bed & Breakfast Inns, Directories, Guide Books.
3. Bed & Breakfast Accommodations - Historic Inns, Directories, Guide Books.
4. Hotel Accommodations - Bed & Breakfast Inns, Directories, Guide Books.
5. Hotel Accommodations - United States, Directories, Guide Books.
I. Title. II. Author. III Bed & Breakfast, The Official Guide to American Historic Inns

ISBN: 1-888050-02-0
Softcover
Printed in the United States of America.
10 9 8 7 6 5 4 3 2 1

Contents

How To Use This Book

Welcome! You hold in your hands the most comprehensive collection of our nation's best historic Bed & Breakfast and Country Inns. Most were built in the 17th, 18th or 19th centuries, but a few inns from the early 20th century have been included. The National Register of Historic Places requires that buildings be constructed prior to 1940 in order to gain historic standing, and we follow this guideline as well.

When you stay at a historic inn, not only do you enjoy a unique getaway, you also promote and support the preservation of our nation's architectural and cultural heritage. Most of these homes are owned privately and have been restored with the private funds of individual families. They are maintained and improved by revenues collected from Bed & Breakfast guests.

With a few exceptions, we have omitted homestays. These are B&Bs with only one or two rooms, often operated casually or as a hobby.

Accommodations

Among the listings, you'll find B&Bs and country inns in converted schoolhouses, lighthouses, 18th-century farmhouses, Queen Anne Victorians, adobe lodges and a variety of other unique places, both new and old.

The majority of inns included in this book were built in the 17th, 18th, 19th or early 20th centuries. We have stated the date each building was constructed at the beginning of each description. Many of the inns are steeped in the traditions of Colonial America, the Victorian Era, The Civil War, Spanish colonization or the Old West. Many are listed in the National Register of Historic Places.

A Variety of Inns

A **Country Inn** generally serves both breakfast and dinner and may have a restaurant associated with it. Many have been in operation for years; some since the 18th century as you will note in our "Inns of Interest" section. Although primarily found on the East Coast, a few country inns are in other regions of the nation.

A **Bed & Breakfast** facility's primary focus is lodging. It can have from three to 20 rooms or more. The innkeepers often live on the premises. Breakfast usually is the only meal served and can be a full-course, gourmet breakfast or a simple buffet. B&B owners often pride themselves on their culinary skills.

As with Country Inns, many B&Bs specialize in providing historic, romantic or gracious atmospheres with amenities such as canopied beds, fireplaces, spa tubs, afternoon tea in the library and scenic views.

Some give great attention to recapturing a specific historic period, such as the Victorian or Colonial eras. Many display antiques and other furnishings from family collections.

A **Homestay** is a room available in a private home. It may be an elegant stone mansion in the best part of town or a charming country farm. Homestays have one to three guest rooms. Because homestays are often operated as a hobby-type business and open and close frequently, only a very few such properties are included in this publication.

A Note About Innkeepers

Your innkeepers are a tremendous resource. Most knowledgeable innkeepers enjoy sharing regional attractions, local folklore, area history, and pointing out favorite restaurants and other special features of their areas. Unlike hotel and motel operators, innkeepers often bring much of themselves into creating an experience for you to long remember. Many have personally renovated historic buildings, saving them from deterioration and often, the bulldozer. Others have infused their inns with a unique style and personality to enliven your experience with a warm and inviting environment.

How to Use This Book

Note: We try to keep the use of codes to a minimum, but they do help us create a more comprehensive listing for each of the inns and B&Bs. We encourage to read this entire section, as it will help plan a getaway that is just right for you.

Area Codes

Although we have made every effort to update area codes throughout the book, new ones do pop up from time to time. The phone companies do provide recordings for several months after a change, but beyond that point, it can be difficult to reach an inn or B&B. Although they are listed by state or province, the new codes were added only in certain sections of the state or province. For example, the 415 area code in California applies only to San Francisco and certain surrounding cities. The following list includes the most recent area code changes that were available at press time.

State/Province	Old Code	New Code	Effective Date of Change
Alabama	205	256	3/23/98
Alberta	403	780	1/25/99
California	415	650	8/2/97
California	916	530	11/1/97
California	510	925	3/14/98
California	714	949	4/18/98
California	213	323	6/13/98
California	408	831	7/11/98
California	209	559	11/14/98
Colorado	303	720	TBD
Florida	813	727	TBD
Georgia	770	678	1/6/98
Kansas	913	785	7/20/97
Massachusetts	617	781	9/1/97
Massachusetts	508	978	9/1/97
Michigan	313	734	12/13/97
Mississippi	601	228	9/15/97
Missouri	816	660	10/12/97
North Carolina	910	336	12/15/97
North Carolina	919	252	TBD
North Carolina	704	828	TBD
Ohio	216	440	8/16/97
Ohio	614	740	12/6/97
Oklahoma	405	580	11/1/97
Pennsylvania	412	724	2/1/98
Quebec	514	450	6/13/98
South Carolina	803	843	3/22/98
Tennessee	615	931	9/15/97
Texas	210	830	7/7/97
Texas	210	956	7/7/97
Utah	801	435	9/21/97
Wisconsin	414	920	7/26/97

Baths

Not all bed & breakfasts and country inns provide a private bath for each guest room. We have included the number of rooms and the number of private baths in each facility. The code "*PB*," indicates how many guest rooms include a private bath. If you must have a private bath, make sure the room reserved for you provides this facility. If a listing indicates that there are suites available, one should assume that a suite includes a private bath. Most cottages also include a private bath, sometimes more than one, but be sure to inquire with the innkeeper about facilities in these units.

Beds

K, Q, D, T, R indicates King, Queen, Double, Twin or Rollaway beds available at the inn. A **C** indicates that a crib is available.

Children

This is always a sensitive subject. We do not list whether children are allowed at inns or B&Bs in this guide because it is illegal in several states to discriminate against persons of any age. However, occasionally innkeepers do "discourage" children as guests. Some innkeepers consider their inn a place for romance or solitude, and often do not think younger guests fit into this scheme. Also, many inns are filled with fine antiques and collectibles, so it may be an inappropriate place for very small children. Some innkeepers discourage children simply because they are not set up to accommodate the needs of a family.

If you plan to bring your children, always ask your innkeeper if children are welcome, and if so, at what age. Many innkeepers go out of their way to provide a wonderful atmosphere for families. In fact, more and more inns are catering to families.

Meals

Continental breakfast: Coffee, juice and toast or pastry.

Continental-plus breakfast: A continental breakfast plus a variety of breads, cheeses and fruit.

Full breakfast: Coffee, juice, breads, fruit and an entree.

Gourmet breakfast: May be a four-course candle-light offering or especially creative cuisine.

Teas: Usually served in the late afternoon with cookies, crackers or other in-between-meal offerings.

Meal Plans

AP: American Plan. All three meals may be included in the price of the room. Check to see if the rate quoted is for two people (double occupancy) or per person (single occupancy).

MAP: Modified American Plan. Breakfast and dinner may be included in the price of the room.

EP: European Plan. No meals are included. We have listed only a few historic hotels that operate on an EP plan.

Always find out what meals, if any, are included in the rates. Not every establishment in this guidebook provides breakfast, although most do. Please do not assume meals are included in the rates featured in the book. Occasionally, an innkeeper has indicated *MAP* and *AP* when she or he actually means that both programs are available and you must specify in which program you are interested.

Payments

MC: MasterCard
VISA
DS: Discover
AX: American Express
DC: Diner's Club
CB: Carte Blanche
TC: Traveler's Cheques
PC: Personal Checks

Pets Allowed

Under some listings, you will note that pets are allowed. Despite this, it is always wise to inform the innkeeper that you have a pet. Some innkeepers charge a fee for pets or only allow certain types and sizes of animals. The innkeeper also may have set aside a specific room for guests with pets, so if this room is booked, you may not be able to bring your pet along this trip.

Rates

Rates are usually listed in ranges, i.e., $45-105. The LOWEST rate is almost always available during off-peak periods and may only apply to the least expensive room. Rates are always subject to change and are not guaranteed. You should always confirm

the rates when making the reservations. Rates for Canadian listings usually are listed in Canadian dollars. Rates are quoted for double occupancy.

Breakfast and other meals MAY or MAY NOT be included in the rates.

Minimum stays

Many inns require a two-night minimum stay on weekends. A three-night stay often is required during holiday periods.

Cancellations

Cancellation policies are individual for each bed & breakfast. It is not unusual to see 7- to 14-day cancellation periods or more. Please verify the inn's policy when making your reservation.

Rooms

Under some listings, you will note that suites are available. We typically assume that suites include a private bath.

Additionally, under some listings, you will note a reference to cottages. A cottage may be a rustic cabin tucked in the woods, a seaside cottage or a private apartment-style accommodation.

Fireplaces

When fireplaces are mentioned in the listing they may be in guest rooms or in common areas. A few have fireplaces that are non-working because of city lodging requirements. Please verify this if you are looking forward to an evening in front of a crackling fire.

Historic Interest

Almost all the inns included have listed items of historic interest nearby that guests can visit. To help you plan your trip, most of the inns also have included the distance to the sites of significant historic interest.

Smoking

The majority of country inns and B&Bs, especially those located in historic buildings, prohibit smoking; therefore, if you are a smoker, we advise you to call and specifically check with each inn to see if and how they accommodate smokers.

State maps

The state maps have been designed to help travelers find an inn's location quickly and easily. Each city shown on the maps contains one or more inns. As you browse through the guide, you will notice coordinates next to each city name, i.e. "C3." The coordinates designate the location of inns on the state map.

Media coverage

Some inns have provided us with copies of magazine or newspaper articles written by travel writers about their establishments and we have indicated that in the listing. Articles written about the inns may be available either from the source as a reprint, through libraries or from the inn itself.

Comments from guests

Over the years, we have collected reams of guest comments about thousands of inns. Our files are filled with these documented comments. At the end of some descriptions, we have included a guest comment received about that inn.

Descriptions

This book contains descriptions of more than 2,300 inns, and each establishment was reviewed carefully prior to being approved for this guide. Although we do charge a listing fee, this is never a guarantee that an inn or B&B will appear in the guide. Many inns and B&Bs were turned away from this guide because they did not meet our standards. We also do not allow innkeepers to write their own descriptions. Our descriptions are created from visits to the inns, interviews with innkeepers and a bulk of other information from ratings to guest comments to articles from top magazines and newspapers.

Inspections

Each year we travel across the country visiting inns. Since 1981, we have had a happy, informal team of inn travelers and prospective innkeepers who report to us about new bed & breakfast discoveries and repeat visits to favorite inns.

Although our staff usually sees hundreds of inns each year, inspecting inns is not the major focus of our travels. We visit as many as possible, photograph them and meet the innkeepers. Some inns are grand mansions filled with classic, museum-quality antiques. Others are rustic, such as reassembled log cabins or renovated barns or stables. We have enjoyed them all and cherish our memories of each establishment, pristine or rustic.

Only rarely have we come across a truly disappointing inn, poorly kept or poorly managed. This type of business usually does not survive because an inn's success depends upon repeat guests and enthusiastic word-of-mouth referrals from satisfied guests. We do not promote these types of establishments.

Traveler or tourist

Travel is an adventure into the unknown, full of surprises and rewards. A seasoned "traveler" learns that even after elaborate preparations and careful planning, travel provides the new and unexpected. The traveler learns to live with uncertainty and considers it part of the adventure.

To the "tourist," whether "accidental" or otherwise, new experiences are disconcerting. Tourists want no surprises. They expect things to be exactly as they had envisioned them. To tourists we recommend staying in a hotel or motel chain where the same formula is followed from one locale to another.

We have found that inngoers are travelers at heart. They relish the differences found at these unique bed & breakfasts and country inns. This is the magic that makes traveling from inn to inn the delightful experience it is.

What if the inn is full?

Ask the innkeeper for recommendations. They may know of an inn that has recently opened or one nearby but off the beaten path. Call the local Chamber of Commerce in the town you hope to visit. They may also know of inns that have recently opened. Please let us know of any new discoveries you make.

We want to hear from you!

We've always enjoyed hearing from our readers and have carefully cataloged all letters and recommendations. If you wish to participate in evaluating your inn experiences, use the Inn Evaluation Form in the back of this book. You might want to make copies of this form prior to departing on your journey.

We hope you will enjoy this book so much that you will want to keep an extra copy or two on hand to offer to friends and family. Many readers have called to purchase our books for hostess gifts, birthday presents, or for seasonal celebrations. It's a great way to introduce your friends to America's enchanting country inns and bed & breakfasts.

① Map coordinates

Easily locate an inn on the state map using these coordinates.

② Inn address

Mailing or street address and all phone numbers for the inn.

③ E-mail address

Contact the inn via the Internet.

④ Description of inn

Descriptions of inns are written by experienced travel writers based on visits to inns, interviews and information collected from inns.

⑤ Drawing of inn

Many listings include artistic renderings.

⑥ Historic Interest

Indicates items of special historic significance near the inn's location.

⑦ Rates, Amenities, Other Information

Rates: Rates are quoted for double occupancy. The rate range includes off-season rates and is subject to change.

Payment types accepted: MC-MasterCard, **VISA**, **DS**-Discover, **AX**-American Express, **DC**-Diner's Club, **CB**-Carte Blanche, **TC**-Traveler's Check, **PC**-Personal Check.

Travel agent commission: Number represents a percentage. Example: **TAC10**=10%

Rooms: Number and types of rooms available. **PB**=Private Bath. **FP**=Fireplace.

Beds: King, **Q**ueen, **D**ouble, **T**win, **R**ollaway, **C**rib

Amenities and activities: Information included here describes the meals that might be included in the rates and other amenities or services available at the inn. Nearby activities are also included.

⑧ Pets allowed

Indicates the inn's policy on pets.

⑨ Location

Location of inn in relation to local landmarks.

⑩ Publicity

Newspapers, magazines and other publications which have featured articles about the inn.

⑪ Guest comments

Comments about the inn from guests.

Anytown ❶ G6

An American Historic Inn

❷ 123 S Main St
Anytown, SC 12345-6789
(123)555-1212 (800)555-1212
Fax:(123)555-2121

❸ E-mail:ahii@ix.netcom.com

❹ **Circa 1907.** Every inch of this breathtaking inn offers something special. The interior is decorated to the hilt with lovely furnishings, plants, beautiful rugs and warm, inviting tones. Rooms include four-poster and canopy beds combined with the modern amenities such ❺ as two-person Jacuzzi tubs, fireplaces, wet bars and stocked refrigerators. Enjoy a complimentary full breakfast at the inn's gourmet restaurant. The chef offers everything from a light breakfast of fresh fruit, cereal and a bagel to heartier treats such as whole grain French toast stuffed with Brie and sundried peaches served with fresh fruit and crisp bacon.

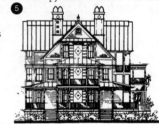

❻ **Historic Interest:** History buffs can visit Secession House, where the first ordinance for Southern secession was drawn up. Penn Center is located on St. Helena Island.

❼ Innkeeper(s): Candice & Sterling Lane. $125-185. MAP. MC VISA AX DC CB DS PC TC. TAC10. 13 rooms with PB, 4 with FP. 1 suite. 1 conference room. Breakfast and afternoon tea included in rates. Types of meals: full breakfast, gourmet breakfast and early coffee/tea. Dinner, picnic lunch, gourmet lunch, banquet service, catering service and room service available. Beds: KQDT. Air conditioning, turn-down service, ceiling fan and cable TV in room. VCR, fax, copier and bicycles on premises. Handicap access. Weddings, small meetings, family reunions and seminars hosted. English and Dutch spoken. Antiques, fishing, parks, shopping, theater and watersports nearby.

❽ Pets Allowed: With advanced notice.

❾ Location: One-half mile from Historic Route 1A.

❿ Publicity: *Anytown News, Southern Living, Country Inns, US Air.*

⓫ *"You have captured a beautiful part of our history."*

Alabama

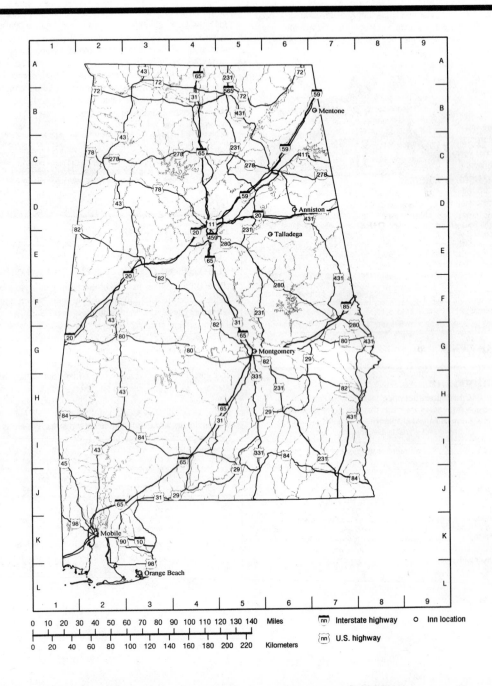

	Miles
0 10 20 30 40 50 60 70 80 90 100 110 120 130 140	
0 20 40 60 80 100 120 140 160 180 200 220	Kilometers

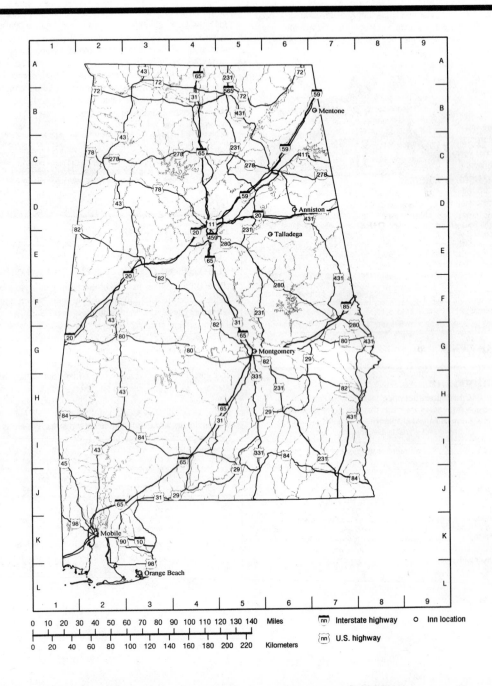 Interstate highway ○ Inn location

  U.S. highway

Anniston D6

The Victoria, A Country Inn & Restaurant

1604 Quintard Ave, PO Box 2213
Anniston, AL 36201-3849
(205)236-0503 (800)260-8781 Fax:(205)236-1138
E-mail: thevic97@aol.com

Circa 1887. This Victorian estate, an Alabama landmark, occupies almost an entire square block on Quintard Avenue, Anniston's major thoroughfare. The first floor of the main house has four dining rooms, a piano lounge and a glass-enclosed veranda. The guest rooms the house are furnished with antiques, while those in the hotel feature reproduction pieces. Covered walkways, verandas and gazebos flow among the massive hardwoods, gardens, courtyard and pool.

Historic Interest: Saint Michaels and All Angels Episcopal Church (1 mile), Tyler Hill Square (2 miles), Olde Mill Antique Mall & Village (4 miles), Grace Episcopal Church (1/2 mile).

Innkeeper(s): Beth & Fain Casey, Jean Ann Oglesby. $64-225. EP. MC VISA AX DC CB DS TC. TAC10. 60 rooms with PB, 4 with FP. 1 cottage. 4 conference rooms. Breakfast included in rates. Types of meals: continental-plus breakfast and early coffee/tea. Banquet service, catering service and room service available. Restaurant on premises. Beds: KQD. Phone, air conditioning and TV in room. VCR, fax, copier and swimming on premises. Handicap access. Weddings, small meetings, family reunions and seminars hosted. Amusement parks, antiques, parks, shopping and theater nearby.

Publicity: *Southern Living, New York Times, Anniston Star, Birmingham Post Herald, Decatur Daily, Birmingham News, Good Housekeeping.*

Mentone B7

Mentone Inn

Hwy 117, PO Box 290
Mentone, AL 35984
(205)634-4836 (800)455-7470

Circa 1927. Mentone is a refreshing stop for those in search of the cool breezes and natural air conditioning of the mountains. Here antique treasures mingle with modern-day conveniences. Sequoyah Caverns, Little River Canyon and DeSoto Falls are moments away.

Innkeeper(s): Frances & Karl Waller. $60-125. MC VISA AX TC. 12 rooms, 11 with PB. Breakfast and afternoon tea included in rates. Types of meals: full breakfast and early coffee/tea. Beds: QT. Air conditioning and ceiling fan in room. TV and VCR on premises. Small meetings, family reunions and seminars hosted. Antiques, parks, downhill skiing and watersports nearby.

Location: On Lookout Mountain in northeast Alabama.

Publicity: *Birmingham News.*

Mobile K2

Malaga Inn

359 Church St
Mobile, AL 36602-2301
(334)438-4701 (800)235-1586 Fax:(334)438-4701

Circa 1862. Malaga Inn is comprised of two townhomes, which were built by two brothers-in-law during the early days of the Civil War, when it looked like the Confederacy might win the fight. One could almost imagine this National Register inn along a street in the French Quarter. The architecture, adorned with first- and second-story verandas and painted a pale salmon, is decidedly French in style. Rooms are elegant with four-poster beds and Oriental rugs. Meals are not included in the rates, but the inn's restaurant serves breakfast and dinner. The inn is adjacent to the Civic Auditorium and easily accessible to everything in downtown Mobile.

Innkeeper(s): Sharon Williams. $69-79. MC VISA AX DS PC. TAC10. 39 rooms with PB. 3 suites. Types of meals: full breakfast and early coffee/tea. Dinner, banquet service, catering service, catered breakfast and room service available. Restaurant on premises. Beds: KQD. Phone, air conditioning, ceiling fan and TV in room. VCR, fax, copier and swimming on premises. Weddings, small meetings, family reunions and seminars hosted. Antiques, fishing, parks, shopping, sporting events, golf, theater and watersports nearby.

Montgomery G5

Lattice Inn B&B

1414 S Hull St
Montgomery, AL 36104-5522
(334)832-9931 (800)525-0652 Fax:(334)264-0075

Circa 1906. Built at the turn-of-the-century in what is known as the Garden District, this Tudor-style cottage offers a relaxing retreat for guests traveling for business or pleasure. The inn's 12-foot ceilings and fireplace greet visitors upon arrival. All rooms are furnished in heirlooms and antiques to enhance the inn's original architectural character. Some rooms boast fireplaces. The main house guest rooms feature four-poster beds and some have clawfoot tubs. The cottage offers the convenience of a complete kitchen and extra sleeping accommodations. Guests can relax on the shady front porch or enjoy a dip in the backyard pool. A wonderful Southern-style full breakfast is served daily. Located in the historic district, the inn is close to shops, restaurants, antiques and parks.

Innkeeper(s): Michael Pierce. $70-85. MC VISA AX DS PC TC. TAC10. 4 rooms, 2 with FP. 1 cottage. Breakfast included in rates. Types of meals: full breakfast and gourmet breakfast. Beds: KQTD. Phone, air conditioning, turn-down service, ceiling fan and TV in room. Fax, copier, spa, swimming, bicycles and library on premises. Handicap access. Small meetings hosted. Sign spoken. Amusement parks, antiques, parks, shopping, sporting events, golf and theater nearby.

Pets Allowed.

Publicity: *Atlanta Journal, Tennessean.*

"The friendly welcome, the cozy creak of the front porch swing, the warm sun in the evening on the back deck, the soft towels in the morning and the wonderful breakfast are just a few of the things that will bring me back again and again!"

Orange Beach
L3

The Original Romar House

23500 Perdido Beach Blvd
Orange Beach, AL 36561-3007
(334)974-1625 (800)487-6627 Fax:(334)974-1163
E-mail: original@gulftel.com

Circa 1924. From the deck of the Purple Parrot Bar, guests at this seaside inn can enjoy a cocktail and a view of the Gulf of Mexico. Each of the guest rooms is named and themed after a local festival and decorated with authentic Art Deco furnishings. Stained- and beveled-glass windows add to the romantic atmosphere. A full Southern breakfast is served each morning, and in the evening, wine and cheese is served in the Purple Parrot Bar.

Innkeeper(s): Darrell Finley. $89-129. MC VISA AX PC. TAC10. 6 rooms with PB. 1 suite. 1 cottage. 1 conference room. Breakfast included in rates. Type of meal: full breakfast. Beds: Q. Air conditioning, turndown service and ceiling fan in room. TV, VCR, spa, swimming, bicycles and library on premises. Weddings, small meetings and family reunions hosted. Amusement parks, antiques, fishing, parks, shopping and watersports nearby.

Talladega
E6

Historic Oakwood B&B

715 North St E
Talladega, AL 35160-2527
(205)362-0662

Circa 1847. This handsome two-story home is one of Alabama's best examples of antebellum Federal architecture. In the National Register, it was built by Talledega's first mayor. It

rests on one acre of grounds. Collectibles and antiques fill the rooms. The favorite accommodation is the master suite with two bathrooms, one with a tub and a bidet, the other with a large shower. Southern breakfasts include grits, biscuits, sausage, bacon and eggs. Nearby is the Alabama Institute for the Deaf and Blind, Talladega College, the Superspeedway and Courthouse Square.

Innkeeper(s): Juanita Woods. $55-95. PC TC. TAC15. 3 rooms, 1 with PB. Breakfast included in rates. Types of meals: continental breakfast and full breakfast. Beds: QDT. Air conditioning, ceiling fan and TV in room. VCR on premises. Antiques and sporting events nearby.

Alaska

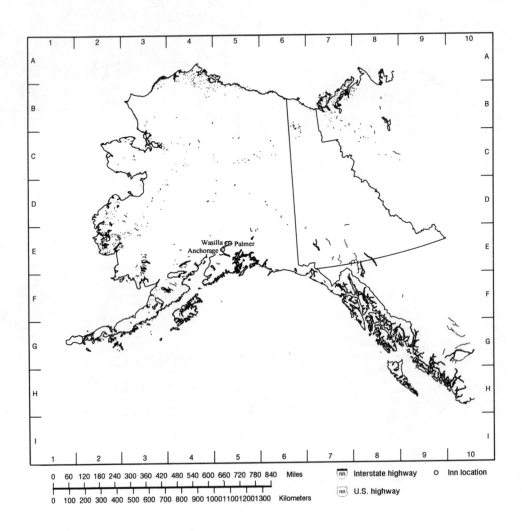

0 60 120 180 240 300 360 420 480 540 600 660 720 780 840 Miles

0 100 200 300 400 500 600 700 800 900 1000 1100 1200 1300 Kilometers

(nn) Interstate highway   o Inn location

(nn) U.S. highway

Anchorage E5

Alaska Private Lodgings

PO Box 200047
Anchorage, AK 99501
(907)258-1717 Fax:(907)258-6613
E-mail: apl@alaska.net

Circa 1900. Alaska Private Lodgings, operated by Mercy Dennis, is a reservation service for private homes. Among the many listed in Anchorage is a charming suite in one of the oldest buildings in town. Additional accommodations are available in apartments. Homes are located in Homer, Kenai, Talkeetna, Alyeska, Seward, Valdez, Wasilla, Willow and Seldovia. Mercy is knowledgeable about tours, sightseeing trips and discount car rentals. $60-75.

"We had a really great time during our eight days in Alaska. We enjoyed all four of our hosts, who were all outstanding in different ways. Thanks for your arrangements."

Alaskan Frontier Gardens

PO Box 24-1881, Hillside & Alatna
Anchorage, AK 99524-1881
(907)345-6556 Fax:(907)562-2923
E-mail: afg@alaska.net

Circa 1982. Secluded on three scenic acres of woods, manicured lawns and gardens, this lodge-style home offers privacy, yet is less than half an hour from downtown Anchorage. The two suites include Jacuzzi tubs, and the Ivory Suite also has a sauna and fireplace. Furnishings are contemporary and comfortable, and guests are encouraged to enjoy the house and relax. The innkeepers can store camping and fishing gear and have a freezer for fish and game. Freshly made Belgian waffles, reindeer sausage, gourmet coffee and homemade pastries are often part of the breakfast fare.

Innkeeper(s): Rita Gittins. $75-175. MC VISA AX DC DS PC TC. TAC10. 3 rooms, 2 with PB, 1 with FP. 2 suites. 1 conference room. Breakfast included in rates. Types of meals: full breakfast, gourmet breakfast and early coffee/tea. Beds: KQDT. Phone, ceiling fan, TV and VCR in room. Fax, copier, spa, sauna, library and pet boarding on premises. Handicap access. Weddings, small meetings, family reunions and seminars hosted. Fishing, parks, shopping, downhill skiing, cross-country skiing, sporting events and golf nearby.

Pets Allowed.

Publicity: *Anchorage Daily News.*

Palmer E5

Colony Inn

325 E Elmwood
Palmer, AK 99645
(907)745-3330 Fax:(907)746-3330

Circa 1935. Historic buildings are few and far between in Alaska, and this inn is one of them. The structure was built to house teachers and nurses in the days when President Roosevelt was sending settlers to Alaska to establish farms. When innkeeper Janet Kincaid purchased it, the inn had been empty for some time. She restored the place, including the wood walls, which now create a cozy ambiance in the common areas. The 12 guest rooms are nicely appointed, and 10 include a whirlpool tub. Meals are not included, but the inn's restaurant offers breakfast and lunch. The inn is listed in the National Register.

Innkeeper(s): Janet Kincaid. $80. MC VISA AX DC PC TC. TAC10. 12 rooms with PB. Type of meal: full breakfast. Lunch available. Restaurant on premises. Beds: QDT. Phone and TV in room. Handicap access. Weddings, small meetings and family reunions hosted. Antiques, fishing, parks, shopping, downhill skiing, cross-country skiing and golf nearby.

"Love the antiques and history."

Wasilla E5

Yukon Don's B&B Inn

1830 E Parks Hwy # 386, 2221 Yukon
Wasilla, AK 99654-7374
(907)376-7472 (800)478-7472 Fax:(907)376-6515
E-mail: yukondon@alaska.com

Circa 1971. Decorated with an Alaskan theme, this comfortable bed & breakfast boasts a second-floor room with a spectacular 360-degree view of the Matanuska Valley. Guests can partake in the continental breakfast bar each morning and also

enjoy use of a sauna and exercise room. The inn is about an hour from Anchorage and is on the direct route to Denali National Park, Fairbanks and Valdez. Among its distinctions, Wasilla is the home of the International Iditarod Dog Sled Race, the Reindeer Farm and the Matanuska and Knik glaciers.

Innkeeper(s): Yukon Don Tanner. $75-125. MC VISA AX DC TC. TAC10. 7 rooms, 1 with FP. 3 suites. 1 cabin. 1 conference room. Breakfast included in rates. Types of meals: continental-plus breakfast and early coffee/tea. Beds: KQT. Phone, ceiling fan, TV and VCR in room. Fax, copier, sauna and library on premises. Weddings, small meetings, family reunions and seminars hosted. Fishing, parks, shopping, downhill skiing, cross-country skiing and golf nearby.

Pets Allowed: Limited.

Arizona

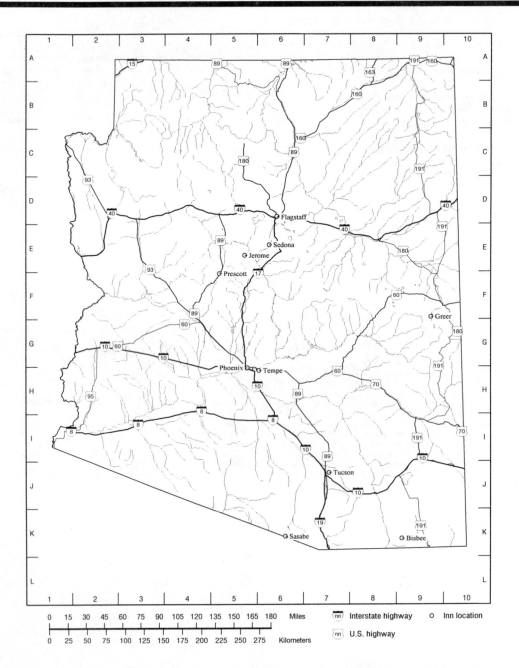

0 15 30 45 60 75 90 105 120 135 150 165 180   Miles

0   25   50   75   100 125 150 175 200 225 250 275   Kilometers

[nn] Interstate highway   ○ Inn location

[nn] U.S. highway

Bisbee K9

Bisbee Grand Hotel, A B&B Inn

61 Main Street, Box 825
Bisbee, AZ 85603
(520)432-5900 (800)421-1909

Circa 1906. This National Register treasure is a stunning example of an elegant turn-of-the-century hotel. The hotel originally served as a stop for mining executives, and it was restored back to its Old West Glory in the 1980s. Each of the rooms is decorated with Victorian furnishings and wallcoverings. The suites offer special items such as clawfoot tubs, an antique Chinese wedding bed, a fountain or four-poster bed. The Grand Western Salon boasts the back bar fixture from the Pony Saloon in Tombstone. After a full breakfast, enjoy a day touring the Bisbee area, which includes mine tours, museums, shops, antiquing and a host of outdoor activities.

Historic Interest: Located in downtown historic Bisbee, features 110 year old back bar fixture.

Innkeeper(s): Bill Thomas. $53-110. MC VISA AX DS. 11 rooms. Breakfast included in rates. Type of meal: full breakfast.

Flagstaff D6

Birch Tree Inn

824 W Birch Ave
Flagstaff, AZ 86001-4420
(520)774-1042 (888)774-1042 Fax:(520)774-8462
E-mail: birch@flagstaff.az.us

Circa 1917. This bungalow is surrounded by a wraparound veranda supported with Corinthian columns. Southwestern and antique decor is featured, including shaker pine and white wicker. Nature-lovers and ski enthu-siasts will appreciate the Ponderosa Pine Forest nearby. Adjacent to the inn, cross-country ski trails are especially popular. A full breakfast and afternoon refreshments are served.

Innkeeper(s): Donna & Rodger Pettinger, Sandy & Ed Znetko. $55-109. MC VISA AX PC TC. TAC10. 5 rooms, 3 with PB. Breakfast and afternoon tea included in rates. Types of meals: full breakfast and early coffee/tea. Beds: KQT. Air conditioning in room. TV, fax, copier and spa on premises. Family reunions hosted. Antiques, fishing, parks, shopping, downhill skiing, cross-country skiing, sporting events and theater nearby.

Publicity: *Daily Sun, Desert Sun, San Francisco Chronicle, Phoenix Gazette.*

"Charming hosts and wonderful food."

Comfi Cottages

1612 N Aztec St
Flagstaff, AZ 86001-1106
(520)774-0731 (888)774-0731 Fax:(520)779-2236

Circa 1920. Each of the six cottages has been refurbished and features a variety of styles. One cottage is decorated in a Southwestern motif, while the oth-ers feature antiques and English-Country decor. Five cottages include fire-places, and all include kitchens stocked with full equipment and all staples. They also have the added luxury of a washer and dryer. Bicycles are available for guest use, as well as picnic tables, a barbecue grill and picnic baskets. The Grand Canyon and national parks are close by, and the cottages are in the per-fect location to enjoy all Flagstaff has to offer.

Historic Interest: The cottages are located near the many activities available in historic downtown Flagstaff. Several Indian ruins are within 50 miles of the cottages.

Innkeeper(s): Ed & Pat Wiebe. $65-195. MC VISA DS. TAC10. 6 cottages. Breakfast included in rates. Type of meal: full breakfast. Beds: KQDT. Phone, ceiling fan, TV and VCR in room. Small meetings and family reunions hosted. French spoken. Antiques, fishing, parks, shopping, downhill skiing, cross-country skiing, sporting events, theater and watersports nearby.

"Beautiful and relaxing. A port in the storm."

Inn at Four Ten

410 N Leroux St
Flagstaff, AZ 86001-4502
(520)774-0088 (800)774-2008 Fax:(520)774-6354

Circa 1894. This inn, once the stately family residence of a wealthy banker, businessman and cattle rancher, has been fre-quented over the years by travelers interested in exploring the Grand Canyon. Today, guests enjoy hospitality, outstanding cuisine and a wonderful home base from which to enjoy Northern Arizona. Each of the guest rooms is individually dec-orated in a unique style. Seven of the guest rooms include a fireplace, and some offer an oversized Jacuzzi tub. Award-win-ning recipes are featured during the gourmet breakfasts, and afternoon cookies and tea are served in the dining room. A two-block walk takes guests to shops, galleries and restaurants in historic downtown Flagstaff. Sedona, Native American sites and the San Francisco Peaks are nearby.

Historic Interest: Riordan Mansion State Park and Lowell Observatory both are located in Flagstaff. Wupatki National Monument (Anasazi Indian Ruins) is 35 miles away. Hopi and Navajo Indian Reservations are within 45 to 100 miles away. Walnut Canyon National Monument (Sinaqua Indian ruins) is seven miles away.

Innkeeper(s): Howard & Sally Krueger. $110-155. MC VISA PC TC. TAC10. 9 rooms with PB, 7 with FP. 4 suites. Breakfast and evening snack included in rates. Type of meal: gourmet breakfast. Beds: KQT. Air conditioning and ceiling fan in room. Library on premises. Handicap access. Weddings, small meetings and family reunions hosted. Antiques, parks, shop-ping, downhill skiing, cross-country skiing and theater nearby.

Publicity: *Westways, Arizona Daily Sun, Mountain Living, Mountain Morning.*

Greer   F9

White Mountain Lodge

PO Box 143
Greer, AZ 85927-0143
(520)735-7568 Fax:(520)735-7498

Circa 1892. This 19th-century lodge affords views of Greer
meadow and the Little Colorado River. The guest rooms are
individually decorated in a Southwestern or country style. The

common rooms are
decorated with peri-
od antiques,
Southwestern art
and Mission-style
furnishings. The
Lodge's living room
is an ideal place to
relax with its stone

fireplace. While dining on the hearty breakfasts, guests not only
are treated to entrees that range from traditional country fare to
the more gourmet, they also enjoy a view from the picture window. The cookie jar is always filled with homemade goodies
and hot drinks are available throughout the day. Small pets are
allowed, although certain restrictions apply. The inn is near
excellent hiking trails.

Innkeeper(s): Charles & Mary Bast. $65-95. MC VISA AX DC DS PC TC. 7
rooms with PB. 3 cottages. Breakfast and evening snack included in rates.
Types of meals: full breakfast and early coffee/tea. Beds: KQDT. TV, VCR, fax,
copier and library on premises. Small meetings and family reunions hosted.
Spanish spoken. Antiques, fishing, shopping, downhill skiing and cross-country skiing nearby.

Pets Allowed: One small pet per unit. Must not be left unattended in room.

Jerome   E5

The Surgeon's House B&B

PO Box 998, 101 Hill St
Jerome, AZ 86331
(520)639-1452 (800)639-1452
E-mail: surghouse1@juno.com

Circa 1917. The innkeeper prides herself in this
Mediterranean-style inn's unique decorator touches and nine-
course gourmet breakfast. Set on two acres with panoramic
views of Verde Valley, guests will enjoy the inn's informal
atmosphere and lush gardens. With advance notice, the
innkeeper will arrange an in-house massage, a personal walking
tour of historic Jerome, a picnic, or cocktail party.

Innkeeper(s): Andrea Jo Prince. $85-125. MC VISA PC TC. 4 rooms, 2 with
PB. 3 suites. 1 cottage. 1 conference room. Breakfast and evening snack
included in rates. Types of meals: gourmet breakfast and early coffee/tea.
Picnic lunch and banquet service available. Beds: QD. Air conditioning, ceiling fan and TV in room. Pet boarding on premises. Weddings, small meetings, family reunions and seminars hosted. Antiques, fishing, parks, shopping, downhill skiing, golf and theater nearby.

Pets Allowed.

Publicity: *Arizona Republic.*

"What a gift to be able to enjoy a weekend in your peaceful home."

Phoenix   H5

La Estancia B&B Inn

4979 E Camelback Rd
Phoenix, AZ 85018-2900
(602)808-9924 (800)410-7655 Fax:(602)808-9925

Circa 1929. Three of the guest rooms at this historic Monterey
Revival home are named for the views guests enjoy from the
windows. All of the guest quarters have whirlpool tubs and
include romantic iron and poster beds dressed in elegant
linens. The home is listed in the National Register and still
maintains original light fixtures and scored cement floors.
Before heading out to dinner, guests are treated to afternoon
wine and cheese. There is a rooftop deck and swimming pool
on the premises.

Innkeeper(s): Ruth & Richard Maloblocki. $165-195. EP. MC VISA AX DC DS
TC. TAC10. 5 rooms with PB. Breakfast and afternoon tea included in rates.
Types of meals: gourmet breakfast and early coffee/tea. Picnic lunch, lunch
and catering service available. Beds: KQ. Air conditioning, turndown service
and ceiling fan in room. VCR, fax, copier, swimming, bicycles and library on
premises. Weddings and small meetings hosted. Antiques, parks, shopping,
sporting events and theater nearby.

Maricopa Manor

15 W Pasadena Ave
Phoenix, AZ 85013
(602)274-6302 (800)292-6403 Fax:(602)266-3904
E-mail: mmanor@getnet.com

Circa 1928. The secluded Maricopa Manor stands amid palm
trees on an acre of land. The Spanish-style house features four
graceful columns in the entry hall, an elegant living room with
a marble mantel and a music room. The spacious suites are
decorated with satins, lace, antiques and leather-bound books.
Guests may relax on the deck, on the patio, by the pool or in
the gazebo spa.

Historic Interest: Arizona Biltmore Resort (2 miles), Heard Museum (3
miles), Pueblo Grand Indian Ruins and Museum.

Innkeeper(s): Mary Ellen & Paul Kelley. $89-229. MC VISA AX DS PC TC.
TAC10. 6 suites, 2 with FP. Breakfast included in rates. Type of meal: continental-plus breakfast. Beds: KQ. Phone, air conditioning, ceiling fan and TV
in room. VCR, fax, copier, spa and swimming on premises. Handicap access.
Antiques, parks, shopping, sporting events and theater nearby.

Location: North central Phoenix near museums, theaters.

Publicity: *Arizona Business Journal, Country Inns, AAA Westways, San
Francisco Chronicle, Focus, Sombrero.*

*"I've stayed 200+ nights at B&Bs around the world, yet have
never before experienced the warmth and sincere friendliness of
Maricopa Manor."*

Prescott   F5

Juniper Well Ranch

PO Box 11083
Prescott, AZ 86304-1083
(520)442-3415

Circa 1991. A working horse ranch sits on the front 15 acres of
this 50-acre, wooded property, which is surrounded by the
Prescott National Forest. Guests are welcome to feed the horses,
and children have been known to take a ride on a tractor with
innkeeper David Bonham. Two log cabins and the ranch house
sit farther back on the land where families can enjoy nature,
"unlimited" hiking and seclusion. A summer house, which can

be reserved by guests staying at the ranch, has no walls, a sloping roof with skylight, and an eight-foot hot tub. Guest pets, including horses, are welcome on an individual basis.

Innkeeper(s): David Bonham & Gail Ball. $100. MC VISA AX DC DS PC TC. TAC10. 3 cottages with PB, 3 with FP. Breakfast included in rates. Type of meal: full breakfast. Beds: QDT. Ceiling fan in room. Spa, stables, library, pet boarding and child care on premises. Handicap access. 50 acres. Weddings, small meetings, family reunions and seminars hosted. Antiques, fishing, parks, shopping, cross-country skiing, golf and theater nearby.

Pets Allowed: Well mannered guest pets, including horses, welcome on an individual basis.

Mount Vernon Inn

204 N Mount Vernon Ave
Prescott, AZ 86301-3108
(520)778-0886 Fax:(520)778-7305
E-mail: mtvrnon@primenet.com

Circa 1900. This inn, listed in the National Register, is known as one of Prescott's "Victorian treasures." Among its architectural features are gables and a Greek Revival porch. In addition to the four spacious guest rooms in the main house, there are three country cottages available. The inn is located in the Mt. Vernon Historic District and is just a few blocks from town square.

Historic Interest: Sharlot Hall Museum, Fort Whipple and Mt. Vernon Avenue's many Victorian homes are among the nearby historic sites.

Innkeeper(s): Michele & Jerry Neumann. $95-125. MC VISA DS TC. TAC10. 4 rooms with PB. 3 cottages. Beds: QDT. Phone in room. Handicap access. Antiques, parks, shopping and theater nearby.

Prescott Pines Inn

901 White Spar Rd
Prescott, AZ 86303-7231
(520)445-7270 (800)541-5374 Fax:(520)778-3665

Circa 1934. A white picket fence beckons guests to the veranda of this comfortably elegant country Victorian inn, originally the Haymore Dairy. There are masses of fragrant pink roses, lavenders and delphiniums, and stately ponderosa pines tower above the inn's four renovated cottages, which were once shelter for farmhands. A three-bedroom, two-bath on-site chalet that sleeps up to eight guests is perfect for a family. The acre of grounds includes a garden fountain and romantic tree swing. A full breakfast is offered at an additional charge.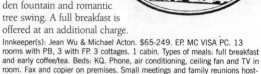

Innkeeper(s): Jean Wu & Michael Acton. $65-249. EP. MC VISA PC. 13 rooms with PB, 3 with FP. 3 cottages. 1 cabin. Types of meals: full breakfast and early coffee/tea. Beds: KQ. Phone, air conditioning, ceiling fan and TV in room. Fax and copier on premises. Small meetings and family reunions hosted. Antiques, parks, shopping and theater nearby.

Location: One-and-a-third miles south of Courthouse Plaza & historic Whiskey Row.

Publicity: *Sunset, Arizona Republic News, Arizona Highways.*

"The ONLY place to stay in Prescott! Tremendous attention to detail."

Sasabe   K6

Rancho De La Osa

PO Box 1
Sasabe, AZ 85633-0001
(520)823-4257 (800)872-6240 Fax:(520)823-4238
E-mail: osagal@aol.com

Circa 1830. This adobe, whose 130,000 acres run along the Mexican border, provides a wondrous glimpse back to the old Southwest. The grounds, first settled by Jesuits in the late 17th century, feature a cantina built in the 1700s, as well as the main hacienda, which dates to the 1830s. The interior, with its exposed log beams, thick adobe walls and authentic decor, is reminiscent of Colonial Mexico. Each room includes a wood-burning fireplace. There is a spa, pool and hiking trails, where guests can enjoy the surrounding Buenos Aires National Wildlife Refuge. Rates include breakfast, a Southwestern lunch and dinner. Guests can opt for horse riding or non-horse riding prices. The historic adobe has hosted such notable guests as Lyndon Johnson, Adlai Stevenson, Tom Mix and Margaret Mitchell.

$250-340. AP. MC VISA DS PC TC. TAC10. 16 rooms with PB, 16 with FP. 6 suites. 2 conference rooms. Breakfast and dinner included in rates. Restaurant on premises. Beds: QDT. Ceiling fan in room. VCR, fax, copier, spa, swimming, stables, bicycles and library on premises. Handicap access. Weddings, small meetings, family reunions and seminars hosted. Spanish spoken. Antiques, fishing, parks, shopping, sporting events, golf and theater nearby.

Sedona   E6

B&B at Saddle Rock Ranch

255 Rock Ridge Dr
Sedona, AZ 86336
(520)282-7640 Fax:(520)282-6829

Circa 1926. Romance and elegance highlight your stay at this historic ranch, which was featured in movies depicting the Old West and Sedona. The unique interior features flagstone floors, beamed ceilings, rock and adobe walls, and 14-foot view windows in the guest parlor. Antique-filled rooms include romantic items such as canopied beds, teddy bears, deluxe linens, woodburning fireplaces and soft, fluffy robes. Coffee, tea, ice and a guest refrigerator are available around the clock. Strolling the grounds, one will be taken in by the beautiful views, gardens and wildlife. Guests have use of a pool and relaxing spa. The innkeepers offer a free concierge service, jeep tours and romance packages.

Historic Interest: Indian ruin sites are interesting day trips.

Innkeeper(s): Fran & Dan Bruno. $120-150. PC TC. 3 rooms with PB, 3 with FP. 1 cottage. Type of meal: full breakfast. Afternoon tea and catering service available. Beds: KQT. Air conditioning, ceiling fan and TV in room. Fax, copier, spa and swimming on premises. Weddings, small meetings and family reunions hosted. Antiques, fishing, parks, shopping, theater and watersports nearby.

Location: On three acres of hillside, one mile from the center of Sedona in the heart of Red Rock Country.

Publicity: *Arizona Republic, Longevity, Sedona Red Rock News, Esquire, Phoenix Home & Garden, ABC, NBC, CBS, Elmer Dills, ABC Radio.*

"Thank you for sharing your ranch with us. It has been the highlight of our trip."

The Lodge at Sedona

125 Kallof Pl
Sedona, AZ 86336-5566
(520)204-1942 (800)619-4467 Fax:(520)204-2128
E-mail: lodge@sedona.net

Circa 1959. This charming lodge, surrounded by the natural wonders of Sedona's red rock and pine trees, was built by the town's first doctor to house his large family. Red rock walls and rough-hewn-beamed ceilings add to the rustic atmosphere of the lodge, which features a glassed-in morning porch, atrium and several fireplaces to enjoy. Expansive, gourmet fare is served each morning, and hors d'oeuvres and desserts are provided later in the day for hungry guests. The Grand Canyon is a two-hour day trip, and the area offers many hiking trails and jeep tours of the surrounding canyons.

Historic Interest: Several Indian ruins are within 40 minutes of the lodge. Prescott, Arizona's first capital and an authentic Western town, is an hour away.

Innkeeper(s): Barb & Mark Dinunzio. $120-225. MC VISA PC. TAC10. 10 rooms with PB, 3 with FP. 3 suites. 1 conference room. Breakfast and evening snack included in rates. Types of meals: gourmet breakfast and early coffee/tea. Picnic lunch available. Beds: KQT. Air conditioning and ceiling fan in room. TV, VCR, fax, copier and library on premises. Handicap access. Small meetings, family reunions and seminars hosted. Antiques, fishing, parks, shopping, downhill skiing, cross-country skiing and theater nearby.

Publicity: *Arizona Republic, Sedona, Red Rock News, San Francisco Examiner, Country Register, New York Post, Sedona, Bon Appetit, Mountain Living.*

"What a wonderful hideaway you have! Everything about your inn was and is fantastic! The friendly service made me feel as if I was home. More importantly, the food made wish that was my home!"

Tempe   H6

Mi Casa-Su Casa Reservation Service

PO Box 950
Tempe, AZ 85280-0950
(602)990-0682 (800)456-0682

Circa 1981. This reservation service represents homes throughout the state, and coordinator Ruth Young knows Arizona like her own backyard. A few of her listings are historic homes and depict the full southwest experience. An American territorial adobe in Tucson is a favorite and has been meticulously restored. Blooming garden courtyards add to its elegance. A directory describes a wide selection of private homestays and historic dude ranches represented by Mi Casa-Su Casa. $50-275.

Location: Covers Arizona as well as New Mexico, Utah, and Nevada.

Tucson   J7

Adobe Rose Inn

940 N Olsen Ave
Tucson, AZ 85719-4951
(520)318-4644 (800)328-4122 Fax:(520)325-0055

Circa 1933. This three-diamond-rated inn is located in the historic Sam Hughes neighborhood just a few blocks from the University of Arizona campus. Airy guest rooms are decorated with a romantic, Southwestern flavor. The Arizona Room includes a fireplace and a huge hand-painted tile tub. The Rainbow's End, which overlooks the pool, offers a beehive fireplace. The innkeepers also offer two cottages, one with a refrigerator and toaster oven and another with a galley kitchen.

Innkeeper(s): Diana Graham. $45-115. MC VISA PC TC. TAC10. 5 rooms with PB, 2 with FP. 2 cottages. Breakfast and evening snack included in

rates. Types of meals: full breakfast, gourmet breakfast and early coffee/tea. Beds: KQT. Phone, air conditioning, ceiling fan, TV and VCR in room. Spa and swimming on premises. Small meetings, family reunions and seminars hosted. Amusement parks, antiques, parks, shopping, downhill skiing, sporting events, theater and watersports nearby.

Casa Alegre B&B

316 E Speedway Blvd
Tucson, AZ 85705-7429
(520)628-1800 (800)628-5654 Fax:(520)792-1880

Circa 1915. Innkeeper Phyllis Florek decorated the interior of this Craftsman-style home with artifacts reflecting the history of

Tucson, including Native American pieces and antique mining tools. Wake to the aroma of fresh coffee and join other guests as you enjoy fresh muffins, fruit and other breakfast treats, such as succulent cheese pancakes with raspberry preserves. The Arizona sitting room opens onto serene gardens, a pool and a Jacuzzi. An abundance of shopping and sightseeing is found nearby.

Historic Interest: The innkeeper serves on the board of directors of the West University Historic District and is full of information about historic sites and the history of the area.

Innkeeper(s): Phyllis Florek. $60-105. MC VISA DS PC TC. TAC10. 5 rooms with PB, 1 with FP. 1 conference room. Breakfast included in rates. Types of meals: full breakfast and gourmet breakfast. Beds: QT. Ceiling fan in room. VCR, fax, spa and swimming on premises. Weddings, small meetings and family reunions hosted. Antiques, parks, shopping, sporting events and theater nearby.

Location: West University Historic District.

Publicity: *Arizona Times, Arizona Daily Star, Tucson Weekly.*

"An oasis of comfort in Central Tucson."

Catalina Park Inn

309 E 1st St
Tucson, AZ 85705-7821
(520)792-4541 (800)792-4885 Fax:(520)792-0838

Circa 1927. Classical music sets the mood as guests linger in front of a roaring fireplace at this inn, located in Tucson's West University Historic District.
The main house offers a spacious room with mountain views and two rooms with private porches that overlook Catalina Park. Colorful rooms are furnished with
antiques and other unique pieces. A bounty of patterned linens, down pillows and comforters dress the beds. The inn is just a few blocks from the University of Arizona and the eclectic shops and restaurants that line Fourth Avenue.

Historic Interest: The San Javier Mission is 10 miles away as is a national park. Closer attractions include the El Presidio and Barrio Historic Districts only a mile away, and the Arizona Historical Society Museum, which is only five blocks from the inn.

Innkeeper(s): Paul Richard & Mark Hall. $75-115. MC VISA TC. TAC10. 6 rooms with PB. 1 suite. 2 cottages. Breakfast and afternoon tea included in rates. Types of meals: gourmet breakfast and early coffee/tea. Beds: QT. Phone, air conditioning and TV in room. Fax on premises. Antiques, parks, sporting events and theater nearby.

Publicity: *Dateline Downtown, Arizona Daily Star, Arizona Illustrated, Tucson Weekly.*

"Our stay here in your beautiful home was wonderful and your hospitality was unsurpassed. Can't wait to return!"

The El Presidio B&B Inn

297 N Main Ave
Tucson, AZ 85701-8219
(602)623-6151 (800)349-6151

Circa 1886. The cobblestone courtyards, fountains, and lush gardens surrounding El Presidio are filled with an old-world Southwestern ambiance. The inn is comprised of a Victorian-Territorial adobe built around a traditional zaguan, or large central hall, plus separate suites in the former carriage house and gate house. Innkeepers Jerry and Patti Toci conducted a 10-year, award-winning restoration of this inn. Rooms are immaculate, romantic and richly appointed. Gourmet breakfasts are served in a dining room that over-

looks the patio. Beverages are served throughout the day. This inn was voted the "Best B&B in Tucson" for 1995-96. Restaurants and museums are nearby.

Innkeeper(s): Patti Toci. $70-115. 3 suites, 1 with FP. 1 conference room. Breakfast included in rates. Beds: Q. Bicycles on premises. Shopping and theater nearby.

Location: Near downtown Tucson in El Presidio Historic District.

Publicity: *Gourmet, Travel & Leisure, Glamour, Tucson Home & Garden, Arizona Highways, Innsider.*

"Thank you again for providing such a completely perfect, pampering, relaxing, delicious, gorgeous vacation 'home' for us."

Hacienda del Sol Ranch

5601 N Hacienda Del Sol
Tucson, AZ 85718
(520)299-1501 (800)728-6514 Fax:(520)299-5554

Circa 1929. What began as a finishing school became a hot spot for Hollywood royalty. In its earlier days as an exclusive resort, Hacienda Del Sol hosted the likes of Clark Gable, Katharine Hepburn and Spencer Tracy. Panoramic views include vistas of mountains, city lights and spectacular Arizona sunrises and sunsets. The lush grounds have a front courtyard with a fountain. Rooms are decorated to look like a Spanish hacienda with Southwestern accents. There is a pool, tennis courts and stables for guests to enjoy, and horseback riding is available in-season. Although no meals are included in the rates, there is a restaurant on the premises featuring regional cuisine.

Innkeeper(s): Richard Fink. $75-345. MC VISA AX. TAC10. 30 rooms with PB, 7 with FP. 5 suites. 3 cottages. 2 conference rooms. Type of meal: continental-plus breakfast. Dinner, banquet service, catering service and catered breakfast available. Restaurant on premises. Beds: KQDT. Phone, air conditioning, ceiling fan and TV in room. Fax, copier, spa, swimming, stables, tennis and library on premises. Handicap access. 34 acres. Weddings, small meetings, family reunions and seminars hosted. Spanish spoken. Amusement parks, antiques, parks, shopping, sporting events, golf and theater nearby.

Publicity: *Travel & Leisure, New York Times.*

La Posada Del Valle

1640 N Campbell Ave
Tucson, AZ 85719-4313
(602)795-3840 Fax:(602)795-3840

Circa 1929. This Southwestern adobe has 18-inch-thick walls, which wraparound to form a courtyard. Ornamental orange trees and lush gardens surround the secluded property. All the rooms have private entrances and open to the patio or overlook the courtyard and foun-

tain. Furnishings include antiques and period pieces from the '20s and '30s. Afternoon tea is served, and breakfasts are served in a dining room that offers a view of the Catalina Mountains. The University of Arizona, University Medical Center, shops, dining and more all are within walking distance.

Innkeeper(s): Karin Dennen. $65-135. MC VISA PC TC. TAC10. 5 rooms with PB. 1 cottage. Breakfast and afternoon tea included in rates. Type of meal: gourmet breakfast. Beds: QT. Phone and air conditioning in room. TV, VCR, fax and library on premises. Weddings, small meetings and family reunions hosted. German spoken. Antiques, parks, shopping, downhill skiing, sporting events and theater nearby.

Location: Walking distance to the University of Arizona.

Publicity: *Gourmet, Los Angeles Times, USA Today, Travel & Leisure, Channel 4 Television.*

"Thank you so much for such a beautiful home, romantic room and warm hospitality."

The Peppertrees B&B Inn

724 E University Blvd
Tucson, AZ 85719-5045
(520)622-7167 (800)348-5763

Circa 1905. Inside this historic home, you will find English antiques inherited from the innkeeper's family. There is a patio filled with flowers and a fountain. Each of two newly built Southwestern-style guest houses features two bedrooms, two bathrooms, a kitchen, laundry and a private patio. Blue-corn pecan pancakes and Scottish shortbread are house specialties. Peppertrees is within walking distance to the university, shops, theaters, museums and restaurants.

Innkeeper(s): Marjorie G. Martin. $68-165. EP. MC VISA DS. 6 rooms, 3 with PB. 2 suites. Breakfast included in rates. Types of meals: full breakfast and gourmet breakfast. Beds: KQT. Phone and ceiling fan in room. Weddings, small meetings and family reunions hosted. Shopping, sporting events, theater and watersports nearby.

Publicity: *Tucson Guide, Travel Age West, Country, Tucson Homes & Gardens, Sunset, Tucson Lifestyle.*

"We have not yet stopped telling our friends what a wonderful experience we shared at your lovely home."

Arkansas

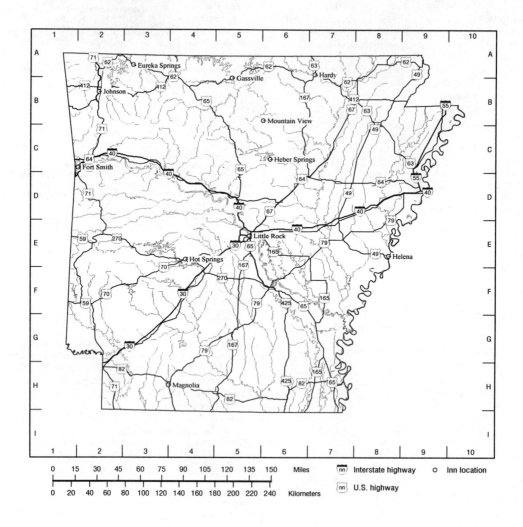

	Miles
0 15 30 45 60 75 90 105 120 135 150	
0 20 40 60 80 100 120 140 160 180 200 220 240	Kilometers

nn Interstate highway   ○ Inn location
nn U.S. highway

Eureka Springs   A3

5 Ojo Inn B&B

5 Ojo St
Eureka Springs, AR 72632-3220
(501)253-6734 (800)656-6734

Circa 1891. Guests at 5 Ojo choose between lodging in cottages or in one of two restored Victorian homes, the Ojo House and the Sweet House. Rooms are decorated with antiques, but

include modern amenities such as refrigerators and coffee makers. Several rooms include whirlpool tubs and two offer fireplaces. The Carriage House Cottage and the Anniversary Suite are ideal places for

honeymooners or those celebrating a special occasion. Among its romantic amenities, the Anniversary Suite includes a private porch with a swing. Gourmet breakfasts are served in the Sweet House's dining room, but private dining can be arranged.

Innkeeper(s): Paula Adkins. $64-139. MC VISA PC TC. TAC10. 10 rooms with PB, 2 with FP. 3 suites. 2 cottages. 1 conference room. Breakfast included in rates. Type of meal: full breakfast. Beds: KDT. Air conditioning, ceiling fan and TV in room. VCR, spa and library on premises. Weddings, small meetings and family reunions hosted. Amusement parks, antiques, fishing, parks, shopping, sporting events, theater and watersports nearby.

Location: Six-minute walk to shops and galleries of America's Victorian Village.

"If this inn hasn't made the Country Inn Magazine, it should be on the list."

Basin Park Hotel

12 Spring St
Eureka Springs, AR 72632
(501)253-7837 (800)643-4972 Fax:(501)253-6985
E-mail: basinprk@ipa.net

Circa 1904. This is a historic hotel, located in the heart of the historic downtown area, in a large multi-storied brownstone building that has operated continuously as a hotel for almost a century. Among the hotel's 61 rooms are both Jacuzzi suites and family rooms furnished with some antiques. Although breakfast is not included in the rate, room service is available, and the hotel has its own balcony restaurant.

Innkeeper(s): Marty & Elise Roeniak. $48-150. EP. MC VISA AX DC DS PC TC. TAC10. 61 rooms with PB. Breakfast included in rates. Type of meal: full breakfast. Lunch, banquet service, catered breakfast and room service available. Restaurant on premises. Beds: KD. Phone, air conditioning, ceiling fan and TV in room. VCR, fax and copier on premises. Handicap access. Weddings, small meetings, family reunions and seminars hosted. Antiques, fishing, parks, shopping, golf, theater and watersports nearby.

Pets Allowed.

Bridgeford House B&B

263 Spring St
Eureka Springs, AR 72632-3154
(501)253-7853 (888)567-2422 Fax:(501)253-5497
E-mail: bridgefordbb@earthlink.net

Circa 1884. This peach-colored Victorian delight is nestled in the heart of the Eureka Springs Historic District and close to many shops. Rooms feature queen-size beds with private baths,

antiques and are decorated in a wonderfully charming Victorian style. Guests will enjoy fresh, hot coffee and a selection of teas in their suites. A bountiful Southern-style breakfast is the perfect way to start the day. Enjoy the horse-drawn carriage rides down Eureka Springs' famed boulevard with its stately Victorian homes.

Historic Interest: Pea Ridge National Park (30 min.), War Eagle Mill & Cavern (30 min.), North Arkansas Railway (1 block).

Innkeeper(s): Henry & Linda Thornton. $85-105. MC VISA AX DS. 4 rooms with PB. 1 suite. Breakfast and afternoon tea included in rates. Types of meals: full breakfast and early coffee/tea. Evening snack and room service available. Beds: QT. Air conditioning, ceiling fan and TV in room. VCR on premises. Weddings, small meetings, family reunions and seminars hosted. Antiques, fishing, shopping, golf, theater and watersports nearby.

Location: North one mile on 62B in Eureka Springs Historic District.

Publicity: *Times Echo Flashlight, Arkansas National Tour Guide.*

"You have created an enchanting respite for weary people."

Candlestick Cottage

6 Douglas St
Eureka Springs, AR 72632-3416
(501)253-6813 (800)835-5184
E-mail: candleci@ipa.net

Circa 1888. Woods and foliage surround this scenic country home, nestled just a few blocks from Eureka Springs historic district. Guests are sure to discover a variety of wildlife strolling by the home, including an occasional deer. Breakfasts are served on the tree-top porch, which overlooks a waterfall and fish pond. The morning meal begins with freshly baked muffins and fresh fruit, followed by an entree. Innkeepers Bill and Patsy Brooks will prepare a basket of sparkling grape juice and wine glasses for those celebrating a special occasion. Guest rooms are decorated in Victorian style, and some include two-person Jacuzzis.

Innkeeper(s): Bill & Patsy Brooks. $65-109. MC VISA AX DS TC. 6 rooms with PB. Breakfast included in rates. Type of meal: full breakfast. Beds: QF. Air conditioning and TV in room. Weddings and small meetings hosted. Antiques, fishing, parks and shopping nearby.

Cliff Cottage & The Place Next Door, A Bed & Breakfast Inn

42 Armstrong St
Eureka Springs, AR 72632-3608
(501)253-7409 (800)799-7409
E-mail: Cliffctg@aol.com

Circa 1892. In the heart of Historic Downtown, this Painted Lady Eastlake Victorian is listed in the National Register of Historic Places. A favorite among honeymooners, accommodations also are available in a Victorian replica named The Place Next Door. Guest rooms include a double Jacuzzi, mini-refrigerator stocked with complimentary champagne and beverages, and all rooms have private decks. The inn offers gourmet candlelight dinners, Victorian picnic lunches and sunset dinner cruises served aboard a 24-foot pontoon boat, which explores the area's romantic coves. Guests enjoy golf and tennis privileges at Holiday Island, which is located five miles away. In 1997, the inn received the "Garden of the Season" award.

Innkeeper(s): Sandra Smith. $105-165. MC VISA PC. TAC10. 5 rooms with PB. 3 suites. Breakfast included in rates. Types of meals: gourmet breakfast and early coffee/tea. Evening snack, picnic lunch and room service available. Beds: KQ. Air conditioning, ceiling fan, TV and VCR in room. Weddings, small meetings, family reunions and seminars hosted. French, Spanish and German spoken. Antiques, fishing, parks, shopping, theater and watersports nearby.

Publicity: *Arkansas Democrat Gazette, Country Inns, Modern Bride.*

Crescent Cottage Inn

211 Spring St
Eureka Springs, AR 72632-3153
(501)253-6022 (800)223-3246 Fax:(501)253-6234
E-mail: raphael@ipa.net

Circa 1881. This Victorian inn was home to the first governor of Arkansas after the Civil War. Two long verandas overlook a

breathtaking valley and two mountain ranges. The home is graced by a beautiful tower, spindlework and coffered ceilings. A huge arch joins the dining and living rooms, which, like the rest of the inn, are filled with antiques. Four of the guest rooms feature whirlpool spas, and two have a fireplace. The inn is situated on the quiet, residential end of the historic loop. A five-minute walk into town takes guests past limestone cliffs, tall maple trees, gardens and refreshing springs. Try a ride on the steam engine train that departs nearby.

Historic Interest: Excluding a few new areas, the entire town of Eureka Springs is a National Historic District and filled with beautiful homes, buildings and shops to explore. The Crescent Cottage is listed on the National Register and designated as a state and city landmark.

Innkeeper(s): Ralph & Phyllis Becker. $94-132. MC VISA DS PC TC. TAC10. 4 rooms with PB, 2 with FP. 1 suite. Breakfast included in rates. Types of meals: full breakfast and early coffee/tea. Beds: Q. Phone, air conditioning, ceiling fan, TV and VCR in room. Fax and copier on premises. Weddings and family reunions hosted. Spanish, some Portuguese and little German spoken. Amusement parks, antiques, fishing, parks, shopping, sporting events, golf, theater and watersports nearby.

Publicity: *Country Homes, Country Inns, Minneapolis Tribune, Fort Lauderdale News, America's Painted Ladies.*

"You gave us a piece of heaven. We will never forget what we dreamed of."

Crescent Hotel

Prospect St
Eureka Springs, AR 72632
(501)253-9766 (800)342-9766 Fax:(501)253-5296
E-mail: basinprk@ipa.net

Circa 1886. This Eureka Springs landmark Victorian inn offers fine lodging and dining to its guests. Guest rooms vary in decor, ranging from historic to Victorian. Some rooms boast king beds, refrigerators and other amenities. The inn is equipped to handle meetings, receptions and weddings, and guests will find many areas for relaxing and socializing, including a swimming pool.

Innkeeper(s): Marty & Elise Roeniak. $45-145. MAP. MC VISA AX DC DS PC TC. TAC10. 68 rooms with PB. Type of meal: full breakfast. Dinner, lunch, banquet service, catering service, catered breakfast and room service available. Restaurant on premises. Beds: KQDT. Phone, air conditioning, ceiling fan and TV in room. VCR, fax, copier, swimming and pet boarding on premises. Handicap access. 13 acres. Weddings, small meetings, family reunions and seminars hosted. Antiques, fishing, parks, shopping, sporting events, golf, theater and watersports nearby.

Pets Allowed.

Heart of The Hills Inn

5 Summit
Eureka Springs, AR 72632
(501)253-7468 (800)253-7468

Circa 1883. Two suites and a Victorian cottage comprise this antique-furnished homestead located just four blocks from

downtown. Suites have been restored and decorating in an 1880s style. The cottage is located beside the inn and is decorated in Victorian-country style. The cottage also offers a private deck that overlooks the garden. The village trolley stops at the inn, but the inn is within walking distance of town.

Innkeeper(s): James & Kathy Vanzandt. $95-125. MC VISA AX PC TC. 3 rooms with PB. 2 suites. 1 cottage. Breakfast and evening snack included in rates. Types of meals: gourmet breakfast and early coffee/tea. Beds: KD. Phone, air conditioning, turndown service, ceiling fan and TV in room. Spa and library on premises. Handicap access. Small meetings and family reunions hosted. Antiques, fishing, shopping, golf, theater and watersports nearby.

Location: On the historic loop.

Publicity: *Carroll County Tribune's Peddler.*

"The decor and atmosphere of your inn was breathtaking; we were able to relax and not want for a thing."

The Heartstone Inn & Cottages

35 King's Hwy
Eureka Springs, AR 72632-3534
(501)253-8916 (800)494-4921 Fax:(501)253-6821

Circa 1903. Described as a "pink and white confection," this handsomely restored Victorian with its wraparound verandas is located in the historic district. The award-winning inn is filled with antiques and artwork from the innkeeper's native England. Live music is featured: in May, a fine arts festival and in September, a jazz festival. Afternoon refreshments are available on the sunny deck overlooking a wooded ravine. Pink roses line the picket fence surrounding the inviting garden.

Historic Interest: Pea Ridge Civil War Battle Ground (20 miles), War Eagle Mill (20 miles).

Innkeeper(s): Iris & Bill Simantel. $65-120. MC VISA AX DS PC TC. TAC10. 12 rooms with PB, 1 with FP. 3 suites. 2 cottages. Breakfast included in rates. Type of meal: gourmet breakfast. Beds: KQ. Air conditioning, ceiling fan and TV in room. Fax and spa on premises. Weddings, small meetings, family reunions and seminars hosted. Amusement parks, antiques, fishing, parks, shopping, theater and watersports nearby.

Location: Northwest Arkansas, Ozarks.

Publicity: *Innsider, Arkansas Times, New York Times, Arkansas Gazette, Southern Living, Country Home, Country Inns.*

"Extraordinary! Best breakfasts anywhere!"

Singleton House B&B

11 Singleton St
Eureka Springs, AR 72632-3026
(501)253-9111 (800)833-3394

Circa 1895. This pink Queen Anne Victorian is highlighted with bird-shaped exterior brackets. Guest rooms are whimsically decorated with an eclectic collection of folk art and antique family treasures. Breakfast is served on the balcony overlooking a wildflower garden, lily-filled goldfish pond and scenic wooded view. Created by a local artist, the garden features a unique birdhouse collection and stone paths that wind through arches and arbors. Guests may stroll one block down a wooded footpath to shops and restaurants, ride the trolley

through town or enjoy a ride to town in the house carriage.

Innkeeper(s): Barbara Gavron. $65-105. MC VISA AX DS PC TC. TAC10. 5 rooms with PB. 2 suites. 1 cottage. Breakfast and afternoon tea included in rates. Types of meals: full breakfast and early coffee/tea. Beds: QDT. Phone, air conditioning, ceiling fan and TV in room. Fax, copier and library on premises. Weddings and family reunions hosted. Spanish spoken. Antiques, fishing, parks, shopping, golf, theater and watersports nearby.

Publicity: *Arkansas Gazette, The Houston Post, The Wichita Eagle-Beacon.*

"All the many little surprises were so much fun. We enjoyed the quietness of sitting on the porch and walking through your garden."

Sleepy Hollow Inn

92 S Main
Eureka Springs, AR 72632
(501)253-5561

Circa 1904. This three-story Victorian cottage with gingerbread trim serves as an ideal accommodation for honeymooners or those in search of privacy and romance. There are two bedrooms, a luxury suite and a third-story guest room with antique furnishings. For the ultimate in intimacy and seclusion,

the cottage is offered to one or two couples at a time, so they are free to relax and enjoy the home. Guests can soak in the antique clawfoot tub or snuggle up on the romantic porch swing. There is a well-equipped kitchen stocked with pastries and other treats. Chilled champagne can be provided for those celebrating a special occasion. The grounds are dotted with gardens. The village's histori-cal museum is across the street, and restaurants, galleries and shops are just a short walk away. The inn offers an ideal setting for weddings, receptions and retreats.

$110. MC VISA DS PC. 3 rooms, 1 with PB. 1 suite. Types of meals: continental breakfast and early coffee/tea. Beds: D. Phone, air conditioning, ceiling fan, TV and VCR in room. Antiques, fishing, parks, shopping, theater and watersports nearby.

"Truly a delightful experience. The love and care going into this journey back in time is impressive."

Sunnyside Inn

5 Ridgeway Ave
Eureka Springs, AR 72632-3024
(501)253-6638

Circa 1883. Beautifully renovated, this National Register Queen Anne Victorian is located three blocks from town. Traditional Victorian decor is especially outstanding in the Rose Room with a carved, high oak bed and original rose stained-glass windows. The Honeymoon Suite features an Abe Lincoln-era carved walnut bed with matching bureau.

Innkeeper(s): Gladys R. Foris. $69-119. TC. 7 rooms with PB. 1 conference room. Breakfast included in rates. Type of meal: continental breakfast. Beds: Q. Air conditioning in room. TV and VCR on premises. Small meetings and family reunions hosted. Antiques, fishing, parks, shopping and theater nearby.

"The best weekend of our lives."

Fort Smith C2

Michael's Mansion

2900 Rogers Ave
Fort Smith, AR 72901
(501)494-3700 Fax:(501)494-5674

Circa 1904. In the National Register, this massive three-story house (10,000 square feet) is a blend of Greek, Romanesque and Renaissance Revival architecture. Located on more than an acre, the inn is known locally as the Horace Franklin Rogers home. Guest rooms are named after the innkeeper's family and decorated accordingly. There are two honeymoon suites with whirlpool tubs for two. One of the suites offers a balcony, while the two-bedroom suite has a fireplace. A continental breakfast features bagels, muffins, fruit, cereal, Danish and a variety of jellys.

Innkeeper(s): Michael & Lynnette "Lynn" Moore. $57-127. MC VISA AX DC CB DS TC. 5 rooms with PB, 1 with FP. 1 suite. 1 conference room. Breakfast included in rates. Type of meal: continental-plus breakfast. Beds: QD. Phone, air conditioning, ceiling fan, TV and VCR in room. Fax, copier and library on premises. Handicap access. Weddings, small meetings, family reunions and seminars hosted. Antiques, fishing, parks, shopping, golf and theater nearby.

Gassville
B5

Lithia Springs B&B

593 Hwy 126 N
Gassville, AR 72635
(870)435-6100

Circa 1890. Set on 39 acres of meadows and woods, this inn with country decor is located between two fishing and boating lakes. Blanchard Springs Caverns, Silver Dollar City, Eureka Springs and the White and Buffalo Rivers are also nearby. Even though the springs are no longer active, the inn gained fame in

the late 1800s because of the supposed cures of the medicinal springs. Breakfast can be enjoyed in the dining room or on the large, screened front porch.

Innkeeper(s): Paul & Reita Johnson. $50-70. MC VISA. 5 rooms, 3 with PB. Breakfast included in rates. Type of meal: full breakfast. Beds: QT. Air conditioning in room. TV and VCR on premises. 36 acres. Small meetings, family reunions and seminars hosted. Antiques, fishing, shopping and watersports nearby.

Publicity: *Good Morning America, Baxter Bulletin.*

"It is so peaceful and quiet and you make us feel so welcome."

Hardy
A7

The Olde Stonehouse B&B Inn

511 Main St
Hardy, AR 72542-9034
(501)856-2983 (800)514-2983 Fax:(501)856-4036
E-mail: oldestonehouse@centuryinter.net

Circa 1928. The stone fireplace gracing the comfortable living room of this former banker's home is set with fossils and unusual stones, including an Arkansas diamond. Lace tablecloths, china and silver make breakfast a special occasion. Each room is decorated to keep the authentic feel of the Roaring '20s. The bedrooms have antiques and ceiling fans. Aunt Jenny's room boasts a clawfoot tub and a white iron bed, while Aunt Bette's room is filled with Victorian-era furniture. Spring River is only one block away and offers canoeing, boating and fishing. Old Hardy Town caters to antique and craft lovers. The innkeepers offer "Secret Suites," located in a nearby historic home. These romantic suites offer plenty of amenities. Breakfasts

in a basket are delivered to the door each morning. The home is listed in the National Register. Murder-mystery weekends and fly-fishing school and guide are available.

Historic Interest: Olde Hardy Town 19th-Century commercial buildings (2 blocks), Old Court House and Jail (2 blocks), Railroad Station/Museum at Mammoth Springs (18 miles), vintage car museum.

Innkeeper(s): Peggy Volland. $69-99. MC VISA AX DS PC TC. TAC10. 7 rooms with PB, 2 with FP. 2 suites. Breakfast and evening snack included in rates. Types of meals: full breakfast and early coffee/tea. Picnic lunch available. Beds: QDT. Phone, air conditioning and ceiling fan in room. VCR, fax, copier, bicycles and library on premises. Small meetings hosted. Antiques, fishing, parks, shopping, theater and watersports nearby.

Location: In a historic railroad town.

Publicity: *Memphis Commercial Appeal, Jonesboro Sun, Vacations.*

"For many years we had heard about 'Southern Hospitality' but never thought it could be this good. It was the best!"

Heber Springs
C6

Anderson House Inn

201 E Main ST
Heber Springs, AR 72543-3116
(501)362-5266 (800)264-5279 Fax:(501)362-2326
E-mail: innkeeper@cswnet.com

Circa 1880. The original section of this welcoming two-story inn was built by one of Heber Springs' founding citizens. The main structure of the inn was built to house a theater, and the home also has enjoyed use as a schoolhouse, doctor's clinic and, when the second story was added, a hotel. Rooms are decorated in a cozy, country motif with bright colors and handmade prints. Historic Spring Park is just across the street offering pleasant scenery

for the inn's guests as well as a variety of activities.

Innkeeper(s): Jim & Susan Hildebrand. $75-120. MC VISA AX DS PC TC. TAC10. 16 rooms with PB, 1 with FP. 2 conference rooms. Breakfast included in rates. Types of meals: full breakfast and early coffee/tea. Banquet service available. Beds: QDT. Air conditioning and ceiling fan in room. TV, VCR, fax and library on premises. Small meetings, family reunions and seminars hosted. French spoken. Antiques, fishing, parks, shopping and watersports nearby.

Helena
E8

Edwardian Inn

317 S Biscoe
Helena, AR 72342
(870)338-9155 (800)598-4749

Circa 1904. In his book Life on the Mississippi, Mark Twain wrote, "Helena occupies one of the prettiest situations on the river." William Short, cotton broker and speculator, agreed and built his stately home here. The Edwardian Inn boasts a large rotunda and two verandas wrapping around both sides of the house. Inside are wood carpets and floor designs imported from Germany that are composed of 36 pieces of different woods arranged in octagon shapes. Polished-oak paneling and woodwork are set off with a Victorian-era decor.

Innkeeper(s): Marjorie Hornbeck & Olive Ellis. $59-85. MC VISA AX DC CB DS PC TC. TAC10. 12 rooms with PB. 5 suites. 1 conference room. Breakfast included in rates. Types of meals: full breakfast and early coffee/tea. Evening snack and catering service available. Beds: KD. Phone, air conditioning, ceiling fan and TV in room. VCR, fax, copier and library on premises. Weddings, small meetings, family reunions and seminars hosted. Antiques, fishing, parks, shopping and watersports nearby.

Publicity: *Arkansas Times, Dallas Morning News, Southern Living, Country Inns, USA.*

"The Edwardian Inn envelopes you with wonderful feelings, smells and thoughts of the Victorian era."

Hot Springs E4

Williams House Inn

420 Quapaw Ave
Hot Springs, AR 71901-5201
(501)624-4275 (800)756-4635

Circa 1891. Williams House is a brownstone and brick Victorian nestled among towering oaks and a 40-foot tulip tree. Light and airy rooms are filled with antiques and plants. The carriage house, hitching

posts and mounting blocks are still on the property, and the inn is listed in the National Register of Historic Places. Raspberry French toast is popular for breakfast.

Historic Interest: The inn is located in the Quapaw-Prospect Historic District, and the National Park Visitors Center and Bathhouse Row are nearby.

Innkeeper(s): Karen & David Wiseman. $75-95. MC VISA AX. 5 rooms with PB. 2 suites. Type of meal: full breakfast. Beds: QDT. Phone in room. Antiques, fishing, theater and watersports nearby.

Location: Fifty miles southwest of Little Rock, three blocks off Hwy 7.

Publicity: *Los Angeles Times, USA Today, Arkansas Times, Arkansas Democrat, Gazette, Hot Springs B&B.*

Johnson B2

The Inn at the Mill

3906 Greathouse Springs Rd
Johnson, AR 72741
(501)443-1800 Fax:(501)521-8091

Circa 1835. Set on 36 acres in the Ozark Mountains; the Inn at the Mill offers visitors a sophisticated combination of modern amenities and historic ambiance. First open for business in 1835 as the Johnson Mill, it was burned down in the Civil War battle at Pea Ridge in 1862. World renowned architect James Lambeth was responsible for the inn's modern renovation; he was inspired by the works of other noted visionary designers such as Frank Lloyd Wright, Walt Disney, Claude Monet and Frederic Remington. Vaulted ceilings, plush modern and reproduction furnishings, and original hand-hewn beams are present in many of the inn's eight suites and 40 guest rooms. The inn's five-star restaurant, the only one in Arkansas, utilizes fresh, local ingredients in many of it recipes created by Chef Miles James, whose culinary skills have gained attention from the New York Times and Southern Living. Upon arrival, guests are invited to enjoy an offering of wine and cheese enjoyed in the historic lobby or on the deck overlooking the waterwheel and pond. An exquisitely prepared complimentary continental breakfast is served daily.

Innkeeper(s): Mr. & Mrs. James Lambeth. $87-175. AP. MC VISA AX DC CB DS TC. TAC10. 40 rooms. 8 suites. Breakfast and evening snack included in rates. Type of meal: continental breakfast. Lunch available. Restaurant on premises. Beds: KQ. Phone, air conditioning, turndown service, ceiling fan and TV in room. Fax and copier on premises. Handicap access. 36 acres. Weddings, small meetings, family reunions and seminars hosted. Shopping and theater nearby.

Publicity: *New York Times, Southern Living, Country Inns.*

Little Rock E5

The Empress of Little Rock

2120 Louisiana St
Little Rock, AR 72206-1522
(501)374-7966 Fax:(501)375-4537

Circa 1888. Day lilies, peonies and iris accent the old-fashioned garden of this elaborate, three-story Queen Anne Victorian. A grand center hall opens to a double staircase, lit by a stained-glass skylight. The 7,500 square feet include a sitting room at the top of the tower. The original owner kept a private poker game going here and the stained-glass windows allowed him to keep an eye out for local authorities, who might close down his gambling activities. The Hornibrook Room features a magnificent Renaissance Revival bedroom set with a high canopy. The Tower bedroom has an Austrian king-size bed. Gourmet breakfasts are served in the dining room.

Historic Interest: At one time it was the first women's college in the state.

Innkeeper(s): Sharon Welch-Blair. $100-140. MC VISA AX. 5 rooms. 2 suites. Breakfast included in rates. Types of meals: continental breakfast, full breakfast and early coffee/tea. Phone, air conditioning, ceiling fan and TV in room. Weddings, small meetings, family reunions and seminars hosted. Antiques, shopping, sporting events and theater nearby.

Hotze House

1619 Louisiana St
Little Rock, AR 72216
(501)376-6563

Circa 1900. Upon its completion, this grand neoclassic mansion was noted as one of the state's finest homes. Opulent restored woodwork, a fireplace and a staircase carved from a South American mahogany tree grace the impressive front entrance. The home is filled with elegant, period pieces and traditional furnishings. Four of the guest rooms include fireplaces, and despite the turn-of-the-century authenticity, modern amenities of television, telephone and climate control are in each room. The innkeepers strive to make their National Register inn a place for both business travelers and those in search of romance or relaxation. Delectables such as frittatas, poached pears and Belgian waffles are served each morning either in the dining room or conservatory. The innkeepers keep a snack area stocked with hot water, soft drinks, beer, wine, cheese, fruit and the like.

Innkeeper(s): Peggy Tooker, Suzanne & Steve Gates. $90. MC VISA AX DC DS PC TC. TAC10. 4 rooms with PB, 4 with FP. 2 conference rooms. Breakfast included in rates. Types of meals: full breakfast and early coffee/tea. Beds: KQ. Phone, air conditioning, turndown service, ceiling fan and TV in room. VCR, fax, copier and library on premises. Weddings, small meetings, family reunions and seminars hosted. Amusement parks, antiques, parks, shopping, sporting events and theater nearby.

Quapaw Inn

1868 S Gaines St
Little Rock, AR 72206-1232
(501)376-6873 (800)732-5591

Circa 1905. Known as Little Rock's original bed and breakfast, Innkeeper Dottie Woodwind says Bill Clinton jogged past her Colonial Revival inn at 7 a.m. each day for 14 years before leaving for Washington, D.C. The roomy pink house offers a Honeymoon Suite with a fireplace and private entrance. Three guests may be accommodated in Aunt Mary's Room, a country charmer with a unique handmade quilts and antique brass bed. Be sure to inquire about dinner and theater packages.

Innkeeper(s): Dottie Woodwind. Call for rates. 1 suite. Type of meal: continental breakfast. Air conditioning and TV in room. Antiques, shopping, sporting events and theater nearby.

Magnolia   *H4*

Magnolia Place B&B

510 E Main St
Magnolia, AR 71753
(501)234-6122 (800)237-6122 Fax:(501)234-1254
E-mail: magnoliaplace@msn.com

Circa 1910. A prominent Magnolia attorney and his wife were the first to reside in this gracious home, and it remained in the family for three generations. The Four-Square-Craftsman-style home is surely as elegant now as it was in its early days. Polished wood floors, original light fixtures, posh draperies and elegant decor enhance the period furnishings, some of which are family heirlooms. Breakfasts are a formal affair served on a beautiful 1820s table once used by President Harding. Entrees such as eggs Benedict get guests off to a good start, and after breakfast, there's plenty to see and do in Magnolia. Guests can tour historic homes or a historic courthouse, and Lake Columbia, Logoly State Park, a unique artificial marsh designed by NASA, museums, restaurants and shops are nearby.

Innkeeper(s): Carolyne Hawley & Ray Sullivent. $89-99. MC VISA AX DC DS. TAC10. 5 rooms with PB. 1 suite. 1 conference room. Breakfast and evening snack included in rates. Types of meals: full breakfast and early coffee/tea. Beds: Q. Phone, air conditioning, ceiling fan and TV in room. Library on premises. Small meetings hosted. Antiques, fishing, parks, shopping, sporting events and watersports nearby.

Publicity: *Southern Living.*

Mountain View   *B6*

Wildflower B&B

100 Washington St, PO Box 72
Mountain View, AR 72560
(870)269-4383 (800)591-4879

Circa 1918. The inn's wraparound porches are a gathering place for local musicians who often play old-time music. If you sit long enough, you're likely to see an impromptu hootenanny in the Courthouse Square across the street. Since there are no priceless antiques, children are welcome.

Historic Interest: For years it was the only painted structure in town.

Innkeeper(s): LouAnne Rhodes. $42-71. MC VISA AX. 8 rooms, 6 with PB. 3 suites. Breakfast included in rates. Types of meals: continental-plus breakfast and early coffee/tea. Beds: DT. Phone, air conditioning, turndown service and ceiling fan in room. Small meetings, family reunions and seminars hosted. Antiques, fishing, parks, shopping, sporting events, theater and watersports nearby.

Location: In the Ozarks.

Publicity: *New York Times, Dan Rather & CBS, Midwest Living, National Geographic Traveler, Travel Holiday.*

"It's the kind of place you'll look forward to returning to."

California

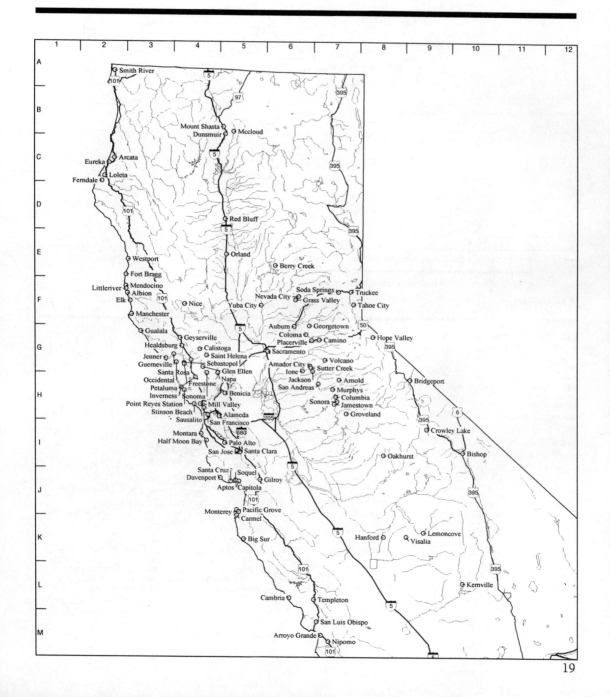

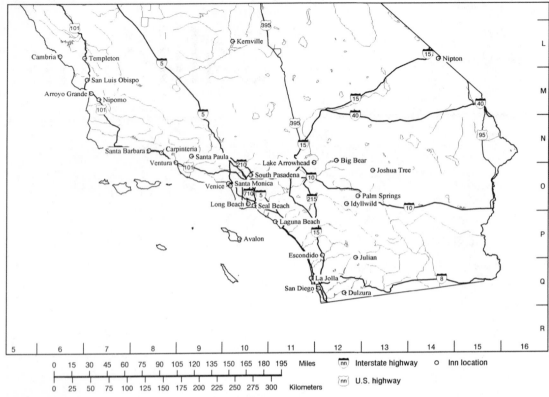

0 15 30 45 60 75 90 105 120 135 150 165 180 195 Miles
0 25 50 75 100 125 150 175 200 225 250 275 300 Kilometers

 Interstate highway   o Inn location
U.S. highway

Alameda   H4

Garratt Mansion

900 Union St
Alameda, CA 94501-4143
(510)521-4779 Fax:(510)521-6796
E-mail: garrattm@pacbell.net

Circa 1893. This handsome, 27-room Colonial Revival mansion was built for industrialist W.T. Garratt. It features walnut
and oak paneling, crystal windows and ornate-manteled fireplaces. The staircase rises three stories with hundreds of
gleaming Jacobean turned balusters. A set of stained-glass windows encircles a bay at the stairwell landing. The elegance of
the mansion is matched by the warmth of its proprietress,
Betty Gladden.

Historic Interest: Unique architecture in neighborhood.

Innkeeper(s): Royce & Betty Gladden. $80-130. MC VISA AX DC PC TC.
TAC10. 7 rooms, 5 with PB, 1 with FP. 1 suite. 1 conference room.
Breakfast and evening snack included in rates. Types of meals: full breakfast
and early coffee/tea. Beds: QDT. Phone and ceiling fan in room. TV, VCR, fax
and library on premises. Weddings and small meetings hosted. Antiques,
parks, sporting events, theater and watersports nearby.

Publicity: *Alameda Times Star, Denver Post.*

"*I can't wait to return as I found an exception to the saying, 'there's
no place like home'.*"

Albion   F3

Fensalden Inn

PO Box 99
Albion, CA 95410-0099
(707)937-4042 (800)959-3850

Circa 1860. Originally a stagecoach station, Fensalden looks
out over the Pacific Ocean as it has for more than 100 years.
The Tavern Room has witnessed many a rowdy scene, and if
you look closely you can see
bullet holes in the
original redwood
ceiling. The inn
provides 20 acres
for walks, whale-
watching, viewing
deer and bicycling.
Relax with wine and
hors d'oeuvres in the evening.

Innkeeper(s): Scott & Frances Brazil. $80-145. MC VISA. TAC10. 8 rooms
with PB, 6 with FP. 3 suites. 2 conference rooms. Breakfast and afternoon
tea included in rates. Types of meals: full breakfast and early coffee/tea.
Beds: KQ. Phone and ceiling fan in room. Handicap access. 20 acres.
Weddings, small meetings, family reunions and seminars hosted. Antiques,
fishing, parks, shopping, theater and watersports nearby.

Location: Seven miles south of Mendocino on Hwy 1.

Publicity: *Sunset, Focus, Peninsula, Country Inns.*

"*Closest feeling to heaven on Earth.*"

Amador City G6

Mine House Inn

PO Box 245
Amador City, CA 95601-0245
(209)267-5900 (800)646-3473

Circa 1870. Mine House Inn was headquarters for one of the most profitable gold mines in the mother lode of 1853, known as the Keystone Mine. Each room in this inn is named for its original function. All are furnished with authentic 19th-century antiques. Rooms include the Vault, Bookkeeping, Directors, Mill Grinding and Assay rooms. Over $24 million of gold was processed into gold bars in the Retort Room. The acre of land surrounding the inn is shaded by 200-year-old oaks and pines. Just steps away is the historic downtown of Amador City with shops and fine restaurants. Within easy driving distance are the towns of Volcano and Columbia.

Historic Interest: Abandoned gold mines, Keystone mine and ruins are across the highway. Knight Foundry in Sutter Creek is two miles away. It is the last operational water-powered foundry in U.S.

Innkeeper(s): Allen & Rose Mendy. $65-110. MC VISA AX DS. 8 rooms with PB. 1 suite. Breakfast included in rates. Type of meal: full breakfast. Beds: KQD. Air conditioning in room. Swimming on premises. Family reunions hosted. Antiques, fishing, shopping, downhill skiing, cross-country skiing, theater and watersports nearby.

Publicity: *Fun Times.*

"We enjoyed the nostalgia and the decor and the challenge of trying to crack the safe."

Aptos J5

Apple Lane Inn

6265 Soquel Dr
Aptos, CA 95003-3117
(408)475-6868 (800)649-8988 Fax:(408)464-5790

Circa 1870. Ancient apple trees border the lane that leads to this Victorian farmhouse set on two acres of gardens and fields.

Built by the Porter brothers, founding fathers of Aptos, the inn is decorated with Victorian wallpapers and hardwood floors. The original wine cellar still exists, as well as the old barn and apple-drying shed used for storage after harvesting the orchard. Miles of beaches are within walking distance of this mini-farm. The innkeepers were married at the inn and later purchased it.

Innkeeper(s): Doug & Diana Groom. $95-150. TAC10. 5 rooms with PB. 2 suites. Breakfast included in rates. Types of meals: full breakfast, gourmet breakfast and early coffee/tea. Afternoon tea and evening snack available. Beds: QDT. Phone in room. TV, fax, library and pet boarding on premises. Handicap access. Weddings, small meetings, family reunions and seminars hosted. Antiques, parks, shopping, sporting events, theater and watersports nearby.

Pets Allowed: Horses in stables, 1 guest room for dogs.

Location: One mile from the beach, five minutes south of Santa Cruz.

Publicity: *Santa Barbara Times, 1001 Decorating Ideas, New York Times.*

"Our room was spotless and beautifully decorated."

Mangels House

570 Aptos Creek Rd, PO Box 302
Aptos, CA 95001
(408)688-7982

Circa 1886. Claus Mangels made his fortune in sugar beets and built this house in the style of a Southern mansion. The inn, with its encircling veranda, stands on four acres of lawns and orchards. It is bounded by the Forest of Nisene Marks, 10,000 acres of redwood trees, creeks and trails. Monterey Bay is three-quarters of a mile away.

Historic Interest: Santa Cruz Mission (6 miles).

Innkeeper(s): Jacquelyn Fisher. $120-160. MC VISA AX. 6 rooms with PB, 1 with FP. 1 conference room. Breakfast included in rates. Types of meals: full breakfast and early coffee/tea. Beds: KQT. Phone in room. Small meetings, family reunions and seminars hosted. Amusement parks, antiques, fishing, shopping, sporting events, theater and watersports nearby.

Location: Central Coast.

Publicity: *Inn Serv, Innviews.*

"Compliments on the lovely atmosphere. We look forward to sharing our discovery with friends and returning with them."

Arcata C2

Hotel Arcata

708 9th St
Arcata, CA 95521-6206
(707)826-0217 (800)344-1221 Fax:(707)826-1737

Circa 1915. This historic landmark hotel is a fine example of Beaux Arts-style architecture. Several rooms overlook Arcata's downtown plaza, which is just across the way. A variety of rooms are available, each decorated in turn-of-the-century style. All rooms include pedestal sinks and clawfoot tubs. The hotel offers a full-service, renown Japanese

restaurant, offering excellent cuisine, and there are many other fine restaurants within walking distance. Guests also enjoy free use of a nearby health club. The starting point of Arcata's architectural homes tour is within walking distance of the hotel.

Innkeeper(s): Virgil Moorehead. $90-180. MC VISA AX DC CB DS TC. 31 rooms with PB. 7 suites. 1 conference room. Breakfast included in rates. Type of meal: continental breakfast. Dinner, lunch, banquet service and room service available. Restaurant on premises. Beds: KQT. Phone and TV in room. Fax and copier on premises. Handicap access. Weddings, small meetings, family reunions and seminars hosted. Antiques, fishing, parks, shopping, sporting events, theater and watersports nearby.

Arnold H7

Lodge at Manuel Mill B&B

PO Box 998
Arnold, CA 95223-0998
(209)795-2622

Circa 1950. Overlooking a three-acre lake that comes right up to the wraparound deck, this log lodge was once the site of a 19th-century lumber mill. Some structures on the property are a century old. The 43 acres of woods include sugar cone pines with 18-inch cones, dogwood and wild blackberries, and traces of the mill's gauge rail system. Sounds of the 24-foot waterfall that cascades over rocks may be heard from the rooms that open to the deck. The Lottie Crabtree Room, named for a spirited performer in the Gold Rush days, is a peaceful, cozy retreat. The Mr. Manuel Room basks in 19th-century ambiance with an oak canopy bed and Victorian decor. The innkeepers prepare a hearty breakfast and present guests with a bottle of wine upon arrival. Martha Stewart-type weddings are popular here. Calaveras Big Trees State Park, known for its giant sequoias, is nearby.

Historic Interest: The surrounding area offers several old gold mining towns to visit.

Innkeeper(s): Linda Johnson. $100-135. MC VISA. 5 rooms with PB. 1 suite. Breakfast included in rates. Type of meal: full breakfast. Picnic lunch and catering service available. Beds: KQD. Swimming on premises. Fishing, downhill skiing, cross-country skiing and watersports nearby.

Arroyo Grande M7

Crystal Rose Inn

789 Valley Rd
Arroyo Grande, CA 93420-4417
(805)481-1854 (800)767-3466 Fax:(805)481-9541

Circa 1890. Once the homestead for a large walnut farm, this picturesque Victorian inn features an acre and a half of gardens. The inn is decorated with period pieces and reproductions. The gardens are a favorite setting for weddings. Guests are pampered with afternoon tea, evening wine and hors d'oeuvres and full, gourmet breakfast. The inn also houses The Hunt Club, a restaurant serving lunch, dinner and Sunday brunch.

Historic Interest: Hearst Castle (1 hour).

Innkeeper(s): Bonnie Royster. $95-185. MAP. MC VISA AX DS. 8 rooms, 5 with PB. 3 suites. 1 conference room. Breakfast, afternoon tea and evening snack included in rates. Type of meal: full breakfast. Dinner, picnic lunch, lunch, catering service and room service available. Restaurant on premises. Beds: KQDT. Phone in room. Handicap access. Weddings hosted. Antiques, fishing, theater and watersports nearby.

Location: Halfway between Los Angeles and San Francisco off Highway 101.

Publicity: *Los Angeles Times, Daughters of Painted Ladies, Travel, Five Cities Times-Press Recorder, Santa Maria Times, Telegram Tribune, Travel & Leisure, Woman's World.*

"What a wonderful magical experience we had at the Crystal Rose. We chose the beautiful Queen Elizabeth room with the enchanted tower. Our romantic interlude was just perfect."

Auburn G6

Powers Mansion Inn

164 Cleveland Ave
Auburn, CA 95603-4801
(530)885-1166 Fax:(530)885-1386

Circa 1898. This elegant Victorian mansion was built by Harold Power with the proceeds from his gold mine. Many prominent people, including engineer Herbert Hoover, visited here. The parlor and the second floor halls contain notes and memorabilia concerning its history. The luxury of the inn is typified by the honeymoon suite, which has a heart-shaped tub and a fireplace at the foot of the brass bed.

Innkeeper(s): Arno & Jean Lejnieks. $79-160. MC VISA AX. 13 rooms with PB, 2 with FP. 1 conference room. Type of meal: full breakfast. Beds: Q. Spa on premises.

Location: In the heart of downtown.

Publicity: *Sierra Heritage Magazine.*

"The rooms are so relaxing and the breakfast is fantastic."

Avalon P10

Catalina Island Seacrest Inn

PO Box 128, 201 Claressa Ave
Avalon, CA 90704-0128
(310)510-0800 Fax:(310)510-1122
E-mail: catisle@catalinas.net

Circa 1910. The unique and romantic setting of Catalina Island is home to this inn, just a block from the ocean. The inn, completely renovated in 1997, enjoys tremendous popularity with honeymooners, who love the in-room whirlpools and tubs for two offered in many of the guest rooms. The inn, home of Catalina Island Weddings, often hosts weddings and offers special packages, including round-trip transportation to the island and many other extras. Many guests enjoy exploring Avalon's shops and sights.

Innkeeper(s): Michele Prevatt. $65-185. MC VISA DC CB DS TC. TAC10. 8 rooms with PB, 4 with FP. 6 suites. Breakfast included in rates. Type of meal: continental breakfast. Beds: KQ. Air conditioning, ceiling fan, TV and VCR in room. Fax on premises. Weddings and family reunions hosted. Fishing, parks, shopping and watersports nearby.

Publicity: *Good Housekeeping.*

Benicia H5

The Painted Lady

141 E F St
Benicia, CA 94510-3226
(707)746-1646

Circa 1898. This folk Victorian, located two blocks from the water, is close to the town's historic landmarks, and you can walk to cafes and shops, or take the paths to the Carquinez Straits and the harbor. The Rosario Room has antique furniture with a soft yellow background and climbing roses. The Daisy Room features a whirlpool tub in its bath. It's 15 minutes to the ferry to San Francisco's waterfront and Napa Valley is a half-hour drive.

Innkeeper(s): Sally Watson. Call for rates. Turndown service and ceiling fan in room. Weddings and family reunions hosted. Amusement parks, antiques and shopping nearby.

Berry Creek E6

Lake Oroville Bed and Breakfast

240 Sunday Dr
Berry Creek, CA 95916-9640
(916)589-0700 (800)455-5253 Fax:(916)589-5313

Circa 1970. Situated in the quiet foothills above Lake Oroville, this country inn features panoramic views from the private porches that extend from each guest room. Two favorite rooms

are the Rose Petal Room and the Victorian Room, both with lake views and whirlpool tubs. The inn's 40 acres are studded with oak and pine trees. Deer and songbirds abound.

Innkeeper(s): Cheryl & Ron Damberger. $75-135. MC VISA AX DS PC TC. 6 rooms with PB. 1 conference room. Breakfast included in rates. Types of meals: full breakfast and early coffee/tea. Banquet service available. Beds: KQ. Phone, air conditioning, turndown service, ceiling fan, TV and VCR in room. Fax, copier, spa, library, pet boarding and child care on premises. Handicap access. 40 acres. Weddings, small meetings, family reunions and seminars hosted. French and Spanish spoken. Antiques, fishing, parks, shopping, golf, theater and watersports nearby.

Pets Allowed: On approval with fee.

Location: Twenty minutes out of Oroville in the foothills above the lake.

Publicity: Oroville Mercury-Register, Chronicle, San Joe Mercury. Ratings: 4 Diamonds.

Big Bear N12

Gold Mountain Manor Historic B&B

1117 Anita, PO Box 2027
Big Bear, CA 92314
(909)585-6997 (800)509-2604 Fax:(909)585-0327
E-mail: goldmtn@bigbear.com

Circa 1928. This spectacular log mansion was once a hideaway for the rich and famous. Eight fireplaces provide a roaring fire in each room in fall and winter. The Lucky Baldwin Room offers a hearth made from stones gathered in the famous Lucky Baldwin mine nearby. In the Clark Gable room is the fireplace Gable and Carole Lombard enjoyed on their honeymoon. Gourmet country breakfasts and afternoon hors d'oeuvres are served. In addition to the guest rooms, there are three cabins.

Historic Interest: Small Historic Museum in Big Bear City (1 mile) and gold mining.

Innkeeper(s): Robert Angilella & Jose Tapia. $125-190. MC VISA DS. TAC10. 6 rooms with PB, 6 with FP. 2 suites. 3 cottages. 1 conference room. Afternoon tea and evening snack included in rates. Types of meals: full breakfast, gourmet breakfast and early coffee/tea. Beds: Q. Ceiling fan in room. TV, VCR, fax, spa, bicycles and library on premises. Weddings,

small meetings, family reunions and seminars hosted. Spanish spoken. Fishing, parks, downhill skiing, cross-country skiing, sporting events and watersports nearby.

Location: Two hours northeast of Los Angeles and Orange counties.

Publicity: Best Places to Kiss, Fifty Most Romantic Places, Kenny G holiday album cover.

"A majestic experience! In this magnificent house, history comes alive!"

Big Sur K5

Deetjen's Big Sur Inn

Highway One
Big Sur, CA 93920
(408)667-2377

Circa 1938. Norwegians Helmut and Helen Deetjen built these casual, rustic rooms on several acres of a redwood canyon. Today they are managed by a non-profit corporation and provide employment for local residents. Two rooms overlook a bubbling stream. Some have fireplaces and down comforters. The inn's restaurant is open daily. The adventurous will appreciate the setting and the whimsy, but the rustic nature of the accommodations may not be for everyone.

Innkeeper(s): Laura Moran. $65-150. EP. 20 rooms, 15 with PB. Beds: QDT. Handicap access.

Location: Twenty-eight miles south of Carmel.

Publicity: New York Times, California Magazine.

"Like stepping back in time, so unique and charming."

Bishop I10

The Matlick House

1313 Rowan Ln
Bishop, CA 93514-1937
(760)873-3133 (800)898-3133

Circa 1906. This gray and pink home with a double veranda was built by Alan Matlick, one of the area's pioneers. The spacious parlor features a clawfoot settee with massive curved arms, antique recliner, European burled-wood armoire and original cherry-wood fireplace. Rooms boast special pieces such as the white iron bed, Eastlake chair and quilted settee in the Lenna room. Guests will enjoy the home's views of both the Sierra Nevadas and the White Mountains. A hearty American breakfast with eggs, bacon and homemade biscuits is served in the dining room. The Eastern Sierras provide a wealth of activities, year-round catch-and-release fly fishing is within 20 minutes from the home.

Historic Interest: Laws Museum is only three miles away. For an entertaining day trip, try Bodie Ghost Town, which is about 90 miles from the inn.

Innkeeper(s): Ray & Barbara Showalter. $79-89. MC VISA AX DS TC. TAC10. 5 rooms with PB. Breakfast and evening snack included in rates. Types of meals: continental-plus breakfast, full breakfast and early coffee/tea. Picnic lunch, lunch and catering service available. Beds: QT. Phone, air conditioning and ceiling fan in room. TV, VCR and fax on premises. Weddings, small meetings, family reunions and seminars hosted. Antiques, fishing, parks, shopping, downhill skiing and cross-country skiing nearby.

Publicity: Inyo Register, Sunset.

"Like sleeping on a nice pink cloud after our Rock Creek Horse drive."

Bridgeport   H9

The Cain House

340 Main St, PO Box 454
Bridgeport, CA 93517
(760)932-7040 (800)433-2246 Fax:(760)932-7419

Circa 1920. The grandeur of the Eastern Sierra Mountains is the perfect setting for evening refreshments as the sun sets, turning the sky into a fiery, purple canvas. The innkeeper's experiences while traveling around the world have influenced The Cain House's decor to give the inn a European elegance with a casual western atmosphere. Travelers can take a short drive to the ghost town of Bodie where 10,000 people once lived in this gold-mining community. Outdoor enthusiasts can find an abundance of activity at Lake Tahoe, which is an hour-and-a-half away.

Innkeeper(s): Chris & Marachal Gohlich. $80-135. MC VISA AX DC CB DS PC TC. TAC10. 7 rooms with PB. Breakfast and evening snack included in rates. Type of meal: full breakfast. Beds: KQ. Air conditioning and TV in room. Fax on premises. Family reunions hosted. Fishing and shopping nearby.
Location: Eastern Sierra Mountains.

Calistoga   G4

Calistoga Wayside Inn

1523 Foothill Blvd
Calistoga, CA 94515-1619
(707)942-0645 (800)845-3632 Fax:(707)942-4169

Circa 1928. The woodsy grounds at this Spanish-style hacienda include a waterfall, which cascades into a picturesque pond. Guests can enjoy the soothing sounds of water fountains from

their rooms, which are decorated in a garden theme. The Delaney Room includes a private balcony with wicker furnishings. Down comforters, special soaps and robes are a few of the thoughtful amenities. The two-course, country breakfast is a perfect start to a day touring the popular Napa Valley. Wine and cheese is served in the afternoon. The Wayside Inn is within walking distance to Calistoga's famed spas. The innkeepers can help guests plan wine-tasting tours as well as glider or hot air balloon rides.

Innkeeper(s): Tom & Jan Balcer. $100-155. MC VISA AX DS PC TC. TAC10. 3 rooms with PB. Breakfast included in rates. Types of meals: full breakfast and early coffee/tea. Beds: KQ. Air conditioning and ceiling fan in room. Fax and library on premises. Weddings, small meetings and family reunions hosted. Antiques, parks and shopping nearby.

"This was my first stay at a B&B and now, certainly the first of many."

Foothill House

3037 Foothill Blvd
Calistoga, CA 94515-1225
(707)942-6933 (800)942-6933 Fax:(707)942-5692

Circa 1892. This country farmhouse overlooks the western foothills of Mount St. Helena. Graceful old California oaks and

pockets of flowers greet guests. Each room features country antiques, a four-poster bed, a fireplace and a small refrigerator. Breakfast is served in the sun room or is delivered personally to your room in a basket. Three rooms offer private Jacuzzi tubs.

Historic Interest: Old Faithful Geyser (1 mile), Petrified Forrest (3 mile).
Innkeeper(s): Doris & Gus Beckert. $150-300. MC VISA AX DS PC TC. TAC10. 4 suites, 4 with FP. Breakfast and evening snack included in rates. Types of meals: full breakfast, gourmet breakfast and early coffee/tea. Beds: KQT. Phone, air conditioning, turndown service, ceiling fan, TV and VCR in room. Fax, copier and library on premises. Weddings, small meetings and family reunions hosted. Amusement parks, antiques, fishing, parks, shopping and watersports nearby.
Location: Napa Valley.
Publicity: Herald Examiner, Baltimore Sun, Sunset, San Francisco Examiner.

"Gourmet treats served in front of an open fire. Hospitality never for a moment flagged."

The Pink Mansion

1415 Foothill Blvd
Calistoga, CA 94515-1617
(707)942-0558 (800)238-7465 Fax:(707)942-0558

Circa 1875. Painted pink in the 1930s by the innkeeper's Aunt Alma, the Pink Mansion as it became known, was originally built by William Fisher, who established Calistoga's first stage line. Here he cleared the mountainside, established vineyards and dug wine caves. Aunt Alma's collections of Victorian and Oriental items, including cherubs and angels, are placed throughout the inn. Views of woodlands and Mount St. Helena may be enjoyed from the guest rooms. There is a heated indoor pool and spa, which are ideal for those who enjoy a late-night swim.

Innkeeper(s): Toppa & Leslie Epps. $95-195. MC VISA AX. 6 rooms with PB, 3 with FP. 3 suites. Breakfast included in rates. Type of meal: full breakfast. Catering service and room service available. Beds: Q. Phone in room. Spa and bicycles on premises.

"Our best B&B find in the USA."

Scarlett's Country Inn

3918 Silverado Trl
Calistoga, CA 94515-9611
(707)942-6669 Fax:(707)942-6669
E-mail: scarletts@aol.com

Circa 1900. Formerly a winter campground of the Wappo Indians, the property now includes a restored farmhouse. There are green lawns and country vistas of woodland and vineyards. Each room has a private entrance. Breakfast is often served beneath the apple trees or poolside.

Historic Interest: Old Bale Mill (2 miles), Beringer and Charles Krug Wineries (4 miles), Schramsberg Champagne Cellars (2 miles), Sharpstein Museum (4 miles), graveyard in Boothe State Park (2 miles).

Innkeeper(s): Scarlett Dwyer. $95-175. PC. TAC10. 3 rooms with PB, 1 with FP. 2 suites. 1 cottage. Breakfast and afternoon tea included in rates. Types of meals: full breakfast, gourmet breakfast and early coffee/tea. Room service available. Beds: Q. Phone, air conditioning and turndown service in room. TV, fax, copier and swimming on premises. Small meetings and family reunions hosted. Spanish spoken. Antiques, fishing, parks, shopping and watersports nearby.

Location: Napa Valley wine country.

Publicity: *Daily News.*

"Wonderful, peaceful, serene."

Trailside Inn

4201 Silverado Trl
Calistoga, CA 94515-9605
(707)942-4106 Fax:(707)942-4702

Circa 1932. This secluded valley farmhouse overlooks Three Palms Vineyard and the distant Sterling Winery. Each accommodation is a tastefully decorated suite with its own porch, private entrance, small kitchen, private bath and fireplace. Furnished with country antiques and old quilts, two suites have an extra bedroom to accommodate a family of four. House specialties are banana and blueberry breads, freshly baked and brought to your room.

Historic Interest: Robert Louis Stevenson State Park (3 miles), Beringer Winery (4 miles), Calistoga (3 miles).

Innkeeper(s): Randy & Lani Gray. $185. MC VISA AX DS. 3 suites, 3 with FP. Breakfast included in rates. Type of meal: continental-plus breakfast. Beds: QDT. Phone in room. Swimming on premises.

Location: Napa Valley.

Publicity: *San Francisco Examiner, Wine Country Review.*

"If Dorothy and Toto were to click their heals together they would end up at the Trailside Inn."

Wisteria Garden B&B

1508 Fair Way
Calistoga, CA 94515-1300
(707)942-5358 Fax:(707)942-6442
E-mail: WisteriaGarden@worldnet.att.net

Circa 1910. Guests at Wisteria Garden stay in one of two spacious rooms, both of which are located in the courtyard away from the historic main house and under the shade of a 150-year-old Wisteria tree. The Fuschia Cottage can accommodate more than four guests and includes a bedroom and living room area. The Wisteria Room can accommodate up to four guests. Both rooms are furnished with antiques, and include modern amenities such as refrigerators and gas fireplaces. The bed & breakfast is within walking distance to downtown Calistoga.

Innkeeper(s): Carmen Maib. $100-150. MC VISA AX. TAC10. 2 rooms with PB. 1 suite. 1 cottage. Breakfast included in rates. Type of meal: continental-plus breakfast. Beds: Q. Phone, air conditioning, ceiling fan, TV and VCR in room. Fax and bicycles on premises. Antiques, parks, shopping and golf nearby. Pets Allowed.

"We thoroughly enjoyed our stay in your beautiful valley and charming home away from home."

Cambria   L6

Olallieberry Inn

2476 Main St
Cambria, CA 93428-3406
(888)927-3222 Fax:(805)927-0202
E-mail: olallieinn@thegrid.net

Circa 1873. This restored Greek Revival home features rooms decorated with fabrics and wall coverings and furnished with

period antiques. Six of the guest rooms feature fireplaces. Butterfly and herb gardens and a 110-year-old redwood grace the front yard. The cheery gathering room boasts a view of the Santa Rosa Creek. Full breakfast with fresh breads, fruits and a special entree start off the day, and wine and hors d'oeuvres are served in the afternoon. The inn is within walking distance to restaurants and shops.

Historic Interest: Hearst Castle is six miles from the inn.

Innkeeper(s): Peter & Carol Ann Irsfeld. $90-175. MC VISA PC TC. TAC10. 9 rooms with PB, 6 with FP. 1 suite. Breakfast and evening snack included in rates. Types of meals: full breakfast, gourmet breakfast and early coffee/tea. Beds: KQ. Fax on premises. Handicap access. Weddings, small meetings, family reunions and seminars hosted. Antiques, fishing, shopping and watersports nearby.

Location: Central coast wine country.

Publicity: *Los Angeles Times, Elmer Dills Radio Show.*

"Our retreat turned into relaxation, romance and pure Victorian delight."

The Squibb House

4063 Burton Dr
Cambria, CA 93428-3001
(805)927-9600

Circa 1877. A picket fence and large garden surround this Victorian inn with its Italianate and Gothic Revival architecture. Guests may relax in the main parlor, stroll the gardens or sit and rock on the porch. The home was built by a Civil War veteran and young school teacher. The downstairs once was used as a classroom while an addition was being made in the town's school. Each guest room has a firestove.

Historic Interest: Heart Castle is six miles away, and further attractions include the San Luis Obispo Mission and San Miguel Mission, both about 35 miles from the home.

Innkeeper(s): Martha. $95-140. MC VISA PC TC. TAC10. 5 rooms with PB, 5 with FP. Breakfast included in rates. Types of meals: continental breakfast and continental-plus breakfast. Beds: Q. Weddings and small meetings hosted. Antiques, fishing, parks, shopping and golf nearby.

Publicity: *Cambrian.*

Camino   G7

The Camino Hotel-Seven Mile House

4103 Carson Rd, PO Box 1197
Camino, CA 95709
(916)644-7740 (800)200-7740 Fax:(916)644-7740

Circa 1888. Once a barracks for the area's loggers, this inn now caters to visitors in the state's famed gold country. Just east of Placerville, historic Camino is on the Old Carson Wagon Trail. Nine guest rooms are available, including the E.J. Barrett Room, a favorite with honeymooners. Other rooms feature names such as Pony Express, Stage Stop and Wagon Train. The family-oriented inn welcomes children, and a local park offers a handy site for their recreational needs. Popular area activities include antiquing, hot air ballooning, white-water rafting,

Llama trekking and wine tasting. The inn also offers a Romance Package, on-site wine tasting and an in-house masseuse.

Innkeeper(s): Paula Nobert. $65-95. AP. MC VISA AX DS PC TC. TAC15. 9 rooms, 3 with PB. 1 conference room. Breakfast and evening snack included in rates. Types of meals: full breakfast and early coffee/tea. Afternoon tea, picnic lunch and banquet service available. Beds: QDT. Turndown service and ceiling fan in room. Fax, copier and library on premises. Weddings, small meetings, family reunions and seminars hosted. Antiques, fishing, parks, shopping, downhill skiing, cross-country skiing, theater and watersports nearby.

Location: In the Apple Hill area of California's Gold Country.

Capitola-By-The-Sea   J5

The Inn at Depot Hill

250 Monterey Ave
Capitola-By-The-Sea, CA 95010-3358
(408)462-3376 (800)572-2632 Fax:(408)462-3697

Circa 1901. Once a railroad depot, this inn offers rooms with themes to represent different parts of the world: a chic auberge in St. Tropez, a romantic French hideaway in Paris, an Italian coastal villa, a summer home on the coast of Holland and a traditional English garden room, to name a few. Most rooms have garden patios with hot tubs. The rooms have many amenities, including a fireplace, white marble bathrooms and featherbeds. Guests are greeted with fresh flowers in their room. Gourmet breakfast, tea, wine, hors d' oeuvres and dessert are offered daily.

Innkeeper(s): Suzie Lankes & Dan Floyd. $165-250. MC VISA AX TC. TAC10. 12 rooms with PB, 8 with FP. 4 suites. 1 conference room. Breakfast and evening snack included in rates. Beds: KQT. Phone, turndown service, TV and VCR in room. Fax and spa on premises. Handicap access. Small meetings, family reunions and seminars hosted. Amusement parks, antiques, fishing, parks, shopping, golf, theater and watersports nearby.

Publicity: Country Inn, Santa Cruz Sentinel, McCalls, Choices & Vacation, San Jose Mercury News, Fresno & Sacramento Bee, San Francisco Focus, American Airline Flight, SF Examiner and Sunset Magazine. Ratings: 4 Stars.

"The highlight of our honeymoon. Five stars in our book!"

Carmel   J5

Happy Landing Inn

PO Box 2619
Carmel, CA 93921-2619
(408)624-7917

Circa 1926. Built as a family retreat, this early Comstock-design inn has evolved into one of Carmel's most romantic places to stay. The Hansel-and-Gretel look is accentuated with a central garden and gazebo, pond and flagstone paths. There are cathedral ceilings and the rooms are filled with antiques. Breakfast is brought to your room.

Innkeeper(s): Robert Ballard and Dick Stewart. $90-165. MC VISA. 7 rooms with PB, 3 with FP. 2 suites. Breakfast included in rates. Type of meal: continental-plus breakfast. Beds: KQD. Phone in room. Handicap access. Shopping nearby.

Publicity: San Francisco Chronicle.

"Just what the doctor ordered!"

Sandpiper Inn-At-The Beach

2408 Bay View Ave
Carmel, CA 93923-9117
(408)624-6433 (800)633-6433 Fax:(408)624-5964

Circa 1929. Only one hundred yards from miles of pristine coastline, this early California-style inn is set in a quiet residential neighborhood of million-dollar estates. There are 13 rooms

individually decorated in English and French antiques. Several of the rooms offer fireplaces or sweeping ocean views. For a more intimate stay, guests can request one of the three cottages. With its beautifully furnished interiors, the inn has been a favorite vacation spot for a host of famous people. A continental breakfast is served in the dining room or on the patio. In the afternoon, guests are invited to enjoy tea or a glass of imported Amontillado sherry.

Innkeeper(s): Graeme & Irene MacKenzie. $95-198. MC VISA AX DS PC TC. TAC10. 16 rooms with PB, 3 with FP. 2 suites. 3 cottages. Breakfast and afternoon tea included in rates. Types of meals: continental-plus breakfast, gourmet breakfast and early coffee/tea. Beds: KQ. TV, fax and copier on premises. Antiques, fishing, parks, shopping, golf, theater and watersports nearby.

Publicity: Country Inns, Sunset.

The Stonehouse Inn

PO Box 2517, 8th Below Monte Verde
Carmel, CA 93921-2517
(408)624-4569 (800)748-6618

Circa 1906. This quaint Carmel country house boasts a stone exterior, made from beach rocks collected and hand shaped by local Indians at the turn of the century. The original owner, "Nana" Foster, was hostess to notable artists and writers from

the San Francisco area, including Sinclair Lewis, Jack London and Lotta Crabtree. The romantic Jack London room features a dramatic gabled ceiling, a brass bed and a stunning view of the ocean. Conveniently located, the inn is a short walk from Carmel Beach and two blocks from the village.

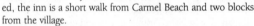

Innkeeper(s): Kevin Navailles. $89-199. MC VISA AX. 6 rooms, 2 with PB. Breakfast included in rates. Type of meal: full breakfast. Beds: KQDT. Weddings and family reunions hosted. Fishing, parks, shopping, theater and watersports nearby.

Location: Two blocks to downtown, 4 blocks to beach.

Publicity: Travel & Leisure, Country Living.

"First time stay at a B&B — GREAT!"

Vagabond's House Inn

PO Box 2747, Dolores & 4th
Carmel, CA 93921-2747
(408)624-7738 (800)262-1262 Fax:(408)626-1243

Circa 1940. Shaded by the intertwined branches of two California live oaks, the stone-paved courtyard of the Vagabond's House sets the tone of this romantic retreat. The inn is comprised of a cluster of white stucco cottages built into a slope. Some include kitchens, but all feature a fireplace and an antique clock. In the morning, continental breakfast is delivered to you near the camellias or in the privacy of your room.

Historic Interest: Carmel Mission (2 miles), Robinson Jeffers' Tor House (1 mile).

Innkeeper(s): Sally Goss. $85-165. MC VISA AX PC TC. TAC10. 11 rooms with PB, 9 with FP. Type of meal: continental-plus breakfast. Beds: KQD. Phone and TV in room. Fax and copier on premises. Weddings hosted. Spanish and Korean spoken. Antiques, fishing, parks, shopping and theater nearby.

Pets Allowed: $10 per night - pet policy.

Location: 4th & Dolores.

Publicity: *Diversion, Cat Fancy.*

"Charming & excellent accommodations and service. Very much in keeping with the character and ambiance of Carmel's historic setting."

Coloma   G6

Coloma Country Inn

PO Box 502
Coloma, CA 95613-0502
(530)622-6919

Circa 1852. Guests at this country farmhouse will want to take advantage of the nearby American River for white-water rafting. Innkeeper Alan Ehrgott is a veteran hot air balloon pilot and offers flights down the river year-round. Bed, Breakfast and Balloon packages are available at the inn, along with white-water rafting packages. The inn is situated on five, private acres in the middle of the 300-acre Gold Discovery State Park, and guests will feel like they've gone back to the Gold Rush days. A duck pond and gazebo are part of the inn's charm, coupled with antique beds, stenciling and country decor.

Historic Interest: Marshall Gold State Historic Park, Sutter's Mill and the south fork of the American River are among the area's historic attractions.

Innkeeper(s): Alan & Cindi Ehrgott. $90-130. PC TC. TAC10. 8 rooms, 4 with PB. 2 suites. 2 cottages. 1 conference room. Breakfast and afternoon tea included in rates. Types of meals: full breakfast and early coffee/tea. Picnic lunch and catering service available. Beds: QD. Air conditioning and ceiling fan in room. Bicycles on premises. Weddings, small meetings, family reunions and seminars hosted. Spanish spoken. Antiques, fishing, parks, downhill skiing, theater and watersports nearby.

Location: Heart of the Gold Country, Coloma, where the Gold Rush began.

Publicity: *Country Living, Los Angeles Times, Country Inns, Sunset, Motorland, New York Times.*

Golden Lotus B&B

1006 Lotus Rd
Coloma, CA 95613
(916)621-4562

Circa 1855. Located on the south fork of the American River, this rustic pre-Victorian inn features large wraparound verandas that look out to an original Indian campground. Much like an old western town, the inn features on-site antique, gift and book stores, gold-panning and a historic restaurant. There are eight rooms, each uniquely decorated around a theme. The Westward Ho, for example, is decorated in relics of the Old West, while the Orient Express will delight guests with its unusual Oriental antiques and furnishings. All rooms offer private baths. A gourmet breakfast of apple sausage, Dutch pancakes and pouched pears is served on-site in Adam's Red Brick Restaurant, once used as a general store for gold miners.

Historic Interest: El Dorado County Historical Site #37.

Innkeeper(s): Bruce & Jill Smith. $85-133. MC VISA TC. TAC10. 8 rooms with PB. 2 suites. 2 cottages. Breakfast included in rates. Types of meals: full breakfast, gourmet breakfast and early coffee/tea. Afternoon tea, dinner, evening snack, picnic lunch, lunch and gourmet lunch available. Restaurant on premises. Beds: KQT. Air conditioning and ceiling fan in room. VCR, fax and library on premises. Weddings, small meetings, family reunions and seminars hosted. Antiques, fishing, parks, shopping, golf, theater and watersports nearby.

Pets Allowed: Well behaved in cottages only - fee & deposit required.

"I rediscovered it is actually possible to sleep, and very well, in a room without TV, phone and mini-bar."

Columbia   H7

City Hotel

PO Box 1870
Columbia, CA 95310-1870
(209)532-1479

Circa 1856. The history of this Victorian hotel dates back to the days when gold miners plunked down bits of their daily work in exchange for room and board. The interior reflects the inn's 19th-century past and Columbia's booming days in the Victorian era. Oriental rugs, antiques and bright, patterned wallcoverings decorate the parlors and guest quarters. Miners found more than $1 billion in gold in the mines around Columbia, and the town has not forgotten. Designated a state historic park, Columbia offers many Gold Rush attractions. Guests can try their luck at gold panning, visit museums or ride a century-old stagecoach. After a day of exploring, the hotel's What Cheer Saloon is the perfect place to enjoy a glass of wine. The saloon still features the original cherry wood bar. The inn also includes a popular full-service restaurant that serves dinner Tuesday through Sunday.

Innkeeper(s): Tom Bender. $85-105. MC VISA AX DS PC TC. TAC10. 10 rooms with PB. Breakfast included in rates. Types of meals: continental-plus breakfast and early coffee/tea. Lunch, gourmet lunch and banquet service available. Restaurant on premises. Beds: QDT. Air conditioning in room. Fax on premises. Weddings, small meetings, family reunions and seminars hosted. Antiques, fishing, parks, shopping, theater and watersports nearby.

Publicity: *Innsider, Bon Appetit, New York Times, Country Inn, Sunset, Motorland, Los Angeles Times.*

"Excellent, by any standard."

Fallon Hotel

PO Box 1870
Columbia, CA 95310-1870
(209)532-1470

Circa 1855. The Fallon Hotel, restored and operated by the State of California Parks and Recreation Department, still boasts the main-floor theater where productions are featured year-round. Original furnishings from the hotel's Gold-Rush days have been repaired, polished and reupholstered, including a fine Turkish loveseat in the parlor. Bradbury & Bradbury redesigned the nine wallpaper patterns featured. The best rooms are upstairs with balconies overlooking the town's four blocks of saloons, cash stores, an ice cream parlor, blacksmith shop and the stage coach that periodically rambles through town.

Innkeeper(s): Tom Bender. $60-105. MC VISA AX PC. TAC10. 14 rooms, 13 with PB. 1 suite. 1 conference room. Breakfast included in rates. Type of meal: continental-plus breakfast. Beds: DT. Phone in room. Handicap access. Antiques, fishing, downhill skiing, theater and watersports nearby.

Publicity: *Home & Garden, Innsider, Motorland, Sunset.*

"Excellent service."

Crowley Lake   I9

Rainbow Tarns B&B at Crowley Lake

Rt 1, PO Box 1053
Crowley Lake, CA 93546-9704
(760)935-4556 (888)588-6269

Circa 1920. Just south of Mammoth Lakes, at an altitude of 7,000 feet, you'll find this secluded retreat amid three acres of ponds, open meadows and the High Sierra Mountains. Country-style here includes luxury touches, such as a double Jacuzzi tub, queen-size bed, down pillows, comforters and a skylight for star-gazing. In the '50s, ponds on the property served as a "U-Catch-Em."
Folks rented fishing poles and paid 10 cents an inch for the fish they caught. Nearby Crowley Lake is still one of the best trout-fishing areas in California. Romantic country weddings are popular here. Guests are free to simply relax in the peaceful setting, but hiking, horseback riding and skiing all are available in the area.

Innkeeper(s): Brock & Diane Thoman. $90-140. 3 rooms. Breakfast included in rates. Types of meals: full breakfast and early coffee/tea. Beds: QD. Phone in room. Handicap access.

Location: Eight-tenths of a mile north of Tom's Place off Crowley Lake Drive on Rainbow Tarns Road.

Publicity: *Mammoth-Sierra, Mammoth Winter, Eastern Sierra Fishing Guide, Mammoth-June Ski Preview, Sunset.*

Davenport   J4

New Davenport B&B

31 Davenport Ave
Davenport, CA 95017
(408)425-1818 (800)870-1817 Fax:(408)423-1160
E-mail: inn@swanton.com

Circa 1906. Captain John Davenport came here to harvest the gray whales that pass close to shore during migration. The oldest building remaining originally was used as a public bath. It

later became a bar, restaurant and dance hall before conversion into a private home. Completely renovated, it now houses four of the inn's rooms. In addition to breakfast, guests also enjoy two complimentary drinks at the bar in the inn's restaurant.

Historic Interest: The Wilder Ranch State Park is five miles away. Davenport Jail, Giovvini Cheesehouse, Old Davenport Pier and the St. Vincent DePaul Catholic Church, built in 1902, are nearby.

Innkeeper(s): Bruce & Marcia McDougal. $75-125. MC VISA AX. 12 rooms with PB. Breakfast included in rates. Type of meal: full breakfast. Dinner, picnic lunch and lunch available. Restaurant on premises. Beds: KQ.

Location: Halfway between Carmel and San Francisco on the coast Highway 1.

Publicity: *Monterey Life, Travel & Leisure, Sacramento Bee, Peninsula Time Tribune.*

"I cannot express the wonderful thrill at the first glimpse of our room with its lovely country appeal and garden."

Dulzura   Q12

Brookside Farm

1373 Marron Valley Rd
Dulzura, CA 91917-2113
(619)468-3043

Circa 1929. Ancient oaks shade terraces leading from the farmhouse to a murmuring brook. Behind a nearby stone barn, there is a grape arbor and beneath it, a spa. Each room in the inn and its cottage is furnished with vintage pieces and handmade quilts. Adventurous hikers can explore mines nearby, which date from the gold rush of 1908. Innkeeper Edd Guishard is a former award-winning restaurant owner.

Innkeeper(s): Sally or Edd Guishard. $75-115. MC VISA AX DC CB DS. 11 rooms with PB, 4 with FP. 2 suites. 1 conference room. Breakfast and dinner included in rates. Type of meal: full breakfast. Beds: Q. Phone in room. Handicap access.

Location: Thirty-five minutes southeast of San Diego.

Publicity: *California, San Diego Home & Garden.*

"Our stay at the farm was the most relaxing weekend we've had in a year."

Dunsmuir   B5

Dunsmuir Inn

5423 Dunsmuir Ave
Dunsmuir, CA 96025-2011
(530)235-4543 (888)386-7684 Fax:(530)235-4154

Circa 1925. Set in the Sacramento River Valley, this country-style inn may serve as a base for an assortment of outdoor activities. At the end of the day, guests can enjoy an old-fashioned soda or ice cream cone. Fishing, available in the crystal-clear waters of the Upper Sacramento River, is within walking distance. The innkeepers can suggest hiking trails and driving tours to mountain lakes, waterfalls, the Castle Crags State Park and Mt. Shasta.

Innkeeper(s): Jerry & Julie Iskra. $60-70. MC VISA AX DC CB DS PC TC. TAC10. 5 rooms with PB. 1 suite. Breakfast included in rates. Types of meals: full breakfast and early coffee/tea. Evening snack and picnic lunch available. Beds: KDT. Air conditioning, turndown service and ceiling fan in room. TV, VCR and fax on premises. Family reunions hosted. Antiques, fishing, parks, downhill skiing, cross-country skiing and watersports nearby.

Location: Sacramento River Valley, Shasta Cascade.

Elk   F3

Elk Cove Inn

6300 S Hwy 1, PO Box 367
Elk, CA 95432
(707)877-3321 (800)275-2967 Fax:(707)877-1808

Circa 1883. This mansard-style Victorian home was built as a guest house for lumber baron L. E. White. Operated as a full-service country inn for more than 27 years, Elk Cove Inn commands a majestic view from atop a scenic bluff. There are four cabins and an addition to the house that features four new suites with large bay windows, skylights and Victorian fireplaces. Most rooms have an ocean view. Antiques, hand-embroidered linens and down comforters add to the amenities. Below the inn is an expansive driftwood-strewn beach. Gourmet breakfasts are served in the ocean-view dining room. Guests can enjoy cocktails or cappuccino in the ocean-front bar. Coffee makers with fresh ground coffee, teas, cider and hot chocolate are available in the rooms.

Historic Interest: Fort Ross original Russian settlement (1 hour away).

Innkeeper(s): Elaine Bryant & Jim Carr. $108-298. MC VISA AX PC. 15 rooms with PB, 14 with FP. 4 suites. 4 cottages. 1 conference room. Breakfast included in rates. Type of meal: gourmet breakfast. Beds: KQ. VCR and fax on premises. Handicap access. Weddings, small meetings, family reunions and seminars hosted. Antiques, fishing, parks, shopping, theater and watersports nearby.

Location: 15 miles south of Mendocino.

"Quiet, peaceful, romantic, spiritual. This room, the inn, and the food are all what the doctor ordered."

Harbor House - Inn By The Sea

5600 S Hwy 1
Elk, CA 95432
(707)877-3203

Circa 1916. Built by a lumber company for executives visiting from the East, the inn is constructed entirely of redwood. The parlor's vaulted, carved ceiling and redwood paneling were sealed by hot beeswax and hand rubbed. Edwardian decor adds elegance to the guest rooms. Views of the ocean and arches carved in the massive rocks that jut from the sea may be seen from the blufftop cottages. Benches nestle along a path edged with wildflowers that winds down the bluff to the sea.

Innkeeper(s): Dean & Helen Turner. $150-285. MAP. 10 rooms with PB, 9 with FP. Breakfast and dinner included in rates. Type of meal: full breakfast. Phone in room.

Publicity: *California Visitor's Review.*

"A window on love, beauty and the sea."

Sandpiper House Inn

5520 S Hwy 1
Elk, CA 95432
(707)877-3587 (800)894-9016

Circa 1916. A garden path leads Sandpiper guests to a bluff overlooking the California coast. The path continues onward to a private beach. The historic home was built by a local lumber company. The living room and dining room have virgin redwood paneling. Guest quarters are appointed to look like rooms in an English country home. Canopied beds, Oriental rugs and polished wood floors create a romantic ambiance. Rooms offer either ocean or countryside views, and three have

a fireplace. Gourmet breakfasts are served on tables set with lace and fresh flowers.

Innkeeper(s): Claire & Richard Melrose. $120-225. MAP. MC VISA AX DS PC TC. 5 rooms with PB, 3 with FP. 1 suite. Breakfast and afternoon tea included in rates. Types of meals: gourmet breakfast and early coffee/tea. Beds: Q. Fishing, parks, shopping, theater and watersports nearby.

Escondido   P12

Zosa Gardens B&B

9381 W Lilac Rd
Escondido, CA 92026
(760)723-9093 (800)771-8361 Fax:(760)723-3460
E-mail: zosa_bb@ramonamall.com

Circa 1940. Escondido, located in northern San Diego County, is the setting for this Spanish Hacienda. The home rests on 22 well-landscaped acres atop a bluff in the Monserate Mountains. Rooms bear flowery themes. Angel-lovers should try the Angel Room. The Master Suite includes a fireplace. The innkeeper is an accomplished chef, and her cuisine has been featured on the TV Food Network, as well as in Bon Appetit. She serves a full customized breakfast for her guests. In the evenings, gourmet tidbits are served with a selection of local wines. Guests are free to enjoy the grounds. There is an outside grill and billiards, and massages are available. Golf courses, restaurants and other sites are just minutes away.

Innkeeper(s): Ted & Connie Vlasis. $80-195. MC VISA AX DC CB DS PC TC. TAC10. 11 rooms, 8 with PB, 1 with FP. 3 suites. 1 cabin. Breakfast and evening snack included in rates. Types of meals: full breakfast, gourmet breakfast and early coffee/tea. Catering service, catered breakfast and room service available. Beds: KQD. Air conditioning, turndown service and TV in room. VCR, fax, copier, spa, swimming and tennis on premises. Handicap access. 22 acres. Weddings, small meetings, family reunions and seminars hosted. Spanish, Filipino, English and Italian spoken. Amusement parks, antiques, fishing, parks, shopping, sporting events, golf, theater and watersports nearby.

Eureka   C2

A Weaver's Inn

1440 B St
Eureka, CA 95501-2215
(707)443-8119 (800)992-8119 Fax:(707)443-7923
E-mail: weavrinn@humboldt1.com

Circa 1883. The stately Queen Anne Colonial Revival house features a spacious fenced garden, parlor and gracious dining room. All four guest rooms are furnished with down comforters, fresh flowers from the garden and are decorated to reflect the genteel elegance of the Victorian era. The Pamela Suite has a sitting room and fireplace, while the Marcia Room includes a window seat. The full breakfast often features home-grown treats from the garden. Honeymooners can enjoy breakfast in their room.

Historic Interest: Redwood Forests (30 miles).

Innkeeper(s): Lea L. & Lee Montgomery, Shoshana McAvoy. $75-125. MC VISA AX DC DS. 1 suite. Breakfast included in rates. Type of meal: full breakfast. Afternoon tea available. Beds: KQDT.

Location: In the historical Victorian seaport of Eureka, in the heart of the Redwoods.

"It's a charming inn, warm ambiance and very gracious hosts!"

Abigail's "Elegant Victorian Mansion" B&B Lodging Accommodations

1406 C St
Eureka, CA 95501-1765
(707)444-3144 Fax:(707)442-5594

Circa 1888. One of Eureka's leading lumber barons built this picturesque home, a National Historic Landmark, from 1,000-year-old virgin redwood. Original wallpapers, wool carpets and antique light fixtures create a wonderfully authentic Victorian ambiance. A tuxedoed butler and your hosts, decked in period attire, greet guests upon arrival. Croquet fields and Victorian gardens surround the inn. The hosts can arrange horse-drawn

carriage rides or boat cruises. Old-fashioned ice cream sodas are served and to top it all off, each morning guests partake in a multi-course, French gourmet breakfast feast. The beds in the well-appointed guest quarters are topped with custom-made mattresses. There is a video library of vintage silent films. The inn has been host to many historic personalities, including actresses Lillie Langtry and Sarah Bernhardt, and many senators and representatives.

Historic Interest: Historic Fort Humboldt State Park, Redwood parks, Clark Historic Museum, Maritime Museum, historic "Old Town" (all within walking distance)

Innkeeper(s): Doug & Lily Vieyra. $95-185. EP. MC VISA. TAC10. 4 rooms, 2 with PB. 1 suite. 1 conference room. Breakfast, afternoon tea and evening snack included in rates. Types of meals: gourmet breakfast and early coffee/tea. Beds: Q. Phone, air conditioning and turndown service in room. TV, VCR, fax, copier, sauna, bicycles and library on premises. Small meetings and seminars hosted. French, Dutch and German and English spoken. Antiques, fishing, shopping, sporting events, theater and watersports nearby.

"A magnificent masterpiece, both in architecture and service. Four-star service and regal opulence."

The Carter House Victorians

301 L St
Eureka, CA 95501
(707)444-8062 (800)404-1390 Fax:(707)444-8067
E-mail: carter52@humboldt1.com

Circa 1884. The Carters found a pattern book in an antique shop and built this inn according to the architectural plans for an 1890 San Francisco Victorian. (The architect, Joseph Newsom, also designed the Carson House across the street.) Three open parlors with bay windows and marble fireplaces provide an elegant

backdrop for relaxing. Guests are free to visit the kitchen in quest of coffee and views of the bay. The inn is famous for its three-course breakfast, including an Apple Almond Tart featured in Gourmet magazine.

Historic Interest: Redwood forests, historic architecture, wildlife/bird sanctuary, Victorian Sawmill (all within 10 miles).

Innkeeper(s): Mark & Christi Carter. $145-350. MAP, AP, EP. MC VISA AX DC CB DS PC TC. TAC10. 31 rooms with PB, 15 with FP. 15 suites. 1 cottage. 2 conference rooms. Breakfast and afternoon tea included in rates. Types of meals: continental breakfast, continental-plus breakfast, full breakfast, gourmet breakfast and early coffee/tea. Dinner, evening snack and room service available. Restaurant on premises. Beds: KQDT. Phone, air conditioning, turndown service, TV and VCR in room. Fax, copier and spa on premises. Handicap access. Small meetings, family reunions and seminars hosted. Italian, Spanish and French spoken. Antiques, fishing, parks, shopping, sporting events, theater and watersports nearby.

Location: Corner of Third & L streets in Old Town.

Publicity: *Sunset, U.S. News & World Report, Country Home, Country Living, Bon Appetit, San Francisco Focus, Northwest Palate, Gourmet, Art Culinare, San Francisco Chronicle.*

"We've traveled extensively throughout the U.S. and stayed in the finest hotels. You've got them all beat!!"

The Daly Inn

1125 H St
Eureka, CA 95501-1844
(707)445-3638 (800)321-9656 Fax:(707)444-3636
E-mail: dalyinn@humboldt1.com

Circa 1905. This 6,000-square-foot Colonial Revival mansion is located in the historic section of Eureka. Enjoy the Belgian antique bedstead, fireplace and view of fish pond and garden from Annie Murphy's Room, or try the former nursery, Miss Martha's Room, with bleached pine antiques from Holland. Breakfast is served fireside in the inn's formal dining room or in the breakfast parlor or garden patio. In the evenings, wine and cheese is served.

Historic Interest: The Carson Mansion, historic Old Town, Fort Humboldt and a Victorian sawmill are among the nearby historic attractions.

Innkeeper(s): Sue & Gene Clinesmith. $80-150. MC VISA AX DS PC TC. 5 rooms, 3 with PB, 1 with FP. 2 suites. Breakfast and evening snack included in rates. Types of meals: gourmet breakfast and early coffee/tea. Beds: QT. Turndown service in room. TV, VCR, fax, copier and library on premises. Weddings, small meetings, family reunions and seminars hosted. Antiques, fishing, shopping and theater nearby.

Location: California's north coast.

"A genuine delight."

Hotel Carter

301 L St
Eureka, CA 95501-0571
(707)444-8062 (800)404-1390 Fax:(707)444-8062

Circa 1880. A new structure that manages to radiate old-time elegance and charm, this sophisticated inn offers a taste of the Victorian era as it also incorporates the modern. Contemporary artwork shares space with marble fireplaces and high ceilings in the inn's lobby. Its 23 guest rooms feature a variety of luxurious touches, including fireplaces, skylights, whirlpool tubs, VCRs, CD stereo systems and mini-refrigerators. Gourmet breakfasts add another element to the Hotel Carter's already impressive

display of hospitality.
Visitors to redwood
country will enjoy
exploring Eureka, home
to more than 1,500
Victorian homes.

Innkeeper(s): Mark & Christi
Carter. Call for rates. 8 suites.
3 conference rooms. Type of
meal: early coffee/tea. Dinner, evening snack, banquet service, catering service, catered breakfast and room service available.

Old Town B&B Inn

1521 3rd St
Eureka, CA 95501-0710
(707)445-3951 (800)331-5098 Fax:(707)268-0231
E-mail: otb-b@humboldt1.com

Circa 1871. This early Victorian/Greek Revival was the original family home of Lumber Baron William Carson. It was constructed of virgin redwood and Douglas fir. This renovated inn has been called a "Humboldt County jewel" by the local visitors' and convention bureau. Try to time your stay on a day when the Timber Beast breakfast menu is served, and be sure to take home a copy of the inn's cookbook.

Innkeeper(s): Leigh & Diane Benson. $75-136. MC VISA AX DC CB DS. 6 rooms, 4 with PB, 1 with FP. Breakfast and afternoon tea included in rates. Types of meals: continental breakfast, continental-plus breakfast, full breakfast, gourmet breakfast and early coffee/tea. Beds: KQDT. Phone in room. Family reunions hosted. Spanish and Italian spoken. Antiques, fishing, parks, sporting events, theater and watersports nearby.

Location: Heart of the Redwood Empire on the Pacific Coast, north of San Francisco.

Publicity: *Times-Standard, Country, San Francisco Chronicle, Sunset.*

"From the moment you opened the door, we knew we had chosen a special place to stay."

Ferndale   C2

Gingerbread Mansion Inn

PO Box 40, 400 Berding St
Ferndale, CA 95536-1380
(707)786-4000 (800)952-4136 Fax:(707)786-4381
E-mail: kenn@humboldt1.com

Circa 1899. Built for Dr. H.J. Ring, the Gingerbread Mansion is now the most photographed of Northern California's inns. Near Eureka, it is in the fairy-tale Victorian village of Ferndale (a California Historical Landmark). Outside the inn are formal English gardens. Gingerbread Mansion is a unique combination of Queen Anne and Eastlake styles with elaborate gingerbread trim. Inside are spacious and elegant rooms including two suites with "his" and "her" bathtubs. There are four parlors.

Historic Interest: Victorian shops and galleries along Main Street, The Ferndale Museum, wilderness park and bird sanctuary (one-half mile).

Innkeeper(s): Ken Torbert. $120-350. MC VISA AX PC TC. TAC10. 10 rooms with PB, 5 with FP. 5 suites. Breakfast and afternoon tea included in rates. Types of meals: full breakfast and early coffee/tea. Beds: KQT. Turndown service in room.

Library on premises. Small meetings and family reunions hosted. Antiques, fishing, parks, shopping and theater nearby.

Location: Five miles west off Hwy 101; 30 minutes south of Eureka.

Publicity: *Travel Holiday, Country Inns, Los Angeles Times, Sunset.* Ratings: 4 Diamonds.

"Absolutely the most charming, friendly and delightful place we have ever stayed."

Shaw House B&B Inn

PO Box 1125, 703 Main St
Ferndale, CA 95536-1125
(707)786-9958 (800)557-7429 Fax:(707)786-9958

Circa 1854. The Shaw House is one of the oldest inns in California. It is an attractive Gothic house with gables, bays and balconies set back on an acre of garden. An old buckeye tree frames the front gate, and in the back, a secluded deck overlooks a creek. Nestled under the wallpapered gables are several guest rooms filled with antiques and fresh flowers.

Historic Interest: Listed in the National Register.

Innkeeper(s): Ken & Norma Bessingpas. $75-135. MC VISA AX. 6 rooms with PB. Breakfast and afternoon tea included in rates. Type of meal: full breakfast. Beds: QD. Phone in room. Antiques, fishing and theater nearby.

Publicity: *Travel & Leisure, New York Times.*

"Lovely place and lovely people—Willard Scott."

Ferndale (Loleta)   C2

Southport Landing

444 Phelan Rd
Ferndale (Loleta), CA 95551
(707)733-5915

Circa 1890. Situated on more than two acres, this early Colonial Revival with its wraparound front porch offers spectacular views of the hills and Humboldt Bay National Wildlife Refuge. Besides the inn's traditional country manor atmosphere with its period antiques, guests will enjoy the uninterrupted silence and the bounty of wildlife. There are five individually decorated guest rooms all with dramatic views of the hillside or the bay. A third-floor game room features a pool table, ping-pong, darts and cards. Fresh farm eggs, homemade sausage, local cheeses and fresh local cider is offered for breakfast, while snacks are provided in the evening. Hiking, bird-watching, bicycling and kayaking are offered.

Historic Interest: Redwood forests, Arcata Marsh, Somoa Dunes, Lost Coast are located nearby.

Innkeeper(s): Judy & Dana Henderson. $85-115. MC VISA. TAC10. 5 rooms, 3 with PB. Breakfast and evening snack included in rates. Types of meals: full breakfast and early coffee/tea. Beds: Q. Turndown service in room. TV, VCR, fax, bicycles and library on premises. Small meetings and family reunions hosted. Antiques, fishing, parks, shopping, golf and theater nearby.

"Our greatest B&B experience!"

Fort Bragg   E2

Annie's Jughandle Beach B&B Inn

32980 Gibney Ln
Fort Bragg, CA 95437-8314
(707)964-1415 (800)964-9957 Fax:(707)961-1473
E-mail: annies@mcn.org

Circa 1883. This inn derives its unusual name from the Jughandle State Preserve, located conveniently right out the inn's front door. There is private beach access, and guests can enjoy watching as the sun sets over the Pacific. The country Victorian decor includes a selection of period antiques. Guests will find special features in each room. The Headlands Room includes a balcony that offers an ocean view. The Enchanted Barn Loft is a spacious affair, with a four-poster bed, sitting area, fireplace, a clawfoot tub and a deck with skylights. The innkeepers hail from New Orleans and put a dash of the South into the gourmet breakfasts, which include items such as frittatas and souffles made with farm-fresh eggs. Young guests are welcome to help the innkeepers collect eggs from the henhouse or pick berries.

Innkeeper(s): Shannon Killilea & Jean LaTorre. $79-159. MC VISA PC TC. TAC10. 5 rooms, 4 with PB, 1 with FP. 1 suite. 1 cottage. 1 conference room. Breakfast included in rates. Types of meals: full breakfast, gourmet breakfast and early coffee/tea. Beds: QT. Ceiling fan in room. Fax and bicycles on premises. Weddings, small meetings, family reunions and seminars hosted. Antiques, fishing, parks, shopping, golf, theater and watersports nearby.

Avalon House

561 Stewart St
Fort Bragg, CA 95437-3226
(707)964-5555 (800)964-5556

Circa 1905. This redwood California Craftsman house was extensively remodeled in 1988 and furnished with a mixture of antiques and willow furniture. Some rooms feature fireplaces, whirlpool tubs, or ocean views and decks. The inn is in a quiet residential area, three blocks from the Pacific Ocean, one block west of Hwy. 1, and two blocks from the Skunk Train depot.

Innkeeper(s): Anne Sorrells. $70-140. MC VISA AX DS PC TC. TAC10. 6 rooms with PB, 4 with FP. Breakfast included in rates. Types of meals: full breakfast and early coffee/tea. Beds: QD. TV and VCR on premises. Weddings, small meetings and family reunions hosted. Antiques, fishing, parks, shopping, theater and watersports nearby.

Location: 150 miles northwest of San Francisco.

Publicity: *Advocate News.*

"Elegant, private and extremely comfortable. We will never stay in a motel again."

Grey Whale Inn

615 N Main St
Fort Bragg, CA 95437-3240
(707)964-0640 (800)382-7244 Fax:(707)964-4408
E-mail: gwhale@mcn.org

Circa 1915. As the name implies, whales can be seen from many of the inn's vantage points during the creatures' migration season along the West Coast. The stately four-story redwood inn features airy and spacious guest rooms with ocean views. Some rooms include a fireplace, whirlpool tub for two or private deck. Near the heart of downtown Fort Bragg, it's an easy walk to the Skunk Train, shops, galleries, a microbrewery and restaurants. There is also a fireside lounge, TV/VCR room and a recreation area with pool table.

Historic Interest: The Georgia Pacific Logging Museum and the Guest House Museum are two blocks away, while the Kelley House Museum and Ford House are a 10-mile drive.

Innkeeper(s): John & Colette Bailey. $90-180. MC VISA AX DS PC TC. TAC10. 14 rooms with PB, 3 with FP. 2 conference rooms. Breakfast included in rates. Type of meal: full breakfast. Beds: KQDT. Phone and TV in room. VCR, fax, copier and library on premises. Handicap access. Weddings, small meetings, family reunions and seminars hosted. German, Spanish and Dutch spoken. Antiques, fishing, parks, shopping, theater and watersports nearby.

Location: Almost in the heart of downtown Fort Bragg on the Mendocino Coast Highway.

Publicity: *Inn Times, San Francisco Examiner, Travel, Fort Bragg Advocate News, Mendocino Beacon, Los Angeles Times, Sunset.*

"We are going to return each year until we have tried each room. Sunrise room is excellent in the morning or evening."

Freestone   G4

Green Apple Inn

520 Bohemian Hwy
Freestone, CA 95472-9580
(707)874-2526

Circa 1860. Located on five acres of redwood trees and meadows, this inn was built by Trowbridge Wells, squire, pundit, grocer and postman for Freestone, the county's first designated historic district. Freestone was once the site of a Russian experimental farm (to grow wheat for Sitka, Alaska, in 1814), a stagecoach stop en route to the coast and a key station on the bootleg Underground Railway. Freestone itself has only one street, and that one is crooked.

Innkeeper(s): Rosemary Hoffman. $85-90. MC VISA. 4 rooms with PB. Type of meal: full breakfast. Beds: QD. Phone in room.

Location: Near Bodega Bay. One hour from San Francisco.

Publicity: *Sonoma Monthly, San Francisco Chronicle, San Jose Mercury, Country Living.*

"The Green Apple is a cozy inn. Not rushed but you can take your time. Emma, age 6."

Georgetown   G6

American River Inn

PO Box 43, Gold Country
Georgetown, CA 95634-0043
(916)333-4499 (800)245-6566 Fax:(916)333-9253
E-mail: ari@pcweb.net

Circa 1853. Just a few miles from where gold was discovered in Coloma stands this completely restored boarding house. Mining cars dating back to the original Woodside Mine Camp are visible. The lode still runs under the inn. Swimmers will enjoy a spring-fed pond on the property. There is also a Jacuzzi, croquet field, putting green and complimentary mountain bikes.

Georgetown is a site for the California sesquicentennial celebration in from 1998 to 2000.

Innkeeper(s): Maria & Will. $85-115. MC VISA AX DS. 25 rooms, 14 with PB, 3 with FP. 1 conference room. Types of meals: full breakfast and gourmet breakfast. Beds: KQ. Phone in room. Fax, copier and spa on premises. Handicap access. Fishing and parks nearby.

Publicity: *Los Angeles Times, Sunset, Gourmet, Westways, 50 Romantic Getaways.*

"Our home away from home. We fell in love here in all its beauty and will be back for our fourth visit in April, another honeymoon for six days."

Geyserville   G4

Hope-Merrill House

21253 Geyserville Ave
Geyserville, CA 95441-9637
(707)857-3356 (800)825-4233 Fax:(707)857-4673

Circa 1885. The Hope-Merrill House is a classic example of the Eastlake Stick style that was so popular during Victorian times. Built entirely from redwood, the house features original wainscoting and silk-screened wallcoverings. A swimming pool, vineyard and gazebo are favorite spots for guests to relax. The Hope-Bosworth House, on the same street, was built in 1904 in the Queen Anne style by an early Geyserville pioneer who lived in the home until the 1960s. The front picket fence is covered with roses. Period details include oak woodwork, sliding doors, polished fir floors and antique light fixtures.

Innkeeper(s): Cosette & Ron Scheiber. $111-164. MC VISA AX PC TC. TAC10. 12 rooms with PB, 4 with FP. 1 suite. Breakfast included in rates. Types of meals: full breakfast, gourmet breakfast and early coffee/tea. Picnic lunch available. Beds: Q. Ceiling fan in room. Fax and copier on premises. Weddings, small meetings and family reunions hosted. Antiques, parks, shopping and watersports nearby.

Publicity: *San Diego Union, Country Homes, Sunset, Sacramento Union, Los Angeles Times.*

Glen Ellen   G4

Gaige House

13540 Arnold Dr
Glen Ellen, CA 95442-9305
(707)935-0237 (800)935-0237 Fax:(707)935-6411
E-mail: gaige@sprynet.com

Circa 1890. This wine country inn, built in the Victorian style, offers 11 individually decorated guest rooms all appointed in a unique Indonesian plantation style. Rattan pieces, beds topped with lacy canopies and plants adorn the bright and airy guest rooms. The most opulent of the rooms, the Gaige Suite, includes an enormous Jacuzzi tub. The lush grounds feature gardens and a creek meanders through the property. Guests enjoy use of a heated swimming pool. Some of the Sonoma Valley's many wineries are within walking distance of the inn. The innkeepers offer a taste of local wines each evening.

Innkeeper(s): Ken Burnet & Greg Nemrow. $135-255. MC VISA AX DS PC TC. TAC10. 11 rooms with PB, 5 with FP. Breakfast and evening snack included in rates. Types of meals: gourmet breakfast and early coffee/tea. Beds: KQ. Phone, air conditioning, ceiling fan, TV and VCR in room. Fax, copier, swimming and library on premises. Small meetings, family reunions and seminars hosted. French and Spanish spoken. Antiques, parks, shopping and golf nearby.

Publicity: *Travel & Leisure.*

Grass Valley   F6

Golden Ore B&B

448 S Auburn St
Grass Valley, CA 95945-7226
(916)272-6872

Circa 1904. This striking country Victorian inn set in the Sierra foothills has five guest rooms, all decorated with antiques gathered from local estates. The Parlour Room and Mistress Mary Room feature elegant antique furniture, showers and clawfoot tubs. Upstairs, via Teddy Bear Row, the sitting room offers a large screen satellite TV, game table and kitchenette. Three rooms feature romantic skylights and antique furnishings. Two rooms offer in-room pedestal sinks and share a bath and shower.

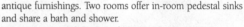

Innkeeper(s): Dave & Gayle Keyte. $65-105. MC VISA PC TC. 5 rooms with PB, 2 with FP. Type of meal: full breakfast. Picnic lunch available. Beds: Q. Turndown service in room. Small meetings, family reunions and seminars hosted. Antiques, fishing, shopping, downhill skiing, cross-country skiing and theater nearby.

"Great charm & Grannies atmosphere."

Murphy's Inn

318 Neal St
Grass Valley, CA 95945-6702
(916)273-6873 (800)895-2488 Fax:(916)273-5157
E-mail: murphys@jps.net

Circa 1866. The Gold Rush turned this home's builder into a wealthy man, and he built this Victorian for his new bride. The home is decorated by century-old ivy, and the grounds include a 140-year-old giant sequoia. Guests can choose from rooms with fireplaces or a skylight, and all rooms are decorated with antiques. One suite is located in a separate house and includes a kitchen and living room. The Victorian is located in a Grass Valley historic district and is within walking distance to many local attractions.

Innkeeper(s): Ted & Nancy Daus. $95-150. MC VISA AX PC. TAC10. 8 rooms with PB, 4 with FP. 3 suites. 1 conference room. Breakfast included in rates. Types of meals: full breakfast, gourmet breakfast and early coffee/tea. Beds: KQHIDEBEDS. Phone, air conditioning, ceiling fan, TV and VCR in room. Fax and library on premises. Small meetings, family reunions and seminars hosted. Antiques, fishing, parks, shopping, downhill skiing, cross-country skiing, golf, theater and watersports nearby.

Groveland H7

The Groveland Hotel

18767 Main St, PO Box 481
Groveland, CA 95321
(209)962-4000 (800)273-3314 Fax:(209)962-6674
E-mail: peggy@groveland.com

Circa 1849. Located 23 miles from Yosemite National Park, the newly restored hotel features both an 1849 adobe building with 18-inch-thick walls constructed during the Gold Rush and a 1914 building erected to house workers for the Hetch Hetchy Dam. Both feature two-story balconies. There is a Victorian parlor, a gourmet restaurant and a Western saloon.

Guest rooms feature European antiques, down comforters and in-room coffee. The feeling is one of casual elegance.

Innkeeper(s): Peggy A. & Grover C. Mosley. $105-125. MC VISA AX DC CB DS PC TC. TAC10. 17 rooms with PB, 3 with FP. 3 suites. 1 conference room. Breakfast included in rates. Types of meals: continental-plus breakfast and early coffee/tea. Picnic lunch, banquet service, catering service and room service available. Restaurant on premises. Beds: QT. Phone, air conditioning and ceiling fan in room. TV, VCR, fax, copier, library, pet boarding and child care on premises. Handicap access. Weddings, small meetings, family reunions and seminars hosted. Antiques, fishing, parks, shopping, downhill skiing, cross-country skiing, golf and watersports nearby.

Publicity: Sonora Union Democrat, Los Angeles Times, Peninsula, Sunset, Stockton Record, Country Inns.

"Hospitality is outstanding."

Gualala G3

North Coast Country Inn

34591 S Hwy 1
Gualala, CA 95445
(707)884-4537 (800)959-4537

Circa 1948. Overlooking the Pacific Ocean, the six guest rooms that comprise North Coast Country Inn are tucked into a pine and redwood forested hillside. Each is furnished with a four-poster bed, private bath and includes a fireplace, wet-bar kitchenette and private deck. There is a hot tub on the hillside or you may relax in the gazebo. Breakfast is served in the common room. In the afternoon, guests are invited to enjoy a glass of sherry. Barking sea lions are often heard in the distance.

Innkeeper(s): Loren & Nancy Flanagan. $140-195. MC VISA AX PC TC. TAC10. 6 rooms with PB, 6 with FP. 1 suite. Breakfast and evening snack included in rates. Type of meal: continental-plus breakfast. Beds: KQ. Ceiling fan in room. TV, VCR, spa and library on premises. Small meetings, family reunions and seminars hosted. Antiques, fishing, parks, shopping, golf and watersports nearby.

Location: On the Mendocino Coast.

Publicity: Wine Trader, Motortrend, Los Angeles Times, San Francisco Chronicle.

"Thank you so much for a very gracious stay in your cozy inn. We have appreciated all the special touches."

Guerneville G3

Applewood Inn & Restaurant

13555 Hwy 116
Guerneville, CA 95446
(707)869-9093 (800)555-8509 Fax:(707)869-9170

Circa 1900. Perched high on a hill amid towering redwoods and an apple orchard, this sophisticated 1920s Mission-style mansion is set in the heart of the Sonoma wine country. Judging from its exquisite architectural features, pristine landscaping and lovely interiors it is impossible to imagine that this gloriously restored estate was a hangout for hippies and Hell Angel's in the 1960s. Each of the inn's nine spacious guest rooms and seven suites are decorated in period and reproduction antiques. Beautiful terra cotta floors, stone fireplaces and wood-cased windows add to the inn's character. Acclaimed Executive Chef David Frakes, once chef at the San Francisco Ritz Carlton, prepares his sumptuous four-course dinner in the inn's on-site restaurant. Guests can relax by the pool surrounded by redwoods or enjoy a sunset wine tasting in the afternoon from the inn's private collection. A gourmet breakfast and Champagne Brunch are included in the rates.

Historic Interest: Located just five minutes from both award-winning wineries and rugged Sonoma Coast in the Russian River Valley. Approximately 1.5 hours from San Francisco.

Innkeeper(s): Jim Caron & Darryl Notter. $100-250. MC VISA AX DC TC. TAC10. 16 rooms with PB, 6 with FP. 7 suites. 1 conference room. Breakfast included in rates. Type of meal: gourmet breakfast. Beds: Q. Phone, turn-down service and TV in room. Fax, copier, spa, swimming and library on premises. Weddings, small meetings, family reunions and seminars hosted. Spanish spoken. Amusement parks, antiques, fishing, parks, shopping, golf, theater and watersports nearby.

Publicity: Bon Appetit, Elle, Country Living, Bride, Travel Holiday, Travel & Leisure, San Francisco Examiner, Coastal Living, Getaways.

Ridenhour Ranch

12850 River Rd
Guerneville, CA 95446-9276
(707)887-1033 Fax:(707)869-2967

Circa 1906. Located on a hill overlooking the Russian River, this ranch house is shaded by redwoods, oaks and laurels. There are seven guest rooms and a cottage overlooking the rose garden. The innkeepers are former restaurateurs from Southern California and provide a changing dinner menu for their guests. The Korbel Champagne cellars are nearby, and it's a five-minute walk to the river.

Innkeeper(s): Fritz & Diane Rechberger. $95-145. MC VISA AX PC TC. TAC10. 8 rooms with PB, 1 with FP. 1 suite. 1 conference room. Breakfast included in rates. Types of meals: full breakfast and early coffee/tea. Catering service available. Restaurant on premises. Beds: QD. Ceiling fan and TV in room. Fax and spa on premises. Handicap access. Weddings, small meetings, family reunions and seminars hosted. German spoken. Antiques, fishing, parks, shopping, theater and watersports nearby.

Location: Thirty minutes from Santa Rosa and 75 minutes north of San Francisco.

Publicity: Los Angeles Times, Orange County Register, Los Altos Town Crier.

"Your hospitality and food will ensure our return!"

Half Moon Bay I4

Old Thyme Inn

779 Main St
Half Moon Bay, CA 94019-1924
(415)726-1616 Fax:(415)726-6394
E-mail: oldthyme@coastside.net

Circa 1899. Located on the historic Main Street of Old Town, this Queen Anne Victorian has a flower and herb garden surrounding it. Seven rooms are named after various herbs that are found in the garden. Guests receive a complimentary book on herbs with each reservation. Most of the rooms have whirlpool baths and/or fireplaces. Resident teddy bears help keep guests in good company. The inn is within walking distance to beaches, restaurants, shops and art galleries.

Historic Interest: San Francisco is just 25 miles away.

Innkeeper(s): George & Maria Dempsey. $85-220. MC VISA PC. 7 rooms with PB, 4 with FP. 1 suite. 1 conference room. Breakfast included in rates. Beds: Q. Phone, TV and VCR in room. Fax and spa on premises. Small meetings and family reunions hosted. Spanish & French spoken. Antiques, fishing, parks, shopping, sporting events, theater and watersports nearby.

Location: Five minutes from ocean.

Publicity: *California Weekends, Los Angeles, San Mateo Times, San Jose Mercury News, Herb Companion, San Francisco Examiner.*

"Furnishings, rooms and garden were absolutely wonderful. Delicious breakfast and great coffee...loved the peaceful neighborhood."

Hanford K8

The Irwin Street Inn

522 N Irwin St
Hanford, CA 93230-3824
(209)583-8000 Fax:(209)583-8793

Circa 1885. Four restored, turn-of-the-century Victorians and gardens decorate the one-and-a-half-acre grounds at this inn. Twelve-foot ceilings, detailed woodwork and period pieces maintain the authentic Victorian flavor. Guest rooms are adorned with antiques, poster beds and clawfoot tubs, creating a romantic environment. Guests needn't venture far to enjoy a special dinner. The inn's full-service restaurant serves up menus with items such as citrus-baked salmon, honey bourbon chicken, domestic lamb and the inn's special Tournedos of Beef. Succulent desserts include French silk pie, bourbon pecan pie and the rich fudge truffle cheesecake.

Innkeeper(s): Peter Klinger.

$69-125. MC VISA AX DC CB DS TC. TAC15. 30 rooms with PB. 3 suites. Breakfast included in rates. Types of meals: continental breakfast, continental-plus breakfast, full breakfast and gourmet breakfast. Dinner, evening snack, lunch, banquet service, catering service, catered breakfast and room service available. Restaurant on premises. Beds: KQDT. Air conditioning, ceiling fan and TV in room. VCR, fax, copier and swimming on premises. Handicap access. Weddings, small meetings, family reunions and seminars hosted. Spanish spoken. Antiques, parks, shopping and theater nearby.

Healdsburg G4

Calderwood Inn

25 W Grant St
Healdsburg, CA 95448-4804
(707)431-1110 (800)600-5444

Circa 1902. This romantic Queen Anne Victorian is surrounded by lush acres of redwoods, cedars and cypress trees. Each of the six rooms has been decorated with elegant, yet comfortable antiques. Two rooms offer clawfoot tubs, while others include relaxing whirlpool tubs. Window seats, antiques, down comforters and four-poster beds are some of the romantic touches guests might find in their rooms. Fresh seasonal fruit and baked goods accompany the morning entree, and afternoon refreshments are served as well.

Historic Interest: Luther Burbank Home & Gardens, Sonoma County Museum, and a Ripley's Believe It Or Not church, constructed entirely out of one redwood tree, are some of the area's historic sites.

Innkeeper(s): Jennifer & Paul Zawodny. $110-185. PC TC. 6 rooms with PB. Breakfast included in rates. Types of meals: full breakfast and early coffee/tea. Beds: Q. Antiques, fishing, theater and watersports nearby.

Camellia Inn

211 North St
Healdsburg, CA 95448-4251
(707)433-8182 (800)727-8182 Fax:(707)433-8130
E-mail: info@cameliainn.com

Circa 1869. An elegant Italianate Victorian townhouse, the Camellia Inn has twin marble parlor fireplaces and an ornate mahogany dining room fireplace. Antiques fill the guest rooms, complementing Palladian windows and classic interior moldings. The award-winning grounds feature 30 varieties of camellias and are accentuated with a swimming pool, which guests may use in summer.

Innkeeper(s): Ray, Del and Lucy Lewand. $75-165. MC VISA AX. 9 rooms with PB, 4 with FP. 1 suite. Breakfast included in rates. Type of meal: full breakfast. Beds: QD. Phone in room. Fax on premises. Antiques and fishing nearby.

Location: Heart of the Sonoma Wine Country, 50 wineries within 10 miles.

Publicity: *Sunset, Travel & Leisure, New York Times, San Fernando Valley Daily News, San Diego Union, Sacramento Bee, Healdsburg Tribune, Washington Post.*

"A bit of paradise for city folks."

Grape Leaf Inn

539 Johnson St
Healdsburg, CA 95448-3907
(707)433-8140 Fax:(707)433-3140

Circa 1900. This magnificently restored Queen Anne home was built in what was considered the "Nob Hill" of Healdsburg. It was typical of a turn-of-the-century, middle-class dream house. It is situated near the Russian River and the town center. Seventeen sky-  lights provide an abun- dance of sunlight, fresh air, and stained glass. Five guest rooms offer whirlpool tubs and showers for two. The innkeepers make the most of their wine country location, host- ing a wine tasting each evening with a display of at least five Sonoma County wines. Each guest room is named for a wine variety, such as Zinfandel or Merlot. The inn is just four blocks from many of Healdsburg's restaurants and shops.

Innkeeper(s): Terry & Karen Sweet. $95-165. MC VISA DS PC TC. TAC10. 7 rooms with PB. Breakfast included in rates. Type of meal: full breakfast. Beds: KQ. Air conditioning in room. Antiques, fishing, shopping and watersports nearby.

"It was our first time at a real one and we were delighted with our lovely accommodations, delicious breakfasts and most of all you graciousness in trying to please your guests. Thank you for making our 38th anniversary a very special one that we will always remember."

Haydon Street Inn

321 Haydon St
Healdsburg, CA 95448-4411
(707)433-5228 (800)528-3703 Fax:(707)433-6637

Circa 1912. Architectural buffs will have fun naming the several architectural styles found in the Haydon House. It has the curving porch and general shape of a Queen Anne Victorian, the expansive areas of siding and unadorned columns of the Bungalow style, and the exposed roof rafters of the Craftsman. The decor is elegant and romantic, with antiques. The Turret Room includes a clawfoot tub and a fireplace. Two rooms are located in the inn's Victorian Cottage, and both have whirlpool tubs. The Pine Room offers a pencil post bed with a Battenburg lace canopy, while the Victorian Room includes fine antiques and a Ralph Lauren wicker bed.

Innkeeper(s): Joanne Claus. $95-165. MC VISA DS PC TC. TAC10. 8 rooms with PB. 1 with FP. 1 cottage. 1 conference room. Breakfast, afternoon tea and evening snack included in rates. Types of meals: full breakfast, gourmet breakfast and early coffee/tea. Beds: QD. Air conditioning and ceiling fan in room. TV, VCR and fax on premises. Family reunions and seminars hosted. Antiques, fishing, parks, shopping and watersports nearby.

Location: Western Sonoma County, heart of the wine country.

Publicity: *Los Angeles.*

"Adjectives like class, warmth, beauty, thoughtfulness with the right amount of privacy, attention to details relating to comfort, all come to mind. Thank you for the care and elegance."

Healdsburg Inn on The Plaza

110 Matheson St, PO Box 1196
Healdsburg, CA 95448-4108
(707)433-6991 (800)431-8663 Fax:(707)433-9513

Circa 1900. A former Wells Fargo building, the inn is a renovated brick gingerbread overlooking the plaza in historic downtown Healdsburg. Ornate bay windows, embossed wood paneling and broad, paneled stairs present a welcome entrance. There are fireplaces and the halls are filled with sunlight from vaulted, glass skylights. A solarium is the setting for breakfast and afternoon tea. A large covered balcony extends along the entire rear of the building. Shops on the premises sell gifts, toys, quilts and fabric. An antique shop and art gallery can be found there as well.

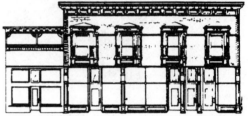

Innkeeper(s): Genny Jenkins & LeRoy Steck. $155-235. MC VISA. 10 rooms with PB, 8 with FP. 1 conference room. Breakfast, afternoon tea and evening snack included in rates. Types of meals: gourmet breakfast and early coffee/tea. Beds: KQT. Phone, air conditioning, ceiling fan, TV and VCR in room. Fax and copier on premises. Small meetings, family reunions and seminars hosted. Antiques, fishing, parks, shopping and watersports nearby.

Publicity: *Healdsburg Tribune, Los Angeles Daily News, New York Times.*

"The first-thing-in-the-morning juice and coffee was much appreciated."

Madrona Manor, A Country Inn

PO Box 818
Healdsburg, CA 95448-0818
(707)433-4231 (800)258-4003 Fax:(707)433-0703

Circa 1881. The inn is comprised of four historic structures in a national historic district. Surrounded by eight acres of manicured lawns and terraced flower and vegetable gardens, the stately mansion was built for John Paxton, a San Francisco businessman. Embellished with turrets, bay windows, porches, and a mansard roof, it provides a breathtaking view of surrounding vineyards. Elegant antique furnishings and a noteworthy restaurant add to the genuine country inn atmosphere. The Gothic-style Carriage House offers more casual lodging.

Historic Interest: Luther Burbank home (15 miles), Simi Winery (3 miles).

Innkeeper(s): John & Carol Muir. $155-250. MC VISA AX DC CB DS PC TC. TAC10. 21 rooms with PB, 17 with FP. 3 suites. 1 cottage. 2 conference rooms. Breakfast included in rates. Type of meal: gourmet breakfast. Dinner and picnic lunch available. Restaurant on premises. Beds: KQDT. Phone and air conditioning in room. Fax, copier and swimming on premises. Handicap access. Weddings, small meetings, family reunions and seminars hosted. Antiques, fishing, parks, shopping, sporting events, theater and watersports nearby.

Pets Allowed: In select buildings.

Location: In the heart of the wine country, Sonoma County.

Publicity: *Gourmet, Woman's Day Home Decorating Ideas, Travel & Leisure, US News, Diversions, Money, Good Housekeeping.*

"Our fourth visit and better every time."

Raford House

10630 Wohler Rd
Healdsburg, CA 95448-9418
(707)887-9573 (800)887-9503 Fax:(707)887-9597

Circa 1880. Situated on more than four acres of rose gardens and fruit trees, this classic Victorian country estate originally was built as a summer home and ranch house in the 1880s. Just 70 miles north of San Francisco, Raford House is nestled in the heart of the Sonoma County wine country, minutes away from award-winning wineries and many fine restaurants. Located close to the Russian River, between Healdsburg and the beautiful Northern California coast, the area has scenic country roads and rugged coastlines.

Innkeeper(s): Carole & Jack Vore. $100-155. MC VISA AX DS. TAC10. 7 rooms with PB. 1 suite. Breakfast and evening snack included in rates. Types of meals: full breakfast and early coffee/tea. Beds: Q. Fax on premises. Small meetings and family reunions hosted. Antiques, fishing, parks, shopping, theater and watersports nearby.

Publicity: *Los Angeles Times, Travel & Leisure, Country.*

"Truly a 'serendipity' experience! Wonderful, welcoming ambiance, great food, lovely hosts. I am 'renewed'."

Hope Valley   G8

Sorensen's Resort

14255 Hwy 88
Hope Valley, CA 96120
(916)694-2203 (800)423-9949

Circa 1876. Where Danish sheepherders settled in this 7,000-foot-high mountain valley, the Sorensen family built a cluster of

fishing cabins. Thus began a century-old tradition of valley hospitality. The focal point of Sorensen's is a "stave" cabin — a reproduction of a 13th-century

Nordic house. Now developed as a Nordic ski resort, a portion of the Mormon-Emigrant Trail and Pony Express Route pass near the inn's 165 acres. In the summer, river rafting, fishing, pony express re-rides, and llama treks are popular Sierra pastimes. Lake Tahoe lies 20 miles to the north. Breakfast is included in the rates for bed & breakfast units only. All the cabins are equipped with kitchens.

Historic Interest: Alpine County Museum (12 miles), Old Indian Trade Ports, Emigrant Road.

Innkeeper(s): John & Patty Brissenden. $65-350. MC VISA AX DS PC TC. TAC10. 30 rooms, 28 with PB, 21 with FP. 28 cottages. 2 conference rooms. Types of meals: continental-plus breakfast, full breakfast and early coffee/tea. Dinner, picnic lunch, lunch and banquet service available. Restaurant on premises. Beds: QD. Copier, sauna and library on premises. Handicap access. 165 acres. Weddings, small meetings, family reunions and

seminars hosted. Spanish spoken. Antiques, fishing, parks, downhill skiing, cross-country skiing and watersports nearby.

Publicity: *Sunset, San Francisco Chronicle, Los Angeles Times, Motorland, Outside.*

"In one night's stay, I felt more comfortable, relaxed, and welcome than any vacation my 47 years have allowed. Thank you for the happiness you have given my children."

Idyllwild   O12

The Pine Cove Inn

23481 Hwy 243, PO Box 2181
Idyllwild, CA 92549
(909)659-5033 (888)659-5033 Fax:(909)659-5034

Circa 1935. These rustic, A-frame cottages offer a variety of amenities in a natural, mountain setting. Refrigerators and microwaves have been placed in each unit, several of which include a wood-burning fireplace. One unit has a full kitchen. A full breakfast is served in a separate lodge which dates back to 1935. The village of Idyllwild is three miles down the road, and the surrounding country offers a variety of activities.

Innkeeper(s): Bob & Michelle Bollmann. $70-100. MC VISA AX DS PC TC. TAC10. 10 rooms with PB, 6 with FP. 3 suites. 1 conference room. Breakfast included in rates. Type of meal: full breakfast. Beds: QT. Ceiling fan in room. TV, VCR and fax on premises. Weddings, small meetings, family reunions and seminars hosted. Antiques, fishing, parks, shopping, cross-country skiing and theater nearby.

Inverness   H4

Hotel Inverness

25 Park Ave, Box 780
Inverness, CA 94937
(415)669-7393 Fax:(415)669-1702
E-mail: desk@hotelinverness.com

Circa 1906. Guests rave about the outdoor breakfasts served in the garden or on the deck. Situated on the edge of a coastal village, Hotel Inverness, near Tomales Bay, is surrounded by the Point Reyes National Seashore. The garden lawn accommodates picnics, lounging or croquet. Boasting one of the best bird-watching areas in the west, the inn has a park-like setting where one can relax and admire the surrounding wooded area. This great natural area reminds many of Yosemite National Park.

Innkeeper(s): Susan & Tom Simms. $100-175. MC VISA AX PC TC. TAC5. 5 rooms with PB. Breakfast included in rates. Type of meal: continental-plus breakfast. Beds: Q. Fax on premises. Parks and watersports nearby.

Publicity: *Los Angeles Times.*

Ione   G6

The Heirloom

214 Shakeley Ln, PO Box 322
Ione, CA 95640-9572
(209)274-4468 (888)628-7896

Circa 1863. A two-story Colonial with columns, balconies and a private English garden, the antebellum Heirloom is true to its name. It has many family heirlooms and a square

grand piano once owned by Lola Montez. The building was dedicated by the Native Sons of the Golden West as a historic site.

Historic Interest: The fourth oldest winery in California (10 miles).

Innkeeper(s): Melisande Hubbs & Patricia Cross. $65-102. MC VISA AX PC TC. TAC10. 6 rooms, 4 with PB, 3 with FP. 2 cottages. Breakfast and afternoon tea included in rates. Meals: full breakfast, gourmet breakfast and early coffee/tea. Room service available. Beds: KQDT. Air conditioning in room. Library on premises. Weddings, small meetings, family reunions, seminars hosted. Antiques, fishing, parks, shopping, golf, theater, watersports nearby.

Location: California Gold Country - halfway between Yosemite & Lake Tahoe.

Publicity: *San Francisco Chronicle, Country Living.*

"Hospitality was amazing. Truly we've never had such a great time."

Jackson   G6

Court Street Inn

215 Court St
Jackson, CA 95642-2309
(209)223-0416 (800)200-0416 Fax:(209)223-5429
E-mail: ct_st_inn@volcano.net

Circa 1872. This cheery yellow and white Victorian-era house is accentuated with a porch stretching across the entire front and decorated with white wicker furniture. Behind the house, a two-story brick structure that once served as a museum for Indian artifacts now houses guests. Afternoon refreshments are served in the dining room under an embossed, carved tin ceiling. Guests relax in front of a marble fireplace in the parlor topped by a gilded mirror. Guest rooms are decorated in antiques. Downtown is only two blocks away.

Historic Interest: Amador County Museum (1/2 block), Kennedy Mine Tailing Wheels (1/2 mile), Chaw Se' Indian Ground Rock State Park (15 miles).

Innkeeper(s): Dave & Nancy Butow. $95-190. MC VISA AX DS PC TC. TAC10. 7 rooms with PB, 4 with FP. 1 suite. 1 cottage. Breakfast and afternoon tea included in rates. Types of meals: full breakfast and early coffee/tea. Beds: KQD. Air conditioning, ceiling fan and TV in room. VCR, fax, copier and spa on premises. Weddings, small meetings, family reunions and seminars hosted. Antiques, fishing, parks, shopping, downhill skiing, cross-country skiing, theater and watersports nearby.

Location: In the center of the Gold Rush Highway 49 & Highway 88.

Publicity: *Amador Dispatch, Sunset, Vacations.*

"Thank you for creating such a warm, relaxing atmosphere. We enjoyed our stay very much and we'll recommend your hospitality."

Gate House Inn

1330 Jackson Gate Rd
Jackson, CA 95642-9539
(209)223-3500 (800)841-1072 Fax:(209)223-1299
E-mail: info@gatehouseinn.com

Circa 1902. This striking Victorian inn is listed in the National Register of Historic Places. Set on a hillside amid lovely gardens, the inn is within walking distance of a state historic park and several notable eateries. The inn's country setting, comfortable porches and swimming pool offer many opportunities for relaxation. Accommodations include three rooms, a suite and a romantic cottage with wood stove and whirlpool tub. All of the guest rooms feature queen beds and elegant furnishings.

Historic Interest: Chaw Se' Indian State Park (8 miles), Kennedy Wheels State Park (one-half mile), Setters Fort/Mill (25 miles).

Innkeeper(s): Keith & Gail Sweet. $95-145. MC VISA AX CB DS PC TC. TAC10. 5 rooms with PB, 3 with FP. 1 suite. 1 cottage. Breakfast included in rates. Types of meals: full breakfast and early coffee/tea. Afternoon tea available. Beds: Q. Air conditioning and ceiling fan in room. Fax, copier and swimming on premises. Weddings, small meetings and family reunions hosted. Antiques, fishing, parks, shopping, skiing, theater and watersports nearby.

"Most gracious, warm hospitality."

Jamestown   H7

The Historic National Hotel B&B

77 Main St, PO Box 502
Jamestown, CA 95327
(209)984-3446 (800)894-3446 Fax:(209)984-5620
E-mail: national@sonnet.com

Circa 1859. One of the 10 oldest continuously operating hotels in California, the inn maintains its original redwood bar where thousands of dollars in gold dust were spent. Electricity and plumbing were added for the first time when the inn was restored a few years ago. It is decorated with Gold Rush period antiques, brass beds and handmade quilts. The restaurant is considered to be one of the finest in the Mother Lode.

Historic Interest: Railtown 1897 State Historic Park, located in Jamestown, is a few blocks from the hotel.

Innkeeper(s): Pamela & Stephen Willey. $80-120. MC VISA AX DC CB DS PC TC. TAC10. 9 rooms with PB. 1 conference room. Breakfast included in rates. Types of meals: continental-plus breakfast and early coffee/tea. Dinner, evening snack, picnic lunch, lunch, gourmet lunch, banquet service and catering service available. Restaurant on premises. Beds: QT. Air conditioning and TV in room. VCR and fax on premises. Weddings, small meetings, family reunions and seminars hosted. Spanish spoken. Antiques, fishing, parks, downhill skiing, cross-country skiing, theater and watersports nearby.

Pets Allowed: By arrangement - credit card or cash deposit required.

Location: Center of town.

Publicity: *Bon Appetit, California Magazine, Focus, San Francisco Magazine, Gourmet, Sunset.*

"Couldn't ask for a more comfortable or peaceful surrounding for resting!"

The Palm Hotel B&B

10382 Willow St
Jamestown, CA 95327-9761
(209)984-3429 (888)551-1852 Fax:(209)984-4929
E-mail: innkeeper@palmhotel.com

Circa 1890. Enjoy Gold Country at this Victorian, which was home to Albert and Amelia Hoyt, publishers of the Mother Lode Magnet. In the 1890s, the home served as a boarding house. Today, it offers eight guest rooms with lacy curtains, fresh flowers, clawfoot tubs, marble showers and robes. The innkeepers also have a soda fountain bar in the parlor. A full, buffet breakfast is served each morning along with The Palm's special blend of coffee. The inn is located two-and-a-half hours from San Francisco and about an hour from Yosemite Valley, and it is within walking distance of Main Street, boutiques, galleries, restaurants and Railtown State Park.

Innkeeper(s): Rick & Sandy Allen. $85-145. MC VISA AX TC. TAC10. 8 rooms with PB. 2 suites. Breakfast included in rates. Type of meal: full breakfast. Beds: KQD. Air conditioning, ceiling fan and TV in room. Fax and copier on premises. Handicap access. Small meetings and family reunions hosted. Antiques, fishing, parks, shopping, golf, theater, watersports nearby.

"The simple elegance of our room and ambiance of the Palm in general was a balm for our souls."

Jenner G3

Jenner Inn & Cottages

10400 Hwy 1, PO Box 69
Jenner, CA 95450
(707)865-2377 (800)732-2377 Fax:(707)865-0829
E-mail: innkeeper@jennerinn.com

Circa 1904. Located on three acres, this New England cottage-style inn began as a hotel with general store and post office to accommodate needs of the local lumber industry. Destroyed by fire and rebuilt by ship builders, the parlor features a beamed ceiling and oak floors and is comfortably furnished. The inn consists of waterside cottages tucked into nooks and crannies of the village. There are suites with fireplaces and kitchenettes, or you may select an entire rental home with panoramic views of the ocean and river. The decor varies from contemporary to rustic or country Victorian. All have sun decks. A favorite meal at the inn's restaurant includes Dungeness Crab Cakes, Sonoma Green Salad, Seared Salmon Filet and Swiss Chocolate Pie. Visit Bodega Bay, wineries, Point Reyes or simply enjoy driving along the scenic country roads. Located close to beautiful sandy beaches.
Historic Interest: Sonoma Coast State Beaches are 15 miles of sandy beaches.
Innkeeper(s): Jenny Carroll, Richard & Sheldon Murphy. $75-195. MC VISA AX PC TC. TAC10. 13 rooms with PB, 7 with FP. 2 suites. 2 cottages. 2 cabins. 1 conference room. Breakfast and afternoon tea included in rates. Types of meals: continental-plus breakfast and early coffee/tea. Beds: KQDB. Ceiling fan in room. Fax, copier and spa on premises. Weddings, small meetings, family reunions and seminars hosted. Antiques, fishing, parks, shopping, golf, theater and watersports nearby.

Joshua Tree O13

Joshua Tree Inn

61259 29 Palms Hwy, PO Box 340
Joshua Tree, CA 92252-0340
(760)366-1188 (800)366-1444 Fax:(760)366-3805

Circa 1940. The hacienda-style inn was once a '50s motel. It now offers Victorian-style rooms with king-size beds. Antiques and Old West memorabilia add to the decor. Throughout the inn, local artists display their creations. The inn is one mile from the gateway to the 467,000-acre Joshua Tree National Park.
Innkeeper(s): Dr. Daniel & Evelyn Shirbroun. $65-175. MAP. MC VISA AX DC CB DS TC. TAC10. 10 rooms with PB. 2 suites. 1 conference room. Type of meal: early coffee/tea. Afternoon tea available. Beds: KQTD. Phone, air conditioning, ceiling fan and TV in room. VCR, fax, copier and swimming on premises. Weddings, small meetings, family reunions and seminars hosted. Antiques, parks, shopping, golf and theater nearby.

Pets Allowed: In designated rooms.

Publicity: *Los Angeles Times, Press Enterprise.*

"Quiet, clean and charming."

Julian P12

Julian Gold Rush Hotel

2032 Main St, PO Box 1856
Julian, CA 92036
(760)765-0201 (800)734-5854

Circa 1897. The dream of a former slave and his wife lives today in this sole surviving hotel in Southern California's "Mother Lode of Gold Mining." This Victorian charmer is listed in the National Register of Historic Places and is a designated State of California Point of Historic Interest (#SDI-09). Guests enjoy the feeling of a visit to Grandma's and a tradition of genteel hospitality.
Historic Interest: Entire townsite is a State Historic Landmark.
Innkeeper(s): Steve & Gig Ballinger. $72-160. MC VISA AX PC TC. TAC10. 14 rooms with PB, 1 with FP. 1 suite. 2 cottages. 1 conference room. Breakfast and afternoon tea included in rates. Type of meal: full breakfast. Beds: QDT. Weddings, small meetings and seminars hosted. Antiques, fishing, parks and theater nearby.
Location: Center of town.
Publicity: *San Diego Union, PSA.*

"Any thoughts you have about the 20th century will leave you when you walk into the lobby of this grand hotel— Westways Magazine."

Orchard Hill Country Inn

2502 Washington St, PO Box 425
Julian, CA 92036-0425
(760)765-1700 (800)672-4273

This Craftsman-style inn is a perfect country getaway for those seeking solace from the city lights. There are three, 1920s cottages, and the newer lodge was built as a companion to the original building.

Expansive, individually appointed guest suites offer amenities such as fireplaces, whirlpool tubs, hand-knitted afghans and down comforters all surrounded by warm, country decor. Gourmet coffee, tea and cocoa also are provided in each suite, as are wet bars. The innkeepers also offer more than 100 games to help pass the time. Guests can enjoy a breakfast of fruits, muffins and a special egg dish in the dining room. Wine and hors d'oeuvres are provided each afternoon. Dinner is served on selected evenings. The expansive grounds boast a variety of gardens highlighting native plants and flowers.
Historic Interest: Orchard Hill is located in the heart of a state historic district, and the innkeepers offer a comprehensive visitors' guide of the Julian area, including maps and a historic walking tour route.
Innkeeper(s): Darrell & Pat Straube. $155-225. MC VISA AX PC TC. TAC10. 22 rooms with PB, 11 with FP. 2 conference rooms. Breakfast and evening snack included in rates. Types of meals: full breakfast and early coffee/tea. Dinner, picnic lunch, banquet service and catering service available. Beds: KQ. Air conditioning, ceiling fan, TV and VCR in room. Fax and copier on premises. Handicap access. Small meetings and seminars hosted. Antiques, fishing, parks, shopping and theater nearby.
Publicity: *San Diego Union Tribune, Los Angeles Times, Orange County Register, Orange Coast, San Francisco Chronicle, San Bernadino Sun, Oceanside Blade-Citizen.* Ratings: 4 Diamonds.

"The quality of the rooms, service and food were beyond our expectations."

Kernville L10

Kern River Inn B&B

119 Kern River Dr
Kernville, CA 93238
(760)376-6750 (800)986-4382 Fax:(760)376-6643
E-mail: kribb@kernvalley.com

Circa 1991. Located across from Riverside Park and the Kern River, this country-style inn boasts a wraparound porch with views and sounds of the river. The Whiskey Flat, Whitewater and Piute rooms include fireplaces. The Big Blue and Greenhorn rooms offer whirlpool tubs. All rooms

afford river views. Breakfast may include the inn's renowned giant home-baked cinnamon rolls, egg and cheese dishes or sweetheart waffles.

Innkeeper(s): Jack & Carita Prestwich. $79-99. MC VISA AX PC TC. TAC10. 6 rooms with PB. Breakfast and afternoon tea included in rates. Types of meals: full breakfast and early coffee/tea. Beds: KQ. Ceiling fan in room. TV, VCR, fax and library on premises. Handicap access. Weddings, small meetings, family reunions and seminars hosted. Antiques, fishing, parks, shopping, downhill skiing, cross-country skiing, golf and watersports nearby.

Location: In the southern Sierra Nevada Mountains, three hours north of L.A.

Publicity: *Kern Valley Sun, Los Angeles Times, Valley News, Westways.*

"For us, your place is the greatest. So romantic."

La Jolla   Q11

Prospect Park Inn

1110 Prospect St
La Jolla, CA 92037-4533
(619)454-0133 (800)433-1609 Fax:(619)454-2056

Circa 1946. Although this is a newer property, built in 1946, the hotel is located within walking distance to many wonderful shops, restaurants and sites in beautiful La Jolla, an upscale suburb of San Diego. Guests enjoy stunning ocean views from some rooms. The decor is done in a modern and pleasing hotel style. Made-to-order continental breakfasts are served on the sundeck, which faces the Pacific and La Jolla Cove. San Diego is just minutes away, but guests can easily spend a whole day enjoying this seaside village.

Innkeeper(s): John Heichman. $100-300. MC VISA AX DC CB DS TC. TAC10. 22 rooms with PB. 2 suites. Breakfast and afternoon tea included in rates. Type of meal: continental breakfast. Beds: KQT. Phone, air conditioning and TV in room. Fax, copier, bicycles and library on premises. Weddings, small meetings, family reunions and seminars hosted. Spanish, German, Russian and Arabic spoken. Amusement parks, fishing, parks, shopping, sporting events, golf, theater and watersports nearby.

Laguna Beach   P11

Eiler's Inn

741 S Coast Hwy
Laguna Beach, CA 92651-2722
(714)494-3004 Fax:(714)497-2215

Circa 1940. This New Orleans-style inn surrounds a lush courtyard and fountain. The rooms are decorated with antiques and wallpapers. Wine and cheese is served during the evening in front of the fireplace. Named after Eiler Larsen, famous town greeter of Laguna, the inn is just a stone's throw from the beach on the ocean side of Pacific Coast Highway.

Innkeeper(s): Nico Wirtz. $100-175. MC VISA AX. 12 rooms with PB, 1 with FP. 1 suite. Breakfast included in rates. Type of meal: continental-plus breakfast. Afternoon tea available. Beds: KQD. Phone in room. Weddings, small meetings and seminars hosted. Amusement parks, antiques, fishing, shopping and theater nearby.

Location: In the heart of the village.

Publicity: *N.Y. Times, L.A. Times, California Magazine, Home & Garden.*

"Who could find a paradise more relaxing than an old-fashioned bed

and breakfast with Mozart and Vivaldi, a charming fountain, wonderful fresh-baked bread, ocean air."

Lake Arrowhead   N11

Bracken Fern Manor

815 Arrowhead Villas Rd, PO Box 100
Lake Arrowhead, CA 92352
(909)337-8557 Fax:(909)337-3323

Circa 1929. Opened during the height of the '20s as Lake Arrowhead's first membership resort, this country inn provided refuge to Silver Screen heroines, the wealthy and the prominent. Old letters from the Gibson Girls found in the attic bespoke of elegant parties, dapper gentlemen, the Depression, Prohibition and homesick hearts. Each room is furnished with antiques collected from a lifetime of international travel. There is also a game parlor, wine tasting cellar, library, art gallery and garden Jacuzzi and sauna. Wine is offered in the afternoon. The Crestline Historical Society has its own museum and curator and a map of historical sites you can visit.

Historic Interest: Lake Arrowhead's first private membership resort with electricity, opened in 1929 by Bugsy Segal.

Innkeeper(s): Cheryl Weaver. $65-228. MC VISA. 10 rooms, 9 with PB. 3 suites. Breakfast included in rates. Types of meals: full breakfast and early coffee/tea. Beds: KQDT. TV and VCR on premises. Weddings, small meetings, family reunions and seminars hosted. Antiques, fishing, shopping, downhill skiing, cross-country skiing, theater and watersports nearby.

Publicity: *Mountain Shopper & Historic B&B, Press Enterprise, Sun, Lava.*

"My husband brought me here for my 25th birthday and it was everything I hoped it would be - peaceful, romantic and so relaxing .... Thank you for the wonderful memories I will hold close to my heart always."

Lemon Cove   K9

Mesa Verde Plantation B&B

33038 Sierra Dr
Lemon Cove, CA 93244-1700
(209)597-2555 (800)240-1466 Fax:(209)597-2551
E-mail: relax@plantationbnb.com

Circa 1908. The history of orange production is deeply entwined in the roots of California, and this home is located on what once was an orange plantation. The original 1908 house burned in the 1960s, but the current home was built on its foundation. In keeping with the home's plantation past, the innkeepers decorated the place with a "Gone With the Wind," theme. The comfortable, country guest rooms sport names

such as the Scarlett O'Hara, the Belle Watling, and of course, the Rhett Butler. A hot tub is located in the orchard, and there also is a heated swimming pool.

Innkeeper(s): Scott & Marie Munger. $70-125. MC VISA AX DC DS PC TC. TAC10. 8 rooms, 6 with PB, 2 with FP. 1 suite. Breakfast and evening snack included in rates. Types of meals: full breakfast, gourmet breakfast and early coffee/tea. Beds: KQD. Air conditioning, ceiling fan, TV and VCR in room.

Fax, spa and swimming on premises. Weddings, small meetings and family reunions hosted. Antiques, fishing, parks, shopping, cross-country skiing, sporting events, golf and watersports nearby.
Publicity: *Exeter Sun, Kaweah Commonwealth.*

"Scarlett O'Hara would be proud to live on this lovely plantation."

Little River   F2

The Victorian Farmhouse

7001 N Hwy 1
Little River, CA 95456
(707)937-0697 (800)264-4723

Circa 1877. Built as a private residence, this Victorian farmhouse is located on two-and-a-half acres in Little River. Two miles south of the historic village of Mendocino, the inn offers a relaxed country setting with deer, quail, flower gardens, an apple orchard and a running creek. Several cottages offer TV and ocean views. A short walk will take you to the shoreline.
Innkeeper(s): Carole Molnar. $85-175. MC VISA AX DS. TAC10. 11 rooms with PB. Breakfast and afternoon tea included in rates. Type of meal: full breakfast. Beds: KQT. Small meetings hosted. Antiques, fishing, parks, shopping, theater and watersports nearby. Pets Allowed.

"This morning when we woke up at home we really missed having George deliver breakfast. You have a lovely inn and you do a super job."

Glendeven

8221 N Highway 1
Littleriver, CA 95456-9502
(707)937-0083

Circa 1867. Lumber merchant Isaiah Stevens built this farmhouse on a two-acre headland meadow with the bay of Little River in the distance. Gray clapboard siding and high-pitched roof lines reflect the architecture of Stevens' native Maine. Stevenscroft is a recent addition of four rooms, each with its own fireplace, views of the bay and breakfast in your room. One can often hear the sound of waves rolling onto the beach.
Innkeeper(s): Jan & Janet deVries. $100-200. MC VISA. 11 rooms, 10 with PB. Breakfast included in rates. Type of meal: full breakfast. Beds: QDT.
Location: One-and-a-half miles to Mendocino.
Publicity: *Arizona Republic, Contra Costa Times, L.A. Times, Country Inns.*

"Thank you for letting us be among those special people who experience the wonderment and joy of Glendeven."

Long Beach   O10

Kennebec Corner Bed & Breakfast

2305 E 2nd ST
Long Beach, CA 90803-5126
(562)439-2705 Fax:(310)518-0616

Circa 1923. This California Craftsman-style home offers a large four-room suite with a sitting room, office, fireplace, bathroom with a double sunken tub and a bedroom with a one-of-a-kind, four-poster king-size bed.
There is an outdoor spa available in the home's courtyard. The innkeepers deliver the morning paper and a tray with coffee or tea to your door an hour prior to breakfast. On weekdays, a healthy

California or continental breakfast is served, and on weekends, guests enjoy a full, gourmet meal. The home is located in Bluff Park, a local historic district two blocks from the beach.
Innkeeper(s): Michael & Marty Gunhus. $95-140. PC TC. TAC20. 1 suite. Breakfast included in rates. Types of meals: continental-plus breakfast, gourmet breakfast and early coffee/tea. Picnic lunch available. Beds: K. Phone in room. TV, VCR, fax, spa, bicycles and library on premises. Antiques, fishing, parks, shopping, sporting events, theater and watersports nearby.

Manchester   F3

Victorian Gardens

14409 S Hwy 1
Manchester, CA 95459-8926
(707)882-3606

Circa 1904. The Caugheys, an Irish-Canadian family, occupied this 92-acre farmland for a century. The family's original home burned in 1904, and this picturesque Victorian farmhouse was built in its place. For those in search of privacy, the inn's location is divine. The inn is tucked beside rolling hills, just off the rocky Pacific coast in a secluded, romantic spot. The eclectic decor is elegant. Beds are topped with down pillows and fluffy comforters, and guests can enjoy a soak in one of the home's original clawfoot tubs. The home is full of interesting things, from paintings by Picasso and Warhol, to artifacts from innkeeper Luciano Zamboni's birthplace of Italy. Gourmet breakfasts are served fireside or perhaps in the garden. In the afternoons, hors d'oeuvres are served, and guests can make arrangements to enjoy a wonderful dinner prepared by Luciano, who specializes in regional Italian cuisine.
Innkeeper(s): Luciano & Pauline Zamboni. $135-185. MC VISA AX PC TC. TAC10. 4 rooms, 2 with PB. Breakfast and evening snack included in rates. Types of meals: full breakfast and early coffee/tea. Picnic lunch and lunch available. Beds: Q. TV, VCR and library on premises. 92 acres. Weddings, small meetings and family reunions hosted. French and Italian spoken. Antiques, fishing, parks, shopping, golf, theater and watersports nearby.
Publicity: *Orange County Coast, News-Herald, North Coast Magazine.*

"This experience is the cream of the crop. You've outdone them all."

McCloud   B5

McCloud River Inn

325 Lawndale Ct
McCloud, CA 96057-1560
(916)964-2130 (800)261-7831 Fax:(916)964-2730
E-mail: mort@snowcrest.net

Circa 1900. Nestled within the beauty of Shasta National Forest, rests this country Victorian. Five serene acres of lawns and woodland create a peaceful setting. The inn once served as the offices for the McCloud River Lumber Company. The town bank and telephone switchboard were located here. The interior has been painstakingly restored, and each of the five guest rooms has its own individual charm. Breakfasts are a treat, and a typical menu might include a savory Greek quiche, homemade bread and a selection of fresh fruits. There is a small cafè at the inn and, for those who must have a gourmet caffeine fix, an espresso bar. Shops and historic sites are within walking distance.

Innkeeper(s): Ron & Marina Mort. $45-76. MC VISA AX DS PC TC. TAC10. 5 rooms, 3 with PB. 1 suite. 1 conference room. Breakfast included in rates. Type of meal: full breakfast. Restaurant on premises. Beds: QDT. Ceiling fan in room. Fax and copier on premises. Weddings, small meetings, family reunions and seminars hosted. Antiques, fishing, parks, shopping, downhill skiing, cross-country skiing, golf and watersports nearby.

Publicity: *Sunset, Berkeley Guide, Siskiyou County Railroad Gazette, Siskiyou County Scene.*

"Thank you for your wonderful hospitality. We thoroughly enjoyed our stay and hope that we will visit again."

Mendocino   F2

Agate Cove Inn

11201 Lansing, PO Box 1150
Mendocino, CA 95460
(707)937-0551 (800)527-3111

Circa 1860. Perched on a blufftop overlooking the Pacific Ocean, the Agate Cove Inn was constructed as a farmhouse by Mathias Brinzing, owner of the first beer brewery in Mendocino. Cottages are lovingly decorated, and some have stunning white water views. All but one of the rooms include a wood-burning stove and a patio with a view. Guests enjoy not only a full breakfast, but at the same time, take in a spectacular view of the shoreline and waves crashing against the rocks.

Innkeeper(s): Scott & Betsy Buckwald. $69-250. MC VISA. 10 rooms with PB, 9 with FP. Type of meal: full breakfast. Beds: KQ. Phone in room.

Publicity: *Travel & Leisure, San Francisco Magazine, San Francisco Examine, Glamour, Sacramento Bee, Travel Holiday.*

"Warmest hospitality, charming rooms, best breakfast and view in Mendocino."

The Headlands Inn

PO Box 132
Mendocino, CA 95460-0132
(707)937-4431 (800)354-4431 Fax:(707)937-0421

Circa 1868. Originally a small barbershop on Main Street, the building later became the elegant "Oyster and Coffee Saloon" in 1884. Finally, horses pulled the house over log rollers to its present location. The new setting provides a spectacular view of the ocean, the rugged coastline and breathtaking sunsets. Antiques, featherbeds and wood-burning fireplaces warm each guest

room. There is a romantic honeymoon cottage, an English-style garden and a parlor. A full gourmet breakfast is brought directly to your room.

Innkeeper(s): Gail Erickson. $110-195. MC VISA AX PC TC. 6 rooms with PB, 6 with FP. 1 cottage. Breakfast and afternoon tea included in rates. Type of meal: gourmet breakfast. Beds: KQ. Fax on premises. Antiques, fishing, parks, shopping, theater and watersports nearby.

Location: Two blocks from village center, within historic preservation district.

Publicity: *Los Angeles Times, New York Times, Innsider, Oakland Tribune, Orange County Register, Contra Costa Times, Palo Alto Times, Alaska Airline, San Jose Mercury, Washington Post.*

"If a Nobel Prize were given for breakfasts, you would win hands down. A singularly joyous experience!!"

John Dougherty House

571 Ukiah St, PO Box 817
Mendocino, CA 95460
(707)937-5266 (800)486-2104
E-mail: jdhbmw@mcn.org

Circa 1867. Early American furnishings and country-style stenciling provide the decor at this welcoming inn. Four rooms have outstanding water views, including the Captain's Room. The water tower room has an 18-foot ceiling and wood-burning stove. The inn's grounds sparkle with an array of beautiful flowers.

The inn has been featured on the cover of Country Homes.

Historic Interest: Located in Mendocino Historic Village.

Innkeeper(s): David & Marion Wells. $95-205. MC VISA DS PC TC. TAC10. 6 rooms with PB, 6 with FP. 3 suites. Breakfast included in rates. Meals: gourmet breakfast and early coffee/tea. Beds: Q. TV in room. Family reunions hosted. Antiques, fishing, parks, shopping, theater, watersports nearby.

Publicity: *Mendocino Beacon, Country Home, Los Angeles Times, San Francisco Times/Tribune.*

"A treasure chest of charm, beauty and views."

Mendocino Hotel

PO Box 587
Mendocino, CA 95460-0587
(707)937-0511 (800)548-0513 Fax:(707)937-0513

Circa 1878. In the heart of Mendocino on Main Street, the Mendocino Hotel originally was established as a temperance hotel for lumbermen. An Old West facade was added. The historic Heeser House, home of Mendocino's first settler, was annexed by the hotel along with its acre of gardens. Many of the guest rooms and suites boast tall, four-poster and canopy beds or fireplaces and coastal

views. The hotel has several dining rooms.

Innkeeper(s): Cynthia Reinhart. $85-225. MC VISA AX. 51 rooms, 37 with PB, 20 with FP. 6 suites. 1 conference room. Type of meal: full breakfast. Dinner, lunch and room service available. Restaurant on premises. Beds: KQDT. Copier on premises. Antiques, fishing, theater and watersports nearby.

Publicity: *Los Angeles Times, Tribune, Wine Spectator, Gourmet, Bon Appetit, Press Democrat, Country Inns.*

"The hotel itself is magnificent, but more importantly, your staff is truly incredible."

Sea Rock B&B Inn

11101 Lansing St
Mendocino, CA 95460
(707)937-0926 (800)906-0926
E-mail: searock@mcn.org

Circa 1930. Enjoy sea breezes and ocean vistas at this inn, which rests on a bluff looking out to the Pacific. Most of the accommodations include a wood-burning Franklin fireplace and featherbed. Four guest rooms are available in the Stratton House and each affords an ocean view. There are six cottages on the grounds, most offering a sea view. The innkeepers also offer deluxe accommodations in four special suites. Each has an ocean view, wood-burning fireplace, private entrance and a deck. The grounds, which now feature gardens, were the site of an 1870s brewery. The inn is less than half a mile from Mendocino.

Innkeeper(s): Susie & Andy Plocher. $85-250. MC VISA AX DS PC TC. 14 rooms with PB, 13 with FP. 4 suites. 6 cottages. Breakfast included in rates. Type of meal: continental-plus breakfast. Beds: KQ. Phone, turndown service, TV and VCR in room. Family reunions hosted. Antiques, fishing, parks, shopping, golf, theater and watersports nearby.

Publicity: *California Visitors Review.*

The Stanford Inn By The Sea

PO Box 487
Mendocino, CA 95460-0487
(707)937-5615 (800)331-8884 Fax:(707)937-0305

Circa 1856. Tucked against a forested hillside, the Stanford Inn, a new building, affords every guest a view of the ocean. Its 10 acres include an expansive lawn studded with flower gardens that slope down to a duck pond and redwood barn where the inn's llamas and horses graze. Each room has a four-poster bed, a wood-burning fireplace and watercolors and paintings by local artists. A '30s cottage is on the premises and there is a turn-of-the-century homestead. Complimentary red and white Mendocino wines are offered.

Historic Interest: Mendocino Village (immediately adjacent).

Innkeeper(s): Joan & Jeff Stanford. $160-190. MC VISA AX DC CB DS. 23 rooms with PB, 26 with FP. 3 suites. 1 conference room. Breakfast and afternoon tea included in rates. Beds: KQT. Spa and sauna on premises. Handicap access. Theater and watersports nearby.

Pets Allowed.

Publicity: *Oakland Tribune, Brides, Contra Costa Times.* Ratings: 4 Diamonds.

"As working parents with young children, our weekends away are so terribly few in number, that every one must be precious. Thanks to you, our weekend in Mendocino was the finest of all."

Whitegate Inn

499 Howard St
Mendocino, CA 95460
(707)937-4892 (800)531-7282 Fax:(707)937-1131

Circa 1883. When it was first built, the local newspaper called Whitegate Inn "one of the most elegant and best appointed residences in town." Its bay windows, steep gabled roof, redwood siding and fishscale shingles are stunning examples of Victorian architecture. The house's original wallpaper and candelabras adorn the double parlors. There, an antique 1827 piano, at one time part of Alexander Graham Bell's collection, and inlaid pocket doors take you back to a more gracious time. French and Victorian antique furnishings and fresh flowers add to the inn's elegant hospitality and old world charm. The

gourmet breakfasts are artfully presented in the inn's sunlit dining room. The inn is just a block from the ocean, galleries, restaurants and the center of town.

Historic Interest: Mendocino Headlands State Park surrounds the village, which was once the property of the original lumber mill.

Innkeeper(s): Carol & George Bechtloff. $119-239. MC VISA AX DS TC. 6 rooms with PB, 6 with FP. 1 conference room. Breakfast and afternoon tea included in rates. Meals: gourmet breakfast and early coffee/tea. Beds: KQT. TV in room. Fax on premises. Weddings, small meetings and family reunions hosted. Antiques, fishing, parks, shopping, theater, watersports nearby.

Publicity: *Innsider, Country Inns, Country Home, Glamour, Santa Rosa Press Democrat, San Francisco Chronicle.*

"Made our honeymoon a dream come true."

Mill Valley   H4

Mountain Home Inn

810 Panoramic Hwy
Mill Valley, CA 94941-1765
(415)381-9000 Fax:(415)381-3615

Circa 1912. At one time the only way to get to Mountain Home was by taking the train up Mount Tamalpais. With 22 trestles and 281 curves, it was called "the crookedest railroad in the world." Now accessible by auto, the trip still provides a spectacular view of San Francisco Bay. Each guest room has a view of the mountain, valley or bay.

Innkeeper(s): Lynn Saggese. $133-249. MC VISA AX PC TC. TAC10. 10 rooms with PB, 5 with FP. 1 conference room. Breakfast included in rates. Type of meal: full breakfast. Dinner and lunch available. Beds: KQ. Phone in room. Fax and copier on premises. Weddings, small meetings and family reunions hosted. Parks and shopping nearby.

Location: Mt. Tamalpais.

Publicity: *San Francisco Examiner, California.*

"A luxurious retreat. Echoes the grand style and rustic feeling of national park lodges — Ben Davidson, Travel & Leisure."

Montara   I4

The Goose & Turrets B&B

835 George St, PO Box 937
Montara, CA 94037-0937
(650)728-5451 Fax:(650)728-0141
E-mail: rhmgt@montara.com

Circa 1908. In the peaceful setting of horse ranches, strawflower farms and an art colony, this Italian villa features beautiful gardens surrounded by a 20-foot-high cypress hedge. The gardens include an orchard, vegetable garden, herb garden,

rose garden, fountains, a hammock, swing and plenty of spots to enjoy the surroundings. The large dining and living room areas are filled with art, collectibles and classical music plays during afternoon tea. Among its many previous uses, the Goose & Turrets once served as Montara's first post office, the town hall, a Sunday school and a grocery store.

Historic Interest: The historic district of Half Moon Bay is eight miles away. Pescadero and a historic mansion and gardens are about 15 miles away.

Innkeeper(s): Raymond & Emily Hoche-Mong. $85-120. MC VISA AX DC DS PC TC. TAC10. 5 rooms with PB, 3 with FP. Breakfast and afternoon tea included in rates. Beds: KQDT. Turndown service in room. Library on premises. French spoken. Antiques, fishing, parks and watersports nearby.

Location: One-half mile from the Pacific Ocean, 20 minutes from San Francisco airport.

Publicity: *San Jose Mercury News, Half Moon Bay Review, Peninsula Times Tribune, San Mateo Times, L.A. Times, Tri-Valley Herald, Contra Costa Times.*

"Lots of special touches. Great Southern hospitality — we'll be back."

Monterey   J5

The Jabberwock

598 Laine St
Monterey, CA 93940-1312
(408)372-4777 (888)428-7253 Fax:(408)655-2946

Circa 1911. Set in a half-acre of gardens, this Craftsman-style inn provides a fabulous view of Monterey Bay with its famous barking seals. When you're ready to settle in for the evening, you'll find huge Victorian beds complete with lace-edged sheets and goose-down comforters. In the late afternoon, hors d'oeuvres and aperitifs are served in an enclosed sun porch. After dinner, guests are tucked into bed with homemade chocolate chip cookies and milk. To help guests avoid long lines, the innkeepers have tickets available for the popular and nearby Monterey Bay Aquarium.

Historic Interest: Historic adobes and Cannery Row are within walking distance of The Jabberwock.

Innkeeper(s): Joan & John Kiliany. $105-190. MC VISA. 7 rooms, 5 with PB, 3 with FP. Types of meals: gourmet breakfast and early coffee/tea. Beds: KQ. Fax and copier on premises. Weddings, small meetings and family reunions hosted. Antiques, fishing, parks, shopping, theater and watersports nearby.

Location: Four blocks above Cannery Row, the beach and Monterey Bay Aquarium; within walking distance to Conference Center.

Publicity: *Sunset, Travel & Leisure, Sacramento Bee, San Francisco Examiner, Los Angeles Times, Country Inns, San Francisco Chronicle, Diablo, Elmer Dill's KABC-Los Angeles TV.*

"Words are not enough to describe the ease and tranquility of the atmosphere of the home, rooms, owners and staff at the Jabberwock."

Monterey Hotel

406 Alvarado St
Monterey, CA 93940-2711
(408)375-3184 (800)727-0960 Fax:(408)373-2899

Circa 1904. Recently saved from demolition and restored in '96, this elegant Victorian hotel offers appealing historic features such as arched doorways and an old hand-painted safe. The original elevator boasts gilt-edged molding and beveled, leaded glass. The lobby is especially inviting with a fireplace, chandeliers, wall sconces and polished woods setting off the tasteful collection of furnishings. There is a two-story atrium. Guest rooms offer plantation shutters, ceiling fans, a handsome collection of antiques and marble baths. Afternoon refreshments are served.

Innkeeper(s): Robin Lemmerman. $99-279. MC VISA AX DC CB DS. TAC10. 45 rooms with PB, 4 with FP. 6 suites. 2 conference rooms. Breakfast, afternoon tea and evening snack included in rates. Type of meal: continental

breakfast. Beds: KQTD. Phone, turndown service, ceiling fan and TV in room. Fax, copier and child care on premises. Handicap access. Weddings, small meetings and family reunions hosted. Amusement parks, antiques, fishing, parks, shopping, sporting events, golf and theater nearby.

Old Monterey Inn

500 Martin St
Monterey, CA 93940-4491
(408)375-8284

Circa 1929. Built in the Tudor style with half-timbers, the ivy-covered Old Monterey Inn looks and feels like an English country house. Brick pathways and a comfortable hammock beckon guests outside to the garden. Redwood, pine and old oak trees shelter an acre of pansies, roses, peonies and rhododendrons. Most of the guest rooms have wood-burning fireplaces, skylights and stained-glass windows. Smoking is permitted in the garden.

Innkeeper(s): Ann & Gene Swett. $150-210. 10 rooms with PB, 8 with FP. Type of meal: full breakfast. Beds: KQT. Phone in room.

Location: Five minutes from Monterey Bay Aquarium.

Publicity: *Los Angeles Times, PSA Magazine, San Francisco Focus, Country Inns, Travel & Leisure, Glamour.*

"Bed and Breakfast Inn of the Year—Hideaway Report."

Mount Shasta   B5

Mount Shasta Ranch B&B

1008 W.A. Barr Rd
Mount Shasta, CA 96067-9465
(530)926-3870 Fax:(530)926-6882
E-mail: alpinere@snowcrest.net

Circa 1923. This large two-story ranch house offers a full view of Mt. Shasta from its 60-foot-long redwood porch. Spaciousness abounds from the 1,500-square-foot living room with a massive rock fireplace to the large suites with private bathrooms that include large tubs and roomy showers. A full country breakfast may offer cream cheese-stuffed French toast or fresh, wild blackberry crepes. Just minutes away, Lake Siskiyou boasts superb fishing, sailing, swimming, and 18 hole golf course with public tennis courts.

Historic Interest: Built in 1923 by HD "Curley" Brown as a thoroughbred horse ranch.

Innkeeper(s): Bill & Mary Larsen. $50-95. MC VISA AX DS PC TC. 9 rooms, 4 with PB. 1 cottage. 1 conference room. Breakfast included in rates. Types of meals: full breakfast and early coffee/tea. Afternoon tea available. Beds: Q. Air conditioning, ceiling fan and TV in room. VCR, fax, copier, spa and library on premises. Small meetings, family reunions and seminars hosted. Antiques, fishing, parks, shopping, downhill skiing, cross-country skiing and watersports nearby. Pets Allowed.

Murphys   H7

Dunbar House, 1880

271 Jones St
Murphys, CA 95247-1375
(209)728-2897 (800)692-6006 Fax:(209)728-1451
E-mail: dunbarhs@goldrush.com

Circa 1880. A picket fence frames this Italianate home, built by Willis Dunbar for his bride. The porch, lined with rocking chairs, is the perfect place to take in the scenery of century-old gardens decorated by fountains, birdhouses and swings. A collection of antiques, family heirlooms and comfortable furnishings fill the interior. The two-room garden suite includes a bed dressed with fine linens and a down comforter and a two-person Jacuzzi spa. Guests can enjoy the morning fare in the dining room, garden or opt for breakfast in their room.

Historic Interest: Columbia State Park (10 miles), Big Trees State Park (14 miles).

Innkeeper(s): Bob & Barbara Costa. $125-175. MC VISA AX PC TC. TAC10. 4 rooms with PB, 4 with FP. 2 suites. Breakfast and afternoon tea included in rates. Types of meals: full breakfast, gourmet breakfast and early coffee/tea. Room service available. Beds: KQ. Phone, air conditioning, turn-down service, ceiling fan, TV and VCR in room. Fax, copier and library on premises. Antiques, fishing, parks, shopping, downhill skiing, cross-country skiing, theater and watersports nearby.

Location: Two blocks from the center of town.

Publicity: *Los Angeles Times, Gourmet, Victorian Homes, Country Inns, Travel & Leisure.*

"Your beautiful gardens and gracious hospitality combine for a super bed & breakfast."

Napa   H4

Beazley House

1910 1st St
Napa, CA 94559-2351
(707)257-1649 (800)559-1649 Fax:(707)257-1518
E-mail: jbeazley@napanet.net

Circa 1902. Nestled in green lawns and gardens, this graceful shingled mansion is frosted with white trim on its bays and balustrades. Stained-glass windows and polished-wood floors set the atmosphere in the parlor. There are six rooms in the main house and the carriage house features five more, many with fireplaces and whirlpool tubs. The venerable Beazley House was Napa's first bed & breakfast inn.

Innkeeper(s): Carol & Jim Beazley. $115-225. MC VISA. 11 rooms with PB, 6 with FP. 5 suites. Breakfast and afternoon tea included in rates. Types of meals: full breakfast and early coffee/tea. Beds: KQDT. Air conditioning and ceiling fan in room. Fax on premises. Handicap access. Weddings and small meetings hosted. Spanish and French spoken. Antiques, fishing, parks and shopping nearby.

Location: In the historic neighborhood of Old Town Napa, at the south end of Napa Valley.

Publicity: *Los Angeles Times, USA Today, Yellow Brick Road, Emergo, Sacramento Bee.*

"There's a sense of peace & tranquility that hovers over this house, sprinkling magical dream dust & kindness."

Belle Epoque

1386 Calistoga Ave
Napa, CA 94559-2552
(707)257-2161 (800)238-8070 Fax:(707)226-6314

Circa 1893. This Queen Anne Victorian has a wine cellar and tasting room where guests can casually sip Napa Valley wines. The inn, which is one of the most unique architectural structures found in the wine country, is located in the heart of Napa's Calistoga Historic District. Beautiful original stained-glass windows include a window from an old church. A selection of fine restaurants and shops are within easy walking distance, as well as the riverfront, city parks and the Wine Train Depot. The train, which serves all meals, takes you just beyond St. Helena and back.

Innkeeper(s): Georgia Jump. $135-195. MC VISA AX DS PC TC. TAC10. 6 rooms with PB, 2 with FP. 1 suite. 1 conference room. Breakfast and evening snack included in rates. Types of meals: gourmet breakfast and early coffee/tea. Beds: KQT. Phone, air conditioning, ceiling fan and TV in room. VCR, fax, copier and spa on premises. Weddings, small meetings, family reunions and seminars hosted. Amusement parks, antiques, parks, shopping, sporting events, golf and theater nearby.

"At first I was a bit leery, how can a B&B get consistent rave reviews? After staying here two nights, I am now a believer!"

Blue Violet Mansion

443 Brown St
Napa, CA 94559-3349
(707)253-2583 (800)959-2583 Fax:(707)257-8205

Circa 1886. English lampposts, a Victorian gazebo, and a rose garden welcome guests to this blue and white Queen Anne Victorian. Listed in the National Register, the house originally was built for a tannery executive. There are three-story bays, and from the balconies guests often view hot air balloons in the early morning. Eight rooms feature two-person spas and 11 have fireplaces. A full breakfast is served in the dining room. The innkeepers offer room service by request, as well as a massage service. In the evenings, desserts are presented. Nearby is the wine train and restaurants.

Historic Interest: Napa County Landmarks prestigious Award of Merit for historical restoration 1993.

Innkeeper(s): Kathy & Bob Morris. $145-285. MC VISA AX DC DS PC TC. TAC10. 14 rooms with PB, 11 with FP. 3 suites. 1 conference room. Breakfast and evening snack included in rates. Type of meal: full breakfast. Dinner, picnic lunch, banquet service, catering service and room service available. Restaurant on premises. Beds: KQ. Phone, air conditioning, turn-down service and ceiling fan in room. TV, VCR, fax, copier, spa and swimming on premises. Handicap access. Weddings, small meetings, family reunions and seminars hosted. Amusement parks, antiques, fishing, parks, shopping, theater and watersports nearby.

Cedar Gables Inn

486 Coombs St
Napa, CA 94559-3343
(707)224-7969 (800)309-7969 Fax:(707)224-4838
E-mail: info@cedargablesinn.com

Circa 1892. This gracious country manor was designed by English architect Ernest Coxhead, who patterned the home after designs prevalent during Shakespeare's time. The innkeepers received an award of merit for their restoration efforts and it's clearly deserved. Guests ascend winding staircases to reach their posh rooms decorated in rich colors and filled with antiques. Each room features its own color scheme and unique touches. The Churchill Chamber, the original master bedroom, is adorned in grays, tans and black and boasts ornate furnishings, a wood-burning fireplace and a two-person whirlpool tub. Four guest rooms include woodburning fireplaces, and others feature claw-foot, whirlpool or Jacuzzi tubs. A complete breakfast is served either in the dining room or in the bright sun room, a perfect start to a full day exploring Napa Valley.

Historic Interest: Aside from the area's bounty of historic wineries, museums and Old Grist Mill are some of the historic sites.

Innkeeper(s): Craig & Margaret Snasdell. $129-189. MC VISA AX DS. 6 rooms with PB, 4 with FP. 1 suite. Breakfast included in rates. Type of meal: full breakfast. Beds: Q.

Publicity: *California Visitor's Review.*

"Charming and elegant, yet strikingly cozy. This place tops the list in atmosphere and hospitality."

Churchill Manor

485 Brown St
Napa, CA 94559-3349
(707)253-7733 Fax:(707)253-8836

Circa 1889. Listed in the National Register of Historic Places, each room of this stately Napa Valley manor is individually decorated with fine European antiques. Five rooms have fireplaces, and the original bath tiles and fireplaces in Edward's Room and Rose's Room are trimmed with 24-karat gold. Guests are treated to delicious breakfasts, freshly baked cookies and refresh-

ments in the afternoons. Each afternoon, cookies and refreshments are offered, and in the evening there is a complimentary two-hour wine and cheese reception. The innkeepers add Victorian flavor by keeping tandem bicycles and a croquet set on hand for their guests. The breakfast buffet offers a glorious selection of fresh fruits, fresh-baked croissants and muffins, gourmet omelets and French toast made-to-order as each guest arrives. Napa Wine Train and balloon ride packages are available to make any vacation memorable.

Historic Interest: Churchill Manor, which is listed in the National Register, is located in the National Register Historic District of Old Town Napa.

Innkeeper(s): Joanna Guidotti & Brian Jensen. $95-185. MC VISA AX DS PC TC. TAC10. 10 rooms with PB, 5 with FP. 3 suites. 3 conference rooms. Breakfast included in rates. Catering service available. Beds: KQ. Phone and air conditioning in room. TV, VCR, fax, copier, bicycles and library on premises. Handicap access. Weddings, small meetings, family reunions and seminars hosted. Spanish spoken. Amusement parks, antiques, fishing, parks, shopping, theater and watersports nearby.

Publicity: *Napa County Record, Food & Beverage Journal, ABC-KGO TV, San Francisco Bay Guardian.*

"Retaining the ambiance of the 1890s yet providing comfort for the 1990s."

The Hennessey House B&B

1727 Main St
Napa, CA 94559-1844
(707)226-3774 Fax:(707)226-2975

Circa 1889. This gracious Queen Anne Eastlake Victorian was once home to Dr. Edwin Hennessey, a Napa County physician. Pristinely renovated, the inn features stained-glass windows and

a curving wraparound porch. A handsome hand-painted, stamped-tin ceiling graces the dining room. All rooms are furnished in antiques. The four guest rooms in the carriage house boast whirlpool baths, fireplaces or patios.

Historic Interest: Historic Old Town Napa.

Innkeeper(s): Alex & Gilda Feit. $85-195. MC VISA AX DS. TAC10. 10 rooms with PB, 4 with FP. Breakfast included in rates. Type of meal: full breakfast. Beds: KQT. Air conditioning, ceiling fan and TV in room. Fax, spa and sauna on premises. Weddings, small meetings, family reunions and seminars hosted. Antiques and shopping nearby.

Location: One hour from San Francisco.

Publicity: *AM-PM Magazine.*

"Thank you for making our stay very pleasant."

Inn on Randolph

411 Randolph St
Napa, CA 94559-3374
(707)257-2886 (800)670-6886 Fax:(707)257-8756
E-mail: randolph@i-cafe.net

Circa 1860. Located just off the Silverado Trail in the heart of Napa Valley, this shuttered Gothic Revival is a city landmark and one of the oldest homes in the valley. Common rooms feature antique Victorian furnishings, hardwood floors and a sweeping spindled staircase. A hand-painted flower mural, white wicker and sleigh bed are just a few of the romantic touches featured in the five guest rooms located in the original house. Besides privacy, the Randolph cottage offers two suites decorated in antiques, fireplaces and whirlpool tubs for two. The Arbor Cottage overlooks a semi-private stone patio and is complete with a fireplace, kitchenette, two-person walk-in shower and whirlpool tub for two. Breakfast begins with freshly ground coffee, tea and juice, followed by peach and strawberry French toast or Mexican quiche served with fresh salsa and jalapeno cheese bread. Wine tasting, shopping, bicycling and golf are nearby.

Innkeeper(s): Deborah Coffee. $99-229. MC VISA AX DS PC. TAC10. 8 rooms with PB, 5 with FP. 2 cottages. Breakfast and evening snack included in rates. Types of meals: full breakfast and early coffee/tea. Picnic lunch available. Beds: KQT. Phone, air conditioning, turndown service, ceiling fan and VCR in room. Fax and library on premises. Weddings hosted. Antiques, parks, shopping, golf and theater nearby.

"You reinforced our reason for staying in lovely bed & breakfasts."

La Residence Country Inn

4066 Saint Helena Hwy
Napa, CA 94558-1635
(707)253-0337 Fax:(707)253-0382

Circa 1870. This inn offers luxurious accommodations for those exploring the enchanting Napa Valley wine country. The uniquely decorated rooms in the French-style farmhouse or Gothic Revival Mansion are spacious and well-appointed, with fine antiques and designer fabrics. Many rooms also feature fireplaces, patios or balconies. Guests will be impressed with the lovely gardens and pool area at the inn, not to mention the discreet but attentive service. Be sure to inquire about excursions into the winery-rich valley.

Innkeeper(s): David Jackson, Craig Claussen. $165-235. MC VISA AX DS TC. TAC10. 16 rooms, 20 with PB, 16 with FP. 4 suites. 1 conference room.

Breakfast and evening snack included in rates. Type of meal: full breakfast. Room service available. Beds: Q. Phone in room. TV, fax, copier, spa, swimming, bicycles and child care on premises. Handicap access. Small meetings and seminars hosted. French, Dutch and German spoken. Antiques, fishing, parks, shopping, golf and theater nearby.

Publicity: *Travel & Leisure.*

Napa Inn

1137 Warren St
Napa, CA 94559-2302
(707)257-1444 (800)435-1144

Circa 1899. Herb and flower gardens frame this Queen Anne Victorian nestled in the heart of a serene wine country neighborhood. Furnished with antiques, the inn has a sitting room with a fireplace. Shaded parks, gourmet and family restaurants are a short stroll from the inn.

Innkeeper(s): Ann & Denny Mahoney. $100-190. MC VISA AX DS PC TC. TAC10. 6 rooms with PB, 2 with FP. 2 suites. Breakfast and evening snack included in rates. Meals: full breakfast and early coffee/tea. Beds: KQ. Phone and air conditioning in room. Weddings, small meetings and family reunions hosted. Amusement parks, antiques, fishing, parks, shopping, theater nearby.

Location: In the historic district.

Publicity: *San Francisco Examiner.*

"You made this a very memorable honeymoon—perhaps we can stay again on our anniversary."

Old World Inn

1301 Jefferson St
Napa, CA 94559-2412
(707)257-0112

Circa 1906. The decor in this exquisite bed & breakfast is second to none. In 1981, Macy's sought out the inn to showcase a new line of fabrics inspired by Scandinavian artist Carl Larrson. Each romantic room is adorned in bright, welcoming colors and includes special features such as canopy beds and clawfoot tubs. The Garden

Room boasts three skylights, and the Anne Room is a must for honeymoons and romantic retreats. The walls and ceilings are painted in a warm peach and blue, bows are stenciled around the perimeter of the room. A decorated canopy starts at the ceiling in the center of the bed and falls downward producing a curtain-like effect. A buffet breakfast is served each morning and a delicious afternoon tea and wine and cheese social will curb your appetite until dinner. After sampling one of Napa's gourmet eateries, return to the inn where a selection of desserts await you.

Innkeeper(s): Sam Van Hoeve. $115-150. MC VISA AX DS PC TC. TAC10. 8 rooms with PB. Breakfast and afternoon tea included in rates. Beds: KQ. Phone in room. Spa and bicycles on premises. Antiques nearby.

Publicity: *Napa Valley Traveller.*

"Excellent is an understatement. We'll return."

Nevada City   F6

Downey House

517 W Broad St
Nevada City, CA 95959-2115
(916)265-2815 (800)258-2815

Circa 1870. This Eastlake Victorian house is one of Nevada City's noted Nabob Hill Victorians. There are six sound-proofed guest rooms, a curved veranda, and in the garden, a pond and

restored red barn. One can stroll downtown where the evening streets are lit by the warm glow of gas lights.

Innkeeper(s): Miriam Wright. $75-100. MC VISA. 6 rooms with PB. Breakfast, afternoon tea and evening snack included in rates. Types of meals: full breakfast, gourmet breakfast and early coffee/tea. Beds: QD. Phone in room. Small meetings hosted. Antiques, fishing, parks, shopping, downhill skiing, cross-country skiing, theater and watersports nearby.

Location: On Nabob Hill close to the Historic District.

Publicity: *San Francisco Examiner, Country Living.*

"The best in Northern California."

The Red Castle Inn Historic Lodgings

109 Prospect St
Nevada City, CA 95959-2831
(916)265-5135 (800)761-4766

Circa 1860. The Smithsonian has lauded the restoration of this four-story brick Gothic Revival known as "The Castle" by townsfolk. Its roof is laced with wooden icicles and the balconies are adorned with gingerbread. Within, there are intricate moldings, antiques, Victorian wallpapers, canopy beds and decorative woodstoves. Verandas provide views of the historic city through cedar, chestnut and walnut trees, and of terraced gardens with a fountain pond.

Historic Interest: Registered state historic site.

Innkeeper(s): Conley & Mary Louise Weaver. $100-135. MC VISA PC TC. TAC10. 7 rooms, 4 with PB. 3 suites. Breakfast and afternoon tea included in rates. Types of meals: gourmet breakfast and early coffee/tea. Catering service available. Beds: QD. Phone, air conditioning and turndown service in room. Library on premises. Weddings, small meetings and family reunions hosted. Antiques, fishing, parks, shopping, skiing, theater and watersports nearby.

Location: Within the Nevada City historic district overlooking the town.

Publicity: *Sunset, Gourmet, Northern California Home & Garden, Sacramento Bee, Los Angeles Times, Travel Holiday, Victorian Homes, Innsider, U.S. News & World Report, USAir, McCalls, New York Times, Brides, San Francisco Focus, Motorland.*

"The Red Castle Inn would top my list of places to stay. Nothing else quite compares with it—Gourmet."

Nice   F4

Featherbed Railroad Company B&B

2870 Lakeshore Blvd, PO Box 4016
Nice, CA 95464
(707)274-4434

Circa 1940. Located on five acres on Clear Lake, this unusual inn features guest rooms in nine luxuriously renovated, painted, and papered cabooses. Each has its own featherbed and private bath, most have Jacuzzi tubs for two. The Southern Pacific cabooses have a bay window alcove, while those from the Santa Fe feature small cupolas.

Innkeeper(s): Lorraine Bassignani. $90-140. MC VISA AX DS. 9 rooms w/ PB. Breakfast included in rates. Meal: full breakfast. Beds: QDT. Spa on premises.

Publicity: *Santa Rosa Press Democrat, Fairfield Daily Republic.*

Nipomo M7

The Kaleidoscope Inn

130 E Dana St
Nipomo, CA 93444-1297
(805)929-5444

Circa 1887. The sunlight that streams through the stained-glass windows of this charming Victorian creates a kaleidoscope effect and thus the name.
The inn is surrounded by gardens. Each romantic guest room is decorated with antiques and the library offers a fireplace. Fresh flowers add a special touch. Breakfast is either served in the dining room, in the gardens, or in your room. L.A. Times readers voted the inn as one of the best lodging spots for under $100 per night.

Historic Interest: Built and lived in by the founding family of Nipomo, the Dana Family.

Innkeeper(s): Patty & Bill Linane. $90. MC VISA AX. TAC10. 3 rooms with PB. 1 conference room. Breakfast included in rates. Types of meals: full breakfast, gourmet breakfast and early coffee/tea. Room service available. Beds: KQ. Turndown service and ceiling fan in room. TV, VCR and library on premises. Weddings, small meetings and family reunions hosted. Antiques, fishing, parks, shopping, theater and watersports nearby.
Location: Twenty miles south of San Luis Obispo, near Pismo Beach.
Publicity: *Santa Maria Times, Los Angeles Times, Country.*

"Beautiful room, chocolates, fresh flowers, peaceful night's rest, great breakfast."

Nipton L14

Hotel Nipton

HC 1, Box 357, 107355 Nipton Rd
Nipton, CA 92364
(760)856-2335
E-mail: hotel@nipton.com

Circa 1904. This Southwestern-style adobe hotel with its wide verandas once housed gold miners and Clara Bow, wife of movie star Rex Bell. It is decorated in period furnishings and historic photos of the area. A 1920s rock and cactus garden blooms, and an outdoor spa provides the perfect setting for watching a flaming sunset over Ivanpah Valley, the New York Mountains and Castle Peaks. Later, a magnificent star-studded sky appears undimmed by city lights.

Historic Interest: Gold mining town started in 1885.

Innkeeper(s): Gerald & Roxanne Freeman. $50. MC VISA DS. TAC7. 4 rooms. Breakfast included in rates. Meals: continental breakfast, early coffee/tea. Beds: DT. Air conditioning in room. Fax, library on premises. 40 acres. Weddings, small meetings, family reunions, seminars hosted. Amusement parks, fishing, parks, shopping, sporting events, golf, theater, watersports nearby.
Location: Mojave National Preserve.
Publicity: *National Geographic Traveler, Town & Country, U.S. News & World Report.*

Oakhurst I8

Chateau Du Sureau

PO Box 577
Oakhurst, CA 93644-0577
(209)683-6860 Fax:(209)683-0800

One of United States' three inns awarded five diamonds, this elegant estate is superb in both lodging and cuisine. Set back from the road off the Southern entrance to Yosemite, the French-country estate features a gathering room with a Monticello-like domed performance area with floor-to-ceiling palladian windows and grand piano, fireplace, beamed ceiling and oak and tile floors. Finely decorated guest rooms may include a canopy bed, whirlpool for two overlooking a garden, antique desk or a fireplace. Beds are dressed in Italian linens and down comforters. There are formal rose gardens and herb gardens. Erna's Elderberry House Restaurant is on the premises but in a separate building.

Innkeeper(s): Erna Kubin-Clanin. $360-430. MC VISA AX. 9 rooms with PB. Breakfast included in rates. Beds: K. Swimming on premises. Fishing and downhill skiing nearby.

Occidental G4

The Inn at Occidental

3657 Church St
Occidental, CA 95465
(707)874-1047 (800)522-6324 Fax:(707)874-1078
E-mail: innkeeper@innatoccidental.com

Circa 1877. Stencilled walls, shiny woodwork and a gracious collection of American and European antiques create the warm, idyllic environment at this 19th-century Victorian. Four of the guest rooms offer fireplaces, and all eight overlook the garden. There are plenty of places to relax, from a wicker-filled veranda to a manicured courtyard with a fountain as its centerpiece. The innkeepers serve gourmet country breakfasts, afternoon refreshments and in the evenings, local wines. The inn offers convenient access to wineries, Point Reyes National Seashore, Bodega Bay and canoeing, swimming and fishing at the Russian River.

Innkeeper(s): Jack Bullard. $135-250. MC VISA AX DC DS PC TC. TAC10. 8 rooms with PB, 4 with FP. 1 conference room. Breakfast, afternoon tea and evening snack included in rates. Types of meals: full breakfast and early coffee/tea. Beds: KQT. Phone and TV in room. Fax and copier on premises. Handicap access. Weddings, small meetings, family reunions and seminars hosted. Limited French and limited Spanish spoken. Antiques, fishing, parks, shopping, cross-country skiing, sporting events, theater, watersports nearby.
Location: Wine country village near Sonoma Coast and Russian River.
Publicity: *Art, Antiques and Collectibles.*

Orland E5

The Inn at Shallow Creek Farm

4712 County Road Dd
Orland, CA 95963-9336
(530)865-4093 (800)865-4093

Circa 1900. This vine-covered farmhouse was once the center of a well-known orchard and sheep ranch. The old barn, adjacent to the farmhouse, was a livery stop. The citrus orchard, now restored, blooms with 165 trees. Apples, pears, peaches, apricots, persimmons, walnuts, figs, and pomegranates are also grown here. Guests can meander about and examine the Polish crested chickens, silver guinea fowl, Muscovy ducks, and African geese. The old caretaker's house is now a four-room guest cottage. Hundreds of narcissus grow along the creek that flows through the property.

Innkeeper(s): Mary & Kurt Glaeseman. $55-75. MC VISA PC. 4 rooms, 2 with PB. 1 suite. Breakfast included in rates. Types of meals: continental-plus breakfast and early coffee/tea. Beds: QT. Phone, air conditioning and ceiling fan in room. Library on premises. French, German and Spanish spoken. Antiques, fishing, parks and theater nearby.

Location: Northern California, 3 miles off Interstate 5.

Publicity: *Adventure Road, Orland Press Register, Focus, Chico Enterprise Record, Minneapolis Star.*

"Now that we've discovered your country oasis, we hope to return as soon as possible."

Pacific Grove J5

Centrella B&B Inn

612 Central Ave
Pacific Grove, CA 93950-2611
(408)372-3372 (800)433-4732 Fax:(408)372-2036
E-mail: concierge@carmelinns.com

Circa 1889. Pacific Grove was founded as a Methodist resort in 1875, and this home, built just after the town's incorporation, was billed by a local newspaper as, "the largest, most commodious and pleasantly located boarding house in the Grove." Many a guest is still sure to agree. The rooms are well-appointed in a comfortable, Victorian style. Six guest rooms include fireplaces. The Garden Room has a private entrance, fireplace, wet bar, Jacuzzi tub and a canopy bed topped with designer linens. Freshly baked croissants or pastries and made-to-order waffles are common fare at the inn's continental buffet breakfast. The inn is within walking distance of the Monterey Bay Aquarium, the beach and many Pacific Grove shops.

Innkeeper(s): Sheryl Walsh. $95-195. MC VISA. TAC10. 26 rooms, 16 with PB, 6 with FP. 5 suites. 5 cottages. Breakfast and evening snack included in rates. Types of meals: continental-plus breakfast and early coffee/tea. Beds: KQDT. Phone in room. TV, VCR, fax, copier and library on premises. Handicap access. Antiques, fishing, parks, shopping, sporting events and watersports nearby.

"I was ecstatic at the charm that the Centrella has been offering travelers for years and hopefully hundreds of years to come. The bed—perfect! I am forever enthralled by the old beauty and will remember this forever!"

Gatehouse Inn

225 Central Ave
Pacific Grove, CA 93950-3017
(408)649-8436 (800)753-1881 Fax:(408)648-8044

Circa 1884. This Italianate Victorian seaside inn is just a block from the Monterey Bay. The inn is decorated with Victorian and 20th-century antiques and touches of Art Deco. Guest rooms feature fireplaces, clawfoot tubs and down comforters. Some rooms have ocean views. The dining room boasts opulent Bradbury & Bradbury Victorian wallpapers as do some of the guest rooms. Afternoon hors d'oeuvres, wine and tea are served. The refrigerator is stocked for snacking.

Innkeeper(s): Lois Deford. $110-150. MC VISA AX DS PC TC. TAC10. 9 rooms with PB, 5 with FP. Breakfast, afternoon tea and evening snack included in rates. Beds: KQT. Phone, turndown service in room. Fax, copier, bicycles on premises. Handicap access. Weddings and family reunions hosted. Antiques, fishing, parks, shopping, theater, watersports nearby.

Location: 1 block from the ocean.

Publicity: *San Francisco Chronicle, Monterey Herald, Time, Newsweek, Inland Empire, Bon Appetit.*

"Thank you for spoiling us."

Grand View Inn

557 Ocean View Blvd
Pacific Grove, CA 93950
(408)372-4341

Circa 1910. Overlooking Lover's Point beach on the edge of Monterey Bay, this site was chosen by noted marine biologist Dr. Julia Platt to build this Edwardian-style home. As the first mayor of Pacific Grove, she was also one of those responsible for preserving the landmark beach and park for future generations. Most of the 10 guest rooms offer unsurpassed ocean views and are elegantly appointed with authentic and reproduction antiques. Guests will delight in strolling the gardens surrounding the inn or venturing outdoors to walk along the seashore. A full breakfast and afternoon tea are served in the ocean-view dining room.

Historic Interest: The world-famous 17-Mile Drive along the ocean to Pebble Beach and Carmel, Cannery Row and Monterey Bay made famous by John Steinbeck. Old Fisherman's Wharf is also located nearby.

Innkeeper(s): Susan & Ed Flatley. $155-275. MC VISA PC TC. TAC10. 10 rooms with PB. Breakfast and afternoon tea included in rates. Meals: full breakfast and early coffee/tea. Beds: Q. Turndown service in room. Handicap access. Antiques, fishing, parks, shopping, golf, theater, watersports nearby.

Martine Inn

255 Ocean View Blvd
Pacific Grove, CA 93950-2914
(408)373-3388 (800)852-5588 Fax:(408)373-3896

Circa 1890. This turn-of-the-century oceanfront manor sits atop a jagged cliff overlooking the coastline of Monterey Bay. Bedrooms are furnished with antiques, and each room contains a fresh rose and a silver Victorian bridal basket filled with fresh fruit. Thirteen rooms also boast fireplaces. Some of the museum-quality antiques were exhibited in the 1893 Chicago World's Fair. Other bedroom sets include furniture that belonged to Edith Head, and there is an 1860 Chippendale Revival four-poster bed with a canopy and side curtains.

Innkeeper Don Martine has a collection of old MGs, three on display for guests. Twilight wine and hors d'oeuvres are served, and Godiva mints accompany evening turndown service. The inn is a beautiful spot for romantic getaways and weddings.

Historic Interest: Pacific Grove Historic Walking Tour.

Innkeeper(s): Marion & Don Martine, Tracy Harris. $125-245. MC VISA AX DS PC TC. TAC10. 20 rooms with PB, 13 with FP. 3 suites. 6 conference rooms. Breakfast included in rates. Types of meals: full breakfast and early coffee/tea. Picnic lunch available. Beds: KQD. Phone and turndown service in room. TV, fax, copier, spa and library on premises. Handicap access. Weddings, small meetings, family reunions and seminars hosted. Antiques, fishing, parks, shopping, sporting events, theater and watersports nearby.

Location: On Monterey Bay, five miles from Monterey airport.

Publicity: *Sunday Oregonian, Bon Appetit, Country Inns, Vacations APAC.*

"Wonderful, can't wait to return."

Old St. Angela Inn

321 Central Ave
Pacific Grove, CA 93950-2934
(408)372-3246 (800)748-6306 Fax:(408)372-8560

Circa 1910. Formerly a convent, this Cape-style inn has been restored and includes a glass solarium where breakfast is served. The ocean is a block away and it's just a short walk to the aquarium or fisherman's wharf.

Innkeeper(s): Lewis Shaefer & Susan Kuslis. $100-150. MC VISA DS PC TC. TAC10. 8 rooms with PB. Breakfast, afternoon tea and evening snack included in rates. Types of meals: gourmet breakfast, early coffee/tea. Beds: KQT. Phone in room. Fax and spa on premises. Small meetings, family reunions hosted. Antiques, fishing, parks, shopping, theater, watersports nearby.

Pets Allowed: Small animals limited to rooms with private entrances.

"Outstanding inn and outstanding hospitality."

Seven Gables Inn

555 Ocean View Blvd
Pacific Grove, CA 93950
(408)372-4341

Circa 1886. At the turn of the century, Lucie Chase, a wealthy widow and civic leader from the East Coast, embellished this Victorian with gables and verandas, taking full advantage of its spectacular setting on Monterey Bay. All guest rooms feature ocean views, and there are elegant antiques, intricate Persian carpets, chandeliers and beveled-glass armoires throughout. Sea otters, harbor seals and whales often can be seen from the inn.

Innkeeper(s): The Flatley Family. $155-295. MC VISA. 14 rooms with PB. Breakfast and afternoon tea included in rates. Type of meal: full breakfast. Picnic lunch available. Beds: Q. Phone in room. Antiques, fishing, theater and watersports nearby.

Publicity: *Travel & Leisure, Country Inns. Ratings: 4 Stars.*

"Our stay was everything your brochure said it would be, and more."

Palm Springs   012

Casa Cody Country Inn

175 S Cahuilla Rd
Palm Springs, CA 92262-6331
(760)320-9346 (800)231-2639 Fax:(760)325-8610

Circa 1920. Casa Cody, built by a relative of Wild Bill Cody and situated in the heart of Palm Springs, is the town's oldest continuously operating inn. The San Jacinto Mountains provide a scenic background for the tree-shaded spa, the pink and purple bougainvillea and the blue waters of the inn's two swimming pools. Each suite has a small kitchen

and features red and turquoise Southwestern decor. Several have wood-burning fireplaces. There are Mexican pavers, French doors and private patios. The area offers many activities,

including museums, a heritage center, boutiques, a botanical garden, horseback riding and golf.

Historic Interest: Village Heritage Center, Village Theater and numerous historic estates within blocks; Mooten Botanic Gardens and Indian Canyons within minutes.

Innkeeper(s): Elissa Goforth. $49-199. MC VISA AX DC CB DS PC TC. TAC10. 23 rooms, 24 with PB, 10 with FP. 8 suites. 2 cottages. Breakfast included in rates. Type of meal: continental-plus breakfast. Beds: KQT. Phone, air conditioning, ceiling fan and TV in room. Fax, copier, spa, swimming and library on premises. Weddings, small meetings, family reunions and seminars hosted. French, Dutch and limited German & Spanish spoken. Antiques and theater nearby. Pets Allowed.

Publicity: *N.Y. Times, Washington Post, L.A. Times, San Diego Union Tribune, Seattle Times, Portland Oregonian, Los Angeles, San Diego Magazine, Pacific Northwest Magazine, Sunset, Westways, Alaska Airlines Magazine.*

"Outstanding ambiance, friendly relaxed atmosphere."

Palo Alto   I5

Adella Villa

PO Box 4528
Palo Alto, CA 94309-4528
(650)321-5195 Fax:(650)325-5121

Circa 1923. This Italian villa is located in an area of one-acre estates five minutes from Stanford University. Two guest rooms feature whirlpool tubs, three guest rooms have showers. The music

room boasts a 1920 mahogany Steinway grand piano. There is a solar-heated swimming pool set amid manicured gardens.

Innkeeper(s): Tricia Young. $115-145. MC VISA AX DC CB PC TC. TAC10. 5 rooms with PB. Breakfast included in rates. Types of meals: full breakfast, gourmet breakfast and early coffee/tea. Afternoon tea and evening snack available. Beds: KQT. Phone and TV in room. VCR, fax, swimming, bicycles, library on premises. Spanish & German spoken. Amusement parks, antiques, fishing, parks, shopping, sporting events, theater, watersports nearby.

Location: Twenty-five miles south of San Francisco at the tip of Silicon Valley.

Publicity: *Los Angeles Times.*

"This place is as wonderful, gracious and beautiful as the people who own it!"

The Victorian on Lytton

555 Lytton Ave
Palo Alto, CA 94301-1538
(415)322-8555 Fax:(415)322-7141

Circa 1896. This Queen Anne home was built for Hannah Clapp, a descendant of Massachusetts Bay colonist Roger Clapp. The house has been graciously restored, and each guest room features its own sitting area. Most rooms boast a canopy or four-poster bed. Stanford University is within walking distance.

Innkeeper(s): Susan & Maxwell Hall. $129-250. EP. MC VISA AX. 10 rooms with PB, 1 with FP. Breakfast and evening snack included in rates. Types of meals: continental-plus breakfast and early coffee/tea. Beds: KQ. Phone, air conditioning and TV in room. Fax on premises. Handicap access. Antiques, parks, shopping and sporting events nearby.

Publicity: *USA Today.*

"A beautiful inn! My favorite."

Petaluma   H4

Cavanagh Inn

10 Keller St
Petaluma, CA 94952-2939
(707)765-4657 (888)765-4658 Fax:(707)769-0466

Circa 1902. Embrace turn-of-the-century California at this picturesque Georgian Revival manor. The garden is filled with beautiful flowers, plants and fruit trees. Innkeeper Jeanne Farris is an award-winning chef and prepares the mouthwatering breakfasts. A typical meal might start off with butterscotch pears and fresh muffins
with honey butter. This
starter would be followed
by an entree, perhaps
eggs served with rosemary
potatoes. The innkeepers
also serve wine at 5:30
p.m. The parlor and
library, which boasts heart-of-redwood panelled walls, is an ideal place to relax. Cavanagh Inn is located at the edge of Petaluma's historic district, and close to shops and the riverfront, including the Petaluma Queen Riverboat.

Innkeeper(s): Ray & Jeanne Farris. $70-125. MC VISA AX PC. TAC10. 7 rooms, 5 with PB. 1 conference room. Breakfast included in rates. Type of meal: gourmet breakfast. Beds: KQDT. Turndown service in room. TV, VCR, fax and library on premises. Small meetings, family reunions and seminars hosted. Spanish spoken. Antiques, parks, shopping and theater nearby.

Publicity: *Argus-Courier.*

"This is our first B&B. . .sort of like learning to drive with a Rolls-Royce!"

Placerville   G6

Chichester-McKee House B&B

800 Spring St
Placerville, CA 95667-4424
(530)626-1882 (800)831-4008

Circa 1892. D.W. Chichester, a partner in the local sawmill, built this house for his wife and the Victorian manor is said to be the first home in Placerville with built-in plumbing. The house is full of places to explore and admire, including the

lovely parlor, library and a conservatory. Guest rooms are filled with family treasures and antiques, and the home is decorated with charming fireplaces and stained glass. Breakfast at the inn includes freshly baked goods and delicious entrees. Evening refreshments are a treat, and the special blends of morning coffee will wake

your spirit. Ask the innkeepers about the discovery of a gold mine beneath the dining room floor.

Historic Interest: Marshall State Historic Gold Discovery Park, Gold Bug Park Mine, Apple Hill.

Innkeeper(s): Doreen & Bill Thornhill. $90-125. MC VISA AX DS PC TC. TAC10. 4 rooms. Breakfast and evening snack included in rates. Types of

meals: full breakfast, gourmet breakfast and early coffee/tea. Beds: QT. TV, VCR and library on premises. Small meetings and family reunions hosted. Antiques, fishing, parks, shopping, downhill skiing, cross-country skiing, theater and watersports nearby.

Publicity: *Hi Sierra, Mount Democrat.*

"The most relaxing and enjoyable trip I've ever taken."

Point Reyes Station   H4

Holly Tree Inn

3 Silverhills Rd, PO Box 642
Point Reyes Station, CA 94956
(415)663-1554 Fax:(415)663-8566

Circa 1939. Innkeepers Diane and Tom Balogh have created an environment to please any guest at their elegant bed & breakfast inn. Located on 19 acres adjoining the Point Reyes National Seashore, the inn is ideal for families. The Vision Cottage is a perfect place for parents and children. The cottage includes two bedrooms, each with a queen-size pine bed dressed with handmade quilts and down comforters. Extra futons are available for children, and there's a wood-burning fireplace and a kitchen. For honeymooners or those seeking solitude, the innkeepers offer Sea Star Cottage, a romantic hamlet for two. The cottage sits at the end of a 75-foot dock on Tomales Bay. Both cottages are several miles from the main inn, but guests also can opt for four, well-appointed rooms in the main inn or the Cottage in the Woods.

Innkeeper(s): Diane & Tom Balogh. $120-250. MC VISA AX PC TC. TAC10. 4 rooms with PB, 4 with FP. 3 cottages. Breakfast included in rates. Types of meals: full breakfast and early coffee/tea. Afternoon tea available. Beds: KQ. Fax, spa and library on premises. 19 acres. Small meetings and seminars hosted. Limited Spanish and limited French spoken. Antiques, fishing, parks, shopping, theater and watersports nearby.

Red Bluff   D5

Faulkner House

1029 Jefferson St
Red Bluff, CA 96080-2725
(916)529-0520 (800)549-6171 Fax:(916)527-4970

Circa 1890. This Queen Anne Victorian stands on a quiet, tree-lined street in the Victorian town of Red Bluff. Furnished in antiques, the house has original stained-glass windows, ornate molding, and eight-foot pocket doors separating the front and back parlors. The Tower Room is a cozy spot or choose the Rose Room with its brocade fainting couch and queen bed.

Historic Interest: Ide Adobe (1 mile), Kelly Griggs Museum (one-half mile).

Innkeeper(s): Harvey & Mary Klingler. $65-90. MC VISA AX. 4 rooms with PB. Breakfast included in rates. Type of meal: full breakfast. Beds: QD. Phone in room. Antiques, fishing, parks and cross-country skiing nearby. Location: 3 1/2 hours north of San Francisco near Lassen National Park.

Publicity: *Red Bluff Daily News.*

"Enjoyed our stay at your beautiful home."

Sacramento   G6

Abigail's

2120 G St
Sacramento, CA 95816-4020
(916)441-5007 (800)858-1568 Fax:(916)441-0621

Circa 1912. This Colonial Revival inn, on an elm-lined street just minutes from the capitol building and convention center, offers gracious surroundings to both business and weekend getaway travelers. The inn's five guest rooms include The Margaret Room, with its four-poster, canopy queen bed, and the maroon and gray "country gentle-man" Uncle Albert Room, with marble-floor bath-room and a queen bed. The inn's secluded garden spa is a favorite spot to relax after a busy day exploring California's capitol city and its surrounding area.

Historic Interest: State Capitol Buildings, Crocker Art Museum (oldest in West), Sutter's Fort (all within one-half-hour walk or 10 minutes by car).

Innkeeper(s): Susanne & Ken Ventura. $105-165. MC VISA AX DC CB DS PC TC. TAC10. 5 rooms with PB. 1 conference room. Breakfast and evening snack included in rates. Meals: full breakfast and early coffee/tea. Catered breakfast available. Beds: KQ. Phone, air conditioning and ceiling fan in room. Fax, copier and spa on premises. Small meetings hosted. Amusement parks, antiques, fishing, parks, shopping, sporting events and theater nearby.

Publicity: *The Times Picayune.*

"Thank you so much for inviting us to rest in your garden of hospitality once again. Each time we visit we find yet another reason to return."

Amber House

1315 22nd St
Sacramento, CA 95816-5717
(916)944-8085 (800)755-6526 Fax:(916)552-6529

Circa 1905. These three historic homes on the city's Historic Preservation Register are in a neighborhood of fine historic homes eight blocks from the capitol. Each room is named for a famous poet, artist or composer and features stained glass, English antiques, and amenities such as bath robes and fresh flowers. Ask about the Van Gogh Room where you can soak in the heart-shaped

Jacuzzi tub-for-two or enjoy one of the rooms with marble baths and Jacuzzi tubs in either the adjacent 1913 Mediterranean man-sion or the 1895 Colonial Revival. A gourmet breakfast can be served in your room or in the dining room at a time you request.

Historic Interest: California State Capitol, State Railroad Museum, Crocker Art Museum, Governor's Mansion, Old Sacramento State Historic Park (all within 8 to 22 blocks).

Innkeeper(s): Michael & Jane Richardson. $119-249. MC VISA AX DC CB DS PC TC. TAC10. 14 rooms with PB, 3 with FP. 1 conference room. Breakfast included in rates. Types of meals: gourmet breakfast and early coffee/tea. Beds: KQ. Phone, air conditioning, turndown service, TV and VCR in room. Fax, bicycles and library on premises. Weddings, small meetings and seminars hosted. Antiques, fishing, parks, shopping, downhill skiing, cross-country skiing, theater and watersports nearby.

Location: Eight blocks to the east of the State Capitol.

Publicity: *Travel & Leisure, Village Crier.*

"Your cordial hospitality, the relaxing atmosphere and delicious breakfast made our brief business/pleasure trip so much more enjoyable."

Inn at Parkside

2116-6th St
Sacramento, CA 95818
(916)658-1818 (800)995-7275 Fax:(916)658-1809
E-mail: gmcgreal@2xtreme.net

Circa 1936. This home was built for the North American ambassador to Nationalist China, and he lived here for 40 years. The architecture is Mediterranean, and in the spirit of its

former owner, the exterior is decorated by several different flags. The interior is elegant and somewhat eclectic, with a mix of antiques and Art Deco stylings, including murals on the hall-way wall, a guest room and in the ballroom. A stained-glass ceiling in one room is another unique item. Two suites offer double Jacuzzi tubs, and one room includes a fireplace. The inn's location affords close access to many attractions in Sacramento, including the convention center and Capitol. The innkeepers specialize in serving low-fat, gourmet vegetarian breakfasts. The inn's conference room and ballroom are popu-lar for groups and special events.

Innkeeper(s): Georgia McGreal & Weldon Reeves. $79-185. MC VISA AX PC TC. TAC10. 7 rooms with PB, 1 with FP. 1 suite. 1 conference room. Breakfast included in rates. Meals: continental-plus breakfast, full breakfast, gourmet breakfast, early coffee/tea. Beds: KQD. Phone, air conditioning, ceil-ing fan, TV, VCR in room. Fax, copier, spa, library on premises. Handicap access. Weddings, small meetings, family reunions hosted. Amusement parks, antiques, fishing, parks, sporting events, golf, theater and watersports nearby.

Sterling Hotel

1300 H St
Sacramento, CA 95814-1907
(916)448-1300 (800)365-7660

Circa 1894. The gables and bays, turrets and verandas of this 20,000-square-foot Queen Anne Victorian home testify to the affluence of its former owners, the Carter-Hawley Hale family of Weinstocks department store fame. The foyer and drawing room boast black marble fireplaces and marble floors, while guest rooms feature writing desks, designer furnishings, private spas and marble baths. A 3,200-square-foot reproduction Victorian ballroom features an elegant stained-glass rotunda and alabaster chandeliers.

Innkeeper(s): Sandi Wasserman. $149-229. MC VISA AX DC. 16 rooms with PB. 3 conference rooms. Restaurant on premises. Beds: KQ. Fax, copier and spa on premises. Publicity: *Sacramento Magazine.*

"Fabulous. Looking forward to my return."

Vizcaya

2019 21st St
Sacramento, CA 95818-1705
(916)455-5243 (800)456-2019 Fax:(916)455-6102

Circa 1899. This 6,500-square-foot, white Colonial Revival is graced with a Victorian tower, massive bays and an impressive columned entrance suitable for its former owner, turn-of-the-century attorney Philip Driver. Crisp white walls and woodwork frame antique fur-nishings upholstered in rose, blue and soft pink. A Victorian gazebo in the back garden is a favorite spot for photographs.

Innkeeper(s): Sandy Wasserman. $125-225. MC VISA AX DC. 9 rooms with PB, 3 with FP. 1 conference room. Type of meal: full breakfast. Beds: KQ. Spa on premises. Publicity: *The Sacramento Bee.*

"Room and breakfast were exquisite! A wonderful place to stay."

Saint Helena   G4

Deer Run Inn

PO Box 311 3995 Spring Mountain Rd
Saint Helena, CA 94574-0311
(707)963-3794 (800)843-3408 Fax:(707)963-9026

Circa 1929. This secluded mountain home is located on four forested acres just up the road from the house used for the television show "Falcon Crest." A fir-tree-shaded deck provides a quiet spot for breakfast while watching birds and deer pass by. Your host, Tom, was born on Spring Mountain and knows the winery area well. There is a watercolorist in residence.

Historic Interest: Robert Louis Stevenson Museum & Library (5 miles), Old Faithful Geyser (12 miles), Petrified Forest (15 miles).

Innkeeper(s): Tom & Carol Wilson. $125-175. MC VISA AX PC TC. TAC10. 4 rooms with PB, 3 with FP. 1 suite. 1 cottage. Breakfast included in rates. Types of meals: gourmet breakfast and early coffee/tea. Beds: KQ. Air conditioning and ceiling fan in room. Fax, copier and swimming on premises. Amusement parks, antiques, fishing, parks, shopping, sporting events, theater and watersports nearby.

Location: Napa Valley.

Publicity: *Forbes, Chicago Tribune, Napa Record.*

"The perfect honeymoon spot! We loved it!"

Ink House

1575 Saint Helena Hwy S
Saint Helena, CA 94574-9775
(707)963-3890
E-mail: inkhousebb@aol.com

Circa 1884. Theron H. Ink, owner of thousands of acres in Marin, Napa and Sonoma counties, was an investor in livestock, wineries and mining. He built his Italianate Victorian with a glass-walled observatory on top, and from this room, visitors can enjoy 360-degree views of the Napa Valley and surrounding vineyards. Listed in the National Register, the Ink House is an elegant, spacious retreat of a time gone by.

Innkeeper(s): Diane Horkheimer. $99-189. 7 rooms, 5 with PB. Type of meal: gourmet breakfast. Evening snack available. Beds: Q. TV on premises.

Location: In the heart of the agricultural preserve in Napa Valley.

Publicity: *Canadian Living, Newsweek, Business Week, Time, Forbes.*

"Your hospitality made us feel so much at home. This is a place and a time we will long remember."

San Andreas

H7

Robin's Nest

PO Box 1408
San Andreas, CA 95249-1408
(209)754-1076 (888)214-9202 Fax:(209)754-3975

Circa 1895. Expect to be pampered from the moment you walk through the door at this three-story Queen Anne Victorian. Guests are greeted with homemade goodies upon arrival, and treated to an elegant, gourmet breakfast. The late 19th-century gem includes many fine architectural features, including eight-foot round windows, 12-foot ceilings on the first floor and gabled ceilings with roof windows on the second floor.

Antiques decorated the guest rooms, with pieces such as a four-poster, step-up bed. One bathroom includes an original seven-foot bathtub. The grounds boast century-old fruit trees, grapevines, a brick well, windmill and the more modern addition of a redwood spa.

Historic Interest: Three large caverns are within 30 minutes of the home.

Innkeeper(s): Karen & Bill Konietany. $55-105. 9 rooms, 7 with PB. 5 suites. Breakfast included in rates. Type of meal: full breakfast. Beds: QDT. Antiques, fishing, skiing, theater and watersports nearby.

Publicity: *Stockton Record, In Flight, Westways.*

"An excellent job of making guests feel at home."

San Diego

Q12

The Cottage

3829 Albatross St
San Diego, CA 92103-3017
(619)299-1564

Circa 1913. The furnishings in this homestead-style inn are an eclectic mix originating from 1840 to 1940. The Garden Room with private entrance is part of the innkeepers' home and is adjacent to the patio. The Cottage is a small house with Victorian decor, a wood burning stove, oak pump organ and fully equipped kitchen. Sages, mints, lavenders, verbenas and 30 more herbs can be found in the unique garden. Guests will find a quiet retreat in the heart of the city.

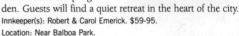

Innkeeper(s): Robert & Carol Emerick. $59-95.

Location: Near Balboa Park.

"The two pictures taken in your garden are wonderful momentos of the restful, restorative time I spent at your B&B."

Heritage Park Inn

2470 Heritage Park Row
San Diego, CA 92110-2803
(619)299-6832 (800)995-2470 Fax:(619)299-9465

Circa 1889. Situated on a seven-acre Victorian park in the heart of Old Town, this inn is two of seven preserved classic structures. The main house offers a variety of beautifully appointed guest rooms, decked in traditional Victorian furnishings and decor. The opulent Manor Suite includes two bedrooms, a Jacuzzi tub and sitting room. Several rooms offer ocean views, and guest also can see the nightly fireworks show at nearby Sea World. A collection of classic movies is available, and a different movie is shown each night in the inn's parlor. Guests are treated to a light afternoon tea, and breakfast is served on fine china on candlelit tables. The home is within walking distance to the many sites, shops and restaurants in the historic Old Town. A small antique shop and Victorian toy store also are located next to the inn.

Innkeeper(s): Nancy & Charles Helsper. $90-225. MAP. MC VISA TC. TAC10. 12 rooms with PB. 1 suite. 1 conference room. Breakfast and afternoon tea included in rates. Types of meals: gourmet breakfast and early coffee/tea. Picnic lunch and catering service available. Beds: KQT. Phone, turndown service and ceiling fan in room. VCR, fax and copier on premises. Small meetings, family reunions and seminars hosted. Antiques, fishing, parks, shopping, sporting events, theater and watersports nearby.

Location: In historic Old Town.

Publicity: *Los Angeles Herald Examiner, Innsider, Los Angeles Times, Orange County Register, San Diego Union, In-Flight, Glamour, Country Inns.*

"A beautiful step back in time. Peaceful and gracious."

San Francisco H4

Archbishop's Mansion

1000 Fulton St (at Steiner)
San Francisco, CA 94117-1608
(415)563-7872 (800)543-5820 Fax:(415)885-3193

Circa 1904. This French Empire-style manor was built for the Archbishop of San Francisco. It is designated as a San Francisco historic landmark. The grand stairway features redwood paneling, Corinthian columns and a stained-glass dome. The parlor has a hand-painted ceiling. Each of the guest rooms is named for an opera. Rooms have antiques, Victorian window treatments and embroidered linens. Breakfast is delivered to your guest quarters or served in the dining room.

Innkeeper(s): Rick Janvier. $129-385. MC VISA AX DC. TAC10. 15 rooms with PB, 11 with FP. 5 suites. Breakfast included in rates. Types of meals: continental-plus breakfast and early coffee/tea. Beds: KQD. Phone, turndown service, TV and VCR in room. Fax and copier on premises. Weddings and small meetings hosted. Parks nearby.

Publicity: *Travel-Holiday, Travel & Leisure.*

"The ultimate, romantic honeymoon spot."

Auberge Des Artistes

829 Fillmore St
San Francisco, CA 94117-1703
(415)776-2530 Fax:(415)441-8242
E-mail: lakpersons@aol.com

Circa 1904. This colorful Victorian row house is located in San Francisco's historic Alamo Square neighborhood. The innkeepers offer a variety of interesting amenities, such as lending out bicycles or allowing guests to use the inn's darkroom. Period antiques, as well as Art Deco and Arts & Crafts furnishings decorate the home. Three guest rooms include a fireplace. Fresh fruit smoothies and cappuccino accompany the inn's full, gourmet breakfasts. The inn's central city location provides close access to many restaurants, shops and sightseeing.

Innkeeper(s): David Novick & Laura Ann Kamm. $75-110. MC VISA AX DS TC. TAC10. 5 rooms with PB, 3 with FP. 2 suites. Breakfast included in rates. Type of meal: gourmet breakfast. Picnic lunch available. Beds: KQT. Fax, copier and library on premises. Weddings, small meetings and family reunions hosted. French and Spanish spoken. Antiques, parks, shopping, sporting events and theater nearby.

"The longer we're here, the harder it is to leave! Your breakfasts are delicious and your home enchanting."

Casa Arguello

225 Arguello Blvd
San Francisco, CA 94118-1406
(415)752-9482 Fax:(415)681-1400
E-mail: 103221.3126@compuserve.com

Circa 1920. This Edwardian flat is located conveniently between San Francisco's Richmond district and Pacific Heights. Public transportation as well as a variety of shops and restaurants are within walking distance. A mix of antiques and contemporary furnishings decorate the rooms, which boast city views. A continental-plus breakfast with fresh fruit, cereals and pastry is served in the dining room.

Innkeeper(s): Marina, Jim & Will McKenzie. $59-89. MC VISA AX DS PC TC. 4 rooms, 2 with PB. 1 suite. Breakfast included in rates. Type of meal: continental-plus breakfast. Beds: KDT. TV on premises. Spanish spoken. Antiques, parks, shopping, sporting events, theater and watersports nearby.

"We just want to say what a wonderful time we had, especially breakfast!"

Golden Gate Hotel

775 Bush St
San Francisco, CA 94108-3402
(415)392-3702 (800)835-1118 Fax:(415)392-6202

Circa 1913. News travels far when there's a bargain. Half of the guests visiting this four-story Edwardian hotel at the foot of Nob Hill are from abroad. Great bay windows on each floor provide many of the rooms with gracious spaces at humble prices. An original bird cage elevator kept in working order floats between floors. Antiques, fresh flowers, and afternoon tea further add to the atmosphere. Union Square is two-and-a-half blocks from the hotel.

Innkeeper(s): John & Renate Kenaston. $65-115. MC VISA AX DC PC TC. TAC10. 23 rooms, 14 with PB. Breakfast and afternoon tea included in rates. Meal: continental breakfast. Beds: QDT. Phone and TV in room. Fax and child care on premises. Family reunions hosted. French, German and Spanish spoken. Amusement parks, antiques and theater nearby.

Pets Allowed: Prior notification $10.00 additional.

Publicity: *Los Angeles Times, Melbourne Sun (Australia), Sunday Oregonian, Globe & Mail.*

"Stayed here by chance, will return by choice!"

The Inn San Francisco

943 S Van Ness Ave
San Francisco, CA 94110-2613
(415)641-0188 (800)359-0913 Fax:(415)641-1701

Circa 1872. Built on one of San Francisco's earliest "Mansion Rows," this 21-room Italianate Victorian is located near the civic and convention centers, close to Mission Dolores. Antiques, marble fireplaces and Oriental rugs decorate the opulent grand double parlors. Most rooms have featherbeds, Victorian wallcoverings and desks, while deluxe rooms offer private spas, fireplaces or bay windows. There is a rooftop deck with a 360-degree view of San Francisco. Complimentary beverages are always available. The inn is close to the opera, symphony, theaters, Mission Dolores, gift and jewelry centers and antique shopping.

Innkeeper(s): Marty Neely & Connie Wu. $85-225. MC VISA AX DC CB DS PC TC. TAC10. 21 rooms, 19 with PB, 3 with FP. 3 suites. 1 cottage. Breakfast included in rates. Type of meal: full breakfast. Afternoon tea available. Beds: QD. Phone in room. Fax on premises. Pets Allowed.

Publicity: *Innsider.*

"...in no time at all you begin to feel a kinship with the gentle folk who adorn the walls in their golden frames."

The Parsonage

198 Haight St
San Francisco, CA 94102
(415)863-3699 Fax:(415)863-8696

Circa 1883. Close your eyes and imagine a 19th-century San Francisco Victorian row house and you'll picture the Parsonage. The inn features Corinthian columned porches, five-sided bay windows with double openings on the front face, second-story bay windows and cornices on top. The original house consisted of 22 rooms, a detached stable, six fireplaces and one bathroom. Today, the inn offers five spacious guest rooms decorated in European and American antiques, down comforters and marble bathrooms. A Historic Landmark, the inn is one of seven Victorian homes on the Hayes Valley Home tour. A complimentary breakfast and afternoon tea is served daily.

Innkeeper(s): Joan Hull & John Phillips. $85-125. PC TC. TAC10. 5 rooms with PB, 1 with FP. Breakfast and afternoon tea included in rates. Types of meals: continental-plus breakfast and full breakfast. Catering service available. Beds: QD. TV, VCR, fax, copier and library on premises. Weddings, small meetings and family reunions hosted. Spanish spoken. Antiques, sporting events and theater nearby.

Spencer House

1080 Haight St
San Francisco, CA 94117-3109
(415)626-9205 Fax:(415)626-9230

Circa 1887. This opulent mansion, which sits on three city lots, is one of San Francisco's finest examples of Queen Anne Victorian architecture. Ornate parquet floors, original wallpapers, gaslights and antique linens are featured. Breakfast is served with crystal and silver in the elegantly paneled dining room.

Innkeeper(s): Barbara Chambers. $115-165. MC VISA AX. 6 rooms with PB. Types of meals: full breakfast and early coffee/tea. Beds: KQD. Phone in room. Antiques and theater nearby.

Location: Ten minutes from the wharf. Golden Gate Park is 8 blocks away.

Stanyan Park Hotel

750 Stanyan St
San Francisco, CA 94117-2725
(415)751-1000 Fax:(415)668-5454
E-mail: info@stanyanpark.com

Circa 1904. Many of the guest rooms of this restored Victorian inn overlook Golden Gate Park. The turret suites and bay suites are popular, but all rooms are decorated in a variety of antiques and color schemes. The suites include kitchens. Museums, horseback riding and biking are available in the park, as well as the Japanese Tea Garden.

Guests enjoy a continental breakfast and evening tea service.

Innkeeper(s): John Brocklehurst. $99-225. MC VISA AX DC CB DS TC. TAC10. 36 rooms with PB. 6 suites. Type of meal: continental breakfast. Beds: QT. Phone in room. Fax, copier and bicycles on premises. Handicap access. Parks, shopping, sporting events and theater nearby.

Publicity: *Metropolitan Home, New York Times, Sunset Magazine.*

Victorian Inn on The Park

301 Lyon St
San Francisco, CA 94117-2108
(415)931-1830 (800)435-1967 Fax:(415)931-1830
E-mail: vicinn@aol.com

Circa 1897. This grand three-story Queen Anne inn, built by William Curlett, has an open belvedere turret with a teahouse roof and Victorian railings. Silk-screened wallpapers, created especially for the inn, are accentuated by intricate mahogany

and redwood paneling. The opulent Belvedere Suite features French doors opening to a Roman tub for two. Overlooking Golden Gate Park, the inn is 10 minutes from downtown.

Innkeeper(s): Lisa & William Benau. $99-169. MC VISA AX DC CB DS PC TC. TAC10. 12 rooms with PB, 3 with FP. 2 suites. Breakfast included in rates. Types of meals: continental-plus breakfast and early coffee/tea. Beds: QT. Phone in room. TV, fax, library and child care on premises. Small meetings and family reunions hosted. Russian and Spanish spoken. Antiques, parks, sporting events and theater nearby.

Location: Adjacent to Golden Gate Park.

Publicity: *Innsider, Country Inns, Good Housekeeping, New York Times, Good Morning America, Country Inns USA, Great Country Inns of America.*

"The excitement you have about your building comes from the care you have taken in restoring and maintaining your historic structure."

The Inn at Union Square

440 Post St
San Francisco, CA 94102-1502
(415)397-3510 (800)288-4346 Fax:(415)989-0529
E-mail: inn@unionsquare.com

Circa 1920. This elegant small non-smoking hotel is tucked away only one-half block from Union Square. The emphasis here is on comfort and European service, from valet parking, to breakfast in bed, to polished shoes at your door each morning, gratuities are included in the rate. Each room is individually decorated with fine fabrics, fresh flowers, Georgian furniture, and lion-head door knockers. The penthouse suite has a whirlpool bath, sauna, fireplace, and wet bar. Each floor features its own lounge and fireplace where, for a modest price, breakfast is served. Early morning complimentary coffee and tea service at begins at 6:30 a.m. Afternoon tea, served between 4:30 and 5:30 p.m., includes scones, cakes, and cucumber sandwiches, followed by evening wine and hors d'oeuvres.

Historic Interest: Pan Pacific Exhibition Pavilion, Golden Gate Park (nearby).

Innkeeper(s): Brooks Bayly. $150-350. MC VISA AX DC DS PC TC. TAC10. 30 rooms with PB, 2 with FP. 7 suites. Breakfast, afternoon tea and evening snack included in rates. Meals: continental-plus breakfast, early coffee/tea. Picnic lunch and room service available. Beds: KQDT. Phone, turndown service and TV in room. VCR, fax, copier, sauna, bicycles on premises. Handicap access. Antiques, parks, shopping, sporting events and theater nearby.

Location: In the heart of San Francisco.

Publicity: *Denver Post, Los Angeles Times, Contra Costa Times, Good Housekeeping.*

"My private slice of San Francisco. I'll always stay here."

San Jose

I5

The Hensley House

456 N 3rd St
San Jose, CA 95112-5250
(408)298-3537 (800)498-3537 Fax:(408)298-4676

Circa 1884. This colorful Queen Anne-style, shingled home is topped off with a Witches' cap. Decorated in rich burgundies and blues, rooms are complemented with lacy curtains, chandeliers, dark woodwork and fine furnishings. Each of the well-appointed rooms is unique with special light fixtures, stained glass and beautiful wall coverings. The Judge's Chamber includes a feather bed, fireplace and the modern amenities of a wet bar and whirlpool bath. Breakfast begins with cof-

fee and an assortment of teas, followed by fresh fruit, muffins, croissants and a hot entree. The innkeepers serve tea in the afternoon on Thursday and Saturday, and wine, teas and hors d'oeuvres are offered every afternoon.

Historic Interest: The Hensley House is located in a National Landmark neighborhood, and San Jose offers numerous historic sites, including parks and homes.

Innkeeper(s): Tony Contreras. $115-225. MC VISA AX. 9 rooms with PB. 2 suites. Breakfast included in rates. Type of meal: full breakfast. Afternoon tea, dinner, picnic lunch, lunch, catering service and room service available. Beds: Q. Antiques, fishing and theater nearby.

Publicity: *Mercury News, New York Times, Metro, Business Journal.*

"Can we move in! Wonderful staff, homey atmosphere, very accommodating. Everything was perfect, breakfast was royal."

San Luis Obispo M7

Garden Street Inn

1212 Garden St
San Luis Obispo, CA 93401-3962
(805)545-9802 Fax:(805)545-9403

Circa 1887. Innkeepers Dan and Kathy Smith restored this elegant home, paying meticulous attention to detail. Each room has a special theme. The Field of Dreams room, dedicated to Kathy Smith's father, includes

memorabilia from his sports reporting days, toy figures from various baseball teams and framed pictures of antique baseball cards. The Cocoon room displays dozens of beautiful butterfly knickknacks. Situated downtown, the inn is within walking distance of shops and restaurants and the San Luis Obispo Mission. Pismo Beach and Hearst Castle are also nearby attractions.

Innkeeper(s): Kathy & Dan Smith. $90-160. MC VISA AX. TAC10. 13 rooms with PB, 5 with FP. 4 suites. 2 conference rooms. Breakfast and afternoon tea included in rates. Types of meals: full breakfast, gourmet breakfast and early coffee/tea. Beds: KQ. Phone, air conditioning and turndown service in room. Fax on premises. Handicap access. Weddings, small meetings and seminars hosted. Antiques, fishing, parks, shopping, sporting events, theater and watersports nearby.

Publicity: *Times-Press-Recorder, Telegram-Tribune, San Francisco Chronicle, Los Angeles Times, Orange County Register, Los Angeles Daily News.*

"We appreciate your warmth and care."

San Martine G4

Country Rose Inn - B&B

455 Fitzgerald Ave, #E
San Martine, CA 95046
(408)842-0441 Fax:(408)842-6646

Circa 1920. Amid five wooded acres, a half-hour's drive south of San Jose, sits the aptly named Country Rose Inn. A roomy Dutch Colonial manor, this inn was once a farmhouse on a chicken ranch. Every room features a rose theme, including wallpaper and quilted bedspreads. Each window offers a relaxing view of horses grazing, fertile fields, or the tranquil grounds, which boast magnificent 100-year-old oak trees.

Historic Interest: San Juan Bautista Mission.

Innkeeper(s): Rose Hernandez. $129-199. MC VISA PC. TAC10. 5 rooms with PB, 2 with FP. 1 suite. 2 conference rooms. Breakfast and afternoon tea included in rates. Types of meals: full breakfast and early coffee/tea. Picnic lunch available. Beds: KQDT. Air conditioning and turndown service in room. Fax and library on

premises. Weddings, small meetings and seminars hosted. Spanish spoken. Antiques, parks, shopping, golf and theater nearby.

Location: Masten Avenue exit off Hwy 101 in San Martin, north of Gilroy.

"The quiet, serene country setting made our anniversary very special. Rose is a delightful, gracious hostess and cook."

Santa Barbara N8

Bath Street Inn

1720 Bath St
Santa Barbara, CA 93101-2910
(805)682-9680 (800)341-2284 Fax:(805)569-1281

Circa 1890. Overlooking the Victorian front veranda, a semicircular "eyelid" balcony on the second floor seems to wink, beckoning guests to come in for an old-fashioned taste of hospitality provided by innkeeper Susan Brown. Originally the home of a merchant tailor,

the inn is within a few blocks of the heart of Old Santa Barbara. Guest chambers upstairs have polished hardwood floors, floral wallpapers and antiques. The back garden deck, surrounded by wisteria and blossoming orange trees, and the more formal dining room are the locations available for enjoying breakfast, afternoon tea and wine and cheese. The Summer House was recently converted to guest rooms that offer Jacuzzis and fireplaces.

Innkeeper(s): Susan Brown, Nan Almstead, Joanne Thorne. $80-195. MC VISA AX PC. TAC10. 10 rooms with PB, 4 with FP. 1 suite. Breakfast, afternoon tea and evening snack included in rates. Types of meals: full breakfast and early coffee/tea. Beds: KQT. Phone, air conditioning and ceiling fan in room. Fax and copier on premises. Handicap access. Antiques, fishing, parks, shopping, sporting events, theater and watersports nearby.

Publicity: *Sunset.*

"Like going to the home of a favorite aunt.—Country Inns."

Casa Del Mar Inn

18 Bath St
Santa Barbara, CA 93101-3803
(805)963-4418 (800)433-3097 Fax:(805)966-4240

Circa 1929. Remodeled between 1994 and 1997, this beautiful Mediterranean-style inn offers grounds with gardens and a courtyard with a Jacuzzi. Guests can choose from spacious, private rooms or one- and two-room suites with kitchens and fireplaces. Business travelers will appreciate the fax service and modem hook-ups. The inn hosts a special social hour each evening with wine and cheese. An all-you-can-eat buffet breakfast is a perfect start to a day

enjoying the Santa Barbara area. The inn is within easy walking distance of shops and fine restaurants. Wedding parties and family reunions are welcome.

Innkeeper(s): Mike & Becky Montgomery. $69-219. MC VISA AX DC DS TC. TAC10. 21 rooms with PB, 6 with FP. 6 suites. Breakfast included in rates. Type of meal: continental-plus breakfast. Beds: KQ. Phone, ceiling fan and TV in room. Fax, copier and spa on premises. Handicap access. German spoken. Watersports nearby.

Pets Allowed: Small, must not be left alone in room.

Cheshire Cat Inn

36 W Valerio St
Santa Barbara, CA 93101-2524
(805)569-1610 Fax:(805)682-1876

Circa 1894. The Eberle family built two graceful houses side by side, one a Queen Anne, the other a Colonial Revival. President McKinley was entertained here on a visit to Santa Barbara. There is a pagoda-like porch, a square and a curved bay, rose gardens, grassy lawns and a gazebo. Laura Ashley wallpapers and furnishings are featured. Outside, guests will enjoy English flower gardens, an outdoor Jacuzzi, a new deck with sitting areas and fountains.

Historic Interest: Santa Barbara Beautiful Award.

Innkeeper(s): Christine Dunstan. $140-300. MC VISA PC TC. 17 rooms with PB. 7 suites. 1 conference room. Breakfast included in rates. Type of meal: full breakfast. Room service available. Beds: KQT. Phone, ceiling fan and TV in room. Spa on premises. Weddings, small meetings, family reunions and seminars hosted. Amusement parks, antiques, fishing, shopping, sporting events, theater and watersports nearby.

Location: Downtown.

Publicity: *Two on the Town, KABC, Los Angeles Times, Santa Barbara, American In Flight, Elmer Dills Recommends.*

"Romantic and quaint."

El Encanto Hotel & Garden Villas

1900 Lasuen Rd
Santa Barbara, CA 93103-1798
(805)687-5000 (800)346-7039 Fax:(805)687-3903
E-mail: elencanto@aol.com

Circa 1913. "El Encanto" means "the enchanted," and this historic hotel, in the National Register, is comprised of a newer two-story building as well as a plethora of villas and cottages tucked into lush gardens overlooking Santa Barbara's red tile roofs and the Pacific Ocean. The cottages, built in a Craftsman style, were the original structures of the hotel. Later structures added to the inn's 10 acres were in the Spanish Colonial Revival style, the predominant architecture for which Santa Barbara is known. The decor is California residential. Several romantic packages are offered including "Some Enchanted Evening," "A Night to Remember," and for midweek, "Romance on the Riviera." Famous guests of the past include Clark Gable and Carole Lombard.

Innkeeper(s): Thomas Narazonick. $150-290. MC VISA AX DC CB PC TC. TAC10. 85 rooms with PB, 42 with FP. 29 suites. 63 cottages. 4 conference rooms. Breakfast included in rates. Types of meals: continental breakfast, continental-plus breakfast, full breakfast and gourmet breakfast. Afternoon tea, dinner, evening snack, picnic lunch, lunch, gourmet lunch, banquet service, catering service, catered breakfast and room service available. Restaurant on premises. Beds: KQ. Phone and TV in room. VCR, fax, copier, spa, swimming, tennis, library and child care on premises. Handicap access. 10 acres. Weddings, small meetings and family reunions hosted. French, Spanish, German and Italian spoken. Antiques, fishing, parks, shopping, golf, theater and watersports nearby.

Publicity: *Business Week, Travel & Leisure, New York Times, Food & Wine.*

Glenborough Inn

1327 Bath St
Santa Barbara, CA 93101-3623
(805)966-0589 (800)962-0589 Fax:(805)564-8610
E-mail: glenboro@silcom.com

Circa 1906. This Craftsman-style inn recreates a turn-of-the-century atmosphere in the Main house and White house. There is also an 1880s cottage reminiscent of the Victorian era. Inside are antiques, rich wood trim and elegant fireplace suites with canopy beds. There's always plenty of hospitality and an open invitation to the secluded garden hot tub. Breakfast is homemade and has been written up in "Bon Appetit" and "Chocolatier."

Historic Interest: Walking distance to historic downtown Santa Barbara, Mission Santa Barbara (1 1/4 mile).

Innkeeper(s): Michael Diaz & Steve Ryan. $100-350. MC VISA AX DC CB DS PC TC. TAC10. 11 rooms with PB, 9 with FP. 5 suites. 1 cottage. Breakfast included in rates. Types of meals: continental breakfast, full breakfast, gourmet breakfast and early coffee/tea. Dinner, picnic lunch and gourmet lunch available. Beds: KQD. Phone and ceiling fan in room. Fax and spa on premises. Spanish and Sign spoken. Antiques, fishing, parks, shopping, sporting events, theater and watersports nearby.

Publicity: *Houston Post, Los Angeles Times, Horizon, Los Angeles, Pasadena Choice.*

"A delightful, elegant and charming suite."

The Mary May Inn

111 W Valerio St
Santa Barbara, CA 93101-2912
(805)569-3398

Circa 1880. These two Victorians are a local and state historical site, and feature many romantic touches. Some guest rooms offer Jacuzzi tubs, some have a fireplace. A few are lit by chandeliers, and each room is different. Open the double doors from the spacious bedchamber in the Brooke Marie room and you'll find a sitting room and bath with a clawfoot tub. The Thimbleberry includes a private entrance, which guests access via a little garden trail. Mexican and Italian influences are prevalent in the breakfast fare. Guests can walk to many Santa Barbara sites from the inn, including the mission, an art museum and shopping.

Innkeeper(s): Kathleen Pohring & Mark Cronin. $100-180. MC VISA AX TC. TAC10. 12 rooms with PB, 4 with FP. Breakfast, afternoon tea and evening snack included in rates. Types of meals: full breakfast and early coffee/tea. Beds: Q. Air conditioning in room. TV on premises. Weddings and family reunions hosted. Antiques, fishing, parks, shopping, sporting events, golf, theater and watersports nearby.

Pets Allowed: Upon innkeeper/owner approval.

Publicity: *Santa Barbara News Press.*

The Old Yacht Club Inn

431 Corona Del Mar
Santa Barbara, CA 93103-3601
(805)962-1277 (800)676-1676 Fax:(805)962-3989

Circa 1912. This California Craftsman house was the home of the Santa Barbara Yacht Club during the Roaring '20s. It was opened as Santa Barbara's first B&B and has become renowned for its gourmet food and superb hospitality. Dinner is offered to guests on Saturday nights. Innkeeper Nancy Donaldson is the author of The Old Yacht Club Inn Cookbook.

Innkeeper(s): Nancy Donaldson. $145-155. MC VISA AX DS. 10 rooms with PB. 1 conference room. Breakfast included in rates. Types of meals: full breakfast, gourmet breakfast and early coffee/tea. Beds: KQ. Phone in room. TV, fax, copier and bicycles on premises. Small meetings and seminars hosted. Antiques, fishing, shopping, sporting events, theater, watersports nearby.

Location: East Beach.

Publicity: Los Angeles, Valley.

"Donaldson is one of Santa Barbara's better-kept culinary secrets."

Olive House Inn

1604 Olive St
Santa Barbara, CA 93101-1115
(805)962-4902 (800)786-6422 Fax:(805)899-2754
E-mail: olivehse@aol.com

Circa 1904. The Craftsman-style home is located a short walk from Santa Barbara's Mission and downtown. The living room is decorated with bay windows, redwood paneling, a fireplace and a studio grand piano. Two guest rooms have a hot tub. Guests can enjoy city and ocean views, private decks and hot tubs. In the afternoon, wine is offered and in the evening, tea, cookies and sherry are presented.

Historic Interest: Santa Barbara Mission, a museum of natural history, Santa Barbara Historical Museum and The Arlington Theatre are all within walking distance.

Innkeeper(s): Lois Gregg & Bharti Singh. $110-180. MC VISA AX DS. 6 rooms with PB, 1 with FP. Breakfast included in rates. Types of meals: gourmet breakfast and early coffee/tea. Evening snack available. Beds: KQ. Phone in room. TV and fax on premises. Small meetings, family reunions and seminars hosted. Antiques, parks, shopping, sporting events and theater nearby.

"Thank you for providing not only a lovely place to stay but a very warm and inviting atmosphere."

The Parsonage

1600 Olive St
Santa Barbara, CA 93101-1115
(805)962-9336 (800)775-0352

Circa 1892. Built for the Trinity Episcopal Church, the Parsonage is one of Santa Barbara's most notable Queen Anne Victorian structures. Each room is elegantly decorated in fine antiques and furnishings distinctive to the period. It is nestled between downtown Santa Barbara and the foothills in a quiet residential, upper eastside neighborhood. The inn has ocean and mountain views and is within walk-

ing distance of the mission, shops, theater and restaurants.

Innkeeper(s): Linda Minke. $130-260. MC VISA AX. TAC10. 6 rooms with PB, 2 with FP. 1 suite. 1 conference room. Breakfast and afternoon tea included in rates. Type of meal: full breakfast. Beds: KQT. Fax on premises. Antiques, fishing, theater and watersports nearby.

Location: Near the Santa Barbara Mission.

Publicity: Los Angeles Times, Epicurean Review, Country Inns B&B, The California Getaway Guide.

"Things were as close to perfect as newlyweds could want. You and your marvelous house played a major role in making it so."

Secret Garden Inn and Cottages

1908 Bath St
Santa Barbara, CA 93101-2813
(805)687-2300 (800)676-1622 Fax:(805)687-4576

Circa 1908. The main house and adjacent cottages surround the gardens and are decorated in American and English-Country style. The Hummingbird is a large cottage guest room with a queen-size white iron bed and a private deck with a hot tub for your exclusive use. The three suites have private outdoor hot tubs. Wine and light hors d'oeuvres are served in the late afternoon, and hot apple cider is served each evening.

Innkeeper(s): Jack Greenwald, Christine Dunstan. $115-225. MC VISA AX PC TC. TAC10. 11 rooms with PB, 1 with FP. 3 suites. 4 cottages. Breakfast, afternoon tea and evening snack included in rates. Types of meals: full breakfast and early coffee/tea. Beds: KQ. TV, fax, copier and bicycles on premises. Weddings, small meetings, family reunions and seminars hosted. Antiques, fishing, shopping, theater and watersports nearby.

Location: Quiet residential area near town and the beach.

Publicity: Los Angeles Times, Santa Barbara, Independant.

"A romantic little getaway retreat that neither of us will be able to forget. It was far from what we expected to find."

Simpson House Inn

121 E Arrellaga
Santa Barbara, CA 93108
(805)963-7067 (800)676-1280 Fax:(805)564-4811
E-mail: Simpsonhouse@compuserve.com

Circa 1874. If you were one of the Simpson family's first visitors, you would have arrived in Santa Barbara by stagecoach or by ship. The railroad was not completed for another 14 years. A stately Italianate Victorian house, the inn is situated on an acre of English gardens hidden behind a 20-foot-tall eugenia hedge. In the evenings, guests are treated to a sampling of local wines, as well as a lavish Mediterranean hors d'oeuvres buffet. The evening turndown service includes delectable chocolate truffles. The innkeepers can arrange for in-room European spa treatments, and guests can workout at a nearby private health club. Guests also receive complimentary passes for the Santa Barbara trolley.

Historic Interest: Santa Barbara Mission, Presidio, El Paseo all within 1 mile.

Innkeeper(s): Linda & Glyn Davies. $145-350. MC VISA AX DS. 14 rooms with PB, 7 with FP. 5 suites. 1 conference room. Breakfast and afternoon tea included in rates. Beds: KQ. Fax, copier and bicycles on premises. Handicap access. Antiques, fishing, theater and watersports nearby.

Location: Five-minute walk to downtown Santa Barbara and historic district.

Publicity: Country Inns, Santa Barbara, LA Magazine, Avenues.

"Perfectly restored and impeccably furnished. Your hospitality is warm and heartfelt and the food is delectable. Whoever said that 'the journey is better than the destination' couldn't have known about the Simpson House."

Tiffany Inn

1323 De La Vina St
Santa Barbara, CA 93101-3120
(805)963-2283

Circa 1898. This Victorian house features a steep front gable and balcony accentuating the entrance. Colonial diamond-paned bay windows and a front veranda welcome guests to an antique-filled inn. The Honeymoon Suite is a favorite with its secluded garden entrance, canopied bed, jacuzzi tub and fireplace. Other rooms are just as interesting, with antique toy collections, floral chintzes and Victorian beds. Fine restaurants and shops are within walking distance.

Innkeeper(s): Carol & Larry Mac Donald. $125-275. MC VISA AX. 7 rooms, 5 with PB, 5 with FP. Type of meal: full breakfast. Beds: Q. Phone in room. Spa on premises.

"We have stayed at a number of B&B's, but this is the best. We especially liked the wonderful breakfasts on the porch overlooking the garden."

The Upham Hotel & Garden Cottages

1404 De La Vina St
Santa Barbara, CA 93101-3027
(805)962-0058 (800)727-0876 Fax:(805)963-2825

Circa 1871. Antiques and period furnishings decorate each of the inn's guest rooms and suites. The inn is the oldest continuously operating hostelry in Southern California. Situated on an acre of gardens in the center of downtown, it's within easy walking distance of restaurants, shops, art galleries and museums. The staff is happy to assist guests in discovering Santa Barbara's varied attractions. Garden cottage units feature porches or secluded patios and several have gas fireplaces.

Innkeeper(s): Jan Martin Winn. $125-360. MC VISA AX DC CB DS TC. TAC10. 50 rooms with PB, 8 with FP. 4 suites. 4 cottages. 4 conference rooms. Breakfast and evening snack included in rates. Types of meals: continental-plus breakfast and early coffee/tea. Banquet service available. Restaurant on premises. Beds: KQD. Phone, ceiling fan and TV in room. VCR, fax and copier on premises. Small meetings, family reunions and seminars hosted. Spanish spoken. Antiques, fishing, parks, shopping, sporting events, theater and watersports nearby.

Publicity: *L.A. Times, Santa Barbara, Westways, Santa Barbara News-Press.*

"Your hotel is truly a charm. Between the cozy gardens and the exquisitely comfortable appointments, The Upham is charm itself."

Santa Barbara (Carpinteria) *N8*

Prufrock's Garden Inn

600 Linden Ave
Santa Barbara (Carpinteria), CA 93013-2040
(805)566-9696 (888)778-3765 Fax:(805)566-9696

Circa 1904. A white picket fence surrounds this California-style cottage, located on a palm-lined small-town main street one block from a beautiful oceanfront state park. The inn has been honored by a number of awards, most recently, the LA Times "Reader's Favorite" poll. The bedrooms offer private sitting areas. Relax on the porch or stroll through the lush gardens. Guest will enjoy the inviting aroma of the inn's busy kitchen in addition to the pleasant ocean breezes.

Historic Interest: The Old Mission and historic county courthouse are about 12 minutes away in Santa Barbara. Other nearby historic attractions include adobes and a state historic park.

Innkeeper(s): Judy & Jim Halvorsen. $99-199. MC VISA DS PC TC. 7 rooms, 5 with PB. Breakfast, afternoon tea and evening snack included in rates. Meals: full breakfast, early coffee/tea. Beds: Q. Turndown service, VCR in room. Bicycles on premises. Small meetings, family reunions, seminars hosted. Antiques, fishing, parks, shopping, sporting events, theater, watersports nearby.

Publicity: *Santa Barbara Independent's "Most Romantic Getaway"; Carpinteria's "Community Beautification" award; pictured in Land's End catalog.*

Santa Clara *I5*

Madison Street Inn

1390 Madison St
Santa Clara, CA 95050-4759
(408)249-5541 (800)491-5541 Fax:(408)249-6676
E-mail: madstinn@aol.com

Circa 1890. This Queen Anne Victorian inn still boasts its original doors and locks, and "No Peddlers or Agents" is engraved in the cement of the original carriageway. Guests, however, always receive a warm and gracious welcome to high-ceilinged rooms furnished in antiques, Oriental rugs and Victorian wallpaper.

Historic Interest: Winchester Mystery House (2 miles), Harns-Lass House (2 miles).

Innkeeper(s): Theresa & Ralph Wigginton. $65-105. MC VISA AX DC DS PC TC. TAC10. 6 rooms, 4 with PB. Breakfast, afternoon tea and evening snack included in rates. Types of meals: gourmet breakfast and early coffee/tea. Picnic lunch, gourmet lunch, banquet service, catering service and catered breakfast available. Beds: QD. Phone and ceiling fan in room. TV, VCR, fax, spa, swimming and bicycles on premises. Weddings, small meetings, family reunions and seminars hosted. Amusement parks, antiques, parks, sporting events, theater and watersports nearby.

Pets Allowed.

Location: Ten minutes from San Jose airport.

Publicity: *Discovery.*

"We spend many nights in hotels that look and feel exactly alike whether they are in Houston or Boston. Your inn was delightful. It was wonderful to bask in your warm and gracious hospitality."

Santa Cruz *J5*

Babbling Brook B&B Inn

1025 Laurel St
Santa Cruz, CA 95060-4237
(408)427-2437 (800)866-1131 Fax:(408)427-2457

Circa 1909. This inn was built on the foundations of an 1870 tannery and a 1790 grist mill. Secluded, yet within the city, the inn features a cascading waterfall, historic waterwheel and meandering creek on one acre of gardens and redwoods. Country French decor, cozy fireplaces, and deep-soaking whirlpool tubs are luxurious amenities of the Babbling Brook. In the evenings, complimentary wine and cheese are served.

Innkeeper(s): Suzie Lankes & Dan Floyd. $105-180. MC VISA AX DC CB DS TC. TAC10. 12 rooms with PB, 10 with FP. 1 conference room. Breakfast, afternoon tea and evening snack included in rates. Types of meals: gourmet breakfast and early coffee/tea. Room service available. Beds: KQ. Phone and TV in room. Fax and spa on premises. Handicap access. Weddings hosted. Amusement parks, antiques, fishing, parks, shopping, sporting events, golf, theater and watersports nearby.

Location: North end of Monterey Bay.

Publicity: *Country Inns, Yellow Brick Road, Times-Press-Recorder.*

"We were impressed with the genuine warmth of the inn. The best breakfast we've had outside our own home!"

Chateau Victorian

118 1st St
Santa Cruz, CA 95060-5402
(408)458-9458

This plum-colored Victorian is within a block of the waterfront and offers seven guest rooms. The romantic Bay Side Room is a favorite of guests, as it offers a marble fireplace and a clawfoot tub with an overhead

shower. Breakfasts, including a variety of tempting fruits, and bread can be enjoyed on the patio, dining room or on the secluded side deck. After a day of exploring Santa Cruz and its surroundings, evening refreshments are a perfect touch. The inn is within

walking distance to downtown, the wharf, a variety of restaurants, the Boardwalk Amusement Park and the beach.

Innkeeper(s): Alice June. $110-140. MC VISA PC. 7 rooms with PB, 7 with FP. 1 cottage. Breakfast included in rates. Meal: continental-plus breakfast. Evening snack available. Beds: Q. Small meetings hosted. Amusement parks, antiques, fishing, parks, shopping, theater and watersports nearby.

Location: One block from the beach.

Publicity: *Times Tribune, Santa Cruz Sentinel, Good Times.*

"Certainly enjoyed our most recent stay and have appreciated all of our visits."

Santa Monica   O10

Channel Road Inn

219 W Channel Rd
Santa Monica, CA 90402-1105
(310)459-1920 Fax:(310)454-9920
E-mail: channel@aol.com

Circa 1910. This shingle-clad building is a variation of the Colonial Revival Period, one of the few remaining in Los Angeles. The abandoned home was saved from the city's wrecking crew by owner Susan Zolla, with the encouragement of the local historical society. The rooms feature canopy beds, fine linens, custom mattresses and private porches. Chile Cheese Puffs served with salsa are a popular breakfast speciality. The Pacific Ocean is one block away, and guests often enjoy borrowing the inn's bicycles to pedal along the 30-mile coastal bike path. In the evening, the inn's spectacular cliffside spa is popular.

Innkeeper(s): Kathy Jensen. $125-245. MC VISA AX PC TC. TAC10. 12 rooms with PB, 2 with FP. 2 suites. Breakfast, afternoon tea and evening snack included in rates. Types of meals: full breakfast and early coffee/tea. Room service available. Beds: KQDT. Phone, ceiling fan, TV and VCR in room. Fax, copier, spa and bicycles on premises. Handicap access. Antiques, fishing, parks, shopping, sporting events, theater and watersports nearby.

Location: One block from the ocean.

Publicity: *Los Angeles Magazine, New York Times, Brides, Country Inns.*

"One of the most romantic hotels in Los Angeles."

Santa Paula   N9

The White Gables Inn

715 E Santa Paula St
Santa Paula, CA 93060-2063
(805)933-3041

Circa 1894. A visit to Santa Paula, a quaint little town about an hour or so out of Los Angeles, is like stepping back into another era. Innkeepers Bob and Ellen Smith have preserved this atmosphere in their Queen Anne

Victorian. Each of the romantic rooms is filled with antiques, vanity tables and unique pieces. The Victorian Room, decked in rose and blue hues, features a clawfoot tub perfect for soaking. The Bear Room boasts oak antique furnishings and a teddy bear collection. The Gables Suite, which encompasses the entire third floor, has a private sitting room, antiques and a clawfoot tub. Freshly baked cookies, chocolate and sherry are just a few of the amenities offered. Breakfasts start out with the house specialty, White Gables Inn Cinnamon Coffeecake, a recipe courtesy of Ellen's mother. The morning meal, which features special entrees such as Macadamia Nut Belgian Waffles, is served in the dining room on a candle-lit table set with fine china, crystal, silver and fresh flowers.

Historic Interest: The inn is a county landmark and is located in Santa Paula's historic district. Several historic sites are nearby, including the Santa Paula Union Oil Museum.

Innkeeper(s): R. L. Bob & Ellen Smith. $85-115. MC VISA AX. 3 rooms with PB. 1 suite. Breakfast included in rates. Type of meal: full breakfast. Beds: KQD. Antiques and theater nearby.

Publicity: *Sunset, Ventura County Star, Los Angeles Times.*

"The house is charming! The street quiet! The breakfast was delicious! We have found our new getaway. We'll be back!!!"

Santa Rosa   G4

The Gables Inn

4257 Petaluma Hill Rd
Santa Rosa, CA 95404-9796
(707)585-7777 (800)422-5376 Fax:(707)584-5634

Circa 1877. Fifteen gables accentuate this striking Gothic Revival house with a French influence. Situated on three-and-a-half acres in the center of Sonoma Wine Country, the inn has 12-foot ceilings, a winding staircase with ornately carved balustrades and three marble fireplaces. The Brookside Suite overlooks Taylor Creek and is decorated in an Edwardian theme. Other rooms feature views of the sequoias, meadows and the barn.

Innkeeper(s): Michael & Judy Ogne. $125-195. MC VISA AX DS. TAC10. 8 rooms with PB, 4 with FP. 1 suite. 1 cottage. Breakfast and afternoon tea included in rates. Types of meals: gourmet breakfast and early coffee/tea. Beds: KQT. Handicap access. Antiques, fishing, parks, shopping, sporting events, theater and watersports nearby.

Publicity: *Press Democrat.*

"You all have a warmth about you that makes it home here."

Melitta Station Inn

5850 Melitta Rd
Santa Rosa, CA 95409-5641
(707)538-7712 (800)504-3099

Circa 1890. Originally built as a stagecoach stop, this rambling structure became a freight depot for the little town of Melitta. Basalt stone, quarried from nearby hills, was sent by rail to San Francisco where it was used to pave the cobblestone streets. Still located down a country lane, the station has been charmingly renovated. Oiled-wood floors, a rough-beam cathedral ceiling and French doors opening to a balcony are features of the sitting room. Wineries and vineyards stretch from the station to the town of Sonoma.

Historic Interest: Jack London State Park & Museum, Luther Burbank Home & Gardens.

Innkeeper(s): Diane Crandon & Vic Amstadter. $95-110. MC VISA. 6 rooms, 4 with PB. 1 suite. Breakfast included in rates. Types of meals: gourmet breakfast and early coffee/tea. Beds: QD. Family reunions hosted. Antiques, fishing, parks and theater nearby.

Publicity: *Los Angeles Times, New York Times, Press Democrat.*

"Warm welcome and great food."

Pygmalion House B&B Inn

331 Orange St
Santa Rosa, CA 95401-6226
(707)526-3407 Fax:(707)526-3407

Circa 1880. This historic Victorian, which has been restored to its 19th-century grandeur, is just a few blocks from Santa Rosa's Old Town, Railroad Square and many antique shops, cafes, coffeehouses and restaurants. The home is filled with a unique mix of antiques, many of which belonged to famed stripper, Gypsy Rose Lee. Each of the Victorian guest rooms includes a bath with a claw-foot tub. Five different varieties of coffee are blended each morning for the breakfast service, which includes homemade entrees, freshly baked breads and fresh fruit.

Innkeeper(s): Caroline Berry. $75-95. MC VISA PC TC. 6 rooms with PB. 1 suite. Breakfast included in rates. Types of meals: full breakfast and early coffee/tea. Afternoon tea and evening snack available. Beds: KQD. Phone, air conditioning and TV in room. Fax and copier on premises. Family reunions and seminars hosted. Antiques, parks, shopping, sporting events, theater and watersports nearby.

Sausalito   H4

Casa Madrona Hotel

801 Bridgeway
Sausalito, CA 94965-2186
(415)332-0502 (800)567-9524 Fax:(415)332-2537

Circa 1885. This Victorian was first used as a lumber baron's mansion. As time went on, additional cottages were added, giving it a European look. A registered Sausalito Historical

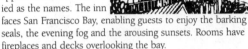

Landmark, it is the oldest building in town. Each room has a unique name, such as "Lord Ashley's Lookout" or "Kathmandu," and the appointments are as varied as the names. The inn faces San Francisco Bay, enabling guests to enjoy the barking seals, the evening fog and the arousing sunsets. Rooms have fireplaces and decks overlooking the bay.

Innkeeper(s): John W. Mays. $125-260. MAP. MC VISA AX DC DS TC. TAC10. 35 rooms with PB. 3 suites. 4 cottages. 1 conference room. Breakfast and evening snack included in rates. Type of meal: continental-plus breakfast. Banquet service, catering service and room service available. Restaurant on premises. Beds: KQT. Phone, turndown service, TV in room. VCR, fax, copier, spa on premises. Weddings, small meetings and family reunions hosted. Parks, shopping, sporting events, theater and watersports nearby.

Location: Downtown Sausalito.

Publicity: *Los Angeles Times, Orange County Register.*

"Had to pinch myself several times to be sure it was real! Is this heaven? With this view, it sure feels like it."

Hotel Sausalito

16 El Portal
Sausalito, CA 94965
(415)332-0700 (888)442-0700 Fax:(415)332-8788

Circa 1915. Just a short drive across the Golden Gate Bridge will take you from San Francisco into the village of Sausalito, the location of this historic Mission Revival-style hotel. Its notorious past includes the possible use of the place as a bordello and a hot spot during Prohibition. However, now the hotel boasts only stylishly, elegant decor in a tranquil setting, meant to appear as a boutique French hotel. There is concierge service and plenty of amenities for business travelers, such as in-room desks, voice mail and modem ports.

Innkeeper(s): William Purdie. $115-250. MC VISA AX DC TC. TAC10. 16 rooms with PB. 2 suites. Breakfast included in rates. Type of meal: continental-plus breakfast. Beds: KQT. Phone, air conditioning and TV in room. Fax and copier on premises. French, Spanish and German spoken. Parks, shopping, theater and watersports nearby.

Seal Beach   O10

The Seal Beach Inn & Gardens

212 5th St
Seal Beach, CA 90740-6115
(562)493-2416 (800)433-3292 Fax:(562)799-0483

Circa 1923. This historic Southern California inn has lush gardens and the look of an oceanside estate. It's a short walk to the Seal Beach pier, shops and restaurants. Major attractions in Orange County and the Los Angeles area are within short driving distances. Business travelers can plan meetings in rooms where 24 people can sit comfortably. The inn has a Mediterranean villa ambiance, and no two rooms are alike.

Historic Interest: The Bauer Museum and Queen Mary are nearby historic attractions, and the inn is within an hour from most of Los Angeles' historic sites. Rancho Los Alamitos, a five-acre historic preserve of an original 1520s Spanish land grant, is just three miles from the inn and includes on its grounds the oldest house in the L.A. area.

Innkeeper(s): Marjorie B. & Harty Schmaehl. $125-275. AP. MC VISA AX DC CB DS TC. 23 rooms with PB, 4 with FP. 11 suites. Breakfast and evening snack included in rates. Types of meals: full breakfast and early coffee/tea. Afternoon tea available. Beds: KQ. Phone and turndown service in room. Fax and copier on premises. Weddings, small meetings, family reunions and seminars hosted. Amusement parks, antiques, fishing, parks, shopping, sporting events, golf, theater and watersports nearby.

Location: 300 yards from the ocean, five minutes from Long Beach.

Publicity: *Brides, Country Inns, Glamour, Country, Long Beach Press Telegram, Orange County Register, L.A. Times, Country Living, Sunset.*

"The closest thing to Europe since I left there. Delights the senses and restores the soul."

Sebastopol
G4

Gravenstein Inn

3160 Hicks Rd
Sebastopol, CA 95472-2413
(707)829-0493 Fax:(707)824-9382
E-mail: gravensteininn@metro.net

Circa 1872. Named for the earliest variety of apple found in the inn's orchard, the Gravenstein is a National Historic Landmark. Shaded by tall redwoods, the three-story inn is in the Victorian style and includes a columned porch and a balcony that overlooks six acres of gardens and lawns. Eighteen varieties of apples grow in the orchard, and there are peaches, apricots, pears, grapes and raspberries. Fragrant rose beds are found near the solar-heated pool, and a new garden offers a gazebo, fish pond and chicken house. Request the Gravenstein Suite and you'll enjoy a fireplace and a summer room surrounded by branches of the inn's buckeye tree. Breakfasts include the freshest seasonal fruits and produce from the property.

Innkeeper(s): Frank & Kathleen Mayhew. $85-125. MC VISA PC TC. TAC10. 5 rooms, 3 with PB, 1 with FP. 1 suite. 1 cottage. Breakfast included in rates. Types of meals: full breakfast, gourmet breakfast and early coffee/tea. Room service available. Beds: QT. Swimming and library on premises. Weddings and family reunions hosted. Antiques, fishing, parks, shopping, golf, theater and watersports nearby.

Smith River
A2

White Rose Inn

149 S Fred Haight Dr
Smith River, CA 95567
(707)487-9260

Circa 1869. Drive through the security gate and up the hill, and you'll feel you are coming home to your own country estate. Built in the style of an Italianate Victorian with large double bay windows, this gracious three-story house is located on more than four acres with fruit and nut trees, a creek, gazebo and green lawns. The Swan Room boasts a king-size canopy bed, a whirlpool for two and antiques original to the Haight family who once lived here. The

Country Cottage Room, recommended for families with children, offers a kitchen, sitting room and bedroom with a four-poster canopy bed. The inn is located in the Smith River Valley, five minutes from the ocean and Smith River.

Innkeeper(s): Candy Gallo. $89-185. PC. 7 rooms with PB. 1 suite. 1 cottage. Breakfast included in rates. Types of meals: continental-plus breakfast and early coffee/tea. Beds: KQDT. Turndown service in room. Fax, copier and swimming on premises. Weddings, small meetings, family reunions, seminars hosted. Antiques, fishing, parks, shopping, golf, theater, watersports nearby.

Pets Allowed: Pet Motel nearby.

Publicity: *Del Norte Triplicate, Humboldt Times.*

"Charming house, your hard work shows."

Soda Springs
F7

Rainbow Lodge

PO Box 1100
Soda Springs, CA 95728-1100
(916)426-3871 (800)500-3871 Fax:(916)426-9221
E-mail: royalg@ix.netcom.com

Circa 1920. Once a stagecoach stop on Donner Summit, this three-story mountain lodge rests on the Yuba River, and some rooms offer river views. A spring on the property provides water for area bottled-water companies. The oldest part of the lodge has knotty pine and stone walls. Guest rooms feature floral spreads, wood paneling and brass beds. Some share a bath down the hall, while others offer private baths. Two-bedroom family suites are available. European and Californian cuisine is offered in the Engadine Cafe located on the premises. Royal Gorge skiing is six miles away.

Innkeeper(s): Jacqui James. $79-129. EP. MC VISA TC. TAC10. 32 rooms, 10 with PB. 2 suites. 1 conference room. Breakfast included in rates. Types of meals: full breakfast, gourmet breakfast and early coffee/tea. Dinner, evening snack, picnic lunch, lunch, gourmet lunch and banquet service available. Restaurant on premises. Beds: QDT. Fax and copier on premises. Weddings, small meetings, family reunions and seminars hosted. French and English spoken. Antiques, fishing, parks, shopping, downhill skiing, cross-country skiing and watersports nearby.

Royal Gorges Rainbow Lodge

9411 Hillside Dr PO Box 1100
Soda Springs, CA 95728
(916)426-3871 (800)500-3871 Fax:(916)426-9221
E-mail: info@royalgorge.com

Circa 1920. Located on a bend of the Yuba River, this old mountain lodge offers a picturesque site to enjoy the area's fishing, hiking and skiing. The lodge is decorated with pictures of Donner Summit and the railroad. The lounge offers an area for playing games. The Historic Rainbow Bar has been refurbished. The lodge has two stone fireplaces, one in the Sierra dining room and another in the guest lounge.

Innkeeper(s): Jacqui James. $79-129. MC VISA TC. 32 rooms, 10 with PB. 2 suites. 1 conference room. Breakfast included in rates. Types of meals: full breakfast and gourmet breakfast. Dinner, lunch, gourmet lunch and banquet service available. Restaurant on premises. Beds: QDT. TV and fax on premises. Weddings, small meetings, family reunions and seminars hosted. Antiques, fishing, parks, shopping, downhill skiing, cross-country skiing, sporting events and watersports nearby.

Location: Located in the Sierras on a bend of the Yuba River.

Publicity: *Sunset, Sacramento News.*

"Enjoyed the cozy feeling of the lodge, particularly evenings by the fireplace in the lounge and the excellent food."

Sonoma   *H4*

Sonoma Hotel

110 W Spain St
Sonoma, CA 95476-5696
(707)996-2996 (800)468-6016 Fax:(707)996-7014

Circa 1879. Originally built as a two-story adobe, a third story
was added in the '20s and it became the Plaza Hotel. The first

floor now boasts an
award-winning restaurant.
The top two floors contain
antique-filled guest rooms.
The Bear Flag Room is
furnished with a beautifully carved rosewood bed-
room suite. In room 21,
Maya Angelou wrote "Gather Together in My Name." A short
walk from the tree-lined plaza are several wineries.

Historic Interest: Mission San Francisco Solano, Bear Flag Revolt, Casa
Grande Indian Servants Quarters (all within walking distance).

Innkeeper(s): Dorene & John Musilli. $60-125. MC VISA AX DC PC TC.
TAC5. 17 rooms, 5 with PB. 1 suite. Breakfast included in rates. Types of
meals: continental breakfast and early coffee/tea. Gourmet lunch available.
Restaurant on premises. Beds: DT. Phone in room. Fax and copier on premises. Weddings and family reunions hosted. Italian spoken. Antiques, parks,
shopping and theater nearby.

Publicity: *Americana, House Beautiful, Press Democrat, California Getaway
Guide.*

*"Great food and service! I was so pleased to see such a warm and
lovable place."*

Sonora   *H7*

Lavender Hill B&B

683 S Barretta St
Sonora, CA 95370-5132
(209)532-9024 (800)446-1333
E-mail: lavender@sonnet.com

Circa 1900. In the historic Gold Rush town of Sonora is this
Queen Anne Victorian inn. Its four guest rooms include the
Lavender Room, which has a mini-suite with desk, sitting area
and clawfoot tub and shower. After a busy day fishing, biking,
river rafting or exploring nearby Yosemite National Park, guests
may relax in the antique-filled parlor or the sitting room.
Admiring the inn's gardens from the wraparound porch is also
a favorite activity. Be sure to ask about dinner theater packages.

Innkeeper(s): Charlie & Jean Marinelli. $75-95. MC VISA AX PC TC. TAC10.
4 rooms with PB. 1 suite. Breakfast included in rates. Types of meals: full
breakfast and early coffee/tea. Beds: KQ. Air conditioning and ceiling fan in
room. TV and library on premises. Weddings, small meetings and family
reunions hosted. Italian spoken. Antiques, fishing, parks, shopping, downhill
skiing, cross-country skiing, golf, theater and watersports nearby.

Lulu Belle's

85 Gold St
Sonora, CA 95370-5028
(209)533-3455 (800)538-3455

Circa 1886. This sturdy home with its spacious lawns, rambling porches and free form picket fence was built for John
Rother, a local builder. "There was always music at the Rother
home - early and late you could hear the piano going," wrote

Ora Morgan in an early Sonora newspaper. Now the music
room is enjoyed by guests for after-dinner entertainment. The
house is filled with Victorian antiques. The historic village, dotted with 1850s store
fronts that house gourmet
restaurants and antique
shops, is two blocks away.
A short drive away is the
Sierra Repertory Theater,
and the inn is just three
miles away from
Columbia State Historic
Park, a beautifully
restored Gold Rush town
and home of the Fallon House Theater. The inn offers night-on-
the-town packages that include dinner and theater.

Historic Interest: Railtown 1897 State Historic Park, featuring different types
of steam train excursions, is located three miles west in historic Jamestown.
Yosemite National Park is just a little more than an hour away by car. Other
area activities include snow and water skiing, fishing, hunting, golfing, river
rafting, boating, gold panning, and horse-back riding.

Innkeeper(s): Denise Morris and Ron & Kate Bush. $85-100. 5 rooms with
PB, 1 with FP. 1 conference room. Type of meal: full breakfast. Beds: KQD.
Phone in room.

Publicity: *California Magazine, Union Democrat-Gadabout.*

*"Hospitality and friendliness matched only by the beautiful accom-
modations! We'll be back for sure."*

Ryan House, 1855

153 S Shepherd St
Sonora, CA 95370-4736
(209)533-3445 (800)831-4897

Circa 1855. This restored homestead is set well back from the
street in a quiet residential area. Green lawns and gardens with
35 varieties of roses surround the house. Each room is individually decorated with handsome antiques. A suite is available
that includes a private parlor with stove and a bathroom with a
two-person tub. An antique-style cookstove sets the mood for a
country breakfast served in the dining room.

Innkeeper(s): Nancy & Guy Hoffman. $85-175. MC VISA AX PC TC. TAC10.
4 rooms with PB, 1 with FP. 1 suite. Breakfast and afternoon tea included in
rates. Types of meals: full breakfast, gourmet breakfast and early coffee/tea.
Beds: Q. Air conditioning and ceiling fan in room. TV, VCR and library on
premises. Small meetings and family reunions hosted. Antiques, fishing,
parks, shopping, downhill skiing, cross-country skiing, theater and watersports nearby.

Location: Two blocks from the heart of historic Sonora.

Publicity: *Home and Garden, Union Democrat, California, Sunset, L.A. Style,
Country Inns.*

*"Everything our friends said it would be: warm, comfortable and
great breakfasts. You made us feel like long-lost friends the moment
we arrived."*

Soquel   *J5*

Blue Spruce Inn

2815 S Main St
Soquel, CA 95073-2412
(408)464-1137 (800)559-1137 Fax:(408)475-0608
E-mail: pobrien@bluespruce.com

Circa 1875. Near the north coast of Monterey Bay, this old
farmhouse has been freshly renovated and refitted with luxurious touches. The Seascape is a favorite room with its private

entrance, wicker furnishings and bow-shaped Jacuzzi for two. The Carriage House offers skylights above the bed, while a heart decor dominates Two Hearts. Local art, Amish quilts and featherbeds are featured throughout. Brunch enchiladas are the inn's speciality. Santa Cruz is four miles away.

Historic Interest: Redwood Forests (5 miles), Santa Cruz Mission (4 miles), Carmel Mission (30 miles), Monterey (20 miles).

Innkeeper(s): Patricia & Tom O'Brien. $85-150. MC VISA AX PC TC. TAC10. 6 rooms with PB, 5 with FP. 1 conference room. Breakfast included in rates. Types of meals: full breakfast and early coffee/tea. Beds: QT. Phone, turndown service, TV and VCR in room. Fax and library on premises. Small meetings and seminars hosted. Spanish spoken. Amusement parks, antiques, fishing, parks, shopping, theater and watersports nearby.

Location: At the edge of Soquel Village, mid-Santa Cruz County, north shore of the Monterey Bay.

Publicity: *Village View.*

"You offer such graciousness to your guests and a true sense of welcome."

South Pasadena 010

The Artists' Inn B&B

1038 Magnolia St
South Pasadena, CA 91030-2518
(818)799-5668 (888)799-5668 Fax:(818)799-3678
E-mail: artistsinn@aol.com

Circa 1895. A poultry farm once surrounded this turn-of-the-century home. Today, the streets are lined with trees and a variety of beautiful homes. Interior designer Janet Marangi restored the historic ambiance of the cheery, yellow home, filling it with antiques and original artwork. Each of the guest rooms captures a different artistic style. Soft, soothing colors enrich the Impressionist room, which includes a clawfoot tub and brass bed. The Italian Suite is decorated in rich hues and includes an adjoining sunroom. The 18th Century English room is filled with pieces by Gainsborough, Reynolds and Constable and includes a romantic, canopied bed. There are plenty of helpful amenities, including hair dryers, toiletries and desks in each room. The innkeeper creates a breakfast menu with freshly made breads, homemade granola, fruit and a special entree. Chef Ray Luna prepares special dinners, teas and luncheons. The home is just a few blocks from South Pasadena's many shops, boutiques, cafes and restaurants.

Historic Interest: The historic Mission West district is a short distance from the inn. The Norton Simon Museum of Art, Old Town Pasadena, Mission San Gabriel and the Huntington Library are other nearby historic attractions.

Innkeeper(s): Janet Marangi. $100-130. MC VISA AX PC TC. TAC10. 9 rooms with PB. 3 suites. Breakfast and afternoon tea included in rates. Types of meals: continental breakfast, continental-plus breakfast, full breakfast, gourmet breakfast and early coffee/tea. Dinner, picnic lunch, gourmet lunch, catered breakfast and room service available. Beds: KQDT. Air conditioning and ceiling fan in room. TV, fax and library on premises. Weddings, small meetings and family reunions hosted. Amusement parks, antiques, parks, shopping, sporting events and theater nearby.

Publicity: *Pasadena Star News, San Marino Tribune, Stanford, Pasadena Weekly, South Pasadena Review,* Recommended by Elmer Dills, *Travel & Leisure, New York Times.*

"Oscar Wilde said in which of our friends homes would we choose to be ill in? The Artist Inn, where we could just rest, relax and be closeted in magic. Everywhere the eye rests is a delight to the mind and the soul and everywhere the body rests is pure peace."

St. Helena

Villa St. Helena

2727 Sulphur Springs Ave
St. Helena, CA 94574-2439
(707)963-2514 Fax:(707)963-2614
E-mail: villash@aol.dam

Circa 1941. This Tuscan-style villa was designed by noted architect Robert M. Carrere, who created stylish mansions and chateaux in Europe and the eastern United States. The peaceful setting, resting on a hill overlooking the Napa Valley, makes it easy to understand why celebrities and politicians chose the site as a retreat in the 1940s and 1950s. The decor is country French, including period antiques. Each of the three guest rooms includes a fireplace. The inn's St. Helena location is close to restaurants, antique shops and dozens of the valley's famed wineries.

Innkeeper(s): Ralph & Carolyn Cotton. $145-245. MC VISA TC. TAC10. 3 suites, 3 with FP. Breakfast included in rates. Type of meal: continental-plus breakfast. Beds: KQ. Phone, turndown service, ceiling fan in room. Library on premises. 20 acres. Antiques, fishing, parks, shopping and golf nearby.

Stinson Beach H4

Casa Del Mar

PO Box 238
Stinson Beach, CA 94970-0238
(415)868-2124 (800)552-2124 Fax:(415)868-2305
E-mail: inn@stinsonbeach

Circa 1920. Enjoy a quick getaway 35 minutes from the Golden Gate Bridge at this quiet coastal village. Casa Del Mar is a Mediterranean villa on a hillside two blocks from the ocean, and guest rooms offer views of both the Pacific Ocean and Mount Tamalpais. Although the original house was built before 1920, all that remains of the home are several fireplaces. The inn's garden, which was started in the '30s, was a teaching garden for the University of California. There are displays of model plots of flowers, succulents and roses, passion flowers and fruit trees. Breakfast is deliciously unique with such specialties as huevos rancheros, black bean and scallion pancakes and lemon walnut bread.

Innkeeper(s): Rick Klein. $125-220. 5 rooms with PB. 1 suite. Type of meal: gourmet breakfast. Evening snack available. Phone in room. Small meetings, family reunions and seminars hosted.

Sutter Creek G6

Foxes In Sutter Creek

77 Main St, PO Box 159
Sutter Creek, CA 95685
(209)267-5882 (800)987-3344 Fax:(209)267-0712

Circa 1857. This Greek Revival home is known for its elegant furnishings. There are canopied beds and handsome armoires, all brought together by the innkeeper's collection of foxes featured in old prints, pillows, plates and even wallpaper. The Fox Den is a favorite upstairs guest room with a private library and wood-burning fireplace. If you choose The Honeymoon Suite with its 16-foot bathroom, fireplace and antique bedstead, opt for breakfast in bed and you'll enjoy a full breakfast presented on silver service.

Innkeeper(s): Pete & Min Fox. $95-160. MC VISA DS. 7 rooms with PB, 4 with FP. Type of meal: full breakfast. Beds: Q.
Location: Downtown historic Sutter Creek.
Publicity: *San Francisco Focus.*

"Foxes is without a doubt the most charming B&B anywhere."

Grey Gables B&B Inn

161 Hanford St, PO Box 1687
Sutter Creek, CA 95685-1687
(209)267-1039 (800)473-9422 Fax:(209)267-0998

Circa 1897. The innkeepers of this Victorian home offer poetic accommodations both in the delightful decor and by the names of their guest rooms. The Keats, Bronte and Tennyson rooms afford garden views, while the Byron and Browning rooms include clawfoot tubs. The Victorian Suite, which encompasses the top floor, affords views of the garden, as well as a  historic churchyard. All of the guest rooms boast fireplaces. Stroll down brick pathways through the terraced garden or relax in the parlor. A proper English tea is served with cakes and scones. Hors d'oeuvres and libations are served in the evenings.

Historic Interest: Property was once owned by Patrick Riordan, Archbishop of San Francisco.
Innkeeper(s): Roger & Susan Garlick. $90-140. MC VISA DS PC TC. TAC10. 8 rooms with PB, 8 with FP. Breakfast, afternoon tea and evening snack included in rates. Types of meals: gourmet breakfast and early coffee/tea. Beds: KQT. Air conditioning and ceiling fan in room. Fax and copier on premises. Handicap access. Antiques, fishing, parks, shopping, downhill skiing, cross-country skiing, theater and watersports nearby.

The Hanford House B&B Inn

61 Hanford St, Hwy 49
Sutter Creek, CA 95685
(209)267-0747 (800)871-5839 Fax:(209)267-1825
E-mail: bobkat@hanfordhouse.com

Circa 1929. When Karen and Bob Tierno purchased this unique Gold Country inn, they were determined to maintain the former innkeepers' standards for hospitality. Karen and Bob went a step further and added many new amenities for their guests, including a conference room, fax machine and providing computer access. While these touches are perfect for the business traveler, the inn is still a place to relax. The inn offers a shaded outdoor patio, charming parlor and a roof-top sundeck. Guests are greeted with freshly baked cookies upon check-in, treated to a homemade breakfast each morning and invited to partake in afternoon refreshments. Wineries, antiquing and historic sites are nearby.

Innkeeper(s): Bob & Karen Tierno. $69-149. MC VISA DS PC TC. TAC10. 10 rooms with PB, 5 with FP. 3 suites. 1 conference room. Breakfast, afternoon tea and evening snack included in rates. Types of meals: gourmet breakfast and early coffee/tea. Beds: KQ. Phone, air conditioning and ceiling fan in room. TV, VCR and fax on premises. Handicap access. Weddings, small meetings, family reunions and seminars hosted. Spanish spoken. Antiques, fishing, shopping, skiing, golf, theater and watersports nearby.

Sutter Creek Inn

PO Box 385
Sutter Creek, CA 95685-0385
(209)267-5606 Fax:(209)267-9287
E-mail: info@suttercreekinn.com

Circa 1859. Nestled among fruit trees, many of the guest rooms open onto latticed enclaves or trellised grapevines.

Columbine and lilacs are part of the lawn and garden's charm. Guests can relax in chaise lounges or in the hammocks. Common areas are decorated with American and European antique furnishings. Also, conversation pieces include collections of memorabilia. There are 12 working fireplaces and just in case, all rooms come with an electric blanket.

Innkeeper(s): Jane Way. $50-175. MC VISA AX DS. 18 rooms with PB. Breakfast included in rates. Type of meal: full breakfast. Beds: QDT. Antiques, fishing, cross-country skiing, theater and watersports nearby.
Publicity: *Fun Times, Motorland, Country Inns.* Ratings: 4 Stars.

"Very pleasant, excellent breakfast, good company."

Tahoe City   F7

Chaney House

4725 W Lake Blvd, PO Box 7852
Tahoe City, CA 96145
(530)525-7333 Fax:(530)525-4413

Circa 1928. Enjoying a wooded lakeside setting, this historic stone house has its own pier and private beach just across the road. The stone walls are 18 inches thick. A massive stone fireplace reaching to the cathedral ceiling, hand-carved woodwork and Gothic arches are reminiscent of Old Tahoe and its European flavor. Breakfast is served on the patio overlooking the lake in the summer and in the formal dining room in the winter. Russell's Suite has pine panelling, a queen bed and lake view.

Historic Interest: Emerald Bay - Viking Home, Erhman Mansion, Bliss Street Park & Sugar Pine Point are about 20 minutes away. Truckee (30 minutes), Donner State Park (30 minutes).
Innkeeper(s): Gary & Lori Chaney. $110-150. 4 rooms with PB. 3 suites. Breakfast included in rates. Type of meal: gourmet breakfast. Beds: KQ. Fax on premises. Antiques, fishing, parks, downhill skiing, cross-country skiing, theater and watersports nearby.
Location: Five miles south of Tahoe City on Highway 89.

"A treat for the quality B&B devotee and a real find for those in search of a grand location."

Mayfield House

236 Grove St, PO Box 5999
Tahoe City, CA 96145
(916)583-1001

Circa 1932. Norman Mayfield, Lake Tahoe's pioneer contractor, built this house of wood and stone, and Julia Morgan, architect of Hearst Castle, was a frequent guest. Dark-stained pine paneling, a beamed ceiling, and a large stone fireplace make an inviting living room. Many rooms have views of mountains, woods, or the golf course.

Innkeeper(s): Cynthia & Bruce Knauss. $85-150. MC VISA AX. 6 rooms, 3 with PB. Breakfast included in rates. Types of meals: full breakfast and early coffee/tea. Evening snack available. Beds: KQD. TV on premises. Weddings hosted. Fishing, parks, shopping, skiing and watersports nearby.
Location: Downtown off Highway 28.
Publicity: *Sierra Heritage, Tahoe Today, San Francisco Chronicle.*

"The place is charming beyond words, complete with down comforters and wine upon checking in. The breakfast is superb."

River Ranch

PO Box 197
Tahoe City, CA 96145-0197
(916)583-4264 (800)535-9900 Fax:(916)583-7237

Circa 1888. This ranch is located, not surprisingly, right along the banks of the Truckee River. In 1888, the Deer Park Inn opened on the site, serving guests as a railroad stop. After the Great Depression hit, the building fell into disrepair and in the mid-1960s, River Ranch was constructed in its place. The comfortable guest rooms feature Early American furnishings, some offer private balconies with river views. After a day on the slopes, enjoy apres-ski in front of a fireplace in the bar. When the snow is gone, river rafting, hiking, golfing and many other outdoor activities fill the day. The restaurant features an excellent wine list and serves up specialties such as mountain rainbow trout, roasted elk flavored with port wine in a bing cherry sauce and filet mignon.

Innkeeper(s): Bric Haley & Pete Friedrichsen. $49-185. MC VISA AX PC TC. TAC10. 21 rooms, 22 with PB. 1 cottage. Breakfast included in rates. Type of meal: continental breakfast. Dinner available. Restaurant on premises. Beds: KQD. Phone and TV in room. Fax and copier on premises. Weddings and family reunions hosted. Fishing, parks, shopping, downhill skiing, cross-country skiing, golf and watersports nearby.

Publicity: *Ski Magazine, San Francisco Weather & Channel 2.*

Templeton   L6

Country House Inn

91 S Main St
Templeton, CA 93465-8701
(805)434-1598 (800)362-6032

Circa 1886. This Victorian home, built by the founder of Templeton, is located in rural wine country. Ancient oak trees shade the grounds. The inn was designated as a historic site in San Luis Obispo County.

Innkeeper(s): Dianne Garth. $95-105. MC VISA DS PC. TAC10. 5 rooms with PB, 1 with FP. 1 suite. Breakfast included in rates. Types of meals: gourmet breakfast and early coffee/tea. Afternoon tea available. Beds: KQ. Ceiling fan in room. Weddings, small meetings and family reunions hosted. Antiques, fishing, parks, shopping, theater and watersports nearby.

Location: Twenty miles north of San Luis Obispo on Hwy 101.

Truckee   F7

Richardson House

10154 High St
Truckee, CA 96161-0110
(916)587-5388 (888)229-0365 Fax:(916)587-0927
E-mail: richardson@ltol.com

Circa 1886. This Victorian bears the name of the prominent lumber baron who built it, Warren Richardson. Each guest room is individually appointed with timely antiques and accessories and the elegant touch of fine linens, feather beds and down comforters. Some rooms offer views of the Sierra Mountains while others have clawfoot tubs. The three deluxe rooms include a fireplace, and some rooms have clawfoot tubs. The gingerbread-adorned gazebo is the highlight of the garden, a perfect setting for a memorable wedding. Meandering paths lead visitors past a cascading waterfall, native aspens, a contemplation bench and a sundial. Guests are welcome to use the inn's outdoor hot tub. Inside, the parlor is set up for relaxation with a player piano, television, VCR, stereo and a well-stocked, 24-hour refreshment center.

Innkeeper(s): Jeannine Karnofsky & Betty Dickens. $75-150. MC VISA AX DS PC TC. TAC15. 8 rooms, 6 with PB, 3 with FP. 3 suites. Breakfast and evening snack included in rates. Types of meals: full breakfast and early cof-

fee/tea. Catering service available. Beds: KQTD. Phone, air conditioning, TV and VCR in room. Copier on premises. Handicap access. Weddings, small meetings, family reunions and seminars hosted. Antiques, fishing, parks, shopping, downhill skiing, cross-country skiing, golf and watersports nearby.

Venice   O10

Venice Beach House

15 30th Ave
Venice, CA 90291-0043
(310)823-1966 Fax:(310)823-1842

Circa 1911. This California Craftsman house was the summer home of relatives Warren Wilson and Abbot Kinney and their families. Wilson founded the Los Angeles Daily News, and Kinney founded the town of Venice, a popular L.A. hot spot for those in search of surf, sand, shopping, food or people watching. The home has been fully restored to its original state. Guest rooms are individually decorated. James Peasgood's Room is especially sweet and spacious for guests in search of romance. It offers a king-size bed, balcony and a double Jacuzzi tub. The Pier Suite is another idyllic choice, offering a partial ocean view, a fireplace and sitting room.

Historic Interest: Mae West's summer home, Charlie Chaplin's home, Venice Canals 1910.

Innkeeper(s): Elayne Alexander. $85-165. MC VISA AX PC TC. TAC10. 9 rooms, 5 with PB, 1 with FP. 2 suites. Breakfast, afternoon tea included in rates. Type of meal: continental breakfast. Beds: KQDT. Phone, TV in room. Fax, library on premises. Small meetings hosted. Amusement parks, antiques, fishing, parks, shopping, sporting events, theater, watersports nearby.

Location: 1/4 block from Venice beach boardwalk, bordering Marina del Rey.

Publicity: *Independent Journal, Sunset, Daily News, Herald Examiner, The Outlook, The Travel Channel, The Argonaut.*

Ventura   N8

Bella Maggiore Inn

67 S California St
Ventura, CA 93001-2801
(805)652-0277

Circa 1926. Albert C. Martin, the architect of the former Grauman's Chinese Theater, designed and built this Spanish Colonial Revival-style hotel. Located three blocks from the beach, it is noted for its richly-carved caste-stone entrance and frieze. An Italian chandelier and a grand piano dominate the parlor. Rooms surround a courtyard with a fountain. Miles of coastal bike paths are nearby, as well as restaurants and antique shops.

Innkeeper(s): Thomas Wood. $60-150. MC VISA AX DC DS. 24 rooms with PB, 6 with FP. 1 conference room. Type of meal: full breakfast. Beds: KQD. Fax, copier and spa on premises. Handicap access.

Publicity: *Ventura County & Coast Reporter, Sunset.*

"Very friendly and attentive without being overly attentive."

La Mer European B&B

411 Poli St
Ventura, CA 93001-2614
(805)643-3600 Fax:(805)653-7329

Circa 1890. This three-story Cape Cod Victorian overlooks the heart of historic San Buenaventura and the spectacular California coastline. Each room is decorated to capture the feeling of a specific European country. French, German, Austrian, Norwegian and English-style accommodations are available.

Gisela, your hostess, is a native of Siegerland, Germany. Midweek specials include romantic candlelight dinners, therapeutic massages and a mineral spa in the country. Horse-drawn antique carriage rides and island cruises are also available.

Historic Interest: The old Mission, Archaeological Dig County Museum and many historical homes, within one-half block.

Innkeeper(s): Gisela Baida. $105-155. MC VISA AX. TAC10. 5 rooms. Breakfast included in rates. Types of meals: full breakfast and early coffee/tea. Beds: KQ. Ceiling fan in room. TV, fax, copier, library and child care on premises. Family reunions hosted. Antiques, fishing, shopping, theater and watersports nearby.

Location: Second house west of City Hall.

Publicity: *Los Angeles Times, California Bride, Los Angeles Magazine, Westways, The Tribune, Daily News.*

Visalia K8

Ben Maddox House B&B

601 N Encina St
Visalia, CA 93291-3603
(209)739-0721 (800)401-9800 Fax:(209)625-0420

Circa 1876. Just 40 minutes away from Sequoia National Park sits this late-19th-century home, constructed completely of gorgeous Sequoia redwood. The parlor, dining room and bedrooms remain in their original state. The house has been tastefully furnished with antiques from the late 1800s to the early 20th century. "Big Bertha," a coal-burning furnace that has been converted to gas, heats the home from her spot in the basement, so no fireplaces are necessary. Breakfast menu choices include fresh fruit, a selection of homemade breads, eggs and meat. The meal, served either in the historic dining room or on the deck, is surrounded by flowers, antique china and goldware.

Historic Interest: Sequoia/King's Canyon National Parks (40 minutes), Tulare Co. Museum (10 minutes), Historical District Walking Tour.

Innkeeper(s): Diane & Al Muro. $75-85. MC VISA AX DS. 4 rooms with PB. Breakfast included in rates. Types of meals: full breakfast and early coffee/tea. Beds: KQ. Phone, air conditioning and TV in room. Spa and swimming on premises. Antiques, fishing, parks, shopping, cross-country skiing, sporting events, theater and watersports nearby.

Publicity: *Southland, Fresno Bee.*

"*Just a very gracious and delightful place and excellent breakfast, also comfortable and a warm and friendly hostess, a delightful experience in all.*"

Volcano G7

St. George Hotel

16104 Pine Grove, PO Box 9
Volcano, CA 95689-0009
(209)296-4458 Fax:(209)296-4458

Circa 1862. This handsome old three-story hotel in the National Register features a double-tiered wraparound porch. There is a dining room, full bar and lounge area with fireplace. It is situated on one acre of lawns. An annex built in 1961 provides rooms with private baths. Volcano is a Mother Lode town that has been untouched by supermarkets and modern motels and remains much as it was during the Gold Rush. Modified American Plan (breakfast and dinner) available.

Innkeeper(s): Marlene & Chuck Inman. $71-94. MAP. MC VISA AX PC TC. 20 rooms, 6 with PB. 1 conference room. Breakfast included in rates. Type of meal: full breakfast. Dinner available. Beds: QDT. Fax and copier on premises. Weddings, small meetings, family reunions and seminars hosted. Antiques, fishing, parks, shopping, downhill skiing, cross-country skiing, theater and watersports nearby.

Location: Sixty-one miles from Sacramento.

"*What is so precious about the hotel is its combination of graciousness and simplicity.*"

Westport E3

Howard Creek Ranch

40501 N Hwy One, PO Box 121
Westport, CA 95488
(707)964-6725 Fax:(707)964-1603

Circa 1871. First settled as a land grant of thousands of acres, Howard Creek Ranch is now a 40-acre farm with sweeping views of the Pacific Ocean, sandy beaches and rolling mountains. A 75-foot bridge spans a creek that flows past barns and outbuildings to the beach 200 yards away. The farmhouse is surrounded by  green lawns, an award-winning flower garden, and grazing cows, horses and llama. This rustic rural location offers antiques, a hot tub, sauna and heated pool.

Innkeeper(s): Charles & Sally Grigg. $55-145. MC VISA AX. 11 rooms, 9 with PB, 5 with FP. 3 suites. 3 cottages. Breakfast included in rates. Types of meals: gourmet breakfast and early coffee/tea. Beds: KQD. Ceiling fan in room. Fax, spa, swimming, sauna and library on premises. 40 acres. German and Spanish spoken. Antiques, fishing, parks, shopping and theater nearby.

Pets Allowed: By prior arrangement.

Location: Mendocino Coast on the ocean.

Publicity: *California, Country, Vacations, Forbes.*

"*Of the dozen or so inns on the West Coast we have visited, this is easily the most enchanting one.*"

Yuba City F5

Harkey House B&B

212 C St
Yuba City, CA 95991-5014
(530)674-1942

Circa 1875. An essence of romance fills this Victorian Gothic house set in a historic neighborhood. Every inch of the home has been given a special touch, from the knickknacks and photos in the sitting room to the quilts and furnishings in the guest quarters. The Harkey Suite features a poster bed with a down comforter and extras such as an adjoining library room and a pellet-burning stove. Breakfasts of muffins, fresh fruit, juice and freshly ground coffee are served in a glass-paned dining room or on the patio.

Historic Interest: Located in the oldest part of Yuba City.

Innkeeper(s): Bob & Lee Jones. $75-100. MC VISA AX DS PC TC. TAC10. 4 rooms with PB, 2 with FP. 1 suite. 1 conference room. Breakfast included in rates. Types of meals: full breakfast and early coffee/tea. Beds: Q. Phone, air conditioning, turndown service, ceiling fan and TV in room. VCR, spa and library on premises. Weddings, small meetings and family reunions hosted. Antiques, fishing, parks, shopping, theater and watersports nearby.

Publicity: *Country Magazine.*

"*This place is simply marvelous...the most comfortable bed in travel.*"

Colorado

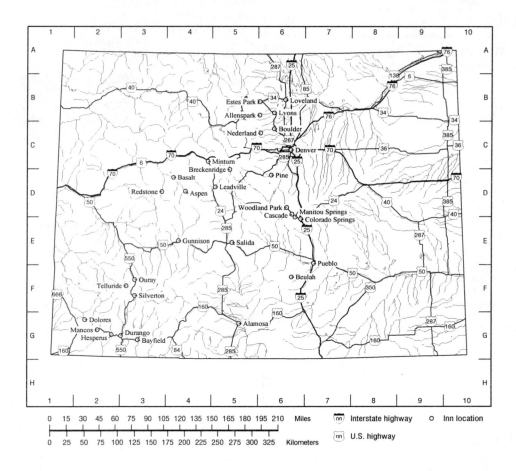

0 15 30 45 60 75 90 105 120 135 150 165 180 195 210   Miles

0 25 50 75 100 125 150 175 200 225 250 275 300 325   Kilometers

(nn) Interstate highway   ○ Inn location

(nn) U.S. highway

Alamosa   G5

Cottonwood Inn

123 San Juan Ave
Alamosa, CO 81101-2547
(719)589-3882 (800)955-2623 Fax:(719)589-6437
E-mail: julie@cottonwoodinn.com

Circa 1908. This refurbished Colorado bungalow is filled with antiques and paintings by local artists. The Stickley dining room set once belonged to Billy Adams, a Colorado governor in the 1920s. Blue-corn blueberry pancakes and flaming Grand Marnier omelets are the inn's specialties. A favorite day  trip is riding the Cumbres-Toltec Scenic Railroad over the La Magna Pass, site of an Indiana Jones movie.

Historic Interest: Cumbres-Toltec Scenic Railroad, highest and longest narrow gauge RR in North America (30 minutes), Fort Garland (20 minutes), San Luis, oldest town in Colorado (45 minutes).

Innkeeper(s): Julie Mordecai & George Sellman. $48-85. MC VISA AX DS PC TC. 9 rooms, 7 with PB. 4 suites. Breakfast and evening snack included in rates. Types of meals: gourmet breakfast and early coffee/tea. Beds: KQTD. Phone in room. TV, VCR, fax and copier on premises. Small meetings, family reunions and seminars hosted. Spanish spoken. Antiques, parks and downhill skiing nearby.

Pets Allowed: In two suites with wood floors. Must be well behaved. Guests pay for all damages.

Location: Close to Great Sand Dunes National Monument.

Publicity: *Rocky Mountain News, Country Inns, Denver Post, Milwaukee Journal, Channel 4 Denver.*

"My husband wants to come over every morning for blueberry pancakes and strawberry rhubarb sauce."

Allenspark   B6

Allenspark Lodge

PO Box 247, 184 Main St
Allenspark, CO 80510-0247
(303)747-2552 Fax:(303)747-2552

Circa 1933. Since its opening in the 1930s, this lodge has welcomed visitors with a combination of beautiful scenery and hospitality. The lodge was constructed out of Ponderosa pine, and its rustic interior still maintains exposed log walls. Rooms are comfortable and country in decor, including antique, handmade pine furnishings. The innkeepers also offer three cabins as accommodations. In the afternoon and early evenings, light fare and spirits can be purchased and enjoyed in the Wilderquest Room. There is plenty to do in the area, no matter the season. Skiing, sleigh rides, hiking, backpacking and birdwatching are among the options.

Innkeeper(s): Mike & Becky Osmun. $50-90. MC VISA PC TC. TAC10. 12 rooms, 5 with PB, 1 with FP. 3 cabins. 1 conference room. Breakfast included in rates. Type of meal: continental-plus breakfast. Evening snack available. Beds: QDT. Ceiling fan in room. TV, fax, spa, stables and library on premises. Weddings, small meetings, family reunions and seminars hosted. Antiques, fishing, parks, shopping, downhill skiing, cross-country skiing, golf, theater and watersports nearby.

Publicity: *New England Hiking Holidays, Travelers Magazine.*

Aspen   D4

Independence Square B&B

404 S Galena St
Aspen, CO 81611-3828
(970)920-2313 (800)633-0336 Fax:(970)920-2548
E-mail: aspenski@rof.net

Circa 1889. Located one block away from Aspen Mountain in the downtown, this completely restored red brick Historic Landmark offers guests the intimacy of an inn, with all the amenities of a large elegant hotel. All 28 guest rooms are decorated in French-country furnishings featuring queen beds, down comforters and wet bars. Guests are invited to enjoy the rooftop Jacuzzi and sundeck or partake in the complimentry apres-ski wine and cheese every afternoon. A continental breakfast buffet is offered every morning. Ski lockers, airport transportation and complimentary use of the Aspen Club are available.

Innkeeper(s): Jami Ryan. $89-310. MC VISA AX PC TC. TAC10. 28 rooms with PB. Breakfast included in rates. Type of meal: continental breakfast. Afternoon tea and catering service available. Beds: Q. Phone, air conditioning and TV in room. Fax, copier, spa and library on premises. Weddings, small meetings and family reunions hosted. Fishing, parks, shopping, downhill skiing, cross-country skiing, golf and theater nearby.

Basalt   D4

Shenandoah Inn

600 Frying Pan Rd
Basalt, CO 81621
(970)927-4991 (800)804-5520 Fax:(970)927-4990
E-mail: shenando@sopris.net

Circa 1897. Once a commune, this inn on the banks of the Frying Pan River has been completely restored into a peaceful country inn. The innkeepers completed an amazing restoration of the house, which was very dilapidated when they discovered the property. In addition to restoring the 1960-era main house, they brought back to life a century-old log cabin. Innkeepers Bob and Terri Ziets can tell an array of fascinating stories about the former occupants, as well as their own exhaustive work. The idyllic setting includes decks for relaxing and a riverside hot tub. On a chilly day, enjoy a hot drink in front of the 16-foot rock fireplace in the living room. Rooms are decorated with antiques, and beds are topped with down quilts. The historic cabin is especially well suited to honeymooners in search of privacy or families, as it sleeps up to six guests. Breakfasts are a treat. Peach-stuffed French toast is a possibility, accompanied by gourmet coffee and a fruit appetizer. Everything is homemade, from the freshly baked breads to the preserves and apple butter. Refreshments are served daily.

Innkeeper(s): Bob & Terri Ziets. $75-150. MC VISA PC TC. TAC10. 5 rooms, 3 with PB. 1 suite. 1 cabin. Breakfast included in rates. Types of meals: full breakfast and early coffee/tea. Beds: KQT. Turndown service in room. TV, VCR, fax, spa and library on premises. Weddings, small meetings and family reunions hosted. French and Spanish spoken. Antiques, fishing, parks, shopping, downhill skiing, cross-country skiing, golf, theater and watersports nearby.

"Your Inn is delightful and both of you were so hospitable. The whole stay was a great experience for us."

Bayfield   G3

Wit's End Guest Ranch

254 Country Rd 500
Bayfield, CO 81122
(970)884-4113 (800)236-9483 Fax:(940)884-3261

Circa 1870. When the owners of this Adirondack-style guest ranch bill their place as "luxury at the edge of the wilderness," it isn't just a snappy slogan, it's true. If a half million acres of wilderness and stunning views of snow capped mountain peaks don't entice you, the historic lodge's interior should. Picture polished exposed beams and wood paneled or log walls, a mix of Victorian and country French furnishings and just enough antlers to create that rustic, lodge atmosphere. Each guest room includes a stone fireplace. There is also an assortment of cabins to consider, some more than a century old. The cabins include a living room, stone fireplace, kitchen and a private porch or deck. There is a full-service, fine-dining restaurant and a tavern often hosting live musical groups from nearby Durango. There's also little shortage of things to do here. Guided wilderness hikes, fly fishing in ponds, rivers and lakes, hayrides, mountain biking, dogsled rides, showshoeing, sleigh rides and watersports are just a few of the possibilities. Horseback and trail riding, of course, are a major part of the fun. The ranch offers a full children's program, with many interesting activities. As is typical of dude ranches, rates below are quoted for weekly visits.

Innkeeper(s): Jim & Lynn Custer. $3650-4385. AP. MC VISA AX DS PC TC. TAC10. 2 rooms with PB. 35 cottages. 4 conference rooms. Breakfast, dinner, evening snack and picnic lunch included in rates. Types of meals: continental-plus breakfast, full breakfast and gourmet breakfast. Lunch, gourmet lunch, banquet service, catering service, catered breakfast and room service available. Restaurant on premises. Beds: Q. Phone, turndown service and VCR in room. TV, fax, copier, spa, swimming, stables, bicycles, tennis and library on premises. Handicap access. 550 acres. Weddings, small meetings, family reunions and seminars hosted. Spanish, French, Italian and German spoken. Antiques, fishing, parks, shopping, downhill skiing, cross-country skiing, sporting events, theater and watersports nearby.

Publicity: *Jeopardy, Wheel of Fortune, Quicksilver, Family Feud, Country Inns, Country Living, Learning Channel.*

Beulah   F6

Beulah House

8733 Pine Dr
Beulah, CO 81023-9719
(719)485-3201

Circa 1900. Nestled on eight wooded acres, this rustic Spanish-style villa features its own chapel, library, museum and gallery. Decorated in authentic Southwestern furniture and artifacts, the inn offers five guest rooms that boast private patios, a well-stocked bar, fireplace, hot tub and luxurious bathrobes. The grounds feature a heated swimming pool, sauna, pool house, barbeque and lush sunken garden. A European-style continental breakfast is served to guest rooms or enjoyed in common rooms depending on the guests preference. Between 11 a.m. and 1 p.m., a buffet brunch featuring baskets of breads, fruits and cheese is served by the pool or in the dining room depending on the weather. Picnic baskets are available by request. In the winter, hot buttered rum is served by the fire. Close to cross-country skiing, fishing and tennis.

Innkeeper(s): Harry & Ann Middelkamp. Call for rates. MC VISA DS PC TC.

TAC10. 5 rooms with PB, 1 with FP. 1 suite. 1 conference room. Breakfast and picnic lunch included in rates. Types of meals: continental breakfast and early coffee/tea. Afternoon tea, dinner, evening snack, lunch, gourmet lunch, banquet service, catering service, catered breakfast and room service available. Restaurant on premises. Beds: KD. Phone, turndown service and TV in room. Copier, spa, swimming, sauna, library and child care on premises. Weddings, small meetings, family reunions and seminars hosted. Fishing, parks, shopping and cross-country skiing nearby.

Publicity: *Pueblo Chieftain, Colorado B&B Cookbook.*

Boulder   C6

The Alps Boulder Canyon Inn

38619 Boulder Canyon Dr # 18298
Boulder, CO 80302-9654
(303)444-5445 (800)414-2577 Fax:(303)444-5522
E-mail: alpsinn@aol.com

Circa 1906. The entrance to this Adirondack-style lodge is through the original log cabin, which dates to 1879 when it was a stagecoach stop. Located on 24 forested acres, the inn adjoins the preserve with miles of scenic trails, picnic and camping areas. Rooms feature mountain views and most have double Jacuzzi tubs, fireplaces and sitting areas. The inviting dining room

boasts polished wood floors and small tables with twig back chairs. The common areas feature lodge and simple English-country decor. Stuffed French toast with apple cider syrup is a popular entree for the inn's breakfast buffet.

Innkeeper(s): John & Jeannine Vanderhart. $118-250. MC VISA AX DC CB DS PC TC. TAC10. 12 rooms with PB, 12 with FP. Breakfast and evening snack included in rates. Types of meals: full breakfast and early coffee/tea. Afternoon tea available. Beds: KQ. Phone and ceiling fan in room. TV, VCR and fax on premises. 24 acres. Weddings and small meetings hosted. Antiques, fishing, parks, shopping, downhill skiing, cross-country skiing, sporting events, golf, theater and watersports nearby.

Publicity: *Country Inns, Geraldo Rivera Show.*

"We felt so personally welcome, at tea time, at every time."

Briar Rose B&B

2151 Arapahoe Ave
Boulder, CO 80302-6601
(303)442-3007 Fax:(303)786-8440

Circa 1896. Known locally as the McConnell House, this English-style brick house is situated in a neighborhood originally composed of bankers, attorneys, miners and carpenters. The inn recently received the Award of Excellence from the City of Boulder. Fresh flowers, handmade feather comforters and turndown service with chocolates add to the atmosphere.

Historic Interest: Historic Boulder offers walking tours of the town, including tours of four historic districts and a cemetery.

Innkeeper(s): Bob & Margaret Weisenbach. $99-150. MC VISA AX DC PC TC. TAC10. 9 rooms with PB, 2 with FP. Breakfast and afternoon tea included in rates. Types of meals: continental-plus breakfast and early coffee/tea. Beds: QDT. Phone, air conditioning, turndown service and ceiling fan in room. TV, fax and copier on premises. Weddings, small meetings and family reunions hosted. Spanish and American Sign Language spoken. Antiques, fishing, parks, shopping, downhill skiing, cross-country skiing, sporting events and theater nearby.

"It's like being at Grandma's; the cookies, the tea, the welcoming smile."

Pearl Street Inn

1820 Pearl St
Boulder, CO 80302-5519
(303)444-5584 (888)810-1302

Circa 1895. Located in downtown Boulder, the Pearl Street Inn is composed of a restored Victorian brick house and a new contemporary-style addition. The guest rooms overlook a tree-shaded courtyard garden where a full gourmet breakfast is served. Antiques, cathedral ceilings, bleached oak floors and fireplaces are featured in all rooms.

Innkeeper(s): Kate Beeman.
$90-145. MC VISA AX DS. 7 rooms with PB, 7 with FP. 1 conference room.
Type of meal: gourmet breakfast. Beds: QDT. Fax and copier on premises.

"Enter the front door and find the sort of place where you catch your breath in awe."

Breckenridge   D5

Bed & Breakfasts on North Main Street

303 N Main St
Breckenridge, CO 80424
(970)453-2975 (800)795-2975

Circa 1880. Within the Breckenridge National Historic District, this miner's home and separate Victorian cottage have been meticulously restored to offer visitors period antiques in a romantic setting. The house has two parlors with mantled fire-

places and a dining room. Ask for the delux room and enjoy mountain views, a fireplace and large whirlpool. The cottage offers three rooms, a fireplace, private parlor, kitchenette, double shower and Jacuzzi for two. Or consider a room in the newly restored "Barn Above the River" with fireplaces, double showers and decks with mountain and river views. Afternoon refreshments are offered each day. A candlelight breakfast, often morning burritos served with stir-fried potatoes, is served in the dining room.

Innkeeper(s): Fred Kinat & Diane Jaynes. $85-245. AX PC. TAC10. 11 rooms with PB, 6 with FP. 1 cottage. Breakfast included in rates. Types of meals: full breakfast and early coffee/tea. Beds: Q. Phone, ceiling fan, TV and VCR in room. Spa and library on premises. Antiques, fishing, parks, shopping, downhill skiing, cross-country skiing, golf, theater and watersports nearby.

Publicity: *Denver Post, Rocky Mountain News, Summit Daily News, Los Angeles Times.*

"We loved the personal touches and superb breakfasts."

The Evans House B&B

102 S French St, PO Box 387
Breckenridge, CO 80424
(970)453-5509

Circa 1886. A view of the famed Breckenridge ski slopes is visible from the windows of this former miner's home. A cornucopia of activities are available to guests who have a love for the outdoors, including rafting, boating and an alpine slide. A ski shuttle is available at the front door, and there is on site parking. This 150-year-old mining town offers many interesting shops and restaurants. In the heart of a historic district with 120 circa 1860-1890 buildings and three museums, tours are available.

Historic Interest: The area is full of abandoned gold mines now open for tours. The Carter Museum was the foundation of the Denver Museum of Natural History, and is now open for tours.

Innkeeper(s): Pete & Georgette Contos. $64-127. PC TC. 4 rooms, 2 with PB. 1 suite. Breakfast and afternoon tea included in rates. Type of meal: full breakfast. Beds: KQDT. Phone in room. TV and VCR on premises. Greek and French spoken. Amusement parks, antiques, fishing, parks, shopping, downhill skiing, cross-country skiing, sporting events, theater and watersports nearby.

Location: In the Breckenridge historic district.

Publicity: *Denver Post.*

"Very clean, outstanding hospitality."

Cascade   D6

Eastholme In The Rockies

PO Box 98, 4445 Haggerman Ave
Cascade, CO 80809
(719)684-9901 (800)672-9901
E-mail: eastholm@rmi.net

Circa 1885. Although Cascade is only six miles from Colorado Springs, guests will feel as though they are staying in a secluded mountain getaway at this Victorian inn. An affluent New Yorker built the historic hotel, which accommodates the many guests traveling the Ute Pass. The most recent innkeeper, Terry Thompson, redecorated the inn and added double Jacuzzi tubs and fireplaces in the two cottages. The decor is Victorian, but rooms are uncluttered and airy. Several rooms are furnished with antiques original to the hotel. Three different homemade breads and entrees such as frittatas with herbed potatoes are served during breakfast service.

Innkeeper(s): Terry Thompson. $69-140. MC VISA AX DS PC TC. TAC10. 6 rooms, 4 with PB, 2 with FP. 2 suites. 2 cottages. Breakfast and evening snack included in rates. Types of meals: gourmet breakfast and early coffee/tea. Beds: QDT. TV, VCR and library on premises. Small meetings, family reunions and seminars hosted. Antiques, fishing, parks, shopping, downhill skiing, cross-country skiing, sporting events, golf, theater and watersports nearby.

Colorado Springs E6

Cheyenne Canon Inn

2030 W Cheyenne Blvd
Colorado Springs, CO 80906
(719)633-0625 (800)633-0625 Fax:(800)633-8826

Circa 1921. World travelers Barbara and John Starr have filled this rustic home with interesting finds from their many visits to foreign lands. The home was built by the wife of a Manitou

Springs sheriff and originally served as an upscale
casino, and more infa-
mously, a bordello. During
the home's heyday as an
inn, guests included the
Marx Brothers and Lon
Cheney. The massive home
features more than 100
windows, all boasting
beautiful views, original
stained glass and silver
wall sconces. Each of the
seven guest rooms and two
cottages captures a unique
international flavor. The
innkeepers recently added
"Le Petit Chateau," a
romantic cottage tucked
beneath 50-foot tall pines trees. Spend the night tucked away in a room reminiscent of a Swiss chalet or enjoy the atmosphere of an Oriental tea room in another guest quarter. The second-floor hot tub affords a view of Cheyenne Mountain. The innkeepers have created a relaxing retreat, but also offer many amenities for the business traveler including in-room phones, TVs and modem outlets.

Historic Interest: Cripple Creek is an hour's drive from the inn, and closer attractions include cliff dwellings, Old Colorado City and the Broadmoor Hotel.

Innkeeper(s): John, Barbara & Josh Starr. $75-175. MC VISA AX DS PC TC. TAC10. 9 rooms, 8 with PB, 3 with FP. 3 suites. 1 cottage. 2 conference rooms. Types of meals: full breakfast and early coffee/tea. Beds: KQT. Phone, air conditioning, turndown service, ceiling fan, TV and VCR in room. Fax, copier, spa and library on premises. Weddings, small meetings and seminars hosted. French spoken. Antiques, fishing, parks, shopping, downhill skiing, cross-country skiing, sporting events and theater nearby.

Publicity: *Denver Post, Colorado Source, Beacon, National Geographic Traveler.*

"It truly was 'home away from home.' You have made it so welcoming and warm. Needless to say our breakfasts at home will never come close to the Cheyenne Canon Inn!!"

Hearthstone Inn

506 N Cascade Ave
Colorado Springs, CO 80903-3327
(719)473-4413 (800)521-1885

Circa 1885. This elegant Queen Anne is actually two houses joined by an old carriage house. It has been restored as a period showplace with six working fireplaces, carved oak staircases and magnificent antiques throughout. A lush lawn, suitable for croquet, surrounds the house, and flower beds match the Victorian colors of the exterior.

Innkeeper(s): Dot Williams & Ruth Williams. $90-170. MC VISA AX. 23 rooms with PB, 3 with FP. 1 conference room. Type of meal: gourmet breakfast. Beds: KQDT. Phone in room.

Location: A resort town at the base of Pikes Peak.

Publicity: *Rocky Mountain News.*

"We try to get away and come to the Hearthstone at least twice a year because people really care about you!"

Holden House-1902 B&B Inn

1102 W Pikes Peak Ave
Colorado Springs, CO 80904-4347
(719)471-3980 Fax:(719)471-4740
E-mail: holdenhouse@worldnet.att.net

Circa 1902. Built by the widow of a prosperous rancher and businessman, this Victorian inn has rooms named after the many Colorado towns in which the Holdens owned mining interests. The main house, adjacent carriage house and Victorian house next door

include the Cripple
Creek, Aspen,
Silverton, Goldfield
and Independence
suites. The inn's
suites boast fire-
places and over-
sized tubs for two.

Guests can relax in the living room with fireplace, front parlor with TV, or veranda with mountain views. There are friendly cats in residence.

Historic Interest: Miramont Castle, McAllister House, Glen Eyrie Castle, The Pioneer's Museum, the Broadmoor Hotel & Carriage House Museum, Cliff Dwellings Museum, Pikes Peak, and Garden of the Gods Park are among the area's many historic attractions.

Innkeeper(s): Sallie & Welling Clark. $115-125. MC VISA AX DC CB DS PC TC. TAC10. 5 suites. Breakfast included in rates. Types of meals: gourmet breakfast and early coffee/tea. Afternoon tea available. Beds: Q. Phone, air conditioning, turndown service and ceiling fan in room. TV, VCR, fax and copier on premises. Handicap access. Seminars hosted. Antiques, fishing, parks, shopping, sporting events and theater nearby.

Location: Near the historic district, "Old Colorado City" in the Pikes Peak Region.

Publicity: *Denver Post, Rocky Mountain News, Victorian Homes, Pikes Peak Journal, Glamour.*

"Your love of this house and nostalgia makes a very delightful experience."

The Husted House

3001 W Kiowa St
Colorado Springs, CO 80904-2118
(719)632-7569
E-mail: 71601.611@compuserve.com

Circa 1884. The highlight of this Gothic Victorian is a grand turret. A gracious wraparound veranda and gingerbread trim are other notable features. There are just two guest rooms at this homestay B&B, and guests have the run of the house. There is an outdoor hot tub to enjoy. The three-course breakfast starts off with a homemade pastry, followed by fresh fruit and a special daily entree. Museums, the zoo and the Rocky Mountains are all at your disposal.

Innkeeper(s): Shirley & Clint Waller. $65-75. MC VISA AX DS TC. 2 rooms with PB. Breakfast included in rates. Types of meals: gourmet breakfast and early coffee/tea. Beds: D. Ceiling fan in room. Spa and bicycles on premises. Amusement parks, antiques, fishing, parks, shopping, sporting events, golf and theater nearby.

The Painted Lady

1318 W Colorado Ave
Colorado Springs, CO 80904-4023
(719)473-3165

Circa 1894. Once a popular restaurant in Old Colorado City, the Painted Lady has been remodeled into a bed & breakfast by its new owners. The three-story Victorian is decorated in a warm, romantic manner with lace and floral fabrics. Antique iron and four-poster beds, clawfoot tubs and brass fixtures fill the guest rooms. Hearty breakfasts, served on the veranda in summer, might include seafood quiche or souffles and homemade breads. Afternoon refreshments can be enjoyed in the parlor or on one of the porches.

Innkeeper(s): Valerie Maslowski. $70-150. MC VISA AX DS PC TC. 2 suites. Breakfast included in rates. Types of meals: full breakfast and early coffee/tea. Beds: QDT. Air conditioning, ceiling fan and TV in room. VCR on premises. Antiques, fishing, parks, shopping, downhill skiing, cross-country skiing, sporting events, theater and watersports nearby.

Location: In historic Old Colorado City.

"Calm, peaceful. Our first B&B, very memorable."

Room at The Inn B&B

618 N Nevada Ave
Colorado Springs, CO 80903-1006
(719)442-1896 (800)579-4621 Fax:(719)442-6802

Circa 1896. A Colorado pioneer built this Queen Anne Victorian, a delightful mix of turret, gables and gingerbread trim. While restoring their century-old Victorian, the innkeepers discovered several hand-painted murals had once decorated the interior. Original fireplace mantels and a collection of antiques add to the nostalgic ambiance. Fresh flowers, turndown service and a bountiful breakfast are just a few of the amenities. Several rooms include a fireplace or double whirlpool tub.

Innkeeper(s): Chick & Jan McCormick. $85-135. MC VISA AX DC CB DS PC TC. TAC10. 7 rooms with PB, 3 with FP. 2 suites. 1 cottage. 1 conference room. Breakfast, afternoon tea and evening snack included in rates. Types of meals: continental breakfast, full breakfast and early coffee/tea. Beds: Q. Phone, air conditioning and turndown service in room. TV, VCR, fax and copier on premises. Handicap access. Small meetings, family reunions and seminars hosted. Antiques, fishing, parks, shopping, sporting events and theater nearby.

"Staying at your Bed & Breakfast was indeed a second honeymoon and rare treat for us. Your kindness, graciousness, and professionalism made our stay at the Room at the Inn the highlight of our trip to Colorado."

Denver

Capitol Hill Mansion

1207 Pennsylvania St
Denver, CO 80203-2504
(303)839-5221 (800)839-9329 Fax:(303)839-9046

Circa 1891. Although only open a few years, owner Kathy Robbins has mastered the art of innkeeping at this beautiful, red sandstone mansion. High turrets, balconies and soaring chimneys create a romantic, elegant almost castle-like appearance. Each of the guest rooms is uniquely decorated. The Gold Banner Suite features a queen brass bed, a fireplace and cozy sitting area. The Pasqueflower Room boasts a six-foot, round whirlpool tub located in the alcove of one of the home's turrets. Enjoy breakfast downstairs or in the privacy of your own room.

Historic Interest: Capitol Hill is one block from the Molly Brown Home and only four blocks from the Governor's Mansion. Guests can walk to several other historic homes, including the Grant-Humphreys Mansion and an art museum and library.

Innkeeper(s): Kathy Robbins. $90-165. MC VISA AX DS. 8 rooms with PB. 3 suites. Breakfast included in rates. Type of meal: full breakfast. Beds: KQ. Antiques, fishing, downhill skiing, cross-country skiing, theater and watersports nearby.

Publicity: *Yellow Brick Road, Life on Capitol Hill, Journal Constitution, Denver Post, Rocky Mountain News.*

Castle Marne - A Luxury Urban Inn

1572 Race St
Denver, CO 80206-1308
(303)331-0621 (800)926-2763 Fax:(303)331-0623

Circa 1889. This 6,000-square-foot fantasy was designed by William Lang and is in the National Register. It is constructed of hand-hewn rhyolite stone. Inside, polished oak, maple and black ash woodwork enhance the ornate fireplaces, period antiques and opulent Victorian decor. For special occasions ask for the Presidential Suite with its tower sitting room, king-size tester bed, whirlpool tub in the solarium and private balcony.

Historic Interest: Downtown Historic District (7 minutes), State Capitol (2 minutes), Byers-Evans Museum (5 minutes), Molly Brown House Museum (3 minutes), State Historical Society (4 minutes), Four Mile House (20 minutes).

Innkeeper(s): The Peiker Family. $85-220. MC VISA AX DC CB DS. 9 rooms with PB. 2 suites. 1 conference room. Breakfast and afternoon tea included in rates. Type of meal: full breakfast. Beds: KQDT. Fax and copier on premises. Antiques, fishing, downhill skiing, cross-country skiing, theater and watersports nearby.

Publicity: *Denver Post, Innsider, Rocky Mountain News, Los Angeles Times, New York Times, Denver Business Journal, Country Inns, Brides, U.S. Air.*

"The beauty, service, friendliness, delicious breakfasts - everything was so extraordinary! We'll be back many times."

Haus Berlin B&B

1651 Emerson St
Denver, CO 80218-1411
(303)837-9527 (800)659-0253 Fax:(303)837-9527
E-mail: haus.berlin@worldnet.att.net

Circa 1892. This brick Victorian townhouse is a delightful place from which to enjoy Denver. The inn is listed in the National Register of Historic Places and located in a neighborhood filled with charming architecture. The cozy guest rooms are well-appointed and feature beds dressed in fine linens and topped with down comforters. The suite is the most luxurious, and it offers a view of downtown Denver, which is a 10-minute walk from the home. The breakfast menu varies, one morning it might be eggs Benedict, the next day could bring a traditional European breakfast with freshly baked rolls, scones with lemon curd and imported hams and cheeses.

Innkeeper(s): Christiana & Dennis Brown. $90-135. MC VISA AX DC DS PC TC. TAC10. 4 rooms with PB. 1 suite. Breakfast included in rates. Types of meals: full breakfast, gourmet breakfast and early coffee/tea. Beds: KQ. Phone, air conditioning, ceiling fan and TV in room. VCR and fax on premises. German spoken. Amusement parks, antiques, fishing, parks, shopping, downhill skiing, cross-country skiing, sporting events, golf, theater and watersports nearby.

Publicity: *Denver Post, Life on Capital Hill.*

"What a beautiful oasis in a big city."

Dolores   G2

Rio Grande Southern Hotel

101 S 5th St, PO Box 516
Dolores, CO 81323
(303)882-7527 (800)258-0434

Circa 1893. Located in the town square, the turn-of-the-century decorated inn has been in continuous use as a hostelry for more than 100 years. Having also served as a railroad hotel, the inn is located at 7,000 feet elevation at the base of the San Juan Mountains and close to the arid desert. This results in an exceptionally diverse environment. Arid and alpine vegetation and wildlife are found in the regions surrounding the Dolores River Valley.

Innkeeper(s): Fred & Cathy Green. $35-130. MC VISA DS. 9 rooms, 2 with PB. 1 suite. Breakfast included in rates. Types of meals: full breakfast and early coffee/tea. Picnic lunch, lunch and banquet service available. Restaurant on premises. Beds: QDT. Turndown service in room. TV and VCR on premises. Weddings, small meetings, family reunions and seminars hosted. Antiques, fishing, shopping, downhill skiing, cross-country skiing and watersports nearby.

Durango   G3

Leland House B&B Suites

721 East Second Ave
Durango, CO 81301-5435
(970)385-1920 (800)664-1920 Fax:(970)385-1967

Circa 1927. The rooms in this Craftsman-style brick building are named after historic figures associated with this former apartment house and Durango's early industrial growth. The decor features unique cowboy and period antiques designed for both comfort and fun. Gourmet breakfasts include inn specialties of homemade granola, cranberry scones, and a variety of entrees like Southwest burritos and multi-grain waffles. Located in the historic district downtown, guests can take walking

tours, enjoy specialty shops, restaurants, galleries and museums nearby.

Innkeeper(s): Kirk & Diane Komick. $95-155. MC VISA AX DS PC TC. TAC10. 10 rooms with PB. 6 suites. Breakfast and afternoon tea included in rates. Type of meal: gourmet breakfast. Picnic lunch and catering service available. Restaurant on premises. Beds: QD. Phone, air conditioning, ceiling fan and TV in room. VCR, fax and copier on premises. Weddings, small meetings, family reunions and seminars hosted. Spanish spoken. Antiques, fishing, parks, shopping, downhill skiing, cross-country skiing, theater and watersports nearby.

"It is great! Charming and warm, friendly staff and superb food. Marvelous historic photo collection."

Lightner Creek Inn Bed & Breakfast

999 County Rd 207
Durango, CO 81301
(970)259-1226 (800)268-9804 Fax:(970)259-9526
E-mail: lci@frontier.net

Circa 1903. With a tree-covered hillside as its backdrop, this French Country estate is a picturesque site to arriving guests. The elegant interior is an uncluttered mix of country and

Victorian styles. The turn-of-the-century home has been well restored and maintains many of its original elements. Guests who opt for the romantic Carriage House enjoy a spacious suite with a sitting area, king-size featherbed and a pellet stove. After a restful sleep, guests enjoy a gourmet breakfast that starts off with a well-presented medley of fruit. From there, a baked egg dish is served, or perhaps stuffed French toast or gingerbread pancakes topped with lemon sauce.

Innkeeper(s): Richard & Julie Houston. $85-195. MC VISA AX DC DS PC TC. TAC10. 8 rooms, 6 with PB, 1 with FP. 1 cottage. Breakfast and afternoon tea included in rates. Types of meals: full breakfast, gourmet breakfast and early coffee/tea. Beds: KQ. VCR, fax and copier on premises. Handicap access. 20 acres. Weddings, small meetings and family reunions hosted. Antiques, fishing, parks, shopping, downhill skiing, cross-country skiing, theater and watersports nearby.

Publicity: *Durango Magazine.*

"Beautiful setting, exquisite decorating, every detail well-planned."

The Rochester Hotel

721 East Second Ave
Durango, CO 81301
(970)385-1920 (800)664-1920 Fax:(970)385-1967

Circa 1892. This Federal-style inn's decor is inspired by many Western movies filmed in and around the town. The building is an authentically restored late-Victorian hotel with the charm and luxury of the Old West, completely furnished in antiques from the period. The inn is situated on a beautifully landscaped setting that features a flower-filled courtyard, and is located just one block from historic Main Avenue downtown. The inn is close to all major attractions, museums, galleries, shops, restaurants, and outdoor activities.

Historic Interest: Listed in National Register of Historic Places.

Innkeeper(s): Kirk & Diane Komick. $125-185. MC VISA AX DS PC TC. TAC10. 15 rooms with PB. 2 suites. 2 conference rooms. Breakfast included in rates. Type of meal: gourmet breakfast. Afternoon tea, picnic lunch and catering service available. Beds: KQ. Phone, air conditioning, ceiling fan and TV in room. VCR, fax and copier on premises. Handicap access. Weddings, small meetings, family reunions and seminars hosted. Spanish spoken. Antiques, fishing, parks, shopping, downhill skiing, cross-country skiing, theater and watersports nearby.

Pets Allowed: Small pets, prior permission needed.

Publicity: *Conde Nast Traveler.*

"In a word — exceptional! Far exceeded expectations in every way."

Eldora   C6

Goldminer Hotel

601 Klandyke Ave
Eldora, CO 80466-9542
(303)258-7770 (800)422-4629 Fax:(303)258-3850

Circa 1897. This turn-of-the-century hotel is a highlight in the Eldora National Historic District. Suites and rooms are decorated with period antiques. The inn provides packages that include guided jeep, horseback, hiking and fishing tours in the summer and back-country ski tours in the winter.

Historic Interest: The surrounding historic district offers many interesting homes and sites. The Goldminer Hotel was dedicated as a Boulder County landmark in 1996.

Innkeeper(s): Scott Bruntjen. $69-129. MC VISA AX TC. 8 rooms, 4 with PB, 1 with FP. 1 suite. 1 cottage. 1 conference room. Breakfast included in rates. Types of meals: full breakfast and early coffee/tea. Beds: KDT. TV, VCR, fax, copier, spa and library on premises. Weddings, small meetings, family reunions and seminars hosted. Antiques, fishing, parks, shopping, downhill skiing, cross-country skiing and sporting events nearby.

Pets Allowed: Cottage only.

Location: Eldora National Historic District.

Publicity: *Daily Camera, Mountain Ear.*

Estes Park   B6

Anniversary Inn

1060 Mary's Lake Rd, Moraine Rt
Estes Park, CO 80517
(970)586-6200

Circa 1890. High in the Colorado Rockies, at 7,600 feet, this authentic log home is surrounded by spectacular views. There are two acres with a pond and river nearby. An exposed-log liv-

ing room is dominated by a massive mossrock fireplace. The guest rooms boast stenciled walls and other country accents. The full breakfasts are served on a glass-enclosed wraparound porch. The inn specializes in honeymoons and anniversaries and features a honeymoon cottage.

Innkeeper(s): Harry & Norma Menke. $95-150. MC VISA PC TC. TAC10. 4 rooms with PB, 1 with FP. 1 cottage. Breakfast included in rates. Types of meals: full breakfast and early coffee/tea. Beds: Q. Turndown service in room. TV, VCR and library on premises. Fishing, shopping, cross-country skiing, golf and theater nearby.

Publicity: *Denver Post, Columbus Dispatch, Rocky Mountain News.*

"The splendor and majesty of the Rockies is matched only by the warmth and hospitality you showed us during our stay."

The Baldpate Inn

PO Box 4445
Estes Park, CO 80517-4445
(970)586-6151
E-mail: baldpatein@aol.com

Circa 1917. This National Register inn is nestled on the side of Twin Sisters Mountain, adjacent to Rocky Mountain National Park. The front porch affords a spectacular view. Guest rooms and private cabins feature country decor with quilts and down comforters. The lobby and library are ideal places to relax, each is flanked with a massive native stone fireplace. The inn also boasts a unique collection of more than 15,000 keys and a notable photo collection. Three-course breakfasts are served, as well as lunch and dinner in the inn's dining room.

Innkeeper(s): Mike, Lois, Jenn & MacKenzie Smith. $95-150. MC VISA DS PC TC. TAC7. 12 rooms, 2 with PB. 3 cottages. 1 conference room. Breakfast and evening snack included in rates. Types of meals: full breakfast, gourmet breakfast and early coffee/tea. Picnic lunch and banquet service available. Restaurant on premises. Beds: KQDT. VCR and library on premises. Weddings, small meetings and seminars hosted. Fishing, parks, shopping and watersports nearby.

Publicity: *The Discovery Channel, Rocky Mountain News, Country Living.*

"This place unlocked my heart!"

Black Dog Inn B&B

PO Box 4659, 650 S Saint Vrain Ave
Estes Park, CO 80517-4659
(970)586-0374

Circa 1910. Imagine relaxing in a private whirlpool bath enjoying a warm fire while surrounded by the majestic Rocky Mountains. Travelers are sure to enjoy this romantic getaway and mountain retreat. All rooms have private baths with two tubs and marble showers. Tasteful family antiques decorate each room. The innkeepers invite guests to visit often to enjoy the many seasons of the Rockies.

Historic Interest: Stanley Hotel (one-half mile), Historical Museum (one-quarter mile), Enos Mills Cabin (8 miles), McGregor Ranch Musuem (3 miles).

Innkeeper(s): Pete & Jane Princehorn. $70-140. MC VISA PC TC. TAC10. 4 rooms with PB, 2 with FP. 2 suites. Breakfast and evening snack included in rates. Types of meals: full breakfast, gourmet breakfast and early coffee/tea. Beds: Q. Ceiling fan in room. TV, VCR and library on premises. Weddings, small meetings, family reunions and seminars hosted. Antiques, fishing, shopping, cross-country skiing and sporting events nearby.

"The peace and tranquility are so refreshing."

Gunnison   E4

Mary Lawrence Inn

601 N Taylor St
Gunnison, CO 81230-2241
(970)641-3343 Fax:(970)641-6719

Circa 1885. A local entrepreneur and saloon owner built this Italianate home in the late 19th century, but the innkeepers named their home in honor of Mary Lawrence, a later resident. Lawrence, a teacher and administrator for the local schools, used the building as a boarding house. The innkeepers have created an inviting interior with touches such as patchwork quilts, antique furnishings and stenciled walls.

The innkeepers serve a variety of treats each morning for breakfast, and keep the cookie jars full. The inn offers convenient access to the area's bounty of outdoor activities.

Historic Interest: In the hills near Gunnison, guests can explore several mining ghost towns. A local museum is open during the summer months. Self-guided tours of the historic buildings are available. The Crested Butte historic district is 30 miles away.

Innkeeper(s): Doug & Beth Parker. $69-109. MC VISA. TAC10. 5 rooms with PB. 2 suites. Breakfast included in rates. Types of meals: full breakfast, gourmet breakfast and early coffee/tea. Beds: KQT. Fax, copier, spa and library on premises. Family reunions hosted. Fishing, parks, shopping, downhill skiing, cross-country skiing, theater and watersports nearby.

Publicity: *Rocky Mountain News, Denver Post, Gunnison Country.*

"You two are so gracious to make our stay a bit of 'heaven' in the snow."

Hesperus   G2

Blue Lake Ranch

16000 Hwy 140
Hesperus, CO 81326
(970)385-4377 Fax:(970)385-4088

Circa 1910. Built by Swedish immigrants, this renovated Victorian farmhouse is surrounded by spectacular flower gardens. The inn is filled with comforts such as down quilts, vases of fresh flowers and family antiques. The property is designated as a wildlife refuge and there is a cabin overlooking trout-filled Blue Lake, cottage on the river and uninterrupted mountain views. Enjoy a European/Southwest buffet breakfast.

Innkeeper(s): David & Shirley Alford. $65-245. PC TC. TAC10. 4 rooms with PB, 4 with FP. 2 suites. 1 conference room. Breakfast and afternoon tea included in rates. Types of meals: gourmet breakfast and early coffee/tea. Beds: KQDT. Phone, turndown service, ceiling fan and VCR in room. Fax, copier and swimming on premises. Handicap access. 100 acres. Weddings, small meetings, family reunions and seminars hosted. German spoken. Antiques, fishing, parks, shopping, downhill skiing, cross-country skiing, theater and watersports nearby.

Location: Twenty minutes from Durango.

Publicity: *Colorado Home & Lifestyles, Durango Herald, Conde Nast Traveler, Country Inns, Beautiful Gardens, Sunset.*

"What a paradise you have created. We would love to return!!"

Leadville   D5

The Apple Blossom Inn Victorian B&B

120 W 4th St
Leadville, CO 80461-3630
(719)486-2141 (800)982-9279

Circa 1879. Originally the home of Leadville banker Absalom Hunter, who lived here with his wife Estelle until 1918, the inn offers a glimpse into the good life of the late 19th century. Brass lights, beautiful crystal, fireplaces with Florentine tile, beveled mirrors, maple and mahogany inlaid floors, and stained-glass windows, including one in a front window that gives The Apple Blossom Inn its name, are evidence to Hunter's prosperity. Innkeeper Maggie Senn invites guests to raid her cookie jar, which can include fresh brownies and chocolate chip cookies.

Innkeeper(s): Maggie Senn. $64-148. MAP. MC VISA AX DC DS PC TC. TAC10. 8 rooms, 3 with PB, 1 with FP. Breakfast and evening snack included in rates. Types of meals: continental breakfast, continental-plus breakfast, full breakfast, gourmet breakfast and early coffee/tea. Afternoon tea, dinner, picnic lunch, lunch, gourmet lunch and catered breakfast available. Beds: KQDT. Weddings, small meetings and family reunions hosted. Antiques, fishing, parks, shopping, downhill skiing, cross-country skiing, theater and watersports nearby.

"You have done a really superb job of creating of a beautiful place to welcome strangers...your warm welcome makes it feel like home!"

Historic Delaware Hotel

700 Harrison Ave
Leadville, CO 80461-3562
(719)486-1418 (800)748-2004 Fax:(719)486-2214

Circa 1886. Often referred to as the Crown Jewel of Leadville, this hotel has served as an architectural cornerstone of the

town's National Historic District. The interior has an elegant Victorian lobby and Callaway's restaurant, which includes period antiques, crystal chandeliers, brass fixtures and oak paneling that reflects Leadville's Boom Days. Adding to the atmosphere are lace curtains, heirloom quilts and bedspreads in the guest rooms.

Innkeeper(s): Susan & Scott Brackett. $68-120. MC VISA AX DC DS. 36 rooms with PB. 4 suites. 1 conference room. Breakfast included in rates. Types of meals: full breakfast and gourmet breakfast. Dinner and lunch available. Restaurant on premises. Beds: QDT. Fax and copier on premises. Antiques, fishing, downhill skiing and cross-country skiing nearby.

Publicity: *Denver Post, Rocky Mountain News, Sunday Summit Daily News.*

"You really did a first-rate job of handling everything, from travel rooms, food, entertainment and snacks. Great job!"

The Ice Palace Inn Bed & Breakfast

813 Spruce St
Leadville, CO 80461-3555
(719)486-8272 (800)754-2840 Fax:(719)486-0345

Circa 1899. Innkeeper Kami Kolakowski was born in this historic Colorado town, and it was her dream to one day return and run a bed & breakfast. Now with husband Giles, she has created a restful retreat out of this turn-of-the-century home built with lumber from the famed Leadville Ice Palace. Giles and Kami have filled the home with antiques and pieces of history from the Ice Palace and the town. Guests are treated to a mouth-watering gourmet breakfast with treats such as stuffed French toast or German apple pancakes.

Historic Interest: The Baby Doe Tabor Museum, National Mining Hall of Fame, Tabor Opera House and Healy House are among Leadville's historic attractions, and all are near the Ice Palace Inn.

Innkeeper(s): Giles & Kami Kolakowski. $69-129. MC VISA AX DS PC TC. TAC10. 6 rooms with PB. Breakfast, afternoon tea and evening snack included in rates. Types of meals: gourmet breakfast and early coffee/tea. Catering service and room service available. Beds: KQDT. Turndown service and ceiling fan in room. TV, VCR, spa and library on premises. Weddings, small meetings, family reunions and seminars hosted. Antiques, fishing, parks, shopping, downhill skiing, cross-country skiing, theater and watersports nearby.

Peri & Ed's Mountain Hide Away

201 W 8th St
Leadville, CO 80461-3529
(719)486-0716 (800)933-3715 Fax:(719)486-2181

Circa 1879. This former boarding house was built during the boom days of Leadville. Families can picnic on the large lawn sprinkled with wildflowers under soaring pines. Shoppers and history buffs can enjoy exploring historic Main Street, one

block away. The surrounding mountains are a natural playground offering a wide variety of activities, and the innkeepers will be happy to let you know their favorite spots and help with directions. The sunny Augusta Tabor room features a sprawling king-size bed with a warm view of the rugged peaks.

Innkeeper(s): Peri & Ed Solder. $45-85. MC VISA AX DS PC TC. TAC10. 9 rooms, 5 with PB, 2 with FP. 2 suites. 2 cottages. Breakfast included in rates. Type of meal: full breakfast. Beds: KQDT. Ceiling fan in room. TV, VCR and library on premises. Family reunions hosted. Antiques, fishing, parks, shopping, downhill skiing, cross-country skiing and theater nearby.

Wood Haven Manor

PO Box 1291, 809 Spruce
Leadville, CO 80461-1291
(719)486-0109 (800)748-2570 Fax:(719)486-0210

Circa 1898. Located on the town's Banker's Row, this Victorian inn is located in a winter wonderland, with cross-country and downhill

skiing nearby, snowmobiling and back-country outings. Gourmet breakfasts include freshly baked bread, sourdough pancakes or eggs Santa Fe, in-season fruits and cool fruit smoothies.

Historic Interest: The area boasts beautiful churches and buildings built before the turn of century. Leadville is in the National Historic Register.

Innkeeper(s): Clint & Christy Burback. $59-129. MC VISA AX DS PC TC. TAC5. 8 rooms with PB. 4 suites. Breakfast, afternoon tea and evening snack included in rates. Types of meals: full breakfast, gourmet breakfast and early coffee/tea. Beds: QDT. TV, VCR, fax, copier and library on premises. Weddings, small meetings, family reunions and seminars hosted. Amusement parks, antiques, fishing, parks, shopping, downhill skiing, cross-country skiing, theater and watersports nearby.

Location: Historic "Bankers Row."

Publicity: *Country Traditional, Country Almanac, Country Decorating Ideas.*

"The room, the food and the hospitality were truly wonderful."

Loveland   B6

The Lovelander B&B Inn

217 W 4th St
Loveland, CO 80537-5524
(970)699-0798 (800)459-6694 Fax:(970)699-0797

Circa 1902. Prepare to be pampered at the Lovelander. Chocolate turndown service, fresh flowers, whirlpool tubs and bubble bath are just a few of the idyllic touches. Guest rooms are appointed in an uncluttered and romantic Victorian style. Three rooms include either a fireplace or whirlpool tub. Enjoy the gentle sounds of a waterfall in the garden or sit back and relax on the wraparound porch. If weather permits, gourmet breakfasts can be enjoyed on the veranda or in the garden. Specialties such as pumpkin apple waffles topped with caramel pecan sauce are the reason why guests will be pleased to note that the inn now offers four-course dinners on Friday and Saturday nights. The inn's memorable cuisine has been featured on the TV shows "Inn Country USA" and "Inn Country Chefs." In addition to these more romantic amenities, there is a fax and copier available, a concierge and tour planning service, and conference facilities, which are located across the street.

Innkeeper(s): Lauren & Gary Smith. $95-150. MC VISA AX DS PC TC. TAC10. 11 rooms with PB, 1 with FP. 1 conference room. Breakfast included in rates. Types of meals: full breakfast, gourmet breakfast and early coffee/tea. Picnic lunch available. Beds: KQDT. Phone, air conditioning and turndown service in room. TV, fax, copier and library on premises. Weddings, small meetings, family reunions and seminars hosted. Antiques, parks, shopping and cross-country skiing nearby.

Lyons
B6

The Inn at Rock 'n River: B&B and Trout Pond Fishing

16858 N Saint Vrain Dr
Lyons, CO 80540-9036
(303)443-4611 (800)448-4611

Circa 1890. Drive under a covered bridge to reach this scenic inn surrounded by woods, ponds, waterfalls and mountain views, all along the banks of the North Saint Vrain River. For lodge guests, pay-by-the-inch trout fishing is the catch of the day at this relaxing retreat. Bait, tackle and license are provided at no extra charge. They'll even clean the catch and show you various ways to cook the fish on an outdoor grill, if desired. The innkeepers ship their gourmet smoked trout throughout the year, and it is available for purchase at the inn. Flowers dot the landscape, and guest rooms are filled with comfortable furnishings. The two-story carriage house boasts a fireplace and private two-person Jacuzzi, and every room offers private baths and beautiful views. After a restful night's sleep, awake to the scent of fresh coffee and enjoy a home-cooked breakfast before heading out for a day of exploring, fishing or antique shopping.
Historic Interest: Rocky Mountain National Park is 18 miles from the inn, while the famed Stanley Hotel is 16 miles away in Estes Park. The City of Lyons is famous for its restaurants and antique shopping, only three miles from the inn.
Innkeeper(s): Marshall & Barbara McCrummen. $89-159. MC VISA AX DS TC. TAC10. 9 rooms with PB, 1 with FP. 1 conference room. Breakfast included in rates. Type of meal: full breakfast. Beds: KQDT. 18 acres. Weddings, small meetings, family reunions and seminars hosted. Amusement parks, antiques, fishing, parks, shopping, cross-country skiing, sporting events and theater nearby.
Publicity: *Country.*

"Tremendous food and fantastic service. Our favorite place to visit in Colorado. I've been coming here for six years and best food and service we've had."

Mancos
G2

Bauer House

100 Bauer Ave, PO Box 1049
Mancos, CO 81328
(970)533-9707 (800)733-9707 Fax:(970)533-7022
E-mail: bauerhse@fone.net

Circa 1890. George Bauer, Mancos' town founder, built this three-story, brick and stone Victorian. Several of the prominent family's possessions are on display, as well as old town newspapers, pictures and bank ledgers. The three guest rooms feature classic decor, and there is a penthouse with a kitchen and bar. All of the guest quarters boast mountain views. There are porches to relax on, and the innkeeper has added a putting green, croquet lawn and a place for bocce ball. Bobbi Black tries a new, creative menu for each day. Breakfast treats include stuffed pancakes, homemade waffles or stratas accompanied by fresh fruit, muffins and granola. The Mancos area offers many activities, including the more unusual stagecoach rides and

llama backpack trips in addition to golfing, hiking and white-water rafting. The inn is seven miles from the entrance to Mesa Verde National Park.
Innkeeper(s): Bobbi Black. $75-125. MC VISA DS TC. TAC10. 4 rooms with PB. 1 suite. Breakfast, afternoon tea and evening snack included in rates. Types of meals: full breakfast and early coffee/tea. Picnic lunch and catering service available. Beds: QT. Phone, turndown service and ceiling fan in room. TV, VCR, fax and copier on premises. Weddings, small meetings, family reunions and seminars hosted. Antiques, fishing, parks, shopping, cross-country skiing, sporting events, theater and watersports nearby.

"Bobbi went out of her way to make our visit to Mancos more enjoyable. She is an excellent ambassador for the Mancos Valley and quite an interesting person to know. The Bauer House should be recommended as the place to stay, to anyone visiting the area!"

Manitou Springs
E6

Onaledge B&B

336 El Paso Blvd
Manitou Springs, CO 80829-2319
(719)685-4265 (800)530-8253

Circa 1912. This Tudor-style home was built to serve as the guest house for an adjacent mansion, which was built by a man who secured his fortune in the Texas oil industry. The home is reminiscent of a European country inn, built out of stone. The interior boasts polished wood floors and dark, exposed beams. Guests drift off to sleep on a feather bed, with the warm glow of the fireplace illuminating their guest room. The Rockledge Suite includes a hot tub. There is also a private carriage house available, with a canopy bed and hot tub. The home is within walking distance of a popular restaurant, located in another historic home.
Innkeeper(s): Adam Kevil. $85-150. MC VISA AX DS PC TC. TAC10. 5 rooms with PB, 5 with FP. 2 suites. 1 cottage. Breakfast, afternoon tea and evening snack included in rates. Types of meals: gourmet breakfast and early coffee/tea. Beds: KQ. Air conditioning and TV in room. Weddings and family reunions hosted. Antiques, fishing, parks, shopping, cross-country skiing, golf and theater nearby.

Red Crags B&B Inn

302 El Paso Blvd
Manitou Springs, CO 80829-2308
(719)685-1920 (800)721-2248 Fax:(719)685-1073
E-mail: info@redcrags.com

Circa 1870. Well-known in this part of Colorado, this unique, four-story Victorian mansion sits on a bluff with a combination of views that includes Pikes Peak, Manitou Valley, Garden of the Gods and the city of Colorado Springs. There are antiques throughout the house. The formal dining room features a rare cherrywood Eastlake fireplace. Two of the suites include double

whirlpool tubs. Outside, guests can walk through beautifully landscaped gardens or enjoy a private picnic area with a barbecue pit and a spectacular view. Wine is served in the evenings.

Innkeeper(s): Howard & Lynda Lerner. $75-165. MC VISA AX DS PC TC. TAC10. 8 rooms with PB. 5 suites. Breakfast, afternoon tea and evening snack included in rates. Types of meals: continental breakfast, gourmet breakfast and early coffee/tea. Beds: K. Fax, spa and bicycles on premises. Weddings, small meetings, family reunions and seminars hosted. Antiques, parks, shopping and theater nearby.

Publicity: *Bridal Guide, Denver Post, Los Angeles Times, Springs Woman, Rocky Mountain News, Colorado Springs Gazette.*

"What a beautiful, historical and well-preserved home - exceptional hospitality and comfort. What wonderful people! Highly recommended!"

Rockledge Country Inn

328 El Paso Blvd
Manitou Springs, CO 80829
(719)685-4515 (888)685-4515 Fax:(719)685-1031
E-mail: rockinn@webcom.com

Circa 1912. Built originally for a wealthy entrepreneur, legend has it that in 1922 a prominent Texas oilman was so taken by the inn's stonework, that he bought the inn as well as the quarry from which the stone had come. Thus, he proceeded to ter-

race and fence this three-acre, 20-room estate. Each of the three spacious luxury suites are distinctively decorated in period reproduction antiques and boast feather beds and sitting rooms. Visitors are invited to enjoy Colorado wines in the afternoon in front of the copperwork fireplace or on the stone patio with a view of Pikes Peak. The inn is minutes from the downtown historic district.

Historic Interest: Minutes from Colorado Springs, Colorado College, U.S. Air Force Academy, and the many attractions of Manitou Springs.

Innkeeper(s): Hartman & Nancy Smith. $200-250. EP. MC VISA AX DS PC TC. TAC10. 3 suites, 2 with FP. 1 conference room. Breakfast, afternoon tea and evening snack included in rates. Type of meal: full breakfast. Beds: K. Phone, turndown service and TV in room. Fax, copier and library on premises. Weddings, small meetings, family reunions and seminars hosted. Amusement parks, antiques, fishing, parks, shopping and sporting events nearby.

Publicity: *The Gazette.*

Minturn C4

Eagle River Inn

PO Box 100
Minturn, CO 81645-0100
(970)827-5761 (800)344-1750 Fax:(970)827-4020
E-mail: eri@vail.net

Circa 1894. Earth red adobe walls, rambling riverside decks, mature willow trees and brilliant flowers enhance the secluded backyard of this Southwestern-style inn. Inside, the lobby features comfortable Santa Fe furniture, an authentic beehive fireplace and a ceiling of traditional latilas and vegas. Baskets, rugs

and weavings add warmth. Guest rooms found on two floors have views of the river or mountains. The innkeepers hold a wine tasting with appetizers each evening. Minturn, which had its beginnings as a stop on the Rio Grande Railroad, is the home of increasingly popular restaurants, shops and galleries.

Innkeeper(s): Patty Bidez. $75-180. MC VISA AX PC TC. TAC10. 12 rooms with PB. Breakfast and evening snack included in rates. Type of meal: full breakfast. Beds: KT. TV in room. Fax and bicycles on premises. Weddings, small meetings and family reunions hosted. Fishing, shopping, downhill skiing, cross-country skiing and sporting events nearby.

Location: Vail Valley.

Publicity: *Rocky Mountain News, Country Accents, National Geographic Traveler.*

"We love this place and have decided to make it a yearly tradition!"

Ouray F3

Damn Yankee B&B Inn

100 Sixth Ave, PO Box 410
Ouray, CO 81427
(970)325-4219 (800)845-7512 Fax:(970)325-4339
E-mail: bigsmac@montrose.net

Circa 1991. Nestled at the foot of mountains, this rustic hideaway affords glorious views from its second-story balcony and sitting room. The parlor boasts leather furniture and a fireplace, and guests will always find something to snack on in the sitting room, which is stocked with fruit, drinks and other treats. Guests planning to hit the nearby slopes will appreciate the inn's expansive, gourmet breakfast, which is served each morning.

Innkeeper(s): Matt & Julie Croce. $72-185. MC VISA AX PC. TAC10. 10 rooms with PB. 3 suites. 1 cottage. Breakfast and afternoon tea included in rates. Types of meals: gourmet breakfast and early coffee/tea. Beds: KQ. Phone, ceiling fan and TV in room. VCR, fax and copier on premises. Handicap access. Weddings and small meetings hosted. Fishing, downhill skiing and golf nearby.

St. Elmo Hotel

426 Main St, PO Box 667
Ouray, CO 81427
(970)325-4951 Fax:(970)325-0348

Circa 1898. The inn was built by Kitty Heit, with views of the amphitheater, Twin Peaks and Mt. Abrams, and it has operated as a hotel for most of its life. Rosewood sofas and chairs covered in red and green velvet, and a player piano furnish the parlor. The Bon Ton Restaurant occupies the stone-walled basement, and it's only a short walk to the hot springs.

Historic Interest: The Town of Ouray is a National Historical District.

Innkeeper(s): Dan & Sandy Lingenfelter. $65-102. MC VISA AX DS. 9 rooms with PB. 2 suites. Breakfast included in rates. Catering service available. Restaurant on premises. Beds: KQ. Phone in room. Spa and sauna on premises. Antiques, fishing, downhill skiing, cross-country skiing and watersports nearby.

Publicity: *Colorado Homes & Lifestyles.*

"So full of character and so homely, it is truly delightful. The scenery in this area is breathtaking."

Wiesbaden Hot Springs Spa & Lodgings

625 5th St
Ouray, CO 81427
(970)325-4347 Fax:(970)325-4358
E-mail: wiesbaden@gwe.net

Circa 1879. Built directly above mineral hot springs, this old lodge has a European flair. In the basement of the inn, into the side of the mountain, is a vapor cave with a soaking pool, the inn's favorite spot. The water here is a consistent 108 to 110 degrees. Chief Ouray had an adobe on the property, and used the cave for its "sacred waters." Therapeutic massage, facials, acupressure and aromatherapy wraps are offered. Guest rooms are simply decorated with wallpapers and country antiques. Breakfast is not provided. Box Canyon Falls and the Ute Indian reservation are spots to visit in the area.

Innkeeper(s): Linda Wright-Minter. $75-145. MC VISA DS TC. TAC10. 19 rooms, 18 with PB, 2 with FP. 2 suites. 2 cottages. Type of meal: early coffee/tea. Beds: KQDT. Phone and TV in room. Spa and swimming on premises. Weddings, small meetings and family reunions hosted. Antiques, fishing, parks, shopping, downhill skiing, cross-country skiing, golf and watersports nearby.
Publicity: *Travel & Leisure, National Geographics Traveler, Shape, Sunset, Lifestyles, New York Times.*

Pine   D6

Meadow Creek B&B Inn

13438 Hwy 285
Pine, CO 80470
(303)838-4167

Circa 1929. This marvelous stone structure, shrouded by pines and aspens, was built as a summer home for Italian Prince Balthasar Gialma Odescalchi, a descendant of rulers of the Holy Roman Empire. Enjoy views of the surrounding mountains as you breath in Colorado's cool, clean air. The lush 35-acre grounds include the main house, barns, a smoke house and a cabin. Although Meadow Creek has been home to royalty, it had been vacant for some time when the current innkeep-

ers found and restored their little treasure. Their restoration efforts have created a truly memorable inn. Rooms are filled with country charm, gracious furnishings and little extras such as teddy bears, flowers, beautiful quilts and lacy curtains. Grandma's Attic, a secluded loft bedroom, offers a sitting area and views at tree-top level. The Colorado Sun Suite offers the modern amenities of a bar, microwave, coffee pot and refrigerator, combined with the romantic amenities of a private sitting room and a Jacuzzi underneath a skylight, perfect for stargazing. Some rooms boast fireplaces, and all guests are pampered with stocked cookie jars and refreshments available throughout the day. A luscious full breakfast with unique entrees, home-baked breads and other treats is served each morning.

Historic Interest: The main house and surrounding structures are listed in the Colorado Historical Register. Meadow Creek is just an hour out of Denver, which offers many historic attractions.

Innkeeper(s): Pat & Dennis Carnahan. $95-180. MC VISA. 7 rooms with PB. 3 suites. Breakfast and evening snack included in rates. Types of meals: full breakfast and early coffee/tea. Beds: KQ. 35 acres. Weddings, small meetings, family reunions and seminars hosted. Antiques, fishing, shopping and cross-country skiing nearby.

Pueblo   E7

Abriendo Inn

300 W Abriendo Ave
Pueblo, CO 81004-1814
(719)544-2703 Fax:(719)542-6544
E-mail: abriendo@rmi.net

Circa 1906. This three-story, 7,000-square-foot four-square-style mansion is embellished with dentil designs and wide porches supported by Ionic columns. Elegantly paneled and carved oak walls and woodwork provide a gracious setting for king-size brass beds, antique armoires and Oriental rugs. Breakfast specialties include raspberry  muffins, sunrise egg enchiladas and nut breads. A 24-hour beverage service is offered. Ask for the music room with its own fireplace and bay window.

Historic Interest: Historic Union Avenue District (within 4 blocks), where Bat Masterson walked the streets & site of "Old Monarch," the Hanging Tree.

Innkeeper(s): Kerrelyn Trent. $59-120. MC VISA AX DC PC TC. TAC10. 10 rooms with PB. 1 suite. Breakfast included in rates. Types of meals: continental breakfast, full breakfast, gourmet breakfast and early coffee/tea. Beds: KQ. Phone, air conditioning, ceiling fan, TV and VCR in room. Fax and copier on premises. Weddings hosted. Antiques, fishing, parks, shopping, cross-country skiing, sporting events, golf and watersports nearby.
Publicity: *Pueblo Chieftain, Rocky Mountain News, Denver Post.*

"Thank you for warm hospitality, cozy environment and fine cuisine! Outstanding!"

Redstone   D3

Cleveholm/The Historic Redstone Castle

0058 Redstone Blvd
Redstone, CO 81623-9498
(970)963-3463 (800)643-4837 Fax:(970)704-1834

Circa 1902. This turn-of-the-century castle combines enchanting decor with the solitude of the Rocky Mountains. The hotel secures its Camelot feel with elegant guest rooms, such as the

Tower Suite with a sleigh bed and sitting room. After a morning of cross-country skiing, guests can bundle up and traverse the grounds by sleigh. In spring and summer months, horseback riding, kayaking and hiking are popular activities. A trip to the village boasts a haven of antique shops, galleries and specialty gift shops. The manor hosts several special events each year, including piano concerts, balls and wine maker dinners.

Historic Interest: Aspen mining town turned tourist mecca (40 miles/1 hour). Surrounded by Snowmass/Maroon Bells Wilderness Area & National Forest, located on West Elk Loop Scenic & Historic Byway.

Innkeeper(s): Cyd Lange. $95-225. MC VISA AX. 16 rooms, 8 with PB. 3 suites. 1 conference room. Breakfast included in rates. Type of meal: continental-plus breakfast. Beds: KQD. Phone in room. Fax and copier on premises. Antiques, fishing and cross-country skiing nearby.
Publicity: *Travel Holiday.*

Salida
E5

River Run Inn

8495 Co Rd 160
Salida, CO 81201
(719)539-3818 (800)385-6925

Circa 1892. This gracious brick home, a National Register build-ing, is located on the banks of the Arkansas River, three miles from town. It was once the poor farm, for folks down on their luck who were willing to work in exchange for food and lodging. The house has been renovated to reflect a country-eclectic style and has seven guest rooms, most enhanced by mountain views. The location is ideal for anglers, rafters, hikers, bikers, skiers. A 13-bed, third-floor is great for groups. A full country breakfast, afternoon cookies and refreshments are offered daily.

Innkeeper(s): Virginia Nemmers. $65-80. MC VISA AX DC DS PC TC. TAC10. 7 rooms, 3 with PB. Type of meal: full breakfast. Beds: KQT. Phone in room.
Publicity: Denver Magazine, Rocky Mountain News, Colorado Country Life.

"We will always remember your generous hospitality in your beautiful home."

Thomas House

307 E 1st St
Salida, CO 81201-2801
(719)539-7104 (888)228-1410

Circa 1888. This home was built as a boarding house to help accommodate the thousands of railroad workers and travelers who passed through Salida. Today, the home still serves as a restful place for weary travelers drawn to the Colorado wilder-ness. The inn is decorated with antiques, collectibles and con-temporary furnishings. Each guest room is named for a moun-tain. The Mt. Princeton suite includes a bedroom, private bath with an antique clawfoot tub and a separate sitting area. The innkeepers keep reading materials on hand, and there is an outdoor hot tub as well. Breakfasts are continental, yet hearty, with a variety of freshly baked breads and muffins, yogurt, gra-nola, cheese and fruit.

Innkeeper(s): Tammy & Steve Office. $45-85. MC VISA PC TC. TAC10. 5 rooms with PB. 1 suite. Breakfast included in rates. Types of meals: conti-nental breakfast and early coffee/tea. Beds: QDT. Ceiling fan in room. Spa and library on premises. Small meetings and family reunions hosted. Antiques, fishing, parks, shopping, downhill skiing, cross-country skiing, the-ater and watersports nearby.

Silverton
F3

The Wyman Hotel & Inn

1371 Greene St
Silverton, CO 81433
(970)387-5372 (800)609-7845 Fax:(970)387-5745

Circa 1902. Silverton, a Victorian-era mining town at the base of the San Juan Mountains, is the location for this National Register hotel. The hotel still maintains an original tin ceiling and an ele-vator. However, the elevator is now housed in one of the guest room, surrounding a Jacuzzi tub. Other unique features include a stone carving of a mule, created by the hotel's builder. The mule is displayed on the roof. Aside from the historic ambiance, the innkeepers offer plenty of amenities. Rooms include a TV

and VCR, and there are hundreds of movies guests can choose, all free of charge. A buffet breakfast is served, featuring fresh fruit, muffins, breads, cereals, special egg dishes and Silverton Spuds, potatoes baked with onions, peppers, tomatoes and cheese. Tea and homemade cookies are served every afternoon.

Innkeeper(s): Lorraine Lewis. $85-139. MC VISA AX DS PC TC. TAC10. 18 rooms with PB. 2 suites. Breakfast and afternoon tea included in rates. Types of meals: gourmet breakfast and early coffee/tea. Picnic lunch available. Beds: KQ. Phone, ceiling fan, TV and VCR in room. Fax, copier and library on premises. Weddings, small meetings and family reunions hosted. Antiques, fishing, parks, shopping, downhill skiing, cross-country skiing, theater and watersports nearby.

Telluride
F3

Johnstone Inn

PO Box 546
Telluride, CO 81435-0546
(970)728-3316 (800)752-1901
E-mail: bschiff@rmii.com

Circa 1891. This Victorian board-ing house is located on Telluride's main street, in view of the San Juan Mountain ski slopes. Guest rooms all have new bathrooms with marble floors and showers. Brass beds are painted with pink and white flowers and topped with fluffy comforters. Laundry use is available. Ski lifts are a short walk away.

Innkeeper(s): Bill Schiffbauer. $80-125. MC VISA AX. 8 rooms with PB. Type of meal: full breakfast. Beds: Q. Spa on premises.
Publicity: Rocky Mountain News.

"Cannot say enough good things, had a great time."

Woodland Park
D6

Pikes Peak Paradise

236 Pinecrest Rd, PO Box 5760
Woodland Park, CO 80863-8432
(719)687-6656 (800)728-8282 Fax:(719)687-9008
E-mail: woodlandco@aol.com

Circa 1987. This three-story Georgian Colonial with stately white columns rises unexpectedly from the wooded hills west of Colorado Springs. The entire south wall of the inn is made of glass to enhance its splendid views of Pikes Peak. A sliding glass door opens from each room onto a patio. Eggs Benedict and Belgian waffles are favorite breakfast dishes.

Innkeeper(s): Priscilla, Martin & Tim. $95-195. MC VISA AX DS PC TC. TAC10. 6 rooms, 2 with PB, 3 with FP. 4 suites. Breakfast included in rates. Type of meal: gourmet breakfast. Beds: KQ. Phone and ceiling fan in room. VCR, fax and spa on premises. Handicap access. Weddings and family reunions hosted. Amusement parks, antiques, fishing, parks, shopping, cross-country skiing, sporting events, theater and water-sports nearby.

Pets Allowed: Small pets with prior approval.

Location: West of Colorado Springs, 25 minutes.

Publicity: Rocky Mountain News.

Connecticut

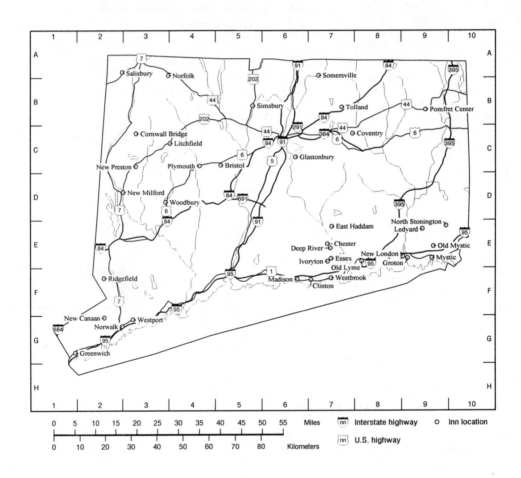

Map of Connecticut showing inn locations.

A — Salisbury, Norfolk, 7, 91, 202, Somersville, 84, 395

B — 44, Simsbury, Tolland, 44, Pomfret Center, 202, 84

C — Cornwall Bridge, Litchfield, 44, 291, 384, 44, Coventry, 6, 395, New Preston, 6, 84, 91, Bristol, 5, Glastonbury, Plymouth

D — New Milford, Woodbury, 84, 691, East Haddam, 395, North Stonington, Ledyard, 6, 84, 91

E — 84, Deep River, Chester, Essex, New London, Old Mystic, Ridgefield, Ivoryton, Old Lyme, 95, Groton, Mystic, 95

F — 7, 95, 1, Madison, Westbrook, Clinton

G — New Canaan, Westport, Norwalk, 684, 95

H — Greenwich

0 5 10 15 20 25 30 35 40 45 50 55 Miles

0 10 20 30 40 50 60 70 80 Kilometers

Interstate highway   Inn location

U.S. highway

Bristol   C5

Chimney Crest Manor

5 Founders Dr
Bristol, CT 06010-5209
(860)582-4219

Circa 1930. This 32-room Tudor mansion possesses an unusual castle-like arcade and a 45-foot living room with a stone fireplace at each end. Many of the rooms are embellished with oak paneling and ornate plaster ceilings. One room includes a thermo spa. The inn is located in the Federal Hill District, an area of large colonial homes.

Historic Interest: American Clock and Watch Museum (3 blocks), New England Carousel Museum (one-half mile).

Innkeeper(s): Dante & Cynthia Cimadamore. $75-155. MC VISA AX. TAC10. 5 rooms with PB, 2 with FP. 3 suites. 1 conference room. Breakfast included in rates. Types of meals: full breakfast and early coffee/tea. Afternoon tea and evening snack available. Beds: KQ. Air conditioning, ceiling fan and TV in room. VCR and library on premises. Weddings and small meetings hosted. Amusement parks, parks and cross-country skiing nearby.

Publicity: Record-Journal.

"Great getaway — unbelievable structure. They are just not made like this mansion anymore."

Chester   E7

The Inn at Chester

318 W Main St
Chester, CT 06412-1026
(860)526-9541 (800)949-7829 Fax:(860)526-4387

Circa 1778. More than 200 years ago, Jeremiah Parmelee built a clapboard farmhouse along a winding road named the Killingworth Turnpike. The Parmelee Homestead stands as a reflection of the past and is an inspiration for the Inn at Chester. Each of the rooms is individually appointed with Eldred Wheeler Reproductions. The Lincoln Suite has a sitting room with a fireplace. Enjoy lively conversation or live music while imbibing your favorite drink at the inn's tavern, Dunk's Landing. Outside Dunk's Landing, a 30-foot fireplace soars into the rafters. Fine dining is offered in the inn's post-and-beam restaurant.

Innkeeper(s): Deborah Moore. $105-215. MC VISA AX DS. 42 rooms with PB, 2 with FP. 1 suite. 3 conference rooms. Breakfast included in rates. Type of meal: continental-plus breakfast. Dinner, lunch and banquet service available. Restaurant on premises. Beds: KQDT. Phone, air conditioning and TV in room. VCR, fax, copier, sauna, bicycles, tennis, library and pet boarding on premises. Handicap access. 12 acres. Weddings, small meetings, family reunions and seminars hosted. Antiques, fishing, parks, shopping, skiing, golf, theater and watersports nearby. Pets Allowed.

Publicity: New Haven Register, Hartford Courant, Pictorial Gazette, Discover Connecticut, New York Times.

Clinton   F7

Captain Dibbell House

21 Commerce St
Clinton, CT 06413-2054
(860)669-1646 Fax:(860)669-2300

Circa 1866. Built by a sea captain, this graceful Victorian house is only two blocks from the harbor where innkeeper Ellis Adams used to sail his own vessel. A ledger of household accounts dating from the 1800s is on display, and there are fresh flowers in each guest room.

Historic Interest: Gillette Castle (20 miles), Stanton House (one-half mile), Essex Steam Train (10 minutes), Yale University (30 miles).

Innkeeper(s): Helen & Ellis Adams. $65-105. MC VISA PC TC. TAC10. 4 rooms with PB. Breakfast included in rates. Meal: full breakfast. Beds: KQT. Air conditioning, turndown service and ceiling fan in room. TV and bicycles on premises. Antiques, fishing, parks, shopping, theater, watersports nearby.

Location: Exit 63 & I-95, south on Rt. 81 to Rt. 1, east for 1 block, right on Commerce.

Publicity: Clinton Recorder, New Haven Register, Hartford Courant.

"This was our first experience with B&Bs and frankly, we didn't know what to expect. It was GREAT!"

Cornwall Bridge   C3

Cornwall Inn & Restaurant

270 Kent Rd # 7
Cornwall Bridge, CT 06754-1607
(203)672-6884

Circa 1810. This country home offers the choice of an inn room or a room in the adjacent country motel. After a restful night's sleep, guests can visit a number of nearby attractions. The Sloane-Stanley museum exhibits many early American artifacts. Hiking and fishing abound at areas such as Kent Falls State Park and Macedonia State Park, which is also an Indian reservation. Car enthusiasts will enjoy Lime Rock, the site of auto racing and a racing school.

Innkeeper(s): Emily Stonat. $50-125. MC VISA AX DC. 13 rooms, 12 with PB. Type of meal: continental breakfast. Restaurant on premises. Beds: KQD.

Coventry   C7

Maple Hill Farm B&B

365 Goose Ln
Coventry, CT 06238-1215
(860)742-0635 (800)742-0635

Circa 1731. This historic farmhouse still possesses its original kitchen cupboards and a flour bin used for generations. Family heirlooms and the history of the former home owners are shared with guests. There is a three-seat outhouse behind the inn. Visitors, of course, are provided with modern plumbing, as well as a screened porch and solarium in which to relax.

Historic Interest: Nathan Hale Homestead (10 miles), Mark Twain, Harriet Beecher Stowe House (22 miles), Brick School (just off property), Sturbridge Village (30 minutes).

Innkeeper(s): Anthony Felice, Jr. & Marybeth Gorke-Felice. $55-85. MC VISA PC TC. TAC10. 4 rooms with PB. Breakfast included in rates. Meals: full breakfast and early coffee/tea. Beds: QDT. Turndown service in room. VCR, fax, copier, spa, swimming, stables, bicycles and library on premises. Weddings, small meetings, family reunions hosted. Antiques, fishing, parks, shopping, cross-country skiing, sporting events, theater, watersports nearby. Pets Allowed: Small dogs with cage.

Location: A good stopping point between Boston and New York.

Publicity: Journal Inquirer, Coventry Journal, Forbes, Hartford Courant, Yankee Traveler, Connecticut Magazine.

Deep River
E7

Riverwind

209 Main St
Deep River, CT 06417-2022
(860)526-2014

Circa 1790. Chosen "most romantic inn in Connecticut" by Discerning Traveler Newsletter, this inn features a wraparound gingerbread porch filled with gleaming white wicker furniture. A happy, informal country decor includes antiques from Barbara's Virginia home. There are fireplaces everywhere, including a 12-foot cooking fireplace in the keeping room.

Innkeeper(s): Barbara Barlow & Bob Bucknall. $95-165. MC VISA AX. 8 rooms with PB. Breakfast included in rates. Type of meal: full breakfast. Beds: QD. Phone in room. Weddings hosted. Antiques and theater nearby.

Publicity: *Hartford Courant, Country Living, Country Inns, Country Decorating, New York, Travel & Leisure, New York Times, Boston Globe, Los Angeles Times.*

"Warm, hospitality, a quiet homey atmosphere, comfortable bed, well thought-out and delightful appointments, delicious light hot biscuits — a great find!"

East Haddam
E7

Bishopsgate Inn

Goodspeed Landing, PO Box 290
East Haddam, CT 06423-0290
(860)873-1677 Fax:(860)873-3898

Circa 1818. This Colonial house is furnished with period antiques, and each floor of the inn has a sitting area where guests often relax with a good book. Four of the guest rooms include a fireplace and the suite has a sauna. The innkeepers serve a hearty breakfast, and for an additional charge, they can prepare picnic lunches and five-course dinners. Although secluded on two acres, the inn is a short walk to the Goodspeed Opera House and shopping.

Innkeeper(s): Kagel Family. $95-140. MAP. MC VISA PC. 6 rooms with PB, 4 with FP. 1 suite. 1 conference room. Breakfast and afternoon tea included in rates. Types of meals: continental breakfast, full breakfast, gourmet breakfast and early coffee/tea. Dinner, evening snack, picnic lunch, lunch and room service available. Beds: QDT. Phone and air conditioning in room. Small meetings and family reunions hosted. Antiques, fishing, parks, shopping, downhill skiing, cross-country skiing, theater and watersports nearby.

Publicity: *Discerning Traveler, Adventure Road, Manhattan Cooperator.*

". . . Attention to detail, ambiance and amenities . . . Bishopsgate is truly outstanding."

Essex
E7

Griswold Inn

36 Main St
Essex, CT 06426-1132
(860)767-1776 Fax:(860)767-0481
E-mail: griswoldin@aol.com

Circa 1776. The main building of the colonial Griswold Inn is said to be the first three-story frame structure built in Connecticut. The Tap Room, just behind the inn, has been called the most handsome barroom in America. The inn is famous for its fine New England fare as well as its English Hunt Breakfast, originally served at the request of the British after they invaded the harbor at Essex during the war of 1812. Ask for a quiet room at the back of the inn unless you'd enjoy a Fife & Drum corps marching by under your window on Main Street.

Historic Interest: Important historic houses line the lanes of Essex. Changing exhibits of early river valley life can be seen at the Connecticut River Museum. Mystic Seaport and Gillette's Castle are also on the "must see" list.

Innkeeper(s): Douglas & Joan Paul. $90-185. MC VISA AX TC. 30 rooms with PB, 6 with FP. 1 conference room. Type of meal: continental breakfast. Dinner and lunch available. Beds: KQDTR. Air conditioning in room. Fax and copier on premises. Weddings, small meetings and family reunions hosted. Antiques, shopping and theater nearby.

Pets Allowed: Certain rooms with advance notice.

Publicity: *Yankee Magazine, House Beautiful.*

"A man in search of the best inn in New England has a candidate in the quiet, unchanged town of Essex, Connecticut — Country Journal."

Glastonbury
C6

Butternut Farm

1654 Main St
Glastonbury, CT 06033-2962
(860)633-7197 Fax:(860)659-1758

Circa 1720. This Colonial house sits on two acres of landscaped grounds amid trees and herb gardens. Prize-winning goats, pigeons, chickens, ducks, pigs and a llama are housed in the old barn on the property. Eighteenth-century Connecticut antiques, including a cherry highboy and cherry pencil-post canopy bed, are placed throughout the inn, enhancing the natural beauty of the pumpkin-pine floors and eight brick fireplaces.

Innkeeper(s): Don Reid. $70-90. AX PC TC. 4 rooms with PB, 3 with FP. 2 suites. Breakfast included in rates. Type of meal: full breakfast. Beds: DT. Phone, air conditioning and VCR in room. Fax on premises. Family reunions hosted. Antiques, fishing, parks, shopping, downhill skiing, cross-country skiing, sporting events and theater nearby.

Location: South of Glastonbury Center, 1.6 miles, 10 minutes to Hartford.

Publicity: *New York Times, House Beautiful, Yankee, Antiques.*

Greenwich
G1

Homestead Inn

420 Field Point Rd
Greenwich, CT 06830-7055
(203)869-7500 Fax:(203)869-7500

Circa 1799. The Homestead began as a typical farmhouse built by a judge and gentleman farmer, Augustus Mead. Later it was remodeled in a fanciful Carpenter Gothic style. The full veranda is filled with wicker furnishings and offers views of rolling lawns and trees. The inn has a fine collection of antiques, an intimate library with fireplace, and a classic French restaurant.

Innkeeper(s): Thomas Henkelmann & Theresa Carroll. $110-350. 23 rooms with PB. 6 suites. 1 conference room. Types of meals: continental breakfast and full breakfast. Dinner and lunch available. Restaurant on premises. Beds: QT. Fax and copier on premises.

Publicity: *Country Inns.*

Ivoryton
E7

The Copper Beech Inn

46 Main St
Ivoryton, CT 06442-1004
(860)767-0330 Fax:(860)767-7840

Circa 1887. The Copper Beech Inn was once the home of ivory importer A.W. Comstock, one of the early owners of the Comstock Cheney Company, which produced ivory combs and keyboards. The village took its name from the ivory trade centered here. An enormous copper beech tree shades the property. Each room in the renovated Carriage House boasts a whirlpool bath and French doors opening onto a deck. The wine list and French-country cuisine at the inn's restaurant have received numerous accolades.

Historic Interest: Connecticut River Museum (4 miles), Goodspeed Opera House (15 miles), Ivoryton Playhouse (1/2 mile), Mystic Seaport (25 miles).
Innkeeper(s): Eldon & Sally Senner. $118-196. MC VISA AX DC CB PC TC. 13 rooms with PB. 1 conference room. Breakfast included in rates. Meal: continental-plus breakfast. Banquet service available. Restaurant on premises. Beds: KQDT. Air conditioning, TV in room. Library on premises. Handicap access. Weddings, small meetings, seminars hosted. Limited Spanish, Portuguese spoken. Antiques, fishing, parks, shopping, theater, watersports nearby.
Location: Lower Connecticut River valley.
Publicity: *L.A. Times, Bon Appetit, Travel & Leisure, Discerning Traveler.*

"The grounds are beautiful ... just breathtaking ... accommodations are wonderful."

Ledyard   E9

Stonecroft

515 Pumpkin Hill Rd
Ledyard, CT 06339-1637
(860)572-0771 Fax:(860)572-9161
E-mail: stoncrft@cris.com

Circa 1807. Although the main portion of this former sea captain's home dates to the early 19th century, the oldest portion was constructed in 1740. The 18th-century portion houses one of the guest rooms, named The Buttery. This room features the original doors and beams. Each bedchamber is delightful. The Stonecroft Room includes a mural, which wraps around the room's walls.

The Westcroft and Orchard rooms are equally pleasing, with polished hardwood floors, elegant wallcoverings and fireplaces. A fancy, four-course breakfast is served by candlelight. Mystic, shopping and casinos are just a short drive away.
Innkeeper(s): Joan & Lynn Egy. $130-200. MAP. MC VISA AX DS PC TC. TAC10. 4 rooms with PB, 3 with FP. Breakfast and afternoon tea included in rates. Types of meals: gourmet breakfast and early coffee/tea. Beds: KQ. Air conditioning in room. Bicycles and library on premises. Handicap access. Weddings, small meetings, family reunions and seminars hosted. Amusement parks, antiques, fishing, parks, shopping, cross-country skiing, sporting events, golf, theater and watersports nearby.
Publicity: *New York Post, Mystic River Press.*

"You added the third R to the perfect R&R weekend...rest, relaxation and romance."

Litchfield   C4

Tollgate Hill Inn

Rt 202 & Tollgate Rd, Box 1339
Litchfield, CT 06759
(860)567-4545 (800)445-3903 Fax:(860)567-8397

Circa 1745. Formerly known as the Captain Bull Tavern, the inn underwent extensive renovations in 1983. Listed in the

National Register, its features include Indian shutters, wide pine-paneled walls, a Dutch door fireplace and an upstairs ballroom. Next door is a historic schoolhouse that contains four of the inn's guest rooms.
Innkeeper(s): Ferdinand J. Zivic. $90-175. EP. AX DC DS PC TC. TAC6. 21 rooms with PB, 9 with FP. 6 suites. 2 conference rooms. Breakfast included in rates. Type of meal: continental breakfast. Dinner, picnic lunch, lunch, gourmet lunch, banquet service, catering service, catered breakfast and room service available. Restaurant on premises. Beds: QDT. Phone, air conditioning and TV in room. VCR, fax, copier and pet boarding on premises. Handicap access. 10 acres. Weddings, small meetings, family reunions and seminars hosted. Amusement parks, antiques, fishing, parks, shopping, skiing, sporting events, theater and watersports nearby.

Pets Allowed.

Publicity: *Food & Wine, Travel & Leisure, New York Times, Bon Appetit.*

Madison   F6

Madison Beach Hotel

PO Box 546, 94 W Wharf Rd
Madison, CT 06443-2905
(203)245-1404 Fax:(203)245-0410

Circa 1800. Since most of Connecticut's shoreline is privately owned, the Madison Beach Hotel is one of the few waterfront lodgings available. It originally was constructed as a stagecoach stop and later became a popular vacation spot for those who stayed for a month at a time with maids and chauffeurs. Art Carney is said to have driven a Madison Beach Hotel bus here when his brother was the manager. Rooms are furnished in a variety of antiques and wall-papers. Many rooms have splendid views of the lawn and the Long Island Sound from private porches.

Innkeeper(s): Lorraine Casula. $70-225. MC VISA AX DC DS TC. 35 rooms with PB. 6 suites. 2 conference rooms. Breakfast included in rates. Types of meals: continental breakfast, continental-plus breakfast and early coffee/tea. Dinner, picnic lunch, lunch, banquet service and room service available. Restaurant on premises. Beds: QT. Phone, air conditioning and TV in room. VCR, fax and copier on premises. Handicap access. Weddings, small meetings, family reunions and seminars hosted. Antiques, fishing, shopping, sporting events, theater and watersports nearby.
Publicity: *New England Travel.*

"The accommodations were wonderful and the service was truly exceptional."

Tidewater Inn

949 Boston Post Rd
Madison, CT 06443-3236
(203)245-8457

Circa 1840. Long ago, this 19th-century home was no doubt a welcome site to travelers needing a rest after a bumpy stagecoach ride. Although its days as a stagecoach stop have long since past, the inn is still a welcoming place for those needing a romantic getaway. The rooms are elegantly appointed with items such as four-poster or canopy beds, Oriental rugs and fine furnishings. The inn's sitting area is a cozy place to relax, with its fireplace and exposed beams. The one-and-a-half-acre grounds include an English garden. The inn is within walking distance to many of Madison's sites, and beaches are just a couple of miles away.
Innkeeper(s): Jean Foy & Rich Evans. $80-160. MC VISA AX PC TC. 9 rooms with PB, 2 with FP. Breakfast included in rates. Meals: continental breakfast, full breakfast and early coffee/tea. Beds: KQDT. Air conditioning and TV in room. Antiques, fishing, parks, shopping, theater and watersports nearby.

Mystic
E9

Harbour Inn & Cottage

15 Edgemont St
Mystic, CT 06355-2853
(860)572-9253

Circa 1898. Known as Charley's Place after its innkeeper, this New England inn located on the Mystic River is comfortably decorated with cedar paneling and hardwood floors throughout. A large stone fireplace and piano are featured in the common room. There is a gazebo, six-person hot tub, picnic area and boat dock on the grounds. The inn is minutes from the Olde Mystic Village, Factory Outlet Stores and casinos.

Innkeeper(s): Charles Lecouras, Jr. $55-250. TC. TAC10. 6 rooms with PB, 1 with FP. 1 cottage. Beds: D. Phone, air conditioning, ceiling fan and TV in room. Spa and pet boarding on premises. Weddings, small meetings and family reunions hosted. Greek spoken. Antiques, fishing, parks, shopping, golf, theater and watersports nearby.

Pets Allowed.

The Inn at Mystic

Jct Rt 1 & 27
Mystic, CT 06355
(203)536-9604

Circa 1904. This is a Colonial Revival mansion built by Katherine Haley, widow of one of the owners of the old Fulton Fish Market. A columned Victorian veranda overlooks the harbor and sound. All the rooms are individually decorated and may include a canopy bed, whirlpool tub or a wood-burning fireplace. There is also a motor inn on the property so be sure to request rooms in the original house. Old Mystic Village, Mystic Seaport Museum and the Aquarium are all nearby. The inn offers a full-service restaurant.

Innkeeper(s): Jody Dyer. $95-250. EP. MC VISA AX DC DS PC TC. TAC10. 68 rooms with PB, 25 with FP. 1 conference room. Restaurant on premises. Beds: KQDT. Fax, copier and spa on premises. Handicap access.

Publicity: Travel & Leisure.

The Whaler's Inn

20 E Main St
Mystic, CT 06355-2646
(860)536-1506 (800)243-2588 Fax:(860)572-1250

Circa 1901. This classical revival-style inn is built on the historical site of the Hoxie House, the Clinton House and the U.S. Hotel. Just as these famous 19th-century inns offered, the Whaler's Inn has the same charm and convenience for today's visitor to Mystic. Once a booming ship-building center, the town's connection to the sea is ongoing and the sailing schooners still pass beneath the Bascule Drawbridge in the center of town. The inn has indoor and outdoor dining available and more than 75 shops and restaurants are within walking distance.

Innkeeper(s): Richard Prisby. $69-145. MC VISA AX TC. 41 rooms with PB. 1 suite. 1 conference room. Type of meal: early coffee/tea. Dinner, lunch and gourmet lunch available. Restaurant on premises. Beds: KQD. Phone, air conditioning and TV in room. Fax, copier and child care on premises. Handicap access. Small meetings, family reunions and seminars hosted. Antiques, fishing, parks, shopping and watersports nearby.

New Canaan
G2

Roger Sherman Inn

195 Oenoke Rd G
New Canaan, CT 06840-4110
(203)966-4541 Fax:(203)966-0503
E-mail: tom1gruezi@aol

Circa 1783. This gracious country inn boasts a traditional center-chimney-style architecture typical of this period of the 18th century. Inviting porches and extended verandas are enjoyed by both inn and restaurant guests. The inn's restaurant is famous locally for its excellent cuisine. The owners have previously managed hotels in Hong Kong, as well as Zurich, Switzerland. Chef Raymond Peron was once the chef for the luxury liner, SS France. The elegant guest rooms of the Roger Sherman Inn reflect a traditional decor.

Innkeeper(s): Thomas, Kay, Rudi, Katie. $110-135. MC VISA AX DC. TAC8. 9 rooms with PB. 1 suite. Breakfast included in rates. Types of meals: continental breakfast and continental-plus breakfast. Gourmet lunch and banquet service available. Restaurant on premises. Beds: Q. Phone, air conditioning and TV in room. Fax and copier on premises. Handicap access. Weddings, small meetings and family reunions hosted. Spanish, French, German and Italian spoken. Antiques, fishing, shopping and golf nearby.

Ratings: 5 Stars.

"*The food was wonderful and the Garden Room looked lovely, but it was the service and attention to detail that made it the relaxed happy evening it was.*"

New London
E9

Queen Anne Inn

265 Williams St
New London, CT 06320-5721
(860)447-2600 (800)347-8818

Circa 1903. Several photographers for historic house books have been attracted to the classic good looks of the Queen Anne Inn. The traditional tower, wraparound verandas and elaborate frieze invite the traveler to explore the interior with its richly polished oak walls and intricately carved alcove. Period furnishings include brass beds and some rooms have their own fireplace.

Historic Interest: The Mystic Seaport, Mystic Marine and an aquarium are a 15-minute drive. Other nearby historic attractions include the Eugene O'Neil Homestead, Goodspeed Opera House and the Nautilus submarine & museum.

Innkeeper(s): Ed Boncich & Janet Moody. $89-185. MC VISA AX DS PC TC. TAC10. 10 rooms, 8 with PB, 2 with FP. Breakfast and afternoon tea included in rates. Types of meals: full breakfast and early coffee/tea. Picnic lunch available. Beds: KQDT. Phone and air conditioning in room. Small meetings and family reunions hosted. Shopping, golf and watersports nearby.

Publicity: New London Day Features.

"*Absolutely terrific — relaxing, warm, gracious — beautiful rooms and delectable food.*"

New Milford   D3

Homestead Inn

5 Elm St
New Milford, CT 06776-2903
(860)354-4080

Circa 1853. Built by the first of three generations of John Prime Treadwells, the inn was established 80 years later. Victorian architecture includes high ceilings, spacious rooms and large verandas. There is a small motel adjacent to the inn.
Innkeeper(s): Rolf & Peggy Hammer. $78-101. MC VISA AX DC DS. 14 rooms with PB. Type of meal: continental-plus breakfast. Beds: KQDT. Phone, air conditioning and TV in room.

Location: In village center, 15 miles north of Danbury.
Publicity: *Litchfield County Times, ABC Home Show, Food & Wine.*

"One of the homiest inns in the U.S.A. with most hospitable hosts. A rare bargain to boot."

New Preston   C3

Boulders Inn

East Shore Rd, Rt 45
New Preston, CT 06777
(203)868-0541 Fax:(203)868-1925

Circa 1895. Outstanding views of Lake Waramaug and its wooded shores can be seen from the living room and many of the guest rooms and cottages of this country inn. The terrace is open in the summer for cocktails, dinner and sunsets over the lake. Antique furnishings, a basement game room, a beach house with a hanging wicker swing and a tennis court are all part of Boulders Inn.
Innkeeper(s): Kees & Ulla Adema. $150-350. MAP. MC VISA AX TC. 17 rooms with PB, 11 with FP. 6 suites. 1 conference room. Breakfast, afternoon tea and dinner included in rates. Types of meals: full breakfast, gourmet breakfast and early coffee/tea. Banquet service available. Restaurant on premises. Beds: KQD. Phone, air conditioning, turndown service and ceiling fan in room. TV, fax, copier and bicycles on premises. Handicap access. 27 acres. Weddings, small meetings and family reunions hosted. Antiques, fishing, parks, shopping, skiing, theater and watersports nearby.
Location: Lake Waramaug.
Publicity: *New York Times, Travel & Leisure, Country Inns.*

"Thank you for a welcome respite from the daily hurly-burly."

The Inn on Lake Waramaug

107 N Shore Rd
New Preston, CT 06777-1105
(203)868-0563 (800)525-3466 Fax:(203)868-9173

Circa 1795. This charming country inn, nestled on beautiful Lake Waramaug, delights its patrons with spectacular views of the Connecticut countryside and of Lake Waramaug. The inn features 23 guest rooms, most with fireplaces, and one two-room suite. All rooms include a private bath, cable TV, telephone and air conditioning. Enjoy creative New American cuisine while dining fireside on a cold winter evening or outside on the canopied deck with views of Lake Waramaug in the summer. Guests can enjoy lake swimming, bicycling and canoe-

ing in the summer and an indoor pool, sauna and game room in cooler months. A beautiful setting for weddings, conferences and retreats, the inn won the Award of Excellence from "The Wine Spectator" in 1993-97. The Boathouse Cafe serves lighter fare Memorial Day through Columbus Day on the water.
Innkeeper(s): Nancy Conant. $128-168. MAP, AP. MC VISA AX. 24 rooms with PB. 1 conference room. Type of meal: early coffee/tea. Dinner and lunch available. Restaurant on premises. Beds: QTD. Phone, air conditioning and TV in room. VCR, swimming and sauna on premises. Handicap access. 25 acres. Weddings, small meetings, family reunions and seminars hosted. Antiques, shopping, cross-country skiing, theater and watersports nearby.
Location: Northwest Connecticut.
Publicity: *Washington Journal, Business Weekly, Record Journal, CT Magazine, Wine Spectator.*

"Guests, innkeepers and a pony all give the Inn on Lake Waramaug the kind of country inn character that most inns can only hope for. — New England Get Aways."

Noank-Mystic   A3

Palmer Inn

25 Church St
Noank-Mystic, CT 06340
(860)572-9000

Circa 1907. This gracious seaside mansion, listed in the National Register, was built for shipbuilder Robert Palmer Jr. by shipyard craftsmen. It features a two-story grand columned entrance, mahogany beams, mahogany staircase, quarter-sawn oak floors and 14-foot ceilings. The Lincrusta wall-covering, original light fixtures and nine stained-glass windows remain. The inn is located two miles to downtown Mystic, and one block to the water in the historic fishing village of Noank.
Historic Interest: Mystic Seaport Museum, Mystic Marinelife Aquarium, Lyman Allyn Museum, Noank Historical Society (all within three miles).
Innkeeper(s): Patricia Ann White. $115-225. FP. MC VISA AX DS PC TC. 6 rooms with PB, 1 with FP. 2 conference rooms. Breakfast and afternoon tea included in rates. Types of meals: continental-plus breakfast and early coffee/tea. Beds: KQDT. Air conditioning, turndown service and ceiling fan in room. Library on premises. Small meetings and seminars hosted. Antiques, fishing, parks, shopping, theater and watersports nearby.
Location: Two miles from Mystic.
Publicity: *Boston Globe, Yankee, Norwalk Hour, Discerning Traveler, Companion, Day, Coastal Cruising, Historic Preservation, New York Times.*

"Your inn is gracious, yet it has the atmosphere of a warm and lovely home."

Norfolk   A3

Blackberry River Inn

Route 44
Norfolk, CT 06058
(860)542-5100

In the National Register, the Colonial buildings that comprise the inn are situated on 27 acres. A library with cherry paneling, three parlors and a breakfast room are offered for guests' relaxation. Guest rooms are furnished with antiques and a Laura Ashley decor. Rooms with Jacuzzis or fireplaces are available. A full country breakfast is served.
Call for rates.

Greenwoods Gate B&B Inn

Greenwoods Rd E, PO Box 491
Norfolk, CT 06058
(860)542-5439

Circa 1797. Luxurious is perhaps the best way to describe this inn. From little touches like providing fresh flowers and soft, fluffy bath robes to the beautiful interior, the innkeepers pamper each guest. Enjoy gourmet breakfast in the formal dining room and refreshments in the late afternoon. Each of the four suites offers something unique. The three-level Levi Thompson Suite offers a romantic sitting area and tiered canopy bed. The E.J. Trescott Suite is full of antiques and doll collections. The Lillian Rose Suite is perfect for couples traveling together as it offers two bedrooms and a library room. A private stairway leads up to the Captain Darius Phelps Suite.

Innkeeper(s): George & Marian Schumaker. $175-235. PC TC. TAC10. 4 suites. Breakfast, afternoon tea and evening snack included in rates. Types of meals: gourmet breakfast and early coffee/tea. Beds: QDT. Air conditioning and ceiling fan in room. TV, VCR and library on premises. Antiques, fishing, parks, shopping, downhill skiing, cross-country skiing, theater and watersports nearby.

Publicity: Yankee, Ladies Home Journal, Country Inns, National Geographic Traveler.

Manor House

69 Maple Ave
Norfolk, CT 06058-0447
(860)542-5690 Fax:(860)542-5690

Circa 1898. Charles Spofford, designer of London's subway, built this home with many gables, exquisite cherry paneling and grand staircase. There are Moorish arches and Tiffany windows. Guests can enjoy hot-mulled cider after a sleigh ride, hay

ride, or horse and carriage drive along the country lanes nearby. The inn was named by "Discerning Traveler" as Connecticut's most romantic hideaway.

Historic Interest: Norfolk is a historic community with many historic homes; the Yale Chamber Music Festival is held at one such historic estate. Litchfield County has many museums and historic homes to tour.

Innkeeper(s): Hank & Diane Tremblay. $120-225. MC VISA AX DS PC TC. TAC10. 8 rooms with PB, 3 with FP. 1 suite. 1 conference room. Breakfast and afternoon tea included in rates. Types of meals: full breakfast, gourmet breakfast and early coffee/tea. Catering service, catered breakfast and room service available. Beds: KQDT. Ceiling fan in room. TV, fax and library on premises. Weddings, small meetings, family reunions and seminars hosted. French spoken. Antiques, fishing, parks, shopping, downhill skiing, cross-country skiing, sporting events, theater and watersports nearby.

Location: Close to the Berkshires.

Publicity: Boston Globe, Philadelphia Inquirer, Innsider, Rhode Island Monthly, Gourmet, National Geographic Traveler, Good Housekeeping.

"Queen Victoria, eat your heart out."

North Stonington E9

Antiques & Accommodations

32 Main St
North Stonington, CT 06359-1709
(860)535-1736 (800)554-7829

Circa 1861. Set amongst the backdrop of an acre of herb, edible flower, perennial and cutting gardens, this Victorian treasure offers a romantic location for a weekend getaway. Rooms filled with antiques boast four-poster canopy beds and fresh flowers surrounded by a soft, pleasing decor. Honeymooners or couples celebrating an anniversary are presented with special amenities such as balloons, champagne and heart-shaped waffles for breakfast. Candlelit breakfasts include unique items such as edible flowers along with the delicious entrees. Historic Mystic Seaport and Foxwood's Casino are just minutes from the inn.

Historic Interest: Historic Mystic and Stonington Village are eight miles from the inn, Newport is a 38-mile drive.

Innkeeper(s): Ann & Tom Gray. $169-229. MC VISA. 5 rooms, 6 with PB. 2 suites. Breakfast included in rates. Type of meal: full breakfast. Beds: Q. Air conditioning, TV and VCR in room. Antiques and fishing nearby.

Publicity: Country Inns, Woman's Day, New London Day.

"The building's old-fashioned welcome-all decor made us feel comfortable the moment we stepped in."

Norwalk G2

Silvermine Tavern

194 Perry Ave
Norwalk, CT 06850-1123
(203)847-4558 Fax:(203)847-9171

Circa 1790. The Silvermine consists of the Old Mill, the Country Store, the Coach House and the Tavern itself. Primitive paintings and furnishings, as well as family heirlooms, decorate the inn. Guest rooms and dining rooms overlook the Old Mill, the waterfall and swans gliding across the millpond. Some guest rooms offer items such as canopy bed or private decks. In the summer, guests can dine al fresco and gaze at the mill pond.

Historic Interest: Lockwood Matthews Mansion (10 miles).

Innkeeper(s): Frank Whitman, Jr. $95-165. MC VISA AX DC CB PC TC. TAC10. 10 rooms with PB. 1 suite. Breakfast included in rates. Meal: continental breakfast. Dinner, lunch, banquet service available. Restaurant on premises. Beds: DT. Air conditioning in room. VCR, fax, copier on premises. Weddings, small meetings, family reunions, seminars hosted. Antiques, fishing, parks, shopping nearby.

Publicity: Advocate, Greenwich Time.

Old Lyme
E8

Bee and Thistle Inn
100 Lyme St
Old Lyme, CT 06371-1426
(860)434-1667 (800)622-4946 Fax:(860)434-3402

Circa 1756. This stately inn is situated along the banks of the Lieutenant River. There are five and one-half acres of trees, lawns and a sunken English garden. The inn is furnished with Chippendale antiques and reproductions. A guitar duo plays in the parlor on Friday, and a harpist performs on Saturday evenings. Bee and Thistle was voted the most romantic inn in the state, the most romantic dinner spot, and for having the best restaurant in the state by readers of "Connecticut Magazine."

Innkeeper(s): Bob, Penny, Lori and Jeff Nelson. $75-215. EP. MC VISA DC DS PC TC. TAC10. 11 rooms with PB, 1 with FP. 1 cottage. Type of meal: gourmet breakfast. Afternoon tea and lunch available. Restaurant on premises. Beds: KQDT. Phone, air conditioning and ceiling fan in room. Weddings, small meetings and family reunions hosted. Antiques, fishing, parks, shopping, theater and watersports nearby.

Location: Historic district next to Florence Griswold Museum.

Publicity: *Countryside, Country Living, Money, New York, U.S. Air, New York Times, Country Traveler.*

Old Mystic
E9

Red Brook Inn
2800 Gold Star Hwy
Old Mystic, CT 06372-0237
(860)572-0349

Circa 1740. If there was no other reason to visit Old Mystic, a charming town brimming with activities, the Red Brook Inn would be reason enough. The Crary Homestead features three

unique rooms, both with working fireplaces, while the Haley Tavern offers seven guest rooms, some with canopy beds and fireplaces. Innkeeper Ruth Keyes has selected a beautiful array of antiques to decorate her inn. Guests are sure to enjoy her wonderful authentic Colonial breakfasts. A special winter meal takes three days to complete and she prepares it over an open hearth. In addition to the full breakfasts, afternoon and evening beverages are provided. The aquarium, Mystic Seaport Museum, a cider mill, casinos and many shops are only minutes away.

Historic Interest: Mystic Seaport Museum.

Innkeeper(s): Ruth Keyes. $95-189. MC VISA AX DS PC TC. 10 rooms with PB, 7 with FP. 3 conference rooms. Breakfast, afternoon tea and evening snack included in rates. Type of meal: full breakfast. Beds: QDT. Phone and air conditioning in room. TV, VCR and library on premises. Small meetings, family reunions and seminars hosted. Amusement parks, antiques, fishing, parks, shopping, sporting events, theater and watersports nearby.

Location: Off route 184 (Gold Star Highway).

Publicity: *Travel & Leisure, Yankee, New York, Country Decorating, Philadelphia Inquirer, National Geographic Traveler, Discerning Traveler.*

"The staff is wonderful. You made us feel at home. Thank you for your hospitality."

Plymouth Village
C4

Shelton House B&B
663 Main St (Rt 6)
Plymouth Village, CT 06782
(860)283-4616 Fax:(860)283-4616
E-mail: sheltonhhb@aol.com

Circa 1825. This home's most famous resident was a carriage maker whose wares were sold as far away as Chicago. The Greek Revival is listed as a city historic site and was a stop on the town's bicentennial homes tour. Antiques and reproductions decorate the interior. Beds are topped with fine quality linens and soft, fluffy comforters. There are three tranquil acres of grounds, shaded by trees. After breakfast, guests can take a trip to historic Litchfield, which is just 12 miles down the road. Antique shops, restaurants, skiing and other activities are all nearby.

Innkeeper(s): Pat & Bill Doherty. $65-95. PC TC. 4 rooms, 2 with PB. Breakfast and afternoon tea included in rates. Type of meal: full breakfast. Beds: QDT. Air conditioning in room. TV and fax on premises. Amusement parks, antiques, fishing, parks, shopping, downhill skiing, cross-country skiing, golf and theater nearby.

"Accommodations were excellent. Breakfast was great. I was pampered and I loved it."

Pomfret Center
B9

Clark Cottage at Wintergreen
354 Pomfret St
Pomfret Center, CT 06259
(860)928-5741 Fax:(860)928-1591
E-mail: qurq@necca.com

Circa 1888. Built for a landscape designer with seven children, this Victorian estate includes more than seven acres of flower and vegetable gardens and 100-year-old towering trees. Innkeeper Doris Geary can help you with your itinerary, which should include a visit to Sturbridge Village. The Williamsburg-like town, a 30-minute drive away, is steeped in Colonial lifestyle with authentic homes and traditional cooking. Doris will prepare breakfast to order if given the request the night before.

Innkeeper(s): Stan & Doris Geary. $60-90. MC VISA PC TC. 4 rooms, 2 with PB, 2 with FP. 1 suite. Breakfast included in rates. Type of meal: full breakfast. Beds: KQT. Phone, air conditioning, ceiling fan, TV and VCR in room. Fax, bicycles and library on premises. Small meetings, family reunions and seminars hosted. Antiques, shopping and cross-country skiing nearby.

Ridgefield
F2

West Lane Inn
22 West Ln
Ridgefield, CT 06877-4914
(203)438-7323 Fax:(203)438-7325

Circa 1849. This National Register Victorian mansion on two acres features an enormous front veranda filled with white whicker chairs and tables overlooking a manicured lawn. A polished oak staircase rises to a third-floor landing and lounge. Chandeliers, wall sconces and floral wallpapers help to establish an intimate atmosphere. Although the rooms do not have antiques, they feature amenities such as heated towel racks, extra-thick towels, air conditioning, remote control cable TVs and desks.

Innkeeper(s): Maureen Mayer & Deborah Prieger. $110-165. MC VISA AX DC CB. 20 rooms with PB, 2 with FP. Breakfast included in rates. Type of meal: continental breakfast. Evening snack and room service available. Beds: KQ. Phone, air conditioning and ceiling fan in room. Handicap access. Small meetings hosted. Antiques, fishing, shopping, cross-country skiing and theater nearby.

Publicity: *Stanford-Advocate, Greenwich Times, Home & Away Connecticut.*

"Thank you for the hospitality you showed us. The rooms are comfortable and quiet. I haven't slept this soundly in weeks."

Salisbury A2

Under Mountain Inn

482 Under Mountain Rd
Salisbury, CT 06068-1104
(860)435-0242 Fax:(860)435-2379

Circa 1732. Situated on three acres, this was originally the home of iron magnate Jonathan Scoville. A thorned locust tree, believed to be the oldest in Connecticut, shades the inn.

*Under Mountain Inn
Salisbury, Connecticut*

Paneling that now adorns the pub was discovered hidden between the ceiling and attic floorboards. The boards were probably placed there in violation of a Colonial law requiring all wide lumber to be given to the king of England. British-born Peter Higginson was happy to reclaim it in the name of the Crown.

Historic Interest: Several Blast Furnaces (6-10 miles), The Salisbury Cannon Museum (5 1/2 miles), Holley-Williams House (5 1/2 miles), Colonel Ashley House (7 miles).

Innkeeper(s): Peter & Marged Higginson. $160-195. TAC10. 7 rooms with PB. Breakfast, afternoon tea and dinner included in rates. Restaurant on premises. Beds: KQD. Air conditioning in room. VCR and fax on premises. Weddings and small meetings hosted.

Publicity: *Travel & Leisure, Country Inns, Yankee, Connecticut, Country Accents.*

"You're terrific!"

Simsbury B5

Simsbury 1820 House

731 Hopmeadow St
Simsbury, CT 06070-2226
(203)658-7658 (800)879-1820 Fax:(203)651-0724

Circa 1820. This graciously restored country manor was originally home to the son of an American Revolutionary War hero. In the heart of the scenic Farmington Valley, it was also home to generations of distinguished American families, including Gifford Pinchot, father of the American Conservation Movement. The rooms are decorated with fabrics, wall hangings and reproductions reminiscent of the 18th and 19th centuries. Charming antiques grace meandering nooks and crannies. Overstuffed chairs and comfortable beds, including many four-posters, invite complete relaxation.

Historic Interest: Hillstead Museum (6 miles), Stanley Whitman House (7 miles), Mark Twain House (12 miles), Massocoh Plantation (one-half mile).

Innkeeper(s): Jeff Brighentil. $109-169. MC VISA AX DC DS. 32 rooms with PB. 3 suites. 4 conference rooms. Breakfast included in rates. Type of meal: continental breakfast. Dinner, banquet service and room service available.

Restaurant on premises. Beds: KQ. Phone, air conditioning and TV in room. Weddings, small meetings, family reunions and seminars hosted. Amusement parks, antiques, fishing, shopping, downhill skiing, cross-country skiing, sporting events, theater and watersports nearby.

Somersville A7

The Old Mill Inn B&B

63 Maple St
Somersville, CT 06072
(860)763-1473

Circa 1860. Giant maples and landscaped grounds create a private, peaceful ambiance at this Greek Revival home, secluded along the banks of the Scantic River. There is a hammock set up for those hoping for a nap among the trees, or perhaps you'd prefer a trip up the river on the inn's canoe. The grounds also are decorated with a gazebo. Rooms feature romantic decor, with comforters, fine linens and furnishings such as a brass bed or a wicker

loveseat. In the evenings, hors d'oeuvres and beverages are served in the fireplaced parlor. One of your innkeepers is an accomplished chef and professional cake decorator, so guests should expect something wonderful during the gourmet breakfast service. The innkeepers provide bicycles for those who wish to tour the area, and there is a spa on premises. The inn is often the site of weddings, parties and family reunions.

Innkeeper(s): Jim & Stephanie D'Amour. $85-95. PC TC. 5 rooms. Types of meals: gourmet breakfast and early coffee/tea. Beds: KD. Phone in room. Spa and bicycles on premises. Weddings and family reunions hosted. Antiques, fishing and shopping nearby.

Location: Five miles east of Exit 47E on I-91, 1 block south of Rt. 190.

"We loved staying here! You are both delightful. P.S. We slept like a log."

Tolland B7

Tolland Inn

63 Tolland Green, PO Box 717
Tolland, CT 06084-3019
(860)872-0800 Fax:(860)870-7958

Circa 1790. This late 18th-century colonial is located on the historic village green. There are seven guest rooms and two suites. One features a fireplace, hot tub and sitting room while another offers a sitting room and hot tub. First-floor rooms offer both a hot tub and fireplace. There are three common rooms. The inn is decorated in antiques and hand-built furniture throughout. The innkeepers are a third-generation innkeeper and a fine furniture maker who's shop is at the inn. Guests are invited to enjoy a wonderful breakfast and afternoon tea by the fire. Convenient to UCONN, Old Sturbridge Village, Brimfield Antique Shows, Caprilands.

Innkeeper(s): Susan & Stephen Beeching. $70-130. MC VISA AX DC CB DS PC TC. TAC10. 7 rooms with PB, 2 with FP. 2 suites. 1 conference room. Breakfast and afternoon tea included in rates. Meals: full breakfast, gourmet breakfast and early coffee/tea. Beds: KQDT. TV, VCR, fax, spa and library on premises. Small meetings, family reunions and seminars hosted. Antiques, fishing, parks, shopping, cross-country skiing, sporting events, theater nearby.

Location: On the village green, one-half mile to exit 68 & I-84.

Publicity: *Journal Inquirer, Hartford Courant, Tolland County Times.*

"The rooms are very clean, the bed very comfortable, the food consistently excellent and the innkeepers very courteous."

Westbrook   F7

Talcott House

PO Box 1016
Westbrook, CT 06498-1016
(860)399-5020

Circa 1890. This restored Newport-style Georgian manor offers an ideal setting on Long Island Sound. From the expansive lawn, guests can enjoy the view as the sun sets over the Atlantic. The home is less than a mile from Pilots Point Marina. The suites all face the oceanfront; one boasts a private veranda. The inn is listed on the local historic register. The Mystic Seaport, Gillette Castle, Essex Village and the Essex Steam Train are among the area's attractions.

Innkeeper(s): Don Correll. $125-135. MC VISA. 4 rooms with PB, 3 with FP. 1 conference room. Breakfast included in rates. Types of meals: continental-plus breakfast and early coffee/tea. Beds: QD. Ceiling fan in room. TV on premises. Handicap access. Weddings, small meetings and family reunions hosted. Antiques, fishing, parks, shopping, theater and watersports nearby.

Westbrook Inn B&B

976 Boston Post Rd
Westbrook, CT 06498-1852
(860)399-4777 Fax:(860)399-8023

Circa 1876. A wraparound porch and flower gardens offer a gracious welcome to this Victorian inn. The innkeeper, an expert in restoring old houses and antiques, has filled the inn with French and American period antiques, handsome paintings and wall coverings. Home-baked breads accompany a variety of breakfast main dishes. Bike rides and walks to the beach are among guests' most popular activities.

Innkeeper(s): Glenn & Chris. $95-135. MC VISA DS PC TC. 4 rooms with PB, 1 with FP. 1 suite. Breakfast, afternoon tea and evening snack included in rates. Type of meal: gourmet breakfast. Banquet service, catered breakfast and room service available. Beds: QDT. Phone, air conditioning, turndown service and TV in room. VCR, fax, copier, bicycles and library on premises. Weddings, small meetings and family reunions hosted. Antiques, fishing, parks, shopping, sporting events, golf, theater and watersports nearby.

Westport   G3

The Inn at National Hall

2 Post Rd W
Westport, CT 06880-4203
(203)221-1351 (800)628-4255 Fax:(203)221-0276

Circa 1873. This exquisite inn is consistently named as one of the nation's best, and it is quite deserving of its four-star and five-diamond rating. The inn, which includes several unique portions, runs along the Saugatuck River and guests can meander by the water on the boardwalk. The renovation of this National Register gem cost upwards of $15 million, and the result is breathtaking. Rooms are masterfully appointed with the finest fabrics and furnishings. The Acorn Room is one stunning example. The walls are painted a deep red hue, and guests slumber atop a massive canopy bed enveloped in luxurious yellow fabrics. Even the conference room is filled with regal touches. Guests can have the European-style continental breakfast delivered to their room. There are ample amenities, valet and room service. During the cocktail hour, guests enjoy an open bar. Gourmet dinners can be enjoyed at the inn's restaurant. Westport's posh boutiques, art galleries and antique shops are a stone's throw away.

Innkeeper(s): Keith Halford. $225-625. MC VISA AX DC TC. TAC10. 15 rooms with PB, 1 with FP. 7 suites. 1 conference room. Breakfast included in rates. Types of meals: continental breakfast, continental-plus breakfast, full breakfast and early coffee/tea. Lunch and room service available. Restaurant on premises. Beds: KQT. Phone, air conditioning, turndown service, TV and VCR in room. Fax and copier on premises. Weddings, small meetings, family reunions and seminars hosted. Antiques, parks, shopping, theater and watersports nearby.

Publicity: *Architectural Digest, Country Inns.* Ratings: 4 Stars.

Woodbury   D3

Merryvale B&B

1204 Main St S
Woodbury, CT 06798-3804
(203)266-0800 Fax:(203)263-4479

Circa 1789. Merryvale, an elegant Colonial inn, is situated in a picturesque New England Village, known as an antique capitol of Connecticut. Guests can enjoy complimentary tea, coffee and biscuits throughout the day. A grand living room invites travelers to relax by the fireplace and enjoy a book from the extensive collection of classics and mysteries. During the week, guests enjoy an ample breakfast buffet and on weekends, the innkeepers prepare a Federal-style breakfast using historic, 18th-century recipes.

Historic Interest: American Indian Archaeology Institute (5 miles), Glebe House & Gardens (1.5 miles), Tapping Reeve House (first law school in U.S.) (12 miles), Bristol Clock & Watch Museum (15 minutes), Carousel Museum (15 minutes).

Innkeeper(s): Gary & Pat Ubaldi Nurnberger. $80-130. MC VISA AX DC. 4 rooms with PB. 2 suites. Breakfast included in rates. Type of meal: full breakfast. Beds: KQT. Phone, air conditioning and TV in room. Weddings, small meetings, family reunions and seminars hosted. Amusement parks, antiques, fishing, shopping, downhill skiing and cross-country skiing nearby.

Publicity: *Voices, Yankee Traveler, Hartford Courant, Newtown Bee.*

"Your hospitality will always be remembered."

Delaware

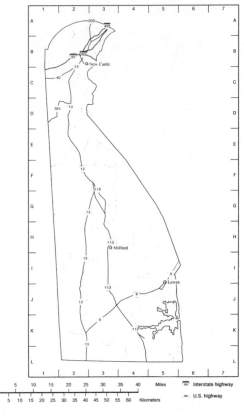

The Bay Moon B&B

128 Kings Hwy
Lewes, DE 19958-1418
(302)644-1802 (800)917-2307 Fax:(302)644-1802

Circa 1887. The exterior of this three-story, cedar Victorian features a front veranda shrouded by the flowers and foliage that also decorate the front walk. The custom-made, hand-crafted beds in the guest rooms are topped with feather pillows and down comforters. Cordials are placed in the room and there is a champagne turndown service is available. During a nightly cocktail hour, appetizers and wine are served. The innkeeper offers plenty of amenities. Beach supplies and an outdoor shower are helpful for guests who want to enjoy the ocean.

Historic Interest: Bay Moon is located in historic Lewes, Del., the first town in the first state.

Innkeeper(s): Laura Beth Kelly. $85-150. EP. MC VISA PC TC. 4 rooms with PB. 1 suite. Breakfast and evening snack included in rates. Meals: full breakfast and early coffee/tea. Beds: KQ. Phone, ceiling fan, TV, VCR in room. Fax, library on premises. Weddings, small meetings, family reunions hosted. Antiques, fishing, parks, shopping, sporting events, theater, watersports nearby.

Kings Inn

151 Kings Hwy
Lewes, DE 19958-1459
(302)645-6438
E-mail: prockett@juno.com

Circa 1888. This nine-bedroom Victorian features high ceilings, stained-glass windows and hardwood floors. The decor is eclectic.

A Jacuzzi tub for two, backyard wisteria arbor, enclosed porch and bicycles are offerings. Breakfast is served in the sunroom and usually includes freshly baked items such as cranberry nut bread or cinnamon scones. Lewes dates from 1631 and offers an interesting collection of historic houses and churches. The Cape May Ferry is here, as well as deep sea charters. One of the largest outlet malls in the United States is nearby.

Innkeeper(s): Patricia & Leon Rockett. $65-85. MC VISA DS PC TC. TAC10. 5 rooms, 3 with PB, 1 with FP. Breakfast included in rates. Types of meals: full breakfast and early coffee/tea. Beds: KQTD. Air conditioning and ceiling fan in room. TV, VCR, spa, sauna, bicycles, tennis, library and pet boarding on premises. Small meetings hosted. German, Spanish and French spoken. Amusement parks, antiques, fishing, parks, shopping, sporting events, golf, theater and watersports nearby. Pets Allowed.

Wild Swan Inn

525 Kings Hwy
Lewes, DE 19958-1421
(302)645-8550 Fax:(302)645-8550

Circa 1900. This Queen Anne Victorian is a whimsical sight, painted in pink with white, green and burgundy trim. The interior is dotted with antiques and dressed in Victorian style. A full, gourmet breakfast and freshly ground coffee are served each morning. The innkeepers have placed many musical treasures in their inn, including an early Edison phonograph and a Victrola. Michael often serenades guests on a 1912 player piano during breakfast. Lewes, which was founded in 1631, is the first town in the first state. Wild Swan is within walking distance of downtown where several fine restaurants await you.

Nearby Cape Henlopen State Park offers hiking and watersports, and the surrounding countryside is ideal for cycling and other outdoor activities. Listed in the National Trust for Historic Preservation, the inn was 3rd place winner in Jones Dairy Farm National Cooking Contest for B&B Inns.

Innkeeper(s): Michael & Hope Tyler. $85-135. PC TC. 3 rooms with PB. Breakfast and evening snack included in rates. Types of meals: gourmet breakfast and early coffee/tea. Beds: Q. Air conditioning and turndown service in room. Swimming, bicycles and library on premises. Antiques, fishing, parks, shopping, theater and watersports nearby.

Publicity: *Washington Post, Country Inns, Delaware Today, Country Collectible, Inn Spots & Special Places CNN Travel Guide.*

"The house is beautiful with lovely detailed pieces. Mike and Hope are gracious hosts. You'll sleep like a baby and wake up to a scrumptious breakfast and a great concert!"

Milford   H3

The Towers B&B

101 N W Front St
Milford, DE 19963-1022
(302)422-3814 (800)366-3814

Circa 1783. Once a simple colonial house, this ornate Steamboat Gothic fantasy features every imaginable Victorian architectural detail, all added in 1891. There are 10 distinct styles of gingerbread as well as towers, turrets, gables, porches and bays. Inside, chestnut and cherry woodwork, window seats and stained-glass windows are complemented with American and French antiques. The back garden boasts a gazebo, porch and swimming pool. Ask for the splendid Tower Room or Rapunzel Suite.

Historic Interest: Historic districts in Milford, town of Lewes, Dickinson Plantation, historic city of Dover.

Innkeeper(s): Daniel & Rhonda Bond. $95-125. MC VISA. TAC15. 6 rooms, 4 with PB. 2 suites. Breakfast included in rates. Beds: QD. Air conditioning and ceiling fan in room. Swimming on premises. Russian spoken. Antiques, fishing, parks, shopping, theater and watersports nearby.

Location: Historic district. A short drive to Delaware Bay & the Atlantic Ocean.

Publicity: *Washington Post, Baltimore Sun, Washingtonian, Mid-Atlantic Country.*

"I felt as if I were inside a beautiful Victorian Christmas card, surrounded by all the things Christmas should be."

New Castle   B2

Armitage Inn

2 The Strand
New Castle, DE 19720-4826
(302)328-6618 Fax:(302)324-1163

Circa 1732. The oldest portion of this historic home was constructed in the early 1730s, but the back wing may have been constructed in the 17th century. For centuries, the Armitage has been a place of elegance, and its current state as a country inn is no exception. Deluxe bed linens, fluffy towels, canopy beds and whirlpool tubs are just a few of the romantic amenities guests might find in their quarters. Gourmet coffee and teas

accompany the breakfasts of fruit, cereal, yogurt, homemade baked goods and a special entree.

Innkeeper(s): Stephen & Rina Marks. $105-175. MC VISA AX DS. TAC10. 5 rooms with PB, 3 with FP. Breakfast included in rates. Type of meal: gourmet breakfast. Beds: KQ. Phone, air conditioning, ceiling fan and TV in room. Fax, copier, tennis and library on premises. Weddings, small meetings and family reunions hosted. Amusement parks, antiques, fishing, parks, shopping and theater nearby.

"I could not have dreamed of a lovelier place to wake up on Christmas morning."

Terry House B&B

130 Delaware St
New Castle, DE 19720-4814
(302)322-2505 Fax:(302)328-1987

Circa 1860. In the center of the historic area, the Terry House is a three-and-a-half-story brick Federal townhouse with long double verandas, overlooking a half acre of beautifully landscaped back gardens that slope down to Battery Park which fronts on the Delaware River. Inside the inn, frieze work, ornately carved woodwork and red pine floors are elegantly set off with Oriental rugs, period antiques and paintings. Guest rooms look out to the park or onto Market Square or the Court House. Breakfast casseroles, breads and fruit are served in the dining room. New Castle was surveyed by Peter Stuyvesant in 1651 and William Penn landed here in 1682. Museums and gardens are abundant and include Longwood Gardens, Winterthur Museum, Brandywine River Museum, and Nemour Mansion and Gardens.

Innkeeper(s): Greg & Margaret Bell, Evelyn Weston. $60-98. MC VISA PC TC. 4 rooms with PB. Breakfast included in rates. Type of meal: continental-plus breakfast. Beds: QT. Phone, air conditioning and TV in room. Fax on premises. Weddings and small meetings hosted. Antiques, parks, sporting events and golf nearby.

William Penn Guest House

206 Delaware St
New Castle, DE 19720-4816
(302)328-7736

Circa 1682. William Penn slept here. In fact, his host Arnoldus de LaGrange witnessed the ceremony in which Penn gained possession of the Three Lower Colonies. Mrs. Burwell, who lived next door to the historic house, "gained possession" of the house one day about 44 years ago while her husband was away. After recovering from his wife's surprise purchase, Mr. Burwell rolled up his sleeves and began restoring the house. Guests may stay in the very room slept in by Penn.

Innkeeper(s): Irma & Richard Burwell. $60-85. MC VISA. 4 rooms, 1 with PB. Type of meal: continental breakfast. Beds: KDT. Phone in room.

Publicity: *Asbury Press.*

"An enjoyable stay, as usual. We'll return in the spring."

Florida

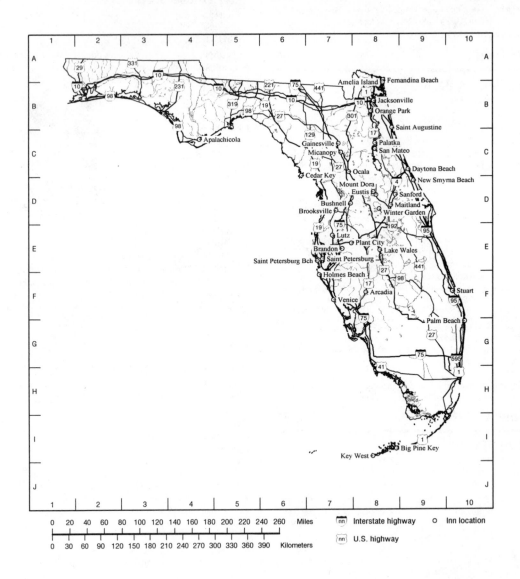

Amelia Island B8

Addison House

614 Ash St
Amelia Island, FL 32034-3933
(904)277-1604 (800)943-1604 Fax:(904)277-8124

Circa 1876. Located in the historic district, this 19th-century Victorian offers guests a comfortable romantic retreat to relax and enjoy the cool ocean breezes. Elegant furnishings highlight the five spacious guest rooms in the main house. The Garden House and Coulter Cottage surrounding the courtyard feature rooms with whirlpools and private porches. Guests will enjoy the inn's fountains and well-manicured secret gardens. A full breakfast and afternoon snack is offered in the dining room or porches. Picnic lunches are available. Located minutes from the ocean, golf, sailing, fishing and hiking.

Innkeeper(s): John, Donna & Jennifer Gibson. $95-175. MC VISA PC. TAC10. 5 rooms with PB, 4 with FP. 1 conference room. Breakfast, afternoon tea and evening snack included in rates. Type of meal: full breakfast. Picnic lunch available. Beds: KQT. Phone, air conditioning, ceiling fan, TV and VCR in room. Fax on premises. Handicap access. Weddings, small meetings, family reunions and seminars hosted. Spanish spoken. Antiques, fishing, parks, shopping, golf, theater and watersports nearby.

"Wow! You exceeded our expectations!"

Amelia Island Williams House

103 S 9th St
Amelia Island, FL 32034-3616
(904)277-2328 (800)414-9257 Fax:(904)321-1325

Circa 1856. It's not this grand Antebellum mansion's first owner, but its second for whom the house is named. Marcellus Williams and his wife, a great-great-granddaughter of the King of Spain, are its most esteemed residents. Among their many influential guests, the two once hosted Jefferson Davis. Ironically, the couple used part of the home for the Underground Railroad. It will be hard for guests to believe that the home was anything but opulent. The innkeepers painstakingly restored the home and the result is fabulous. Antiques from nine different countries decorate the home. The guest rooms are romantic; the gourmet breakfast served on the finest china; and the lush, fragrant grounds are shaded by a 500-year-old oak tree. The innkeepers also have restored the historic home next door, which was used as an infirmary during the Civil War. Four of the guest rooms are housed here, complete with clawfoot or Jacuzzi tubs.

Innkeeper(s): Dick Flitz & Chris Carter. $135-175. MC VISA PC. TAC10. 8 rooms with PB, 5 with FP. 2 suites. Breakfast and afternoon tea included in rates. Type of meal: gourmet breakfast. Beds: KT. Phone, air conditioning, turndown service, ceiling fan, TV and VCR in room. Fax, copier and bicycles on premises. Handicap access. Family reunions hosted. Antiques, fishing, parks, shopping, sporting events, golf, theater and watersports nearby.

Publicity: *Country Inns, Southern Living, Southern Accents, Victoria, Veranda, Palm Beach Life.*

Elizabeth Pointe Lodge

98 S Fletcher Ave
Amelia Island, FL 32034-2216
(904)277-4851 (800)772-3359 Fax:(904)277-6500

Circa 1991. Situated directly on the ocean, this newly constructed inn is in an 1890s Nantucket shingle-style design. Guest rooms feature king-size beds and oversized tubs. Several rooms have private whirlpools. Lemonade is served on the porch, which is filled with rockers for viewing the sea and its treasures of pelicans, dolphins and sea birds. Touring bikes, beach equipment and airport pickup are available.

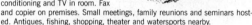

Innkeeper(s): David & Susan Caples. $125-215. MC VISA AX DS. 25 rooms with PB. 2 suites. 1 conference room. Breakfast included in rates. Picnic lunch, lunch, catering service and room service available. Beds: KQ. Phone, air conditioning and TV in room. Fax and copier on premises. Small meetings, family reunions and seminars hosted. Antiques, fishing, shopping, theater and watersports nearby.

Location: Oceanfront on Barrier Island.

Publicity: *Money, Country, Ladies Home Journal, Florida Living, Elegant Bride, United Air's Hemispheres, Brides, Travel Holiday, Hideaways.*

"The innkeeper's labor of love is evident in every detail. Outstanding. Superb accommodations and service."

The Fairbanks House

227 S 7th St
Amelia Island, FL 32034-3924
(904)277-0500 (800)261-4838 Fax:(904)277-3103
E-mail: fairbanks@net-magic.net

Circa 1885. The living and dining room fireplace tiles of this Italianate-style mansion bring to life scenes from Shakespeare's works and "Aesop's Fables." Other features include polished hardwood floors, intricately carved moldings and eight other fireplaces that grace spacious rooms. Each of the guest rooms is furnished with a four-poster or canopied king, queen or twin bed, Jacuzzi and clawfoot tubs or showers. Guests can step outside to enjoy an inviting courtyard, swimming pool and gardens bursting with roses, palms and magnolias. The Fairbanks was named one of the "Top 10 Luxury Inns In America" by Country Inns Magazine.

Innkeeper(s): Nelson & Mary Smelker. $110-200. EP. MC VISA AX DS. TAC10. 12 rooms with PB, 9 with FP. 3 suites. 3 cottages. 1 conference room. Breakfast included in rates. Meals: gourmet breakfast, early coffee/tea. Picnic lunch available. Beds: KQT. Phone, air conditioning, ceiling fan and TV in room. VCR, fax, copier, swimming, bicycles on premises. Handicap access. Weddings, small meetings and seminars hosted. Amusement parks, antiques, fishing, parks, shopping, sporting events, theater, watersports nearby.

Publicity: *Amelia Now, Islander, Country Inns, Florida Living, New York Times.*

Florida House Inn

PO Box 688, 22 S 3rd St
Amelia Island, FL 32034-4207
(904)261-3300 (800)258-3301 Fax:(904)277-3831
E-mail: inkeepers@floridahouseinn.com

Circa 1857. Located in the heart of a 50-block historic National Register area, the Florida House Inn is thought to be the oldest continuously operating tourist hotel in Florida. Recently renovated, the inn features a small pub, a guest parlor, a library and a New Orleans-style courtyard in which guests may enjoy the shade of 200-year-old oaks. Rooms are decorated with country pine and oak antiques, cheerful handmade rugs and quilts. The Carnegies, Rockefellers and Ulysses S. Grant have been guests.

Innkeeper(s): Bob & Karen Warner. $70-130. MC VISA AX. 15 rooms with PB, 10 with FP. 1 suite. 1 conference room. Breakfast included in rates.

Types of meals: full breakfast and early coffee/tea. Dinner, picnic lunch, lunch and catering service available. Restaurant on premises. Beds: KQT. Phone, air conditioning, ceiling fan and TV in room. Fax and copier on premises. Handicap access. Small meetings, family reunions and seminars hosted. Antiques, fishing, sporting events and theater nearby.

Publicity: *Amelia Now, Tampa Tribune, Miami Herald, Toronto Star, Country Living, Ft. Lauderdale Sun Sentinel.*

Hoyt House B&B

804 Atlantic Ave
Amelia Island, FL 32034-3629
(904)277-4300 (800)432-2085 Fax:(904)277-9626
E-mail: hoythouse@net-magic.net

Circa 1905. A wraparound veranda welcomes guests to this three-story, yellow Victorian. Trimmed in blue and white and shaded by large trees, the house is in the National Register. Exuberant color schemes accent the interior architectural features. There are heart-pine floors, handsome woodwork and carved fireplace mantels. Breakfast is served in the lavender and teal dining room under the crystal chandelier. A garden gazebo surrounded by white azaleas boasts a porch swing and old school bell.

Innkeeper(s): Rita & John Kovacevich. $79-139. MC VISA AX DS PC TC. TAC10. 9 rooms with PB, 3 with FP. 1 conference room. Breakfast included in rates. Types of meals: full breakfast, gourmet breakfast and early coffee/tea. Afternoon tea, picnic lunch, gourmet lunch, banquet service, catering service and catered breakfast available. Beds: KQDT. Phone, air conditioning, turndown service, ceiling fan and TV in room. VCR, fax, copier and bicycles on premises. Handicap access. Weddings, small meetings, family reunions and seminars hosted. Amusement parks, antiques, fishing, parks, shopping, sporting events, golf, theater and watersports nearby.

Apalachicola   C4

The Coombs House Inn

80 6th St
Apalachicola, FL 32320-1750
(850)653-9199

Circa 1905. This Victorian manor was built for James N. Coombs, a wealthy lumber baron who served in the Union Army. Despite his Yankee roots, Coombs was an influential figure in Apalachicola. The home has been lovingly restored to reflect its previous grandeur. Co-owner Lynn Wilson is a renown interior designer and her talents accent the inn's high ceilings, tiled fireplaces and period antiques. Bright English fabrics decorate windows and Oriental rugs accentuate the hardwood floors.

Historic Interest: The inn is close to a variety of historic attractions, including the Raney Home, Trinity Church, Gorrie Museum and Chestnut Hill Cemetery.

Innkeeper(s): Marilyn & Charlie Schubert. $89-129. MC VISA AX PC TC. 18 rooms with PB. 3 suites. 1 conference room. Breakfast included in rates. Types of meals: continental breakfast and early coffee/tea. Catering service available. Beds: KQDT. Phone, air conditioning, ceiling fan and TV in room. Fax, copier and bicycles on premises. Handicap access. Weddings, small meetings, family reunions and seminars hosted. German spoken. Antiques, fishing, parks, shopping and watersports nearby.

Pets Allowed: With prior arrangements.

Arcadia   F8

Historic Parker House

427 W Hickory St
Arcadia, FL 34266-3703
(941)494-2499 (800)969-2499

Circa 1895. Period antiques, including a wonderful clock collection, grace the interior of this turn-of-the-century home, which was built by a local cattle baron. Along with two charm-

ing rooms and a bright, "yellow" suite, innkeepers Shelly and Bob Baumann added the spacious Blue Room, which offers a white iron and brass bed and clawfoot bathtub. An expanded continental breakfast with pastries, fresh fruits, cereals, muffins and a variety of beverages is offered each morning, and afternoon teas can be prepared on request.

Historic Interest: The home, listed in the National Register, is within walking distance of downtown Arcadia with more than 350 buildings on the register.

Innkeeper(s): Bob & Shelly Baumann. $60-75. MC VISA AX TC. 4 rooms, 2 with PB, 2 with FP. 1 conference room. Breakfast and afternoon tea included in rates. Types of meals: continental-plus breakfast and early coffee/tea. Room service available. Beds: QDT. Phone, air conditioning, ceiling fan and TV in room. Small meetings and family reunions hosted. Antiques, fishing, parks, shopping and watersports nearby.

Publicity: *Tampa Tribune, Desoto Sun Herald, Florida Travel & Life, Miami Herald (Palm Beach Edition), WINK-TV News.*

Sandusky Manor B&B

606 E Oak St
Arcadia, FL 34266-4630
(941)494-7338 (800)348-5057 Fax:(941)494-2372
E-mail: d-ccoc@desoto.net

Circa 1913. This bungalow is named for its first resident, Carl Sandusky. The interior is comfortable and eclectic. There are collectibles, photographs, quilts, lanterns and old clocks throughout. Breakfasts with freshly baked biscuits, sweet rolls, fruit and egg dishes are served in the dining room or on the front porch. In the evenings, the innkeepers serve coffee, tea and dessert. Antique shops in historic downtown Arcadia, swamp buggy tours, golf and horseback riding are among the area attractions.

Innkeeper(s): Wayne & Judy Haligus. $65-75. AP. MC VISA AX DC DS TC. 5 rooms, 3 with PB. Breakfast and evening snack included in rates. Types of meals: full breakfast and early coffee/tea. Dinner, picnic lunch and lunch available. Beds: KQDT. Phone, air conditioning, ceiling fan and VCR in room. Fax, bicycles and child care on premises. Weddings, small meetings and family reunions hosted. Antiques, fishing, shopping and golf nearby.

"The Southern hospitality you provided was to die for!"

Big Pine Key   I8

Deer Run B&B on The Atlantic

PO Box 431, Long Beach Dr
Big Pine Key, FL 33043
(305)872-2015 Fax:(305)872-2842
E-mail: deerrunbb@aol.com

Circa 1984. Located oceanfront, this Florida Cracker-Style house is decorated in a tropical flavor with light colors, wicker, rattan, watercolors and Bahama fans. Guest rooms offer French doors opening to ocean views. Homemade biscuits and egg dishes are served on the inn's wide veranda, in full view of the ocean. There's a seaside spa, a perfect spot from which to see one of the Key deer that walk along the beach. Guests enjoy water sports such as diving and taking advantage of local boat charters for fishing the Gulfstream.

Innkeeper(s): Sue Abbott. $85-135. PC TC. TAC10. 3 rooms with PB. 1 suite. Breakfast included in rates. Meals: full breakfast and early coffee/tea. Beds: KQ. Air conditioning, ceiling fan, TV in room. Spa, swimming and bicycles on premises. Fishing, parks, shopping, golf, theater, watersports nearby. Publicity: *Soundings.*

"The beautiful view, the lovely breezes, the peacefulness and the adorable key deer will never be forgotten."

Brandon   E7

Behind The Fence B&B Inn

1400 Viola Dr at Countryside
Brandon, FL 33511-7327
(813)685-8201 (800)448-2672

Circa 1976. Experience the charm of New England on
Florida's west coast at this secluded country inn surrounded
by tall pines and oaks. Although the frame of the home was
built in the mid-1970s, the innkeepers searched Hillsborough
County for 19th-century and turn-of-the-century artifacts,
including old stairs, doors, windows, a pantry and the back
porch. Guests can stay either in the main house or in a two-
bedroom cottage. All rooms are filled with antique Amish-
county furniture. The innkeepers serve fresh popcorn on cool
nights in front of the fireplace. Breakfast includes fresh fruit,
cereals, juices, coffees and delicious Amish sweet rolls.

Historic Interest: The inn is a short distance from historic Ybor City, known
as Tampa's second city.

Innkeeper(s): Larry & Carolyn Yoss. $59-79. PC TC. TAC7. 5 rooms, 3 with
PB. 1 suite. 1 cottage. 1 conference room. Breakfast, afternoon tea and
evening snack included in rates. Meals: continental-plus breakfast and early
coffee/tea. Beds: DT. Phone, air conditioning, TV, VCR in room. Swimming on
premises. Small meetings and seminars hosted. Amusement parks, antiques,
fishing, parks, shopping, sporting events, theater and watersports nearby.

Publicity: *Brandon News, Travel Host, Country Living.*

"One of the best kept secrets in all of Tampa! Thanks again!"

Brooksville   D7

Verona House

201 S Main St
Brooksville, FL 34601-3337
(352)796-4001 (800)355-6717 Fax:(352)799-0612
E-mail: veronabb@gate.net

Circa 1925. In the 1920s, the Verona was one of several styles
of homes available to buyers through the Sears-Roebuck catalog. This inn arrived by train along with an instruction book.
Obviously, its builder follow the directions, and now guests
enjoy this charming Dutch Colonial. There are four rooms
inside the house, and the innkeepers also offer a cottage with a
kitchen and covered deck. Antique shopping and many outdoor activities are all nearby.

Innkeeper(s): Bob & Jan Boyd. $55-80. MC VISA AX DS PC TC. TAC10. 4
rooms with PB. 1 cottage. Breakfast and afternoon tea included in rates.
Types of meals: continental breakfast, continental-plus breakfast, full breakfast and early coffee/tea. Room service available. Beds: QT. Air conditioning
and ceiling fan in room. VCR, fax, copier and spa on premises. Handicap
access. Weddings, small meetings and family reunions hosted. Antiques, fishing, parks, shopping, golf, theater and watersports nearby.

Bushnell   D7

Veranda House B&B

202 W Noble Ave
Bushnell, FL 33513-5414
(352)793-3579

Circa 1888. For innkeepers Barbara and Bill Pownall, this inn
was love at first sight. The two spent thousands of long hours
restoring their Queen Anne gem back to period condition, and
because of their work, the home is now listed in the National
Register. Verandas wrap around the two stories, giving the

home an almost riverboat-like appearance. There are just two
rooms available, decorated with antiques. Bushnell is close to
many attractions, from the Webster Flea Market to antique
shops in Dade City or enjoying nearby rivers and lakes.

Innkeeper(s): Barbara & Bill Pownall. $68. PC TC. 2 rooms, 2 with FP.
Breakfast included in rates. Types of meals: continental-plus breakfast and
early coffee/tea. Afternoon tea and dinner available. Beds: KT. Air conditioning and ceiling fan in room. TV, VCR and bicycles on premises. Weddings,
small meetings and family reunions hosted. German spoken. Antiques, fishing, parks and golf nearby.

Publicity: *Sumter County Then & Now, Sumter County Times.*

"Our guardian angels led us to your heavenly abode."

Cedar Key   C6

Island Hotel

2nd & B St
Cedar Key, FL 32625
(352)543-5111 (800)432-4640
E-mail: ishotel@gnv.fdt.net

Circa 1859. The history of Island Hotel begins at about the same
time as the history of Cedar Key. The hotel is constructed for
seashell tabby with oak supports. Its walls have withstood wind
and weather for 150 years and its sloping
wooden floors have survived the
passage of innumerable feet.
Current innkeepers Dawn and
Tony Cousins have worked to
restore the home's traditional
charm. Some rooms boast views of the Gulf or Back
Bayou. All rooms include access to the inn's balcony, an ideal
spot for relaxation. A gourmet seafood restaurant is located on the
premises promising a delightful array of local catch.

Historic Interest: 1859 building has original murals from 1915 and 1948.

Innkeeper(s): Dawn & Tony Cousins. $75-110. MC VISA DS TC. 13 rooms
with PB. Breakfast included in rates. Types of meals: full breakfast and
gourmet breakfast. Restaurant on premises. Beds: KQD. Air conditioning and
ceiling fan in room. Weddings, small meetings, family reunions and seminars
hosted. Antiques, fishing, parks, sporting events and watersports nearby.

*"A delight! Ernst Hemmingwayish or Humphery Bogartish - what
atmosphere!"*

Daytona Beach   C9

Live Oak Inn

444 S Beach St
Daytona Beach, FL 32114-5004
(904)252-4667 (800)881-4667 Fax:(904)239-0068

Circa 1871. Overlooking the Halifax Harbor Marina, the inn is
actually two carefully restored homes joined by a large deck.
Both listed on the National Register of Historic Places, they
originally stand where Mathias Day founded Daytona. Each of
the inn's 12 rooms is decorated in memorabilia and furnishings significant to Florida's history. The inn is located one mile
from the beach.

Innkeeper(s): Jessie & Del Glock. $80-200. MC VISA PC TC. TAC10. 12
rooms with PB. Breakfast and afternoon tea included in rates. Types of
meals: continental-plus breakfast and early coffee/tea. Restaurant on premises. Beds: KQD. Phone, air conditioning, ceiling fan, TV and VCR in room.
Fax, copier and library on premises. Weddings, small meetings and family
reunions hosted. Japanese spoken. Amusement parks, antiques, fishing,
parks, shopping, sporting events, golf and watersports nearby.

The Villa

801 N Peninsula Dr
Daytona Beach, FL 32118-3724
(904)248-2020 Fax:(904)248-2020

Circa 1926. This Spanish Revival manor is listed in the National Register of Historic Places and is located within walking distance of the beach. The acre-and-a-half grounds are tropical, highlighted by soaring palm trees. The interior boasts many original elements, as well as stenciled ceilings and artwork. Rooms, with names such as the Queen Isabella and Christopher Columbus, honor the state's history of Spanish exploration. Within an hour of Daytona Beach, guests can reach Orlando, St. Augustine and Cape Canaveral or stay and explore Daytona, which offers plenty of shopping and restaurants, as well as the ocean.

Innkeeper(s): Jim Camp. $60-250. AP. MC VISA AX TC. TAC10. 4 rooms with PB. Breakfast included in rates. Types of meals: continental-plus breakfast and early coffee/tea. Beds: KQ. Air conditioning, ceiling fan and TV in room. VCR, fax, copier, spa and swimming on premises. Weddings, small meetings and family reunions hosted. Antiques, fishing, parks, shopping, sporting events, golf, theater and watersports nearby.

Eustis

D8

Dreamspinner Historic Moses Taylor Home

117 Deidrich St
Eustis, FL 32726-4322
(352)589-8082 (888)474-1229 Fax:(352)589-8860

Original black onyx fireplaces, a wraparound porch and candlelight dinners are a few of the reasons guests return to this white-shuttered Victorian. Situated on more than an acre, the inn's surrounding gardens feature antique roses, camellias, azaleas, benches and ponds shaded by romantic moss-covered oaks. The

wide, spacious lawn is perfect for an afternoon game of croquet. Each guest room is individually decorated with antiques, English fabrics, fireplaces and fresh flowers. Breakfast fare includes Confetti Quiche, baked sausage links, banana waffles with maple pecan syrup, scalloped apples or creole-diced potatoes. Mystery weekends are available.

Historic Interest: Moses Taylor, who built the home, was the first town clerk of Eustis.

Innkeeper(s): Jeano & Lee Broome. $95-115. PC TC. TAC10. 5 rooms, 4 with PB, 2 with FP. Breakfast and afternoon tea included in rates. Types of meals: gourmet breakfast and early coffee/tea. Beds: QT. Turndown service and ceiling fan in room. TV, VCR, fax and bicycles on premises. Weddings, small meetings, family reunions and seminars hosted. Amusement parks, antiques, fishing, parks, shopping, golf, theater and watersports nearby.

Publicity: *Orlando/Lake Sentinel.*

Fernandina Beach

A8

Bailey House

28 S 7th St
Fernandina Beach, FL 32034-3960
(904)261-5390 (800)251-5390 Fax:(904)321-0103

Circa 1895. This elegant Queen Anne Victorian was a wedding present that steamship agent Effingham W. Bailey gave to his bride. He shocked the locals by spending the enormous sum of $10,000 to build the house with all its towers, turrets, gables and verandas. The parlor and dining room open to a fireplace in a reception hall with the inscription "Hearth Hall - Welcome All." A spirit of hospitality has reigned in this home from its beginning.

Historic Interest: The historic seaport is within walking distance, Fort Clinch (2 miles).

Innkeeper(s): Tom & Jenny Bishop. $95-135. AP. MC VISA AX PC. TAC10. 9 rooms with PB, 7 with FP. Breakfast included in rates. Type of meal: full breakfast. Beds: KQD. Air conditioning, ceiling fan and TV in room. Fax, copier and bicycles on premises. Handicap access. Weddings hosted. Antiques, fishing, parks, shopping and watersports nearby.

Location: In historic district on Amelia Island.

Publicity: *Innsider, Southern Living, Victorian Homes, Saint Petersburg Times, Jacksonville.*

"Well, here we are back at Mickey Mouse land. I think we prefer the lovely Bailey House!"

Gainesville

C7

Magnolia Plantation

309 SE 7th St
Gainesville, FL 32601-6831
(352)375-6653 Fax:(352)338-0303

Circa 1885. This restored French Second Empire Victorian is in the National Register. Magnolia trees surround the house. Six guest rooms are filled with family heirlooms. All bathrooms feature clawfoot tubs and candles. Guests may enjoy the gardens, reflecting pool with waterfalls and gazebo.

Bicycles are also available. Evening wine and snacks are included. The inn is two miles from the University of Florida.

Innkeeper(s): Joe & Cindy Montalto. $75-125. AP. MC VISA AX. TAC10. 5 rooms with PB, 5 with FP. 1 cottage. Breakfast, afternoon tea and evening snack included in rates. Types of meals: full breakfast and early coffee/tea. Beds: Q. Air conditioning, turndown service and ceiling fan in room. TV, VCR, fax, bicycles and library on premises. Antiques, parks, shopping, sporting events and theater nearby.

"This has been a charming, once-in-a-lifetime experience."

Holmes Beach   F7

Harrington House Beachfront B&B Inn

5626 Gulf Dr N
Holmes Beach, FL 34217-1666
(941)778-5444 Fax:(941)778-0527

Circa 1925. A mere 40 feet from the water, this gracious home is set among pine trees and palms. Constructed of 14-inch-thick coquina blocks, the house features a living room with a 20-foot-high beamed ceiling, fireplace, '20s wallpaper and French doors. Many of the guest rooms have four-poster beds, antique wicker furnishings and French doors opening onto a deck overlooking the swimming pool and Gulf of Mexico. Kayaks are available for dolphin watching.

Innkeeper(s): Jo & Frank Davis. $109-225. MC VISA. 13 rooms with PB. Breakfast included in rates. Meal: full breakfast. Beds: KQDT. Phone, air conditioning, ceiling fan, TV, VCR in room. Handicap access. Weddings, small meetings, family reunions, seminars hosted. Amusement parks, antiques, fishing, shopping, sporting events, theater and watersports nearby.
Publicity: *Sarasota Herald Tribune, Island Sun, Palm Beach Post, Tampa Tribune, Glamour, Atlantic Monthly, Southern Living.*

"Elegant house and hospitality."

Jacksonville   B8

House on Cherry St

1844 Cherry St
Jacksonville, FL 32205-8702
(904)384-1999 Fax:(904)384-5013
E-mail: houseoncherry@compuserve.com

Circa 1909. Seasonal blooms fill the pots that line the circular entry stairs to this Federal-style house on tree-lined Cherry Street. It was moved in two pieces to its present site on St. Johns River in the historic Riverside area. Traditionally decorated rooms include antiques, collections of hand-carved decoy ducks and old clocks that chime and tick. Most rooms overlook the river. A canoe and kayak are available for guest use. Your hosts are a social worker and family doctor.
Innkeeper(s): Carol Anderson. $85. MC VISA AX PC TC. TAC10. 4 suites. Breakfast and evening snack included in rates. Meal: continental breakfast. Beds: QT. Phone, air conditioning, ceiling fan in room. TV, VCR, fax, copier on premises. Small meetings, family reunions, seminars hosted. Antiques, fishing, parks, shopping, sporting events, theater, watersports nearby.
Location: Historic Avondale.
Publicity: *Florida Wayfarer, Tampa Tribune, New York Times.*

Key West   I8

Blue Parrot Inn

916 Elizabeth St
Key West, FL 33040-6406
(305)296-0033 (800)231-2473

Circa 1884. This Bahamian-style inn is decorated in a pleasing, tropical style. The grounds are lush and peaceful. Continental-plus breakfasts of fresh fruit, bagels, muffins and quiche are served poolside. There is plenty of space around the pool to relax and tan, but for those who prefer, the innkeepers also offer a private, clothing-optional sun deck. The inn is located in a historic neighborhood and is near shops and restaurants. The ocean is just a few blocks away.
Innkeeper(s): Larry Rhinard & Frank Yaccino. $70-165. MC VISA AX DC CB DS TC. TAC10. 10 rooms with PB. Breakfast included in rates. Type of meal: continental breakfast. Beds: QDT. Phone, air conditioning, ceiling fan and TV in room. Fax, copier, swimming and bicycles on premises. Handicap access. Weddings, small meetings and family reunions hosted. Antiques, fishing, parks, shopping, theater and watersports nearby.

Center Court-Historic Inn & Cottages

916 Center St
Key West, FL 33040
(305)296-9292 (800)797-8787 Fax:(305)294-4104
E-mail: centerct@aol

Circa 1873. The main house at Center Court was built by a ship's captain around 1873. Two circa 1880 cottages also are located on the property, and all three buildings are listed in the National Register. In all, guests can choose from four rooms in the main guest house and eight private cottages. The decor is modern with a tropical touch. Most of the cottages include a full or efficiency kitchen, and some have private decks or verandas. Several cottages can accommodate four guests. The Family House and Conch Cottage both accommodate up to six guests. There is a pool, Jacuzzi and exercise area for guest use.

Innkeeper(s): Naomi R. Van Steelandt. $88-298. MC VISA AX DS PC TC. TAC10. 14 rooms, 6 with PB. 8 cottages. Breakfast included in rates. Type of meal: continental-plus breakfast. Beds: KQD. Phone, air conditioning, ceiling fan, TV and VCR in room. Fax, copier, spa and swimming on premises. Weddings, small meetings and family reunions hosted. Antiques, fishing, parks, shopping, golf, theater and watersports nearby.
Pets Allowed: In cottages, $10 pet fee per night.
Publicity: *Town & Country, Florida Keys.*

"The insights you shared saved us time and expense, allowing us to make the most of our vacation."

Conch House Heritage Inn

625 Truman Ave
Key West, FL 33040-3233
(305)293-0020 (800)207-5806 Fax:(305)293-8447
E-mail: conchinn@conch.net

Circa 1889. This restored Victorian is located in a historic Key West neighborhood and is listed in the National Register. In 1895, the home was purchased by Lance and Herminia Lester, and it has remained in the family ever since. The inn is surrounded by a picturesque white picket fence. The interior is light, airy and elegant. Walls are painted in bright colors and the home has a spacious, uncluttered feel. Rooms are appointed with elegant antiques. The continental-plus breakfast includes locally made Cuban bread.
Innkeeper(s): W. Sam Holland Jr. $88-168. MC VISA AX DC DS PC TC. TAC10. 6 rooms with PB, 1 with FP. Breakfast included in rates. Type of meal: continental-plus breakfast. Beds: KQT. Phone, air conditioning, ceiling fan and TV in room. Fax, copier, swimming and bicycles on premises. Handicap access. Weddings and family reunions hosted. Spanish spoken. Antiques, fishing, parks, shopping, golf, theater and watersports nearby.

Duval House

815 Duval St
Key West, FL 33040-7405
(305)294-1666 (800)223-8825 Fax:(305)292-1701

Circa 1890. The Duval House's seven Victorian houses surround a garden and a swimming pool. French doors open onto the tropical gardens. Guests may relax on the balconies. Continental Plus breakfast is served in the pool lounge. Rooms have wicker and antique furniture and Bahamian fans.

Historic Interest: Hemingway House (1 block).

Innkeeper(s): Richard Kamradt. $80-260. MC VISA AX DC DS TC. TAC10. 25 rooms. 4 suites. Breakfast included in rates. Beds: QD. Phone, air conditioning and ceiling fan in room. Swimming on premises. Antiques, fishing, shopping and watersports nearby.
Publicity: Newsday, Palm Beach Post, Cleveland Plain-Dealer, Roanoke Times, Brides, Vacations.

"*You certainly will see us again.*"

Eden House

1015 Fleming St
Key West, FL 33040-6962
(305)296-6868 (800)533-5397 Fax:(305)294-1221
E-mail: mike@edenhouse.com

Circa 1924. This Art Deco hotel was once a hot spot for writers, intellectuals and European travelers. Innkeeper Mike Eden improved the home, adding a 10-person Jacuzzi, decks, gazebos, an elevated sundeck and hammocks. Ceiling fans and wicker furniture complete the tropical atmosphere found in each room. The home was the site for the Goldie Hawn movie, "Criss Cross."

Next door, Martin's Cafe boasts delicious cuisine by chef and owner Martin Busam. Breakfast is not included in the room price, but the restaurant offers gourmet entrees such as Shrimp Eggs Benedict and cinnamon coffee. For lunch and dinner, enjoy the "Island" and German-style cuisine. Guests are served cold refreshments upon arrival, and there is a complimentary happy hour.

Innkeeper(s): Mike Eden. $55-250. EP. MC VISA TC. 42 rooms, 26 with PB. 6 suites. Restaurant on premises. Beds: QDT. Air conditioning and ceiling fan in room. TV, fax, swimming and bicycles on premises. Fishing, shopping and watersports nearby. Pets Allowed: Restrictions apply.
Publicity: Chicago Tribune, Woman's Day, Southern Living, Miami Herald.

"*We feel lucky to have found such a relaxing place, and we look forward to returning.*"

Heron House

512 Simonton St
Key West, FL 33040-6832
(800)294-1644 Fax:(305)294-5692

Circa 1856. One of the oldest homes remaining in Key West,

this house is an early example of Conch architecture. The inn showcases many beautiful features, including hand-crafted woodwork, marble baths and stained-glass transoms. The orchid gardens add to the inn's beauty.

Innkeeper(s): Fred Geibelt. $99-268. MC VISA AX DC CB. 20 rooms. Breakfast included in rates. Type of meal: continental-plus breakfast. Beds: KQD. Phone in room.
Location: One block from Duval St. in center of Historic District.
Publicity: Sun Sentinel.

"*The common pool and garden area gave us the feeling that we were in a tropical paradise.*"

Island City House

411 William St
Key West, FL 33040-6853
(305)294-5702 (800)634-8230 Fax:(305)294-1289

Circa 1889. This house was built for a wealthy Charleston merchant who later converted it to a small hotel, anticipating the arrival of the railroad in 1912. Restored by two active preservationists, Island City House and Arch House provide suites in beautifully restored environs with turn-of-the-century decor. Private porches and ceiling fans are historical amenities that remain.

Innkeeper(s): Stanley & Janet Corneal. $95-210. MC VISA DC CB DS TC. TAC10. 24 suites. Breakfast included in rates. Type of meal: continental-plus breakfast. Beds: KQD. Phone, air conditioning, ceiling fan and TV in room. VCR, fax, copier, spa, swimming and bicycles on premises. Weddings hosted. Antiques, fishing, parks, shopping, theater and watersports nearby.
Publicity: Palm Beach Daily News, London Times, Miami Herald, Palm Beach Post.

"*We really enjoyed our stay and have decided we're going to visit the Keys every year and stay at our new-found 'home,' apartment #4.*"

Nassau House

1016 Fleming St
Key West, FL 33040-6908
(305)296-8513 (800)296-8513 Fax:(305)293-8423
E-mail: nassau@conch.net

Circa 1894. This century-old home, located in Key West's historic Old Town, has been completely restored. The grounds are beautifully landscaped and the area around the pool is a tropical delight. The porch is lined with wicker rockers and loveseats topped with pillows, and paddle fans provide added comfort. Guest rooms are elegant, yet comfortable with wicker and fine linens. The Treetop Suites also include living rooms and kitchens.

Innkeeper(s): Damon Leard. $75-200. MC VISA AX TC. TAC10. 9 rooms, 7 with PB. 2 suites. Breakfast and evening snack included in rates. Type of meal: continental-plus breakfast. Beds: KQD. Phone, air conditioning, ceiling fan and TV in room. VCR, fax, copier, spa, swimming, bicycles, library, pet boarding on premises. Handicap access. Weddings and small meetings hosted. German, Dutch spoken. Fishing, shopping, theater, watersports nearby. Pets Allowed: Small dogs only.

"*Our stay has been absolutely delightful!*"

The Popular House, Key West B&B

415 William St
Key West, FL 33040-6853
(305)296-7274 (800)438-6155 Fax:(305)293-0306

Circa 1890. This pink and white Victorian sits elegantly behind a white picket fence. It was constructed by shipbuilders with sturdy heart-pine walls and 13-foot ceilings. With two stories of porches, the inn is located in the center of the Historic District.

Innkeeper(s): Jody Carlson. $59-250. MC VISA AX DC CB DS PC TC. TAC10. 8 rooms, 4 with PB. 1 suite. Breakfast included in rates. Types of meals: continental-plus breakfast and early coffee/tea. Beds: KQDT. Air conditioning and ceiling fan in room. Fax, copier, spa, swimming, sauna, bicycles and library on premises. Weddings, small meetings, family reunions and seminars hosted. Antiques, fishing, shopping, theater and watersports nearby.

Location: Two blocks from the Gulf.

Publicity: *Palm Beach Life, South Florida, Food Arts, London House & Gardens, Conde Nast Traveler, New York Times.*

"*The essence of charming.*"

Seascape

420 Olivia St
Key West, FL 33040-7411
(305)296-7776 (800)765-6438 Fax:(305)296-7776

Circa 1889. This restored inn offers privacy among the hustle and bustle of Key West's Old Town. It features a tropical garden, heated pool-spa and sundecks. Bright, airy guest rooms

are filled with wicker and fresh flowers. Seascape offers close access to the Atlantic Ocean and the Gulf of Mexico and is within walking distance to restaurants and shops. Breakfast is served under the shade of the sapodilla tree on a private patio deck. As the sun sets, guests may join the hosts for the complimentary wine hour in season.

Innkeeper(s): Alan Melnick. $69-119. MC VISA AX DS. 5 rooms with PB. Breakfast included in rates. Type of meal: continental-plus breakfast. Beds: QT. Antiques, fishing, theater and watersports nearby.

Publicity: *New York Times.*

The Watson House

525 Simonton St
Key West, FL 33040-6872
(305)294-6712 (800)621-9405 Fax:(305)294-7501

Circa 1860. Purchased by an Ohio couple during the Civil War, this home was remodeled as a Bahamian-style home, ideal for its sub-tropical climate. In 1986, after two years of restoration, the house became the recipient of the Excellence in Rehabilitation award granted by the Historic Florida Keys Preservation Board. Guest apartments, featuring many modern amenities, also are available, and guests have access to a heated swimming pool, spa and sun decks.

Innkeeper(s): Joe Beres & Ed Czaplicki. $105-400. AP. MC VISA AX. 3 suites. Breakfast included in rates. Type of meal: continental-plus breakfast. Beds: KQD. Fax, copier and spa on premises. Antiques, fishing, theater and watersports nearby.

Publicity: *Travel South, Palm Beach Post, Country Inns, Washington Post.*

"*Our stay at the Watson House was a Christmas dream.*"

Westwinds

914 Eaton St
Key West, FL 33040-6923
(305)296-4440 (800)788-4150 Fax:(305)293-0931

Circa 1921. The verdant flora that surrounds this historic inn will make guests feel as though they have left the city and entered a tropical paradise. However, Westwinds is located in the historic seaport district of Old Town Key West, and shops, restaurants and galleries are just steps away. Wicker and bright floral prints decorate the guest rooms. The grounds include a pool and a waterfall.

Innkeeper(s): Ingrid Ford. $50-250. MC VISA AX DS TC. TAC10. 22 rooms, 20 with PB. 4 suites. Breakfast included in rates. Meal: continental-plus breakfast. Beds: KQD. Phone, air conditioning, ceiling fan in room. TV, fax, copier and swimming on premises. Weddings, small meetings, family reunions, seminars hosted. Antiques, fishing, shopping, golf, theater nearby.

Lake Wales E8

Chalet Suzanne Country Inn & Restaurant

3800 Chalet Suzanne Dr
Lake Wales, FL 33853-7060
(941)676-6011 (800)433-6011 Fax:(941)676-1814

Circa 1924. Situated on 70 acres adjacent to Lake Suzanne, this country inn's architecture includes gabled roofs, balconies, spires and steeples. The superb restaurant has a glowing reputation, and places of interest on the property include the Swiss Room, Wine Dungeon, Gift Boutique, Autograph Garden, Chapel Antiques, Ceramic Salon, Airstrip and the Soup Cannery. The inn has been transformed into a village of cottages and miniature chateaux, one connected to the other seemingly with no particular order.

Historic Interest: This wonderful inn is located in a National Historic District.

Innkeeper(s): Carl & Vita Hinshaw. $139-195. MC VISA AX DC CB DS TC. TAC10. 30 rooms with PB. Breakfast included in rates. Types of meals: full breakfast and early coffee/tea. Dinner, lunch and room service available. Restaurant on premises. Beds: KDT. Phone, air conditioning, ceiling fan and TV in room. VCR, fax, copier, swimming and library on premises. Handicap access. 70 acres. Weddings, small meetings, family reunions and seminars hosted. German spoken. Amusement parks, antiques, fishing, parks, shopping, sporting events, golf, theater and watersports nearby.

Location: Four miles north of Lake Wales. US Hwy 27 & Chalet Suzanne Rd.

Publicity: *Southern Living, Country Inns, National Geographic Traveler. Uncle Ben's 1992 award.*

"*I now know why everyone always says, 'Wow!' when they come up from dinner. Please don't change a thing.*"

Lutz E7

The White House B&B

20320 Mid Ct
Lutz, FL 33549-5116
(813)949-6079 (800)775-4166 Fax:(423)496-9778

Circa 1898. This Queen Anne Victorian boasts a wraparound porch with a swing. Rooms are decorated in traditional style with family antiques. Innkeepers pamper their guests with Tennessee hospitality, a hearty country breakfast and a mouth-watering sundae bar in the evenings. The innkeepers also help guests plan daily activities, and the area is bursting with possibilities. Hiking, horseback riding, panning for gold and driving tours are only a few choices. The Ocoee River is the perfect place for a river float trip or take on the challenge of roaring rapids. The river was selected as the site of the 1996 Summer Olympic Whitewater Slalom events.

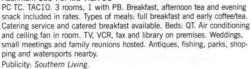

Historic Interest: The Ducktown Mining Museum is a popular local attraction. Fields of the Wood, a biblical theme park, is 20 minutes away and free of charge.

Innkeeper(s): Dan & Mardee Kauffman. $60-70. MC VISA DS PC TC. TAC10. 3 rooms, 1 with PB. Breakfast, afternoon tea and evening snack included in rates. Types of meals: full breakfast and early coffee/tea. Catering service and catered breakfast available. Beds: QT. Air conditioning and ceiling fan in room. TV, VCR, fax and library on premises. Weddings, small meetings and family reunions hosted. Antiques, fishing, parks, shopping and watersports nearby.
Publicity: *Southern Living.*

"We wanted a relaxing couple of days in the mountains and that's what we got. Thank you."

Maitland D8

Thurston House

851 Lake Ave
Maitland, FL 32751-6306
(407)539-1911 (800)843-2721 Fax:(407)539-0365
E-mail: jball54@aol.com

Circa 1885. Just minutes from busy Orlando and the many attractions found nearby, this classic Queen Anne Victorian inn boasts a lakefront, countryside setting. Two of the inn's screened porches provide views of Lake Eulalia. Two parlors provide additional relaxing spots, and many guests like to stroll the grounds, which feature fruit trees and several bountiful gardens.

Innkeeper(s): Carole Ballard. $100-110. MC VISA AX. TAC10. 4 rooms with PB. Breakfast and evening snack included in rates. Types of meals: continental-plus breakfast and early coffee/tea. Beds: Q. Phone, air conditioning and ceiling fan in room. TV, VCR, fax, copier and library on premises. Antiques, fishing, parks, shopping, sporting events and theater nearby.
Publicity: *Fort Lauderdale Sun Sentinel, Orlando Sentinel, Florida Living, Country Almanac.*

"Gracious hosts. What a jewel of a place. We couldn't have enjoyed ourselves more!"

Micanopy C7

Herlong Mansion

402 NE Cholokka Blvd, PO Box 667
Micanopy, FL 32667
(352)466-3322 (800)437-5664 Fax:(352)466-3322

Circa 1845. This mid-Victorian mansion features four two-story carved-wood Roman Corinthian columns on its veranda. The mansion is surrounded by a garden with statuesque old oak and pecan trees. Herlong Mansion features leaded-glass windows, mahogany inlaid oak floors, 12-foot ceilings and floor-to-ceiling windows in the dining room. Guest rooms have fireplaces and are furnished with antiques.

Historic Interest: St. Augustine is about one and one-half hours from the mansion. The Marjorie Kennan Rawlings Home is eight miles away. Micanopy is the oldest inland town in Florida, and has been the site for several movies.

Innkeeper(s): H.C. (Sonny) Howard, Jr. $50-170. MC VISA. TAC10. 12 rooms with PB, 6 with FP. 4 suites. 2 cottages. 1 conference room. Breakfast and evening snack included in rates. Types of meals: full breakfast and early coffee/tea. Catering service available. Beds: KQD. Air conditioning and ceiling fan in room. TV, VCR, fax, copier and bicycles on premises. Handicap access. Weddings, small meetings, family reunions and seminars hosted. Antiques, fishing, parks, sporting events and watersports nearby.
Publicity: *Country Inns, Travel & Leisure, National Geographic Traveler, Southern Living, Florida Living.*

Mount Dora D8

Lakeside Inn

100 N Alexander St
Mount Dora, FL 32757-5570
(352)383-4101 (800)556-5016 Fax:(352)735-2642

Circa 1883. A stay at the Lakeside Inn is like being transported back in time to a grand old hotel. The inn was a hot spot during the Roaring '20s and has served guests since its creation in 1883. Set on the water's edge, many of the historic hotel's guests enjoy simply taking in the view on the veranda while lounging in a rocker. The hotel offers tennis courts, a pool, lakefront rooms, water sports, boat

rentals, hot air ballooning, verandas and courtyard gardens. Gourmet chefs prepare delectable meals featuring an abundance of seasonal fare and a popular Sunday brunch. The Lakeside Inn hosts many special events and festivals, as well as tea dances and sunset cruises on Lake Dora. Only 25 miles from Orlando, the village of Mount Dora offers plenty of shops, galleries, flea markets and antiquing.

Historic Interest: The Lakeside Inn is listed in the National Register, and Mount Dora offers several museums, including the Royellou Museum, which is located in a former jail and firehouse.

$95-250. MC VISA AX DC DS TC. TAC10. 88 rooms with PB. 17 suites. 5 conference rooms. Breakfast included in rates. Meals: continental breakfast, continental-plus breakfast, full breakfast, gourmet breakfast and early coffee/tea. Afternoon tea, dinner, evening snack, picnic lunch, lunch, gourmet lunch, banquet service, catering service, catered breakfast and room service available. Restaurant on premises. Beds: KDT. Phone, air conditioning and TV in room. VCR, fax, copier, swimming, tennis, child care on premises. Handicap access. Weddings, small meetings, family reunions, seminars hosted. Dutch, German, French and Spanish spoken. Amusement parks, antiques, fishing, parks, shopping, sporting events, theater, watersports nearby.
Publicity: *Orvis, AAA World, AAA Going Places, USA Today, Orlando, Miami Herald.*

Magnolia Inn

347 E 3rd Ave
Mount Dora, FL 32757-5654
(352)735-3800 (800)776-2112 Fax:(352)735-0258

Circa 1926. This Mediterranean-style inn in Central Florida offers elegant accommodations to its guests, who will experience the Florida Boom furnishings of the 1920s. Guests will enjoy the convenience of early coffee or tea before sitting down to the inn's full breakfasts. Guests can take a soak in the inn's spa, relax in the hammock by the garden wall or swing beneath the magnolias. Lake Griffin State Recreational Area and Wekiwa Springs State Park are within easy driving distance. Just an hour from Disneyworld and the other Orlando major attractions, Mount Dora is the antique capital of Central Florida. Known as the Festival City, it is also recommended by "Money" Magazine as the best retirement location in Florida and is the site of Renninger's Winter Antique Extravaganzas. Romantic carriage rides and historic trolley tours of the downtown, two blocks from the inn, are available.

Innkeeper(s): Gerry & Lolita Johnson. $90-160. MC VISA AX PC TC. TAC10. 4 rooms with PB. Breakfast included in rates. Types of meals: full breakfast and early coffee/tea. Beds: KQT. Air conditioning and ceiling fan in room. TV, VCR, fax, copier and spa on premises. Weddings hosted. Amusement parks, antiques, fishing, parks, shopping, theater and watersports nearby.

Publicity: *Mount Dora Topic.*

"I love the way you pamper your guests."

New Smyrna Beach   D9

Night Swan Intracoastal B&B

512 S Riverside Dr
New Smyrna Beach, FL 32168-7345
(904)423-4940 (800)465-4261 Fax:(904)427-2814

Circa 1906. From the 140-foot dock at this waterside bed & breakfast, guests can gaze at stars, watch as ships pass or perhaps catch site of dolphins. The turn-of-the-century home is

decorated with period furnishings, including an antique baby grand piano, which guests are invited to use. Several guest rooms afford views of the Indian River, which is part of the Atlantic Intracoastal Waterway. The

innkeepers have created several special packages, featuring catered gourmet dinners, boat tours or romantic baskets with chocolate, wine and flowers.

Innkeeper(s): Martha & Chuck Nighswonger. $80-150. MC VISA AX DS PC TC. TAC10. 8 rooms with PB. 4 suites. 1 conference room. Breakfast and evening snack included in rates. Types of meals: full breakfast and early coffee/tea. Catering service available. Beds: KQ. Phone, air conditioning, ceiling fan and TV in room. Fax and library on premises. Weddings, small meetings, family reunions and seminars hosted. Antiques, fishing, parks, shopping, theater and watersports nearby.

Ocala   C7

Seven Sisters Inn

820 SE Fort King St
Ocala, FL 34471-2320
(352)867-1170 Fax:(352)867-5266
E-mail: sistersinn@aol.com

Circa 1888. This highly acclaimed Queen Anne-style Victorian is located in the heart of the town's historic district. In 1986, the house was judged ìBest Restoration Projectî in the state by Florida Trust Historic Preservation Society. Guests

may relax on the large covered porches or visit with other guests in the club room. A gourmet breakfast features a different entree daily, which include blueberry French bread, three-cheese stuffed French toast, egg pesto and raspberry-oatmeal pancakes.

Historic Interest: Marjorie Kinan Rawlings House, who authored "The Yearling," is 30 minutes away.

Innkeeper(s): Ken Oden & Bonnie Morehardt. $105-165. 8 rooms with PB, 3 with FP. 4 suites. 1 conference room. Breakfast, afternoon tea and evening snack included in rates. Types of meals: full breakfast, gourmet breakfast and early coffee/tea. Dinner and picnic lunch available. Beds: KQT. Phone, air conditioning, turndown service, ceiling fan and TV in room. Fax and copier on premises. Weddings, small meetings, family reunions and seminars hosted. Amusement parks, antiques, fishing, parks, shopping, sporting events, theater and watersports nearby.

Pets Allowed: Off grounds pet boarding available.

Publicity: *Southern Living Feature, Glamour, Conde Nast Traveler, Country Inns (one of twelve best).*

Orange Park   B8

The Club Continental Suites

2143 Astor St
Orange Park, FL 32073-5624
(904)264-6070 (800)877-6070 Fax:(904)264-4044

Circa 1923. This lavish waterfront estate was constructed for the Palmolive family and overlooks the St. Johns River. The architecture is Italian Renaissance with stucco and clay tile roof.

Formal grounds include gardens with fountains, giant oaks and an elegant courtyard. Riverfront views are enjoyed from several guest rooms. The French Room and The English Room are favorites. There are seven tennis courts, a marina and the pre-Civil War River House Pub, as well as the Club Continental Restaurant, a dinner club. A complimentary breakfast is served daily. Lunch is served Tuesday through Friday; brunch is available on Sunday.

Innkeeper(s): Caleb Massee & Karrie Stevens. $75-160. MC VISA AX DC PC TC. TAC10. 22 rooms with PB, 2 with FP. 4 suites. 2 conference rooms. Breakfast included in rates. Type of meal: continental breakfast. Dinner and gourmet lunch available. Beds: KQ. Phone, air conditioning, ceiling fan and TV in room. Fax, copier, swimming and tennis on premises. Weddings, small meetings, family reunions and seminars hosted. Antiques, fishing, parks, shopping, sporting events and theater nearby.

Pets Allowed: In two rooms only.

Location: On the St. Johns River, 20 miles to many Florida beaches and 30 miles to St. Augustine.

Publicity: *Miami Herald, Sun Sentinel, Tampa Tribune.*

"Superb dining with spectacular grounds."

Orlando (Winter Garden)   D8

Meadow Marsh B&B

940 Tildenville School Rd
Orlando (Winter Garden), FL 34787
(407)656-2064 (888)656-2064

Circa 1877. Meadow Marsh is located on 12 acres just outside the quiet village of Winter Garden, an Orlando suburb. One of the town's settlers built the Victorian manor, which is highlighted by verandas on the first and second stories. The home remained in

the original family until the 1980s. Today, guest rooms appear much as they probably did in the 19th century, filled with country Victorian pieces. However, there have been some pleasant additions, including whirlpool tubs in three of the guest rooms and cottage. A three-course breakfast is served daily. Guests will enjoy a variety of afternoon and evening treats. The innkeeper moved her gift shop and tea room to Meadow Marsh in late 1996. The tea room serves luncheons by reservation Wednesday through Saturday. The inn is a favorite spot for small weddings.

Innkeeper(s): Cavelle & John Pawlack. $95-199. MC VISA TC. TAC6. 5 rooms with PB, 1 with FP. 2 suites. 1 cottage. Breakfast and evening snack included in rates. Dinner, picnic lunch, lunch and catering service available. Beds: QD. Air conditioning, turndown service and ceiling fan in room. TV, VCR, fax, copier and library on premises. 12 acres. Amusement parks, antiques, parks, sporting events, theater and watersports nearby.

"What a beautiful home with such warm, gracious Southern hospitality."

Palatka
C8

Minute Maid Bed & Breakfast

220 Madison St
Palatka, FL 32177
(904)325-4547 Fax:(904)325-4547
E-mail: azalea0001@aol.com

Circa 1878. Located within the Palatka Historic District, this beautifully embellished Queen Anne Victorian, also known as the Azalea House, is yellow with green shutters. Bay windows, gables and verandas have discrete touches of royal blue, gold, white and aqua on the gingerbread trim, a true "Painted Lady." It sits on a green lawn graced with lavish perennial gardens, azaleas and camellias. There are oak, magnolia and palm trees and an 85-year-old, grafted camellia tree with both pink and white blossoms. Double parlors are furnished with period antiques including an arched, floor-to-ceiling mirror. A three-story heart and curly pine staircase leads to the guest rooms. Ask for the Camellia Room and you'll enjoy a king-size canopy bed draped in white gauze. Breakfast is served on fine china in the formal dining room or deck. Two blocks away is the mile-wide north flowing St. John's River. An unaltered golf course designed by Donald Ross in 1925 is nearby, as well as the Ravine State Botanical Garden.

Innkeeper(s): Bland Holland/Norman Gill. $55-95. MC VISA DS PC TC. TAC10. 4 rooms, 2 with PB. Breakfast included in rates. Meals: continental-plus breakfast and early coffee/tea. Evening snack, picnic lunch and catering service available. Beds: KQ. Phone, air conditioning and turndown service in room. TV, VCR, fax, spa and swimming on premises. Weddings, small meetings and family reunions hosted. Amusement parks, antiques, fishing, parks, shopping, sporting events, golf, theater and watersports nearby.
Publicity: *American Treasures.*

Palm Beach
G10

Plaza Inn

215 Brazilian Ave
Palm Beach, FL 33480-4620
(561)832-8666 (800)233-2632 Fax:(561)835-8776
E-mail: plazainn@aol.com

Circa 1940. Located just one block from the beach, this classic European-style inn has been immaculately renovated and maintained throughout the years. Gleaming wood floors and antique

and reproduction furniture are featured in all of the common rooms. Deluxe guest rooms is individually decorated with hand-crafted comforters, fresh flowers and four-poster or canopy beds. The inn features the Stray Fox Pub, twice a week entertainment and a Charleston-style courtyard.

Innkeeper(s): Ajit Asrani & Patrick Connolly. $105-255. MC VISA AX. 47 rooms with PB. 2 suites. Breakfast included in rates. Type of meal: full breakfast. Beds: KQDT. Phone, air conditioning, ceiling fan and TV in room. VCR, copier, spa and swimming on premises. Weddings, small meetings and family reunions hosted. French and Spanish spoken. Antiques, fishing, parks, sporting events, golf, theater and watersports nearby.
Pets Allowed: Small.
Publicity: *USAir, Palm Beach Life, Sun Sentinel, Travel & Leisure, Daily News, Pittsburgh Post Gazette, Miami Herald, Globe & Mail, USA Today.*

Plant City
E7

Rysdon House

702 W Reynolds St
Plant City, FL 33566-4814
(813)752-8717 Fax:(813)752-8717

Circa 1910. A lumber baron built this stately home, which features a wide front veranda lined with rocking chairs. The interior still boasts the elegant decor one would expect in the home of a prominent lumberman. The parlor features exposed stone walls, a fireplace, red velvet Victorian furniture and a 200-year-old grand piano. Bedchambers are tastefully appointed, from the masculine hunter green walls in the Kensington room to the iron bed and floral appointments in the Queen Anne suite. There is a pool and spa for guests to use. The home is located in a town historic district.

Innkeeper(s): Claudia Rysdon. $65-105. MC VISA AX DS PC TC. TAC10. 4 rooms with PB, 2 with FP. 1 suite. 1 conference room. Breakfast included in rates. Meal: continental-plus breakfast. Beds: KQDT. Air conditioning, turndown service, ceiling fan, TV in room. Fax, spa, swimming, bicycles on premises. Weddings, small meetings, seminars hosted. Antiques, golf nearby.

Saint Augustine
B8

Casa de la Paz Bayfront Inn

22 Avenida Menendez
Saint Augustine, FL 32084-3644
(904)829-2915 (800)929-2915

Circa 1915. Overlooking Matanzas Bay, Casa de la Paz was built after the devastating 1914 fire leveled much of the old city. An ornate stucco Mediterranean Revival house, it features clay barrel tile roofing, bracketed eaves, verandas and a lush walled courtyard. The home is listed in the National Register of Historic Places. Guest rooms offer ceiling fans, central air, hardwood floors, antiques, a decanter of sherry, chocolates and complimentary beverages and snacks.

Historic Interest: Fountain of Youth, Castillo de San Marcos, Lightner Museum, Flagler College (walking distance).

Innkeeper(s): Bob & Donna Marriott. $89-179. MC VISA AX PC TC. 6 rooms with PB, 1 with FP. Breakfast included in rates. Meals: full breakfast, early coffee/tea. Beds: KQ. Phone, air conditioning, ceiling fan, TV in room. Antiques, fishing, parks, shopping, sporting events, theater, watersports nearby.
Publicity: *Innsider, US Air Magazine, PBS.*

"We will always recommend your beautifully restored, elegant home."

Casa De Solana, B&B Inn

21 Aviles St
Saint Augustine, FL 32084-4441
(904)824-3555 (800)760-3556 Fax:(904)824-3316
E-mail: solana@aug.com

Circa 1776. Spanish military leader Don Manuel Solana built this home in the early European settlement, and Spanish records show that a Solana child was the first European child

born in America. The thick coquina-shell walls (limestone formed of broken shells and corals cemented together), high ceilings with dark, hand-hewn beams and polished hand-pegged floors are part of the distinctive

flavor of this period. Two Majorcan fireplaces are in the carriage house. A Southern breakfast is served at an elegant 10-foot-long mahogany table.

Innkeeper(s): Faye' Lang-McMurray. $125-145. MC VISA AX DS PC. 4 suites. Breakfast included in rates. Meal: full breakfast. Beds: KQD. Phone, air conditioning, TV in room. Fax on premises. Amusement parks, antiques, fishing, parks, shopping, sporting events, theater and watersports nearby.

Location: In the Historic District.

Publicity: *House Beautiful, Palm Beach Post, Innsider, North Florida Living, Jacksonville Today.*

Castle Garden B&B

15 Shenandoah St
Saint Augustine, FL 32084-2817
(904)829-3839

Circa 1860. This newly-restored Moorish Revival-style inn was the carriage house to Warden Castle. Among the seven guest rooms are three bridal suites with in-room Jacuzzi tubs and sunken bedrooms with cathedral ceilings. The innkeepers offer packages including carriage rides, picnic lunches, gift baskets and other enticing possibilities. Guests enjoy a homemade full, country breakfast each morning.

Historic Interest: Castle Warden next door, Fort Mantanza's (200 yards to south), Alligator Farm, Saint Augustine Lighthouse (nearby).

Innkeeper(s): Bruce & Kimmy Kloeckner. $75-150. MC VISA AX DS. 7 rooms with PB. 3 suites. Breakfast included in rates. Types of meals: full breakfast and early coffee/tea. Picnic lunch available. Beds: KQT. Air conditioning and ceiling fan in room. TV on premises. Antiques, fishing, shopping, golf, theater and watersports nearby.

Cedar House Inn

79 Cedar St
Saint Augustine, FL 32084-4311
(904)829-0079 (800)233-2746 Fax:(904)825-0916
E-mail: russ@aug.com

Circa 1893. A player piano entertains guests in the parlor of this restored Victorian, which offers plenty of relaxing possibilities. Enjoy refreshments on the veranda or simply curl up with a good book in the library. Innkeepers Russ and Nina Thomas have preserved the home's luxurious heart-of-pine floors and

10-foot ceilings. They highlighted this architectural treasure with period furnishings and reproductions. Guests rooms are decked in Victorian decor and boast either claw-foot or Jacuzzi tubs. The

innkeepers also offer an outdoor Jacuzzi spa. Elegant breakfasts are served either in the dining room or on the veranda. Guests may borrow bicycles perfect for exploring historic Saint Augustine or nearby beaches.

Historic Interest: The inn is within walking distance of the Lightner Museum, downtown historical sites and the historic district.

Innkeeper(s): Russ & Nina Thomas. $79-150. MC VISA AX DS PC. TAC5. 6 rooms with PB, 3 with FP. 1 suite. 1 conference room. Breakfast and evening snack included in rates. Types of meals: gourmet breakfast and early coffee/tea. Dinner and picnic lunch available. Beds: Q. Air conditioning and ceiling fan in room. Fax, spa and bicycles on premises. Weddings, small meetings, family reunions and seminars hosted. Antiques, fishing, parks, shopping, theater and watersports nearby.

Publicity: *Palm Beach Post, Halifax Magazine.*

"What a special 'home' to spend our honeymoon! Everything was terrific! We feel this is our place now and will be regular guests here! Thank you!"

Kenwood Inn

38 Marine St
Saint Augustine, FL 32084-4439
(904)824-2116 Fax:(904)824-1689

Circa 1865. Originally built as a summer home, the Kenwood Inn has taken in guests for more than 100 years. Early records show that it was advertised as a private boarding house as early as 1886. Rooms are decorated in periods ranging from the simple Shaker decor to more formal colonial and Victorian styles.

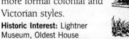

Historic Interest: Lightner Museum, Oldest House Museum, Bridge of Lions (walking distance).

Innkeeper(s): Mark & Kerrianne Constant. $85-150. MC VISA DS PC TC. 14 rooms with PB. 4 suites. Breakfast included in rates. Meal: continental breakfast. Beds: KQD. Air conditioning, ceiling fan in room. TV, fax, swimming on premises. Antiques, fishing, shopping, theater, watersports nearby.

Location: One block from the bay front.

Publicity: *Palm Beach Post, Florida Living, Southern Living, Seabreeze.*

"It's one of my favorite spots for a few days of relaxation and recuperation."

Old City House Inn & Restaurant

115 Cordova St
Saint Augustine, FL 32084-4413
(904)826-0113 Fax:(904)829-3798

Circa 1873. Saint Augustine is a treasure bed of history and this inn is strategically located in the center. A red-tile roof covers this former stable, and a veranda and courtyard add to the Spanish atmosphere. Gourmet breakfasts are prepared by innkeeper John Compton, whose recipes have been printed in Food Arts magazine. Inn guests are privy to the expansive breakfasts, but can join others for lunch and dinner in the restaurant. Appetizers include baked brie and Alligator Fritters.

For lunch, unique salads, fresh fish and chicken create the menu, while dinner choices include gourmet standards such as Filet Mignon or a more unusual Seafood Strudel.

Historic Interest: Castillo de San Marcos (one-fourth miles), Ripley's Believe It or Not Museum (one-half mile), Lightner Museum (across street).

Innkeeper(s): John & Darcy Compton. $75-150. MC VISA AX DC CB DS. 7 rooms with PB. Breakfast included in rates. Types of meals: full breakfast and early coffee/tea. Dinner and catering service available. Restaurant on premises. Beds: Q. Air conditioning, ceiling fan and TV in room. VCR, fax, copier and bicycles on premises. Handicap access. Antiques, fishing, shopping, theater and watersports nearby.

Location: Heart of St. Augustine, within walking distance of all the sights.

Publicity: *Florida Times Union, Florida Trend, Ft. Lauderdale Sun Sentinal.*

Old Powder House Inn

38 Cordova St
Saint Augustine, FL 32084-3629
(904)824-4149 (800)447-4149 Fax:(904)825-0143
E-mail: ahowes@aug.com

Circa 1899. This inn's name comes from the property's history. In the 18th century, the Spanish housed gunpowder for a fort in a building on the grounds. It eventually burned, and at the turn of the century, this Victorian was built in its place. Many original features remain, and guests can relax on the veranda much as they did in 1899. However, the addition of a 10-person, outdoor Jacuzzi provides a relaxing and modern option. Each room is different, but all feature Victorian decor. Sunken and Jacuzzi tubs are among the possibilities. The innkeepers serve wine and hors d'oeuvres in the early evening, and after a restful night's sleep, breakfast is served at intimate tables for two. There is off-street parking, and guests can borrow the innkeeper's bicycles. For a special getaway, ask about the different inn packages.

Innkeeper(s): Al & Eunice Howes. $79-165. MC VISA DS TC. TAC10. 8 rooms with PB. 2 suites. Breakfast and evening snack included in rates. Types of meals: gourmet breakfast and early coffee/tea. Picnic lunch available. Beds: KQDT. Phone, air conditioning and ceiling fan in room. TV, fax and copier on premises. Weddings, small meetings, family reunions and seminars hosted. Antiques, fishing, parks, shopping, golf, theater and watersports nearby.

"If you're looking for a retreat into a world of elegance and repose, try The Old Powder House Inn. - West Palm Beach Post."

Penny Farthing Inn

83 Cedar St
Saint Augustine, FL 32084
(904)824-2100 (800)395-1890
E-mail: penny@.com

Circa 1890. This Victorian, located in the oldest U.S. city, has been restored to its 18th-century ambiance. The inn is decorated in period decor with antiques. Some rooms offer a whirlpool tub. The two-room suite, popular with those seeking a romantic getaway, includes a clawfoot tub. The porches offer swings

and comfortable chairs, and the huge, namesake bicycle is displayed outside the front door. The day begins with a homemade full breakfast, with items such as cinnamon pecan pancakes. The innkeepers offer several biking packages, as well as packages that include carriage rides, canoe trips or tickets to the theater.

Innkeeper(s): Pam & Walt James. $90-175. MC VISA DS PC TC. 5 rooms with PB, 1 with FP. 3 suites. Breakfast included in rates. Type of meal: gourmet breakfast. Picnic lunch available. Beds: QT. Air conditioning, ceiling fan and TV in room. Bicycles and library on premises. Weddings, small meetings and seminars hosted. Antiques, fishing, parks, shopping, sporting events, golf, theater and watersports nearby.

St. Francis Inn

279 Saint George St
Saint Augustine, FL 32084-5031
(904)824-6068 (800)824-6062 Fax:(904)810-5525
E-mail: innceasd@aug.com

Circa 1791. Long noted for its hospitality, the St. Francis Inn is nearly the oldest house in town. A classic example of Old World architecture, it was built by Gaspar Garcia, who received a Spanish grant to the plot of land. Coquina was the main building material. A buffet breakfast is served. Some rooms have whirlpool tubs and fireplaces. The city of Saint Augustine was founded in 1565.

Historic Interest: The nation's oldest house (free admission for guests at the St. Francis Inn), Saint Augustine Antigua.

Innkeeper(s): Joe Finnegan. $75-175. MC VISA AX PC. TAC10. 14 rooms, 8 with PB, 4 with FP. 6 suites. 1 cottage. 2 conference rooms. Breakfast included in rates. Type of meal: early coffee/tea. Beds: KQDT. Air conditioning, ceiling fan and TV in room. Fax, copier, swimming and bicycles on premises. Weddings, small meetings, family reunions and seminars hosted. American Sign Language spoken. Antiques, fishing, parks, shopping, sporting events and watersports nearby.

Location: In the Saint Augustine Historic District, the nation's oldest city.

Publicity: *Orlando Sentinel.*

"We have stayed at many nice hotels but nothing like this. We are really enjoying it."

Victorian House B&B

11 Cadiz St
Saint Augustine, FL 32084-4431
(904)824-5214

Circa 1894. Enjoy the historic ambiance of Saint Augustine at this turn-of-the-century Victorian, decorated to reflect the grandeur of that genteel era. The heart-of-pine floors are topped with hand-hooked rugs, stenciling highlights the walls, and the innkeepers have filled the guest rooms with canopy beds and period furnishings. The expanded continental breakfast includes homemade granola, fruit and a variety of freshly made breads.

Innkeeper(s): Daisy Morden. $80-115. MC VISA AX TC. 8 rooms with PB. 2 suites. Breakfast included in rates. Type of meal: continental-plus breakfast. Beds: KQTD. Air conditioning and ceiling fan in room. TV on premises. Antiques, parks, shopping and theater nearby.

Westcott House

146 Avenida Menendez
Saint Augustine, FL 32084-5049
(904)824-4301 Fax:(904)824-4301
E-mail: westcotth@aol.com

Circa 1890. Dr. John Westcott, a man notable for his part in
building the St. John Railroad and linking the Intracoastal
Waterway from St. John's River to Miami, built this stunning
vernacular Victorian. The elegant inn overlooks Matanzas bay,
affording guests an enchanting view both inside and out. The
interior is filled with Victorian furnishings, from marble-topped
tables to white iron beds. The inn is located in St. Augustine's
historic district, and plenty of historic sites, restaurants and
shops are within walking distance.

Innkeeper(s): Janet & Tom Murray. $95-175. MC VISA AX DS PC TC. 9
rooms with PB, 3 with FP. Breakfast included in rates. Type of meal: continental breakfast. Beds: KQ. Air conditioning, turndown service, ceiling fan
and TV in room. Antiques, fishing, shopping and golf nearby.

Publicity: *Country Homes, AAA Magazine.*

Saint Petersburg   E7

Bayboro House B&B on Old Tampa

1719 Beach Dr SE
Saint Petersburg, FL 33701-5917
(813)823-4955 Fax:(813)823-4955

Circa 1905. Victorian decor and beautiful antique furnishings
fill the Bayboro House, a charming turn-of-the-century manor.
The veranda is set up for relaxation with a variety of rockers,
swings, wicker chairs and chaise lounges. Breakfasts, served in
the formal dining room, feature what every Florida breakfast
should, freshly squeezed juices and in-season fruits. Before
heading out to one of Saint Petersburg's many restaurants, relax
and sip a glass of wine in the parlor.

Historic Interest: The Bayboro House is only minutes from six museums and
downtown Saint Petersburg.

Innkeeper(s): Antonia & Gordon Powers. $85-145. MC VISA PC TC. 4 rooms
with PB. 1 suite. Breakfast included in rates. Type of meal: continental-plus
breakfast. Beds: QD. Air conditioning, ceiling fan and VCR in room. Fax, spa
and swimming on premises. Amusement parks, antiques, fishing, parks,
shopping, sporting events, theater and watersports nearby.

Location: Off exit 9 (I-275), downtown Saint Petersburg.

Publicity: *Miami Herald, Sun Sentinal.*

*"Made our anniversary very special; got the feeling I could be a new
bride, a celebrity or even a princess."*

McCarthy Hotel

326 1st Ave N
Saint Petersburg, FL 33701-3811
(813)822-4141 Fax:(813)821-0122

Circa 1925. This historic hotel is listed in the National Register
and has received a city award for its renovation. Rooms are
pleasant with modern decor and amenities such as in-room
refrigerators and ceiling fans. Each of the 64 rooms has been
individually decorated, and each features a different style of tile.
Meals are not included, but the hotel is close to a variety of
restaurants, as well as shops and museums.

Innkeeper(s): Terence McCarthy. $35-59. MC VISA PC TC. TAC10. 64 rooms
with PB. 1 conference room. Type of meal: early coffee/tea. Beds: TD. Phone,
air conditioning, ceiling fan and TV in room. Fax on premises. Small meetings
hosted. Antiques, fishing, parks, shopping, sporting events, golf, theater and
watersports nearby. Pets Allowed: Very short term.

Saint Petersburg Beach   E7

Island's End

1 Pass A Grille Way
Saint Petersburg Beach, FL 33706-4326
(813)360-5023 Fax:(813)367-7890

Circa 1950. This collection of cottages is truly at the edge of
the beach, where the Gulf of Mexico and Intracoastal Waterway
merge. Guests enjoy beach access and can walk along a boardwalk and through a gazebo to reach water and a fishing dock.
The six cottages are comfortable, with contemporary decor.
Each comes with a full kitchen. A few cottages date back half a
century. Unit A is the largest of the accommodations, offering
three bedrooms, a water view and a private pool. Breakfast is
provided three times each week.

Innkeeper(s): Jone & Millard Gamble. $65-175. MC VISA PC TC. 6 cottages
with PB. Breakfast included in rates. Type of meal: continental breakfast.
Beds: KQT. Phone, air conditioning, ceiling fan, TV and VCR in room. Fax and
copier on premises. Weddings hosted. Lithuanian and Latvian spoken.
Amusement parks, antiques, fishing, parks, shopping, sporting events, golf,
theater and watersports nearby.

Publicity: *Vanity Fair.*

San Mateo   C8

Ferncourt B&B

150 Central Ave, PO Box 758
San Mateo, FL 32187
(904)329-9755

Circa 1889. This Victorian "painted lady," is one of the few
remaining relics from San
Mateo's heyday in the early
1900s. Teddy Roosevelt once
visited the elegant
home. The current
innkeepers have
restored the
Victorian atmos-
phere with rooms decorated with bright, floral prints and gracious furnishings. Awake to the smells of brewing coffee and the
sound of a rooster crowing before settling down to a full gourmet
breakfast. Historic Saint Augustine is a quick, 25-mile drive.

Innkeeper(s): Jack & Dee Morgan. $55-75. MC VISA PC TC. TAC10. 6
rooms, 5 with PB. Breakfast included in rates. Meals: gourmet breakfast and
early coffee/tea. Beds: KQD. Air conditioning and ceiling fan in room. TV,
bicycles and library on premises. Handicap access. Small meetings and family reunions hosted. Antiques, fishing, parks, shopping, golf, theater nearby.

*"First class operation! A beautiful house with an impressive history
and restoration. Great company and fine food."*

Sanford   D8

The Higgins House

420 S Oak Ave
Sanford, FL 32771-1826
(407)324-9238 (800)584-0014 Fax:(407)324-5060

Circa 1894. This inviting blue Queen Anne-style home features cross gables with patterned wood shingles, bay windows
and a charming round window on the second floor. Pine floors,
paddle fans and a piano in the parlor, which guests are encouraged to play, create Victorian ambiance. The second-story bal-

cony affords views not only of a charming park and Sanford's oldest church, but of Space Shuttle launches from nearby Cape Canaveral. The Queen Anne room looks out over a Victorian box garden, while the Wicker Room features a bay window sitting area. The Country Victorian room boasts a 19th-century brass bed. Guests also can opt to stay in Cochran's Cottage, which features two bedrooms and baths, a living room, kitchen and porch. Nature lovers will enjoy close access to Blue Spring State Park, Ocala National Forest, Lake Monroe and the Cape Canaveral National Seashore. And of course, Walt Disney World, Seaworld and Universal Studios aren't far away.

Historic Interest: Historic downtown Sanford offers a variety of early Cracker and Victorian architecture and many book stores, antique shops, cafes and art galleries. Twenty-two buildings in the district are in the National Register.

Innkeeper(s): Walter & Roberta Padgett. $85-165. MC VISA AX DS PC TC. TAC10. 3 rooms. 1 cottage. Breakfast and evening snack included in rates. Types of meals: continental-plus breakfast and early coffee/tea. Picnic lunch available. Beds: QD. Air conditioning, turndown service and ceiling fan in room. TV, VCR, spa and bicycles on premises. Weddings, small meetings, family reunions and seminars hosted. Antiques, fishing, parks, shopping and watersports nearby.

Location: In the historic district.

Publicity: *Southern Living, Sanford Herald, Connecticut Traveler, LifeTimes, Orlando Sentinel, Southern Accents, Country Inns, Florida Living.*

"The Higgins House is warm and friendly, filled with such pleasant sounds, and if you love beauty and nature, you're certain to enjoy the grounds."

Stuart F10

Homeplace

501 Akron Ave
Stuart, FL 34994-2950
(561)220-9148 (800)251-5473 Fax:(561)221-3265

Circa 1913. This two-story Victorian with its pink clapboard and white trim was the personal home of the builder responsible for constructing many of the important buildings in the newly restored downtown historic district, which once served as a pineapple plantation. The inn boasts gleaming Dade

County pine floors, Oriental rugs, a wicker-filled sunroom and a formal dining room. The Captain's Quarters features an antique brass bed, while Opal's Room is furnished in golden oak. Overlooking the pool, Prissy's Room features white eyelet and pastel flowers. Coffee, fruit and cereal are offered first thing in the morning followed by a full breakfast served in the dining room or on a tray by the pool. The inn offers an intimate environment for weddings, showers, parties or meeting. Shopping, theater and antiques are just a short walk from the inn.

Innkeeper(s): Suzanne & Michael Pescitelli. $85-110. MC VISA PC TC. TAC10. 4 rooms with PB. Breakfast included in rates. Types of meals: full breakfast and early coffee/tea. Room service available. Beds: KQDT. Air conditioning and ceiling fan in room. TV, fax, copier, spa and swimming on premises. Weddings, small meetings, family reunions and seminars hosted. Antiques, fishing, parks, shopping, golf, theater and watersports nearby.

Publicity: *Country Inns.*

"You certainly have the right idea about how to pamper your guests and make them feel welcome."

Venice F7

Banyan House

519 Harbor Dr S
Venice, FL 34285-2812
(941)484-1385 Fax:(941)484-8032

Circa 1926. Spanish and Mediterranean influences are prominent in the design of this European-style inn. The grounds are lush, sporting tropical plants, trees and flowers. There is a hot

tub tucked beneath a banyan tree, and the first swimming pool built in Venice. Guests can opt for one of four guest rooms in the main mansion. Maid service and breakfast are included in the rates. The innkeepers offer bicycles for those who wish to explore the area, and there are plenty of nearby activities, including the beach, shops and restaurants. There are laundry facilities on the premises.

Innkeeper(s): Ian & Suzie Maryan. $70-120. MC VISA TC. 4 rooms with PB. Breakfast included in rates. Type of meal: continental-plus breakfast. Afternoon tea available. Beds: KQT. Air conditioning, ceiling fan and TV in room. Fax, copier, spa, swimming, bicycles and library on premises. Weddings, small meetings and family reunions hosted. Amusement parks, antiques, fishing, parks, shopping, theater and watersports nearby.

Georgia

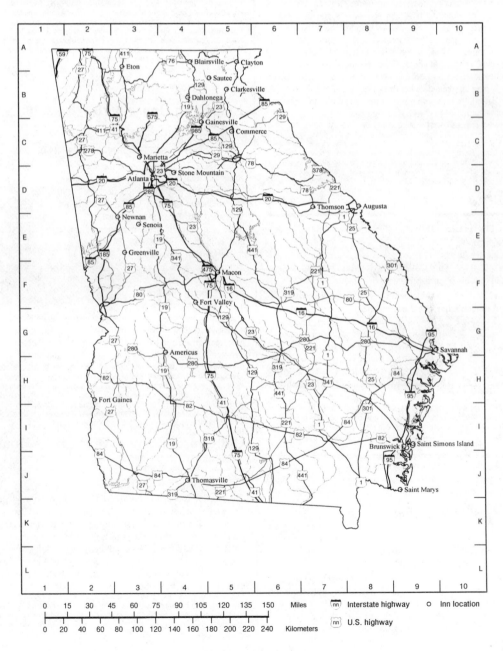

	Miles
0 15 30 45 60 75 90 105 120 135 150	
0 20 40 60 80 100 120 140 160 180 200 220 240	Kilometers

(nn) Interstate highway   o Inn location

(nn) U.S. highway

Americus G4

1906 Pathway Inn B&B

501 S Lee St
Americus, GA 31709-3919
(912)928-2078 (800)889-1466 Fax:(912)928-2078

Circa 1906. This turn-of-the-century inn is located along the Andersonville Trail and not far from the city of Andersonville, a Civil War village. Located between Andersonville and Plains, the home of former President Jimmy Carter, where you may attend and hear him teach Sunday school. The gracious, wrap-around porch is a perfect spot for relaxation. The innkeepers plan the morning meal to accommodate their guests' schedules, serving up a candle-lit breakfast with freshly baked breads using silver, crystal and china. The guest rooms offer romantic amenities such as whirlpools and snug down comforters. Two of the rooms are named in honor of Jimmy and Rosalynn Carter. Late afternoons are reserved for wine and refreshments. Several restaurants are within walking distance.

Innkeeper(s): Sheila & David Judah. $70-117. MC VISA AX DS PC TC. TAC10. 5 rooms with PB, 2 with FP. Breakfast included in rates. Types of meals: gourmet breakfast and early coffee/tea. Evening snack and room service available. Beds: KQ. Phone, air conditioning, turndown service, ceiling fan, TV and VCR in room. Fax and copier on premises. Small meetings hosted. Antiques, parks and theater nearby. Pets Allowed: With prior approval.
Location: Ten miles from Andersonville and Plains.

Atlanta D3

Beverly Hills Inn

65 Sheridan Dr N E
Atlanta, GA 30305-3121
(404)233-8520 (800)331-8520 Fax:(404)233-8659
E-mail: mit-bhi@mindspring.com

Circa 1929. Period furniture and polished-wood floors decorate this inn located in the Buckhead neighborhood. There are

private balconies, kitchens and a library with a collection of newspapers and books. The governor's mansion, Neiman-Marcus, Saks and Lord & Taylor are five minutes away.

Innkeeper(s): Mit Amin. $90-160. MC VISA AX DC DS PC TC. TAC10. 18 suites. Breakfast included in rates. Type of meal: continental-plus breakfast. Beds: QD. Phone, air conditioning and TV in room. Small meetings and family reunions hosted. French, Italian and Spanish spoken. Antiques, parks and shopping nearby. Pets Allowed: With kennels.
Location: North on Peachtree 15 minutes then one-half block off Peachtree.
Publicity: *Country Inns, Southern Living, Time.*

"Our only regret is that we had so little time. Next stay we will plan to be here longer."

The Gaslight Inn B&B

1001 St Charles Ave NE
Atlanta, GA 30306-4221
(404)875-1001 Fax:(404)876-1001
E-mail: innkeeper@gaslightinn.com

Circa 1913. Flickering gas lanterns outside, original gas lighting inside and five working fireplaces add to the unique quality of this inn. Beautifully appointed guest rooms offer individual decor. The Ivy Cottage is a romantic bungalow with a living room and kitchen. The regal English Suite boasts a four-poster

bed covered in rich blue hues and a private deck. The Rose Room features a fireplace and four-poster bed covered with lace. Located in the Virginia Highlands neighborhood, the inn is approximately five minutes from downtown and is served by Atlanta's public transportation system.

Innkeeper(s): Jim Moss. $95-195. MC VISA AX DS PC TC. TAC10. 6 rooms with PB, 3 with FP. 3 suites. 2 cottages. 1 conference room. Breakfast included in rates. Types of meals: continental-plus breakfast and early coffee/tea. Beds: KQ. Phone, air conditioning, ceiling fan, TV and VCR in room. Fax, copier, spa, sauna and library on premises. Handicap access. Weddings, small meetings, family reunions and seminars hosted. Amusement parks, antiques, parks, shopping, sporting events and theater nearby.
Publicity: *Travel Channel.*

"Best B&B I've ever stayed in."

King-Keith House B&B

889 Edgewood Ave NE
Atlanta, GA 30307
(404)688-7330 (800)728-3879 Fax:(404)584-0730

Circa 1890. This beautifully restored and preserved Queen Anne Victorian features many wonderful elements, including a whimsical chimney that vividly declares "1890," the year the home was built. Inside, the hardwood floors and intricate woodwork glisten. Walls are painted in deep, rich hues and antiques fill the rooms. Marble-topped tables and delicate love seats decorate the parlor. Each guest room is special, and beds are topped with luxury linens. One room is lit by a colorful stained-glass window, another features a Victorian dollhouse. The opulent home is located in an Atlanta historic district listed in the National Register. It's just two blocks from the subway station.

Innkeeper(s): Jan & Windell Keith. $65-125. MC VISA AX PC TC. TAC10. 5 rooms, 4 with PB, 1 with FP. 1 suite. Breakfast included in rates. Types of meals: full breakfast, gourmet breakfast and early coffee/tea. Afternoon tea, catering service and room service available. Beds: KQDT. Phone, air conditioning, ceiling fan and TV in room. Fax on premises. Weddings, small meetings, family reunions and seminars hosted. Amusement parks, antiques, parks, shopping, sporting events, golf and theater nearby.

Old Consulate Inn F.W. Hastings House

133 Peachtree St, NE #4600
Atlanta, GA 30303
(800)300-6753 Fax:(360)385-2097

Circa 1889. This handsome red Victorian, once the residence of the German consul, commands expansive views of Port Townsend Bay from its blufftop setting. Fine antiques, a grand piano, elegant stairway and Victorian wallcoverings create a romantic fantasy that is continued in the Tower Suite, where five curved turret windows afford majestic water and mountain views. There is also a hot tub and a gazebo on the premises.

Innkeeper(s): Rob & Joanna Jackson. $96-195. MAP. MC VISA AX PC TC. TAC10. 8 rooms with PB, 1 with FP. 3 suites. 1 conference room. Breakfast, afternoon tea and evening snack included in rates. Types of meals: gourmet breakfast and early coffee/tea. Catering service and catered breakfast available. Beds: KQ. Turndown service in room. TV, VCR, fax, copier, spa, tennis and library on premises. Weddings, small meetings, family reunions and seminars hosted. Antiques, fishing, parks, shopping, cross-country skiing, theater and watersports nearby.

Publicity: *Pacific Northwest, Seattle Weekly. Ratings: 4 Diamonds.*

"Beautiful in every way."

Augusta   D8

Perrin Guest House Inn

208 Lafayette Dr
Augusta, GA 30909-2104
(706)731-0920 (800)668-8930 Fax:(706)731-9009

Circa 1863. Massive brick and iron front gates welcome guests to the lush grounds that surround this elegant white cotton plantation home. Within the three-acre estate are tree-shaded brick pathways leading to secluded gardens that boast century-old magnolia trees and a romantic arbor. The inn's expansive front porch entry opens to a beautifully appointed parlor and dining room. The 10 guest rooms are decorated in period antiques and feature sitting areas with fireplaces and private baths; many of the rooms include Jacuzzis. A hearty continental breakfast is offered every morning. Romantic getaway packages with champagne and roses are available. Golf, shopping, restaurants, museums and historic Old Town are located nearby.

Historic Interest: Within driving distance of Aiken, South Carolina, the home of the famed Triple Crown of horse-racing.

$75-125. MC VISA AX. 10 rooms with PB, 10 with FP. Breakfast included in rates. Meal: continental-plus breakfast. Beds: KQ. Phone, air conditioning, TV in room. Fax on premises. Weddings and small meetings hosted. Antiques, fishing, shopping, sporting events, golf, theater and watersports nearby.

Pets Allowed: Rare exceptions.

Publicity: *Georgia Journal. Ratings: 4 Diamonds.*

Blairsville   A4

Misty Mountain Inn & Cottages

4376 Misty Mountain Ln
Blairsville, GA 30512-5604
(706)745-4786 (888)647-8966 Fax:(706)781-1002

Circa 1890. This Victorian farmhouse is situated on a four-acre compound that features six mountain-side cottages, three inviting ponds and a picnic area. There are four spacious guest rooms in the main house, all appointed with private baths and

fireplaces. All are decorated in country antiques with hand-crafted accessories, quilts and green plants. Two cottages boast antique beds and Jacuzzi tubs. The lofted bedroom cottages can comfortably sleep more than two people, while offering separate bedrooms, living rooms and eat-in kitchens. Flea markets, festivals, antique shops and arts and crafts are located nearby.

Historic Interest: Close to Lake Winfield Scott, Lake Nottely, Lake Chatuge, Young Harris College, Georgia Mountain Fair, Vogel State Park and the Appalachian Trail.

$50-85. MC VISA TC. TAC10. 4 rooms with PB, 10 with FP. 6 cottages. Breakfast included in rates. Types of meals: continental breakfast, continental-plus breakfast, full breakfast and early coffee/tea. Beds: QT. Air conditioning and ceiling fan in room. TV, fax and copier on premises. Handicap access. Weddings, small meetings and family reunions hosted. Antiques, fishing, parks, shopping, golf and watersports nearby. Pets Allowed: in cottages.

Brunswick   I9

Brunswick Manor

825 Egmont St
Brunswick, GA 31520-7825
(912)265-6889

Circa 1866. Nestled in the heart of historic Old Town Brunswick, this Victorian inn features the original carved oak staircase, high ceilings and Victorian mantels with beveled mirrors, antiques and period reproductions. Guests may relax on the rockers or wicker swing on the columned porch and enjoy the moss-draped oaks and tall palm trees. A stroll through the gardens leads to the greenhouse, fish pond, fountain, verandah and arbor-covered hot tub. The inn boasts a Country Inns/Waverly Fabrics award-winning room. Captained day charters are available. A full, complimentary breakfast is offered each morning.

Historic Interest: Fort Frederica, Coastal Historic Museum, Jekyll Island Historic District.

Innkeeper(s): Claudia & Harry Tzucanow. $65-90. MC VISA PC TC. 7 rooms with PB. 3 suites. Breakfast and afternoon tea included in rates. Type of meal: gourmet breakfast. Picnic lunch and catering service available. Beds: QT. Phone in room. Antiques, fishing, golf, theater and watersports nearby.

Publicity: *Southern Homes, Bon Appetit, Country Inns.*

"Your great charm and warm hospitality is your legacy. We've never stayed in such a room & house full of such treasures before. We'd say one of the best B&Bs in the country!"

Clarkesville   B5

The Burns-Sutton Inn

855 Washington St
Clarkesville, GA 30523
(706)754-5565

Circa 1901. Located in Clarkesville's historic district, this three-story Queen Anne Victorian inn is listed in the National Register of Historic Places. Furnished with antiques and period pieces, the inn also boasts a beautiful exterior. Magnificent magnolia trees are found in the front yard, adding to its elegant setting. Stained-glass windows, wrap-around porches and four-poster canopy beds add

to guests' enjoyment. A full country breakfast is served.

Innkeeper(s): Jaime Huffman. $55-95. MC VISA. 7 rooms, 5 with PB, 3 with FP. 2 suites. 1 conference room. Breakfast included in rates. Type of meal: full breakfast. Beds: QDT. Phone, air conditioning and ceiling fan in room. TV on premises. Weddings, family reunions and seminars hosted. Antiques, fishing, parks, shopping and watersports nearby.

Location: Northeast Georgia mountain foothills.

Publicity: *Southern Living, Gwinnett Daily Post, Blue Ridge County.*

Glen-Ella Springs Hotel

1789 Bear Gap Rd
Clarkesville, GA 30523
(706)754-7295

Circa 1875. This renovated hotel just south of the new Tallulah Gorge State Park is an outstanding example of early 19th- and 20th-century inns that dotted the Georgia countryside. The luxury of private baths and a plethora of porches have been added. A great stone fireplace is the focal point of the parlor, decorated in bright chintzes. Local hand-crafted pieces and antiques furnish the guest rooms. Two suites feature stone fireplaces. Bordered by Panther Creek, the property includes a swimming pool, 17 acres of meadows, flower and herb gardens and original mineral springs. The dining room features gourmet breakfast and dinner by reservation.

Historic Interest: Listed in the National Register of Historic Places.

Innkeeper(s): Barrie & Bobby Aycock. $120-180. EP. MC VISA AX. 16 rooms with PB, 2 with FP. 1 conference room. Type of meal: gourmet breakfast. Dinner available. Restaurant on premises. Beds: KQT. Fax, copier and swimming on premises. Handicap access.

Publicity: *Atlanta, Georgia Journal, Country Inns.*

"Quality is much talked about and too seldom found. With you folks it's a given."

Clayton   A5

English Manor
Hwy 76 E, PO Box 1605
Clayton, GA 30525
(706)782-5789 (800)782-5780 Fax:(706)782-5780

Circa 1912. Seven wooded acres serve as the location for this unique collection of inns. The main inn was purchased as a kit from a Sears Roebuck catalog and assembled on the property. The remaining six inns are just under a decade old. All seven have individually decorated guest rooms filled with antiques and reproductions. Suites offer the added amenities of a Jacuzzi tub and fireplace, and 14 rooms have fireplaces. There is an outdoor pool and oversized hot tub for guest use and verandas lined with rockers. The inn boasts extensive libraries. Guests are greeted by the inn's friendly, feline innkeepers.

Innkeeper(s): Juanita Shope. $79-219. PC TC. TAC10. 42 rooms with PB, 14 with FP. 7 suites. Breakfast included in rates. Type of meal: gourmet breakfast. Beds: KQD. Air conditioning and TV in room. Fax and copier on premises. Handicap access. Weddings, small meetings, family reunions and seminars hosted. Spanish and French spoken. Antiques, fishing, parks, shopping, downhill skiing and golf nearby.

Commerce   C5

Magnolia Inn
206 Cherry St
Commerce, GA 30529
(706)335-7257 (800)989-5548

Circa 1909. You'd never know by looking at this cozy Queen Anne Victorian that a host of murders have been solved right behind its wraparound porch and elegant front entry. In fact, the home with its six fireplaces, 12-foot-high ceilings and hardwood floors is the ideal setting for the inn's Mystery Weekend packages where guests are invited to spend a weekend solving a thrilling crime. Antiques, collectibles and a rose garden with a Dogwood tree enhance the inn's natural charm. Just one block from main street and the historic downtown.

Historic Interest: A short drive from North Georgia Mountains, University of Georgia, outlet malls and the racetrack.

Innkeeper(s): Annette & Jerry Potter. $60-75. MC VISA PC. TAC10. 4 rooms, 3 with PB, 1 with FP. 1 conference room. Breakfast and dinner included in rates. Types of meals: full breakfast, gourmet breakfast and early coffee/tea. Evening snack, picnic lunch, banquet service, catering service and room service available. Beds: QDT. Air conditioning, turndown service and TV in room. Child care on premises. Weddings, small meetings, family reunions and seminars hosted. Amusement parks, antiques, fishing, parks, shopping, sporting events, golf and theater nearby.

The Pittman House B&B
81 Homer Rd
Commerce, GA 30529-1806
(706)335-3823

Circa 1890. An hour's drive from Atlanta is this four-square Colonial inn, found in the rolling hills of Northeast Georgia. The inn has four guest rooms, furnished in antiques. The surrounding area offers many activities, including Lake Lanier, Lake Hartwell, Hurricane Shoals, Crawford W. Long Museum, an outlet mall, a winery and a championship golf course. Innkeeper Tom Tomberlin, a woodcarver, has items for sale in an antique shop next to the inn.

Innkeeper(s): Tom & Dot Tomberlin. $55-65. MC VISA PC TC. TAC10. 4 rooms, 2 with PB. Breakfast included in rates. Meals: full breakfast and early coffee/tea. Beds: D. Air conditioning and ceiling fan in room. TV and VCR on premises. Weddings, small meetings, family reunions and seminars hosted. Antiques, fishing, parks, shopping, sporting events and watersports nearby.

Dahlonega   B4

The Royal Guard Inn
65 Park St South
Dahlonega, GA 30533
(706)864-1713

Circa 1938. Shaded by tall magnolias, a large wraparound veranda surrounds this Cape Cod-style house, located a half block from downtown. Guest rooms are furnished in a contemporary style with plantation shutters. Afternoon wine and cheese is offered. There is a full breakfast with egg casseroles, pancakes and plenty of fresh fruit served in the dining room.

Innkeeper(s): John & Farris. $70-85. MC VISA AX. 5 rooms with PB. Breakfast and evening snack included in rates. Type of meal: gourmet breakfast. Beds: Q. Air conditioning, ceiling fan and TV in room. VCR and library on premises. Antiques, fishing, parks, shopping, golf, theater and watersports nearby.

The Smith House
84 Chestatee St SE
Dahlonega, GA 30533
(706)867-7000 (800)852-9577 Fax:(706)864-7564

Circa 1885. This inn in the Blue Ridge Mountains stands on a vein of gold. (In 1884 the landowner tried, without success, to get permission from city officials to set up a mining operation.) The inn features original woodwork, dry-rock fireplaces and a large wraparound porch with rocking chairs. Family-style dining is offered.

Innkeeper(s): The Welch Family. $65-150. MC VISA AX DS TC. 16 rooms with PB. 1 conference room. Breakfast included in rates. Type of meal: continental breakfast. Dinner and lunch available. Restaurant on premises. Beds: KQD. Phone, air conditioning, ceiling fan and TV in room. Fax, copier and swimming on premises. Small meetings and family reunions hosted. Antiques, parks, shopping and theater nearby.

Location: One block south of town square.

Publicity: *Atlanta Constitution, Atlanta Magazine, Southern Living, CNN Travel Guide.*

Worley Homestead Inn

168 Main St W
Dahlonega, GA 30533-1640
(707)864-7002

Circa 1845. Two blocks from the historic town square is this beautiful old Colonial Revival inn. Several guest rooms are equipped with fireplaces, adding to the romantic atmosphere and Victorian ambiance. All the rooms have private baths, and feature antique beds. A popular spot for honeymooners and couples celebrating anniversaries, Dahlonega is close to the lures of the Chattahoochee National Forest.

Innkeeper(s): Bill, Francis & Christine. $85-95. MC VISA. 7 rooms. Breakfast included in rates. Types of meals: full breakfast and early coffee/tea. Air conditioning and TV in room. Weddings and small meetings hosted. Antiques and shopping nearby.

Eton
A3

Ivy Inn B&B

245 Fifth Ave E
Eton, GA 30724
(706)517-0526 (800)201-5477 Fax:(706)517-0526

Circa 1908. Dr. S.A. Brown, an Eton town founder, built this country home, and the house has changed hands only four times in its near-century of existence. There are three guest rooms, each with its own personality. The Woodbine includes the home's rustic original beaded board walls and ceiling. Another room, the Needlepoint, is full of its namesake works and affords a view of Grassy Mountain. Regional dishes, such as grits and Southern tomato pie accompany fresh fruits, muffins and other treats on the breakfast table. The area offers a variety of activities, from horseback riding to hiking or shopping.

Innkeeper(s): Gene & Juanita Twiggs. $87. MC VISA AX PC. TAC10. 3 rooms with PB. Breakfast and evening snack included in rates. Types of meals: full breakfast and early coffee/tea. Beds: TD. Phone, air conditioning and TV in room. Fax, copier, bicycles and library on premises. Small meetings hosted. Antiques, fishing, parks, golf, theater and watersports nearby.

Publicity: *Dalton Daily Citizen, Georgia Journal, Chattanooga Free Press.*

"The service was incredible and the stay was very pleasant. We love your inn and your gracious hospitality."

Fort Gaines
H2

The John Dill House

PO Box 8
Fort Gaines, GA 31751-0008
(912)768-2338 Fax:(912)768-2338

Circa 1820. This stately homestead, once a stagecoach stop, is just two blocks from the Chattahoochee River in the state's Southwest region. The inn, listed with the national, state and local historic registers, boasts a fireplace in each of its nine guest rooms. Rooms have a queen size bed and a private bath,

all tastefully furnished in Adams mantels, imported Italian tile, cypress wainscoting and hand-carved antiques. Features include a 600-square-foot kitchen and more than $500,000 worth of antiques. Proceeds of the Elizabeth Dill Gift Shop, also on the grounds, go toward the costs of restoring the inn.

Innkeeper(s): Philip & Ramona Kurland. $50-70. PC TC. 9 rooms with PB, 9 with FP. Breakfast included in rates. Type of meal: gourmet breakfast. Catering service available. Beds: Q. Turndown service in room. TV, VCR and fax on premises. Handicap access. Weddings, small meetings and family reunions hosted. Antiques, fishing, parks and watersports nearby.

Publicity: *Georgia Journal, Atlanta Constitution, Southern Living.*

Fort Valley
F4

The Evans-Cantrell House

300 College St
Fort Valley, GA 31030-3415
(912)825-0611

Circa 1916. Innkeepers Norman and Cyriline Cantrell are only the second owners of this majestic home, which was constructed by A.J. Evans, who built an empire reaching into agriculture, commerce and finance. The Italian Renaissance Revival-style architecture is the perfect package for what guests discover inside. Brightly painted walls, traditional furnishings and glorious woodwork create an atmosphere reminiscent of early America. The dining room boasts the table and chairs that were built originally for the home. A beautiful mahogany-stained staircase leads up to the guest rooms, each of which is named for one of A.J. Evans' children. The innkeepers are happy to accommodate special culinary needs during the breakfast service. The inn is a 1995 recipient of the Georgia Historic Preservation Award.

Historic Interest: The Evans-Cantrell House is located in Fort Valley's Everett Square Historic District, and innkeepers will provide guests with a walking tour map. Historic Macon, Indian mounds, several historic homes and Andersonville's National Memorial is about 35 minutes away.

Innkeeper(s): Norman & Cyriline Cantrell. $75-95. MC VISA AX PC TC. 4 rooms with PB. 1 suite. Breakfast, afternoon tea and evening snack included in rates. Type of meal: early coffee/tea. Dinner available. Beds: QD. Phone, air conditioning, turndown service, ceiling fan and TV in room. Amusement parks, antiques and shopping nearby.

Publicity: *Georgia Journal, Macon.*

"Award Winning! We must get your efforts a Georgia Trust Award!! Keep up the good work!!!"

Gainesville
C4

Dunlap House

635 Green St NW
Gainesville, GA 30501-3319
(770)536-0200 (800)264-6992 Fax:(404)503-7857

Circa 1910. Located on Gainesville's historic Green Street, this inn offers 10 uniquely decorated guest rooms, all featuring period furnishings. Custom-built king or queen beds and remote-controlled cable TV are found in all of the rooms, several of which have romantic fireplaces. Guests may help themselves to coffee, tea and light refreshments in the inn's common area. Breakfast may be enjoyed in guests' rooms or on the picturesque veranda, with its comfortable wicker furniture. The Quinlan Art Center and Lake Sidney Lanier are nearby.

Innkeeper(s): Ann & Ben Ventress. $105-155. MC VISA DC. 10 rooms, 9 with PB, 2 with FP. Type of meal: full breakfast. Beds: KQ. Phone, air conditioning, turndown service and TV in room. Handicap access. Weddings, small meetings and family reunions hosted. Amusement parks, antiques, fishing, shopping, sporting events and theater nearby.

Publicity: *Southern Living, Atlanta Journal Constitution.*

Greenville E3

Samples Plantation

15380 Roosevelt Hwy
Greenville, GA 30222
(706)672-4765 Fax:(706)672-9966

Circa 1832. The romance of the South lives on at this Antebellum mansion. The manor originally was part of the Render Plantation, and among the Render family were a Georgia governor, a congressman and a Supreme Court justice. Each guest room has been individually decorated with antiques, lace, satin and romance in mind. Guests are pampered with a homemade plantation-style breakfast. Shopping and other attractions, including Franklin Roosevelt's Little White House, are nearby. Atlanta is 50 miles away, and Callaway Gardens are 17 miles away.

Innkeeper(s): Marjorie Samples. $149-289. MC VISA PC TC. TAC10. 7 suites, 6 with FP. Breakfast, afternoon tea, evening snack, picnic lunch included in rates. Meals: full breakfast, early coffee/tea. Beds: KQDT. Air conditioning, turndown service, ceiling fan in room. TV, VCR, fax, copier, bicycles, library on premises. 25 acres. Weddings hosted. Amusement parks, antiques, fishing, parks, shopping, sporting events, theater, watersports nearby.
Publicity: Columbia Ledger, Atlanta Journal.

"Outstanding."

Macon F5

1842 Inn

353 College St
Macon, GA 31201-1651
(912)741-1842 (800)336-1842 Fax:(912)741-1842

Circa 1842. Judge John J. Gresham, cotton merchant and founder of the Bibb Manufacturing Company, built this antebellum Greek Revival house. It features graceful columns, elaborate

mantels, crystal chandeliers and oak parquet floors inlaid with mahogany. Guest rooms boast cable television discreetly tucked into antique armoires. There are whirlpool baths available in the main house and in an adjoining Victorian cottage. All rooms are accented with fine English antiques, Oriental rugs and working fireplaces.

Historic Interest: The inn is located in a designated Historic District with museum houses within walking distance. Guided riding tours are available.
Innkeeper(s): Phillip Jenkins & Richard Meils. $105-165. MC VISA AX. 21 rooms with PB, 8 with FP. 1 conference room. Breakfast included in rates. Type of meal: continental-plus breakfast. Afternoon tea and room service available. Beds: KQDT. Copier and spa on premises. Handicap access. Antiques, golf and theater nearby.
Publicity: Christian Science Monitor, Southern Living, Daily News, Touring USA, Country Inns, PBS.

"The best B&B we've seen! Deserves all four stars!"

Marietta C3

Whitlock Inn

57 Whitlock Ave
Marietta, GA 30064-2343
(770)428-1495 Fax:(770)919-9620

Circa 1900. This cherished Victorian has been restored and is located in a National Register Historic District, one block from the Marietta Square. Amenities even the Ritz doesn't provide

are in every room, and you can rock on the front verandas. An afternoon snack also is served. There is a ballroom grandly suitable for weddings and business meetings.

Historic Interest: Kennesaw Mtn. Battlefield & Civil War National Park (3 miles), historic homes, several from Civil War era (within 6 blocks).

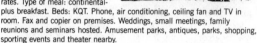

Innkeeper(s): Alexis Edwards. $100. MC VISA AX DS. TAC10. 5 rooms with PB. 3 conference rooms. Breakfast included in rates. Type of meal: continental-plus breakfast. Beds: KQT. Phone, air conditioning, ceiling fan and TV in room. Fax and copier on premises. Weddings, small meetings, family reunions and seminars hosted. Amusement parks, antiques, parks, shopping, sporting events and theater nearby.
Publicity: Marietta Daily Journal.

"This is the most beautiful inn in Georgia and I've seen nearly all of them."

Newnan E3

Southern Comfort B&B Inn

66 La Grange St
Newnan, GA 30263-2649
(770)254-9266 (800)818-0066

Circa 1883. Four thirty-foot-tall Corinthian columns mark the stately elegance of this Greek Revival style bed & breakfast. Located 20 minutes south of Atlanta, it is situated in a neighborhood of historic houses. The veranda and wraparound porch are shaded by tall trees. An upstairs library, stained glass windows, handsome stairway, thick carpets, fireplaces and a canopy bed are special features. Breakfast, served in the dining room, includes items such as hash browns,

Eggs Benedict and biscuits. Old Mill Museum, the Lewis Grizzard Museum and Courthouse Square are nearby.

Innkeeper(s): Barbara & Lawrence Opal. $69-89. MC VISA AX DS PC TC. TAC10. 4 rooms, 2 with PB, 4 with FP. Breakfast and evening snack included in rates. Types of meals: full breakfast and early coffee/tea. Room service available. Beds: QD. Phone, turndown service, ceiling fan and TV in room. Small meetings hosted. Amusement parks, antiques, fishing, parks, shopping, sporting events, golf, theater and watersports nearby.

"A beautiful home with a character of its own."

Rabun Gap

Sylvan Falls Mill

Box 548, Taylors Chapel Rd
Rabun Gap, GA 30568
(706)746-7138

Circa 1840. The Sylvan Falls Mill Site has been the location of a working gristmill for more than 150 years. The mill was constructed in 1840 from wormy chestnutwood. The original waterwheel was

replaced in 1946 by a steel waterwheel from Tennessee. The mill is still powered by the waterfall that cascades over one side of the property that overlooks picturesque Wolffork Valley. The property has been a home since then, offering three antique-filled guest rooms with private baths. High tea is served at 4 p.m.; check-in and a full, gourmet breakfast is served at 9 a.m. Outdoor activities are the highlight of the inn. Guest will delight in hiking the Bartram Trail or rafting down the Chatooga River.

Innkeeper(s): Jan & Ruth Ann Cort. $95. MC VISA PC TC. 3 rooms with PB. Breakfast and afternoon tea included in rates. Types of meals: gourmet breakfast and early coffee/tea. Evening snack and catered breakfast available. Beds: KQD. Ceiling fan in room. Library on premises. Weddings, small meetings and family reunions hosted. Antiques, fishing, parks, shopping, downhill skiing, golf and watersports nearby.

Publicity: *Country Inns, Mountain Review, The Atlanta Journal-Constitution.*

Saint Marys
J9

Spencer House Inn B&B

101 E Bryant St
Saint Marys, GA 31558-4501
(912)882-1872 Fax:(912)882-9427

Circa 1872. A white picket fence surrounds this Greek Revival house, painted a pleasant pink with white trim on the wide two-level veranda. The inn is in the St. Mary's Historic District and is in the National Register. Heart-pine floors, original mold-

ings and high ceilings are features of the rooms. Carefully selected reproductions, fine antiques, coordinated fabrics and rugs have been combined to create a sunny, fresh decor. There are four-poster

beds and clawfoot soaking tubs. Breakfast is buffet style with cranberry pecan bread pudding or frittatas as specialties. The inn is one block to the ferry to Georgia's largest barrier island, Cumberland Island, with 17 miles of white sand beaches, live oak forests, salt marshes and wild horses. Okefenokee National Wildlife Refuge is 45 minutes away.

Innkeeper(s): Mary & Mike Neff. $65-115. MC VISA AX DS PC TC. 14 rooms with PB. 1 suite. Breakfast included in rates. Types of meals: full breakfast and early coffee/tea. Picnic lunch available. Beds: KQTD. Phone, air conditioning, ceiling fan and TV in room. Fax and library on premises. Handicap access. Weddings, small meetings, family reunions and seminars hosted. Antiques, fishing, parks, shopping, sporting events and watersports nearby.

Publicity: *Seabreeze.*

"I don't see how it could be improved!"

Saint Simons Island
I9

The Lodge on Little St. Simons Island

PO Box 21078
Saint Simons Island, GA 31522-0578
(912)638-7472 (888)733-5774 Fax:(912)634-1811
E-mail: lssi@mindspring.com

Once a part of Butler Plantation, Little St. Simons Island was purchased at the turn of the century by the Berolzheimer family. Deer roam freely and birds soar over 10,000 acres of pristine forests, fresh water ponds, isolated beaches and marshland. There are more than 220 species of birds, and guests can enjoy horseback riding on miles of private trails. As well, there are seven miles of isolated beach to enjoy. All activities are included in the rates. The

Hunting Lodge, filled with books and memorabilia, is the gathering spot for the island. To ensure solitude and privacy, the innkeepers allow only 30 overnight guests at a time. Full-Island rates, ranging from $3,400 to $5,800 are available. Breakfast, lunch and dinner, served family style, are included in the rates.

Historic Interest: Fort Frederica National Monumet (neighboring Island), Fort George (13 miles), Jekyll Club and historic district homes of turn-of-the-century millionaires (Jekyll Island).

Innkeeper(s): Debbie & Kevin McIntyre. $300-540. AP. MC VISA PC. TAC10. 13 rooms with PB. 1 suite. 3 conference rooms. Breakfast and dinner included in rates. Types of meals: full breakfast and early coffee/tea. Lunch available. Beds: KQT. Air conditioning and ceiling fan in room. Fax, copier, swimming, stables and bicycles on premises. Handicap access. Weddings, small meetings, family reunions and seminars hosted.

Location: A privately owned island 20 minutes offshore from St. Simons.

Publicity: *Conde Nast, Country Inns, Meeting Destinations, Savannah Magazine, Chattanooga News Free Press, Gourmet, Today Show, CNN Travel, Great Country Inns.*

Sautee
B5

The Stovall House

1526 Hwy 255 N
Sautee, GA 30571
(706)878-3355

Circa 1837. This house, built by Moses Harshaw and restored in 1983 by Ham Schwartz, has received two state awards for its restoration. The handsome farmhouse has an extensive wrap-

around porch providing vistas of 28 acres of cow pastures, meadows and creeks. High ceilings, polished walnut woodwork and decorative stenciling provide a pleasant backdrop for the inn's collec-

tion of antiques. Victorian bathroom fixtures include pull-chain toilets and pedestal sinks. The inn has its own restaurant.

Historic Interest: Sautee Nacoochee Arts and Community Center (1 mile), Museum of Indian and local history, Stovall Covered Bridge (1 mile).

Innkeeper(s): Ham Schwartz. $68-80. MC VISA PC TC. 5 rooms with PB. Breakfast included in rates. Type of meal: continental breakfast. Dinner and catering service available. Restaurant on premises. Beds: KQDT. Air conditioning and ceiling fan in room. Library on premises. 26 acres. Weddings, small meetings and family reunions hosted. Amusement parks, antiques, fishing, parks, shopping, theater, watersports nearby. Publicity: *Atlanta Journal.*

Savannah
G9

Eliza Thompson House

5 W Jones St
Savannah, GA 31401-4503
(912)236-3620 (800)348-9378 Fax:(912)238-1920

Circa 1847. Spared General Sherman's wrath during the Civil War, this elegantly restored Federalist-style mansion built by Eliza Thompson is one of Savannah's oldest operating inns. Set on a brick-paved street in the heart of the historic district, this architectural landmark built around a magnificent courtyard consists of 23 spacious guest rooms, all featuring gleaming heart-pine floors and period antiques. Many of the rooms offer fireplaces. Richly brewed coffee, freshly baked croissants, pastries and homemade muffins along with fresh seasonal fruits and cereals are offered each morning. Guests can explore the historic downtown just a few minutes away by foot.

Innkeeper(s): Carol Day. $89-189. MC VISA PC TC. TAC10. 23 rooms with PB, 12 with FP. 1 conference room. Breakfast, afternoon tea and evening snack included in rates. Types of meals: full breakfast and early coffee/tea. Beds: KQD. Phone, turndown service, ceiling fan and TV in room. Fax on premises. Weddings, small meetings and seminars hosted. Antiques, fishing, parks, shopping, golf and theater nearby.

Foley House Inn

14 W Hull St
Savannah, GA 31401-3903
(912)232-6622 (800)647-3708 Fax:(912)231-1218

Circa 1896. Fine craftsmen have faithfully restored the inn, and there is a fireplace in each room of the main house. Its antiques, silver, china, Oriental rugs and hand-colored engravings come from around the world. A variety of hors d'oeuvres are served in the evening. Churches, museums, galleries and the riverfront are within walking distance.

Innkeeper(s): Inge Svensson Moore. $120-225. MC VISA AX DC CB DS. 19 rooms with PB. Meal: continental-plus breakfast. Evening snack available. Beds: KQD. Phone, air conditioning, turndown service, TV, VCR in room. Small meetings, family reunions hosted. Antiques, shopping, theater nearby.

Forsyth Park Inn

102 W Hall St
Savannah, GA 31401-5519
(912)233-6800

Circa 1893. This graceful yellow and white three-story Victorian features bay windows and a large veranda overlooking Forsyth Park. Sixteen-foot ceilings, polished parquet floors of oak and maple, and a handsome oak stairway provide an elegant background for the guest rooms. There are several whirlpool tubs, marble baths, four-poster beds, fireplaces and there is a walled garden courtyard.

Historic Interest: In the heart of historic district, overlooking the largest park in the District Two Historic Forts. A lighthouse and beach are nearby.
Innkeeper(s): Hal & Virginia Sullivan. $125-200. MC VISA AX DS PC TC. 10 rooms, 9 with PB, 8 with FP. 1 cottage. Breakfast included in rates. Type of meal: continental breakfast. Beds: KQT. Air conditioning in room. French spoken. Antiques, fishing, parks, shopping, theater and watersports nearby.
Location: Savannah's historic district, opposite Forsyth Park.
Publicity: *Savannah Morning News, Land's End, Vis-A-Vis, Learning Channel.*

"Breathtaking, exceeded my wildest dreams."

Lion's Head Inn

120 E Gaston St
Savannah, GA 31401-5604
(912)232-4580 (800)355-5466 Fax:(912)232-7422

Circa 1883. All of the guest rooms in this Southern 19th-century mansion have working fireplaces and four-poster beds. Because the inn is situated in a historic district, guests can enjoy strolls among mansions, lush gardens and restored homes. Considered a living museum, this Federal-style inn was constructed by J.R. Hamlet for the William Wade family. Guests may want to relax in the well-stocked library, draped in classic motif or enjoy an afternoon wine and cheese reception in the double parlor or sit on the wicker swing on the large veranda.

Innkeeper(s): Christy Dell'Orco. $95-190. MC VISA AX DS. 6 rooms with PB. 3 suites. Breakfast included in rates. Type of meal: continental-plus breakfast. Beds: KQD. Antiques, fishing, theater and watersports nearby.
Publicity: *Country Inns, Brides, Ladies Home Journal, Southern Living.*

Olde Harbour Inn

508 E Factors Walk
Savannah, GA 31401-1200
(912)234-4100

Circa 1892. Located in the historic district, this building once housed the offices, warehouse and shipping center of the Tidewater Oil Company and in 1930, the Alexander Blue Jean Manufactory. Now converted to suites, are all richly decorated in a traditional style and all boast river views. Within walking distance are some of the South's finest restaurants.

Innkeeper(s): Susan Steinhauser. $99-200. MC VISA AX. 24 rooms with PB. Type of meal: continental-plus breakfast. Beds: QDT. Phone in room.

The President's Quarters

225 E President St
Savannah, GA 31401-3806
(912)233-1600 (800)233-1776

Circa 1855. Situated in the heart of Savannah's Historic District, the President's Quarters is located on quiet Oglethorpe Square. Tour stops and restaurants are literally at the inn's front door. In 1985, these two twin townhouses were used as a backdrop for the Alex Haley's film Roots. In 1870 Robert E. Lee paid a call here to confederate General Alexander R. Lawton, lawyer and American charge d' affaires to the Court of Vienna. Each room has period furnishings, a fireplace, four-poster rice beds or brass beds and balconies. Special services include a complimentary fruit basket and a chilled bottle of wine, afternoon tea with cakes, cheeses, salads, and wine. A nightly turndown service features juice, port or sherry at your bedside along with a mint chocolate. Breakfast is served in your room or in our private courtyard. The inn offers its own parking to guests.

Innkeeper(s): S.K. Stephens. $137-200. MC VISA DC DS. 16 rooms with PB, 16 with FP. Type of meal: continental-plus breakfast. Beds: KQD. Fax and copier on premises. Handicap access.
Publicity: *Country Inns, Southern Homes.*

"President's Quarters was truly a home away from home-Karl Malden."

Remshart-Brooks House

106 W Jones St
Savannah, GA 31401-4508
(912)234-6928

Circa 1853. Guests at this Savannah-style home enjoy complete privacy as the single accommodation is a spacious terrace-garden suite. The home is the second house of a four-house row that was constructed for William Remshart and his family, and it is surrounded by a neighborhood of restored homes. The furnishings include country antiques gathered from Virginia and Georgia. The suite offers a bedroom, living room, private bath and butler's pantry.

Innkeeper(s): Anne & Ewing Barnett. $75. PC TC. 1 suite. Breakfast included in rates. Meal: continental breakfast. Beds: Q. Phone, air conditioning, TV in room. Antiques, fishing, parks, sporting events, theater, watersports nearby.

The Veranda

252 Seavy St, PO Box 177
Senoia, GA 30276-0177
(770)599-3905 Fax:(770)599-0806

Circa 1906. Doric columns adorn the verandas of this 9,000-square-foot Neoclassical hotel. William Jennings Bryan stayed

here, and it is said that Margaret Mitchell, who wrote "Gone With the Wind" came here to interview Georgia veterans of the Civil War who held their annual reunion at the hotel. Furnishings include walnut bookcases owned by President William McKinley and a rare Wurlitzer player piano-pipe organ. There are Victorian collections of hair combs, walking canes, books and one of the largest assortments of kaleidoscopes in the Southeast. The inn offers a five course gourmet candlelight dinner by reservation.

Historic Interest: Male Academy Museum (19 miles), Little White House of FDR (35 miles), Reconstruction of Civil War Stockade for TNT mini-series "Andersonville" (10 miles), Joel Chandler Harris Home/Museum (40 miles).
Innkeeper(s): Jan & Bobby Boal. $99-150. MC VISA AX DS PC TC. TAC10. 9 rooms with PB. 1 conference room. Meals: gourmet breakfast, early coffee/tea. Afternoon tea, evening snack available. Beds: KQ. Air conditioning, turndown service in room. VCR, fax, copier on premises. Handicap access. Weddings, small meetings, family reunions, seminars hosted. Amusement parks, antiques nearby. Location: 30 miles south of Atlanta airport.
Publicity: *Glamour, Southern Homes, Southern Living, Atlanta Journal/Const.*

Stone Mountain D4

The Village Inn B & B

992 Ridge Ave
Stone Mountain, GA 30083-3676
(770)469-3459 (800)214-8385 Fax:(770)469-1051

Circa 1850. This city historic site was built as hotel, but served as a Confederate hospital during the Civil War. Rooms are decorated with period antiques and in a nostalgic country style that will take guests back in time to the mid-19th century. Although the inn has a decidedly historic feel, two of the guest rooms offer a whirlpool tub. The spacious Ballroom Suite includes a refrigerator, coffee maker, TV and VCR. Southern-style breakfasts are served, popular regional fare such as cheese grits or baked

buttermilk biscuits are a staple. Ask any resident of Atlanta, and they are sure to place a visit to Stone Mountain at the top of the sightseeing list. There are shops to explore in this charming village, and guests can walk or ride a tram up to the top of the mountain for a memorable view. The attractions of Atlanta are nearby.

Innkeeper(s): Rob & Deandra Bailey. $75-125. MC VISA AX DS PC TC. TAC10. 6 rooms, 5 with PB, 1 with FP. 1 suite. Breakfast and evening snack included in rates. Meals: full breakfast, early coffee/tea. Beds: KQDT. Phone, air conditioning, turndown service, ceiling fan, TV, VCR in room. Fax on premises. Handicap access. Weddings, small meetings, family reunions hosted. Amusement parks, antiques, fishing, parks, shopping, golf, theater nearby.
Publicity: *Southern Living, Campus Live, Inn Route.*

Thomasville J4

Serendipity Cottage

339 E Jefferson St
Thomasville, GA 31792-5108
(912)226-8111 (800)383-7377 Fax:(912)226-2656

Circa 1906. A wealthy Northerner hand picked the lumber used to build this four-square house for his family. The home still maintains its original oak pocket doors and leaded-glass

windows. The decor in guest rooms ranges from Victorian with antiques to rooms decorated with wicker furnishings. Honeymooners will find a bottle of champagne placed in the room. Breakfasts are hearty and made from scratch, including freshly baked breads and homemade jams. The home is located in a neighborhood of historic houses.

Innkeeper(s): Kathy & Ed Middleton. $75. MC VISA AX DS PC TC. TAC10. 3 rooms with PB, 2 with FP. Breakfast included in rates. Meals: continental breakfast, full breakfast and early coffee/tea. Beds: QD. Phone, air conditioning, turndown service, ceiling fan, TV and VCR in room. Bicycles on premises. Antiques, fishing, parks, shopping, sporting events and theater nearby.

Susina Plantation Inn

1420 Meridian Rd
Thomasville, GA 31792
(912)377-9644

Circa 1841. Four towering columns support the enormous portico of this Greek Revival plantation home designed by John Wind. Its commanding position provides a view of 115 acres of lawns, woodlands and ancient oak and magnolia trees. The dining room, drawing rooms and verandas are graciously furnished with fine antiques. A deep well on the property is noted for its superb drinking water. Fishing the stocked pond is a popular plantation activity. In addition to breakfast, the rates also include a four-course, gourmet dinner.

Innkeeper(s): Anne-Marie Walker. $150. MAP. 8 rooms with PB. 1 conference room. Breakfast and dinner included in rates. Restaurant on premises. Beds: KQDT. Phone in room. Publicity: *The Palm Beach Post.*

Thomson D7

1810 West Inn

254 N Seymour Dr
Thomson, GA 30824-7851
(706)595-3156 (800)515-1810

Circa 1810. Restoration expert and now innkeeper Virginia White refurbished this plantation farmhouse as well as the several turn-of-the-century tenant houses that adjoin the main property. Virginia had the historic houses moved to the 11-acre farm and has restored them into quaint country dwellings. Peacocks and other farm creatures mingle on the grounds, which are dotted with magnolias and lush gardens. The Whites' "continental" morning fare is more akin to a hearty country breakfast, with items such as individual quiche, freshly baked biscuits and fresh fruit. Virginia was born in Thomson and has named each of the richly decorated guest quarters after her local ancestors. Rooms offer cozy fireplaces, shiny pine paneled walls, antique beds and handmade Native American rugs. The country kitchen is stocked with snacks and guests are welcome to peruse the cupboards for a cup of tea or a small treat. The grounds offer a jogging trail, and guests are allowed privileges at a nearby golf and tennis club.

Historic Interest: Nearby Wrightsborough, one of Georgia's first communities, includes the historic Rock House, which was built in 1785. Other historic attractions in the area include the site of a Quaker settlement and part of the Bartram Trail.
Innkeeper(s): Virginia White. $55-105. MC VISA AX. 10 rooms with PB. 3 suites. Meals: continental-plus breakfast, early coffee/tea. Picnic lunch, catering service available. Beds: QDT. 12 acres. Antiques, fishing, shopping nearby.

Hawaii

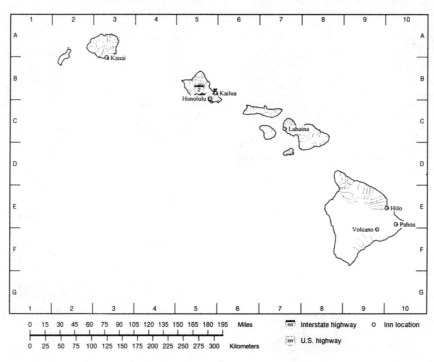

	Miles
0 15 30 45 60 75 90 105 120 135 150 165 180 195	

	Kilometers
0 25 50 75 100 125 150 175 200 225 250 275 300	

[nn] Interstate highway   ○ Inn location

[nn] U.S. highway

Hilo   *E10*

Shipman House Bed & Breakfast Inn

131 Ka'iulani St
Hilo, HI 96720
(808)934-8002 (800)627-8447 Fax:(808)934-8002
E-mail: bighouse@bigisland.com

Circa 1899. Locals know Shipman House as "The Castle," no doubt because of both its size and grandeur. The manor, a mix of Italianate and Queen Anne styles, is listed on both the state and national historic registers. The home's former mistress, Mary Shipman, not only was the granddaughter of a Hawaiian chiefess, but a friend of Queen Lili'uokalani. Jack London and his wife once stayed here for a month as guests of the Shipmans. The grounds still feature many of the plants, palms and flowers nurtured by the Shipmans. Inside, the innkeeper has decorated the home with a mix of antiques and traditional furnishings, many pieces original to the house. There is a cottage available as well, secluded by trees and foliage. A lav-ish, continental-plus breakfast buffet is served on the home's lanai, offering such items as homemade granola, local fruit (and there are 20 different varieties of fruit trees on the property), freshly baked breads, home-

made passionfruit butter, and pancakes, waffles or French toast. With advance notice, the innkeeper is happy to accommodate any special dietary needs.

Innkeeper(s): Barbara & Gary Andersen. $140-150. MC VISA AX TC. TAC10. 5 rooms with PB. 1 cottage. 2 conference rooms. Breakfast, afternoon tea and evening snack included in rates. Types of meals: continental-plus breakfast and early coffee/tea. Banquet service available. Beds: QT. Phone, turn-down service and ceiling fan in room. TV, VCR, fax, copier and library on premises. Weddings, small meetings, family reunions and seminars hosted. Limited French spoken. Antiques, fishing, parks, shopping, sporting events, theater and watersports nearby.

Honolulu   B5

The Manoa Valley Inn

2001 Vancouver Dr
Honolulu, HI 96822-2451
(808)947-6019 (800)535-0085 Fax:(808)946-6168
E-mail: marc@aloha.net

Circa 1915. This exquisite home offers the best of two worlds, a beautiful, country home surrounded by a tropical paradise. Each restored room features lavish decor with ornate beds, ceiling fans and period furniture. Little amenities such as the his and her robes create a romantic touch. Breakfasts with kona coffee, juices and fresh fruits are served, and after a day of sightseeing, evening wine and cheese are served. The inn's common rooms offer unique touches such as a nickelodeon and antique Victrola. The Manoa Valley is a perfect location to enjoy Hawaii and is only blocks away from the University of Hawaii.

Historic Interest: The Honolulu Art Academy, founded by an early missionary, features a unique architectural mix of Polynesian design and missionary style. The Iolani Place was built by King David Kalakaua and was the home of Hawaiian royalty until the demise of the monarchy in 1893.

Innkeeper(s): Herb Fukushima. $99-190. MC VISA AX DC TC. TAC10. 8 rooms, 3 with PB. 1 suite. 1 cottage. Breakfast and evening snack included in rates. Type of meal: continental breakfast. Beds: KQD. Phone and ceiling fan in room. TV, fax, copier and library on premises. Weddings, small meetings and seminars hosted. Fishing, parks, shopping, sporting events, theater and watersports nearby.

Location: On the island of Oahu.

Publicity: *Travel & Leisure, LA Style.*

"A wonderful place!! Stepping back to a time of luxury!"

Kailua   B5

Hale Mali`e

137 Mookua Street
Kailua, HI 96734
(808)261-1755 Fax:(808)261-9420
E-mail: mgm@aloha.net

Circa 1936. The name of this traditional plantation home means "House of Tranquility," and the inn was once the residence of Hawaii's first governor, John Burns. Away from the hustle and bustle of Waikiki but within driving distance of local attractions, this B&B is located a block from the water and a five-minute walk from the three-mile-long Kailua beach (the second-best beach in America, according to Holiday Magazine). Each of the air-conditioned rooms has a television, phone and refrigerator.

Innkeeper(s): Geoffrey Paterson, Maureen McDonough. $70-95. MC VISA AX PC TC. TAC10. 4 rooms, 3 with PB. Breakfast included in rates. Type of meal: continental-plus breakfast. Beds: KQT. Phone, air conditioning, TV and VCR in room. Fax on premises. Parks, golf and watersports nearby.

Kauai   B3

Poipu B&B Inn & Gallery

2720 Hoonani Rd, Poipu Beach
Kauai, HI 96756
(808)742-1146 (800)552-0095 Fax:(808)742-6843
E-mail: poipu@aloha.net

Circa 1933. This restored plantation house preserves the character of old Kauai, while providing for every modern convenience. The handcrafted wood interiors and old-fashioned lanais provide the perfect backdrop for the ornate white Victorian wicker,

carousel horses, pine antiques and tropical color accents. Several of the units are oceanfront, while others offers expansive views of the sea. Most of the rooms feature whirlpool tubs. Local art and handcrafts abound as one of the innkeepers is an avid collector and artist. The beach is one block away, and the innkeepers can help you arrange every detail of your stay including helicopter tours, short-term health spa membership and dinner reservations.

Innkeeper(s): Dotti Cichon. $80-350. MC VISA AX DC CB DS PC TC. TAC10. 9 rooms with PB. 2 suites. 3 cottages. Breakfast and afternoon tea included in rates. Types of meals: continental-plus breakfast and early coffee/tea. Beds: KQT. Ceiling fan, TV and VCR in room. Fax, copier and library on premises. Weddings, small meetings, family reunions and seminars hosted. French and German spoken. Fishing, parks, shopping and watersports nearby.

Location: Poipu Beach.

Publicity: *Travel & Leisure, Smart Money, Country Inns, Travel-Holiday.*

"Thank you for sharing your home as well as yourself with us. I'll never forget this place, it's the best B&B we've stayed at."

Lahaina   C7

The Lahaina Inn

127 Lahainaluna Rd
Lahaina, HI 96761-1502
(808)661-0577 (800)669-3444 Fax:(808)667-9480

Circa 1938. After a fire in 1963, the inn was rebuilt in a frontier storefront style. Recently renovated by Rick Ralston, founder of Crazy Shirts, the inn has been appointed in furnishings chosen from Ralston's warehouse of 12,000 antiques. Each of the stunning guest rooms boasts balconies with views of the harbor or mountains. The 12 rooms feature individual decor with coordinating bed covers and linens, Oriental rugs, antique beds made from iron, brass or wood, and ceiling fans. An antique sideboard outside the guest rooms is stocked each morning with steaming Kona coffee. The inn's restaurant, David Paul's Lahaina Grill, features a variety of gourmet fare and was named "Maui's Best Restaurant" four years in a row by Honolulu Magazine.

Historic Interest: A walking tour of this charming Hawaiian town includes such sites as the Government Market, a courthouse, fort and canal. The Hauola Stone, a stop of the tour, was believed to have been used by Hawaiians as a healing place.

Innkeeper(s): Tyler Ralston. $89-149. MC VISA AX DS. 12 rooms with PB. 3 suites. Breakfast included in rates. Type of meal: continental breakfast. Restaurant on premises. Beds: KQDT. Fax and copier on premises. Antiques, shopping and watersports nearby.

Publicity: *Tour & Travel News, Hawaii Magazine, Honolulu, Pacific Business News, Glamour.*

"Outstanding lodging and service. Ahhh! Paradise. Fantastic. Excellent. Exquisite."

Pahoa   E10

Kalani Oceanside Retreat

RR 2 Box 4500, Pahoa Beach Rd
Pahoa, HI 96778-9724
(808)965-7828 (800)800-6886 Fax:(808)965-9613
E-mail: kalani@kalani.net

Circa 1880. Set on more than 100 lush tropical acres, this oceanside retreat is the only coastal lodging within Hawaii's largest conservation area. Guest cottages and lodges are comfortable and some offer ocean views. Guests enjoy the multitude of outdoor activities that include swimming in the inn's luxurious olympic-sized pool, snorkeling, therapeutic massage, nature treks, Yoga and a variety of on-site educational seminars. The inn also features Hawaiian mythology, hula lessons and dancing. Three tropical buffets are served daily in an open-air, ocean-view lanai. Meals are not included in the rate.

Historic Interest: Located close to orchid farms, botanical gardens, thermal springs, Volcanoes National Park, a crater lake and five parks.

Innkeeper(s): Richard Koob, Carol Magee, Delton Johnson. $75-130. MC VISA AX DC TC. TAC10. 45 rooms, 22 with PB. 8 cottages. 5 conference rooms. Meals: continental-plus breakfast, full breakfast, early coffee/tea. Afternoon tea, dinner, picnic lunch, lunch available. Restaurant on premises. Beds: KQDT. Turndown service, ceiling fan in room. VCR, fax, copier, spa, swimming, sauna, bicycles, tennis, library, child care on premises. Handicap access. 113 acres. Weddings, small meetings, family reunions, seminars hosted. German, French, Japanese and Spanish spoken. Antiques, fishing, parks, shopping, sporting events, golf, theater and watersports nearby.

Publicity: *New York Times.*

"My feet have yet to touch the ground as I'm still floating from delicious Kalani."

Volcano   F9

Chalet Kilauea - The Inn at Volcano

PO Box 998
Volcano, HI 96785-0998
(808)967-7786 (800)937-7786 Fax:(808)577-1849
E-mail: reservations@volcano-hawaii.com

Circa 1945. From elegant guest rooms to private cottages and vacation homes, this collection of properties offers something for everyone. The vacation homes are perfect for families. The inn itself offers five rooms, each with a special theme. The rooms sport names such as the Out of Africa, Treehouse or Oriental Jade. The Bridal and  Treehouse suites include Jacuzzi tubs. Inn guests are treated to a two-course, gourmet breakfast served by candlelight.

Historic Interest: Hawaii Volcanoes National Park (1 1/2 mile).

Innkeeper(s): Lisha & Brian Crawford. $125-395. MC VISA AX DS PC. TAC10. 2 rooms with PB, 2 with FP. 4 suites. 6 cottages. 1 conference room. Breakfast and afternoon tea included in rates. Type of meal: gourmet breakfast. Catering service available. Beds: KQT. Phone, ceiling fan, TV and VCR in room. Fax, copier, spa and library on premises. Weddings, small meetings, family reunions and seminars hosted. French, Dutch and Spanish spoken. Antiques, fishing, parks, shopping, theater and watersports nearby.

Hale Ohia Cottages

PO Box 758
Volcano, HI 96785-0758
(808)967-7986 (800)455-3803 Fax:(808)967-8610

Circa 1931. These country cottages, nestled in the quaint Volcano Village area, are surrounded by Hawaiian gardens and lush forest. You can stroll the serene property on paths made of lava rock and enjoy the many orchids and native plants. The gardens are some of the finest in Volcano. Volcano National Park is only one mile from the cottage.

Historic Interest: The home is a historic estate, built by locals, and preserving Hawaii's heritage. Volcano Village itself has more than 150 historic homes or buildings. The historic town of Hilo is 23 miles away.

Innkeeper(s): Michael Tuttle. $75-115. MC VISA DC CB DS PC TAC10. 2 rooms with PB, 2 with FP. 1 suite. 3 cottages. 1 conference room. Breakfast included in rates. Type of meal: continental breakfast. Beds: QDT. VCR, fax, copier and spa on premises. Handicap access. Weddings, small meetings, family reunions and seminars hosted. Antiques, fishing, parks, shopping, theater and watersports nearby.

Publicity: *National Geographic Traveler, N.Y. Times, Hawaii Bride, Pacific Connection, Travel & Leisure.*

Kilauea Lodge

PO Box 116
Volcano, HI 96785-0116
(808)967-7366 Fax:(808)967-7367
E-mail: k-lodge@aloha.net

Circa 1938. Guests are pampered at this gorgeous tropical paradise, only a mile from the entrance to Volcanoes National Park. Fluffy towels, towel warmers, cozy, comfortable beds and rich decor create a feeling of warmth and romance in each of the guest rooms. Fresh flowers and original art  add to the majesty of the lodge. The wonderful, gourmet meals are served in front of the lodge's historic Fireplace of Friendship, which is decked with all sorts of artifacts. The innkeepers offer truly memorable meals, praised by such publications as Bon Appetit and Gourmet Magazine. The inn has an interesting history. Built as a YMCA, it later was used during World War II as offices and a military bivouac.

Historic Interest: Historical Hilo Town is 26 miles away and the Volcano Art Center and original Volcano House, built in the 1890s, are two miles away.

Innkeeper(s): Lorna & Albert Jeyte. $95-145. MC VISA AX PC TC. 11 rooms with PB, 7 with FP. 3 suites. 2 cottages. Breakfast included in rates. Type of meal: full breakfast. Dinner available. Restaurant on premises. Beds: KQT. VCR and library on premises. Handicap access. 10 acres. Weddings and family reunions hosted. German spoken. Antiques and golf nearby.

Publicity: *National Geographic Traveler, Bon Appetit, Conde Nast.*

My Island B&B Inn

PO Box 100
Volcano, HI 96785-0100
(808)967-7216   E-mail: myisland@ilhawaii.net

Circa 1886. Once home to the Lyman family of missionaries, this three-story shiplap house was built in the style of a Connecticut farmhouse. It is located amid flower gardens atop one of the world's most active volcanoes. Furnishings include family heirlooms and  koa pieces. The five-acre grounds include three landscaped acres with more than 150 varieties of flowers, shrubs and trees. The Morses operated Hawaii Island Safaries for 23 years and have an extensive collection of volcano books and maps. The speciality of the house is all the macadamia nuts you can eat.

Innkeeper(s): Gordon & Joann Morse. $60-100. 6 rooms, 3 with PB. Type of meal: full breakfast. Beds: QT. Publicity: *Good Housekeeping, Sunset.*

Volcano B&B

PO Box 998
Volcano, HI 96785-0998
(808)967-7779 (800)736-7140 Fax:(808)967-8660
E-mail: reservations@volcano-hawaii.com

Circa 1912. This three-story historic home, one of Volcano's oldest, has been renovated into a relaxing bed & breakfast. The six, comfortable guest rooms are decorated in a casual, country style. Tropical fruit and sweet breads highlight the continental buffet. The inn is just five minutes from Volcanoes National Park.

Innkeeper(s): Brian & Lisha Crawford. $45-65. 6 rooms. 2 suites.
Publicity: *Travel Weekly.*

Idaho

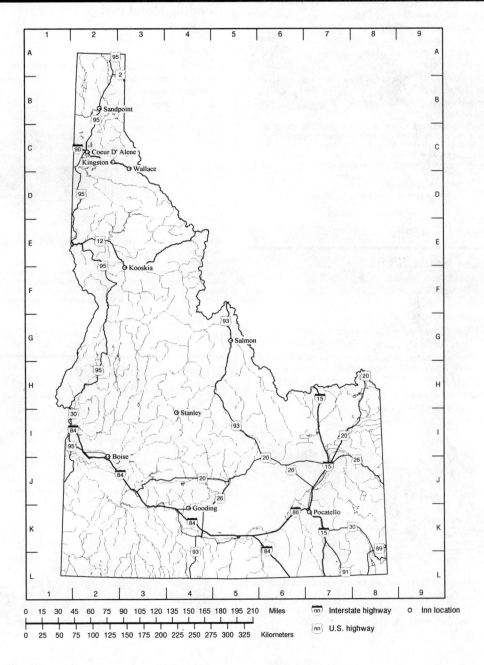

0 15 30 45 60 75 90 105 120 135 150 165 180 195 210 Miles

0 25 50 75 100 125 150 175 200 225 250 275 300 325 Kilometers

[nn] Interstate highway   O Inn location

[nn] U.S. highway

Boise I2

Idaho Heritage Inn

109 W Idaho St
Boise, ID 83702-6122
(208)342-8066 Fax:(208)343-2325

Circa 1904. This Colonial Revival home, set back on a tree-lined street near downtown, was once the home of Senator Frank Church and is in the National Register. Because of its location in the historic Warm Springs district, geothermal water is used for heating and bathing.
Period furnishings and
wall coverings are found
throughout. Bicycles
are available for enjoy-
ing the nearby green-
belt, which winds
along the Boise River.

Innkeeper(s): Phyllis Lupher. $60-95. MC VISA AX DS PC TC. TAC10. 6 rooms with PB. 2 suites. 1 cottage. Breakfast included in rates. Types of meals: full breakfast, gourmet breakfast and early coffee/tea. Beds: Q. Phone, air conditioning and TV in room. VCR, fax and bicycles on premises. Antiques, fishing, parks, shopping, downhill skiing, cross-country skiing and watersports nearby.

Location: Six blocks from downtown.

Publicity: *Idaho Statesman, American West, Idaho Business Review.*

"Thanks so much for the hospitality and warmth."

Coeur D' Alene C2

Baragar House B&B

316 Military Dr
Coeur D' Alene, ID 83814-2137
(208)664-9125 (800)615-8422 Fax:(208)765-2427
E-mail: baragar@dmi.net

Circa 1926. This expansive Craftsman-style bungalow was built by a lumber baron. Each of the rooms is individually decorated. The Honeymoon Suite, decorated in Victorian style, is especially appealing with its oversized bathroom offering a clawfoot tub under a bay window. The Country Cabin room includes murals of a mountain stream and clouds. The floral-themed Garden Room has a canopied window seat and

antique vanity. All rooms include private use of an indoor spa and sauna. Be sure to ask the innkeeper to describe how all guests can "sleep under the stars." The innkeeper prepares "wreck your diet breakfasts" and will accommodate special dietary needs.

Innkeeper(s): Bernie & Carolyn Baragar. $95-125. MC VISA AX DS PC TC. TAC10. 3 rooms, 1 with PB. Breakfast and evening snack included in rates. Types of meals: gourmet breakfast and early coffee/tea. Beds: Q. Air conditioning, ceiling fan, TV and VCR in room. Fax, spa, sauna and library on premises. Amusement parks, antiques, fishing, parks, shopping, downhill skiing, cross-country skiing, sporting events, theater and watersports nearby.

Location: Downtown by city park, beach and college in historic Ft. Sherman.

"Thank you for the hospitality and most exquisite honeymoon setting."

Gooding K4

Gooding Hotel Bed & Breakfast

112 Main St
Gooding, ID 83330-1102
(208)934-4374

Circa 1906. An early Gooding settler, William B. Kelly, built this historic hotel, which is the oldest building in town. Each of the guest rooms is named in honor of someone significant in the history of Gooding or the hotel. A buffet breakfast is served every morning in the William Kelly Room. The area offers many activities, from golfing and fishing to exploring ice caves or visiting wineries and museums.

Historic Interest: Shoshone Ice Caves, 1000 Springs, Craters of the Moon, Snake River Canyon, Sun Valley.

Innkeeper(s): Dean & Judee Gooding. $45-60. MC VISA AX PC TC. TAC10. 3 suites. Breakfast included in rates. Types of meals: continental breakfast, full breakfast and gourmet breakfast. Room service available. Beds: QDT. Air conditioning and ceiling fan in room. TV, copier and bicycles on premises. Small meetings hosted. Antiques, fishing, parks, shopping, downhill skiing, cross-country skiing and golf nearby.

Pets Allowed: $25 deposit on pets.

Kingston C2

Kingston 5 Ranch B&B

42297 Silver Valley Rd
Kingston, ID 83839-0130
(208)682-4862 (800)254-1852 Fax:(208)682-9445
E-mail: k5ranch@nidlink.com

Circa 1930. With the Coeur D' Alene Mountains as its backdrop, this picturesque country farmhouse is a wonderful place to escape and relax. Lazy mornings begin as the scent of freshly ground coffee wafts through the home. Then a hearty country breakfast is served with cured ham, bacon, Belgian waffles topped with fresh fruit, omelets and plenty of other treats.

Many of the ingredients are grown on the farm. The original owners built a garage on the property first and lived there until the Pennsylvania Dutch barn and the farmhouse were built. Innkeepers Walt and Pat Gentry have refurbished the home completely, filling the guest rooms with lace, down comforters and charming furnishings. Rooms also offer romantic amenities such as an in-room fireplace, mountain views, a four-poster bed, private veranda, jetted tub and private decks with an outdoor hot tub.

Historic Interest: The Historic Cataldo Mansion, the oldest building in Idaho, is just five minutes away. Wallace, a town listed on the historic register, is 20 minutes from the farmhouse.

Innkeeper(s): Walter & Pat Gentry. $99-125. MC VISA PC TC. TAC10. 2 rooms with PB, 2 with FP. 1 suite. Breakfast included in rates. Types of meals: full breakfast and early coffee/tea. Evening snack available. Beds: Q. Air conditioning, turndown service, ceiling fan and TV in room. VCR, fax, copier, spa, stables and bicycles on premises. Small meetings hosted. Amusement parks, antiques, fishing, parks, shopping, downhill skiing, cross-country skiing, theater and watersports nearby.

"The food was fabulous and so much!"

Kooskia   F3

Three Rivers Resort

Hwy 12 in Lowell, Idaho
Kooskia, ID 83539-9500
(208)926-4430 Fax:(208)962-7526

Circa 1927. Once a meeting ground for the Nez Perce Indians, the campground and rustic hand-hewn log cabins overlook the Lochsa river. Each of the 15 cabins is decorated in western antiques and feature ceiling fans and outdoor barbeques. Old #1 Log Cabin, a former ranger's cabin, offers a Jacuzzi, VCR, full breakfast and champagne. Set on 200 wooded acres, Three Rivers Resort boasts a heated swimming pool, three Jacuzzis, a gift shop and small grocery store. There is an on-site restaurant, and Lochsa Louie's Bar serves cocktails every night. White-water rafting, fish and game licenses are available.

Innkeeper(s): Mike & Marie Smith. $100. MC VISA AX DC CB DS PC TC. TAC15. 1 room. Breakfast included in rates. Type of meal: full breakfast. Restaurant on premises. Beds: Q. VCR in room. TV, fax, copier, spa and stables on premises. 200 acres. Weddings, small meetings and family reunions hosted. Spanish/Chinese spoken. Antiques, fishing and watersports nearby.

Pets Allowed.

Publicity: *Grizzly Bear, Wolf Recovery Wilderness Specials, Lewis & Clark (Ken Burns).*

Pocatello   K7

Back O' Beyond Victorian Inn

404 S Garfield
Pocatello, ID 83204
(208)232-3825 (888)232-3820 Fax:(208)232-2771
E-mail: backbeyond@gemstate.net

Circa 1893. This Queen Anne Victorian is located on a quiet residential street shaded by trees and decorated with window boxes and gingerbread trim. The home was built by the Ifft family, who published a local newspaper. Three generations of the family lived in the home. Innkeeper Sherrie Mennenga has decorat-

ed the city historic site with a collection of antiques. The decor is reminiscent of a turn-of-the-century family home. Innkeeper Jay Mennenga is an author and has written a book about Pocatello, as well as one documenting the life of pioneers traveling the Oregon Trail. He often hosts lectures about the latter. The two offer murder-mystery theater events at the inn. Shops, restaurants and the university are all nearby.

Innkeeper(s): Jay & Sherrie Mennenga. $60-70. MC VISA AX DC DS PC TC. TAC10. 4 rooms with PB, 1 with FP. Breakfast and afternoon tea included in rates. Types of meals: full breakfast and early coffee/tea. Picnic lunch and room service available. Beds: D. Ceiling fan in room. TV, VCR, fax, copier and library on premises. Weddings, small meetings, family reunions and seminars hosted. Antiques, fishing, parks, shopping, cross-country skiing, sporting events, golf and theater nearby.

Pets Allowed: With prior permission.

Publicity: *Idaho State Journal, City Calendar.*

Salmon   G5

Greyhouse Inn B&B

H C 61, Box 16
Salmon, ID 83467
(208)756-3968 (800)348-8097

Circa 1894. The scenery at Greyhouse is nothing short of wondrous. In the winter, when mountains are capped in white and the evergreens are shrouded in snow, this Victorian appears as a safe haven from the chilly weather. In the summer, the rocky peaks are a contrast to the whimsical house, which looks like something out of an Old West town. The historic home is known around town as the old maternity hospital, but there is nothing medicinal about it now. The rooms are Victorian in style with antique furnishings. The parlor features deep red walls and carpeting, floral overstuffed sofas and a dressmaker's model garbed in a black Victorian gown. Outdoor enthusiasts will find no shortage of activities, from facing the rapids in nearby Salmon River to fishing to horseback riding. The town of Salmon is just 12 miles away.

Innkeeper(s): David & Sharon Osgood. $65-80. MC VISA PC TC. TAC10. 4 rooms, 2 with PB. Breakfast included in rates. Types of meals: full breakfast and early coffee/tea. Afternoon tea and evening snack available. Beds: KQDT. TV, VCR, bicycles, library and pet boarding on premises. Weddings, small meetings and family reunions hosted. Antiques, fishing, parks, shopping, downhill skiing, cross-country skiing, golf and watersports nearby.

Pets Allowed: We have a kennel.

"To come around the corner and find the Greyhouse, as we did, restores my faith! Such a miracle. We had a magical evening here, and we plan to return to stay for a few days. Thanks so much for your kindness and hospitality. We love idaho!"

Sandpoint   B2

Coit House B&B

502 N Fourth St
Sandpoint, ID 83864
(208)265-4035 Fax:(208)265-4035
E-mail: Lodgecenresnidlink.com

Circa 1907. Period, Victorian furnishings, polished wood floors, fine woodwork and a wraparound porch are some of the charming elements at this bed & breakfast. There are four guest rooms, each decorated with unique antiques. Two rooms include clawfoot tubs. Breakfast features a changing menu: Homemade breads, French toast, savory quiches and soufflés are among the possibilities. The inn is located near the Schweitzer Mountain Resort, walking distance to downtown Sandpoint and is less than 50 miles from Coeur D' Alene.

Innkeeper(s): Julie & Seth Coit. $55-85. MC VISA PC TC. TAC10. 4 rooms with PB. Breakfast included in rates. Types of meals: full breakfast and early coffee/tea. Beds: Q. Phone, air conditioning and TV in room. VCR, fax and copier on premises. Small meetings hosted. Amusement parks, antiques, fishing, parks, shopping, downhill skiing, cross-country skiing, golf, theater and watersports nearby.

"The antiques are exquisite, your home is beautiful, we look forward to our next visit."

Stanley   I4

Idaho Rocky Mountain Ranch

HC 64 Box 9934
Stanley, ID 83278
(208)774-3544 Fax:(208)774-3477
E-mail: idrocky@cyberhighway.net

Circa 1930. This large cattle ranch is situated at the 6,600-foot level in the Sawtooth Valley. A rustic lodge dining room overlooks the Salmon River, a mile away, to the spectacular ragged ridges of the Sawtooth Mountains. Near the edge of the river,

the inn has a pool constructed from natural hot springs. Rustic accommodations in lodgepole pine cabins feature handmade log furniture and fieldstone fireplaces. The lodge and cabins recently were listed in the National Register of Historic Places.

Historic Interest: Ghost towns of Vienna, Boulder, Bonanza and Custer (within 50 miles), Stanley Historical Museum (10 miles), Yankee Fork Dredge/Museum (30 miles).

Innkeeper(s): Bill Leavell. $134-224. MAP. MC VISA DS PC TC. 21 rooms with PB, 17 with FP. 9 cottages. Breakfast and dinner included in rates. Type of meal: full breakfast. Picnic lunch available. Beds: QT. Fax, copier, swimming, stables, bicycles and library on premises. 1000 acres. Spanish spoken. Fishing, parks, downhill skiing, cross-country skiing and watersports nearby.

Location: Fifty miles north of Sun Valley.

Publicity: *Washington Post, National Geographic Traveler.*

"We had such a great time! The kids loved it! Can't you adopt us so we can stay longer?"

Wallace   C3

21 Bank Street B&B

21 Bank St
Wallace, ID 83873-2149
(208)752-1292 (888)846-5051 Fax:(208)752-1291

Circa 1916. A former mayor built this home, which is a mixture of Mission and Victorian styles. It was used for several years as a convent. The home has an old-fashioned ambiance

and features light Victorian decor. Guest rooms feature beds topped with flowery prints and a canopy sash at the headboard. The town of Wallace is listed in the National Register and offers interesting mining sites, museums, antique shops and plenty of outdoor activities.

Innkeeper(s): Doug & Terri Austin. $65-75. MC VISA DS PC. TAC10. 3 rooms. Breakfast included in rates. Types of meals: continental breakfast, full breakfast and early coffee/tea. Beds: Q. Turndown service in room. TV, VCR, fax and library on premises. Weddings, small meetings and family reunions hosted. Antiques, fishing, shopping, downhill skiing and cross-country skiing nearby.

The Beale House

107 Cedar St
Wallace, ID 83873-2115
(208)752-7151

Circa 1904. This attractive, three-story Colonial Revival home is listed in the National Register, as is the town of Wallace. Original parquet wood floor, antiques and memorabilia combine to lend an authentic aura of the past. Each of the five guest rooms offers a unique feature, such as a fireplace, balcony or wall of windows. The innkeepers are well versed in their home's history and guests are welcome to look over a photographic record of the house and its former owners. A backyard hot tub provides views of the mountains and creek. Recreational activities abound in the vicinity, famous for its silver mines.

Historic Interest: Town of Wallace, Cataldo Mission.

Innkeeper(s): Jim & Linda See. $75-125. PC TC. TAC10. 5 rooms, 1 with PB, 1 with FP. Breakfast included in rates. Types of meals: continental breakfast, full breakfast and early coffee/tea. Beds: DT. Turndown service in room. TV, VCR, spa and library on premises. Weddings hosted. Antiques, fishing, parks, shopping, downhill skiing, cross-country skiing, theater and watersports nearby.

Publicity: *Shoshone News Press, Spokesman Review, Silver Valley Voice.*

"Thank you for the fine hospitality."

Illinois

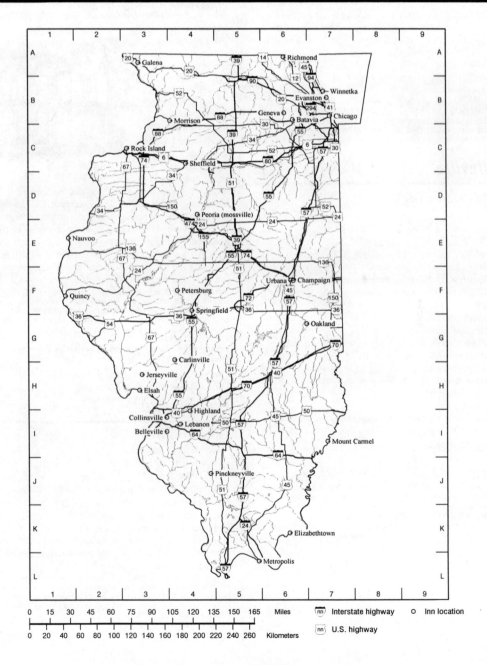

	Miles
0 15 30 45 60 75 90 105 120 135 150 165	
0 20 40 60 80 100 120 140 160 180 200 220 240 260	Kilometers

[nn] Interstate highway   ○ Inn location

[nn] U.S. highway

Batavia B6

Villa Batavia

1430 S Batavia Ave
Batavia, IL 60510
(630)406-8182

Circa 1844. This historic home is a mix of Greek Revival and Italianate styles. The manor is set on seven acres, which include a meadow, a Christmas tree farm and a quaint path that winds its way down to the Fox River. There are two guest rooms at this intimate bed & breakfast, each decorated in Victorian style. The Caroline Room includes an impressive four-poster bed with a lace canopy. Gourmet breakfasts are served on a table set with china and sterling silver. The home is close to a variety of outdoor activities, as well as antique shops and riverboat casinos.

Innkeeper(s): Dick Palmer & Fran Steiner. $90-150. MC VISA DS PC. 2 rooms with PB, 2 with FP. 1 suite. Breakfast included in rates. Types of meals: full breakfast and gourmet breakfast. Beds: Q. Phone, air conditioning and TV in room. Weddings and small meetings hosted. Limited French and German spoken. Antiques, fishing, parks, shopping, cross-country skiing and watersports nearby.

Belleville I3

Swans Court B&B

421 Court St
Belleville, IL 62220-1201
(618)233-0779

Circa 1883. This home, designated by the Department of the Interior as a certified historic structure, was once home to David Baer, known as the "mule king of the world." Baer sold more than 10,000 mules each year to British troops in World War I and Americans in World War II. The home is furnished almost entirely in antiques. Innkeeper Monty Dixon searched high and low to fill her B&B with authentic pieces, creating a nostalgic ambiance. The library offers a selection of books, games and puzzles for guests to enjoy. The home is located in a historic neighborhood, within walking distance to shops and restaurants. Belleville is convenient to St. Louis, and there are casinos, historic sites, a racetrack and a state park nearby.

Innkeeper(s): Ms. Monty Dixon. $65-80. MC VISA AX DS PC TC. TAC10. 4 rooms, 2 with PB, 2 with FP. Breakfast and evening snack included in rates. Type of meal: full breakfast. Beds: DT. Phone, air conditioning and ceiling fan in room. VCR and library on premises. Handicap access. Weddings, small meetings, family reunions and seminars hosted. Spanish spoken. Antiques, shopping, sporting events, golf and theater nearby.

Publicity: *News Democrat, Country Register.*

"*We feel like we have made a new friend. We appreciated all of the nice little touches, such as the fresh flowers.*"

Carlinville G4

Victoria Tyme Inn

511 E First South St
Carlinville, IL 62626-1827
(217)854-8689 Fax:(217)854-5122
E-mail: victyme@accunet.net

Circa 1857. This National Register home actually is comprised of two historic homes, one was built in the 1850s and the other home in 1876. The structures eventually were joined together. Noted author Mary Hunter Austin was born in the home. The inn's spacious suite is named for her, and it includes a whirlpool tub. The decor is an understated Victorian with antiques, and two rooms display pressed tin ceilings. The verandas offer rocking chairs for those who wish to relax, and the half-acre grounds are decorated with gardens. In the morning, the innkeeper's signature waffles or perhaps a rich, stuffed French toast are accompanied by homemade jams and marmalade, fresh fruit and muffins straight from the oven. Carlinville boasts the country's largest collection of Sears catalog homes, as well as shops, antiquing and festivals throughout the year. The town is midway between Springfield, Ill., and St. Louis.

Innkeeper(s): Jeff & Jodie Padgett. $68-130. MC VISA DS PC TC. 4 rooms with PB. 1 suite. Breakfast and evening snack included in rates. Types of meals: full breakfast, gourmet breakfast and early coffee/tea. Beds: Q. Air conditioning, turndown service and ceiling fan in room. TV, VCR, fax and library on premises. French and Spanish spoken. Antiques, fishing, parks, shopping and golf nearby.

Publicity: *State Journal-Register, Belleville News-Democrat, St. Louis Post-Dispatch.*

"*The warmth, beauty and charm of this beautiful home is certainly reflected through both of you.*"

Champaign F6

Golds B&B

2065 County Road 525 E
Champaign, IL 61821-9521
(217)586-4345

Circa 1874. Visitors to the University of Illinois area may enjoy a restful experience at this inn, west of town in a peaceful farmhouse setting. Antique country furniture collected by the innkeepers over the past 25 years is showcased in the inn and is beautifully offset by early American stenciling on its walls. An apple tree and garden are on the grounds, and seasonal items are sometimes used as breakfast fare.

Innkeeper(s): Rita & Bob Gold. $45-50. PC TC. TAC10. 3 rooms, 1 with PB. Breakfast included in rates. Types of meals: continental-plus breakfast and early coffee/tea. Beds: QDT. Air conditioning in room. TV and VCR on premises. Antiques, fishing, parks, shopping, cross-country skiing, sporting events, theater and watersports nearby.

Location: near University of Illinois.

Publicity: *News Gazette.*

Chicago   B7

Amber Creek's Chicago Connection

1260 N Dearborn
Chicago, IL
(815)777-8400 Fax:(815)777-8446

Located in the heart of Chicago's Gold Coast, this early 20th-century flat offers lake views and privacy. The apartment has a spacious living room, antique-decorated bedroom, complete kitchen and bath. Situated directly above one of Chicago's favorite coffee houses, it is within walking distance of the lake, restaurants, night life and Michigan Avenue shopping.
Call for rates.

Gold Coast Guest House

113 W Elm St
Chicago, IL 60610-2805
(312)337-0361 Fax:(312)337-0362
E-mail: Sally@bbchicago.com

Circa 1873. Built just after the Great Chicago Fire, this 19th-century brick row house is situated in the heart of the Gold Coast in one the city's most exclusive neighborhoods. The inn is only one of three historic buildings still standing on Elm Street. Recently restored, the inn is decorated in a combination of antiques and contemporary furnishings. Four tastefully appointed guest rooms offer private baths, TV and ceiling fans. The two upstairs guest rooms feature whirlpool tubs, while one offers a bay window and the original brick fireplace. Fresh bagels, fruit, apple-cinnamon coffee cake, English muffins and assorted cereals are served in the second-floor dining room. The inn is a five-minute walk to the shops on the "Magnificent Mile" and to the lakeshore, public transportation, restaurants, museums and theaters.
Innkeeper(s): Sally Baker. $99-179. MC VISA AX DS PC TC. TAC10. 4 rooms with PB. 1 conference room. Breakfast included in rates. Types of meals: continental breakfast, continental-plus breakfast and early coffee/tea. Beds: QT. Phone, air conditioning, ceiling fan and TV in room. Fax on premises. Small meetings and family reunions hosted. Amusement parks, antiques, parks, shopping, sporting events, golf, theater and watersports nearby.
Publicity: *Mexico City Times, Kansas City Magazine, Michigan Living, Country Inns, "HUS" Sweden.*

Wooded Isle Suites & Apts

5750 S Stony Island Ave
Chicago, IL 60637-2051
(773)288-6305 (800)290-6844 Fax:(773)288-8972
E-mail: chavenswi@aol.com

Circa 1914. Although neither bed & breakfast nor country inn, this collection of two- and three-room apartment suites serves as a convenient, relaxing alternative to hotel travel. The suites are located in Chicago's Hyde Park area and are convenient to the many museums, shops, restaurants and attractions in the downtown area and Lake Michigan. The early 20th-century complex originally served as housing for employees of the Illinois Central Railroad Hospital. Each suite includes a long list of practical amenities, such as a kitchen stocked with pots, pans, dishes, coffee makers, coffee, tea bags and more. The decor is a pleasant, contemporary style.
Innkeeper(s): Charlie Havens & Sara Pitcher. $108-136. MC VISA AX DS PC. TAC10. 13 suites. Beds: Q. Phone, air conditioning, ceiling fan and TV in room. Fishing, parks, sporting events, theater and watersports nearby.

"We have all had very positive experiences at Wooded Isle. Everyone has been pleasant and tuned in to our joy."

Collinsville   I3

Maggie's B&B

2102 N Keebler Ave
Collinsville, IL 62234-4713
(618)344-8283

Circa 1900. A rustic two-acre wooded area surrounds this friendly Victorian inn, once a boarding house. Rooms with 14-foot ceilings are furnished with exquisite antiques and art objects collected on worldwide travels. Downtown St. Louis, the Gateway Arch and the Mississippi riverfront are just 10 minutes away.
Historic Interest: Cahokia Indian Mounds (3 miles), Gateway Arch (15 miles).
Innkeeper(s): Maggie Leyda.
$40-85. PC TC. 5 rooms, 3 with PB, 2 with FP. 1 suite. 1 conference room. Breakfast included in rates. Types of meals: full breakfast and early coffee/tea. Beds: QDT. Air conditioning, turndown service, ceiling fan, TV and VCR in room. Spa and library on premises. Handicap access. Weddings, small meetings and family reunions hosted. Amusement parks, antiques, fishing, parks, shopping, sporting events and theater nearby.
Publicity: *Collinsville Herald Journal, Innsider, Belleville News, Democrat, Saint Louis Homes & Gardens, Cooking Light, USA Today.*

"We enjoyed a delightful stay. You've thought of everything. What fun!"

Elizabethtown   K6

River Rose Inn B&B

1 Main St PO Box 78
Elizabethtown, IL 62931-0078
(618)287-8811

Circa 1914. Large, shade trees veil the front of this Greek Gothic home, nestled along the banks of the Ohio River. From the grand front entrance, guests look out to polished woodwork and a staircase leading to shelves of books. Rooms are cheerful and nostalgic, decorated with antiques. Each guest room offers something special. One has a four-poster bed, another offers a fireplace. The Scarlet Room has its own balcony, and the Rose Room has a private patio. The Magnolia Cottage is ideal for honeymooners and includes a whirlpool tub for two, fireplace and a deck that overlooks the river. Breakfasts are served either in the dining room or in the glass atrium room, where guests can enjoy the water views.
Innkeeper(s): Don & Elisabeth Phillips. $59-90. MC VISA PC TC. 5 rooms with PB, 1 with FP. 1 cottage. Breakfast included in rates. Types of meals: gourmet breakfast and early coffee/tea. Beds: Q. Air conditioning, ceiling fan and TV in room. VCR, swimming and library on premises. English, French and German spoken. Antiques, fishing, parks, shopping and watersports nearby.

Elsah   H3

Corner Nest B&B

3 Elm St, PO Box 220
Elsah, IL 62028
(618)374-1892 (800)884-3832

Circa 1883. In the National Register, this country houses eclectic architecture of includes a glassed-in porch and several dormers. Surrounding limestone bluffs rise 400 feet above the inn and the Mississippi River. It is one block from the Great River Road in the village. Rooms are decorated in various antique themes such as Primitive, Country Victorian and the Twenties. Nearby are 80 antique shops. Ham, eggs, biscuits and gravy are offered for breakfast as well as lighter items. American Bald Eagles roost in the surrounding area, and guests often enjoy spotting them during breakfast.

Innkeeper(s): Judy & Bob Doerr. $70-90. MC VISA DS PC TC. TAC10. 4 rooms, 2 with PB. Breakfast included in rates. Types of meals: full breakfast and early coffee/tea. Beds: D. Air conditioning and TV in room. VCR and bicycles on premises. Weddings, small meetings and seminars hosted. Amusement parks, antiques, fishing, parks, sporting events, golf, theater and watersports nearby.

Evanston B7

The Homestead

1625 Hinman Ave
Evanston, IL 60201
(847)475-3300 Fax:(847)570-8100
E-mail: office@homesteadev.com

Circa 1927. This hotel, the only lodging in Evanston's Lakeshore Historic District, was built by a local architect and his Colonial structure is very much unchanged from its beginnings in the 1920s.

Several rooms offer views of Lake Michigan, which is just two blocks away. Northwestern University also is just a two-block walk from the hotel. The inn's much-renown restaurant, Trio, serves specialties such  as grilled pheasant with pinenut bread pudding or perhaps roasted Maine sea scallops served with a black truffle and parmesan risotto.

Innkeeper(s): David Reynolds. $85-150. MC VISA AX DC DS PC TC. 35 rooms. 1 suite. 1 conference room. Breakfast included in rates. Type of meal: continental breakfast. Restaurant on premises. Beds: QDT. Phone, air conditioning and TV in room. Fax, copier and library on premises. Small meetings and seminars hosted. Parks, sporting events, theater and watersports nearby.

Margarita European Inn

1566 Oak Ave
Evanston, IL 60201-4234
(847)869-2273 Fax:(847)869-2353

Circa 1927. This stately inn, once the proper home to young area working women, has a proud tradition in the city's history. The Georgian architecture is complemented by an impressive interior, featuring arched French doors, vintage period molding and a large parlor with floor-to-ceiling windows. Near the lakefront and Northwestern University, it also boasts, a library, large-screen TV room and VaPenisero, a restaurant serving regional Italian specialties. Guests often enjoy renting a bike and exploring the area's many attractions, including 24 nearby art galleries.

Innkeeper(s): Barbara & Tim Gorham. Call for rates. 1 conference room. Phone and ceiling fan in room. Weddings, small meetings, family reunions and seminars hosted. Antiques, shopping, sporting events and theater nearby.

Galena A3

Aldrich Guest House

900 3rd St
Galena, IL 61036-2627
(815)777-3323

Circa 1845. This elegant Greek Revival home is listed in the National Register of Historic Places. Victorian antiques decorate the interior. Guest rooms include antiques and handmade quilts. Clawfoot tubs and pedestal sinks in the private bathrooms add to the nostalgic charm of the inn. A multi-course, gourmet breakfast is prepared daily served on fine china and linens. The screened porch overlooks the yard where General Grant once drilled Union soldiers. The home is within walking distance of shops and restaurants.

Innkeeper(s): Sandy & Herb Larson. $85-155. MC VISA DS PC. 5 rooms with PB. Type of meal: full breakfast. Beds: Q. Air conditioning in room. Publicity: *Chicago Tribune, Telegraph Herald.*

"Thank you for the 'personal touch' you give to your guests."

Avery Guest House

606 S Prospect St
Galena, IL 61036-2520
(815)777-3883

Circa 1848. Avery Guest House is named for Major George Avery, who served in the Civil War and later led parades through Galena each year. The house originally was owned by a steamboat captain and later by a wagon-maker. There is a porch swing for leisurely evenings. Breakfast is served in the sunny dining room where bay windows overlook the Galena River Valley. It's an easy walk to the historic downtown area.

Historic Interest: General Grant's Home, Old Market House (walking distance), Museums, Trolley Tour.

Innkeeper(s): Gerry & Armon Lamparelli. $60-85. MC VISA. 3 rooms. Breakfast included in rates. Type of meal: full breakfast. Beds: Q. Phone in room. Antiques and theater nearby.

Publicity: *Galena Gazette, Chicago Tribune.*

"We've stayed in several B&Bs, and this one is the most pleasant and friendly."

Captain Gear Guest House

1000 S Bench St, PO Box 1040
Galena, IL 61036-1040
(815)777-0222 (800)794-5656 Fax:(815)777-3210

Circa 1855. Lead miner Captain Hezekiah H. Gear chose this picturesque spot overlooking the Galena River Valley to build his gracious estate. The lush, four-acre grounds create a secluded, country atmosphere paralleled by the romantic, country guest rooms, each of which contains a fireplace and a view of the grounds. One room also includes a whirlpool tub. The home has been carefully

decorated with carved rosewood and mahogany furnishings. The formal breakfasts at this National Register home are served on silver and china in the dining room.

Historic Interest: Galena has been designated a historic district and is listed in the National Register. The area is full of 19th- and early 20th-century architecture.

Innkeeper(s): Susan Pettey. $135-175. MC VISA DS PC. 3 rooms with PB, 3 with FP. 1 suite. Breakfast included in rates. Type of meal: full breakfast. Beds: KQ. Air conditioning and VCR in room. Antiques, parks, shopping, downhill skiing, cross-country skiing, theater and watersports nearby.

Hellman Guest House

318 Hill St
Galena, IL 61036-1836
(815)777-3638

Circa 1895. A corner tower and an observatory turret rise above the gabled roof line of this Queen Anne house built of Galena brick. The house was constructed from designs drawn by Schoppel of New York. An antique telescope in the parlor is a favorite of guests who wish to view the town. Stained glass, pocket doors and antique furnishings add to the inn's charms. The Tower Room with its brass bed, fireplace and village views is recommended.

Historic Interest: Market House, Grants Home and Washburn House. Most of Galena is in the National Register of Historic Places.

Innkeeper(s): Merilyn Tommaro. $89-149. MC VISA DS PC. 4 rooms with PB. Breakfast included in rates. Types of meals: full breakfast and early coffee/tea. Beds: Q. Air conditioning in room. Library on premises. Small meetings and family reunions hosted. Amusement parks, antiques, parks, shopping, downhill skiing, cross-country skiing, theater and watersports nearby.

Publicity: *Innsider, Midwest Living, Chicago Tribune.*

"We found your home a treasure, the breakfast delicious and your company superb."

Park Avenue Guest House

208 Park Ave
Galena, IL 61036-2306
(815)777-1075

Circa 1893. A short walk from Grant Park sits this attractive Queen Anne Victorian with turret and wraparound porch. Gardens and a gazebo add to this peaceful neighborhood charm, as does the original woodwork throughout. The Helen Room features a gas fireplace, TV, tub and shower, while Miriam Room's brass bed highlights a cheerful floral decor and a fireplace. The Anna Suite also has a fireplace and boasts a comfortable sitting room in the inn's turret area and the Lucille Room is tastefully furnished in mauve, gray and white tones. The holiday decorations, including twelve Christmas trees, are not to be missed.

Innkeeper(s): Sharon & John Fallbacher. $85-105. MC VISA DS PC TC. 4 rooms with PB, 3 with FP. 1 suite. Evening snack included in rates. Types of meals: continental-plus breakfast and early coffee/tea. Beds: QT. Air conditioning, ceiling fan and TV in room. VCR on premises. Weddings, small meetings and family reunions hosted. Antiques, fishing, shopping, downhill skiing, cross-country skiing and theater nearby.

Publicity: *Country Inns.*

Geneva

The Oscar Swan Country Inn

1800 W State St
Geneva, IL 60134-1002
(630)232-0173

Circa 1902. This turn-of-the-century Colonial Revival house rests on seven acres of trees and lawns. Its 6,000 square feet are filled with homey touches. There is a historic barn on the

property and a gazebo on the front lawn. A pillared breezeway connects the round garage to the house. The stone pool is round, as well. Nina is a retired home economics teacher and Hans speaks German and was a professor of business administration at Indiana University.

Innkeeper(s): Nina Heymann. $65-139. MC VISA AX. 8 rooms, 4 with PB. 3 conference rooms. Breakfast included in rates. Type of meal: full breakfast. Lunch and catering service available. Beds: KQD. Phone, air conditioning and VCR in room. Weddings, small meetings, family reunions and seminars hosted. Antiques, shopping, cross-country skiing and theater nearby.

Publicity: *Chicago Tribune, Windmill News.*

"Thank you for making our wedding such a beautiful memory. The accommodations were wonderful, the food excellent."

Highland

Tibbetts House

801 9th St
Highland, IL 62249-1521
(618)654-4619

Circa 1914. Local doctor Mose Tibbetts built this home as his family residence in a town known as the oldest and largest Swiss settlement in Illinois. There are five guest rooms, each named in honor of a member of the Tibbets family. Each room is individually decorated, and antiques such as the beautifully carved, rich wood pieces add to the country appeal. Fluffy robes and slippers are placed in each guest room, and guests sometimes will find little extras such as chocolates or fresh flowers. Guests enjoy breakfast on a table set with china and crystal in the home's dining room, which features a built-in oak buffet with leaded-glass panes. The grounds, are lush with trees and flowers, and guests can relax and enjoy the peaceful surroundings on the sun deck or on an enclosed front porch. The innkeeper's brother and sister-in-law run a successful restaurant across the street in a mid-19th-century home. Tibbetts House is close to antique shops, restaurants, historic sites and plenty of outdoor activities.

Historic Interest: The Kaeser Park house, a former stagecoach house and now a museum, is nearby. Other historic sites include the Latzer Homestead, home of the man who founded Pet Inc.

Innkeeper(s): Ruth Ann Ernst. $65-80. MC VISA. 5 rooms, 3 with PB. Type of meal: full breakfast. Beds: KQDT. Phone, air conditioning and turndown service in room. TV on premises. Small meetings and family reunions hosted. Antiques, fishing, shopping and sporting events nearby.

Location: Twenty-five minutes from St. Louis.

Jerseyville H3

The Homeridge B&B

1470 N State St
Jerseyville, IL 62052-1127
(618)498-3442

Circa 1867. This red brick Italianate Victorian features ornate white trim, a stately front veranda and a cupola where guests often take in views of sunsets and the surrounding 18 acres.

The home was constructed by Cornelius Fisher, just after the Civil War. In 1891, it was purchased by Senator Theodore Chapman and remained in his family until the 1960s. The innkeepers have filled the 14-room manor with traditional and Victorian furnishings, enhancing the high ceilings and ornate woodwork typical of the era. Guests are invited to take a relaxing dip in the inn's swimming pool or relax with a refreshment on the veranda.

Innkeeper(s): Sue & Howard Landon. $75-85. MC VISA AX PC TC. 4 rooms with PB. Breakfast included in rates. Types of meals: full breakfast and early coffee/tea. Afternoon tea available. Beds: KDT. Air conditioning and ceiling fan in room. TV, VCR, copier, swimming, bicycles and library on premises. 20 acres. Weddings, small meetings, family reunions and seminars hosted. Amusement parks, antiques, fishing, parks, shopping, cross-country skiing, sporting events, theater and watersports nearby.

"A most beautiful, entertaining, snow-filled few days."

Lebanon I4

Landmark on Madison B&B

118 S Madison St
Lebanon, IL 62254-1504
(618)537-9532 (800)226-6632

Circa 1906. Lebanon's first hotel once rested where this manor now stands. Eventually, it was torn down to make room for the impressive Greek Revival, which was to be the home of a prominent Lebanon family. The ionic columns that grace the exterior were brought here from the St. Louis World's Fair. The interior is gracious with Oriental rugs and traditional furnishings. Each room has its name painted on the door. The Mill Pond Room can be transformed into a suite with a private library. The Veranda Room includes antiques and a brass bed.

Breakfasts are artfully presented on a table set with lace and china. Strawberry parfaits, freshly baked muffins or breads and entrees such as a soufflé might be the fare. Weddings, and proposals, are quite com-

mon here. The inn is a half-hour from St. Louis, and near to shops, a lake, riverboat casinos and more.

Innkeeper(s): Betty & John Carter. $75-95. MC VISA DS PC TC. TAC10. 3 rooms with PB. Breakfast, afternoon tea and evening snack included in rates. Types of meals: gourmet breakfast and early coffee/tea. Beds: KQT. Air conditioning, turndown service and ceiling fan in room. TV, VCR and library on premises. Weddings and small meetings hosted. Antiques, fishing, parks, shopping, sporting events, golf, theater and watersports nearby.

"This B&B is a place of warmth and beauty. Its charm is reflective of the talent and hospitality of our hosts."

Metropolis L5

Isle of View B&B

205 Metropolis St
Metropolis, IL 62960-2213
(618)524-5838 Fax:(618)524-2978

Circa 1889. Metropolis, billed as the "home of Superman," is not a bustling concrete city, but a quaint, country town tucked along the Ohio River. The Isle of View, a stunning Italianate manor, is just a short walk from shops, restaurants and the Players Riverboat Casino. All the guest rooms are appointed in Victorian design with antiques. The Master Suite was originally the

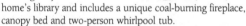

home's library and includes a unique coal-burning fireplace, canopy bed and two-person whirlpool tub.

Innkeeper(s): Kim & Gerald Offenburger. $65-115. MC VISA AX DC CB DS TC. 5 rooms with PB. Breakfast included in rates. Types of meals: gourmet breakfast and early coffee/tea. Beds: KQD. Phone, air conditioning, ceiling fan and TV in room. Small meetings and family reunions hosted. Antiques, fishing, parks, shopping, theater and watersports nearby.

Pets Allowed.

"You may never want to leave."

Morrison B4

Hillendale B&B

600 W Lincolnway
Morrison, IL 61270-2058
(815)772-3454 Fax:(815)772-7023
E-mail: hillend@clinton.net

Circa 1891. Guests at Hillendale don't simply spend the night in the quaint town of Morrison, Ill., they spend the night in France, Italy, Hawaii or Africa. Each of the guests rooms in this Tudor manor reflects a different theme from around the world. Travelers and innkeepers Barb and Mike Winandy cleverly decorated each of the guest quarters. The Kimarrin room reflects Mayan culture with photographs of antiquities. The Outback, a private cottage, boasts a fireplace and whirlpool spa along with Australian decor. The Failte room includes a rococo Victorian antique highback bed, fireplace and Irish-themed decor. And these are just a few of the

possibilities. Barb creates wonderful breakfasts full of muffins, breads and special entrees. Stroll the two-acre grounds and you will encounter a three-tier water pond, which sits in front of a teahouse, built by the original owner after a trip to Japan. One of the tiers houses Japanese Koi and another a water garden. The area has riverboat gambling and plenty of outdoor activities. Carriage, hay and sleigh rides, and massages can be arranged.

Historic Interest: The home is near several historic sites, including Albany Indian Burial Mounds, Dillion Home Museum and Carlton House, Morrison Historic Society. Hillendale is part of the Northwest Illinois Chocolate Trail.

Innkeeper(s): Barb & Mike Winandy. $55-150. MC VISA AX DC DS TC. 10 rooms with PB. Breakfast included in rates. Type of meal: full breakfast. Beds: QDT. Phone, air conditioning, ceiling fan, TV and VCR in room. Fax and copier on premises. Small meetings hosted. Antiques, fishing, parks, cross-country skiing and theater nearby.

Location: On the historic original Lincoln Highway.

Publicity: *New York Times, Sterling Gazette, Whiteside News Sentinel, Midwest Living, Home & Away.*

"We've never been any place else that made us feel so catered to and comfortable. Thank you for allowing us to stay in your beautiful home. We feel very privileged."

Mount Carmel I7

The Poor Farm B&B

Poor Farm Rd
Mount Carmel, IL 62863-9803
(618)262-4663 (800)646-3276 Fax:(618)262-8199
E-mail: poorfarm@midwest.net

Circa 1915. This uniquely named inn served as a home for the homeless for more than a century. Today, the stately Federal-style structure hosts travelers and visitors to this area of Southeastern Illinois, offering a "gracious glimpse of yester-year." An antique player piano and VCRs add to guests' comfort, and the inn also has bicycles available for those wishing to explore the grounds. The Poor Farm B&B sits adjacent to a recreational park with a well-stocked lake and is within walking distance of an 18-hole golf course and driving range. Riverboat gambling is 45 minutes away in Evansville, Ind.

Historic Interest: Historic New Harmony, Indiana (40 Minutes).

Innkeeper(s): Liz & John Stelzer. $45-85. MC VISA AX DS PC TC. TAC10. 5 rooms with PB, 2 with FP. 2 suites. 2 conference rooms. Breakfast included in rates. Types of meals: full breakfast and early coffee/tea. Afternoon tea, dinner, evening snack, lunch, banquet service and catering service available. Restaurant on premises. Beds: QDT. Phone, air conditioning, turndown service, ceiling fan and VCR in room. Fax, copier, bicycles and library on premises. Handicap access. Weddings, small meetings, family reunions and seminars hosted. Amusement parks, antiques, fishing, parks, shopping, cross-country skiing, sporting events, theater and watersports nearby.

Pets Allowed: None inside-outside enclosure.

"Delightful. Oatmeal supreme. Best in Illinois. Enjoyed every moment. Hi Yo Silver!"

Nauvoo E1

The Ancient Pines B&B

2015 Parley St
Nauvoo, IL 62354
(217)453-2767

Circa 1900. This turn-of-the-century home is surrounded by 140-year-old pines, and the grounds boast flower and herb gardens as well as a lawn set up for croquet games. Guest rooms are decorated with lacy curtains, restored pine floors and

unique decor. Fresh coffees and herbal teas complement the breakfasts of homemade breads, fruit, eggs and ham or sausage. The innkeepers also offer heart-healthy meals upon request. The area boasts many places to visit, including a  steamboat casino, biennial passion play, the Nauvoo Blue Cheese Factory and Baxterís Vineyard and Winery.

Historic Interest: Civil War re-enactments and historic Mormon homes are among the areaís historic attractions.

Innkeeper(s): Genevieve Simmens. $45-49. 3 rooms. Breakfast included in rates. Type of meal: full breakfast. Beds: QDT. Antiques, fishing and watersports nearby.

Publicity: *Midwest Living, Country Inns and B&B's.*

Oakland G6

The Inn on The Square

3 Montgomery
Oakland, IL 61943
(217)346-2289

Circa 1878. This inn features hand-carved beams and braided rugs on wide pine flooring. The Tea Room has oak tables, fresh flowers and a hand-laid brick fireplace. Guests may wander in the forest behind the inn or relax in the library with a book or jigsaw puzzle. Guest rooms have oak poster beds and handmade quilts. The Pine Room boasts an heirloom bed with a carved headboard. In addition to guest rooms, the inn houses shops selling ladies apparel, gifts and antiques.

Innkeeper(s): Linda & Gary Miller. $50-60. MC VISA. 3 rooms with PB, 1 with FP. 1 conference room. Type of meal: full breakfast. Restaurant on premises. Beds: D. Phone in room. Fishing and golf nearby.

Publicity: *Amish Country News, PM, Midwest Living, Country Living.*

Peoria (Mossville) D4

Old Church House Inn

1416 E Mossville Rd
Peoria (Mossville), IL 61552
(309)579-2300

Circa 1869. Once a church sanctuary, this restored Colonial-style home now features Victorian ambiance highlighted by the 18-foot wooden ceilings, arched windows and period furnishings. Each of the guest rooms offers something unique, such as an 1860s carved bedstead, featherbeds, handmade quilts and lacy curtains.

Guests can enjoy a relaxing stroll through flower, herb and vegetable gardens, or sip afternoon tea.

Innkeeper(s): Dean & Holly Ramseyer. $75-105. MC VISA DS. 2 rooms, 1 with PB. Breakfast and afternoon tea included in rates. Types of meals: continental-plus breakfast and early coffee/tea. Picnic lunch and room service available. Beds: Q. Air conditioning and turndown service in room. Weddings and small meetings hosted. Antiques, fishing, shopping, cross-country skiing, sporting events, theater and watersports nearby.

Location: Peoria's northside.

Publicity: *Chillicothe Bulletin, Journal Star.*

"Your hospitality, thoughtfulness, the cleanliness, beauty, I should just say everything was the best."

Petersburg   F4

The Oaks Bed & Breakfast

510 W Sheridan St
Petersburg, IL 62675-1358
(217)632-5444

Circa 1875. More than five acres of manicured gardens and grand oak trees surround this brick Italianate Victorian, complete with tower and gables. Inside, a three-story walnut staircase with finely carved newel post, seven fireplaces, ornate plasterwork, walnut woodwork and interior shutters set an elegant tone. The Edward Laning Suite provides an excellent view of historic Petersburg and the Sangamon River. A fireplace and antique furnishings complement its black, gold and ivory decor. Seven-course dinners and picnic lunches are available with advance arrangement. Nearby is Lincoln's New Salem with its reconstructed 1830s village.

Innkeeper(s): Susan & Ken Rodger. $70-115. MC VISA DS PC TC. 5 rooms, 3 with PB. Breakfast and afternoon tea included in rates. Type of meal: gourmet breakfast. Dinner and picnic lunch available. Beds: QD. Library on premises. Weddings, small meetings, family reunions and seminars hosted. Antiques, fishing, parks and watersports nearby.

Pinckneyville   J4

Oxbow B&B

R R 1 Box 47
Pinckneyville, IL 62274-9711
(618)357-9839

Circa 1929. Several of the guest rooms at this unique brick veneer farmhouse feature beds designed and built by innkeeper Al Doughty, who among his other trades has been a rural veterinarian, Civil War historian and coal miner. His wife, innkeeper Peggy Doughty, raises prize Arabian horses, some of which have gone on to reach Top Ten Championships. Each of the antique-filled guest rooms features names from the Civil War. The Shiloh room boasts a seven-foot headboard, marble-top dresser and quaint wash stand with a pitcher and mirror, while the Pilot Knob room features a four-poster, canopy bed made from aged barn timbers. There's is a large parking area at the B&B.

Historic Interest: Oxbow B&B is near several historic sites, including Fort Kaskaskia, St. Mary River Covered Bridge, Charter Oak Schoolhouse, Pierre Menard Home, The Old Slave House and Fort De Chartes. The Perry County Historical Jail is only one mile from the home.

Innkeeper(s): Al & Peggy Doughty. $50-65. MC VISA. 5 rooms with PB. 1 suite. Breakfast included in rates. Type of meal: full breakfast. Beds: Q. Antiques, fishing and watersports nearby.

Quincy   F1

The Kaufmann House B&B

1641 Hampshire St
Quincy, IL 62301-3143
(217)223-2502

Circa 1885. Gardens, tall trees and a fountain are part of the setting for this Queen Anne-style inn. Ask for the Gray Antique Room with walnut antiques, a sleigh couch and a bay window offering views of the terraced gardens. The Patriot Room features a sitting area and trundle bed, private bath and a balcony. Breakfast by candlelight and on antique china often features freshly baked scones and ham and cheese roll-ups. Borrow the inn's bicycle built for two and ask for directions to a scenic route.

Innkeeper(s): Emery & Bettie Kaufmann. $70. PC. 3 rooms with PB. 2 suites. 1 conference room. Breakfast included in rates. Types of meals: gourmet breakfast and early coffee/tea. Beds: QDT. Air conditioning in room. TV, VCR, bicycles and library on premises. Weddings, small meetings, family reunions and seminars hosted. Antiques, fishing, parks, shopping, golf, theater and watersports nearby.

Richmond   A6

Gazebo House B&B

10314 East St
Richmond, IL 60071
(815)678-2505

Circa 1893. This intimate, homestay B&B is located in a charming "Painted Lady," whimsically painted and set on a fragrant five acres with gardens and trees. The well-designed interior has a hint of the Victorian era, with a few flowery touches, but mostly elegant and understated decor. One room offers a brass bed and a unique rocking horse, the other has a four-poster bed. The Richmond room also has a whirlpool tub. Guests can relax on the veranda, stroll the scenic grounds or relax with a good book. The innkeepers have more than 1,000 volumes on bookshelves around the home.

Innkeeper(s): Sandy & Jeff Heaney. $89-109. MC VISA DS PC. TAC5. 2 rooms with PB, 1 with FP. Breakfast included in rates. Type of meal: continental-plus breakfast. Beds: Q. Air conditioning, ceiling fan and TV in room. VCR, fax, spa and library on premises. Antiques, fishing, parks, shopping, downhill skiing, cross-country skiing, golf, theater and watersports nearby.

Publicity: *Classic Cars Magazine, Chicago Tribune, NW Herald, Lakeland.*

"The quiet and calm atmosphere was just what I needed!"

Rock Island   C3

Victorian Inn

702 20th St
Rock Island, IL 61201-2638
(309)788-7068

Circa 1876. Built as a wedding present for the daughter of a Rock Island liquor baron, the inn's striking features include illuminated stained-glass tower windows. Other examples of the Victorian decor are the living room's beveled-plate-glass French doors and the dining room's Flemish Oak ceiling beams and paneling, crowned by turn-of-the-century tapestries. Standing within sight of three other buildings listed in the National Register, the inn's wooded grounds are home to many songbirds from the area. A glassed-in Florida porch is perfect for relaxing during any season and a patio table in the gardens

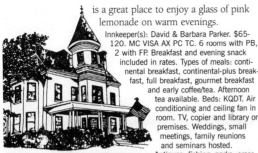

is a great place to enjoy a glass of pink lemonade on warm evenings.

Innkeeper(s): David & Barbara Parker. $65-120. MC VISA AX PC TC. 6 rooms with PB, 2 with FP. Breakfast and evening snack included in rates. Types of meals: continental breakfast, continental-plus breakfast, full breakfast, gourmet breakfast and early coffee/tea. Afternoon tea available. Beds: KQDT. Air conditioning and ceiling fan in room. TV, copier and library on premises. Weddings, small meetings, family reunions and seminars hosted. Antiques, fishing, parks, cross-country skiing, sporting events, theater and watersports nearby.

Sheffield   C4

Chestnut Street Inn

301 E Chestnut St
Sheffield, IL 61361
(815)454-2419

Circa 1854. Originally built in Italianate style, this mid-19th-century reborn Colonial Revival is the dream-come-true for innkeeper Gail Bruntjen. She spent more than 15 years searching for just the right country home to open a bed & breakfast. With its gracious architectural character and well-organized interior spaces, the Chestnut Street Inn fit

the bill. Classic French doors open to a wide foyer with gleaming chandeliers and a floating spindle staircase. Sophisticated chintz fabrics and authentic antiques highlight each room. The four guest rooms offer down comforters, four-poster beds and private baths. Guests will be delighted by the gourmet selections offered every morning such as broccoli mushroom quiche, homemade breads and fresh fruit, all exquistly presented by candlelight on fine China and crystal. Afternoon tea and evening snacks are served in the public rooms. Antiquing, shops, golf and fishing are located nearby.

Innkeeper(s): Gail Bruntjen. $75-150. MC VISA PC TC. TAC10. 4 rooms with PB, 1 with FP. 1 suite. 1 conference room. Breakfast, afternoon tea and evening snack included in rates. Types of meals: full breakfast and early coffee/tea. Beds: KQT. Air conditioning, turndown service, TV and VCR in room. Library on premises. Weddings and small meetings hosted. Antiques, fishing, parks, shopping and golf nearby.

Publicity: *The Illinois Review.*

"Without a doubt, the best B&B I've ever been to."

Springfield   F4

The Inn on Edwards B&B

810 E Edwards St
Springfield, IL 62703
(217)528-0420

Circa 1865. The cheerful blue Italianate Victorian displays many original features, from its curving walnut staircase, fine woodwork and fireplace mantel with faux marbling. The home was appointed by a local interior

design firm, and rooms feature antiques. The home is adjacent to the Lincoln Home National Historic Site, which includes Abraham Lincoln's family home and several blocks of Springfield.

Innkeeper(s): Charles Kirchner. $65-75. MC VISA PC. TAC10. 4 rooms with PB. Breakfast included in rates. Type of meal: full breakfast. Beds: QT. Air conditioning and ceiling fan in room. Amusement parks, antiques, fishing, parks, shopping, sporting events, golf, theater and watersports nearby.

Publicity: *State Journal Register.*

Urbana   F6

Lindley House

312 W Green St
Urbana, IL 61801-3222
(217)384-4800 Fax:(217)384-8280
E-mail: lindley@shout.net

Circa 1895. Designed by architect Rudolph Zachariah Gill from the University of Illinois for a prominent physician, this classic Queen Anne Victorian displays many of the whimsical architectural details popular during this era. The facade features imposing gables, an octagonal turret and a curved porch supported by four carved wooden columns. Gleaming parquet floors in the four public rooms, a magnificent oak gingerbread staircase, beveled- and stained-glass windows are all part of the many Victorian detailing on the inside. All second-floor guest rooms are decorated in period antiques, while the spacious attic suite offers a sitting area and private bath. Guests are invited to enjoy a cup of tea in the parlor or library. Fresh fruit, homemade breads and Columbian coffee are offered in the morning. Lindley House is located close to antiques, parks, sports activities and the University of Illinois.

Innkeeper(s): Catherine Cutter. $75-150. MC VISA PC TC. 4 rooms, 1 with PB. 1 suite. 1 cottage. Breakfast included in rates. Types of meals: continental-plus breakfast and early coffee/tea. Beds: KQ. Phone, air conditioning, ceiling fan, TV and VCR in room. Bicycles and library on premises. Weddings, small meetings, family reunions and seminars hosted. Antiques, fishing, parks, shopping, sporting events, golf and theater nearby.

Winnetka   B7

Chateau Des Fleurs

552 Ridge Rd
Winnetka, IL 60093-3926
(847)256-7272 Fax:(847)256-7272

Circa 1936. This is an authentic French-style country home near Lake Michigan. The lawn and terraced English gardens are shaded by cottonwood, willow and apple trees. A Steinway baby grand piano is in the living room, and there is a library available to guests. The Northwestern Train to the Chicago Loop is four blocks away. Chicago is 30 minutes away.

Innkeeper(s): Sally H. Ward. $115-125. 3 rooms with PB. 1 conference room. Breakfast included in rates. Type of meal: full breakfast. Beds: KQT. Spa on premises. Antiques, fishing, cross-country skiing, theater and watersports nearby.

Publicity: *Pioneer Press.*

"We will always remember your wonderful hospitality and your delightful gardens."

Indiana

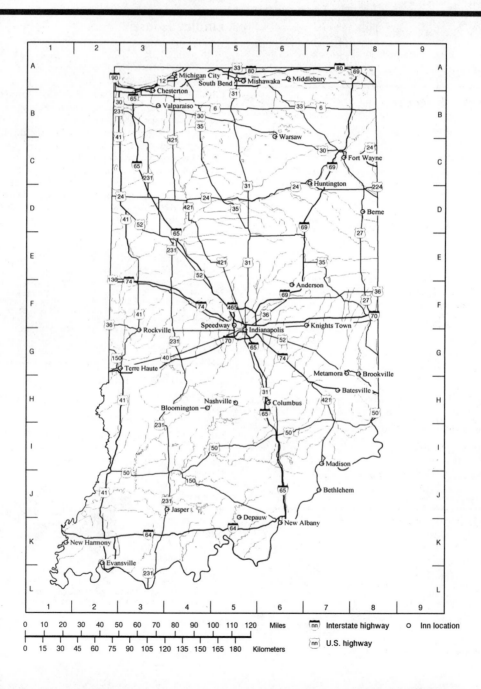

Anderson   F6

Plum Retreat B&B

926 Historical W Eighth St
Anderson, IN 46016
(765)649-7586 Fax:(765)649-9928

Circa 1892. This Queen Anne Victorian, so named because of
its light purple hue, is surrounded by a wrought-iron fence,
roses and foliage. The
front doors, fashioned
out of a rich wood,
feature an intricate
glass pattern. The
veranda offers wicker
furnishings so guests
can enjoy the scenery
and relax. The three
guest rooms include
antiques such as a
high-back walnut bed.
The home was built

by the vice president of a local loan association, and at one
time the grounds included a racetrack. Antique shops, museums, horse racing and wilderness areas are nearby.

$70-120. PC. 3 rooms, 1 with PB, 1 with FP. 1 suite. 2 conference rooms.
Breakfast, afternoon tea and evening snack included in rates. Types of meals:
full breakfast, gourmet breakfast and early coffee/tea. Beds: QDT. Air conditioning in room. TV, VCR and library on premises. Weddings, small meetings,
family reunions and seminars hosted. Antiques, parks, shopping, sporting
events, golf and theater nearby.

Publicity: *Madison County Monthly, Midwest Living, Victorian Homes.*

*"This house was a life long dream of my wife, we both fell in love
with it. We appreciate you letting us have this most wonderful experience in your home."*

Batesville   H7

Sherman House Restaurant & Inn

35 S Main St
Batesville, IN 47006-1278
(812)934-2407 (800)445-4939

Circa 1852. This hotel has been in business for more than 145
years. During this century it acquired a Tudor facade. The inn's
restaurant is the focal point of town, with business meetings and
frequent banquets in the Chalet Room. Antique shopping and
nearby covered bridges are also a highlight of this quaint town.

Innkeeper(s): Neal Rudolf. $44-66. MC VISA AX DC. 23 rooms with PB. 3
conference rooms. Types of meals: full breakfast and early coffee/tea. Dinner
and lunch available. Beds: KQD. Phone in room.

Berne   D8

Schug House Inn

706 W Main St
Berne, IN 46711-1328
(219)589-2303

Circa 1907. This Queen Anne home was built in 1907 by
Emanuel Wanner. It was constructed for the Schug family,
who occupied the home for 25 years, and whom the innkeepers chose the name of their inn. Victorian features decorate

the home, including inlaid floors, pocket doors and a wraparound porch. Guest rooms boast walnut, cherry and oak furnishings. Fruit, cheeses and pastries are served on antique
china each morning in the dining room. Horse-drawn carriages from the nearby Old Order Amish community often
pass on the street outside.

Innkeeper(s): John Minch. $35-40. MC VISA. 9 rooms, 8 with PB. 1 confer-
ence room. Breakfast included in rates. Type of meal: continental breakfast.
Beds: KQDT.

Bethlehem   J7

The Inn at Bethlehem

101 Walnut St
Bethlehem, IN 47104
(812)293-3975

Circa 1830. This two-story, Federal-style inn sits atop a bluff
overlooking the Ohio River. In its long history, it has seen uses
as a grocery, jail and possibly a stop on the Underground
Railroad. Rocking chairs and hammocks are ready for those
who wish to relax, and there's 26 acres to explore. The inn is
furnished with elegant pieces, including some period antiques.
One of the innkeepers is an accomplished chef, so the breakfasts are a treat. Guests can make a reservation for a gourmet
dinner in the inn's Rustic Lodge. Your menu might include saffron shrimp bisque, garden salad dressed with a balsamic vinaigrette, an appetizer of wild mushroom cream in a beggars
purse, then bourbon pecan chicken or perhaps a beef tenderloin wrapped in smoky bacon and served with a Merlot sauce.
Guests finish off the meal with a succulent dessert. Sunday
brunch also is served.

Innkeeper(s): Lawrence & Debbie Llana. $90-150. MAP. AP. MC TC. TAC10.
10 rooms with PB. 1 suite. 2 conference rooms. Breakfast included in rates.
Types of meals: full breakfast, gourmet breakfast and early coffee/tea. Dinner,
evening snack, picnic lunch, gourmet lunch and banquet service available.
Restaurant on premises. Beds: KQDT. Air conditioning and ceiling fan in
room. VCR, fax and bicycles on premises. 26 acres. Weddings, small meetings, family reunions and seminars hosted. Antiques, fishing, parks and shopping nearby.

"We love this place! It is now our little getaway."

Bloomington   H4

Grant Street Inn

310 N Grant St
Bloomington, IN 47408-3736
(812)334-2353 (800)328-4350 Fax:(812)331-8673

Circa 1883. Built originally before the turn of the century for
the Zeigler family, the home remained with the family for more
than 100 years until 1987. It was moved to its present location
at 7th and Grant Street in the historic district and restored to
its original elegance of hardwood flooring, crown moldings and
raised porches. There are 24 individually decorated rooms all
featuring antique-style furnishings. All of the rooms offer private baths, TV and phones. Some of the rooms feature fireplaces and separate entrances. Suites offer the romance of
Jacuzzi tubs and fireplaces. Guests can enjoy a leisurely full
breakfast in the breakfast room. The inn is located within walking distance of Indiana's largest antique mall and cultural
events at Indiana University.

Historic Interest: The inn is a short drive to Lake Monroe, Brown County and
McCormick's Creek State Park.

Innkeeper(s): Bob Bohler. $90-160. MC VISA AX DS PC. TAC10. 24 rooms with PB, 14 with FP. 2 suites. 1 conference room. Breakfast included in rates. Type of meal: full breakfast. Beds: KQT. Phone, air conditioning and TV in room. Fax and copier on premises. Handicap access. Antiques, fishing, parks, shopping, sporting events, golf, theater and watersports nearby.

Scholars Inn

801 N College
Bloomington, IN 47404
(812)332-1892 (800)765-3466 Fax:(812)335-1490

Circa 1892. This five-room bed & breakfast features Victorian architecture inside and out. The woodwork, mantels, transoms and other features have been maintained and restored. One room includes a hand-carved fountain, another offers a Jacuzzi tub. The innkeepers offer a variety of packages, including specials for those in search of romance or perhaps a great game of Hoosier football. The gourmet breakfasts include delectables such as Belgian waffles or perhaps an egg souffle. The cinnamon rolls are a specialty.

Innkeeper(s): Lyle & Kerry Feigenbaum. $69-150. MC VISA AX DS TC. 5 suites, 1 with FP. 1 conference room. Breakfast and evening snack included in rates. Types of meals: gourmet breakfast and early coffee/tea. Beds: K. Phone, air conditioning, ceiling fan, TV and VCR in room. Fax and library on premises. Weddings, small meetings, family reunions and seminars hosted. Antiques, fishing, parks, shopping, downhill skiing, cross-country skiing, sporting events, golf, theater and watersports nearby.

Publicity: *Herald Times.*

Brookville   G8

Sulina Farm B&B

10052 US 52
Brookville, IN 47012
(765)647-5944 (800)486-8079

Circa 1913. The innkeepers of this elegantly renovated turn-of-the-century brick farmhouse take pride in offering guests the best in bed & breakfast accommodations in Southeast Indiana. In 1913, a devastating flood ravaged the Indiana and Ohio valleys, sweeping away the original home in just a few hours. Today, this third-generation farm is still home to the old cemetery and Indian burial mounds. The inn's sitting room and porches have a pleasant valley view, while the first floor Deweese Suite is complete with queen and twin beds. Upstairs, guests have their choice of the Wiley Suite or George's room. All guest rooms offer private baths with clawfoot tubs. A full breakfast is served family-style on the large country table. The inn is close to shopping, antiques, water sports and universities.

Innkeeper(s): Triston Ariens. $55-75. MC VISA AX DS PC TC. 4 rooms with PB. Breakfast included in rates. Type of meal: full breakfast. Beds: QDT. Air conditioning and ceiling fan in room. VCR and library on premises. 190 acres. Antiques, fishing, parks, shopping, golf and watersports nearby.

Pets Allowed: Outside only.

Chesterton   B3

The Gray Goose

350 Indian Boundary Rd
Chesterton, IN 46304-1511
(219)926-5781 (800)521-5127 Fax:(219)926-4845

Circa 1939. Situated on 100 wooded acres, just under one hour from Chicago, this English country inn overlooks a private lake. Guests can see Canadian geese and ducks on the lake and surrounding area. Rooms are decorated in 18th-century

English, Shaker and French-country styles. Some of the rooms feature fireplaces and poster beds. Complimentary snacks, soft drinks, coffee and tea are available throughout the day. Strains of Mozart or Handel add to the ambiance.

Historic Interest: The Dunes State and National Lakeshore is less than three miles from the inn.

Innkeeper(s): Tim Wilk & Chuck Ramsey. $80-156. MC VISA AX DS PC TC. 8 rooms with PB, 3 with FP. 3 suites. 1 conference room. Breakfast, afternoon tea and evening snack included in rates. Types of meals: full breakfast, gourmet breakfast and early coffee/tea. Beds: KQ. Phone, air conditioning, ceiling fan and VCR in room. Fax, copier and library on premises. 100 acres. Weddings, small meetings, family reunions and seminars hosted. Antiques, fishing, parks, shopping, downhill skiing, cross-country skiing, sporting events, theater and watersports nearby.

Publicity: *Insider, Post-Tribune, Glamour, Country Inns, Midwest Living.*

"Extremely gracious! A repeat stay for us because it is such a wonderful place to stay."

Columbus   H6

The Columbus Inn

445 5th St
Columbus, IN 47201-6206
(812)378-4289 Fax:(812)378-4289

Circa 1895. Dances, basketball games and poultry shows once convened in the auditorium of the old Columbus City Hall during its years as the focal point of town. The original terra-cotta floors, enormous brass chandeliers and hand-carved oak woodwork now welcome overnight guests. Lavishly decorated rooms feature reproduction antiques such as cherry sleigh beds. Twelve-foot-high windows and 21-foot ceilings grace the Charles Sparrell Suite with its separate sleeping level. A horse and buggy stops at the inn's front door. Awarded the AAA four-diamond rating.

Historic Interest: In the National Register.

Innkeeper(s): Paul A. Staublin. $96. MC VISA AX DC CB DS PC TC. 34 rooms with PB. 5 suites. 3 conference rooms. Breakfast and evening snack included in rates. Types of meals: full breakfast, gourmet breakfast and early coffee/tea. Afternoon tea, dinner, picnic lunch, lunch, gourmet lunch, banquet service and catering service available. Beds: QD. Phone, air conditioning, turndown service, TV and VCR in room. Fax, copier, library and child care on premises. Handicap access. Weddings, small meetings, family reunions and seminars hosted. Amusement parks, antiques, fishing, parks, shopping, downhill skiing, sporting events, theater and watersports nearby.

Publicity: *Chicago Sun-Times, Country Inns, Home & Away, Cincinnati Enquirer, Glamour, Innsider, InnReview.*

"A delicious and beautifully served breakfast was the crowning glory of our stay."

Evansville   K2

Cool Breeze Estate B&B

1240 SE 2nd St
Evansville, IN 47713-1304
(812)422-9635

Circa 1906. This prairie school home is surrounded by more than an acre of grounds, ideal for those in search of peace and quiet. Truck and automobile maker Joseph Graham once lived here, as well as philanthropist Giltner Igleheart. One room features the wallpaper mural, "Scenic America." The same mural was chosen by Jacqueline Kennedy to decorate the White House. The sunny rooms have names such as Margaret Mitchell or Bronte. A zoo, art museum and riverboat casino are among the nearby attractions.

Innkeeper(s): Katelin & David Hills. $75. AX DC CB DS PC TC. 4 rooms with PB. 2 suites. 2 conference rooms. Breakfast included in rates. Type of meal: full breakfast. Beds: QD. Phone and air conditioning in room. TV, VCR and library on premises. Weddings, small meetings, family reunions and seminars hosted. Antiques, parks, shopping, sporting events, theater and watersports nearby.

Pets Allowed: Must be well trained.

Location: Old Ohio River city.

Publicity: *Evansville Courier, Midwest Living.*

"It was so much like discovering something wonderful from the past and disappearing into the warmth of childhood again."

Fort Wayne C7

The Carole Lombard House B&B

704 Rockhill St
Fort Wayne, IN 46802-5918
(219)426-9896

Circa 1895. Jane Alice Peters, a.k.a. Carole Lombard, spent her first six years in this turn-of-the-century home located in Ft. Wayne's historic West-Central neighborhood. The innkeepers named two guest rooms in honor of Lombard and her second husband, Clark Gable. Each of these rooms features memorabilia from the Gable-Lombard romance. A video library with a collection of classic movies is available, including many of Lombard's films. The innkeepers provide bicycles for exploring Fort Wayne and also provide information for a self-guided architectural tour of the historic area.

Historic Interest: On Oct. 6, 1908, Jane Alice Peters was born in the handsome house at the foot of Rockhill Street. The world knew her as Carole Lombard.

Innkeeper(s): Bev Fiandt. $55-75. MC VISA DS PC TC. TAC5. 4 rooms with PB. Breakfast included in rates. Types of meals: full breakfast and early coffee/tea. Beds: KQDT. Phone, air conditioning and TV in room. VCR and bicycles on premises. Small meetings hosted. Antiques, parks, sporting events and theater nearby.

Publicity: *Michigan Living.*

"The elegance and ambience are most appreciated."

Huntington C7

Purviance House

326 S Jefferson St
Huntington, IN 46750-3327
(219)356-4218

Circa 1859. This Italianate-Greek Revival house is listed in the National Register of Historic Places. The inn features a winding cherry staircase, parquet floors,

original interior shutters, tile fireplaces, ornate ceiling designs, antiques and period reproductions. The gold parlor offers well-stocked bookshelves.

Historic Interest: Forks of the Wabash Historic Park is three miles away, and the Dan Quayle Center also is nearby.

Innkeeper(s): Bob & Jean Gernand. $45-55. MC VISA DS TC. TAC5. 5 rooms, 2 with PB, 2 with FP. 2 conference rooms. Breakfast and snack included in rates. Types of meals: full breakfast and early coffee/tea. Banquet service and room service available. Beds: QDT. Air conditioning and ceiling fan in room. Library on premises. Weddings, small meetings, family reunions and seminars hosted. Antiques, fishing, parks, shopping and watersports nearby.

Location: One-half hour from Ft. Wayne.

Publicity: *Huntington County TAB, Purdue Alumnus, Richmond Palladium-Item.*

"A completely delightful experience!"

Indianapolis G5

The Nuthatch B&B

7161 Edgewater Pl
Indianapolis, IN 46240-3020
(317)257-2660 Fax:(317)257-2677
E-mail: nuthatch@netride.com

Circa 1928. "Breakfast." That's the only word it should take to draw guests to this 1920s, cottage-like home. Innkeeper Joan Morris is a cooking instructor and creator of the inn's memorable breakfasts. Each morning brings with it a different culinary style, from down-home fare to a goat-cheese omelet with peppers and shiitake mushrooms or poached pears with rosemary honey. The two guest rooms are decorated with an eclectic mix of styles. Guests walk down a circular staircase to reach The Adirondack Suite, which includes a fireplace and a greenhouse. The Wren's Nest is decorated with stained glass and a wren motif, and the bath includes a clawfoot tub.

Innkeeper(s): Joan & Bernie Morris. $80-95. MC VISA AX DS PC TC. TAC10. 2 rooms with PB, 1 with FP. Breakfast, afternoon tea and evening snack included in rates. Types of meals: full breakfast, gourmet breakfast and early coffee/tea. Beds: Q. Phone, air conditioning, turndown service and ceiling fan in room. Fax and library on premises. Yiddish and some Spanish spoken. Antiques, fishing, parks, shopping, cross-country skiing, sporting events, theater and watersports nearby.

Pets Allowed: In one room only, must be crated, crate provided.

"We had a wonderful night for our sixth anniversary."

Renaissance Tower Historic Inn

230 E 9th St
Indianapolis, IN 46204-1151
(317)261-1652 (800)676-7786 Fax:(317)262-8648

Circa 1922. Nestled in the heart of the Historic St. Joseph District, this inn is listed in the National Register of Historic Places. The inn features distinctive construction details. Guest rooms have cherry four-poster beds, Queen Anne furniture, elegant sitting rooms and scenic bay windows. Each suite has a fully equipped kitchen and free local calls. Complimentary adjacent parking is available.

Innkeeper(s): Jeffrey Bowling. $75-85. MC VISA AX PC TC. TAC10. 80 suites. Beds: QD. Phone, air conditioning and TV in room. Fax and copier on premises. Shopping, sporting events and theater nearby.

Publicity: *Indianapolis Business Journal, New York Times, Indianapolis Star, Muncie Star, TWA's Ambassador.*

"We were so pleased with your lovely decor in the rooms."

Jasper J4

Powers Inn B&B

325 W 6th St
Jasper, IN 47546
(812)482-3018

Circa 1880. This B&B's location was meant for hospitality. A local attorney built this Second Empire Victorian on this spot, but it once was the site of a local log cabin inn. The innkeepers painstakingly restored their Victorian, which included rebuilding the foundation. They managed to save many original elements along the way. The rooms are elegant, decorated with antiques and reproductions. Antique dressers house the bathroom sinks, and one bathroom includes an original clawfoot tub.

Innkeeper(s): Alice & Larry "Joe" Garland. $60. MC VISA PC. 3 rooms with PB. Breakfast included in rates. Type of meal: full breakfast. Beds: DT. Air conditioning in room. TV and VCR on premises. Amusement parks, antiques, fishing, parks, shopping, downhill skiing, golf, theater and watersports nearby.

Publicity: *Chicago Tribune, Dubois County Daily Herald.*

"Warm, cozy and very friendly!"

Knightstown F7

Old Hoosier House

7601 S Greensboro Pike
Knightstown, IN 46148-9613
(765)345-2969 (800)775-5315

Circa 1840. The Old Hoosier House was owned by the Elisha Scovell family, who were friends of President Martin Van Buren, and the president stayed overnight in the home. Features of the Victorian house include tall, arched windows and a gabled entrance. Rooms are decorated with antiques and lace curtains. Hearty Hoosier breakfasts include such specialties as a breakfast pizza of egg, sausage and cheese, and Melt-Away Puff  Pancakes. The inn's eight acres are wooded, and the deck overlooks a pond on the fourth hole of the adjacent golf course.

Historic Interest: Wilbur Wright Memorial and birthplace (20 miles), Metamora restored canal village (40 miles), Noblesville Transportation Museum (25 miles), James Whitcomb Riley birthplace & museum (10 miles).

Innkeeper(s): Jean & Tom Lewis. $60-70. PC. TAC10. 4 rooms with PB, 1 with FP. 1 suite. Breakfast, afternoon tea and evening snack included in rates. Types of meals: full breakfast and early coffee/tea. Beds: KQT. Phone, air conditioning and ceiling fan in room. TV, VCR and library on premises. Handicap access. Weddings, small meetings and family reunions hosted. Antiques, fishing, parks, shopping, sporting events and theater nearby.

Location: Greensboro Pike & Rd. 750 S.

Publicity: *Indianapolis Star News, New Castle Courier-Times, Indianapolis Monthly.*

"We had such a wonderful time at your house. Very many thanks."

Madison I7

Schussler House B&B

514 Jefferson St
Madison, IN 47250
(812)273-2068 (800)392-1931

Circa 1849. This Federal-style home was built by a local doctor who used it as both house and office. The three guest rooms include antiques and reproductions. The innkeepers pamper guests with a delectable full breakfast, served by candlelight. Madison, a picturesque Ohio River town surrounded by rolling hills, has more than 100 blocks listed in the National Register and designated a National Trust Historic District. The B&B is within walking distance to many shops and sites, and the river is just five blocks away.

Innkeeper(s): Judy & Bill Gilbert. $90-120. MC VISA DS PC TC. TAC10. 3 rooms with PB. Breakfast and evening snack included in rates. Types of meals: full breakfast and early coffee/tea. Beds: QT. Air conditioning and turndown service in room. Small meetings and family reunions hosted. Antiques, fishing, parks, shopping and golf nearby.

Publicity: *Update, Cincinnati Magazine, The Downtowner.*

"Five star all the way!"

Metamora G7

The Thorpe House Country Inn

19049 Clayborne St, PO Box 36
Metamora, IN 47030
(765)647-5425 (888)427-7932

Circa 1840. The steam engine still brings passenger cars and the gristmill still grinds cornmeal in historic Metamora. The Thorpe House is located one block from the canal. Rooms feature original pine and poplar floors, antiques, stenciling and country accessories. Enjoy a hearty breakfast selected from the inn's restaurant menu. (Popular items include homemade biscuits, egg dishes and sourdough pecan rolls.) Walk to the village to explore more than 100 shops.

Historic Interest: Indian mounds, historic Brookville, Laurel, and "village of spires" Oldenburg are within 10 minutes. Historic Connersville and Batesville are within one-half hour.

Innkeeper(s): Jean Owens. $70-125. MC VISA AX DS. 5 rooms with PB. 1 suite. Breakfast included in rates. Types of meals: full breakfast and early coffee/tea. Dinner, evening snack, picnic lunch, lunch and catering service available. Restaurant on premises. Beds: DT. Phone and air conditioning in room. Small meetings and family reunions hosted. Antiques, fishing, shopping and watersports nearby.

Pets Allowed.

Location: One block from the Whitewater Canal State Historic Site.

Publicity: *Cincinnati Enquirer, Chicago Sun-Times.*

"Thanks to all of you for your kindness and hospitality during our stay."

Michigan City   A4

The Hutchinson Mansion Inn

220 W 10th St
Michigan City, IN 46360-3516
(219)879-1700

Circa 1875. Built by a lumber baron in 1875, this grand, red-brick mansion features examples of Queen Anne, Classic Revival and Italianate design. The mansion boasts 11 stained-glass panels and the front parlor still has its original plaster friezes, ceiling medallion
and a marble fireplace.
The dining room's oak-paneled walls include a
secret panel. The library
is stocked with interest-ing books and games,
and classical composi-tions and Victorian par-lor music are piped in.
The second floor offers a

host of places perfect for relaxation, including a small game room, mini library and a sun porch. Rooms are filled with antiques and unusual pieces such as the Tower Suite's octagon, Gothic-style bed. The carriage house suites include a sitting room, refrigerator and either a whirlpool or large, soaking tub.

Historic Interest: The mansion is nestled in Michigan City's historic district and a short distance from other gracious homes. The Barker Mansion, a house museum, is only three blocks away. A lighthouse museum is less than a mile from the inn. Bailly Homestead and Chellberg Farm, a turn-of-the-century Swedish farm, are 15 minutes away.

Innkeeper(s): Ben & Mary DuVal. $68-140. MC VISA AX. 10 rooms with PB. 5 suites. Breakfast included in rates. Beds: QD. Antiques, fishing, shopping, cross-country skiing and theater nearby.

Publicity: *Midwest Living, Midwest Motorist, Heritage Country, Indianapolis Star, Michigan Living, South Bend Tribune.*

"Beautiful, romantic inn, exceptional hospitality, your breakfasts were fabulous."

Middlebury   A6

Patchwork Quilt Country Inn

11748 CR 2
Middlebury, IN 46540
(219)825-2417 Fax:(219)825-5172
E-mail: rgminn@aol.com

Circa 1800. Located in the heart of Indiana's Amish country, this inn offers comfortable lodging and fine food. Some of the recipes are regionally famous, such as the award-winning Buttermilk Pecan Chicken. All guest rooms feature handsome quilts and country decor, and The Loft treats visitors to a whirlpool tub and kitchenette. Ask about the four-hour guided tour of the surrounding Amish area. The alcohol- and smoke-free inn also is host to a gift shop.

Innkeeper(s): Ray & Rosetta Miller. $70-100. MC VISA PC TC. TAC10. 15 rooms with PB. 2 suites. 2 conference rooms. Breakfast included in rates. Types of meals: full breakfast and early

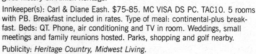

coffee/tea. Dinner, evening snack, lunch and banquet service available. Restaurant on premises. Beds: KQT. Air conditioning and TV in room. VCR, fax and copier on premises. Handicap access. 18 acres. Weddings, small meetings, family reunions and seminars hosted. Antiques, fishing, parks, shopping, downhill skiing, cross-country skiing, sporting events, golf and theater nearby.

Tiffany Powell's Bed & Breakfast

523 South Main Street
Middlebury, IN 46540
(219)825-5951

Circa 1914. The porch of this B&B is a favorite spot for guests to sit and watch Amish buggies pass by, especially on Saturday nights. The inn features leaded and beveled glass and original oak floors and woodwork. Guest rooms reflect a fresh country decor with bright handmade quilts sewn by Judy's grandmother. Known locally and acknowledged nationally on the Oprah show for her hospitality, the innkeeper offers a full breakfast. Amish Sausage Casserole is a speciality of the house and is served in the dining room. Shipshewana is seven minutes away, and Amish markets and craft shops are nearby.

Innkeeper(s): Judy Powell. $65. 3 rooms with PB. Breakfast included in rates. Beds: Q. Turndown service and ceiling fan in room. VCR on premises.

Varns Guest House

PO Box 125, 205 S Main St
Middlebury, IN 46540-0125
(219)825-9666 (800)398-5424

Circa 1898. Built by the innkeepers' great-grandparents, this home has been in the family for nearly a century. Recently restored, it is located on the
town's tree-shaded main
street. Guests enjoy gliding
on the front porch swing
while they watch Amish
horses and buggies clip-clop past the inn. The
Kinder Room features a
whirlpool tub.

Historic Interest: Welcome center in Shipshewana (7 miles) gives history on Amish heritage.

Innkeeper(s): Carl & Diane Eash. $75-85. MC VISA DS PC. TAC10. 5 rooms with PB. Breakfast included in rates. Type of meal: continental-plus breakfast. Beds: QT. Phone, air conditioning and TV in room. Weddings, small meetings and family reunions hosted. Parks, shopping and golf nearby.

Publicity: *Heritage Country, Midwest Living.*

"In terms of style, decor, cleanliness and hospitality, there is none finer!"

Mishawaka   A5

The Beiger Mansion Inn

317 Lincoln Way E
Mishawaka, IN 46544-2012
(219)256-0365 (800)437-0131 Fax:(219)259-2622
E-mail: beiger@michiana.org

Circa 1907. This Neoclassical limestone mansion was built to satisfy Susie Beiger's wish to copy a friend's Newport, R.I. estate. Palatial rooms that were once a gathering place for local society now welcome guests who seek gracious accommodations. Notre Dame, St. Mary's and Indiana University in South Bend are nearby.

Innkeeper(s): Ron Montandon & Phil Robinson. $65-125. MC VISA AX DC CB DS. 8 rooms with PB, 2 with FP. 1 conference room. Types of meals: full breakfast and gourmet breakfast. Dinner and lunch available. Restaurant on premises. Beds: Q. Fax on premises.

Location: Northern Indiana.

Publicity: *Tribune*.

"Can't wait until we return to Mishawaka to stay with you again!"

Nashville H5

Allison House

PO Box 1625
Nashville, IN 47448
(812)988-0814

Circa 1883. This inviting yellow home was restored to include cozy, comfortable furnishings in a relaxed atmosphere. A full breakfast begins a day of browsing through the village's hundreds of shops and famed arts and crafts colony. Indiana's largest state park is less than two miles from Allison House. **Historic Interest:** T.C. Steele's studio and home is nine miles away. Architectural tours are available in Columbus, 17 miles away.

Innkeeper(s): Tammy Galm. $85-95. 5 rooms with PB. Breakfast included in rates. Beds: QDT. Antiques, fishing, downhill skiing, cross-country skiing and theater nearby.

New Albany K6

Honeymoon Mansion B&B & Wedding Chapel

1014 E Main St
New Albany, IN 47150-5843
(812)945-0312 (800)759-7270

Circa 1850. The innkeepers at Honeymoon Mansion can provide guests with the flowers, wedding chapel and honeymoon suite. All you need to bring is a bride or groom. An ordained minister is on the premises and guests can marry or renew their vows in the inn's Victorian wedding chapel. However, one need not be a newlywed to enjoy this bed & breakfast. Canopy beds, stained-glass windows and heart-shaped rugs are a few of the romantic touches. Several suites include marble Jacuzzis flanked on four sides with eight-foot-high marble columns, creating a dramatic and elegant effect. The home itself, a pre-Civil War Italianate-style home listed in the state and national historic registers, boasts many fine period features. Gingerbread trim, intricate molding and a grand staircase add to the Victorian ambiance. Guests are treated to an all-you-can-eat country breakfast with items such as homemade breads, biscuits and gravy, eggs, sausage and potatoes.

Innkeeper(s): J. Franklin & Beverly Dennis. $70-140. MC VISA PC TC. TAC10. 6 suites. 2 conference rooms. Breakfast included in rates. Type of meal: full breakfast. Catering service available. Beds: Q. Air conditioning,

ceiling fan, TV and VCR in room. Copier on premises. Handicap access. Weddings, small meetings, family reunions and seminars hosted. Amusement parks, antiques, fishing, parks, shopping, downhill skiing, cross-country skiing, sporting events, theater and watersports nearby.

Location: On the Ohio Scenic Route in Southern Indiana.

Publicity: *Indianapolis Star, Courier-Journal, Evening News, Tribune.* Ratings: 4 Stars.

New Harmony K1

Raintree Inn B&B

503 West St, PO Box 566
New Harmony, IN 47631
(812)682-5625
E-mail: raintree@evansville.net

Circa 1899. This uniquely designed Colonial Revival brick house is replete with rotunda, porch, gabled dormers and arched windows, all with finely detailed trim. The interiors are elaborately gilded with Victorian wall and ceiling papers that enhance the mansion's golden-oak, paneled woodwork, stained-glass windows, columns, arches and interior fret work. Bed chambers are appointed with four-poster or canopied beds, and there are clawfoot tubs and heated towel racks in the bathrooms. Breakfasts are served in the dining room or elegant back parlor, and may feature eggs baked in filo pastry with hollandaise sauce or brandied cream crepes with orange marmalade sauce. On the weekend, afternoon tea is offered to the public, but is complimentary for guests.

Innkeeper(s): Scott & Nancy McDonald. $85-95. MC VISA DS PC TC. 4 rooms with PB. Breakfast included in rates. Types of meals: full breakfast, gourmet breakfast and early coffee/tea. Beds: KQ. Air conditioning and turndown service in room. Library on premises. Antiques, fishing, parks, shopping and theater nearby.

Publicity: *Evansville Courier, Chicago Tribune*.

"The Raintree is a great bed & breakfast...one to be counted among our many cherished memories."

Rockville G3

Billie Creek Inn

RR 2, Box 27, Billie Creek Village
Rockville, IN 47872
(765)569-3430 Fax:(765)569-3582

Circa 1996. Although this inn was built recently, it rests on the outskirts of historic Billie Creek Village. The village is a non-profit, turn-of-the-century living museum, complete with 30 historic buildings and three covered bridges. Guests can explore an 1830s cabin, a farmstead, a general store and much more to experience how Americans lived in the 19th century. The innkeepers take part in the history, dressing in period costume. The inn is decorated in a comfortable, country style. The nine suites include the added amenity of a whirlpool tub. All inn guests receive complimentary admission to Billie Creek Village. Coffee and continental breakfast fare are available around the clock. Special packages include bike tours, Civil War Days and Covered Bridge Festivals.

Innkeeper(s): Carol Gum & Doug Weisheit. $49-99. MC VISA AX DS PC TC. TAC10. 31 rooms with PB. 9 suites. 2 conference rooms. Breakfast included in rates. Type of meal: continental breakfast. Catering service available. Restaurant on premises. Beds: KD. Phone, air conditioning and TV in room. VCR, fax, copier, stables and pet boarding on premises. Handicap access. 100 acres. Weddings, small meetings, family reunions and seminars hosted. Antiques, fishing, parks, shopping, sporting events, golf, theater and watersports nearby.

Pets Allowed: Home to Scott Pet Hotel.

Owl Nest B&B

303 Howard Ave
Rockville, IN 47872
(765)569-1803

Circa 1889. You'll feel like you're stepping back in time when you walk through the doors of this gracious Queen Anne home situated in Parke County, the covered bridge capitol of Indiana. High ceilings, natural walnut woodwork, a carved staircase, two fireplaces and the original chandelier are featured in the common rooms and add to the warm family atmosphere. A hearty full breakfast is served every morning. Snacks are offered in the evening. Located in the historic district, the inn is close to antiques, shopping, sporting activities and theater.

Innkeeper(s): Richard & Tulie Ann Jadzak. $65-85. PC TC. 4 rooms. Breakfast, afternoon tea and evening snack included in rates. Types of meals: gourmet breakfast and early coffee/tea. Catered breakfast available. Air conditioning, turndown service and ceiling fan in room. TV, VCR and bicycles on premises. Small meetings and family reunions hosted. Antiques, fishing, parks, shopping, golf, theater and watersports nearby.

Suits Us B&B

514 N College St
Rockville, IN 47872-1511
(765)569-5660 (888)478-4878

Circa 1883. Sixty miles west of Indianapolis is this stately Colonial Revival inn, where Woodrow Wilson, Annie Oakley and James Witcomb Riley were once guests of the Strause Family. The inn offers a fireplace and library, bicycles and an exercise room. Turkey Run State Park are nearby. The Ernie Pyle State Historic Site, Raccoon State Recreation Area and four golf courses are within easy driving distance.

Historic Interest: There are 32 covered bridges in the area.

Innkeeper(s): Marty & Bev Rose. $55-125. TC. 4 rooms with PB. 1 suite. Breakfast included in rates. Types of meals: full breakfast and early coffee/tea. Beds: KQD. Air conditioning, ceiling fan, TV and VCR in room. Bicycles on premises. Antiques, fishing, parks, shopping, golf and watersports nearby.

Publicity: *Touring America, Traces Historic Magazine.*

South Bend A5

The Book Inn B&B

508 W Washington St
South Bend, IN 46601-1528
(219)288-1990 Fax:(219)234-2338
E-mail: bookinn@aol.com

Circa 1872. Hand-hewn, butternut woodwork and 12-foot ceilings accentuate the rich decor at this Second Empire-style home. Among the many impressive architectural features are entry doors with double leaf wood and applied decorations. The Cushing Suite boasts a bay window, hand-painted walls and four-poster bed. Other rooms, which are named in honor of famous female authors, feature delightful decor. Bookworms will delight not only in the name of this inn, but also the inn's own used bookstore.

Innkeeper(s): Peggy & John Livingston. $80-120. MC VISA AX PC TC. TAC10. 5 rooms with PB. 2 suites. 1 conference room. Breakfast included in rates. Types of meals: full breakfast and early coffee/tea. Beds: KQT. Phone and air conditioning in room. VCR, fax, copier and library on premises. Small meetings, family reunions and seminars hosted. Antiques, fishing, parks, shopping, cross-country skiing, sporting events, theater and watersports nearby.

Oliver Inn

630 W Washington St
South Bend, IN 46601-1444
(219)232-4545 (888)697-4466 Fax:(219)288-9788

Circa 1886. This stately Queen Anne Victorian sits amid 30 towering maples and was once home to Josephine Oliver Ford, daughter of James Oliver, of chilled plow fame. Located in South Bend's historic district, this inn offers a comfortable library and nine inviting guest rooms, some with built-in fireplaces or double Jacuzzis. The inn is within walking distance of downtown, and public transportation is available.

Innkeeper(s): Richard & Venera Monahan. $85-192. MC VISA AX DS PC TC. 9 rooms with PB, 2 with FP. 3 suites. 1 conference room. Breakfast and evening snack included in rates. Types of meals: continental-plus breakfast and early coffee/tea. Beds: KQ. Phone, air conditioning, turndown service, ceiling fan and TV in room. Fax on premises. Handicap access. Weddings, small meetings, family reunions and seminars hosted. Antiques, fishing, parks, shopping, cross-country skiing, sporting events, theater and watersports nearby.

Speedway F5

Speedway Inn B&B

1829 Cunningham Dr
Speedway, IN 46224
(317)487-6531 (800)975-3412

Circa 1906. This two-story white columned inn reflects a plantation-style architecture. The inn is situated on an acre of lawn and trees. The bed & breakfast has a homey decor that includes a wood-paneled common room and simply furnished guest rooms. Breakfast includes items such as homemade coffee cake and Danish or sausage and egg casserole. Nearby attractions include President Harrison's home, the Hall of Fame Museum and the largest city park in the nation, Eagle Creek Park.

Innkeeper(s): Robert & Pauline Grothe. $68. PC TC. 6 rooms, 5 with PB. 1 conference room. Breakfast included in rates. Type of meal: continental-plus breakfast. Beds: KD. Air conditioning and TV in room. VCR, fax and bicycles on premises. Antiques, fishing, parks, shopping, sporting events, golf and theater nearby.

"It is people like you who have given B&Bs such a good reputation."

Terre Haute G3

Sycamore Farm B&B

5001 E Poplar Dr
Terre Haute, IN 47803-9792
(812)877-9288 Fax:(812)877-3930

Circa 1862. This farmhouse served as a family home for five generations, and the grounds still include the barn. Each room has its own charm with antiques, such as a hand-carved oak bed. For those in search of romance, try the Master's Room, a

spacious suite with its own private porch where guests can enjoy an intimate breakfast. The innkeepers have won a local beautification award for their bed & breakfast. There is a tea room on the premises, which serves lunch. Covered bridges, parks, historic sites and golf courses are all nearby.

$74-79. MC VISA. 5 rooms, 3 with PB. Breakfast included in rates. Types of meals: full breakfast and early coffee/tea. Restaurant on premises. Beds: KQD. Air conditioning in room. TV on premises. Weddings and small meetings hosted. Antiques, fishing, parks, shopping, sporting events and golf nearby.

Publicity: *Tribune-Star.*

Valparaiso   B3

The Inn at Aberdeen

3158 South SR 2
Valparaiso, IN 46385
(219)465-3753 Fax:(219)465-9227
E-mail: innaberd@netnitco.net

Circa 1890. An old stone wall borders this inn, once a dairy farm, horse farm and then hunting lodge. Recently renovated and expanded, this Victorian farmhouse is on more than an acre. An elegant getaway, there's a solarium, library, dining room and parlor for relaxing. The inn offers traditional Queen Anne furnishings in the guest rooms. The Timberlake Suites include fireplaces, Jacuzzi tubs and balconies. A conference center on the property is popular for executive meetings and special events, and there is 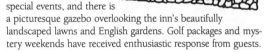 a picturesque gazebo overlooking the inn's beautifully landscaped lawns and English gardens. Golf packages and mystery weekends have received enthusiastic response from guests.

Innkeeper(s): Gary Atherton. $90-150. MC VISA AX DC CB DS TC. 11 suites, 10 with FP. 1 conference room. Breakfast and evening snack included in rates. Type of meal: gourmet breakfast. Afternoon tea, dinner, picnic lunch, lunch, gourmet lunch and banquet service available. Beds: KQ. Phone, air conditioning, ceiling fan, TV and VCR in room. Fax, copier, spa, swimming, bicycles, tennis and library on premises. Handicap access. Weddings, small meetings, family reunions and seminars hosted. Antiques, fishing, parks, shopping, downhill skiing, cross-country skiing, sporting events, golf, theater and watersports nearby.

Publicity: *The Times, Post-Tribune.*

"Everytime we have the good fortune to spend an evening here, it is like a perfect fairy tale, transforming us into King and Queen."

Warsaw   B6

Candlelight Inn

503 E Fort Wayne St
Warsaw, IN 46580-3338
(219)267-2906 (800)352-0640 Fax:(219)269-4646

Circa 1860. Canopy beds, pedestal sinks, clawfoot tubs and period antiques carry out the inn's "Gone With the Wind" theme. Scarlett's Chamber features rose wallpaper, a queen bed and mauve carpeting, while Rhett Butler's Chamber boasts navy walls, hardwood floors, a walnut canopy bed, burgundy velvet sofa and a whirlpool tub.

Historic Interest: Built in 1860 and 1865, has old fashion wraparound porch, restored woodwork in butternut, walnut oak, staircase, antiques in each room.

Innkeeper(s): Deborah Hambright. $74-129. MC VISA AX. 10 rooms with PB. Breakfast included in rates. Types of meals: full breakfast and early coffee/tea. Room service available. Phone, air conditioning, turndown service, ceiling fan and TV in room. Fax on premises. Family reunions hosted. Antiques, fishing, shopping and theater nearby.

Location: Two miles south on State Road 15 off Highway 30.

White Hill Inn

2513 E Center St
Warsaw, IN 46580-3819
(219)269-6933 Fax:(219)268-1936

Circa 1934. This elegantly crafted 4,500-square-foot English Tudor was constructed during the Depression when fine artisans were available at low cost. Handsome arched entryways and ceilings, crown molding and mullioned windows create a gracious intimate atmosphere. The mansion has been carefully renovated and decorated with a combination of traditional furnishings and contemporary English fabrics.

Innkeeper(s): Zoyla Henderson. $80-120. MC VISA AX DC DS. 8 rooms with PB. Breakfast included in rates. Type of meal: continental-plus breakfast. Beds: KQ. Handicap access. Fishing, downhill skiing and cross-country skiing nearby.

Publicity: *Indiana Business, USA Today.*

"It's the perfect place for an at-home getaway."

Iowa

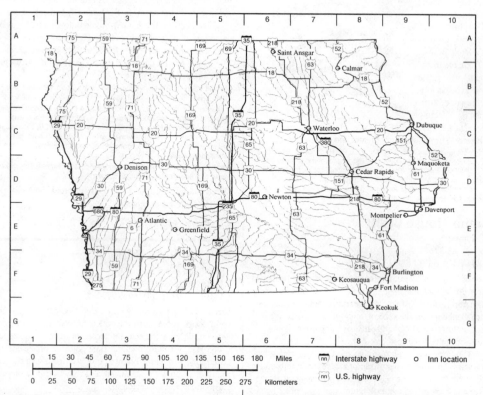

Atlantic E3

Chestnut Charm B&B

1409 Chestnut St
Atlantic, IA 50022-2547
(712)243-5652

Circa 1898. The charm doesn't end at this richly appointed bed & breakfast. Guests first will be taken by the expansive manicured lawn and the Victorian design of the manor. Inside, natural hardwood floors, ornate woodwork and original, hand-painted linen wall coverings are exquisite. Relax in one of the sunrooms, or enjoy the view by the fountained patio or on the romantic gazebo. Each of the rooms features something fun and unique, from the private sunroom in the Master Suite to the Battenburg lace and ruffles in Tabitha's Quarters. The innkeeper offers upscale suites in a newly remodeled carriage house, as well. The wafting scent of fresh coffee leads hungry guests into the dining room for a delectable breakfast. Formal dinners are available with prior reservations.

Historic Interest: Explore the bevy of historical day trips, including the historic bridges of Madison County. A Danish Windmill and museum, Pellett Memorial Gardens and plenty of antiquing are also within driving distance.

Innkeeper(s): Barbara Stensvad. $75-250. MC VISA PC. TAC10. 9 rooms with PB, 7 with FP. 6 suites. Breakfast included in rates. Type of meal: gourmet breakfast. Dinner available. Beds: KQD. Air conditioning in room. Library on premises. Antiques, fishing, parks and shopping nearby.

Location: Halfway between Omaha, Neb., and Des Moines, Iowa.

Publicity: *Atlantic News Telegraph, Midwest Living, Iowan, Iowa Lady, Home & Away, Omaha World Herald.*

"We truly had a wonderful weekend. Your hospitality was unsurpassed!"

Burlington   F9

Mississippi Manor

809 N 4th St
Burlington, IA 52601
(319)753-2218

Circa 1877. Located just two blocks from the Mississippi River
in the National Landmark District, this Italianate Victorian
manor house was built by a lumber baron who incorporated
European craftsmanship
into the fine architectural detailing. Inside, the
inn is elegantly decorat-
ed with a Mark Twain
theme. There are five
guest rooms with private
baths and two spacious
suites with wood burn-
ing fireplaces. A conti-

nental breakfast is included in the rates. The inn is close to
parks, the arboretum, shopping, theater and entertainment.
Innkeeper(s): Linda Lentine Clark. $75. MC VISA PC TC. 5 rooms with PB, 2
with FP. 2 conference rooms. Breakfast included in rates. Type of meal: continental-plus breakfast. Beds: QT. Phone, air conditioning, ceiling fan and TV in
room. VCR on premises. Weddings, small meetings, family reunions and
seminars hosted. German spoken. Antiques, fishing, parks, shopping, cross-
country skiing, golf, theater and watersports nearby.

Schramm House B&B

616 Columbia St
Burlington, IA 52601
(319)754-0373 (800)683-7117 Fax:(319)754-0373

Circa 1866. "Colossal" would be an excellent word to describe
this Queen Anne Victorian. The home is an impressive site in
this Burlington historic district. The exterior is brick on the first
story with clapboard on the second, and a third-story tower is
one of the architectural highlights. Inside, the parquet floors
and woodwork have been restored to their 19th-century
grandeur. The home was built just after the Civil War ended by
a local department store owner. Additions were made in the
1880s. Eventually, the home was converted into apartments, so
the innkeepers took on quite a task refurbishing the place back
to its original state. The Victorian is decorated with the
innkeepers collection of antiques. One particularly appealing
guest room includes an exposed brick wall and tin ceiling.
Breakfast might begin with a baked pear topped with toasted
almonds and a raspberry sauce. From there, freshly baked
muffins arrive, followed by an entree, perhaps a frittata or
French toast. All courses are served with fine china and crystal.
The home is just six blocks from the Mississippi, and don't
pass up a walk down historic Snake Alley.
Innkeeper(s): Sandy & Bruce Morrison. $75. MC VISA AX DS PC TC. TAC10.
3 rooms with PB. Breakfast included in rates. Types of meals: full breakfast
and early coffee/tea. Beds: QDT. Turndown service and ceiling fan in room.
TV, VCR, fax and library on premises. Weddings and small meetings hosted.
Antiques, fishing, parks, shopping and golf nearby.
Publicity: *Hawk Eye.*

*"This historically interesting home has been restored to a charming
B&B. I was raised in Burlington, Iowa, and I am especially pleased
to see this handsome old family home used in such an enjoyable way."*

Calmar   B8

Calmar Guesthouse

103 W North St
Calmar, IA 52132-9801
(319)562-3851

Circa 1890. This beautifully restored Victorian home was built
by John B. Kay, a lawyer and poet. Stained-glass windows,
carved moldings, an oak-and-walnut staircase and gleaming
woodwork highlight the gracious interior. A grandfather clock
ticks in the living room. In the foyer, a friendship yellow rose is
incorporated into the stained-glass window pane. Breakfast is
served in the formal dining room. The Laura Ingalls Wilder
Museum is nearby in Burr Oak. The Bily Brothers Clock
Museum, Smallest Church, Luther College and Norweigian
Museum are located nearby.
Historic Interest: The Norwegian Museum is 10 minutes away. The Smallest
Church, Bily Brothers Clocks Museum and Luther College are nearby.
Innkeeper(s): Lucile Kruse. $45-50. MC VISA PC TC. 5 rooms, 1 with PB.
Breakfast included in rates. Types of meals: full breakfast and early
coffee/tea. Beds: Q. Air conditioning and TV in room. VCR, bicycles and
library on premises. Small meetings hosted. Antiques, fishing, parks, shop-
ping, downhill skiing, cross-country skiing, sporting events, theater and
watersports nearby.
Publicity: *Iowa Farmer Today, Calmar Courier, Minneapolis Star-Tribune,
Home and Away, Iowan.* Ratings: 5 Stars.

*"What a delight it was to stay here. No one could have made our
stay more welcome or enjoyable."*

Cedar Rapids   D8

Gwendolyn's B&B

1809 2nd Ave S E
Cedar Rapids, IA 52403-2307
(319)363-9731 (800)760-9731

Circa 1917. This recently remodeled Georgian inn features air-
conditioned rooms with the added convenience of ceiling fans.
Guests will enjoy the eclectic decor, courtesy of innkeeper
Gwen Hall, who also prepares their gourmet breakfasts.
Gwendolyn's, a family-oriented inn, also features a conference
room for its guests' use. Guests also may borrow a bicycle for a
close-up view of Cedar Rapids.
Innkeeper(s): Gwen Hall. $70-100. MC VISA AX PC TC. TAC10. 3 rooms. 1
suite. Breakfast included in rates. Types of meals: full breakfast, gourmet
breakfast and early coffee/tea. Beds: Q. Phone, air conditioning, ceiling fan,
TV and VCR in room. Spa, bicycles and library on premises. Family reunions
hosted. Antiques, fishing, parks, shopping, cross-country skiing, sporting
events, golf and theater nearby.
Pets Allowed.

Davenport   E9

Fulton's Landing Guest House

1206 E River Dr
Davenport, IA 52803-5742
(319)322-4069 Fax:(319)322-8186

Circa 1871. Enjoy views of the Mississippi River from the
porches of this stone, Italianate home, which is listed in the
National Register. The guest rooms are decorated with antiques,
including ceiling fans. After enjoying the morning meal, guests
have a variety of activities to choose. Riverboat gambling, shopping and downtown Davenport all are nearby.

Innkeeper(s): Pat & Bill Schmidt. $60-125. MC VISA AX. 5 rooms with PB. 1 suite. 2 conference rooms. Breakfast included in rates. Types of meals: full breakfast and gourmet breakfast. Beds: Q. Phone, air conditioning, ceiling fan and TV in room. Fax, copier and bicycles on premises. Antiques, fishing, parks, shopping, cross-country skiing, sporting events, theater and watersports nearby.

"I have never felt more pampered and cared for staying away from home."

Denison
D3

Queen Belle Country Inn

1430 3rd Ave S
Denison, IA 51442
(712)263-6777

Circa 1889. The wide front veranda of this historic Victorian provides wicker chairs and other furnishings for those who wish to relax. The interior is decorated in country Victorian style with flowery wallpapers. The front parlor features an antique organ and piano. Guests will enjoy plenty of homemade food. The innkeepers provide breakfast, afternoon and evening snacks for guests. Gourmet dinner is also an option.

Innkeeper(s): Paul & Arleeta Lenz. $65-150. MC VISA PC TC. TAC10. 4 rooms, 3 with PB, 1 with FP. 1 suite. 1 conference room. Breakfast, afternoon tea and evening snack included in rates. Types of meals: full breakfast, gourmet breakfast and early coffee/tea. Dinner and room service available. Beds: KQT. Phone, air conditioning, turndown service, TV and VCR in room. Fax, spa and library on premises. Handicap access. Weddings, small meetings, family reunions and seminars hosted. Antiques, fishing, parks, shopping, cross-country skiing, golf, theater and watersports nearby.

Dubuque
C9

The Hancock House

1105 Grove Ter
Dubuque, IA 52001-4644
(319)557-8989 Fax:(319)583-0813

Circa 1891. Victorian splendor can be found at The Hancock House, one of Dubuque's most striking examples of Queen Anne architecture. Rooms feature period furnishings and offer views of the Mississippi River states of Iowa, Illinois and Wisconsin. The Hancock House, listed in the National Register, boasts several unique features, including a fireplace judged blue-ribbon best at the 1893 World's Fair in Chicago. Visitors also will enjoy the inn's authentic bathrooms, featuring clawfoot tubs and pull-chain water closets.

Innkeeper(s): Chuck & Susan Huntley. $75-150. MC VISA AX DS PC TC. TAC10. 9 rooms with PB, 3 with FP. 1 suite. 1 cottage. Breakfast included in rates. Type of meal: full breakfast. Beds: Q. Air conditioning and TV in room. Fax, copier and spa on premises. Family reunions hosted. Antiques, fishing, parks, shopping, downhill skiing, cross-country skiing, theater and watersports nearby.

Juniper Hill Farm B&B

15325 Budd Rd
Dubuque, IA 52002
(319)582-4405 (800)572-1449 Fax:(319)583-6607
E-mail: jhbandb@aol.com

Circa 1939. Stationed on 40 acres in the hills of the Mississippi River Valley, eight miles from downtown, this cedar shingle house overlooks wide vistas, and it is adjacent to Sundown Ski

Area. There are seven acres of lawns and grounds. Guest rooms are furnished with country oak pieces and Mennonite quilts, and one has a double whirlpool tub. The inn's common room with dark pine floors and walls and a brick fireplace, has a cast-iron stove that serves as a buffet. Heritage Bike Trail is nearby, but guests often elect to hike through the woods, fish for largemouth bass in the pond or enjoy the hot tub. Breakfast may includes berries from the inn's bushes.

Innkeeper(s): Bill & Ruth McEllhiney. $70-145. MC VISA DS PC TC. TAC10. 3 rooms, 1 with PB. 2 suites. Breakfast and evening snack included in rates. Types of meals: full breakfast, gourmet breakfast and early coffee/tea. Beds: KQT. Air conditioning, turndown service and ceiling fan in room. TV, VCR, fax, copier, spa, bicycles and library on premises. 40 acres. Small meetings and family reunions hosted. Antiques, fishing, parks, shopping, downhill skiing, cross-country skiing, golf and theater nearby.

The Mandolin Inn

199 Loras Blvd
Dubuque, IA 52001-4857
(319)556-0069 (800)524-7996 Fax:(319)556-0587

Circa 1908. This three-story brick Edwardian with Queen Anne wraparound veranda boasts a mosaic-tiled porch floor. Inside are in-laid mahogany and rosewood floors, bay windows and a turret that starts in the parlor and ascends to the second-floor Holly Marie Room, decorated in a wedding motif. This room features a seven-piece French Walnut bedroom suite and a crystal chandelier. A three-course gourmet breakfast is served in the dining room with Italian tile depicting women's work at the turn-of-the-century. There is an herb garden outside the kitchen. A church is across the street and riverboat gambling is 12 blocks away.

Innkeeper(s): Jan Oswald. $75-135. MC VISA AX DC DS PC TC. TAC10. 7 rooms, 5 with PB. 2 conference rooms. Breakfast included in rates. Types of meals: gourmet breakfast and early coffee/tea. Beds: KQD. Air conditioning, ceiling fan and TV in room. Fax on premises. Weddings, small meetings, family reunions and seminars hosted. Antiques, fishing, parks, shopping, downhill skiing, cross-country skiing, sporting events, theater and watersports nearby.

"From the moment we entered the Mandolin, we felt at home. I know we'll be back."

The Richards House

1492 Locust St
Dubuque, IA 52001-4714
(319)557-1492

Circa 1883. Owner David Stuart estimates that it will take several years to remove the concrete-based brown paint applied by a bridge painter in the '60s to cover the 7,000-square-foot, Stick-style Victorian house. The interior, however, only needed a tad of polish. The varnished cherry and bird's-eye maple woodwork is set aglow under electrified gaslights. Ninety stained-glass windows, eight pocket doors with stained glass and a magnificent entryway reward those who pass through.

Historic Interest: Five historic districts are in Dubuque.

Innkeeper(s): Michelle A. Delaney. $40-95. MC VISA AX DC CB DS TC. 6 rooms, 3 with PB, 5 with FP. 1 suite. 1 conference room. Breakfast included in rates. Types of meals: full breakfast and early coffee/tea. Afternoon tea and evening snack available. Beds: Q. Phone, TV and VCR in room. Fax on premises. Weddings, small meetings and family reunions hosted. Antiques, fishing, parks, shopping, downhill skiing, cross-country skiing, theater and watersports nearby.

Pets Allowed.

Location: In the Jackson Park National Register Historic District.

Publicity: *Collectors Journal, Telegraph Herald.*

"Although the guide at the door had warned us that the interior was incredible, we were still flabbergasted when we stepped into the foyer of this house."

Fort Madison   F8

Kingsley Inn

707 Avenue H (Hwy 61)
Fort Madison, IA 52627
(319)372-7074 (800)441-2327 Fax:(319)372-7096

Circa 1858. Overlooking the Mississippi River, this century-old inn is located in downtown Fort Madison. Though furnished with antiques, all 14 rooms offer modern amenities and private baths (some with whirlpools) as well as river views. There also is a two-bedroom, two-bath suite. The suite includes a living room, dining area, kitchen and a whirlpool tub in one bathroom. A riverboat casino and a variety of shops are within a few blocks of the inn. There is a restaurant, Alphas on the Riverfront, and a gift shop on the premises.

Historic Interest: A museum and historic fort are nearby. Historic Nauvoo, Ill., known as the "Williamsburg of the Midwest," is only 11 miles from the inn.

Innkeeper(s): Nannette Evans. $65-115. MC VISA AX DC DS. 14 rooms with PB. 1 suite. 1 conference room. Breakfast included in rates. Types of meals: continental-plus breakfast and early coffee/tea. Restaurant on premises. Beds: KQD. Phone, air conditioning and TV in room. Fax on premises. Handicap

access. Weddings, small meetings, family reunions and seminars hosted. Antiques, fishing, shopping and theater nearby.

Location: US Highway 61 in downtown Fort Madison.

Publicity: *Hawkeye.*

"Wow, how nice and relaxing, quiet atmosphere, great innkeeper, so personal, kind and friendly."

Greenfield   E4

The Brass Lantern

2446 State Hwy 92
Greenfield, IA 50849-9757
(515)743-2031 (888)743-2031 Fax:(515)343-7500
E-mail: info@brasslantern.com

Circa 1918. Located on 20 acres, just minutes from the famous bridges of Madison County, this B&B is highlighted by

an indoor pool complex with a curving 40-foot pool. Spacious, luxuriously appointed guest rooms overlook the pool and rolling countryside and share the use of a fully furnished kitchenette. A hearty breakfast is served next door in the formal dining room of the antique-filled 1918 farm house.

Historic Interest: The antique aircraft museum, the Warren Opera House and the original Mormon Trail are located nearby.

Innkeeper(s): Terry & Margie Moore. $85-145. PC TC. 3 rooms, 2 with PB. Breakfast included in rates. Types of meals: full breakfast and early coffee/tea. Evening snack available. Beds: Q. Phone, air conditioning and TV in room. Fax and copier on premises. 20 acres. Antiques, fishing, shopping and golf nearby.

Pets Allowed: Advance notice required.

"Iowa is a beautiful place and The Brass Lantern is its crown jewel!"

Keokuk   G8

The Grand Anne

816 Grand Ave
Keokuk, IA 52632
(319)524-6310 (800)524-6310 Fax:(319)524-6310
E-mail: grandann@interl.net

Circa 1897. Situated high on a hill overlooking the Mississippi River on Keokuk's historic Grand Avenue, this exquisitely restored Queen Anne Victorian is a dramatic testimony to the craftsmanship of the renowned turn-of-the-century architect, George F. Barber. Modern-day architect Bob Diefenbach and his wife, Dana McCready, left their corporate jobs in California to transform this 6,000-square-foot, 22-room mansion into the magnificent bed & breakfast that it is today. The candle-snuffer porch and tower rooms with bent-glass windows, an impressive oak-paneled reception hall with a coffered ceiling and a gleaming oak staircase with hand-turned spindles are a few of George Barber's signature architectural details. The two spacious parlors, music room, formal dining room and conservatory feature wainscoting and intricately detailed moldings. The music room opens to a screened porch overlooking the formal gardens and expansive lawns where guests can enjoy a game of croquet or practice golf on the putting green. Each of the inn's four individually decorated rooms features plush terry robes and designer towels, Crabtree & Evelyn toiletries, down comforters and fresh flowers. Guests will appreciate Judge Huiskamp's Chamber, located in the spacious third-floor tower, for its separate sitting room and spectacular views of the Mississippi River. Morning fare includes baked herb cheese eggs, quiche, souffle, Starbucks coffee and the innkeeper's famous cinnamon rolls.

Historic Interest: Located close to fishing, boating, bicycling and golfing. Historic Nauvoo, Ill., is a 20-minute drive via the scenic river route. The inn is listed in the National Register of Historic Places.

Innkeeper(s): Dana McCready & Bob Diefenbach. $70-95. MC VISA AX PC. TAC10. 5 rooms, 3 with PB. 1 suite. Breakfast included in rates. Types of meals: full breakfast and early coffee/tea. Picnic lunch and room service available. Beds: Q. Phone, air conditioning, ceiling fan and VCR in room. Fax, bicycles and library on premises. German and Spanish spoken. Antiques, fishing, parks, shopping, cross-country skiing, golf, theater and watersports nearby.

Publicity: *Country Inns, The Iowan, Des Moines Register.*

Keosauqua   F7

Hotel Manning

100 Van Buren St
Keosauqua, IA 52565
(319)293-3232 (800)728-2718 Fax:(319)293-9960

Circa 1899. This historic riverfront inn offers a peek at bygone days. Its steamboat gothic exterior is joined by an interior that

strives for historic authenticity. All bedrooms are furnished with antiques. Lacey-Keosauqua State Park and Lake Sugema are within easy driving distance. Inn guests enjoy a full breakfast. There is a 19-room, modern motel adjacent to the inn.

Innkeeper(s): Ron & Connie Davenport. $35-72. MC VISA DS PC. 18 rooms, 10 with PB. 2 suites. 1 conference room. Breakfast included in rates. Banquet service, catering service and catered breakfast available. Beds: QD. Air conditioning and ceiling fan in room. VCR, fax and copier on premises. Weddings, small meetings, family reunions and seminars hosted. Antiques, fishing, parks and shopping nearby.

Maquoketa   D9

Squiers Manor B&B

418 W Pleasant St
Maquoketa, IA 52060-2847
(319)652-6961

Circa 1882. Innkeepers Virl and Kathy Banowetz are ace antique dealers, who along with owning one of the Midwest's largest antique shops, have refurbished this elegant, Queen Anne Victorian. The inn is furnished with period antiques that are beyond compare. Guest rooms boast museum-quality

pieces such as a Victorian brass bed with lace curtain wings and inlaid mother-of-pearl or an antique mahogany bed with carved birds and flowers. Six guest rooms include whirlpool tubs, and one includes a unique Swiss shower. The innkeepers restored the home's original woodwork, shuttered-windows, fireplaces, gas and electric chandeliers and stained- and engraved-glass windows back to their former glory. They also recently renovated the mansion's attic ballroom into two luxurious suites. The Loft, which is made up of three levels, features pine and wicker furnishings, a sitting room and gas-burning wood stove. On the second level, there is a large Jacuzzi, on the third, an antique queen-size bed. The huge Ballroom Suite boasts 24-foot ceilings, oak and pine antiques, gas-burning wood stove and a Jacuzzi snuggled beside a dormer window. Suite guests enjoy breakfast delivered to their rooms. Other guests feast on an array of mouth-watering treats, such as home-baked breads, seafood quiche and fresh fruits. Evening desserts are served by candlelight.

Historic Interest: The area has 70 sites listed in the National Register.

Innkeeper(s): Virl & Kathy Banowetz. $75-185. MC VISA AX. 8 rooms with PB. 3 suites. Breakfast included in rates. Types of meals: full breakfast and gourmet breakfast. Beds: KQT. Small meetings hosted. Antiques, fishing, parks, shopping, downhill skiing, cross-country skiing and watersports nearby.

Publicity: *Des Moines Register Datebook, Daily Herald.*

"We couldn't have asked for a more perfect place to spend our honeymoon. The service was excellent and so was the food! It was an exciting experience that we will never forget!"

Montpelier   E9

Varners' Caboose

204 E 2nd, Box 10
Montpelier, IA 52759
(319)381-3652

Circa 1956. Located halfway between Davenport and Muscatine, this original Rock Island Lines caboose rests on its own track behind the Varners' home, the former Montpelier Depot. The caboose is decorated in simple, country style. The innkeepers prepare a full breakfast and deliver it to their guests. Llamas, ducks and geese are available for petting.

Innkeeper(s): Bob & Nancy Varner. $60. PC. 1 room with PB. Breakfast included in rates. Type of meal: full breakfast. Beds: QT. Air conditioning, TV and VCR in room. Fishing and parks nearby.

Pets Allowed.

Location: Located on Route 22, halfway between Davenport and Muscatine.

Newton   D6

La Corsette Maison Inn

629 1st Ave E
Newton, IA 50208-3305
(515)792-6833 Fax:(515)792-6597

Circa 1909. This unusual Mission-style building has an arts-and-crafts interior. All the woodwork is of quarter-sawn oak, and the dining room furniture was designed by Limbert. Stained and beveled glass is found throughout. French bedchambers feature reproduction and antique furnishings. One of the suites includes a fireplace and double whirlpool tub. The inn's restaurant has received four-and-one-half stars from the Des Moines Register's Grumpy Gourmet. The mansion also has three working wood-burning fireplaces.

Historic Interest: Jasper County Courthouse (7 blocks), Saint Stevens Episcopal Church (3 blocks).

Innkeeper(s): Kay Owen. $70-190. AP. MC VISA AX. 7 rooms with PB, 3 with FP. 2 suites. Breakfast included in rates. Type of meal: full breakfast. Dinner and picnic lunch available. Restaurant on premises. Beds: KQD. Fax and bicycles on premises. Antiques, fishing, downhill skiing and cross-country skiing nearby.

Pets Allowed: by prior arrangements.

Location: One mile from I-80 on Highway 6, seven blocks east of city square.

Publicity: *Cedar Rapids Gazette, American Airlines, Innsider, Midwest Living, AAA Home and Away, Des Moines Register, Bon Appetit.*

"We shall return. You and your house are an inspiration."

St. Ansgar   A6

Blue Belle Inn B&B

PO Box 205, 513 W 4th St
St. Ansgar, IA 50472
(515)736-2225 Fax:(515)736-4024
E-mail: bluebelle@deskmedia.com

Circa 1896. This home was purchased from a Knoxville, Tenn., mail-order house. It's difficult to believe that stunning features, such as a tin ceiling, stained-glass windows, intricate woodwork and pocket doors could have come via the mail, but these original items are still here for guests to admire. Rooms are named after books special to the innkeeper. Four of the rooms include a Jacuzzi  tub, and the Never Neverland room has a clawfoot tub. Other rooms offer a skylight, fireplace or perhaps a white iron bed. During the Christmas season, every room has its own decorated tree. The innkeeper hosts a variety of themed luncheons, dinners and events, such as the April in Paris cooking workshop. Mother's Day brunches, the "Some Enchanted Evening" dinner or the posh "Pomp and Circumstance" dinner are some of the possibilities.

Innkeeper(s): Sherrie Hansen. $60-130. MC VISA AX DS PC TC. TAC10. 6 rooms, 5 with PB, 2 with FP. 2 suites. 2 conference rooms. Breakfast included in rates. Types of meals: continental breakfast, continental-plus breakfast, full breakfast, gourmet breakfast and early coffee/tea. Afternoon tea, dinner, evening snack, lunch, gourmet lunch, banquet service and room service available. Restaurant on premises. Beds: KQT. Air conditioning, TV and VCR in room. Fax and library on premises. Weddings, small meetings, family reunions and seminars hosted. German spoken. Antiques, fishing, parks, shopping, golf and watersports nearby.

Publicity: *Minneapolis Star Tribune, Post-Bulletin, Midwest Living, Country, AAA Home & Away, Des Moines Register.*

Waterloo   C7

Wellington B&B

800 W Fourth St
Waterloo, IA 50702-2149
(319)234-2993

Circa 1900. This sturdy Colonial Revival/Queen Anne Victorian home has bay windows, porches and a balcony, and it is in the National Register. A garden filled with perennials is behind the inn's stately Buckeye tree. Lavish Victorian interiors include polished curly birch woodwork, a handsome oak staircase, stained glass, a crystal chandelier and Victorian antiques. In all, 11 varieties of wood were used to form  moldings, balustrades and other woodwork in the house. Guest rooms are spacious and accommodate the full breakfasts that are brought to each room in the morning.

Innkeeper(s): Jim & Reatha Aronson. $75-115. MC VISA AX DS PC TC. TAC10. 4 rooms with PB, 1 with FP. 3 suites. 1 conference room. Breakfast included in rates. Types of meals: continental breakfast, continental-plus breakfast, full breakfast, gourmet breakfast and early coffee/tea. Beds: Q. Phone, air conditioning, ceiling fan and TV in room. Copier, bicycles and library on premises. Weddings, small meetings, family reunions and seminars hosted. Antiques, fishing, parks, cross-country skiing, sporting events, golf and theater nearby.

Publicity: *Midwest Living.*

"Your love is evident in the splendid restoration you have done. Meals were world class and unsurpassed."

Kansas

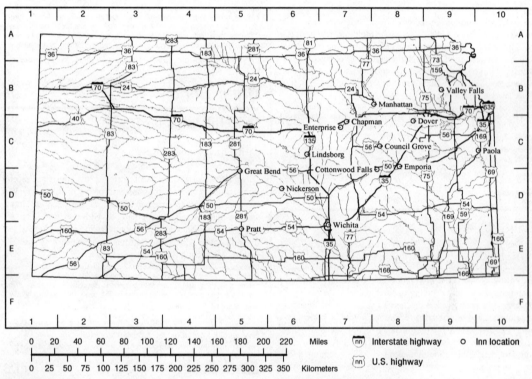

		Miles
0 20 40 60 80 100 120 140 160 180 200 220		Miles
0 25 50 75 100 125 150 175 200 225 250 275 300 325 350		Kilometers

- 🛈 Interstate highway   o Inn location
- 🛈 U.S. highway

Chapman   C7

Windmill Inn B&B

1787 Rain Rd
Chapman, KS 67431-9317
(913)263-8755

Circa 1917. The Windmill Inn is a place of memories. Many were created by the innkeeper's grandparents, who built the home. Others are the happy remembrances guests take home. The home is filled with antiques, family heirlooms. Stained glass and a window seat add to the charm. Evening meals or picnic lunches are also available. The wraparound porch offers a relaxing swing, and on starry nights, the outdoor spa is the place to be. Historic Abilene is just a few miles down the road, offering a glimpse of an authentic Old West town, located on the Chisolm Trail.

Innkeeper(s): Deb Sanders. $65-85. 4 rooms. Breakfast included in rates.
Type of meal: full breakfast.

Cottonwood Falls   D8

1874 Stonehouse B&B on Mulberry Hill

Rt 1, Box 67A
Cottonwood Falls, KS 66845
(316)273-8481 Fax:(316)273-8481
E-mail: shmh1874@aol.com

Circa 1874. More than 100 acres surround this historic home, which is one of the state's oldest native stone homes that is still in use. Each guest room offers something special. The Rose Room includes a sleigh bed, while the Blue Room and Yellow Room offer views either of the quarry pond or the Flint Hills. Explore the property and you'll see wildlife, an old stone barn and corral ruins. The Cottonwood River runs through the property at one point, offering fishing. The innkeepers can arrange for guests to fish in a stocked pond, too.

Innkeeper(s): Diane Ware. $75-95. MC VISA TC. 3 rooms with PB. Breakfast included in rates. Types of meals: full breakfast and gourmet breakfast. Beds:

KQT. Air conditioning and ceiling fan in room. VCR, fax, copier and library on premises. 120 acres. Antiques, fishing, parks, shopping and watersports nearby.

Pets Allowed: Kennel for dogs.

"I have never felt so pampered. Our walk around the countryside was so peaceful and beautiful."

Council Grove   C8

The Cottage House Hotel

25 N Neosho St
Council Grove, KS 66846-1633
(316)767-6828

Circa 1872. The inn is located in Council Grove, the rendezvous point on the Santa Fe Trail. The building grew from a boarding house to an elegant home before it became the hotel of a local banker. Listed in the National Register of Historic Places, the inn has been completely renovated and is a beautiful example of Victorian architecture in a prairie town.

Historic Interest: National Register.

Innkeeper(s): Connie Essington. $50-130. MC VISA AX DC DS. 26 rooms with PB. 1 cottage. 2 conference rooms. Type of meal: continental breakfast. Beds: KQDW. Spa and sauna on premises. Handicap access. Fishing nearby.

Location: Northeast Kansas, intersection of 56 & 177.

Publicity: *Manhattan Mercury, Gazette, Globe & Mail, Kansas City Star, Wichita Eagle, Midwest Living, Kansas Magazine.*

"A walk back into Kansas history; preserved charm and friendliness."

Dover   C8

Historic Sage Inn

13553 SW K-4 Hwy
Dover, KS 66420-0013
(913)256-6336 (888)256-6566

Circa 1882. Constructed from limestone, this country inn is a unique and rustic sight. The inn opened in 1882 as a hotel, housing stagecoach travelers on their way to and from Topeka. The inn is located on the historic Southwest Trail, a link which connected the Oregon Trail to the Santa Fe Trail. Original pine floors and 18-inch limestone walls remain. The three guest rooms are decorated in Southwestern style. One room includes a bath with an antique copper soaking tub. The inn is within a 30-minute drive of Topeka.

Innkeeper(s): Robert & Janice Dunwell. $65-75. PC. 3 rooms with PB. Breakfast included in rates. Types of meals: gourmet breakfast and early coffee/tea. Gourmet lunch available. Beds: KQ. Phone and air conditioning in room. TV and VCR on premises. Weddings, small meetings and family reunions hosted. Amusement parks, antiques, fishing, parks, shopping, golf, theater and watersports nearby.

Pets Allowed: with advance notice.

Enterprise   C7

Ehrsam Place B&B

103 S Grant
Enterprise, KS 67441
(785)263-8747 Fax:(785)263-8548

Circa 1879. In its early days, this home and the family who lived in it were the talk of the town. The family held an abundance of well-attended parties, and many rumors were spread about why the Ehrsam company safe was kept in the home's basement. Rumors aside, the home features a variety of architectural styles, leaning toward Georgian, with columns gracing the

front entrance. The 20-acre grounds are fun to explore, offering a windmill, silo, stables, a carriage house and creek. The innkeepers encourage guests to explore the home as well, which rises three stories. The basement still houses the illusive safe. Rooms are decorated to reflect the area's history. Guests can enjoy breakfast in bed if they choose. With advance notice, the innkeepers will prepare hors d'oeuvres, picnic lunches and dinners for their guests. Candlelight dinners for two also are available, and turn-down service is one of the romantic amenities.

Historic Interest: Located five minutes from Abilene.

Innkeeper(s): Mary & William Lambert. $55-85. MC VISA PC TC. 4 suites. 1 conference room. Breakfast, afternoon tea and evening snack included in rates. Types of meals: full breakfast and early coffee/tea. Dinner, picnic lunch, catering service and room service available. Beds: Q. Air conditioning, turn-down service, ceiling fan and TV in room. VCR, fax and library on premises. 17 acres. Weddings, small meetings, family reunions and seminars hosted. Antiques, fishing, parks, shopping, sporting events, golf and theater nearby.

"Thank you for history, laughs and most all sharing your treasures with us."

Great Bend   D5

Peaceful Acres B&B

RR 5 Box 153
Great Bend, KS 67530-9805
(316)793-7527

Circa 1899. A casual country setting greets guests at Peaceful Acres, a comfortable farmhouse with plenty of calves, chicken, dogs and cats to entertain all visitors, especially children, who are more than welcome here. Activities abound for the youngsters and they also will enjoy the zoo in Great Bend, five miles away. Cheyenne Bottoms and Pawnee Rock are within easy driving distance.

Innkeeper(s): Dale & Doris Nitzel. $30. 2 rooms. 1 conference room. Breakfast included in rates. Type of meal: full breakfast. Beds: QDT. Air conditioning and ceiling fan in room. VCR and library on premises. 10 acres. Family reunions and seminars hosted. Antiques, fishing, parks and shopping nearby.

Pets Allowed.

"Thank you for the charming accommodations. The food was very good and filling, and the place is peaceful, just like the name. We enjoyed the company at breakfast! It felt like staying with family."

Lindsborg   C6

Swedish Country Inn

112 W Lincoln St
Lindsborg, KS 67456-2319
(913)227-2985 (800)231-0266

Circa 1904. Founded in the 1860s by Swedish immigrants, the town of Lindsborg is still known as "Little Sweden," maintaining its heritage through a variety of cultural events, festivals, galleries, shops and restaurants. The Swedish Country Inn adds to the town's ethnic flavor. All the furnishings have been imported from Sweden. Bright, airy rooms feature pine furnishings, handmade quilts and hand-painted cupboards. A Swedish-style buffet breakfast is served each morning, with items such as meatballs, lingonberries, herring, knackebread, fruit, cheese, cold meats and fresh baked goods. The Christmas season is an especially festive time to visit this inn and picturesque small town.

Innkeeper(s): Becky Anderson. $50-75. MC VISA AX DS PC TC. 19 rooms with PB. 2 suites. Breakfast, afternoon tea and evening snack included in rates. Types of meals: full breakfast, gourmet breakfast and early coffee/tea. Beds: QD. Phone, air conditioning and TV in room. Sauna and bicycles on premises. Weddings, small meetings, family reunions and seminars hosted. Antiques, parks and shopping nearby.

Manhattan
B8

Colt House Inn B&B

617 Houston St
Manhattan, KS 66502
(785)776-7500 Fax:(785)776-7775

Circa 1906. This Queen Anne Transition-style house with its wraparound porch has recently been renovated, having served as a rental for half a century. The inn is furnished in antiques and turn-of-the-century photographs and memorabilia of the Colt family. Most rooms have a two-person whirlpool, and there are brass beds, carved walnut Eastlake beds and iron beds. All the guest rooms are named after women's flower names: Daisy, Rose, Iris, Lillie and Violet. These flowers also are found in the English garden and the cutting gardens. In the morning, a continental breakfast is served on the second floor from 7-8:30 a.m., while a full breakfast is served in the dining from 8-9:30 a.m. Located 10 blocks from the university, Colt House is also close to McCall's Patterns and Ft. Riley.

Innkeeper(s): Michael Cody. $80-100. MC VISA PC. 5 rooms with PB. Breakfast and evening snack included in rates. Types of meals: continental breakfast, continental-plus breakfast, full breakfast, gourmet breakfast and early coffee/tea. Afternoon tea, dinner, picnic lunch, lunch, gourmet lunch and catering service available. Beds: QD. Phone, air conditioning and ceiling fan in room. TV, VCR, fax and library on premises. Handicap access. Weddings, small meetings, family reunions and seminars hosted. Antiques, fishing, parks, shopping, golf, theater and watersports nearby.

Nickerson
D6

Hedrick's Exotic Animal Farm and B&B

7910 N Roy L Smith Rd
Nickerson, KS 67561-9049
(316)422-3245 (888)489-8039 Fax:(316)422-3766

Circa 1993. There are few places where one can say they've been properly greeted by a giraffe, and Hedrick's is one of them. You may reread the first sentence if you wish. That's right, a giraffe is among the many unusual animals that inhabit the grounds at this exotic animal farm. Guests are welcome to pet camels, kiss giraffes, hop with kangaroos or hug a llama. Even the exterior of this bed & breakfast is entrancing. It appears as the facade of an Old West town. The rooms are a wild, exotic mix of decor, that is both whimsical and strangely elegant at the same time. Local artists have painted murals in each of the themed guest quarters, and each room is named in honor of one of the animals who reside at the farm. The innkeepers offer vacation options for groups, and this farm is an ideal place for a family vacation. Children can enjoy pony rides and even help bottle feed baby animals.

Innkeeper(s): Joe & Sondra Hedrick. $59-120. MC VISA DS PC TC. 7 rooms with PB. 2 suites. 2 conference rooms. Breakfast and evening snack included in rates. Types of meals: full breakfast and early coffee/tea. Banquet service available. Beds: QDB. Phone, air conditioning, ceiling fan and TV in room. VCR, fax, copier and spa on premises. Handicap access. 40 acres. Weddings, small meetings, family reunions and seminars hosted. Antiques, fishing, parks, shopping, sporting events and golf nearby.

"This is fantastic—great service, food, animals, room—just everything!"

Paola
C10

The Victorian Lady B&B

402 S Pearl
Paola, KS 66071
(913)294-4652 (888)842-5239 Fax:(913)294-6996
E-mail: vladyy@msn.com

Circa 1894. For a century, this Victorian was owned by the same family. The gracious home was designed by a notable Kansas architect, and the innkeepers have restored the home back to its original glory. Common rooms are decorated in Victorian style, but each guest room reflects a different era. The 1920s Room is a whimsical retreat with red and white striped wallpaper, a colorful handmade quilt and a carousel horse. The 1940s room is elegant, the bed is topped with  Battenburg lace and the bathroom includes a unique tub made of tin. The Eastlake Room, filled with its namesake furnishings, reflects the home's 19th-century beginnings. For an extra fee, guests can create a special package with a massage, Victorian tea or perhaps roses and champagne. Paola offers a variety of shops, and the downtown square is just a few blocks away.

Innkeeper(s): Harry & Lue Ann Hellyer. $69-89. MC VISA AX DS PC TC. TAC10. 3 rooms, 2 with PB. Breakfast included in rates. Types of meals: gourmet breakfast and early coffee/tea. Afternoon tea, dinner, evening snack, picnic lunch, lunch and room service available. Beds: Q. Phone, air conditioning, turndown service and TV in room. VCR, fax and bicycles on premises. Weddings, small meetings and seminars hosted. Antiques, fishing, parks, shopping, golf, theater and watersports nearby.

Publicity: *Olathe Daily News, Miami County Republic.*

"Looking for a romantic, relaxing getaway and we found the perfect place."

Pratt
E5

Pratt Guest House B&B Inn

PO Box 326, 105 N Iuka St
Pratt, KS 67124-0326
(316)672-1200

Circa 1910. This three-story Colonial Revival was built by Samuel Gebhart, who not only founded a town newspaper, but also served as a mayor and councilman. The innkeeper painstakingly restored the three-story manor, which is the only property in Pratt listed in both the state and national historic registers. William Jennings Bryan was once a guest here. Family heirlooms and antiques are the furnishings that decorate the interior, giving the home a nostalgic atmosphere. However, two of the rooms include the modern amenity of a whirlpool tub. Stuffed French toast or a frittata are among the breakfast specialties, served along with freshly ground coffee, fruit and homemade muffins or breads.

Innkeeper(s): Marguerite Flanagan. $55-90. MC VISA PC. 5 rooms with PB. Breakfast and evening snack included in rates. Types of meals: full breakfast, gourmet breakfast and early coffee/tea. Beds: KQD. Air conditioning in room. Weddings, small meetings and family reunions hosted. Antiques, fishing, parks and shopping nearby.

"Beautiful B&B. A+ from a couple of school folks."

Valley Falls B9

The Barn B&B

14910 Bluemound Rd
Valley Falls, KS 66088-9529
(913)945-3225

Circa 1892. This century-old barn tucked in the rolling countryside of northeast Kansas has been modernized and converted to a bed & breakfast inn. King-size beds, an exercise room,
a delicious, homecooked supper and hearty farm-style breakfast
are among The Barn's special amenities.Swimmers will appreciate the indoor heated pool available all year. The inn also has
its own fishing ponds and walking trail.

Innkeeper(s): Tom & Marcella Ryan. $89-99. AP. MC VISA AX. 20 rooms
with PB. 2 conference rooms. Type of meal: full breakfast. Beds: K. Copier
on premises.

Publicity: *Manhattan Mercury, Kansas Magazine, Kansas City Star, Wichita
Eagle.*

"Great place, great time, great people! Our seventh visit."

Wichita E7

The Castle Inn Riverside "The Historic Campbell Castle"

1155 N River Blvd
Wichita, KS 67203
(316)263-9300 (800)580-1131 Fax:(316)263-4998

Circa 1886. Camelot lives on at this breathtaking castle, a
stunning example of classic Richardsonian Romanesque architecture. Built by cattle baron Colonel Burton Campbell, the
home offers 14 bedchambers to choose from, each carefully
restored and individually appointed with antiques. Six guest
rooms include Jacuzzi tubs, 12 offer a fireplace, and still another is located inside the castle turret. The stately interior also
includes a library, parlor, turret and gift shop all fashioned like
a Scottish country castle. The innkeepers maintain a sense of

romance, but still provide several amenities for their business
travelers. Chef Andrea Cowley fills the breakfast menu with
fresh fruits, juices, freshly baked muffins and specialty entrees
such as berry-stuffed French toast with spice raspberry honey
or perhaps an apple- and brie-filled omelet. Paula also serves
afternoon refreshments, an assortment of sinful delights that
might include mocha cheesecake or lemon-blueberry shortcake.

Historic Interest: The area offers several historic attractions, including nearby
Old Town, a Native American center and several museums.

Innkeeper(s): Terry & Paula Lowry. $125-225. MC VISA AX DS PC TC.
TAC10. 14 rooms with PB, 12 with FP. 1 suite. 1 cottage. 1 conference
room. Breakfast and evening snack included in rates. Type of meal: gourmet
breakfast. Beds: KQ. Phone, air conditioning, ceiling fan, TV and VCR in
room. Fax and copier on premises. Handicap access. Weddings, small meetings, family reunions and seminars hosted. Antiques, fishing, parks, shopping, sporting events, theater and watersports nearby.

The Inn at The Park

3751 E Douglas Ave
Wichita, KS 67218-1002
(316)652-0500 (800)258-1951 Fax:(316)652-0610

Circa 1910. This popular three-story brick mansion offers
many special touches, including unique furnishings in each of
its 11 guest rooms, three of which are suites. Some of the
rooms feature fireplaces, refrigerators or hot tubs. The inn's
convenient location makes it ideal for business travelers or
those interested in exploring Wichita at length. The inn's park-
side setting provides additional opportunities for relaxation or
recreation. Ask for information about shops and restaurants in
Wichita's Old Town.

Innkeeper(s): Michelle Hickman. $85-145. MC VISA AX DS. 12 rooms with
PB, 8 with FP. 3 suites. 1 conference room. Breakfast included in rates.
Types of meals: continental-plus breakfast and early coffee/tea. Catering ser-
vice available. Beds: KQ. Phone, air conditioning, turndown service, TV and
VCR in room. Fax, copier and spa on premises. Antiques, shopping and the-
ater nearby.

Publicity: *Wichita Business Journal.*

*"This is truly a distinctive hotel. Your attention to detail is surpassed
only by your devotion to excellent service."*

Kentucky

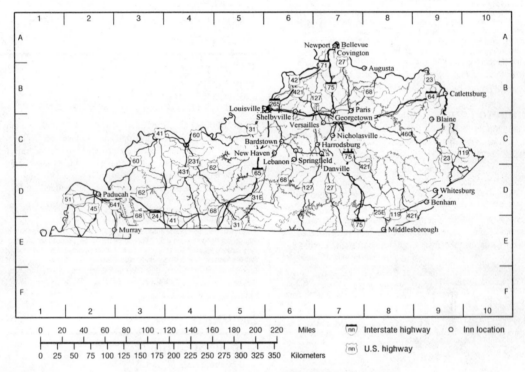

| | | | | | | | | | |
|1|2|3|4|5|6|7|8|9|10|

Newport ■ Bellevue
Covington
71 27
Augusta
42
75 68 23
421 Catlettsburg
127 64
Louisville 265 Paris
Shelbyville Georgetown
Versailles Blaine
41 60 31 Nicholasville 460
Bardstown Harrodsburg
60 231 New Haven 75 23
431 62 Lebanon Springfield 421 119
65 Danville
Paducah 62 68
51 641 31E 127 27 Whitesburg
45 Benham
68 24 68 25E 119 421
41 31 75 Middlesborough
Murray

| | | | | | | | | | |
|1|2|3|4|5|6|7|8|9|10|

```
0   20   40   60   80  100  120  140  160  180  200  220   Miles
0  25  50  75 100 125 150 175 200 225 250 275 300 325 350  Kilometers
```

(nn) Interstate highway   o Inn location
(nn) U.S. highway

Augusta   B8

Doniphan Home
302 E 4th St
Augusta, KY 41002-1120
(606)756-2409

Circa 1825. This brick Georgian-style house, with porch and
white shutters, was built around a core constructed of logs in
the late 18th century. There are 14-inch-thick walls. Antiques
are featured in the wallpapered guest rooms. An antique dish
collection and handsome sideboard add to the warmth of the
bed & breakfast's decor. Full breakfasts are served in the formal
dining room, which features a chandelier and polished walnut
woodwork. An old ferry boat still plies the river.

Innkeeper(s): Ruth & George Cummins. $65. PC TC. 3 rooms, 1 with FP. 1
suite. Breakfast and evening snack included in rates. Types of meals: full breakfast and gourmet breakfast. Beds: KD. Phone, air conditioning and TV in room.
VCR and library on premises. Antiques, fishing, parks and shopping nearby.
Pets Allowed.

Publicity: *Country Home, Southern Living.*

*"Everywhere I look I see the beauty in this home and in this town.
Augusta is forever in my heart."*

Bardstown   C6

Jailer's Inn
111 W Stephen Foster Ave
Bardstown, KY 40004-1415
(502)348-5551 (800)948-5551 Fax:(502)348-1852

Circa 1819. As the innkeepers say, guests can come and "do
time" at this inn, which was used as a jail as late as 1987.
However, today, accommodations are bit less restrictive. Each
of the elegant guest rooms is individually appointed. From the
Victorian Room to the Garden Room, each captures a different
theme. Two guest rooms include a double Jacuzzi tub. Only
one guest room resembles a jail cell, it contains two bunks, as
well as the more luxurious addition of a waterbed. In the summer, the full breakfasts are served in a courtyard. The inn is
located in the heart of historic Bardstown.

Historic Interest: Tours of "My Old Kentucky Home," conducted by guides in antebellum costumes, are a popular attraction. Lincoln's birthplace and boyhood home and the oldest cathedral west of Alleghany are nearby, as is the Getz Museum of Whiskey History.

Innkeeper(s): Paul McCoy. $65-95. MC VISA AX DS PC TC. TAC10. 6 rooms with PB. 1 conference room. Breakfast included in rates. Types of meals: full breakfast and early coffee/tea. Evening snack available. Beds: KQD. Air conditioning, turndown service, ceiling fan and TV in room. VCR on premises. Weddings, small meetings and family reunions hosted. Antiques, parks, shopping and theater nearby.

Location: South of Louisville 35 miles.

Publicity: *Vacations, New Choices, Kentucky Standard, USA Weekend.*

"Wonderful experience! A very special B&B."

Kenmore Farms

1050 Bloomfield Rd # 62 E
Bardstown, KY 40004-9711
(502)348-8023 (800)831-6159 Fax:(502)348-0617

Circa 1860. This stately home was established as a prominent Kentucky horse farm. Antiques, Oriental rugs and cherry stairway add to the home's charm. Guest rooms are furnished with pieces such as four-poster or Lincoln beds. Among the linens are vintage, antique pieces. Guests are encouraged to relax, and can enjoy the fresh air either on the front porch or in the gazebo. The innkeepers prepare a hearty, country breakfast each morning.

Historic Interest: The area offers many historic sites, including Maker's Mark Distillery, The Kentucky Railway Museum and St. Joseph's Proto-Cathedral.

Innkeeper(s): Dorothy & Bernie Keene. $80-100. 4 rooms with PB. 1 suite. Breakfast and evening snack included in rates. Types of meals: full breakfast and early coffee/tea. Beds: QDT. Antiques, golf and theater nearby.

Publicity: *Kentucky Standard, Nelson County Record, Midwest Motorist, Country Roads of Kentucky.*

"Your hospitality and the extras you provided help to make our first anniversary a special one."

The Mansion Bed & Breakfast

1003 N 3rd St
Bardstown, KY 40004-2616
(502)348-2586 (800)399-2586 Fax:(502)349-6098

Circa 1851. The Confederate flag was raised for the first time in Kentucky on this property. The beautifully crafted Greek Revival mansion is in the National Register of Historic Places. Period antiques and hand-crocheted bedspreads, dust ruffles and shams are featured in the guest rooms. There are more than three acres of tall trees and gardens. The Courthouse in historic Bardstown is nine blocks away.

Innkeeper(s): Joseph & Charmaine Downs. $80-125. MC VISA DS. 8 rooms with PB. 1 conference room. Breakfast included in rates. Type of meal: continental-plus breakfast. Beds: KD. Air conditioning and ceiling fan in room. TV and VCR on premises. Small meetings and seminars hosted. Antiques, fishing, shopping and theater nearby.

Old Talbott Tavern

107 W Stephen Foster Ave, PO Box 365
Bardstown, KY 40004
(502)348-3494 (800)482-8376 Fax:(502)348-0673

Circa 1779. Old Talbott Tavern is the oldest continuously operating "western" stagecoach inn in America. The stone building is filled with antiques, and there are murals painted by Prince Philippe of France and his entourage. If you look closely, you'll find bullet holes left by Jesse James. There are six guest rooms, and in addition to the pub, three public dining rooms to include group bookings.

Innkeeper(s): The Kelley Family. $70-125. EP. MC VISA. 6 rooms with PB.

Bellevue A7

Weller Haus B&B

319 Poplar St
Bellevue, KY 41073-1108
(606)431-6829 (800)431-4287 Fax:(606)431-4332

Circa 1880. Set in historic Taylor Daughter's District, five minutes from downtown Cincinnati, these two Victorian Gothic homes sit side by side. Special features include original millwork antique appointed suites and a newly added, sky-lit great room with cathedral ceilings and an ivy-covered gathering kitchen.One suite offers a Jacuzzi for two. A secluded garden adjoins the great room.

Innkeeper(s): Mary & Vernon Weller. $75-145. MC VISA AX DC DS PC. 5 rooms with PB. 4 suites. 1 conference room. Breakfast included in rates. Types of meals: full breakfast and early coffee/tea. Beds: QDT. Air conditioning, ceiling fan and TV in room. VCR on premises. Small meetings and seminars hosted. Amusement parks, antiques, fishing, shopping, downhill skiing, sporting events, theater and watersports nearby.

Location: Directly across the Ohio River from Cincinnati.

Publicity: *Downtowner, Bellevue Community News, Cincinnati Enquirer.*

"You made B&B believers out of us."

Benham D9

Schoolhouse Inn

100 Central Ave, PO Box B
Benham, KY 40807
(606)848-3000 (800)231-0627 Fax:(606)848-3820

Circa 1928. Guests imagine children traipsing down the halls of this enormous brick school, refurbished to include a restaurant and banquet room. The inn was a working school until 1993 and now features the cozy comforts of a country home in a unique setting. Most of the floors are still covered with original wood, and lockers still line the hallways. However, the new decor features elegant touches such as the chandelier that graces the entry. Meals at the Schoolhouse offer anything but what guests might remember from their own school days. A full-service bakery creates the many fresh breads and other treats. The restaurant features an array of cuisine, from country cooking to gourmet dishes.

Historic Interest: The Schoolhouse is within walking distance to the historic district of Benham.

Innkeeper(s): Jim Whitaker. $60-85. MC VISA AX DS. 27 rooms with PB. 3 suites. Types of meals: continental breakfast and full breakfast. Afternoon tea, dinner, picnic lunch, lunch, catering service and room service available. Restaurant on premises. Beds: KD. Antiques, fishing and theater nearby.

Publicity: *Tri-City News, Harlan Daily Enterprise.*

"What a wonderful feeling to return to my old school. The many wonderful memories of days gone by. I shall cherish forever. Thanks for the opportunity to recall and share these with my daughter. We shall return."

Blaine
C9

The Gambill Mansion

PO Box 98, S R 32 & 201
Blaine, KY 41124
(606)652-3120

Circa 1923. For guests who wish to personalize their stay, the innkeepers at Gambill Mansion offer a variety of unique packages. The most popular is "The Romantic," which includes a special cake, fresh flowers and non-alcoholic champagne all served by candlelight. Other themes include Hawaiian, 1950s, English, Mother's Day, Country and Nostalgic. There are three guest rooms in the main house, which was built by twin doctors Harry and John Gambill. The third-floor suite includes an antique bath. Guests also can stay in a restored guest house, which includes a kitchen, bedroom and a bath with a clawfoot tub. Elaborate trays of coffee are delivered to the rooms prior to breakfast, which sometimes is served in front of the fireplace. For an extra charge, guests can enjoy a theme breakfast.

Innkeeper(s): Art & Ella Seals. $60-125. MC VISA PC. 4 rooms. 1 suite. 1 cottage. Breakfast included in rates. Types of meals: continental breakfast, full breakfast and early coffee/tea. Beds: DT. Phone, air conditioning, turn-down service, TV and VCR in room. Weddings, small meetings and family reunions hosted. Amusement parks, antiques, fishing, parks, shopping, golf, theater and watersports nearby.

Publicity: *Ashland Daily Independent, Big Sandy News.*

Catlettsburg
B9

Levi Hampton House B&B

2206 Walnut St, US Rt 23
Catlettsburg, KY 41129
(606)739-8118 (888)538-4426 Fax:(606)739-6148
E-mail: bnb@ramlink.net

Circa 1847. Levi J. Hampton was one of the area's first settlers, and he built this pre-Civil War, Italianate-style home. Guest rooms are decorated with poster beds, candles and just a touch of lace. The innkeepers offer plenty of amenities for their business travelers, including computer jacks and fax or copier service. Guests enjoy early morning coffee or tea service in their rooms before joining the hosts for a full breakfast with treats such as home-made breads and per-haps a Southwestern-style quiche with tomatoes and salsa.

Innkeeper(s): Dennis & Kathy Stemen. $77-138. MC VISA. TAC10. 5 rooms with PB, 3 with FP. 2 suites. 2 cottages. Breakfast

and evening snack included in rates. Type of meal: full breakfast. Beds: QDT. Phone, air conditioning and TV in room. VCR, fax and copier on premises. Small meetings hosted. Amusement parks, antiques, fishing, parks, shopping, golf, theater and watersports nearby.

Publicity: *Ashland Daily Independent.*

"Having been in other B&Bs I know they all have their own unique qualities, but this one experience will be used to compare all others."

Covington
A7

Amos Shinkle Townhouse

215 Garrard St
Covington, KY 41011-1715
(606)431-2118 (800)972-7012 Fax:(606)491-4551

Circa 1854. This restored mansion has won several preservation awards. It features a Greco-Italianate facade with a cast-iron filigree porch. Inside there are lavish crown moldings and Italianate mantels on the fireplaces. Sixteen-foot ceilings and Rococo Revival chandeliers add to the formal elegance. Guest rooms boast four-poster or massive Victorian-style beds and period furnishings. Here, Southern hospitality is at its finest.

Historic Interest: National Register.

Innkeeper(s): Don Nash & Bernie Moorman. $77-130. MC VISA AX DC DS PC TC. 7 rooms with PB, 1 with FP. 1 conference room. Breakfast included in rates. Type of meal: full breakfast. Beds: QD. Phone and air conditioning in room. Fax and copier on premises.

Location: Fifteen-minute walk to downtown Cincinnati.

Publicity: *Executive Lifestyles, Bluegrass Magazine, Cincinnati Magazine, Cincinnati Post, Lexington Herald-Leader, Globe & Mail, Everybody's News, Plain Dealer, New York Times, Country Inn, Washington Post, Southern Living, ComAir Wing Tips.*

"It's like coming home to family and friends."

Sandford House B&B

1026 Russell St
Covington, KY 41011-3065
(606)291-9133 (888)291-9133
E-mail: danrrmiles@aol.com

Circa 1820. Originally a fine example of Federal architecture, the inn underwent reconstruction after a fire in the 1880s and changed to a more Victorian style. The inn once served as a finishing school for young ladies, and was the President's home for the Western Baptist Theological Seminary. The home now offers two full apart-ments, a suite and one guest room. Guests enjoy a gourmet breakfast. The inn is in the heart of the Old Seminary Historic District, listed in the National Register. The Basilica is two blocks away.

Historic Interest: Oldenberg Brewery (3 miles), Cincinnati Union Terminal, now a natural history museum, (3 miles), Cincinnati's old buildings (2 miles), Main Strasse (7 blocks).

Innkeeper(s): Dan & Linda Carter. $55-95. MC VISA PC TC. TAC10. 5 rooms with PB. 1 suite. 1 cottage. Breakfast included in rates. Type of meal: gourmet breakfast. Beds: QT. Phone, ceiling fan, TV and VCR in room. Weddings, small meetings, family reunions and seminars hosted. Amusement parks, antiques, parks, shopping, sporting events, theater and watersports nearby.

Pets Allowed.

Publicity: *Cincinnati Post, Country Inns.*

Danville   C7

Randolph House

463 W Lexington Ave
Danville, KY 40422-1455
(606)236-9594

Circa 1860. This Georgian-style inn is situated on a half-acre in the heart of the historic district in this quiet college town. Decorated in period antiques, the inn is inviting, and guests may browse the shelves in the library or relax in the afternoon on the front porch. Guest rooms feature antiques, private baths and TVs. A gourmet breakfast is served in the cozy dining room or in guest rooms by request. Dinner is available by prior reservation. Randolph House is close to shopping, town center, theater, colleges and antiques.

Innkeeper(s): Georgie Heizer. $55-65. MC VISA AX PC TC. TAC10. 3 rooms with PB. Breakfast and dinner included in rates. Type of meal: gourmet breakfast. Room service available. Beds: QT. Phone, air conditioning, ceiling fan, TV and VCR in room. Library on premises. Antiques, parks, sporting events and theater nearby.

Pets Allowed: only with prior arrangements.

"I have stayed in numerous bed & breakfasts and recently found a jewel in Danville."

Georgetown   B7

Bourbon House Farm

584 Shropshire Lane
Georgetown, KY 40324
(606)987-8669 Fax:(606)987-6292

Circa 1820. This home was built by a colonel who received the land for his services during the War of 1812. Equestrians will especially love this 25-acre horse farm, and guests are encouraged to watch and enjoy the animals. The farm has an excellent and far-reaching reputation, in the past its horses have been sold to the czar of Russia. Guests can fish in the four-acre pond or just relax on a hammock with a good book. The decor is elegant and uncluttered with just a few collectibles placed here and there. Each guest room has a fireplace. Gourmet breakfasts include entrees such as an asparagus and fresh herb frittata with roasted potatoes, fresh fruit, homemade breads and lemon curd. Antique stores, flea markets and plenty of equestrian points of interest are within a half-hour of the farm.

Innkeeper(s): Peter Van Andel & Mary Lewis. $85-125. MC VISA PC. TAC10. 2 rooms with PB, 2 with FP. Breakfast included in rates. Type of meal: full breakfast. Beds: KT. Air conditioning in room. Fax, copier, bicycles and library on premises. 25 acres. Antiques, fishing, parks, shopping, golf and theater nearby.

"Perfection and then some!"

Pineapple Inn

645 S Broadway St # 25
Georgetown, KY 40324-1135
(502)868-5453

Circa 1876. White gingerbread trim decorates the yellow Victorian Pineapple Inn, highlighting its gables, large front porch, dentil trim and bay window. In the Kentucky Historic Register and the Bluegrass historic list, the house provides a cheerful welcome to guests visiting Kentucky's antique center. Polished antiques throughout, a country French dining room and handsome wallcoverings make the interiors pristine and inviting. A full Kentucky breakfast is served.

Innkeeper(s): Muriel & Les. $65-95. MC VISA. 4 rooms with PB. Breakfast included in rates. Type of meal: full breakfast. Beds: QD. Antiques and fishing nearby.

Publicity: *Country Extra.*

"Your hospitality was wonderful. The food was fantastic."

Harrodsburg   C7

Bauer Haus

362 N College
Harrodsburg, KY 40330
(606)734-6289

Circa 1880. This Queen Anne Victorian, sans gingerbread, features a wicker-filled front porch, complete with swing. In the National Register, it was built on one of the first lots in Harrodsburg. Inside, archways open to the parlor. Roomy guest rooms are furnished in a traditional decor with antiques. Coffee or tea is served to your room a half hour before the breakfast seating. Low-fat ham or sausage and an egg dish is complemented with non-fat, made-from-scratch breakfast cakes or muffins.

Innkeeper(s): Dick & Marian Bauer. $60-70. MC VISA DS. 4 rooms, 2 with PB, 3 with FP. Breakfast and evening snack included in rates. Types of meals: full breakfast and early coffee/tea. Beds: QDT. Air conditioning in room. TV and VCR on premises. Small meetings, family reunions and seminars hosted. Antiques, fishing, shopping, golf, theater and watersports nearby.

Canaan Land Farm B&B

700 Canaan Land Rd.
Harrodsburg, KY 40330-9220
(606)734-3984 (888)734-3984

Circa 1795. This National Register farmhouse, one of the oldest brick houses in Kentucky, is appointed with antiques, quilts and featherbeds. Your host is a shepherd/attorney and your hostess is a handspinner artist. A large flock of sheep, goats and other assorted barnyard animals graze the pastures at this working farm. In 1995, the innkeepers reconstructed an 1815, historic log house on the grounds. The log house includes three guest rooms and two working fireplaces.

Historic Interest: In 1992, Canaan Land Farm was named a Kentucky historic farm. Nearby Shakertown, a restored Shaker village, features daily craft demonstrations, riverboat rides and tours.

Innkeeper(s): Theo & Fred Bee. $75-125. PC TC. 7 rooms with PB, 2 with FP. Breakfast included in rates. Types of meals: full breakfast and early coffee/tea. Beds: DT. Phone in room. VCR, spa and swimming on premises. 189 acres. Weddings, family reunions and seminars hosted. Antiques, fishing, parks, shopping, golf and watersports nearby.

Location: Two miles from Shakertown.

Publicity: *Danville Advocate, Lexington Herald Leader.*

"You truly have a gift for genuine hospitality."

Shaker Village of Pleasant Hill

3501 Lexington Rd
Harrodsburg, KY 40330-8846
(800)734-5611

Circa 1805. A non-profit organization preserves this 19th-century Shaker village set atop a pleasant meadow. Guest rooms are in 15 restored buildings. The entire village is a National Historic Landmark and is restricted to foot traffic. Reproductions of authentic Shaker furnishings fill the guest rooms. Air conditioning is hidden, and there are no closets. Instead, clothes (and sometimes chairs and lamps) are hung on Shaker pegs spaced one foot apart on all four walls.

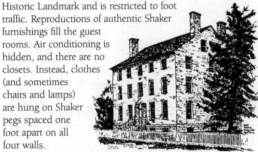

Costumed interpreters in the craft buildings describe Shaker culture and craft.

Innkeeper(s): James Thomas. $50-100. EP. 81 rooms with PB. 2 conference rooms. Type of meal: full breakfast. Dinner and lunch available. Restaurant on premises. Beds: DT. Fax on premises.

Location: Twenty-five miles southwest of Lexington on US Hwy 68.

Publicity: *Southern Living, Traveler, Richmond Times-Dispatch.*

"We can't wait to return! We treasure our memories here of peaceful, pleasant days."

Lebanon

C6

Myrtledene B&B

370 N Spalding Ave
Lebanon, KY 40033-1563
(502)692-2223 (800)391-1721

Circa 1833. Once a Confederate general's headquarters at one point during the Civil War, this pink brick inn, located at a bend in the road, has greeted visitors entering Lebanon for more than 150 years. When General John Hunt Morgan returned in 1863 to destroy the town, the white flag hoisted to signal a truce was flown at Myrtledene. A country breakfast usually features ham and biscuits as well as the innkeepers' specialty, peaches and cream French toast.

Historic Interest: Headquarters of confederate General John Hunt Morgan. Morgan rode his mare up to front hall stairs.

Innkeeper(s): James F. Spragens. $65. MC VISA PC TC. TAC10. 4 rooms, 1 with FP. 1 conference room. Breakfast included in rates. Types of meals: full breakfast, gourmet breakfast and early coffee/tea. Afternoon tea available. Beds: DT. Air conditioning and turndown service in room. TV, VCR and library on premises. Weddings, small meetings, family reunions and seminars hosted. Antiques, fishing, parks, shopping, theater and watersports nearby.

Publicity: *Lebanon Enterprise, Louisville Courier-Journal, Lebanon/Marion County Kentucky.*

"Our night in the Cabbage Rose Room was an experience of another time, another culture. Your skill in preparing and presenting breakfast was equally elegant! We'll be back!"

Louisville

B6

Ashton's Victorian Secret B&B

1132 S 1st St
Louisville, KY 40203-2804
(502)581-1914 (800)449-4691
E-mail: sroosa@ix.netcom.com

Circa 1883. This three-story Queen Anne Victorian has 11 fireplaces. Antiques and period furnishings are featured throughout the brick inn, located in Historic Old Louisville. Guest amenities include sundecks, washer-dryer facilities and a workout room with a bench press, rowing machine and stationary bicycle.

Innkeeper(s): Nan & Steve Roosa. $48-89. PC. TAC7. 4 rooms, 1 with PB, 4 with FP. 1 suite. Breakfast included in rates. Type of meal: continental-plus breakfast. Beds: KQD. Air conditioning and ceiling fan in room. VCR on premises. Small meetings and family reunions hosted. Amusement parks, antiques, parks, shopping, downhill skiing, sporting events and theater nearby.

Old Louisville Inn

1359 S 3rd St
Louisville, KY 40208-2378
(502)635-1574 Fax:(502)637-5892

Circa 1901. This 12,000-square-foot, three-story Beaux Arts inn boasts massive ornately carved mahogany columns in the lobby. Rooms are filled with antiques gathered from local auctions and shops, and three rooms have whirlpool tubs. The third-floor Celebration Suite, with its whirlpool bath, fireplace and king-size canopy bed, offers perfect honeymoon accommodations. The morning meal, including the inn's famous popovers, is served in the breakfast room, courtyard or in the guest rooms. The inn's location, in the heart of Louisville's Victorian district, makes sightseeing inviting.

Historic Interest: Churchill Downs (2 miles), Kentucky Derby Museum (2 miles).

Innkeeper(s): Marianne Lesher. $65-195. MC VISA AX DS PC TC. 10 rooms with PB, 2 with FP. Breakfast and afternoon tea included in rates. Type of meal: gourmet breakfast. Beds: KQDT. Air conditioning in room. VCR, fax and copier on premises. Weddings, small meetings, family reunions and seminars hosted. Antiques, parks, shopping, sporting events and theater nearby.

"My most enjoyable, relaxed business trip!"

The Inn at the Park

1332 S 4th St
Louisville, KY 40208-2314
(502)637-6930 (800)700-7275 Fax:(502)637-2796
E-mail: innatpark@aol.com

Circa 1886. An impressive sweeping staircase is one of many highlights at this handsome Richardsonian Romanesque inn, in the historic district of Old Louisville. Guests also will appreciate the hardwood floors, 14-foot ceilings and stone balconies on the second and third floors. The seven guest rooms offer a variety of amenities and a view of Central Park.

Innkeeper(s): John & Sandra Mullins. $79-149. MC VISA AX PC TC. TAC10. 7 rooms with PB, 5 with FP. 3 suites. Breakfast included in rates. Types of meals: full breakfast and early coffee/tea. Beds: KQ. Phone, air conditioning, ceiling fan and TV in room. VCR, fax and spa on premises. Small meetings and seminars hosted. German spoken. Amusement parks, antiques, parks, shopping, sporting events and theater nearby.

The Inn at Woodhaven

401 S Hubbard Lane
Louisville, KY 40208
(502)895-1011 (888)895-1011

Circa 1853. This Gothic Revival, painted in a cheerful shade of yellow, is still much the same as it was in the 1850s, when it served as the home on a prominent local farm. The rooms still feature the outstanding woodwork, and guest quarters are tastefully appointed with antiques. All seven guest rooms include a fireplace. Criss-cross window designs, winding staircases, decorative mantels and hardwood floors are other notable elements. The National Register home is close to all of Louisville's attractions.

Innkeeper(s): Marsha Burton. $70-90. MC VISA PC. 7 rooms with PB, 7 with FP. 2 suites. Breakfast included in rates. Types of meals: full breakfast and gourmet breakfast. Dinner and picnic lunch available. Beds: KQDT. Phone, air conditioning, ceiling fan and TV in room. Fax, copier and library on premises. Handicap access. Weddings, small meetings, family reunions and seminars hosted. Amusement parks, antiques, parks, shopping, sporting events, golf, theater and watersports nearby.
Publicity: *Courier Journal.*

Middlesborough   E8

The Ridge Runner B&B

208 Arthur Hts
Middlesborough, KY 40965-1728
(606)248-4299

Circa 1890. Bachelor buttons, lilacs and wildflowers line the white picket fence framing this 20-room brick Victorian mansion. Guests enjoy relaxing in its turn-of-the-century library and parlor filled with Victorian antiques. Ask for the President's

Room and you'll enjoy the best view of the Cumberland Mountains. (The innkeeper's great, great-grandfather hosted Abe Lincoln the night before his Gettysburg address, and the inn boasts some heirlooms from that home.) A family-style breakfast is provided and special diets can be accommodated if notified in advance. Cumberland Gap National Park is five miles away, and the inn is two miles from the twin tunnels that pass through the Cumberland Gap. Pine Mountain State Park is 12 miles away.

Historic Interest: Restoration of a P-38 fighter plane, Abraham Lincoln artifacts and museum.

Innkeeper(s): Susan Richards & Irma Gall. $55-65. PC. 4 rooms, 2 with PB. Breakfast and evening snack included in rates. Type of meal: early coffee/tea. Beds: DT. Turndown service and ceiling fan in room. Small meetings and family reunions hosted. Antiques, parks and shopping nearby.

Publicity: *Lexington Herald Leader, Blue Ridge Country, Indianapolis Star, Daily News, Courier Journal, Country Inn.*

Murray   E2

The Diuguid House B&B

603 Main St
Murray, KY 42071-2034
(502)753-5470 (888)261-3028

Circa 1895. This Victorian house features eight-foot-wide hallways and a golden oak staircase with stained-glass window. There is a sitting area adjoining the portico. Guest rooms are generous in size.

Historic Interest: Listed in the National Register.

Innkeeper(s): Karen & George Chapman. $40. MC VISA DC PC TC. 3 rooms. Breakfast included in rates. Types of meals: full breakfast and early coffee/tea. Beds: QT. Phone, air conditioning and turndown service in room. TV on premises. Weddings, small meetings and family reunions hosted. Antiques, fishing, parks, theater and watersports nearby.

Pets Allowed: Advance approval.

Location: Downtown Murray, near state university.

Publicity: *Murray State News.*

"We enjoyed our visit in your beautiful home, and your hospitality was outstanding."

New Haven   C6

The Sherwood Inn

138 S Main St
New Haven, KY 40051-6355
(502)549-3386

Circa 1914. Since 1875, the Johnson family has owned the Sherwood Inn. A week after the original building burned in

1913, construction for the current building began. In the National Register, the inn catered to passengers of the nearby L & N (Louisville and Nashville) Railroad. Antiques and reproductions complement some of the inn's original furnishings. The restaurant is open for dinner Wednesday through Saturday. The inn's slogan, first advertised in 1875 remains, "first class table and good accommodations."

Innkeeper(s): Cecilia Johnson. $45-65. MC VISA DS. 5 rooms, 3 with PB. Breakfast included in rates. Type of meal: full breakfast. Restaurant on premises. Beds: D. Air conditioning and ceiling fan in room. TV on premises. Small meetings, family reunions and seminars hosted. Shopping nearby.

Location: Eleven miles south from Bardstown on US 31-E.

Publicity: *Kentucky Standard.*

"A memorable stop."

Newport   A7

Gateway B&B

326 E 6th St
Newport, KY 41071-1962
(606)581-6447 (888)891-7500

This charming Italianate won a National Trust for Historic Preservation award after current owners/innkeepers Ken and Sandra Clift turned a labor of love into a successful bed & breakfast. The inn is located in East Newport's historic district, Kentucky's second-largest. An antique organ and phonograph sit on either side of the fireplace in the music room. A view of the Tri-City area is enjoyed from the rooftop deck. Guests may opt to eat their full

breakfast in the dining room or kitchen. Downtown Cincinnati is just a five-minute drive from the inn.

Innkeeper(s): Ken & Sandra Clift. Call for rates. Phone, air conditioning and turndown service in room. TV and VCR on premises. Weddings, small meetings and seminars hosted. Antiques, shopping, sporting events and theater nearby.

Nicholasville   C7

Sandusky House & O'Neal Log Cabin B&B

1626 Delaney Ferry Rd
Nicholasville, KY 40356-8729
(606)223-4730
E-mail: humphlin@aol.com

Circa 1855. This Greek Revival inn rests in the tree-lined countryside, surrounded by horse farms and other small farms. Its tranquil setting offers a perfect getaway from busy nearby Lexington. The inn, which is listed on Kentucky's state register,

boasts six porches, seven fireplaces and impressive brick columns. The three guest rooms feature desks, private baths and turndown service. The innkeepers also offer lodging in a two-bedroom, 180-year-old log cabin. Although historic, the National Register cabin includes modern amenities such as a full kitchen and whirlpool tub. Area attractions include Asbury College, Keeneland Race Course, the Mary Todd Lincoln House and the University of Kentucky.

Innkeeper(s): Jim & Linda Humphrey. $75-95. MC VISA PC TC. 3 rooms with PB. 1 cottage. Breakfast included in rates. Types of meals: full breakfast and early coffee/tea. Beds: D. Air conditioning and turndown service in room. TV and VCR on premises. 10 acres. Amusement parks, antiques, fishing, parks, shopping, sporting events and theater nearby.

Location: Eight miles from downtown Lexington.

Publicity: *Lexington Herald-Leader, Country Inns.*

Paducah   D2

The 1857's B&B

PO Box 7771
Paducah, KY 42001-0789
(502)444-3960 (800)264-5607 Fax:(502)444-6751

Circa 1857. Paducah's thriving, history-rich commercial district is home to this Folk Victorian inn, located in Market House Square. Guests choose from rooms such as the Master Bedroom, a suite featuring a king-size, four-poster bed or perhaps the Hunt Room, which includes a four-poster, queen-size canopy bed. The popular third-floor game room boasts an impressive mahogany billiard table. There is an outdoor hot tub on the deck. The Ohio River is an easy walk from the inn, and guests also will enjoy an evening stroll along the gas-lit brick sidewalks. The inn occupies the second and third floors of a former clothing store, with an Italian restaurant at street level.

Innkeeper(s): Deborah Bohnert. $65-95. MC VISA PC TC. TAC10. 3 rooms. 1 suite. Breakfast included in rates. Types of meals: continental-plus breakfast and early coffee/tea. Room service available. Restaurant on premises. Beds: KQDT. Phone, air conditioning, ceiling fan and TV in room. VCR, fax, copier and library on premises. Small meetings and family reunions hosted. Antiques, fishing, shopping, theater and watersports nearby.

Paris   B7

Pleasant Place B&B

515 Pleasant St
Paris, KY 40361
(606)987-5546 (800)890-5094 Fax:(606)987-8804

Circa 1889. Pleasant is an apt description for this Queen Anne Victorian, located in a historic Paris neighborhood. The innkeepers are just the third family to occupy this elegant home, which maintains many original architectural features, including a showpiece staircase. The three guest rooms each are furnished with a variety of fine antiques. Breakfasts feature Kentucky specialties of homemade breads and gourmet

casseroles. After a hearty breakfast, guests can explore Kentucky's famed horse country.

Innkeeper(s): Jeanine & Berkeley Scott. $55-75. MC VISA DS PC TC. 3 rooms, 2 with PB, 3 with FP. Breakfast included in rates. Types of meals: full breakfast, gourmet breakfast and early coffee/tea. Beds: KQ. Air conditioning and TV in room. VCR, fax and library on premises. Antiques, fishing, parks, shopping and golf nearby.

Publicity: *Bourbon Times.*

"Pleasant Place is beautiful and the food was wonderful."

Rosedale B&B

1917 Cypress St
Paris, KY 40361-1220
(606)987-1845 (800)644-1862

Circa 1862. Once the home of Civil War General John Croxton, this low-roofed Italianate inn was voted prettiest B&B in the Bluegrass area by the Lexington Herald-Leader in 1994.

The four decorated guest rooms feature Colonial touches and are filled with antiques and paintings. Fresh flowers, down comforters and ceiling fans add to the rooms' comfort and charm. The Henry Clay Room, with its twin four-poster beds, is one option for visitors. Guests may relax with a game of croquet, bocce, horseshoes, on benches found on the inn's three-acre lawn or on the screened porch. Duncan Tavern Historic Shrine is nearby, as well as beautiful horse farms.

Historic Interest: Hopewell Museum, Kentucky Garden Club Headquarters, Cane Ridge Shrine, Keeneland Race Course, Rupp Arena, the Kentucky Horse Park and many historic homes are nearby.

Innkeeper(s): Katie & Jim Haag. $65-100. MC VISA PC TC. 4 rooms, 2 with PB. 2 suites. Breakfast and evening snack included in rates. Types of meals: full breakfast and early coffee/tea. Beds: DT. Air conditioning and ceiling fan in room. TV, VCR and library on premises. Small meetings, family reunions and seminars hosted. Antiques, fishing, parks, shopping, sporting events and theater nearby.

"Your hospitality has been lovely and your home is a fine example of tradition and comfort."

Shelbyville   B6

The Wallace House

613 Washington St
Shelbyville, KY 40065
(502)633-2006

Circa 1804. This Federal-style house, midway between Louisville and Frankfort, is listed in the National Register of Historic Places. Its four well-appointed guest suites all feature kitchenettes.

Historic Interest: Kentucky Horse Park (50 miles), Shakertown (50 miles), Churchill Downs Derby Museum (30 miles).

Innkeeper(s): Evelyn Laurent. $70-95. MC VISA AX. 4 suites. Type of meal: continental-plus breakfast. Beds: Q. Air conditioning and TV in room. Antiques, fishing, shopping and theater nearby.

Springfield   C6

Maple Hill Manor

2941 Perryville Rd
Springfield, KY 40069-9611
(606)336-3075 (800)886-7546

Circa 1851. This brick Revival home with Italianate detail is a Kentucky Landmark home and is listed in the National Register of Historic Places. It features 13-1/2-foot ceilings, 10-foot doors, nine-foot windows, a cherry spiral staircase, stenciling in the foyer, a large parlor, period furnishings and a dining room with a fireplace. The library has floor-to-ceiling mahogany bookcases and the

Honeymoon Room features a canopy bed and Jacuzzi. A large patio area is set among old maple trees.

Historic Interest: Bardstown (20 miles), Danville (23 miles), Perryville Battlefield (15 miles).

Innkeeper(s): Kathleen Carroll. $50-90. MC VISA PC TC. 7 rooms with PB. 1 conference room. Breakfast included in rates. Types of meals: full breakfast and early coffee/tea. Evening snack available. Beds: QDT. Phone, air conditioning and ceiling fan in room. VCR on premises. 14 acres. Weddings, small meetings, family reunions and seminars hosted. Antiques, fishing, shopping and theater nearby.

Publicity: *Danville's Advocate-Messenger, Springfield Sun, Eastside Weekend, Courier Journal.*

"Thank you again for your friendly and comfortable hospitality."

Versailles   C7

B&B at Sills Inn

270 Montgomery Ave
Versailles, KY 40383-1427
(606)873-4478 (800)526-9801 Fax:(606)873-7099
E-mail: sillsinn@aol.com

Circa 1911. Innkeeper Tony Sills and Glenn Blind didn't miss a detail with this restored Victorian Inn, located only a short distance from the state capitol and many other attractions, including the Keeneland race course, a restored Shaker village and plenty of interesting shops, cafes and art studios. A fully stocked guest kitchen is available to guests craving a midnight snack, and three of the suites feature wet bars. Breakfast is served on fine china and crystal in the sun porch. There are plenty of places to relax, including three common areas and a wraparound porch.

Historic Interest: Shakertown Village (30 minutes), Mary Todd Lincoln Home (15 minutes), Historic Horse Farm Region (5 minutes).

Innkeeper(s): Tony Sills & Glenn Blind. $69-159. MC VISA AX DS TC. TAC10. 12 rooms with PB. 9 suites. 1 conference room. Breakfast and evening snack included in rates. Type of meal: gourmet breakfast. Beds: KQ. Phone, air conditioning, ceiling fan, TV and VCR in room. Fax, copier and library on premises. Handicap access. Small meetings, family reunions and seminars hosted. Antiques, fishing, parks, shopping, sporting events and theater nearby.

Rose Hill Inn

233 Rose Hill
Versailles, KY 40383-1223
(606)873-5957 (800)307-0460
E-mail: rosehillbb@aol.com

Circa 1820. Both Confederate and Union troops used this manor during the Civil War. The home maintains many elegant features, including original woodwork, 14-foot ceilings and floors fashioned from timber on the property. The decor is comfortable, yet elegant. One guest bath includes a clawfoot bathtub, another includes a double marble Jacuzzi. The innkeepers restored the

home's summer kitchen into a private cottage, which now includes a private porch, kitchen and two full-size beds. Three generations of the Amberg family live and

work here, including friendly dogs. The mother/daughter innkeepers serve a hearty, full breakfast, and in the afternoon, appetizers are presented. Among the sites are a Shaker Village, antique shops, horse farms, Keeneland Race Track and a wildlife sanctuary.

Innkeeper(s): Sharon Amberg & Marianne Ruano. $59-99. MC VISA AX TC. TAC10. 4 rooms with PB. 1 suite. 1 cottage. Breakfast and afternoon tea included in rates. Types of meals: full breakfast and early coffee/tea. Beds: KQDT. Phone, air conditioning, turndown service, ceiling fan and TV in room. VCR, bicycles, library and child care on premises. Small meetings and family reunions hosted. Antiques, fishing, parks, shopping, sporting events and golf nearby.

Pets Allowed: In cottage with prior approval.

"Everything was top-notch and we really enjoyed our stay in Miss Lucy's room."

Shepherd Place

31 Heritage Rd
Versailles, KY 40383-9211
(606)873-7843 (800)278-0864
E-mail: sylviayawn@msn.com

A pre-Civil War, two-story federal house, this bed & breakfast is set on five acres. The front porch with its swing and rocking chairs is a favorite spot for enjoying natural colored Romey sheep grazing. You may commission Sylvia to knit a sweater, or purchase the yarn to make your own. The innkeeper will hand-knit custom sweaters for you from yarn she has spun. Two pet ewes, Abigail and Victoria, are kept on the property. Kentucky breakfasts include whole wheat walnut pancakes.

Innkeeper(s): Marlin & Sylvia Yawn. $75. MC VISA. 3 rooms with PB. Breakfast included in rates. Type of meal: early coffee/tea. Beds: QDT. Air conditioning and ceiling fan in room. Antiques, shopping, sporting events and golf nearby.

Whitesburg D9

Salyers House

126 Hays
Whitesburg, KY 41858
(606)633-2532

Circa 1932. This comfortable Victorian-styled inn, named after its original owner who lived here until 1992, is located in the tranquil mountains of Kentucky. Guest rooms are appointed with antiques, family memorabilia, collectibles and

clawfoot tubs. A hearty breakfast of croissants, omelets, rice pudding and fresh fruit add to the homey atmosphere. Hiking in the mountains and shopping for local crafts are a favorite among guests.

Innkeeper(s): Faith Gullett. $65-90. MC VISA AX PC TC. 5 rooms with PB. 1 suite. Breakfast and evening snack included in rates. Types of meals: continental-plus breakfast and early coffee/tea. Beds: KQ. Phone, air conditioning, ceiling fan, TV and VCR in room. Small meetings hosted. Parks and shopping nearby.

"The house is beautiful, we couldn't have stayed at a more beautiful, comfortable and homey place."

Louisiana

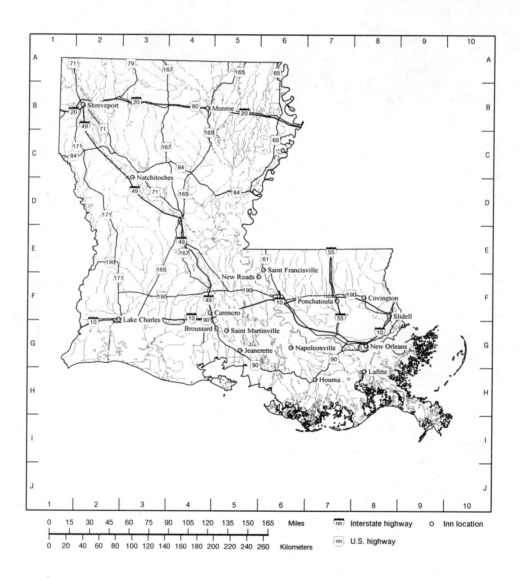

0 15 30 45 60 75 90 105 120 135 150 165 Miles

0 20 40 60 80 100 120 140 160 180 200 220 240 260 Kilometers

⌐nn⌐ Interstate highway   ○ Inn location

⌐nn⌐ U.S. highway

Broussard   G5

La Grande Maison

302 E Main St
Broussard, LA 70518
(318)837-4428 (800)837-5633 Fax:(318)837-5733

Circa 1911. This aptly named bed & breakfast boasts many Victorian architectural elements, including gables, gingerbread trim, a wide veranda and a turret that soars above the roofline. The National Register home is painted an inviting shade of pale blue and the grounds are dotted with flowers and old oak trees. Guest rooms feature Victorian furnishings and decor, such as a canopy bed topped with a floral comforter. The full breakfast is served on well-appointed tables in the dining room, which is highlighted by a bay window with stained glass.

Innkeeper(s): Norman & Brenda Fakier. $85-195. MC VISA PC TC. 5 rooms with PB. Breakfast included in rates. Type of meal: full breakfast. Beds: KQD. Turndown service and ceiling fan in room. TV, VCR and fax on premises. Handicap access. Small meetings and family reunions hosted.

"Highest standards and best in cajun hospitality."

Jeanerette   G5

Alice Plantation B&B

9217 Old Jeanerette Hwy
Jeanerette, LA 70544
(318)276-3187 Fax:(318)276-3187

Circa 1796. Bayou Teche fronts the property of this West Indies Colonial-style plantation, built during the terms of George Washington and Thomas Jefferson. Two 250-year-old oaks shade the inn. Now in the National Register, the house once served as a Civil War hospital. There are two dining areas, one with brick walls and cypress beams, the other with a glassed-in gallery. Guest rooms are in the cottages on the grounds, and one is a two-story house, reminiscent of the architecture of the main house. The inn's 16 acres include a pool and tennis courts. There is always something in bloom along the brick paths that meander throughout the extensive grounds, including the azalea and camellia gardens. If you can manage to pull yourself away from the plantation, take a swamp tour or visit the Live Oak Gardens, the Konriko rice mill, or the Tabasco plant and gardens.

Innkeeper(s): Stan & Rachel Rodgers. $100-125. MC VISA PC TC. TAC10. 1 room with PB. 2 cottages. 1 conference room. Breakfast included in rates. Types of meals: full breakfast, gourmet breakfast and early coffee/tea. Beds: QD. Phone, air conditioning, ceiling fan, TV and VCR in room. Fax, copier, swimming and tennis on premises. 16 acres. Weddings, small meetings, family reunions and seminars hosted. Antiques, fishing, parks, shopping, sporting events, golf and watersports nearby.

Publicity: *Southern Living, Country Living.*

Lafayette   G4

La Maison de Campagne, Lafayette

825 Kidder Rd
Lafayette, LA 70520-9119
(318)896-6529 Fax:(318)896-1494

Circa 1871. Built by a successful plantation owner, this turn-of-the-century Victorian has once again found a new life with innkeepers Fred and Joeann McLemore. The McLemores turned what was an almost dilapidated old home into a welcoming B&B, surrounded by nine acres of manicured lawns dotted with flowers and trees. The home is filled with antiques and treasures Joeann collected during Fred's three decades of military service, which took them around the world. Fine Victorian pieces are accented by lace and Oriental rugs. The innkeepers offer accommodations in the main house, or for longer stays, in an adjacent sharecropper's cottage. The cottage includes kitchen and laundry facilities. Joeann prepares the Cajun-style breakfasts. Several different homemade breads or pastries accompany items such as banana-strawberry soup, sweet potato biscuits, spicy Cajun eggs souffles or a potato and sausage quiche. Many of the recipes served are featured in Joeann's new cookbook, Lache Pas La Patate (Don't Drop the Potato).

Innkeeper(s): Joeann & Fred McLemore. $100-140. AP. MC VISA AX DS PC TC. TAC10. 4 rooms with PB. 1 cottage. Breakfast included in rates. Types of meals: gourmet breakfast and early coffee/tea. Evening snack available. Beds: KQ. Air conditioning, turndown service and ceiling fan in room. TV, fax, copier and swimming on premises. Small meetings hosted. Cajun French spoken. Antiques, fishing, parks, shopping, sporting events, theater and watersports nearby.

Location: Heart of Cajun Country.

Publicity: *Los Angeles Times, Boston Globe, Country, Texas Monthly, Country Inns.*

Lafitte   H8

Victoria Inn

Hwy 45, Box 545 B
Lafitte, LA 70067
(504)689-4757 (800)689-4797 Fax:(504)689-3399

Circa 1884. Located on the site of the Mulligan Plantation, this inn consists of three West Indies-style homes on more than six acres of landscaped gardens. The grounds include an antique rose garden, a parterre herb garden and an iris pond. A private pier and sea water pool extend out into the lake, which was once the field of this Louisiana sugar plantation. All of the rooms are uniquely furnished and the galleries offer a place to relax and enjoy the tropical breezes. Swamp tours, fishing charters, hiking or canoeing in the National Park are available.

Innkeeper(s): Roy & Dale Ross. $85-125. MC VISA AX DS. 14 rooms with PB. 5 suites. Breakfast included in rates. Types of meals: full breakfast and early coffee/tea. Beds: QDT. Fishing and watersports nearby.

Publicity: *Times Picayune, Shreveport Times, San Francisco Examiner.*

"You contributed greatly to the fine memories of our 35th wedding anniversary."

Lake Charles F2

Ramsay-Curtis Mansion Guest House

626 Broad St
Lake Charles, LA 70601-4337
(318)439-3859 (800)522-4276 Fax:(318)439-3859
E-mail: rcm626@aol.com

Circa 1885. This Queen Anne Revival-style manor is graced by
sweeping wraparound verandas on its first and second floors.

Inside, parquet floors
and fine woodwork are
set off by Oriental rugs,
walls painted in deep,
rich hues and period fur-
nishings. All four guest
rooms have a fireplace,
and furnishings such as a
four-poster canopy bed
that adds a romantic
touch. A lumber baron
built the home, which is
now listed in the National Register of Historic Places.

Innkeeper(s): Michael & Judy Curtis. $90-225. MC VISA AX DC DS PC TC.
TAC10. 4 rooms with PB, 4 with FP. 2 suites. 1 cottage. Breakfast included
in rates. Type of meal: continental-plus breakfast. Beds: QD. Phone, air conditioning, turndown service, ceiling fan, TV and VCR in room. Fax, bicycles
and library on premises. Weddings and small meetings hosted. Antiques,
fishing, parks, shopping, golf and watersports nearby.

Publicity: *Southern Living.*

"Wonderful conclusion to our 10th Anniversary weekend."

Monroe B4

Boscobel Cottage

185 Cordell Ln
Monroe, LA 71202-9225
(318)325-1550 (800)254-3529 Fax:(318)325-7505

Circa 1820. Boscobel Cottage is in the heart of cotton country
on the Ouachita River and is surrounded by century-old pecan
trees. Guest rooms are on the grounds of the cottage. A quaint
chapel was once the plantation overseer's office. It features a
Victorian bed, down pillows and European-style bedding and
quilts. The Garconniere is a bachelor's apartment with a balcony overlooking a New Orleans-style courtyard. Breakfast is
served in your room, on the front porch or under the gazebo.
The innkeepers offer an 1894 house with two guest rooms and
a gallery across the front with rocking chairs set up for guests
who wish to relax and enjoy a view of the grounds.

Historic Interest: Monroe (15 miles north), Columbia (15 miles south).

Innkeeper(s): Kay & Cliff LaFrance. $75-95. MC VISA AX DS. 4 rooms with
PB. Breakfast included in rates. Type of meal: full breakfast. Beds: Q. Phone
in room. Fishing nearby.

Publicity: *New Orleans
Times, Louisiana.*

*"Words like exquisite
just don't convey
enough of the grati-
tude I feel for being
allowed to visit here."*

Napoleonville G6

Madewood Plantation

4250 Highway 308
Napoleonville, LA 70390-8737
(504)369-7151 (800)375-7151 Fax:(504)369-9848

Circa 1846. Six massive ionic columns support the central
portico of this striking Greek Revival mansion, a National
Historic Landmark. Framed by

live oaks and ancient magnolias, Madewood, on 20
acres, across from Bayou
Lafourche. It was
designed by Henry
Howard, a noted
architect from Cork,
Ireland. There are ele-
gant double parlors, a ballroom, library,
music room and dining room where regional specialties are
served by candlelight.

Historic Interest: Swamp tours, other plantations (one-half hour).

Innkeeper(s): Keith Marshall. $185. MAP. MC VISA AX DS. 8 rooms with PB,
1 with FP. 2 suites. 1 conference room. Breakfast and dinner included in
rates. Type of meal: full breakfast. Beds: QDT. Phone in room. Copier on
premises.

Location: Seventy-five miles from New Orleans.

Publicity: *Travel & Leisure, National Geographic Traveler, Travel Holiday, Los
Angeles Times, Country Home, Country Inns (1 of 12 best inns in 1993).*

*"We have stayed in many hotels, other plantations and English
manor houses, and Madewood has surpassed them all in charm, hospitality and food."*

Natchitoches C3

Fleur de Lis B&B

336 Second St
Natchitoches, LA 71457
(318)352-6621 (800)489-6621

Circa 1903. A prosperous lumberman built this Victorian so
that his children could attend a nearby college. The home is
located in a National Historic

Landmark District, and it
features original wood-
work and a pressed-tin
roof. The guest rooms
are decorated with
period antiques. A
full breakfast is
served, perhaps
French toast or
Southern fare, such
as ham and freshly
made biscuits.

Innkeeper(s): Tom & Harriette Palmer. $65-80. MC VISA AX DS. 5 rooms
with PB. 1 conference room. Breakfast included in rates. Types of meals: full
breakfast, gourmet breakfast and early coffee/tea. Beds: KQ. Air conditioning
and ceiling fan in room. TV and VCR on premises. Small meetings and family
reunions hosted. Antiques, fishing, parks, shopping, sporting events, golf and
watersports nearby.

*"Each time I come, I feel more and more at home. It is a gift you
have given me."*

New Orleans   G8

A Hotel, The Frenchman

417 Frenchmen St
New Orleans, LA 70116-2022
(504)948-2166 (800)831-1781 Fax:(509)948-2258

Circa 1860. Two town houses built by Creole craftsmen have been totally renovated, including the slave quarters. The original site was chosen to provide convenient access to shops and Jackson Square. The location today is still prime. Historic homes, quaint shops, and fine restaurants are immediately at hand. The Old Mint and French Market are across the way. Most rooms are furnished with period antiques. There is a hot tub and swimming pool on the premises, and free limited parking is available.

Innkeeper(s): Brent A. Kovach. $59-245. MC VISA AX PC TC. TAC10. 27 rooms with PB. 6 suites. Breakfast included in rates. Types of meals: continental breakfast and continental-plus breakfast. Restaurant on premises. Beds: QDT. Phone, air conditioning, ceiling fan and TV in room. Swimming on premises. Amusement parks, antiques, fishing, parks, sporting events and theater nearby.

Location: The French Quarter.

"Still enjoying wonderful memories of my stay at your charming hotel...such a delightful respite from the frantic pace of the Quarter."

A Villa B&B-New Orleans

3336 Gentilly Blvd
New Orleans, LA 70122
(504)945-4253 (800)973-1020

Circa 1939. Close to the French Quarter and the Mississippi River, this Spanish Colonial Revival home offers a unique blend of privacy and romance. The innkeepers' two great-great-great-grandfathers fought the battle of New Orleans. Rooms feature oak floors and are decorated with antiques and original art. Guest rooms all have ceiling fans, refrigerators, and there are breakfast nooks to enjoy the fresh pastry, juice and coffee  that is served in your room. Guests will delight in walking or jogging beneath the beautiful oak trees that populate the area. Free parking is available on the premises.

Innkeeper(s): Ann & Walter Hingle. $69-125. MC VISA TC. TAC10. 2 rooms with PB. Breakfast included in rates. Type of meal: continental-plus breakfast. Beds: KQD. Air conditioning, ceiling fan and TV in room. Antiques, fishing, parks, shopping, sporting events, golf, theater and watersports nearby.

"Thank you so much for a great room and great service!"

Beau Sejour

1930 Napoleon Ave
New Orleans, LA 70115-5542
(504)897-3746 Fax:(504)897-3746

Circa 1906. On an avenue lined with grand oaks hung with Spanish moss, Beau Sejour recently has undergone a complete renovation. Its uptown location places the inn in a neighborhood of grand mansions. Stained-glass, an ornate staircase, 12-foot ceilings and elegant fireplaces fill the three-story house, which once held seven apartments. Original moldings, floor-to-ceiling windows and gleaming wood floors provide the background for the four-poster beds and American and European antiques. During Mardi Gras more than 12 parades pass by and guest line the inn's balconies to watch. Several fine New Orleans restaurants are nearby, and a short ride on the St. Charles Avenue streetcar will take you to the French Quarter. The innkeepers are local preservationists and are also knowledgeable about area activities such as bayou swamp tours and visiting Mississippi River Road plantations.

Innkeeper(s): Gilles & Kim Gagnon. $95-175. PC. 6 rooms, 5 with PB. 1 suite. Breakfast included in rates. Type of meal: continental-plus breakfast. Beds: KQT. Antiques, fishing, parks, theater and watersports nearby.

"You have a very friendly and warm inn and we enjoyed getting to know you. We'll be back."

Bougainvillea House

841 Bourbon St
New Orleans, LA 70116-3106
(504)525-3983 Fax:(504)283-7777

Circa 1822. Originally built by a plantation owner, and located directly in the French Quarter, this French Townhouse served as a hospital during the Civil War. The Riverboat Suite faces the courtyard and has French doors that open onto a balcony. It offers a living room and full kitchen. The inn is furnished with Victorian antiques and traditional pieces. The courtyard and patio are behind private locked gates. Bourbon Street is one block away, while Royal Street and its restaurants and museums is two blocks away. Guests can walk to Antoines for dinner.

Innkeeper(s): Flo Cairo. $90-250. VISA AX. TAC10. 3 suites. Beds: KQD. Phone, air conditioning, ceiling fan and TV in room. Fax on premises. Antiques, parks, shopping, sporting events, golf and theater nearby.

"We love your home and always enjoy our visits here so much!"

Columns Hotel

3811 Saint Charles Ave
New Orleans, LA 70115-4638
(504)899-9308 (800)445-9308 Fax:(504)899-8170

Circa 1883. The Columns was built by Simon Hernsheim, a tobacco merchant, who was the wealthiest philanthropist in New Orleans. The two-story columned gallery and portico provide a grand entrance into this restored mansion. The estate was selected by Paramount Studios for the site of the movie "Pretty Baby," with Brooke Shields. The hotel is in the National Register of Historic Places.

Historic Interest: Garden District (one-half mile), aquarium (two miles), zoo (one-half mile), universities (one-half mile), French Quarter (two miles on streetcar).

Innkeeper(s): Claire & Jacques Creppel. $65-300. MC VISA AX. 19 rooms, 11 with PB. 3 suites. 1 conference room. Breakfast included in rates. Type of meal: continental breakfast.

Pets Allowed.

Publicity: *Good Housekeeping, New York Times, Vogue, Good Morning America, Elle, Forbes FYI, Travel Holiday, Conde Nast.*

"...like experiencing life of the Old South, maybe more like living in a museum. We came to New Orleans to learn about New Orleans, and we did... at The Columns."

Fairchild House

1518 Prytania St
New Orleans, LA 70130-4416
(504)524-0154 (800)256-8096 Fax:(504)568-0063

Circa 1841. Situated in the oak-lined Lower Garden District of New Orleans, this Greek Revival home was built by architect L.H. Pilie. The house maintains its Victorian ambiance with elegantly appointed guest rooms. Wine and cheese is served upon guests' arrival. Excluding holidays and Sundays, afternoon tea can be served upon request. The inn, which is on the Mardi Gras parade route, is 17 blocks from the French Quarter and eight blocks from the convention center. Streetcars are nearby, as are many local attractions, including paddleboat cruises, Canal Place and Riverwalk shopping, an aquarium, zoo, the Charles Avenue mansions and Tulane and Loyola universities.

Innkeeper(s): Rita Olmo & Beatriz Aprigliano. $75-125. MC VISA AX TC. 7 rooms with PB. 1 suite. Breakfast included in rates. Type of meal: continental-plus breakfast. Beds: KQDT. Phone, air conditioning and ceiling fan in room. Fax and copier on premises. Weddings and family reunions hosted. Antiques, shopping and theater nearby.

Location: Lower Garden District.

"Accommodations were great; staff was great...Hope to see ya'll soon!"

La Maison à l' Avenue Jackson

1740 Jackson Ave
New Orleans, LA 70113
(504)522-1785 (888)840-2331 Fax:(504)566-0405

Circa 1858. Enjoy the excitement of New Orleans at this four-suite guest house located on the Carnival parade route. The structure represents the classical double-galley, two-story framed house with side bay windows. Each suite is appointed with antique furnishings, collectibles, Oriental rugs, paintings and prints collected over the last 40 years. The suites also boast  a private entrance, offering the ultimate in privacy and romance. The morning begins with the daily newspaper, fresh cut flowers, and a La Maison breakfast that includes a bowl of fresh fruit, juice crush (granita), a silver tray of breads, muffins and danishes, a choice of cereal and tea or coffee.

Historic Interest: The Garden District is only two blocks away and guests can take the St. Charles streetcar into the historic French Quarter or the Warehouse District.

Innkeeper(s): Jessie Smallwood. $125-325. MC VISA PC TC. TAC10. 4 suites. Breakfast included in rates. Type of meal: continental breakfast. Beds: QT. Air conditioning, turndown service, ceiling fan and TV in room. VCR, fax and copier on premises. Antiques, shopping and theater nearby.

Publicity: *Times Picayune/States Item, Essence, American Vision, Upscale, Black Colleague.*

"Thank you for a very pleasant stay. You have a lovely place—it radiates all the care and dedication you have put into it. I hope we will have a chance to come back."

Lafitte Guest House

1003 Bourbon St
New Orleans, LA 70116-2707
(504)581-2678 (800)331-7971 Fax:(504)581-2678

Circa 1849. This elegant French manor house has been meticulously restored. The house is filled with fine antiques and paintings collected from around the world. Located in the heart of the French Quarter, the inn is near world-famous restaurants, museums, antique shops and rows of Creole and Spanish cottages. Wine and hors d'oeuvres are served.

Historic Interest: Historic New Orleans Collection, Keyes House, Beauregard House, Gallier House (few blocks away), famous Jackson Square and Saint Louis Cathedral (4 blocks), French Market (3 blocks).

Innkeeper(s): Bobby L'Hoste, Manager, Robert D. Guyton, Owner. $99-179. MC VISA AX DC DS TC. 14 rooms with PB, 8 with FP. Breakfast and evening snack included in rates. Type of meal: continental-plus breakfast. Beds: KQ. Phone, air conditioning and ceiling fan in room. Fax and copier on premises. Weddings, small meetings, family reunions and seminars hosted. Amusement parks, antiques, fishing, parks, shopping, sporting events, theater and watersports nearby.

Publicity: *Glamour, Antique Monthly, McCall's, Dixie, Country Living.*

"This old building offers the finest lodgings we have found in the city — McCall's Magazine."

Lamothe House

621 Esplanade Ave
New Orleans, LA 70116-2018
(504)947-1161 (800)367-5858 Fax:(504)943-6536

Circa 1830. A carriageway that formerly cut through the center of many French Quarter buildings was enclosed at the Lamothe House in 1866, and it is now the foyer. Splendid Victorian furnishings enhance moldings, high ceilings and hand-turned mahogany stairway railings. Gilded opulence goes unchecked in the Mallard and Lafayette suites. Registration takes place in the second-story salon above the courtyard.

Historic Interest: National Register.

Innkeeper(s): Carol Chauppette. $75-250. MC VISA AX PC TC. TAC10. 20 rooms with PB, 1 with FP. 9 suites. 2 cottages. 1 conference room. Breakfast included in rates. Type of meal: continental-plus breakfast. Afternoon tea available. Beds: QTD. Phone, air conditioning, turndown service, ceiling fan and TV in room. VCR, fax, copier, swimming and child care on premises. Weddings, small meetings and family reunions hosted. Amusement parks, antiques, fishing, parks, shopping, sporting events and theater nearby.

Publicity: *Houston Post, Travel & Leisure.*

Maison Esplanade

1244 Esplanade Ave
New Orleans, LA 70116-1978
(504)523-8080 (800)290-4233 Fax:(504)527-0040

Circa 1846. Experience the splendor of New Orleans in this Creole-style inn, which is located within walking distance of the French Quarter. Polished wood floors, ceiling fans and 13-foot ceilings highlight this historic district home, which is furnished with antiques and replicas. Bedchambers honor New Orleans' jazz tradition, bearing names such as the Jelly Roll Norton Suite or Count Basie Suite. Breakfast service begins about 7:45 a.m., but continues until nearly noon, a pleasure for late risers. The hosts welcome guests with a refreshment and are full of information about the myriad of tours available in the city, including tours of the French Quarter, plantation homes, swamps, historic homes or the city itself. They can also help arrange cooking classes and other outings.

Innkeeper(s): Bonnie Leigh and Michael Dandy. $69-179. MC VISA AX DC DS TC. 9 rooms with PB. 2 suites. Breakfast included in rates. Type of meal:

continental-plus breakfast. Beds: Q. Phone, air conditioning and ceiling fan in room. Fax and copier on premises. Weddings, small meetings and family reunions hosted. Shopping nearby.

Pets Allowed.

Location: Two blocks to French Quarter.

"I had a marvelous visit to New Orleans and your delightful hospitality and friendship made it even more special."

The Melrose Mansion

937 Esplanade Ave
New Orleans, LA 70116-1942
(504)944-2255 Fax:(504)945-1794

Circa 1884. It's little wonder why this dramatic Italianate Victorian has been named a top accommodation. Aside from its gracious exterior, the interior has been carefully restored and filled with the finest of furnishings. Antique-filled guest rooms offer amenities such as down pillows, private patios, fresh flowers, whirlpool tubs and bathrooms stocked with fine soaps. Despite the elegance, guests are encouraged to relax and enjoy the New Orleans' tradition of hospitality. Fresh fruit laced with cognac and a regional favorite, Creole "lost bread," are among the memorable breakfast fare. The National Register home is located in the French Quarter.

Innkeeper(s): Melvin & Rosemary Jones. $225-425. MC VISA AX DS PC TC. TAC10. 8 rooms with PB. 4 suites. Breakfast included in rates. Types of meals: gourmet breakfast and early coffee/tea. Beds: KQT. Phone, air conditioning, ceiling fan and TV in room. Fax, copier and swimming on premises. Antiques, fishing, parks, shopping, sporting events and theater nearby.

"The Melrose Mansion is more than a hotel. It is a rare sanctum of style and grace, the personification of true southern gentility."

The Olivier Estate, a B&B

1839 Esplanade Ave
New Orleans, LA 70116
(504)949-9600 (800)429-3240 Fax:(504)948-2219
E-mail: bnbolivier@aol.com

Circa 1855. The expansive parlor at this Spanish Colonial boasts a hand-crafted, marble-topped bar with a roulette wheel embedded in it, which was made for gangster Al Capone. This eclectic room also includes a mahogany, three-slate pool table with leather pockets, a handmade Italian gaming table and a 1950s vintage quarter slot machine. The spacious bedchambers include private entrances, and some offer working fireplaces and marble baths. During the week, a full breakfast is the morning fare, while on the weekends, the innkeepers offer a full, Creole-style brunch. An open bar, nightly turndown service, airport transfers, and a 9 a.m. to 9 p.m. car service is offered daily. A hot tub, swimming pool and fresh flowers are just a few of the amenities guest will enjoy during their stay.

Innkeeper(s): Richard Saucier. $79-450. MC VISA AX. 5 rooms with PB. 4 suites. Breakfast included in rates. Type of meal: full breakfast. Beds: KQ. Antiques, fishing, theater and watersports nearby.

"The courtesy, hospitality and friendliness of the staff was incredible. We'll return again."

The Prytania Park Hotel

1525 Prytania St
New Orleans, LA 70130-4415
(504)524-0427 (800)862-1984 Fax:(504)522-2977

Circa 1850. This hotel consists of a historic Greek Revival building and a new building, located in a National Historic Landmark District. Request the older rooms to enjoy the

English Victorian reproduction furnishings, garden chintz fabrics and 14-foot ceilings. Some of these rooms have fireplaces. Rooms in the new section feature refrigerators, microwaves and contemporary furnishings. Prytania Park, reminiscent of a small European hotel, is located on the historic St. Charles Avenue streetcar line. Free off-street parking is available.

Innkeeper(s): Edward Halpern. $99-229. MC VISA AX DC DS PC TC. TAC10. 62 rooms with PB. 6 suites. Breakfast included in rates. Type of meal: continental-plus breakfast. Lunch available. Beds: KQDT. Phone, air conditioning, ceiling fan and TV in room. Fax and copier on premises. Small meetings and family reunions hosted. Spanish spoken. Antiques, parks, shopping and sporting events nearby.

Location: Lower Garden District.

"A little jewel—Baton Rouge Advocate."

Soniat House

1133 Chartres St
New Orleans, LA 70116-2504
(504)522-0570 (800)544-8808

Circa 1830. Located in one of the French Quarter's quiet byways, the Soniat House combines Creole style with classic Greek Revival detail. The courtyard features a fountain, magnolia trees, hibiscus and wisteria vines that climb the ancient walls. The inn is furnished with fine English, French and Louisiana antiques, antique Oriental rugs and paintings on loan from the New Orleans Museum of Art. Guests may enjoy freshly baked buttermilk biscuits with homemade preserves, fresh orange juice and rich Creole coffee. Conde Nast Traveler chose Soniat House as one of the 10 best small hotels in the United States.

Innkeeper(s): Rodney & Frances Smith. $145-475. MC VISA AX DC. 33 rooms with PB. 1 conference room. Type of meal: continental breakfast. Beds: KQDT. Handicap access.

Publicity: Travel & Leisure, New York Magazine, Vis a Vis.

"Beautiful, peaceful and relaxing."

St. Peter Guest House Hotel

1005 Saint Peter St
New Orleans, LA 70116-3014
(504)524-9232 (800)535-7815 Fax:(504)523-5198

Circa 1800. The St. Peter House, which is ideally situated in the middle of the French Quarter, offers a delightful glance at New Orleans French heritage and 18th-century charm. From the lush courtyards to the gracious balconies, guests will enjoy the view of the busy quarter. Rooms are individually appointed, some with period antiques.

Innkeeper(s): Brent Kovach. $49-225. MC VISA AX DS PC TC. TAC10. 28 rooms with PB. 11 suites. Breakfast included in rates. Type of meal: continental-plus breakfast. Beds: KQDT. Phone, air conditioning, ceiling fan and TV in room. Fax on premises. Amusement parks, antiques, fishing, parks, shopping and theater nearby.

Sully Mansion - Garden District

2631 Prytania St
New Orleans, LA 70130-5944
(504)891-0457 Fax:(504)899-7237

Circa 1890. This handsome Queen Anne Victorian, designed by its namesake, Thomas Sully, maintains many original features common to the architecture. A wide veranda, stained glass, heart-of-pine floors and a grand staircase are among the notable items. Rooms are decorated in a comfortable mix of antiques and more modern pieces. This is a place where people can relax and enjoy New Orleans' Garden District.

Innkeeper(s): Maralee Prigmore. $98-225. MC VISA AX DS PC TC. TAC10. 7 rooms with PB. Breakfast included in rates. Type of meal: continental-plus breakfast. Beds: KQT. Phone and air conditioning in room. Fax on premises. Antiques and parks nearby.

Publicity: *Houston Chronicle, Travel & Leisure.*

"I truly enjoyed my stay at Sully Mansion—the room was wonderful, the pastries memorable and so enjoyed your conversation."

Sun Oak Inn B&B

2020 Burgundy St
New Orleans, LA 70116-1606
(504)945-0322 Fax:(504)945-0322

Circa 1836. This historic home was restored to its former glory as an early 19th-century manor by innkeeper Eugene Cizek. Cizek heads the preservation program at Tulane University and has won awards for historic preservation. His expertise has turned a dilapidated home into a beautiful showplace. Rooms feature a variety of French, Creole, Acadian and mid-French Louisiana antiques, Oriental rugs, ceiling fans, fine fabrics and beautiful light fixtures. Behind the home lie lush, landscaped patios, gardens and the Sun Oak tree.

Historic Interest: The edge of the French Quarter is five minutes from the historic Sun Oak, and the inn itself is located in a local and national historic district.

Innkeeper(s): Eugene D. Cizek & Lloyd L. Sensat, Jr. $75-175. PC TC. TAC10. 2 rooms with PB. 1 conference room. Breakfast included in rates. Type of meal: continental breakfast. Beds: D. Phone, air conditioning and ceiling fan in room. Fax and library on premises. Weddings, small meetings, family reunions and seminars hosted. Some Spanish spoken. Antiques, fishing, parks, shopping, sporting events, theater and watersports nearby.

Publicity: *Colonial Homes, Better Homes & Gardens, Traditional Home, Old House Interiors, Classic New Orleans, New Orleans Elegance and Decadence.*

"From A-Z we loved our visit to Sun Oak. The house is so warm and charming."

New Roads   F5

Pointe Coupee B&B
(Samson-Claiborne House)

405 Richey St
New Roads, LA 70760
(504)638-6254 Fax:(504)638-6060

Circa 1835. A wealthy landowner built this creole plantation house, located in the heart of the historic downtown. Its 10-foot-high double French doors open into the front and rear galleries that are just steps away from a cypress covered brick patio with a fireplace. The host, a veteran of the U.S. Air Force and Cape Kennedy Missile Program, is an adept blacksmith artisan and creates F.P. Tools and carriage lamps. The inn's hostess is an interior designer with a love of history. Both have combined their talents to create a warm and relaxing atmosphere. Refreshments are served on the gallery in the afternoon. A full Southern-style gourmet breakfast is offered every morning. Buggy rides are available seasonally by reservation. The inn is available for weddings, receptions, brunches, meetings and luncheons. The B&B is close to shopping, restaurants and False River. Listed in the National Register of Historic Places.

Innkeeper(s): Mr. & Mrs. J. B. McVea. $100. MC VISA TC. TAC10. 2 rooms with PB. Breakfast included in rates. Types of meals: continental breakfast, continental-plus breakfast, full breakfast, gourmet breakfast and early coffee/tea. Evening snack, catering service and room service available. Beds: DT. Phone, air conditioning, turndown service and ceiling fan in room. TV, VCR, bicycles and library on premises. Weddings, small meetings, family

reunions and seminars hosted. Antiques, fishing, shopping, sporting events and watersports nearby.

Publicity: *Country Roads, Country Victoria.*

Ponchatoula   F7

Bella Rose Mansion

225 N 8th St
Ponchatoula, LA 70454-3209
(504)386-3857 Fax:(504)386-3857

Circa 1942. This Georgian-style mansion boasts a three-story spiral staircase that rises up to a stained-glass dome. Master craftsmen detailed this luxurious manor with mahogany paneling, parquet floors, Waterford crystal chandeliers and a marble-walled solarium with a fountain.

The home once served as a monastery for Jesuit priests. The mansion includes an indoor terrazzo shuffleboard court and heated swimming pool. Gourmet breakfasts feature entrees such as eggs Benedict complemented with fresh fruits and juices. Ponchatoula's many antique shops have earned its nickname as America's Antique City.

Historic Interest: The Belle Rose is a state historic site and located only 30 minutes or so from New Orleans and its bounty of historic buildings and museums.

Innkeeper(s): Rose James & Michael-Ray Britton. $125-225. MC VISA. TAC10. 4 rooms with PB. 2 suites. Breakfast included in rates. Type of meal: gourmet breakfast. Beds: KQ. Air conditioning and ceiling fan in room. VCR, fax, copier, swimming, bicycles and library on premises. Antiques, fishing, parks, shopping, sporting events, theater and watersports nearby.

Publicity: *Houston Chronicle, Sunday Star.*

"What a fabulous place! Your warmth is truly an asset. The peacefulness is just what we needed in our hectic lives."

Ramsay/Covington   F8

Mill Bank Farms

75654 River Rd
Ramsay/Covington, LA 70435
(504)892-1606

Circa 1832. This home was built to house offices for a lumber mill. After all but one tree had been cut down, the innkeeper's father purchased the house in 1915 and transformed the place into a farm. There are just two bedchambers, and guests have run of the living and dining rooms. Beds are topped with quilts, and robes and fresh flowers appear in each guest room. Before breakfast is presented, guests can relax on the porch with coffee or perhaps a mimosa. The morning meal is always fabulous, the innkeeper studied at the famed Cordon Bleu school. New Orleans is just 40 minutes away.

Innkeeper(s): Mrs. Katie Planche Friedrichs. $100-125. MC VISA AX DS PC TC. TAC10. 2 rooms with PB. Breakfast and afternoon tea included in rates. Types of meals: continental-plus breakfast, gourmet breakfast and early coffee/tea. Beds: D. Phone, air conditioning, turndown service, ceiling fan and TV in room. Swimming, bicycles and library on premises. 70 acres. Some French and Spanish spoken. Antiques, fishing, parks, shopping, sporting events, golf, theater and watersports nearby.

Pets Allowed: If house broken and de-fleaed.

Publicity: *Country Roads, North Shore Life, New Orleans Times.*

Saint Francisville   E6

Barrow House Inn

9779 Royal, Drawer 2550
Saint Francisville, LA 70775
(504)635-4791 Fax:(504)635-4769
E-mail: staff@topteninn.com

Circa 1800. This saltbox with a Greek Revival addition was built during Spanish colonial times. Antiques dating from 1840-1860 include a Mississippi plantation bed with full canopy and a massive rosewood armoire crafted by the famous New Orleans cabinet-maker, Mallard. One room has a Spanish-moss mattress, traditional Louisiana bedding material used for more than 200 years. Six nearby plantations are open for tours.

Innkeeper(s): Shirley Dittloff. $95-150. MC VISA PC. TAC10. 8 rooms with PB. 3 suites. Breakfast included in rates. Types of meals: continental breakfast, full breakfast, gourmet breakfast and early coffee/tea. Dinner available. Beds: KQDT. Air conditioning in room. VCR, fax and copier on premises. Weddings, small meetings and family reunions hosted. Antiques, parks and shopping nearby.
Publicity: Gourmet, Chicago Tribune, Southern Living.

"This was the icing on the cake."

Green Springs B&B

7463 Tunica Trace
Saint Francisville, LA 70775-5716
(504)635-4232 (800)457-4978 Fax:(504)635-3355
E-mail: madeline@bsf.net

Circa 1990. Although this replica of a bluffland cottage, in the Feliciana style, was constructed just several years ago, its historic roots run deep. The inn rests on 150 acres that were

owned by the innkeeper's family for 200 years, and on the grounds is a 2,000-year-old Indian mound. The inn's name comes from a natural spring found in a glen on the property, and Big Bayou Sara Creek is on the property borders. Visitors can choose from three guest rooms, decorated in an attractive blend of antique and contemporary furnishings or four cottages with king or queen beds, Jacuzzi tubs and fireplaces. A full plantation breakfast is served.

Innkeeper(s): Ivan & Madeline Nevill. $85. MC VISA. 3 rooms with PB. 1 suite. 4 cottages. Breakfast included in rates. Types of meals: full breakfast and early coffee/tea. Beds: KQT. Air conditioning, ceiling fan and TV in room. VCR on premises. 150 acres. Antiques, fishing, shopping and sporting events nearby.

Publicity: Houston Chronicle, Saint Francisville Democrat, Star Telegram, Country Roads, Advocate.

"The most picturesque setting in Louisiana."

Rosedown Plantation & Historic Garden

12501 Hwy 10
Saint Francisville, LA 70755
(504)635-3332

Circa 1835. Century-old oaks line the drive up to this stunning plantation home, which truly looks like something out of "Gone With the Wind." The surrounding 1,000 acres include 14 buildings that were once part of this thriving cotton plantation. The original family lived here for more than a century. The grounds boast 28 acres of spectacular gardens. Guests will experience the best of 19th-century plantation life, and the rates include a tour of the home. Guests also enjoy use of a swimming pool and tennis court.

Innkeeper(s): Rosedown Plantation Staff. $95-145. MC VISA AX DS PC TC. 11 rooms with PB. Breakfast included in rates. Type of meal: continental breakfast. Beds: Q. Air conditioning in room. TV and swimming on premises. 1000 acres. Weddings, small meetings, family reunions and seminars hosted. Antiques, fishing, shopping, sporting events, golf, theater and watersports nearby.

Shadetree

9704 Royal St at Ferdinand
Saint Francisville, LA 70775
(504)635-6116 Fax:(504)635-0072
E-mail: hilltopinn@aol.com

Circa 1840. A collection of romantic retreats comprises this bed & breakfast. One is a pre-Civil War cottage nestled on

three acres in the town's historic district. The innkeeper is a noted interior designer and creates a decor that blends beautifully into the natural surroundings. The Gardener's Cottage features 12 stained-glass windows and a canopy draped bed. All rooms offer stereos and telephones. Camp Mon Soleil is another idyllic option, a cabin surrounded by woods of oaks, magnolias and dogwoods. The 20-foot-tall fireplace is decorated and lit by candles, a place ideal for a romantic evening in front of the fire. It's the perfect little hideaway. The kitchen would fancy any gourmet cook, and the master suite includes a clawfoot tub.

Innkeeper(s): Ellen & KW Kennon. $145-475. MC VISA DS PC TC. TAC10. 2 suites. 1 cottage. 1 cabin. Breakfast and evening snack included in rates. Types of meals: continental breakfast and continental-plus breakfast. Catering service available. Beds: K. Phone, air conditioning, ceiling fan and TV in room. Fax, copier, bicycles and library on premises. Weddings, small meetings, family reunions and seminars hosted. Antiques, fishing, parks, shopping, sporting events, golf, theater and watersports nearby.

Publicity: Southern Living, Times Picayune, Country Roads, Weekends Getaways, Louisiana Off the Beaten Path.

"If I had to describe this place in a single word, I would say it's magical."

Saint Martinville G5

The Old Castillo Hotel

PO Box 172
Saint Martinville, LA 70582-0172
(318)394-4010 (800)621-3017 Fax:(318)394-7983

Circa 1825. Ionic columns and a second-story veranda grace the exterior of this Greek Revival home, which was used originally as an inn. From the turn of the century until the mid 1980s, the home served as a Catholic girls' school. Today, the home once again serves travelers, both as hotel and restaurant. Guest rooms are furnished with antiques and reproductions. The restaurant serves up Bayou favorites such as fried alligator, catfish, crawfish, frog legs, as well as other seafood and steak specialties.

Innkeeper(s): Peggy Hulin. $50-80. MC VISA AX. TAC10. 5 rooms with PB. 3 suites. 1 conference room. Breakfast included in rates. Types of meals: continental breakfast, continental-plus breakfast, full breakfast and early coffee/tea. Dinner and lunch available. Restaurant on premises. Beds: QD. Air conditioning in room. Fax on premises. Small meetings, family reunions and seminars hosted. French spoken. Amusement parks, antiques, fishing, parks, shopping, sporting events, theater and watersports nearby.

Shreveport B2

The Columns on Jordan

615 Jordan St
Shreveport, LA 71101-4748
(318)222-5912 (800)801-4950 Fax:(318)459-1155

Circa 1898. This Classical Revival house in the historic district features four Gothic columns, and it is surrounded by stately magnolia trees whose white blooms reach to the upstairs porch in the spring. Guest rooms are decorated in period furnishings. The pool was constructed in the shape of a femur bone by order of the owner, an orthopedic surgeon.

Innkeeper(s): Judith Simonton. $85-125. MC VISA AX DS TC. TAC10. 5 rooms, 4 with PB. 1 conference room. Beds: KDT. Phone in room. Spa on premises.
Publicity: *Shreveport Times, Travel Times CBS.*

Slattery House B&B

2401 Fairfield Ave
Shreveport, LA 71104
(318)222-6977 Fax:(318)222-7539

Circa 1903. This National Register Victorian is one of few remaining structures designed by noted Shreveport architect N.S. Allen. The home has had only three owners, so much of the original period features are still intact. The Victorian decor

includes antiques, some of which belonged to the first owner, J.B. Slattery. Guests can relax by the pool or on the veranda. Southern breakfasts with eggs, bacon, grits and freshly made biscuits and pastries are served each morning.

Innkeeper(s): Bill & Adrienne Scruggs. $85-165. AP. MC VISA AX DC DS PC TC. TAC10. 6 rooms with PB. 2 suites. Breakfast included in rates. Types of meals: full breakfast, gourmet breakfast and early coffee/tea. Beds: Q. Phone, air conditioning, ceiling fan, TV and VCR in room. Fax, copier and swimming on premises. Spanish spoken. Amusement parks, antiques, parks, shopping, golf and theater nearby.
Publicity: *Shreveport Times.*

Slidell F8

Salmen-Fritchie House B&B

127 Cleveland Ave
Slidell, LA 70458
(504)643-1405 (800)235-4168 Fax:(504)643-2251
E-mail: sfritbb@communique.net

Circa 1895. At one time, most of the residents in Slidell worked for the owner of this Victorian home at his lumber and brickworks business. Eventually, the home passed on to innkeeper Homer Fritchie's grandmother and then to him. He

and his wife, Sharon, spent hundreds of thousands of dollars restoring the place and transforming it into a B&B. The home is decorated with period antiques, including family heirlooms from both the Salmen and Fritchie families. Guests are offered two different breakfast options, one might be a Belgian waffle topped with fresh strawberries and cream or perhaps a Creole omelet. New Orleans is a half-hour away.

Innkeeper(s): Homer & Sharon Fritchie. $85-150. MC VISA AX DS PC TC. TAC10. 6 rooms with PB, 3 with FP. 3 suites. 1 cottage. 1 conference room. Breakfast and afternoon tea included in rates. Types of meals: full breakfast and early coffee/tea. Beds: QDT. Phone, air conditioning, ceiling fan and TV in room. Fax and library on premises. Small meetings, family reunions and seminars hosted. Antiques, fishing, parks, shopping, golf and theater nearby.
Publicity: *Times Picayune News, Slidell Sentry News, Southern Living.*

"Never again shall I sit down to breakfast without wishing I were in the Salmen-Fritchie House."

Maine

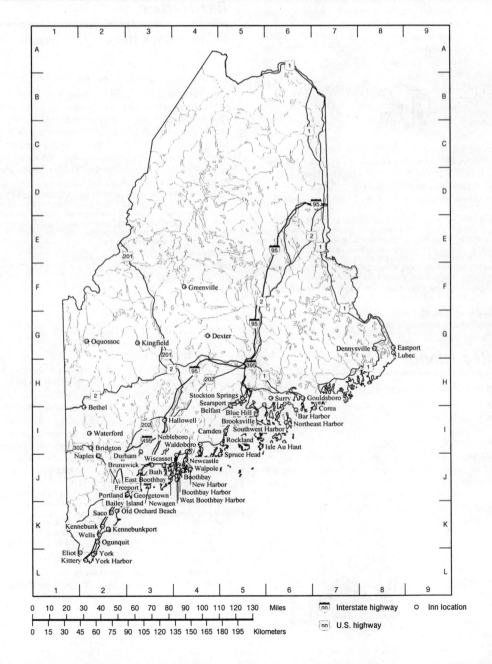

Interstate highway — Inn location

U.S. highway

| 0 | 10 | 20 | 30 | 40 | 50 | 60 | 70 | 80 | 90 | 100 | 110 | 120 | 130 | Miles |
| 0 | 15 | 30 | 45 | 60 | 75 | 90 | 105 | 120 | 135 | 150 | 165 | 180 | 195 | Kilometers |

Augusta (Hallowell)　I3

Maple Hill Farm B&B Inn

RR 1 Box 1145, Outlet Rd
Augusta (Hallowell), ME 04347
(207)622-2708 (800)622-2708 Fax:(207)622-0655
E-mail: maple@mint.net

Circa 1890. Visitors to Maine's capitol city have the option of staying at this nearby inn, a peaceful farm setting adjacent to a 550-acre state wildlife management area that is available for canoeing, fishing, hiking and hunting. This Victorian Shingle-style inn was once a stagecoach stop and dairy farm. The inn's suite includes a double whirlpool tub. The inn, with its 130-acre grounds, easily accommodates conferences, parties and receptions. Guests are welcome to visit the many farm animals. Cobbossee Lake is a five-minute drive from the inn. The center portion of Hallowell is listed as a National Historic District and offers antique shops and restaurants.

Historic Interest: State capitol building, state museum, archives, & Fort Western (5 miles).

Innkeeper(s): Scott Cowger. $50-125. MC VISA AX DC CB DS PC TC. 7 rooms, 4 with PB. 1 suite. 1 conference room. Breakfast and afternoon tea included in rates. Types of meals: full breakfast and early coffee/tea. Evening snack, picnic lunch, banquet service and catering service available. Beds: QD. Phone in room. VCR on premises. Handicap access. 130 acres. Weddings, small meetings, family reunions and seminars hosted. Antiques, shopping, cross-country skiing, theater and watersports nearby.

Publicity: *Family Fun, An Explorer's Guide to Maine, The Forecaster, Portland Press Herald, Kennebec Journal, Maine Times.*

"You add many thoughtful touches to your service that set your B&B apart from others, and really make a difference. Best of Maine, hands down! Maine Times"

Bailey Island　J3

Captain York House B&B

Route 24, PO Box 298
Bailey Island, ME 04003
(207)833-6224
E-mail: athorn7286@aol.com

Circa 1906. Bailey Island is the quaint fisherman's village of stories, poems and movies. Guests cross the world's only cribstone bridge to reach the island, where beautiful sunsets and dinners of fresh Maine lobster are the norm. This shingled, turn-of-the-century, Mansard-style B&B was the home of a famous Maine sea captain, Charles York. Now a homestay-style bed & breakfast, the innkeepers have restored the home to its former glory, filling it with many antiques. Guests at

Captain York's enjoy water views from all the guest rooms. Wild Maine blueberries often find a significant place on the breakfast menu.

Innkeeper(s): Alan & Jean Thornton. $68-100. PC TC. TAC10. 5 rooms, 3 with PB. Breakfast included in rates. Type of meal: full breakfast. Beds: QT. TV and VCR on premises. Weddings, small meetings, family reunions and seminars hosted. Antiques, parks, shopping, sporting events, theater and watersports nearby.

"Bailey Island turned out to be the hidden treasure of our trip and we hope to return for your great hospitality again."

Bar Harbor　I6

Balance Rock Inn on The Ocean

21 Albert Meadow
Bar Harbor, ME 04609-1702
(207)288-2610 (800)753-0494 Fax:(207)288-5534

Circa 1903. Built for a Scottish railroad tycoon, the Shingle-style structure was designed by a prestigious Boston architectural firm often used by wealthy summer residents of Bar Harbor. The inn is set on a secluded tree-covered property with views of the islands and Frenchman's Bay. Bar Harbor is two short blocks away. Off the back veranda, overlooking the pool, and past nearly an acre of sweeping lawns is the Historic Shore Path that winds its way around the waterfront.

Innkeeper(s): Mike & Nancy Cloud. $135-425. MC VISA AX DS PC TC. TAC10. 14 rooms with PB, 6 with FP. 3 suites. Breakfast included in rates. Types of meals: full breakfast and early coffee/tea. Afternoon tea available. Beds: KQ. Phone, air conditioning, turndown service and TV in room. VCR, fax, swimming and pet boarding on premises. Weddings hosted. Antiques, parks, theater and watersports nearby.

Pets Allowed.

Location: Acadia National Park.

Ratings: *4 Diamonds.*

Bar Harbor Inn

Newport Dr
Bar Harbor, ME 04609-0007
(800)248-3351 (207)288-3351
E-mail: bhinn@acadia.net

Circa 1887. Once known as the Oasis Club, this historic waterfront inn was the first social club on Mt. Desert Island. A Bar Harbor landmark, it survived the 1947 fire that destroyed many of the town's famous hotels. Overlooking Frenchman Bay, in summer the yellow umbrellas of the inn's Terrace Grille-Cafe dot the lawns in view of the fishing vessels and windjammers that frequent the harbor. The inn's private pier is home to a four-masted schooner, Margaret Todd, and day sails are offered. Choose between rooms in the historic main inn, the Oceanfront Lodge or Newport Building.

Innkeeper(s): David J. Witham. $59-395. MC VISA AX DC DS PC TC. TAC5. 153 rooms with PB. 1 conference room. Breakfast included in rates. Types of meals: continental-plus breakfast, full breakfast and early coffee/tea. Dinner, lunch, banquet service and room service available. Restaurant on premises. Beds: KQDT. Phone, air conditioning, turndown service, TV and VCR in room. Fax, copier and swimming on premises. Handicap access. Weddings, small meetings, family reunions and seminars hosted. French and German spoken. Antiques, fishing, shopping, cross-country skiing, golf and watersports nearby.

Pets Allowed: Limited number of designated rooms.

Publicity: *New York Times, Boston Globe, Chicago Tribune. Ratings: 4 Stars.*

Bayview Inn

111 Eden St
Bar Harbor, ME 04609-1105
(207)288-5861 (800)356-3585 Fax:(207)288-3173

Circa 1930. This inn's location is stunning, set just yards off Frenchman Bay with mountains and woods as a backdrop. The six-room Georgian inn was built by George McMurty, who was one of Theodore Roosevelt's Rough Riders. McMurty was awarded the Medal of Honor for his service during World War I. Among his influential friends and guests was Winston Churchill. Four of the rooms offer ocean views, and two include a fireplace. Elegant accommodations also are available in an adjacent hotel and townhomes, so for a historic experience, be sure to ask for rooms in the 1930s inn.

Innkeeper(s): Trish Nolan. $75-275. MC VISA AX DC CB PC TC. TAC10. 6 rooms with PB, 2 with FP. 1 suite. 3 conference rooms. Breakfast included in rates. Type of meal: continental-plus breakfast. Beds: KQD. Phone, air conditioning, turndown service and TV in room. Fax, copier, swimming, tennis and library on premises. Small meetings, family reunions and seminars hosted. Antiques, fishing, parks, shopping, golf, theater and watersports nearby.

Black Friar Inn

10 Summer St
Bar Harbor, ME 04609-1424
(207)288-5091 Fax:(207)288-4197
E-mail: blackfriar@acadia.net

Circa 1900. When this three-story house was renovated in 1981, the owners added mantels, hand-crafted woodwork and windows gleaned from old Bar Harbor mansions that had been torn down. Victorian and country furnishings are accentuated with fresh flowers and soft carpets. Breakfast is presented in the greenhouse, a room that boasts cypress paneling and embossed tin recycled from an old country church.

Historic Interest: Acadia National Park, the second most popular park in the U.S. (nearby).

Innkeeper(s): Perry & Sharon Risley & Falke. $55-140. MC VISA DS PC TC. 7 rooms with PB, 1 with FP. 1 suite. Breakfast and afternoon tea included in rates. Type of meal: gourmet breakfast. Beds: KQ. Air conditioning and ceiling fan in room. TV and VCR on premises. Antiques, fishing, parks, shopping, cross-country skiing, theater and watersports nearby.

"A great place and great innkeepers!"

Breakwater

45 Hancock St
Bar Harbor, ME 04609-1700
(207)288-2313 (800)238-6309 Fax:(207)288-2377

Circa 1904. This is an oceanfront English Tudor estate on more than four acres of lawns, gardens and woods. It is located at the end of Bar Harbor's historic Shore Path. There are plenty of common areas and 11 working fireplaces. Bedchambers feature queen beds, walk-in closets and most have ocean views. The inn also offer two carriage house apartments. Guests may play billiards in the library. The inn offers a full breakfast, afternoon tea and evening hors d'oeuvres.

Innkeeper(s): Margaret Eden. $145-335. MC VISA AX PC TC. TAC10. 6 rooms with PB, 6 with FP. 2 cottages. Breakfast, afternoon tea and evening snack included in rates. Type of meal: full breakfast. Banquet service available. Beds: KQ. Turndown service in room. Fax and library on premises. Weddings, small meetings and family reunions hosted. Antiques, parks, shopping, theater and watersports nearby.

Publicity: *Country Inns, Down East, Discerning Traveler, B&B of the Year, Harper's Hideaway Report.*

"There's no place like home, unless it's here at Breakwater! It was beautiful, delicious, and our every 'want' was anticipated by the outstanding staff. The most outstanding inn we've ever visited."

The Inn at Canoe Point

Rt 3 Box 216R-Hull's Cove
Bar Harbor, ME 04609
(207)288-9511

Circa 1889. This oceanfront inn has served as a summer residence for several generations of families escaping city heat. Guests are treated to the gracious hospitality of the past, surrounded by the ocean and pine forests. They can relax on the deck overlooking Frenchman's Bay, or pursue outdoor activities in Acadia National Park.

Innkeeper(s): Tom & Nancy. $80-245. 5 rooms with PB, 1 with FP. Type of meal: full breakfast. Beds: KQ. Phone in room.

Publicity: *New York Times, Travel-Holiday, Travel & Leisure, Conde Nast.*

Castlemaine Inn

39 Holland Ave
Bar Harbor, ME 04609-1433
(207)288-4563 (800)338-4563 Fax:(207)288-4525

Circa 1886. This Queen Anne charmer was once the summer home to the Austro-Hungarian ambassador to the United States. Rooms are decorated in a light, comfortable Victorian style. Two

guest rooms include a whirlpool tub and most include a private balcony or deck and a fireplace. In the mornings, a generous breakfast buffet is presented, with freshly baked scones, muffins, breads and coffee cake, as well as bagels, cream cheese, fresh fruit, cereals and a variety of beverages.

Innkeeper(s): Terence O'Connell & Norah O'Brien. $65-175. MC VISA PC TC. 15 rooms with PB, 11 with FP. 5 suites. Breakfast included in rates. Type of meal: continental-plus breakfast. Beds: KQ. Air conditioning, ceiling fan, TV and VCR in room. Fax and copier on premises. Antiques, fishing, parks, shopping, golf, theater and watersports nearby.

Publicity: *Country Inns.*

"This year we celebrate our tenth anniversary in our relationship with Castlemaine."

Graycote Inn

40 Holland Ave
Bar Harbor, ME 04609-1432
(207)288-3044 Fax:(207)288-2719
E-mail: graycote@acadia.net

Circa 1881. This Victorian inn was built by the first rector of St. Saviour's Episcopal Church. Some of the guest rooms have fireplaces, while others have sun rooms or balconies. A full, hot breakfast is served on a sunny, glass-enclosed porch with tables set for two or four. Afternoon refreshments also are served. The inn is located on a one-acre lot with lawns, large trees, flower gardens, a croquet court and a double-size hammock. Guests can also relax on the veranda, which is furnished with wicker. The innkeepers are happy to make activity and dining recommendations. Guests can walk to restaurants, and Acadia National Park is nearby.

Historic Interest: Acadia National Park is less than two miles from the inn.
Innkeeper(s): Pat & Roger Samuel. $65-150. MC VISA DS PC TC. 12 rooms with PB, 3 with FP. Breakfast included in rates. Type of meal: full breakfast. Beds: KQ. Air conditioning and ceiling fan in room. Small meetings and seminars hosted. Antiques, parks, shopping, cross-country skiing, theater and watersports nearby.
Location: Bar Harbor and Acadia National Park.
Publicity: *Victorian Decorating & Lifestyle.*

"Thank you for the honeymoon of our dreams! The decor and the atmosphere combine to make this one of the most romantic places we've ever been."

Heathwood Inn

Rte 3, Box 1938
Bar Harbor, ME 04609
(207)288-5591 Fax:(207)288-4862

Circa 1910. This Victorian farmhouse offers something special in each of the guest quarters. The Honeymoon suite is a romantic retreat with a lace canopied bed and double French doors, which open onto a six-foot Jacuzzi tub. Other rooms feature four-poster beds or special amenities such as a fireplace, private balcony or Finnish dry sauna. Home-baked treats fill the breakfast buffet and guests are treated to afternoon refreshments, as well. Heathwood Inn is only a few miles from downtown Bar Harbor and Acadia National Park.

Innkeeper(s): Richard & Cindy Cassey. $60-148. MC VISA. 5 rooms with PB. Type of meal: continental-plus breakfast. Beds: KQ. Antiques, fishing, cross-country skiing, theater and watersports nearby.
Publicity: *Best Places to Kiss in New England.*

Holbrook House

74 Mount Desert St
Bar Harbor, ME 04609-1323
(207)288-4970

Circa 1876. This Victorian inn is located on the historic corridor of Bar Harbor. Antiques, lace, chintz and flowers enhance the inn's nostalgic ambiance. Guests can enjoy a full breakfast offering fruit flans, blueberry buckle or egg savories in the sunroom. The porch, that runs the length of the inn, offers guests a relaxing option for enjoying refreshments. The inn is a short walk to restaurants, shops and the harbor.

Historic Interest: Located one mile from Acadia National Park.
Innkeeper(s): Carol & Bill Deike. $95-135. MC VISA. 10 rooms with PB. 2 suites. Type of meal: full breakfast. Beds: QDT. Phone in room.
Location: Mt. Desert Island.
Publicity: *The Discerning Traveler.*

"When I selected Holbrook House all my dreams of finding the perfect inn came true."

Ledgelawn Inn

66 Mount Desert St
Bar Harbor, ME 04609-1324
(207)288-4596 (800)274-5334 Fax:(207)288-9968

Circa 1904. Gables, bays, columns and verandas are features of this rambling three-story summer house located on an acre of wooded land within walking distance to the waterfront. The red clapboard structure sports black shutters and a mansard roof. Filled with antiques and fireplaces, the inn features a sitting room and library.

Innkeeper(s): Nancy & Mike Cloud. $65-250. MC VISA AX DS PC TC. TAC10. 33 rooms with PB, 12 with FP. 1 suite. Breakfast included in rates. Types of meals: full breakfast and early coffee/tea. Afternoon tea available. Beds: KQD. Phone, turndown service and TV in room. Fax, swimming, pet boarding and child care on premises. Family reunions hosted. Antiques, parks, theater and watersports nearby.
Pets Allowed.
Location: Acadia National Park.
Publicity: *New York Times.*

"A lovely place to relax and enjoy oneself. The area is unsurpassed in beauty and the people friendly."

Manor House Inn

106 West St
Bar Harbor, ME 04609-1856
(207)288-3759 (800)437-0088 Fax:(207)288-2974

Circa 1887. Colonel James Foster built this 22-room Victorian mansion, now in the National Register. It is an example of the tradition of gracious summer living for which Bar Harbor was and is famous. In addition to the main house, there are several charming cottages situated in the extensive gardens on the property.

Innkeeper(s): Mac Noyes. $55-175. MC VISA. TAC10. 14 rooms, 7 with PB, 6 with FP. 7 suites. Breakfast and afternoon tea included in rates. Types of meals: full breakfast and early coffee/tea. Beds: KQT. Ceiling fan in room. TV, fax and copier on premises. Weddings, small meetings, family reunions and seminars hosted. Antiques, fishing, parks, shopping and watersports nearby.

Location: Close to Acadia National Park.

Publicity: *Discerning Traveler.*

"Wonderful honeymoon spot! Wonderful inn, elegant, delicious breakfasts, terrific innkeepers. We loved it all! It's our fourth time here and it's wonderful as always."

Mira Monte Inn & Suites

69 Mount Desert St
Bar Harbor, ME 04609-1327
(207)288-4263 (800)553-5109 Fax:(207)288-3115
E-mail: mburns@acadia.net

Circa 1864. A gracious 18-room Victorian mansion, the Mira Monte has been newly renovated in the style of early Bar Harbor. It features period furnishings, pleasant common rooms, a library and wraparound porches. Situated on estate grounds, there are sweeping lawns, paved terraces and many gardens. The inn was one of the earliest of Bar Harbor's famous summer cottages. The two-room suites each feature canopy beds, two-person whirlpools, a parlor with a sleeper sofa, fireplace and kitchenette unit. The two-bedroom suite includes a full kitchen, dining area and parlor. The suites boast private decks with views of the gardens.

Historic Interest: Acadia National Park is nearby. Many estates are still visible by water tours around the island.

Innkeeper(s): Marian Burns. $125-185. MC VISA AX DC DS TC. TAC10. 16 rooms, 15 with PB, 11 with FP. 3 suites. Breakfast and afternoon tea included in rates. Types of meals: full breakfast and early coffee/tea. Beds: KQT. Phone, air conditioning, TV and VCR in room. Fax and library on premises. Handicap access. Small meetings hosted. Antiques, fishing, parks, shopping and theater nearby.

Location: Five-minute walk from the waterfront, shops and restaurants.

Publicity: *Los Angeles Times.*

"On our third year at your wonderful inn in beautiful Bar Harbor. I think I enjoy it more each year. A perfect place to stay in a perfect environment."

Stratford House Inn

45 Mount Desert St
Bar Harbor, ME 04609-1748
(207)288-5189

Circa 1900. Lewis Roberts, Boston publisher of Louisa Mae Alcott's "Little Women" constructed a 10-bedroom cottage for his guests. It was modeled on Shakespeare's birthplace in an English Tudor style with Jacobean period furnishings and motifs throughout. The rooms are all furnished with antiques such as four-poster mahogany and brass bow-bottom beds. The entrance and dining room are paneled in ornate black oak.

Innkeeper(s): Barbara & Norman Moulton. $75-150. MC VISA. 10 rooms, 8 with PB. Type of meal: continental breakfast. Beds: KQD. Phone in room.

"Marvelous visit. Love this house. Great hospitality."

The Tides

119 West St
Bar Harbor, ME 04609-1430
(207)288-4968
E-mail: thetides@acadia.net

Circa 1887. As innkeeper Joe Losquadro might explain, The Tides has endurance. The gracious Victorian survived a 10-day firestorm that destroyed more than 17,000 acres and 60 of Mt. Desert Island's grand summer homes. The Tides still stands as testament to local resilience. Each of the suites offers something special. The Master Suite includes an ocean view, a king-size bed and working fireplace. The Ocean Suite boasts water views from every window, including the bath. The suite includes a parlor with cable TV, bedroom with a working fireplace and balcony. Guests in the Captain's Suite enjoy a bubble bath in a clawfoot tub and the view of the historic, tree-lined West Street as well as the bay. Joe has been an innkeeper on the island for more than five years and is full of local information and plenty of ideas for vacationers.

Historic Interest: Acadia National Park, the first national park established east of the Mississippi River, is nearby and includes the Abbe Museum, with its vast collection of Native American artifacts. The Islesford Museum on Little Cranberry Island offers many maritime exhibits. The Bar Harbor Historical Museum provides documents and photographs from Bar Harbor's heyday as grand resort for the country's wealthiest citizens.

Innkeeper(s): Joe & Judy Losquadro. $150-275. AP. MC VISA TC. 4 rooms with PB, 2 with FP. 3 suites. Breakfast included in rates. Types of meals: full breakfast and early coffee/tea. Beds: KQ. Ceiling fan and TV in room. Weddings, small meetings and family reunions hosted. Antiques, parks, shopping, cross-country skiing, theater and watersports nearby.

"Your hospitality made us feel very welcome. Thank you once again."

Bath   J3

Donnell House B&B

251 High St
Bath, ME 04530
(207)443-5324 (888)595-1664

Circa 1860. From the cupola atop the roof of this Italianate home, guests may enjoy a moon lit view of the Kennebec River. The inn's exterior is elegantly painted in gray with white on the columns and trim. Inside are hardwood floors and antiques, set against cheerful wall colors and white woodwork. There are two front parlors, one a sunny yellow and white, and the other with marble fireplace, Oriental rug and a rose-patterned wallpaper. Guest bedrooms offer four-poster beds, and some have fireplaces. One room boasts a Roman tub. A three-course breakfast is served on Blue Willow china in the formal dining room .

Innkeeper(s): Kenneth & Rachel Parlin. $70-130. PC TC. 4 rooms with PB, 1 with FP. 1 suite. Breakfast included in rates. Types of meals: full breakfast and early coffee/tea. Beds: Q. Phone and TV in room. Library on premises. Small meetings hosted. Antiques, fishing, parks, shopping, cross-country skiing, theater and watersports nearby.

"Your beautiful home offered the space and energy we all needed."

Fairhaven Inn

RR 2 PO Box 85, N Bath Rd
Bath, ME 04530
(207)443-4391 (888)443-4391

Circa 1790. With its view of the Kennebec River, this site was so attractive that Pembleton Edgecomb built his Colonial house where a log cabin had previously stood. His descendants occupied it for the next 125 years. Antiques and country furniture

fill the inn. Meadows and lawns, and woods of hemlock, birch and pine cover the inn's 16 acres.

Innkeeper(s): Susie & Dave Reed. $80-120. MC VISA DS PC TC. TAC10. 8 rooms, 6 with PB. 1 suite. 1 cottage. 1 conference room. Breakfast included in rates. Types of meals: full breakfast and early coffee/tea. Beds: KQT. TV, fax and library on premises. 16 acres. Small meetings and family reunions hosted. Antiques, parks, shopping, cross-country skiing, sporting events, theater and watersports nearby.

Publicity: *The State, Coastal Journal.*

"The Fairhaven is now marked in our book with a red star, definitely a place to remember and visit again."

The Galen C. Moses House

1009 Washington St
Bath, ME 04530-2759
(207)442-8771 (888)442-8771
E-mail: galencmoses@clinic.net

Circa 1874. This Victorian mansion is filled with beautiful architectural items, including stained-glass windows, wood-carved and marble fireplaces and a grand staircase. The innkeepers have filled the library, a study, morning room and the parlor with antiques. A corner fireplace warms the dining room, which overlooks the lawns and gardens. Tea is presented in the formal drawing room.

Historic Interest: Brandywine Valley, Longwood Gardens, Winterthuer.

Innkeeper(s): James Haught, Larry Kieft. $69-99. MC VISA PC TC. 4 rooms with PB. Breakfast and afternoon tea included in rates. Types of meals: continental breakfast and gourmet breakfast. Beds: QDT. Turndown service in room. TV, VCR and library on premises. Family reunions and seminars hosted. Antiques, fishing, parks, shopping, cross-country skiing, theater and watersports nearby.

Publicity: *Philadelphia, Back Roads USA.*

"For our first try at B&B lodgings, we've probably started at the top, and nothing else will ever measure up to this. Wonderful food, wonderful home, grounds and wonderful hosts!"

Packard House

45 Pearl St
Bath, ME 04530-2746
(207)443-6069 (800)516-4578
E-mail: packardhouse@clinic.net

Circa 1790. Shipbuilder Benjamin F. Packard purchased this handsome home in 1870. The inn reflects the Victorian influence so prominent in Bath's busiest shipbuilding years. The Packard family, who lived in the house for five generations, left many family mementos. Period furnishings, authentic colors and shipbuilding memorabilia all reflect Bath's romantic past. The

mighty Kennebec River is just a block away. A full breakfast is served daily.

Historic Interest: The inn is situated in a historic district, and nearby historic Front Street offers many antique stores and other commercial businesses in historic buildings. Maine Maritime Museum, 10-acre site on original shipyard (1 mile), Front Street (one-half mile); forts and lighthouses at Mouth of Kennebec River (12 miles south).

Innkeeper(s): Debby & Bill Hayden. $60-90. MC VISA PC TC. 2 rooms with PB. 1 suite. Breakfast included in rates. Type of meal: full breakfast. Beds: KQT. TV and library on premises. Family reunions hosted. Some French spoken. Antiques, parks, shopping, theater and watersports nearby.

Location: Historic district.

Publicity: *Times Record, Maine Sunday Telegram, Coastal Journal.*

"Thanks for being wonderful hosts."

Belfast H5

Inn on Primrose Hill

212 High St
Belfast, ME 04915-1542
(207)338-6982 (888)338-6982
E-mail: primroseh@aol.com

Circa 1812. Located on two acres that include a rhododendron garden, a white rose hedge and a Japanese garden, this Federal-Colonial-style inn features an unusual addition of six

enormous Ionic columns added by the original builder. The home was once owned by Admiral William V. Pratt, former Chief of Naval Operations. The inn's formal dining room boasts wood panelings and Waterford crystal chandeliers. There is a pine-paneled library and a 30-foot-long sunroom. Some of the guest rooms have views of the bay.

Innkeeper(s): Linus & Pat Heinz. $80-90. PC TC. 4 rooms, 3 with PB, 2 with FP. 2 suites. 1 conference room. Breakfast and afternoon tea included in rates. Types of meals: gourmet breakfast and early coffee/tea. Beds: QDT. TV, VCR and library on premises. Small meetings hosted. Antiques, fishing, parks, shopping, golf, theater and watersports nearby.

Publicity: *Travel Today, Bride's, Women's Day, Down East, Republican Journal, Yankee, Waterville Sunday Sentinel.*

"We just love your home and this beautiful town of Belfast. It has been a 'quiet oasis' in the midst of our vacation travels."

The Jeweled Turret Inn

40 Pearl St
Belfast, ME 04915-1907
(207)338-2304 (800)696-2304

Circa 1898. This grand Victorian is named for the staircase that winds up the turret, lighted by stained- and leaded-glass panels and jewel-like embellishments. It was built for attorney James Harriman. Dark pine beams adorn the ceiling of the den, and the fireplace is constructed of bark and rocks from every state in the Union. Elegant antiques furnish the guest rooms. Guests can relax in one of the inn's four parlors, which are furnished with period antiques, wallpapers, lace and boast fire-

places. The verandas feature wicker and iron bistro sets and views of the historic district. The inn is within walking distance of the town and its shops, restaurants and the harbor.

Historic Interest: The home, which is listed in the National Register, is near many historic homes. Walking tours are available.

Innkeeper(s): Cathy & Carl Heffentrager. $75-95. MC VISA PC TC. TAC10. 7 rooms with PB, 1 with FP. Breakfast and afternoon tea included in rates. Types of meals: gourmet breakfast and early coffee/tea. Beds: QDT. Phone and ceiling fan in room. Small meetings and family reunions hosted. Antiques, fishing, shopping, downhill skiing, cross-country skiing, theater and watersports nearby.

Publicity: *Republican Journal, Waterville Sentinel, Los Angeles Times, Country Living, Victorian Homes, The Saturday Evening Post.*

"The ambiance was so romantic that we felt like we were on our honeymoon."

The Thomas Pitcher House B&B

19 Franklin St
Belfast, ME 04915-1105
(207)338-6454 (888)338-6454

Circa 1873. This richly appointed home was considered state-of-the-art back in 1873, for it was one of only a few homes offering central heat and hot or cold running water. Today, innkeepers have added plenty of modern amenities, but kept the ambiance of the Victorian era. Some vanities include original walnut and marble, while another bathroom includes tin ceilings and a step-down bath. Some rooms have cozy reading areas. Guests enjoy a full breakfast each morning with menus that feature specialties such as Maine blueberry buttermilk pancakes or a French toast puff made with homemade raisin bread.

Historic Interest: A short walk from the Thomas Pitcher House will take you into the center of historic Belfast, which includes a variety of shops and galleries and the harbor. Walking tours through historic tree-lined streets are available and nearby Searsport offers plenty of antiquing. The Penobscot Marine Museum is 10 miles away, Fort Knox and Montpelier are easy day trips, as is the Owl's Head Transportation Museum.

Innkeeper(s): Fran & Ron Kresge. $70-90. MC VISA PC TC. TAC10. 4 rooms with PB. Breakfast included in rates. Types of meals: gourmet breakfast and early coffee/tea. Beds: QDT. TV, VCR and library on premises. German and limited French spoken. Antiques, fishing, parks, shopping, downhill skiing, cross-country skiing, theater and watersports nearby.

Publicity: *Boston Herald, Jackson Clarion-Ledger, Toronto Sunday Sun, Bride's, Knoxville News-Sentinel, Saturday Evening Post.*

"A home away from home."

Bethel 12

Chapman Inn

PO Box 206
Bethel, ME 04217-0206
(207)824-2657

Circa 1865. As one of the town's oldest buildings, this Federal-style inn has been a store, a tavern and a boarding house known as "The Howard." It was the home of William Rogers Chapman, composer, conductor and founder of the Rubenstein Club and the Metropolitan Musical Society, in addition to the Maine Music Festival. The inn is a convenient place to begin a walking tour of Bethel's historic district. A private beach, located on Songo Pond, is just five miles away and is available in the summer and fall complete with canoe, picnic table and beach chairs.

Innkeeper(s): Sandra & "Bub" Wight, Ada & "Pip" Cummings. Call for rates. MC VISA AX DS PC TC. 2 suites. Breakfast, afternoon tea and evening snack included in rates. Types of meals: full breakfast and early coffee/tea. Catering service available. TV, VCR, fax, sauna and child care on premises. Weddings, small meetings, family reunions and seminars hosted. Antiques, fishing, parks, shopping, downhill skiing, cross-country skiing, golf, theater and watersports nearby.

Pets Allowed.

Holidae House, A Country Inn

Main St
Bethel, ME 04217
(207)824-3400 (800)882-3306

Circa 1906. The friendly, pristine front porch of Holidae House is festooned with mauve awnings and shutters, handsome balustrades and pots of impatiens. Painted in a deep teal blue, creme and mauve accents highlight the Victorian Revival-style inn with hipped roofline. Guest rooms are furnished in period and reproduction pieces and Oriental rugs in keeping with its Victorian atmosphere. The dining room has individual couples' tables. A historical museum and walking tour is nearby.

Innkeeper(s): Tom McGinniss. $30-125. MC VISA AX PC. 9 rooms with PB. Breakfast included in rates. Type of meal: continental-plus breakfast. Beds: Q. Phone, air conditioning and TV in room. Weddings and family reunions hosted. Antiques, fishing, parks, shopping, downhill skiing, cross-country skiing and golf nearby.

Publicity: *Boston Globe.*

"You put so much love into your home that it always makes it such a pleasure to be here."

Sudbury Inn

Lower Main St
Bethel, ME 04217
(207)824-2174 (800)395-7837 Fax:(207)824-2329

Circa 1873. After a day of skiing at one of the many local ski areas, guests will enjoy the warmth and comfort that this late 19th-century Colonial inn has to offer. There are 10 spacious guest rooms and six suites, some geared to accommodate families. Although visitors may appreciate the inn's original architectural details such as its coffered ceilings and wraparound porch, the inn is most famous for its restaurant and pub that occupies the entire first floor. The menu offers a selection of fresh seafood, steaks and pasta and features an extensive wine list. After dinner, guests can retire to the Suds Pub where they can enjoy late-night dancing, a wide variety of draft beer or an after-supper snack. Located in the foothills of the White Mountains, the inn is close to hiking trails, golf and wildlife.

Historic Interest: The Appalachian Trail and Sunday River are located nearby. Innkeeper(s): Don Paddock. $50-150. MC VISA AX TC. 16 rooms with PB. 6 suites. 1 cottage. Breakfast included in rates. Types of meals: continental breakfast, continental-plus breakfast, full breakfast and early coffee/tea. Dinner, banquet service and catering service available. Restaurant on premises. Beds: KQDT. Phone and TV in room. Fax and copier on premises. Family reunions hosted. Amusement parks, antiques, fishing, parks, shopping, downhill skiing, cross-country skiing, golf and watersports nearby.

Pets Allowed.

Publicity: *Yankee Traveler, Boston Globe.*

Blue Hill   H5

The Blue Hill Inn

Union St Rt 177
Blue Hill, ME 04614-0403
(207)374-2844 (800)826-7415 Fax:(207)374-2829
E-mail: bluhilin@downeast.net

Circa 1830. This Federalist-style inn set on an acre in the heart of the historic town center has operated continuously as an inn for more than 150 years. Located near Blue Hill Bay, the inn is distinguished by its shuttered windows, clapboards, brick ends, five chimneys and wide pumpkin-pine floors. These architectural features are set off by the inn's antique period furnishings. There are two common rooms for guests to read, relax or enjoy the company of other guests. Each of the 12 guest rooms is individually decorated to provide comfort and romance. Several rooms offer fireplaces or sitting areas, and all come with private bathrooms. Although a full breakfast and hors d'oeuvres are offered, the inn is known for its elegant five-course dinners prepared by chef Andre Strong and served by candlelight. Shopping, antiquing, parks, golf, fishing, boating and skiing are available.

Historic Interest: Located close to Acadia National Park and the Maine coast. Innkeeper(s): Mary & Don Hartley. Call for rates. MAP. MC VISA DS TC. TAC10. 12 rooms with PB, 4 with FP. 3 suites. 1 cottage. Breakfast and dinner included in rates. Types of meals: full breakfast, gourmet breakfast and early coffee/tea. Room service available. Restaurant on premises. Beds: KQDT. Fax on premises. Handicap access. Family reunions hosted. Antiques, fishing, parks, cross-country skiing and golf nearby.

Boothbay   J4

Kenniston Hill Inn

Rt 27, PO Box 125
Boothbay, ME 04537-0125
(207)633-2159 (800)992-2915 Fax:(207)633-2159

Circa 1786. The elegant clapboard home is the oldest inn at Boothbay Harbor and was occupied by the Kenniston family for more than a century. Five of the antique-filled bedrooms have fireplaces. After a walk through the gardens or woods, warm up in the parlor next to the elegant, open-hearthed fireplace. Boothbay Harbor offers something for everybody, including whale-watching excursions and dinner theaters.

Innkeeper(s): Susan & David Straight. $69-110. MC VISA DS PC TC. TAC10. 10 rooms with PB, 5 with FP. Breakfast and afternoon tea included in rates. Types of meals: full breakfast and early coffee/tea.

Beds: KQDT. Ceiling fan in room. Fax on premises. Weddings and family reunions hosted. Antiques, fishing, parks, shopping, downhill skiing, cross-country skiing, theater and watersports nearby.

Publicity: *Boothbay Register.*

"England may be the home of the original bed & breakfast, but Kenniston Hill Inn is where it has been perfected!"

Boothbay Harbor   J4

1830 Admiral's Quarters Inn

71 Commercial St
Boothbay Harbor, ME 04538-1003
(207)633-2474 Fax:(207)633-5904
E-mail: loon@admiralsquartersinn.com

Circa 1830. Set on a rise looking out to the sea, this handsome sea captain's house commands a splendid harbor view. The inn is decorated with white wicker and antiques and each accommodation features French doors or sliding glass doors that open to a private deck or terrace to take advantage of the view of the harbor. Guests may walk a short distance to the wharf.

Historic Interest: Maine Maritime Museum.

Innkeeper(s): Les & Deb Hallstrom. $65-125. MC VISA DS TC. 6 rooms with PB. 4 suites. Breakfast and afternoon tea included in rates. Beds: KQT. Phone, ceiling fan and TV in room. Library on premises. Family reunions hosted. Amusement parks, antiques, fishing, parks, shopping, theater and watersports nearby.

Location: On the point of Commercial, facing up the harbor.

Publicity: *Franklin Business Review, Down East Magazine, Yankee Traveler.*

"If you're looking to put down stakes in the heart of Boothbay Harbor, the Admiral's Quarters Inn provides an eagle's eye view on land and at sea —Yankee Traveler."

Harbour Towne Inn on the Waterfront

71 Townsend Ave
Boothbay Harbor, ME 04538-1158
(207)633-4300 (800)722-4240 Fax:(207)633-4300
E-mail: mainco@gwi.net

Circa 1880. This Victorian inn's well-known trademark boasts that it is "the finest B&B on the waterfront." Most of the inn's 12 rooms offer an outside deck and the Penthouse has an outstanding view of the harbor from its private deck. Breakfast is served in the inn's Sunroom, and guests also may relax in the parlor, which has a miniature antique library and a beautiful antique fireplace. A conference area is available for meetings. The inn's meticulous grounds include flower gardens and well-kept shrubs and trees. It's an easy walk to the village and its art galleries, restaurants, shops and boat trips. Special off-season packages are available. Ft. William Henry and the Fisherman's Memorial are nearby.

Historic Interest: Boothbay Region Historical Building (3 blocks), lighthouses (5 to 50 minutes).
Innkeeper(s): George Thomas. $69-275. MC VISA AX DS PC TC. TAC10. 12 rooms with PB. 1 conference room. Breakfast included in rates. Type of meal: continental-plus breakfast. Beds: KQDT. Phone and TV in room. Fax and copier on premises. Handicap access. Weddings, small meetings, family reunions and seminars hosted. Antiques, fishing, parks, shopping, downhill skiing, cross-country skiing, theater and watersports nearby.

Bridgton 12

Noble House

PO Box 180
Bridgton, ME 04009-0180
(207)647-3733 Fax:(207)647-3733

Circa 1903. Located on Highland Lake, this inn is tucked among three acres of old oaks and a grove of pine trees, providing an estate-like view from all guest rooms. The elegant parlor contains a library, grand piano and hearth. Bed chambers are furnished with antiques, wicker and quilts. Three rooms have whirlpool tubs, and family suites are available. A hammock placed at the water's edge provides a view of the lake and Mt. Washington. The inn's lake frontage also allows for canoeing at sunset and swimming. Restaurants are nearby.

Historic Interest: Shaker Village (30 minutes), Willowbrook, a restored 19th-century village (45 minutes), Narramissic, unspoiled early 19th-century rural farm homestead (15 minutes), Songo River Queen, replica of the Mississippi River Stern paddle wheelers (15 minutes).
Innkeeper(s): The Starets Family. $64-125. MC VISA AX. 9 rooms, 6 with PB. 3 suites. Breakfast included in rates. Type of meal: full breakfast. Beds: QDT. Phone in room. Antiques, fishing, downhill skiing, cross-country skiing, theater and watersports nearby.
Location: Forty miles northwest of Portland.
Publicity: *Bridgton News.*

"It's my favorite inn."

Tarry-A-While Resort

Box A, Highland Ridge Rd
Bridgton, ME 04009
(207)647-2522 Fax:(207)647-5512

Circa 1897. Tarry-A-While offers a variety of comfortable accommodations, including a Victorian inn and cottages. There is also a social hall. The resort is located on a 25-acre hillside

and there are plenty of outdoor activities. Tennis and boating are included in the rates, and sailing or waterskiing is available. An 18-hole golf course is a walk away. The inn's dining room, which overlooks Highland Lake and Pleasant Mountain, serves fine cuisine as you gaze at the sunset.

Innkeeper(s): Marc & Nancy Stretch. $70-130. MC VISA PC. 27 rooms, 22 with PB. Breakfast included in rates. Type of meal: continental breakfast. Beds: KQDT. Air conditioning in room. Bicycles and tennis on premises. Weddings, small meetings and family reunions hosted. Antiques, shopping and theater nearby.

"A definite return trip to romantic peaceful memories."

Brooksville 15

Buck's Harbor Inn

Rt 176 Box 268
Brooksville, ME 04617
(207)326-8660 Fax:(207)326-0730

Circa 1901. It was during the days of the steamship that South Brooksville enjoyed its heyday as a vacation resort town. The Buck's Harbor Inn was built at the turn of the century as a bed-

room annex for the Bay View Hotel and eventually became a private residence. Today, it offers six comfortable rooms and close access to the area's bounty of activities. Antiquing and craft shopping abound, and the area boasts wonderful boating and sailing. Acadia National Park offers plenty of outdoor activities.

Historic Interest: The historic towns of Bar Harbor, Camden, Castine, Bangor and Stonington offer plenty of historic sites. Castine, 20 miles from Buck's Harbor Inn, includes an early fort and was the site of several battles. Bangor, once known as the "Queen City," includes many attractions.
Innkeeper(s): Peter & Ann Ebeling. $65-75. MC VISA. 6 rooms. 1 suite. Breakfast included in rates. Type of meal: full breakfast. Beds: QT. Antiques, fishing and cross-country skiing nearby.

Oakland House Seaside Inn & Cottages

Herrick Rd, RR 1 Box 400
Brooksville, ME 04617
(207)359-8521 (800)359-7352
E-mail: littlefield@acadia.net

Guests at this seaside getaway spot enjoy the best of Maine, from the half-mile of private ocean front to the miles of hiking trails. The innkeeper is a descendant of John Billings, who received the property's original land grant from King George of England in the 18th century, and the land has remained in the family since that time. Bed & breakfast

guests stay at a more recent addition to the property, Shore Oaks, a 1907 Craftsman-style home. The interior of this bed & breakfast is decorated with Craftsman-style furnishings and Victorian pieces. The living room has a large stone fireplace, original wicker furnishings, huge multi-paned windows and offers a panoramic view of Penobscot Bay. Breakfasts are served in the dining room, and dinner is served in the on-premises hotel dining rooms. In addition to the bed & breakfast rooms in Shore Oaks, more than a dozen cottages dot the 50-acre property, offering from one to five bedrooms. Many of the cottages include amenities such as kitchenettes and living rooms with fireplaces, and most boast panoramic views of Penobscot Bay. Each of the cottages are unique, a few are more than 100 years old. In-season guests at Shore Oaks are treated to both breakfast and dinner.

Historic Interest: The Brooksville area was a trading post of the Puritans of Plymouth in the early 1600s and was taken by the French in 1635, then captured by the Dutch and later abandoned. Fort George was the largest fort built by the British during the Revolutionary War. In the waters off nearby Castine, America suffered its greatest naval disaster until Pearl Harbor.

Innkeeper(s): Jim & Sally Littlefield. $51-172. MAP. PC TC. TAC10. 10 rooms, 7 with PB, 2 with FP. 15 cottages. 2 conference rooms. Breakfast and dinner included in rates. Types of meals: continental breakfast, continental-plus breakfast, full breakfast and early coffee/tea. Picnic lunch, banquet service, catering service and catered breakfast available. Beds: QDT. VCR, fax, copier, swimming and library on premises. 50 acres. Weddings, small meetings, family reunions and seminars hosted. Antiques, fishing, parks, shopping, cross-country skiing and watersports nearby.

Pets Allowed: In some cottages, not in the inn.

Publicity: *Country Living, Down East.*

"We thoroughly enjoyed the peace, quiet and wonderful smells of pines and salt water. Thanks again for a wonderful get-away place!"

Brunswick J3

Brunswick B&B

165 Park Row
Brunswick, ME 04011-2000
(207)729-4914

Circa 1860. The Brunswick, a Greek Revival-style home, overlooks the town green. Guests often relax in one of the two front parlors, with their inviting fireplaces. Summertime guests enjoy the wraparound front porch. Rooms are filled with antiques, collectibles and quilts. In the years that the bed & breakfast served as a family home for law professor Daniel Stanwood, the home was host to an array of famed personalities, including Edna St. Vincent Millay, Thornton Wilder and Admiral Richard Byrd. Ice skating in the "mall" across the street is a popular winter activity. Freeport, only a 10-minute drive, is perfect for shoppers, and several state parks are nearby. Bowdin College is a short walk away from the inn.

Innkeeper(s): Mercie & Steve Normand. $87-117. MC VISA. 8 rooms with PB. Breakfast included in rates. Types of meals: full breakfast and early coffee/tea. Beds: KQDT. TV, fax and copier on premises. Weddings, small meetings and family reunions hosted. Antiques, fishing, parks, shopping, sporting events and theater nearby.

Publicity: *Times Record, Coastal Journal, Atlanta Journal.*

"Good bed, great shower, fine breakfast (nice mix of substance and sweets and excellent java) and of course convivial hosts."

Camden I5

A Little Dream

66 High St
Camden, ME 04843-1735
(207)236-8742

Circa 1888. This Victorian was built as a guest cottage on an estate that is the home to Norumberg Castle, a vast manor built by the inventor of the dual teletype, J.B. Stearns. The rooms are wonder-  fully romantic, displaying a divine English-country ambiance. One room features a pencil-post bed decorated with dried flowers. Another boasts a cozy sitting area with a fireplace. Whimsical touches include a collection of teddy bears and antique toys. Views of the bay and islands add to the romance. Breakfasts are artfully displayed on fine china. Edible flowers decorate plates with items such as an apple-brie omelet or lemon-ricotta pancakes with a raspberry sauce. Guests, if they can tear themselves away from the inn, are sure to leave rejuvenated.

Innkeeper(s): JoAnna Ball & Bill Fontana. $95-159. MC VISA AX PC TC. 7 rooms with PB, 1 with FP. 2 suites. Breakfast and afternoon tea included in rates. Types of meals: gourmet breakfast and early coffee/tea. Beds: KQ. Phone, air conditioning, turndown service, TV and VCR in room. Library on premises. French, German and Italian spoken. Antiques, fishing, parks, shopping, downhill skiing, cross-country skiing, golf, theater and watersports nearby.

Publicity: *Country Inns, Glamour, Yankee Magazine, Country Living.*

Abigail's B&B By The Sea

8 High St
Camden, ME 04843-1611
(207)236-2501 (800)292-2501 Fax:(207)230-0657
E-mail: abigails@midcoast.com

Circa 1847. This Federal home was the former residence of Maine senator E.K. Smart. Each guest room is decorated with poster beds, antiques, quilts, fireplaces and Jacuzzis. English chintzes and wicker abound. Enjoy breakfast in bed or share it with other guests in the sunny dining room. Everything from French toast, scones and fresh fruit to souffles and quiche highlight the meal. An afternoon tea is served in the parlor, which boasts two fireplaces. Unique shops, galleries and musical festivals and craft fairs are but a few ways to enjoy this harbor-side town.

Innkeeper(s): Donna & Ed Misner. $85-145. MC VISA AX. 4 rooms with PB. 2 suites. Breakfast and afternoon tea included in rates. Type of meal: full

breakfast. Beds: QT. Phone in room. Antiques, fishing, downhill skiing, cross-country skiing, golf, theater and watersports nearby.

Location: Historic district.

"Wonderful, romantic place for our eighth wedding anniversary."

Captain Swift Inn

72 Elm St
Camden, ME 04843-1907
(207)236-8113 (800)251-0865 Fax:(207)230-0464
E-mail: swiftinn@midcoast.com

Circa 1810. This inviting Federal-style home remains much as it did in the 19th century, including the original 12-over-12

windows and a beehive oven. The innkeepers have worked diligently to preserve the historic flavor, and the home's original five fireplaces, handsome wide pine floors, restored moldings and exposed beams add to the warm and cozy interior. Guest rooms are filled with period antiques and reproductions and offer down pillows, handmade quilts and comfortable beds. The only addition to the home was a new section, which includes the innkeeper's quarters, a kitchen and a guest room entirely accessible for guests with wheelchairs. A gourmet, three-course breakfast includes items that sound decadent, but are truly low in fat and cholesterol, such as an apple pancake soufflé.

Innkeeper(s): Tom & Kathy Filip. $75-110. MC VISA PC TC. TAC10. 4 rooms with PB. Breakfast and afternoon tea included in rates. Types of meals: full breakfast, gourmet breakfast and early coffee/tea. Beds: QT. Air conditioning in room. TV, VCR, fax, copier and library on premises. Handicap access. Small meetings and family reunions hosted. Antiques, fishing, parks, shopping, downhill skiing, cross-country skiing, golf, theater and watersports nearby.

Publicity: *Maine Boats & Harbors, Boston Patriot Ledger, Tea-Time Journeys, Secrets of Entertaining, Wake Up & Smell the Coffee.*

"We came intending to stay for one night and ended up staying for five. . .need we say more!"

Castleview By The Sea

59 High St
Camden, ME 04843-1733
(207)236-2344 (800)272-8439

Circa 1856. This classic American cape house is the only B&B located on the waterside of the ocean view section of Camden's flowered historic district. Guest rooms feature wide pine floors, beamed ceilings, stained glass and balconies. The inn reflects the owner's world-wide travel in its eclectic decorating. Guests can literally enjoy views of the ocean right from their bed. Rooms offer cable TV and air conditioning.

Historic Interest: Tennis is located next to the property. Antiques, fishing, hiking, shopping, theater, museums, downhill and cross-country skiing, boating and sailing are located nearby.

Innkeeper(s): Bill Butler. $75-175. MC VISA PC. TAC10. 3 rooms with PB. Breakfast included in rates. Types of meals: continental-plus breakfast and full breakfast. Beds: KQ. Phone, air conditioning, ceiling fan, TV and VCR in room. Library on premises. Family reunions hosted. Antiques, fishing, parks, shopping, downhill skiing, cross-country skiing, theater and watersports nearby.

"Wonderful food, wonderful view, wonderful host."

Elms B&B

84 Elm St, Rt 1
Camden, ME 04843-1907
(207)236-6250 (800)755-3567 Fax:(207)236-7330
E-mail: theelms@midcoast.com

Circa 1806. Captain Calvin Curtis built this Colonial a few minutes' stroll from the picturesque harbor. Candlelight shimmers year round from the inn's windows. A sitting room, library and parlor are open for guests. Tastefully appointed bed chambers scattered with antiques are available in both the main house and the carriage house. A cottage garden can be seen beside the carriage house. A lighthouse theme permeates the decor, and there is a wide selection of lighthouse books, collectibles and artwork.

Historic Interest: Guests can take a boat tour and view Camden's Curtis Island lighthouse, which has been in operation since the late 19th century. There are a variety of lighthouses and maritime museums within an hour to an hour and a half of Camden, including active lighthouses that date back to the 1820s.

Innkeeper(s): Ted & Jo Panayotoff. $65-95. MC VISA PC TC. 6 rooms with PB, 1 with FP. Breakfast and afternoon tea included in rates. Types of meals: continental breakfast, full breakfast and early coffee/tea. Beds: QDT. Phone in room. Handicap access. Antiques, fishing, parks, shopping, downhill skiing, cross-country skiing and theater nearby.

"If something is worth doing, it's worth doing first class, and your place is definitely first class."

Hartstone Inn

41 Elm St
Camden, ME 04843-1910
(207)236-4259 (800)788-4823

Circa 1835. A third story, mansard roof and large bay windows were added to this house at the turn-of-the-century, changing it to a stately Victorian. Both the parlor and dining room feature fireplaces. A carriage house with barn beams, kitchen, skylights and sleeping loft is available as well as the comfortable rooms in the main house. Located in the village, the inn is a block away from the harbor with its fleet of windjammers.

Innkeeper(s): Sunny & Peter Simmons. $70-135. MC VISA AX PC TC. TAC10. 10 rooms with PB, 2 with FP. 2 suites. Breakfast included in rates. Types of meals: full breakfast, gourmet breakfast and early coffee/tea. Afternoon tea available. Beds: KQDT. Phone and air conditioning in room. TV and library on premises. Weddings, small meetings and family reunions hosted. Antiques, fishing, parks, shopping, downhill skiing, cross-country skiing, theater and watersports nearby.

Publicity: *Bangor Daily News, Newsday.*

"When can I move in?"

Hawthorn Inn

9 High St
Camden, ME 04843-1610
(207)236-8842 Fax:(207)236-6181
E-mail: hawthorn@midcoast.com

Circa 1894. This handsome yellow and white turreted
Victorian sits on an acre and a half of sloping lawns with a view
of the harbor. The interior boasts a grand,
three-story staircase and original
stained-glass windows.
The inn has 10 rooms
all with private baths.
The carriage house
rooms offer private
decks, double
Jacuzzi tubs and
fireplaces. Breakfasts with fresh
fruit, coffeecakes and egg dishes are served by fireside, or during warm weather, guests are invited to eat on the deck overlooking the harbor.

Historic Interest: Downtown Camden has been restored and features many
shops, galleries and restaurants nestled around its beautiful harbor.

Innkeeper(s): Nicholas & Patricia Wharton. $80-185. MC VISA AX PC TC.
TAC10. 10 rooms with PB, 3 with FP. Breakfast included in rates. Types of
meals: full breakfast and early coffee/tea. Beds: QDT. Phone, TV and VCR in
room. Fax on premises. Small meetings hosted. Antiques, fishing, parks, shopping, downhill skiing, cross-country skiing, theater and watersports nearby.

Publicity: *Glamour, Country Inns, Outside, Yankee, Down East, Cleveland
Plain Dealer, Minneapolis Tribune.*

*"The outstanding location, excellent rates and marvelous innkeepers
make this one of the B&Bs we will be frequenting for years to come."*

Lord Camden Inn

24 Main St
Camden, ME 04843-1704
(207)236-4325 (800)336-4325 Fax:(207)236-7141
E-mail: lordcam@midcoast.com

Circa 1893. Lord Camden Inn, housed in a century-old brick
building, offers the gentle warmth of a seaside inn with all the
comforts and services of a modern downtown hotel. Located in
the midst of Camden's fine shops and restaurants, the bustling
waterfront and beautiful parks, Lord Camden Inn offers splendid views of the harbor, Camden Hill and the village. Amenities
include private baths, cable TV, air conditioning, phones and
elevator services.

Historic Interest: Conway House (1 mile), Fort Knox (45 minutes), Children
Chapel (1 1/2 mile), Owls Head Museum Montpelier (8 miles), Lime Klins
Rockport Harbor.

Innkeeper(s): Stuart & Marianne Smith. $88-178. MC VISA PC. TAC10. 31
rooms with PB. 4 suites. 2 conference rooms. Breakfast included in rates.
Types of meals: continental-plus breakfast and early coffee/tea. Beds: KQD.
Phone in room. Fax and copier on premises. Weddings, small meetings, family reunions and seminars hosted. Antiques, fishing, parks, shopping, downhill
skiing, cross-country skiing, theater and watersports nearby.

The Maine Stay Inn

22 High St
Camden, ME 04843-1735
(207)236-9636

Circa 1802. The innkeepers of this treasured colonial, that is
one of the oldest of the 66 houses which comprise the High
Street Historic District, take great pleasure in making guests

feel at home. One of the trio of innkeepers is known for his
ìdown-eastî stories told in a heavy ìdown-eastî accent.
Antiques from the 17th, 18th and 19th centuries adorn the
rooms. The center of the village and the Camden Harbor are a
short five-minute walk away.

Historic Interest: The Camden Opera House, historic mill and manufacturing
buildings, and the First Congregational Church are among the area's historic sites.

Innkeeper(s): Peter & Donny Smith & Diana Robson. $95-140. MC VISA AX. 8
rooms with PB, 4 with FP. Breakfast included in rates. Beds: QT. Phone in room.

Publicity: *Miami Herald, Lewiston Sun-Journal, Country Inns, Glamour,
Country Living, Rand McNally's Best B&Bs, Discerning Traveler, Bazaar,
Boston Globe, Down East Magazine.*

*"We've traveled the East Coast from Martha's Vineyard to Bar
Harbor and this is the only place we know we must return to."*

The Swan House

49 Mountain St
Camden, ME 04843-1635
(207)236-8275 (800)207-8275 Fax:(207)236-0906
E-mail: swanhse@midcoast.com

Circa 1870. Nestled on just under an acre of wooded grounds
at the foot of Mt. Battie, this Victorian is a welcoming site
inside and out. Antique-filled guest rooms are comfortable,

each named for a different variety of swan. Four of the rooms
offer private entrances. The Lohengrin Suite is a spacious
room with its own sitting area, while the Trumpeter Room
offers a private deck. Hearty breakfasts include country-style
fare, fruit, homemade granola and special pastry of the day.
The village of Camden and the surrounding area offer plenty of
activities, and the innkeepers are happy to point guests in an
interesting direction.

Innkeeper(s): Lyn & Ken Kohl. $70-125. MC VISA PC TC. 6 rooms with PB. 1
suite. Breakfast included in rates. Types of meals: full breakfast and early cof-
fee/tea. Afternoon tea available. Beds: QD. Phone in room. Fax on premises.
Small meetings and family reunions hosted. Antiques, fishing, parks, shopping, downhill skiing, cross-country skiing, theater and watersports nearby.

*"We loved our stay at the Swan House and our breakfast there was
by far the most excellent breakfast we have ever had."*

Corea   17

The Black Duck Inn on Corea Harbor

PO Box 39
Corea, ME 04624-0039
(207)963-2689 Fax:(207)963-7495
E-mail: bduck@acadia.net

Circa 1890. Two of the guest rooms at this turn-of-the-century
farmhouse boast harbor views, while another offers a wooded
scene out its windows. The innkeepers have decorated the
home in an eclectic mix of old and new with antiques and contemporary pieces. There are two waterfront cottages for those
who prefer more privacy. The full, gourmet breakfasts include

house specialties, such as "eggs Black Duck" or items such as orange glazed French toast, blintzes or perhaps eggs Benedict.
Innkeeper(s): Barry Canner & Bob Travers. $70-140. MC VISA PC TC. TAC10. 4 rooms, 2 with PB. 1 suite. 2 cottages. Breakfast included in rates. Types of meals: gourmet breakfast and early coffee/tea. Beds: QDT. TV, VCR, fax, bicycles and library on premises. 12 acres. Weddings and family reunions hosted. Danish spoken. Antiques, fishing, parks, shopping, cross-country skiing and watersports nearby.

"Never could we have known how warmly received we would all feel and how really restored we would be by the end of the week."

Damariscotta Mills

Mill Pond Inn

50 Main St
Damariscotta Mills, ME 04555
(207)563-8014

Circa 1780. The one acre of grounds surrounding this 18th-century home are packed with scenery. A pond with a waterfall flows into the adjacent Damariscotta Lake and trees offer plenty of shade. Rooms are decorated in a whimsical country style and they have pond views and fresh flowers. Breakfasts are served in a room that overlooks the pond and grounds. Innkeeper Bobby Whear is a registered Maine guide, and the innkeepers offer private fishing trips. Complimentary canoeing and biking are available.
Innkeeper(s): Bobby & Sherry Whear. $80. 6 rooms with PB, 3 with FP. 1 suite. Breakfast and afternoon tea included in rates. Types of meals: full breakfast and early coffee/tea. Beds: KQT. TV, VCR, fax, copier and bicycles on premises. Weddings, small meetings, family reunions and seminars hosted. Antiques, fishing, parks, shopping, downhill skiing, cross-country skiing, sporting events, theater and watersports nearby.

Dennysville   G8

Lincoln House Country Inn

Rts 1 & 86
Dennysville, ME 04628
(207)726-3953 Fax:(207)726-0654

Circa 1787. Theodore Lincoln, son of General Benjamin Lincoln, who accepted the sword of surrender from Cornwallis after the American Revolution, built this house. The four-

square Colonial looks out to the Dennys River and its salmon pools. John James Audubon stayed here on his way to Labrador. He loved the house and family so much that he named the Lincoln Sparrow in their honor.
Historic Interest: Listed in the National Register.
Innkeeper(s): Mary & Jerry Haggerty. $68-85. MC VISA PC TC. TAC10. 6 rooms, 2 with PB, 2 with FP. 1 conference room. Breakfast included in rates. Types of meals: full breakfast, gourmet breakfast and early coffee/tea. Beds: QDT. Library on premises. 100 acres. Antiques, fishing, parks, shopping, cross-country skiing and watersports nearby.
Location: On the Dennys River.
Publicity: *Good Housekeeping, Washington Post, New York Times.*

"The food was delicious, the ambiance special."

Dexter   G4

Brewster Inn of Dexter, Maine

37 Zions Hill Rd
Dexter, ME 04930-1122
(207)924-3130
E-mail: brewster@nconline.net

Circa 1935. Located on two acres with rose and perennial gardens, this handsome Colonial Revival-style house was built by architect John Calvin  Stevens for Governor Ralph Brewster. It is in the National Register. Some guest rooms offer fireplaces, window seats, original tile bathrooms and views of the gardens. One has a whirlpool tub. Furnishings include antiques and reproductions. A breakfast buffet includes hot entrees such as quiche, gingerbread pancakes or stuffed apples.
Innkeeper(s): Ivy & Michael Brooks. $59-89. MC VISA PC TC. TAC10. 5 rooms with PB, 3 with FP. 2 suites. Breakfast and afternoon tea included in rates. Types of meals: full breakfast and early coffee/tea. Picnic lunch available. Beds: KQDT. Air conditioning and TV in room. Fax, bicycles and tennis on premises. Handicap access. Weddings, small meetings, family reunions and seminars hosted. Spanish spoken. Antiques, fishing, parks, shopping, downhill skiing, cross-country skiing, golf and watersports nearby.

Durham   I3

The Bagley House

1290 Royalsborough Rd
Durham, ME 04222-5225
(207)865-6566 (800)765-1772 Fax:(207)353-5878

Circa 1772. Six acres of fields and woods surround the Bagley House. Once an inn, a store and a schoolhouse in town. Guest rooms are decorated with colonial furnishings and hand-sewn Maine quilts. For breakfast, guests gather in the country kitchen in front of a huge brick fireplace and beehive oven.
Historic Interest: Bowdoin College, Maritime Museum and Old Sea Captain Homes.

Innkeeper(s): Suzanne O'Connor & Susan Backhouse. $70-125. MC VISA AX DS. 5 rooms with PB, 1 with FP. 1 conference room. Breakfast and afternoon tea included in rates. Types of meals: full breakfast and early coffee/tea. Evening snack and picnic lunch available. Beds: QDT. Phone in room. Fax on premises. Small meetings and family reunions hosted. Antiques, shopping, downhill skiing, cross-country skiing, sporting events and theater nearby.
Location: Route 136, Durham.
Publicity: *Los Angeles Times, New England Getaways, Lewiston Sun, Springfield Register.*

"I had the good fortune to stumble on the Bagley House. The rooms are well-appointed and the innkeeper is as charming a host as you'll find."

East Boothbay
J4

Ocean Point Inn

Shore Rd
East Boothbay, ME 04544
(207)633-4200 (800)552-5554

Circa 1890. Ocean Point Inn is comprised of a white clapboard main house, lodge, cottages, apartments and motel units located on three oceanfront acres. There are gardens and a lovely road along the bay where guests watch lobstermen, seals and passing windjammers. Four lighthouses may be viewed among the nearby islands. Boothbay Harbor is six miles away, but right at hand is the pier and the inn's restaurant with a view of the ocean. In addition to lobster dishes and crabcakes, the specialty of the house is fresh Maine salmon poached in Court Boullion served with dill sauce. Select from a wide choice of activities such as swimming, fishing and hiking, or simply settle into the Adirondack chairs and watch the soothing sea. Guests can rent motor boats or kayaks in Boothbay Harbor.

Innkeeper(s): Beth & Dave Dudley. $67-154. EP. MC VISA AX DS TC. 61 rooms with PB, 3 with FP. 10 suites. 7 cottages. Type of meal: full breakfast. Dinner available. Beds: KQTD. Phone, air conditioning and TV in room. Swimming on premises. Family reunions hosted. Antiques, fishing, parks, shopping, golf, theater and watersports nearby.

Eastport
G8

The Milliken House

29 Washington St
Eastport, ME 04631-1324
(207)853-2955

Circa 1846. This inn is filled with beautiful furnishings and knickknacks, much of which belonged to the home's first owner, Benjamin Milliken. Ornately carved, marble-topped pieces and period decor take guests back in time to the Victorian Era. Milliken maintained a wharf on Eastport's waterfront from which he serviced the tall trading ships that used the harbor as a port of entry to the United States. An afternoon glass of port or sherry and chocolate turn-down service are among the amenities. Breakfasts are a gourmet treat, served in the dining room with its carved, antique furnishings.

Historic Interest: The waterfront historic district is just two blocks away as is the Barracks Historical Museum.

Innkeeper(s): Joyce Weber. $40-60. MC VISA AX PC TC. 5 rooms. 1 conference room. Breakfast included in rates. Type of meal: full breakfast. Beds: QT. Phone in room.

"Your lovely place is so homey - fantastic breakfast!"

Weston House

26 Boynton St
Eastport, ME 04631-1305
(207)853-2907 (800)853-2907

Circa 1810. Jonathan Weston, an 1802 Harvard graduate, built this Federal-style house on a hill overlooking Passamaquoddy Bay. John Audubon stayed here as a guest of the Westons while awaiting passage to Labrador in 1833. Each guest room is furnished with antiques and Oriental rugs. The Weston and Audubon rooms boast views of the bay and gardens. Breakfast menus vary, including such delectables as heavenly pancakes with hot apricot syrup or

freshly baked muffins and coddled eggs. Seasonal brunches are served on weekends and holidays. The area is full of outdoor activities, including whale watching. Nearby Saint Andrews-by-the-Sea offers plenty of shops and restaurants.

Historic Interest: Nearby historic attractions include Campobello Island, where Franklin D. Roosevelt spent his summers. King's Landing, a restored Loyalist settlement dating back to 1780, is two hours away.

Innkeeper(s): Jett & John Peterson. $55-75. PC TC. 5 rooms, 1 with FP. 1 suite. 1 conference room. Breakfast and afternoon tea included in rates. Type of meal: gourmet breakfast. Picnic lunch and catering service available. Beds: KQDT. TV in room. Weddings, small meetings and family reunions hosted. Fishing, shopping and theater nearby.

Publicity: *Down East, Los Angeles Times, Boston Globe, Boston Magazine, New York Times.*

"All parts of ourselves have been nourished."

Eliot
L2

Moses Paul Inn

270 Goodwin Rd
Eliot, ME 03903-1204
(207)439-1861 (800)552-6058

Circa 1780. This Colonial farmhouse is charming and hard to miss, with its barn-red exterior and white trim. The home is truly welcoming. Restored wood floors and woodwork gleam, and rooms, some with exposed beams, are decorated with treasures the innkeepers found at local auctions. Quilts, antiques and country furnishings are among the finds. The restored barn serves as an antique shop. Be sure to ask the innkeepers about a French soldier who may still inhabit the halls in ghostly form. Kittery Outlet Malls and historic Portsmouth are just a few minutes away, as is the coastline.

Innkeeper(s): Joanne Weiss & Larry James. $55-75. MC VISA DS PC TC. 5 rooms, 2 with PB. Breakfast included in rates. Type of meal: full breakfast. Beds: QDT. Ceiling fan in room. TV, VCR, fax and library on premises. Weddings, small meetings, family reunions and seminars hosted. American Sign Language spoken. Amusement parks, antiques, fishing, parks, shopping, downhill skiing, cross-country skiing, sporting events, theater and watersports nearby.

Freeport J3

Atlantic Seal B&B

PO Box 146
Freeport, ME 04032-0146
(207)865-6112

Circa 1850. The Atlantic Seal is situated in a seaside neighborhood overlooking South Freeport Harbor. The guest rooms, all

with harbor views, are named after sailing vessels built in local shipyards long ago. The Cape Cod-style home is furnished with antiques and nautical collections of the hosts, Captain Thomas Ring. There is an old-fashioned parlor with a fireplace and a private deck overlooking the harbor. L.L. Bean and other outlet stores are nearby.

Innkeeper(s): Captain Thomas Ring. $75-135. 4 rooms with PB. Breakfast included in rates. Type of meal: full breakfast. Beds: KQD.

Publicity: *Yankee.*

Captain Josiah Mitchell House

188 Main St
Freeport, ME 04032-1407
(207)865-3289

Circa 1789. Captain Josiah Mitchell was commander of the clipper ship "Hornet." In 1866, en route from New York to San Francisco it caught fire, burned and was lost. The passengers and crew survived in three longboats, drifting for 45 days. When the boats finally drifted into one of the South Pacific Islands, Samuel Clemens was there, befriended the Captain and wrote his first story, under the name of Mark Twain and about the captain. The diary of Captain Mitchell parallels episodes of "Mutiny on the Bounty." Flower gardens and a porch swing on the veranda now welcome guests to Freeport and Captain Mitchell's House.

Historic Interest: Henry Wadsworth Longfellow house (13 miles), Admiral McMillan, polar explorer with Perry, Bowdoin College (7 miles) and Freeport.

Innkeeper(s): Alan & Loretta Bradley. $69-95. MC VISA PC TC. TAC10. 7 rooms with PB. Breakfast included in rates. Type of meal: full breakfast. Beds: QDT. Air conditioning and ceiling fan in room. Amusement parks, antiques, fishing, parks, shopping, downhill skiing, cross-country skiing, sporting events and theater nearby.

Publicity: *Famous Boats and Harbors.*

"Your wonderful stories brought us all together. You have created a special place that nurtures and brings happiness and love. This has been a dream!"

Country at Heart B&B

37 Bow St
Freeport, ME 04032-1519
(207)865-0512

Circa 1870. This cozy country home is decorated with handmade crafts and antiques. The Shaker Room has a hand-stenciled border with Shaker accents throughout. A Shaker peg rack surrounds the room. The Quilt Room has a heart stenciled border with quilt related wall hangings and antique quilts. The

Teddy Bear Room is full of, you guessed it, bears of all shapes and sizes. Breakfast is served on an eight-foot oak dining room table.

Innkeeper(s): Roger & Kim Dubay. $65-85. MC VISA PC TC. TAC10. 3 rooms with PB. Breakfast and afternoon tea included in rates. Types of meals: full breakfast and early coffee/tea. Beds: QDT. Ceiling fan in room. TV and VCR on premises. Antiques, fishing, parks, shopping, cross-country skiing, sporting events, theater and watersports nearby.

"Thank you for your genuine hospitality! Wonderful breakfast too!"

Harraseeket Inn

162 Main St
Freeport, ME 04032-1311
(207)865-9377 (800)342-6423 Fax:(207)865-1684

Circa 1889. The tavern and drawing room of this inn are decorated in the Federal style. Guest rooms are furnished with antiques and half-canopied beds. Some have whirlpools and fireplaces. The L.L. Bean store is just two blocks away, with other outlet stores such as Ralph Lauren, Neiman Marcus and Anne Klein nearby.

Innkeeper(s): Gray Family. $95-225. EP. MC VISA AX DC DS. TAC10. 84 rooms, 54 with PB, 16 with FP. 3 suites. 5 conference rooms. Breakfast and afternoon tea included in rates. Type of meal: gourmet breakfast. Dinner, lunch and room service available. Restaurant on premises. Beds: KQD. Fax, copier and spa on premises. Handicap access. Antiques, fishing, cross-country skiing and theater nearby.

Ratings: *4 Diamonds.*

The Isaac Randall House

5 Independence Dr
Freeport, ME 04032-1110
(207)865-9295 (800)865-9295 Fax:(207)865-9003
E-mail: ikesspot@aol.com

Circa 1823. Isaac Randall's Federal-style farmhouse was once a dairy farm and a stop on the Underground Railway for slaves escaping into Canada. Randall was a descendant of John Alden

and Priscilla Mullins of the Mayflower. Longfellow immortalized their romance in "The Courtship of Miles Standish." The inn is located on six wooded acres with a pond. Guest rooms are air-conditioned.

Innkeeper(s): Cindy Wellito. $65-125. MC VISA DS. TAC10. 10 rooms with PB, 5 with FP. 1 conference room. Breakfast and evening snack included in rates. Type of meal: full breakfast. Beds: KQT. Phone and air conditioning in room. TV, VCR, fax, copier, spa, library and child care on premises. Weddings, small meetings, family reunions and seminars hosted. French and Spanish spoken. Antiques, fishing, parks, shopping, cross-country skiing, sporting events, golf, theater and watersports nearby.

Pets Allowed: Not to be left alone in rooms uncrated.

Location: At the south edge of Freeport Village.

Publicity: *Toronto Star, Early American Life, Newsday.*

"Enchanted to find ourselves surrounded by all your charming antiques and beautiful furnishings."

John Briggs House B&B

8 Maple Ave
Freeport, ME 04032-1315
(207)865-1868 (800)217-2477

Circa 1853. This mid-19th-century home's most notable resident was John A. Briggs, a shipbuilder whose ancestors arrived in America via the Mayflower. There are five comfortable guest rooms, offering beds topped with quilts and country decor. A full breakfast prepares guests for a day of outlet shopping in Freeport. The famous L.L. Bean factory store and about a hundred more outlets are just minutes away. Harbor cruises, fishing, whale watching, hiking and just enjoying the scenery in this coastal town are other options.

Innkeeper(s): Frank Family. $66-96. MC VISA PC TC. 5 rooms with PB. Breakfast included in rates. Type of meal: full breakfast. Beds: KQDT. Phone and air conditioning in room. TV and VCR on premises. Small meetings and family reunions hosted. Antiques, fishing, parks, shopping, downhill skiing, cross-country skiing, sporting events, golf, theater and watersports nearby.

Georgetown   J3

The Grey Havens

PO Box 308
Georgetown, ME 04548-0308
(207)371-2616 Fax:(207)371-2274

Circa 1904. For more than 20 summers, members of the Texas-based Hardcastle family have returned to welcome guests to this handsome shingle-style hotel on Georgetown Island. From the wraparound porch and many of the rooms, guests may view the harbor, the inn's deep-water dock, rowboats, islands, lighthouses and the open ocean. The lounge features a huge rock fireplace and a 12-foot-tall window. Furnishings are antique. Ask for one of the four turret rooms for a 180-degree ocean view. Reid State Park, Bath, the Maine Maritime Museum and Freeport are nearby.

Innkeeper(s): Bill & Haley Eberhart. $100-195. MC VISA PC TC. 12 rooms with PB. 1 suite. 1 conference room. Breakfast and evening snack included in rates. Types of meals: continental-plus breakfast and early coffee/tea. Beds: KQD. Fax, copier and bicycles on premises. Weddings, small meetings, family reunions and seminars hosted. Antiques, fishing, parks, shopping and watersports nearby.

Greenville   F4

Greenville Inn

Norris St, PO Box 1194
Greenville, ME 04441
(207)695-2206 (888)695-6000 Fax:(207)695-2206

Circa 1895. Lumber baron William Shaw built this inn, which sits on a hill overlooking Moosehead Lake and the Squaw Mountains. The inn includes many unique features. Ten years were needed to complete the embellishments on the cherry and mahogany paneling, which is found throughout the inn. A spruce tree is painted on one of the leaded-glass windows on the stairway landing. The inn's six fireplaces are adorned with carved mantels, English tiles and mosaics. The inn's dining room is ideal for a romantic dinner. Fresh, seasonal ingredients fill the ever-changing menu, and the dining room also offers a variety of wine choices.

Historic Interest: SS Katahdin, restored steamship offering daily cruises, in season (nearby), Moosehead Marine Museum (nearby), Evelyn Craft-Sheridan Historical House Museum (2 miles).

Innkeeper(s): Elfi, Michael and Susie Schnetzer. $95-195. MC VISA DS PC TC. TAC10. 5 rooms, 12 with PB, 2 with FP. 1 suite. 6 cottages. Type of meal: continental-plus breakfast. Dinner available. Restaurant on premises. Beds: KQDT. Weddings, small meetings and family reunions hosted. German & French spoken.

Location: Moosehead Lake, Greenville.

Publicity: *Maine Times, Portland Monthly, Bangor Daily News, Grays Sporting Journal.*

"The fanciest place in town. It is indeed a splendid place."

Isle Au Haut   I5

The Keeper's House

PO Box 26
Isle Au Haut, ME 04645-0026
(207)367-2261

Circa 1907. Designed and built by the U.S. Lighthouse Service, the handsome 48-foot-high Robinson Point Light guided vessels into this once-bustling island fishing village. Guests arrive on the mailboat. Innkeeper Judi Burke, whose father was a keeper at the Highland Lighthouse on Cape Cod, provides picnic lunches so guests may explore the scenic island trails. Dinner is served in the keeper's dining room. The lighthouse is adjacent to the most remote section of Acadia National Park. It's not uncommon to hear the cry of an osprey, see deer approach the inn, or watch seals and porpoises cavorting off the point. Guest rooms are comfortable and serene, with stunning views of the island's ragged shore line, forests and Duck Harbor.

Historic Interest: Acadia National Park, adjacent 18th-century one-room school house, church & town hall (1-mile walk away).

Innkeeper(s): Jeff & Judi Burke. $250-285. PC TC. 6 rooms. 1 cottage. Breakfast, dinner and picnic lunch included in rates. Types of meals: full breakfast, gourmet breakfast and early coffee/tea. Afternoon tea, lunch and gourmet lunch available. Beds: D. Swimming, bicycles and library on premises. Weddings, small meetings, family reunions and seminars hosted. Spanish spoken. Parks and shopping nearby.

Location: A small island six miles south of Stonington, reached by mailboat.

Publicity: *New York Times, USA Today, Los Angeles Times, Ladies Home Journal, Christian Science Monitor, Down East, New York Woman, Philadelphia Inquirer, McCalls, Country, Men's Journal, Travel & Leisure.*

"Simply one of the unique places on Earth."

Kennebunk K2

Arundel Meadows Inn

PO Box 1129
Kennebunk, ME 04043-1129
(207)985-3770
E-mail: docmy@aol.com

Circa 1827. This expansive farmhouse features seven bedrooms, each with their own sitting areas. Three rooms boast
fireplaces. A gourmet breakfast is prepared by innkeeper Mark
Bachelder, who studied under Madeleine Kamman, a popular

chef on PBS. Mark's freshly baked delicacies also are served
during afternoon teas. Antiques and paintings by innkeeper
Murray Yaeger decorate the house. Nearby Kennebunkport provides excellent shopping at factory outlets, antique galleries and
a variety of restaurants.

Historic Interest: Rachel Carson Reserve and Laud Holm Farm (5 miles),
Brick Stone Museum (2 miles), Kennebunkport Historical Society (Nott
House, etc.), tours of homes and Historical Landmarks (5 miles), Strawberry
Bank Restorations (18 miles south).

Innkeeper(s): Mark Bachelder & Murray Yaeger. $65-125. 7 rooms with PB.
3 with FP. 2 suites. Breakfast and afternoon tea included in rates. Type of
meal: full breakfast. Beds: KQDT. Antiques, theater and watersports nearby.

Publicity: *York County Coast Star.*

"The room was beautiful. Breakfast wonderful."

William Lord Mansion

20 Summer St
Kennebunk, ME 04043-1823
(207)985-6213

Circa 1760. Positioned on four handsomely landscaped acres
within the historic district, this rambling white clapboard colonial inn is in the National Register. Stately homes in the neighborhood add to the gracious atmosphere. High ceilings, fine
woodwork, hardwood floors and beautifully crafted fireplaces
are features of the inn. For a special celebration, request the
room with the king-size Austrian wedding bed, whirlpool tub
and fireplace in both the bedroom and bath. Stroll the village,
or relax and enjoy the inn's gardens. Breakfasts are offered in
the elegantly appointed dining room.

Innkeeper(s): Shirley Loewy. $150-175. PC. 2 rooms with PB. Breakfast
included in rates. Type of meal: gourmet breakfast. Beds: KQ. Phone, turndown
service and TV in room. VCR on premises. Weddings hosted. Antiques, fishing,
parks, shopping, cross-country skiing, golf, theater and watersports nearby.

Kennebunk Beach K2

The Ocean View

171 Beach Ave
Kennebunk Beach, ME 04043-2524
(207)967-2750

Circa 1900. This brightly painted Victorian is literally just
steps to the beach. Nine oceanfront guest rooms are located
either in the turn-of-the-century Victorian or in the Ocean View
Too, a wing of the main house with four suites. Hand-painted
furniture and colorful fabrics decorate the whimsical, eclectic
guest rooms. Breakfast is served in an oceanfront breakfast
room. Specialties, which are served on colorful china, include
baked pears with yogurt, honey and slivered almonds, followed
by Belgian waffles topped with seasonal fresh fruit and a dollop
creme fraiche. Suite guests also can opt to enjoy breakfast in
bed. The village of Kennebunkport is just one mile away.

Historic Interest: National Register Historic Walk.

Innkeeper(s): Carole & Bob Arena. $95-225. MC VISA AX DS TC. 9 rooms
with PB. 5 suites. Breakfast and afternoon tea included in rates. Types of
meals: gourmet breakfast and early coffee/tea. Beds: KQT. Phone, ceiling fan,
TV and VCR in room. Fax and library on premises. French spoken. Antiques,
fishing, parks, shopping, sporting events, theater and watersports nearby.

Location: National Wildlife Refuge.

Publicity: *Boston Magazine, New York Times Syndicated, Entree, Elegance.*

Kennebunkport K2

Captain Jefferds Inn

PO Box 691, 5 Pearl St
Kennebunkport, ME 04046-0691
(207)967-2311 (800)839-6844 Fax:(207)967-0721
E-mail: captjeff@captainjefferdsinn

Circa 1804. This Federal-style home was given as a wedding
gift from a father to his daughter and new son-in-law. It was
constructed the same year Thomas Jefferson was re-elected to
the presidency. Each
guest room is differ-
ent. Several offer
clawfoot tubs, six
have a fireplace.
Canopy, four-poster
and sleigh beds
are among the fur-
nishings. In the afternoons, tea is served in the garden room.

The breakfasts feature gourmet fare and are served by candlelight. The inn is located in a local historic district, just minutes
from shops and restaurants.

Innkeeper(s): Pat & Dick Bartholomew. $105-240. MC VISA PC TC. TAC10.
16 rooms with PB, 6 with FP. 5 suites. Breakfast and afternoon tea included
in rates. Types of meals: continental breakfast, gourmet breakfast and early
coffee/tea. Beds: KQDT. Turndown service and ceiling fan in room. TV, VCR,
fax and library on premises. Weddings, small meetings and family reunions
hosted. Antiques, fishing, parks, shopping, downhill skiing, cross-country skiing, golf and watersports nearby.

Pets Allowed: Dogs with prior approval.

The Captain Lord Mansion

Corner Pleasant & Green, PO Box 800
Kennebunkport, ME 04046
(207)967-3141 Fax:(207)967-3172
E-mail: captain@biddeford.com

Circa 1812. In the National Register, the Captain Lord Mansion was built during the War of 1812 and is one of the finest examples of Federal architecture on the coast of Maine. A four-story spiral staircase winds up to the cupola where one can view the town and the Kennebunk River and Yacht Club. The inn is furnished with elegant antiques. Many bedchambers have gas fireplaces, and there's a room with a fireplace in the bathroom. A family-style breakfast is served in the country kitchen.

Innkeeper(s): Bev Davis & Rick Litchfield. $100-350. MC VISA DS. TAC7. 16 rooms with PB, 15 with FP. 2 conference rooms. Breakfast included in rates. Types of meals: full breakfast and early coffee/tea. Afternoon tea available. Beds: KQ. Phone and air conditioning in room. TV, fax, copier and library on premises. Small meetings, family reunions and seminars hosted. Antiques, fishing, shopping, cross-country skiing and theater nearby.

Publicity: Andrew Harper's Hideaway Report, Colonial Homes, Yankee, New England Getaways. Ratings: 4 Stars.

"A showcase of elegant architecture. Meticulously clean and splendidly appointed. It's a shame to have to leave."

Cove House

11 S Maine St
Kennebunkport, ME 04046-6313
(207)967-3704

Circa 1793. This roomy Colonial Revival farmhouse overlooks Chick's Cove on the Kennebunk River. The inn's peaceful setting offers easy access to beaches, shops and the town. Three guest rooms serve visitors of this antique-filled home. Guests enjoy full breakfasts, which often include the inn's famous blueberry muffins, in the Flow Blue dining room. A popular gathering spot is the book-lined living room/library. Bicycles may be borrowed for a leisurely ride around the town. A cozy, secluded cottage with a screened front porch is another lodging option.

Innkeeper(s): Katherine Jones. $70-95. MC VISA PC TC. TAC10. 3 rooms with PB. 1 cottage. Breakfast and afternoon tea included in rates. Types of meals: full breakfast and early coffee/tea. Beds: QT. TV, VCR, bicycles and library on premises. Small meetings hosted. Antiques, fishing, parks, shopping, cross-country skiing, theater and watersports nearby.

English Meadows Inn

141 Port Rd
Kennebunkport, ME 04043
(207)967-5766 (800)272-0698

Circa 1860. Bordered by century-old lilac bushes, this Queen Anne Victorian inn and attached carriage house offer 13 guest rooms. The inn's well-tended grounds, which include apple trees, gardens and lush lawns, invite bird-lovers or those who desire a relaxing stroll. Four-poster beds, afghans and hand-sewn quilts are found in many of the guest rooms. Visitors also will enjoy the talents of local artists, whose works are featured throughout the inn. Guests may eat breakfast in bed before heading out to explore Kennebunkport.

Historic Interest: Walkers Pointe, President Bush's summer residence (2 miles).

Innkeeper(s): Charles Doane. $85-115. MC VISA AX DS PC TC. 13 rooms with PB. 1 suite. 1 cottage. Breakfast and afternoon tea included in rates. Types of meals: full breakfast and early coffee/tea. Room service available. Beds: KQDT. TV on premises. Small meetings and family reunions hosted. Amusement parks, antiques, fishing, parks, shopping, cross-country skiing, theater and watersports nearby.

"Thanks for the memories! You have a warm Yankee hospitality here!"

Kennebunkport Inn

1 Dock Sq
Kennebunkport, ME 04046-6012
(207)967-2621 (800)248-2621 Fax:(207)967-3705

Circa 1899. The Kennebunkport Inn offers a wonderful combination of elegance and relaxation. The main lounge is furnished with velvet loveseats and chintz sofas. Guest rooms are decorated with mahogany queen-size beds, wing chairs and Queen Anne writing desks. Innkeeper Martha Griffin is a graduate of Paris' prestigious La Varenn Ecole de Cuisine and London's Elizabeth Pomeroy Cooking School. Her culinary creations are unforgettable and award-winning. Maine lobster is a dinner staple, but save room for dessert. The inn also includes a fire-lit lounge with a piano bar.

Historic Interest: Knott House.

Innkeeper(s): Rick & Martha Griffin. $69-269. MAP, AP, EP. MC VISA AX PC TC. TAC10. 34 rooms with PB, 1 with FP. 1 suite. Type of meal: full breakfast. Dinner and lunch available. Beds: KQDT. Phone, air conditioning and TV in room. Fax, copier and swimming on premises. Small meetings hosted. Amusement parks, antiques, fishing, shopping, cross-country skiing, theater and watersports nearby.

Location: In the center of Kennebunkport.

Publicity: Getaways for Gourmets, Coast Guide.

"From check-in, to check-out, from breakfast through dinner, we were treated like royalty."

Kylemere House 1818

6 South St, PO Box 1333
Kennebunkport, ME 04046-1333
(207)967-2780

Circa 1818. Located in Maine's largest historic district, this Federal-style house was built by Daniel Walker, a descendant of an original Kennebunkport family. Later, Maine artist and architect Abbot Graves purchased the property and named it "Crosstrees" for its maple trees. The inn features New England antiques and brilliant flower gardens in view of the formal dining  room in spring and summer. A full breakfast is provided. Art galleries, beaches, antiquing and golf are nearby.

Historic Interest: Built in 1818, a Federal Style home built by one of the first four families in Kennebunkport.

Innkeeper(s): Ruth Toohey. $90-150. MC VISA. 4 rooms with PB, 1 with FP. Breakfast included in rates. Types of meals: full breakfast and early coffee/tea. Beds: KQT. Phone in room. Weddings, small meetings and family reunions hosted. Antiques, fishing, shopping and theater nearby.

Publicity: Boston Globe, Glamour Magazine, Regis and Kathie Lee Show.

"Beautiful inn. Outstanding hospitality. Thanks for drying our sneakers, fixing our bikes. You are all a lot of fun!"

Lake Brook Bed & Breakfast

PO Box 762, Lower Village Rt 9
Kennebunkport, ME 04046
(207)967-4069

Circa 1900. This pleasant old farmhouse is situated on a tidal brook. Comfortable rockers offer an inviting rest on the wrap-around porch where you can enjoy the inn's flower gardens that trail down to the marsh and brook. Gourmet breakfasts are served. Walk to Kennebunkport's Dock Square and lower village to visit fine galleries, shops and restaurants.

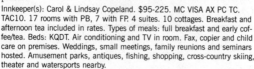

Historic Interest: The Brick Store Museum and other historical sites are nearby.

Innkeeper(s): Carolyn A. McAdams. $85-120. MC VISA. TAC10. 3 rooms with PB. Breakfast included in rates. Types of meals: gourmet breakfast and early coffee/tea. Beds: QD. Ceiling fan in room. Small meetings and family reunions hosted. Spanish spoken. Antiques, fishing, parks, shopping, cross-country skiing, theater and watersports nearby.

"Truly wonderful atmosphere."

Maine Stay Inn & Cottages

PO Box 500-A
Kennebunkport, ME 04046-6174
(207)967-2117 (800)950-2117 Fax:(207)967-8757
E-mail: innkeeper@mainestayinn.com

Circa 1860. In the National Register, this is a square-block Italianate contoured in a low hip-roof design. Later additions reflecting the Queen Anne period include a suspended spiral staircase, crystal windows, ornately carved mantels and moldings, bay windows and porches. A sea captain built the handsome cupola that became a favorite spot for making taffy. In the '20s, the cupola was a place from which to spot offshore rumrunners. Guests enjoy afternoon tea with stories of the Maine Stay's heritage. Two suites and one room in the main building and five of the cottage rooms have working fireplaces.

Innkeeper(s): Carol & Lindsay Copeland. $95-225. MC VISA AX PC TC. TAC10. 17 rooms with PB, 7 with FP. 4 suites. 10 cottages. Breakfast and afternoon tea included in rates. Types of meals: full breakfast and early coffee/tea. Beds: KQDT. Air conditioning and TV in room. Fax, copier and child care on premises. Weddings, small meetings, family reunions and seminars hosted. Amusement parks, antiques, fishing, shopping, cross-country skiing, theater and watersports nearby.

Location: In the Kennebunkport National Historic District.

Publicity: *Boston Globe, Discerning Traveler, Montreal Gazette, Innsider, Tourist News, Down East, Staten Island Advance, Birmingham News, Delaware County Times, Family Travel Times.*

"We have traveled the East Coast from Martha's Vineyard to Bar Harbor, and this is the only place we know we must return to."

Old Fort Inn

Old Fort Ave, PO Box M 1
Kennebunkport, ME 04046
(207)967-5353 (800)828-3678 Fax:(207)967-4547

Circa 1880. The Old Fort Inn is a luxurious country inn located in a secluded setting, minutes away from Kennebunkport's shops, art galleries and beaches. The inn's gracious interiors feature antiques, canopy and four-poster beds. There is an antique shop, a tennis court and a fresh-water pool on the property. The ocean is just a block away.

Historic Interest: Trolly Car Museum, Brick Store Museum, historic homes and landmarks.

Innkeeper(s): Sheila & David Aldrich. $95-280. MC VISA AX DS PC TC. TAC10. 16 rooms with PB. 1 conference room. Breakfast included in rates. Type of meal: full breakfast. Beds: KQD. Phone, air conditioning and TV in room. Fax, copier, swimming and tennis on premises. 15 acres. Small meetings hosted. Antiques, fishing, parks, shopping and theater nearby.

Publicity: *Country Inns. Ratings: 4 Diamonds.*

"My husband and I have been spending the last two weeks in August at the Old Fort Inn for years. It combines for us a rich variety of what we feel a relaxing vacation should be."

The Inn on South Street

PO Box 478A
Kennebunkport, ME 04046-1778
(207)967-5151 (800)963-5151

Circa 1806. This early 19th-century Greek Revival manor is within walking distance of Kennebunkport's many shops, restaurants and the ocean. A unique "Good Morning" staircase will

be one of the first items guests will notice upon entering the inn. Richly appointed rooms are full of beautiful furnishings, lovely window dressings and pine plank floors. Guests will enjoy such amenities as telephones, fireplaces and fresh flowers in the guest rooms. Breakfasts are a treat, served up in the second-floor or country kitchen with views of the river and ocean, and they feature special dishes with herbs from the inn's herb garden.

Historic Interest: Kennebunkport boasts many two- and three-story wooden Federal-style dwellings, which date back to the early 19th century. Cape Arundel, one mile away, features the work of John Calvin Stevens, a noted 19th-century architect. Among the roomy summer cottages he created was the home of former President Bush.

Innkeeper(s): Jacques & Eva Downs. $105-225. MC VISA. 4 rooms with PB, 2 with FP. 1 suite. Breakfast and afternoon tea included in rates. Types of meals: gourmet breakfast and early coffee/tea. Beds: QT. Phone in room. German, Spanish and Russian spoken. Antiques, fishing, parks, theater and watersports nearby.

Publicity: *Summertime, Country Inns, Down East.*

"Superb hospitality. We were delighted by the atmosphere and your thoughtfulness."

Tides Inn By The Sea

252 King's Hwy, Goose Rocks Beach
Kennebunkport, ME 04046
(207)967-3757

Circa 1899. This spacious Victorian mansion is located oceanfront on Goose Rocks Beach. Interior murals set off the inn's hardwood floors, antique furnishings, over-stuffed couches and

whimsical accents. The breakfast room, as well as several guest rooms, offers ocean views. Lamb, lobster and salmon are features of the dining room and Sandy Bottom Pub is on the premises. Enjoy the adjacent sandy beach, or watch the harbor seals or lobster men hauling traps. Whale-watching cruises and sailboat charters are nearby. Teddy Roosevelt and Sir Arthur Conan Doyle were among the celebrities hosted here.

Innkeeper(s): Marie & Kristin Henriksen. $85-225. EP. MC VISA AX. 22 rooms, 19 with PB. 3 suites. Type of meal: gourmet breakfast. Restaurant on premises. Beds: KQDT. Ceiling fan in room. TV, fax and swimming on premises. Weddings, small meetings and family reunions hosted. Amusement parks, antiques, fishing, parks, shopping, sporting events, golf, theater and watersports nearby.

Publicity: *Down East, Boston Sunday Herald, Conde Nast Traveler, Tourist News.*

"*Always a treat to visit here—so unique and pleasant.*"

Kingfield   G3

Herbert Inn

PO Box 67
Kingfield, ME 04947-0067
(207)265-2000 (800)843-4372 Fax:(207)265-4594
E-mail: www.byme.com/

Circa 1917. This three-story, Beaux-Arts-style hotel with its original terrazzo marble floors, brass fixtures and oak floors was built by Maine legislator Herbert Wing. A sink remaining on the dining room wall once provided stagecoach patrons a place to wash up before dining. A moosehead is the focal point above the fireplace. Simply furnished rooms are equipped with jacuzzis or steam baths.

Innkeeper(s): Bud Dick, Faye Boyce. $49-90. MAP, EP. MC VISA AX DC DS PC TC. TAC10. 32 rooms, 23 with PB. 4 suites. 1 conference room. Breakfast included in rates. Types of meals: continental breakfast and continental-plus breakfast. Dinner available. Restaurant on premises. Beds: KQDT. TV, VCR, fax, copier, spa and sauna on premises. Weddings, small meetings and seminars hosted. Antiques, fishing, shopping, downhill skiing, cross-country skiing and golf nearby.

Pets Allowed: well-behaved, not to be left for extended periods of time.

Publicity: *New England Monthly, Portland Press Herald.*

Kittery   L2

Enchanted Nights B&B

29 Wentworth St
RT 103
Kittery, ME 03904-1720
(207)439-1489

Circa 1890. The innkeepers bill this unique inn as a "Victorian fantasy for the romantic at heart." Each of the guest rooms is unique, from the spacious rooms with double whirlpool tubs to the cozy turret room. A whimsical combination of country French and Victorian decor permeates the interior. Wrought-iron beds and hand-painted furnishings add to the ambiance.

Breakfasts, often with a vegetarian theme, are served with gourmet coffee in the morning room on antique floral china.

Historic Interest: There are museums, forts, churches, historic homes and buildings all within five miles of the home.

Innkeeper(s): Nancy Bogerberger & Peter Lamandia. $47-180. MC VISA AX DS. 6 rooms with PB. Breakfast included in rates. Types of meals: full breakfast

and gourmet breakfast. Beds: QD. Air conditioning, ceiling fan, TV and VCR in room. Pet boarding on premises. Handicap access. Weddings, small meetings, family reunions and seminars hosted. Antiques, fishing, parks, shopping, theater and watersports nearby. Pets Allowed.

"*The atmosphere was great. Your breakfast was elegant. The breakfast room made us feel we had gone back in time. All in all it was a very enjoyable stay.*"

Lubec   G8

Peacock House

27 Summer St
Lubec, ME 04652-1134
(207)733-2403

Circa 1860. Built by a sea captain from Bedford, England, the inn is nestled in the country's most northeastern town. Six generations of the Peacock family have lived here, hosting some prominent people. Guests included Margaret Chase Smith, several governors, Donald McMillen (Arctic explorer), Sen. Edmund Muskie and members of the Roosevelt family and their staff. The house originally was constructed as a Victorian with later updates making it more of a mixture of Federal and Greek Revival architectural styles. The Bay of Fundy is two blocks away. The Peacock House is the county's only three-diamond rated B&B.

Historic Interest: The island home of Franklin Delano Roosevelt is a nearby historic attraction.

Innkeeper(s): Chet & Veda Childs. $60-80. MC VISA. 5 rooms with PB. 1 suite. Breakfast and afternoon tea included in rates. Type of meal: full breakfast. Beds: QDT. Phone in room. Fax on premises. Handicap access. Antiques nearby.

Publicity: *Quoddy Tides, Downeast Coastal Press.*

"*A perfect B&B — great beds, fantastic breakfast and a hospitable family.*"

Naples   J2

Augustus Bove House

Corner Rts 302 & 114, RR 1 Box 501
Naples, ME 04055
(207)693-6365

Circa 1830. A long front lawn nestles up against the stone foundation and veranda of this house, once known as the Hotel Naples, one of the area's summer hotels in the 1800s. The guest rooms are decorated in a Colonial style and modestly furnished with antiques. Many rooms provide a view of Long Lake. A fancy country breakfast is provided.

Innkeeper(s): David & Arlene Stetson. $49-135. MC VISA AX DS PC TC. TAC10. 11 rooms, 7 with PB. 1 suite. Breakfast and afternoon tea included in rates. Types of meals: full breakfast and early coffee/tea. Beds: KQT. Phone, air conditioning and TV in room. VCR, fax and spa on premises.

Weddings, small meetings and family reunions hosted. Antiques, fishing, parks, shopping, downhill skiing, cross-country skiing, theater and watersports nearby.

Pets Allowed.

Location: Corner of routes 302 & 114.

Publicity: *Brighton Times.*

"Beautiful place, rooms, and people."

Inn at Long Lake

Lake House Rd, PO Box 806
Naples, ME 04055
(207)693-6226 (800)437-0328

Circa 1906. Reopened in 1988, the inn housed the overflow guests from the Lake House resort about 90 years ago. Guests traveled to the resort via the Oxford-Cumberland Canal, and

each room is named for a historic canal boat. The cozy rooms offer fluffy comforters and a warm, country decor in a romantic atmosphere. Warm up in front of a crackling fire in the great room, or enjoy a cool Long Lake breeze on the veranda while watching horses in nearby pastures. Murder-mystery weekends offer a spooky alternative to your getaway plans.

Historic Interest: Sungo Lock, Shaker Museum, Jones Glass Museum.

Innkeeper(s): Maynard & Irene Hincks. $69-150. MC VISA DS PC TC. TAC10. 16 rooms with PB. 2 suites. 1 conference room. Breakfast included in rates. Types of meals: continental-plus breakfast and early coffee/tea. Beds: QDT. Air conditioning in room. Library on premises. Weddings, family reunions and seminars hosted. Spanish and French spoken. Antiques, fishing, parks, shopping, downhill skiing, cross-country skiing and watersports nearby.

Location: Sebago Lakes Region.

Publicity: *Bridgton News, Portland Press Herald.*

"Convenient location, tastefully done and the prettiest inn I've ever stayed in."

Lamb's Mill Inn

RR 1, Box 676, Lambs Mill Rd
Naples, ME 04055
(207)693-6253
E-mail: lambsmil@pivot.net

Circa 1800. This cheery, yellow farmhouse offers six guest rooms, each filled with comfortable furnishings. Guests are pampered with down comforters, a hot tub and 20 peaceful acres of woods, fields and perennial gardens. Fresh vegetable frittata with items picked from the garden and raspberry

Belgian waffles are among the breakfast entrees. Evening snacks are served as well. The home is close to cross-country and alpine skiing, golf, tennis, parasailing, shopping, restaurants and antiquing.

Innkeeper(s): Laurel Tinkham & Sandy Long. $75-105. MC VISA PC TC. TAC10. 6 rooms with PB. Breakfast, afternoon tea and evening snack included in rates. Types of meals: gourmet breakfast and early coffee/tea. Beds: KQ. Turndown service in room. TV, VCR, spa and library on premises. 20 acres. Weddings and family reunions hosted. Antiques, fishing, parks, shopping, downhill skiing, cross-country skiing, theater and watersports nearby.

"We really enjoyed our week in your lovely home."

New Harbor   J4

Bradley Inn at Pemaquid Point

Rt 130, HC 61, Box 361
New Harbor, ME 04554
(207)677-2105 Fax:(207)677-3367

Circa 1900. The history-rich region of Pemaquid is home to this large Victorian Shingle inn, which offers 16 guest rooms. Many rooms sport views of St. John's Bay. Guests may enjoy bicycling, canoeing, exploring the tidal pools of the Rachel Carson Salt Pond, lawn games and swimming, and they also are free to play the inn's baby grand piano. There is a restaurant-pub on the premises. Be sure to inquire about arrangements for boating excursions, clambakes, picnic lunches and fishing charters.

Innkeeper(s): Warren & Beth Busteed. $110-175. MC VISA AX. 12 rooms with PB. 1 suite. 1 conference room. Type of meal: continental breakfast. Dinner and banquet service available. Restaurant on premises. Beds: QT. Phone and ceiling fan in room. TV, fax, copier and child care on premises. Weddings, small meetings, family reunions and seminars hosted. Antiques, fishing, shopping, cross-country skiing and theater nearby.

Location: Pemaquid Point Lighthouse.

Gosnold Arms

Route 32
New Harbor, ME 04554
(207)677-3727 Fax:(207)677-2662

Circa 1840. Located on the historic Pemaquid peninsula, the Gosnold Arms includes a remodeled, saltwater farmhouse situated on a rise above the harbor. There are several cottages and many accommodations with views. A cozy lounge offers two large stone fireplaces and a glassed-in dining porch overlooking the water.

Historic Interest: Pemaquid archaeological dig at Pemaquid Beach; Pemaquid Lighthouse and Fisherman's Museum (1 mile), Summer boat to Monhegan Island from New Harbor (1 hour ride).

Innkeeper(s): The Phinney Family. $75-134. MC VISA PC TC. 26 rooms with PB. Breakfast included in rates. Type of meal: full breakfast. Dinner available. Restaurant on premises. Beds: QDT. Phone in room. Antiques, fishing and theater nearby.

Publicity: *New York, Down East.*

Newagen   J4

Newagen Seaside Inn

PO Box 68, Rt 27
Newagen, ME 04552
(207)633-5242 (800)654-5242 Fax:(207)633-5242
E-mail: seaside@wiscasset.net

Circa 1903. Europeans have inhabited Cape Newagen since the 1620s, and a fort built on this property was destroyed in a skirmish with Native Americans. Rachel Carson sought refuge at this seaside inn, and it is here that her final resting place is located. The peaceful scenery includes vistas of islands and lighthouses, and guests can enjoy the view from an oceanside gazebo. There are both freshwater and saltwater swimming pools, nature trails, tennis courts and a mile of rocky shoreline to enjoy. Some rooms offer private decks, and each is decorated in traditional style. The innkeepers also offer four cottages. Maine Lobster is a specialty at the inn's restaurant.

Innkeeper(s): Herdi & Peter Larsen. $85-175. EP. MC VISA PC TC. TAC10. 26 rooms with PB. 3 suites. 4 cottages. 1 conference room. Breakfast included in rates. Types of meals: full breakfast and early coffee/tea. Dinner, picnic lunch, lunch, banquet service and catered breakfast available. Restaurant on premises. Beds: KQT. TV, VCR, fax, copier, swimming, tennis and library on premises. Handicap access. 85 acres. Weddings, small meetings, family reunions and seminars hosted. Antiques, fishing, parks, shopping, golf, theater and watersports nearby.

Publicity: *Down East, Yankee, New England Travel.*

Newcastle   I4

The Newcastle Inn

60 River Rd
Newcastle, ME 04553-9802
(207)563-5685 (800)832-8669 Fax:(207)563-6877
E-mail: newcastinn@aol.com

Circa 1860. The Newcastle Inn is a Federal-style colonial picturesquely situated on a lawn that slopes down to the Damariscotta River. Most rooms feature antique beds and water views. Honeymooners like the room with the old-fashioned canopy bed. Breakfast consists of four courses and may include eggs with caviar on puff pastry or brioche with lemon curd. A three- or five-course dinner is available.

Innkeeper(s): Howard & Rebecca Levitan. $75-225. MC VISA AX PC. 15 rooms with PB, 5 with FP. 1 suite. 1 conference room. Breakfast included in rates. Types of meals: full breakfast and early coffee/tea. Afternoon tea and banquet service available. Restaurant on premises. Beds: KQDT. Fax, copier and library on premises. Weddings, small meetings, family reunions and seminars hosted. French and limited Spanish spoken. Antiques, parks, shopping, downhill skiing, cross-country skiing, sporting events, theater and watersports nearby.

Location: Tidal Damariscotta River.

Publicity: *Yankee Magazine, Down East, Romantic Hideaways.*

"To eat and stay here is to know life to the fullest."

Northeast Harbor   I6

Asticou Inn

Route 3
Northeast Harbor, ME 04662
(207)276-3344 (800)258-3373 Fax:(207)276-3373
E-mail: asticou@acadia.net

Circa 1883. Offering splendid vistas of the mountains and the blue waters of Northeast Harbor, this treasured old inn is one of Mount Desert Island's two remaining luxury Victorian hotels. In the National Register, the gray-shingled and gabled inn was rebuilt after a fire in 1899. Asticou is the name of a chief of the Penobscot Native American tribe who lived in the area in 1613 when Champlain first came. Guest rooms are decorated with summer furniture, wicker and antiques. Across the road is the Asticou Azalea Gardens, dazzling in spring but inviting in all seasons. The inn offers a game room, TV room, lobby, bar, deck and covered porch. The dining room boasts a large menu, which includes lamb, filet mignon, salmon and Maine lobster.

Innkeeper(s): Joseph J. Joy. $120-349. MAP. MC VISA PC TC. TAC10. 45 rooms, 32 with PB, 10 with FP. 13 suites. 2 conference rooms. Breakfast and dinner included in rates. Types of meals: full breakfast, gourmet breakfast and early coffee/tea. Afternoon tea, picnic lunch, gourmet lunch, banquet service, catering service and room service available. Restaurant on premises. Beds: KQDT. Phone and turndown service in room. TV, VCR, fax, copier, swimming, tennis, library and child care on premises. 38 acres. Weddings, small meetings, family reunions and seminars hosted. Antiques, fishing, parks, shopping, golf and watersports nearby.

Publicity: *Down East.*

Harbourside Inn

Northeast Harbor, ME 04662
(207)276-3272

Circa 1888. This country inn is an appealing version of the New England shingle style. Continuously operating since it was constructed in 1888, the inn has been the favorite summer vacation spot for many famous people throughout its history. Situated on more than four wooded acres, the grounds feature gardens, a greenhouse with a vegetable and cutting garden and nostalgic gravel driveways. Glimpses of the harbor may be seen through the woods. Guest rooms are clean, bright and decorated with antiques. Rooms on the first and second floors feature working fireplaces. There are several suites with private glassed-in porches. Some kitchenettes are available. The inn is adjacent to Acadia National Park.

Innkeeper(s): The Sweet Family. $90-175. 14 rooms with PB, 10 with FP. Type of meal: continental breakfast. Beds: KQDT. Phone in room.

Publicity: *The New York Times.*

"We so much appreciate your long hours of work mostly unseen by us except for the spotless results."

Ogunquit   K2

Chestnut Tree Inn

PO Box 2201
Ogunquit, ME 03907-2201
(207)646-4529 (800)362-0757

Circa 1870. Gable roofs peak out from the top of this Victorian inn, which has greeted guests for more than a century. A smattering of antiques and Victorian decor creates a 19th-century atmosphere. Guests can relax on the porch or head out for a stroll on Marginal Way, a mile-long path set along Maine's scenic coastline. The beach, shops, Ogunquit Playhouse and a variety of restaurants are just a few minutes down the road.

Innkeeper(s): Cynthia Diana & Ronald St. Laurent. $35-125. MC VISA AX TC. TAC10. 22 rooms, 15 with PB. 1 suite. Type of meal: continental-plus breakfast. Beds: QDT. Phone, air conditioning and TV in room. Family reunions hosted. French spoken. Amusement parks, antiques, fishing, parks, shopping, downhill skiing, cross-country skiing, sporting events, theater and watersports nearby.

"Your inn was absolutely beautiful and peaceful. Your kindness will not be forgotten."

Rockmere Lodge

40 Stearns Rd
Ogunquit, ME 03907
(207)646-2985 Fax:(207)646-6947
E-mail: rockmere@cybertours.com

Circa 1899. Offering an outstanding view of the Atlantic from its site on Marginal Way (the town's oceanside path), this shingle-style Victorian is enhanced by gardens, fountains and a wraparound veranda filled with white wicker. The inn is furnished with period antiques and Victorian collectibles. Every room except one enjoys an ocean view. Walk to galleries, boutiques and fine restaurants. Ten miles south is Kittery, a center for factory outlets.

Innkeeper(s): Andy Antoniuk & Bob Brown. $60-150. MC VISA AX DS TC. 8 rooms with PB. Type of meal: continental-plus breakfast. Beds: QTD. TV in room. VCR, fax and library on premises. Antiques, fishing, parks, shopping, cross-country skiing, sporting events, golf, theater and watersports nearby.

Publicity: *York County Coast Star.*

Scotch Hill Inn

PO Box 87, 175 Main St, US Rt 1
Ogunquit, ME 03907
(207)646-2890 Fax:(207)646-4324

Circa 1898. This Victorian is ideally situated just minutes from the beach. Everything about the interior is bright and cheery. The parlor features yellow and white striped wallcoverings and a mix of traditional and Victorian furnishings. Head up the staircase, which is covered in rich hunter green carpeting and highlighted by yellow walls and a flowered border, to reach the guest rooms. Each is decorated differently. One might encounter a four-poster bed topped with a white comforter. In the mornings, a three-course breakfast begins with homemade scones. If weather permits, the meal is served on the inn's veranda. There are also two carriage houses on the premises, which are rented by the week. The homes are spacious with three to four bedrooms, living rooms and kitchens. Scotch Hill Inn is open from April until mid-October.

Innkeeper(s): Donna & Dick Brown. $60-110. MC VISA TC. 8 rooms, 5 with PB, 1 with FP. 2 cottages. Breakfast and afternoon tea included in rates. Types of meals: full breakfast, gourmet breakfast and early coffee/tea. Beds: KQTD. Air conditioning in room. TV, VCR and fax on premises. Weddings, small meetings and family reunions hosted. Amusement parks, antiques, fishing, parks, shopping, golf, theater and watersports nearby.

"The best B&B in this country! And I've stayed in a few!!!"

Old Orchard Beach   K2

Atlantic Birches Inn

20 Portland Ave Rt 98
Old Orchard Beach, ME 04064-2212
(207)934-5295 (888)934-5295
E-mail: dancyn@aol.com

Circa 1903. The front porch of this Shingle-style Victorian is shaded by white birch trees. Badminton and croquet are set up on the lawn. The house is a place for relaxation and enjoyment, an uncluttered, simple haven filled with comfortable furnishings. The guest rooms are decorated with a few antiques and pastel wallcoverings. Maine's coast offers an endless

amount of activities, from boating to whale watching. It is a five-minute walk to the beach and the pier.

Innkeeper(s): Dan & Cyndi Bolduc. $59-95. EP. MC VISA AX DS TC. TAC10. 8 rooms with PB. Breakfast included in rates. Type of meal: continental-plus breakfast. Beds: KQDT. Air conditioning and ceiling fan in room. TV, VCR, copier, swimming and library on premises. Small meetings and family reunions hosted. French spoken. Amusement parks, antiques, fishing, parks, shopping, sporting events and watersports nearby.

"Your home and family are just delightful! What a treat to stay in such a warm & loving home."

Oquossoc   G2

Oquossoc's Own B&B

Rangeley Ave, PO Box 27
Oquossoc, ME 04964
(207)864-5584

Circa 1903. The recreation-rich mountains of Western Maine are home to this Victorian inn, which offers five guest rooms and easy access to local outdoor attractions. The inn's living room offers a cozy spot for guests to read or watch TV. Basketball and tennis courts are nearby, and a grocery store and post office are within easy walking distance of the inn. Innkeeper Joanne Conner Koob is well-known in the area for her catering skills. The Saddleback Mountain Ski Area, elevation 4,116 feet, is nearby. Three popular restaurants and the marina cove are within distance.

Innkeeper(s): Joanne Conner Koob. $68. 5 rooms. Types of meals: full breakfast and early coffee/tea. Picnic lunch and catering service available. VCR on premises. Small meetings and family reunions hosted. Antiques, shopping, downhill skiing and cross-country skiing nearby.

Portland   J3

Inn at St John

939 Congress St
Portland, ME 04102-3031
(207)773-6481 (800)636-9127 Fax:(207)756-7629

Circa 1897. Tucked on a city street, this Victorian inn is conveniently located near many Portland sites, including museums, restaurants and shops. The guest rooms feature antiques and traditional furnishings, and hardwood floors are topped with Oriental rugs. Pictures showcasing Portland's railroad history are on display. The inn is European in style, and some rooms have a shared bath. Children are welcome, and those younger than 12 can stay for free.

Innkeeper(s): Paul Hood. $36-124. MC VISA AX DC CB DS PC TC. TAC15. 31 rooms, 17 with PB. Breakfast included in rates. Types of meals: continental-plus breakfast and early coffee/tea. Beds: KQDT. Phone, air conditioning and TV in room. Fax, copier, library and child care on premises. Weddings and family reunions hosted. Amusement parks, antiques, fishing, parks, shopping, cross-country skiing, sporting events, golf, theater and watersports nearby.

Pets Allowed: Not to be left unattended in guest room.

Publicity: *Down East, Portland Press Herald.*

"We were surprised at how much charm there is tucked in to this building."

Pomegranate Inn

49 Neal St
Portland, ME 04102-3506
(207)772-1006 (800)356-0408 Fax:(207)773-4426

Circa 1884. This three-story inn is furnished with a mix of contemporary art and antiques. Faux-finished woodwork painted by the innkeeper's daughter includes moldings, fireplace mantels and columns. Another local artist handpainted the guest room walls.

Historic Interest: Greater Portland landmark.

Innkeeper(s): Isabel Smiles. $95-165. MC VISA AX DS. 8 rooms with PB. 1 suite. 1 conference room. Breakfast and afternoon tea included in rates. Type of meal: full breakfast. Beds: KQT. Air conditioning in room. Fax on premises. Antiques, cross-country skiing and theater nearby.

Publicity: *Portland Monthly, Portland Press Herald, New England Living, Country Inns, Travel & Leisure.*

"The most wonderful inn I have ever been in! — Irish visitor."

West End Inn

146 Pine St
Portland, ME 04102-3541
(207)772-1377 (800)338-1377

Circa 1871. Located in Portland's Western Promenade Historic District, this Georgian-style inn is one of many Victorian-era homes found there. Rooms are decorated with

four-poster, canopy beds. The inn's full, New England-style breakfasts include such items as blueberry pancakes, sausage, eggs and fruit. The menu changes daily and guests may opt for lighter fare. An afternoon tea also is  served and provides a perfect opportunity to relax after an activity-filled day. The inn also offers facilities for meetings, reunions and wedding receptions. The Museum of Art and the University of South Maine are nearby.

Innkeeper(s): Teri Dizon. $79-169. MC VISA AX PC. TAC10. 6 rooms with PB. Breakfast included in rates. Type of meal: full breakfast. Beds: KQT. Phone, ceiling fan and TV in room. Bicycles and library on premises. Small meetings hosted. Spanish spoken. Antiques, fishing, parks, shopping, downhill skiing, cross-country skiing, sporting events, theater and watersports nearby.

Rockland   I5

Lakeshore Inn Bed & Breakfast

184 Lakeview Dr (RT 17)
Rockland, ME 04841-5705
(207)594-4209 Fax:(207)596-6407

Circa 1767. Surrounded by an 200-year-old apple orchard, hemlock and pine trees, this recently renovated farmhouse is one of the most historic buildings in the area. Providing pleasant vistas, the inn's green lawns slope down toward the lake. It was built by one of the 23 children of Isaiah Tolman. Each of the guest rooms offer a view of Lake Chickawaukie, and two have decks. Guests are invited to enjoy the outdoor hot tub

spa or come indoors to sit by the cozy fireplace. Breakfast includes an entree such as feta omelets and Belgium waffles.

Innkeeper(s): Joseph McCluskey & Paula Nicols. $90-95. MC VISA PC TC. TAC10. 4 rooms with PB. Breakfast and evening snack included in rates. Types of meals: gourmet breakfast and early coffee/tea. Dinner and picnic lunch available. Beds: Q. Air conditioning in room. TV, VCR, fax, copier and library on premises. Weddings, small meetings and family reunions hosted. Greek spoken. Antiques, fishing, shopping, golf and watersports nearby.

Publicity: *Bangor Daily News.*

"We'll pass on the word - satisfaction indeed!"

Saco   K2

Crown 'n' Anchor Inn

121 North St, PO Box 228
Saco, ME 04072-0228
(207)282-3829 (800)561-8865 Fax:(207)282-7495

Circa 1827. This Greek Revival house, listed in the National Register, features both Victorian baroque and colonial antiques. A collection of British coronation memorabilia displayed

throughout the inn includes 200 items. Guests gather in the Victorian parlor or the formal library. The innkeepers, a college librarian and an acad-  emic bookseller, lined the shelves with several thousand volumes, including extensive Civil War and British royal family collections and travel, theater and nautical books. Royal Dalton china, crystal and fresh flowers create a festive breakfast setting.

Historic Interest: Kennebunkport, The George Bush Estate, The Victorian Mansion, Portland Head Lighthouse.

Innkeeper(s): John Barclay & Martha Forester. $60-95. MC VISA AX PC TC. TAC10. 5 rooms with PB, 2 with FP. Breakfast included in rates. Types of meals: full breakfast, gourmet breakfast and early coffee/tea. Afternoon tea available. Beds: KQDT. TV in room. VCR and library on premises. Weddings, small meetings, family reunions and seminars hosted. Limited French spoken. Amusement parks, antiques, fishing, parks, shopping, downhill skiing, cross-country skiing, sporting events, theater and watersports nearby.

Pets Allowed: Small or caged.

Publicity: *Lincoln County News, Yankee, Saco, Biddeford, Old Orchard Beach Courier, Country, Portland Press Herald.*

"A delightful interlude! A five star B&B."

Searsport   H5

Brass Lantern Inn

PO Box 407, 81 W Main St
Searsport, ME 04974-3501
(207)548-0150 (800)691-0150
E-mail: brasslan@agate.net

Circa 1850. This Victorian inn is nestled at the edge of the woods on a rise overlooking Penobscot Bay. Showcased throughout the inn are many collectibles, antiques and family heirlooms, as well as artifacts from innkeeper Maggie Zieg's home in England. Enjoy breakfast by candlelight in the dining room with its ornate tin ceiling, where you'll feast on Maine blueberry pancakes and other sumptuous treats. Centrally located between Camden and Bar Harbor, Searsport is known as the antique capital of Maine. There are many local attrac-

tions, including the Penobscot Marine Museum, fine shops and restaurants, as well as a public boat facility.

Historic Interest: Fort Knox (8 miles).

Innkeeper(s): Maggie & Dick Zieg. $65-90. MC VISA PC TC. TAC5. 4 rooms with PB. Breakfast included in rates. Types of meals: full breakfast and early coffee/tea. Beds: DT. TV and library on premises. Small meetings and family reunions hosted. Antiques, fishing, parks, shopping, cross-country skiing and theater nearby.

Publicity: *Country Living, Republication Journal, Travel Today, Down East.*

"Very elegant surrounding, cozy atmosphere. We felt really spoiled. It was my daughter's first stay at a B&B and she's still praising the blueberry pancakes. Everything was just perfect!"

Homeport Inn

RR 1 Box 647
Searsport, ME 04974-9728
(207)548-2259 (800)742-5814 Fax:(978)443-6682

Circa 1861. Captain John Nickels built this home on Penobscot Bay. On top of the two-story historic landmark is a widow's walk. A scal-

loped picket fence frames the property. Fine antiques, black marble fireplaces, a collection of grandfather clocks and elaborate ceiling medallions add to the

atmosphere. Landscaped grounds sweep out to the ocean's edge. Some rooms have an ocean view. There are Victorian cottages available for weekly rental.

Historic Interest: Fort Knox, Owl's Head Lighthouse, historical architecture homes.

Innkeeper(s): Dr. & Mrs. F. George Johnson. $55-85. MC VISA AX DS. 10 rooms, 7 with PB. Breakfast included in rates. Type of meal: full breakfast. Beds: QT. Phone in room. TV on premises. Handicap access. Small meetings and family reunions hosted. Antiques, fishing, parks, shopping, downhill skiing, cross-country skiing, sporting events and theater nearby.

Publicity: *Yankee, Down East.*

"Your breakfast is something we will never forget."

Thurston House B&B

PO Box 686, 8 Elm St
Searsport, ME 04974-3368
(207)548-2213 (800)240-2213
E-mail: thurston@acadia.net

Circa 1831. The innkeepers of this Colonial home proudly serve their "Forget About Lunch" breakfast, which consists of three courses, fresh prepared fruit, baked hot breads and then a sumptuous entree course. Special diets are happily accommo-

dated, as well. Stephen Thurston was the pastor of the first Congregational Church in Searsport for the heart of the 19th century. He was one of the town's most prominent citizens. In 1853, the 242-ton brig named after Thurston was launched.

Innkeeper(s): Carl Eppig. $45-65. MC VISA AX. 4 rooms, 2 with PB, 2 with FP. 1 suite. Breakfast included in rates. Types of meals: full breakfast and early coffee/tea. Afternoon tea available. Beds: DT. Small meetings hosted. Antiques, fishing, shopping, downhill skiing, cross-country skiing, sporting events, theater and watersports nearby.

Publicity: *Yankee, Evening Times-Globe, Clarion-Ledger.*

"When we again travel in the Maine area, there is no doubt that we will make certain to stay at Thurston House. They deserve the best accolades!"

Searsport (Waldo County)   H5

Watchtide, B&B by the Sea

190 W Main St, US Rte. 1
Searsport (Waldo County), ME 04974-3514
(207)548-6575 (800)698-6575
E-mail: watchtyd@agate.net

Circa 1795. Built for a sea captain, this New England Cape-style inn with its nearly four acres of lawns and gardens, has a spectacular view of Penobscot Bay. There are four individually decorated rooms, two with private baths. The innkeeper's motto is "we love to spoil our guests." Breakfast is served on the wicker furnished porch, which overlooks the inn's bird sanctuary and the bay. An antique shop, with a large collection of angels made by the resident artist, is located in the adjacent barn. Guests can receive a discount at this shop.

Historic Interest: Considered by visitors to have the best antique shopping in Maine. Near Acadia National Park, lighthouses, ocean and lakes, water sports, skiing, golf, theater and excellent restaurants.

Innkeeper(s): Nancy-Linn Nellis & Jack Elliott. $65-100. MC VISA DS PC TC. TAC15. 4 rooms, 2 with PB. Breakfast and afternoon tea included in rates. Types of meals: gourmet breakfast and early coffee/tea. Beds: KDT. Turndown service in room. TV and library on premises. Limited French spoken. Antiques, fishing, parks, shopping, downhill skiing, cross-country skiing, sporting events, theater and watersports nearby.

Pets Allowed: Non-smoking inn.

Publicity: *Republican Journal, Daily Item, Courier Weekend, Bangor Daily News, Pilot Tribune, Clarion-Ledger, Sunday Patriot News, Sunday Herald-Times.*

"Talk of spoiling folks, you have spoiled us for any other B&B - nothing compares! There is no place else that I would rather be than at Watchtide! You won our 'best hotel in New England' award! This is our considered opinion after staying many other hotels."

Southwest Harbor   I6

Inn at Southwest

371 Main St, PO Box 593
Southwest Harbor, ME 04679
(207)244-3835
E-mail: innatsw@acadia.net

Circa 1884. This pristine Second Empire Victorian boasts three stories, two towers and a wraparound porch, and it was built originally as an inn. Rooms are named after Maine lighthouses. For instance, the Cape Elizabeth features a king-size bed, antique writing desk, bay window and sitting area. Down comforters, ceiling fans, vibrant designer fabrics and luxury linens are appointments in the guest rooms, and some have views of the harbor. Breakfast offerings include items such as crab potato bake, poached pears in wine sauce and raspberry coffee cake. Acadia National Park is five minutes away.

Innkeeper(s): Jill Lewis. $60-135. MC VISA DS PC TC. 9 rooms with PB. Breakfast and afternoon tea included in rates. Types of meals: full breakfast, gourmet breakfast and early coffee/tea. Beds: KQDT. Ceiling fan in room. Library on premises. Family reunions hosted. Antiques, fishing, parks, shopping, golf, theater and watersports nearby.

Publicity: *Yankee Travel Guide.*

"How could any place that serves dessert for breakfast be bad?"

The Island House

PO Box 1006
Southwest Harbor, ME 04679-1006
(207)244-5180

Circa 1830. The first guests arrived at Deacon Clark's door as early as 1832. When steamboat service from Boston began in the 1850s, the Island House became a popular summer hotel. Among the guests was Ralph Waldo Emerson. In 1912, the hotel was taken down and rebuilt as two separate homes using much of the woodwork from the original building.

Innkeeper(s): Ann and Charles Bradford. $50-165. MC VISA. 5 rooms. 2 suites. Breakfast included in rates. Type of meal: full breakfast. Beds: KQDT. Phone in room. Antiques, fishing, theater and watersports nearby.

Location: Mount Desert Island (Acadia National Park).

Publicity: *Bangor Daily News.*

"Island House is a delight from the moment one enters the door! We loved the thoughtful extras. You've made our vacation very special!"

Kingsleigh Inn

PO Box 1426   373 Main St
Southwest Harbor, ME 04679-1426
(207)244-5302

Circa 1904. Your first introduction to the inn will be its cozy, country kitchen where an assortment of teas, coffee, and cocoa are available throughout the day. The living room offers guests the warmth of the crackling fireplace and a wonderful collection of antiques and fine art. The inn's dining room library features a wide variety of books, magazines and games while the sitting room offers comfortable over-stuffed chairs. A flower-filled wrap-around porch offers a compelling view of the harbor. The inn offers eight distinctively decorated rooms, many with harbor views, that boast a comfortable blend of wall coverings with matching window treatments and peri-

od furnishings. A secluded third-floor suite offers a separate bedroom, fireplace and a panoramic view from its private turret. Fresh flowers and candlelight make breakfast at the inn an especially memorable experience.

Innkeeper(s): Ken & Cyd Champagne Collins. $90-175. 8 rooms with PB. Type of meal: full breakfast. Beds: KQ.

Publicity: *McCall's.*

"Very romantic and wonderfully decorated. We'll always treasure our stay with you."

The Lambs Ear Inn

60 Clark Point Rd, PO Box 30
Southwest Harbor, ME 04679
(207)244-9828 Fax:(207)244-9924

Circa 1857. This stately colonial inn was built by Captain Mayo, one of the town's earliest settlers. Guests can view lobster boats, sailing ships and all the other activities of Southwest Harbor. The harbor is surrounded by Acadia National Park with its pristine pine forests, lakes and mountains. Breakfasts at the inn are known to be as artistic as they are excellent.

Innkeeper(s): Elizabeth Hoke. $85-165. MC VISA PC TC. 8 rooms with PB, 2 with FP. 1 suite. Breakfast and afternoon tea included in rates. Types of meals: gourmet breakfast and early coffee/tea. Beds: QDT. TV in room. Amusement parks, antiques, fishing, parks, shopping, cross-country skiing, theater and watersports nearby.

"The food is delicious, the presentation is beautiful."

Lindenwood Inn

PO Box 1328
Southwest Harbor, ME 04679-1328
(207)244-5335

Circa 1906. Sea Captain Mills named his home "The Lindens" after stately linden trees in the front lawn. Elegantly refurbished, this historic house features many items collected from the new innkeeper's world travels. The rooms have sun-drenched balconies overlooking the harbor and its sailboats and lobster boats. A hearty full breakfast is served in the dining room with a roaring fireplace in the winter. The inn has a heated, in-ground swimming pool and a spa. From the inn you may take a tree-lined path down to the wharf.

Innkeeper(s): James King. $55-195. MC VISA DS. 11 rooms with PB. 5 suites. Breakfast included in rates. Types of meals: full breakfast and early coffee/tea. Dinner available. Beds: QDT. Phone, ceiling fan and TV in room. Spa, swimming, bicycles and child care on premises. Weddings, small meetings, family reunions and seminars hosted. Amusement parks, antiques, fishing, shopping, cross-country skiing and watersports nearby.

Location: Mt. Desert Island.

Publicity: *McCall's.*

"We had a lovely stay at your inn. Breakfast, room and hospitality were all first-rate. You made us feel like a special friend instead of a paying guest."

Spruce Head   J5

Craignair Inn
533 Clark Island Rd
Spruce Head, ME 04859
(207)594-7644 (800)320-9997 Fax:(207)596-7124

Circa 1930. Craignair originally was built to house stonecutters working in nearby granite quarries. Overlooking the docks of the Clark Island Quarry, where granite schooners

once were loaded, this roomy, three-story inn is tastefully decorated with local antiques.

Historic Interest:
General Knox (Washington's Secretary of War) Mansion, called Montpelier (8 miles).

Innkeeper(s): Theresa E. Smith. $74-102. MC VISA AX PC TC. TAC10. 24 rooms, 8 with PB. Breakfast included in rates. Types of meals: full breakfast and early coffee/tea. Banquet service, catering service and catered breakfast available. Restaurant on premises. Beds: KDT. Phone in room. Fax, copier and swimming on premises. Weddings, small meetings, family reunions and seminars hosted. Antiques, fishing, parks, shopping, downhill skiing, cross-country skiing, theater and watersports nearby.

Pets Allowed.

Location: Clark Island ocean view.

Publicity: *Boston Globe, Free Press, Tribune.*

"A coastal oasis of fine food and outstanding service with colonial maritime ambiance!"

Stockton Springs   H5

Hichborn Inn
Church St
Stockton Springs, ME 04981
(207)567-4183 (800)346-1522

Circa 1850. This graceful Italianate-style Victorian home, built by shipbuilder N. G. Hichborn, boasts a cupola and seven dormer windows. It is in the National Register. Inside are high ceilings, Oriental carpets, polished pine floors, a handsome Eastlake walnut fireplace and antiques. There is a "gentleman's parlor" and a music room for relaxing. In the guest rooms are down comforters, old-fashioned oil lamps, antique beds and fine linens. Some rooms have views of the harbor. Breakfast often features raspberry crepes with berries that are picked on the property.

Innkeeper(s): Nancy, Bruce & Morgan Suppes. $51-95. PC TC. TAC10. 5 rooms, 2 with PB. 1 conference room. Breakfast included in rates. Types of meals: full breakfast, gourmet breakfast and early coffee/tea.

Afternoon tea available. Beds: TD. Air conditioning in room. Small meetings hosted. Antiques, fishing, parks, shopping, cross-country skiing, golf, theater and watersports nearby.

Publicity: *Down East.*

"I have but one complaint: I'm afraid you set the standard so high that other B&Bs may pale in comparison. I will have nothing but praise for your inn and high recommendations."

Surry   H6

Surry Inn
Contention Cove, Rt 172
Surry, ME 04684
(207)667-5091 (800)742-3414

Circa 1832. Two colonial buildings comprise the Surry Inn. Set on three-and-a-half acres with lawns that slope down to the ocean, the main house originally served as a steamboat/stagecoach stop. Located on Contenton Cove, the inn offers beautiful sunsets from its waterfront site. The dining room is notable for its expansive menu and provides a fine fireside setting. Cocktails are served on the long glassed-in porch. Croquet,

horseshoes, bird watching, seal watching and taking out the canoe and rowboat are favored activities. Nearby is Bar Harbor, Deer Isle, Arcadia National Park and Mt. Desert Island.

Innkeeper(s): Peter Krinsky. $48-72. MC VISA DS PC TC. 13 rooms, 11 with PB. Breakfast included in rates. Type of meal: full breakfast. Dinner, banquet service and catered breakfast available. Restaurant on premises. Beds: D. TV, VCR and swimming on premises. Handicap access. Weddings, small meetings, family reunions and seminars hosted. Antiques, fishing, parks, shopping, cross-country skiing, golf and watersports nearby.

Publicity: *New York Times.*

Waldoboro   I4

Broad Bay Inn & Gallery
PO Box 607
Waldoboro, ME 04572-0607
(207)832-6668 (800)736-6769

Circa 1830. This Colonial inn lies in the heart of an unspoiled coastal village. You'll find Victorian furnishings throughout and some guest rooms have canopy beds. An established art gallery displays works by renowned artists, as well as limited-edition prints. Television, games and an art library are available in the common room. It's a short walk to restaurants, tennis, churches and the historic Waldo Theatre.

Innkeeper(s): Libby Hopkins. $45-75. MC VISA. 5 rooms. Breakfast included in rates. Types of meals: full breakfast and early coffee/tea. Beds: DT. TV, VCR and copier on premises. Weddings, small meetings, family reunions and seminars hosted. Antiques, fishing, parks, shopping, downhill skiing, cross-country skiing, theater and watersports nearby.

Publicity: *Boston Globe, Ford Times, Courier Gazette, Princeton Packet, Better Homes & Gardens Cookbook.*

"Breakfast was so special - I ran to get my camera. Why, there were even flowers on my plate."

Walpole J4

Brannon-Bunker Inn

349 S St Rt 129
Walpole, ME 04573
(207)563-5941 (800)563-9225

Circa 1820. This Cape-style house has been a home to many generations of Maine residents, one of whom was captain of a ship that sailed to the Arctic. During the '20s, the barn served as a dance hall. Later, it was converted into comfortable guest rooms. Victorian and American antiques are featured, and there are collections of military and political memorabilia.

Innkeeper(s): Joe & Jeanne Hovance. $55-75. MC VISA AX PC TC. TAC10. 8 rooms, 5 with PB. 1 suite. Breakfast included in rates. Type of meal: continental-plus breakfast. Beds: QDT. TV, VCR, library and child care on premises. Handicap access. 28 acres. Weddings, small meetings and family reunions hosted. Antiques, fishing, parks, shopping, cross-country skiing, golf, theater and watersports nearby.

Publicity: *Times-Beacon Newspaper.*

"Wonderful beds, your gracious hospitality and the very best muffins anywhere made our stay a memorable one."

Waterford I2

Kedarburn Inn

Rt 35 Box 61
Waterford, ME 04088
(207)583-6182 Fax:(207)583-6424

Circa 1858. The innkeepers of this Victorian establishment invite guests to try a taste of olde English hospitality and cuisine at their inn, nestled in the foothills of the White Mountains in Western Maine. Located in a historic village, the inn sits beside the flowing Kedar Brook, which runs to the shores of Lake Keoka. Each of the spacious rooms is decorated with handmade quilts and dried flowers. Explore the inn's shop and you'll discover a variety of quilts and crafts, all made by innkeeper Margaret Gibson. Ask about special quilting weekends. With prior reservation, the innkeepers will prepare an English afternoon tea.

Innkeeper(s): Margaret & Derek Gibson. $71-125. MC VISA AX DS PC TC. 7 rooms, 3 with PB. 1 suite. 1 conference room. Breakfast included in rates. Types of meals: full breakfast and early coffee/tea. Afternoon tea, dinner, evening snack, banquet service, catering service, catered breakfast and room service available. Restaurant on premises. Beds: KQDT. Air conditioning in room. TV, VCR, fax and pet boarding on premises. Weddings, small meetings, family reunions and seminars hosted. Antiques, fishing, shopping, downhill skiing, cross-country skiing, theater and watersports nearby.

Pets Allowed.

Location: In the White Mountains.

Publicity: *Maine Times.*

Lake House

Rts 35 & 37
Waterford, ME 04088
(207)583-4182 (800)223-4182 Fax:(207)583-6078

Circa 1780. Situated on the common, the Lake House was first a hotel and stagecoach stop. In 1817, granite baths were constructed below the first floor. The inn opened as "Dr.

Shattuck's Maine Hygienic Institute for Ladies." It continued as a popular health spa until the 1890s. Now noted for excellent country cuisine, there are two dining rooms for non-smokers. Four guest rooms are upstairs. The spacious Grand Ballroom Suite features curved ceilings and a sitting room. Views of Lake Keoka are enjoyed from the inn's veranda. A cozy guest bungalow with private porch sits behind the inn.

Innkeeper(s): Michael Myers. $84-130. MAP. MC VISA AX. 5 rooms with PB. 1 suite. Type of meal: full breakfast. Restaurant on premises. Beds: QDT. Phone in room. Weddings, small meetings, family reunions and seminars hosted. Antiques, fishing, shopping, downhill skiing, cross-country skiing and theater nearby.

Publicity: *Country Inns, Yankee Travel Magazine.*

"Your hospitality was matched only by the quality of dinner that we were served."

Wells K2

Sand Dollar Inn

50 Rachel Carson Ln
Wells, ME 04090
(207)646-2346 (888)545-5451

Circa 1924. This Dutch Colonial house sits oceanfront on Wells Beach, offering guests a seaside experience of glistening waves, shore birds, sunrises and waters lit by moonlight. There is an enclosed porch and an upper sun deck. Traditional furnishings, billowing curtains and soft colors in the guest rooms add to the serenity. Ask for the oceanfront Peach Room. Pancakes rolled over apples, egg entrees and a fresh fruit medley with custard sauce are favorite breakfast items. In cool weather a "Winter Soup Pot" is provided, and guests enjoy the warmth of the wood stove.

Innkeeper(s): Bob & Carolyn Della Pietra. $85-145. MAP. MC VISA PC. 6 rooms, 4 with PB. 2 suites. Breakfast and afternoon tea included in rates. Types of meals: full breakfast, gourmet breakfast and early coffee/tea. Picnic lunch available. Beds: QT. Ceiling fan in room. TV and VCR on premises. Handicap access. Weddings, small meetings and seminars hosted. Amusement parks, antiques, fishing, shopping, cross-country skiing, golf, theater and watersports nearby.

"The Sand Dollar Inn is not a B&B, it is heaven, a place to rejuvenate and refresh the mind and body. There are no words to adequately express our appreciation."

The Victorian House Inn

1616 Post Rd, PO Box 1644
Wells, ME 04090
(207)646-5355

Circa 1898. This comfortable 19th-century Victorian offers a cozy retreat for guests looking to enjoy the miles of sandy beaches located just minutes away. Each of the three guest rooms features antiques and Victorian memorabilia. Breakfast includes such items as juice, muffins, assorted sweet breads, peachy French toast, scrambled eggs with chives or broccoli and Canadian bacon quiche served with sausage on the side.

Historic Interest: Neighboring towns of Kennebunkport and Oqunquit offer art galleries, museums, whale watching, deep sea fishing and cruises.

Innkeeper(s): Kathy Wright. $75-100. MC VISA PC TC. 3 rooms with PB, 1 with FP. Breakfast included in rates. Types of meals: full breakfast and early coffee/tea. Beds: D. Turndown service in room. Weddings hosted. Antiques, fishing, shopping, cross-country skiing, golf and theater nearby.

"It's like visiting your own family. I felt right at home!"

West Boothbay Harbor J4

Lawnmeer Inn

PO Box 505
West Boothbay Harbor, ME 04575-0505
(800)633-7645

Circa 1899. This pleasant inn sits by the shoreline, providing a picturesque oceanfront setting. Located on a small, wooded island, it is accessed by a lift bridge. Family-oriented rooms are clean and homey, and there is a private honeymoon cottage in the Smoke House. The dining room is waterside and serves continental cuisine with an emphasis on seafood. Boothbay Harbor is two miles away.

Innkeeper(s): Lee & Jim Metzger. $68-175. MC VISA. TAC10. 32 rooms with PB. 1 suite. 1 cottage. Types of meals: full breakfast and early coffee/tea. Dinner and banquet service available. Restaurant on premises. Beds: KQD. Weddings, small meetings and family reunions hosted. Antiques, fishing, shopping, theater and watersports nearby.

Pets Allowed: Small pets-one per room.

Publicity: *Los Angeles Times, Getaways for Gourmets.*

"Your hospitality was warm and gracious and the food delectable."

West Gouldsboro H6

Sunset House

Rt 186 HCR 60, Box 62
West Gouldsboro, ME 04607
(207)963-7156 (800)233-7156

Circa 1898. This coastal country farm inn is situated near Acadia National Park. Naturalists can observe rare birds and

other wildlife in an unspoiled setting. Seven spacious bedrooms are spread over three floors. Four of the bedrooms have ocean views; a fifth overlooks a freshwater pond behind the house. During winter, guests can ice skate on the pond, while in summer it is used for swimming. The innkeepers have a resident cat and poodle, and they also raise goats. Guests enjoy a full country breakfast cooked by Carl, who has been an executive chef for more than 20 years.

Innkeeper(s): Kathy & Carl Johnson. $69-79. MC VISA AX DC CB DS PC TC. 7 rooms, 3 with PB. Breakfast included in rates. Types of meals: full breakfast and early coffee/tea. Beds: KDT. VCR on premises. Weddings and family reunions hosted. Antiques, fishing, parks, shopping and cross-country skiing nearby.

Location: Only 6.5 miles from the Schoodic Peninsula, which is the quiet side of Acadia National Park.

Wiscasset J4

The Squire Tarbox Inn

Box 1181 Westport Island
Wiscasset, ME 04578-3501
(207)882-7693 Fax:(207)882-7107

Circa 1763. North of Bath, deep into the country and woods, Squire Tarbox built his rambling farmhouse around a building originally constructed in 1763. Today, the rooms are warm and

comfortable in the inn and in the remodeled hayloft. The innkeepers raise Nubian goats, all photogenic, that have become part of the entertainment (milking and goat cheese). A house-party atmosphere pervades the inn.

Historic Interest: Maritime Museum, old forts, lighthouses, sea captain's homes, abundant antique shops, fishing museums, windjammers, beaches, lobster shacks, etc. (30 minutes). World's finest Music Box Museum.

Innkeeper(s): Bill & Karen Mitman. $85-171. MC VISA AX DS PC TC. TAC10. 11 rooms with PB, 4 with FP. Breakfast included in rates. Types of meals: full breakfast and early coffee/tea. Afternoon tea and dinner available. Restaurant on premises. Beds: DT. Air conditioning in room. Bicycles and library on premises. 12 acres. Antiques, fishing, parks, shopping and theater nearby.

Location: Route 144, 8 1/2 miles on Westport Island.

Publicity: *Washington Post, New York Times, Yankee, Bon Appetit.*

"Your hospitality was warm, friendly, well-managed and quite genuine. That's a rarity, and it's just the kind we feel best with."

York L2

Dockside Guest Quarters

PO Box 205
York, ME 03909-0205
(207)363-2868 Fax:(207)363-1977
E-mail: info@docksidegq.com

Circa 1900. This small resort provides a panoramic view of the Atlantic Ocean and harbor activities. Guest rooms are located in the classic, large New England home, which is the Maine House, and modern multi-unit cottages. Most rooms have private balconies or porches with unobstructed views of the water. Some suites have fireplaces. The resort is available for weddings. The on-premise restaurant is bi-level with floor to ceiling windows, affording each table a view of the harbor. Child-care services are available.

Historic Interest: The York Historic District offers several interesting sites.

Innkeeper(s): Lusty Family. $73-149. MC VISA DS PC. TAC10.

21 rooms, 2 with FP. 6 suites. 1 conference room. Types of meals: continental-plus breakfast and early coffee/tea. Afternoon tea and lunch available. Restaurant on premises. Beds: KQDT. TV in room. Fax, bicycles, library and child care on premises. Weddings, small meetings and family reunions hosted. French spoken. Amusement parks, antiques, fishing, parks, shopping, cross-country skiing, theater and watersports nearby.

Location: York Harbor, Maine Rt. 103.

Publicity: *Boston Globe, Yankee Travel Guide.*

"We've been back many years. It's a paradise for us, the scenery, location, maintenance, living quarters."

York Harbor   L2

Bell Buoy B&B

570 York St
York Harbor, ME 03911
(207)363-7264

Circa 1884. Just a short walk to Long Sands Beach, this Victorian inn is located in prestigious York Harbor. You may want to stroll the Marginal Way along the ocean shore or catch the scenic trolley that stops across the street and takes you to points of interest while giving you a narrative about the town. After your day of enjoying the area, check out one of the many outstanding restaurants in the area, some within walking distance. Breakfasts can be relished in the family dining room or on the porch.

Innkeeper(s): Wes & Kathie Cook. $60-85. PC TC. 4 rooms, 3 with PB. 1 suite. Breakfast included in rates. Types of meals: full breakfast and early coffee/tea. Beds: KQDT. Turndown service and ceiling fan in room. TV and VCR on premises. Amusement parks, antiques, fishing, parks, shopping, theater and watersports nearby.

The Inn at Harmon Park

415 York St
York Harbor, ME 03911
(207)363-2031 Fax:(207)351-2948

Circa 1899. The innkeeper of this turn-of-the-century inn has worked hard to maintain the home's Victorian ambiance. Rooms are decorated with wicker furnishings and ceiling fans. Fresh flowers add extra color. The inn includes several fireplaces, one of which is found in a guest room. The inn is within walking distance of York Harbor Beach.

Innkeeper(s): Sue Antal. $69-109. PC TC. TAC10. 5 rooms with PB, 1 with FP. 1 suite. Breakfast included in rates. Types of meals: full breakfast and early coffee/tea. Beds: KQDT. Ceiling fan in room. TV, VCR, fax, copier, bicycles and library on premises. Weddings, small meetings, family reunions and seminars hosted. Amusement parks, antiques, fishing, parks, shopping, cross-country skiing, sporting events, theater and watersports nearby.

Location: Three-block walk to beaches and historic district.

York Harbor Inn

PO Box 573, Rt 1A
York Harbor, ME 03911-0573
(207)363-5119 (800)343-3869 Fax:(207)363-7151
E-mail: garyinkeep@aol.com

Circa 1800. The core building of the York Harbor Inn is a small log cabin constructed on the Isles of Shoals. Moved and reassembled at this dramatic location overlooking the entrance to York Harbor, the cabin is now a gathering room with a handsome stone fireplace. There is an English-style pub in the cellar,

a large ballroom and five meeting rooms. The dining room and some guest rooms overlook the ocean. Several guest rooms have ocean view decks, working fireplaces and Jacuzzi spas. One three-room suite is available.

Historic Interest: Old York Historical Society Museum buildings (1.5 miles), Strawberry Banke Colonial Village Museum (6 miles).

Innkeeper(s): Joseph & Garry Dominguez. $89-219. MAP. MC VISA AX DC CB PC TC. 33 rooms with PB, 4 with FP. 1 suite. 4 conference rooms. Breakfast included in rates. Types of meals: continental breakfast, continental-plus breakfast and early coffee/tea. Dinner, lunch, banquet service, catering service and room service available. Restaurant on premises. Beds: KQD. Phone, air conditioning and TV in room. VCR, fax, copier, spa, swimming and child care on premises. Weddings, small meetings, family reunions and seminars hosted. Amusement parks, antiques, fishing, parks, shopping, cross-country skiing, theater and watersports nearby.

Location: York Harbor's historic district.

Publicity: *New York Times, Down East, Food & Wine, The Learning Channel, Ladies Home Journal.*

"It's hard to decide where to stay when you're paging through a book of country inns. This time we chose well."

Maryland

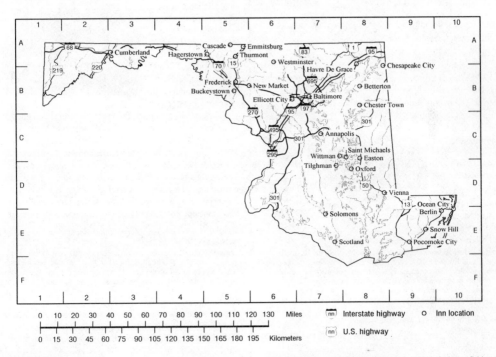

1	2	3	4	5	6	7	8	9	10

Cascade, Emmitsburg, Thurmont, Westminster, Havre De Grace, Chesapeake City, Frederick, New Market, Betterton, Buckeystown, Ellicott City, Baltimore, Chester Town, Annapolis, Saint Michaels, Wittman, Easton, Tilghman, Oxford, Vienna, Ocean City, Berlin, Solomons, Snow Hill, Scotland, Pocomoke City, Cumberland, Hagerstown

0 10 20 30 40 50 60 70 80 90 100 110 120 130 Miles
0 15 30 45 60 75 90 105 120 135 150 165 180 195 Kilometers

Interstate highway   o Inn location
U.S. highway

Annapolis   C7

The Barn on Howard's Cove

500 Wilson Rd
Annapolis, MD 21401-1052
(410)266-6840 Fax:(410)266-7293
E-mail: gdgutsche5@aol.com

Circa 1850. This renovated 1850 horse barn is located just
outside Annapolis on a cove of the Severn River. The six-and-a-
half-acre grounds create a restful environment. The two guest
rooms, which are decorated with antiques and handmade
quilts, offer water and garden views. There is also a small
kitchen area between the two guest rooms for preparing snacks
and coffee. A private balcony adjoins one guest room. The
innkeepers, a U.S. Naval Academy professor and an artist also
keep a unique Noah's Ark collection on display. The innkeepers have canoes and a kayak on the premises for guests.
Historic Interest: U.S. Naval Academy, the Paca House, Saint Johns College.
Innkeeper(s): Graham & Libbie Gutsche. $90. PC. TAC10. 2 rooms with PB.
Breakfast included in rates. Types of meals: continental breakfast and full
breakfast. Beds: Q. Phone, air conditioning, ceiling fan and TV in room. Fax

and swimming on premises. Small meetings hosted. Antiques, fishing, parks,
shopping, sporting events, theater and watersports nearby.

Location: Dock for boaters located nearby.

Publicity: *Baltimore Sun, New York Times, Mid-Atlantic Country, Christian
American.*

*"Thank you so much for your gracious hospitality and for making
our wedding night special."*

Georgian House B&B

170 Duke of Gloucester St
Annapolis, MD 21401-2517
(410)263-5618 (800)557-2068
E-mail: georgian@erols.com

Circa 1747. Walk to
all the city's historic
locations from this
elegant old red brick
Georgian home, once
the meeting place of
the Forensic Society
with three of its
members signers of

the Declaration of Independence. Dark green shutters grace the exterior and there are six fireplaces and original pine floors inside. Period furniture, reproductions and original art furnish the guest rooms. Breakfast served before the fireplace in the dining room or in summer, on the patio, often features a baked vegetable frittata and homemade breads.

Innkeeper(s): Dan & Michele Brown. $95-120. MC VISA PC TC. TAC15. 3 rooms with PB, 2 with FP. Breakfast included in rates. Types of meals: full breakfast, gourmet breakfast and early coffee/tea. Beds: KQ. Air conditioning and ceiling fan in room. TV, VCR and copier on premises. Antiques, fishing, parks, shopping, sporting events, golf, theater and watersports nearby.

Publicity: *National Geographic Traveler.*

Gibson's Lodgings

110 Prince George St
Annapolis, MD 21401-1704
(410)268-5555

Circa 1786. This Georgian house in the heart of the Annapolis Historic District was built on the site of the Old Courthouse, circa 1680. Two historic houses make up the inn, and there was a new house built in 1988.

All the rooms, old and new, are furnished with antiques. Only a few yards away is the City Dock Harbor and within two blocks is the Naval Academy visitor's gate. There is parking on premises.

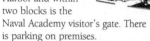

Historic Interest: U.S. Naval Academy, Chesapeake Bay.

Innkeeper(s): Claude & Jeanne Schrift. $68-125. MC VISA AX TC. TAC10. 21 rooms, 7 with PB. 2 suites. 2 conference rooms. Breakfast, afternoon tea and evening snack included in rates. Type of meal: continental-plus breakfast. Beds: QDT. Phone, air conditioning, ceiling fan and TV in room. Fax on premises. Handicap access. Weddings, small meetings, family reunions and seminars hosted. Antiques, fishing, parks, shopping, sporting events, theater and watersports nearby.

Publicity: *Mid-Atlantic Country, New York.*

"We had a delightful stay! We enjoyed the proximity to the waterfront, the fun atmosphere and the friendly people."

Historic Inns of Annapolis

58 State Circle
Annapolis, MD 21401-1917
(410)263-2641

Circa 1727. Five beautifully restored historic inns comprise Paul Pearson's Historic Inns of Annapolis: Robert Johnson House, State House, Maryland Inn, Reynolds Tavern and the Governor Calvert House. The Tavern, for instance, took seven years to restore. During that time, workers confirmed local legends that the tavern was once a center for smuggling and included a network of tunnels extending to the Annapolis waterfront. Architectural styles include Victorian, Georgian and Colonial with furnishings of the same period. (The Maryland Inn has been in continuous operation for more than 200 years.) There is also a new hotel attached to the State House.

Innkeeper(s): William Burrurs, Jr. $85-175. EP. MC VISA AX DC. 141 rooms with PB. 1 conference room. Type of meal: continental breakfast. Restaurant on premises. Beds: KQDT. Fax, copier and spa on premises. Handicap access.

Publicity: *Washingtonian, Historic Preservation, Boating.*

Jonas Green House B&B

124 Charles St
Annapolis, MD 21401-2621
(410)263-5892 Fax:(410)263-5895
E-mail: jghouse@erols.com

Circa 1690. For those seeking a truly historic vacation, Jonas Green House is a perfect starting place. The kitchen building of this historic home was completed in the 1690s and still houses the original cooking fireplace and an original crane. From this point, more was added until its completion sometime in the 1740s. Much of the home's original floors, wainscoting, fireplace surrounds and a corner cabinet with original glass has survived through the years. The home is named for one of innkeeper Randy Brown's relatives, who was a colonial patriot and printer. Jonas Green brought his bride to Annapolis and in 1738 settled at the home where the current innkeeper's family has resided ever since. Restoration of the home uncovered many interesting artifacts, which guests are sure to enjoy. Traditional furnishings fill the home, adding to its historic flavor. The innkeepers have kept the decor simple and authentic.

Historic Interest: The National Landmark home rests in the middle of a historic district. The Colonial Capitol Building is three blocks north and all of Annapolis' historic structures and the U.S. Naval Academy are within five or six blocks of the inn.

Innkeeper(s): Randy & Dede Brown. $85-115. MC VISA AX DS PC TC. 3 rooms, 1 with PB, 2 with FP. Breakfast included in rates. Type of meal: continental-plus breakfast. Beds: KDT. Air conditioning in room. Fax and copier on premises. Small meetings hosted. Danish spoken. Antiques, fishing, parks, shopping, sporting events, theater and watersports nearby.

Pets Allowed: Stay with owner in room.

Publicity: *Annapolitan, Capital, Washington Post, National Geographic Traveler, New York Times.*

"Thank you for your hospitality in a wonderful house so full of personal and American history."

Prince George Inn

232 Prince George St
Annapolis, MD 21401-1632
(410)263-6418 Fax:(410)626-0009

Circa 1884. The Prince George Inn is a three-story restored Victorian town house comfortably furnished with antiques. The guest parlor, breakfast room, porch and courtyard offer areas for relaxing. In the heart of the colonial city, the inn is near restaurants, museums, shops and the City Dock. The Naval Academy is two blocks away.

Historic Interest: Listed in the National Register.

Innkeeper(s): Janet & Dennis Coughlin. $85-110. MC VISA DS PC. TAC10. 4 rooms, 2 with PB. Breakfast included in rates. Type of meal: gourmet breakfast. Beds: KQT. Air conditioning, ceiling fan, TV and VCR in room. Fax and copier on premises. Antiques, fishing, shopping, sporting events, theater and watersports nearby.

Location: Historic District of Annapolis.

Publicity: *WMAR TV, Country Inns, Annapolitan.*

"Thoroughly enjoyed our six days in your lovely home!"

William Page Inn B&B

8 Martin St
Annapolis, MD 21401-1716
(410)626-1506 (800)364-4160
E-mail: WmPageInn@aol.com

Circa 1908. For more than 50 years, this immaculately renovated turn-of-the-century Four Square house served as the
Democratic Club in the historic district. The inn now offers visitors five distinctively appointed guest rooms furnished with
antiques and period reproductions. Common areas feature an
open stairway flanked by crystal chandeliers and period artwork. Guests can enjoy a breakfast of freshly baked breads and
Colonial egg casserole on the wraparound porch or in one of
the common rooms.

Innkeeper(s): Robert L. Zuchelli. $105-200. MC VISA PC. 5 rooms, 3 with
PB. Type of meal: full breakfast. Beds: Q. Phone in room.

Publicity: *The Evening Capital Newspaper, Country Inns.*

*"It was such a pleasure to see such a very elegantly appointed
Victorian inn."*

Baltimore   B7

Betsy's B&B

1428 Park Ave
Baltimore, MD 21217-4230
(410)383-1274 (800)899-7533 Fax:(410)728-8957
E-mail: amandars@aol.com

Circa 1870. This four-story townhouse features a hallway floor laid
with alternating strips of oak and walnut, ceiling medallions, large windows
and marble mantels. Walls are decked
with family heirlooms and other collectibles. Breakfast is served in the formal dining room, with a unique
carved marble mantel. Each of the
comfortably decorated guest rooms is
spacious, with a private bath.

Historic Interest: The home is located in the
historic Bolton Hill section of Baltimore, which
offers plenty of activities, including the simple
pleasure of exploring neighborhoods of row
houses, Antique Row, museums and plenty of
good restaurants.

Innkeeper(s): Betsy Grater. $85-150. MC VISA AX DS PC TC. TAC10. 3
rooms with PB. Breakfast included in rates. Type of meal: full breakfast.
Beds: KQ. Phone and air conditioning in room. TV, VCR, fax and copier on
premises. Weddings hosted. Antiques, parks, shopping, sporting events and
theater nearby.

Location: Inner Harbor, about 1.5 miles north.

Publicity: *Peabody Reflector, Nation's Business, Times Herald, Baltimore
Sun, Working Woman, WJZ-TV.*

*"What hotel room could ever compare to a large room in a 115-year-
old house with 12-foot ceilings and a marble fireplace with hosts that
could become dear longtime friends?"*

The Inn at Government House

1125 N Calvert St
Baltimore, MD 21202-3801
(410)539-0566

Circa 1897. This is the official guest house for Baltimore's visiting dignitaries, as well as the general public. Three town

houses comprise the inn, located in the Mt. Vernon historic
district. Features include chandeliers, ornate wallpapers and
Victorian antiques. Each bedchamber has its own view.

Innkeeper(s): Barbara Hunter. $95-140. MC VISA AX. 18 rooms with PB.
1 conference room. Type of meal: continental breakfast. Beds: KQD.
Handicap access.

Gramercy B&B

1400 Greenspring Valley Rd, Box 119
Baltimore, MD 21153-0119
(410)486-2405 Fax:(410)486-1765

Circa 1902. This English Tudor mansion was built as a wedding
present for the daughter of Alexander Cassatt, president of
Pennsylvania Railroad and brother to Mary Cassatt, famous
impressionist. A mother and daughter team runs the B&B. There
is a music room, library and parlors, all decorated with antiques

and Oriental rugs. Most of the guest rooms have fireplaces and a
few have Jacuzzi baths. Cookie, the inn's collie, loves taking
guests on nature walks along the woodland trails to flush deer
and fox out for viewing. There are commercial herb gardens, an
orchard, a stream and flower gardens. The house was featured as
the Decorator Showhouse to benefit the Baltimore Symphony.
The inn is known for its delectable breakfasts.

Historic Interest: Carroll Family Museums (20 minutes), Fort McHenry (20
minutes), Babe Ruth birthplace (18 minutes), Westminster Hall (Edgar Allen
Poe burial site).

Innkeeper(s): Anne & Cristin Pomykala. $145-250. MC VISA AX DS PC TC.
10 rooms, 5 with PB, 3 with FP. 2 suites. 2 conference rooms. Breakfast and
evening snack included in rates. Types of meals: full breakfast and gourmet
breakfast. Beds: KD. Phone, air conditioning, turndown service and VCR in
room. Fax, copier, swimming, tennis and library on premises. 45 acres.
Weddings, small meetings, family reunions and seminars hosted. Antiques,
parks and shopping nearby.

Location: 20 minutes from Baltimore Inner Harbor.

Publicity: *Mid-Atlantic B&B Guide, Washington Post.*

"The hospitality, atmosphere, food, etc. were top-notch."

Mr. Mole B&B

1601 Bolton St
Baltimore, MD 21217-4317
(410)728-1179 Fax:(410)728-3379

Circa 1869. Set on a quiet, up-scale street in the historic
Bolton Hill neighborhood, this beautifully restored brick town
house, named after the fastidious character in The Wind in the
Willows, is a combination of whimsical romantic ambiance and
old Baltimore society. Throughout the house, 18th- and 19th-
century antiques enhance wainscoting, painted draped ivy and
14-foot ceilings. Each guest room and suite features a different
theme. The Garden Suite, blooming with sunny floral prints

and plaid, offers a bright, third-floor sun room, sitting room and a spacious private bath. The Explorer Suite features sophisticated leopard-print fabrics and a zebra-skin rug. The only Mobil four-star B&B in Maryland, the inn is located six blocks from the Meyerhoff Symphony Hall, the Lyric Opera House, the Metro and the beginning of Baltimore's Antique Row.

Historic Interest: On historic Bolton Hill. Located close to Johns Hopkins University and the University of Baltimore. Downtown Baltimore, the Inner Harbor and Fells Point are five minutes away by car, Metro or trolley.

Innkeeper(s): Paul Bragaw & Collin Clarke. $99-145. MC VISA AX DC DS PC TC. TAC8. 5 rooms with PB, 4 with FP. 2 suites. Breakfast included in rates. Type of meal: continental-plus breakfast. Beds: Q. Phone, air conditioning and turndown service in room. Fax and library on premises. Antiques, parks, shopping, sporting events, golf and theater nearby.

Publicity: *Baltimore Magazine, Maryland Magazine, Travel Holiday, Mid-Atlantic, Washingtonian.* Ratings: 4 Stars.

The Paulus Gasthaus

2406 Kentucky Ave
Baltimore, MD 21213-1014
(410)467-1688 Fax:(410)467-1688

Circa 1927. The Gasthaus serves as a good home base from which to enjoy Baltimore. The three-story home is comfortably furnished, and fresh flowers and chocolates pamper guests. German and American specialties are prepared for the morning meal. Mass transit is just a block away, as is Johns Hopkins University and the football stadium.

Innkeeper(s): Lucie & Ed Paulus. $80. PC TC. TAC10. 2 rooms, 1 with PB. Breakfast, afternoon tea and evening snack included in rates. Type of meal: gourmet breakfast. Beds: QDT. Air conditioning and ceiling fan in room. Fluent German and some French spoken. Antiques, parks, shopping, sporting events and theater nearby.

Location: Four and one half miles from Inner Harbor.

"We ran across this extra copy of a picture of your lovely home. It brings back memories of gracious hospitality and great plentiful meals and snacks. We enjoyed our visit with you last spring."

Union Square House B&B

23 S Stricker St
Baltimore, MD 21223-2490
(410)233-9064 Fax:(410)233-4046

Circa 1870. This restored Victorian Italianate townhouse is situated in "Millionaires' Row" of the Union Square Historic District. It faces Union Square Park with its gardens, trees, gracious domed gazebo and fountain. Rooms feature original plaster moldings, handsome woodwork and period furnishings. The University of Maryland, B&O Railroad Museum, Convention Center and the Inner Harbor are just a few blocks away.

Historic Interest: B&O Train Museum (2 blocks), Fort McHenry (1 mile), H.L. Menchen Museum (one-half block).

Innkeeper(s): Joseph & Patrice Debes. $90-125. MC VISA AX DS TC. TAC10. 4 rooms with PB, 3 with FP. 2 suites. 1 conference room. Breakfast and afternoon tea included in rates. Types of meals: continental-plus breakfast, full breakfast and early coffee/tea. Beds: D. Air conditioning in room. Fax on premises. Weddings and small meetings hosted. Antiques, parks, shopping, sporting events, theater and watersports nearby.

Pets Allowed: Seeing eye dogs only.

"It is apparent that much care and thoughtfulness have gone into making your house a memorable and delightful place for your guests."

Berlin E10

Atlantic Hotel Inn & Restaurant

2 N Main St
Berlin, MD 21811-1043
(410)641-3589 (800)814-7672 Fax:(410)641-4928

Circa 1895. The exterior of this stunning Victorian hotel is a red brick wonder, decked with ornate trim. The hotel was built by Horace and Ginny Harmonson, and it was Ginny who ran the hotel until passing it on to her daughter. Through the years, the inn has had a succession of owners, the current of which refurbished the hotel back to its 19th-century glory. Rich fabrics cover the period antiques, which are set on polished wood floors and Oriental rugs. Bedchambers are awash in color with lacy touches and canopy or poster beds. The hotel has established a grand culinary tradition, carried on today by chef Larry Wilgus, a graduate of the Baltimore International Culinary College. Subtle lighting, linen tablecloths and soft decor create a romantic environment in the hotel dining room, where guests can choose from a variety of seasonal cuisine.

Innkeeper(s): Larry Wilgus. $55-140. MC VISA AX TC. 17 rooms, 16 with PB. 1 suite. 1 conference room. Breakfast included in rates. Type of meal: continental breakfast. Dinner, lunch and banquet service available. Restaurant on premises. Beds: QD. Phone, air conditioning, turndown service and TV in room. Weddings, small meetings, family reunions and seminars hosted. Amusement parks, antiques, fishing, parks, golf and watersports nearby.

Merry Sherwood Plantation

8909 Worcester Hwy
Berlin, MD 21811-3016
(410)641-2112 (800)660-0358 Fax:(410)641-9528

Circa 1859. This magnificent pre-Civil War mansion is a tribute to Southern plantation architecture. The inn features antique period furniture, hand-woven, Victorian era rugs and a

square grand piano. The ballroom, now a parlor for guests, boasts twin fireplaces and pier mirrors. (Ask to see the hidden cupboards behind the fireside bookcases in the library.) Nineteen acres of grounds are beautifully landscaped and feature azaleas, boxwoods and 125 varieties of trees.

Innkeeper(s): Kirk Burbage. $95-175. MC VISA. 8 rooms, 6 with PB, 4 with FP. 1 suite. Breakfast included in rates. Types of meals: full breakfast and gourmet breakfast. Afternoon tea available. Beds: QD. Air conditioning in room. TV on premises. 19 acres. Weddings, small meetings, family reunions and seminars hosted. Amusement parks, antiques, fishing, shopping and watersports nearby.

Publicity: *Washington Post, Baltimore Sun, Southern Living.*

"Pure elegance and privacy at its finest."

Betterton
B8

Lantern Inn

115 Ericsson Ave, PO Box 29
Betterton, MD 21610-9746
(410)348-5809 (800)499-7265

Circa 1904. Framed by a picket fence and a wide front porch, this four-story country inn is located one block from the nettle-free public beach on Chesapeake Bay. Comfortable rooms are furnished with antiques and handmade quilts. The surrounding area is well-known for its wildlife preserves. Antique shops and restaurants are nearby. Kent County offers plenty of cycling possibilities, and there are detailed maps available at the inn for trips that start at the inn and go for 10 to 90 miles. Tennis courts are two blocks away.

Historic Interest: Historic Chestertown (12 miles), Chesapeake Bay (1 block).

Innkeeper(s): Ken & Ann Washburn. $70-90. MC VISA. 13 rooms, 4 with PB. Breakfast included in rates. Type of meal: continental-plus breakfast. Beds: KDT. Phone in room. Antiques and fishing nearby.

Location: On the Chesapeake Bay.

Publicity: *Richland Times-Dispatch, North Carolina Outdoorsman, Washingtonian, Mid-Atlantic Country.*

"Thanks for your warm hospitality."

Buckeystown
B5

The Inn at Buckeystown

3521 Buckeystown Pike Gen Del
Buckeystown, MD 21717
(301)874-5755 (800)272-1190

Circa 1897. Gables, bay windows and a wraparound porch are features of this grand Victorian mansion located on two-and-a-half acres of lawns and gardens (and an ancient cemetery). Nearby St. John's Reformed Church, built in 1884, has been refurbished as a cottage. The inn features a polished staircase, antiques and elegantly decorated guest rooms. Ask for the Winter Suite, which boasts a lavish queen oak bed. At dinner, cream of garlic soup, German duck and ginger cream cake are house specialties. The village of Buckeystown is in the National Register.

Historic Interest: Frederick, Barbara Fritchie and Francis Scott Key grave sites (4 miles), National Battle of the Monocacy Civil War Battlefield Park (3 miles), Camp David (15 miles).

Innkeeper(s): Daniel R. Pelz & Chase Barnett. $140-300. MAP. MC VISA AX. 7 rooms with PB, 3 with FP. 1 conference room. Breakfast, afternoon tea and dinner included in rates. Types of meals: full breakfast and early coffee/tea. Beds: QDT. Phone and air conditioning in room. Weddings, small meetings, family reunions and seminars hosted. Antiques, fishing, shopping, downhill skiing, cross-country skiing, sporting events and watersports nearby.

Publicity: *Mid-Atlantic, Innsider, The Washingtonian, Washington Post.*

"The courtesy of you and your staff were the glue that bound the whole experience together."

Catoctin Inn & Antiques

3613 Buckeystown Pike
Buckeystown, MD 21717
(301)874-5555 (800)730-5550
E-mail: catoctin@fred.net

Circa 1780. The inn's four acres of dogwood, magnolias, maples and sweeping lawns overlook the village and the Catoctin Mountains range. Some special features of the inn include a library with marble fireplaces and a handsome wraparound veranda. A Victorian carriage house marks the site for weddings, showers and receptions for up to 150 guests. Fifteen of the guest rooms include a fireplace and a whirlpool tub. Nearby villages to visit include Harper's Ferry, Antietam and New Market. Buckeystown's Monocacy River provides canoeing and fishing.

Innkeeper(s): Terry & Sarah MacGillivray. $85-150. MC VISA AX DS PC. 20 rooms with PB, 15 with FP. 8 suites. 3 cottages. 3 conference rooms. Breakfast included in rates. Type of meal: continental breakfast. Afternoon tea and catering service available. Beds: KQ. Phone, air conditioning, turndown service, TV and VCR in room. Library on premises. Weddings, small meetings, family reunions and seminars hosted. Antiques, fishing, shopping, downhill skiing, cross-country skiing, sporting events and theater nearby.

Cascade
A5

Bluebird on The Mountain

14700 Eyler Ave
Cascade, MD 21719-1938
(301)241-4161 (800)362-9526

Circa 1900. In the mountain village of Cascade, this gracious shuttered Georgian manor is situated on two acres of trees and

wildflowers. Three suites have double whirlpool tubs. There is an outdoor hot tub as well. The Rose Garden Room and Mt. Magnolia suites have fireplaces and porches overlooking the back garden. The inn is appointed with antiques, lace and white linens, and white wicker. On Sundays, a full breakfast is served.

Innkeeper(s): Eda Smith-Eley. $105-125. MC VISA AX PC. TAC10. 5 rooms with PB, 3 with FP. 2 suites. Breakfast included in rates. Types of meals: continental-plus breakfast, full breakfast, gourmet breakfast and early coffee/tea. Room service available. Beds: KQT. Air conditioning, turndown service, ceiling fan, TV and VCR in room. Spa on premises. Small meetings, family reunions and seminars hosted. Antiques, fishing, parks, shopping, downhill skiing, sporting events, theater and watersports nearby.

Publicity: *Warm Welcomes, Baltimore Sun, Frederick News, Washington Post.*

"A wonderful balance of luxury and at-home comfort."

Chesapeake City   B8

Inn at The Canal

104 Bohemia Ave
Chesapeake City, MD 21915-1218
(410)885-5995 Fax:(410)885-3585

Circa 1870. A favorite activity here is watching the parade of boats and ships from the waterfront porch. The Inn at the Canal was built by the Brady family who owned the tugboats that operated on the canal. Rooms are furnished in antiques and quilts, set off by original hand-painted and elaborately designed ceilings. Guests enjoy European soaking tubs. The historic canal town offers a fine collection of restaurants and shops.

Innkeeper(s): Mary & Al Ioppolo. $75-130.
MC VISA AX DC CB DS PC TC. TAC10. 7 rooms with PB. 1 suite. 1 conference room. Breakfast and evening snack included in rates. Types of meals: full breakfast and early coffee/tea. Beds: KQDT. Phone, air conditioning and TV in room. Fax on premises. Small meetings hosted. Antiques, fishing, parks, shopping, sporting events, golf, theater and watersports nearby.

Chestertown   B8

Great Oak Manor

10568 Cliff Rd
Chestertown, MD 21620-4115
(410)778-5943 (800)504-3098 Fax:(410)778-5943

Circa 1938. This elegant Georgian mansion anchors vast lawns at the end of a long driveway. Situated directly on the

Chesapeake Bay, it is a serene and picturesque country estate. A library with fireplace, den and formal parlors are available to guests. With its grand circular stairway, bayside gazebo, and nearby beach and marina, the Manor is a remarkable setting for events such as weddings and reunions. Chestertown is eight miles away.

Innkeeper(s): Don & Dianne Cantor. $76-145. MC VISA PC TC. TAC10. 11 rooms with PB, 5 with FP. 1 suite. 2 conference rooms. Breakfast included in rates. Types of meals: continental-plus breakfast and early coffee/tea. Beds: KT. Phone and air conditioning in room. VCR, fax, copier, bicycles and library on premises. 12 acres. Weddings, small meetings, family reunions and seminars hosted. Antiques, fishing, parks, shopping, sporting events, theater and watersports nearby.

Publicity: *Country Inns, Southern Living.*

"The charming setting, professional service and personal warmth we experienced at Great Oak will long be a pleasant memory. Thanks for everything!"

The Inn at Mitchell House

8796 Maryland Pkwy
Chestertown, MD 21620-4209
(410)778-6500

Circa 1743. This pristine 18th-century manor house sits as a jewel on 12 acres overlooking Stoneybrook Pond. The guest rooms and the inn's several parlors are preserved and appointed in an authentic Colonial mood, heightened by handsome polished wideboard floors. Eastern Neck Island National Wildlife

Refuge, Chesapeake Farms, St. Michaels, Annapolis and nearby Chestertown are all delightful to explore. The Inn at Mitchell House is a popular setting for romantic weddings and small corporate meetings.

Innkeeper(s): Tracy & Jim Stone. $75-110. MC VISA PC. 6 rooms, 5 with PB, 3 with FP. Breakfast included in rates. Types of meals: full breakfast and early coffee/tea. Restaurant on premises. Beds: KQD. Air conditioning and turndown service in room. VCR on premises. 12 acres. Weddings, small meetings, family reunions and seminars hosted. Antiques, fishing, shopping, sporting events, theater and watersports nearby.

Publicity: *Washingtonian, New York Magazine, Glamour, Philadelphia Inquirer, Baltimore Sun, Kent County News, Ten Best Inns in the Country, New York Times. Washington Post, National Geographic Traveler.*

The Parker House

108 Spring Ave
Chestertown, MD 21620-1343
(410)778-9041

This gracious yellow Colonial features a beautifully crafted staircase, high ceilings and a lovely location in the Historic District of Chestertown. Guest rooms are furnished with interesting antiques. The innkeepers' cocker spaniel, Half Pint, is an integral part of the inn staff, and there is a large barn

on the property where you may keep your own pet, if arrangements are made in advance. Nearby is the campus of Washington College.

Innkeeper(s): Marcy & John Parker. Call for rates.

White Swan Tavern

231 High St
Chestertown, MD 21620-1517
(410)778-2300

Circa 1730. During the 1978 restoration of this inn, an archeological dig made an interesting discovery. Before 1733, the site was a tannery operated by the Shoemaker of Chestertown. His one-room dwelling is now a converted guest room. After additions to the building, it became a tavern in 1793 and was described as "situated in the center of business...with every attention given to render comfort and pleasure to such as favor it with their patronage."

Innkeeper(s): Mary Susan Maisel. $100-195. 6 rooms with PB. 2 conference rooms. Type of meal: continental-plus breakfast. Afternoon tea available. Beds: QDT. Phone in room.

Location: Eastern shore of Maryland. Downtown historic district.

"You could not find a more authentic, atmospheric sleeping room in Colonial Williamsburg."

Cumberland
A3

The Inn at Walnut Bottom

120 Greene St
Cumberland, MD 21502-2934
(301)777-0003 (800)286-9718 Fax:(301)777-8288

Circa 1820. Two historic houses comprise the Inn at Walnut Bottom: the 1815 Cowden House and the 1890 Dent House. There are two guest parlors. Country antiques and reproduction furnishings decorate the charming rooms. The Oxford House Restaurant serves meals Monday through Saturday.

Historic Interest:
George Washington Headquarters, Fort Cumberland, Allegany County Courthouse and the scenic railroad are all within walking distance. Frank Lloyd Wright's Fallingwater is nearby.

Innkeeper(s): Grant M. Irvin & Kirsten O. Hansen. $79-180. MAP. MC VISA AX DS PC TC. 12 rooms, 8 with PB. 2 suites. Breakfast included in rates. Types of meals: continental breakfast, full breakfast and early coffee/tea. Dinner, lunch and room service available. Restaurant on premises. Beds: KQDT. Phone, air conditioning, ceiling fan and TV in room. Fax, copier and bicycles on premises. Weddings, small meetings, family reunions and seminars hosted. Danish, German and French spoken. Antiques, fishing, parks, shopping, downhill skiing, cross-country skiing and theater nearby.

Publicity: *Washington Post, Mid-Atlantic Country, Southern Living.*

"Delightful!! Thank you!! Delicious food & gracious service."

Easton
C8

The Bishop's House B&B

214 Goldsborough St
Easton, MD 21601
(410)820-7290 (800)223-7290 Fax:(410)820-7290
E-mail: bishopshouse@skipjack.bluecrab.org

Circa 1880. The innkeepers of this in-town Victorian lovingly restored it in 1988. The three-and-a-half-story clapboard and gabled roof home includes three spacious first-floor rooms with 14-foot-high ceilings and generously sized second- and third-floor guest rooms. With its

period-style furnishings, working fireplaces and whirlpool tubs, the inn offers its guests both romance and the ambiance of the Victorian era. A hot breakfast is served every morning. Located in Easton's Historic District, it is within three blocks of boutiques, antique shops, restaurants and historic sites. The inn provides off-street parking.

Historic Interest: Within 10 miles of historic Oxford and St. Michaels.

Innkeeper(s): John & Diane Ippolito. Call for rates. Breakfast included in rates. Type of meal: early coffee/tea.

Ellicott City
B6

Wayside Inn

4344 Columbia Rd
Ellicott City, MD 21042-5910
(410)461-4636 Fax:(410)750-2070

Circa 1800. This stone farmhouse is situated on two acres and has a small pond. A parlor, music room and a recreation room are available for guests. There are two suites with private baths, while the two other guest rooms feature fireplaces and a shared bath. The guest rooms are decorated in a combination of antiques and reproduction furniture. The innkeepers continue the tradition of lighting a candle in each window where a room is still available for the night.

Historic Interest: Ellicott City Historic District (2 miles).

Innkeeper(s): Margo & John Osantowski. $75-95. MC VISA AX DS PC TC. TAC10. 4 rooms, 2 with PB, 2 with FP. 2 suites. Breakfast and evening snack included in rates. Types of meals: continental-plus breakfast, gourmet breakfast and early coffee/tea. Beds: QD. Air conditioning and turndown service in room. Fax and copier on premises. Small meetings hosted. Antiques, parks, shopping and theater nearby.

Publicity: *Mid-Atlantic, Howard County Sun, Maryland, Country Magazine.*

"Thank you! So much for such a wonderful experience! You make your guests feel extra special!"

Emmitsburg
A5

Stonehurst Inn B&B

9436 Waynesboro Rd, Rt 140 W
Emmitsburg, MD 21727
(301)447-2880 (800)497-8458 Fax:(301)447-3521
E-mail: stonehurstbbmd

Circa 1875. This mansion, reminiscent of a European villa, was once the home of the first national Episcopal bishop. The landscaped eight acres afford a peaceful getaway. The front veranda, lined with wicker chairs, is a perfect spot to relax. Guests enjoy a warm greeting from canine innkeeper, Lucky, a handsome sheltie. There are seven guests rooms, decorated in a homey, traditional style. The suite includes a fully equipped kitchen. There's much to do in the area, which boasts the Cacotin and Blue Ridge mountains. Gettysburg and other Civil War sites are just a few miles away. Breakfasts are served family-style on a table set with china and crystal.

Innkeeper(s): Marie & Don Sanderson. $65-95. MC VISA AX PC TC. TAC10. 8 rooms, 3 with PB. 1 suite. 1 cottage. 1 conference room. Breakfast, afternoon tea and evening snack included in rates. Types of meals: continental breakfast, continental-plus breakfast, full breakfast, gourmet breakfast and early coffee/tea. Room service available. Beds: KQDT. Phone, air conditioning, turndown service, TV and VCR in room. Fax, copier, library and pet boarding on premises. Handicap access. Weddings, small meetings, family reunions and seminars hosted. Antiques, fishing, parks, shopping, downhill skiing, cross-country skiing, sporting events, golf and watersports nearby.

Pets Allowed: In kennel on premises on grounds.

Publicity: *Fredrick Post.*

"The house reflects a lot of tender loving care and hard work. The breakfast was a meal fit for a king."

Frederick B5

Tyler-Spite House

112 W Church St
Frederick, MD 21701-5411
(301)831-4455

Circa 1814. This three-story, Federal-style house was built literally overnight by Dr. John Tyler who hoped the home's construction would prevent the extension of a local road. Thus, Tyler's home also bears the nickname, "Spite" house. Inside, elaborate woodwork, high ceilings with raised paneling and eight working fireplaces, some with marble mantels, create an elegant, inviting atmosphere. A winding staircase, lit by a beautiful chandelier, leads guests up to the five, well-appointed bedchambers decorated with Oriental rugs and antiques. Multi-course breakfasts are served in the formal dining room or on the patios in warm weather. High tea is served each afternoon. For an extra charge, the innkeepers offer romantic carriage rides through the park and historic district.

Historic Interest: The Brunswick R.R. Museum, in nearby Brunswick, offers a look at the history of the railroad in the United States. Mount Olivet Cemetery in Frederick is the final resting place of such esteemed Americans as Francis Scott Key and Barbara Fritchie. Fritchie, who angrily confronted General Stonewall Jackson in 1862, was memorialized in a poem.

Innkeeper(s): Bill & Andrea Myer. $100-180. MC VISA AX. 6 rooms, 4 with PB. 1 suite. Type of meal: full breakfast. Afternoon tea and catering service available. Beds: QD. Antiques, fishing and cross-country skiing nearby.

Publicity: *Potomac.*

Hagerstown A5

Beaver Creek House B&B

20432 Beaver Creek Rd
Hagerstown, MD 21740-1514
(301)797-4764

Circa 1905. History buffs enjoy this turn-of-the-century inn located minutes away from Antietam and Harpers Ferry National Historical Parks. The surrounding villages house antique shops and some hold weekend auctions. The inn features a courtyard with a fountain and a country garden. Innkeepers Don and Shirley Day furnished the home with family antiques and memorabilia. Guests can sip afternoon tea or complimentary sherry in the elegant parlor or just relax on the porch and take in the view of South Mountain.

Historic Interest: Antietam National Battlefield (12 miles), Gettysburg (34 miles), Fort Frederick (16 miles), Appalachian Trail (4 miles).

Innkeeper(s): Donald & Shirley Day. $75-95. MC VISA AX PC TC. TAC10. 5 rooms with PB. 1 conference room. Breakfast included in rates. Types of meals: full breakfast and gourmet breakfast. Beds: DT. Air conditioning and ceiling fan in room. Copier on premises. Small meetings, family reunions and seminars hosted. Amusement parks, antiques, fishing, parks, shopping, downhill skiing, cross-country skiing, sporting events, theater and watersports nearby.

Publicity: *Baltimore Sun, Hagerstown Journal, Herald Mail, Washington Post, Frederick.*

"Thanks so much for your hospitality. You're wonderful hosts and breakfast was delicious as usual. Don't change a thing."

Sunday's B&B

39 Broadway
Hagerstown, MD 21740-4019
(301)797-4331 (800)221-4828

Circa 1890. This Queen Anne Victorian is appropriately appointed with period antiques. Fresh flowers and fruit baskets are provided and guests are pampered with a full breakfast, afternoon tea, evening wine and cheese and for late evening, bedside cordials and chocolates. Antietam, Harpers Ferry and the C&O Canal are nearby.

Innkeeper(s): Robert Ferrino. $75-115. MC VISA DC. 4 rooms, 3 with PB. Breakfast included in rates. Types of meals: full breakfast and early coffee/tea. Afternoon tea, dinner, picnic lunch and catering service available. Beds: QD. Air conditioning and TV in room. Weddings, small meetings and family reunions hosted. Antiques, fishing, parks, shopping, downhill skiing and theater nearby.

Location: Twenty minutes from Antietam Battlefields.

"A four star inn! Every detail perfect, decor and atmosphere astounding."

Havre De Grace A8

Spencer Silver Mansion

200 S Union Ave
Havre De Grace, MD 21078-3224
(410)939-1097 (800)780-1485

Circa 1896. This elegant granite Victorian mansion is graced with bays, gables, balconies, a turret and a gazebo veranda. The Victorian decor, with antiques and Oriental rugs, complements the house's carved-oak woodwork, fireplace mantels and parquet floors. The Concord Point Lighthouse (oldest continuously operated lighthouse in America) is only a walk away. In addition to the four rooms in the main house, a romantic carriage house suite is available, featuring an in-room fireplace, TV, whirlpool bath and kitchenette.

Historic Interest: Fort McHenry (45 minutes), Concord Point Lighthouse (1 minute).

Innkeeper(s): Carol Nemeth. $65-125. MC VISA AX DS PC TC. TAC10. 5 rooms, 3 with PB, 1 with FP. 1 cottage. Breakfast included in rates. Types of meals: full breakfast and early coffee/tea. Beds: QDT. Phone, air conditioning, turndown service and TV in room. Weddings, small meetings and family reunions hosted. German spoken. Antiques, fishing, parks, shopping and watersports nearby.

Pets Allowed: In Carriage House only.

Location: In the heart of the historic district, 2 blocks from the waterfront.

Publicity: *Mid-Atlantic Country, Maryland.*

"A fabulous find. Beautiful house, excellent hostess. I've stayed at a lot of B&Bs, but this house is the best."

New Market
B6

National Pike Inn

PO Box 299, 9 W Main St
New Market, MD 21774-0299
(301)865-5055

Circa 1796. This red-shuttered, brick Federal-style home is one of the few inns remaining on the National Pike, an old route that carried travelers from Baltimore to points west. The inn's Colonial decor includes wingback chairs, Oriental rugs and four-poster beds. Azalea gardens border a private courtyard and fountain. New Market, founded in 1793, offers more than 30 antique shops and other charming points of interest, including an old-fashioned general store and fine dining, all within walking distance of the inn.

Historic Interest: Frederick Museums (7 miles), Civil War Medical Museum (nearby), Harpers Ferry, Va. (25 minutes drive).

Innkeeper(s): Tom & Terry Rimel. $85-125. MC VISA PC TC. 6 rooms, 4 with PB, 3 with FP. 1 suite. 1 conference room. Breakfast included in rates. Type of meal: full breakfast. Beds: QD. Air conditioning in room. TV and VCR on premises. Small meetings hosted. Antiques, shopping, sporting events and theater nearby.

Location: Exit 62 off interstate 70, 6 miles east of Frederick, Md.

Publicity: *Mid-Atlantic Country, Country.*

"A total joy! A relaxed, charming and romantic setting."

Strawberry Inn

17 Main St, PO Box 237
New Market, MD 21774
(301)865-3318

Circa 1860. Strawberry Inn is a restored Maryland farmhouse located in the center of a 200-year-old historic National Register town. The white Victorian clapboard house is furnished with antiques, of course, since New Market is the antique capital of Maryland.

Innkeeper(s): Jane Rossig. $85-125. 5 rooms with PB. Beds: KQT.

"A tiny jewel in a Victorian setting. — New York Times."

Ocean City
E10

Atlantic House B&B

501 N Baltimore Ave
Ocean City, MD 21842-3926
(410)289-2333
E-mail: atlanticho.aol.com

Circa 1927. From the front porch of this bed & breakfast, guests can partake in ocean views. The rooms are decorated in antique oak and wicker complementing a relaxing beach

stay. The morning breakfast buffet includes such items as freshly baked breads, fruit, egg casseroles, cereals and yogurt. In the afternoons, light refreshments also are served. The inn, nestled in the original Ocean City, is a short walk to the beach, boardwalk and shopping.

Innkeeper(s): Paul & Debi Cook. $55-145. MC VISA AX DS TC. TAC10. 14 rooms, 8 with PB. 1 suite. Breakfast, afternoon tea and evening snack included in rates. Types of meals: full breakfast and early coffee/tea. Beds: QD. Air conditioning, ceiling fan and TV in room. Weddings, small meetings, family reunions and seminars hosted. Amusement parks, antiques, fishing, parks, shopping, sporting events, theater and watersports nearby.

"We were anxious to see if we made the right choice, we definitely did."

Oxford
D8

1876 House

PO Box 658, 110 N Morris St
Oxford, MD 21654-0658
(410)226-5496

Circa 1876. This early Victorian house has a welcoming front porch, 10-foot ceilings and wide-planked pine floors. A queen-size, four-poster bed is in the master suite, which looks out over North Morris Street. A continental breakfast is served in a formal dining room.

Historic Interest: Chesapeake Bay Maritime Museum.

Innkeeper(s): Eleanor & Jerry Clark. $97. PC TC. 3 rooms with PB. Type of meal: continental-plus breakfast. Beds: QD. Phone in room. Fishing, golf and watersports nearby.

Publicity: *Discerning Traveler, New York Times.*

"Every detail is perfect and certainly marks you as pure royalty in the hospitality area."

The Robert Morris Inn

314 N Morris St PO Box 70
Oxford, MD 21654
(410)226-5111 Fax:(410)226-5744

Circa 1710. Once the home of Robert Morris Sr., a representative of an English trading company, the house was constructed by ship carpenters with wooden-pegged paneling, ship's nails and hand-hewn beams. Bricks brought to Oxford as ballast in trading ships were used to build the fireplaces. Robert Morris Jr., a partner in a Philadelphia law firm, used his entire savings to help finance the Continental Army. He signed the Declaration of Independence, Articles of Confederation and United States Constitution. James A. Michener, author of "Chesapeake," rated the inn's crab cakes as his favorite.

Historic Interest: Talbot Historic Society (15 minutes), Chesapeake Maritime Museum (25 minutes).

Innkeeper(s): Jay Gibson. $70-240. EP. MC VISA PC. TAC10. 35 rooms with PB. Restaurant on premises. Beds: KQDT. Air conditioning in room. Fax, copier and library on premises. Handicap access. Small meetings and seminars hosted. Antiques, fishing, parks, shopping, theater and watersports nearby.

Publicity: *Southern Accents, The Evening Sun, Maryland, Mid-Atlantic Country, Bon Appetite.*

"Impressed! Unbelievable!"

Pocomoke City E9

Littletons Bed & Breakfast

407 2nd St
Pocomoke City, MD 21851-1417
(410)957-1645 Fax:(410)957-1645

Circa 1860. Recently awarded its place in the National Register of Historic Places, this classic Second Empire-style home was built by two prominent merchants. Completely renovated in 1994, guests will take

pleasure in the warmth and hospitality offered by innkeepers Walter and Pamela Eskiewicz. Upon arrival, guests are treated to a refreshing beverage. All rooms are decorated in a combination of antiques and traditional furnishings. An accomplished gourmet cook,
Pamela prides herself on her unique breakfast specialties such as Gingerbread Pancakes with Currant Pear Maple Syrup, Chocolate Walnut Butter Bread, potato pancakes with sausage and Carmella's Omelet. Pocomoke River, creeks and tributaries are located nearby.

Historic Interest: Located close to the View Trail 100 that offers a unique cycling experience through the Worcester County countryside and historic district.

Innkeeper(s): Walter & Pam Eskiewicz. $60-95. MC VISA DS PC. 4 rooms, 3 with PB. Breakfast included in rates. Types of meals: full breakfast and gourmet breakfast. Beds: QDT. Air conditioning and ceiling fan in room. Fax, bicycles and library on premises. Small meetings hosted. Amusement parks, antiques, fishing, parks, shopping, sporting events, golf and watersports nearby.

Publicity: *The Daily Times.*

"Very pretty and cozy atmosphere. It was so nice to feel safe over the night. The accommodations were as comfortable as being at home. Thanks for good conversation!"

Saint Michaels C8

Kemp House Inn

412 Talbot St, PO Box 638
Saint Michaels, MD 21663
(410)745-2243

Circa 1807. This two-story Georgian house was built by Colonel Joseph Kemp, a shipwright and one of the town forefathers. The inn is appointed in period furnishings accentuated by candlelight. Guest rooms include patchwork quilts, a collection of four-poster rope beds and old-fashioned nightshirts. There are several working fireplaces. Robert E. Lee is said to have been a guest.

Historic Interest: Listed in the National Register.

Innkeeper(s): Diane M. Cooper. $75-115. MC VISA DS. 8 rooms, 6 with PB, 4 with FP. Breakfast included in rates. Types of meals: continental breakfast and early coffee/tea. Catered breakfast available. Beds: QDT. Air conditioning in room. Antiques, fishing, shopping and watersports nearby.

Pets Allowed.

Location: Historic town on the eastern shore of the Chesapeake.

Publicity: *Gourmet, Philadelphia.*

"It was wonderful. We've stayed in many B&Bs, and this was one of the nicest!"

Parsonage Inn

210 N Talbot St
Saint Michaels, MD 21663-2102
(410)745-5519 (800)394-5519

Circa 1883. A striking Victorian steeple rises next to the wide bay of this brick residence, once the home of Henry Clay

Dodson, state senator, pharmacist and brickyard owner. The house features brick detail in a variety of patterns and inlays, perhaps a design statement for brick customers. Porches are decorated with filigree and spindled columns. Laura

Ashley linens, late Victorian furnishings, fireplaces and decks add to the creature comforts. Four bikes await guests who wish to ride to Tilghman Island or to the ferry that goes to Oxford. Gourmet breakfast is served in the dining room.

Historic Interest: Maritime Museum & Historic Boats (2 blocks), Town of Oxford (10 miles), Town of Easton (9 miles).

Innkeeper(s): Gayle Lutz. $100-160. MC VISA PC TC. TAC10. 8 rooms with PB, 3 with FP. Breakfast included in rates. Type of meal: gourmet breakfast. Beds: KQD. Air conditioning and ceiling fan in room. TV and bicycles on premises. Handicap access. Small meetings and family reunions hosted. Antiques, fishing, shopping and watersports nearby.

Location: In the historic district.

Publicity: *Wilmington, Delaware News Journal, Philadelphia Inquirer.*

"Striking, extensively renovated."

The Inn at Perry Cabin

308 Watkins Ln
Saint Michaels, MD 21663-2114
(410)745-2200 (800)722-2949 Fax:(410)745-3348
E-mail: perrycbn@friend.ly.net

Circa 1812. Built around an early 19th-century farmhouse, this pristine waterside escape is one of the Laura Ashley Company's signature inns. A private boat dock, indoor swimming pool and excellent food service are all among the amenities that may be expected. Of course, fabulous fabrics and wall coverings are featured throughout.

Innkeeper(s): Stephen Creese. $150-575. MC VISA AX DC CB PC TC. TAC10. 41 rooms with PB. 1 conference room. Breakfast and afternoon tea included in rates. Types of meals: continental breakfast, continental-plus breakfast, full breakfast, gourmet breakfast and early coffee/tea. Dinner, evening snack, picnic lunch, lunch, gourmet lunch, banquet service, catering service, catered breakfast and room service available. Restaurant on premises. Beds: KQDT. Phone, air conditioning, turndown service, TV and VCR in room. Fax, copier, spa, swimming, sauna, bicycles, tennis, library and child care on premises. Handicap access. 25 acres. Weddings, small meetings, family reunions and seminars hosted. French, Spanish and German spoken. Antiques, fishing, parks, shopping, sporting events, golf, theater and watersports nearby.

Pets Allowed.

Ratings: *4 Stars.*

"The Inn at Perry Cabin is a little piece of heaven on earth."

Wades Point Inn on the Bay

PO Box 7, Wades Point Rd, McDaniel
Saint Michaels, MD 21663
(410)745-2500 (888)923-3466 Fax:(410)745-3443

Circa 1819. This waterfront estate is located on 120 acres and was named for Zachary Wade, who received the land grant in 1657. Thomas Kemp, a notable ship builder, built the house in  1819. The Kemp families' burial grounds are adjacent to the inn's mile-long walking trail. The trail passes the farm's crops and cultivated flowers and fishing ponds. Deer rabbit, fox, raccoons, bald eagles, blue heron, swans and osprey are often seen. There is a boat dock and fishing pier. Rooms are available in the historic main house and in an adjoining building with balconies and screened porches overlooking the Chesapeake Bay. Innkeeper(s): Betsy & John Feiler. $95-230. AP. MC VISA TC. 24 rooms, 17 with PB. 1 suite. 1 conference room. Breakfast included in rates. Types of meals: continental-plus breakfast and early coffee/tea. Beds: QDT. Air conditioning and ceiling fan in room. Fax, copier and library on premises. Handicap access. 120 acres. Small meetings, family reunions and seminars hosted. Antiques, fishing, parks, shopping, sporting events, golf, theater and watersports nearby.

Publicity: *Maryland Magazine, Travel & Leisure, Chesapeake Bay Magazine, Washingtonian, Mid-Atlantic Country.*

Scotland   E7

St. Michael's Manor B&B

50200 St Michael's Manor Way
Scotland, MD 20687
(301)872-4025 Fax:(301)872-4025

Circa 1805. Twice featured on the Maryland House and Garden Tour, St. Michael's Manor is located on Long Neck Creek, a half-mile from Chesapeake Bay. The original hand-

crafted woodwork provides a handsome backdrop for the inn's antique collection. A three-acre vineyard and swimming pool are on the property.

Historic Interest: Saint Mary's City, Sotterly Mansions, Old Mill & Country Store, Solomon's Island and Calvert Marine Museum, US Air Museum, Civil War Museum and Point Lookout State Park.

Innkeeper(s): Joe & Nancy Dick. $45-70. PC TC. 4 rooms. Breakfast included in rates. Types of meals: full breakfast and early coffee/tea. Beds: QDT. Phone and air conditioning in room. TV, fax, swimming and bicycles on premises. 10 acres. Weddings, small meetings, family reunions and seminars hosted. Antiques, fishing, parks, shopping, cross-country skiing, sporting events, theater and watersports nearby.

Location: Near Point Lookout State Park.

Publicity: *Washington Post.*

"Your B&B was so warm, cozy and comfortable."

Snow Hill   E9

Chanceford Hall Inn

209 W Federal St
Snow Hill, MD 21863-1159
(410)632-2231

Circa 1759. This pre-Revolutionary War inn is listed in the National Register and Smithsonian's "Guide to Historic America." The home maintains many original features, including woodwork, floors and mantels. Rooms feature romantic,

CIRCA 1759

canopy beds and the home boasts 10 wood-burning fireplaces and Oriental rugs throughout. Wine and hors d'oeuvres are served after guests check in, and a full breakfast is served each morning in the inn's formal dining room. Spend the day exploring the Snow Hill area, or simply relax by the lap pool. The innkeepers offer bicycles for their guests.

Historic Interest: Built in 1759 by Robert Morris.

Innkeeper(s): Michael & Thelma C. Driscoll. $115-135. PC TC. TAC10. 5 rooms with PB, 4 with FP. 1 suite. Breakfast included in rates. Types of meals: full breakfast, gourmet breakfast and early coffee/tea. Beds: Q. Air conditioning in room. TV, VCR, copier, swimming and bicycles on premises. Antiques, fishing, parks, shopping, sporting events and watersports nearby.

River House Inn

201 E Market St
Snow Hill, MD 21863-2000
(410)632-2722 Fax:(410)632-2866

Circa 1860. This picturesque Gothic Revival house rests on the banks of the Pocomoke River and boasts its own dock. Its two acres roll  down to the river over long tree-studded lawns. Lawn furniture and a hammock add to the invitation to relax as do the inn's porches. Some guest rooms feature marble fireplaces. The 17th-century village of Snow Hill boasts old brick sidewalks and historic homes. Canoes can be rented two doors from the inn or you may wish to take a river cruise on the innkeeper's pontoon boat.

Innkeeper(s): Larry & Susanne Knudsen. $100-175. MC VISA AX DS TC. TAC10. 8 rooms with PB, 6 with FP. 1 suite. 2 cottages. Breakfast and evening snack included in rates. Types of meals: full breakfast and early coffee/tea. Beds: KQT. Air conditioning and ceiling fan in room. TV, VCR, fax, copier, bicycles, library and child care on premises. Handicap access. Weddings, small meetings and family reunions hosted. Amusement parks, antiques, fishing, shopping and watersports nearby.

Publicity: *Daily Times, Washington Times, Washingtonian.*

"Thank you for making our first B&B an exceptional one."

Solomons Island   E7

Solomons Victorian Inn

125 Charles Street
Solomons Island, MD 20688-0759
(410)326-4811 Fax:(410)326-0133

Circa 1906. The Davis family, renowned for their shipbuilding talents, constructed this elegant Queen Anne Victorian at the

turn of the century. Each of the inn's elegant common rooms and bedchambers boasts special touches such as antiques, Oriental rugs and lacy curtains. The inn's suites include whirlpool tubs. The home affords views of Solomons Harbor and its entrance into the picturesque Chesapeake Bay. Guests are treated to an expansive breakfast in a dining room, which overlooks the harbor.

Historic Interest: Historic Saint Mary's City is a half hour from the inn, while Washington, D.C., is just an hour away.

Innkeeper(s): Richard & Helen Bauer. $90-165. MC VISA PC. 8 rooms with PB. 3 suites. Breakfast and evening snack included in rates. Types of meals: full breakfast and early coffee/tea. Beds: KQ. Air conditioning in room. TV, fax and library on premises. Small meetings hosted. Antiques, fishing, parks, shopping, theater and watersports nearby.

"Instead of guests at a place of lodging, you made us feel like welcome friends in your home."

Thurmont   A5

Cozy Country Inn

103 Frederick Rd
Thurmont, MD 21788-1813
(301)271-4301 Fax:(301)271-4301

Circa 1929. This Country Victorian-style inn has evolved into a unique destination point for travelers throughout the years. The six-acre compound includes the inn, a restaurant with seating capacity for 700 and a craft and antique village. Still operated by the founding family, the Cozy features lodging that should please a variety of travelers. Many of the rooms are themed after past presidents. Memorabilia from nearby Camp David, past presidents and political dignitaries are displayed throughout.

Innkeeper(s): Jerry & Beeby Freeze. $44-130. EP. MC VISA AX DS TC. 21 rooms with PB, 5 with FP. 3 suites. 5 cottages. 5 conference rooms. Breakfast included in rates. Types of meals: continental breakfast and full breakfast. Dinner, picnic lunch, lunch, banquet service, catering service and room service available. Restaurant on premises. Beds: KQD. Phone, air

conditioning, TV and VCR in room. Fax, copier and spa on premises. Handicap access. Weddings, small meetings, family reunions and seminars hosted. Antiques, fishing, parks, shopping, downhill skiing, cross-country skiing, sporting events and golf nearby.

Tilghman   D7

Black Walnut Point Inn

Black Walnut Rd, PO Box 308
Tilghman, MD 21671
(410)886-2452 Fax:(410)886-2053

Circa 1843. Located on 57 beautiful acres set aside as a wildlife sanctuary, this handsome Colonial Revival manor commands waterfront views from its private peninsula location. Charter fishing and island river cruises can be arranged by the innkeepers. From its bayside hammock to its nature walk, swimming pool and lighted tennis court, the inn provides an amazingly private getaway. Accommodations are in the main house as well as the Riverside Cottage. The Cove Cottage has its own kitchen and screened porch facing the river.

Innkeeper(s): Tom & Brenda Ward. $120-140. MC VISA PC TC. 7 rooms with PB. 2 cottages. 1 conference room. Breakfast included in rates. Types of meals: continental-plus breakfast and early coffee/tea. Beds: Q. Air conditioning in room. Fax, copier, spa, swimming, bicycles, tennis and library on premises. 57 acres. Small meetings, family reunions and seminars hosted. Antiques, fishing, parks, shopping and watersports nearby.

Vienna   D8

Tavern House

111 Water St, PO Box 98
Vienna, MD 21869
(410)376-3347

Circa 1760. River views are available from the guest rooms of this home which was a popular tavern, popular during colonial days. The inn has been restored and the polished wood floors and white plaster walls provide the backdrop for simple antique furnishings and reproductions. Five fireplaces at the inn include a cooking hearth in the cellar.

Innkeeper(s): Harvey & Elise Altergott. $60-75. MC VISA. 4 rooms. Type of meal: full breakfast.

Location: On Nanticoke River at the Maryland Eastern Shore.

Westminster   A6

The Winchester Country Inn

111 Stoner Ave
Westminster, MD 21157-5451
(410)876-7373 (800)887-3950 Fax:(410)848-7409

Circa 1760. William Winchester, the founder of Westminster, built this unusual English-style house. It has a steeply slanted roof similar to those found in the Tidewater area. A central fireplace opens to both the parlor and the central hall. Colonial-period furnishings prevail, with some items loaned by the local historic society. Community volunteers, historians, craftsmen and designers helped restore the inn. A non-profit agency provides some of the housekeeping and gardening staff from its developmentally disabled program.

Historic Interest: Gettysburg, Penn. (35 minutes), Washington, D.C., (90 minutes), Baltimore (45 minutes).

Innkeeper(s): Sarah Martin. $40-75. AP. MC VISA AX DS. 5 rooms, 3 with PB. Breakfast included in rates. Type of meal: full breakfast. Catering service available. Beds: KQDT. Air conditioning, TV and VCR in room. Handicap access. Weddings and small meetings hosted. Antiques, fishing, parks, shopping and theater nearby.

Publicity: *Country Living, Evening Sun, The Towson Flier, The Itinerary, Cracker Barrell, Carroll County Sun.*

"We give your inn an A+. Our stay was perfect."

Wittman C7

The Inn at Christmas Farm

8873 Tilghman Island Rd
Wittman, MD 21676
(410)745-5312 (800)987-8436 Fax:(410)745-5618

Circa 1893. Set on the water's edge at Cummings Creek, the Inn at Christmas Farm offers a combination of wildlife, farm animals and four exquisitely restored suites. The kitchen, dining room and two suites make up the main house originally built around 1800. One guest room, the Brother's Palmer's Still suite, is named for a still that had been concealed in a false ceiling during prohibition. The adjacent Christmas Cottage features a private entrance and two-person Jacuzzi. Each suite in the St. James Chapel includes a refrigerator and sink in the sitting room and deck or patio that overlooks the pond. A gourmet breakfast is served in the enclosed sun porch of the farm house overlooking the inn's "toy farm" that features horses, sheep, chickens and peacocks.

Innkeeper(s): Paul Curtis & Sue Rockwell. $105-165. MC VISA PC TC. TAC10. 5 rooms with PB. 3 suites. 1 cottage. Breakfast included in rates. Type of meal: gourmet breakfast. Beds: K. Air conditioning and ceiling fan in room. Fax, swimming and stables on premises. 50 acres. Weddings, small meetings, family reunions and seminars hosted. Antiques, fishing, parks, shopping, golf, theater and watersports nearby.

Massachusetts

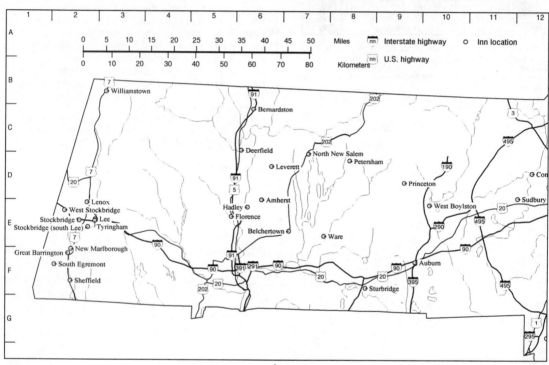

| | | 0 5 10 15 20 25 30 35 40 45 50 | Miles |  Interstate highway | o Inn location |
| | | 0 10 20 30 40 50 60 70 80 | Kilometers | U.S. highway | |

Amherst   D6

Allen House Victorian Inn

599 Main St
Amherst, MA 01002-2409
(413)253-5000

Circa 1886. This stick-style Queen Anne is much like a
Victorian museum with guest rooms that feature period reproduction wallpapers, pedestal sinks, carved golden oak and
brass beds, painted wooden floors and plenty of antiques.
Among its many other treasures include Eastlake fireplace mantels. Unforgettable breakfasts include specialties such as Eggs
Benedict or French toast stuffed with rich cream cheese.
Afternoon tea is a treat, and the inn offers plenty of examples of
poetry from Emily Dickinson, whose home is just across the
street from the inn.

Historic Interest: Aside from the Dickinson home, the area offers many
museums and the inn is within walking distance of Amherst College,
Hampshire College and the University of Massachusetts. Emily Dickinson
Homestead (less than one-fourth mile), historic Deerfield (18 miles north),

Norman Rockwell
Museum and Tanglewood
(less that 1 hour away).

Innkeeper(s): Alan & Ann
Zieminski. $55-135.
MAP, AP, EP. MC VISA DS
PC TC. 7 rooms with PB.
Breakfast, afternoon tea
and evening snack includ-
ed in rates. Types of
meals: full breakfast,
gourmet breakfast and
early coffee/tea. Beds:
QDT. Phone, air condi-
tioning and ceiling fan in room. TV and library on premises. Amusement
parks, antiques, fishing, parks, shopping, downhill skiing, cross-country skiing, sporting events, theater and watersports nearby.
Location: Old Sturbridge Village, Historic Deerfield and Hancock Shaker
Village (less than 1 hour away).

Publicity: *New York Times, Boston Globe, Bon Appetit, Yankee Travel, Boston.*

*"Our room and adjoining bath were spotlessly clean, charming, and
quiet, with good lighting. Our meals were delicious and appetizing,
and the casual, family-like atmosphere encouraged discussions among
the guests."*

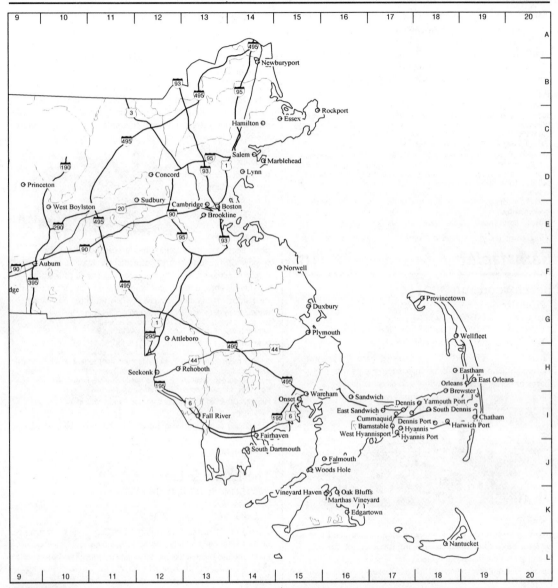

| | 9 | 10 | 11 | 12 | 13 | 14 | 15 | 16 | 17 | 18 | 19 | 20 |

Newburyport
Rockport
Essex
Hamilton
Salem
Marblehead
Concord
Lynn
Princeton
Sudbury
West Boylston
Cambridge Boston
Brookline
Auburn
Norwell
Provincetown
Wellfleet
Duxbury
Plymouth
Eastham
Attleboro
Orleans East Orleans
Brewster
Seekonk
Rehoboth
Wareham
Sandwich
Dennis Yarmouth Port
Onset
East Sandwich
South Dennis
Fall River
Cummaquid
Dennis Port
Chatham
Barnstable
Hyannis
Harwich Port
Fairhaven
West Hyannisport
Hyannis Port
South Dartmouth
Falmouth
Woods Hole
Vineyard Haven Oak Bluffs
Marthas Vineyard
Edgartown
Nantucket

Attleboro   G12

Colonel Blackinton Inn
203 N Main St
Attleboro, MA 02703-1749
(508)222-6022 (800)734-2487

Circa 1850. This Greek Revival home, once known as the historic Blackinton Double House, has been renovated to include modern amenities in old-fashioned style. The grounds create a romantic environment. Rooms are simple with elegant touches. The breakfast buffet at the Col. Blackinton is a treat, and lunch is served Monday through Friday. Situated between Boston and Providence, there is no shortage of places to visit, or guests can simply relax with a book in the library or enjoy the parlor.

Innkeeper(s): Joe Supinski. $75-125. MC VISA AX DC CB DS. 12 rooms, 11 with PB. Breakfast included in rates. Type of meal: full breakfast. Afternoon tea and catering service available. Beds: KQDT. Antiques and theater nearby.

Publicity: *Blackstone Valley and the Attleboros, Providence Sunday Journal.*

"You treated us so well! The meals were delicious, and the room was so comfortable."

Auburn   F9

Captain Samuel Eddy House B&B
609 Oxford St S
Auburn, MA 01501-1811
(508)832-7282

Circa 1765. This Georgian-style house was once the home of a Revolutionary War captain. The B&B is decorated in period

215

style with handmade quilts, antiques, stenciling, hooked rugs and four-poster beds in the guest rooms. The Captain's Attic Suite has a king-size bed and couch in one room and Chinese decor. The suite also has a double bed with brass headboard and an antique maple twin bed in the other room. The Common Room is a popular place for guests to relax, especially in front of a warm fire. The sunroom is another relaxing spot, boasting views of woods, a pond and the garden.

Historic Interest: The area has a variety of historic attractions, including Old Sturbridge Village, Clara Barton Museum, Higgins Armory, Salisbury Mansion, Blackstone River National Heritage Corridor, the Tower Hill Botanical Garden, Worcester Historical Museum and more.

Innkeeper(s): Diedre & Mike Meddaugh. $70-90. PC TC. TAC10. 3 rooms with PB. 1 suite. 1 conference room. Breakfast included in rates. Types of meals: full breakfast, gourmet breakfast and early coffee/tea. Afternoon tea available. Beds: KQDT. Air conditioning in room. TV, VCR, bicycles and library on premises. Weddings, small meetings and family reunions hosted. Antiques, shopping, downhill skiing, cross-country skiing, sporting events and theater nearby.

Publicity: *Boston Herald, Auburn News, New York Times, Country.*

"Hosts warm and professional, a remarkable and oft overlooked area."

Barnstable   I17

Beechwood Inn

2839 Main St, Rt 6A
Barnstable, MA 02630-1017
(508)362-6618 (800)609-6618 Fax:(508)362-0298
E-mail: bwdinn@virtualcapecod.com

Circa 1853. Beechwood is a beautifully restored Queen Anne Victorian offering period furnishings, some rooms with fireplaces or ocean views. Its warmth and elegance make it a

favorite hideaway for couples looking for a peaceful and romantic return to the Victorian era. The inn is named for rare old beech trees that shade the veranda.

Historic Interest: Plymouth Rock (30 minutes), Kennedy Compound and JFK Monument (10 minutes), Oldest library in USA (walking distance).

Innkeeper(s): Debbie & Ken Traugot. $90-175. MC VISA AX PC TC. TAC10. 6 rooms with PB, 3 with FP. Breakfast and afternoon tea included in rates. Types of meals: full breakfast and early coffee/tea. Beds: KQD. Fax, copier and bicycles on premises. Weddings, small meetings and family reunions hosted. French spoken. Antiques, fishing, parks, shopping, sporting events, theater and watersports nearby.

Location: Cape Cod's historic North Shore.

Publicity: *National Trust Calendar, New England Weekends, Rhode Island Monthly, Cape Cod Life.*

"Your inn is pristine in every detail. We concluded that the innkeepers, who are most hospitable, are the best part of Beechwood."

Crocker Tavern B&B

3095 Main St
Barnstable, MA 02630-1119
(508)362-5115 (800)773-5359 Fax:(508)362-5562
E-mail: crocktav@capecod.net

Circa 1754. This historic Cape Cod inn once served as a head-quarters for the Whigs during the Revolutionary era. The inn is part of the Olde Kings Highway Historic District and also is listed on the National Register. Visitors choose from five guest rooms in this two-story, Georgian-style inn, each with a four-poster or canopy bed, sitting area and antiques. Several rooms include working fireplaces. Many of this home's Colonial elements have been beautifully restored, such as the wood

plank floors, exposed beams, window seats and the elegant woodwork. The inn's hearty continental breakfasts are served on candle-lit tables set with china and crystal. The B&B is within walking distance to restaurants, antique shops, historic sites and the harbor, where guests can enjoy whale-watching excursions.

Historic Interest: Sturgis Library, oldest public library in U.S., built in 1644 (across the street), Old Colonial Courthouse (one-eighth mile), Winslow Crocker House (4 miles), Trayser Museum (1/4 mile).

Innkeeper(s): Sue & Jeff Carlson. $80-115. MC VISA PC TC. TAC10. 5 rooms with PB, 2 with FP. Breakfast and evening snack included in rates. Types of meals: continental-plus breakfast and early coffee/tea. Afternoon tea available. Beds: QD. Air conditioning in room. Fax and library on premises. Handicap access. Small meetings and family reunions hosted. Antiques, fishing, parks, shopping, theater and watersports nearby.

Publicity: *Cape Cod Times, Society for the Preservation of New England Antiquities.*

"Thank you so much for your wonderful hospitality. You have a lovely home, and your attention to detail made our stay all the more pleasant. We will always remember fondly our stay at Crocker Tavern."

The Lamb & Lion

2504 Main St, Rt 6A, PO Box 511
Barnstable, MA 02630
(508)362-6823 Fax:(508)362-0227

Circa 1740. This rambling collection of Cape-style buildings sits on four acres overlooking the Old King's highway. Newly decorated, the inn offers a feeling of casual elegance. The Innkeeper's Pride is a romantic suite with sunken tub, fireplace, kitchenette and a deck overlooking a garden and woods. The Barn-stable is one of the original buildings and now offers three bedrooms, a living and dining area and French doors to a private patio.

A large central courtyard houses a generous sized pool.

Innkeeper(s): Donald P. McKeag. $75-165. MC VISA AX PC TC. 12 rooms, 10 with PB, 3 with FP. 2 suites. 2 cottages. 1 conference room. Breakfast included in rates. Type of meal: continental-plus breakfast. Catering service available. Beds: KQDT. Air conditioning, turndown service and TV in room. VCR and swimming on premises. Weddings, small meetings, family reunions and seminars hosted. Antiques, fishing, parks, shopping, golf, theater and watersports nearby.

Barnstable, Cape Cod   I17

Ashley Manor Inn

3660 Olde Kings Hwy PO Box 856
Barnstable, Cape Cod, MA 02630
(508)362-8044

Circa 1699. This manor house has lived through a succession of expansions, the first addition built in 1750. The final effect is wonderful and mysterious. The inn, thought to be a hiding place for Tories during the Revolutionary War, features huge open-hearth fireplace with beehive oven and a secret passage-

way connecting the upstairs and downstairs suites. The inn is reminiscent of a gracious English country house and is filled with Oriental rugs and antiques. Each of the guest rooms boasts fireplaces, and three have large whirlpool baths. Two acres of manicured lawns include a regulation-size tennis court. Nature- lovers will enjoy the landscape, dotted with cherry and apple trees. The romantic gazebo is the perfect location to view the fountain garden. A full gourmet breakfast is served on the brick terrace or fireside in the formal dining room.

Historic Interest: Nantucket and Martha's Vineyard, Chatham, the National Seashore and Provincetown on the Cape.

Innkeeper(s): Donald Bain. $120-180. MC VISA DS PC TC. TAC10. 6 rooms with PB, 5 with FP. 4 suites. 1 cottage. Breakfast included in rates. Type of meal: gourmet breakfast. Beds: KQD. Air conditioning in room. Bicycles, tennis and library on premises. French spoken. Antiques, fishing, parks, theater and watersports nearby.

Location: In the heart of Cape Cod's historic district.

Publicity: *Chicago Tribune, Boston Globe, Bon Appetit, Tennis, New York Times, Pittsburgh Press, Gourmet, GBH, Newsday.*

"This is absolutely perfect! So many very special, lovely touches."

Belchertown   E7

Ingate Farms B&B

60 Lamson Ave
Belchertown, MA 01007-9710
(413)253-0440 Fax:(413)253-0440

Circa 1740. This Cape-style home was built as a bobbin factory, and eventually it was moved and reassembled at its current location on a 400-acre equestrian center. The interior is homey, with an emphasis on early American decor. Guests can relax on

the enclosed porch, which is filled with comfortable furnishings. From the porch, guests can watch horses and enjoy the country-side. The grounds

offer hiking trails, and guests can rent a boat and fish at nearby Quabbin Reservoir.

Innkeeper(s): Virginia Kier & Bill McCormick. $55-85. MC VISA AX PC TC. 5 rooms, 3 with PB. 1 suite. Breakfast and afternoon tea included in rates. Types of meals: continental-plus breakfast and early coffee/tea. Beds: KQT. Air conditioning, ceiling fan and TV in room. VCR, fax, copier, swimming, stables, library and pet boarding on premises. Handicap access. 400 acres. Family reunions hosted. Amusement parks, antiques, fishing, parks, shopping, downhill skiing, cross-country skiing, sporting events, golf and theater nearby.

"I've felt so at home here this week and also charmed by the calm and loveliness of this place."

Bernardston   C6

Falls River Inn

1 Brattleboro Rd
Bernardston, MA 01337-9532
(413)648-9904 Fax:(413)648-0538

Circa 1905. Guests have been welcomed to this site since the late 18th century. The first inn burned down in the 1800s, and the current Federal-style Victorian inn was built in its place. Guests will find various styles of antiques in their comfortable, country rooms, three of which include a fireplace. During the week, a continental breakfast is served, and on weekends, guests are treated to a full breakfast. The inn's restaurant is open Wednesday through Sunday, and features everything from

chicken pot pie to pepper shrimp served on a bed of angel hair pasta and surrounded by an orange cream sauce. Don't forget to try the restaurant's signature "Vampire Chasers."

Innkeeper(s): Kerber Family. $66-85. MC VISA AX PC TC. TAC10. 7 rooms with PB, 3 with FP. 1 conference room. Breakfast included in rates. Types of meals: gourmet breakfast and early coffee/tea. Dinner, lunch, banquet service, catering service and room service available. Restaurant on premises. Beds: KQDT. Ceiling fan in room. TV, fax and copier on premises. Weddings, small meetings, family reunions and seminars hosted. French spoken. Antiques, fishing, parks, shopping, downhill skiing, cross-country skiing, sporting events, golf, theater and watersports nearby.

Pets Allowed: $7 per day boarding kennel 5 miles from us.

Publicity: *Snow Country Magazine, America's Favorite, Franklin County Magazine.*

"The food was excellent, the rooms charming and clean, the whole atmosphere so relaxing."

Boston   E13

Beacon Hill B&B

27 Brimmer St
Boston, MA 02108-1013
(617)523-7376

Circa 1869. This six-story Victorian rowhouse overlooks the Charles River in a quiet residential area of downtown Boston. Rooms are spacious and each has a fireplace. Two of the comfortably furnished guest rooms and the dining room have views of the river. There's an elevator for toting luggage. The Boston Common and Freedom Trail, Quincy Market, conference hotels and the Back Bay are all within easy walking distance. The neighborhood can't be beat, but you'll have to pay extra for parking a few blocks away.

Historic Interest: Freedom Trail neighborhood, brick sidewalks, gas lights, no exterior changes to buildings permissible.

Innkeeper(s): Susan Butterworth. $135-200. PC TC. 3 rooms with PB. Breakfast included in rates. Type of meal: full breakfast. Beds: QT. Phone and air conditioning in room. French spoken. Antiques, parks, shopping, sporting events and theater nearby.

"Enjoyed your lovely home, your cooking, your friendliness and the vibrant, alive decor."

Host Homes of Boston

PO Box 117-Waban Branch
Boston, MA 02168-0001
(617)244-1308

Circa 1864. One of the many fine homes available through this reservation service includes a stately townhouse on Commonwealth Avenue in Boston's chic Back Bay, less than one block away from the Boston Common and a short walk to Copley Square. Host Homes offers a variety of vacation possibilities throughout the Boston area and its suburbs. Country and coastal locations also are available.

Historic Interest: Boston and its surrounding areas are full of historic sites. Each of the accommodations is near something unique.

Innkeeper(s): Marcia Whittington. $68-175. MC VISA AX PC. Breakfast included in rates. Type of meal: continental-plus breakfast. Beds: KQDT. Antiques, historic sites, museums, shopping, sporting events, theater and whale watching nearby.

Location: Additional homes in Beacon Hill, Back Bay, Cambridge, Greater Boston.

Publicity: *Changing Times, USA Today, What's Doing in Boston, BBC Holiday, Marie Claire.*

"Very special. I have never stayed at such an excellent, elegant B&B. Our hosts were delightful, the place, magnificent!"

Brewster   H18

Candleberry Inn

1882 Main St
Brewster, MA 02631-1827
(508)896-3300 (800)573-4769

Circa 1750. The one-and-a-half-acre grounds of this 250-year-old inn feature gardens complete with lawn swings. Wainscoting is dominant in the guest rooms, which feature Oriental rugs on top of pine-planked floors. Antiques and family heirlooms decorated the inn. Three rooms include working fireplaces. A full, gourmet breakfast is served in the dining room, which is also the inn's oldest room. The beach is less than a mile away, and Brewster offers many shops and restaurants.

Innkeeper(s): Gini & David Donnelly. $80-165. MC VISA AX. 9 rooms with PB, 3 with FP. 2 suites. Type of meal: full breakfast. Beds: TD.
Publicity: *Brewster Oracle.*

"Wonderful, relaxing time, don't want to leave."

Captain Freeman Inn

15 Breakwater Rd
Brewster, MA 02631-1311
(508)896-7481 (800)843-4664 Fax:(508)896-5618
E-mail: visitus@capecod.net

Circa 1866. This Cape Cod mansion was designed with the architectural detail befitting its original owner's expensive taste. Captain William Freeman, an aristocratic shipmaster, imported the inn's ornate plaster moldings from Italy, and the floors were laid in a light and dark herringbone pattern. A commanding center staircase with a hand-carved banister leads to the inn's luxurious guest rooms, all decorated with period reproductions. Many of the rooms offer fireplaces, balconies and whirlpool tubs. Guests are invited to swim in the inn's pool surrounded by flower and herb gardens or play croquet and badminton on more than an acre of sweeping lawns. The inn offers a full breakfast served poolside in the warmer months or fireside in the dining room. Tea or hot chocolate is offered on cool days in the fall and spring. Walk to the beach on Cape Cod Bay or borrow a bicycle and explore the miles of bike paths. Tennis, golf, horseback riding, theater, antiquing, art galleries and shopping are located nearby.

Historic Interest: Close to the Museum of Natural History, Nickerson State Park, Cape Playhouse and many other historic seaside attractions.

Innkeeper(s): Carol & Tom Edmondson. $100-245. MC VISA AX DC PC TC. TAC8. 13 rooms with PB, 7 with FP. 7 suites. Breakfast and afternoon tea included in rates. Types of meals: gourmet breakfast and early coffee/tea. Beds: Q. Phone, air conditioning, ceiling fan, TV and VCR in room. Fax, swimming and bicycles on premises. Weddings, small meetings and seminars hosted. Antiques, parks, shopping, golf, theater and watersports nearby.

Location: Cape Cod, Mass.

"We were in awe when we entered our room, and the charm, elegance and romantic decor instilled in us a memory we will cherish always."

Greylin House

2311 Main St
Brewster, MA 02631-1813
(508)896-0004 (800)233-6662

Circa 1837. Once home to Brewster's poor, this historic Greek Revival inn now offers comfortable quarters to inn visitors. Rooms are furnished with antiques and other eclectic stylings. Guests will find shops and outstanding eateries within easy walking distance. Roland C. Nickerson State Park is in the immediate vicinity. Hiking and bike trails are nearby.

Innkeeper(s): Skip & Gerri Caplan. Call for rates. Family reunions hosted. Antiques, shopping and theater nearby.

"Thank you for super food, pristine surroundings and warm friendship."

Old Manse Inn

1861 Main St PO Box 745
Brewster, MA 02631-1826
(508)896-3149

Circa 1800. This completely renovated sea captain's house is tucked behind tall trees and has a gracious mansard roof. It was built by Captain Winslow F. Lewis Knowles and served as a link in the Underground Railroad during the Civil War.
Innkeeper(s): David & Suzanne Plum. $95-115. MC VISA AX DS. 8 rooms with PB. Type of meal: full breakfast. Dinner available. Restaurant on premises. Beds: QTD. Phone, air conditioning and TV in room. Small meetings and family reunions hosted. Antiques, fishing, shopping and theater nearby.

Location: Cape Cod.

Publicity: *Travel & Leisure, Boston Herald, Boston Globe.*

"Our stays at the Old Manse Inn have always been delightful. The innkeepers are gracious, the decor charming and the dining room has a character all its own."

Old Sea Pines Inn

2553 Main St, PO Box 1026
Brewster, MA 02631-1959
(508)896-6114 Fax:(508)896-7387

Circa 1900. This turn-of-the-century mansion on three-and-one-half acres of lawns and trees was formerly the Sea Pines School of Charm and Personality for Young Women, established

in 1907. Recently renovated, the inn displays elegant wallpapers and a grand sweeping stairway. It is located near beaches and bike paths, as well as village shops and restaurants.
Historic Interest: Local Historic Registry.
Innkeeper(s): Michele Rowan. $55-115. MC VISA AX DC DS. 21 rooms, 14 with PB, 3 with FP. 2 suites. 1 conference room. Breakfast and afternoon tea included in rates. Types of meals: full breakfast and early coffee/tea. Evening snack, picnic lunch, banquet service, catering service and room service available. Beds: QDT. Phone, air conditioning and TV in room. Handicap access. Weddings, small meetings, family reunions and seminars hosted. Antiques, fishing, shopping, theater and watersports nearby.

Location: Cape Cod.

Publicity: *New York Times, Cape Cod Oracle, For Women First, Home Office, Entrepreneur.*

"The loving care applied by Steve, Michele and staff is deeply appreciated."

Pepper House Inn

2062 Main St (Rt 6A)
Brewster, MA 02631
(508)896-4389 Fax:(508)896-5012
E-mail: pepper@capecod.net

Circa 1793. This handsome two-story, red Federal-style home has the typical five-window facade with a fanlight over the centered door. A sea captain's house now in the National Register, it has been handsomely restored. Guest rooms offer four-poster beds, antiques, reproductions, original wide pine floors, wallpapers, chandeliers and colonial fireplaces. An outdoor deck with market umbrellas is a favored spot in good weather for breakfast. Located near the center of the village, the inn is convenient to the historic district, galleries, antique shops and craft studios. Bike trails and beaches are a short walk or drive away.
Innkeeper(s): Bill & Cheri Metters. $89-125. MC VISA AX. 4 rooms with PB, 4 with FP. Breakfast and evening snack included in rates. Types of meals: gourmet breakfast and early coffee/tea. Beds: Q. Air conditioning and TV in room. Fax on premises. Antiques, fishing, parks, shopping, golf, theater and watersports nearby.

"We weren't quite sure if we were B&B compatible, but after this most hospitable five days, we are hooked!"

Ruddy Turnstone B&B

463 Main St
Brewster, MA 02631-1049
(508)385-9871 (800)654-1995

Circa 1810. This Cape-style home once served as a salt works. Guests opt for rooms in the main house or in the restored car-

riage house, which was brought to the property from Nantucket. Each guest room offers something special. The Bayview Suite include a fireplace and boasts ocean views. Both carriage house rooms includes canopy beds. Guests to this Cape Cod retreat can relax and enjoy views of the marsh and the bay or stroll to shops, museums and restaurants.
Innkeeper(s): Gordon & Sally Swanson. $75-150. MC VISA AX PC TC. TAC10. 5 rooms with PB, 1 with FP. 2 suites. 1 cottage. 2 conference rooms. Breakfast included in rates. Types of meals: full breakfast and early coffee/tea. Beds: Q. Air conditioning and turndown service in room. TV on premises. Weddings, small meetings, family reunions and seminars hosted. Antiques, fishing, parks, shopping, golf, theater and watersports nearby.
Publicity: *National Geographic Traveler, Victoria, Cape Cod Life.*

"Here lies the true New England, warm, comfortable and welcoming."

Brookline · E13

The Bertram Inn

92 Sewall Ave
Brookline, MA 02146-5327
(617)566-2234 (800)295-3822 Fax:(617)277-1887

Circa 1907. Antiques and authenticity are the rule at this turn-of-the-century Gothic Revival inn, found on a peaceful, tree-lined street two miles from central Boston. The Bertram Inn

features old-English stylings and Victorian decor. Guests can enjoy breakfast or afternoon tea by the fire in the common room or, if weather permits, on the front porch overlooking the garden. Boston College, Boston University, Fenway Park and the F.L. Olmstead National Historic Site all are nearby. Shops and restaurants are within walking distance, and the Boston area's many attractions are nearby. Parking is included in the rates.

Historic Interest: Faneuil Hall and the Freedom Trail (10 minutes).

Innkeeper(s): Bryan Austin & Jennifer Liu. $69-194. MC VISA AX PC TC. TAC10. 14 rooms with PB, 2 with FP. Breakfast included in rates. Type of meal: continental-plus breakfast. Afternoon tea available. Beds: KQDT. Phone, air conditioning and TV in room. Fax on premises. German, French, Spanish and Italian and Mandarin Chinese spoken. Antiques, parks, shopping, sporting events and theater nearby.

Pets Allowed.

"This B&B is just wonderful, I can't imagine a nicer place. Thank you for your warm generosity, a fine substitute for home."

Cambridge   E13

A Cambridge House B&B Inn

2218 Massachusetts Ave
Cambridge, MA 02140-1836
(617)491-6300 (800)232-9989 Fax:(617)868-2848
E-mail: innach@aol.com

Circa 1892. Listed in the National Register, Cambridge House has been restored to its turn-of-the-century elegance. A remarkable carved cherry fireplace dominates the den, and some rooms have four-poster canopy beds and fireplaces. The

library is often the setting for mulled cider, hors d'oeuvres or tea served fireside on brisk afternoons. Parking is available and the subway is two blocks away.

Historic Interest: National Register.

Innkeeper(s): Ellen Riley & Tony Femmino. $99-275. MC VISA AX DC DS PC TC. TAC10. 14 rooms with PB, 2 with FP. Breakfast included in rates. Type of meal: full breakfast. Beds: KQDT. Phone, air conditioning and TV in room. Fax and copier on premises. Italian & Portuguese spoken. Antiques, fishing, parks, shopping, sporting events and theater nearby.

Location: Minutes from downtown Boston.

Publicity: *Glamour, Los Angeles Times, Entrepreneur, Working Woman, Oprah Winfrey show.*

"I'm afraid you spoiled us quite badly! Your home is elegant, charming and comfortable. Breakfasts were delicious and beautifully served."

A Friendly Inn

1673 Cambridge St
Cambridge, MA 02138-4316
(617)547-7851 Fax:(617)547-7851

Circa 1893. With Harvard Square less than three blocks away, this three-story Victorian is conveniently close to many of the area's most famous historic sites. All rooms have private baths, air conditioning and TV. Rates include a continental breakfast and free parking. A tennis court, swimming pool, library and museums are across the street.

Innkeeper(s): Alice & Arnold. $87-107. MC VISA AX DC DS PC TC. TAC10. 17 rooms with PB. Breakfast included in rates. Type of meal: continental breakfast. Beds: QDT. Phone, air conditioning and TV in room. Fax, copier, swimming and library on premises. Antiques, parks, shopping, sporting events and theater nearby.

The Mary Prentiss Inn

6 Prentiss St
Cambridge, MA 02140-2212
(617)661-2929 Fax:(617)661-5989

Circa 1843. Only a half-mile from Harvard Square, this restored Greek Revival Inn features ionic fluted columns and Doric trim. During summer months, guests are treated to breakfast under umbrella-covered tables on the outdoor deck, while wintertime guests enjoy their morning fare in front of a roaring fire in the parlor room. Several of the unique guest rooms feature kitchenettes, three suites include a working fireplace. The inn is winner of the 1995 Massachusetts Historic Commission Preservation Award.

Historic Interest: Cambridge offers no shortage of activities, including the Cambridge Common where George Washington took command of the Continental Army, and the church where he and wife, Martha, worshiped. Historic battlefields and Walden Pond are only a short drive away.

Innkeeper(s): Jennifer & Nicholas Fandetti. $109-300. MC VISA AX. 20 rooms with PB. 5 suites. Breakfast and afternoon tea included in rates. Types of meals: continental breakfast and full breakfast. Catering service available. Beds: QT. Phone, air conditioning and TV in room. Small meetings and family reunions hosted. Antiques, shopping, sporting events, theater and watersports nearby.

Publicity: *Cambridge Chronicle, Travel & Leisure, Discerning Traveler, Cambridge Current.*

"We thank you for the special privilege of staying at such a magnificent inn. We had a wonderful time, and you helped to make it so."

Cape Cod (Harwich Port)   I18

Dunscroft By The Sea Inn & Cottage

24 Pilgrim Rd
Cape Cod (Harwich Port), MA 02646
(508)432-0810 (800)432-4345 Fax:(508)432-5134
E-mail: alyce@capecod.net

Circa 1920. The innkeepers at this Colonial Revival inn pride themselves on creating a quiet, romantic retreat for their guests. The Victorian decor includes special touches such as romantic poetry books placed in the rooms, candles, chocolates and other surprises. Canopy and four-poster beds decorate the graciously appointed bedchambers. Rooms with a fireplace or double Jacuzzi tub also are available. In addition to the inn rooms, the King Suite is located in what was the chauffer's cottage and includes a fireplace. The inn is located just steps away from a association beach that stretches more than a mile between two harbors. Built as a private summer estate in 1920, the inn has been welcoming guests for nearly half a century.

Innkeeper Alyce Cunningham prepares a sumptuous full, country breakfast on a lace-covered table set with elegant china. A short walk will take you to restaurants and shops.

Historic Interest: Cape Cod National Seashore (15 minutes), Plymouth Plantation (30 minutes), Plymouth Rock (30 minutes).

Innkeeper(s): Alyce & Wally Cunningham. $95-225. MAP. MC VISA AX PC. TAC10. 9 rooms with PB, 2 with FP. 1 suite. 1 cottage. 1 conference room. Breakfast included in rates. Type of meal: full breakfast. Catering service available. Beds: KQ. Air conditioning, ceiling fan and TV in room. Fax, copier, swimming, tennis and library on premises. Handicap access. Weddings, small meetings, family reunions and seminars hosted. Amusement parks, antiques, fishing, parks, shopping, cross-country skiing, sporting events, theater and watersports nearby.

Location: Ten miles east of Hyannis.

Publicity: *Cape Codder.*

"A quaint and delightful slice of New England. Your generous hospitality is greatly appreciated. Your place is beautiful."

Chatham   119

The Azubah Atwood Inn

177 Cross St
Chatham, MA 02633
(508)945-0714 (888)242-8426 Fax:(508)945-9652
E-mail: azubah@ capecod.net

Circa 1789. A sea captain built this 18th-century home, and additions were made to the home in 1838. The innkeepers, who own two other Chatham inns, live on the premises of this historic home. Guests can enjoy the peaceful grounds from the porch or, perhaps, from a bench tucked in the side yard. The inn is open from May 15 until Nov. 1.

Innkeeper(s): William & Audrey Gray. $149. MC VISA AX DS PC TC. TAC10. 3 rooms with PB. Breakfast and afternoon tea included in rates. Types of meals: full breakfast and early coffee/tea. Beds: Q. Phone, air conditioning and TV in room. Fax and library on premises. Antiques, fishing, parks, shopping, golf, theater and watersports nearby.

"What a wonderful adventure - the charm of the room and its perfect blend of history, a feeling of tranquility, and modern conveniences."

Carriage House Inn

407 Old Harbor Rd
Chatham, MA 02633-2322
(508)945-4688 (800)355-8868 Fax:(508)945-4688

Circa 1890. This Colonial Revival inn is an easy find as it is located adjacent to Chatham's tallest flagpole. Antiques and family pieces decorate the interior. Chintzes and floral prints

permeate the six guest rooms, and the three carriage house rooms each include a fireplace and an entrance to an outside sitting area. Breakfast items such as fresh fruit, juices,

cereals, homemade muffins, scones and breads are presented on a sideboard buffet, and guests can enjoy the fare either in the dining room or on the sun porch. Borrow a bike for a tour of the area, or relax in front of the fireplace. Beach towels are furnished for trips to the shore, just a quarter mile away.

Historic Interest: Cape Cod National Seashore (30 minutes).

Innkeeper(s): Patty & Dennis O'Neill. $125-175. MC VISA AX PC TC. TAC10. 6 rooms with PB, 3 with FP. Breakfast and evening snack included in rates. Types of meals: continental-plus breakfast and early coffee/tea. Beds: Q. Air conditioning and ceiling fan in room. TV, VCR, fax and bicycles on premises. Antiques, fishing, parks, shopping, theater and watersports nearby.

"This might well have been our best B&B experience ever. It was the hosts who made it so memorable."

Chatham Town House Inn

11 Library Ln
Chatham, MA 02633-2310
(508)945-2180 (800)242-2180

Circa 1881. This sea captain's unique estate was built by Daniel Webster Nickerson, a direct descendant of William Nickerson who came over on the Mayflower. Resting on two acres at the village center, the inn is a complex of four buildings that feature canopy beds and balconies with water views. Two cottages offer fireplaces.

Innkeeper(s): Russell & Svea Peterson. $165-275. MC VISA AX DC CB DS. 28 rooms with PB, 2 with FP. 2 cottages. 2 conference rooms. Breakfast included in rates. Type of meal: full breakfast. Dinner and lunch available. Beds: KQ. Air conditioning in room. Fax, copier, spa and swimming on premises. Handicap access.

Publicity: *New York Times, Boston Globe, Yankee, Cape Cod Life, Modern Bride.*

The Cranberry Inn at Chatham

359 Main St
Chatham, MA 02633-2425
(508)945-9232 (800)332-4667 Fax:(508)945-3769

Circa 1830. Continuously operating for over 150 years, this inn originally was called the Traveler's Lodge, then the Monomoyic after a local Indian tribe. A cranberry bog adjacent to the property inspired the current name. Recently restored, the inn is located in the heart of the historic district. It's within walking distance of the lighthouse, beaches, shops and restaurants. Guest rooms feature four-poster beds, wide-planked floors and coordinated fabrics. A tap room is on the premises.

Innkeeper(s): Ray & Brenda Raffurty. $85-260. MC VISA AX DS PC TC. TAC10. 18 rooms with PB, 8 with FP. 2 suites. Breakfast and afternoon tea included in rates. Type of meal: full breakfast. Beds: QDT. Phone, air conditioning and TV in room. VCR, fax and library on premises. Weddings and family reunions hosted. Antiques, fishing, parks, shopping, theater and watersports nearby.

Location: Near many Cape Cod attractions.

Publicity: *Country Inns, Cape Cod Life, Glamour.*

Cyrus Kent House

63 Cross St
Chatham, MA 02633-2207
(508)945-9104 (800)338-5368 Fax:(508)945-9104

Circa 1877. A former sea captain's home, the Cyrus Kent House was built in the Greek Revival style. The award-winning restoration retained many original features such as wide pine floorboards, ceiling rosettes, and marble fireplaces. Although furnished with antiques and reproductions, all modern amenities are available. Most bedrooms have four-poster beds. Suites feature sitting rooms with fireplaces. Chatham's historic district is a short stroll away.

Innkeeper(s): Sharon Mitchell-Swan. $85-250. MC VISA. 10 rooms with PB. Breakfast and afternoon tea included in rates. Types of meals: continental-plus breakfast and early coffee/tea. Beds: QD. Phone and TV in room. Fax on premises. Weddings, small meetings, family reunions and seminars hosted. Antiques, fishing, shopping and watersports nearby.

Location: Located on a quiet side street within easy walking distance of the historic village of Chatham.

Publicity: *Country Inns.*

Moses Nickerson House

364 Old Harbor Rd
Chatham, MA 02633-2374
(508)945-5859

Circa 1839. This historic, rambling sea captain's house, built in 1839, features wide pine floors, many fireplaces and colorful gardens. Unforgettably charming, the inn is decorated with antique furnishings and Oriental rugs, retaining the character of by-gone days. Each of the rooms offers its own distinctive decor. Breakfast is served in a glass-enclosed dining area that radiates morning sunlight. The inn provides an ambiance of simple elegance.

Innkeeper(s): Lind & George Watts. $95-169. MC VISA AX DS. 7 rooms with PB, 3 with FP. Types of meals: continental-plus breakfast and full breakfast. Beds: Q. Phone, air conditioning and TV in room.

Publicity: *Cape Cod Life, The Discerning Traveler.*

"The attention to detail in unsurpassed."

Port Fortune Inn

201 Main St
Chatham, MA 02633-2423
(508)945-0792 (800)750-0792 Fax:(508)945-0792

Circa 1930. The front of this charming Cape Cod home is decorated with colorful flowers and plants. The interiors of each of the inn's two historic buildings is elegant and inviting with traditional furnishings, and many of the guest rooms are decorated with poster beds. The grounds include perennial gardens and a patio set up with furniture for those who wish to relax and catch a few sea breezes. The inn is featured on the walking tour through the historic Old Village, which is Chatham's oldest neighborhood.

Innkeeper(s): Michael & Renee Kahl. $85-170. MC VISA AX. 14 rooms with PB. Breakfast included in rates. Type of meal: continental-plus breakfast. Beds: QDT. Phone and air conditioning in room. TV on premises. Antiques, fishing, parks, shopping, sporting events, theater and watersports nearby.

"Excellent. The entire experience was wonderful as usual."

Concord D12

Colonel Roger Brown House

1694 Main St
Concord, MA 01742-2831
(508)369-9119 (800)292-1369 Fax:(508)369-1305

Circa 1775. This house was the home of Minuteman Roger Brown, who fought the British at the Old North Bridge. The frame for this center-chimney Colonial was being raised on April 19, the day the battle took place. Some parts of the house were built as early as 1708. The adjacent Damon Mill houses a fitness club available to guests. Both buildings are in the National Register.

Historic Interest: Thoreau's Walden Pond, Concord Museum, Alcott House, Wayside, Old Manse, Old North Bridge (all 3 miles), Lexington, National Heritage Museum (11 miles), Lowell Mills and natural historic district (15 miles).

Innkeeper(s): Lauri Berlied. $75-100. MC VISA AX DC PC TC. TAC10. 5 rooms with PB. 1 suite. Breakfast and afternoon tea included in rates. Type of meal: continental-plus breakfast. Beds: QDT. Phone and air conditioning in room. Fax, copier, spa, swimming, sauna and library on premises. Family reunions and seminars hosted. Antiques, fishing, parks, shopping, downhill skiing, cross-country skiing, theater and watersports nearby.

Publicity: *Middlesex News, Concord Journal, Washingtonian.*

"The Colonel Roger Brown House makes coming to Concord even more of a treat! Many thanks for your warm hospitality."

Hawthorne Inn

462 Lexington Rd
Concord, MA 01742-3729
(978)369-5610 Fax:(978)287-4949

Circa 1870. The Hawthorne Inn is situated on land that once belonged to Ralph Waldo Emerson, the Alcotts and Nathaniel Hawthorne. It was here that Bronson Alcott planted his fruit trees, made pathways to the Mill Brook, and erected his Bath House. Hawthorne purchased the land and repaired a path leading to his home with trees planted on either side. Two of these trees still stand. Across the  road is Hawthorne's House, The Wayside. Next to it is the Alcott's Orchard House and Grapevine Cottage where the Concord grape was developed. Nearby is Sleepy Hollow Cemetery where Emerson, the Alcotts, the Thoreaus and Hawthorne were laid to rest.

Historic Interest: Old North Bridge (1 1/2 miles), Walden Pond (2 miles).

Innkeeper(s): Marilyn Mudry & Gregory Burch. $140-215. MC VISA AX DS PC TC. TAC10. 7 rooms with PB. Breakfast and afternoon tea included in rates. Type of meal: continental-plus breakfast. Beds: QDT. Air conditioning in room. Fax and library on premises. Weddings, small meetings and family reunions hosted. Antiques, fishing, parks, shopping and cross-country skiing nearby.

Location: On the famed "Battle Road" of 1775. East of Town Green by eight-tenths of a mile.

Publicity: *New York Times, Boston Globe, Yankee.*

"Surely there couldn't be a better or more valuable location for a comfortable, old-fashioned country inn."

Cummaquid 117

The Acworth Inn

4352 Old Kings Hwy, PO Box 256
Cummaquid, MA 02637
(508)362-3330 (800)362-6363

Circa 1860. This inn, located on the Olde Kings Highway on the north side of Cape Cod, offers a strategic midway point for those exploring the area. The historic Cape-style farmhouse features six guest rooms, each with a private bath. Hand-painted, restored furniture adds charm to the inn's interior. Guests select from the Cummaquid, Chatham, Yarmouth Port, Barnstable, Wellfleet and Orleans rooms, all named for Cape Cod villages. Visitors will find the shore just a half-mile from the inn.

Historic Interest: Sturgis Library (2 miles away in Barnstable), Old Colonial Courthouse. Route 6A is part of America's largest historic district.

Innkeeper(s): Cheryl & Jack Ferrell. $85-125. MC VISA AX DS PC TC. TAC10. 6 rooms with PB, 1 with FP. Breakfast and afternoon tea included in rates. Types of meals: full breakfast and early coffee/tea. Beds: QDT. Turndown service in room. TV and library on premises. German spoken. Antiques, fishing, parks, shopping, theater and watersports nearby.

Publicity: *Boston, Connecticut.*

"...*great accommodations, food, tour guiding, local flavor, etc...We will be back.*"

Deerfield C6

Deerfield Inn

81 Old Main St
Deerfield, MA 01342-0305
(413)774-5587 (800)926-3865 Fax:(413)773-8712

Circa 1884. The village of Deerfield was settled in 1670. Farmers in the area still unearth bones and ax and arrow heads from French/Indian massacre of 1704. Now, 50 beautifully restored 18th- and 19th-century homes line mile-long main street, considered by many to be the loveliest street in New England. Fourteen of these houses are museums of Pioneer Valley decorative arts and are open year-round to the public. The Memorial Hall Museum, open from May to November, is the oldest museum in New England and full of local antiquities. The inn is situated at the center of this peaceful village, and for those who wish to truly experience New England's past, this is the place. The village has been designated a National Historic Landmark.

Innkeeper(s): Jane & Karl Sabo. $141-261. MC VISA AX. 23 rooms with PB. 1 conference room. Breakfast and afternoon tea included in rates. Type of meal: full breakfast. Dinner and lunch available. Restaurant on premises. Beds: QT. Fax and copier on premises. Handicap access. Antiques, fishing, cross-country skiing and theater nearby.

Location: Middle of historic village.

Publicity: *Travel Today, Country Accents, Colonial Homes, Country Living, Country Inns B&B, Yankee.*

"*We've stayed at many New England inns, but the Deerfield Inn ranks among the best.*"

Dennis 118

The Four Chimneys Inn

946 Main St, Rt 6 A
Dennis, MA 02638-1406
(508)385-6317 (800)874-5502

Circa 1881. Large lawns and gardens enhance this award-winning Victorian inn, which is located across from Scargo Lake on Historic Route 6A near Dennis Village. The inn is furnished with marble fireplaces, decorative woodwork, high ceilings with medallions and paddle fans. Guests can relax by the fireplace in the living room or library. Breakfast can be enjoyed in the dining room or on the large screened porch. The innkeepers will help you plan your day from this centrally located inn.

Historic Interest: Dennis Manse Historic House is within one mile of the inn. Other area attractions include Scargo Lake shore, an Indian burial ground.

Innkeeper(s): Russell & Kathy Tomasetti. $80-120. MC VISA AX DS. 8 rooms with PB. 1 suite. 1 conference room. Breakfast included in rates. Types of meals: continental breakfast and continental-plus breakfast. Afternoon tea available. Beds: QDT. Phone in room. Antiques, fishing, and watersports nearby.

Location: Cape Cod.

Publicity: *Littleton Independent, Cape Cod Life.*

"*We enjoyed a special homely welcome, home away from home. We loved to stay here. Thanks to the most charming innkeepers.*"

Isaiah Hall B&B Inn

152 Whig St, PO Box 1007
Dennis, MA 02638
(508)385-9928 (800)736-0160 Fax:(508)385-5879

Circa 1857. Adjacent to the Cape's oldest cranberry bog is this Greek Revival farmhouse built by Isaiah Hall, a cooper. His brother was the first cultivator of cranberries in America and Isaiah designed and patented the original barrel for shipping cranberries. In 1948, Dorothy Gripp, an artist, established the inn. Many examples of her artwork remain.

Historic Interest: Cape Playhouse (one-third mile), Old Kings Highway (one-third mile), Old Salt Works (2 miles).

Innkeeper(s): Marie Brophy. $89-149. MC VISA AX TC. 9 rooms, 10 with PB, 1 with FP. 1 suite. Breakfast included in rates. Types of meals: continental-plus breakfast and early coffee/tea. Beds: QDT. Air conditioning in room. TV and fax on premises. Small meetings and seminars hosted. Antiques, fishing, parks, shopping, theater and watersports nearby.

Location: Cape Cod.

Publicity: *Cape Cod Life, New York Times, Golf, National Geographic Traveler.*

"*Your place is so lovely and relaxing.*"

Dennisport 118

Rose Petal B&B

152 Sea St PO Box 974
Dennisport, MA 02639-2404
(508)398-8470

Circa 1872. This Cape Cod-style home was built for Almond Wixon, whose seafaring family was among the original settlers of

Dennisport. In 1918, Wixon was lost at sea with all on board. The Wixon homestead was completely restored in 1986. Surrounded by a white picket fence and attractively land-scaped yard, the Rose Petal is situated in the

heart of Cape Cod, a short walk from the beach. Home-baked pastries highlight a full breakfast in the dining room.

Historic Interest: JFK Museum, family compound (10 miles).

Innkeeper(s): Gayle & Dan Kelly. $59-96. MC VISA AX. TAC10. 3 rooms, 2 with PB. Breakfast included in rates. Types of meals: gourmet breakfast and early coffee/tea. Beds: QT. Air conditioning in room. TV on premises. Family reunions hosted. Some French spoken. Antiques, fishing, parks, shopping, theater and watersports nearby.

"Perfect. Every detail was appreciated."

Duxbury G15

The Winsor House Inn

390 Washington St
Duxbury, MA 02332-4552
(781)934-0991 Fax:(781)934-5955

Circa 1803. A visit to this inn is much like a visit back in time to our early Colonial days. The early 19th-century home was built by a prominent sea captain and merchant Nathaniel Winsor as a wedding gift for his daughter, Nancy. With an eye for the authentic, the innkeepers have restored parts of the inn

to look much the way it might have when the young bride and groom took up residence. Rooms are decorated with Colonial furnishings,

canopied beds, fresh flowers, and each has a fireplace. The Carriage House offers lunch fare, and guests might enjoy a drink at the inn's English-style pub. For a romantic dinner, try the inn's Dining Room, which serves everything from roasted venison with a juniper berry and mushroom crust to herb-seared salmon with plum tomato saffron vinaigrette.

Historic Interest: Plymouth Plantation, Mayflower and Plymouth Rock, 15 minutes away. Twenty miles to Cape Cod.

Innkeeper(s): Mr & Mrs David M O'Connell. $130-210. MC VISA AX DS PC TC. 3 rooms with PB, 3 with FP. 1 suite. Breakfast included in rates. Types of meals: full breakfast and early coffee/tea. Dinner, evening snack, picnic lunch, banquet service, catering service and catered breakfast available. Restaurant on premises. Beds: QT. Air conditioning in room. Fax and copier on premises. Small meetings and family reunions hosted. Antiques, fishing, shopping, cross-country skiing and watersports nearby.

East Orleans H19

The Nauset House Inn

143 Beach Rd, PO Box 774
East Orleans, MA 02643
(508)255-2195

Circa 1810. Located a short distance from Nauset Beach, this inn is a renovated farmhouse set on three acres, which include an old apple orchard. A Victorian conservatory was purchased from a Connecticut estate and reassembled here, then filled with wicker furnishings, Cape flowers and stained glass. Hand-stenciling, handmade quilts, antiques and more bouquets of flowers decorate the rooms. The breakfast room features a fire-place, brick floor and beamed ceiling. Breakfast includes treats such as ginger pancakes or waffles with fresh strawberries. Wine and cranberry juice are served in the evenings.

Innkeeper(s): Al & Diane Johnson, John & Cindy Vessella. $75-128. MC VISA DS PC TC. 14 rooms, 8 with PB. 1 cottage. Breakfast and evening snack included in rates. Types of meals: full breakfast and early coffee/tea. Afternoon tea available. Beds: KQDT. Antiques, fishing, parks, shopping, sporting events, theater and watersports nearby.

Publicity: *Country Living, Glamour, West Hartford News, Travel & Leisure.*

"The inn provided a quiet, serene, comforting atmosphere."

The Parsonage Inn

202 Main St, PO Box 1501
East Orleans, MA 02643
(508)255-8217 (888)422-8217 Fax:(508)255-8216
E-mail: parsinn@capecod.net

Circa 1770. Originally a parsonage, this Cape-style home is now a romantic inn nestled in the village of East Orleans and only a mile and a half from Nauset Beach. Rooms are decorated with antiques, quilts, Laura Ashley fabrics and stenciling, and they include the original pine floors and low ceilings. Freshly baked breakfasts are served either in the dining room or on the brick patio. The innkeepers keep a selection of menus from local restaurants on hand and serve appetizers and refreshments each evening while guest peruse their dining choices. The Parsonage is the perfect location to enjoy nature, with the national seashore, Nickerson State Park and whale-watching opportunities available to guests.

Historic Interest: Cape Cod offers plenty of historic homes and sites.

Innkeeper(s): Ian & Elizabeth Browne. $85-125. MC VISA AX. TAC10. 8 rooms with PB. 2 suites. Breakfast included in rates. Beds: QDT. Phone, air conditioning and ceiling fan in room. Fax on premises. Family reunions hosted. Antiques, shopping, theater and watersports nearby.

Publicity: *Conde Nast Traveler.*

"Your hospitality was as wonderful as your home. Your home was as beautiful as Cape Cod. Thank you!"

Ship's Knees Inn

186 Beach Rd, PO Box 756
East Orleans, MA 02643
(508)255-1312 Fax:(508)240-1351

Circa 1820. This 175-year-old restored sea captain's home is a three-minute walk to the ocean. Rooms are decorated in a nautical style with antiques. Several rooms feature authentic ship's

knees, hand-painted trunks, old clipper ship models and four-poster beds. Some rooms boast ocean views and the Master Suite has a working fireplace. The inn offers swimming and tennis facilities on the grounds. About three miles away, the innkeepers also offer a one-bedroom efficiency apartment and two heated cottages on the Cove. Head into town or spend the day basking in the beauty of Nauset Beach with its picturesque sand dunes.
Innkeeper(s): Jean & Ken Pitchford. $45-110. MC VISA. 11 rooms with PB, 3 with FP. Breakfast included in rates. Type of meal: continental breakfast. Beds: KQDT. Weddings, small meetings and family reunions hosted. Amusement parks, antiques, fishing, parks, shopping, theater and watersports nearby.

Location: One-and-a-half hours from Boston.

Publicity: *Boston Globe.*

"Warm, homey and very friendly atmosphere. Very impressed with the beamed ceilings."

East Sandwich   I17

Spring Garden

578 Route 6a # 867
East Sandwich, MA 02537-1437
(508)888-0710 (800)303-1751 Fax:(508)833-2849
E-mail: skauf@tiac

Circa 1940. Nestled on 11 rural acres, this shingled Cape Cod cottage offers guests panoramic views of the Great Sandwich Salt Marsh, the Tidal Scorton River and the New England country side. Surrounded by a 1,000-acre wildlife sanctuary, the inn is located along one of America's 10 most scenic highways. Each of the 11 spacious rooms is equipped with two double beds, refrigerators and a sundeck or patio. A freshly-baked continental breakfast is offered in the morning. The beach, fine dining, shopping and golf are nearby.
Innkeeper(s): Steve & Betty Kauffman. $67-90. MC VISA DS PC TC. 11 rooms with PB. 3 suites. Breakfast included in rates. Type of meal: continental breakfast. Beds: D. Phone, air conditioning and TV in room. Fax and swimming on premises. Handicap access. 11 acres. Family reunions hosted. Antiques, fishing, parks, shopping, golf, theater and watersports nearby.

Wingscorton Farm Inn

Rt 6a, Olde Kings Hwy
East Sandwich, MA 02537
(508)888-0534

Circa 1763. Wingscorton is a working farm on thirteen acres of lawns, gardens and orchards. It adjoins a short walk to a private ocean beach. This Cape Cod manse, built by a Quaker

family, is a historical landmark on what once was known as the King's Highway, the oldest historical district in the United States. All the rooms are furnished with antiques and working fireplaces (one with a secret compartment where runaway slaves hid). Breakfast features fresh produce with eggs, meats and vegetables from the farm's livestock and gardens. Pets and children welcome.
Innkeeper(s): Sheila Weyers & Richard Loring. $115-150. MC VISA AX PC TC. TAC10. 7 rooms, 7 with FP. 4 suites. 2 cottages. Breakfast included in rates. Types of meals: full breakfast and gourmet breakfast. Beds: QDT. Swimming, library and child care on premises. 13 acres. Weddings, small meetings, family reunions and seminars hosted. Antiques, fishing, parks, shopping, downhill skiing, cross-country skiing, sporting events, theater and watersports nearby.

Pets Allowed.

Location: North Side of Cape Cod, off Route 6A.

Publicity: *Boston Globe, New York Times.*

"Absolutely wonderful. We will always remember the wonderful time."

Eastham   H18

Over Look Inn, Cape Cod

3085 County Rd, PO Box 771
Eastham, MA 02642
(508)255-1886 Fax:(508)240-0345
E-mail: stay@overlookinn.com

Circa 1869. Schooner Captain Barnabus Chipman built this three-story home for his wife. In 1920 it opened as an inn and was frequented by author and naturalist Henry Beston as he wrote "The Outermost House." Located on three acres of grounds, the inn is furnished with Victorian antiques. A collection of Winston Churchill books fills the inn's library. The Aitchisons, from Edinburgh, are known for their warm Scottish charm and occasional bagpipe serenades.
Historic Interest: Coast Guard Beach (1 mile), Nauset Lighthouse (2 miles), Cape Cod National Seashore Museum (one-fourth mile).
Innkeeper(s): Ian & Nan Aitchison. $95-165. MC VISA AX DC CB DS. 10 rooms with PB. 1 conference room. Breakfast and afternoon tea included in rates. Type of meal: full breakfast. Beds: QDT. Antiques, fishing, parks, theater and watersports nearby.

Location: Across from Cape Cod National Seashore on the bike trail.

Publicity: *Conde Nast Traveler, Victorian Homes, New York Times, Cape Code Life, Outside.*

"A delightful experience—Max Nichols, Oklahoma City Journal Record."

Penny House Inn

4885 County Rd, PO Box 238
Eastham, MA 02651
(508)255-6632 (800)554-1751 Fax:(508)255-4893

Circa 1690. Captain Isaiah Horton built this house with a shipbuilder's bow roof. Traditional wide-planked floors and 200-year-old beams buttress the ceiling of the public room. The Captain's Quarters, the largest guest room with its own fireplace, bears the motto: Coil up your ropes and anchor here, Til better weather doth appear.
Innkeeper(s): Margaret Keith. $115-175. MC VISA AX DS PC TC. TAC10. 11 rooms with PB, 3 with FP. 1 conference room. Breakfast and afternoon tea

included in rates. Types of meals: full breakfast and early coffee/tea. Beds: KQDT. Air conditioning and ceiling fan in room. TV, VCR, fax, copier and library on premises. Weddings, small meetings, family reunions and seminars hosted. Antiques, fishing, parks, shopping, theater and watersports nearby.

Location: One mile from National Seashore, Cape Cod.

Publicity: *Cape Cod Life, Cape Codder.*

"Enjoyed my stay tremendously. My mouth waters thinking of your delicious breakfast."

The Whalewalk Inn

220 Bridge Rd
Eastham, MA 02642-3261
(508)255-0617 Fax:(508)240-0017

Circa 1830. Three acres of meadow and lawn surround the Whalewalk, originally a whaling captain's house. An old picket fence frames the elegant house and there is a widow's walk. In

addition to the main house, suites are available in a separate guest house, a renovated barn, a carriage house and a salt-box cottage. Common rooms boast 19th-century antiques from England, France and Denmark, and guest rooms boast antique low-post beds, country furnishings and lovely linens. Start off the day with a delectable full breakfast including crepes, waffles or Grand Marnier French toast. The inn is within walking distance of Cape Cod's bayside beaches and the Cape Cod Rail Trail, a 27-mile bike path.

Historic Interest: Cape Cod National Seashore is 10 minutes away, as is First Encounter Beach. Pilgrim Monument Provincetown is a 30-minute drive.

Innkeeper(s): Carolyn & Richard Smith. $120-245. MC VISA PC TC. TAC10. 16 rooms with PB, 8 with FP. 5 suites. Breakfast and evening snack included in rates. Types of meals: full breakfast, gourmet breakfast and early coffee/tea. Beds: KQT. Air conditioning in room. Fax, copier, bicycles and library on premises. Small meetings, family reunions and seminars hosted. Antiques, fishing, shopping, theater and watersports nearby.

Location: Near the warm bay-side beaches, but only a 10-minute drive to the Atlantic side.

Publicity: *New York Times, Glamour, Yankee Traveler, Conde Nast Traveler.*

"Your hospitality will long be remembered."

Edgartown   K16

The Arbor

222 Upper Main St, PO Box 1228
Edgartown, MA 02539
(508)627-8137

Circa 1880. Originally built on the adjoining island of Chappaquiddick, this house was moved over to Edgartown on a barge at the turn of the century. Located on the bicycle path, it is within walking distance from downtown and the harbor. Guests may relax in the hammock, have

tea on the porch, or walk the unspoiled island beaches of Martha's Vineyard.

Historic Interest: Methodist Camp Meeting Ground.

Innkeeper(s): Peggy Hall. $80-150. MC VISA PC TC. TAC10. 10 rooms, 8 with PB. 1 cottage. Breakfast and afternoon tea included in rates. Type of meal: continental breakfast. Beds: QD. Air conditioning in room. Antiques, fishing, shopping, theater and watersports nearby.

Location: Martha's Vineyard.

Publicity: *Herald News, Yankee Traveler.*

"Thank you so much for your wonderful hospitality! You are a superb hostess. If I ever decide to do my own B&B, your example would be my guide."

Charlotte Inn

27 S Summer St
Edgartown, MA 02539
(508)627-4751

Circa 1864. Shaded by linden and chestnut trees and just minutes from the historic town center, this white clapboard merchant's house is a combination of old-world charm and modern-day elegance. To maintain its historic character, the inn remains purposely behind the times. The inn features 19th-century American and English art, Oriental rugs and crystal chandeliers. Richly paneled mahogany walls, antique fixtures, standing clocks and converted gas lamps add to the inn's natural romantic ambiance. Guest rooms are accented with late 19th-century English antiques, down comforters and four-poster beds. The inn's restaurant features a combination of continental cooking with traditional New England ingredients from the fields, streams and sea.

Innkeeper(s): Gery & Paula Conover. $165-750. 23 rooms. 2 suites. Type of meal: full breakfast. Phone, air conditioning and TV in room.

Colonial Inn of Martha's Vineyard

38 N Water St, PO Box 68
Edgartown, MA 02539-0068
(508)627-4711 (800)627-4701 Fax:(508)627-5904

Circa 1911. This impressive Colonial structure has served as an inn since opening its doors in 1911. Somerset Maugham and Howard Hughes were among the regulars at the inn. Guests at Colonial Inn can sit back and relax on a porch lined with rockers as they gaze at the harbor and enjoy refreshing sea breezes. Flowers, an atrium and courtyards decorate the grounds. The inn has a full-service restaurant and seven boutiques on the premises. Some guest rooms boast harbor views, and all are decorated in an elegant country style. The inn is located in the heart of the town's historic district.

Innkeeper(s): Linda Malcouronne. $90-250. MC VISA AX PC TC. TAC10. 43 rooms with PB. 4 suites. 3 conference rooms. Breakfast included in rates. Type of meal: continental-plus breakfast. Dinner and lunch available. Restaurant on premises. Beds: QD. Phone, air conditioning and TV in room. Fax and library on premises. Handicap access. Small meetings and seminars hosted. Portuguese, Spanish and German spoken. Antiques, fishing, parks, shopping, theater and watersports nearby.

Location: Overlooking the harbor.

Publicity: *Glamour.*

"Everyone very friendly and very efficient."

Edgartown Inn

56 N Water
Edgartown, MA 02539
(508)627-4794

Circa 1798. The Edgartown Inn originally was built as a home for whaling Captain Thomas Worth. (Fort Worth, Texas, was

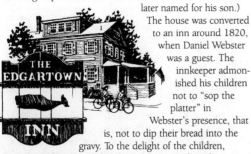

later named for his son.) The house was converted to an inn around 1820, when Daniel Webster was a guest. The innkeeper admonished his children not to "sop the platter" in Webster's presence, that is, not to dip their bread into the gravy. To the delight of the children, Webster himself "sopped the platter." Later, Nathaniel Hawthorne stayed here and proposed to the innkeeper's daughter Eliza Gibbs (who turned him down).

Innkeeper(s): Liliane & Earle Radford. $78-185. 20 rooms, 16 with PB. Types of meals: continental breakfast and full breakfast. Restaurant on premises. Beds: KQD. Phone in room. Antiques, fishing, theater and watersports nearby.

Location: Martha's Vineyard.

Publicity: *Vineyard Gazette.*

"Breakfast in the garden is unbeatable and your staff couldn't be friendlier."

Tuscany Inn The Lodgings

22 N Water
Edgartown, MA 02539
(508)627-5999 Fax:(508)627-6605
E-mail: 70632.3363@compuserve.com

Circa 1893. This Italianate Victorian inn overlooking Edgartown Harbor is located in the heart of this quaint sea-side village. Originally a sea captain's home, the inn has been lovingly restored to reflect the art, interior design and culinary skills of the current innkeepers. There are eight spacious rooms with private baths individually decorated in sophisticated country antiques. Guests

are invited to relax in the garden with a cappuccino and enjoy one of the innkeeper's homemade biscotti. A full breakfast features fresh fruit, homemade frittata and freshly baked

breads. La Cucina ristorante, the inn's on-site restaurant, is open for dinner. Beaches, bicycle paths, museums and art galleries are a short walk away.

Historic Interest: The island is home to Goldie Hawn, John Kennedy Jr., James Taylor, Carly Simon, and a favorite vacation spot for President Bill Clinton.

Innkeeper(s): Laura Scheuer. $90-325. MC VISA AX DC DS TC. TAC10. Breakfast included in rates. Types of meals: full breakfast and gourmet breakfast. Beds: KQT. Air conditioning and TV in room. Fax and library on premises. Italian spoken. Antiques, fishing, parks, shopping, golf and watersports nearby.

Essex   C15

George Fuller House

148 Main St, Rt 133
Essex, MA 01929-1304
(508)768-7766 (800)477-0148 Fax:(508)768-6178

Circa 1830. This three-story, Federal-style home is situated on a lawn that reaches to the salt marsh adjoining the Essex River. Original Indian shutters and Queen Anne baseboards remain. All the guest accommodations boast Boston rockers, and some feature canopy beds and fireplaces. For a view of the water, ask for the Andrews Suite. Belgian waffles and cranberry muffins are a house specialty. Many of the town's 50 antique shops are within walking distance of the inn.

Innkeeper(s): Cindy & Bob Cameron. $75-150. MC VISA AX DC DS PC. TAC10. 7 rooms with PB, 4 with FP. 2 suites. Breakfast and afternoon tea included in rates. Type of meal: full breakfast. Beds: KQDT. Phone, air conditioning and TV in room. VCR and fax on premises. Weddings, small meetings, family reunions and seminars hosted. Antiques, fishing, shopping, cross-country skiing, theater and watersports nearby.

Publicity: *Gloucester Times, Yankee Traveler, Discerning Traveler.*

"Thank you for the wonderful time we had at your place. We give you a 5-star rating!"

Fairhaven   I14

Edgewater B&B

2 Oxford St
Fairhaven, MA 02719-3310
(508)997-5512

Circa 1760. On the historic Moby Dick Trail, Edgewater overlooks the harbor from the grassy slopes of the Acushnet River. The inn is in the charming, rambling, eclectic-style of the area. Its lawns and porches provide water views. Across the harbor in New Bedford, is Herman Melville's "dearest place in all New England." There, visitors immerse themselves in the history and lore of whaling. Near the B&B is the Gothic Revival-style Unitarian Church with stained glass by Tiffany.

Innkeeper(s): Kathy Reed. $70-95. MC VISA AX. 5 rooms with PB. Type of meal: continental-plus breakfast. Beds: KQDT. Phone in room.

Location: Close to ferries to Martha's Vineyard and Cuttyhunk Island, Plymouth, Cape Cod, and Newport, R.I.

Publicity: *Standard Times, Fairhaven Advocate.*

Fall River   I13

Lizzie Bed & Breakfast - Museum

92/230 Second St
Fall River, MA 02721-2006
(508)675-7333
E-mail: Lizziebnb@aol.com

Circa 1845. For those who remember the infamous line, "Lizzie Borden took an ax . . ." here's your chance to find out more about this unsolved crime. Yes, this is where the murders of Lizzie Borden's father and stepmother occurred. Borden was acquitted of the crime, but the real killer was never discovered. Despite its ominous history, the home offers charming Victorian decor. Floors are covered with flowery carpets, walls with cheerful wallpaper, and a collection of Victorian furnishings fills the inn. Homemade biscuits and cornbread, fresh fruit, eggs and sausage are among the breakfast fare.

Innkeeper(s): Ron Evans & Martha McGinn. $150-200. MC VISA AX DS. TAC10. 6 rooms, 1 with PB. Breakfast and evening snack included in rates. Types of meals: full breakfast and early coffee/tea. Beds: QD. Air conditioning in room. TV, VCR, fax, copier and library on premises. Weddings, small meetings and family reunions hosted. Antiques, fishing, parks, shopping and golf nearby.

Publicity: *People Magazine, USA Today, New York Times.*

Falmouth   J16

Captain Tom Lawrence House

75 Locust St
Falmouth, MA 02540-2658
(508)540-1445 (800)266-8139 Fax:(508)457-1790

Circa 1861. After completing five whaling trips around the world, each four years in length, Captain Lawrence retired at 40 and built this house. There is a Steinway piano here now and elegantly furnished guest rooms, some with canopied beds. The house is near the beach, bikeway, ferries and bus station. Freshly ground organic grain is used to make Belgian waffles with warm strawberry sauce, crepes Gisela and pancakes. German is spoken here.

Historic Interest: Hyannisport (Kennedy compound) (20 miles), birthplace of Kathryn Lee Bates who wrote "America the Beautiful" (in Falmouth).

Innkeeper(s): Barbara Sabo-Feller. $85-160. MC VISA PC TC. 6 rooms with PB. 1 suite. Breakfast included in rates. Type of meal: full breakfast. Beds: KQT. Air conditioning and ceiling fan in room. Family reunions hosted. Antiques, fishing, parks, shopping, theater and watersports nearby.

Location: Cape Cod.

Publicity: *Country Inns.*

"This is our first B&B experience. Better than some of the so-called 4-star hotels!! We loved it here."

Elms

PO 895, 495 Rte 28a
Falmouth, MA 02574
(508)540-7232 Fax:(508)540-7295

Circa 1739. The breezes of Buzzards Bay, quality accommodations and a full continental breakfast greet guests at this Queen Anne Victorian inn. Chapoquoit Beach is a short walk and the grounds sport herb gardens and a romantic gazebo. Guests enjoy their 4 p.m. daily meeting time in the living room, where they may sample a complimentary glass of sherry. The Saconesset Homestead Museum is nearby, and South Cape Beach and Washburn Island State Parks are within easy driving distance.

Innkeeper(s): Joe & Betty Mazzucchelli. $65-100. MC VISA AX. 9 rooms, 7 with PB. Breakfast included in rates. Type of meal: continental-plus breakfast. Beds: QDT. TV on premises. Weddings, small meetings, family reunions and seminars hosted. Antiques, fishing, shopping, theater and watersports nearby.

Hewins House B&B

Village Green
Falmouth, MA 02540
(508)457-4363 (800)555-4366

Circa 1820. Built by a wealthy merchant and sea captain, this handsomely restored Federal-style home overlooks Falmouth's Historic Village Green and is a short walk to the Woods Hole

Ferry to Martha's Vineyard. Both the house and the green are in the National Register. The inn's back porch overlooks formal gardens. Inside is a new country kitchen. Although all the guest rooms are decorated attractively, ask for the room with the four poster canopy bed and French armoire for a truly romantic setting. Breakfast is served in the formal dining room.

Innkeeper(s): Virginia Price. $80-100. MC VISA AX DS PC TC. TAC10. 2 rooms with PB, 2 with FP. Breakfast included in rates. Type of meal: full breakfast. Beds: QDT. Phone and air conditioning in room. TV, VCR and copier on premises. Antiques, fishing, parks, shopping, sporting events, golf, theater and watersports nearby.

The Moorings Lodge

207 Grand Ave
Falmouth, MA 02540-3742
(508)540-2370 (800)398-4007

Circa 1905. Captain Frank Spencer was a clever man. He built this wood-shingled Victorian, but first made sure that his ocean view would always be unobstructed. Spencer convinced the town to purchase the beach directly across the street from his home. Guests can relax and enjoy a view of Martha's Vineyard and Vineyard Sound from the inn's glassed-in front porch. Rooms are comfortable and some can accommodate more than two guests. Start off the day with a Vineyard view and breakfasts of

homemade granola, freshly baked breads and entrees such as quiche, soufflés or French toast topped with strawberries. The inn is open from May 15 to Oct. 15.

$85-139. MC VISA AX. 8 rooms with PB. TV and VCR on premises. Fishing and golf nearby.

Mostly Hall B&B Inn

27 Main St
Falmouth, MA 02540-2652
(508)548-3786 (800)682-0565 Fax:(508)457-1572
E-mail: mostlyhl@cape.com

Circa 1849. Albert Nye built this Southern plantation house with wide verandas and a cupola to observe shipping in Vineyard Sound. It was a wedding gift for his New Orleans bride. Because of the seemingly endless halls on every floor (some 30 feet long), it was whimsically called Mostly Hall. The inn recently was placed in the National Register. All rooms have queen-size canopy beds. Bicycles are available for guest use, and the inn is near the bicycle path to Woods Hole.

Historic Interest: The birthplace of Kathryn Lee Bates, author of "America the Beautiful," is across the street. Plymouth and Plimoth Plantation is 35 miles, and the Kennedy Museum and Monument in Hyannisport is 23 miles.

Innkeeper(s): Caroline & Jim Lloyd. $90-130. MC VISA AX DS PC TC. 6

rooms with PB. Breakfast and afternoon tea included in rates. Types of meals: full breakfast, gourmet breakfast and early coffee/tea. Beds: Q. Air conditioning and ceiling fan in room. TV, VCR, fax, bicycles and library on premises. German spoken. Antiques, fishing, parks, shopping, theater and watersports nearby.

Location: In the historic district across from the village green.

Publicity: *Bon Appetit, Boston Globe.*

"Of all the inns we stayed at during our trip, we enjoyed Mostly Hall the most. Imagine, Southern hospitality on Cape Cod!!"

The Inn at One Main Street

1 Main St
Falmouth, MA 02540-2652
(508)540-7469 (888)281-6246

Circa 1892. In the historic district, where the road to Woods Hole begins, is this shingled Victorian with two-story turret, an open front porch and gardens framed by a white picket fence. It first became a tourist house back in the '50s. Cape Cod cranberry pecan waffles and gingerbread pancakes with whipped cream are favorite specialties. Within walking distance, you'll find the Shining Sea Bike Path, beaches, summer theater, tennis, ferry shuttle and bus station. The innkeepers are Falmouth natives and are available to offer their expertise on the area.

Innkeeper(s): Karen Hart & Mari Zylinski. $70-115. MC VISA AX PC TC. 6 rooms with PB. Breakfast included in rates. Type of meal: full breakfast. Beds: QT. Air conditioning and ceiling fan in room. TV on premises. Family reunions hosted. Antiques, shopping, theater and watersports nearby.

"The art of hospitality in a delightful atmosphere, well worth traveling 3,000 miles for."

Palmer House Inn

81 Palmer Ave
Falmouth, MA 02540-2857
(508)548-1230 (800)472-2632 Fax:(508)540-1878

Circa 1901. Just off the village green in Falmouth's historic district, lies this turn-of-the-century Victorian and its adjacent guest house. The polished woodwork, stained-glass windows and collection of antiques tie the home to a romantic, bygone era. Innkeeper Joanne Baker prepares an opulent feast for the morning meal, which is served in traditional Victorian style, by candlelight on tables set with fine china and crystal. Creamed eggs in puff pastry and chocolate-stuffed French toast are two of the reasons why the cuisine has been featured in Gourmet and Bon Appetit. Joanne also offers heart-healthy fare for those monitoring their fat and cholesterol. Afternoon refreshments quell those before-dinner hunger pangs.

Innkeeper(s): Ken & Joanne Baker. $78-185. MC VISA AX DC CB DS PC TC. TAC10. 12 rooms with PB. 1 suite. Breakfast and afternoon tea included in rates. Types of meals: gourmet breakfast and early coffee/tea. Beds: KQDT. Air conditioning, turndown service and ceiling fan in room. TV, fax, copier and bicycles on premises. Handicap access. Small meetings, family reunions and seminars hosted. Antiques, fishing, parks, shopping, theater and watersports nearby.

Location: In the historic district of Falmouth.

Publicity: *Country Inns, Gourmet, Runners World, Yankee Traveler, Bon Appetit.*

"Exactly what a New England inn should be!"

Village Green Inn

40 Main St
Falmouth, MA 02540-2667
(508)548-5621 (800)237-1119 Fax:(508)457-5051
E-mail: vgi40@aol.com

Circa 1804. The inn, listed in the National Register, originally was built in the Federal style for Braddock Dimmick, son of Revolutionary War General Joseph Dimmick. Later, "cranberry king" John Crocker moved the house onto a granite slab foundation, remodeling it in the Victorian style. There are inlaid floors, large porches and gingerbread trim.

Historic Interest: Plimoth Plantation and Heritage Plantation are nearby.

Innkeeper(s): Diane & Don Crosby. $85-150. MC VISA AX PC TC. 5 rooms with PB, 2 with FP. 1 suite. Breakfast and afternoon tea included in rates. Types of meals: full breakfast and early coffee/tea. Beds: Q. Air conditioning, ceiling fan and TV in room. Bicycles on premises. Family reunions hosted. Antiques, fishing, parks, shopping, sporting events, theater and watersports nearby.

Location: Falmouth's historic village green.

Publicity: *Country Inns, Cape Cod Life, Yankee.*

"Tasteful, comfortable and the quintessential New England flavor ... You have turned us on to the B&B style of travel and we now have a standard to measure our future choices by."

Wildflower Inn

167 Palmer Ave
Falmouth, MA 02540-2861
(508)548-9524 (800)294-5459 Fax:(508)548-9524
E-mail: wldflr167@aol.com

Circa 1898. This three-story Victorian, combines modern amenities with the inn's original architectural character. Gleaming woods floors throughout are topped by Oriental rugs and period antiques. All second-floor and third-floor guest rooms are individually decorated for warmth and comfort. For a more intimate stay, the inn offers its Loft-Cottage that boasts a private entrance, porch, a full kitchen and a spiral staircase leading to a romantic loft bedroom. Breakfast includes edible flowers and features Stuffed Lemon Pancakes, Blueberry Country Flower Muffins and Pansy Butter. The inn is a short walk to the Village Green, restaurants and the shuttle to island ferries.

Innkeeper(s): Phil & Donna Stone. $90-160. MC VISA AX TC. TAC10. 5 rooms, 6 with PB. 1 cottage. Breakfast, afternoon tea and evening snack included in rates. Types of meals: gourmet breakfast and early coffee/tea. Beds: QT. Air conditioning and ceiling fan in room. TV, VCR, fax and bicycles on premises. Antiques, fishing, parks, shopping, theater and watersports nearby.

Publicity: *Cape Cod Times, Journal of Bed & Breakfast, PBS, Cape Cod Travel Guide.*

"This was a magical stay, everything was perfect — hospitality, room, food. It was everything we hoped for, and way beyond what we expected."

Woods Hole Passage B&B Inn

186 Woods Hole Rd
Falmouth, MA 02540-1670
(508)548-9575 (800)790-8976 Fax:(508)540-4771
E-mail: woods.hole.inn@usa.net

Circa 1890. This Cape Cod-style carriage house was moved more than 50 years ago to its present site, surrounded by trees and wild berry bushes. The home's common area provides a spacious, comfortable setting, while guest quarters feature country decor. Breakfasts often are served on the patio, which overlooks the one-and-a-half-acre grounds or in the garden. Items such as homemade breads, fresh fruit and quiche are among the fare. It's just a short walk through the woods to the beach. A bike path, Martha's Vineyard, an aquarium, shopping and restaurants are just a few of the nearby attractions.

Innkeeper(s): Deb Pruitt. $75-115. MC VISA AX DC DS PC TC. TAC10. 5 rooms with PB. Breakfast and afternoon tea included in rates. Types of meals: full breakfast and early coffee/tea. Picnic lunch available. Beds: QD. Air conditioning and ceiling fan in room. Fax, bicycles, tennis and library on premises. Weddings and family reunions hosted. Amusement parks, antiques, fishing, parks, shopping, theater and watersports nearby.

Falmouth Heights   J16

Grafton Inn

261 Grand Ave S
Falmouth Heights, MA 02540-3784
(508)540-8688 (800)642-4069 Fax:(508)540-1861

Circa 1870. If you want to enjoy grand ocean views while staying at an inn in Cape Cod, this is the place. Oceanfront and within walking distance to the ferries, the inn is an ideal place to hop on board a ferry and spend a day on Nantucket Island or Martha's Vineyard and return that evening to relax and watch the moon over the ocean from your bedroom window. Snacks of wine and cheese are served in the after-  noon. The inn is often seen on television and ESPN because of its unique location at the final leg of the Falmouth Road Race.

Historic Interest: Plimoth Plantation (30 miles), Heritage Plantation (15 miles), Bourne Farm (6 miles).

Innkeeper(s): Liz & Rudy Cvitan. $75-169. MC VISA AX DS TC. TAC10. 11 rooms with PB. Breakfast included in rates. Types of meals: gourmet breakfast and early coffee/tea. Beds: KQDT. Air conditioning, ceiling fan and TV in room. Fax, swimming and library on premises. Small meetings hosted: Antiques, fishing, parks, shopping, theater and watersports nearby.

Publicity: *Enterprise, At Your Leisure, Cape Cod Life.*

"You have certainly created a lovely inn for those of us who wish to escape the city and relax in luxury."

Great Barrington   F2

Baldwin Hill Farm B&B

121 Baldwin Hill Rd N/S
Great Barrington, MA 01230-9061
(413)528-4092 (888)528-4092 Fax:(413)528-6365

Circa 1840. Several barns, dating back to the mid-18th century are still to be found on this 450-acre farm. The main house,

a Victorian-style, New England farmstead, features a screened-in front porch where guests can enjoy the tranquil scenery of hills, fields, valleys, mountains, gardens and orchards. As the home has been in the family since 1912, the four guest rooms include many family antiques. Homemade country breakfasts are served in the formal dining room. The inn is 30 minutes or less from many attractions, including museums, golf courses, ski areas, Tanglewood and antique shops.

Innkeeper(s): Richard & Priscilla Burdsall. $75-100. MC VISA PC TC. TAC10. 4 rooms, 2 with PB, 1 with FP. 2 conference rooms. Breakfast and afternoon tea included in rates. Type of meal: full breakfast. Beds: KQT. TV, VCR, copier, swimming, stables and library on premises. 450 acres. Weddings, small meetings and family reunions hosted. Antiques, fishing, parks, shopping, downhill skiing, cross-country skiing, sporting events, theater and watersports nearby.

"We enjoyed your home immensely - from the wonderful views to your beautiful perennial flower beds to your sumptuous breakfasts."

Seekonk Pines

142 Seekonk Cross Rd
Great Barrington, MA 01230-1571
(413)528-4192 (800)292-4192 Fax:(413)528-1076

Circa 1832. Known as the Crippen Farm from 1835-1879, Seekonk Pines Inn now includes both the original farmhouse and a Dutch Colonial wing. Green lawns, gardens and meadows surround the inn. The name "Seekonk" was the local Indian name for the Canadian geese which migrate through this part of the Berkshires. The inn is an easy drive to Tanglewood.

Historic Interest: Chesterwood (8 miles), Colonel Ashley House (10 miles), Norman Rockwell Museum (8-9 miles), Hancock Shaker Village (35-40 minutes, approximately 19 miles).

Innkeeper(s): Bruce, Roberta & Rita Lefkowitz. $80-135. MC VISA AX. TAC10. 6 rooms with PB. Breakfast included in rates. Type of meal: full breakfast. Beds: QDT. Air conditioning and ceiling fan in room. TV, VCR, fax, copier, swimming, bicycles and library on premises. Weddings and family reunions hosted. Antiques, fishing, shopping, downhill skiing, cross-country skiing, golf, theater and watersports nearby.

Location: Near Tanglewood.

Publicity: *Los Angeles Times, Boston Sunday Globe, Country Inns, New York Newsday.*

"Of all the B&Bs we trekked through, yours was our first and most memorable! This has been our best ever Berkshire escape...thanks to your wonderful B&B."

Hadley E6

Clark Tavern Inn B&B

98 Bay Rd
Hadley, MA 01035-9718
(413)586-1900 Fax:(413)587-9788
E-mail: mrcallhn@aol.com

Circa 1740. Gardens of perennials and wildflowers frame this pre-revolutionary Colonial home, which once served as a toll-house and tavern. To preserve it from demolition when I-91 was built, local men disassembled it and meticulously reassembled and restored it. Furnished with colonial pieces in keeping with the pristine simplicity of the wide pine plank floors, original woodwork and 12-over-12 windows, rooms are enhanced by lavish canopy beds in the guest rooms. Two rooms have fireplaces.

Innkeeper(s): Mike & Ruth Callahan. $100-145. MC VISA AX DS PC TC. 3 rooms with PB, 2 with FP. Breakfast, afternoon tea and evening snack included in rates. Types of meals: full breakfast and early coffee/tea. Room service available. Beds: Q. Phone, air conditioning, TV and VCR in room. Fax and swimming on premises. Spanish spoken. Amusement parks, antiques, fishing, parks, shopping, downhill skiing, cross-country skiing, sporting events, golf, theater and watersports nearby.

Publicity: *New York Times, Boston Herald.*

Hamilton C14

Miles River Country Inn

823 Bay Rd, Box 149
Hamilton, MA 01936
(508)468-7206 Fax:(508)468-3999

Circa 1789. This rambling colonial inn sits on more than 30 acres of magnificent curving lawns bordered by trees and formal gardens that lead to the Miles River. There are meadows,

woodlands and wetlands surrounding the property and available for exploring. The river flows through the property, which is a haven for a wide variety of wildlife. Many of the inn's 12 fireplaces are in the guest rooms. Family heirloom antiques compliment the interior.

Historic Interest: Ipswich, which features the nation's largest collection of homes built prior to 1800, is one of the area's many historic attractions. Salem, home to the House of Seven Gables, is another interesting destination.

Innkeeper(s): Gretel & Peter Clark. $80-210. MC VISA AX PC TC. 8 rooms, 6 with PB, 4 with FP. 1 suite. 2 conference rooms. Breakfast and afternoon tea included in rates. Types of meals: full breakfast and early coffee/tea. Beds: QDT. TV, VCR, fax, copier, bicycles and library on premises. 30 acres. Weddings, small meetings, family reunions and seminars hosted. Spanish and French spoken. Antiques, fishing, parks, shopping, downhill skiing, cross-country skiing, sporting events, theater and watersports nearby.

Publicity: *Boston Globe, Salem Evening News.*

Harwich Port I18

Augustus Snow House

528 Main St
Harwich Port, MA 02646-1842
(508)430-0528 (800)320-0528 Fax:(508)432-7995

Circa 1901. This gracious, Queen Anne Victorian is a turn-of-the-century gem, complete with a wide, wraparound veranda, gabled windows and a distinctive turret. Victorian wallpapers, stained glass and rich woodwork complement the interior, which is appropriately decorated in period style. Each of the romantic guest quarters offers something special. One room has a canopy bed and a fireplace, while another includes a relaxing clawfoot tub. Three rooms have Jacuzzi tubs. The king-size beds are dressed in fine linens. As is the Victorian way, afternoon refreshments are served each day. The breakfasts include delectables, such as banana chip muffins, baked pears in raspberry cream sauce or, possibly, baked French toast with layers of homemade cinnamon bread, bacon and cheese.

Innkeeper(s): Joyce & Steve Roth. $105-160. MC VISA AX DS PC TC. 5 rooms with PB, 1 with FP. Breakfast included in rates. Types of meals: gourmet breakfast and early coffee/tea. Beds: KQ. Phone, air conditioning, ceiling fan and TV in room. Fax and copier on premises. Weddings, small meetings and family reunions hosted. Antiques, fishing, parks, shopping, golf and watersports nearby.

"Being able to walk to the beach early in the morning before breakfast was the perfect start to our stay. Breakfast was more than we ever thought we could eat."

Captain's Quarters B&B Inn

85 Bank St
Harwich Port, MA 02646-1903
(508)432-1991 (800)992-6550

Circa 1850. This romantic Victorian inn features a classic wrap-around porch and a graceful, curving front stairway. Guest rooms include brass beds and charming decor. A continental breakfast is served each morning. The inn is a three-minute walk to the beach or the village.

Innkeeper(s): Ed Kenney. $89-109. MC VISA AX DS. 5 rooms with PB. Breakfast included in rates. Type of meal: continental-plus breakfast. Beds: QT. Phone and TV in room. Antiques and shopping nearby.

Location: One-and-a-half hours from Boston.

"A great romantic getaway with lovely rooms."

Hyannis I17

The Inn on Sea Street

358 Sea St
Hyannis, MA 02601-4509
(508)775-8030 Fax:(508)771-0878
E-mail: innonsea@capecod.net

Circa 1849. This white Victorian inn is comprised of two homes, both are listed in the town's register of historic buildings. Guest rooms are decorated with four-poster canopy beds. Its charm includes Colonial portraits, Persian carpets and a grand curved staircase. Breakfast is served on the sun porch or elegant dining room on tables set with sterling silver, china, crystal and fresh flowers from the garden. A log book in the living room is open for guests to rate local restaurants and get opinions before going out on the town.

Historic Interest:
Kennedy Library &
Compound is less than
one mile from the home.
Innkeeper(s): Lois M.
Nelson & J.B.
Whitehead. $78-125.
MC VISA AX DS. 9
rooms, 7 with PB. 1 cot-
tage. Breakfast included
in rates. Type of meal:
full breakfast. Beds:
QDT. Phone, air condi-
tioning and TV in room. Small meetings and family reunions hosted.
Antiques, fishing, shopping, theater and watersports nearby.

Publicity: *Journal*.

"A lot of people really don't know how much they are missing, until they visit you."

Hyannis Port   117

The Simmons Homestead Inn

288 Scudder Ave
Hyannis Port, MA 02647
(508)778-4999 (800)637-1649 Fax:(508)790-1342

Circa 1820. This former sea captain's home features period
decor and includes huge needlepoint displays and lifelike
ceramic and papiermache animals that give the inn a country

feel. Some rooms boast canopy beds, and each is individually
decorated. Traditional full breakfasts are served in the formal
dining room. Evening wine helps guests relax after a day of
touring the Cape. There is a billiard room on the premises.

Innkeeper(s): Bill Putman & Betsy Reney. $120-200. MC VISA AX DS TC.
TAC10. 12 rooms with PB. 1 suite. Breakfast included in rates. Type of
meal: full breakfast. Beds: KQT. Ceiling fan in room. TV, fax, copier and bicycles on premises. Small meetings and family reunions hosted. Antiques, fishing, parks, shopping and watersports nearby.

Location: In heart of Cape Cod.

Publicity: *Bon Appetit, Cape Code Life, Yankee.*

"I want to say that part of what makes Cape Cod special for us is the inn. It embodies much of what is wonderful at the Cape. By Sunday, I was completely rested, relaxed, renewed, and restored."

Lee   E2

Applegate

279 W Park St
Lee, MA 01238-1718
(413)243-4451 (800)691-9012 Fax:(413)243-4451

Circa 1920. This romantic bed & breakfast is an ideal accommodation for those visiting the Berkshires. Well-dressed, four-
poster beds rest atop polished wood floors. Gracious furnishings, Oriental rugs and soft lighting add to the ambiance. Two
guest rooms offer fireplaces, and several offer views of woods or
gardens. Fresh flowers, brandy and Godiva chocolates are just a
few extras that await guests. In the early evening, wine and

cheese is served. Breakfasts are served by candlelight, with
crystal stemware and antique china. The innkeepers offer several special getaway packages, such as a wine-tasting dinner
weekends and "renew your vows" weekends. Golf and tennis
facilities are located across the street.

Historic Interest: Norman Rockwell Museum is nearby.

Innkeeper(s): Richard & Nancy Begbie-Cannata. $95-230. MC VISA PC TC.
6 rooms with PB, 2 with FP. 1 cottage. Breakfast included in rates. Type of
meal: continental-plus breakfast. Beds: KQD. Air conditioning in room. TV,
VCR, fax, copier, swimming, bicycles and library on premises. Weddings,
small meetings, family reunions and seminars hosted. Antiques, parks, shopping, downhill skiing, cross-country skiing, theater and watersports nearby.

Publicity: *Country Inns.*

"The house is decorated beautifully—cozy dolls decorate all the little nooks and crannies."

Devonfield

85 Stockbridge Rd
Lee, MA 01238-9308
(413)243-3298 (800)664-0880 Fax:(413)243-1360

Circa 1800. The original section of this Colonial inn was
built by a Revolutionary War soldier. Guest rooms are spacious with charming furniture and patterned wallcoverings.
Three of the rooms feature fireplaces. The one-bedroom cottage has both a fireplace and an efficiency kitchen. Guests are
treated to a full breakfast. One need not wander far from the
grounds to find something to do. The innkeepers offer a tennis court, swimming pool and bicycles for guests, and a nine-
hole golf course is just across the way. Inside, guests can relax
in the living room with its fireplace and library or in the television room. The area is full of boutiques, antique shops and
galleries to explore,
as well as hiking,
fishing and skiing.
Tanglewood, sum-
mer home of the
Boston Symphony,
is close by.

Historic Interest: Among the many historic sites offered in this part of
Massachusetts are the Norman Rockwell Museum and the Hancock Shaker
Village. There's no shortage of historic homes to visit.

Innkeeper(s): Sally & Ben Schenck. $70-260. MC VISA AX DS PC TC.
TAC10. 10 rooms with PB, 4 with FP. 4 suites. 1 cottage. Beds: KQT. Air
conditioning in room. TV, fax, copier, swimming, bicycles, tennis and library
on premises. 40 acres.

Publicity: *Discerning Traveler.*

"A special thank you for your warm and kind hospitality. We feel as though this is our home away from home."

Morgan House Inn

33 Main St
Lee, MA 01238-1611
(413)243-0181

Circa 1817. This classic Colonial inn reflects the stagecoach
era with its stenciled wall coverings, comfortable antique-filled
rooms and country prints. The innkeepers, Lenora and Stuart,
are former owners of a Berkshire inn, a Cambridge fine dining
restaurant, a wine and specialty food store and have years of
experience in corporate dining. Lenora prepares contemporary
and traditional New England cuisine. Her favorites include
warm popovers, barbecue glazed pork tenderloin with Boston
baked beans and sweet potato chips, duckling with cinnamon-

spiced orange sauce, plum conserve, and wild rice pancakes. Lighter "tavern" fare is served throughout the day. The inn is just one mile from the Berkshire Outlet Village.

Historic Interest: Norman Rockwell Museum (5 miles), Home of Daniel Chester French, Chesterwood (5 miles), Herman Melville home, Arrowhead (8 miles).

Innkeeper(s): Lenora & Stuart Bowen. $50-155. EP. MC VISA AX DC DS TC. 11 rooms, 5 with PB. 1 conference room. Breakfast included in rates. Type of meal: full breakfast. Dinner, picnic lunch, lunch and catering service available. Restaurant on premises. Beds: KQDT. Air conditioning in room. TV on premises. Weddings, small meetings, family reunions and seminars hosted. Antiques, fishing, parks, shopping, downhill skiing, cross-country skiing and theater nearby.

Publicity: *Berkshire Book, Union News, Golden Ages, Restaurants of New England, Country Inns.*

"*Charming and friendly—5-star rating.*"

The Parsonage on The Green

20 Park Pl
Lee, MA 01238-1618
(413)243-4364

Circa 1851. As the former parsonage to the first Congregational Church (known as having the highest wooded steeple in the country), this white colonial inn is tucked behind a white picket fence. A pleasant wicker-filled side porch is shaded by the boughs of an old apple tree. Family heirlooms, 18th-century American antiques and Oriental rugs are set against polished maple and oak hardwood floors. An elegant afternoon tea is served graciously from the tea cart in the parlor and includes freshly made sweets such as Victorian lace cookies and scones. A candlelight breakfast is provided or cross the street and enjoy a cup of coffee at McClellands Drug Store for 16 cents. Walk to restaurants, galleries and shops. Stockbridge and Lenox are nearby.

Innkeeper(s): Barbara & Don Mahony. $60-100. MC VISA PC TC. 4 rooms. Breakfast and afternoon tea included in rates. Types of meals: continental-plus breakfast and early coffee/tea. Dinner and picnic lunch available. Beds: D. Turndown service and ceiling fan in room. TV, VCR, bicycles and library on premises. Antiques, fishing, parks, shopping, downhill skiing, cross-country skiing, sporting events, golf, theater and watersports nearby.

Publicity: *Berkshire Eagle.*

"*Our dream came true, the perfect romantic getaway.*"

Lenox   E2

Amadeus House

15 Cliffwood St
Lenox, MA 01240-2026
(413)637-4770 (800)205-4770 Fax:(413)637-4484

Circa 1820. Named to capture the feeling of Lenox as the nation's summer music capital, this original Colonial house, which was later updated during the Victorian era, is close to several performing arts companies. The area is the summer home of the Boston Symphony Orchestra, Shakespeare & Co., who perform stage classics and modern repertoire, and the Berkshire Performing Arts Center. Besides the love for music reflected at the inn, with its rooms named after great composers and a library of recordings and books, you can spend a relaxing summer afternoon on the porch, reading a good book and sipping lemonade.

Historic Interest:
Tanglewood, summer house of Boston Symphony (1 1/2 miles), Arrowhead, home of Herman Melville (5 miles), the mountain home of Edith Wharton (2 miles).

Innkeeper(s): John Felton & Martha Gottron. $60-175. MC VISA AX. 8 rooms, 5 with PB. 1 suite. Breakfast and afternoon tea included in rates. Types of meals: full breakfast and early coffee/tea. Picnic lunch available. Beds: KQT. Ceiling fan in room. Small meetings and family reunions hosted. Antiques, fishing, shopping, downhill skiing, cross-country skiing, theater and watersports nearby.

Publicity: *Discerning Traveler, Yankee.*

"*Your gracious attention to every detail at Amadeus House made it one of the best stays we've had anywhere. It was all your special touches that made our stay so special.*"

Birchwood Inn

7 Hubbard St, Box 2020
Lenox, MA 01240-2329
(413)637-2600 (800)524-1646 Fax:(413)637-2600
E-mail: detoner@bcn.net

Circa 1767. This inn, which is the only privately owned Lenox building listed in the National Register, is situated on a hilltop and overlooks the village. The gardens and lawns are surrounded by old New England stone fences. Guests can enjoy the wood burning fireplaces and large library. Full international breakfasts are changed daily and include items such as Eggs Benedict, huevos rancheros, omelets and New England pancakes. For a small fee, the innkeepers can arrange for guests to use a local health club, which includes tennis courts and a swimming pool.

Historic Interest: Edith Wharton's home is two miles away, while Herman Melville's home is three miles from the inn. The Norman Rockwell Museum is about four miles away.

Innkeeper(s): Joan, Dick & Dan Toner. $60-210. MC VISA AX DC CB DS. 12 rooms, 10 with PB, 6 with FP. 2 suites. 1 conference room. Breakfast included in rates. Types of meals: full breakfast and early coffee/tea. Evening snack available. Beds: KQDT. Phone, air conditioning, ceiling fan and TV in room. VCR on premises. Small meetings, family reunions and seminars hosted. Antiques, fishing, shopping, downhill skiing, cross-country skiing, theater and watersports nearby.

Location: Berkshires.

"*Inn-credible! Inn-viting! Inn-spiring! Inn-comparable! Our ultimate getaway. Wonderful ambiance, great food and the finest hosts we ever met. We have been going to the Birchwood Inn for more than 15 years and each time we enjoy it even more.*"

Blantyre

16 Blantyre Rd, PO Box 995
Lenox, MA 01240
(413)637-3556 Fax:(413)637-4282
E-mail: hide@blantyre.com

Circa 1902. Situated on manicured lawns near Tanglewood, this Tudor manor is entered through a massive portico. Grandly-sized rooms include the Great Hall and an elegantly paneled dining room. Breakfast is graciously served in the conservatory. Formal grounds offer four tennis courts, two championship croquet courts, a pool and carriage house.

Historic Interest: Hancock Shaker Village (10 miles), Norman Rockwell Museum (7 miles), Chesterwood (7 miles).

Innkeeper(s): Roderick Anderson, Managing Director. $250-750. MC VISA AX DC PC TC. TAC10. 23 rooms, 7 with FP. 10 suites. 2 cottages. 1 conference room. Breakfast included in rates. Types of meals: continental breakfast, full breakfast and gourmet breakfast. Dinner, picnic lunch, lunch, banquet service and room service available. Restaurant on premises. Beds: KQD. Phone, air conditioning, turndown service and TV in room. VCR, fax, copier, swimming, sauna and tennis on premises. Handicap access. 100 acres. Weddings, small meetings, family reunions and seminars hosted. French spoken. Antiques, fishing, shopping, golf, theater and watersports nearby.

Publicity: *Hideaway Report, Country Inns, Conde Nast Traveler, Zagat, Victoria Magazine, Discovery Channel-Great Country Inns. Ratings: 4 Stars.*

"There was not a single aspect of our stay with you that was not worked out to total perfection."

Brook Farm Inn

15 Hawthorne St
Lenox, MA 01240-2404
(413)637-3013 (800)285-7638 Fax:(413)637-4751
E-mail: innkeeper@brookfarm.com.

Circa 1870. Brook Farm Inn is named after the original Brook Farm, a literary commune that sought to combine thinker and worker through a society of intelligent, cultivated members. In keeping with that theme, this gracious Victorian inn offers poetry and writing seminars and has a 650-volume poetry library. Canopy beds, Mozart and a swimming pool tend to the spirit.

Historic Interest: Home of Edith Wharton (the Mount), home of Herman Melville (Arrowhead), home of Daniel Chester French, Lincoln Memorial (Chesterwood).

Innkeeper(s): Joe & Anne Miller. $80-200. MC VISA DS PC TC. 12 rooms with PB, 6 with FP. Breakfast and afternoon tea included in rates. Types of meals: full breakfast and early coffee/tea. Beds: KQT. Air conditioning and ceiling fan in room. Fax, copier and swimming on premises. Family reunions hosted. Antiques, fishing, parks, shopping, downhill skiing, cross-country skiing, sporting events, theater and watersports nearby.

Location: In the heart of Berkshire County.

Publicity: *Berkshire Eagle, Country Inns, Travel & Leisure, Boston.*

"We've been traveling all our lives and never have we felt more at home."

Cornell Inn

203 Main St
Lenox, MA 01240
(413)637-0562 (800)637-0562 Fax:(413)637-0927

Circa 1880. This graceful Queen Anne Victorian first welcomed guests in the '30s. Back then, it was a guest house with a speakeasy in the adjacent carriage house. Today, the inn is a full-service country inn with a restaurant, pub and health spa. Choose between a cozy bedroom with a fireplace in the main house, a fully equipped suite with a fireplace and kitchen in the carriage house, or a room with a four-poster bed, fireplace and Jacuzzi in the MacDonald House. Carriage house suites include a fireplace and a kitchen. The lush grounds have a Japanese garden. Packages are available.

Innkeeper(s): Jack D'Elia. $59-195. MC VISA AX DC CB DS PC. TAC5. 30 rooms with PB, 18 with FP. Breakfast included in rates. Type of meal: continental-plus breakfast. Beds: KQDT. Phone in room. Spa and sauna on premises. Downhill skiing, cross-country skiing, golf and watersports nearby.

Garden Gables Inn

PO Box 52
Lenox, MA 01240-0052
(413)637-0193 Fax:(413)637-4554
E-mail: gardeninn@aol.com

Circa 1780. Several distinctive gables adorn this home set on five wooded acres. Deer occasionally wander into the garden to help themselves to fallen apples. Breakfast is served in the

dining room, which overlooks tall maples, flower gardens and fruit trees. The swimming pool was the first built in the county and is still the longest. Guests will find many special amenities including in-room phones, fireplaces and whirlpool tubs. There is a Baby Grand Steinway Piano in the living room.

Innkeeper(s): Mario & Lynn Mekinda. $80-250. MC VISA AX DS PC TC. 18 rooms with PB, 8 with FP. 2 suites. 4 cottages. Breakfast and afternoon tea included in rates. Types of meals: full breakfast and early coffee/tea. Beds: KQFT. Phone, air conditioning and TV in room. VCR, fax and swimming on premises. Weddings, small meetings, family reunions and seminars hosted. French and German spoken. Antiques, fishing, parks, shopping, downhill skiing, cross-country skiing, theater and watersports nearby.

Location: In the Berkshires.

Publicity: *National Geographic Traveler, Berkshire Eagle, Los Angeles Times, Long Island News.*

"Charming and thoughtful hospitality. You restored a portion of my sanity and I'm very grateful—Miami Herald."

The Kemble Inn

2 Kemble St
Lenox, MA 01240-2813
(413)637-4113 (800)353-4113

Circa 1881. Named for a famous 19th-century actress, Fanny Kemble, this three-story Georgian-style inn boasts an incredible view of the mountains in the Berkshires. The inn's 15 luxurious guest rooms are named for American authors, including Nathaniel Hawthorne, Henry Wadsworth Longfellow, Herman Melville, Mark Twain and Edith Wharton. The impressive Fanny Kemble Room, which features mountain views,

includes two fireplaces, a Jacuzzi tub and a king-size, four-poster bed. The inn is within minutes of five major ski areas, and Tanglewood is less than two miles away.

Historic Interest: Norman Rockwell Museum, Edith Wharton Restoration.

Innkeeper(s): J. Richard & Linda Reardon. $85-275. MC VISA DC CB DS PC TC. 15 rooms with PB, 6 with FP. Breakfast included in rates. Type of meal: continental breakfast. Phone, air conditioning and TV in room. Handicap access. Antiques, fishing, parks, shopping, downhill skiing, cross-country skiing, theater and watersports nearby.

Publicity: *Country Inns.*

"Kemble Inn was a showcase B&B - just what we had hoped for."

Rookwood Inn

11 Old Stockbridge Rd PO Box 1717
Lenox, MA 01240-1717
(413)637-9750 (800)223-9750
E-mail: innkeepers@rookwoodinn.com

Circa 1885. This turn-of-the-century Queen Anne Victorian inn offers 21 elegant guest rooms, including two suites. Among the amenities in the air-conditioned guest rooms are antiques and fireplaces. The public rooms and halls are decorated with the innkeepers' collection of antique handbags and Wallace Nutting prints. The day begins with a bountiful breakfast, prepared by innkeeper Steve Lindner-Lesser. The beautiful Berkshires are famous for cultural and recreational opportunities, and guests can walk to shops and restaurants. Tanglewood is one mile away.

Innkeeper(s): Amy & Stephen Lindner-Lesser. $85-275. MC VISA AX DS PC TC. TAC10. 21 rooms with PB, 8 with FP. 2 suites. 2 conference rooms. Breakfast and afternoon tea included in rates. Type of meal: full breakfast. Beds: KQTD. Air conditioning and ceiling fan in room. TV and child care on premises. Handicap access. Weddings, small meetings, family reunions and seminars hosted. Antiques, fishing, parks, shopping, downhill skiing, cross-country skiing, theater and watersports nearby.

Location: One-half block from town center.

Publicity: *New York Times, Boston Globe, London Times.*

"Of all the inns I've visited, Rookwood, by far, was the most comfortable, with personable, friendly and obliging innkeepers, excellent breakfasts and cozy atmosphere."

Seven Hills Country Inn & Restaurant

40 Plunkett St
Lenox, MA 01240-2704
(413)637-0060 (800)869-6518 Fax:(413)637-3651

Circa 1911. Descendants of those who sailed on the Mayflower built this rambling, Tudor-style mansion. The inn's 27 acres often serve as the site for weddings, receptions and meetings. The grounds include two tennis courts and a swimming pool. Guest rooms are elegantly appointed with antiques, and the mansion still maintains its hand-carved fireplaces and leaded glass windows. In addition to the original elements, some rooms contain the modern amenity of a jet tub. The inn's chef, whose cuisine has been featured in Gourmet magazine, prepares creative, continental specialties. Seven Hills offers close access to many attractions in the Berkshires.

Innkeeper(s): Patricia & Jim Eder. $65-250. MAP, EP. MC VISA AX DC CB DS PC TC. TAC10. 52 rooms with PB, 5 with FP. 2 suites. 4 conference rooms. Breakfast included in rates. Types of meals: continental-plus breakfast and full breakfast. Dinner available. Beds: KQTD. Phone and air conditioning in room. TV, VCR, fax, copier, swimming, tennis, library and child care on premises. Handicap access. 27 acres. Weddings, small meetings, family reunions and seminars hosted. Spanish and French spoken. Antiques, fishing, parks, shopping, downhill skiing, cross-country skiing, theater and watersports nearby.

Pets Allowed: Pets sometimes allowed.

Summer Hill Farm

950 East St
Lenox, MA 01240-2205
(413)442-2059 (800)442-2059
E-mail: innkeeper@summerhillfarm.com

Circa 1796. Situated on a scenic 19 acres, this Colonial home was once part of a 300-acre farm deeded to the Steven family just after the French & Indian War. Several rooms include fireplaces or brass beds. The Loft and Mountain View rooms both offer superb views. The Cottage, an old hay barn, includes a bedroom as well as sitting, dining and cooking areas. Fresh fruit, homemade granola, and home-baked bread accompany

the morning's special breakfast entree. After a hearty breakfast, guests should have no trouble finding something to do. Arts and sports activities are nearby, as are museums, Hancock Shaker Village, antique shops, Tanglewood, theatres and many other cultural attractions.

Innkeeper(s): Sonya & Michael Wessel. $55-150. MC VISA AX PC. TAC10. 7 rooms with PB, 3 with FP. 1 cottage. Breakfast included in rates. Type of meal: full breakfast. Beds: KQDT. Air conditioning and TV in room. VCR, stables and library on premises. 19 acres. Family reunions hosted. Limited French and limited Spanish spoken. Antiques, fishing, parks, downhill skiing, cross-country skiing, sporting events, theater and watersports nearby.

"You and your home are wonderfully charming."

Walker House

64 Walker St
Lenox, MA 01240-2718
(413)637-1271 (800)235-3098 Fax:(413)637-2387
E-mail: phoudek@vgernet.net

Circa 1804. This beautiful Federal-style house sits in the center of the village on three acres of graceful woods and restored gardens. Guest rooms have fireplaces and private baths. Each is named for a favorite composer such as Beethoven, Mozart or Handel. The innkeepers' musical backgrounds include associations with the San Francisco Opera, the New York City Opera, and the Los Angeles Philharmonic. Walker House concerts are scheduled from time to time. The innkeepers offer film and opera screenings nightly on a twelve-foot screen. With prior approval, some pets may be allowed.

Historic Interest: Tanglewood, The Mount.

Innkeeper(s): Peggy & Richard Houdek. $70-200. PC. 8 rooms with PB, 5 with FP. 1 conference room. Breakfast and afternoon tea included in rates. Types of meals: continental-plus breakfast and early coffee/tea. Beds: QDT. Phone and air conditioning in room. TV, VCR, fax, copier and library on premises. Handicap access. Weddings, small meetings and family reunions hosted. French and Spanish spoken. Antiques, fishing, parks, shopping, downhill skiing, cross-country skiing, theater and watersports nearby.

Pets Allowed: With prior approval.

Location: Route 183 & 7A.

Publicity: *Boston Globe, PBS, Los Angeles Times, New York Times, Dog Fancy.*

"We had a grand time staying with fellow music and opera lovers! Breakfasts were lovely."

Whistler's Inn

5 Greenwood St
Lenox, MA 01240-2029
(413)637-0975 (888)820-0123 Fax:(413)637-2190
E-mail: rmears3246@aol.com

Circa 1820. Whistler's Inn is an English Tudor home surrounded by eight acres of woodlands and gardens. Inside, elegance is abundant. In the impressive Louis XVI music room, you'll find a Steinway piano, chandeliers and gilt palace furniture. There is

an English library with chintz-covered sofas, hundreds of volumes of books and a fireplace of black marble. Here, guests have sherry or tea and perhaps engage in conversation with their well-traveled hosts, both authors. A baronial dining room features a Baroque candelabrum.

Innkeeper(s): Richard & Joan Mears. $70-225. MC VISA AX DS PC TC. TAC10. 12 rooms with PB, 2 with FP. 3 conference rooms. Breakfast included in rates. Type of meal: full breakfast. Afternoon tea available. Beds: KQDT. Phone, air conditioning and ceiling fan in room. TV, fax, copier and library on premises. Small meetings, family reunions and seminars hosted. Antiques, parks, shopping, downhill skiing, cross-country skiing, theater and watersports nearby.

Publicity: *Berkshire Book.*

Leverett   D6

Hannah Dudley House Inn

114 Dudleyville Rd
Leverett, MA 01054-9713
(413)367-2323

Circa 1797. Each season brings with it a new reason to visit this 18th-century Colonial, which is named for a member of the first family to inhabit this home. In autumn, the home's 110 acres explode in color. In winter, snow-capped pines add to the festive atmosphere, and guests snuggle up in front of a roaring fire. Two guest rooms include fireplaces, and the house offers four others. The guest room refrigerators are always stocked with drinks. At certain times of the year, dinner

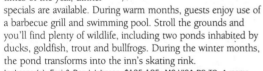

specials are available. During warm months, guests enjoy use of a barbecue grill and swimming pool. Stroll the grounds and you'll find plenty of wildlife, including two ponds inhabited by ducks, goldfish, trout and bullfrogs. During the winter months, the pond transforms into the inn's skating rink.

Innkeeper(s): Erni & Daryl Johnson. $125-185. MC VISA PC TC. 4 rooms with PB, 2 with FP. 1 suite. Breakfast and evening snack included in rates. Types of meals: full breakfast and early coffee/tea. Dinner available. Beds: QD. Turndown service in room. Swimming and library on premises. 110 acres. Weddings, small meetings, family reunions and seminars hosted. Antiques, fishing, parks, shopping, downhill skiing, cross-country skiing, sporting events and theater nearby.

"Your generosity, hospitality, and friendliness made an already special time in our lives just that much more so. We look forward to our next visit to the welcome oasis you have created in Leverett."

Lynn   D14

Diamond District Breakfast Inn

142 Ocean St
Lynn, MA 01902-2007
(617)599-4470 (800)666-3076 Fax:(617)595-2200

Circa 1911. This 17-room Georgian house was built for shoe manufacturer P.J. Harney-Lynn. The Charles Pinkham family (son of Lydia Pinkham, a health tonic producer) later purchased it. Many of the original fixtures remain, and the inn is

suitably furnished with Oriental rugs and antiques. The parlor features a collection of antique musical instruments. There are several views of the ocean from the house, but the porch is the most popular spot for sea gazing. Two romantic suites feature fireplaces, whirlpool tubs, ocean view and deck. Candlelight breakfast is served in the dining room or on the porch. Fresh fruits, homemade breads and hot coffee, tea or cider start off the meal, followed by a special entree.

Historic Interest: The Lynn Historical Museum, Mary Baker Eddy home, the founder of Christian Science, Grand Army of the Republic meeting hall and museum are within walking distance. Located eight miles north of Boston.

Innkeeper(s): Sandra & Jerry Caron. $95-235. MC VISA AX DC CB DS PC TC. TAC10. 11 rooms, 7 with PB. 2 suites. 1 conference room. Breakfast included in rates. Type of meal: full breakfast. Beds: KQDT. Phone, air conditioning, ceiling fan and TV in room. Fax and copier on premises. Antiques, fishing, cross-country skiing and watersports nearby.

"The room was spectacular and breakfast was served beautifully. Bed and breakfast were both outstanding! Thanks so much for your hospitality."

Marblehead   D14

Brimblecomb Hill

33 Mechanic St
Marblehead, MA 01945-3448
(617)631-3172

Circa 1721. This gracious pre-Revolutionary War Colonial home is a fun place to soak in New England's history and charm. The home was host to a variety of tradesmen including a cooper and a wigmaker, not to mention a friend of Benjamin Franklin. The bed & breakfast is only about 20 miles from Boston and the town of Marblehead offers many fine galleries, shops and restaurants, and of course, Marblehead Harbor.

Historic Interest: Marblehead was incorporated in 1649 and features an array of historic buildings and churches. Some of the highlights include the town's Old North Church, Abbot Hall. A walking tour can be arranged. The American Navy began in Marblehead's historic harbor, and the original painting "Spirit of '76," hangs in the town hall.

Innkeeper(s): Gene Arnould. $65-85. MC VISA. 3 rooms, 1 with PB. Breakfast included in rates. Types of meals: continental breakfast and continental-plus breakfast. Beds: QD. Air conditioning in room. Antiques, fishing, theater and watersports nearby.

"Thank you for such wonderful hospitality. We really enjoyed our stay & loved the B&B atmosphere! We will definitely plan a trip back!"

Harbor Light Inn

58 Washington
Marblehead, MA 01945
(617)631-2186 Fax:(617)631-2216
E-mail: hliatshore.net

Circa 1729. This early 18th-century inn is an elegant New England retreat. Oriental rugs, refined furnishings, fine paintings and items such as four-poster beds create a warm, inviting character. A dozen of the guest rooms include a fireplace, and some offer sunken Jacuzzi tubs. For three years, Vacations magazine ranked the inn as one of the nation's most romantic. The inn is located within walking distance of shops and restaurants, as well as Marblehead Harbor.

Innkeeper(s): Peter & Suzanne Conway. $95-245. MC VISA AX PC TC. 22 rooms with PB, 12 with FP. 2 suites. 1 cabin. 1 conference room. Breakfast included in rates.
Type of meal: continental breakfast.
Beds: KQT. Phone, air conditioning, TV and VCR in room.
Fax, copier, swimming and sauna on premises.
Weddings, small meetings, family reunions and seminars hosted.
Publicity: *Vacations.*

Harborside House B&B

23 Gregory St
Marblehead, MA 01945-3241
(781)631-1032
E-mail: swliving@shore.net

Circa 1840. Enjoy the Colonial charm of this home, which overlooks Marblehead Harbor on Boston's historic North Shore. Rooms are decorated with antiques and period wallpaper. A third-story sundeck offers excellent views. A generous continental breakfast of home-baked breads, muffins and fresh fruit is served each morning in the well-decorated dining room or on the open porch. The village of Marblehead provides many shops and restaurants. Boston and Logan airport are 30 minutes away.

Historic Interest: Lee Mansion (1768), King Hooper Mansion (1745) and St. Michael's Church (1714).

Innkeeper(s): Susan Livingston. $70-85. PC TC. TAC10. 2 rooms. Breakfast, afternoon tea and evening snack included in rates. Type of meal: continental-plus breakfast. Beds: DT. Bicycles on premises. Antiques, parks, shopping and watersports nearby.

Publicity: *Marblehead Reporter.*

"Harborside Inn is restful, charming, with a beautiful view of the water. I wish we didn't have to leave."

The Nesting Place B&B

16 Village St
Marblehead, MA 01945-2213
(781)631-6655
E-mail: louisehire@aol.com

Circa 1890. Conveniently located one-half hour away from Boston and Cape Ann, this turn-of-the-century house offers as much privacy as you require. Discover the world of the early clipper ships as you walk the narrow winding streets and the beaches of Marblehead's renowned harbor, only minutes away. There's a relaxing hot tub to top off a day of browsing through art galleries, antique shops and quaint boutiques. Massages and facials also are available off premises.

Innkeeper(s): Louise Hirshberg. $65-75. MC VISA PC TC. 2 rooms. Breakfast included in rates. Types of meals: continental-plus breakfast and early coffee/tea. Beds: KQT. VCR and spa on premises. Antiques, fishing, parks, shopping, cross-country skiing, sporting events, theater and watersports nearby.

Spray Cliff on The Ocean

25 Spray Ave
Marblehead, MA 01945-2746
(617)631-6789 (800)626-1530 Fax:(617)639-4563

Circa 1910. Panoramic views stretch out in grand proportions from this romantic English Tudor mansion set high above the Atlantic. The inn provides a spacious and elegant atmosphere inside. The grounds of the inn include a brick terrace surrounded by lush flower gardens where eider ducks, black cormorants and seagulls gather. Spray Cliff is the only Marblehead B&B inn located directly on the ocean.

Historic Interest: Old Town Marblehead (within 5 minutes), Historic Salem (10-15 minute drive).

Innkeeper(s): Roger Plauche. $175-200. MC VISA AX. 7 rooms with PB, 3 with FP. Breakfast included in rates. Type of meal: continental-plus breakfast. Beds: KQ. Phone in room. Antiques, fishing, shopping, cross-country skiing, sporting events, theater and watersports nearby.

Location: Fifteen miles north of Boston.

Publicity: *New York Times, Glamour.*

"I prefer this atmosphere to a modern motel. It's more relaxed and love is everywhere!"

Martha's Vineyard   K16

Captain Dexter House of Edgartown

35 Pease's Point Way, Box 2798
Martha's Vineyard, MA 02539
(508)627-7289 Fax:(508)627-3328

Circa 1843. Located just three blocks from Edgartown's harbor and historic district, this black-shuttered sea merchant's house has a graceful lawn and terraced flower gardens. A gentle Colonial atmosphere is enhanced by original wooden beams, exposed floorboards, working fireplaces, old-fashioned dormers and a collection of period antiques. Luxurious canopy beds are featured, and some rooms include fireplaces.

Historic Interest: The marine biology laboratories at Woods Hole (45 minutes by ferry).

Innkeeper(s): Rick Fenstemaker. $85-175. MC VISA AX PC TC. TAC10. 8 rooms with PB, 2 with FP. 1 suite. Breakfast included in rates. Type of meal: continental-plus breakfast. Afternoon tea available. Beds: QD. Air conditioning and ceiling fan in room. Fax on premises. Weddings, small meetings, family reunions and seminars hosted. Antiques, fishing, parks, theater and watersports nearby.

Location: On a tree-lined residential street in downtown Edgartown on the island of Martha's Vineyard.

Publicity: *Island Getaways, Vineyard Gazette, Martha's Vineyard Times, Cape Cod Life.*

"Since we were on our honeymoon, we were hoping for a quiet, relaxing stay, and the Captain Dexter House was perfect!"

Captain Dexter House of Vineyard Haven

92 Main St, PO Box 2457
Martha's Vineyard, MA 02568
(508)693-6564 Fax:(508)693-8448

Circa 1840. Captain Dexter House was the home of sea captain Rodolphus Dexter. Authentic 18th-century antiques and reproductions are among the inn's appointments. There are Count Rumford fireplaces and handstencilled walls in several rooms. Located on a street of historic homes, the inn is a short stroll to the beach, town and harbor. The innkeepers offer an evening aperitif and in the summer, lemonade is served.

Historic Interest: Marine Biology Laboratories at Woods Hole (45 minutes by ferry). Many of the buildings in this quaint Martha's Vineyard locale are historic.
Innkeeper(s): Rick Fenstemaker. $75-175. MC VISA AX PC TC. TAC10. 8 rooms with PB, 2 with FP. Breakfast included in rates. Type of meal: continental-plus breakfast. Afternoon tea available. Beds: QD. Air conditioning and ceiling fan in room. Fax on premises. Weddings, small meetings, family reunions and seminars hosted. Antiques, fishing, parks, shopping, theater and watersports nearby.

Location: Martha's Vineyard.

Publicity: *Martha's Vineyard Times, Cape Cod Life.*

"The house is sensational. Your hospitality was all one could expect. You've made us permanent bed & breakfast fans."

Nancy's Auberge

98 Main St, PO Box 4433
Martha's Vineyard, MA 02568
(508)693-4434

Circa 1840. This 1840 Greek Revival home affords harbor views from its spot in a historic neighborhood once home to early settlers and whaling captains. Three of the antique-filled rooms include fireplaces, and one of the bedchambers boasts a harbor view. The inn is just a few blocks from the local ferry. Bicycle paths and beaches are nearby, as well as restaurants and a variety of shops.

Innkeeper(s): Nancy Hurd. $88-118. MC VISA. 3 rooms. Breakfast included in rates. Type of meal: continental-plus breakfast. VCR on premises. Family reunions hosted. Antiques, shopping and theater nearby.

"It's so picturesque. It's like living on a postcard."

Thorncroft Inn

460 Main St, PO Box 1022
Martha's Vineyard, MA 02568
(508)693-3333 (800)332-1236 Fax:(508)693-5419
E-mail: kgb@tiac.net

Circa 1918. The Thorncroft Estate is a classic craftsman bungalow with a dominant roof and neo-colonial details. It was built by Chicago grain merchant John Herbert Ware as the guest house of a large oceanfront estate. Most guest rooms include working fireplaces and canopied beds. Some also boast two-person whirlpool tubs or private 300-gallon hot tubs. The inn is situated in three buildings on three-and-one-half acres of lawns and woodlands. In its naturally romantic setting, the

Thorncroft provides the perfect ambiance for honeymooners, anniversaries and special couples' getaways. Full breakfasts and afternoon teas are served in the dining rooms, but guests can opt for a continental breakfast served in their room.

Innkeeper(s): Karl & Lynn Buder. $150-450. MC VISA AX DC CB DS. 14 rooms with PB, 10 with FP. 1 cottage. Breakfast and afternoon tea included in rates. Types of meals: full breakfast and gourmet breakfast. Room service available. Beds: KQD. Fax and copier on premises. Antiques, fishing, theater and watersports nearby.

Location: Martha's Vineyard Island.

Publicity: *Cape Cod Life, Glamour, Travel & Leisure.* Ratings: 4 Stars.

"It's the type of place where we find ourselves falling in love all over again."

Nantucket   **L18**

The Carlisle House Inn

26 N Water St
Nantucket, MA 02554-3548
(508)228-0720

Circa 1765. For more than 100 years, the Carlisle House has served as a notable Nantucket lodging establishment. Three floors of picture-perfect rooms provide accommodations from the simple to the deluxe. Polished pine wide-board floors, handsome color schemes and carpets fill each room. The ferry is a five-minute walk.

Innkeeper(s): Peter Conway. $60-175. MC VISA AX PC TC. 14 rooms, 10 with PB, 4 with FP. 1 suite. Breakfast included in rates. Type of meal: continental-plus breakfast. Afternoon tea available. Beds: KQDT. Air conditioning, ceiling fan and TV in room. Weddings, small meetings, family reunions and seminars hosted. Antiques, shopping, theater and watersports nearby.

Publicity: *Cape Cod Life, Boston Globe, Los Angeles Times, Innsider.*

"Outstanding hospitality."

Century House

10 Cliff Rd
Nantucket, MA 02554-3640
(508)228-0530

Circa 1833. Captain Calder built this Federal-style house and supplemented his income by taking in guests when the whaling industry slowed down. According to late historian Edouard Stackpole, the house is the oldest continually operating inn on the island. It is surrounded by other large homes on a knoll in the historic district. Museums, beaches and restaurants are a short walk away. The inn's motto for the last 100 years has been, "An inn of distinction on an island of charm." Cottages are also available.

Innkeeper(s): Husband & wife, Gerry Connick & Jeane Heron. $95-195. 14 rooms with PB. Type of meal: continental-plus breakfast. Beds: KQDTW. Phone in room.

Publicity: *Palm Beach Daily News, Boston Globe, Spur Magazine.*

"Thanks so much for the warm hospitality. Century House is beautiful!"

Cobblestone Inn

5 Ash St
Nantucket, MA 02554-3515
(508)228-1987 Fax:(508)228-6698

Circa 1725. Located on a cobbled side street, the Cobblestone Inn boasts four fireplaces, wide floorboards, curved-corner support posts from the frame of a ship and a quiet outside sitting area. Guest rooms have period decorations and canopy beds. A third-floor suite offers a good view of the boats sailing in the harbor. Guests may relax in the living room and enjoy the collection of Nantucket books around the fireplace.

Innkeeper(s): Robin Hammer-Yankow & Keith Yankow. $50-250. MC VISA. 6 rooms with PB. Breakfast included in rates. Type of meal: continental-plus breakfast. Phone in room. Antiques, fishing, theater and watersports nearby.

Publicity: *Yankee, Woman's Day.*

"Your warmth and hospitality made our stay all the more pleasureful!"

Corner House

49 Center St, PO Box 1828
Nantucket, MA 02554-3666
(508)228-1530
E-mail: cornerhs@nantucket.net

Circa 1790. The Corner House is a charming 18th-century village inn. Architectural details such as the original pine floors, paneling and fireplaces have been preserved. A screened porch overlooks the English perennial garden, where guests often take afternoon tea. Many of the romantically appointed bedchambers feature canopy beds.

Innkeeper(s): John & Sandy Knox-Johnston. $65-185. AP. MC VISA TC. 15 rooms with PB, 3 with FP. 2 suites. Breakfast and afternoon tea included in rates. Type of meal: continental-plus breakfast. Beds: QDT. Phone, air conditioning and TV in room. Fax and library on premises. Limited French and German spoken. Antiques, fishing, golf, theater and watersports nearby.

Publicity: *Detroit Free Press, Atlanta Journal, Newsday, Gourmet, Elle Decor.*

"Thank you so much for the care, atmosphere, cleanliness and peace you provided for us this week."

House of The Seven Gables

32 Cliff Rd
Nantucket, MA 02554-3644
(508)228-4706

Circa 1865. Originally the annex of the Sea Cliff Inn, one of the island's oldest hotels, this three-story Queen Anne Victorian inn offers 10 guest rooms. Beaches, bike rentals, museums, restaurants, shops and tennis courts are all found nearby. The guest rooms are furnished with king or queen beds and period antiques. Breakfast is served each morning in the guest rooms, and often include homemade coffee cake, muffins or Portuguese rolls.

Innkeeper(s): Sue Walton. $65-175. MC VISA AX. 10 rooms, 8 with PB. Breakfast included in rates. Type of meal: continental breakfast. Beds: KQF. TV on premises. Antiques, fishing, shopping, theater and watersports nearby.

"You have a beautiful home and one that makes everyone feel relaxed and at home."

Jared Coffin House

29 Broad St
Nantucket, MA 02554-3502
(508)228-2400

Circa 1845. Jared Coffin was one of the island's most successful ship owners and the first to build a three-story mansion. The house's brick walls and slate roof resisted the Great Fire of 1846 and, in 1847, it was purchased by the Nantucket Steamship Company for use as a hotel. Additions were made and a century later, the Nantucket Historical Trust purchased and restored the house. Today, the inn consists of five historic houses and a 1964 building. The oldest is the Swain House.

Innkeeper(s): Phil and Peg Read. $100-200. MC VISA AX DC. 60 rooms with PB. 3 conference rooms. Type of meal: continental breakfast. Dinner and lunch available. Restaurant on premises. Beds: QDT. Fax and copier on premises.

Publicity: *Coast & Country.*

"The dining was superb, the atmosphere was gracious and the rooms were charming and spotless."

Martin House Inn

61 Centre St PO Box 743
Nantucket, MA 02554
(508)228-0678 Fax:(508)325-4798
E-mail: martinn@nantucket.net

Circa 1803. Known as Wonoma Inn in the '20s, this shingled mariner's house in the historic district is tucked behind a picket fence. In summer, roses climb to the six-over-six windows and the hammock gently sways on the side veranda. Authentic period pieces include Chippendale chests, Windsor rockers and Victorian settlers, and there are four-poster and canopy beds in the guest rooms. Three fireplace rooms are available during the off season. The cobblestone streets of Nantucket's Main Street are a stroll away.

Historic Interest: Located within Nantucket's Historic District.

Innkeeper(s): Channing & Cecilia Moore. $65-160. MC VISA AX PC TC. 13 rooms, 9 with PB, 3 with FP. Breakfast included in rates. Types of meals: continental-plus breakfast and early coffee/tea. Beds: QDT. Phone in room. TV and library on premises. Weddings and family reunions hosted. Antiques, fishing, parks, shopping, theater and watersports nearby.

Publicity: *Cape Cod Life.*

"A wonderful weekend filled with warm hospitality. We enjoyed it all."

Pineapple Inn

10 Hussey St
Nantucket, MA 02554-3612
(508)228-9992 Fax:(508)325-6051
E-mail: pineappl@nantucket.net

Circa 1838. Built for a prominent whaling ship captain, this classic colonial has been restored and refurnished to inspire the gracious and elegant standard of a time in history that most of us only read about in books. Reproduction and authentic 19th-century antiques, artwork and Oriental rugs are featured throughout the inn. Luxurious goose down comforters and Ralph Lauren linens top beautiful handmade, four-poster canopy beds in all of the 12 guest rooms. The innkeepers, seasoned restaurateurs, offer guests a delightful combination of steaming cappuccinos, freshly squeezed orange juice, a fresh fruit plate and a selection of pastries served restaurant-style in the formal dining room or on the bricked garden patio.

Innkeeper(s): Caroline & Bob Taylor. $75-225. MC VISA AX PC TC. 12 rooms with PB. Breakfast included in rates. Types of meals: continental breakfast, continental-plus breakfast, gourmet breakfast and early coffee/tea. Beds: KQ. Phone, air conditioning and TV in room. Fax and copier on premises. Handicap access. Weddings, small meetings, family reunions and seminars hosted. Antiques, fishing, shopping, golf, theater and watersports nearby.

"Our time here was more than just a lovely room. The patio breakfast was heavenly... and you always took time to chat and make us feel welcome. In a word — wonderful! Gracious hosts, delicious breakfasts and a cozy bed."

Quaker House

5 Chestnut St
Nantucket, MA 02554
(508)228-0400 Fax:(508)228-2967

Circa 1847. The recently renovated Quaker House is situated in the Nantucket Historic District on a quiet side street once

known as Petticoat Lane. During the whaling era, women operated most of the businesses on this street. Guest rooms are furnished with Oriental rugs and period antiques that include brass, iron and carved wood. Its restaurant is recommended for reasonable rates and outstanding breakfasts.

Innkeeper(s): Stephanie Silva. $80-170. EP. MC VISA AX. 8 rooms with PB. Breakfast included in rates. Restaurant on premises. Beds: Q. Phone in room.

Publicity: *Boston, Yesterday's Island.*

"From two Quakers, it was enlightening and grand."

The White House

48 Center St
Nantucket, MA 02554-3664
(508)228-4677

Circa 1800. For more than 40 years a favorite hostelry of visitors to Nantucket, The White House is situated ideally in the heart of the historic district and a short walk to the beach and ferry terminal. The first floor houses an antique shop. Guests stay in rooms on the second floor or a housekeeping apartment. Afternoon wine and cheese is served in the garden.

Innkeeper(s): Nina Hellman. $70-120. MC VISA AX. 3 rooms with PB. 1 suite. Breakfast included in rates. Type of meal: continental breakfast. Beds: Q. Phone in room. Antiques, fishing, shopping, theater and watersports nearby.

The Woodbox Inn

29 Fair St
Nantucket, MA 02554-3798
(508)228-0587

Circa 1709. Nantucket's oldest inn was built by Captain George Bunker. In 1711, the captain constructed an adjoining house. Eventually, the two houses were made into one by cutting into the sides of both. Guest rooms are furnished with period antiques. The inn's gourmet dining room features an

Early American atmosphere with low-beamed ceilings and pine-paneled walls. The restaurant received an award of excellence from Wine Spectator magazine.

Innkeeper(s): Dexter Tutein. $140-230. PC TC.
9 rooms with PB, 6 with FP. 6 suites. Type of meal: full breakfast. Restaurant on premises. Beds: KQDT. Phone in room. Weddings, small meetings and family reunions hosted. French, German and Spanish spoken. Antiques, fishing, parks, shopping, theater and watersports nearby.

Location: Historic district.

Publicity: *Wharton Alumni, Cape Cod Life, Boston Magazine.*

"Best breakfast on the island, Yesterday's Island."

New Marlborough   F2

Old Inn on The Green

Rt 57
New Marlborough, MA 01230
(413)229-3131 (800)286-3139 Fax:(413)229-2053

Circa 1760. This former stagecoach stop, tavern, store and post office offers guest rooms in two locations. Gedney Farm, on 300 acres, is a short walk away from the main house. It accommodates the guest suites in two enormous Normandy-style barns, where Percheron stallions and Jersey cattle were once housed. The elegant country decor is warmed by hardwood floors, handhewn beams and granite fireplaces. There are tiled whirlpool tubs in all the rooms. The dining room offers colonial elegance in candle-lit rooms. "Superb" is the most frequently stated complement about the inn's fine dining experience.

Innkeeper(s): Leslie Miller & Brad Wagstaff. $120-285. MC VISA AX PC TC. TAC10. 21 rooms with PB, 13 with FP. 2 suites. 3 conference rooms. Breakfast included in rates. Types of meals: continental-plus breakfast and early coffee/tea. Dinner, lunch and banquet service available. Restaurant on premises. Beds: KQT. Phone, air conditioning, turndown service and ceiling fan in room. Fax and library on premises. 300 acres. Weddings, small meetings and family reunions hosted. Antiques, fishing, parks, shopping, downhill skiing, cross-country skiing, golf and theater nearby.

Pets Allowed.

Newburyport   B14

Clark Currier Inn

45 Green St
Newburyport, MA 01950-2646
(508)465-8363 (800)360-6582

Circa 1803. Once the home of shipbuilder Thomas March Clark, this three-story Federal-style inn provides gracious accommodations to visitors in the Northeast Massachusetts area. Visitors will enjoy the inn's details added by Samuel McEntire, one of the nation's most celebrated home builders and woodcarvers. Breakfast is served in the garden room, with an afternoon tea offered in the parlor. The inn's grounds also boast a picturesque garden and gazebo. Parker River National Wildlife Refuge and Maudslay State Park are nearby.

Historic Interest: The Cushing House Museum, Firehouse Center, Custom House Museum and Market Square are within walking distance. Lowell's Boat Shop, a museum across the river, houses the Amesbury dory and high-

lights more than 200 years of boat building.
Innkeeper(s): Mary & Bob Nolan. $65-145. MC VISA AX DS PC TC. 8 rooms with PB. Breakfast and afternoon tea included in rates. Type of meal: continental breakfast. Beds: QDT. Phone, air conditioning, TV and VCR in room. Bicycles, library and child care on premises. Handicap access.
Weddings, small meetings, family reunions and seminars hosted. Amusement parks, antiques, fishing, parks, shopping, downhill skiing, cross-country skiing, sporting events, theater and watersports nearby.

"We had a lovely stay in your B&B! We appreciated your hospitality!"

Windsor House

38 Federal St
Newburyport, MA 01950-2820
(978)462-3778 (888)879-5896 Fax:(978)465-3443
E-mail: tintagel@greennet.net

Circa 1786. This brick Federal-style mansion was designed as a combination home and chandlery (a ship's outfitter and brokerage company for cargo). The third floor served as a warehouse and the Merchant Suite was once the main office. This suite fea-

tures a 14-foot ceiling with handhewn, beveled beams. It is appointed with a wing-back chair from the Old Boston Opera, a sleigh bed and an antique hope chest. The English innkeeper serves a hearty English-country breakfast and a full English tea in the afternoon.
Historic Interest: William Lloyd Garrison birthplace (across the street), Newburyport Custom's House and Caleb Cushing House (walking distance).
Innkeeper(s): Judith & John Harris. $110-135. MC VISA AX DS. 4 rooms with PB. Breakfast and afternoon tea included in rates. Type of meal: full breakfast. Beds: KQD. Phone in room. TV and VCR on premises. Small meetings, family reunions and seminars hosted. Antiques, fishing, parks, shopping, cross-country skiing, theater and watersports nearby.
Pets Allowed.
Location: Thirty-eight miles north of Boston.
Publicity: *New York Times, Boston, Boston Herald Sunday, Globe.*

"You will find what you look for and be met by the unexpected too. A good time!"

North New Salem
D7

Bullard Farm B&B

89 Elm St
North New Salem, MA 01355-9502
(978)544-6959 Fax:(978)544-6959

Circa 1793. This inn's four guest rooms are found in a farmhouse containing six working fireplaces. The farm has been in the family of the innkeeper's mother since 1864, and guests are welcome to hike the inn's grounds, observing its history as a lumber mill and tannery. The inn features many original pieces used in its country-style decor. Full breakfasts may include banana sour cream coffee cake. Winter visitors may

enjoy a sleigh ride or cross-country skiing on the inn's 300 acres. Quabbin Resevoir is a one-mile drive from the inn.
Innkeeper(s): Janet F. Kraft. $70-80. MC VISA. 4 rooms, 2 with FP. 1 conference room. Type of meal: full breakfast. Phone and air conditioning in room. VCR and fax on premises. 300 acres. Weddings, small meetings, family reunions and seminars hosted. Antiques, fishing, shopping, downhill skiing, cross-country skiing, sporting events and theater nearby.
Publicity: *Boston Globe, Worcester Telegram.*

Northampton (Florence)
E5

Lupine House

185 N Main St
Northampton (Florence), MA 01062-0483
(413)586-9766 (800)890-9766

Circa 1872. This Colonial offers a comfortable setting for those enjoying a New England getaway. Rooms are simply furnished with antiques adding to the ambiance. Light, continental-plus fare is served in the mornings, including homemade granola, fresh fruit, cereals, breads and muffins. The B&B is a short drive from downtown Northampton and many area schools, including Amherst, Smith, Hampshire and Mount Holyoke colleges and the University of Massachusetts.
Historic Interest: Old Deerfield is just a few minutes drive away.
Innkeeper(s): Evelyn & Gil Billings. $70. MC VISA PC TC. 3 rooms with PB. Breakfast included in rates. Types of meals: continental-plus breakfast and early coffee/tea. Beds: QDT. TV and library on premises. Antiques, fishing, parks, shopping, downhill skiing, cross-country skiing, sporting events and theater nearby.

"You certainly provide 'the extra mile' of hospitality and service. Thank you."

Norwell
F15

1810 House B&B

147 Old Oaken Bucket Rd
Norwell, MA 02061-1320
(781)659-1810
E-mail: tuttle1810@aol.com

Circa 1810. Exposed beams, original to this early 19th-century house, add a rustic touch to the 1810 House. Guest rooms are simply furnished in a traditional country decor. One includes a canopy bed and another offers an antique spool bed. Savory New England breakfasts with fresh fruit, yogurt, muffins, egg dishes, sausage, bacon and ham are served in the fireside dining room or on the screened-in porch. Guests can take a tour of the village via the innkeeper's restored 1915 Model T. The 1810 house is located midway between Plymouth and Boston.
Innkeeper(s): Susanne & Harold Tuttle. $75-85. PC TC. TAC10. 3 rooms, 2 with PB. 1 suite. Breakfast included in rates. Types of meals: full breakfast and early coffee/tea. Beds: QT. Air conditioning, turndown service and ceiling fan in room. TV, VCR and copier on premises. Antiques, fishing, shopping, theater and watersports nearby.

"We will remember the warmth of your welcome and hospitality."

Oak Bluffs

K16

The Oak Bluffs Inn

Circuit and Pequot Ave
Oak Bluffs, MA 02557
(508)693-7171 (800)955-6235

Circa 1870. A widow's walk and gingerbread touches were added to this graceful home to enhance the Victorian atmosphere already prevalent throughout the inn. Rooms are decorated in Victorian style with antiques. Home-baked breads and fresh fruits start off the day. After enjoying the many activities Martha's Vineyard has to offer, return for a scrumptious afternoon tea with scones, tea sandwiches and pastries. Oak Bluffs originally was named Cottage City, and is full of quaint, gingerbread homes to view. Nearby Circuit Avenue offers shopping, ice cream parlors, eateries and the nation's oldest carousel.

Innkeeper(s): Maryann Mattera. $100-200. MC VISA AX DC DS. TAC10. 9 rooms with PB. Breakfast included in rates. Type of meal: continental-plus breakfast. Beds: QD. Air conditioning and ceiling fan in room. TV on premises. Antiques, fishing, parks, shopping, golf, theater and watersports nearby.

The Tucker Inn

46 Massasoit Ave, PO Box 2680
Oak Bluffs, MA 02557
(508)693-1045

Circa 1872. Located on a quiet residential park within walking distance of retail establishments and the town beach, this two-story Victorian Stick/Shingle inn offers visitors to Martha's Vineyard a choice of suites and guest rooms with shared and private baths. The former doctor's residence boasts an attractive veranda that is ideal for reading or relaxing after a busy day  exploring the island's many attractions, or a trip to nearby Chappaquiddick. Public transportation and boat lines are a five-minute walk from the inn.

Innkeeper(s): William Reagan. $55-135. MC VISA. 8 rooms, 5 with PB. 2 suites. Breakfast included in rates. Type of meal: continental breakfast. Beds: QDT. Ceiling fan in room. TV and VCR on premises. Antiques, fishing, shopping, theater and watersports nearby.

Onset

I15

Onset Pointe Inn

9 Eagle Way, PO Box 1450
Onset, MA 02558
(508)295-8442 (800)356-6738 Fax:(508)295-5241

Circa 1880. This restored Victorian mansion is surrounded by the ocean on Point Independence. Its casually elegant decor is enhanced by sea views, sunlight, bright colors and florals. Spacious verandas, an enclosed circular sun porch and a bayside gazebo are available to guests. Accommodations are divided among the main house and two additional buildings. An all-you-can-eat hearty continental breakfast is available in the waterfront dining room. The Onset Pointe Inn received the National Trust first prize for preservation in its B&B category.

Innkeeper(s): Debi & Joe Lopes. $55-175. MC VISA AX DS PC TC. 15 rooms with PB. 6 suites. Breakfast included in rates. Beds: QDT. Phone in room. TV, fax, copier and swimming on premises. Weddings, small meetings, family reunions and seminars hosted. Antiques, fishing, parks, shopping, theater and watersports nearby.

Location: Village of Onset, at the gateway to Cape Cod.

"We've found the B&B we've been looking for!"

Orleans

H19

The Farmhouse at Nauset Beach

163 Beach Rd
Orleans, MA 02653-2732
(508)255-6654

Circa 1870. Feel the intimacy of Orleans and capture the flavor of Cape Cod at this quiet country inn resting in a seashore setting. Rooms in this Greek Revival-style inn are comfortably furnished to depict their 19th-century past. Some rooms offer ocean views, and one includes a decorated fireplace. Nauset Beach is a short walk away. Spend a day charter fishing in Cape Cod Bay or the Atlantic. To make your stay complete, your itinerary can include antiquing, shopping, exploring quiet country lanes or a day at the beach. The inn is open year-round.

Innkeeper(s): Dorothy Standish. $42-105. MC VISA PC. 8 rooms with PB, 1 with FP. Breakfast included in rates. Type of meal: continental-plus breakfast. Beds: KQD. Ceiling fan and TV in room. Family reunions hosted. Antiques, fishing, shopping, theater and watersports nearby.

Petersham

D8

Winterwood at Petersham

19 N Main St
Petersham, MA 01366-9500
(978)724-8885

Circa 1842. The town of Petersham is often referred to as a museum of Greek Revival architecture. One of the grand houses facing the common is Winterwood. It boasts fireplaces in almost every room. Private dining is available for groups of up to 70 people.

Historic Interest: Listed in the National Register.

Innkeeper(s): Jean & Robert Day. $80. MC VISA AX DS. 6 rooms with PB, 5 with FP. 1 conference room. Type of meal: continental-plus breakfast. Beds: QTF. Phone in room. Weddings, small meetings, family reunions and seminars hosted. Antiques, downhill skiing and cross-country skiing nearby.

Publicity: *Boston Globe.*

"Between your physical facilities and Jean's cooking, our return to normal has been made even more difficult. Your hospitality was just a fantastic extra to our total experience."

Plymouth G15

Foxglove Cottage

101 Sandwich Rd
Plymouth, MA 02360-2503
(508)747-6576 (800)479-4746 Fax:(508)747-7622

Circa 1820. Follow tree-lined Sandwich Road, the original Colonial highway to Boston, as it meanders to Foxglove Cottage, a pink 1820 Cape-style house. There are 40 acres of meadow, woodland, and a lawn with rhododendron and parts of an old stone fence. Across the street, horses graze in a pasture. Wideboard floors, Victorian antiques, six working fireplaces and coordinating fabrics and wallpapers create a warm, welcoming environment. Ask for the Rose Room for a handsomely decorated retreat with a four-poster canopy bed or the Canopy Room for two twin-size canopy beds. Baked French toast with blueberries or a sausage, egg and cheese casserole are popular breakfast items. Plimoth Plantation is nearby.

Innkeeper(s): Mr. & Mrs. Charles K. Cowan. $80. DS PC TC. TAC10. 3 rooms with PB, 3 with FP. Breakfast and afternoon tea included in rates. Type of meal: full breakfast. Beds: KQT. Air conditioning in room. TV, VCR, fax and copier on premises. Antiques, fishing, parks, shopping, theater and watersports nearby.

"A very charming place."

Princeton D9

Fernside B&B

PO Box 303, 162 Mountain Rd
Princeton, MA 01541
(978)464-2741 (800)545-2741 Fax:(978)464-2065
E-mail: fernside@msn.com

Circa 1835. Originally built by Capt. Benjamin Harrington, this elegant Federal mansion was transformed in 1870 into a tavern and boarding house for Harvard professors and students. In

1890, the home changed owners and served as a vacation house for working women for more than 100 years. In 1994, the Morrisons transformed it once again and meticulously restored it. Situated on the eastern slope of Mount Wachusett, the inn is nestled on seven acres with breathtaking sunrise views. Designed for entertaining, there are eight cozy fireplaces, numerous sitting rooms and a variety of porches. The common rooms as well as the guest rooms are elegantly decorated with antiques and period reproductions and Oriental rugs. A home-cooked breakfast includes fresh fruit, pastries and a variety of entrees.

Innkeeper(s): Jocelyn & Richard Morrison. $105-155. MC VISA AX PC TC. TAC10. 6 rooms with PB, 4 with FP. 2 suites. 1 conference room. Breakfast included in rates. Types of meals: gourmet breakfast and early coffee/tea. Evening snack, lunch and room service available. Beds: QT. Phone and turndown service in room. Fax and copier on premises. Handicap access. Weddings, small meetings, family reunions and seminars hosted. Antiques, parks, shopping, downhill skiing, cross-country skiing and golf nearby.

"You cannot help but feel at ease the moment you walk into the inn."

Provincetown G18

Bradford Gardens Inn

178 Bradford St
Provincetown, MA 02657-2423
(508)487-1616 (800)432-2334

Circa 1820. Framed by a split-rail fence, this Cape Cod house is conveniently located within a short walk of all of Provincetown. Behind the inn is the Loft Lodge with cathedral ceilings, a kitchen and its own fireplace. An informal New England decor with period furnishings is enhanced by a collection of original paintings. If your visit is in the spring, request the Cherry Tree Room and enjoy the delicate blossoms from your window. In addition, the innkeeper also offers accommodations in five, two-bedroom townhomes and a penthouse with a view of Cape Cod Bay. The townhomes sleep six and include kitchens, working fireplaces and decks off the master bedroom.

Innkeeper(s): Susan Culligan. $69-118. EP. MC VISA AX. 12 rooms with PB, 10 with FP. 5 cottages. Type of meal: full breakfast. Beds: QD. Phone in room.

Publicity: Country Inns.

"We return year after year for the gourmet breakfasts, incredibly beautiful gardens and the warm atmosphere."

Land's End Inn

22 Commercial St
Provincetown, MA 02657-1910
(508)487-0706 (800)276-7088

Circa 1904. Built originally as a summer bungalow for Charles Higgins, a Boston merchant, Lands End commands a panoramic view of Provincetown and Cape Cod Bay. It still houses part of the Higgins' collection of Oriental wood carvings and stained glass. While David Schoolman was the inn's owner, he enhanced it by decorating with an eclectic array of wonderful antiques. Amid luxuriant gardens, the inn successfully retains an air of quiet and relaxation.

Innkeeper(s): Anthony Arakelian. $87-285. MC VISA PC TC. 16 rooms with PB. Breakfast included in rates. Types of meals: continental breakfast and early coffee/tea. Beds: QD. Ceiling fan in room. Weddings, small meetings, family reunions and seminars hosted. Antiques, fishing, parks, shopping, theater and watersports nearby.

Location: At the tip of Cape Cod.

Publicity: Travel Magazine, Cape Cod Review, Cape Cod Life.

Rehoboth   H12

Gilbert's Tree Farm B&B

30 Spring St
Rehoboth, MA 02769-2408
(508)252-6416
E-mail: jeanneg47@aol.com

Circa 1835. This country farmhouse sits on 100 acres of woodland that includes an award-winning tree farm. Cross-country skiing, hiking, and pony-cart rides are found right outside the door. If they choose to, guests can even help with the farm chores, caring for horses and gardening. A swimming pool is open during summer. Three antique-filled bedrooms share a second-floor sitting room. The nearby town of Rehoboth is 350 years old.

Historic Interest: Battleship Massachusetts (8 miles), Museum of Lizzie Borden artifacts (8 miles), Carpenter Museum (4 miles), Plymouth Plantations (1 hour), Newport mansions (45 minutes).

Innkeeper(s): Jeanne Gilbert. $55. PC TC. TAC10. 3 rooms. Breakfast, afternoon tea and evening snack included in rates. Types of meals: full breakfast and early coffee/tea. Beds: KDT. VCR, copier, swimming, stables, bicycles, library and pet boarding on premises. 100 acres. Antiques, fishing, parks, shopping, cross-country skiing, sporting events, theater and watersports nearby.

Location: Twelve miles east of Providence.

Publicity: *Attleboro Sun Chronicle, Country, Somerset Spectator, Country Gazette, Pawtucket Times.*

"This place has become my second home. Thank you for the family atmosphere of relaxation, fun, spontaneity and natural surroundings."

Perryville Inn

157 Perryville Rd
Rehoboth, MA 02769-1922
(508)252-9239

Circa 1820. The Perryville Inn was a dairy farm for more than 140 years. During that time, in 1897, the original two-story colonial was remodeled into a handsome three-story Victorian, now in the National Register. (The house was raised and an additional floor added underneath.) The pasture is now a public golf course, but the icehouse remains. There are old stone walls, a mill pond, trout stream and wooded paths. Inside the inn, cozy rooms are decorated with comfortable antiques.

Innkeeper(s): Tom & Betsy Charnecki. $65-95. MC VISA AX DS PC TC. 4 rooms with PB. 1 suite. 1 conference room. Breakfast included in rates. Type of meal: continental-plus breakfast. Beds: KQDT. Phone and air conditioning in room. Bicycles on premises. Antiques, fishing and cross-country skiing nearby.

Location: Within 20 minutes of Providence, one hour of Boston, Newport, Plymouth, & Cape Cod.

Publicity: *Providence Journal-Bulletin, Evening.*

"The family voted the Perryville the best place we stayed on our entire trip, without hesitation!"

Rockport   C15

Addison Choate Inn

49 Broadway
Rockport, MA 01966-1527
(978)546-7543 (800)245-7543 Fax:(978)546-7638

Circa 1851. Antiques and reproductions decorate the interior of this mid-19th-century home. The guest rooms feature antique and wicker furnishings, artwork and polished, pine floors. Freshly ground coffee, homemade baked breads, fruit and cereals are served each morning in the inn's dining room, which still contains the original fireplace with a beehive oven. If weather permits, breakfasts are served on the inn's wraparound porch, offering a view of the garden. Shops, restaurants and art galleries all are nearby.

Innkeeper(s): Knox & Shirley Johnson. $85-130. MC VISA DS PC TC. TAC10. 5 rooms with PB. 1 suite. 2 cottages. Breakfast and afternoon tea included in rates. Types of meals: continental-plus breakfast and early coffee/tea. Beds: KQT. TV, VCR, fax, copier and swimming on premises. Antiques, fishing, parks, shopping and theater nearby.

The Inn on Cove Hill

37 Mount Pleasant St
Rockport, MA 01966-1727
(978)546-2701 (888)546-2701

Circa 1791. Pirate gold found at Gully Point paid for this Federal-style house. A white picket fence and granite walkway welcome guests. Inside, an exquisitely crafted spiral staircase, random-width, pumpkin-pine floors and hand-forged hinges display the original artisan's handiwork. Furnishings include family heirlooms, four-poster canopy beds, and paintings by area artists. Muffin Du Jour is baked fresh each day by John. Bicycles can be rented, and you can enjoy whale watching, fishing the local waters, or simply exploring the antique shops and village streets.

Historic Interest: For historic sites, Gloucester is just five miles away, offering tours of Beauport, a historic 1907 home and the Hammond Castle Museum.

Innkeeper(s): John & Marjorie Pratt. $47-107. MC VISA PC TC. 11 rooms, 9 with PB. Breakfast included in rates. Types of meals: continental breakfast and early coffee/tea. Beds: QDT. Air conditioning in room. Antiques, fishing, parks and theater nearby.

Linden Tree Inn

26 King St
Rockport, MA 01966-1444
(978)546-2494 (800)865-2122
E-mail: ltree@shore.net

Circa 1840. The breakfasts at this Victorian-style inn keep guests coming back year after year. Guests feast on home-baked treats such as pumpkin chocolate chip bread, blueberry cake or Sunday favorites, lemon nut bread and sour cream chocolate chip coffee cake. Each of the bedchambers features individual decor, and the innkeepers offer a formal living room and sun room for relaxation. The cupola affords a view of Mill Pond and Sandy Bay.

Historic Interest: Motif No. 1 is less than one mile from the home, and Boston is about 40 miles away.

Innkeeper(s): Dawn & Jon Cunningham. $75-107. MC VISA PC TC. TAC10. 18 rooms with PB. 1 suite. Breakfast and afternoon tea included in rates. Types of meals: continental breakfast and continental-plus breakfast. Beds: KQDT. Air conditioning, ceiling fan and TV in room. VCR and copier on premises. Weddings, small meetings, family reunions and seminars hosted. Antiques, fishing, parks, shopping, theater and watersports nearby.

Publicity: *Gloucester Daily Times.*

"Great coffee! Love that apple walnut bread. Thank you for making this home."

Ralph Waldo Emerson Inn

Phillips Ave
Rockport, MA 01966
(798)546-6321 Fax:(798)546-7043
E-mail: emerson@cove.com

Circa 1840. This Greek Revival inn's namesake once called the place, "the proper summer home." As it is the oldest continuously operated inn on Cape Ann, decades of travelers agree with his sentiment. The guest rooms are comfortable, yet tastefully furnished, and some boast ocean views. The grounds

include a heated, saltwater swimming pool as well as a sauna and whirlpool. Although breakfasts are not included in the rates, guests can enjoy the morning meal or dinner at the inn's dining room, an area added to the 19th-century inn in 1912.

Innkeeper(s): Gary Wemyss. $88-140. EP. MC VISA DS PC TC. TAC10. 36 rooms with PB. 3 suites. 3 conference rooms. Types of meals: continental breakfast, continental-plus breakfast, full breakfast and early coffee/tea. Afternoon tea, dinner, catered breakfast and room service available. Restaurant on premises. Beds: KQDT. Phone and air conditioning in room. TV, VCR, fax, copier, spa, swimming and sauna on premises. Handicap access. Weddings, small meetings, family reunions and seminars hosted. Antiques, fishing, parks, theater and watersports nearby.

"We were very impressed with every aspect of the Emerson Inn."

Romantik Hotel Yankee Clipper Inn

PO Box 2399
Rockport, MA 01966-3399
(508)546-3407 (800)545-3699 Fax:(508)546-9730

Circa 1840. This white clapboard oceanfront mansion features sweeping views of the sea and the rocky shoreline. Gleaming mahogany woodwork and fireplaces combined with fine antiques create an old-fashioned, elegant ambiance in the main building. Some accommodations offer canopy beds and balconies. The Bulfinch House, a Greek Revival building housing extra guest rooms, is situated away from the water uphill from the main inn. A heated salt water pool is in view of the ocean.

Historic Interest: Town of Salem - House of Seven Gables, etc. (one-half hour), Concord, Lexington - Revolutionary War sites (one hour). Rockport and Gloucester founded in 1600s.

Innkeeper(s): Robert & Barbara Ellis. $120-259. MAP. MC VISA AX DS PC TC. TAC10. 26 rooms with PB. 6 suites. 1 cottage. 1 conference room. Breakfast included in rates. Types of meals: continental-plus breakfast and gourmet breakfast. Dinner and room service available. Restaurant on premises. Beds: KQDT. Phone and air conditioning in room: TV, VCR, fax, copier, swimming and library on premises. Weddings, small meetings, family reunions and seminars hosted. German spoken. Antiques, fishing, parks, shopping, theater and watersports nearby.

Publicity: *Gloucester Daily Times, Los Angeles Times, North Shore Life, Country Living, Discerning Traveler, Country Inns, Travel Holidays, Great Country Inns TV Show.*

"The rooms were comfortable, the views breathtaking from most rooms, and the breakfasts delicious, with prompt and courteous service."

Sally Webster Inn

34 Mount Pleasant St
Rockport, MA 01966-1713
(508)546-9251

Circa 1832. William Choate left this pre-Civil War home to be divided by his nine children. Sally Choate Webster, the ninth child, was to receive several first-floor rooms and the attic chamber, but ended up owning the entire home. Innkeepers Tiffany and David Muhlenberg have filled the gracious home with antiques and period reproductions, which comple-  ment the original pumpkin pine floors, antique door moldings and six fireplaces. Shops, restaurants, the beach and the rocky coast are all within three blocks of the inn. Whale watching, kayaking, antique shop, music festivals, island tours and museums are among the myriad of nearby attractions. In addition to these, Salem is just 15 miles away, and Boston is a 35-mile drive.

Innkeeper(s): Tiffany Traynor-Muhlenberg. $60-98. MC VISA DS PC TC. 8 rooms with PB. Breakfast included in rates. Type of meal: continental-plus breakfast. Beds: KQDT. Phone and air conditioning in room.

"All that a bed and breakfast should be."

Seacrest Manor

99 Marmion Way
Rockport, MA 01966-1927
(978)546-2211

Circa 1911. After more than two decades of serving guests, the innkeepers at this estate inn have achieved "ace" status, welcoming travelers with well-polished hospitality. Their inn was once summer home to a prominent restaurateur and looks out to the sea. The two-and-a-half acres include gardens to stroll through, and inside there is a well-stocked library. Fresh flowers are placed in each guest room, and some rooms are further enhanced with decorative fireplaces. Various types of berry pan-  cakes, Irish oatmeal topped with dates, corn fritters and French toast are just a few of the items that might be found on the morning table. The inn is located across the street from the nine-acre John Kieran Nature Reserve. This is a non-smoking inn.

Innkeeper(s): Leighton Saville & Dwight MacCormack, Jr. $98-142. PC TC. 8 rooms, 6 with PB. Breakfast and afternoon tea included in rates. Types of meals: gourmet breakfast and early coffee/tea. Beds: KQDT. Turndown service and TV in room. Bicycles and library on premises. French spoken. Antiques, fishing, parks, shopping, theater and watersports nearby.

Publicity: *Yankee.*

"We'll always have many fond memories."

Tuck Inn

17 High St
Rockport, MA 01966-1644
(508)546-7260 (800)789-7260
E-mail: tuckinn@shore.net

Circa 1790. Two recent renovations have served to make this charming Colonial inn all the more enticing. Period antiques and paintings by local artists are featured throughout the spacious inn. A favorite gathering spot is the living room with

its fireplace, wide pine floors, tasteful furnishings and a piano available for guest use. Buffet breakfasts feature homemade breads, muffins, cakes and scones, granola accompanied by fresh fruit and yogurt. Guests may take a dip in the swimming pool or at local beaches. Within easy walking distance are the many art galleries, restaurants and shops of Bearskin Neck. A nearby train station offers convenient access to Boston.

Historic Interest: The inn is 10 minutes from Gloucester. Other historic towns, such as Salem, Boston, Lexington and Concord, are within an hour's drive of the inn.

Innkeeper(s): Liz & Scott Wood. $55-115. MC VISA PC TC. 11 rooms with PB. 1 suite. Breakfast included in rates. Types of meals: continental-plus breakfast and early coffee/tea. Afternoon tea available. Beds: KQDT. Air conditioning, ceiling fan and TV in room. VCR, swimming, bicycles and library on premises. Small meetings and family reunions hosted. Antiques, fishing, parks, shopping, downhill skiing, cross-country skiing, sporting events, theater and watersports nearby.

Publicity: *Fall River Herald News, North Shore News, Cape Ann Weekly, San Francisco Chronicle.*

"Wonderful people, lovely scenery, and great food, all good for the soul! Your hospitality and service was wonderful and we look forward to returning very soon!"

Salem   D14

Amelia Payson House

16 Winter St
Salem, MA 01970-3807
(978)744-8304
E-mail: bbamelia@aol.com

Circa 1845. This elegantly restored two-story house features four white columns and is a prime example of Greek Revival architecture. Period antiques and wallpapers decorate the guest rooms and the formal dining room. Located in the heart of the Salem Historic District, it is a short walk to shops, museums, Pickering Wharf and waterfront restaurants. Train service to

Boston is four blocks away. This is a non-smoking establishment.

Historic Interest: House of Seven Gables (2 blocks), Peabody Museum (1 block), Witch Museum (1 block), Maritime Historic Site (2 blocks).

Innkeeper(s): Ada & Donald Roberts. $65-105. MC VISA AX. 4 rooms with PB. Breakfast included in rates. Type of meal: continental-plus breakfast. Beds: QT. Phone in room. Antiques and watersports nearby.

Location: Thirteen miles north of Boston.

"Your hospitality has been a part of my wonderful experience."

Coach House Inn

284 Lafayette St
Salem, MA 01970-5462
(978)744-4092 (800)688-8689 Fax:(978)745-8031

Circa 1879. Captain Augustus Emmerton was one of the last Salem natives to earn his living from maritime commerce. He was master of the barkentine Sophronia and the ship Neptune's Daughter that sailed to Zanzibar and the Orient. Emmerton's house is an imposing example of Second Empire architecture situated two blocks from the harbor. The House of Seven Gables and the Salem Witch Museum are nearby.

$72-98. MC VISA AX DS. 11 rooms, 9 with PB, 7 with FP. Beds: DT. Phone in room.

Publicity: *The North Shore, Gourmet.*

The Salem Inn

7 Summer St
Salem, MA 01970-3315
(508)741-0680 (800)446-2995 Fax:(508)744-8924

Circa 1834. This picturesque Federal-style inn is located in the heart one of America's oldest cities is comprised of three houses: The West House, circa 1834; The Curwen House, circa 1854; and The Peabody House, circa 1874. These homes are just a short walk to galleries, antiques, museums, the wharf and harbor. The inn's individually decorated guest rooms feature an array of amenities such as antiques, Jacuzzi tubs, fireplaces and canopy beds. The Peabody House, the latest addition, features two large, luxury suites, as well as comfortable and spacious two-and-three-bedroom family suites with kitchenettes. Both of the large luxury suites enjoy a fireplace in the living room and bedroom and double whirlpool baths. The dining area, with its brick walls and cozy atmosphere, is the perfect place to enjoy a light breakfast.

Historic Interest: Located 18 miles from Boston, the inn is the perfect base to explore nearby Concord and Lexington, as well as the coastal towns of Rockport and Gloucester. Historic Salem is home to the Salem Witch Museum, the Peabody Essex Museum, the House of Seven Gables, Salem Maritime National Historic Site, Pickering Wharf and whale watching cruises.

Innkeeper(s): Richard & Diane Pabich. $99-175. MC VISA AX DC CB DS TC. TAC10. 39 rooms with PB, 18 with FP. 11 suites. 1 conference room. Breakfast included in rates. Type of meal: early coffee/tea. Restaurant on premises. Beds: KQT. Phone, air conditioning and TV in room. Fax on premises. Weddings and small meetings hosted. Antiques, fishing, parks, shopping, sporting events, theater and watersports nearby.

Pets Allowed.

Location: Historic downtown.

Publicity: *New York Times, Boston Sunday Globe.*

"Delightful, charming. Our cup of tea."

The Inn at Seven Winter Street

7 Winter St
Salem, MA 01970-3806
(508)745-9520 Fax:(508)745-5052

Circa 1871. Historic sites, museums, the waterfront, unique shops and quaint restaurants are all within walking distance of this French Second Empire Victorian manor. Some of the guest rooms have a working marble fireplace, canopy bed, Victorian bath, Jacuzzi, or open onto a large sundeck overlooking the inn's gardens. Breakfast is served in the main parlor and evening tea is served fireside.

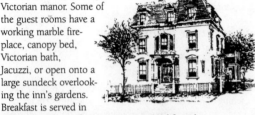

Innkeeper(s): D.L. and Jill Cote, Sally Flint. $95-165. MC VISA AX. 10 rooms with PB. 2 suites. Breakfast and afternoon tea included in rates. Type of meal: continental-plus breakfast. Beds: QDT. Phone, air conditioning and TV in room. Antiques, fishing, shopping, cross-country skiing, sporting events, theater and watersports nearby.

Stephen Daniels House

1 Daniels St
Salem, MA 01970-5214
(508)744-5709

Circa 1667. This lovely 300-year-old captain's house is one of the few three-story homes of this vintage still intact. Two large walk-in fireplaces grace the common rooms and each guest room includes antique furnishings, a canopy bed, and a woodburning fireplace. A pleasant English garden is filled with colorful blooms. Children and well-behaved pets are welcome.

Innkeeper(s): Catherine Gill. $60-85. 5 rooms, 3 with PB, 4 with FP. 1 conference room. Types of meals: continental breakfast and full breakfast. Beds: DT.

Publicity: *Country Living.*

"Like going back to earlier times."

Suzannah Flint House

98 Essex St
Salem, MA 01970-5225
(978)744-5281 (800)893-9973

Circa 1808. Adjacent to Salem Common and the historic district, this fine example of a Federal-style home is completely restored both inside and out. Antiques, Oriental rugs and original hardwood floors add to the inn's natural charm. The inn's original 1808 fireplaces, featured in each room, although not operating, add to the inn's architectural character. Muffins, croissants, bagels and fresh fruit are the morning fare.

Innkeeper(s): Scott Eklind. $50-100. MC VISA AX DS PC TC. 3 rooms with PB. Breakfast included in rates. Type of meal: continental-plus breakfast. Beds: QD. Air conditioning, TV and VCR in room. Antiques, fishing, parks, shopping, sporting events, golf, theater and watersports nearby.

Publicity: *Washington Post.*

Bay Beach B&B

PO Box 151, 1-3 Bay Beach Ln
Sandwich, MA 02563
(508)888-8813 (800)475-6398 Fax:(508)888-5416

Beautiful grounds bursting with gardens and a heavenly view of the sea attract many guests to this peaceful Cape Cod bed & breakfast, located in historic Sandwich. Rooms are tastefully appointed with contemporary furnishings and include amenities such as ceiling fans, mini refrigerators stocked with a few choice refreshments and private decks. The inn has received a four-diamond rating from AAA.

Innkeeper(s): Emily & Reale Lemieux. $160-225. MC VISA PC. 6 rooms with PB, 2 with FP. 3 suites. Breakfast and afternoon tea included in rates. Type of meal: continental-plus breakfast. Room service available. Beds: KD. Phone, air conditioning, turndown service, ceiling fan and TV in room. Fax, copier, swimming, bicycles and library on premises. French spoken. Antiques, fishing, parks, shopping, golf, theater and watersports nearby.

Ratings: *4 Diamonds.*

Captain Ezra Nye House

152 Main St
Sandwich, MA 02563-2232
(508)888-6142 (800)388-2278 Fax:(508)833-2897
E-mail: captnye@aol.com

Circa 1829. Captain Ezra Nye built this house after a record-shattering Halifax to Boston run, and the stately Federal-style house reflects the opulence and romance of the clipper ship era. Hand-stenciled walls and museum-quality antiques decorate the interior. Within walking distance are the Doll Museum, the Glass Museum, restaurants, shops, the famous Heritage Plantation, the beach and marina.

Innkeeper(s): Elaine & Harry Dickson. $85-110. MC VISA AX DS PC TC. TAC10. 6 rooms with PB, 1 with FP. 1 suite. Breakfast included in rates. Types of meals: full breakfast, gourmet breakfast and early coffee/tea. Beds: QDT. TV, VCR, fax and library on premises. Small meetings and family reunions hosted. Spanish spoken. Antiques, fishing, parks, shopping, theater and watersports nearby.

Location: In the heart of Sandwich Village, the oldest town on Cape Cod.

Publicity: *Glamour, Innsider, Cape Cod Life, Toronto Life, Yankee.*

"The prettiest room and most beautiful home we have been to. We had a wonderful time."

The Dan'l Webster Inn

149 Main St
Sandwich, MA 02563-2271
(508)888-3622

Circa 1692. Originally built as a parsonage in the late 17th century, the inn offers the essence of Colonial charm and elegance. Each of the 47 guest rooms is individually appointed with period furnishings. Suites offer canopy and four-poster beds, working fireplaces and whirlpool tubs. Guests are invited to enjoy

their meals by the fireside, in the sun room or moon-lit conservatory. The inn is recognized for its outstanding service and innovative cuisine, and it holds a Mobil four-star rating.

Innkeeper(s): Steve Catania. $99-199. MAP. EP. MC VISA AX DC CB DS. 47 rooms with PB, 7 with FP. 1 conference room. Types of meals: continental-plus breakfast, full breakfast and gourmet breakfast. Restaurant on premises. Beds: KQDT. Fax and copier on premises. Handicap access. Fishing nearby.

Publicity: *Bon Appetit, New York Times, Great Weekends, Los Angeles Times, Good Housekeeping.*

"Excellent accommodations and great food."

The Dunbar House

1 Water St
Sandwich, MA 02563-2303
(508)833-2485 Fax:(508)833-4713
E-mail: dunbar@capecod.net

Circa 1741. This Colonial-style house overlooks a pond in the charming setting of Cape Cod's oldest town. The three guest rooms are appointed in Colonial style, and all boast a view of the pond. The Ennerdale rooms has a four-poster bed. Each morning, guests are pampered with a homemade breakfast, and afternoon tea is served in the innkeeper's English tea shop. The inn is within walking distance to many historic sites and the beach.

Innkeeper(s): Nancy Iribarren & David Bell. $65-95. MC VISA PC TC. TAC10. 3 rooms with PB, 3 with FP. Breakfast and afternoon tea included in rates. Types of meals: continental breakfast, continental-plus breakfast, full breakfast, gourmet breakfast and early coffee/tea. Lunch available. Restaurant on premises. Beds: QT. VCR, fax, copier, bicycles and library on premises. Weddings, small meetings, family reunions and seminars hosted. Limited Spanish spoken. Antiques, fishing, parks, shopping, theater and watersports nearby.

Inn at Sandwich Center

118 Tupper Rd
Sandwich, MA 02563-1828
(508)888-6958 (800)249-6949 Fax:(508)833-2770
E-mail: innsan@aol.com

Circa 1750. In the National Register, this Federal salt-box-style home is said to have been on the Underground Railway. This is the third family to have owned the inn since 1750. The inn is situated in Cape Cod's most historic town, Sandwich, founded in 1637. Guest rooms have a French touch thanks to the innkeepers' country of origin. There are antiques, fireplaces, four-poster beds and paintings. Robes, hair dryers and chocolates are special amenities. Guests gather in the Keeping Room for a candlelight breakfast served next to the inn's beehive oven and 1750 fireplace. Everything served is homemade including the scones, croissants and jams. Across the street is the Sandwich Glass Museum and within walking distance, the Heritage Plantation's Antique Car and Live Art Museums with 76 acres of gardens.

Innkeeper(s): Eliane & Al Thomas. $75-110. MAP. MC AX DS PC TC. 5 rooms with PB, 3 with FP. Breakfast included in rates. Types of meals: continental breakfast, continental-plus breakfast and gourmet breakfast. Beds: KQ. Turndown service in room. Small meetings and family reunions hosted. English, French, Italian and some Spanish. spoken. Antiques, fishing, parks, shopping, golf, theater and watersports nearby.

Publicity: *The Sandwich Broadsider.*

"We agreed that we were treated more like honored family rather than hotel guests. As Eliane would say, 'Our home is your home' and that's exactly what we experienced."

The Summer House

158 Main St
Sandwich, MA 02563-2232
(508)888-4991 (800)241-3609

Circa 1835. The Summer House is a handsome Greek Revival in a setting of historic homes and public buildings. (Hiram Dillaway, one of the owners, was a famous mold maker for the Boston & Sandwich Glass Company.) The house is fully restored and decorated with antiques and hand-stitched quilts. Four of the guest rooms have fireplaces. The breakfast room and parlor have black marble fireplaces. The  sunporch overlooks an old-fashioned perennial garden, antique rose bushes, and a 70-year-old rhododendron hedge. The inn is open year-round.

Historic Interest: Sandwich Glass Museum (1 block), Thornton Burgess Museum (1 block), Heritage Plantation Museum (1 mile).

Innkeeper(s): Marjorie & Kevin Huelsman. $65-95. MC VISA AX DS PC TC. 5 rooms with PB, 4 with FP. Breakfast and afternoon tea included in rates. Types of meals: full breakfast, gourmet breakfast and early coffee/tea. Beds: KQT. Library on premises. Weddings, small meetings and family reunions hosted. Antiques, fishing, parks, shopping, cross-country skiing, theater and watersports nearby.

Location: Center of village, Cape Cod.

Publicity: *Country Living, Boston, Cape Cod Times.*

"An absolutely gorgeous house and a super breakfast. I wish I could've stayed longer! Came for one night, stayed for three! Marvelous welcome."

The Village Inn at Sandwich

PO Box 951, 4 Jarves St
Sandwich, MA 02563-0951
(508)833-0363 (800)922-9989
E-mail: capecodinn@aol.com

Circa 1836. Located in the heart of the historic district, this 19th-century Federal-style inn offers guests more than just its lovely interiors and convenient location. The innkeepers have taken advantage of the area's scenic marshes, beaches and cranberry bogs to offer a series of artist's workshops and bed & breakfast/workshop packages conducted by professional artists at the inn's private art studio. Designed for the beginner as well as the more advanced student, the workshops run from April through October. Guests not attending a workshop will find plenty to do while staying at the Village Inn. Besides the inn's gardens, guests can stroll to the village, the oldest town on

Cape Cod, where they'll find museums, galleries, restaurants and antique shops. Home-baked muffins and breads, fresh fruit, a hot entree and gourmet French toast are just a sampling of the morning fare.

Historic Interest: Nearby Shawme Pond is surrounded by landmark homes, a working gristmill and an English tea room. Walking distance to Cape Cod beaches.

Innkeeper(s): Susan Fehlinger. $70-110. MC VISA AX DS PC TC. 8 rooms, 6 with PB, 2 with FP. Breakfast included in rates. Types of meals: continental-plus breakfast, full breakfast and early coffee/tea. Beds: QT. Ceiling fan in room. Fax, bicycles and library on premises. Small meetings, family reunions and seminars hosted. Antiques, fishing, parks, shopping, golf, theater and watersports nearby.

Sandwich (Cape Cod)　　　I16

Isaiah Jones Homestead

165 Main St
Sandwich (Cape Cod), MA 02563-2283
(508)888-9115 (800)526-1625

Circa 1849. This fully restored Victorian homestead is situated on Main Street in the village. Eleven-foot ceilings and two bay windows are features of the Gathering Room. Guest rooms contain antique Victorian bedsteads such as the half-canopy

bed of burled birch in the Deming Jarves Room, where there is an over-sized whirlpool tub and a fireplace. Candlelight breakfasts are highlighted with the house speciality, freshly baked cornbread, inspired by nearby Sandwich Grist Mill.

Innkeeper(s): Jan & Doug Klapper. $75-155. MC VISA AX DS PC TC. TAC10. 5 rooms with PB, 3 with FP. Breakfast and afternoon tea included in rates. Types of meals: full breakfast and early coffee/tea. Beds: QDT. TV on premises. Weddings, small meetings, family reunions and seminars hosted. Antiques, fishing, parks, shopping, theater and watersports nearby.

Publicity: *Cape Cod Life, New England Travel, National Geographic Travel.*

"Excellent! The room was a delight, the food wonderful, the hospitality warm & friendly. One of the few times the reality exceeded the expectation."

Seekonk　　　H12

Historic Jacob Hill Farm B&B/Inn

120 Jacob St
Seekonk, MA 02771
(508)336-9165 (888)336-9165 Fax:(508)336-0951

Circa 1722. This historic Colonial home overlooks 50 acres and is located three miles outside Providence. In the '20s and '30s, it was the Jacob Hill Hunt Club and hosted the Vanderbilts during hunts and horse shows. Beamed ceilings, wall paintings of horse and hunting scenes and rare Southern longleaf pine floors create the gracious setting. Guest rooms may include a canopy bed, fireplace or whirlpool tub. Enjoy

the inn's stable of horses or take a riding lesson, then relax in the gazebo at sunset. Stuffed French toast with whipped cream and strawberries is often served in the original kitchen area with its large beehive fireplace.

Innkeeper(s): Bill & Eleonora Rezek. $95-175. MC VISA AX DS PC TC. TAC10. 7 rooms, 5 with PB, 3 with FP. 2 suites. Breakfast included in rates. Types of meals: full breakfast, gourmet breakfast and early coffee/tea. Afternoon tea available. Beds: KQDT. Air conditioning and turndown service in room. TV, VCR, fax, swimming, stables and tennis on premises. Weddings, small meetings and family reunions hosted. Polish spoken. Amusement parks, antiques, fishing, parks, shopping, downhill skiing, cross-country skiing, sporting events, theater and watersports nearby.

Sheffield　　　F2

Race Brook Lodge

864 S Undermountain Rd
Sheffield, MA 01257-9641
(413)229-2916 Fax:(413)229-6629

Circa 1790. This beautifully restored 18th-century barn features a rustic, country decor. Charming rooms boast exposed, hand-hewn beams and polished wooden floors. The Barn Suite, Hayloft Suite and Harness barn are well-suited to families or groups traveling together. Other rooms are tucked away in lofts, and all feature warm, inviting interiors. Hearty buffet breakfasts start off with a cup of tea or specially blended coffees, and includes fresh fruit, cereals, homemade muffins and bagels.

Historic Interest: Chesterwood estate and gardens is 18 miles, Edith Warton's Mount is 20 miles, and Herman Melville's Arrowhead is about 30 miles away.

Innkeeper(s): David Rothstein. $79-149. MC VISA AX. 22 rooms with PB. Breakfast included in rates. Beds: KQDT. Antiques, fishing, downhill skiing, cross-country skiing, theater and watersports nearby.

Publicity: *New York Post, Berkshires Weekend, Boston Globe, Newsday.*

"A real hidden treasure."

Staveleigh House

59 Main St, PO 608
Sheffield, MA 01257
(413)229-2129

Circa 1821. The Reverend Bradford, minister of Old Parish Congregational Church, the oldest church in the Berkshires, built this home for his family. Afternoon tea is served and the inn is especially favored for its four-course breakfasts and gracious hospitality. Located next to the town green, the house is in a historic district in the midst of several fine antique shops. It is also near Tanglewood, skiing and all Berkshire attractions.

Innkeeper(s): Dorothy Marosy & Marion Whitman. $80-105. TC. 5 rooms, 2 with PB. Breakfast and afternoon tea included in rates. Types of meals: full breakfast and early coffee/tea. Beds: KQDT. Turndown service and ceiling fan in room. Handicap access. Weddings, small meetings, family reunions and seminars hosted. Antiques, fishing, parks, shopping, downhill skiing, cross-country skiing, theater and watersports nearby.

Publicity: *Los Angeles Times, Boston Globe.*

"Our annual needlework workshops are so much fun, we have a waiting list to join our group."

South Dartmouth J14

Salt Marsh Farm

322 Smith Neck Rd
South Dartmouth, MA 02748-1441
(508)992-0980

Circa 1770. In 1665, John Smith traded his house in
Plymouth for this land in Dartmouth, so he could escape the

overcrowding in
Plymouth. The land
was called Smith's
Neck. Later, Isaac
Howland built this
two-story, hip-
roofed colonial
house. The farm
has 90 acres of salt
meadows, tidal marshes, hay fields and woodlands. Organic
vegetable and flower gardens are enjoyed by guests. The
innkeeper is a descendant of John Smith and enjoys sharing
local history.

Historic Interest: The New Bedford Whaling Historic National Park is nearby,
as is the ancestral home of Hetty Green ("the witch of Wall Street").

Innkeeper(s): Larry & Sally Brownell. $65-90. MC VISA. 2 rooms with PB.
Breakfast and afternoon tea included in rates. Type of meal: full breakfast.
Beds: DT. Phone in room. Bicycles and library on premises. Antiques and
theater nearby.

Location: Southeastern Massachusetts.

Publicity: *New Bedford Standard-Times, Dartmouth/Westport Chronicle,
Country Living, Boston Sunday Globe, A Better Tomorrow, Journal Inquirer.*

"A peaceful setting for the refreshment of both body & spirit."

South Dennis I18

Captain Nickerson Inn

333 Main St
South Dennis, MA 02660-3643
(508)398-5966 (800)282-1619

Circa 1828. This Queen Anne Victorian inn is located in the
mid-Cape area. Guests can relax on the front porch with white
wicker rockers and tables. The guest rooms are decorated with
period four-poster or white iron queen beds and
hand-woven or Oriental-style
rugs. The dining room
has a fireplace and a
stained-glass picture
window. The
Cape Cod bike
Rail Trail, which
is more than 20

miles long, is less than a mile away.

Historic Interest: Jericho House is one mile away, while Scargo Tower is a
five-mile drive.

Innkeeper(s): Pat & Dave York. $65-95. MC VISA DS PC. TAC10. 5 rooms, 3
with PB. Breakfast included in rates. Type of meal: full breakfast. Beds: QDT.
Air conditioning and ceiling fan in room. TV, VCR, fax and bicycles on premises. Small meetings and family reunions hosted. Antiques, fishing, parks,
shopping, theater and watersports nearby.

"Your inn is great!"

South Egremont F2

Egremont Inn

Old Sheffield Rd
South Egremont, MA 01258
(413)528-2111 (800)859-1780 Fax:(413)528-3284

Circa 1780. This three-story inn, listed in the National
Register, was once a stagecoach stop. Guest rooms are furnished with country antiques. Dinner is available Wednesday
through Sunday in the formal dining room, and there is a historic tavern room. Five fireplaces are found in the common
rooms. A wraparound porch, tennis courts and a swimming
pool are on the premises.

Historic Interest: Minutes from the site of Shays Rebellion. Formerly a mus-
tering-in location and hospital during the Revolutionary War.

Innkeeper(s): Karen & Steven Waller. $80-165. MAP. MC VISA AX PC TC.
TAC10. 20 rooms with PB. 1 suite. 1 conference room. Breakfast included in
rates. Types of meals: continental breakfast and full breakfast. Dinner available. Restaurant on premises. Beds: KQDT. Phone, air conditioning and ceiling fan in room. VCR, swimming, tennis and library on premises. Weddings,
small meetings, family reunions and seminars hosted. Antiques, fishing,
parks, shopping, downhill skiing, cross-country skiing, sporting events and
theater nearby.

Location: In the heart of the Berkshires.

*"All the beauty of the Berkshires without the hassle, the quintessen-
tial country inn."*

Weathervane Inn

Rt 23, Main St
South Egremont, MA 01258
(413)528-9580 (800)528-9580 Fax:(413)528-1713
E-mail: weathervaneinn.com

Circa 1785. The original post-and-beam New England farmhouse with its beehive oven was added on to throughout its history. It has been restored to combine today's modern amenities
with the charm of the inn's historic past. The inn's historic architectural features include broad plank floors, tree trunk supports
and granite columns. A full breakfast is offered every morning.

Historic Interest: Norman Rockwell Museum, Berkshire Museum, The Clark
Museum and Hoosac Railroad Tunnel built during the Civil War.

Innkeeper(s): Vincent & Anne Murphy. $125-215. MC VISA AX. 11 rooms
with PB. 1 suite. 1 conference room. Breakfast included in rates. Type of
meal: full breakfast. Restaurant on premises. Beds: KQD. Phone in room.
Antiques, fishing, downhill skiing, cross-country skiing, golf, theater and
watersports nearby.

Location: Main Street, Route 23.

Publicity: *New York Times, Berkshire Eagle, Boston Herald, Newsday.*

*"The Murphy family exemplifies the best tradition of New England
hospitality—Berkshire Business Journal."*

Stockbridge E2

Arbor Rose B&B

8 Yale Hill, Box 114
Stockbridge, MA 01262
(413)298-4744

Circa 1810. This New England farmhouse overlooks an 1800s
mill, pond and gardens with the mountains as a backdrop.
During the winter months, guests often relax in front of the
wood stove in the inn's cozy front parlor. Four-poster beds,
antiques and rural-themed paintings decorate the rooms. The
inn's 19th-century mill now houses guests. The mill was one of

five in the vicinity and was still in operation as late as the 1930s. The Berkshire Theatre, open for the summer season, is across the street. The Norman Rockwell Museum, Tanglewood Music Festival, ski areas and antique, outlet and specialty shops are all within a seven-mile radius.

Historic Interest: Mission House, the first mission set up for the Stockbridge Indians, and the historic Main Street of Stockbridge are among the nearby historic sites.

Innkeeper(s): Christina Alsop. $85-175. MC VISA AX PC TC. TAC10. 5 rooms with PB. 1 conference room. Breakfast included in rates. Types of meals: full breakfast, gourmet breakfast and early coffee/tea. Beds: KQT. Air conditioning and ceiling fan in room. Weddings, small meetings, family reunions and seminars hosted. Antiques, parks, shopping, downhill skiing, cross-country skiing and theater nearby.

Location: One-half mile from center of Stockbridge.

Publicity: *Yankee Traveler.*

"If houses really do exude the spirit of events and feelings stored from their history, it explains why a visitor feels warmth and joy from the first turn up the driveway."

The Red Lion Inn

Main St
Stockbridge, MA 01262
(413)298-5545 Fax:(413)298-5130
E-mail: Innkeeper@redlioninn.com

Circa 1773. The venerable white clapboard Red Lion Inn has been continuously operated as a tavern and inn since it's inception. The originator Salas Pepoon is said to have initiated a rally to protest the use of British goods. This meeting resulted in a letter said to have been the first Declaration of Independence. A vital part of the area's history, the inn is the last of the 18th-century Berkshire hotels still in operation. The collection of fine antique furnishings, colonial pewter and Staffordshire china found in the inn's parlor was gathered in the late 19th century by proprietor Mrs. Charles Plumb. The inn is part of the Norman Rockwell "Mainstreet Stockbridge" painting. Traditional decor extends to the comfortable guest rooms and some have four-poster and canopy beds, fireplaces, antique vanities and desks. The inn is home to four restaurants. Rocking on the long front porch is a favored activity, and one wonders if former visitors such as presidents Cleveland, McKinley, Theodore Roosevelt, Coolidge and Franklin Roosevelt enjoyed the privilege. Roast turkey dinners and New England bread pudding are among the specialties of the inn's restaurants.

Innkeeper(s): Brooks Bradbury. $87-165. EP. MC VISA AX DC CB DS PC TC. TAC10. 111 rooms, 88 with PB. 23 suites. 7 cottages. 4 conference rooms. Types of meals: continental breakfast, continental-plus breakfast, full breakfast and early coffee/tea. Dinner, picnic lunch, lunch, banquet service and room service available. Restaurant on premises. Beds: KQDT. Phone, turndown service and TV in room. VCR, fax, copier, swimming and library on premises. Handicap access. Weddings, small meetings, family reunions and seminars hosted. Antiques, fishing, shopping, downhill skiing, cross-country skiing, golf and theater nearby.

Publicity: *Country Folk Art, The Age, USA Today.*

"My family and I travel quite a bit and your facility and employees top them all."

Roeder House B&B

Rt 183
Stockbridge, MA 01262
(413)298-4015 (800)245-6011 Fax:(413)298-4015

Circa 1856. Shaded by tall trees, this Federal-style farmhouse sits on a knoll overlooking four acres of grounds that include carefully tended perennial beds, an old carriage barn and green lawns. Decorated in a country-cottage style, there is a library and sitting room with fireplace and a screened porch. Four-poster canopy beds are features of the guest rooms. Breakfast specialties include blueberry muffins, malted waffles and pure maple syrup. In cool weather, hot cider is offered before the fire.

Innkeeper(s): Diane & Vernon Reuss. $120-230. MC VISA AX DS PC TC. TAC10. 7 rooms with PB. Breakfast included in rates. Types of meals: full breakfast and early coffee/tea. Picnic lunch and catered breakfast available. Beds: QT. Air conditioning and ceiling fan in room. TV, VCR, fax, copier and swimming on premises. Small meetings and family reunions hosted. Antiques, fishing, shopping, downhill skiing, cross-country skiing, golf and theater nearby.

"A wonderful experience, please adopt me."

The Inn at Stockbridge

PO Box 618
Stockbridge, MA 01262-0618
(413)298-3337 Fax:(413)298-3406
E-mail: innkeeper@stockbridgeinn.com

Circa 1906. Giant maples shade the drive leading to this Southern-style Georgian Colonial with its impressive pillared entrance. Located on 12 acres, the grounds include a reflecting pool, a fountain, meadows and woodland as well as wide vistas of the rolling hillsides. The guest rooms feature antiques and handsome 18th-century reproductions. Breakfast is graciously presented with fine china, silver and linens.

Innkeeper(s): Alice & Len Schiller. $85-260. MC VISA AX DS. TAC10. 12 rooms, 8 with PB. 4 with FP. 4 suites. 1 conference room. Breakfast and evening snack included in rates. Types of meals: full breakfast, gourmet breakfast and early coffee/tea. Beds: KQDT. Phone, air conditioning, ceiling fan, TV and VCR in room. Fax, copier and swimming on premises. Handicap access. 12 acres. Weddings, small meetings, family reunions and seminars hosted. Antiques, parks, shopping, downhill skiing, cross-country skiing, golf, theater and watersports nearby.

Publicity: *Vogue, New York, New York Daily News, Country Inns Northeast, Arts & Antiques.*

"Classy & comfortable."

Stockbridge (South Lee)　　　E2

Historic Merrell Inn

1565 Pleasant St, Rt 102
Stockbridge (South Lee), MA 01260
(413)243-1794 (800)243-1794 Fax:(413)243-2669
E-mail: merey@bcn.net

Circa 1794. This elegant stagecoach inn was carefully preserved under supervision of the Society for the Preservation of New England Antiquities. Architectural drawings of Merrell Inn have been preserved by the Library of Congress. Eight fireplaces in the inn include two with original beehive and warming ovens. An antique circular birdcage bar serves as a check-in desk.

Comfortable rooms feature canopy and four-poster beds with Hepplewhite and Sheraton-style antiques.

Historic Interest: Hancock Shaker Village (15 miles), Norman Rockwell Museum (3 miles).

Innkeeper(s): Charles & Faith Reynolds. $75-165. MC VISA. 9 rooms with PB, 3 with FP. Breakfast included in rates. Type of meal: full breakfast. Beds: KQDT. Phone and air conditioning in room. TV, fax and copier on premises. Family reunions and seminars hosted. Antiques, fishing, parks, shopping, cross-country skiing and theater nearby.

Publicity: *Americana, Country Living, New York Times, Boston Globe, Country Accents, Travel Holiday, USA Today.*

"We couldn't have chosen a more delightful place to stay in the Berkshires. Everything was wonderful. We especially loved the grounds and the gazebo by the river."

Sturbridge   F8

Commonwealth Cottage

11 Summit Ave
Sturbridge, MA 01566-1225
(508)347-7708

Circa 1873. This 16-room Queen Anne Victorian house, on an acre near the Quinebaug River, is just a few minutes from Old Sturbridge Village. Both the dining room and parlor have fireplaces. The Baroque theme of the Sal Raciti room makes it one of the guest favorites and it features a queen mahogany bed. Breakfast may be offered on the gazebo porch or in the

formal dining room. It includes a variety of homemade specialties, such as freshly baked breads and cakes.

Historic Interest: Old Sturbridge Village (1 1/2 mile).

Innkeeper(s): Robert & Wiebke Gilbert. $85-145. PC TC. 5 rooms, 4 with PB. Types of meals: full breakfast and early coffee/tea. Evening snack available. Beds: QDT. Ceiling fan in room. Library on premises. Weddings and family reunions hosted. German spoken. Antiques, fishing, parks, shopping, theater and watersports nearby.

Publicity: *Long Island Newsday, Villager.*

"Your home is so warm and welcoming we feel as though we've stepped back in time. Our stay here has helped to make the wedding experience extra special!"

Publick House Historic Inn & Country Motor Lodge

PO Box 187, Common Route 131
Sturbridge, MA 01566-0187
(800)PUBLICK Fax:(508)347-5073

Circa 1771. This property includes four lodging facilities, three restaurants, 12 meeting rooms and 60 acres of countryside.

Many special events take place throughout the year, including a New England Lobster Bake, a Beer and Wine Maker's Dinner, Harvest Weekend, Yankee Winter Weekends and Murder-Mystery Weekends. All the rooms in the main building are decorated with period furnishings.

Innkeeper(s): Albert Cournoyer. $74-155. MC VISA AX DC CB PC TC. TAC10. 14 rooms with PB. 7 suites. Types of meals: continental breakfast, continental-plus breakfast, full breakfast, gourmet breakfast and early coffee/tea. Afternoon tea, dinner, evening snack, picnic lunch, lunch, gourmet lunch, banquet service, catering service, catered breakfast and room service available. Restaurant on premises. Beds: KQDT. Phone, air conditioning and TV in room. VCR, fax and swimming on premises. Handicap access. 60 acres. Weddings, small meetings, family reunions and seminars hosted. Spanish and French spoken. Antiques, fishing, parks, shopping, cross-country skiing, sporting events and theater nearby.

Sturbridge Country Inn

PO Box 60, 530 Main St
Sturbridge, MA 01566-0060
(508)347-5503 Fax:(508)347-5319

Circa 1840. Shaded by an old silver maple, this classic Greek Revival house boasts a two-story columned entrance. The

attached carriage house now serves as the lobby and displays the original post-and-beam construction and exposed rafters. All guest rooms have individual fireplaces and whirlpool tubs. They are appointed gracefully in reproduction colonial furnishings, including queen-size, four-posters. A patio and gazebo are favorite summertime retreats.

Innkeeper(s): Patricia Affenito. $59-159. MC VISA AX DS PC TC. TAC10. 9 rooms with PB, 9 with FP. 1 suite. 1 conference room. Breakfast included in rates. Types of meals: continental breakfast and early coffee/tea. Room service available. Restaurant on premises. Beds: KQ. Phone, air conditioning, ceiling fan, TV and VCR in room. Fax, copier and spa on premises. Weddings, small meetings, family reunions and seminars hosted. Spanish spoken. Antiques, fishing, parks, shopping, downhill skiing, cross-country skiing, theater and watersports nearby.

Location: Near Old Sturbridge Village.

Publicity: *Southbridge Evening News, Worcester Telegram & Gazette.*

"Best lodging I've ever seen."

Sudbury   D12

Arabian Horse Inn

277 Old Sudbury Rd
Sudbury, MA 01776-1842
(508)443-7400 (800)272-2426 Fax:(508)443-0234
E-mail: joanbeers@aol.com

Circa 1880. Nestled on nine wooded acres, this Queen Anne Victorian offers visitors the ultimate in privacy and romance. In fact, the inn offers a popular honeymoon and anniversary suite.

Once part of a 225-acre apple farm, the inn still retains the original four-story barn with its post and beam ceiling and huge cupola. Guests are invited to enjoy the tranquillity of the lovely pastures, pond and wildlife surrounding the inn. A complimentary gourmet breakfast includes fresh strawberries, Rosemary eggs and the innkeeper's homemade Rosemary bread. Tea is served daily. The inn is close to restaurants, shopping, theater and sporting activities.

Innkeeper(s): Joan & Richard Beers. $99-249. MC VISA TC. TAC10. 3 rooms, 1 with PB, 1 with FP. 1 suite. Breakfast and afternoon tea included in rates. Types of meals: continental breakfast, continental-plus breakfast, full breakfast, gourmet breakfast and early coffee/tea. Room service available. Beds: KDT. Phone, air conditioning, ceiling fan, TV and VCR in room. Fax, copier, stables, library and pet boarding on premises. Weddings, small meetings, family reunions and seminars hosted. Amusement parks, antiques, fishing, parks, shopping, downhill skiing, cross-country skiing, sporting events, golf, theater and watersports nearby.

Pets Allowed: use of pen, booked with reservation.

Tyringham E2

Golden Goose

123 Main Rd # 336
Tyringham, MA 01264-9700
(413)243-3008

Circa 1800. This white colonial house rests on six acres in the peaceful valley of Tyringham. The innkeeper has gathered antiques for the inn from her shopkeeping days in Manhattan, where she sold Victorian oak pieces. Cheery wallpapers and wide-plank floors create a fresh country decor. The inn features one suite with a kitchen, private bath and entrance. From the dining room, beveled French doors lead to a deck that overlooks the back grounds. Across the road is Hop Brook, a trout fishing spot and the Tyringham Cobble, part of the Appalachian Trail. Guests can enjoy a full or continental breakfast and evening and afternoon snack.

Historic Interest: Norman Rockwell Museum (6 miles), Hancock Shaker Village (12 miles), Sterling-Clark Museum (30 miles).
Innkeeper(s): Lilja & Joseph Rizzo. $80-125. MC VISA AX TC. 6 rooms, 4 with PB. 1 suite. Breakfast, afternoon tea and evening snack included in rates. Types of meals: continental-plus breakfast, full breakfast and early coffee/tea. Beds: KQD. Air conditioning in room. Small meetings, family reunions and seminars hosted. Antiques, fishing, parks, shopping, downhill skiing, cross-country skiing, sporting events and theater nearby.
Location: In the Berkshires on the Appalachian Trail.
Publicity: *Boston Sunday Globe, Travel & Leisure, Food & Wine.*

"The classical music puts the final touch on a classic inn and two classic hosts!"

Vineyard Haven K16

The Look Inn

Box 2195, 25 Look St
Vineyard Haven, MA 02568-2195
(508)693-6893

Circa 1806. Located three blocks from the ferry and in the Vineyard Haven Historic District, the Look Inn is a restored farmhouse, bordered by a fieldstone wall. Rooms are furnished with antiques and country pieces and have queen beds and private sinks. Guests can enjoy a good book from the library with its cozy fireplace or enjoy the night sky in the on-site hot tub. Breakfast is served on the sun porch overlooking an acre of lawn and gardens. There's a fishpond and hammock. Photo/hiking tours are offered, and massages can be scheduled

with the innkeeper.

Innkeeper(s): Freddy Rundlet, Catherine Keller. $80-100. MC VISA PC TC. TAC5. 3 rooms. Breakfast included in rates. Types of meals: continental-plus breakfast and early coffee/tea. Beds: Q. Bicycles and library on premises. Family reunions hosted. French and Spanish spoken. Amusement parks, antiques, fishing, parks, shopping, cross-country skiing, sporting events, golf, theater and watersports nearby.

Lothrop Merry House

Owen Park, PO Box 1939
Vineyard Haven, MA 02568
(508)693-1646

Circa 1790. Eight yoke of oxen moved this house to its present beach-front location. A wedding gift from father to daughter, the house has a classic center chimney and six fireplaces. Breakfast is served in season on the flower-bedecked patio overlooking stunning harbor views. A private beach beckons at the end of a sloping lawn.

Innkeeper(s): John & Mary Clarke. $68-205. MC VISA PC TC. 7 rooms, 4 with PB, 3 with FP. Breakfast included in rates. Type of meal: continental breakfast. Beds: QDT. Phone and air conditioning in room. Child care on premises. Weddings, small meetings, family reunions and seminars hosted. Antiques, fishing, shopping, cross-country skiing, golf, theater and watersports nearby.
Location: Martha's Vineyard.
Publicity: *Cape Cod Life, Sailing, Martha's Vineyard Times.*

"It is the nicest place we've ever stayed."

Ware E7

The Wildwood Inn

121 Church St
Ware, MA 01082-1203
(413)967-7798 (800)860-8098

Circa 1880. This yellow Victorian has a wraparound porch and a beveled-glass front door. American primitive antiques include a collection of New England cradles and heirloom quilts, a saddlemaker's bench and a spinning wheel. The inn's two acres are 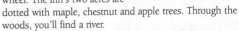 dotted with maple, chestnut and apple trees. Through the woods, you'll find a river.

Historic Interest: Old Sturbridge Village (15 miles), Old Deerfield (30 miles), Amherst College (15 miles).
Innkeeper(s): Fraidell Fenster & Richard Watson. $50-85. MC VISA AX DC DS PC TC. TAC10. 9 rooms, 7 with PB. 1 suite. 2 conference rooms. Breakfast and afternoon tea included in rates. Types of meals: full breakfast and early coffee/tea. Banquet service, catering service and catered breakfast available. Beds: KQDT. Air conditioning and turndown service in room. Bicycles, tennis and library on premises. Handicap access. Weddings, small meetings, family reunions and seminars hosted. Amusement parks, antiques, fishing, parks, shopping, downhill skiing, cross-country skiing, sporting events and theater nearby.
Publicity: *Boston Globe, National Geographic Traveler, Country, Worcester Telegram-Gazette.*

"Excellent accommodations, not only in rooms, but in the kind and thoughtful way you treat your guests. We'll be back!"

Wareham I15

Mulberry B&B

257 High St
Wareham, MA 02571-1407
(508)295-0684 Fax:(508)291-2909

Circa 1847. This former blacksmith's house is in the historic district of town and has been featured on the local garden club house tour. Frances, a former school teacher, has decorated the guest rooms in a country style with antiques. A deck, shaded by a tall mulberry tree, looks out to the back garden.

Historic Interest: Plymouth (18 miles), New Bedford Whaling Capitol (17 miles), Provincetown/Eastham, where Pilgrims first landed (70 miles).
Innkeeper(s): Frances Murphy. $50-65. MC VISA AX DS PC TC. TAC10. 3 rooms. Breakfast included in rates. Type of meal: full breakfast. Afternoon tea available. Beds: KDT. Air conditioning and turndown service in room. TV and VCR on premises. Antiques, fishing, parks, shopping, cross-country skiing, sporting events, theater and watersports nearby.
Publicity: *Brockton Enterprise, Wareham Courier.*

"Thank you for your hospitality. The muffins were delicious."

Wellfleet G18

The Inn at Duck Creeke

70 Main St, PO Box 364
Wellfleet, MA 02667-0364
(508)349-9333 Fax:(508)349-0234
E-mail: duckinn@capecod.net

Circa 1815. The five-acre site of this sea captain's house features both a salt-water marsh and a duck pond. The Saltworks house and the main house are appointed in an old-fashioned style with antiques, and the rooms are comfortable and cozy. Some have views of the nearby salt marsh or the pond. The inn is favored for its two restaurants; Sweet Seasons and the Tavern Room. The latter is popular for its jazz performances.

Historic Interest: Marconi Station (first wireless Trans Atlantic radio transmission). Wellfleet Historical Museum.
Innkeeper(s): Bob Morrill & Judy Pihl. $50-100. MC VISA AX PC TC. 25 rooms, 17 with PB. 1 conference room. Breakfast included in rates. Types of meals: continental-plus breakfast and early coffee/tea. Dinner available. Restaurant on premises. Beds: QDT. Ceiling fan in room. Weddings, small meetings, family reunions and seminars hosted. Antiques, fishing, parks, shopping, theater and watersports nearby.
Publicity: *New York Times, Provincetown, Providence Journal, Cape Cod Life, Conde Nast Traveler.*

"Duck Creeke will always be our favorite stay!"

West Boylston E10

The Rose Cottage

24 Worcester St
West Boylston, MA 01583-1413
(508)835-4034

Circa 1850. Overlooking the placid water of Wachusett Reservoir, this yellow Gothic Revival house features dormers and a gabled roof trimmed with gingerbread. Inside, wideboard floors, floor-to-ceiling windows and marble fireplaces remain. Guest rooms are decorated with small print wallpapers, quilts and antiques. There are two apartments for longer stays that feature skylights in the cathedral ceilings, fully equipped kitchens and private entrances.

Innkeeper(s): Michael & Loretta Kittredge. $70. PC TC. 5 rooms, 1 with PB. 1 conference room. Types of meals: full breakfast and gourmet breakfast. Beds: DT. Phone in room.
Publicity: *The Evening Gazette.*

"Your concern, your caring, your friendliness made me feel at home!"

West Hyannisport I17

B&B Cape Cod

PO Box 341
West Hyannisport, MA 02672-0341
(800)686-5252
E-mail: bedandb@capecod.net

Circa 1709. This reservation service represents many exquisitely restored historic houses in almost every nook and cranny on the Cape, Nantucket and Martha's Vineyard. Many are in the National Register. One of the oldest, an Early American home, is two blocks from Cape Cod Bay. Furnished in an early 1700s decor, the home has four-poster beds and period antiques. A hearty country breakfast is served. All homes (115 locations) are inspected and approved by the agency.

Innkeeper(s): General manager Clark Diehl. $55-195. MC VISA AX.
Publicity: *Innsider Magazine.*

"Clean, orderly and comfortable."

West Stockbridge E2

Card Lake Inn

PO Box 38
West Stockbridge, MA 01266-0038
(413)232-0272 Fax:(413)232-0272

Circa 1880. Located in the center of town, this Colonial Revival inn features a popular local restaurant on the premises. Norman Rockwell is said to have frequented its tavern. Stroll around historic West Stockbridge then enjoy the inn's deck cafe with its flower boxes and view of the sculpture garden of an art gallery across the street. Original lighting, hardwood floors and antiques are features of the inn. Chesterwood and Tanglewood are within easy driving distance.

Historic Interest: Norman Rockwell Museum (2 miles).
Innkeeper(s): Ed & Lisa Robbins. $60-140. MC VISA AX DS. 8 rooms. Breakfast included in rates. Types of meals: continental breakfast and early coffee/tea. Restaurant on premises. Beds: KQ. Air conditioning and ceiling fan in room. TV and VCR on premises. Weddings, small meetings, family reunions and seminars hosted. Amusement parks, antiques, shopping and sporting events nearby.

Marble Inn

4 Stockbridge Rd
West Stockbridge, MA 01266-0268
(413)232-7092

Circa 1835. This Georgian Colonial was built as the city's marble quarries and limestone works were expanding. Rooms are decorated with an impressive collection of primitive antiques. The innkeepers accent the restored white pine floors with handmade rugs. The country-style guest rooms feature furnishings such as a pencil four-poster bed or an antique white iron bed. One room includes a bath with a clawfoot tub. As a night cap, guests are treated to sherry and home baked cookies. Breakfasts include a wide variety of juices, homemade breads, fresh fruit and a selection of gourmet entrees, such as speciality  omelets, asparagus crepes or oats n' applesauce pancakes. The inn is close to Tanglewood, the Shaker Village, antique shops and much more.

Innkeeper(s): Yvonne & Joe Kopper. $85-135. MC VISA AX DS PC TC. 4 rooms with PB, 1 with FP. Breakfast included in rates. Type of meal: gourmet breakfast. Picnic lunch available. Beds: QD. Air conditioning in room. Weddings, small meetings and family reunions hosted. Antiques, fishing, downhill skiing, cross-country skiing, theater and watersports nearby.

Shaker Mill Inn

5 Albany Rd
West Stockbridge, MA 01266-9206
(413)232-8596 Fax:(413)232-4644

Circa 1987. Originally a stagecoach stop in the early 1800s, this immaculately renovated barn became the home of inventor Anson Clark, famous for the glass slide used in early photography. In 1987, the barn was renovated and additions were built to create this cozy inn. Situated on more than three acres in the heart of the Berkshires, the inn offers all of the modern amenities of luxury lodging, while maintaining many of the characteristics of the original building. The on-site restaurant, the Cafe, offers a 125-seat outdoor deck with its own pavilion kitchen and bar. The Cafe is known for its great barbecue, salad bar, grilled fish and unique pizza concoctions.

Innkeeper(s): Jonathan Rick. $85-250. EP. MC VISA AX PC. TAC10. 10 rooms with PB, 3 with FP. 4 suites. Breakfast and picnic lunch included in rates. Type of meal: continental-plus breakfast. Phone, air conditioning, ceiling fan, TV and VCR in room. Fax, copier and swimming on premises. Handicap access. Weddings, small meetings, family reunions and seminars hosted. Amusement parks, antiques, fishing, parks, shopping, downhill skiing, cross-country skiing, sporting events, golf, theater and watersports nearby.

Pets Allowed: Deposit for damage.

Williamsville Inn

Rt 41
West Stockbridge, MA 01266
(413)274-6118 Fax:(413)274-3539

Circa 1797. At the foot of Tom Ball Mountain is this Federalstyle inn, formerly the Tom Ball farm. Some guest rooms feature fireplaces or woodstoves. The inn's grounds sport gardens, a

swimming pool and tennis court. Guests often enjoy relaxing in a swing that hangs from an ancient elm. Chesterwood, Mission House, The Norman Rockwell Museum and  Tanglewood are within easy driving distance.

Innkeeper(s): Gail & Kathleen Ryan. $120-185. MC VISA AX PC. TAC10. 16 rooms with PB, 2 with FP. 1 suite. 1 conference room. Breakfast included in rates. Type of meal: full breakfast. Dinner available. Beds: KQDT. Air conditioning in room. Fax, copier, swimming and tennis on premises. 10 acres. Weddings, small meetings, family reunions and seminars hosted. Spanish, French and Some Japanese spoken. Antiques, fishing, parks, shopping, downhill skiing, cross-country skiing, theater and watersports nearby.

Pets Allowed: By special arrangement, subject to availability.

Location: Heart of the Berkshires.

Williamstown   B3

Steep Acres Farm

520 White Oaks Rd
Williamstown, MA 01267-2227
(413)458-3774

Circa 1900. Built at the turn of the century, Steep Acres was constructed as a chicken farm. The hilltop home, secluded on 50 peaceful acres, offers a view of the Berkshire Hills and the Green Mountains in Vermont. Guests are free to enjoy canoeing, fishing or swimming in the 1.5-acre pond. The interior is decorated in country style with antiques. Breakfast includes homemade maple syrup and honey.

$85-100. PC TC. 4 rooms, 1 with PB. Breakfast and afternoon tea included in rates. Types of meals: full breakfast, gourmet breakfast and early coffee/tea. Beds: TD. Ceiling fan in room. Swimming on premises. 50 acres. Weddings and family reunions hosted. Antiques, fishing, parks, shopping, downhill skiing, cross-country skiing, sporting events, golf and theater nearby.

Woods Hole   J15

The Marlborough B&B

PO Box 238
Woods Hole, MA 02543-0238
(508)548-6218 (800)320-2322 Fax:(508)457-7519

Circa 1942. This is a faithful reproduction of a Cape-style cottage complete with picket fence and rambling roses. An English paddle-tennis court and swimming pool are popular spots in summer. In winter, breakfast is  served beside a roaring fire. The inn is the closest bed & breakfast to the ferries to Martha's Vineyard and Nantucket.

Innkeeper(s): Al Hammond. $65-125. MC VISA AX PC. TAC10. 6 rooms with PB. 1 cottage. Breakfast included in rates. Types of meals: gourmet breakfast and early coffee/tea. Beds: QD. Air conditioning in room. TV, fax, swimming and tennis on premises. Antiques, fishing, shopping, theater and watersports nearby.

Location: Near Falmouth historic district.

Publicity: *Cape Cod Life.*

"Our stay at the Marlborough was a little bit of heaven."

Yarmouth Port 117

Colonial House Inn

Rt 6 A, 277 Main St
Yarmouth Port, MA 02675
(508)362-4348 (800)999-3416 Fax:(508)362-8034

Circa 1730. Although the original structure was built in pre-revolutionary times, a third floor was later added and another section was shipped in from Nantucket. The innkeepers reno-

vated the carriage house, creating 10 new rooms. Dining areas include the Colonial Room with hand-stenciled walls and a fireplace, and the Common Room, a recent glass-enclosed addition with a view of the veranda and town green. A traditional Thanksgiving dinner is served every year, and guests may enjoy other specialties, including murder-mystery, Las Vegas and wine-tasting weekends.

Innkeeper(s): Malcolm Perna. $70-95. MAP, AP, EP. MC VISA AX DS PC TC. TAC10. 21 rooms with PB, 3 with FP. 2 suites. 3 conference rooms. Breakfast and dinner included in rates. Type of meal: continental breakfast. Restaurant on premises. Beds: KQDT. Phone, air conditioning and ceiling fan in room. VCR, fax, copier, spa, swimming, sauna, library and child care on premises. Handicap access. Weddings, small meetings, family reunions and seminars hosted. French, Spanish and Italian spoken. Antiques, fishing, parks, shopping, cross-country skiing, sporting events, theater and watersports nearby.

Pets Allowed: Certain rooms.

Publicity: *New York Times, Yankee, Cape Cod Life, Boston Globe, Newsday.*

"The nicest place I've ever stayed."

Liberty Hill Inn

77 Main St, Rt 6a
Yarmouth Port, MA 02675-1709
(508)362-3976 (800)821-3977

Circa 1825. Just back from historic Old King's Highway, this country inn is a restored Greek Revival mansion. It is located on the site of the original Liberty

Pole dating from Revolutionary times. A romantic decor includes fine antiques and thick carpets, enhancing the tall windows and high ceilings. Guests can request rooms

with a fireplace or double whirlpool tub. The innkeepers now offer four guest rooms in a restored historic barn. Stroll past the inn's flower-edged lawns for a brief walk to antique shops, auctions and restaurants. The house was built by shipwrights.

Historic Interest: Two historic restorations from the 18th century are within a half mile. Maritime history is celebrated each May with tours of historic buildings.

Innkeeper(s): Jack & Beth Flanagan. $85-185. MC VISA AX PC TC. TAC10. 9 rooms with PB. Types of meals: gourmet breakfast and early coffee/tea. Beds: KQT. Phone, air conditioning and ceiling fan in room. Small meetings and seminars hosted. Antiques, fishing, parks, shopping, theater and watersports nearby.

Location: On Cape Cod, 10 minutes north of Hyannis, 90 minutes from Boston.

Publicity: *Cape Cod Life, Colonial Homes.*

"Immaculate and incredibly clean. Plenty of information for one and all. Thank you for a delightful stay."

Olde Captain's Inn on the Cape

101 Main St Rt 6A
Yarmouth Port, MA 02675-1709
(508)362-4496 (888)407-7161

Circa 1835. Located in the historic district and on Captain's Mile, this house is in the National Register. It is decorated in a traditional style, with coordinated wallpapers and carpets, and there are two suites that include kitchens and living rooms. Apple trees, blackberries and raspberries grow on the acre of grounds and often contribute to the breakfast menus. There is a summer veranda overlooking the property. Good restaurants are within walking distance.

Historic Interest: Plymouth Rock and Plantation (30 miles).

Innkeeper(s): Sven Tilly. $40-100. 3 rooms, 1 with PB. 2 suites. Breakfast included in rates. Type of meal: continental-plus breakfast. Beds: KQD. TV in room. Antiques, fishing, shopping, sporting events, theater and watersports nearby.

Location: Cape Cod.

One Centre Street Inn

1 Center St
Yarmouth Port, MA 02675-1342
(508)362-8910 (888)407-1653

Circa 1824. A rustic cookstove warms the dining room where such items as freshly baked scones, homemade granola and Orange French toast topped with a Strawberry-Grand Marnier sauce get the morning off to a perfect start. This National Register inn was used as a church parsonage when it was built in the 1820s. Four-poster or brass beds decorated the guest rooms, appointed in a mix of styles, from Queen Anne to Colonial.

Innkeeper(s): Karen Iannello. $75-130. MC VISA PC TC. TAC10. 6 rooms, 4 with PB, 1 with FP. Breakfast included in rates. Types of meals: full breakfast and gourmet breakfast. Beds: QDT. Bicycles on premises. Small meetings and family reunions hosted. Antiques, fishing, parks, shopping, theater and watersports nearby.

Michigan

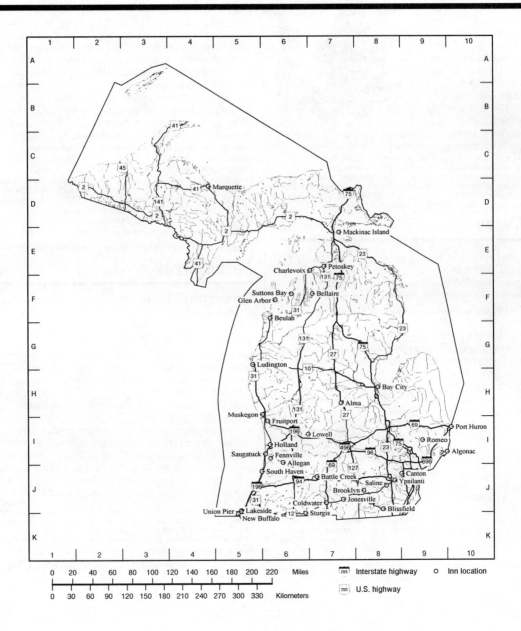

(nn) Interstate highway	○ Inn location
(nn) U.S. highway	

Miles: 0 20 40 60 80 100 120 140 160 180 200 220

Kilometers: 0 30 60 90 120 150 180 210 240 270 300 330

Algonac I9

Linda's Lighthouse Inn

5965 Pointe Tremble Rd Box 828
Algonac, MI 48001-4229
(810)794-2992 Fax:(810)794-2992

Circa 1909. Overlooking Dickerson Island, on the north branch of the St. Clair River, is this two-story Colonial inn, which once aided bootleg-

gers who brought in liquor from Canada during Prohibition. Guests who arrive by boat and use the inn's 100 feet of dockage will have transportation to restaurants provided for them. Guests choose from the Jacuzzi, Lighthouse, Rose and Duck rooms, all featuring feather pillows. St. John's Marsh is less than a half-mile away.

Innkeeper(s): Ron & Linda (Russell) Yetsko. $75-125. MC VISA AX TC. 4 rooms with PB. Breakfast and evening snack included in rates. Types of meals: gourmet breakfast and early coffee/tea. Picnic lunch available. Beds: QD. Phone, air conditioning, turndown service and ceiling fan in room. TV, VCR, copier and bicycles on premises. Antiques, fishing, parks, shopping, cross-country skiing and watersports nearby. Pets Allowed.

Allegan I6

Winchester Inn

524 Marshall St M-89
Allegan, MI 49010-1632
(616)673-3620 (800)582-5694

Circa 1864. This neo-Italian Renaissance mansion was built of double-layer brick and has been restored to its original beauty. Surrounded by a unique, hand-poured iron fence, the inn is decorated with period antiques, including antique toys and trains. The innkeeper's love for Christmas and other holidays is evident. Many christmas decorations remain up throughout the year. The tree in the dining

room is decorated for whatever holiday is near. For instance, around Halloween, pumpkins and gourds decorate the tree. Each guest room has it's own theme. One is a Christmas room, another features an angel theme, and one is decorated for the current holiday.

Historic Interest: Historical bridge (one-half mile), located in middle of a historic district.

Innkeeper(s): Denise & Dave Ferber. $70-90. MC VISA AX PC TC. TAC10. 4 rooms with PB. Breakfast included in rates. Types of meals: continental-plus breakfast, full breakfast and early coffee/tea. Beds: KQD. Phone and ceiling fan in room. TV on premises. Weddings, small meetings and family reunions hosted. Antiques, fishing, parks, shopping, downhill skiing, cross-country skiing, sporting events, theater and watersports nearby.

Location: Near Grand Rapids, Kalamazoo, Holland, Saugatuck and Lake Michigan State Forest.

Publicity: *Architectural Digest, Home and Away, Midwest Living, Detroit Free Press, Cleveland Plain Dealer, Grand Rapids Press.*

"*This is one of Michigan's loveliest country inns.*"

Alma H7

Saravilla

633 N State St
Alma, MI 48801-1640
(517)463-4078

Circa 1894. This 11,000-square-foot Dutch Colonial home with its Queen Anne influences was built as a magnificent wedding gift for lumber baron Ammi W. Wright's only surviving child, Sara. Wright spared no expense building this mansion for his daughter, and the innkeepers have spared nothing in restoring the home to its former prominence. The foyer and dining room boast imported English oak woodwork. The foyer's hand-painted canvas wallcoverings and the ballroom's embossed wallpaper come from France. The home still features original leaded-glass windows, built-in bookcases, window seats and light fixtures. In 1993, the innkeepers added a sunroom with a hot tub that overlooks a formal garden. The full, formal breakfast includes such treats as homemade granola, freshly made coffeecakes, breads, muffins and a mix of entrees.

Historic Interest: Alma is within three hours of almost every portion of Michigan's lower peninsula and plenty of historic sites.

Innkeeper(s): Linda and Jon Darrow. $55-110. MC VISA DS PC TC. 7 rooms with PB, 3 with FP. Breakfast and afternoon tea included in rates. Type of meal: full breakfast. Room service available. Beds: KQDT. Antiques, fishing, cross-country skiing and theater nearby.

Location: Twenty minutes from Michigan's largest casino.

Publicity: *Morning Sun, Saginaw News, Sault Sunday.*

"*I suggest we stay longer next time. We are looking forward to that visit.*"

Battle Creek J7

Greencrest Manor

6174 Halbert Rd E
Battle Creek, MI 49017-9449
(616)962-8633 Fax:(616)962-7254

Circa 1934. Once used as monestary, this 13,000-square-foot French Normandy mansion rests on 20 acres. Extensive gardens are lush with apple orchards, tiered gardens, herb gardens, reflecting pools, Japanese maples and cherry trees. It is in the National Register as a rare example of Norman-style architecture in the United States. The inn's inviting drawing room boasts egg-and-dart molding, sofas and drapes in an English cabbage-rose print and floor-to-ceiling French windows. The dining room has a white marble fireplace, Parisian chandelier and Oriental carpet. Ask for the VIP Suite for a king bed, white marble fireplace and double whirlpool showers.

Innkeeper(s): Tom & Kathy VanDaff. $75-200. MC VISA AX DC PC TC. 8 rooms, 6 with PB, 1 with FP. 6 suites. 3 conference rooms. Breakfast included in rates. Type of meal: continental breakfast. Banquet service and catering service available. Beds: KQD. Phone, air conditioning, ceiling fan and TV in room. Fax, copier and library on premises. 20 acres. Weddings and small meetings hosted. Antiques, parks, shopping, cross-country skiing, golf nearby.

Publicity: *Country Inns, Lifestyles.*

"*I've been in Normandy many times, I've never seen anything like your French Chateau.*"

Greencrest Manor

6174 Halbert Rd E
Battle Creek, MI 49017-9449
(616)962-8633 Fax:(616)962-7254

Circa 1934. Once used as monestary, this 13,000-square-foot French Normandy mansion rests on 20 acres. Extensive gardens are lush with apple orchards, tiered gardens, herb gardens, reflecting pools, Japanese maples and cherry trees. It is in the National Register as a rare example of Norman style architecture in the United States. The inn's inviting drawing room boasts egg-and-dart molding, sofas and drapes in an English cabbage-rose print and floor-to-ceiling French windows. The dining room has a white marble fireplace, Parisian chandelier and Oriental carpet. Ask for the VIP Suite for a king bed, white marble fireplace and double whirlpool showers.

Innkeeper(s): Tom & Kathy VanDaff. $75-200. MC VISA AX DC PC TC. 8 rooms, 6 with PB, 1 with FP. 6 suites. 3 conference rooms. Breakfast included in rates. Type of meal: continental breakfast. Banquet service and catering service available. Beds: KQD. Phone, air conditioning, ceiling fan and TV in room. Fax, copier and library on premises. 20 acres. Weddings, small meetings hosted. Antiques, parks, shopping, cross-country skiing and golf nearby.

Publicity: *Country Inns, Lifestyles.*

"I've been in Normandy many times, I've never seen anything like your French Chateau."

Bay City　　　　　H8

Clements Inn

1712 Center Ave M-25
Bay City, MI 48708-6122
(517)894-4600 (800)442-4605 Fax:(517)895-8535

Circa 1886. The amber-paned windows and oak ceilings of this three-story Queen Anne Victorian inn are just a few of its impressive features. Built by William Clements, the home joined a number of other impressive estates on Center Avenue, most of which were owned by lumber barons. The inn's well-appointed guest rooms are named for famous authors or fictional characters, continuing a strong tradition started by Clements, a collector of rare books. A winding staircase, original gas lighting fixtures and hand-carved woodwork have impressed many visitors.

Innkeeper(s): Brian & Karen Hepp. $70-175. MC VISA AX DC DS TC. 6 rooms with PB. 2 suites. Breakfast and evening snack included in rates. Type of meal: continental-plus breakfast. Beds: KQD. Phone, air conditioning, TV and VCR in room. Fax on premises. Antiques, fishing, parks, shopping, downhill skiing, cross-country skiing and theater nearby.

Bellaire　　　　　F7

Bellaire B&B

212 Park St
Bellaire, MI 49615-9595
(616)533-6077 (800)545-0780

Circa 1879. Maple trees line the drive to this American Gothic home. Relax on the porch swing, or enjoy the warmth of a crackling fire in the parlor. The fresh, family-style continental-plus breakfast is a treat. A nearby park offers swimming, tennis, basketball, shuffleboard and a playground. Browse through the downtown shops or hunt for

antiques. Bellaire hosts several fun events during the year, including a Rubber Ducky Race in August.

Innkeeper(s): David Schulz & Jim Walker. $65-95. 4 rooms, 2 with PB. Type of meal: continental-plus breakfast. Afternoon tea available. Beds: QF.

Grand Victorian B&B Inn

402 N Bridge St
Bellaire, MI 49615-9591
(616)533-6111 (800)336-3860 Fax:(616)533-8197

Circa 1895. It's hard to believe that anything but joy has ever been associated with this beautiful Queen Anne Victorian inn, but its original owner, who built it in anticipation of his upcoming nuptials, left town broken-hearted when his wedding plans fell through. The eye-pleasing inn, with its gables, square corner towers, bays and overhangs, is listed in the National Register of Historic Places. There is much to do in this popular area of Northern Michigan, with its famous nearby skiing and fishing spots, but the  inn's impressive interior may entice guests to stay on the premises. Guest rooms are well-appointed with period antiques and lavish touches. Visitors may borrow a bicycle built for two for a relaxing tour of town.

Innkeeper(s): Jill Watson. $95-135. MC VISA AX. 4 rooms with PB. Breakfast and afternoon tea included in rates. Types of meals: full breakfast and early coffee/tea. Picnic lunch available. Beds: QD. Air conditioning in room. VCR on premises. Weddings, small meetings, family reunions and seminars hosted. Antiques, fishing, shopping, downhill skiing, cross-country skiing and watersports nearby.

Publicity: *Featured on Nabisco Crackers/Cookies Boxes Promotion, Midwest Living, Country Inns.*

"We certainly enjoyed our visit to the Grand Victorian. It has been our pleasure to stay in B&Bs in several countries, but never one more beautiful and almost never with such genial hosts."

Beulah　　　　　F6

Brookside Inn

115 N Michigan, PO Box 506
Beulah, MI 49617
(616)882-9688

Circa 1939. Antiques and country furnishings decorate the interior of Brookside Inn, located near Crystal Lake. King-size canopy waterbeds, Polynesian spas and wood-burning stoves are just a few of the romantic amenities. The inn also boasts a 100,000-bottle wine cellar. Both breakfast and dinner are included in the rates, and guests may dine on the outdoor deck or by the fireplace. The inn's seven-acre grounds include a bridge to an herb and flower garden. Private sauna, steam bath and tanning bed are available.

Innkeeper(s): Pam & Kirk Lorenz. $205-265. MAP. MC VISA AX DC DS. 20 rooms with PB, 19 with FP. 1 conference room. Type of meal: full breakfast. Dinner available. Restaurant on premises. Beds: KW. Spa and sauna on premises. Handicap access. Downhill skiing and cross-country skiing nearby.

Publicity: *Detroit Free Press.*

"Michigan's romantic retreat...works a spell, Rick Sylvain, Detroit Free Press."

Blissfield J8

Hiram D. Ellis Inn

415 W Adrian St US Hwy 223
Blissfield, MI 49228-1001
(517)486-3155

Circa 1883. This red brick Italianate house is in a village setting directly across from the 1851 Hathaway House, an elegant historic restaurant. Rooms at the Hiram D. Ellis Inn feature handsome antique bedsteads, armoires and floral wallpapers. Breakfast is served in the inn's common room, and the innkeeper receives rave reviews on her peach and apple dishes. (There are apple and peach trees on the property.) Bicycles are available for riding around town, or you can walk to the train station and board the murder-mystery dinner train that runs on weekends.
Innkeeper(s): Christine Webster & Frank Seely. $75-95. MC VISA AX PC TC. TAC10. 4 rooms with PB. Breakfast included in rates. Types of meals: continental-plus breakfast, full breakfast and early coffee/tea. Beds: QD. Phone, air conditioning and TV in room. Bicycles on premises. Small meetings, family reunions and seminars hosted. Antiques, fishing, parks, shopping, cross-country skiing, golf and theater nearby. Pets Allowed: small pets only.
Publicity: *Ann Arbor News, Michigan Living.*

"*I have now experienced what it is truly like to have been treated like a queen.*"

Brooklyn J8

Dewey Lake Manor

11811 Laird Rd
Brooklyn, MI 49230-9035
(517)467-7122

Circa 1868. This Italianate house overlooks Dewey Lake and is situated on 18 acres in the Irish Hills. The house is furnished in a country Victorian style with antiques. An enclosed porch is a favorite spot to relax and take in the views of the lake while having breakfast. Favorite pastimes  include lakeside bonfires in the summertime and ice skating or cross-country skiing in the winter.
Historic Interest: The Great Saulk Trail (2 miles from U.S. 12), Walker Tavern, a stagecoach stop on the trail (2 miles), Saint Joseph Catholic Shrine (5 miles).
Innkeeper(s): Barb & Joe Phillips. $55-75. MC VISA AX. 5 rooms with PB. 1 conference room. Breakfast included in rates. Meals: full breakfast and early coffee/tea. Evening snack and picnic lunch available. Beds: QDT. Phone, air conditioning, ceiling fan and TV in room. VCR on premises. 18 acres. Weddings, small meetings, family reunions hosted. Antiques, fishing, shopping, cross-country skiing, sporting events, golf, theater, watersports nearby. Location: In Irish Hills of southern Michigan.
Publicity: *Ann Arbor News.*

"*I came back and brought my friends. It was wonderful.*"

Canton J9

Willow Brook Inn

44255 Warren Rd
Canton, MI 48187-2147
(313)454-0019 (888)454-1919

Circa 1929. Willow Brook winds its way through the backyard of this aptly named inn, situated on a lush, wooded acre. Innkeepers Bernadette and Michael Van Lenten filled their home with oak

and pine country antiques and beds covered with soft quilts. They also added special toys and keepsakes from their own childhood to add a homey touch. After a peaceful rest, guests are invited to partake in the morning meal either in the "Teddy Bear" dining room, in the privacy of their rooms or in the sun room. Breakfasts consist of luscious treats such as homemade breads, scones topped with devon cream and a rich, egg dish.
Historic Interest: The Henry Ford Museum and historic Greenfield Village are just 20 minutes away.
Innkeeper(s): Bernadette & Michael Van Lenten. $85-115. MC VISA. TAC10. 4 rooms with PB. 2 suites. Breakfast and evening snack included in rates. Types of meals: gourmet breakfast and early coffee/tea. Afternoon tea, picnic lunch and catering service available. Beds: KQDT. Phone, turndown service, ceiling fan and VCR in room. Fax, copier, bicycles, pet boarding and child care on premises. Weddings, small meetings and family reunions hosted. French spoken. Antiques, parks, shopping, cross-country skiing, sporting events, theater and watersports nearby.
Pets Allowed: Not permitted in bedrooms.
Publicity: *Canton Observer, Canton Eagle, Detroit News.*

"*We've stayed in B&B's in Europe, Australia and New Zealand, and we put yours at the top of the list for luxury, friendly care and delicious food (especially the scones). We're glad we found you. Thanks.*"

Charlevoix E7

Bridge Street Inn

113 Michigan Ave
Charlevoix, MI 49720-1819
(616)547-6606 Fax:(616)547-1812

Circa 1895. This three-story Colonial Revival structure recalls the bygone era when Charlevoix was home to many grand hotels. Originally a guest "cottage" of one of those large hotels, this inn boasts nine gracious guest rooms, many of which are available with private bath. The rooms sport antique furnishings, floral rugs and wooden floors and offer stunning views of the surrounding lakes. Guests are within walking distance of Lake Michigan's beaches, Round Lake's harbor and Lake  Charlevoix's boating and fishing. Be sure to inquire in advance about the inn's many discounts and special rate for small groups.
Innkeeper(s): Vera & John McKown. $64-180. MC VISA PC TC. TAC10. 9 rooms, 3 with PB. Breakfast included in rates. Type of meal: continental-plus breakfast. Beds: QT. Ceiling fan in room. TV, VCR and fax on premises. Family reunions hosted. German spoken. Antiques, fishing, parks, shopping, skiing, sporting events, theater and watersports nearby.

Coldwater J7

Chicago Pike Inn

215 E Chicago St
Coldwater, MI 49036-2001
(517)279-8744

Circa 1903. This exquisite colonial mansion was built by an architect who designed many of the homes on Mackinac Island. Furnished with period antiques, the inn features chandeliers, stained glass, parquet flooring and a stunning cherry staircase. Its name is derived from Coldwater's midway location

on the old Detroit-Chicago turnpike. Guests will enjoy exploring Coldwater's historic buildings or perhaps a visit to the Victorian-style Tibbits Opera House built in 1882.

Innkeeper(s): Becky Schultz. $90-180. MC VISA AX PC TC. 8 rooms with PB, 1 with FP. 2 suites. 1 conference room. Breakfast included in rates. Types of meals: full breakfast and early coffee/tea. Beds: QT. Phone, turn-down service, ceiling fan, TV and VCR in room. Fax, copier, bicycles and library on premises. Weddings, small meetings, family reunions and seminars hosted. Antiques, fishing, parks, shopping, cross-country skiing, sporting events, theater and watersports nearby.

"Your warmth and hospitality added so much to the time we spent with you."

Fennville   I6

The Kingsley House

626 W Main St
Fennville, MI 49408-9442
(616)561-6425 Fax:(616)561-2593
E-mail: garyking@accn.org

Circa 1886. Construction of this Queen Anne Victorian, with a three-story turret, was paid for in silver bricks by the Kingsley family. Mr. Kingsley is noted for having introduced the apple tree to the area. In recognition of him, guest rooms are named Dutchess, Golden Delicious, Granny Smith, McIntosh and Jonathan. The Northern Spy, complete with hot tub, is nestled in the third-floor suite. A winding oak staircase leads to the antique-filled guest chambers. Family heirlooms and other period pieces add to the inn's elegance.

Historic Interest: Historic Saugatuck and Holland just minutes away.

Innkeeper(s): Gary & Kari King. $80-145. MC VISA AX DS PC TC. TAC10. 8 rooms with PB, 3 with FP. 3 suites. Breakfast and evening snack included in rates. Types of meals: continental-plus breakfast, full breakfast and early coffee/tea. Picnic lunch available. Beds: KQD. Air conditioning, ceiling fan and TV in room. Fax, bicycles and library on premises. Small meetings and seminars hosted. Antiques, fishing, parks, shopping, downhill skiing, cross-country skiing, sporting events, theater and watersports nearby.

Location: 196 South of Holland to Exit 34 then East 5 miles.

Publicity: *Innsider, Battle Creek Enquirer, Fennville Herald, Commercial Record, Glamour, Country, Country Victorian Decorating Ideas, National Geographic Traveler.*

"It was truly enjoyable. You have a lovely home and a gracious way of entertaining."

Fruitport   I6

Village Park B&B

60 Park St
Fruitport, MI 49415-9668
(616)865-6289 (800)469-1118

Circa 1873. Located in the midst of Western Michigan's Tri-Cities area, this inn's small-town village location offers comfort and relaxation to those busy partaking of the many nearby activities.

This country classic farmhouse-style inn overlooks Spring Lake and a park where guests may picnic, play tennis, use a pedestrian/bike path and boat launch. There also is a hot tub and exercise room on the premises. The inn offers six guest rooms, all with private bath. A library is just across the street. P.J. Hoffmaster State Park, the Gillette Nature Sand Dune Center are nearby.

Innkeeper(s): John Hewett. $60-95. MC VISA PC TC. TAC10. 6 rooms with PB. Breakfast included in rates. Types of meals: continental breakfast, continental-plus breakfast, full breakfast and early coffee/tea. Beds: KDT. Air conditioning in room. TV, VCR, fax, spa, sauna and bicycles on premises. Small meetings and family reunions hosted. Amusement parks, antiques, fishing, parks, shopping, cross-country skiing, theater and watersports nearby.

Glen Arbor   F6

The Sylvan Inn

PO Box 648, 6680 Western (M-109)
Glen Arbor, MI 49636-0309
(616)334-4333

Circa 1885. During restoration, innkeepers Jenny and Bill Olson worked diligently to maintain their 19th-century farmhouse's historic flavor. The older portion of the inn is furnished with antiques, and guest rooms feature brass or iron beds dressed with fine linens and down comforters. In the newer "Great House," there are six additional guest rooms with more contemporary decor and furnishings. There are plenty of things to see and do in the Glen Arbor area, including winery tours, activities at Lake Michigan, hiking, skiing, golf and more.

Innkeeper(s): Jenny & Bill Olson. $60-120. MC VISA PC TC. TAC10. 14 rooms, 7 with PB. 1 suite. Breakfast included in rates. Types of meals: continental-plus breakfast and early coffee/tea. Beds: QT. Phone, ceiling fan and TV in room. Spa and sauna on premises. Handicap access. Weddings and family reunions hosted. Antiques, fishing, parks, shopping, downhill skiing, cross-country skiing, theater and watersports nearby.

"Your wonderful service and luxurious accommodations helped to make our wedding a very memorable occasion."

White Gull Inn

PO Box 351, 5926 SW Manitou Trl
Glen Arbor, MI 49636-9702
(616)334-4486 Fax:(616)334-3546

Circa 1900. One of Michigan's most scenic areas is home to the White Gull Inn. With the Sleeping Bear Dunes and alluring Glen Lake just minutes away, visitors will find no shortage of sightseeing or recreational activities during a stay here. The inn's farmhouse setting, country decor and five comfortable guest rooms offer a relaxing haven no matter what the season. Lake Michigan is a block away, and guests also will enjoy the area's fine dining and shopping opportunities.

Innkeeper(s): Bill & Dotti Thompson. $65-75. MC VISA AX DS TC. 6 rooms, 1 with FP. Breakfast included in rates. Type of meal: continental-plus breakfast. Beds: QDT. Air conditioning, TV and VCR in room. Family reunions hosted. Antiques, fishing, parks, shopping, downhill skiing, cross-country skiing, theater and watersports nearby.

Holland   I6

Bonnie's Parsonage 1908 B&B

6 E 24th St/Central Ave
Holland, MI 49423-4817
(616)396-1316

Circa 1908. Built as the parsonage by one of Holland's Dutch churches, this American Four-Square home housed seven ministers and their families through the years. Since 1984, it has

served as a bed & breakfast. The inn features restored woodwork, leaded glass and pocket doors. Holland recently celebrated its sesquicentennial. Close to fine dining, shops and bike trails.

Historic Interest: Cappon House (a few blocks), Lake Michigan beaches, the historic Saugatuck Resort (12-mile drive).

Innkeeper(s): Bonnie McVoy-Verwys. $80-100. PC TC. TAC10. 3 rooms, 2 with PB. Breakfast included in rates. Types of meals: full breakfast and gourmet breakfast. Beds: DT. Air conditioning, turndown service and ceiling fan in room. VCR and library on premises. Antiques, parks, shopping, cross-country skiing and theater nearby.

Location: Close to Hope College.

Publicity: *Detroit Free Press Travel Tales, Midwest Living.*

"Charming. We slept so well! Thank you again for a pleasant visit to a beautiful city in Michigan. And our special thanks to Ms. Verwys and her wonderful home."

Dutch Colonial Inn

560 Central Ave
Holland, MI 49423-4846
(616)396-3664 Fax:(616)396-0461

Circa 1928. Romantic rooms at this Dutch-inspired home include the Hideaway Suite with a Battenberg lace coverlet and whirlpool tub for two. Another choice is the Jenny Lind suite with a king bed, raspberry and creme decor and a whirlpool tub for two. A few prized family heirlooms from the Netherlands are featured.

Historic Interest: The Cappon House Museum (5 minutes).

Innkeeper(s): Bob & Pat Elenbaas. $60-150. MC VISA AX DS PC. 4 rooms with PB. 2 suites. Breakfast included in rates. Types of meals: full breakfast and early coffee/tea. Beds: KQ. Phone, air conditioning and TV in room. VCR and fax on premises. Antiques, fishing, parks, shopping, cross-country skiing and watersports nearby.

Publicity: *Shoreline Living, Country Folk Art.*

"Thank you again for your generous hospitality, Dutch cleanliness and excellent breakfasts."

The Old Holland Inn

133 W 11th St
Holland, MI 49423-3205
(616)396-6601

Circa 1895. Innkeeper Dave Plaggemars is a descendant of one of Holland's 10 original founding families. The entrance hall to his National Register Victorian home opens to an oak staircase. Grecian columns support an elaborate fireplace with brass inlays and an 1895 heat-reflecting insert. The oak pocket doors were crafted by first-generation Dutch woodworkers. Now, family collections and period antiques are scattered throughout the spacious guest rooms. A pear hedge on the property provided the inspiration for Dave Plaggemars' poached pears in cranberry sauce. The inn is within walking distance to downtown Holland.

Innkeeper(s): Dave & Fran Plaggemars. $75-115. DS. 5 rooms, 2 with PB. 1 conference room. Type of meal: continental-plus breakfast. Beds: DT.

Publicity: *The Ann Arbor News, Holland Evening Sentinel, Country Inn Cookbook, Chicago Sun-Times.*

"We enjoyed the touches of live flowers, a selection of books and the wonderful deck."

Jonesville
J7

Horse & Carriage B&B

7020 Brown Rd
Jonesville, MI 49250-9720
(517)849-2732 Fax:(517)849-2732

Circa 1898. Enjoy a peaceful old-fashioned day on the farm. Milk a cow, gather eggs and cuddle baby lambs. In the winter, families are treated to a horse-drawn sleigh ride at this 18th-century home, which is surrounded by a 700-acre dairy farm. In the warmer months, horse-drawn carriage rides pass down an old country lane past Buck Lake. The innkeeper's family has lived on the property for more than 150 years. The home itself was built as a one-room schoolhouse. A mix of contemporary and country furnishings decorate the interior. The Rainbow Room, a perfect place for children, offers twin beds and a playroom. Guests are treated to hearty breakfasts made with farm-fresh eggs and fresh fruits and vegetables.

Innkeeper(s): Keith Brown & family. $55-100. PC. 3 rooms, 1 with PB. 1 suite. Breakfast and evening snack included in rates. Types of meals: continental breakfast, continental-plus breakfast, full breakfast, gourmet breakfast and early coffee/tea. Beds: QT. Phone in room. Fax and copier on premises. 700 acres. Small meetings and family reunions hosted. Portuguese spoken. Antiques, fishing, parks, shopping, cross-country skiing, sporting events, theater and watersports nearby.

Munro House B&B

202 Maumee St
Jonesville, MI 49250-1247
(517)849-9292

Circa 1840. Ten fireplaces are found at the historic Munro House, named for George C. Munro, a Civil War brigadier general. The Greek Revival structure, Hillsdale County's first brick house, also served as a safe haven for slaves on the Underground Railroad. Visitors can still see a secret room, once used for hiding slaves. Many guests enjoy selecting one of the library's special-interest books and spend a quiet evening in front of a  fireplace in their room. Seven guest rooms include a fireplace, and two rooms have a Jacuzzi tub. Breakfast is eaten overlooking the inn's gardens. Hillsdale College is just five miles away.

Innkeeper(s): Joyce Yarde. $75-150. MC VISA. 7 rooms with PB, 5 with FP. Breakfast included in rates. Type of meal: full breakfast. Evening snack available. Phone, air conditioning, ceiling fan and TV in room. VCR on premises. Weddings, small meetings, family reunions and seminars hosted. Antiques, shopping, cross-country skiing, sporting events and theater nearby.

"What a delightful stay. Beautiful house, wonderful history and a delightful hostess. Felt like we knew her forever. We will tell all our friends."

Lakeside
J5

Lakeside Inn

15281 Lakeshore Rd
Lakeside, MI 49116
(616)469-0600 Fax:(616)469-1914

Circa 1890. Totally renovated in 1995, the Lakeside Inn and Spa features original wood pillars and rustic stone fireplaces in the lobby and ballroom. The inn overlooks Lake Michigan located just across the street. Each individually decorated room combines the special ambiance of comfortable antique furnishings with modern amenities like TVs, air conditioning and private baths. Many of the rooms feature lake views and/or Jacuzzi tubs. Besides board games or cards for indoor recreation, the inn offers a spa, complete with sauna, exercise equipment and massage. Hiking, horseback riding, swimming or sailing located nearby.

Historic Interest: Located one hour from Chicago.

Innkeeper(s): Connie Williams. $75-150. MC VISA DS PC TC. TAC10. 30 rooms with PB. 1 suite. 1 conference room. Breakfast included in rates. Meals: continental breakfast, continental-plus breakfast and full breakfast. Picnic lunch, lunch, catering service and catered breakfast available. Restaurant on premises. Beds: KQDT. Air conditioning and TV in room. Fax, copier, spa, swimming, sauna and bicycles on premises. Handicap access. Weddings, small meetings, family reunions and seminars hosted. Antiques, fishing, parks, shopping, cross-country skiing, golf and watersports nearby.

Pets Allowed: Restricted to certain conditions.

Publicity: *Chicago Tribune.*

Lowell   I6

McGee Homestead B&B

2534 Alden Nash NE
Lowell, MI 49331
(616)897-8142

Circa 1880. Just 18 miles from Grand Rapids, travelers will find the McGee Homestead B&B, an Italianate farmhouse with four antique-filled guest rooms. Surrounded by orchards, it is one of the largest farmhouses in the area. Breakfasts feature the inn's own fresh eggs. Guests may golf at an adjacent course or enjoy

nearby fishing and boating. Lowell is home to Michigan's largest antique mall, and many historic covered bridges are found in the surrounding countryside. Travelers who remain on the farm may relax in a hammock or visit a barn full of petting animals.

Innkeeper(s): Bill & Ardie Barber. $38-58. MC VISA AX DS PC TC. 4 rooms with PB. 1 conference room. Breakfast, afternoon tea and evening snack included in rates. Types of meals: full breakfast and early coffee/tea. Beds: KDT. Phone, air conditioning, turndown service, ceiling fan and VCR in room. Library and child care on premises. Small meetings hosted. Antiques, fishing, parks, shopping, downhill skiing and cross-country skiing nearby.

Ludington   G5

Lamplighter B&B

602 E Ludington Ave
Ludington, MI 49431-2223
(616)843-9792 (800)301-9792 Fax:(616)845-6070
E-mail: catsup@aol.com

Circa 1895. This Queen Anne home offers convenient access to Lake Michigan's beaches, the Badger Car Ferry to Wisconsin and Michigan state parks. A collection of European antiques, original paintings and lithographs decorate the inn. The home's centerpiece, a golden oak curved staircase, leads guests up to their rooms. Two rooms feature whirlpool tubs, one a fireplace.

The innkeepers have created a mix of hospitality and convenience that draws both vacationers and business travelers. A full, gourmet breakfast is served each morning. Freddy, the inn's resident cocker spaniel, is always available for a tour of the area. The innkeepers are fluent in German.

Innkeeper(s): Judy & Heinz Bertram. $89-129. MC VISA AX DS PC TC. TAC10. 5 rooms with PB, 1 with FP. Breakfast included in rates. Types of meals: gourmet breakfast and early coffee/tea. Beds: QD. Phone, air conditioning, turndown service and TV in room. VCR, fax and copier on premises. German spoken. Amusement parks, antiques, fishing, parks, shopping, cross-country skiing, golf and watersports nearby.

"For my husbands first bed and breakfast experience, it couldn't have been better."

The Inn at Ludington

701 E Ludington Ave
Ludington, MI 49431-2224
(616)845-7055 (800)845-9170

Circa 1890. This Queen Anne Victorian was built during the heyday of Ludington's lumbering era by a local pharmacist and doctor. Despite its elegant exterior with its three-story turret, the innkeepers stress relaxation at their inn. The rooms are filled with comfortable, vintage furnishings. Guests can snuggle up with a book in front of a warming fireplace or enjoy a soak in a clawfoot tub. A hearty, buffet-style breakfast is served each morning. The innkeepers take great pride in their cuisine and are always happy to share some of their award-winning recipes with guests. After a day of beachcombing, antiquing, cross-country skiing or perhaps a bike ride, guests return to the inn to find a chocolate atop their pillow. Don't forget to ask about the innkeepers' murder-mystery weekends.

Innkeeper(s): Diane Shields & David Nemitz. $70-90. MC VISA AX PC TC. TAC10. 6 rooms with PB, 2 with FP. 1 suite. Breakfast included in rates. Types of meals: full breakfast and early coffee/tea. Picnic lunch available. Beds: QD. Air conditioning, turndown service, ceiling fan and TV in room. Fax, copier and library on premises. Weddings, small meetings and seminars hosted. Amusement parks, antiques, fishing, parks, shopping, downhill skiing, cross-country skiing, theater and watersports nearby.

Location: Near Lake Michigan.

Publicity: *Ludington Daily News, Detroit Free Press, Chicago Tribune, Country Accents.*

"Loved the room and everything else about the house."

Mackinac Island   E7

Haan's 1830 Inn

PO Box 123
Mackinac Island, MI 49757-0123
(906)847-6244

Circa 1830. The clip-clopping of horses is still heard from the front porches of this inn as carriages and wagons transport visitors around the island. In the Michigan Register of Historic Places, Haan's 1830 Inn is the oldest Greek Revival-style home in the Northwest Territory. It is behind a picket fence and just across the street from Haldiman Bay. Victorian and early American antiques include a writing desk used by Colonel Preston, an officer at Fort Mackinac at the turn of the century, and a 12-foot breakfast table formerly used by Amish farmers when they harvested each other's crops. The inn is open from May to October.

Historic Interest: Original British Fort Mackinac, Indian dormitory, Dr. Beaumont Memorial (discoverer of human digestion), John Jacob Astor Fur Trading Warehouse.

Innkeeper(s): Nicholas & Nancy Haan. $80-145. 7 rooms, 5 with PB. 2 suites. Breakfast included in rates. Types of meals: continental-plus breakfast and early coffee/tea. Beds: QD. Phone in room. Antiques, fishing and shopping nearby.

Publicity: *Detroit Free Press, Chicago Tribune, Innsider, Chicago Sun-Times, Good Housekeeping.*

"The ambiance, service and everything else was just what we needed."

Metivier Inn

PO Box 285, Market St
Mackinac Island, MI 49757-0285
(906)847-6234

Circa 1877. The Metivier Inn is perched on a bluff overlooking the downtown historic district where horse-drawn carriages and bicyclists preside in the absence of motorized vehicles. French and English decor is found throughout the turreted Victorian home. Guests can relax in the living room before the fire or out on the wicker-filled porch.

Innkeeper(s): Ken & Diane Neyer, Jane & Mike Bacon. $115-250. MC VISA DS. 21 rooms with PB. 1 suite. 1 conference room. Breakfast included in rates. Type of meal: continental breakfast. Beds: QT. TV on premises. Small meetings, family reunions and seminars hosted. Fishing, downhill skiing, cross-country skiing, theater and watersports nearby.

Location: On Market Street in the downtown historic district.

Publicity: *Travel & Leisure, Michigan Living, Detroit News, New York Times.*

"The accommodations were more than expected and our hosts made it even better."

Marquette   D4

The Bayou Place

2361 US 41 South
Marquette, MI 49855
(906)249-3863

Circa 1857. This home was built by the man who engineered the first above-ground rail system in Chicago and New York. The rooms are decorated with antiques, and one suite offers a Jacuzzi tub and fireplace. Turndown service, evening desserts, fluffy robes, a sauna and a hot tub are a few of the amenities. There is an exercise room on the premises and the innkeepers offer a concierge service. Plenty of seasonal activities are nearby, from cross-country and downhill skiing in the winter, to canoeing, kayaking and fishing in the warmer months.

Innkeeper(s): Bonnie & Bob Maki. $65-145. MC VISA TC. TAC5. 4 rooms, 2 with PB, 1 with FP. 1 conference room. Breakfast and evening snack included in rates. Types of meals: full breakfast, gourmet breakfast and early coffee/tea. Beds: QD. Air conditioning and turndown service in room. Spa, swimming and sauna on premises. Weddings, small meetings, family reunions and seminars hosted. Antiques, fishing, parks, shopping, skiing, sporting events, golf, theater and watersports nearby.

Muskegon   H6

Port City Victorian Inn

1259 Lakeshore Dr
Muskegon, MI 49441-1659
(616)759-0205 (800)274-3574 Fax:(616)759-0205

Circa 1877. Lumber baron and industrialist Alexander Rodgers, Sr. built this Queen Anne-style home. Among its impressive features are the grand entryway with a natural oak staircase and paneling, carved posts and spindles. The cuved, leaded-glass windows in the inn's parlor offer a view of Muskegon Lake. Beveled-glass doors enclose the natural wood fireplace in the sitting room, and high ceilings, intricate molding, polished oak floors and antiques further enhance the charm of this house. Guest rooms offer views of the lake, as well as double whirlpool tubs. A full breakfast is served either on the sun porch, in the dining room or guests can enjoy the meal in the privacy of their room.

Innkeeper(s): Fred & Barbara Schossau. $65-125. MC VISA AX DS. TAC10. 5 rooms, 3 with PB. 2 suites. Breakfast included in rates. Meals: full breakfast and early coffee/tea. Beds: QD. Phone, air conditioning, turndown service and TV in room. VCR, fax, copier, bicycles on premises. Amusement parks, fishing, parks, shopping, cross-country skiing, theater, watersports nearby.

"The inn offers only comfort, good food and total peace of mind."

New Buffalo   K5

Sans Souci Euro Inn

19265 S Lakeside Dr
New Buffalo, MI 49117-9276
(616)756-3141 Fax:(616)756-5511
E-mail: sans-souci@worldnet.att.net

Circa 1940. Located on 50 acres of woodland, meadows and spring-fed lakes, and bordered by the Galien River, Sans Souci (French for "without a care") is in a pristine setting. The decor is a crisp European contemporary style featuring king-size beds. For a family or two couples there is a separate cottage, The Dutch House, with two bedrooms, a whirlpool, sunken den and kitchen.

Innkeeper(s): Angelika Siewert. $98-185. MC VISA AX PC TC. 9 rooms with PB, 6 with FP. 1 conference room. Type of meal: full breakfast. Beds: K. Spa on premises. Handicap access.

Publicity: *Midwest Living, Lake Forest Review.*

"A little piece of heaven."

Petoskey · E7

Stafford's Perry Hotel

Bay & Lewis Streets
Petoskey, MI 49770
(616)347-4000 (800)456-1917 Fax:(616)347-0636

Circa 1899. This gracious, Victorian Italianate hotel has been welcoming guests since the turn of the century. At one point in its history, the hotel almost was converted into a hospital. It has remained a place for hospitality instead. Some of the pleasant, period-style guest rooms boast balconies overlooking Little Traverse Bay. Guests can enjoy live music, from jazz to folk, at the hotel's Noggin Room Pub. The H.O. Rose Room serves breakfast, lunch and dinner, and The Salon serves appetizers in the afternoon and evening. In season, the Rose Garden veranda is a great place for enjoying lunch, appetizers and cocktails. For guests seeking relaxation after a day exploring the area, there is a hot tub on the premises.
Innkeeper(s): Stephen Hooley. $75-185. EP. MC VISA AX DS. TAC10. 80 rooms with PB. 2 conference rooms. Meals: continental breakfast, continental-plus breakfast, full breakfast and early coffee/tea. Dinner, evening snack, picnic lunch, lunch, banquet service, catering service, catered breakfast, room service available. Restaurant on premises. Beds: KQD. Phone, air conditioning, TV in room. VCR, fax, copier, spa, library on premises. Handicap access. Weddings, small meetings, family reunions, seminars hosted. Antiques, fishing, parks, shopping, skiing, golf, theater, watersports nearby.

Petoskey (Bay View) · E7

Terrace Inn

1549 Glendale
Petoskey (Bay View), MI 49770
(616)347-2410 (800)530-9898 Fax:(616)347-2407
E-mail: terracei@freeway.net

Circa 1911. This late Victorian inn is located on what began as a Chautauqua summer resort, and more than 400 Victorian cottages have sprung up in this lakeside vacation spot. Terrace Inn was built in 1911, and most of its furnishings are original to the property. Guests will enjoy stunning views of Lake Michigan and Little Traverse Bay, and they can enjoy the shore at the private Bay View beach. In keeping with the surrounding homes, the guest rooms are decorated in a romantic-country cottage style. To take guests back in time, there are no televisions or telephones in the rooms. This historic resort town offers many attractions, from swimming and watersports to hiking to summer theater. During the summer season, the inn's restaurant is a great spot for dinner.
Innkeeper(s): Tom & Denise Erhart. $49-103. MC VISA AX. TAC10. 44 rooms with PB. 2 conference rooms. Breakfast included in rates. Types of meals: continental-plus breakfast and early coffee/tea. Dinner, picnic lunch and banquet service available. Restaurant on premises. Beds: QDT. Air conditioning in room. TV, VCR, fax, copier, swimming, bicycles, tennis and child care on premises. Handicap access. Weddings, small meetings, family reunions and seminars hosted. Antiques, fishing, parks, shopping, downhill skiing, cross-country skiing, golf, theater and watersports nearby.
Publicity: *Oakland Press & Observer Eccentric, Michigan Magazine.*

Port Huron · I10

Victorian Inn

1229 7th St
Port Huron, MI 48060-5303
(810)984-1437

Circa 1896. This finely renovated Queen Anne Victorian house has both an inn and restaurant. Gleaming carved-oak woodwork, leaded-glass windows and fireplaces in almost every

room reflect the home's gracious air. Authentic wallpapers and draperies provide a background for carefully selected antiques. At the Pierpont's Pub & Wine Cellar, Victorian-inspired menus include such entrees as partridge with pears and filet of beef Africane, all served on antique china.
Innkeeper(s): Randall Shannon. $65-75. MC VISA AX DC CB DS PC TC. 4 rooms, 2 with PB, 2 with FP. 1 suite. Breakfast included in rates. Room service available. Restaurant on premises. Beds: QDT. Air conditioning in room. TV on premises. Weddings and small meetings hosted. Antiques, fishing, parks, shopping, cross-country skiing, theater and watersports nearby.
Publicity: *Detroit Free Press.*

"In all of my trips, business or pleasure, I have never experienced such a warm and courteous staff."

Romeo · I9

Hess Manor B&B

186 S Main St
Romeo, MI 48065-5128
(810)752-4726 Fax:(810)752-6456

Circa 1854. This pre-Civil War home is located in a town listed in the National Register. The inn boasts a fireplace and Victorian decor. The innkeepers also renovated the inn's 110-year-old carriage house into an antique and gift shop. At night, guests are encouraged to enjoy the inn's complimentary soda pop and wine while viewing a wide selection free movies. For stargazers, there is a wonderful outdoor Jacuzzi. Much of Romeo's historic sites are within walking distance of Hess Manor, including galleries, antique shops, bookstores and restaurants. Frontier Town, a collection of Old West-style buildings, is a popular attraction.

Innkeeper(s): John & Ilene Hess. $59-70. MC VISA AX PC. TAC15. 4 rooms, 2 with PB. Breakfast included in rates. Meal: gourmet breakfast. Beds: Q. Air conditioning in room. TV, VCR and copier on premises. Small meetings hosted. Antiques, fishing, parks, shopping, golf, theater and watersports nearby.

Saline · J8

The Homestead B&B

9279 Macon Rd
Saline, MI 48176-9305
(313)429-9625

Circa 1851. The Homestead is a two-story brick farmhouse situated on 50 acres of fields, woods and river. The house has 15-inch-thick walls and is furnished with Victorian antiques and family heirlooms. This was a favorite camping spot for Native Americans while they salted their fish, and many arrowheads have been found on the farm. Activities include long walks through meadows of wildflowers and cross-country skiing in season. It is 40 minutes from Detroit and Toledo and 10 minutes from Ann Arbor.

Innkeeper(s): Shirley Grossman. $60-70. MC VISA AX DS TC. 5 rooms. 1 conference room. Breakfast and evening snack included in rates. Types of meals: full breakfast and early coffee/tea. Beds: DT. Air conditioning in room. VCR on premises. 50 acres. Small meetings, family reunions, seminars hosted. Antiques, parks, shopping, cross-country skiing, sporting events nearby.

Location: Southeastern Michigan, within six miles of I-94 & US 23.

Publicity: *Ann Arbor News, Country Focus, Saline Reporter.*

"It is so nice to be back after three years and from 5,000 miles away!"

Saugatuck   I6

Bayside Inn

618 Water St Box 1001
Saugatuck, MI 49453
(616)857-4321 Fax:(616)857-1870

Circa 1926. Located on the edge of the Kalamazoo River and across from the nature observation tower, this downtown inn was once a boathouse.

The common room now has a fireplace and view of the water. Each guest room has its own deck. The inn is near several restaurants, shops and beaches. Fishing for salmon, perch and trout is popular.

Innkeeper(s): Kathy Wilson. $60-225. MC VISA AX DS. 10 rooms with PB, 4 with FP. 4 suites. 1 conference room. Breakfast included in rates. Type of meal: continental-plus breakfast. Beds: KQD. Phone, air conditioning, TV and VCR in room. Fax, copier and spa on premises. Weddings, small meetings, family reunions and seminars hosted. Antiques, fishing, shopping, cross-country skiing, theater and watersports nearby.

Location: On the water in downtown Saugatuck.

"Our stay was wonderful, more pleasant than anticipated, we were so pleased. As for breakfast, it gets our A 1 rating."

Beechwood Manor B&B

736 Pleasant St # 876
Saugatuck, MI 49453-9781
(616)857-1587 Fax:(616)857-3909

Circa 1874. This late 19th-century Victorian was once home to the U.S. Consul General to Mexico. Vacant for many years,

the inn was Lovingly restored by James and Sherron Lemons. The inn is highlighted by heirloom antiques, gleaming wood floors and beautifully refurbished pine wood work. Each individually decorated guest room is named after the original owner's children. There are more than 100 unique shops located in the historic town.

Historic Interest: Located close to Lake Michigan and the Historic Pump House Museum.

Innkeeper(s): James & Sherron Lemons. $125-160. MC VISA TC. 5 suites, 2 with FP. 2 cottages. 1 conference room. Breakfast included in rates. Types of meals: continental-plus breakfast, gourmet breakfast and early coffee/tea. Beds: Q. Air conditioning, turndown service and ceiling fan in room. TV, VCR, fax, copier and bicycles on premises. Small meetings hosted. Amusement parks, antiques, fishing, parks, shopping, downhill skiing, cross-country skiing, sporting events, golf, theater and watersports nearby.

Publicity: *The Commercial Record, Country Inns,.*

"Thank you for allowing us to experience a whole new world in accommodations."

Kemah Guest House

633 Allegan St
Saugatuck, MI 49453-0339
(616)857-2919 (800)445-3624

Circa 1906. Stained-glass windows, beamed ceilings, and stone and tile fireplaces are trademarks of this house. There is a billiard room, and a Bavarian rathskeller has German inscriptions on the wall and original wine kegs. Deco Dormer, a guest room with a mahogany bedroom suite, was featured in a 1926 Architectural Digest. That same year, a Frank Lloyd Wright-style solarium with its own waterfall was added to the house. Kemah is situated on one wooded acre in a residential setting. Guests will want to explore the man-made grotto, which was used during prohibition.

Innkeeper(s): Cindi & Terry Tatsch. $85-140. MC VISA AX DS TC. 6 rooms, 4 with PB. 1 conference room. Breakfast included in rates. Type of meal: continental-plus breakfast. Beds: KQD. Air conditioning and ceiling fan in room. TV and VCR on premises. Weddings, small meetings, family reunions and seminars hosted. Antiques, fishing, parks, shopping, cross-country skiing, theater and watersports nearby.

Publicity: *Innsider, West Michigan, Grand Rapids Press.*

"What a wonderful time we had at Kemah. Thank you for a delightful stay. Your home is very special."

The Park House

888 Holland St
Saugatuck, MI 49453-9607
(616)857-4535 (800)321-4535 Fax:(616)857-1065
E-mail: parkhouse@softhouse.com

Circa 1857. This Greek Revival-style home is the oldest residence in Saugatuck and was constructed for the first mayor. Susan B. Anthony was a guest here for two weeks in the 1870s, and the local Women's Christian Temperance League was established in the parlor. A country theme pervades the inn, with antiques, old woodwork and pine floors. A cottage with a hot tub and a river-front guest house are also available.

Historic Interest: Listed in the National Register.

Innkeeper(s): Lynda & Joe Petty, Susan Bentley, Dan Osborn. $70-225. MC VISA AX DS PC TC. TAC10. 8 rooms with PB, 6 with FP. 3 suites. 4 cottages. Breakfast included in rates. Types of meals: full breakfast and early coffee/tea. Beds: KQT. Phone, air conditioning, TV and VCR in room. Fax and copier on premises. Handicap access. Small meetings, family reunions and seminars hosted. Antiques, fishing, parks, shopping, cross-country skiing, theater and watersports nearby.

Publicity: *Detroit News, Innsider, Gazette, South Bend Tribune.*

"Thanks again for your kindness and hospitality during our weekend."

The Red Dog B&B

132 Mason St
Saugatuck, MI 49453
(616)857-8851 (800)357-3250

Circa 1879. This comfortable, two-story farmhouse is located in the heart of downtown Saugatuck and is just a short walk away from shopping, restaurants and many of the town's seasonal activities. Rooms are furnished with a combination of traditional and antique furnishings. One room includes a fireplace and Jacuzzi tub for two. Guests can relax and enjoy views of the garden from the B&B's second-story porch, or warm up next to the fireplace in the living room. The full breakfast includes treats such as baked apple cinnamon French toast or a ham and cheese strata. The innkeepers offer special golf and off-season packages.

Innkeeper(s): Patrick & Kristine Clark. $60-110. MC VISA AX DC DS PC TC. TAC10. 6 rooms with PB, 1 with FP. 1 suite. Breakfast included in rates. Types of meals: full breakfast and early coffee/tea. Beds: QD. Air conditioning, ceiling fan and TV in room. VCR, fax and copier on premises. Weddings, small meetings and family reunions hosted. Antiques, fishing, parks, shopping, cross-country skiing, theater and watersports nearby.

Publicity: *South Bend Trio, Michigan Cyclist, Restaurant and Institutions.*

Twin Oaks Inn

PO Box 867, 227 Griffith St
Saugatuck, MI 49453-0867
(616)857-1600

Circa 1860. This large Queen Anne Victorian inn was a boarding house for lumbermen at the turn of the century. Now an old-English-style inn, it offers a variety of lodging choices, including three suites. One room has a Jacuzzi. Guests also

may stay in the inn's cozy cottage, which boasts an outdoor hot tub. There are many diversions at Twin Oaks, including a collection of videotaped movies numbering more than 700. An English garden with a pond and fountain provides a relaxing setting, and guests also may borrow bicycles or play horseshoes on the inn's grounds.

Innkeeper(s): Jerry & Nancy Horney. $65-125. MC VISA DS TC. 7 rooms with PB. 3 suites. 1 conference room. Breakfast and evening snack included in rates. Types of meals: continental-plus breakfast, full breakfast and early coffee/tea. Beds: KQ. Air conditioning, TV and VCR in room. Weddings, small meetings and family reunions hosted. Antiques, fishing, parks, shopping, cross-country skiing, theater and watersports nearby.

Location: Downtown.

Publicity: *Home & Away, Cleveland Plain Dealer, South Bend Tribune, Shape, AAA Magazine.*

Saugatuck (Douglas)   I6

Sherwood Forest B&B

938 Center St
Saugatuck (Douglas), MI 49453
(800)838-1246 Fax:(616)857-1996

Circa 1904. As the name suggests, this gracious Victorian is surrounded by woods and flanked with a large wraparound porch. Each guest room features antiques, one room offers a Jacuzzi and another an oak-manteled fireplace with a unique mural that transforms the room into a tree-top loft. A breakfast of delicious coffees or teas and homemade treats can be enjoyed either in the dining room or on the

porch. The heated pool includes a mural of dolphins riding on ocean waves. White-sand beaches and the eastern shore of Lake Michigan are only a half block away.

Innkeeper(s): Keith & Susan Charak. $60-140. MC VISA DS PC. TAC10. 4 rooms with PB, 1 with FP. 1 cottage. 1 conference room. Breakfast and after-

noon tea included in rates. Types of meals: continental-plus breakfast and early coffee/tea. Catering service available. Beds: Q. Air conditioning and ceiling fan in room. TV, VCR, fax, swimming and bicycles on premises. Weddings, small meetings, family reunions and seminars hosted. Antiques, fishing, parks, shopping, cross-country skiing, theater, watersports nearby.

Publicity: *Commercial Record, Chicago SunTimes, New York Times.*

"We enjoyed our weekend in the forest, the atmosphere was perfect, and your suggestions on where to eat and how to get around was very appreciated. Thanks for remembering our anniversary."

South Haven   J5

Carriage House at The Park & Harbor

233 Dyckman - 118 Woodman
South Haven, MI 49090-1471
(616)639-1776 Fax:(616)639-2409

Circa 1896. Fashioned in the style of a turn-of-the-century Victorian farmhouse, this inn features all the comforts of its modern amenities while maintaining a nostalgic atmosphere with its use of antiques and Amish furnishings. The inn consists of two separate locations: The Carriage House at the Park and The Carriage House at the Harbor. Both inns feature individually decorated rooms with fireplaces and private baths. Many of the rooms offer views and separate balconies. Breakfast specialties at both houses include spice peaches, homemade muffins, stuffed French toast and honey-baked coffee cake.

Historic Interest: One block from Lake Michigan. The inn is walking distance to the downtown.

Innkeeper(s): Jay & Joyce Yelton. Call for rates.

The Seymour House

1248 Blue Star Hwy
South Haven, MI 49090-9696
(616)227-3918 Fax:(616)227-3010
E-mail: seymour@cybersol.com

Circa 1862. Less than half a mile from the shores of Lake Michigan, this pre-Civil War, Italianate-style home rests upon 11 acres of grounds, complete with nature trails and a stocked fishing pond. Each of the guest rooms is named for a state significant in the innkeepers' lives. The Arizona Room, popular with honeymooners, includes a double Jacuzzi tub. Poached pears with raspberry sauce, buttermilk blueberry pancakes and locally made sausages are a few of

the items that might appear on the breakfast menu. The inn is midway between Saugatuck and South Haven, which offer plenty of activities. Beaches, Kal-Haven Trail, shopping, horseback riding and winery tours are among the fun destination choices.

Innkeeper(s): Tom & Gwen Paton. $80-135. MC VISA PC TC. TAC10. 5 rooms with PB, 2 with FP. 1 cabin. Breakfast and evening snack included in rates. Types of meals: gourmet breakfast and early coffee/tea. Picnic lunch available. Beds: KQD. Air conditioning, ceiling fan and VCR in room. TV, fax, copier and swimming on premises. 11 acres. Antiques, fishing, parks, shopping, downhill skiing, cross-country skiing, theater and watersports nearby.

"As one who comes from the land that invented B&Bs, I hope to say that this is a truly superb example."

Yelton Manor Bed & Breakfast

140 N Shore Dr
South Haven, MI 49090-1135
(616)637-5220

Circa 1872. Sunsets over Lake Michigan, award-winning gardens and gourmet breakfasts are just a sampling of what guests will partake of at this restored Victorian. There are 11 guest rooms from which to choose, each named for a flower. The anniversary and honeymoon suites offer lakeside views. Several rooms include a Jacuzzi tub. Each of the guest rooms includes

a TV and VCR, and there is a large video library to peruse. Bountiful breakfasts include items such as blueberry pancakes or a homemade egg strata with salsa. Yelton Manor guests also enjoy evening hors d'oeuvres, and don't forget to sample one of the inn's signature chocolate chip cookies. During the Christmas season, a tree is placed in every room, and more than 15,000 lights decorate the inn. The innkeepers also offer six additional rooms in the new Manor Guest House, a Victorian home built in 1993. Those staying at the guest house enjoy a continental breakfast delivered to their room door.

Innkeeper(s): Elaine Herbert & Robert Kripaitis. $95-230. MC VISA AX. 17 rooms with PB, 7 with FP. 1 conference room. Type of meal: full breakfast. Beds: KQ. Phone, TV and VCR in room. Library on premises.

Publicity: *Great Lakes Getaway, Adventure Roads, Chicago Tribune, New York Times, Hour Detroit, Chicago Sun Times, Country Living.*

"The Yelton Manor is a lovely place to unwind and enjoy the special amenities provided by the very friendly staff. We appreciate all your hard work and will definitely plan to be back! Thank You!"

Sturgis K6

Christmere House

110 Pleasant St
Sturgis, MI 49091-1751
(616)651-8303 (888)651-8303 Fax:(616)651-3860

Circa 1869. This Queen Anne Victorian was built by Dr. Nelson Packard, who served as a surgeon in the Civil War, and its original purpose was to serve as a hospital. Guest rooms feature elegant decor, and special touches, such as a whirlpool tub, clawfoot tub or an Austrian stove. The Roosevelt Room, located in the inn's turret, includes a whirlpool tub and fireplace. The Country Squire Suite includes a small kitchen and stained-glass windows.

Innkeeper(s): Janette Parr Johns. $65-125. MC VISA AX DS PC TC. TAC15. 11 rooms, 1 with PB, 4 with FP. 3 suites. 3 conference rooms. Breakfast

included in rates. Type of meal: full breakfast. Banquet service and catering service available. Restaurant on premises. Beds: KQDT. Phone, air conditioning, ceiling fan and TV in room. Fax and library on premises. Weddings, small meetings, family reunions and seminars hosted. Antiques, fishing, shopping, cross-country skiing, golf, theater and watersports nearby.

Suttons Bay F6

Century Farm

2421 N Jacobson Rd
Suttons Bay, MI 49682-9274
(616)271-2421 (800)252-8480

Circa 1895. This picturesque, two-story, white farmhouse sits on 30 acres, a mile from Grand Traverse Bay. There are seven outbuildings of wood and stone construction, a brook, fruit trees, and a Jacuzzi on the deck. Guests enjoy views of the bay from the top of the hill. One guest room is located in a stone cottage furnished in antiques, while another is a two-room log cabin. Breakfasts consist of fruit, quiche and fresh sweet bread, or you are welcome to request special items when making your reservations.

Innkeeper(s): Julie Jacobs. $75-125. PC TC. 7 rooms, 3 with PB. 1 cottage. 1 cabin. Breakfast included in rates. Types of meals: full breakfast and early coffee/tea. Beds: KQDT. Ceiling fan in room. TV, VCR, fax, spa, stables, bicycles, library and pet boarding on premises. Handicap access. 30 acres. Weddings, small meetings, family reunions and seminars hosted. Antiques, fishing, parks, shopping, downhill skiing, cross-country skiing, sporting events, golf, theater and watersports nearby.

Pets Allowed.

Union Pier J5

Garden Grove B&B

9549 Union Pier Rd
Union Pier, MI 49129-9411
(616)469-6346 Fax:(616)469-3419
E-mail: gardenbnb@aol

Circa 1925. This vintage, cottage-style home originally was built using plans from a Sears-Roebuck catalog. The innkeepers have constructed an addition, keeping the home's cottage style in mind. Two guest rooms include fireplaces and whirlpool tubs, while the others have clawfoot tubs. Rooms have a garden theme with names such as The Sunflower or The Violet. The home is secluded on a lush acre near the shore of Lake Michigan. The breakfasts here are hearty, and in keeping with the romance of the place, the innkeepers serve the morning meal at tables for two. For callers in the midwest, the innkeepers offer a toll-free number, (800) 613-2872.

Innkeeper(s): Mary Ellen & Ric Postlewaite. $80-150. MC VISA DS TC. TAC10. 4 rooms with PB, 2 with FP. Breakfast and evening snack included in

rates. Types of meals: full breakfast and early coffee/tea. Beds: KQT. Phone, air conditioning, ceiling fan, TV and VCR in room. Fax, copier, spa, bicycles and library on premises. Antiques, fishing, parks, shopping, cross-country skiing and watersports nearby.

"What a wonderful, tranquil slice of heaven you have here. This has been such a romantic way to spend our first anniversary. An incredible escape to a timeless place."

Pine Garth B&B

15790 Lakeshore Rd
Union Pier, MI 49129-9340
(616)469-1642 Fax:(616)469-0418

Circa 1905. The seven rooms and five guest cottages at this charming bed & breakfast inn are decorated in a country style and each boasts something special. Some have a private deck and a wall of windows that look out to Lake Michigan. Other rooms feature items such as an unusual twig canopy bed, and several have whirlpool tubs. The deluxe cottages offer two queen-size beds, a wood-burning fireplace, VCR, cable TV and

an outdoor tub on a private deck with a gas grill. Rates vary for the cottages. The inn has its own private beach and there are sand dunes, vineyards, forests and miles of beaches in the area.
Innkeeper(s): Paula & Russ Bulin. $115-170. MC VISA DS PC. 7 rooms with PB, 1 with FP. 5 cottages. 1 conference room. Breakfast included in rates. Types of meals: full breakfast and gourmet breakfast. Afternoon tea, evening snack and banquet service available. Beds: Q. Ceiling fan and VCR in room. TV, fax, copier, swimming, bicycles and library on premises. Shopping nearby.
Location: On the shores of Lake Michigan with private beach.

"Your warm and courteous reception, attentiveness and helpfulness will never be forgotten."

The Inn at Union Pier

9708 Berrien
Union Pier, MI 49129-0222
(616)469-4700 Fax:(616)469-4720

Circa 1920. Set on a shady acre across a country road from Lake Michigan, this inn features unique Swedish ceramic wood-burning fireplaces, a hot tub and sauna, a veranda ringing the house and a large common room with comfortable overstuffed furniture and a grand piano. Rooms offer such amenities as private balconies and porches, whirlpools, views of the English garden and furniture dating from the early 1900s. Breakfast includes fresh fruit and homemade jams made of fruit from surrounding farms.
Innkeeper(s): Joyce & Mark Pitts. $125-195. MC VISA DS PC TC. 16 rooms with PB, 12 with FP. 2 suites. 1 conference room. Breakfast and evening snack included in rates. Types of meals: continental breakfast, full breakfast, gourmet breakfast and early coffee/tea. Catering service available. Beds: KQT. Phone, air conditioning and ceiling fan in room. TV, VCR, fax, copier, spa, swimming, sauna, bicycles and library on premises. Handicap access. Weddings, small meetings, family reunions and seminars hosted. Antiques, parks, cross-country skiing, sporting events and watersports nearby.

Publicity: *Chicago Tribune, Chicago, Midwest Living, Chicago Sun Times, Country Living, Romantic Inns, The Travel Channel.*

"The food, the atmosphere, the accommodations, and of course, the entire staff made this the most relaxing weekend ever."

Ypsilanti   J8

Parish House Inn

103 S Huron St
Ypsilanti, MI 48197-5421
(313)480-4800 (800)480-4866 Fax:(313)480-7472

Circa 1893. This Queen Anne Victorian was named in honor of its service as a parsonage for the First Congregational Church. The home remained a parsonage for more than 50 years after its construction and then served as a church office and Sunday school building. It was moved to its present site in Ypsilanti's historic district in the late 1980s. The rooms are individually decorated with Victorian-style wallpapers and antiques. One guest room includes a two-person Jacuzzi tub. Those in search of a late-night snack need only venture into the kitchen to find drinks and the cookie jar. For special occasions, the innkeepers can arrange trays with flowers, non-alcoholic champagne, chocolates, fruit or cheese. The terrace overlooks the Huron River.
Innkeeper(s): Mrs. Chris Mason. $89-124. MC VISA AX PC TC. TAC10. 9 rooms with PB, 2 with FP. 1 conference room. Breakfast and evening snack included in rates. Types of meals: continental breakfast, full breakfast, gourmet breakfast and early coffee/tea. Afternoon tea, picnic lunch, catering service and catered breakfast available. Beds: QDT. Phone, air conditioning, ceiling fan, TV and VCR in room. Fax and library on premises. Handicap access. Small meetings, family reunions and seminars hosted. Amusement parks, antiques, fishing, parks, shopping, cross-country skiing, sporting events, theater and watersports nearby.

Minnesota

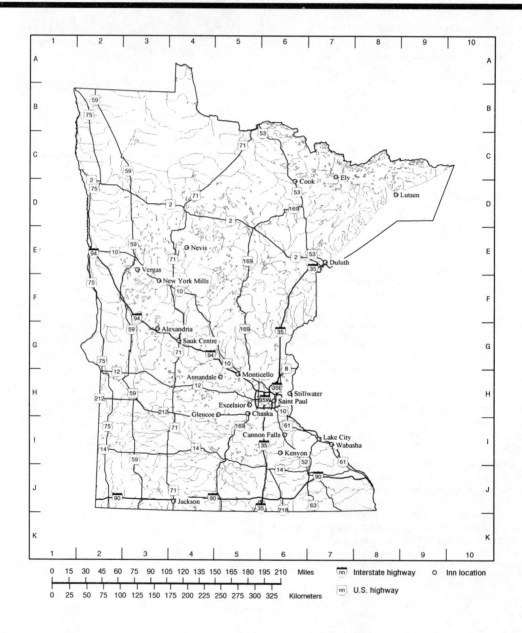

0   15   30   45   60   75   90   105 120 135 150 165 180 195 210   Miles

0   25   50   75   100 125 150 175 200 225 250 275 300 325   Kilometers

(nn) Interstate highway   o Inn location

(nn) U.S. highway

Alexandria G3

Cedar Rose Inn

422 - 7th Ave W
Alexandria, MN 56308
(320)762-8430 Fax:(320)762-8044

Circa 1903. Diamond-paned windows, gables, a wraparound porch and stained glass enhance the exterior of this handsome three-story Tudor Revival home. Located in what was once referred to as the "Silk Stocking District," the home was built by the town's mayor. Arched doorways, Tiffany chandeliers, a glorious open staircase, maple floors and oak woodwork set the atmosphere. There's a library, a parlor with fireplace and window seat, and a formal dining room. Request the Noah P. Ward room and enjoy the king-size bed and double whirlpool with mood lights for a special celebration. Wake to the aroma of freshly baked caramel rolls, scones or cinnamon buns. Entrees of sausage and quiche are favorites. In the evening, enjoy watching the sunset over Lake Winona from the veranda. Reserve a mountain bike ahead of time with the innkeeper, or enjoy a day of lake activities, shopping, antiquing or horseback riding.

Innkeeper(s): Aggie & Florian Ledermann. $75-120. MC VISA PC. TAC10. 4 rooms with PB. 1 suite. Breakfast and evening snack included in rates. Types of meals: full breakfast and early coffee/tea. Beds: KQD. Air conditioning in room. TV, VCR, fax, bicycles and library on premises. Amusement parks, antiques, fishing, parks, shopping, downhill skiing, cross-country skiing, theater and watersports nearby.

"The Cedar Rose Inn was more than we imagined it would be. We felt like royalty in your beautiful dining room."

Annandale H5

Thayer Bed & Breakfast Inn

PO Box 246 Hwy 55 60 West Elm St
Annandale, MN 55302
(320)274-8222 (800)944-6595 Fax:(320)274-8222

Circa 1895. Gus Thayer, the town constable, school bus driver, thresher and mill operator, originally built this old railroad-style hotel to accommodate weary road and rail travelers. At that time, the inn epitomized the unique turn-of-the-century gaiety of dining, dancing, singing and sleeping all under one roof. Although there have been many changes throughout its 100 years, innkeeper, and psychic, Sharon Gammell has restored the inn to its original intended purpose. Richly appointed rooms feature authentic period furnishings, four-poster beds and hot tubs. Visitors can take advantage of several packages including: Romantic Hide-A-Way, Honeymoon, Murder Mystery or Psychic. All visitors will enjoy gourmet breakfast with specialties such as raspberry cheese blintzes served on smoked bacon strips and hand-dipped chocolate covered strawberries. Dining is available and a lounge features 38 varieties of Scotch and a wide selection of beers. The inn is listed on the National Register of Historic Places.

Innkeeper(s): Sharon Gammell. $49-150. MC VISA AX DS PC TC. TAC10. 11 rooms with PB, 1 with FP. 1 conference room. Breakfast included in rates. Types of meals: continental breakfast, continental-plus breakfast, full breakfast, gourmet breakfast and early coffee/tea. Afternoon tea, dinner, evening snack, picnic lunch, lunch, gourmet lunch, banquet service, catering service and catered breakfast available. Restaurant on premises. Beds: QDT. Air conditioning, TV and VCR in room. Fax, copier, spa and sauna on premises. Weddings, small meetings, family reunions and seminars hosted. Amusement parks, antiques, fishing, parks, shopping, downhill skiing, cross-country skiing, theater and watersports nearby.

Pets Allowed: prior approval necessary.

Cannon Falls I6

Quill & Quilt

615 Hoffman St W
Cannon Falls, MN 55009-1923
(507)263-5507 (800)488-3849

Circa 1897. This three-story, gabled Colonial Revival house has six bay windows and several porches and decks. The inn features a well-stocked library, a front parlor with a fireplace, and handsomely decorated guest rooms. A favorite is the room with a double whirlpool tub, two bay windows, a king-size oak canopy bed and Victorian chairs.

Innkeeper(s): Staci Smith. $55-130. AP. MC VISA. 4 rooms with PB. 1 suite. Breakfast included in rates. Types of meals: continental breakfast and full breakfast. Beds: KQD. Spa on premises. Antiques, downhill skiing, cross-country skiing and watersports nearby.

Location: Forty-five miles from Minneapolis/St. Paul and Rochester.

Publicity: *Minneapolis Tribune, Country Quilts.*

"What a pleasure to find the charm and hospitality of an English country home while on holiday in the United States."

Chaska H5

Bluff Creek Inn

1161 Bluff Creek Dr
Chaska, MN 55318-9515
(612)445-2735

Circa 1860. This two-story brick Victorian folk home was built on land granted by Abe Lincoln to one of the earliest settlers in the area. It boasts a wide veranda and three summer porches. Family antiques are accentuated by Laura Ashley and Merrimekko quilts and linens. A three-course breakfast is served at individual tables with Bavarian crystal and old English china in the country dining room.

Historic Interest: Located minutes away from the Mall of America, Chanhassen Dinner Theater and Minnieapolis Arboretum. Thirty minutes from downtown Minneapolis.

Innkeeper(s): Anne & Gary Delaney. $75-175. MC VISA. 5 rooms with PB, 2 with FP. Types of meals: full breakfast and gourmet breakfast. Beds: KQD. Phone in room. Fishing nearby.

Location: In the bluffs of the Minnesota River Valley.

Publicity: *Star & Tribune, Chicago Tribune, Sailor.*

"Thank you for your wonderful hospitality and extra special considerations."

Cook D6

Ludlow's Island Lodge

PO Box 1146
Cook, MN 55723-1146
(218)666-5407 (800)537-5308 Fax:(218)666-2488
E-mail: info@ludlowsresort.com

Circa 1945. A collection of 18 rustic cabins is spread across two shores of the lake and a private island. They range in style and size and are from one to five bedrooms. All have fireplaces, kitchens and outdoor decks. All cabins have multiple baths and are equipped with tubs and showers. This resort is very private with many activities on the property that are free of charge including tennis, racquetball, canoeing and sailboating. A 24-hour convenience grocery store is also on premises. Children may enjoy watching movies that are shown every evening in the lodge.

Innkeeper(s): Mark & Sally Ludlow. $165-370. MC VISA AX PC. TAC10. 51 rooms. 18 cottages. 2 conference rooms. Catering service available. Beds: KQDT. Ceiling fan, TV, VCR in room. Fax, copier, swimming, sauna, tennis, library, child care on premises. 10 acres. Weddings, small meetings, family reunions, seminars hosted. Fishing, shopping, skiing, golf, watersports nearby.
Publicity: *Family Circle, Midwest Living, USA Today, Parents, Country Inns, Architecture Minnesota.*

Duluth E7

Manor on The Creek

2215 E 2nd St
Duluth, MN 55812-1864
(218)728-3189 (800)428-3189 Fax:(218)724-3915
E-mail: manor@cp.duluth.mn.us

Circa 1907. This exquisite mansion is one of Duluth's five largest homes. As you enter this cherished home, you will first be taken by its remarkable woodwork. The home's architects, the team of Bray and Nystrom, were originally influenced by, and early associates, of Frank Lloyd Wright. The interior design is magnificent, and the innkeepers complement its beauty by filling the home with period furnishings. The suites include whirlpool tubs, and guests will find fresh flowers and candies in their rooms. The inn's grounds also are noteworthy, two acres set along Oregon Creek and overlooking woods and a ravine. The gourmet breakfasts include such items as blueberry pancakes (a secret recipe) or perhaps three-cheese scrambled eggs with fresh herbs and roasted baby potatoes. Special event dining is available.

Innkeeper(s): Ken, Mona, Casey Knutson. $98-189. MC VISA DS PC TC. TAC8. 8 rooms with PB, 2 with FP. 4 suites. 1 cottage. 2 conference rooms. Breakfast included in rates. Types of meals: continental breakfast, full breakfast, gourmet breakfast and early coffee/tea. Picnic lunch and banquet service available. Beds: KQD. Phone and ceiling fan in room. TV, VCR and fax on premises. Weddings, small meetings, family reunions and seminars hosted. Antiques, fishing, parks, shopping, downhill skiing, cross-country skiing, sporting events, golf, theater and watersports nearby.
Pets Allowed: Not allowed alone in rooms, must be leashed, must be good with people, $10 a night charge, damage deposit.
Publicity: *MN Monthly, Rochester Press, St Paul Pioneer Press.*

Ely C7

Burntside Lodge

2755 Burntside Lodge Rd
Ely, MN 55731-8402
(218)365-3894

Circa 1913. "Staying here is like taking a vacation 60 years ago," states innkeeper Lou LaMontagne. Families have come

here for more than 80 years to enjoy the waterfront and woodside setting. The lodge and its cabins are in the National Register and much of the original hand-carved furnishings remain from the jazz age. Fishing, listening to the cry of the loon and boating around the lake's 125 islands are popular activities. Breakfast and dinner are available in the waterside dining room.

Innkeeper(s): Lou & Lonnie LaMontagne. $90-165. MAP, EP. MC VISA AX DS PC TC. TAC5. 24 cottages. Meals: full breakfast and early coffee/tea. Dinner and lunch available. Beds: KDT. VCR, fax, copier, swimming, sauna and library on premises. 20 acres. Weddings, small meetings, family reunions and seminars hosted. Antiques, fishing, parks, shopping, watersports nearby.
Location: Six miles southwest of Ely.

"Unforgettable."

Excelsior H5

James H. Clark House B&B

371 Water St
Excelsior, MN 55331-3039
(612)474-0196

Circa 1858. This pre-Civil War, Italianate-style home is named for its first owner, and it is listed in the local historic register. There are four guest rooms and a suite to choose from that include amenities such as whirlpool or clawfoot tubs. The Garden Room is especially unique, as it features a trompe l'oeil painting on the walls and stained glass. The home's decor is meant to be like an English garden, and to add extra romance, the innkeeper has placed candles in the windows. Breakfast is an appetizing affair, guests are pampered with a French banana pancake topped with caramel sauce or perhaps Belgian waffles with strawberries and cream. The inn offers close access to Minneapolis and sites such as the Mall of America. Located in historic Excelsior, the inn is located near the Old Log Theater, Chanhassen Dinner Theater and the University of Minnesota Arboratum.

Innkeeper(s): Skip & Betty Welke. $85-145. PC. 4 rooms with PB, 2 with FP. 1 suite. Breakfast included in rates. Meals: full breakfast and early coffee/tea. Beds: QT. Air conditioning in room. Library on premises. Antiques, fishing, parks, shopping, cross-country skiing, golf, theater and watersports nearby.
Publicity: *Minnesota Monthly, Midwest Traveler, Minneapolis Star & Tribune.*

Glencoe H5

Glencoe Castle B&B

831 13th St E
Glencoe, MN 55336-1503
(320)864-3043 (800)517-3334
E-mail: schoenr@hutchtel.net

Circa 1895. Glencoe Castle was built as a wedding promise to lure a bride from New York to Minnesota. She would move to Glencoe only if her husband built her a castle. This grand manor did the trick, with its carved woodwork, stained glass and ornate wood floors. The third floor originally was built as a ballroom. The home is decorated with antiques, Oriental and country pieces. Guests are treated to a lavish candlelight breakfast with such items as baked eggs in cream and Havarti cheese, Canadian bacon, blueberry French toast, homemade bread, pastries and fresh fruit. In the evenings, tea and dessert are served. There is a Victorian gift shop on the premises. For an extra charge, guests can arrange small meetings, parties, group teas, dinner or teas for two. The teas range from a light breakfast tea to the more extravagant Victorian High Tea. Murder-Mystery events also can be arranged.

Innkeeper(s): Becky & Rick Schoeneck. $65-175. MC VISA AX DS PC. 4 rooms, 1 with PB, 1 with FP. Breakfast and evening snack included in rates. Type of meal: gourmet breakfast. Afternoon tea available. Beds: KD. Air conditioning in room. TV, VCR, fax and copier on premises. Weddings and small meetings hosted. Amusement parks, antiques, fishing, parks, shopping, downhill skiing, cross-country skiing, sporting events and theater nearby.

Jackson   J4

Old Railroad Inn

219 Moore St
Jackson, MN 56143-1101
(507)847-5348 (888)844-5348

Circa 1888. This inn was built as a small hotel and also served as housing for railroad employees. Innkeeper Joann Neuenschwander's parents bought the place in the 1940s, and she grew up in it, helping out when it was used as a boarding house for railroad workers. The atmosphere is homey and comfortable, with a country appeal. Each guest room is named in honor of a different railroad line, such as the Soo Line or the Rock Island. Candles and a display of wedding gowns create a romantic feel. Breakfasts include quiche, fresh fruit, homemade bagels and other treats.

Innkeeper(s): Joann & Don Neuenschwander. $45-55. MC VISA DS PC TC. 4 rooms, 1 with PB. Breakfast and evening snack included in rates. Types of meals: full breakfast and early coffee/tea. Beds: QD. Ceiling fan and TV in room. VCR and bicycles on premises. Amusement parks, antiques, fishing, parks, shopping, cross-country skiing, sporting events, golf, theater and watersports nearby.

Publicity: *Minneapolis Star Tribune.*

"What a grand place! The room is gorgeous and comfortable, the breakfasts are superb and the visiting is therapeutic!"

Kenyon   I6

Grandfather's Woods

3640 450th St
Kenyon, MN 55946-3626
(507)789-6414

Circa 1860. This sprawling 440-acre farm boasts a handsome two-story Scandinavian clapboard home, and off in the woods, the original log cabin built six generations ago by the Langemo family. Abraham Lincoln personally endorsed the original homestead document displayed in the house. Old photos include one of Grandfather Jorgen next to a tiny tree in 1861.

The same tree has grown to giant proportions and now shades the entire house. An antique rocking chair, now in the parlor, is seen in an ancient photo of great-grandmother Karen. The Solarium, one of the rooms, has a brass bed and wicker furniture, and it looks out over the fish pond and garden to the fields and woods along the river. There are 65 acres of wooded trails on the property. Guests enjoy the farm's horses and sheep, and in springtime, the young lambs. The inn offers hay and sleigh rides, cross-country skiing, croquet, a garden swing and a nine-hole golf course across from the hay field. A fancy farm breakfast may include homemade caramel rolls and oven eggs with sausage.

Innkeeper(s): Judy & George Langemo. $65-70. PC TC. 3 rooms, 2 with PB, 1 with FP. 1 suite. Breakfast and evening snack included in rates. Types of meals: continental breakfast, continental-plus breakfast, full breakfast and early coffee/tea. Dinner, picnic lunch and lunch available. Beds: QD. Ceiling fan in room. Bicycles on premises. 440 acres. Small meetings and family reunions hosted. Antiques, parks, shopping, cross-country skiing, sporting events, golf and watersports nearby.

Publicity: *Life & Leisure.*

"This has been a precious gift we'll never forget."

Lake City   I7

Red Gables Inn

403 N High St
Lake City, MN 55041-1325
(612)345-2605

Circa 1865. This red Victorian features a Greek Revival center section with Italianate styling and a veranda that wraps around two sides of the house. Lace curtains and floral wallpapers provide a background for antiques, Oriental rugs and the inn's handsome black walnut staircase. Guest rooms are named for the old riverboats of the area and are furnished with iron and brass beds and antique armoires. Breakfast is served in the formal dining room. Hors d'oeuvres are served in the parlor at twilight. Bicycles are available.

Innkeeper(s): Mary & Doug De Roos. $85-95. MC VISA DS PC TC. TAC10. 5 rooms, 2 with PB. Breakfast, dinner and evening snack included in rates. Types of meals: full breakfast, gourmet breakfast and early coffee/tea. Beds: KQD. Air conditioning, turndown service and ceiling fan in room. TV and bicycles on premises. Small meetings and family reunions hosted. Antiques, fishing, parks, shopping, downhill skiing, cross-country skiing, sporting events, golf, theater and watersports nearby.

Publicity: *Red Wing Eagle, Chicago Sun-Times, San Francisco Examiner, Star-Tribune.*

"You made it very personal and special by doing small things, and those things are what count!"

The Victorian B&B

620 S High St
Lake City, MN 55041-1757
(612)345-2167 (888)345-2167

Circa 1896. This Victorian stick-style was built by a wealthy local banker and landowner. Fine, carved woodwork and stained-glass windows are among the home's architectural features. All offer views of Lake Pepin. Antique furnishings decorate the interior. The innkeepers are adding a guest house with two guest rooms. Lake Pepin's riverwalk is across the street from the B&B. Area attractions include skiing, shopping and hiking.

Innkeeper(s): Bernard & Ione Link. $65-150. PC. TAC10. 5

rooms with PB, 2 with FP. Breakfast and evening snack included in rates. Type of meal: full breakfast. Beds: KQ. Air conditioning and ceiling fan in room. TV and VCR on premises. Antiques, fishing, parks, shopping, downhill skiing, cross-country skiing, golf and watersports nearby.

"You've attended to every detail to make sure our stay was perfect. We'd come back in a heartbeat!"

Lutsen   D8

Cascade Lodge

3719 W Hwy 61
Lutsen, MN 55612-9705
(218)387-1112 (800)322-9543 Fax:(218)387-1113
E-mail: cascade@cascadelodgemn.com

Circa 1938. A main lodge and 10 cabins (including log cabins), a four-unit motel and a nearby house, comprise Cascade Lodge. The lodge is tucked away in the midst of Cascade River

State Park, which overlooks Lake Superior. Cascade Creek meanders between the cabins toward the lake. The lodge has a natural-stone fireplace and the living room and restaurant areas are decorated with hunting trophies of moose, coyote, wolves and bear. Canoeing, hiking to Lookout Mountain, walking along Wild Flower Trail and watching the sunset from the lawn swing are favorite summer activities. The lodge is open all year.
Historic Interest: Grand Portage National Monument, Superior National Forest.
Innkeeper(s): Gene & Laurene Glader. $35-170. MAP, EP. MC VISA AX DS PC TC. TAC10. 11 cottages, 12 with PB, 9 with FP. 1 suite. 1 conference room. Type of meal: early coffee/tea. Restaurant on premises. Beds: QDT. Phone in room. VCR, fax, copier, bicycles and library on premises. 14 acres. Small meetings, family reunions and seminars hosted. German spoken. Antiques, fishing, parks, shopping, skiing, golf, theater and watersports nearby.
Location: Overlooking Lake Superior on Highway 61.
Publicity: *Country Inns, Lake Superior.*

"We needed to get away and recharge ourselves. This was the perfect place."

Lindgren's B&B on Lake Superior

County Rd 35, PO Box 56
Lutsen, MN 55612-0056
(218)663-7450

Circa 1926. This '20s log home is in the Superior National Forest on the north shore of Lake Superior. The inn features massive stone fireplaces, a baby grand piano, wildlife decor and a Finnish-style sauna. The

living room has tongue-and-groove, Western knotty cedar wood paneling and seven-foot windows offering a view of the lake. The innkeeper's homemade jams, freshly baked breads

and entrees such as French Toast topped with homemade chokecherry syrup, eggs Benedict or Danish pancakes get the day off to a pleasant start. In addition to horseshoes and a volleyball court, guests can gaze at the lake on a swinging love seat.
Innkeeper(s): Shirley Lindgren. $85-125. MC VISA PC. TAC10. 4 rooms with PB, 1 with FP. Breakfast included in rates. Types of meals: full breakfast and early coffee/tea. Afternoon tea, evening snack and picnic lunch available. Beds: KDT. VCR, sauna and library on premises. Antiques, fishing, parks,

shopping, skiing, golf, theater and watersports nearby.
Location: On the Lake Superior Circle Tour.
Publicity: *Brainerd Daily Dispatch, Duluth News-Tribune, Tempo, Midwest Living, Minnesota Monthly, Lake Superior, Country, Minneapolis-St. Paul.*

"Your delectable dessert with anniversary cooler made a perfect end to a most memorable day for us."

Monticello   H5

The Historic Rand House

One Old Territorial Rd
Monticello, MN 55362
(612)295-6037 Fax:(612)295-6037
E-mail: randhaus@aol.com

Circa 1884. Located in the Monticello Historic District on more than three secluded acres, this three-story Queen Anne country Victorian is in the National Register as one of the last remaining Victorian country estates of its kind. There is a library and drawing room, and the winter parlor features arched windows and a stone fireplace. A favorite guest room is the Turret Room with clawfoot tub, tiled fireplace and an

octagonal sitting area with views of the grounds and the city. Breakfast is served in the solarium, wraparound porch or in the dining room with linen, china, silver, flowers and candlelight. Specialties at breakfast include items such as fruit plate, freshly baked scones and a frittata or quiche with sausage.
Innkeeper(s): Duffy & Merrill Busch. $85-135. MC VISA AX PC. TAC10. 4 rooms with PB, 2 with FP. 1 suite. Breakfast and afternoon tea included in rates. Types of meals: continental-plus breakfast, full breakfast, gourmet breakfast and early coffee/tea. Beds: KQ. Phone, air conditioning and turn-down service in room. Fax and library on premises. Family reunions hosted. Antiques, fishing, parks, shopping, cross-country skiing, sporting events, golf, theater and watersports nearby.
Publicity: *The Old Times, Country Register.*

"We're glad we discovered the Rand House and are looking forward to visiting again."

Nevis   E4

The Park Street Inn

R R 1 Box 254
Nevis, MN 56467-9704
(218)652-4500 (800)797-1778

Circa 1912. This late Victorian home was built by one of Minnesota's many Norwegian immigrants, a prominent businessman. He picked an ideal spot for the home, which overlooks Lake Belle Taine and sits across from a town park. The three comfortable guest rooms feature country antiques and beds topped with handmade quilts. Oak lamposts light the foyer, and the front parlor is highlighted by a Mission oak fireplace. Homemade fare such as waffles, pancakes, savory meats, egg dishes and French toast are served during the inn's daily country breakfast.
Innkeeper(s): Irene & Len Hall. $60-125. MC VISA PC TC. TAC10. 3 rooms, 4 with PB. 1 suite. Breakfast included in rates. Types of meals: full breakfast and early coffee/tea. Beds: QD. VCR, bicycles and library on premises. Weddings, small meetings and family reunions hosted. Antiques, fishing, parks, shopping, cross-country skiing and watersports nearby.
Pets Allowed: By arrangement only.

"Our favorite respite in the Heartland, where the pace is slow, hospitality is great and food is wonderful."

New York Mills   F3

Whistle Stop Inn B&B

RR 1 Box 85
New York Mills, MN 56567-9704
(218)385-2223 (800)328-6315

Circa 1903. A choo-choo theme permeates the atmosphere at this signature Victorian home. Antiques and railroad memorabilia decorate guest rooms
with names such as Great
Northern or Burlington
Northern. The Northern
Pacific room includes a bath
with a clawfoot tub. For
something unusual, try a
night in the Cozy Caboose,
which is exactly that, a
restored 19th-century
caboose. Despite the rustic nature, the caboose offers a double whirlpool tub. Freshly baked breads and seasonal fruit accompany the mouth-watering, homemade breakfasts.

Innkeeper(s): Roger & Jann Lee. $49-79. MC VISA AX DS PC. TAC10. 4 rooms with PB. 1 suite. 1 cottage. 1 conference room. Breakfast included in rates. Meals: continental breakfast, full breakfast and early coffee/tea. Afternoon tea available. Beds: QD. Phone, ceiling fan, TV in room. Bicycles on premises. Weddings, small meetings, family reunions and seminars hosted. Antiques, fishing, parks, shopping, cross-country skiing and golf nearby.

Saint Paul   H6

Chatsworth B&B

984 Ashland Ave
Saint Paul, MN 55104-7001
(612)227-4288

Circa 1902. This three-story Victorian is framed by maple and basswood trees, a tranquil setting for those in search of peace and relaxation. Each room is individually appointed. The Four
Poster Room is a romantic
retreat with a lace canopy
bed and marble bath.
Other rooms include
Scandanavian, Victorian,
Oriental and garden
themes. Specialty soaps,
kimonos, robes and luxurious towels are among the
amenities. The inn offers
close access to downtown St. Paul and Minneapolis, as well as the airport and the Mall of America.

Innkeeper(s): Casey Peterson & Neelie Forrester. $70-190. MC VISA AX DS. 5 rooms, 3 with PB. 1 conference room. Meals: continental-plus breakfast and full breakfast. Beds: KQDT. Phone in room. Bicycles on premises.
Publicity: St. Paul Pioneer Press and Dispatch.

"All that one needs, plus peace, quiet and space in such a creative and wonderful atmosphere."

The Garden Gate B&B

925 Goodrich Ave
Saint Paul, MN 55105-3127
(612)227-8430 (800)967-2703

Circa 1907. One of the most striking of the city's Victoria Crossing neighborhood homes is this recently redecorated

Prairie-style Victorian. The large duplex features guest rooms named Gladiolus, Rose and Delphinium, and the rooms are as lovely as they sound. Visitors to
the Garden Gate will be
enthralled with the treats within walking distance, including
other beautiful homes in the
neighborhood and along historic Summit Ave. and the
many shops, restaurants and
coffee shops on Grand Ave.
After a busy day of exploring, guests may want to request a therapeutic massage or soak in a clawfoot tub.

Historic Interest: St. Paul's Cathedral is one-and-one-half miles away, Governor's Mansion is two blocks away and the State Capitol is 2 miles away.
Innkeeper(s): Miles & Mary Conway. $55-75. PC TC. 4 rooms. Breakfast included in rates. Types of meals: continental-plus breakfast and early coffee/tea. Beds: QT. Air conditioning in room. Family reunions hosted. Antiques, parks, shopping, cross-country skiing and theater nearby.

"I couldn't have felt more at home!"

Sauk Centre   G4

Palmer House Hotel

228 Main St
Sauk Centre, MN 56378
(630)352-3431 (888)222-3431 Fax:(320)352-5602
E-mail: palmerhouse@saukherald.com

Circa 1901. Stained-glass windows, antique furnishings and paneled ceilings are among the features of this hotel, located on the old main street of town. There is a pub with a fireplace and a pianist plays the baby grand in the lobby. Some rooms offer Jacuzzis. The inn's restaurant offers homemade soups, prime rib, salads and breads in a setting with white table cloths and candles.

$59. AP. MC VISA AX DC CB DS PC TC. 22 rooms with PB. 8 suites. 1 conference room. Breakfast included in rates. Meals: continental breakfast and full breakfast. Lunch available. Restaurant on premises. Beds: QDT. Phone, air conditioning and TV in room. VCR, fax, copier and library on premises. Handicap access. Small meetings and family reunions hosted. Antiques, fishing, parks, shopping, cross-country skiing, golf and watersports nearby.
Publicity: Minnesota Seasons Magazine.

Stillwater   H6

Elephant Walk

801 Pine St W
Stillwater, MN 55082-5685
(612)430-0359 (888)430-0359 Fax:(612)351-9080
E-mail: elphantbb@aol.com

Circa 1886. Innkeeper Rita Graybill has filled her unusually named bed & breakfast with items she collected during 20 years in the diplomatic corp. Each room is named for a different place in the world, such as the Rangoon Room or Cadiz Garden Suite. The suite includes a rooftop garden, fireplace and whirlpool tub. For breakfast, homemade scones and tropical fruit accompany a special entree. Guests will
enjoy strolling the streets of
Stillwater, Minnesota's oldest
town, which features many
restored Victorian homes.
Elephant Walk is a 35-minute
drive from the Twin Cities.

Innkeeper(s): Rita Graybill. $109-219. MC VISA DS PC TC. 4 rooms with PB, 4 with FP. 1 suite. Breakfast and evening snack included in rates. Meals: gourmet breakfast, early coffee/tea. Beds: QD. Air conditioning, ceiling fan in room. Fax, copier, spa on premises. Small meetings hosted. Thai and Spanish spoken. Antiques, fishing, parks, shopping, skiing, golf, theater nearby.

Publicity: *Midwest Living, Discover.*

"You made our visit at the Elephant Walk incredibly delightful. Thank you for sharing your world with us."

Rivertown Inn

306 Olive St W
Stillwater, MN 55082-4932
(612)430-2955 (800)562-3632 Fax:(612)430-0034

Circa 1882. This three-story Victorian was built by lumbermill owner John O'Brien. Framed by an iron fence, the home has a wraparound veranda. Each guest room has been decorated with care, but we suggest the honeymoon suite or Patricia's Room with its giant whirlpool and white iron bed. A burl-wood buffet in the dining room is laden each morning with home-baked breads and cakes. The St. Croix River is a short walk away.

Innkeeper(s): Chuck & Judy Dougherty. $79-179. MC VISA AX DC DS PC TC. TAC10. 12 rooms with PB, 9 with FP. 4 suites. 1 conference room. Breakfast and evening snack included in rates. Types of meals: full breakfast, gourmet breakfast and early coffee/tea. Beds: QD. Phone, air conditioning, ceiling fan and TV in room. Fax on premises. Handicap access. Small meetings and seminars hosted. Antiques, fishing, parks, shopping, skiing, theater nearby.
Location: Four blocks from historic main street.
Publicity: *Country.*

"Fantastic place for a romantic getaway!"

The William Sauntry Mansion

626 4th St N
Stillwater, MN 55082-4827
(612)430-2653 (800)828-2653 Fax:(612)351-7872
E-mail: sauntryinn@aol.com

Circa 1890. This Queen Anne Victorian is stunning inside and out. Its exterior is that of a true "Painted Lady," done in shades of goldenrod and a deep green, with intricate trim. The palatial interior has been painstakingly restored, including the near dozen fireplaces, shining parquet floors and beautiful woodwork. Stained-glass windows add to the Victorian ambiance, as do the variety of fine antiques that fill the home. Each bedchamber has a fireplace, and some have whirlpool tubs. William Sauntry, a prominent lumber baron, built the 25-room manor, and it is listed in the National Register. With the many historic homes, Stillwater is a perfect town for those who wish to bask in all that is Victoriana. Minneapolis and the Mall of America are nearby.

Innkeeper(s): Art & Elaine Halbardier. $99-159. MC VISA PC TC. 7 rooms with PB, 6 with FP. Breakfast, afternoon tea and evening snack included in rates. Types of meals: gourmet breakfast and early coffee/tea. Beds: KQ. Air conditioning in room. Fax on premises. Small meetings, family reunions and seminars hosted. Fishing, parks, shopping, downhill skiing, sporting events, golf, theater and watersports nearby.

"The history here is intriguing, the rooms very nicely done and your cooking is superb."

Vergas   E3

The Log House & Homestead on Spirit Lake

PO Box 130
Vergas, MN 56587-0130
(218)342-2318 (800)342-2318

Circa 1889. Either a 19th-century family log house or a turn-of-the-century homestead greets guests at this inn, situated on 115

acres of woods and fields. The inn overlooks Spirit Lake in the heart of Minnesota's lake country. Both houses have been carefully restored in a romantic, country style. Guest rooms are light and airy with colorful  quilts, poster beds and elegant touches. Three rooms include fireplaces and whirlpool baths for two. The innkeepers recently added a penthouse suite, perfect for a romantic getaway. During the summer months, guests enjoy use of small boats and canoes equipped with parasols, and in the winter, snowshoes are available. Guests are welcomed with a tray filled with goodies. For an additional charge, the innkeepers offer a picnic lunch.

Historic Interest: Two state parks (30 miles), Itasca, source of the Mississippi (1 1/2 hours).

Innkeeper(s): Yvonne & Lyle Tweten. $95-145. MC VISA AX DS PC TC. 5 rooms with PB, 3 with FP. 1 suite. 1 conference room. Breakfast included in rates. Types of meals: gourmet breakfast and early coffee/tea. Picnic lunch available. Beds: KQ. Air conditioning and ceiling fan in room. Swimming on premises. 115 acres. Weddings, small meetings and seminars hosted. French spoken. Antiques, parks, shopping, cross-country skiing, sporting events, theater and watersports nearby.

Publicity: *Forum, News Flashes, Minneapolis/St. Paul, Minnesota Monthly, House To Home, St. Paul Pioneer Press, Midwest Living, Mpls/St. Paul Magazine.*

"Our stay here has made our anniversary everything we hoped for!"

Wabasha   17

Bridgewaters B&B

136 Bridge Ave
Wabasha, MN 55981-1211
(612)565-4208

Circa 1903. Located a block and a half from the Mississippi River, this inn features gardens and a massive wraparound veranda, often the site for weddings and reunions. Originally

built by a lumber executive, the house boasts beautiful woodwork including polished parquet floors. Guest chambers are named after various Mississippi River bridges. The Lafayette Room has a whirlpool tub, fireplace and an antique bed. On weekends, a full breakfast is served by candlelight and may include wild rice sausage and a hot entree.

Innkeeper(s): Bill & Carole Moore. $75-145. MC VISA. 5 rooms, 2 with PB, 1 with FP. 1 suite. Breakfast included in rates. Types of meals: continental-plus breakfast, full breakfast and early coffee/tea. Beds: QDT. Phone and air conditioning in room. Weddings, small meetings and family reunions hosted. Antiques, fishing, parks, shopping, downhill skiing, cross-country skiing, golf and watersports nearby.

Publicity: *Minnesota Monthly.*

Mississippi

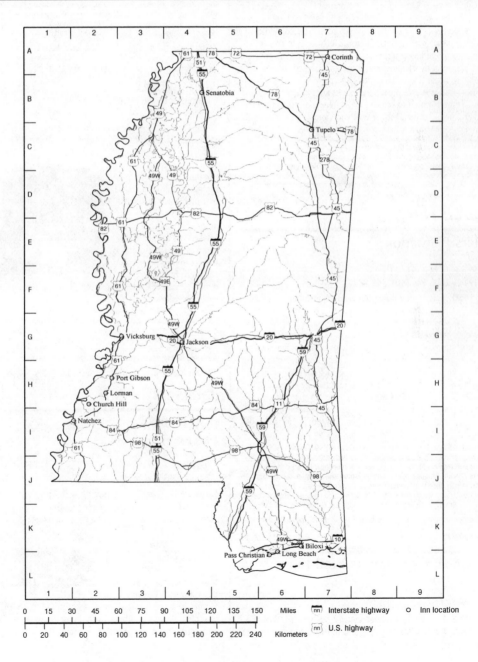

	1	2	3	4	5	6	7	8	9

A — 61, 78, 72 — 72, Corinth
45
51
55

B — Senatobia — 78
49

C — 61 — Tupelo, 78
49W, 49 — 45
55 — 278

D — 49W, 49 — 82, 82 — 45

E — 82, 61 — 55 — 49W, 49
45

F — 61 — 49E — 45
55

G — 49W — 20 — 20
Vicksburg, 20, Jackson — 45
59

H — 61 — 55 — 49W
Port Gibson — 84, 11 — 45
Lorman
Church Hill
59

I — Natchez — 84 — 84 — 59
84, 98, 51, 55 — 98

J — 61 — 49W — 98
59

K — 49W, 10
Pass Christian, Long Beach, Biloxi

L

| 0 | 15 | 30 | 45 | 60 | 75 | 90 | 105 | 120 | 135 | 150 | Miles |
| 0 | 20 | 40 | 60 | 80 | 100 | 120 | 140 | 160 | 180 | 200 | 220 | 240 | Kilometers |

nn Interstate highway   ○ Inn location

nn U.S. highway

277

Biloxi K6

Father Ryan House B&B

1196 Beach Blvd
Biloxi, MS 39530-3631
(228)435-1189 (800)295-1189 Fax:(228)436-3063
E-mail: frryan@datasync.com

Circa 1841. Father Abram Ryan, once the Poet Laureate of the Confederacy and a friend of Jefferson Davis, lived in this Antebellum manor. The inn is in the National Historic Registry and one of the oldest homes on the Gulf Coast. The Gulf of Mexico sparkles just across the way, and guests can enjoy the view from several guest rooms. There are 11 rooms to choose, four include a whirlpool tub. Several offer a porch or balcony. Rooms are elegantly appointed, and the antique beds are dressed with luxury linens. Down comforters and pillows are other amenities. Father Ryan's poetry and books are placed throughout the inn. There is much to see and do in Biloxi; guests can tour historic homes, charter a fishing boat and shop at an outlet mall.
Innkeeper(s): Alicia Stanley & Dina Davis. $85-150. MC VISA AX DS TC. TAC10. 11 rooms with PB, 2 with FP. 3 suites. 2 cottages. Breakfast included in rates. Meals: full breakfast, gourmet breakfast, early coffee/tea. Beds: KQ. Phone, air conditioning, turndown service, ceiling fan, TV in room. VCR, fax, swimming, library on premises. Handicap access. Weddings, small meeting,s family reunions hosted. Italian and Spanish spoken. Amusement parks, antiques, fishing, parks, shopping, golf, theater and watersports nearby.
Publicity: *Travel & Leisure, Southern Living.*

Church Hill H2

Cedars Plantation

Route 553
Church Hill, MS 39120
(601)445-2203 Fax:(601)445-2372

Circa 1830. This National Register estate is a testament to the fact that getting married in the South has its advantages. The 1830 home was built by Colonel James Wood as a wedding gift for his daughter. It also was home to actor George Hamilton. The home started out as a Federal-style planters cottage, but 1854 additions added the impressive Greek Revival architecture and Doric columns. The inn's 176 acres include a lake and rolling lawns dotted with cedars and flowers. The elegant, Antebellum decor captures the spirit of the 19th century. In regal Southern style, guests are treated to a gourmet breakfast served on antique china with silver and crystal. Regional breakfast essentials, such as cheese grits and freshly baked biscuits, accompany eggs and bacon or perhaps stuffed French toast.
Innkeeper(s): Glenda & Dick Robinson. $160-200. MC VISA DS PC. TAC18. 4 rooms with PB, 4 with FP. 1 suite. Breakfast included in rates. Types of meals: full breakfast and early coffee/tea. Dinner and banquet service available. Beds: KQ. Phone, air conditioning, turndown service and ceiling fan in room. TV, VCR and fax on premises. 176 acres. Weddings and small meetings hosted. Antiques, fishing, parks, shopping, golf and theater nearby.

"It was a wonderful expression of southern living in a most beautiful setting."

Corinth A7

The Generals' Quarters B&B Inn

924 Fillmore St
Corinth, MS 38834-4125
(601)286-3325 Fax:(601)287-8188

Circa 1872. History buffs will enjoy this inn, located 22 miles from Shiloh National Military Park and in the historic district of Corinth, a Civil War village. Visitors to this Queen Anne Victorian, with its quiet, tree-lined lot, enjoy a full breakfast and grounds decorated with a pond and flowers. Three guest rooms and two suites are available. Fort Robinette and Corinth National Cemetery are nearby. The inn is within walking distance to shops, museums, historic sites, restaurants and more.
Innkeeper(s): Charlotte Brandt & Luke Doehner. $75-90. MC VISA DS TC. 5 rooms with PB, 4 with FP. 2 suites. 1 conference room. Breakfast and evening snack included in rates. Types of meals: full breakfast, gourmet breakfast and early coffee/tea. Dinner, picnic lunch, gourmet lunch, banquet service, catering service, catered breakfast and room service available. Restaurant on premises. Beds: KQDT. Phone, air conditioning, turndown service, ceiling fan, TV and VCR in room. Fax and bicycles on premises. Handicap access. Weddings, small meetings, family reunions and seminars hosted. Antiques, fishing, parks, shopping, theater and watersports nearby.

"Ranks with the best, five stars. You have thought of many comforts."

Robbins Nest Bed & Breakfast

1523 E Shiloh Rd
Corinth, MS 38834-3632
(601)286-3109

Circa 1869. This gracious columned plantation-style mansion rests on two acres of grounds with tall oaks and a pink, red and white hedge of dog-wood. Azaleas bloom on the inn's grounds in spring. A walnut staircase, two-inch-thick plank walls and pine floors are among the features of the house. The formal dining room or the back porch is the setting for hearty Southern breakfasts, which consist of cheese grits, hash brown potatoes, eggs, pancakes or waffles.
Innkeeper(s): Anne & Tony Whyte. $80-90. MC VISA PC TC. 3 rooms with PB. 1 suite. Breakfast and afternoon tea included in rates. Types of meals: continental breakfast, continental-plus breakfast, full breakfast and gourmet breakfast. Beds: QDT. Phone, air conditioning, turndown service, ceiling fan and TV in room. VCR on premises. Weddings and small meetings hosted. Antiques, fishing, parks, shopping, golf, theater and watersports nearby.

"We felt like we were visiting a favorite cousin."

Jackson G4

Fairview Inn

734 Fairview St
Jackson, MS 39202-1624
(601)948-3429 (888)948-1908 Fax:(601)948-1203
E-mail: fairview@teclink.net

Circa 1908. There's little question why this magnificent Colonial Revival mansion has been chosen as one of the United States' premiere inns. Designed by an associate of Frank Lloyd Wright, the home boasts unfor-gettable polished hardwood floors, a beautiful marble floor, fine furnishings and tasteful decor. The innkeepers, Carol and William Simmons, pamper guests with a plentiful cook-to-order breakfast, fresh flowers and have hosted many a wedding reception and party. History buffs will appreciate William's knowledge of

Mississippi's past. There are helpful business amenities here, including in-room dataports. The inn has been hailed for its hospitality and cuisine by Country Inns magazine and the James Beard Foundation.

Historic Interest: The home, one of few of its kind remaining in Jackson, is listed in the National Register. The Old Capitol Museum is just over a mile from Fairview. Historic Manship House is only half a mile, and an art museum and agriculture and forestry museum are two miles away.

Innkeeper(s): Carol & William Simmons. $115-165. EP. MC VISA AX DS PC TC. TAC10. 8 rooms with PB. 5 suites. 4 conference rooms. Breakfast included in rates. Types of meals: continental breakfast, full breakfast, gourmet breakfast and early coffee/tea. Dinner, evening snack, lunch, gourmet lunch, banquet service, catering service and catered breakfast available. Beds: KQ. Phone, air conditioning, turndown service, ceiling fan, TV and VCR in room. Fax, copier and library on premises. Handicap access. Weddings, small meetings, family reunions and seminars hosted. French spoken. Antiques, parks, shopping, sporting events and theater nearby.

Publicity: *Country Inns.*

"Elegant and comfortable."

Millsaps-Buie House

628 N State St
Jackson, MS 39202-3303
(601)352-0221

Circa 1888. Major Millsaps, founder of Millsaps College, built this stately mansion more than 100 years ago. Today the house remains in the family. A handsome, columned entrance, bays and gables are features of the house decorated by Berle Smith, designer for Mississippi's governor's mansion. The parlor features a grand piano. The guest rooms are appointed in antiques and canopied beds.

Historic Interest: Listed in the National Register.

Innkeeper(s): Nancy Fleming, Harriet Brewer & Rodger Ownby. $100-170. MC VISA AX DC DS. 11 rooms with PB. 1 conference room. Meal: full breakfast. Beds: KQ. Fax, copier on premises. Handicap access. Theater nearby.

Publicity: *New York Times, Jackson Clarion Ledger, Mississippi Magazine, Travel & Leisure.*

Long Beach
L6

Red Creek Inn, Vineyard & Racing Stables

7416 Red Creek Rd
Long Beach, MS 39560-8804
(601)452-3080 (800)729-9670 Fax:(601)452-4450

Circa 1899. This inn was built in the raised French cottage-style by a retired Italian sea captain, who wished to entice his bride to move from her parents' home in New Orleans. There

are two swings on the 64-foot front porch and one swing that hangs from a 300-year-old oak tree. Magnolias and ancient live oaks, some registered with the Live Oak Society of the Louisiana Garden Club, dot 11 acres. The inn features a parlor, six fireplaces, ceiling fans and antiques, including a Victorian organ, wooden radios and a Victrola. The inn's suite includes a Jacuzzi tub.

Historic Interest: The inn is near Beauvoir, Jefferson Davis' last home.

Innkeeper(s): Karl & "Toni" Mertz. $49-124. PC. TAC10. 6 rooms, 4 with PB, 1 with FP. 1 suite. 1 conference room. Breakfast included in rates. Types of meals: continental-plus breakfast and early coffee/tea. Beds: DT. Air conditioning in room. TV, VCR, fax, copier, stables and library on premises. 11 acres. Weddings, small meetings, family reunions and seminars hosted.

Spanish spoken. Amusement parks, antiques, fishing, parks, shopping, theater and watersports nearby.

Publicity: *Jackson Daily News, Innviews, TV Channel 13, Mississippi ETV, Men's Journal, The Bridal Directory.*

"We loved waking up here on these misty spring mornings. The Old South is here."

Lorman
H2

Rosswood Plantation

Hwy 552 East
Lorman, MS 39096
(601)437-4215 (800)533-5889 Fax:(601)437-6888
E-mail: whylander@aol.com

Circa 1857. Rosswood is a stately, columned mansion in an original plantation setting. Here, guests may find antiques, buried treasure, ghosts, history of a slave revolt, a Civil War battleground, the first owner's diary and genuine southern hospitality. Voted the "prettiest place in the country" by Farm & Ranch Living, the manor

is a Mississippi Landmark and is in the National Register.

Innkeeper(s): Jean & Walt Hylander. $99-125. MC VISA AX DS PC TC. TAC10. 4 rooms with PB, 4 with FP. Breakfast included in rates. Types of meals: gourmet breakfast and early coffee/tea. Beds: QDT. Phone, air conditioning, ceiling fan and VCR in room. Fax, copier, spa, swimming and library on premises. 100 acres. Weddings and small meetings hosted. Antiques, fishing, parks and shopping nearby.

Publicity: *Southern Living, The New York Times, Mississippi Magazine, Conde Nast Traveler, Inn Country USA.*

Natchez
I2

The Briars Inn & Garden

PO Box 1245
Natchez, MS 39121-1245
(601)446-9654 (800)634-1818 Fax:(601)446-6037
E-mail: w&cint@bkbank.com

Circa 1814. Set on 19 wooded acres overlooking the Mississippi River, the Briars is most noted for having been the family home of Varina Howell where she married Jefferson Davis in 1845. One can only imagine the romance evoked from the simple ceremony in the parlor in front of the carved wood Adam-style mantel. Everything about this elegant and sophisticated Southern

Planter-style home brings to life glorious traditions of the Old South, from the 48-foot drawing room with its twin staircases, five Palladian arches and gallery to the lush gardens with more than 1,000 azaleas and camellias. The current owners are interior designers, which is evident in their fine use of fabrics, wall coverings, tastefully appointed guest rooms decorated in period antiques, Oriental rugs and selected art. A gourmet breakfast is served each morning.

Innkeeper(s): R E Canon-Newton Wilds. $135-150. MC VISA AX PC TC. TAC10. 14 rooms with PB, 6 with FP. 2 suites. 1 cottage. Breakfast included in rates. Meals: full breakfast, gourmet breakfast and early coffee/tea. Beds: KQT. Phone, air conditioning, turndown service, ceiling fan and TV in room. Fax, copier and swimming on premises. Handicap access. 19 acres. Antiques, fishing, parks, shopping, cross-country skiing, golf, theater nearby.

"We so enjoyed the splendor of your beautiful gardens. Breakfast was superb and the service outstanding! Thanks!"

Dunleith

84 Homochitto St
Natchez, MS 39120-3905
(601)446-8500 (800)433-2445

Circa 1856. This Greek Revival plantation house is listed as a National Historic Landmark. During the Civil War, the Davis family raised thoroughbred horses here, and the story goes that when they heard Union officers were coming to take their horses, they hid their favorites in the cellar under the dining room. The officers ate dinner and heard nothing so the horses were saved. Rare French Zuber mural wallpaper decorates the dining room.

Innkeeper(s): Nancy Gibbs. $95-140. MC VISA DS TC. 11 rooms with PB, 11 with FP. 1 conference room. Breakfast included in rates. Type of meal: full breakfast. Beds: QDT. Phone, air conditioning and TV in room. 40 acres. Antiques nearby.

Publicity: *Southern Accents, Unique Homes, Good Housekeeping, Country Inns.*

"The accommodations at the mansion were wonderful. Southern hospitality is indeed charming and memorable!"

Highpoint

215 Linton Ave
Natchez, MS 39120-2315
(601)442-6963 (800)283-4099

Circa 1890. This Queen Anne Victorian, just a block from the Mississippi River, was named the 1997 Property of the Year by the Natchez Convention and Visitors Bureau. The home was the first residence built in the state's first planned subdivision. Guests enjoy a tour of the historic home upon arrival. A plentiful, plantation-style breakfast is  served each morning. The inn is in the National Register.

Innkeeper(s): Frank Bauer, John Davis. $80-125. MC VISA PC TC. TAC10. 3 rooms with PB, 2 with FP. Breakfast and evening snack included in rates. Types of meals: full breakfast, gourmet breakfast and early coffee/tea. Beds: KQT. Phone, air conditioning and turndown service in room. TV and library on premises. Small meetings and family reunions hosted. Antiques, shopping and theater nearby.

"You have a special gift for making others feel welcome. Thank you for such a good time."

Linden

1 Linden Pl
Natchez, MS 39120-4077
(601)445-5472 (800)254-6336 Fax:(601)442-7548

Circa 1800. Mrs. Jane Gustine purchased this elegant white Federal plantation home in 1849, and it has remained in her family for six generations. Nestled on seven wooded acres, the inn boasts one of the finest collections of Federal antique furnishings in the South. The stately dining room contains an original Hepplewhite banquet table, set with a many pieces of family coin silver and heirloom china. Three Havell editions of John James Audubon's bird prints are displayed on the walls. Throughout the years, the inn has served as a respite for famous Mississippi statesmen, including the wife of Senator Percy Quinn. Each of the seven guest rooms features canopy beds and authentic Federal antiques. A full Southern breakfast is included in the rates. The Linden is on the Spring and Fall Pilgrimages.

Historic Interest: The inn is in the National Register.

Innkeeper(s): Jeanette Feltus. $90-115. PC TC. TAC10. 7 rooms with PB. Breakfast included in rates. Types of meals: full breakfast, gourmet breakfast and early coffee/tea. Beds: KQDT. Air conditioning, turndown service and ceiling fan in room. TV, fax, copier and library on premises. Handicap access. Antiques, fishing, parks, shopping, golf, theater and watersports nearby.

Location: Off Melrose Avenue.

Monmouth Plantation

36 Melrose Ave
Natchez, MS 39120-4005
(601)442-5852 (800)828-4531 Fax:(604)446-7762

Circa 1818. Monmouth was the home of General Quitman who became acting Governor of Mexico, Governor of Mississippi, and a U.S. Congressman. In the National Historic Landmark, the inn features antique four-poster and canopy beds, turndown service and an evening cocktail hour. Guests Jefferson Davis and Henry Clay enjoyed the same acres of gardens, pond and walking paths available today.

Innkeeper(s): Jim Anderson. $130-350. MC VISA AX DC CB DS PC TC. 28 rooms with PB, 18 with FP. 13 suites. 4 cottages. 1 conference room. Breakfast included in rates. Types of meals: full breakfast and early coffee/tea. Dinner available. Restaurant on premises. Beds: KQDT. Air conditioning, turndown service and TV in room. Fax and copier on premises. 26 acres. Weddings, small meetings, family reunions and seminars hosted. French spoken. Antiques and shopping nearby.

"The best historical inn we have stayed at anywhere."

Oakland Plantation

1124 Lower Woodville Rd
Natchez, MS 39120-8657
(601)445-5101 (800)824-0355 Fax:(601)442-5182

Circa 1785. Andrew Jackson courted his future wife, Rachel Robards, at this gracious 18th-century home. This working cattle plantation includes nature trails and a game preserve, fishing ponds, a tennis court and canoeing. Rooms are filled with antiques, and the innkeepers provide guests with a tour of the main home and plantation. They also will arrange tours of Natchez.

Historic Interest: The historic mansions of Natchez are all within 10 miles of the inn.

Innkeeper(s): Jean & Andy Peabody. $65-75. AP. MC VISA AX TC. TAC10. 3 rooms, 2 with PB, 3 with FP. 1 conference room. Breakfast included in rates. Type of meal: full breakfast. Beds: KT. Air conditioning in room. TV and tennis on premises. 360 acres. Small meetings hosted. Antiques, fishing, parks, theater and watersports nearby.

Publicity: *Southern Living, Country Inns.*

"Best kept secret in Natchez! Just great!"

Ravennaside

601 S Union St
Natchez, MS 39120-3521
(601)442-8015 (888)442-8015 Fax:(601)446-7441

Circa 1899. In the Greek Revival style, this mansion's four acres are set off with a wrought-iron fence and include giant live oaks, huge camellias and magnolias and a path lined with crepe myrtle. Hosting writers, foreign dignitaries, politicians and the social elite of Natchez, the home belonged to "Sweet Auntie," Mrs. Roane Fleming Byrnes, originator of the Natchez Trace. The original master plan for the parkway is displayed, brought here by Eleanor Roosevelt. The Gold Room offers unique parquet floors, a handsome gilded mirror, marble fireplace, chandeliers, gold-finished furnishings and a white baby grand piano. Ask for the room with the grand canopy bed and purple seatee. Garlic cheese grits, fresh biscuits, and sausage and egg strata are breakfast specialties. Enjoy billiards, bocci, croquet and horseshoes.

Innkeeper(s): Sara & Jack Coleman. $85-135. MC VISA PC TC. TAC10. 8 cabins, 1 with FP. 1 conference room. Breakfast included in rates. Types of meals: full breakfast and early coffee/tea. Banquet service available. Beds: QT. Air conditioning and TV in room. VCR, fax, copier, spa, stables, bicycles, library and child care on premises. Weddings, small meetings, family reunions and seminars hosted. Antiques, fishing, parks, shopping, golf, theater and watersports nearby. Pets Allowed.

Weymouth Hall

1 Cemetery Rd
Natchez, MS 39120-2028
(601)445-2304 Fax:(601)445-0602

Circa 1855. Situated on a bluff overlooking the Mississippi, this National Registry Greek Revival mansion boasts sweeping panoramic views of the river and lush grounds surrounding it. Recessed porches, fine millwork and brickwork are a few of the architectural features of the original design. Common rooms as well as guest rooms are decorated in period antiques. A complimentary breakfast features eggs, ham, grits, fresh fruit and muffins is served daily.

$95-120. MC VISA AX TC. TAC10. 5 rooms with PB. Breakfast included in rates. Types of meals: full breakfast and early coffee/tea. Catering service available. Beds: QD. Air conditioning and VCR in room. Fax on premises. 12 acres. Weddings, small meetings, family reunions and seminars hosted. Antiques, golf and theater nearby.

Pass Christian   L6

Harbour Oaks Inn

126 W Scenic Dr
Pass Christian, MS 39571-4420
(228)452-9399 (800)452-9399 Fax:(228)452-9321
E-mail: harbour@ibm.net

Circa 1860. Three dormers rise from the roof of this two-and-a-half-story coastal cottage, listed in the National Register. Shaded by massive live oaks draped with Spanish moss, this is the only 19th-century hotel still operating in the area. It was formerly known as the Live Oaks House and later the Crescent Hotel. A double veranda stretches gracefully across the width of the inn. Decorated with interesting antiques and family heirlooms, the inn's white woodwork, French doors and multi-paned windows bring light and air to the guest rooms. Surviving both Union shelling and 200-mile Hurricane Camille, the inn stands beautifully maintained overlooking the harbor

and Gulf of Mexico. Enjoy the Jacuzzi room or stroll to galleries and antique shops.

Innkeeper(s): Tony & Diane Brugger. $83-108. MC VISA AX PC TC. TAC10. 5 rooms with PB, 2 with FP. Breakfast included in rates. Types of meals: full breakfast and early coffee/tea. Beds: KD. Air conditioning in room. TV, VCR, fax and copier on premises. Small meetings hosted. Antiques, fishing, parks, shopping, golf, theater and watersports nearby.

"The last few days have been a marvelous experience. You welcomed me into your home and made me feel like family."

Port Gibson   H2

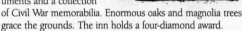

Oak Square Plantation

1207 Church St
Port Gibson, MS 39150-2609
(601)437-5300 (800)729-0240 Fax:(601)437-5768

Circa 1850. Six 22-foot-tall fluted Corinthian columns support the front gallery of this 30-room Greek Revival plantation. The owners furnished the mansion with Mississippi heirloom antiques, some as old as 200 years. The parlor holds a carved rosewood Victorian suite, original family documents and a collection of Civil War memorabilia. Enormous oaks and magnolia trees grace the grounds. The inn holds a four-diamond award.

Historic Interest: Listed in the National Register.

Innkeeper(s): Ms. William D. Lum. $85-125. MC VISA AX DS TC. 12 rooms with PB. Breakfast included in rates. Type of meal: full breakfast. Beds: QT. Phone, air conditioning, turndown service and TV in room. VCR, fax and copier on premises. Small meetings hosted.

Location: US 61 between Natchez & Vicksburg.

Publicity: *Quad-City Times, Dallas Morning News.*

"We just cannot say enough about the wonderful ambiance of Oak Square...except it is even better than four stars."

Senatobia   B4

Spahn House B&B

401 College St
Senatobia, MS 38668-2128
(601)562-9853 (800)400-9853 Fax:(601)562-8160

Circa 1904. Originally built by a cotton and cattle baron, this 5,000-square-foot Neoclassical house sits on two acres and is listed in the National Register. Professionally decorated, it features

fine antiques and luxuriously furnished rooms with elegant bed linens and Jacuzzi tubs. Private candlelight dinners are available by advance request. Breakfasts feature gourmet cuisine as the inn also manages a full-time catering business. (Guests sometimes are invited to sample food in the kitchen before it makes its way to local parties and events.) Memphis is 30 minutes north.

Historic Interest: Graceland, Sun Studio, Clarksdale's Delta Blues Museum.

Innkeeper(s): Daughn & Joe Spahn. $60-110. MC VISA AX DS PC TC. TAC10. 4 rooms with PB. 1 suite. 5 conference rooms. Breakfast included in rates. Meals: full breakfast, gourmet breakfast and early coffee/tea. Afternoon tea, dinner, evening snack, picnic lunch, lunch, gourmet lunch, banquet service, catering service, catered breakfast, room service available. Beds: Q. Phone, air conditioning, ceiling fan, TV in room. VCR, fax and library on premises. Weddings, small meetings, family reunions, seminars hosted. Limited French, German, Spanish spoken. Amusement parks, antiques, fishing, parks, shopping, sporting events, theater, watersports nearby.

Publicity: *South Florida Magazine, Mississippi Magazine.*

"I hope everyone gets to experience that type of Southern hospitality just once in their lifetime."

Tupelo   C7

The Mockingbird Inn B&B

305 N Gloster St
Tupelo, MS 38801-3623
(601)841-0286 Fax:(601)840-4158

Circa 1925. This inn's architecture incorporates elements of Colonial, Art Deco and Arts and Crafts styles. The interior is decorated with white sofas, a plethora of green plants and antiques. Guest rooms include Paris with a pewter canopy wedding bed and Victorian wicker chaise, and the Athens, which boasts a lavish Grecian decor including columns and an L-shaped whirlpool for two. Other rooms and corresponding themes offered are Africa, Bavaria, Venice, Mackinac Island and Sansabel Island. Several romantic packages are available including a Sweetheart Gift Basket. A porch, gazebo and back garden invite relaxing conversation. Cross the street to three of the area's favorite restaurants. Children 10 and over are welcome.

Innkeeper(s): Jim & Sandy Gilmer. $65-125. MC VISA AX DS TC. TAC10. 7 rooms with PB, 1 with FP. 2 suites. Breakfast and evening snack included in rates. Types of meals: gourmet breakfast and early coffee/tea. Beds: Q. Phone, air conditioning, ceiling fan and TV in room. Fax, copier and pet boarding on premises. Handicap access. Antiques, fishing, parks, shopping, golf and theater nearby.

Pets Allowed: With $10 donation to Humane Society.

Vicksburg   G3

Annabelle

501 Speed St
Vicksburg, MS 39180-4065
(601)638-2000 (800)791-2000 Fax:(601)636-5054

Circa 1868. From the outside, Annabelle looks like a friendly mix of Victorian and Italianate architecture set on an unassuming lawn of magnolias and pecan trees. It is the gracious interior and hospitality that has earned this bed & breakfast consistently high ratings. Walls are painted in deep, rich hues, highlighting the polished wood floors, Oriental rugs and beautiful antiques. Some of the furnishings are family heirlooms. Innkeepers George and  Carolyn Mayer spent many years in the restaurant business and offer delicious Southern fare during the morning meal. George, a native of Moravia, speaks German, Portuguese and some Spanish.

Historic Interest: Antebellum homes and civil war history sites.

Innkeeper(s): Carolyn & George Mayer. $90-150. MC VISA AX DC CB DS PC TC. TAC10. 8 rooms with PB, 2 with FP. 1 suite. 1 cottage. Breakfast and afternoon tea included in rates. Types of meals: gourmet breakfast and early coffee/tea. Beds: KQ. Phone, air conditioning, turndown service and TV in

room. Fax, swimming and library on premises. Family reunions hosted. German and Portuguese spoken. Amusement parks, antiques, fishing, parks, shopping, theater and watersports nearby.

Pets Allowed: Small.

"You have a beautiful home. The history and decor really give the place flavor."

Balfour House

1002 Crawford St
Vicksburg, MS 39181-0781
(601)638-7113 (800)294-7113

Circa 1835. Writer and former resident Emma Balfour witnessed the Siege of Vicksburg from the window of this Greek Revival home. Until the Civil War, the home was the site of elegant balls attended by Southern belles in ornate gowns accompanied by Confederate beaus. Innkeepers Bob and Sharon Humble brought back these grand affairs during several re-enactment dances, in which guests dress up in period costume. The National Register home is a piece of history, with stunning architectural features, such as the showpiece, three-story elliptical spiral staircase. The home is an official site on the Civil War Discovery Trail, as well as a Vicksburg and Mississippi landmark.

Innkeeper(s): Bob & Sharon Humble. $85-150. MC VISA AX PC TC. 4 rooms with PB, 1 with FP. 1 conference room. Breakfast included in rates. Type of meal: gourmet breakfast. Catering service available. Beds: KQDT. Phone, air conditioning and TV in room. Weddings, small meetings, family reunions and seminars hosted. Amusement parks, antiques, fishing, parks, shopping and theater nearby.

Belle of The Bends

508 Klein St
Vicksburg, MS 39180-4004
(601)634-0737 (800)844-2308

Circa 1876. Located in Vicksburg's Historic Garden District, this Victorian, Italianate mansion was built by Mississippi State Senator Murray F. Smith and his wife, Kate. It is nestled on a bluff overlooking the Mississippi River. The decor includes period antiques, Oriental rugs and memorabilia of the steamboats that plied the river waters in the 1880s and early 1900s. Two bedrooms and the first- and second-story wrap-around verandas provide views of the river. A plantation breakfast is served and a tour of the house and history of the steamboats owned by the Morrissey Line is given. A tour of the Victorian Gardens also is available to guests.

Historic Interest: A military park and Old Courthouse Museum are less than one mile from the home.

Innkeeper(s): Wallace & Josephine Pratt. $95-135. MC VISA AX DS. 4 rooms with PB. Breakfast and afternoon tea included in rates. Type of meal: full breakfast. Beds: KQDT. Air conditioning, TV, VCR in room. Antiques nearby.

Publicity: *Natchez Trace News Explorer, Victorian Style, Victoria.*

"Thank you for the personalized tour of the home and area. We greatly enjoyed our stay. This house got us into the spirit of the period."

Cedar Grove Mansion Inn

2200 Oak St
Vicksburg, MS 39180-4008
(601)636-1000 (800)862-1300 Fax:(601)634-6126

Circa 1840. It's easy to relive "Gone With the Wind" at this grand antebellum estate built by John Klein as a wedding present for his bride. Visitors sip mint juleps and watch gas chandeliers flicker in the finely appointed parlors. The children's rooms and master bedroom contain their original furnishings. Although Cedar Grove survived the Civil War, a Union cannonball is still lodged in the parlor wall. There is a magnificent view of the Mississippi from the terraces and front galleries. Four acres of gardens include fountains and gazebos. There is a bar, and the inn's restaurant opens each evening at 6 p.m.

Historic Interest: National Military Park (5 miles) and museums.

Innkeeper(s): Rhonda Abraham. $68-165. MC VISA AX DS TC. TAC10. 28 rooms with PB, 3 with FP. 11 suites. 8 cottages. 4 conference rooms. Breakfast included in rates. Type of meal: full breakfast. Banquet service and room service available. Restaurant on premises. Beds: KQDT. Phone, air conditioning, turndown service and TV in room. Fax, copier, swimming, bicycles, tennis and library on premises. Handicap access. Weddings, small meetings and family reunions hosted. Amusement parks, antiques, fishing, parks, shopping, theater and watersports nearby.

Publicity: *Vicksburg Post, Southern Living, Victorian Homes, Country Inns.*

"Love at first sight would be the best way to describe my feelings for your home and the staff."

The Duff Green Mansion

PO Box 75, 1114 First East St
Vicksburg, MS 39180
(601)636-6968 (800)992-0037

Circa 1856. The 12,000-square-foot Duff Green Mansion is considered one of the finest examples of Palladian architecture in Mississippi. It was a wedding gift to Mary Lake Green from her parents, Judge and Mrs. William Lake, who built the adjacent house, Lakemont. During the siege of Vicksburg, Mary Green gave birth in one of the caves next to the mansion and named her son Siege Green. Handsome furnishings highlight the spacious and elegantly renovated common rooms where guests are invited to enjoy afternoon tea or an evening cocktail.

Innkeeper(s): Mr & Mrs Harry Carter Sharp (Alicia). $75-160. MC VISA AX DS PC TC. TAC10. 7 rooms with PB, 7 with FP. 3 suites. 2 conference rooms. Breakfast included in rates. Types of meals: continental-plus breakfast, full breakfast and early coffee/tea. Afternoon tea, dinner, evening snack, picnic lunch, lunch, gourmet lunch and banquet service available. Restaurant on premises. Beds: QD. Phone, air conditioning and turndown service in room. TV, VCR, fax, copier, swimming and pet boarding on premises. Handicap access. Weddings, small meetings, family reunions and seminars hosted. Amusement parks, antiques, fishing, parks, shopping, sporting events, golf, theater and watersports nearby.

Pets Allowed: Small pets.

Publicity: *Southern Living.*

Stained Glass Manor - Oak Hall

2430 Drummond St
Vicksburg, MS 39180
(601)638-8893 (888)VICKBNB Fax:(601)636-3055
E-mail: vickbnb@magnolia.net

Circa 1902. Billed by the innkeepers as "Vicksburg's historic Vick inn," this restored, Mission-style manor boasts 38 stained-glass windows, original woodwork and light fixtures. Period furnishings create a Victorian flavor. George Washington Maher, who employed a young draftsman named Frank Lloyd Wright, probably designed the home, which was built from 1902 to 1908. Lewis J. Millet did the art for 36 of the stained-glass panels. The home's first owner, Fannie Vick Willis Johnson, was a descendent of the first Vick in Vicksburg. All but one guest room has a fireplace, and all are richly appointed with antiques, reproductions and Oriental rugs. "New Orleans" breakfasts begin with cafe au lait, freshly baked bread, Quiche Lorraine and other treats.

Innkeeper(s): Bill & Shirley Smollen. $60-185. MC VISA DS TC. TAC10. 6 rooms, 4 with PB, 10 with FP. 1 suite. 1 cottage. 3 conference rooms. Breakfast included in rates. Types of meals: continental-plus breakfast, gourmet breakfast and early coffee/tea. Beds: KQDT. Air conditioning and TV in room. VCR, fax and library on premises. Weddings, small meetings, family reunions and seminars hosted. Amusement parks, antiques, fishing, parks, shopping, theater and watersports nearby.

Pets Allowed: If kept under control.

Missouri

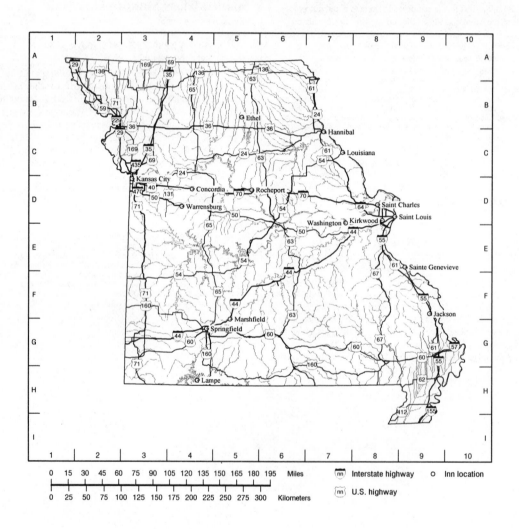

0 15 30 45 60 75 90 105 120 135 150 165 180 195 Miles

0 25 50 75 100 125 150 175 200 225 250 275 300 Kilometers

Interstate highway   o Inn location

U.S. highway

Concordia   D4

Fannie Lee B&B Inn

902 Main St
Concordia, MO 64020
(816)463-7395

Circa 1882. Framed by a handsome iron fence, this three-story Victorian is one of three houses on the inn's one acre. Rooms are furnished with antiques and European paintings. There is a double oak stairway. Breakfast is served by candlelight with china. The gardens at the inn include 650 rose bushes and 25,000 tulips.

Innkeeper(s): John Campbell. $40-65. MC VISA AX DC CB DS PC TC. TAC10. 4 rooms, 3 with PB. 1 cottage. Breakfast, afternoon tea and evening snack included in rates. Types of meals: continental-plus breakfast, full breakfast and early coffee/tea. Beds: Q. Phone, air conditioning, ceiling fan, TV and VCR in room. Copier and library on premises. Weddings hosted. Amusement parks, antiques, fishing, parks, shopping, golf, theater nearby.
Pets Allowed.

Ethel   B5

Recess Inn

203 E Main St
Ethel, MO 63539-1109
(816)486-3328 (800)628-5003 Fax:(816)486-3382

Circa 1909. This two-story brick schoolhouse has a bell tower and an arched entry. Antique furnishings are accentuated with school memorabilia throughout. There are collections of trophies, yearbooks and a scattering of desks. The library features antique books and children's readers. The innkeepers will prepare picnic lunches for excursions to local lakes and country roads. Southern breakfasts of biscuits, sausages and eggs are served.

Innkeeper(s): Ralph & Sandra Clark. $55. PC TC. 3 rooms with PB. Breakfast, afternoon tea and evening snack included in rates. Types of meals: full breakfast, gourmet breakfast and early coffee/tea. Room service available. Beds: KQ. Phone, air conditioning, turndown service and ceiling fan in room. Fax, copier and library on premises. Weddings, small meetings, family reunions and seminars hosted. Antiques, fishing, parks, shopping, golf and watersports nearby.

Hannibal   C7

Fifth Street Mansion B&B

213 S 5th St
Hannibal, MO 63401-4421
(573)221-0445 (800)874-5661 Fax:(573)221-3335

Circa 1858. This 20-room Italianate house listed in the National Register displays extended eaves and heavy brackets, tall windows and decorated lintels. A cupola affords a view of the town. Mark Twain was invited to dinner here by the Garth family and joined Laura Frazer (his Becky Thatcher) for the evening. An enormous stained-glass window lights the stairwell. The library features a stained-glass window with the family crest and is paneled with hand-grained walnut.

Innkeeper(s): Donalene & Mike Andreotti. $65-110. MC VISA AX DS TC. 7 rooms with PB. 1 conference room. Breakfast included in rates. Type of meal:

full breakfast. Beds: Q. Phone and air conditioning in room. TV, VCR and fax on premises. Weddings, small meetings, family reunions and seminars hosted. Antiques, fishing and shopping nearby.
Location: North of St. Louis 100 miles.
Publicity: *Innsider, Country Inns.*

"We thoroughly enjoyed our visit. Terrific food and hospitality!"

Garth Woodside Mansion

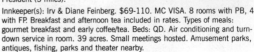

RR 3 Box 578
Hannibal, MO 63401-9634
(573)221-2789

Circa 1871. This Italian Renaissance mansion is set on 39 acres of meadow and woodland. Original Victorian antiques fill the house. An unusual flying staircase with no visible means of support vaults three stories. Best of all, is the Samuel Clemens Room where Mark Twain slept. Afternoon beverages are served, and there are nightshirts tucked away in your room.

Historic Interest: Mark Twain Boyhood Home (3 miles), a rare inland lighthouse, lit by the President (3 miles).

Innkeeper(s): Irv & Diane Feinberg. $69-110. MC VISA. 8 rooms with PB, 4 with FP. Breakfast and afternoon tea included in rates. Types of meals: gourmet breakfast and early coffee/tea. Beds: QD. Air conditioning and turndown service in room. 39 acres. Small meetings hosted. Amusement parks, antiques, fishing, parks and theater nearby.
Location: Along the Mississippi River just off highway 61.
Publicity: *Country Inns, Chicago Sun-Times, Glamour, Victorian Homes, Midwest Living, Innsider, Country Living, Conde Nast Traveler, Bon Appetit.*

"So beautiful and romantic and relaxing, we forgot we were here to work—Jeannie and Bob Ransom, Innsider."

Jackson   F9

Trisha's B&B

203 Bellevue
Jackson, MO 63755
(314)243-7427

Circa 1905. This inn offers a sitting room, tea room and spacious guest rooms. Some rooms have bay windows and are furnished with antiques and family heirlooms. Trisha provides unique teas and serves hand-picked fruits and homemade baked goods.

Innkeeper(s): Trisha Wischmann. $55-80. MC VISA AX DS. 4 rooms with PB. 2 conference rooms. Breakfast included in rates. Types of meals: full breakfast and gourmet breakfast. Beds: KQD. Phone in room.
Publicity: *Cash-Book Journal, Southeast Missourian.*

"You have created a beautiful home so naturally. Your B&B is filled with love and care—a really special place."

Kansas City   D3

The Doanleigh Inn

217 E 37th St
Kansas City, MO 64111-1473
(816)753-2667 Fax:(816)531-5185

Circa 1907. This three-story Georgian inn overlooks Hyde Park and is a perfect spot to enjoy the best of Kansas City. American and European antiques grace the guest rooms.  Jacuzzis, fireplaces and decks are among the amenities. A gourmet breakfast is served each morning, and in the evenings, wine and cheese are served.

Innkeeper(s): Terry Maturo & Cynthia Brogdon. $90-150. MC VISA AX DS PC TC. 5 rooms with PB, 2 with FP. 1 suite. 1 conference room. Breakfast and evening snack included in rates. Types of meals: gourmet breakfast and early coffee/tea. Beds: KQ. Phone, air conditioning, turndown service, TV and VCR in room. Fax and copier on premises. Weddings, small meetings, family reunions and seminars hosted. Antiques, parks, shopping, sporting events, theater and watersports nearby.

Location: Five minutes from Crown Center and Country Club Plaza.

Southmoreland on The Plaza

116 E 46th St
Kansas City, MO 64112-1702
(816)531-7979 Fax:(816)531-2407

Circa 1913. Located just two blocks off the illustrious Country Club Plaza, this four-star inn blends classic New England B&B ambience with small hotel amenities. Paired glass doors flank the foyer and original stair designs and fireplaces have been restored. Each of the inn's twelve guest rooms include private baths, and each has something special. Eight guest rooms include treetop decks. Fireplaces and Jacuzzi tubs are other possibilities. In the afternoon, guests are pampered with wine and hors d'oeuvres. Guests are invited to enjoy privileges at a Plaza athletic club. Explore the elegant shops that line the Plaza or visit Crown Center, an elaborate enclosed area featuring specialty shops and gourmet restaurants. The inn is a four-block walk from the Nelson-Atkins Museum of Art.

Innkeeper(s): Susan Moehl & Penni Johnson. $120-170. MC VISA AX PC TC. 12 rooms with PB, 3 with FP. 2 conference rooms. Breakfast included in rates. Types of meals: full breakfast and gourmet breakfast. Beds: KQ. Phone, air conditioning, turndown service and ceiling fan in room. TV, VCR, fax and copier on premises. Handicap access. Small meetings hosted. Antiques, parks, shopping, sporting events and theater nearby.

Location: Two blocks off the Country Club Plaza and four blocks from the Nelson-Atkins Museum of Art.

Publicity: Inn Business Review, Country Inns, Kansas City Business Journal, Southern Living, American West Airlines Magazines, Midwest Living, Better Homes and Gardens. Ratings: 4 Stars.

"Southmoreland on the Plaza goes beyond just setting new standards for an emergent class of inns in the European tradition. It is a uniquely Kansas City interpretation of an ancient form of roadside respite- Lawrence Goldblatt, Kansas City Business Journal."

Kirkwood   D8

Fissy's Place

500 N Kirkwood Rd
Kirkwood, MO 63122-3914
(314)821-4494

Circa 1939. The innkeeper's past is just about as interesting as the history of this bed & breakfast. A former Miss Missouri, the innkeeper has acted in movies with the likes of Burt Reynolds and Robert Redford, and pictures of many movie stars decorate the home's interior. A trained interior designer, she also shares this talent in the cheerfully decorated guest rooms. Historic downtown Kirkwood is within walking distance to the home, which also offers close access to St. Louis.

Innkeeper(s): Fay Haas. $69-76. MC VISA PC TC. TAC10. 3 rooms with PB. 1 conference room. Breakfast and evening snack included in rates. Types of meals: continental-plus breakfast, full breakfast and early coffee/tea. Catering service available. Beds: QDT. Phone, air conditioning, turndown service, ceiling fan, TV and VCR in room. Copier on premises. Handicap access. Small meetings, family reunions and seminars hosted. Antiques, parks, shopping, sporting events and theater nearby.

Lampe   H4

Grandpa's Farm B&B

HC 3, PO Box 476
Lampe, MO 65681-0476
(417)779-5106 (800)280-5106

Circa 1891. This limestone farmhouse in the heart of the Ozarks offers guests a chance to experience country life in a relaxed farm setting. Midway between Silver Dollar City and Eureka Springs, Ark., and close to Branson, the inn boasts several lodging options, including a duplex with suites and a honeymoon suite. The innkeepers are known for their substantial country breakfast and say guests enjoy comparing how long the meal lasts before they eat again. Although the inn's 116 acres are not farmed extensively, domesticated farm animals are on the premises.

Innkeeper(s): Keith & Pat Lamb. $65-95. MC VISA DS PC TC. TAC15. 4 suites. Breakfast included in rates. Meal: full breakfast. Beds: KD. Air conditioning and ceiling fan in room. VCR, fax, spa on premises. Handicap access. 116 acres. Small meetings, family reunions, seminars hosted. Amusement parks, antiques, fishing, parks, shopping, theater and watersports nearby.

Louisiana   C7

Serando's House

918 Georgia St, PO Box 205
Louisiana, MO 63353-1812
(573)754-4067 (800)754-4067

Circa 1876. Southerners traveling up the Mississippi River discovered this lush area in the early 19th century, founded it and named their little town Louisiana. The town still features many of the earliest structures in the downtown historic district. Serando's House still showcases much of its original woodwork and stained glass. The two guest rooms are comfortably furnished, and one includes a balcony. Guests select their breakfast from a variety of menu items.

Innkeeper(s): Tom & Jeannie Serandos. $65-85. MC VISA AX PC TC. TAC5. 2 rooms, 1 with PB. Breakfast included in rates. Types of meals: full breakfast and early coffee/tea. Dinner, picnic lunch and lunch available. Beds: Q. Air conditioning, ceiling fan, TV and VCR in room. Spa on premises. Small meetings hosted. Antiques, fishing, parks, shopping and watersports nearby. Publicity: *Discover Mid-America.*

Marshfield   G5

Dickey House

331 S Clay St
Marshfield, MO 65706-2114
(417)468-3000 Fax:(417)859-5478

Circa 1913. This Greek Revival mansion is framed by ancient oak trees and boasts eight massive two-story Ionic columns.

Burled woodwork, beveled glass and polished hardwood floors accentuate the gracious rooms. Interior columns soar in the parlor, creating a suitably elegant setting for the innkeeper's outstanding collection of antiques. A queen-size canopy bed, fireplace and balcony are featured in the Heritage Room. Some rooms offer amenities such as Jacuzzi tubs, a fireplace and cable TV.

Innkeeper(s): William & Dorothy Buesgen. $60-105. MC VISA DS PC TC. TAC10. 6 rooms with PB. 2 suites. 1 cottage. Breakfast included in rates. Meals: full breakfast and gourmet breakfast. Beds: KQD. Phone, air conditioning, ceiling fan, VCR in room. TV, fax, copier, library on premises. Handicap access. Weddings, small meetings, family reunions, seminars hosted.

"Thanks so much for all that you did to make our wedding special."

Rocheport   D5

Roby River Run, A B&B

201 N Roby Farm Rd
Rocheport, MO 65279-9315
(573)698-2173 (888)762-9786

Circa 1854. Moses Payne, known as Boone County's "Millionaire Minister," chose these wooded, 10-acre grounds nestled near the banks of the Missouri River, on which to build his home. The Federal-style manor, which is listed in the National Register, offers three distinctive guest rooms. The Moses U. Payne room offers a cherry, Queen Anne poster bed and a fireplace. The Sarah Payne room, named for Moses' second wife, boasts a rice bed and antique wash-stand.

The Hattie McDaniel, named for the Academy Award-winning actress who portrayed Mammy in "Gone With the Wind," offers a peek at the inn's extensive collection of memorabilia from the movie. Homemade breakfasts include eggs, biscuits, country-cured ham and specialties such as marmalade-cream cheese stuffed French toast. Rocheport, a National Register town, offers several antique shops to explore, as well as the Katy Trail, a path for hikers and bikers that winds

along the river. As the evening approaches, guests can head up to Les Bourgeois Vineyards and purchase a picnic basket, a bottle of Missouri wine and watch the sun set over the river.

Innkeeper(s): Gary Smith & Randall Kilgore. $80-90. MC VISA AX DS PC. TAC5. 3 rooms, 1 with PB, 1 with FP. Type of meal: full breakfast. Beds: Q. Phone, air conditioning and turndown service in room. VCR and stables on premises. 10 acres. Weddings and small meetings hosted. Antiques nearby.

School House B&B Inn

504 Third St
Rocheport, MO 65279
(573)698-2022

Circa 1914. This three-story brick building was once a schoolhouse. Now luxuriously appointed as a country inn, it features 13-foot-high ceilings, small print wallpapers and a bridal suite with Victorian furnishings and a private spa. The basement

houses an antique shop. Nearby is a winery and a trail along the river providing many scenic miles for cyclists and hikers.

Historic Interest: Historic Katy Trail (2 blocks), Missouri River (4 blocks), local museum (4 blocks), Rocheport has 80 buildings in the National Register.

Innkeeper(s): Vicki Ott & Penny Province. $85-155. MC VISA. TAC10. 10 rooms with PB. 1 suite. 1 conference room. Breakfast and evening snack included in rates. Types of meals: continental breakfast, continental-plus breakfast, full breakfast and early coffee/tea. Afternoon tea available. Beds: KQDT. Phone, air conditioning and ceiling fan in room. TV, VCR, bicycles and library on premises. Small meetings and family reunions hosted. Antiques, fishing, parks, shopping, sporting events and theater nearby.

Publicity: *Midwest Motorist, Successful Farming, Hallmark Greeting Cards, Romance of Country Inns, Southern Living, New York Times.*

"We are still talking about our great weekend in Rocheport. Thanks for the hospitality, the beautiful room and delicious breakfasts, they were really great."

Saint Charles   D8

Boone's Lick Trail Inn

1000 S Main St
Saint Charles, MO 63301-3514
(314)947-7000

Circa 1840. This Federal-style brick and limestone house, overlooking the wide Missouri and Katy Trail, is situated in this old river settlement with its brick street and green spaces, at the start of the Booneslick Trail. V'Anne's delicate lemon biscuits, fresh fruit, and hot entrees are served amidst regional antiques and Paul's working duck decoy collection. Because

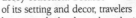

of its setting and decor, travelers have remarked at how close the inn resembles a European inn.

Historic Interest: Goldenrod Showboat (one-fourth miles), Missouri First State Capitol (one-half miles), Daniel Boone Homestead (25 miles), Gateway Arch (20 minutes), Jefferson Memorial Courthouse.

Innkeeper(s): V'Anne & Paul Mydler. $75-175. MC VISA AX DC CB DS. 5 rooms with PB. 1 suite. Breakfast included in rates. Meals: continental-plus breakfast, full breakfast. Beds: QDT. Phone in room. Antiques, shopping, golf nearby.

Location: 8 minutes from St. Louis airport.

Publicity: *Saint Louis Post-Dispatch, Midwest Motorist, Midwest Living.*

"Makes your trip back in time complete. A wonderful stay, one to which others should be graded."

Saint Louis   D8

Fleur-De-Lys Inn, Mansion at The Park

3500 Russell Blvd
Saint Louis, MO 63104
(314)773-3500 (888)969-3500 Fax:(314)773-6546

Circa 1912. The innkeepers at Fleur-De-Lys are ace decorators, creating bed chambers that are both warm and inviting, yet bright and cheerful at the same time. The Botanical Garden room features creamy yellow walls, a bed piled high with pillows and dressed with a puffy comforter and yellow gingham bed skirt. Another room, the Reservoir Park, is highlighted by a carved, four-poster plantation bed and masculine hues of burgundy and pale green. Other rooms include a king-size, antique iron and brass bed and a huge double bath, while another has a double Jacuzzi tub. Guests are pampered with amenities such as Turkish towels placed on heated towel racks, fresh flowers and a hot tub. There is a library, a cigar porch, a parlor and a gallery featuring works for sale by local artists. The inn is perfect for those seeking romance, but there are plenty of amenities for the business traveler. Fax, copying and printing services are available, as well as same-day dry cleaning, desks in each guest room and a selection of national and local papers available daily. Guests will enjoy the inn's gourmet breakfast. Downtown St. Louis and many area attractions are five minutes away.

Innkeeper(s): Kathryn Leep. $85-175. MC VISA AX DC CB DS PC TC. TAC10. 2 suites. 1 conference room. Breakfast included in rates. Types of meals: gourmet breakfast and early coffee/tea. Dinner available. Beds: KQD. Phone, air conditioning, turndown service, ceiling fan, TV and VCR in room. Fax, copier, spa and library on premises. Small meetings hosted. Amusement parks, antiques, parks, shopping, sporting events and theater nearby.

Lafayette House

2156 Lafayette Ave
Saint Louis, MO 63104-2543
(314)772-4429 (800)641-8965 Fax:(314)664-2156

Circa 1876. Captain James Eads, designer and builder of the first trussed bridge across the Mississippi River, built this

Queen Anne mansion as a wedding present for his daughter Margaret. The rooms are furnished in antiques, and there is a suite with a kitchen on the third floor. The house overlooks Lafayette Park.

Innkeeper(s): Nancy Buhr, Anna Millet. $60-150. MC VISA AX DC CB DS PC TC. TAC10. 6 rooms, 3 with PB. 1 suite. Breakfast included in rates. Types of meals: gourmet breakfast and early coffee/tea. Beds: QDT. Phone, air conditioning and TV in room. VCR, fax and copier on premises. Weddings, small meetings, family reunions and seminars hosted. Antiques, parks, shopping, sporting events and theater nearby.

Pets Allowed: Check with innkeepers, cats on premises.

Location: In the center of St. Louis.

"We had a wonderful stay at your house and enjoyed the furnishings, delicious breakfasts and friendly pets."

Lehmann House B&B

10 Benton Pl
Saint Louis, MO 63104-2411
(314)231-6724

Circa 1893. This National Register manor's most prominent resident, former U.S. Solicitor General Frederick Lehmann, hosted Presidents Taft, Theodore Roosevelt and Coolidge at this gracious home. Several key turn-of-the-century literary figures also visited the Lehmann family. The inn's formal dining room, complete with oak paneling and a fireplace, is a stunning place to enjoy the formal breakfasts. Antiques and gracious furnishings dot the well-appointed guest rooms. The home is located in St. Louis' oldest historic district, Lafayette Square.

Historic Interest: Presidents Taft, Roosevelt, Coolidge visited Lehmann House.
Innkeeper(s): Marie & Michael Davies. $65-80. MC VISA AX DC DS PC TC. TAC10. 4 rooms, 2 with PB, 3 with FP. 3 conference rooms. Breakfast included in rates. Types of meals: full breakfast and early coffee/tea. Evening snack available. Beds: KQDT. Air conditioning and ceiling fan in room. Swimming, tennis and library on premises. Weddings, small meetings, family reunions and seminars hosted. Amusement parks, antiques, parks, shopping, sporting events and theater nearby.

"Wonderful mansion with great future ahead. Thanks for the wonderful hospitality."

The Winter House

3522 Arsenal St
Saint Louis, MO 63118-2004
(314)664-4399
E-mail: rmwinter@swbell.net

Circa 1897. Original brass hardware, three fireplaces and a turret provide ambiance at this turn-of-the-century brick Victorian. Embossed French paneling adds elegance. The suite features a balcony, and the bedroom has a pressed-tin ceiling. The Rose

Room is decorated with its namesake flower and a king-size bed. The home is ideally located three miles from the downtown area. Exotic restaurants are within walking distance. Breakfast is served on antique Wedgewood china and includes hand-squeezed orange juice, gourmet coffees, teas and a full breakfast. With special reservations, guests can enjoy breakfast accompanied by professional piano music.

Historic Interest: Tower Grove Park (one-half block), Missouri Botanical Garden (1 mile).
Innkeeper(s): Kendall Winter. $80-115. MC VISA AX DC CB DS PC TC. TAC10. 3 rooms with PB. 1 suite. Breakfast included in rates. Type of meal: full breakfast. Beds: KQDR. Air conditioning and ceiling fan in room. Amusement parks, antiques, fishing, parks, shopping, sporting events and theater nearby.

Publicity: *Inssider, St. Louis Post Dispatch.*

"A delightful house with spotless, beautifully appointed rooms, charming hosts. Highly recommended."

Sainte Genevieve   E9

Inn St. Gemme Beauvais

78 N Main St
Sainte Genevieve, MO 63670-1336
(573)883-5744 (800)818-5744 Fax:(573)883-3899

Circa 1848. This three-story, Federal-style inn is an impressive site on Ste. Genevieve's Main Street. The town is one of the oldest west of the Mississippi River, and the St. Gemme Beauvais is the oldest operating Missouri bed & breakfast. The rooms are nicely appointed in period style, but there are modern amenities here, too. The Jacuzzi tubs in some guest rooms are one relaxing example. There is an outdoor hot tub as well. Guests are pampered with all sorts of cuisine, from full breakfasts to luncheons with sinfully rich desserts, and in the late afternoons, wine, hors d'oeuvres and refreshments are served.
Innkeeper(s): Janet Joggerst. $69-125. AP. MC VISA PC TC. 7 rooms with PB, 1 with FP. 5 suites. 2 conference rooms. Breakfast and afternoon tea included in rates. Types of meals: full breakfast, gourmet breakfast and early coffee/tea. Evening snack, picnic lunch, lunch, gourmet lunch, banquet service, catering service, catered breakfast and room service available. Restaurant on premises. Beds: QDT. Air conditioning, turndown service, ceiling fan and TV in room. VCR, fax, copier, spa and bicycles on premises. Weddings, small meetings, family reunions and seminars hosted. Antiques, parks and shopping nearby.

Main Street Inn

221 North Main St
Sainte Genevieve, MO 63670
(573)883-9199 (800)918-9199
E-mail: msinn@ldd.net

Circa 1883. This exquisite inn is one of Missouri's finest bed & breakfast establishments. Built as the Meyer Hotel, the inn has welcomed guests for more than a century. Now completely renovated, each of the individually appointed rooms includes amenities such as bubble bath and flowers. Rooms are subtly decorated, and some have stenciled walls. Beds are topped with vintage quilts and tasteful linens. Two rooms include a whirlpool tub. The morning meal is prepared in a beautiful brick kitchen, which features an unusual blue cookstove, and is served in the elegant dining room. The menu changes from day to day, caramelized French toast is one of the inn's specialties.
Innkeeper(s): Ken & Karen Kulberg. $65-115. MC VISA AX DS PC TC. TAC10. 7 rooms with PB. Breakfast and evening snack included in rates. Types of meals: gourmet breakfast and early coffee/tea. Beds: QDT. Air conditioning in room. Copier on premises. Small meetings, family reunions and seminars hosted. Antiques, parks and shopping nearby.

The Southern Hotel

146 S 3rd St
Sainte Genevieve, MO 63670-1667
(573)883-3493 (800)275-1412 Fax:(573)883-9612

Circa 1790. This Federal building is the largest and oldest brick home west of the Mississippi. It features a long front porch, large parlors and a spacious dining room. Highlights of the guest rooms include cedar bedposts carved in the shape of Old Man River, a hand-painted headboard and a delicately carved Victorian bed. The clawfoot tubs are

hand-painted. Guests are invited to add their names to a quilt-in-progress, which is set out in the parlor.
Innkeeper(s): Mike & Barbara Hankins. $80-125. MC VISA PC TC. 8 rooms with PB, 4 with FP. 1 conference room. Breakfast included in rates. Meals: full breakfast, gourmet breakfast and early coffee/tea. Beds: KQD. Air conditioning and ceiling fan in room. Bicycles on premises. Small meetings, family reunions and seminars hosted. Antiques, fishing, parks and shopping nearby.
Publicity: *Innsider, St. Louis Gourmet, River Heritage Gazette.*

"I can't imagine ever staying in a motel again! It was so nice to be greeted by someone who expected us. We felt right at home."

Springfield   G4

The Mansion at Elfindale

1701 S Fort Ave
Springfield, MO 65807-1280
(417)831-5400

Circa 1800. The Mansion at Elfindale once served as the St. de Chantel Academy for girls. The gray stone structure features a turret observation room, ornate fireplaces, stained-glass windows, vaulted ceilings, marble-finish furnishings, wicker furniture and antiques. Breakfast includes foods from around the world.
Innkeeper(s): Jef Wells. $75-125. MC VISA AX DC DS. TAC10. 13 rooms with PB, 2 with FP. 1 conference room. Breakfast included in rates. Dinner, banquet service and catering service available. Beds: KQDT. Phone in room. Handicap access. Weddings, small meetings, family reunions and seminars hosted. Antiques, shopping and sporting events nearby.

"Many thanks for your warm hospitality."

Virginia Rose B&B

317 E Glenwood St
Springfield, MO 65807-3543
(417)883-0693 (800)345-1412

Circa 1906. Three generations of the Botts family lived in this home before it was sold to the current innkeepers, Virginia and Jackie Buck. The grounds still include the rustic red barn.
Comfortable, country rooms are named after Buck family members and feature beds covered with quilts. The innkeepers also offer a two-bedroom suite, the Rambling Rose, which is decorated in a sportsman theme in honor of

the nearby Bass Pro. Hearty breakfasts are served in the dining room, and the innkeepers will provide low-fat fare on request.
Historic Interest: Wild Bill Hickok shot Dave Tutt on the public square in Springfield, which is about two miles from the inn. Wilson's Creek National Battlefield is about eight miles away. Other Springfield attractions include Springfield National Cemetery, The Frisco Railroad Museum and the History Museum for Springfield and Greene County.
Innkeeper(s): Jackie & Virginia Buck. $50-90. MC VISA AX DS PC TC. TAC10. 5 rooms, 3 with PB. 1 suite. Breakfast included in rates. Types of meals: full breakfast and early coffee/tea. Evening snack and picnic lunch available. Beds: QD. Phone, air conditioning and turndown service in room. TV, VCR and fax on premises. Family reunions and seminars hosted. Amusement parks, antiques, fishing, parks, shopping, sporting events, theater and watersports nearby.
Publicity: *Auctions & Antiques, Springfield Business Journal, Today's Women Journal.*

"The accommodations are wonderful and the hospitality couldn't be warmer."

Walnut Street Inn

900 E Walnut St
Springfield, MO 65806-2603
(417)864-6346 (800)593-6346 Fax:(417)864-6184
E-mail: walnutstinn@pcis.net

Circa 1894. This three-story Queen Anne gabled house has cast-iron Corinthian columns and a veranda. Polished wood floors and antiques are featured throughout.
Upstairs you'll find the gathering room with a fireplace. Ask for the McCann guest room with two bay windows. A full breakfast is served, including items such as peach-stuffed French toast.

Historic Interest: Springfield History Museum (3 blocks), Laura Ingalls Wilder Museum (40 minutes), Wilson's Creek National Battlefield (20 minutes), General Sweeney's Civil War Museum (20 minutes).

Innkeeper(s): Gary & Paula Blankenship. $69-159. MC VISA AX DC DS PC TC. 12 rooms with PB, 8 with FP. 1 suite. Breakfast included in rates. Types of meals: gourmet breakfast and early coffee/tea. Afternoon tea available. Beds: QD. Phone, air conditioning, turndown service, ceiling fan, TV and VCR in room. Fax and copier on premises. Handicap access. Amusement parks, antiques, fishing, parks, shopping, sporting events, theater and watersports nearby.

Publicity: *Southern Living, Women's World, Midwest Living, Victoria, Country Inns, Innsider, Glamour, Midwest Motorist, Missouri, Saint Louis Post, Kansas City Star, USA Today.*

"Rest assured your establishment's qualities are unmatched and through your commitment to excellence you have won a life-long client."

Warrensburg   D4

Cedarcroft Farm B&B

431 SE County Rd Y
Warrensburg, MO 64093-8316
(660)747-5728 (800)368-4944
E-mail: bwayne@cedarcroft.com

Circa 1867. John Adams, a Union army veteran, and Sandra's great grandfather, built this house. There are 80 acres of woodlands, meadows and creeks where deer, fox, coyotes and wild turkeys still roam. Two original barns remain. Guests stay in a private, two-bedroom suite, which can accommodate couples or families. Bill participates in Civil War reenactments and is

happy to demonstrate clothing, weapons and customs of the era. Sandra cares for her four horses and provides the home-baked, full country breakfasts.

Innkeeper(s): Sandra & Bill Wayne. $75-90. MC VISA AX DS PC TC. TAC10. 1 room. Breakfast and evening snack included in rates. Type of meal: full breakfast. Beds: D. Air conditioning in room. TV and VCR on premises. 80 acres. Antiques, fishing, parks, shopping and theater nearby.

Location: About six miles southeast of Warrensburg, Mo., 60 miles from Kansas City.

Publicity: *Kansas City Star, Higginsville Advance, Midwest Motorist, KCTV, KMOS TV, Territorial Small Farm Today, Country America, Entrepreneur.*

"We enjoyed the nostalgia and peacefulness very much. Enjoyed your wonderful hospitality and great food."

Washington   D7

Schwegmann House

438 W Front St
Washington, MO 63090-2103
(314)239-5025 (800)949-2262

Circa 1861. John F. Schwegmann, a native of Germany, built a flour mill on the Missouri riverfront. This stately three-story home was built not only for the Miller and his family but also to provide extra lodging for overnight customers who traveled long hours to the town. Today weary travelers enjoy the formal gardens and warm atmosphere of this restful home. Patios overlook the river, and the gracious rooms are decorated with antiques

and handmade quilts. The new Miller Suite boasts a tub for two, and guests receive a bottle of Missouri wine delivered to their door. Guests enjoy full breakfasts complete with house specialties such as German apple pancakes or a three-cheese strata accompanied with homemade breads, meat, juice and fresh fruit. There are 11 wineries nearby, or guests can visit one of the historic district, many galleries, historic sites, antique shops, excellent restaurants and riverfront park located nearby.

Historic Interest: The home is part of the historic downtown Washington area and full of homes and buildings to admire. Daniel Boone's home is 20 miles away. Old Bethel Church and Anna Belle Chapel are short drives. The house is 10 blocks from the Washington Historical Museum.

Innkeeper(s): Catherine & Bill Nagel. $85-150. MC VISA AX PC TC. TAC10. 9 rooms with PB. 1 suite. Breakfast and evening snack included in rates. Types of meals: gourmet breakfast and early coffee/tea. Beds: QD. Phone, air conditioning and ceiling fan in room. TV and bicycles on premises. Weddings, small meetings, family reunions and seminars hosted. Antiques nearby.

Location: One hour west of St. Louis.

Publicity: *St. Louis Post-Dispatch, West County Journal, Midwest Living, Country Inns, Midwest Motorist, Ozark.*

"Like Grandma's house many years ago."

Montana

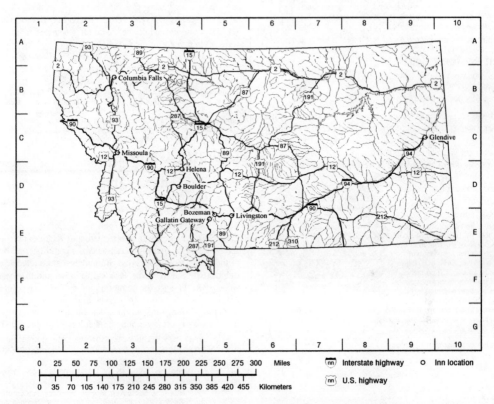

	1	2	3	4	5	6	7	8	9	10	

0 25 50 75 100 125 150 175 200 225 250 275 300   Miles

0 35 70 105 140 175 210 245 280 315 350 385 420 455   Kilometers

(nn) Interstate highway   o Inn location

(nn) U.S. highway

Boulder   D4

Boulder Hot Springs B&B

PO Box 930
Boulder, MT 59632-0930
(406)225-4339 Fax:(406)225-4345

Circa 1888. This Spanish-style hotel with its peaked Moorish gables and red roofline is under restoration. In the National Register, the 33 rooms in the east wing, the pool and bathhouse have been renovated. Forty springs are on the inn's 274 acres. There are hotel rooms as well as B&B rooms, which offer antiques and original paintings. A comfortable lobby with wood stove provides a variety of games. Breakfast is generous with omelets and sausage or French toast and pancakes. Enjoy the geothermal baths or hike along Deerlodge National Forest. An abundant wildlife includes bear, deer, fox, antelope and moose. Some guests enjoy exploring the area's radon mines which are nearby.

Innkeeper(s): Barb Reiter, Manager. $70-90. MC VISA PC TC. 7 rooms with PB. 2 conference rooms. Breakfast included in rates. Meal: full breakfast. Beds: TD. Fax, copier, spa, sauna, library on premises. Handicap access. 274 acres. Weddings, small meetings, family reunions, seminars hosted. Antiques, fishing, parks, cross-country skiing, theater, watersports nearby.
Location: Three miles south of Boulder on Route 69.

Bozeman   E5

Lehrkind Mansion

719 N Wallace Ave
Bozeman, MT 59715-3063
(406)585-6932 (800)992-6932 Fax:(406)585-6932
E-mail: lehrkindmansion@imt.net

Circa 1897. Peaked gables, gingerbread trim and captivating corner tower are among the fanciful architectural elements found in this Queen Anne Victorian. Inside, beautifully restored woodwork and leaded- and stained-glass windows marry with period antiques and elegant decor. The home is located in

Bozeman's historic Brewery District, and the first owner built it next to his brewery. In the afternoons, enjoy refreshments in the parlor as you listen to melodies from an antique music box. Excellent local skiing is a short drive away at Bridger Bowl, and Bozeman's charming historic downtown area offers a variety of shops and restaurants. Yellowstone National Park is an hour away. Ask the innkeepers about the home's secret tunnel.

Innkeeper(s): Jon Gerster & Christopher Nixon. $65-155. MC VISA AX DS PC TC. TAC10. 4 rooms, 1 with PB. 1 suite. 2 conference rooms. Breakfast and afternoon tea included in rates. Types of meals: full breakfast and early coffee/tea. Beds: QD. Phone and turndown service in room. Fax, spa and library on premises. Weddings, small meetings, family reunions and seminars hosted. German spoken. Antiques, fishing, parks, shopping, downhill skiing, cross-country skiing, sporting events, golf and theater nearby.

Publicity: *Bozeman Daily Chronicle.*

"The entire mansion is beautiful and each room so nicely decorated."

Torch & Toes B&B

309 S 3rd Ave
Bozeman, MT 59715-4636
(406)586-7285 (800)446-2138

Circa 1906. This Colonial Revival home, three blocks from the center of town, boasts an old-fashioned front porch with porch swing and a carriage house. Antique furnishings in the dining room feature a Victrola and a pillared and carved oak fireplace. Ron is a professor of architecture at nearby Montana State University and Judy is a weaver. Her loom and some of her colorful work are on display at this artisan's inn.

Innkeeper(s): Ron & Judy Hess. $80-90. MC VISA PC TC. TAC10. 4 rooms with PB. Breakfast included in rates. Types of meals: full breakfast and gourmet breakfast. Beds: KQT. Ceiling fan in room. TV and VCR on premises. Small meetings, family reunions and seminars hosted. Antiques, fishing, parks, shopping, downhill skiing, cross-country skiing, sporting events, theater and watersports nearby.

Location: North of Yellowstone National Park.

Publicity: *Bozeman Chronicle, San Francisco Peninsula Parent, Northwest.*

"Thanks for your warm hospitality."

Voss Inn

319 S Willson Ave
Bozeman, MT 59715-4632
(406)587-0982 Fax:(406)585-2964

Circa 1883. The Voss Inn is a restored two-story house with a large front porch and a Victorian parlor. Old-fashioned furnishings include an upright piano and chandelier. Two of the inn's six rooms include air conditioning. A full breakfast is served, with freshly baked rolls kept in a unique warmer that's built into an ornate 1880s radiator.

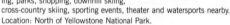

Historic Interest: Little Big Horn (Custer battle site, 18 miles), Virginia City and Nevada City (60 miles), Madison Buffalo Jump (30 miles).

Innkeeper(s): Bruce & Frankee Muller. $85-95. MC VISA AX PC TC. TAC7. 6 rooms with PB. Breakfast and afternoon tea included in rates. Meal: gourmet breakfast. Picnic lunch available. Beds: KQ. Phone, air conditioning in room. TV, fax on premises. Weddings, small meetings, family reunions hosted. Spanish, some Dutch spoken. Antiques, fishing, parks, skiing, watersports nearby.

Location: Four blocks south of downtown.

Publicity: *Sunset, Cosmopolitan, Gourmet, Countryside.*

Columbia Falls   B3

Bad Rock Country B&B

480 Bad Rock Dr
Columbia Falls, MT 59912-9213
(406)892-2829 (800)422-3666 Fax:(406)892-2930
E-mail: jalper@digisys.net

This inn features four guest rooms in two newly constructed log buildings that are replicas of an old settler's home. Hand-hewn square logs with dove-tail corners were fashioned to create the buildings, using the original building techniques of Montana settlers 150 years ago. The main house is furnished in Old West antiques while the log building features handmade lodge-pole pine furniture. Grizzly Big Bite, an egg casserole served on jalapeno biscuits and Montana Potato Pie or Sundance eggs are specialties created by Sue. The inn is a great place to stay while visiting Glacier National Park.

Innkeeper(s): Jon & Sue Alper. $98-155. MC VISA AX DC CB DS PC TC. TAC10. 7 rooms with PB, 4 with FP. Breakfast included in rates. Meals: full breakfast and gourmet breakfast. Beds: KQT. Phone, air conditioning, turndown service, ceiling fan in room. VCR, fax, copier, spa on premises. 30 acres. Family reunions hosted. Antiques, fishing, parks, shopping, skiing, golf, theater and watersports nearby. Publicity: *Country Inns.*

Gallatin Gateway   E5

Gallatin Gateway Inn

Hwy 191, PO Box 376
Gallatin Gateway, MT 59730
(406)763-4672

Circa 1927. Just outside of Bozeman, and 75 miles north of Yellowstone National Park, lies one of the grand railroad hotels of the Rocky Mountains West. Stunningly restored in 1927, the original hand-hewn beams, Paladian windows and mahogany woodwork still grace the common rooms. The inn is located in the heart of Yellowstone Country amid spectacular scenery, hiking and fly-fishing opportunities. The inn has its own casting pond, tennis court, swimming pool and outdoor Jacuzzi. The rooms are comfortable and well appointed and a gourmet continental breakfast is served every morning. The inn's historic dining room offers fine dining and a casual pub.

Innkeeper(s): Martha Riley. $60-145. MC VISA AX DS. 35 rooms. 1 conference room. Dinner available. Beds: KQT. Spa on premises.

Publicity: *Travel & Leisure, Conde Nast Traveler, Bon Appetite, Country Living, House & Garden, Diversions, Bon Appetit, Historic Gourmet, Travel Holiday, Adventure West.*

Glendive   C9

The Hostetler House B&B

113 N Douglas St
Glendive, MT 59330-1619
(406)365-4505 (800)965-8456 Fax:(406)365-8456

Circa 1912. Casual country decor mixed with handmade and heirloom furnishings are highlights at this two-story inn. The inn features many comforting touches, such as a romantic hot tub and gazebo, enclosed sun porch and sitting room filled with books. The two guest rooms share a bath, and are furnished by Dea, an interior decorator. The full breakfasts may be enjoyed on Grandma's china in the dining room or on the sun

porch. The Yellowstone River is one block from the inn, and downtown shopping is two blocks away. Makoshika State Park, home of numerous fossil finds, is nearby.

Historic Interest: Guests are invited to tour Glendive's historic district on the innkeeper's tandem mountain bike.

Innkeeper(s): Craig & Dea Hostetler. $50. MC VISA DS PC TC. TAC10. 2 rooms. Breakfast included in rates. Meals: gourmet breakfast, early coffee/tea. Beds: D. Air conditioning and ceiling fan in room. TV, VCR, fax, spa, bicycles, library on premises. Small meetings hosted. German spoken. Antiques, fishing, parks, shopping, x-country skiing, sporting events, theater, watersports nearby. Publicity: *Ranger Review*.

Helena   D4

Appleton Inn B&B

1999 Euclid Ave, Hwy 12 West
Helena, MT 59601-1908
(406)449-7492 (800)956-1999 Fax:(406)449-1261
E-mail: appleton@ixi.net

Circa 1890. Montana's first resident dentist called this Victorian his home. It remained in his family until the 1970s when it was transformed into apartments. Fortunately, the innkeepers bought and restored the home, bringing back the original beauty. The innkeepers have their own furniture-making company and have created many of the pieces that decorate the guest rooms. Rooms range from the spacious Master Suite, with its oak, four-poster bed and bath with a clawfoot tub, to the quaint and cozy Attic Playroom.  The inn is a convenient place to enjoy the Helena area, and there are mountain bikes on hand for those who wish to explore.

Historic Interest: West Mansion District, Montana Historic Society Museum and the state capitol building all are nearby historic sites.

Innkeeper(s): Tom Woodall & Cheryl Boid. $60-125. AP. MC VISA AX DS PC TC. TAC10. 5 rooms with PB. 1 suite. Breakfast included in rates. Afternoon tea and picnic lunch available. Beds: Q. Phone, air conditioning in room. TV, VCR, fax, copier, bicycles on premises. Weddings, small meetings, family reunions, seminars hosted. Antiques, fishing, parks, shopping, skiing, sporting events, theater, watersports nearby. Pets Allowed: Need prior approval.

The Sanders - Helena's Bed & Breakfast

328 N Ewing St
Helena, MT 59601-4050
(406)442-3309 Fax:(406)443-2361
E-mail: folks@sandersbb.com

Circa 1875. This historic inn is filled with elegantly carved furnishings, paintings and collections that are original to the house. Wilbur Sanders, an attorney and a Montana senator, built his house near the Governor's Mansion, in the heart of Helena. The three-story house features a front and side porch, and balconies and bay windows that provide views of the mountains and downtown Helena. In addition to the rich interior and hospitality, guests are pampered with gourmet breakfasts, featuring such items as freshly ground, organically grown coffee, orange-banana juice, Grand Marinier French toast and mixed fruit topped with a yogurt-nutmeg sauce.

Historic Interest: Montana State Historical Museum, Cathedral of St. Helena, Reeders Alley & Capital.

Innkeeper(s): Bobbi Uecker & Rock Ringling. $85-105. MC VISA AX PC TC. 7 rooms with PB, 1 with FP. 2 conference rooms. Breakfast included in rates. Meals: full breakfast, gourmet breakfast and early coffee/tea. Afternoon tea, catering service, room service available. Beds: Q. Phone, air conditioning,

turndown service, ceiling fan in room. Fax and library on premises. Weddings, small meetings, family reunions, seminars hosted. Antiques, fishing, parks, shopping, skiing, sporting events, theater, watersports nearby. Publicity: *National Geographic Traveler, Country Travels, Pacific Northwest, Washington Post, Boston Globe, New York Times*.

Livingston   E5

The River Inn on The Yellowstone

4950 Hwy 89 S
Livingston, MT 59047
(406)222-2429

Circa 1895. Crisp, airy rooms decorated with a Southwestern flavor are just part of the reason why this 100-year-old farmhouse is an ideal getaway. There are five acres to meander, including more than 500 feet of riverfront, and close access to a multitude of outdoor activities. Two rooms have decks boasting views of the river, and the third offers a canyon view. Guests also can stay in Calamity Jane's, a rustic riverside cabin. For an unusual twist, summer guests can opt for Spangler's Wagon and experience life as it was on the range. This is a true, turn-of-the-century sheepherders' wagon and includes a double bed and woodstove.  The innkeepers guide a variety of interesting hikes, bike and canoe trips in the summer and fall. The inn is close to many outdoor activities. Don't forget to check out Livingston, just a few miles away. The historic town has been used in several movies and maintains an authentic Old West spirit.

Historic Interest: Yellowstone National Park is located nearby.

Innkeeper(s): Dee Dee VanZyl & Ursula Neese. $50-90. MC VISA. TAC10. 3 rooms with PB. 1 cottage. Breakfast included in rates. Types of meals: full breakfast, gourmet breakfast and early coffee/tea. Picnic lunch available. Beds: QDT. VCR and bicycles on premises. Weddings, small meetings, family reunions and seminars hosted. Limited Spanish spoken. Antiques, fishing, parks, shopping, skiing, sporting events, theater and watersports nearby. Pets Allowed: Horses. Dogs in cabin, wagon only. Other, by arrangement.

Missoula   C3

Goldsmith's B&B

809 E Front St
Missoula, MT 59802-4704
(406)721-6732 Fax:(406)543-0095

Circa 1911. Missoula, made famous for its "A River Runs Through It" connection, is the site of this Four-Square-style inn originally the home of the president of the University of Montana, Clyde Duniway. It would be difficult for the inn to offer a better view of the Clark Fork River, the waterway is just a few feet from the home's front door. Guest quarters are a mixture of turn-of-the-century country and romantic whimsy with bright flowery patterns and quilts dressing the sleigh, pewter, porcelain or wicker beds. Several rooms boast river views. There is a full-service restaurant in an adjoining building, and guests are treated to a memorable full breakfast. Omelets and ice cream batter pancakes are famed specialties of the house. The restaurant includes a bagel bakery and has homemade ice cream.

Innkeeper(s): Dick & Jeana Goldsmith. $69-119. MC VISA AX TC. TAC10. 7 rooms with PB, 2 with FP. 4 suites. Breakfast included in rates. Types of meals: full breakfast and early coffee/tea. Dinner and lunch available. Restaurant on premises. Beds: QD. Phone, air conditioning, ceiling fan and TV in room. Library on premises. Small meetings, family reunions and seminars hosted. Fishing, parks, shopping, skiing, sporting events, theater nearby.

Nebraska

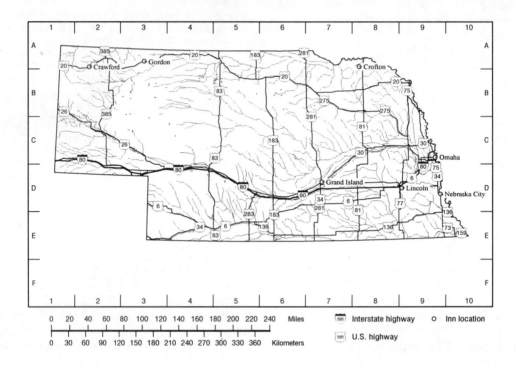

0 20 40 60 80 100 120 140 160 180 200 220 240 Miles

0 30 60 90 120 150 180 210 240 270 300 330 360 Kilometers

[nn] Interstate highway   o Inn location

[nn] U.S. highway

Crawford   A2

Fort Robinson Inn
PO Box 392
Crawford, NE 69339-0392
(308)665-2900 Fax:(308)665-2906

Circa 1909. This collection of lodge rooms, cabins, adobes and a ranch-style home are located within Fort Robinson State Park. Accommodations are comfortable and simple, available from early April until the third weekend in November. The real draw here is the park, which was a former U.S. Army fort and dates to the Indian Wars. It was here that Sioux Chief Crazy Horse was killed. The park offers a wealth of exciting American history and activities. Horseback and jeep tours, stagecoach rides, fishing and RV camping are available. Some activities are scheduled for summer months only. "Cabins" have kitchen facilities, and the Fort Robinson Inn offers a full-service restaurant during the summer months. The park also offers souvenirs, cross-country skiing and theater.

Innkeeper(s): Jim Lemmon. $26-520. MC VISA PC TC. 23 rooms. 32 cottages. 1 conference room. Types of meals: continental breakfast, continental-plus breakfast, full breakfast and early coffee/tea. Dinner, picnic lunch, lunch, banquet service, catering service and catered breakfast available. Restaurant on premises. Beds: QDT. Air conditioning and ceiling fan in room. Fax, copier, swimming, stables, bicycles and tennis on premises. Handicap access. Weddings, small meetings, family reunions and seminars hosted. Fishing, parks, shopping, cross-country skiing and theater nearby.

Pets Allowed: In cabins, not in lodge. Must be on leash when outside.

Crofton   A8

Historic Argo Hotel
211 W Kansas St
Crofton, NE 68730
(402)388-2400 (800)607-2746 Fax:(402)388-2525

Circa 1912. This hotel's first owner named the historic building after the ship that brought him to America. In its heyday as a lodging for those traveling by train, the Argo hosted several governors. Eventually the hotel served other purposes, as a sanitarium and then as offices for a Crofton family doctor. The brother and sister team of Sandra McDonald and Jerry Bogner, both Crofton natives, returned to their hometown to purchase and restore this historic gem after it had fallen into disrepair. The two did an amazing job, including things guests won't see, such as replacing the electrical and plumbing systems. What

guests will find are well-appointed rooms, fine woodwork and a sense of turn-of-the-century nostalgia. As is traditional of an Old West hotel, several of the bathrooms are shared, but robes are provided for guests. The honeymoon suite includes a private bath with a whirlpool tub. There is a popular restaurant on the premises, where guests can enjoy excellent cuisine at reasonable prices, as well as live entertainment.

Innkeeper(s): Sandra McDonald & Jerry Bogner. $45-120. MC VISA AX DS PC TC. TAC10. 12 rooms, 8 with PB, 3 with FP. 2 suites. 1 conference room. Breakfast included in rates. Types of meals: continental-plus breakfast and early coffee/tea. Dinner and banquet service available. Restaurant on premises. Beds: QT. Phone, air conditioning, ceiling fan and TV in room. VCR, fax and copier on premises. Weddings, small meetings, family reunions and seminars hosted. Antiques, fishing, parks, shopping, golf, theater and watersports nearby.

Publicity: *Town & Country Weekly News, Sioux City Journal, Omaha World-Herald, Gowrie News.*

Gordon   A3

Meadow View Ranch B&B Bunkhouse

HC 91 Box 29
Gordon, NE 69343-9111
(308)282-0679

Circa 1920. For an added charge, guests at this working ranch can take the saddle horses for a ride across the 5,000-acre grounds. The unpretentious guest quarters at Meadow View originally served as a bunkhouse for ranch hands. The simple guest rooms feature country decor and comfortable antiques. Innkeepers Clyde and Billie Lefler serve up a full country breakfast and can arrange cookouts. The

Leflers also host a country music jamboree each August.

Historic Interest: The Gordon area is full of historic attractions within a half-hour drive, including Old-Time Cowboyís Museum and Mari Sandoz Museum. The Fur Trade Museum and Red Cloud Indian National Art Show are about an hour from the ranch.

Innkeeper(s): Clyde & Billie Lefler. $45-75. 4 rooms with PB. Breakfast included in rates. Meal: full breakfast. Beds: QT. Antiques and fishing nearby. Pets Allowed.

Publicity: *Rural Electric Nebraskan, Sunday World Herald, Omaha World Herald.*

"Great scenery. Nice people. What a great experience, we'll be back again."

Grand Island   D7

Kirschke House B&B

1124 W 3rd St
Grand Island, NE 68801-5834
(308)381-6851 (800)381-6851

Circa 1902. A steeply sloping roofline and a two-story tower mark this distinctive, vine-covered brick Victorian house. Meticulously restored, there are polished wood floors, fresh wallpapers and carefully chosen antiques. The Roses Roses

Room is a spacious accommodation with a lace canopy bed, wicker rocking chair and decorating accents of roses and vines. In the old brick wash house is a wooden hot tub. In winter and spring, the area is popular for viewing the migration of sandhill cranes and whooping cranes.

Innkeeper(s): Lois Hank & Kiffani Smith. $55-145. MC VISA AX DS PC TC. TAC10. 5 rooms, 2 with PB. 1 cottage. Breakfast included in rates. Types of meals: gourmet breakfast and early coffee/tea. Lunch and room service available. Beds: QDT. Air conditioning and ceiling fan in room. TV, VCR, spa and library on premises. Weddings, small meetings and family reunions hosted. Antiques, fishing, parks, shopping and watersports nearby.

Location: In the historic district near downtown.

Publicity: *Grand Island Daily Independent.*

"We have been to many B&Bs in England, Canada and America. The Kirschke House ranks with the finest we've stayed in."

Lincoln   D9

The Atwood House B&B

740 S 17th St
Lincoln, NE 68508-3708
(402)438-4567 (800)884-6554 Fax:(402)477-8314

Circa 1894. Located two blocks from the state capitol, this 7,000-square-foot mansion, in the Neoclassical Georgian Revival style, features four massive columns. Interior columns are repeated throughout such as on the dressing room vanity, on the staircase and on the parlor fireplace. Classically appointed, the parlor and entranceway set an elegant yet inviting tone. Guest suites are large and feature spacious sitting rooms, fireplaces, massive bedsteads and Oriental carpets. The 800-square-foot bridal suite consists of three rooms, and it includes a fireplace, a carved walnut bed and a large whirlpool tub set off by columns. Breakfast is served on bone china with Waterford crystal and sterling flatware.

Innkeeper(s): Ruth & Larry Stoll. $78-165. MC VISA AX DS PC TC. 3 suites, 1 with FP. 1 conference room. Breakfast and evening snack included in rates. Meals: gourmet breakfast and early coffee/tea. Beds: KQ. Phone, air conditioning, turndown service, TV and VCR in room. Fax, copier and library on premises. Weddings, small meetings hosted. Antiques, fishing, parks, shopping, cross-country skiing, sporting events, golf, theater, watersports nearby.

Publicity: *Lincoln Journal Star.*

"Such a delightful B&B! It is such a nice change in my travels."

Nebraska City   D9

Whispering Pines

21st St & 6th Ave
Nebraska City, NE 68410-9802
(402)873-5850

Circa 1892. An easy getaway from Kansas City, Lincoln or Omaha, Nebraska City's Whispering Pines offers visitors a relaxing alternative from big-city life. Fresh flowers in each bedroom greet guests at this two-story brick Italianate, furnished with Victorian and country decor. Situated on more than six acres of trees, flowers and ponds, the inn is a birdwatcher's delight. Breakfast is served formally in the dining room, or guests may opt to eat on the deck with its view of the garden and pines. The inn is within easy walking distance to Arbor Lodge, home of the founder of Arbor Day.

Historic Interest: Nebraska City is the home of Arbor Day. Guests can take a short walk from the B&B and tour Arbor Lodge, a 52-room mansion owned by J. Sterling Morton, founder of Arbor Day. The mansion is located on a 64-acre state park. Wildwood Historic Home, built in 1869, also is open for tours. There also are several museums in town, as well.

Innkeeper(s): W.B. Smulling. $50-75. MC VISA DS. 5 rooms, 2 with PB. Breakfast included in rates. Type of meal: gourmet breakfast.

Omaha   C9

Offutt House

140 N 39th St
Omaha, NE 68131-2307
(402)553-0951

Circa 1894. This two-and-a-half-story, 14-room house is built like a chateau with a steep roof and tall windows. During the 1913 tornado, although almost every house in the neighborhood was leveled, the Offutt house stood firm. It is said that a decanter of sherry was blown from the dining room to the living room without anything spilling. The large parlor features a handsome fireplace, a wall of books and an inviting sofa. A bridal suite is tucked under the gables of the third floor. A continental-plus breakfast is served during the week and a full breakfast is offered on the weekends.

Historic Interest: Historic Old Market (5 minutes), Joslyn Castle (across street).

Innkeeper(s): Janet & Paul Koenig. $65-105. MC VISA AX DS. 6 rooms with PB. 2 suites. Breakfast included in rates. Types of meals: continental-plus breakfast and full breakfast. Beds: KQD. Antiques, golf and theater nearby. Pets Allowed.

Location: Central Omaha.

Publicity: *Midwest Living, Innsider, Bon Appetit, Innovations.*

"Hospitable, comfortable, lovely. A wonderful place to stay and great central location."

Nevada

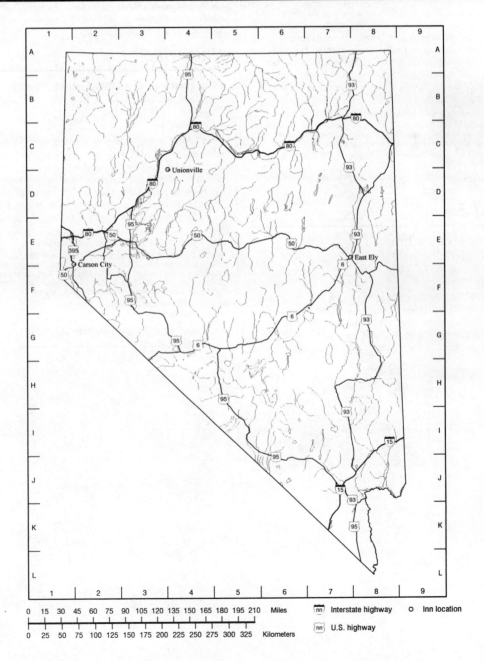

0	15 30 45 60 75 90 105 120 135 150 165 180 195 210	Miles	[nn] Interstate highway	o Inn location
0	25 50 75 100 125 150 175 200 225 250 275 300 325	Kilometers	[nn] U.S. highway	

Carson City
E2

Bliss Mansion B&B

710 W Robinson St
Carson City, NV 89703-3865
(702)887-8988 (800)320-0627 Fax:(702)887-0540

Circa 1879. Although one might assume that this beautifully restored mansion is so named because of the joy guests experience upon entering the home, it actually is named for its builder and owner. Duane Bliss, owner of the successful Carson-Tahoe Lumber and Fluming Company, created the home, which was at one time the largest in Nevada. The innkeepers have renovated the manor so successfully that it rivals its former elegance. Guest rooms feature hand-crafted mahogany fireplaces. In the afternoons, the innkeepers serve refreshments on the veranda. Although Nevada is known for gambling, Carson City offers a great deal more, including museums and historic homes. Skiing is available in nearby Lake Tahoe.

$195-245. MC VISA AX DS PC TC. TAC12. 4 rooms with PB. Breakfast and afternoon tea included in rates. Types of meals: gourmet breakfast and early coffee/tea. Beds: KQ. Phone and air conditioning in room. TV, VCR, fax, copier and library on premises. Antiques, fishing, parks, downhill skiing, golf and watersports nearby.

"A Hearst Castle with air-conditioning, pillowtop mattresses and instant hot water."

East Ely
E7

Steptoe Valley Inn

220 E 11th St, PO Box 151110
East Ely, NV 89315-1110
(702)289-8687

Circa 1907. Originally a grocery store at the turn of the century, this inn has been lovingly reconstructed and resembles a fancy, Old West-style store. The interior is decorated in Victorian country-cottage style. Five uniquely decorated guest rooms are named for local pioneers. The rooms also have views

of the inn's scenic surroundings, and three of them feature queen beds. A nearby railroad museum offers train rides and Great Basin National Park is 70 miles away. This inn is open from June to October. During the off-season, guests may inquire about the inn at (702) 435-1196.

Historic Interest: Nevada Northern Railway Museum (one-half block), Ward Charcoal Ovens (12 miles), Liberty Copper Pit (3 miles).

Innkeeper(s): Jane & Norman Lindley. $84-95. MC VISA AX PC TC. TAC10. 5 rooms with PB. 1 conference room. Breakfast and evening snack included in rates. Type of meal: full breakfast. Beds: QT. Phone, air conditioning, ceiling fan and TV in room. VCR and library on premises. Weddings, small meetings and family reunions hosted. Spanish spoken. Fishing and parks nearby.

Publicity: *Las Vegas Review Journal, Great Getaways, Yellow Brick Road.*

"Everything was so clean and first-rate."

Unionville
D4

Old Pioneer Garden Guest Ranch

2805 Unionville Rd
Unionville, NV 89418-8204
(702)538-7585

Circa 1861. Once a bustling silver mining town, Unionville now has only a handful of citizens, and Old Pioneer Garden Guest Ranch is just down the road from town. Accommodations are in a renovated blacksmith's house, a farmhouse and across the meadow in the Hadley House. A Swedish-style gazebo rests beside a bubbling stream, and there are orchards, grape arbors, vegetable gardens, sheep and goats. A country supper is available. The innkeepers can accommodate visiting horses in their barn and corrals.

Innkeeper(s): Mitzi & Lew Jones. $65-75. 12 rooms, 4 with PB, 1 with FP. 1 suite. 1 conference room. Breakfast included in rates. Types of meals: full breakfast, gourmet breakfast and early coffee/tea. Dinner, picnic lunch, lunch, gourmet lunch, banquet service and catering service available. Beds: D. Handicap access. 114 acres. Antiques and fishing nearby.

Location: 139 miles east of Reno.

Publicity: *Denver Post.*

"An array of charm that warms the heart and delights the soul."

New Hampshire

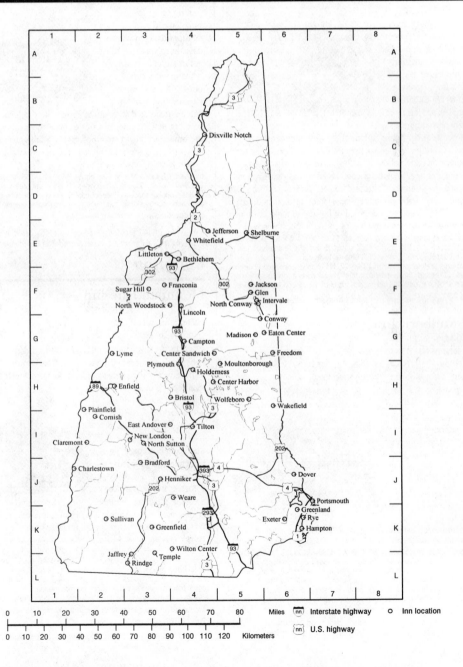

Map legend:

0 10 20 30 40 50 60 70 80 Miles [nn] Interstate highway o Inn location

0 10 20 30 40 50 60 70 80 90 100 110 120 Kilometers (nn) U.S. highway

Map locations:
- Dixville Notch — 3
- Jefferson
- Shelburne
- Whitefield
- Littleton
- Bethlehem
- Sugar Hill
- Franconia
- Jackson
- Glen
- North Woodstock
- North Conway
- Intervale
- Lincoln
- Conway
- Madison
- Eaton Center
- Campton
- Center Sandwich
- Freedom
- Lyme
- Moultonborough
- Plymouth
- Holderness
- Center Harbor
- Enfield
- Bristol
- Wolfeboro
- Plainfield
- Wakefield
- Cornish
- East Andover
- Tilton
- New London
- North Sutton
- Claremont
- Bradford
- Dover
- Charlestown
- Henniker
- Portsmouth
- Weare
- Greenland
- Rye
- Sullivan
- Exeter
- Hampton
- Greenfield
- Jaffrey
- Wilton Center
- Temple
- Rindge

Bethlehem E4

Adair A Country Inn

80 Guider Lane
Bethlehem, NH 03574
(603)444-2600 (888)444-2600 Fax:(603)444-4823

Circa 1927. Adair represents all that a New England country inn is supposed to be. From its Georgian Colonial architecture to its elegant decor to rooms warmed by fireplaces, the inn is picturesque enough that  Sears chose to highlight its exterior on the cover of the 1995 Wish Book. The four-diamond-rated inn originally served as a wedding gift from Frank Hogan to his daughter, Dorothy Adair Hogan. Dorothy hosted many famed guests at her home, among them were presidents, Supreme Court justices and actors. Freshly baked popovers start off the morning fare, followed by fresh fruit, granola and specialty dishes such as eggs Benedict accompanied by hash brown potatoes and a fried tomato. Cakes and cookies are served during the complimentary afternoon tea service. The inn also offers dinner service at Tim-Bir Alley restaurant, but be sure to make advance reservations as the dining room is open to the public, as well.

Innkeeper(s): Hardy, Pat & Nancy Banfield. $135-220. MC VISA AX PC TC. TAC10. 9 rooms with PB, 6 with FP. 2 suites. Breakfast and afternoon tea included in rates. Types of meals: full breakfast and early coffee/tea. Restaurant on premises. Beds: KQ. TV, VCR, fax, copier, tennis and library on premises. 200 acres. Small meetings, family reunions and seminars hosted. Antiques, shopping, downhill skiing, cross-country skiing and theater nearby.

"What can we say, we expected a lot - and got much more."

The Mulburn Inn

2370 Main St, Rt 302
Bethlehem, NH 03574
(603)869-3389 (800)457-9440 Fax:(603)869-5633
E-mail: the.mulburn.inn@connriver.net

Circa 1908. This summer cottage was known as the Ivie Estate, and many of the Ivie and Woolworth (as in the famed five and dime store) family members vacationed here in summer. Cary Grant and Barbara Hutton spent their honeymoon at the mansion. Polished oak staircases and stained-glass windows add to the atmosphere.

Historic Interest: Crawford Notch State Park, Franconia Notch State Park, Heritage, Mount Washington.

Innkeeper(s): The Skeels Family. $60-90. MC VISA AX DS PC TC. TAC10. 7 rooms with PB. Breakfast and afternoon tea included in rates. Types of meals: full breakfast and early coffee/tea. Catered breakfast available. Beds: KQDT. TV, VCR, fax, copier and library on premises. Weddings and small meetings hosted. Amusement parks, antiques, fishing, parks, shopping, downhill skiing, cross-country skiing and golf nearby.

Publicity: The Record, Yankee, Boston Globe.

"You have put a lot of thought, charm, beauty and warmth into the inn. Your breakfasts were oh, so delicious!!"

Bradford J3

Candlelite Inn

5 Greenhouse Ln
Bradford, NH 03221-3505
(603)938-5571 (888)812-5571

Circa 1897. Nestled on three acres of countryside in the valley of the Lake Sunapee region, this Victorian inn has all of the grace and charm of an era gone by. The inn offers a gazebo porch perfect for sipping lemonade on a summer day. On winter days, keep warm by the parlor's fireplace while relaxing with a good book. All guest rooms have mountain views  and are decorated with quilts, cross stitch pillows and tole painting that includes plaques to table-top decorations from the innkeeper's own creations. Enjoy a full gourmet breakfast, down to the dessert, in the sun room overlooking the pond.

Historic Interest: Close to the John Hay.

Innkeeper(s): Les & Marilyn Gordon. $65-95. MC VISA AX DS. 6 rooms with PB. Breakfast included in rates. Types of meals: full breakfast and early coffee/tea. Evening snack available. Beds: Q. Antiques, shopping, downhill skiing, cross-country skiing, sporting events and theater nearby.

Publicity: Grapevine, InterTown News.

"We had a perfect night of sleep and an incredible breakfast. We are planning another trip next summer and The Candlelite is on our list."

Campton G4

Mountain-Fare Inn

Mad River Rd, PO Box 553
Campton, NH 03223
(603)726-4283

Circa 1830. This white farmhouse is surrounded by flower gardens in the summer and unparalleled foliage in the fall. This early 19th-century village inn is an ideal spot from which to enjoy New Hampshire's many offerings. Each season brings with it different activities, from skiing to biking and hiking or simply taking in the beautiful scenery. Skiers will enjoy the inn's lodge atmosphere during the winter, as well as the close access to ski areas. The inn  is appointed in a charming New Hampshire style with country-cottage decor. The hearty breakfast is a favorite of returning guests.

Historic Interest: Franconia Notch (Old Man of the Mountain), Squam Lake (Golden Pond), and drive the Scenic Kancamagus Highway.

Innkeeper(s): Susan & Nick Preston. $65-95. MAP, EP. 10 rooms, 8 with PB. Breakfast and afternoon tea included in rates. Type of meal: full breakfast. Beds: QDT. Phone in room. TV, VCR and child care on premises. Weddings, small meetings and family reunions hosted. Antiques, fishing, parks, downhill skiing, cross-country skiing, sporting events, theater and watersports nearby.

Location: Two hours north of Boston in the White Mountains.

Publicity: Ski, Skiing, Snow Country.

"Thank you for your unusually caring attitude toward your guests."

Center Harbor H4

Kona Mansion Inn

PO Box 458
Center Harbor, NH 03226-0458
(603)253-4900 Fax:(603)253-7350

Circa 1900. Located in the state's scenic lake region, this family-oriented Tudor inn sports a waterfront location on 125 acres. Six of the guest rooms boast kitchenettes, and some rooms are able to accommodate
visitors' pets. The inn
also hosts meetings,
reunions and weddings, and it offers a
variety of food services. Antiquing and
fishing are other popular guest activities.

Innkeeper(s): The Crowleys. Call for rates. 1 conference room. Picnic lunch, banquet service, catering service available. Air conditioning in room. TV, VCR on premises. 125 acres. Weddings, small meetings, family reunions, seminars hosted. Amusement parks, antiques, shopping, sporting events, theater nearby.

Red Hill Inn

RR 1 Box 99m
Center Harbor, NH 03226-9603
(603)279-7001 (800)573-3445 Fax:(603)279-7003

Circa 1904. The mansion was once the centerpiece of a 1,000-acre estate. It was called "keewaydin" for the strong north wind that blows across Sunset Hill. When the Depression was over,
the inn was sold. New owners included
European royalty escaping from Nazi
Germany. Now the mansion is a restored country
inn with spectacular
views of the area's lakes
and mountains. From
your room you can see
the site of the filming of
"On Golden Pond." Eighteen of the rooms boast woodburning fireplaces, and 10 rooms have private whirlpool baths.

Historic Interest: The White Mountains are a 45-minute drive from the inn.

Innkeeper(s): Don Leavitt & Rick Miller. $105-175. EP. MC VISA AX DC CB DS. TAC15. 25 rooms with PB, 18 with FP. Breakfast included in rates. Type of meal: full breakfast. Dinner and lunch available. Restaurant on premises. Beds: KQDT. Phone in room. VCR and copier on premises. 60 acres. Weddings, small meetings, family reunions and seminars hosted. Amusement parks, antiques, fishing, shopping, downhill skiing, cross-country skiing, theater and watersports nearby.

Location: Central New Hampshire in the Lakes Region.

Publicity: *New England Getaways, Yankee, Yankee Traveler, Boston, New Hampshire Profiles, Country Living.*

"Our stay was very enjoyable."

Center Sandwich G4

Overlook Farm B&B

14 Mountain Rd
Center Sandwich, NH 03227
(603)284-6485

Circa 1783. If one were to conjure up an image of a representative New England farmhouse, Overlook Farm might spring to mind. Nestled on 15 rolling acres with mountains as a backdrop, the bed & breakfast offers four comfortable guest rooms

with Colonial decor and antiques. Among the historical artifacts of this 18th-century house is a wheel for the original well
bucket, an old barn and
granite walls. Innkeeper
Phyllis Olafsen prepares a
different, homemade
breakfast every day, and
also varies the table settings. Squam Lake is nearby, as is Lake Winnipesaukee and the White Mountains.

Innkeeper(s): Phyllis Olafsen. $65-85. PC TC. 4 rooms, 2 with PB. 1 suite. Breakfast included in rates. Types of meals: full breakfast, gourmet breakfast and early coffee/tea. Beds: QDT. Turndown service in room. TV, VCR and library on premises. 15 acres. Family reunions hosted. Amusement parks, antiques, fishing, parks, shopping, golf, theater and watersports nearby.

"When we look back on our trip, your lovely home and warm hospitality is one of the things we remember the most."

Charlestown J1

MapleHedge B&B

355 Main St, PO Box 638
Charlestown, NH 03603
(603)826-5237 (800)962-7539 Fax:(603)826-5237
E-mail: debrine@fmis.net

Circa 1820. This elegantly restored home is set among acres of lawn and 200-year-old maple trees. The bed & breakfast boasts five distinctive bedrooms. The Beale Room is named for the
innkeeper's grandparents and
is full of sentimental treasures
such as milk bottles from her
grandfather's dairy and family
photos. The Butterfly Suite is
filled with white wicker,
including an antique, glass-topped hamper and Victorian
butterfly trays. The rooms are furnished in antiques, including some of the linens. A delectable three-course breakfast is served and may include fresh fruit salads and scones. Evening refreshments include California wine with New Hampshire cheese. Guests can go on antiquing tours or attend country auctions, and many historical attractions are nearby.

Historic Interest: Located within the longest National Historic District in the state, Fort Number Four (1 mile), Saint Gauden's National Historic Site (20 minutes), and Dartmouth College (35 minutes).

Innkeeper(s): Joan & Dick DeBrine. $80-100. MC VISA PC. TAC10. 5 rooms with PB. 1 suite. Breakfast and evening snack included in rates. Meals: gourmet breakfast and early coffee/tea. Beds: QT. Air conditioning, turndown service in room. Fax, copier, library on premises. Small meetings and family reunions hosted. Antiques, fishing, shopping, theater, watersports nearby.

Location: Connecticut River Valley of New Hampshire.

Publicity: *L.A. Times, Buffalo News, Country Living, Yankee Traveler, Newsday.*

"The highlight of my two weeks in New England. A breakfast worth jumping out of bed for."

Claremont I2

Goddard Mansion B&B

25 Hillstead Rd
Claremont, NH 03743-3399
(603)543-0603 (800)736-0603 Fax:(603)543-0001

Circa 1905. This English-style manor house and adjacent garden tea house is surrounded by seven acres of lawns and gardens. Each of the guest rooms is decorated in a different style.

One features French Country decor, another sports a Victorian look. The living room with its fireplace, window seats and baby grand piano is a perfect place to relax. Homemade breakfasts, made using natural ingredients and fresh produce, include items such as souffles, pancakes, freshly baked muffins and fruit. The hearty meals are served in the wood paneled dining room highlighted by an antique Wurlitzer jukebox.

Innkeeper(s): Debbie Albee. $65-125. MC VISA AX DC CB DS PC TC. 10 rooms, 3 with PB. 1 suite. 2 conference rooms. Breakfast included in rates. Types of meals: continental-plus breakfast, full breakfast and gourmet breakfast. Beds: KQDT. Phone, air conditioning and turndown service in room. TV, VCR, fax, bicycles and library on premises. Weddings, small meetings, family reunions and seminars hosted. Antiques, fishing, parks, shopping, downhill skiing, cross-country skiing and theater nearby.

Publicity: *Eagle Times, Yankee.*

"Our trip would not have been as enjoyable without having stayed at your inn."

Conway   G5

The Darby Field Inn

Bald Hill, PO Box D
Conway, NH 03818-4003
(603)447-2181 (800)426-4147 Fax:(603)447-5726
E-mail: marc@darbyfield.com

Circa 1826. This rambling, blue clapboard farmhouse has a huge fieldstone fireplace, stone patio and outstanding views of the Mt. Washington Valley and the Presidential Mountains. For many years it was called the Bald Hill Grand View Lodge but was renamed to honor the first man to climb Mt. Washington, Darby Field. Modified American Plan rates are

$65 to $100 per person, double occupancy. For those wanting bed & breakfast only, rates range from $45 to $80 per person, double occupancy.

Innkeeper(s): Marc & Maria Donaldson. $45-100. MC VISA AX. 16 rooms, 14 with PB. 1 suite. Beds: KQDT. Air conditioning and ceiling fan in room. TV and VCR on premises. Weddings, small meetings, family reunions and seminars hosted. Amusement parks, antiques, shopping, downhill skiing, cross-country skiing and theater nearby.

Location: Half a mile south of Conway.

"If an inn is a place for a weary traveler to relax, recover and feel the hospitality and warmth of the innkeeper, then the Darby Field Inn is one of the finest."

Cornish   I2

Chase House B&B Inn

Rt 12A, RR 2 Box 909
Cornish, NH 03745
(603)675-5391 (800)401-9455 Fax:(603)675-5010

Circa 1776. Cornish's first English settler, Dudley Chase, built this Federal house noted for its fine architecture. In 1845, it was moved to accommodate the Sullivan County Railroad. Designated a National Historic Landmark, it was the birthplace

of Salmon Chase, Governor of Ohio, Secretary of the Treasury for President Lincoln and Chief Justice of the Supreme Court. The Chase Manhattan Bank was named after him.

Historic Interest: Saint Gauden's Historic Site (5 minutes), Fort Number Four (30 minutes), American Precision Museum (5 minutes), Dartmouth College (30 minutes).

Innkeeper(s): Barbara Lewis & Ted Doyle. $95-125. MC VISA. 8 rooms, 7 with PB. 2 suites. Breakfast included in rates. Type of meal: full breakfast. Beds: QDT. Phone in room. Antiques, fishing, downhill skiing, cross-country skiing, theater and watersports nearby.

Location: Two-and-a-half hours from Boston.

Publicity: *Hartford Courant, The Philadelphia Inquirer, USA Today.*

Dixville Notch   C4

The Balsams Grand Resort Hotel

Lake Gloriette, Rt 26
Dixville Notch, NH 03576-9710
(603)255-3400 (800)255-0600 Fax:(603)255-4221
E-mail: thebalsams@aol.com

Circa 1866. Guests aren't likely to be disappointed by this four-star resort, which has been in continuous operation since 1866. Since 1960, the result of the New Hampshire primary, and the first vote for a presidential election, has been announced from the Notch's 25 voters. The location is stunning, surrounded by mountain views and bordering Lake Gloriette. Among the 15,000 acres of grounds, guests will find 27 holes of golf, tennis courts, an Olympic-size heated pool that rests just off the lakeshore, Alpine and cross-country ski trails, snowboarding, an ice skating rink and much more. The hotel, itself, is a Victorian masterpiece. Guest rooms are individually and tastefully decorated, and family suites are available. The two most opulent suites are located in the hotel's tower. The rates include everything, including made-to-order breakfasts, a summer-season lunch buffet and gourmet dinners. Picnic are offered during the summer season. The hotel is open from mid-May to mid-October and again from mid-December to March.

Innkeeper(s): Steve Barba & Warren Pearson. $150-205. AP. MC VISA AX DS PC TC. TAC10. 208 rooms with PB. 18 suites. 19 conference rooms. Breakfast and dinner included in rates. Types of meals: full breakfast, gourmet breakfast and early coffee/tea. Lunch, gourmet lunch, banquet service and room service available. Restaurant on premises. Beds: KDT. Phone and turndown service in room. TV, VCR, fax, copier, swimming, bicycles, tennis, library and child care on premises. Handicap access. Weddings, small meetings, family reunions and seminars hosted. French spoken. Fishing, parks, shopping, downhill skiing and cross-country skiing nearby.

Publicity: *Travel Guide to New England, Golfer, Golf, Money, Providence Sunday Journal, Atlantic Monthly.* Ratings: 4 Stars.

Dover   J6

Silver Street Inn

103 Silver St
Dover, NH 03820-3923
(603)743-3000 Fax:(603)749-5673

Circa 1880. For nearly a century, this stately Victorian remained in the Frank B. Williams family, owners of the I.B. Williams Belt & Lace Factory. They decorated their mansion with imported Honduran mahogany, Italian slate, and Austrian crystal, all of which remains intact today. Ornate molded plas-

ter ceilings, covered bois-
erie wall panels and
Oriental rugs further
enhance the classic
European elegance.
Original fixtures such as
pedestal sinks and claw-

foot tubs have been preserved in some of the bedrooms, but all
modern conveniences have been added.

Innkeeper(s): Lorene Cook. $69-89. MC VISA DC CB DS TC. 10 rooms, 9
with PB. 1 suite. Breakfast included in rates. Meal: full breakfast. Beds: QDT.
Phone, air conditioning and TV in room. Fax and copier on premises.
Weddings and small meetings hosted. Antiques, parks and theater nearby.

"Extremely pleasant atmosphere, quiet and clean."

East Andover   I4

Highland Lake Inn B&B

Maple St
East Andover, NH 03231-0164
(603)735-6426 Fax:(603)735-5355

Circa 1767. This early Colonial-Victorian inn overlooks three
mountains, and all the rooms have views of either the lake or
the mountains. Many guest rooms feature handmade quilts and
some have four-poster beds. Guests
may relax with a book from the
inn's library in front of the sitting room fireplace or walk
the 12-acre grounds and
enjoy old apple and maple
trees, as well as the shore-

line of the lake. Adjacent to a 21-acre nature conservancy, there
are scenic trails and a stream to explore. Highland Lake is
stocked with bass and also has trout. Fresh fruit salads, hot
entrees, and homemade breads are featured at breakfast.

Historic Interest: Two Shaker Villages, old one-room school house.

Innkeeper(s): Mary Petras. $85-125. MC VISA AX. 10 rooms with PB.
Breakfast included in rates. Type of meal: full breakfast. Beds: KQT. Ceiling
fan in room. TV and VCR on premises. 10 acres. Weddings, small meetings,
family reunions and seminars hosted. Amusement parks, antiques, fishing,
shopping, skiing, sporting events, theater and watersports nearby.
Publicity: Andover Beacon.

"Place is very close to heaven."

Eaton Center   G6

The Inn at Crystal Lake

Rt 153 PO Box 12
Eaton Center, NH 03832
(603)447-2120 (800)343-7336 Fax:(603)447-3599

Circa 1884. Balconies with flower boxes, a veranda and shutters
add an inviting warmth to this three-story, yellow and white,
Greek Victorian Revival inn. A cheerful dining room is just one
of the inn's common rooms. There is a library and parlor, as
well. An old-fashioned country decor extends throughout the
inn. The innkeepers provide a canoe or paddle boat to explore
the shoreline of Crystal Lake. In winter, there is ice skating, ice
fishing and sleigh rides. Five major ski areas and the National
Forest are all nearby, and Conway is six miles away.

Historic Interest: Built in 1884, it was a stagecoach stop and the first post office.

Innkeeper(s): Richard & Janice Octeau. $60-100. MC VISA AX DC DS PC
TC. TAC10. 11 rooms with PB. 1 suite. Breakfast included in rates. Types of

meals: full breakfast and early coffee/tea. Banquet service available. Beds:
QDT. Phone and VCR in room. TV, fax, copier and swimming on premises.
Small meetings and family reunions hosted. Amusement parks, antiques,
fishing, parks, shopping, skiing, golf, theater and watersports nearby.

Rockhouse Mountain Farm Inn

PO Box 90
Eaton Center, NH 03832-0090
(603)447-2880

Circa 1900. This handsome old house is framed by maple
trees on 450 acres of forests, streams, fields and wildflowers.
Milking cows, pigs, geese, peacocks and llamas provide entertainment for city young-
sters of all ages. Three
generations of the Edges
have operated this inn
and some guests have
been coming since 1946,
the year it opened. A
250-year-old barn bulges
at times with new-mown

hay, and there is a nearby beach with swimming and boating
for the exclusive use of guests.

Innkeeper(s): Johnny & Alana Edge. $50-60. MAP. PC TC. 18 rooms, 8 with
PB, 1 with FP. 2 cottages. Breakfast and dinner included in rates. Type of
meal: full breakfast. Restaurant on premises. Beds: DT. Swimming, sauna,
stables and library on premises. Handicap access. 450 acres. Small meetings
and family reunions hosted. French spoken. Antiques, fishing, parks, shopping, golf, theater and watersports nearby.

Location: Near the White Mountains.

Publicity: New York Times, Family Circle, Woman's Day, Boston Globe,
Country Vacations.

*"We have seen many lovely places, but Rockhouse remains the real
high spot, the one to which we most want to return."*

Enfield   H2

Mary Keane House

PO Box 5, Rt 4 A
Enfield, NH 06748
(603)632-4241 (888)239-2153

Circa 1930. This lakeside Queen Anne Victorian is pristinely
restored and painted mauve with white trim. It adjoins a
chapel, all encircled with a white picket fence. Views from the
porches and balconies include the inn's flower beds, Lake
Mascoma and 1,200
acres of woodland
and meadow. A
handsome drawing
room with antiques
and fireplace,

mahogany paneling, stained and beveled glass, and a gracious
front staircase are featured. Mini frittatas with salsa, rhubarb
coffee cake and hot oatmeal scones are among the items
offered on the inn's bountiful table. Walk to the Shaker
Museum, herb gardens, Shaker Village and the Dana Robes
Woodcraftsmen Workshop where Shaker furniture is fashioned.

Innkeeper(s): Sharon & David Carr. $75-125. MC VISA AX PC TC. TAC10. 5
rooms with PB. 3 suites. Breakfast included in rates. Types of meals: full
breakfast and early coffee/tea. Beds: KQTD. Turndown service and TV in
room. VCR, copier, swimming and library on premises. Weddings, small
meetings and family reunions hosted. Antiques, fishing, shopping, downhill
skiing, cross-country skiing, sporting events, golf and theater nearby.
Pets Allowed: If well behaved.

Exeter
K6

Inn of Exeter

90 Front St
Exeter, NH 03833-2723
(603)772-5901 (800)782-8444 Fax:(603)778-8757

Circa 1932. For more than 60 years, guests have been enjoying New England hospitality at this inn. A mix of fine antiques and reproductions are found in the traditionally appointed guest rooms. The inn is often the site of weddings and receptions, as well as business meetings. Although meals are not included in the rates, the inn's restaurant serves breakfast, lunch, dinner and Sunday brunch. The location is within walking distance of museums, historical sites and shops.

Innkeeper(s): Carl G. Jensen. $89-114. MC VISA AX DC CB DS TC. TAC10. 47 rooms with PB, 1 with FP. 1 suite. 7 conference rooms. Types of meals: continental breakfast, continental-plus breakfast, full breakfast, gourmet breakfast and early coffee/tea. Dinner, evening snack, picnic lunch, lunch, gourmet lunch and banquet service available. Restaurant on premises. Beds: KQDT. Phone, air conditioning and TV in room. VCR, fax and copier on premises. Handicap access. Weddings, small meetings, family reunions and seminars hosted. Danish and Italian spoken. Antiques, fishing, parks, shopping, cross-country skiing, sporting events, theater and watersports nearby.

Franconia
F3

The Inn at Forest Hills

Rt 142, PO Box 783
Franconia, NH 03580
(603)823-9550 (800)280-9550 Fax:(603)823-8701
E-mail: innfhills@connriver.net

Circa 1890. This Tudor-style inn in the White Mountains offers a solarium, a living room with fireplace and a large common room with fireplace and cathedral ceilings. Breakfast is served with a quiet background of classical music in the dining room,

where in the winter there's a blazing fireplace, and in summer the French doors open to the scenery. Guest rooms feature a casual country decor with quilts, flowered wall coverings and some four-poster beds. Cross-country ski for free on the inn's property and at the local touring center. Downhill facilities are found at Bretton Woods, Cannon or Loon Mountain. Nearby Franconia Notch Park and the White Mountains feature trails designed for cycling and hiking. Innkeepers are justices of the peace, and will do weddings or a renewal of vows.

Historic Interest: Mount Washington Hotel (20 minutes), Franconia Notch State Park (5 minutes), Robert Frost Museum (10 minutes).

Innkeeper(s): Gordon & Joanne Haym. $85-145. MC VISA AX DC PC TC. 7 rooms with PB. Breakfast included in rates. Type of meal: full breakfast. Evening snack available. Beds: KQ. TV, VCR, fax, tennis and library on premises. Weddings, small meetings, family reunions and seminars hosted. Antiques, fishing, parks, shopping, downhill skiing, cross-country skiing and watersports nearby.

"What a delightful inn! I loved the casual country elegance of your B&B and can understand why you are so popular with brides and grooms."

Franconia Inn

1300 Easton Rd
Franconia, NH 03580-4921
(603)823-5542 (800)473-5299 Fax:(603)823-8078
E-mail: info@franconiainn.com

Circa 1934. Beautifully situated on 117 acres below the White Mountain's famous Franconia Notch, this white clapboard inn is three stories high. An oak-paneled library, parlor, rathskeller lounge and two verandas offer relaxing retreats. The inn's rooms are simply decorated in a pleasing style and there is a special honeymoon suite with private Jacuzzi. Bach, classic wines and an elegant American cuisine are featured in

the inn's unpretentious dining room. There's no shortage of activity here. The inn offers four clay tennis courts, horseback riding, a heated swimming pool, croquet, fishing, cross-country ski trails and glider rides among its outdoor amenities.

Innkeeper(s): Alec Morris. $75-135. MAP, EP. MC VISA AX. 34 rooms, 29 with PB, 3 with FP. 4 suites. 1 conference room. Breakfast included in rates. Types of meals: gourmet breakfast and early coffee/tea. Dinner, picnic lunch and catering service available. Restaurant on premises. Beds: KQDT. Phone in room. VCR, copier, spa, swimming, bicycles, tennis and child care on premises. 107 acres. Weddings, small meetings, family reunions and seminars hosted. Amusement parks, antiques, fishing, parks, shopping, downhill skiing, cross-country skiing, sporting events and theater nearby.

Location: Exit 38 off I-93, two-and-a-half miles south on Route 116.

Publicity: *Philadelphia Inquirer, Boston Globe, Travel & Leisure, Powder.*

"The piece de resistance of the Franconia Notch is the Franconia Inn—Philadelphia Inquirer."

Freedom
G6

Freedom House B&B

13 Old Portland Rd
Freedom, NH 03836
(603)539-4815

Circa 1855. Freedom House, set in a peaceful New England village, is a rambling two- and three-story Victorian farmhouse. It features two double bays, and there's an antique shop on the premises. Gathering places include the inn's two porches, a parlor and library, but often guests stroll out to the woodland meadow or the mill pond. Decorated with Victorian country pieces, Freedom House is a welcome location for afternoon tea, served at 4 p.m. each day. Breakfast offerings include cereal, freshly baked muffins and dishes such as stuffed French toast.

Innkeeper(s): Patrick J. Miele & Dean Balch. $65-85. MC VISA. 4 rooms. Breakfast included in rates. Types of meals: full breakfast and early coffee/tea. Afternoon tea available. Beds: DT. TV, VCR and library on premises. Small meetings and family reunions hosted. Spanish spoken. Antiques, fishing, parks, shopping, downhill skiing, cross-country skiing, golf, theater and watersports nearby.

"The breakfasts were the best!"

Glen F5

Bernerhof Inn

Rt 302, PO Box 240
Glen, NH 03838-0240
(603)383-9132 (800)548-8007 Fax:(603)383-0809
E-mail: stay@bernerhofinn.com

Circa 1880. This historic inn is located in the foothills of the White Mountains. Several of the nine guest rooms include a double whirlpool tub. Guests can dine on gourmet cuisine at the inn's award-winning restaurant. The inn's Black Bear Pub is a perfect place for a more casual meal, including a taste from the pub's ample beer selection. Novice chefs should try the inn's "Taste of the Mountains Cooking School," where they can pick up many tricks of the trade.

Innkeeper(s): Sharon Wroblewski. $75-150. MAP. MC VISA AX DS PC TC. 9 rooms with PB. 2 suites. Breakfast included in rates. Type of meal: full breakfast. Dinner, lunch, catering service and room service available. Beds: KQD. Air conditioning, ceiling fan and TV in room. Fax and copier on premises. 10 acres. Weddings, small meetings and family reunions hosted. Amusement parks, antiques, fishing, parks, shopping, downhill skiing, cross-country skiing and theater nearby.

Publicity: *Bon Appetit, New Hampshire Profiles, Boston Globe, Yankee, Skiing, National Geographic Traveler.*

"When people want to treat themselves, this is where they come."

Greenfield K3

The Greenfield Inn

Forest Rd at Rts 31 N & 136
Greenfield, NH 03047
(603)547-6327 Fax:(603)547-2418
E-mail: innkeeper@greenfieldinn.com

Circa 1817. In the 1850s this inn was purchased by Henry Dunklee, innkeeper of the old Mayfield Inn across the street. When there was an overflow of guests at his tavern, Mr. Dunklee accommodated them here. This totally renovated Victorian mansion features veranda views of Crotched, Temple and Monadnock Mountains. There is a conference room with a lovely mountain view. The gracious innkeepers and comfortable interiors have been enjoyed by many well-traveled guests, including Dolores and Bob Hope.

Historic Interest: The inn is located near the historic town graveyard and the first town hall in New Hampshire.

Innkeeper(s): Barbara & Vic Mangini. $49-119. MC VISA AX PC TC. TAC10. 11 rooms, 8 with PB. 2 suites. 1 cottage. 1 conference room. Breakfast included in rates. Type of meal: full breakfast. Beds: KQDT. Phone, air conditioning, ceiling fan and VCR in room. Fax, copier and library on premises. Small meetings, family reunions and seminars hosted. Antiques, fishing, parks, shopping, downhill skiing, cross-country skiing, theater and watersports nearby.

Location: Southern New Hampshire, 45 minutes from Manchester Airport, 90 minutes from Boston.

Publicity: *Manchester Union Leader, Innsider.*

"I'm coming back for more of this New Hampshire therapy—Bob Hope."

Greenland K6

Captain Folsom Inn

Rt 151, PO Box 396
Greenland, NH 03840-0396
(603)436-2662

Circa 1758. George Washington is said to have stopped at this former tavern along the Boston to Portland stage coach route, where he gave a speech on the front lawn. Located on six acres, the inn was an active American Revolution site and one of the most prominent inns in the state. A three-story federal building, it still has the original kitchen fireplaces with brick ovens. The innkeeper has taught

open hearth cooking classes and has a collection of old colonial recipes. In the tavern at the back of the inn, guests can experience the atmosphere and life of colonial times. Guest rooms feature canopy beds, antiques and reproductions. There are wraparound porches on the back of the house on two levels.

Innkeeper(s): Faith & Bob McTigue. $45-85. MC VISA AX DS PC TC. 6 rooms, 2 with PB, 6 with FP. Breakfast and afternoon tea included in rates. Types of meals: full breakfast and early coffee/tea. Beds: QT. Air conditioning in room. TV, VCR, swimming and child care on premises. Weddings, small meetings, family reunions and seminars hosted. Antiques, fishing, downhill skiing, golf, theater and watersports nearby.

Publicity: *Lifestyles, Salmon Falls Stoneware.*

Hampton K6

The Inn at Elmwood Corners

252 Winnacunnet Rd
Hampton, NH 03842-2726
(603)929-0443 (800)253-5691

Circa 1870. This old sea captain's house boasts a wide wraparound porch, filled with wicker in the summer. The inn is decorated with stenciled walls, braided rugs and collections such as thimbles and dolls. Mary has stitched the quilts that top the beds. The library is jammed and guests may borrow a book and finish reading it at home. A

favorite breakfast is John's poached brook trout or Eggs Benedict.

Innkeeper(s): John & Mary Hornberger. $65-85. MC VISA TC. 7 rooms, 2 with PB. 2 suites. Breakfast included in rates. Beds: QT. Air conditioning in room. TV and library on premises. Limited French spoken. Amusement parks, antiques, fishing, parks, shopping, x-country skiing, theater, watersports nearby.

Location: Three miles east of I-95, one mile west of the ocean.

Publicity: *Portsmouth Herald, Hampton Union, Boston Globe, Country.*

"Very hospitable, can't think of a thing you need to add."

The Oceanside Inn

365 Ocean Blvd
Hampton, NH 03842-3633
(603)926-3542 Fax:(603)926-3549
E-mail: oceansid@nh.ultranet.com

Circa 1900. This two-story hotel with upper veranda is located directly across the street from the ocean and adjacent to the Oceanside Mall. Elegant interiors include a pillared living room/library with fireplace, comfortable sitting areas, Oriental rugs and paintings. A
sample guest room, the
Patriot Gove Room, has
two double beds, wicker
chairs and views of the
ocean. Other rooms,
such as the Moses Leavitt

Room, offer a canopy bed. A simple continental breakfast is available, and there is nightly turndown service. Beach chairs and towels are offered for enjoying the sandy beaches.

Innkeeper(s): Skip & Debbie Windemiller. $120-145. MC VISA AX DS TC. TAC5. 10 rooms with PB. 1 cottage. Breakfast included in rates. Type of meal: continental-plus breakfast. Beds: KQTD. Phone, air conditioning and turndown service in room. TV, VCR, fax, copier and library on premises. Amusement parks, antiques, shopping, golf, theater and watersports nearby.

"We went back in time to find our true free spirits & delight in the cozy & warm yesteryears, magnificent!"

Henniker J3

Colby Hill Inn

3 The Oaks, PO Box 779
Henniker, NH 03242-0779
(603)428-3281 (800)531-0330 Fax:(603)428-9218
E-mail: colbyhillinn@conknet.com

Circa 1797. This 18th-century Colonial and its surrounding five acres is a classic example of an old New England Farm. There are still old barns on the grounds, as well as a restored carriage house. Stroll the
grounds and you'll also
find gardens, a swimming
pool and a picturesque
gazebo. Antiques fill the
guest rooms, each of
which is individually
appointed in an elegant, tradi-

tional style. Four rooms have working fireplaces. Guests and others can enjoy a romantic dinner by candlelight at the inn's dining room. Specialties of the house include items such as baked brie with toasted almonds, poached salmon in a mustard cream sauce and rich desserts, including maple walnut pie. Dinner is served every night.

Innkeeper(s): Ellie & John Day, Laurel Day Mack. $85-175. MC VISA AX DC CB DS PC TC. TAC10. 16 rooms with PB, 4 with FP. 3 suites. 1 conference room. Breakfast included in rates. Types of meals: full breakfast, gourmet breakfast and early coffee/tea. Dinner, evening snack, banquet service and room service available. Restaurant on premises. Beds: KQDT. Phone and air conditioning in room. TV, VCR, fax, copier and swimming on premises. Weddings, small meetings, family reunions and seminars hosted. Antiques, fishing, parks, downhill skiing and cross-country skiing nearby.

Holderness H4

The Inn on Golden Pond

Rt 3, PO Box 680
Holderness, NH 03245
(603)968-7269

Circa 1879. Framed by meandering stone walls and split-rail fences more than 100 years old, this inn is situated on 50 acres of woodlands. Most rooms overlook picturesque countryside and nearby is Squam Lake, setting for the film "On Golden Pond." An inviting, 60-foot screened porch provides a place to relax during the summer.

Innkeeper(s): Bill & Bonnie Webb. $85-140. MC VISA AX. TAC10. 8 rooms with PB. 1 suite. Breakfast included in rates. Types of meals: full breakfast and early coffee/tea. Beds: KQT. Phone and turndown service in room. TV on premises. 50 acres. Antiques, fishing, shopping, downhill skiing, cross-country skiing, sporting events, theater and watersports nearby.

Location: In the lakes region, close to Squam Lake.

Publicity: *Boston Globe, Baltimore Sun, Los Angeles Times.*

"Another sweet flower added to my bouquet of life."

Manor on Golden Pond

Rt 3 Box T
Holderness, NH 03245
(603)968-3348

Circa 1903. An Englishman and land developer had a boyhood dream of living in a beautiful mansion high on a hill overlooking lakes and mountains. After he discovered these beautiful 13 acres, he brought craftsmen from around the world to build an English-style country mansion. Old world charm is reflected at this manor by marble fireplaces and the hand-carved mahogany lobby.

Innkeeper(s): David & Bambi Arnold. $190-325. EP. MC VISA AX PC TC. TAC10. 21 rooms with PB, 13 with FP. Breakfast, afternoon tea and dinner included in rates. Meal: gourmet breakfast. Beds: DT. Phone and air conditioning in room. Fax and copier on premises. Fishing and watersports nearby.

Location: On Squam Lake, under two hours north of Boston.

Publicity: *Summer Week. Ratings: 4 Diamonds.*

"The setting, the inn itself, the dining, the staff, the fascinating boat tour. Everything was outstanding!"

Intervale F5

The Forest - A Country Inn *

PO Box 37
Intervale, NH 03845-0037
(603)356-9772 (800)448-3534 Fax:(603)356-5652
E-mail: forest@moose.ncia.net

Circa 1830. This spacious Second Empire Victorian offers easy access to the many attractions of the Mt. Washington Valley. The inn's guest rooms are uniquely decorated with country antique charm. Honeymooners often enjoy the privacy of the inn's turn-of-the-century stone cottage. A stream runs through the inn's 25 wooded acres, and guests may cross-country ski right on the property. The inn also boasts a built-in swimming pool. Breakfast fare could include apple pancakes, cinnamon French toast or spiced Belgian waffles. Conway Scenic Railroad nearby.

Innkeeper(s): Bill & Lisa Guppy. $60-169. MC VISA AX DS PC TC. TAC10. 12 rooms, 10 with PB, 5 with FP. 2 suites. 3 cottages. Breakfast and evening snack included in rates. Type of meal: full breakfast. Beds: QDT. Ceiling fan in room. TV, fax and swimming on premises. 25 acres. Family reunions and seminars hosted. Amusement parks, antiques, fishing, parks, shopping, skiing, sporting events, theater and watersports nearby.

Jackson   F5

Carter Notch Inn

Carter Notch Rd, Box 269
Jackson, NH 03846
(603)383-9630 (800)794-9434

Circa 1900. This turn-of-the-century home rests on a wooded acre, offering views of the surrounding mountains and valley, as well as the Wildcat River. Guest rooms are charming, with painted wood floors, beds topped with quilts and furnishings made from oak and wicker. The innkeepers prepare a multi-course breakfast that always includes a fresh fruit dish, home-made muffins or coffee cake and an entree, such as Grand Marnier French toast. Cross-country ski trails begin right out the front door; golfing, hiking and other outdoor activities abound in the area. After a day of enjoying fall foliage or hunting down antique bargains, return for a soak in the outdoor hot tub.

Innkeeper(s): Jim & Lynda Dunwell. $59-109. MC VISA AX DS PC TC. TAC10. 7 rooms, 5 with PB. 1 suite. Breakfast and afternoon tea included in rates. Types of meals: full breakfast, gourmet breakfast and early coffee/tea. Beds: QD. Air conditioning in room. TV, VCR, fax, spa, swimming and tennis on premises. Weddings, small meetings, family reunions and seminars hosted. Antiques, fishing, parks, downhill skiing, cross-country skiing, golf, theater and watersports nearby.

Dana Place Inn

Rt 16, Pinkham Notch Rd
Jackson, NH 03846
(603)383-6822 (800)537-9276 Fax:(603)383-6022
E-mail: dpi@ncia.net

Circa 1860. The original owners received this Colonial farm-house as a wedding present. The warm, cozy atmosphere of the inn is surpassed only by the spectacular mountain views.
During autumn, the fall leaves explode with color, and guests can enjoy the surroundings while tak-
ing a hike or bike ride through the area. The beautiful Ellis River is the perfect place for an afternoon of fly-fishing or a picnic. After a scrumptious country breakfast, winter guests can step out the door and into skis for a day of cross-country skiing.

Historic Interest: Mount Washington Auto Road (5 miles), 1860s Cog. Railroad (30 miles).

Innkeeper(s): The Levine Family. $135-225. MC VISA AX DC CB DS PC TC. TAC10. 33 rooms, 29 with PB. 4 suites. Breakfast and afternoon tea included in rates. Type of meal: full breakfast. Dinner, picnic lunch, banquet service and room service available. Restaurant on premises. Beds: KQDT. Phone, air conditioning, ceiling fan and TV in room. VCR, fax, copier, spa, swimming, tennis and library on premises. 300 acres. Weddings, small meetings, family reunions and seminars hosted. French and Spanish spoken. Amusement parks, antiques, fishing, parks, shopping, downhill skiing, cross-country skiing, golf, theater and watersports nearby.

Pets Allowed: Exterior rooms.

Location: At the base of Mt. Washington, White Mountain National Forest.

Publicity: *Travel & Leisure, Inn Spots, Bon Appetit, Country Journal.*

"We had such a delightful time at Dana Place Inn. We will recommend you to everyone."

Ellis River House

Rt 16, Box 656
Jackson, NH 03846
(603)383-9339 (800)233-8309 Fax:(603)383-4142
E-mail: 76073,1435@compuserve.com

Circa 1893. Andrew Harriman built this farmhouse, as well as the village town hall and three-room schoolhouse where the innkeepers' children attended school. Classic antiques and Laura Ashley prints decorate the guest rooms and riverfront "honeymoon" cottage, and each window reveals
views of magnificent mountains, the vineyard or spectacular Ellis River. In 1993, the innkeepers added 18 rooms, 13 of which feature fireplaces
and three offer two-person Jacuzzis. They also added four family suites, a heated, outdoor pool, an indoor Jacuzzi and a sauna.

Historic Interest: The White Mountains School of Art is nearby. Artists such as Albert Bierstadt and Benjamin Champney were among the many to attend this school.

Innkeeper(s): Barry & Barbara Lubao. $79-229. MAP. MC VISA AX DC CB DS PC TC. TAC5. 20 rooms with PB, 13 with FP. 4 suites. 1 cottage. 1 conference room. Breakfast included in rates. Types of meals: full breakfast and early coffee/tea. Afternoon tea, dinner and picnic lunch available. Beds: KQDT. Phone, air conditioning and TV in room. Fax, spa, swimming and sauna on premises. Handicap access. Weddings, small meetings, family reunions and seminars hosted. Polish spoken. Amusement parks, antiques, fishing, parks, shopping, downhill skiing, cross-country skiing, sporting events, theater and watersports nearby.

Location: White Mountain area.

Publicity: *Philadelphia Inquirer.*

"We have stayed at many B&Bs all over the world and are in agreement that the beauty and hospitality of Ellis River House is that of a world-class bed & breakfast."

The Inn at Jackson

PO Box 807, Main St at Thornhill Rd
Jackson, NH 03846
(603)383-4321 (800)289-8600 Fax:(603)383-4085
E-mail: innjack@ncia.net

Circa 1902. Architect Stanford White designed this inn for the Baldwin family of New York (of piano fame) and served as their
summer residence. The inn offers a grand foyer, spacious guest rooms, some with TV and air conditioning, private baths, hardwood floors, fire-places and an outdoor hot tub Jacuzzi. A full breakfast
is served in our sunporch overlooking the mountains.

Historic Interest: Mount Washington (15 minutes); Cog Railway (45 minutes).

Innkeeper(s): Lori Tradewell. $69-169. MC VISA AX DC CB DS PC TC. TAC10. 14 rooms with PB, 3 with FP. Breakfast included in rates. Type of meal: full breakfast. Beds: KQT. Air conditioning in room. TV, VCR, fax, spa and library on premises. Fishing, parks, shopping, downhill skiing, cross-country skiing and theater nearby.

"We had a terrific time and found the inn warm and cozy and most of all relaxing."

Nestlenook Farm Resort

Dinsmore Rd
Jackson, NH 03846
(603)383-9443 (800)659-9443 Fax:(603)383-4515

Circa 1790. This 200-year-old Victorian is decorated with white gingerbread trim on windows, balustrades and porches. Each guest room has its own Jacuzzi and antique furnishings. In the dining room is a handsome Victorian bird cage complete with two love birds. The Murdoch Suite boasts a double Jacuzzi, original art  and views of the inn's 65 acres of grounds. Sleigh rides and mountain bikes are available.

Innkeeper(s): Robert Cyr. $125-299. MC VISA DS. TAC10. 7 rooms with PB, 1 with FP. Breakfast included in rates. Type of meal: full breakfast. Evening snack available. Beds: KQ. Phone in room. Fax, copier, swimming and bicycles on premises. 65 acres. Weddings hosted. Antiques, fishing, parks, shopping, downhill skiing, cross-country skiing, theater and watersports nearby.

Location: Cross the historic Jackson covered bridge then take the first right onto Dinsmore Road. In the Mount Washington Valley.

Publicity: *Ski, Friends, Manage Quebec, Discerning Traveler.*

Village House

Rt 16 A Box 359
Jackson, NH 03846
(603)383-6666 (800)972-8343 Fax:(603)383-6464

Circa 1860. Village House was built as an annex to the larger Hawthorne Inn, which eventually burned. It is a colonial building, with a porch winding around three sides. The Wildcat River flows by the inn's seven acres, and there is a swimming pool, outdoor Jacuzzi, clay tennis court and shuffleboard set in view of the White Mountains. In the afternoons, snacks are  served, and beverages always are available.

Innkeeper(s): Robin Crocker. $65-145. MC VISA DS PC TC. TAC10. 15 rooms with PB. 2 suites. 1 conference room. Breakfast included in rates. Types of meals: continental-plus breakfast, full breakfast and early coffee/tea. Beds: KQDT. TV, fax, copier, spa, swimming and tennis on premises. Weddings, small meetings, family reunions and seminars hosted. Antiques, fishing, parks, shopping, downhill skiing, cross-country skiing, theater and watersports nearby.

Pets Allowed: In one building.

Publicity: *Foxboro Reporter.*

"Your hospitality and warmth made us feel right at home. The little extras, such as turndown service, flowers and baked goods, are all greatly appreciated."

Whitneys' Inn

Rt 16B, PO Box 822
Jackson, NH 03846
(603)383-8916 (800)677-5737 Fax:(603)383-6886

Circa 1842. This country inn offers romance, family recreation and a lovely setting at the base of the Black Mountain Ski Area. The inn specializes in recreation, as guests enjoy cookouts, cross-country and downhill skiing, hiking, lawn games, skating, sledding, sleigh rides, swimming and tennis. Popular nearby activities include trying out Jackson's two golf courses and picnicking at Jackson Falls.

Innkeeper(s): David Linne. $76-170. MAP. MC VISA AX DS PC TC. TAC10. 29 rooms with PB, 3 with FP. 9 suites. 2 cottages. 1 conference room. Breakfast and dinner included in rates. Type of meal: full breakfast. Afternoon tea, picnic lunch and banquet service available. Restaurant on premises. Beds: KQDT. TV, VCR, swimming, tennis and library on premises. 14 acres. Weddings, small meetings, family reunions and seminars hosted. Amusement parks, antiques, fishing, parks, downhill skiing, cross-country skiing, theater and watersports nearby.

Pets Allowed.

Jaffrey   L3

The Benjamin Prescott Inn

Rt 124 E, 433 Turnpike Rd
Jaffrey, NH 03452
(603)532-6637 Fax:(603)532-6637

Circa 1853. Colonel Prescott arrived on foot in Jaffrey in 1775 with an ax in his hand and a bag of beans on his back. The family built this classic Greek Revival many years later. Now, candles light the windows, seen from the stonewall-lined lane adjacent to the inn.  Each room bears the name of a Prescott family member and is furnished with antiques.

Innkeeper(s): Jan & Barry Miller. $65-140. EP. MC VISA AX PC TC. TAC10. 9 rooms with PB. 2 suites. 1 conference room. Breakfast included in rates. Type of meal: full breakfast. Beds: KQDT. Phone and ceiling fan in room. VCR, fax and library on premises. Weddings, small meetings, family reunions and seminars hosted. Antiques, fishing, parks, shopping, downhill skiing, cross-country skiing, sporting events, theater and watersports nearby.

"The coffee and breakfasts were delicious and the hospitality overwhelming."

Jefferson   E4

Applebrook B&B

Rt 115A, PO Box 178
Jefferson, NH 03583-0178
(603)586-7713 (800)545-6504
E-mail: applebrk@aol.com

Circa 1797. Panoramic views surround this large Victorian farmhouse nestled in the middle of New Hampshire's White Mountains. Guests can awake to the smell of freshly baked muffins made with locally picked berries. A comfortable, fire-lit sitting room boasts stained glass, a goldfish pool and a beautiful view of Mt. Washington. Test your golfing skills at the nearby 18-hole championship course, or spend the day antique hunting. A trout  stream and spring-fed rock pool are nearby. Wintertime guests can ice skate or race through the powder at nearby ski resorts or by way of snowmobile, finish off the day with a moonlight toboggan ride. After a full day, guests can enjoy a soak in the hot tub under the stars, where they might see shooting stars or the Northern Lights.

Historic Interest: The area boasts several covered bridges within 10 miles of the bed & breakfast. The Cog Railroad is 15 miles away, while the Jefferson Historical Museum is only one mile from the inn.

Innkeeper(s): Sandra Conley & Martin Kelly. $40-75. MC VISA AX PC TC. TAC10. 14 rooms, 7 with PB. 1 conference room. Breakfast included in rates. Types of meals: full breakfast and early coffee/tea. Beds: KQDT. Ceiling fan in room. Spa and library on premises. 35 acres. Weddings, small meetings, family reunions and seminars hosted. Amusement parks, antiques, fishing, parks, shopping, downhill skiing, cross-country skiing, theater and watersports nearby.

Pets Allowed: Two rooms kept pet-free; $5.00/night per pet-half of which is donated to Lancaster Humane Society.

Publicity: *PriceCostco Connection, New Hampshire Outdoor Companion, Outdoor.*

"We came for a night and stayed for a week."

Jefferson Inn

R R 1 Box 68 A, Rt 2
Jefferson, NH 03583
(603)586-7998 (800)729-7908 Fax:(603)586-7808
E-mail: jeffinn@moose.ncia.net

Circa 1896. This rambling Victorian house features a turret, gables and wraparound verandas. Nestled in the White Mountain National Forest, the inn overlooks the Jefferson Meadows to Franconia Notch, Mt. Washington and the northern Presidential range. All rooms have views and period antiques. There is an 18-hole championship golf course across the street. Cycling trips depart from the driveway. Trails for Mt. Waumbek and Starr King lead from the inn. Nearby, the Weathervane Summer Theater provides nightly entertainment. An afternoon tea with homemade baked goods is served daily.

Innkeeper(s): Marla Mason & Don Garretson. $70-150. EP. MC VISA AX DS PC TC. 11 rooms with PB. Breakfast, afternoon tea and evening snack included in rates. Types of meals: gourmet breakfast and early coffee/tea. Beds: KQDT. Fax, copier and swimming on premises. Handicap access. Weddings, family reunions and seminars hosted. German spoken. Amusement parks, antiques, parks, downhill skiing, cross-country skiing, theater and watersports nearby.

"Marvelous breakfast and a warm, comfortable atmosphere."

Lincoln   F4

Red Sleigh Inn

PO Box 562
Lincoln, NH 03251-0562
(603)745-8517

Circa 1900. This house was built by J. E. Henry, owner of the Lincoln Paper Mill, a huge lumber business and dairy farm. The foundation was constructed of stones taken from the Pemigawasset River. Loretta's blueberry muffins are a guest favorite.

Innkeeper(s): Bill & Loretta Deppe. $55-85. MC VISA TC. 6 rooms, 2 with PB. Breakfast included in rates. Type of meal: full breakfast. Beds: KQ. TV and VCR on premises. Weddings and family reunions hosted. Amusement parks, antiques, fishing, parks, shopping, downhill skiing, cross-country skiing, sporting events, theater and watersports nearby.

Publicity: *Newsday, Ski, Skiing.*

"Your ears must be ringing because we haven't stopped talking about the Red Sleigh Inn and its wonderful, caring owners."

Littleton   E3

Beal House Inn

2 W Main St
Littleton, NH 03561-3502
(603)444-2661 Fax:(603)444-6224
E-mail: beal.house.inn@connriver.net

Circa 1833. This Federal Renaissance farmhouse has been an inn since 1938. The original barn still stands, now covered with white clapboard. The inn is furnished with handsome antiques, canopy beds and down comforters. Some of the rooms feature fireplaces. Candlelight breakfasts are served fireside and you can choose from three entrees offered daily including pancakes, sausage or bacon, omelets, waffles, or eggs any style. The has reopened its popular restaurant where it provides fine dining and a full-service bar to its guests. Beal House is a Main Street landmark.

Historic Interest: Located in the heart of the White Mountains. Littleton Opera House, Robert Frost House (1 mile).

Innkeeper(s): Pat & Michael McGuinn. $60-85. MC VISA AX DS. 10 rooms, 8 with PB. 1 suite. 1 conference room. Breakfast and afternoon tea included in rates. Type of meal: full breakfast. Beds: KQDT. Fax on premises. Small meetings hosted. Antiques, fishing, parks, shopping, downhill skiing, cross-country skiing, theater and watersports nearby.

Publicity: *Country Inns, Glamour, Le Soleil, Star Ledger, New Jersey, Yankee.*

"These innkeepers know and understand people, their needs and wants. Attention to cleanliness and amenities, from check-in to check-out, is a treasure."

Thayers Inn

136 Main St
Littleton, NH 03561-4014
(603)444-6469 Fax:(800)634-8179

Circa 1843. Ulysses Grant is said to have spoken from the inn's balcony in 1869. In those days, fresh firewood and candles were delivered to guest rooms each day as well as a personal thunder-jug. The handsome facade features four 30-foot, hand-carved pillars and a cupola with views of the surrounding mountains.

Innkeeper(s): Don & Carolyn Lambert. $33-70. AP. MC VISA AX DC CB DS. 41 rooms, 38 with PB. 6 suites. Dinner and lunch available. Restaurant on premises. Beds: KQDT. Fax and copier on premises. Antiques, fishing, downhill skiing, cross-country skiing, theater and watersports nearby.

Publicity: *Business Life, Vacationer, Bon Appetit, Yankee.*

"This Thanksgiving, Russ and I spent a lot of time thinking about the things that are most important to us. It seemed appropriate that we should write to thank you for your warm hospitality as innkeepers."

Lyme   G2

Alden Country Inn

One Market St
Lyme, NH 03768
(603)795-2222 (800)794-2296 Fax:(603)795-9436

Circa 1809. This early 19th-century inn features unusual architecture and has served weary travelers since the 1820s. First, it served as a tavern, then a stagecoach stop. The building then was used for a variety of business, eventually welcoming guests again in 1918. The 15 guest rooms are decorated in country style. Guests enjoy a full country breakfast six days a week, and brunch is served on Sundays. The inn's restaurant serves regional New England cuisine, and is known for its Shaker cranberry pot roast.

Innkeeper(s): Mickey Dowd. $95-160. MC VISA AX DC DS PC TC. 15 rooms with PB, 3 with FP. 2 suites. 1 conference room. Breakfast and afternoon tea included in rates. Types of meals: full breakfast and early coffee/tea. Dinner, picnic lunch, lunch, banquet service and catering service available. Restaurant on premises. Beds: KQT. Phone, air conditioning and ceiling fan in room. TV, fax, copier, bicycles and child care on premises. Weddings, small meetings, family reunions and seminars hosted. Antiques, fishing, parks, shopping, downhill skiing, cross-country skiing, sporting events, golf, theater and watersports nearby.

Madison   G5

Maple Grove House

21 Maple Grove Rd
Madison, NH 03849
(603)367-8208

Circa 1911. Alongside a quiet country road and across from an apple orchard, this white Victorian farmhouse offers a spacious wraparound porch with views of the White Mountains. A wood burning stove warms the living room, and there is an original guest register from the home's early years. Common rooms include a library and sunny dining room. Polished hardwood floors are highlights of the bedrooms. North Conway outlet shops and restaurants are nearby.

Innkeeper(s): Celia & Don Pray. $75-85. MC VISA AX DS PC TC. 6 rooms, 4 with PB. 1 suite. Breakfast and evening snack included in rates. Types of meals: full breakfast and early coffee/tea. Beds: QT. Ceiling fan, TV and VCR in room. Library on premises. 216 acres. Small meetings and family reunions hosted. Antiques, fishing, parks, shopping, skiing, golf and theater nearby.

Moultonborough   H5

Olde Orchard Inn

RR 1 Box 256, Lee Rd & Lees Mill
Moultonborough, NH 03254-9502
(603)476-5004 (800)598-5845 Fax:(603)476-5419
E-mail: innkeep1@aol.com

Circa 1790. This farmhouse rests next to a mountain brook and pond in the midst of an apple orchard. Nine guest rooms are available, all with private baths. Three rooms have a Jacuzzi tub. After enjoying a large country breakfast,

guests may borrow a bicycle for a ride to Lake Winnipesaukee, just a mile away. The inn is within an hour's drive of five downhill skiing areas, and guests also may cross-country ski nearby. The Castle in the Clouds and the Audubon Loon Center are nearby.

Innkeeper(s): Jim & Mary Senner. $70-125. MC VISA PC TC. TAC10. 9 rooms with PB, 3 with FP. 1 cottage. Breakfast included in rates. Type of meal: full breakfast. Beds: QDT. Air conditioning in room. TV, VCR, fax, child care on premises. 12 acres. Small meetings, family reunions, seminars hosted. Antiques, fishing, parks, shopping, skiing, theater, watersports nearby.
Pets Allowed: In cottage or kennel/barn.

New London   13

New London Inn

PO Box 8
New London, NH 03257-0008
(603)526-2791

Circa 1792. This classic New England inn is situated right on Main Street next to the town green and features a two-story veranda. Inside are bedchambers decorated in colonial furnishings. Guests may dine beside the fire at the inn's popular restaurant. Colby-Sawyer College is nearby.

Innkeeper(s): Kim & Terry O'Mahoney. $80-130. MC VISA AX. 30 rooms with PB. 1 conference room. Meal: continental-plus breakfast. Restaurant on premises. Beds: KQDT. Fax and copier on premises. Theater nearby.
Publicity: *Boston Globe, New Hampshire Profiles.*

The Inn at Pleasant Lake

125 Pleasant St, PO Box 1030
New London, NH 03257-1030
(603)526-6271 (800)626-4907 Fax:(603)526-4111

Circa 1790. In its early days, this inn served as a farmhouse. By the late 1870s, it was serving guests as a summer resort. Its tradition of hospitality continues today with relaxing guest rooms, which offer lake or wood views. The five-acre grounds face Pleasant Lake, which has a private beach. Guests may enjoy the lake on their own rowboat or canoe, but the innkeepers will lend

theirs if requested. Meander over wooded trails or take a stroll around New London. Innkeeper and Culinary Institute of America graduate Brian McKenzie prepares the inn's five-course, prix fixe dinners.

Innkeeper(s): Linda & Brian MacKenzie. $95-135. MC VISA DS PC TC. TAC10. 12 rooms with PB. 2 suites. Breakfast and afternoon tea included in rates. Types of meals: continental-plus breakfast and full breakfast. Dinner and banquet service available. Beds: KQDT. Ceiling fan in room. Copier and swimming on premises. Weddings, small meetings and family reunions hosted. Antiques, fishing, shopping, downhill skiing, cross-country skiing, sporting events, golf and theater nearby.

"What a perfect setting for our first ever visit to New England."

Newfound Lake

The Inn on Newfound Lake

1030 Mayhew Tpke
Newfound Lake, NH 03222-5108
(603)744-9111 (800)745-7990 Fax:(603)744-3894

Circa 1840. This inn was the mid-way stop on the stage coach route from Boston to Montreal and formerly was known as the Pasquaney Inn. A full veranda overlooks the lake with its spectacular sunsets. Located in the foothills of the White Mountains, the inn is situated on more than seven acres of New Hampshire countryside.

Historic Interest: Cantebury, an authentic Shaker village, is just 20 minutes away. Daniel Webster's birthplace and the state capital are about a half-hour drive from the inn.

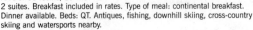

Innkeeper(s): Phelps C. Boyce II. $55-105. MAP, AP. MC VISA AX DS. 31 rooms, 23 with PB. 2 suites. Breakfast included in rates. Type of meal: continental breakfast. Dinner available. Beds: QT. Antiques, fishing, downhill skiing, cross-country skiing and watersports nearby.

Publicity: *The Record Enterprise.*

"The rooms were quaint and cozy with just the right personal touches, and always immaculate. The bed and pillows were so comfortable, it was better than sleeping at home! The inn itself is magnificent, elegance never felt so warm and homey."

North Conway F5

Buttonwood Inn

Mount Surprise Rd
North Conway, NH 03860
(603)356-2625 (800)258-2625 Fax:(603)356-3140
E-mail: button_w@ moose.ncia.net

Circa 1820. This center-chimney, New England-style inn was once a working farm of more than 100 acres on the mountain. Of the original outbuildings, only the granite barn foundation remains. Through the years, the house has been extended to a total of 20 rooms.

Historic Interest: Mount Washington (20 minutes), Cog Railway (40 minutes), Heritage, N.H. (10 minutes).

Innkeeper(s): Claudia & Peter Needham. $70-150. MC VISA AX DS PC TC. TAC10. 9 rooms, 5 with PB, 1 with FP. 2 suites. 1 conference room. Breakfast and afternoon tea included in rates. Types of meals: full breakfast, gourmet breakfast and early coffee/tea. Beds: KQDT. TV, VCR, fax, swimming, bicycles and library on premises. Weddings, small meetings, family reunions and seminars hosted. Amusement parks, antiques, fishing, parks, shopping, downhill skiing, cross-country skiing, theater and watersports nearby.

Location: Tucked away on Mt. Surprise, two miles from town.

Publicity: *Northeast Bound, Skiing, Boston Globe, Yankee Travel, The Mountain Ear.*

"The very moment we spotted your lovely inn nestled midway on the mountainside in the moonlight, we knew we had found a winner."

Nereledge Inn

River Rd, Off Main St, PO Box 547
North Conway, NH 03860
(603)356-2831 Fax:(603)356-7085

Circa 1787. This big white house is decorated simply in a New England style featuring cozy English eiderdowns and rocking chairs in many of the guest rooms. Woodstoves warm the breakfast room and the sitting room. There is an English-style pub room with a fireplace, darts and backgammon. For breakfast you may be served apple crumble with ice cream as a

dessert after the main course. Innkeeper Valerie Halpin grew up in Burnley, England. The area is bursting with activity for those who wish to bask in the outdoors. The river, a perfect place to enjoy swimming, canoeing and fishing, is within walking distance, as are shopping and restaurants in the village. The area boasts wonderful rock and ice climbing. Nereledge Inn is a non-smoking inn.

Historic Interest: Dartmouth College is two- and one-half hours away.

Innkeeper(s): Valerie & Dave Halpin. $59-109. MC VISA AX DS. 11 rooms, 5 with PB. 1 suite. Breakfast included in rates. Type of meal: full breakfast. Beds: QDT. Phone in room. Antiques, fishing, downhill skiing, cross-country skiing and theater nearby.

Location: In the heart of Mt. Washington Valley.

Publicity: *White Mountain Region Newspaper, Outside, Men's Journal.*

"Our home away from home."

Stonehurst Manor

Rt 16
North Conway, NH 03860-1937
(603)356-3113 (800)525-9100 Fax:(603)356-3217

Circa 1876. This English-style manor stands on lush, landscaped lawns and 30 acres of pine trees. It was built as the summer home for the Bigelow family, founder of the Bigelow Carpet Company. Inside the tremendous front door is an elegant display of leaded- and stained-glass windows, rich oak woodwork, a winding staircase and a massive, hand-carved oak fireplace.

Innkeeper(s): Peter Rattay. $106-176. MAP. MC VISA AX PC TC. 24 rooms, 22 with PB, 7 with FP. Breakfast and dinner included in rates. Type of meal: full breakfast. Beds: KQDT. Air conditioning, ceiling fan and TV in room. Fax, copier, spa, swimming and tennis on premises. Handicap access. 33 acres. Weddings, small meetings, family reunions and seminars hosted. German spoken. Antiques, fishing, shopping, downhill skiing, sporting events, theater and watersports nearby.

Location: In White Mountains.

Publicity: *Boston Globe, New York Daily News, Bon Appetit, Boston Magazine, Gourmet.*

"An architecturally preserved replica of an English country house, a perfect retreat for the nostalgic-at-heart—Phil Berthiaume, Country Almanac."

Victorian Harvest Inn

28 Locust Ln, Box 1763
North Conway, NH 03860
(603)356-3548 (800)642-0749 Fax:(603)356-8430

Circa 1853. Perched atop a hill in the Mt. Washington Valley, this Folk Victorian inn features comfortable surroundings and attention to detail. The country Victorian furnishings are highlighted by homemade quilts and teddy bears that visitors may adopt during their stay. The Victoria Station Room boasts its own carousel horse, and the Nook & Cranny Room offers a view of the entire Moat Range. Cotswold Hideaway offers a skylight and gas fireplace. Guests also enjoy strolling the grounds, which include a footbridge, gardens and a Victorian decorated pool.

Innkeeper(s): Linda & Robert Dahlberg. $75-120. MC VISA DS TC. 6 rooms, 4 with PB. Breakfast and afternoon tea included in rates. Type of meal: full breakfast. Air conditioning and ceiling fan in room. TV, VCR, fax and copier on premises. Family reunions hosted. Antiques, fishing, parks, shopping, downhill skiing, cross-country skiing, theater and watersports nearby.

Wyatt House Country Inn

PO Box 777
North Conway, NH 03860-0777
(603)356-7977 (800)527-7978

Circa 1880. This rambling Victorian is surrounded by acres of manicured grounds and trees on the banks of the Saco River. The mountain view, double Jacuzzi suite is an inspiration for romance. Rooms are decorated with antiques in Country Victorian style, and guests are pampered with in-room sherry, canopy beds and views of the river and mountains. The delightful, multi-course breakfasts are served on fine English Wedgwood and lace. Everything is fresh and homemade, including granola, muffins and squeezed orange juice. Apple cobbler with vanilla ice cream, cheese souffles, shirred eggs, spinach and Vermont cheese quiche, chocolate chip pancakes and New England breakfast pie are among the memorable treats.

Innkeeper(s): Arlene & Bill Strickland. $50-175. MC VISA AX DS PC TC. TAC10. 7 rooms, 5 with PB. 5 suites. Breakfast and afternoon tea included in rates. Types of meals: full breakfast, gourmet breakfast and early coffee/tea. Room service available. Beds: QDT. Air conditioning, ceiling fan and TV in room. Swimming, bicycles and library on premises. Small meetings and family reunions hosted. Antiques, fishing, parks, shopping, downhill skiing, cross-country skiing, sporting events, theater and watersports nearby.

North Sutton   I3

Follansbee Inn

PO Box 92
North Sutton, NH 03260-0092
(603)927-4221 (800)626-4221

Circa 1840. This New England farmhouse was enlarged in 1929, becoming an inn, no doubt because of its attractive location on the edge of Kezar Lake. It has a comfortable porch, sitting rooms with fireplaces, and antique-furnished bedrooms. Enjoy the best of the past while nestled in a small country village. The inn offers boating and swimming. Cross-country skiing starts at the doorstep. The inn is popular for small seminars and family reunions.

Historic Interest: The inn is located in the area of the John Hay Estate, "The Fells," Muster Field Farm Museum, Kearsarge Indian Museum and the Saint Gauden's National Historic Site.

Innkeeper(s): Sandy & Dick Reilein. $75-105. MC VISA. 23 rooms, 11 with PB. Breakfast included in rates. Type of meal: full breakfast. Beds: KQDT. Phone in room. Small meetings, family reunions and seminars hosted. Watersports nearby.

Location: 95 miles from Boston, four miles south of New London.

Publicity: Country Inns.

"Bravo! A great inn experience. Super food."

North Woodstock   F4

Wilderness Inn

RFD 1, Box 69, Rts 3 & 112
North Woodstock, NH 03262-9710
(603)745-3890

Circa 1912. Surrounded by the White Mountain National Forest, this charming shingled home offers a picturesque getaway for every season. Guest rooms are furnished with antiques and Oriental rugs, and the innkeepers also offer family suites and a private cottage with a fireplace and a view of Lost River. Breakfast is a delightful affair with choices ranging from fresh muffins to brie cheese omelets, French toast topped with homemade apple syrup, crepes or specialty pancakes. For the children, the innkeepers create teddy bear pancakes or French toast. If you have room, an afternoon tea also is prepared.

Innkeeper(s): Michael Yarnell. $40-105. MAP. MC VISA AX PC TC. 7 rooms, 5 with PB. 1 cottage. Breakfast included in rates. Type of meal: gourmet breakfast. Beds: QDT. Phone in room.

"The stay at your inn, attempting and completing the 3D jig-jaw puzzle, combined with those unforgettable breakfasts, and your combined friendliness, makes the Wilderness Inn a place for special memories."

Plainfield   H2

Home Hill Country Inn

River Road
Plainfield, NH 03781
(603)675-6165

Circa 1812. Tall maples shade this massive white brick Federal house located on the banks of the Connecticut River. Its 25 acres of grounds include a private golf course bordered by whitewashed fences, a clay tennis court, swimming pool, pool house, ski trails and riding paths. Guest rooms are furnished with country French and American antiques and hand-stenciled walls. A notable French restaurant fills three fireplaced dining rooms.

Innkeeper(s): Victoria & Stephane du Roure. $150. MC VISA AX. 9 rooms with PB. Type of meal: continental breakfast. Beds: KQD. Phone in room.

Publicity: Country Living, Bon Appetit, Discerning Traveler, Outside.

"What a wonderful memory maker."

Plymouth   H4

Colonel Spencer Inn

RR 1, Box 206
Plymouth, NH 03264
(603)536-3438

Circa 1764. This pre-Revolutionary Colonial boasts Indian shutters, gleaming plank floors and a secret hiding place. Joseph Spencer, one of the home's early owners, fought at Bunker Hill and with General Washington. Within view of the river and the mountains, the inn is now a cozy retreat with warm Colonial decor. A suite with a kitchen is also available.

Innkeeper(s): Carolyn & Alan Hill. $45-65. PC TC. TAC10. 7 rooms with PB. 1 suite. Breakfast and evening snack included in rates. Type of meal: full breakfast. Beds: D. Small meetings and family reunions hosted. Antiques, fishing, parks, shopping, downhill skiing, cross-country skiing, sporting events, theater and watersports nearby.

Location: Near lake and mountain district.

"You have something very special here and we very much enjoyed a little piece of it!"

Crab Apple Inn B&B

PO Box 188
Plymouth, NH 03264-0188
(603)536-4476

Circa 1835. Behind an immaculate, white picket fence is a brick Federal house beside a small brook at the foot of Tenney Mountain. Rooms are appointed with antiques. The two-room suite includes an antique clawfoot tub and a canopy bed. The grounds have gardens and, of course, many crab apple trees.

Innkeeper(s): Christine DeCamp. $70-105. MC VISA PC TC. 5 rooms, 3 with PB. Breakfast and afternoon tea included in rates. Types of meals: gourmet breakfast and early coffee/tea. Beds: QDT. Air conditioning in room. Weddings, small meetings, family reunions and seminars hosted. Amusement parks, antiques, fishing, parks, shopping, downhill skiing, cross-country skiing, sporting events, theater and watersports nearby.

Location: Gateway to White Mountains in the Baker River Valley.

"We are still excited about our trip. The Crab Apple Inn was the unanimous choice for our favorite place to stay."

Portsmouth   J7

The Inn at Christian Shore

335 Maplewood Ave
Portsmouth, NH 03801-3536
(603)431-6770 Fax:(603)431-7743

Circa 1800. This handsome Federal-style house combines the convenience of in-town lodging with the charm of a country inn. Minutes from downtown Portsmouth, the inn is located in a diverse neighborhood with historic homes and attractions nearby. The inn offers six tastefully decorated rooms, two of which feature fireplaces. Guests can enjoy a full gourmet breakfast served in our open-beamed dining room appointed with a Harvest table and Windsor chairs.

Innkeeper(s): Mariaelena Koopman. $75-95. MC VISA AX TC. 6 rooms, 4 with PB. Breakfast and afternoon tea included in rates. Types of meals: continental-plus breakfast, full breakfast and early coffee/tea. Beds: QDT. Air conditioning and TV in room. VCR on premises. Spanish/English spoken. Antiques, fishing, parks and shopping nearby.

Rindge   L3

Woodbound Inn

Woodbound Rd
Rindge, NH 03461
(603)532-8341 (800)688-7770 Fax:(603)532-8341
E-mail: woodbound@aol.com

Circa 1819. Vacationers have enjoyed the Woodbound Inn since its opening as a year-round resort in 1892. The main inn actually was built in 1819, and this portion offers 19 guest rooms, all appointed with classic-style furnishings. The innkeepers offer more modern accommodations in the Edgewood Building, and there are eleven cabins available. The one- and two-bedroom cabins rest along the shore of Lake Contoocook. The inn's 162 acres include a private  beach, fishing, hiking, nature trails, tennis courts, a volleyball court, a game room and a golf course. There is a full service restaurant, a cocktail lounge and banquet facilities on premises. If for some reason one would want to venture away from the inn, the region is full of activities, including ski areas, more golf courses and Mount Monadnock.

Innkeeper(s): Kohlmorgen Family. $79-135. EP. MC VISA AX PC. TAC10. 44 rooms, 34 with PB, 6 with FP. 5 suites. 11 cottages. 5 conference rooms. Breakfast included in rates. Type of meal: full breakfast. Dinner, lunch, banquet service and catering service available. Restaurant on premises. Beds:

QDT. Phone and air conditioning in room. VCR, copier, swimming, tennis, library and child care on premises. Handicap access. 162 acres. Weddings, small meetings, family reunions and seminars hosted. Amusement parks, antiques, fishing, parks, shopping, downhill skiing, cross-country skiing, theater and watersports nearby. Pets Allowed: In cabins only.

Rye   K6

Rock Ledge Manor B&B

1413 Ocean Blvd
Rye, NH 03870-2207
(603)431-1413

Circa 1860. In a simple Gambrel style, this white Victorian with wraparound porch boasts panoramic views of the Isle of Shoal from its oceanfront location at Concord Point. Some rooms have views and all have brass and iron beds, ceiling fans and wallpapers. Breakfast may include fruit pancakes and sausage, or omelets and sweet rolls, served in the dining room, with a water view. After watching  the sunrise over the Atlantic from the front porch plan to explore the tidepools, the harbor park or enjoy some local salt-water fishing. Five miles away is historic Portsmouth, and there are cruises for whale watching and visiting off shore islands.

Innkeeper(s): Stan & Sandi Smith. $80-90. PC. 4 rooms, 2 with PB. Breakfast included in rates. Type of meal: full breakfast. Beds: QD. Phone and ceiling fan in room. Antiques, fishing, shopping, golf and theater nearby.

"A lovely peaceful oasis."

Shelburne   E5

Philbrook Farm Inn

881 North Rd
Shelburne, NH 03581
(603)466-3831

Circa 1834. The Philbrook family has lived in this home since 1853 and run the place as an inn since 1861. Through the years, additions have been added, and now guests can choose from 19 guest rooms and seven summer cottages. What once was a simple farmhouse, now appears as a rambling New England country inn. New rooms are decorated in a comfortable early American style. In traditional country inn style, both breakfast and dinner are included in the rates. The surrounding wilderness offers a variety of outdoor activities, from hiking to snowshoeing.

Innkeeper(s): Philbrook/Leger Family. $110-140. MAP. PC TC. 19 rooms, 10 with PB. 7 cottages. Breakfast and dinner included in rates. Type of meal: full breakfast. Picnic lunch available. Beds: KDT. TV, VCR and swimming on premises. 1000 acres. Weddings, small meetings, family reunions and seminars hosted. Amusement parks, antiques, fishing, parks, skiing, golf nearby. Pets Allowed: In summer cottages.

Sugar Hill   F3

Foxglove, A Country Inn

Rt 117 at Lovers Ln
Sugar Hill, NH 03585
(603)823-8840 Fax:(603)823-5755
E-mail: 76651.1757@compuserve.com

Circa 1898. Three acres, dotted with trees, gardens, fountains and a spring-fed pond, surround Foxglove. The turn-of-the-century home originally served as a summer house for an heiress.

Upscale French-country decor permeates the six guest rooms, which include designer linens and fine furnishings. Guests can relax and enjoy the peaceful surroundings on a hammock for

two. Gourmet breakfasts are served on the sun porch, the posh setting includes antique china, crystal and fine linens. A menu might include a vegetable frittata with fresh herbs, sliced tomato and fresh asparagus dressed in a light vinaigrette and sunflower whole wheat toast. The innkeepers also will prepare gourmet candlelight dinners by request. Skiing, biking, fishing and outlet shopping are among the nearby attractions.

Innkeeper(s): Janet & Walter Boyd. $85-165. MC VISA PC. TAC10. 6 rooms, 5 with PB, 1 with FP. Breakfast included in rates. Types of meals: full breakfast, gourmet breakfast and early coffee/tea. Afternoon tea and picnic lunch available. Beds: KQTD. Turndown service in room. TV, VCR, fax, copier, bicycles, tennis and library on premises. Weddings, small meetings, family reunions and seminars hosted. Antiques, fishing, parks, shopping, downhill skiing, cross-country skiing, golf, theater and watersports nearby.
Publicity: *New Hampshire Magazine, Yankee Traveler.*

"We were extremely fortunate to be able to stay in a home that sparkles from the obvious attention given to all aspects of housekeeping."

Sullivan   K2

The Post and Beam B&B

HCR 33, Box 380 Centre St
Sullivan, NH 03445
(603)847-3330 (888)766-2623 Fax:(603)847-3306
E-mail: postandbeam@top.monad.net

Circa 1797. Situated on a hill above Otter Brook and the Sullivan countryside, this late 18th-century Colonial post-and-beam farmhouse was home to the Union Store and first town telephone company. Today, the inn's rustic hand-hewn exposed beams are a prominent architectural feature of the main living room. The guest rooms feature fireplaces, wide pine floors and antiques collected throughout the area. A family-style, three-course New England breakfast is served in the dining room each morning.

Historic Interest: There are nearby covered bridges and nine state parks are a short drive away. Nearby Keene and Peterborough offers 30 local craft and gift shops.
Innkeeper(s): Darcy Bacall & Priscilla Hardy. $45-85. MC VISA AX DS PC TC. 7 rooms, 2 with PB, 5 with FP. Breakfast and afternoon tea included in rates. Types of meals: continental breakfast, full breakfast and early coffee/tea. Room service available. Beds: KQTD. Air conditioning in room. TV, VCR, fax, copier and library on premises. Handicap access. Family reunions and seminars hosted. French spoken. Antiques, fishing, parks, shopping, skiing, sporting events, golf, theater and watersports nearby.
Publicity: *Keene Shopper, Sunday Sentinel.*

"Warm, cozy, beautiful B&B run by special people! Thanks for taking such good care of us! We'll be back."

Temple   K3

Birchwood Inn

Rt 45
Temple, NH 03084
(603)878-3285 Fax:(603)878-2159
E-mail: virtualcities.com

Circa 1775. For more than 200 years, this Federalist-style gable-roofed farmhouse, located on the original stagecoach route, provided a comfortable refuge for many an overnight

guest, Henry David Thoreau among them. Considered the oldest inn in New Hampshire, the Birchwood is in the National Register of Historic Places. Although it has operated as an inn, tavern and dining establishment since it was built, the Birchwood has also

housed the Temple post office, a small general store and most recently, an antique shop. One of the most noted features of the inn is the fresco mural in the dining room painted by 19th-century artist Rufus Porter. Period antiques, a grand piano and cozy fireplaces add to the ambiance. A full breakfast features the innkeeper's specialties of freshly-baked muffins and homemade jams. Dinner, served by candlelight, is made-to-order and designed to please a variety of palates. Summer theater, Monadnock Music Series, horseback riding and hay rides are nearby.

$60-70. EP. PC TC. 7 rooms, 5 with PB. Breakfast included in rates. Type of meal: full breakfast. Dinner available. Restaurant on premises. Beds: QDT. TV, VCR, fax and copier on premises. Small meetings hosted. Antiques, parks, shopping, cross-country skiing, golf and theater nearby.
Publicity: *USA Today, New Hampshire Sunday News.*

Tilton   I4

Tilton Manor

40 Chestnut St
Tilton, NH 03276-5546
(603)286-3457 Fax:(603)286-3308

Circa 1884. This turn-of-the-century Folk Victorian inn is just two blocks from downtown Tilton. The inn's comfortable guest rooms are furnished with antiques and sport handmade afghans. Guests are treated to a hearty country breakfast featuring freshly baked muffins, and dinner is available with advance reservations. Visitors enjoy relaxing in the sitting room, where they may play games, read or watch TV after a busy day exploring the historic area. Gunstock and Highland ski resorts are nearby and the Daniel Webster Birthplace and Shaker Village are within easy driving distance. Shoppers will enjoy Tilton's latest addition — an outlet center.

Historic Interest: Historic Concord is just 15 minutes from the manor.
Innkeeper(s): Chip & Diane. $60-70. MC VISA AX DS PC TC. 4 rooms, 2 with PB, 1 with FP. 2 suites. Breakfast included in rates. Type of meal: full breakfast. Beds: KDT. TV, library and child care on premises. Weddings, small meetings, family reunions and seminars hosted. Antiques, fishing, shopping, downhill skiing, cross-country skiing and watersports nearby.
Pets Allowed: Small pets with responsible owners.

"A home away from home."

Wakefield   H6

Wakefield Inn

2723 Wakefield Rd
Wakefield, NH 03872-4374
(603)522-8272 (800)245-0841

Circa 1804. Early travelers pulled up to the front door of the Wakefield Inn by stagecoach, and while they disembarked, their luggage was handed up to the second floor. It was brought in through the door, which is still visible over the porch roof. A spiral staircase, ruffled curtains, wallpapers and a wraparound porch all create the romantic ambiance of days gone by. In the living room, an original three-sided fireplace casts a warm glow on guests as it did more than 190 years ago.

Historic Interest: New Hampshire Farm Museum, Museum of Childhood.

Innkeeper(s): Harry & Lou Sisson. $50-75. MC VISA PC TC. 7 rooms with PB. Breakfast included in rates. Types of meals: full breakfast and early coffee/tea. Beds: QDT. Ceiling fan in room. VCR on premises. Antiques, fishing, shopping, cross-country skiing and golf nearby.

Location: Historic district.

"Comfortable accommodations, excellent food and exquisite decor highlighted by your quilts."

Weare   J4

Weare-House B&B

76 Quaker St
Weare, NH 03281-4513
(603)529-2660

Circa 1819. This home was the town's first two-story home and was utilized as a working farm until the late 1960s. It has since been transformed into a comfortable bed & breakfast, offering four guests rooms decorated with antiques. Beds are topped with down comforters. The home still maintains its original hand-hewn beams and pine floors. Guests can explore the 12-acre grounds and visit  the donkeys, horses and hens that live in the barn. After a homemade country breakfast, guests can head out and enjoy antique shops, auctions, skiing and other outdoor activities.

Innkeeper(s): Ellen & Curt Goldsberry. $55-70. MC VISA. 4 rooms, 1 with PB. Breakfast included in rates. Meals: full breakfast, early coffee/tea. Beds: QTD. 12 acres. Antiques, parks, shopping, skiing, watersports nearby. Pets Allowed: Dogs & cats, downstairs only (not in guest rooms - only in "Pet Room")

"We couldn't ask for more. The food was delicious and the beds were like clouds!"

Whitefield   E4

Spalding Inn & Club

Mountain View Rd
Whitefield, NH 03598
(603)837-2572 (800)368-8439 Fax:(603)837-3062
E-mail: mflinder@Moose.ncia.

Circa 1865. Guests have enjoyed New England hospitality at this charming country inn since 1865. Guest rooms are located in the main inn and in the carriage house. There are several private cottages as well, each with one or more bedrooms, a living room, fireplace and private bath. Laura Ashley decor and

antiques create a romantic atmosphere. The inn is noted for its cuisine, but the dining room's mountain views are memorable, too. Breakfasts won't leave you hungry, a variety of country goodies are prepared. Dinners, served by candlelight, feature a menu which changes daily. The innkeepers offer a variety of packages, with golf, tennis, family vacation and theater-lovers as themes.

Historic Interest: Mount Washington Cog Railway, Mount Washington Museum, New England Ski Museum, Robert Frost's Mountain Farm, Heritage New Hampshire.

Innkeeper(s): Diane, April Cockrell, Mike Flinder. $109-119. MC VISA PC TC. TAC15. 36 rooms with PB, 6 with FP. 6 suites. 6 cottages. 2 conference rooms. Breakfast included in rates. Types of meals: full breakfast and early coffee/tea. Afternoon tea, dinner and banquet service available. Restaurant on premises. Beds: KT. Phone in room. VCR, fax, copier, swimming, tennis and library on premises. 220 acres. Weddings, small meetings and family reunions hosted. Amusement parks, antiques, fishing, parks, theater nearby.

Pets Allowed: In cottages only.

"A special spot in an enchanting setting."

Wilton Center   K4

Stepping Stones B&B

Bennington Battle Tr
Wilton Center, NH 03086
(603)654-9048 (888)654-9048 Fax:(603)654-6821

Circa 1790. Decks and terraces overlook the enormous gardens of this Greek Revival house, listed in the local historic register. Guest rooms feature white-washed pine, cherry or Shaker-style country pieces accented with botanical prints, handwoven throws, rugs, pillows and fresh flowers. Poached eggs on asparagus with hollandaise sauce, blueberry Belgian waffles and jumbo apple muffins with streusel topping are guests' favorite breakfast choices. The innkeeper is both a garden designer and weaver, and there is a handweaving studio on the premises.

Innkeeper(s): D. Ann Carlsmith. $55-60. PC TC. 3 rooms with PB. Breakfast included in rates. Afternoon tea available. Beds: QDT. Library on premises. Weddings and family reunions hosted. Antiques, parks, skiing and theater nearby.

Pets Allowed: If well-behaved.

"A very relaxing and beautiful getaway. The color and fragrance of the gardens is stunning."

Wolfeboro   H5

Tuc' Me Inn B&B

118 N Main St, PO Box 657, Rt 109 N
Wolfeboro, NH 03894-4310
(603)569-5702

This 1850 Federal Colonial-style house features a music room, parlor and screen porches. Chocolate chip or strawberry pancakes are often presented for breakfast in the  dining room. The inn is a short walk to the quaint village of Wolfeboro and the shores of Lake Winnipesaukee.

Innkeeper(s): Ernie & Terrille Foutz. $65-90. MC VISA. 7 rooms, 3 with PB. Breakfast included in rates. Types of meals: full breakfast and early coffee/tea. Afternoon tea available. Beds: QT. Phone in room. TV and VCR on premises. Weddings, small meetings, family reunions and seminars hosted. Antiques, fishing, shopping, skiing and theater nearby.

Publicity: *Granite State News, Wolfeboro Times.*

"Super in every detail."

New Jersey

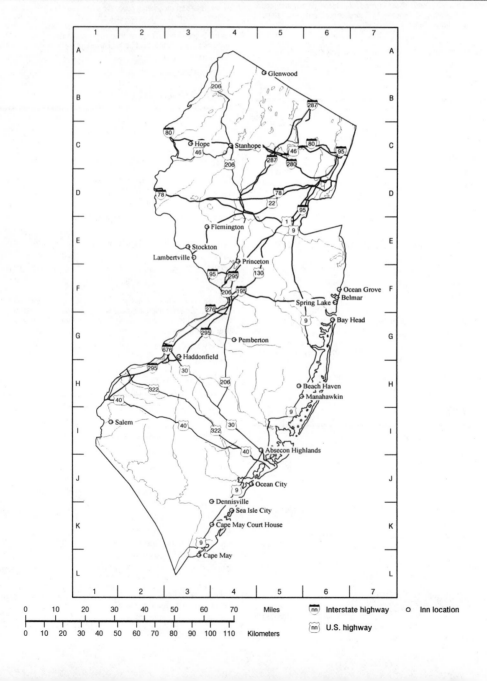

0 10 20 30 40 50 60 70	Miles
0 10 20 30 40 50 60 70 80 90 100 110	Kilometers

Interstate highway   ○ Inn location

U.S. highway

Absecon Highlands I5

White Manor Inn

739 S 2nd Ave
Absecon Highlands, NJ 08201-9542
(609)748-3996 Fax:(609)652-0073

Circa 1932. This quiet country inn was built by the innkeeper's father and includes unique touches throughout, many created by innkeeper Howard Bensel himself, who became a master craftsman from his father's teachings and renovated the home extensively. Beautiful flowers and plants adorn both the lush grounds and the interior of the home.
Everything is comfortable and cozy at this charming B&B, a relaxing contrast to the glitz of nearby Atlantic City.

Historic Interest: A short drive will take guests to a number of historic sites, including the Towne of Smithville, Atlantic City Boardwalk, Renault Winery, Wharton State Forest, the Somers Mansion, and Margate, home of Lucy the Elephant, a National Historic Landmark.

Innkeeper(s): Anna Mae & Howard R. Bensel Jr. $65-105. PC TC. 7 rooms, 5 with PB. 1 suite. 1 conference room. Breakfast and evening snack included in rates. Types of meals: continental breakfast, continental-plus breakfast and early coffee/tea. Beds: QDT. Air conditioning and ceiling fan in room. VCR on premises. Small meetings, family reunions and seminars hosted. Amusement parks, antiques, fishing, parks, shopping, sporting events, theater and watersports nearby.

"We felt more like relatives than total strangers. By far the most clean inn that I have seen — spotless!"

Bay Head G6

Bentley Inn

694 Main Ave
Bay Head, NJ 08742-5346
(732)892-9589 Fax:(732)701-0030

Circa 1887. Located three houses away from the beach, this blue shingled inn has a large white wraparound, double-tiered porch with flower boxes filled with geraniums. Rooms are decorated in an eclectic fashion, and the main parlor offers wicker furnishings and some antiques. A full breakfast is served in the dining room or screened-in porch. There is
also a restaurant on the premises. Specialties of the house include Filet Mignon and Chicken Saltimbocca.

Innkeeper(s): Anthony & Alessandra Matteo. $50-165. MC VISA AX DC DS PC TC. TAC10. 20 rooms, 6 with PB. 6 suites. 1 conference room. Breakfast included in rates. Type of meal: full breakfast. Dinner, banquet service and catering service available. Restaurant on premises. Beds: KQDT. Phone and air conditioning in room. Library on premises. Weddings, small meetings, family reunions and seminars hosted. Amusement parks, antiques, fishing, parks, shopping, golf and watersports nearby.

"Many thanks for your thoughtful hospitality. The very best of luck (although you two will not need it.)"

Beach Haven H5

Green Gables Inn, Restaurant & Tea Room

212 Centre St
Beach Haven, NJ 08008-1714
(609)492-3553 (800)492-0492 Fax:(609)492-2507

Circa 1880. This Queen Anne Victorian located in the Beach Haven Historic District is in the National Register. Decorated in an elegant Victorian style, the inn's dining room provides romantic candlelight dinners rated "four-star" nationally. (If you plan to dine here, be sure to make reservations at the same time you reserve your room.) Among some guest favorites are enjoying the inn's flower gardens from front porch rockers, strolling on the beach a block and a half away, and walking to shops, concerts in the park and nearby clubs. New Broadway plays may be seen at the summer stock theater, Surflight, just around the corner.

Innkeeper(s): Rita & Aldolfo De Martino. $85-135. MC VISA AX DC TC. 6 rooms, 2 with PB. Breakfast included in rates. Meals: continental-plus breakfast and early coffee/tea. Afternoon tea, picnic lunch, lunch, gourmet lunch and catering service available. Restaurant on premises. Beds: D. Ceiling fan in room. Handicap access. Weddings, small meetings, family reunions and seminars hosted. Italian and French spoken. Amusement parks, antiques, fishing, parks, shopping, sporting events, theater and watersports nearby.

Belmar F6

The Inn at The Shore

301 4th Ave
Belmar, NJ 07719-2104
(732)681-3762 Fax:(732)280-1914

Circa 1880. This country Victorian actually is near two different shores. Both the ocean and Silver Lake are within easy walking distance of the inn. From the inn's windows, guests can view swans on the lake or people perusing Belmar's boardwalk. The innkeepers decorated their Victorian home in period style. The inn's patio is set up for barbecues.

Innkeeper(s): Rosemary & Tom Volker. $55-125. MC VISA AX. 12 rooms, 3 with PB. 1 conference room. Breakfast included in rates. Type of meal: continental-plus breakfast. Phone, air conditioning and TV in room. VCR and bicycles on premises. Weddings, small meetings, family reunions and seminars hosted. Amusement parks, antiques, fishing, parks, shopping, sporting events, theater and watersports nearby.

Location: Sixty miles from Atlantic City, twenty miles from Six Flags Great Adventure Theme Park.

Cape May L3

The Abbey Bed & Breakfast

34 Gurney St at Columbia Ave
Cape May, NJ 08204
(609)884-4506 Fax:(609)884-2379

Circa 1869. This inn consists of two buildings, one a Gothic Revival villa with a 60-foot tower, Gothic arched windows and shaded verandas. Furnishings include floor-to-ceiling mirrors, ornate gas chandeliers, marble-topped dressers and beds of carved walnut, wrought iron and brass. The cottage adjacent to the villa is a Second Empire-style home with a mansard roof. A full breakfast is served in the dining room in spring and fall and on the veranda in the summer. Late afternoon refreshments and tea are served each day at 5 p.m. The beautiful inn is featured in the town's Grand Christmas Tour, and public tours and tea are offered three times a week in season.

Innkeeper(s): Jay & Marianne Schatz. $100-275. MC VISA DS TC. 14 rooms with PB. 2 suites. 2 conference rooms. Breakfast and afternoon tea included in rates. Types of meals: full breakfast and early coffee/tea. Beds: KQD. Small meetings and seminars hosted. Antiques, fishing, parks, shopping, theater and watersports nearby.

Location: In the heart of Cape May's historic district.

Publicity: *Richmond Times-Dispatch, New York Times, Glamour, Philadelphia Inquirer, National Geographic Traveler.*

"Staying with you folks really makes the difference between a 'nice' vacation and a great one!"

Abigail Adams B&B By The Sea

12 Jackson St
Cape May, NJ 08204-1418
(609)884-1371 (888)827-4354

Circa 1888. This charming Victorian is only 100 feet from the beach which affords refreshing sea breezes and ocean views. There is a free-standing circular staircase, as well as original fireplaces and woodwork throughout. The decor is highlighted with flowered chintz and antiques, and the dining room is hand-stenciled. A full breakfast features the inn's homemade baked sweets.

Historic Interest: One of the "Seven Sisters of Cape May" built by Stephen Decatur Button.

Innkeeper(s): Kate Emerson. $75-185. MC VISA AX. 5 rooms, 3 with PB. Breakfast included in rates. Type of meal: full breakfast. Afternoon tea available. Beds: QD. Phone, air conditioning and ceiling fan in room. Amusement parks, antiques, fishing, theater and watersports nearby.

Location: In the primary historic district, 100 feet from the beach and a half block from the mall.

"What a wonderful time. Comfortable & homey."

Alexander's Inn

653 Washington St
Cape May, NJ 08204-2324
(609)884-2555 Fax:(609)884-8883

Circa 1883. This mansard-roofed Victorian has been recently renovated and fitted with private baths and central air conditioning, yet the inn still maintains its elegant Victorian atmosphere. There are Oriental rugs, antiques and oil paintings in abundance. The gourmet dining room provides white-glove ser-

vice with silver, crystal, linen and lace. Located on Washington Street are the trolley tours, horse-and-carriage rides, bicycle rentals, museums and shops. Saturday night guests at the inn are treated to a five-course Sunday brunch. During the rest of the week, guests are pampered with a continental-plus breakfast and buffet-style afternoon tea service.

Innkeeper(s): Larry & Diane Muentz. $110-160. MC VISA AX DC CB DS PC TC. 7 rooms with PB. 1 conference room. Breakfast and afternoon tea includ-

ed in rates. Type of meal: continental-plus breakfast. Dinner and banquet service available. Restaurant on premises. Beds: QD. Phone, air conditioning, ceiling fan, TV and VCR in room. Fax and copier on premises. Weddings, small meetings, family reunions and seminars hosted. Antiques, fishing, shopping, theater and watersports nearby.

Barnard-Good House

238 Perry St
Cape May, NJ 08204-1447
(609)884-5381

Circa 1865. The Barnard-Good House is a Second Empire Victorian with a mansard roof and original shingles. A wraparound veranda adds to the charm of this lavender, blue and tan cottage along with the original picket fence and a concrete-formed flower garden. The inn was selected by New Jersey Magazine as the No. 1 spot for breakfast in New Jersey, and breakfasts are a special, four-course, gourmet feast.

Innkeeper(s): Nan & Tom Hawkins. $100-150. MC VISA PC. 5 rooms with PB. 2 suites. Breakfast included in rates. Types of meals: full breakfast and gourmet breakfast. Beds: KQD. Air conditioning and ceiling fan in room. Antiques, fishing, parks, shopping, theater and watersports nearby.

Publicity: *N.Y. Times, New Jersey Monthly, McCalls, Philadelphia Inquirer.*

"Even the cozy bed can't hold you down when the smell of Nan's breakfast makes its way upstairs."

Bedford Inn

805 Stockton Ave
Cape May, NJ 08204-2446
(609)884-4158 Fax:(609)884-0533

Circa 1880. The Bedford, decked in gingerbread trim with verandas on both of its two stories, has welcomed guests since its creation in the 19th century. Electrified gaslights, period wallcoverings and rich, Victorian furnishings create an air of nostalgia. The inn is close to many of Cape May's shops and restaurants, as well as the beach, which is just half a block away. Guests are pampered with breakfasts of quiche, gourmet egg dishes, French toast and freshly baked breads.

Innkeeper(s): Cindy & Al Schmucker. $90-195. MC VISA AX DS PC TC. TAC10. 11 rooms, 8 with PB. 3 suites. Breakfast and afternoon tea included in rates. Type of meal: gourmet breakfast. Beds: QDT. Air conditioning, ceiling fan and TV in room. Library on premises. Weddings hosted. Antiques, fishing, parks, theater and watersports nearby.

Captain Mey's B&B Inn

202 Ocean St
Cape May, NJ 08204-2322
(609)884-7793

Circa 1890. Named after Dutch explorer Capt. Cornelius J. Mey, who named the area, the inn displays its Dutch heritage with table-top Persian rugs, Delft china and imported Dutch lace curtains. The dining room features chestnut and oak Eastlake paneling and a fireplace. The charming exterior is painted in shades of lavender and cream. A hearty breakfast is served by candlelight, or on the wraparound veranda in the summertime.

Historic Interest: Cold Spring Village and the Cape May Lighthouse are five minutes away. Lewes, Del., is one hour by ferry.

Innkeeper(s): George & Kathleen Blinn. $75-210. MC VISA AX PC TC. TAC10. 7 rooms with PB. 1 suite. Breakfast and afternoon tea included in rates. Type of meal: full breakfast. Beds: QT. Air conditioning and ceiling fan in room. Small meetings and family reunions hosted. Amusement parks, antiques, fishing, parks, shopping, theater and watersports nearby.

Publicity: *Atlantic City, Americana, Country Living, New Jersey Monthly, WKYW News (CBS) Philadelphia, WNJN (N.J. Network News Trenton).*

"The innkeepers pamper you so much you wish you could stay forever."

The Carroll Villa B&B

19 Jackson St
Cape May, NJ 08204-1417
(609)884-9619 Fax:(609)884-0264

Circa 1882. This Victorian hotel is located one-half block from the ocean on the oldest street in the historic district of Cape May. Breakfast at the Villa is a memorable event, featuring dishes acclaimed by the New York Times and Frommer's. Homemade fruit breads, Italian omelets and Crab Eggs Benedict are a few specialties. Meals are served in the Mad Batter Restaurant on a European veranda, a secluded garden terrace or in the sky-lit Victorian dining room. The restaurant serves breakfast, lunch and dinner daily. The decor of this inn is decidedly Victorian with period antiques and wallpapers.

Innkeeper(s): Mark Kulkowitz & Pamela Ann Huber. $75-160. MC VISA AX DS PC. TAC10. 22 rooms with PB. 2 conference rooms. Breakfast included in rates. Type of meal: early coffee/tea. Dinner, lunch, banquet service, catering service and catered breakfast available. Beds: QD. Phone, air conditioning and ceiling fan in room. TV, VCR, fax and copier on premises. Weddings, small meetings, family reunions and seminars hosted. Amusement parks, antiques, fishing, parks, shopping and theater nearby.

Location: One-half block from the ocean.

Publicity: *Atlantic City Press, Asbury Press, Frommer's, New York Times, Washington Post.*

"Mr. Kulkowitz is a superb host. He strives to accommodate the diverse needs of guests."

The Chalfonte

301 Howard St, PO Box 475
Cape May, NJ 08204-2430
(609)884-8409 Fax:(609)884-4588
E-mail: chalfontnj@aol.com

Circa 1876. This 108-room hotel was built by Civil War hero Colonel Henry Sawyer. The hotel features wrap-around porches, simply appointed rooms with marble-topped dressers and other original antiques. The fare in the Magnolia Room is Southern-style with fresh fish daily and vegetarian options. Children of all ages are welcome, and there is a supervised children's dining room for six-year-olds and under. Much of the hotel's restoration and preservation is accomplished by dedicated volunteers who have adopted the hotel as their own. Painting workshops, Elderhostel educational programs, weekly events and entertainment, group retreats, weddings, family reunions are offered. An early continental breakfast is provided to those guests who may be heading out to go birding, cycling or walking.

Historic Interest: Cold Springs Village (4 miles).

Innkeeper(s): Anne LeDuc & Judy Bartella. $89-184. MAP. MC VISA AX. TAC10. 108 rooms, 11 with PB. 2 cottages. 2 conference rooms. Breakfast and dinner included in rates. Meals: full breakfast and early coffee/tea.

Afternoon tea available. Restaurant on premises. Beds: KQDT. Ceiling fan in room. TV, VCR, fax, copier, child care on premises. Weddings, small meetings, family reunions and seminars hosted. Amusement parks, antiques, fishing, parks, shopping, sporting events, golf, theater and watersports nearby.

Location: Centrally located in the historic district, three blocks from city center and from beaches.

Publicity: *Travel & Leisure, Washingtonian, Philadelphia Inquirer, New York Times, Country Inns, Richmond Times, Mid-Atlantic Country, Star and Wave, Virginian Pilot & Ledger-Star, USA Today.*

Dormer House

800 Columbia Ave
Cape May, NJ 08204-2310
(609)884-7446 (800)884-5052

Circa 1899. This Colonial Revival estate is three blocks from the ocean and the historic walking mall. It was built by marble-dealer John Jacoby and retains much of the original marble and furniture.

Innkeeper(s): Lucille & Dennis Doherty. $80-210. MC VISA AX PC TC. 10 rooms with PB, 1 with FP. 2 suites. 2 cottages. Breakfast and afternoon tea included in rates. Type of meal: full breakfast. Beds: Q. Air conditioning, ceiling fan and TV in room. Bicycles on premises. Amusement parks, antiques, fishing, parks, shopping, theater and watersports nearby.

Location: Corner of Franklin & Columbia in the historic district.

Publicity: *Cape May Star & Wave.*

"Our 7th year here. We love it."

Fairthorne B&B

111 Ocean St
Cape May, NJ 08204-2319
(609)884-8791 (800)438-8742 Fax:(609)884-1902
E-mail: WEHFAIR@aol.com

Circa 1892. Antiques abound in this three-story Colonial Revival. Lace curtains and a light color scheme complete the charming decor. The signature breakfasts include special daily entrees along with an assortment of home-baked breads and muffins. A light afternoon tea also is served with refreshments. The proximity to the beach will be much appreciated by guests, and the innkeepers  offer the use of beach towels, bicycles and sand chairs. The nearby historic district is full of fun shops and restaurants.

Innkeeper(s): Diane & Ed Hutchinson. $90-230. MC VISA AX DS TC. 7 rooms. 1 suite. Breakfast and afternoon tea included in rates. Meals: full breakfast, early coffee/tea. Beds: KQ. Air conditioning, ceiling fan in room. Fax on premises. Antiques, fishing, parks, shopping, theater, watersports nearby.

Publicity: *New Jersey Women's Magazine.*

"I feel as if I have come to stay with a dear old friend who has spared no expense to provide me with all that my heart can desire! ... I will savor the memory of your hospitality for years to come. Thanks so much."

Frog Hollow Inn

819 Kearney Ave
Cape May, NJ 08204-2451
(609)884-1426 Fax:(609)884-1638

Circa 1919. This State Register home is just two blocks from the ocean and right in the middle of all the action in this historic Victorian town. The inn is decorated in a comfortable Victorian style with Oriental rugs, period-style furnishings and flowery wallcoverings. Breakfasts are homemade and include several courses, with a fresh fruit dish, pastries and perhaps a soufflé or French toast as an entree. The innkeepers offer several getaway packages, and provide beach passes for their guests.

Innkeeper(s): Jane & Carl Buck. $80-150. MC VISA AX. TAC10. 5 rooms with PB. Breakfast and afternoon tea included in rates. Meals: full breakfast and early coffee/tea. Beds: KQDT. Air conditioning and ceiling fan in room. TV, VCR, fax, copier on premises. Weddings, small meetings, family reunions hosted. Amusement parks, antiques, fishing, parks, golf, theater nearby.

Publicity: *New York Times.*

Gingerbread House

28 Gurney St
Cape May, NJ 08204
(609)884-0211

Circa 1869. The Gingerbread is one of eight original Stockton Row Cottages, summer retreats built for families from

Philadelphia and Virginia. It is
a half-block from the ocean
and breezes waft over the
wicker-filled porch. The inn is
listed in the National Register.
It has been meticulously
restored and decorated with
period antiques and a fine collection of paintings. The inn's
woodwork is especially
notable, guests enter through
handmade teak double doors.

Historic Interest: Historic tours are available.

Innkeeper(s): Fred & Joan Echevarria. $90-220. MC VISA PC TC. 6 rooms, 2 with PB. 1 suite. Breakfast, afternoon tea included in rates. Meal: full breakfast. Beds: QD. Air conditioning in room. Small meetings, family reunions hosted. Antiques, fishing, parks, shopping, theater, watersports nearby.

Location: Historic District, one-half block from the beach.

Publicity: *Philadelphia Inquirer, New Jersey Monthly, Atlantic City Press.*

"*The elegance, charm and authenticity of historic Cape May, but more than that, it appeals to us as `home'.*"

The Henry Sawyer Inn

722 Columbia Ave
Cape May, NJ 08204-2332
(609)884-5667 (800)449-5667

Circa 1877. This fully restored three-story ecru Victorian home boasts a gingerbread embellished veranda, brick-colored shutters and brown trim. Inside, the parlor features Victorian antiques, a marble fireplace, polished wood floors, an Oriental rug, formal wallcoverings, a crystal chandelier and fresh flowers. Guest rooms have been decorated with careful attention to a romantic and fresh Victorian theme, as well. One room includes a whirlpool tub, another includes a private porch. Ask for the Mary Macrissic Sawyer room.

Innkeeper(s): Mary & Barbara Morris. $85-185. MC VISA AX DS PC TC. TAC10. 3 rooms with PB, 1 with FP. 2 suites. 1 conference room. Breakfast and afternoon tea included in rates. Types of meals: full breakfast, gourmet breakfast and early coffee/tea. Beds: KQT. Air conditioning, ceiling fan, TV and VCR in room. Small meetings and family reunions hosted. Antiques, fishing, parks, shopping, theater and watersports nearby.

Humphrey Hughes House

29 Ocean St
Cape May, NJ 08204-2411
(609)884-4428 (800)582-3634

Circa 1903. Stained-glass windows mark each landing of the staircase, and intricately carved American chestnut columns add to the atmosphere in this 30-room mansion. The land was

purchased by the Captain
Humphrey Hughes family
in the early 1700s. The
majestic grandfather clock
remains as one of many
late-Victorian antiques.

Historic Interest: The inn is listed in National Register.

Innkeeper(s): Lorraine & Terry Schmidt. $85-215. MC VISA PC. 7 rooms with PB. 4 suites. Breakfast and afternoon tea included in rates. Beds: KQ. Air conditioning and ceiling fan in room. Handicap access. Antiques, shopping, theater and watersports nearby.

Publicity: *New York Times.*

"*Thoroughly enjoyed our stay.*"

John Wesley Inn

30 Gurney St
Cape May, NJ 08204
(609)884-1012

Circa 1869. The innkeepers of this graciously restored Carpenter Gothic home have won awards for their captivating exterior Christmas decorations, and holidays at the inn are a seasonal delight. The interior decor preserves the Victorian era so treasured in this seaside village. Antiques are set in rooms decorated with bright, patterned wallpapers and windows decked in lace. The innkeepers also offer a restored carriage house, featuring the same period decor, but the modern amenity of a stocked kitchen.

Innkeeper(s): John & Rita Tice. $75-165. PC TC. 6 rooms, 4 with PB. 2 cottages. 1 conference room. Breakfast included in rates. Meal: continental-plus breakfast. Beds: QD. Phone, air conditioning and ceiling fan in room. Weddings, small meetings, family reunions and seminars hosted. Amusement parks, antiques, fishing, parks, shopping, theater and watersports nearby.

Mainstay Inn

635 Columbia Ave
Cape May, NJ 08204-2305
(609)884-8690

Circa 1872. This was once the elegant and exclusive Jackson's Clubhouse popular with gamblers. Many of the guest rooms and the grand parlor look much as they did in the 1870s. Fourteen-foot-high ceilings, elaborate chandeliers, a sweeping veranda and a cupola add to the atmosphere. Tom and Sue Carroll received the American Historic Inns award in 1988 for their preservation efforts, and have been making unforgettable memories for guests for decades. A writer for Conde Nast Traveler once wrote, "architecturally, no inn, anywhere, quite matches the Mainstay."

Historic Interest: Cape May Lighthouse & State Park Museum (2 miles).

Innkeeper(s): Tom & Sue Carroll. $95-250. PC TC. 16 rooms with PB, 4 with FP. 7 suites. Breakfast and afternoon tea included in rates. Types of

meals: continental-plus breakfast, full breakfast and early coffee/tea. Beds: KQD. Phone, air conditioning, ceiling fan, TV and VCR in room. Library on premises. Handicap access. Small meetings and seminars hosted. Amusement parks, antiques, fishing, parks, shopping, sporting events, theater and watersports nearby.

Location: Cape May National Landmark District.

Publicity: *Washington Post, Good Housekeeping, New York Times, Conde Nast Traveler, Smithsonian, Americana, Travel & Leisure, National Geographic Traveler.*

"*By far the most lavishly and faithfully restored guesthouse...run by two arch-preservationists—Travel & Leisure.*"

The Mason Cottage

625 Columbia Ave
Cape May, NJ 08204-2305
(609)884-3358 (800)716-2766

Circa 1871. Since 1946, this elegant seaside inn has been open to guests. The curved-mansard, wood-shingle roof was built by local shipyard carpenters. Much of the original furniture remains in the house, and it has endured both hurricanes and the 1878 Cape May fire. Two of the inn's suites include a fireplace and whirlpool tub.

Historic Interest: The inn is listed in the New Jersey Historic Register.

Innkeeper(s): Dave & Joan Mason. $85-265. MC VISA AX TC. 9 rooms with PB, 2 with FP. 4 suites. 1 conference room. Breakfast and afternoon tea included in rates. Type of meal: full breakfast. Beds: QD. Air conditioning and ceiling fan in room. Weddings, small meetings, family reunions and seminars hosted. Antiques, fishing, parks, shopping, theater and watersports nearby.

Location: In the historic district.

"*We relaxed and enjoyed ourselves. You have a beautiful and elegant inn, and serve great breakfasts. We will be back on our next trip to Cape May.*"

The Inn on Ocean

25 Ocean St
Cape May, NJ 08204-2411
(609)884-7070 (800)304-4477 Fax:(609)884-1384

Circa 1880. Pansies and petunias blossom in front of this Second Empire Victorian and accentuate the green, white and yellow color scheme and strawberry pink roof. Inside, a light Victorian decor creates a bright and airy, yet elegant atmosphere. The inn boasts the only Victorian billiard room in town.

Innkeeper(s): Jack & Katha Davis. $99-295. MC VISA AX DC CB DS PC TC. TAC10. 4 rooms with PB. 1 suite. Breakfast and afternoon tea included in rates. Types of meals: full breakfast and early coffee/tea. Beds: KQ. Air conditioning, ceiling fan and TV in room. Antiques, fishing, parks, shopping, theater and watersports nearby.

Publicity: *Delta Airlines In-Flight Magazine, Washington Post Sunday Magazine.*

"*The food was fabulous and served with a delicate flair. We enjoyed the family warmth and Victorian elegance.*"

Poor Richard's Inn

17 Jackson St
Cape May, NJ 08204-1417
(609)884-3536

Circa 1882. The unusual design of this Second-Empire house has been accentuated with five colors of paint. Arched gingerbread porches tie together the distinctive bays of the house's facade. The combination of exterior friezes, balustrades and fretwork has earned the inn an individual listing in the National Register. Some rooms sport an eclectic country Victorian decor with patchwork quilts and pine furniture, while others tend toward a more traditional turn-of-the-century ambiance. An apartment suite is available.

Innkeeper(s): Richard Samuelson. $59-135. EP. MC VISA. 10 rooms with PB. 1 suite. Breakfast included in rates. Types of meals: continental-plus breakfast and early coffee/tea. Beds: QDT. Air conditioning and TV in room. Copier on premises. Small meetings and family reunions hosted. Amusement parks, antiques, fishing, parks, theater and watersports nearby.

Publicity: *Washington Post, New York Times, National Geographic Traveler, New Jersey.*

"*Hold our spot on the porch. We'll be back before you know it.*"

The Queen Victoria

102 Ocean St
Cape May, NJ 08204-2320
(609)884-8702

Circa 1881. Christmas is a special festival at these beautifully restored Victorians. Special tours, Charles Dickens' feasts and costumed carolers crowd the calendar. The rest of the year, well-stocked libraries, and long porches lined with antique rocking chairs provide for more sedate entertainment. "Victorian Homes" featured 23 color photographs of The Queen Victoria. Amenities include afternoon tea and mixers, a fleet of bicycles, and evening turndown service. The innkeepers also offer complimentary beach tags and towels for their summer guests. Suites feature a whirlpool tub, fireplace or private porch. Guest rooms are spread among three, adjacent Victorian homes, all beautifully appointed in Victorian country style.

Historic Interest: National Landmark District.

Innkeeper(s): Joan & Dane Wells. $90-270. EP. PC. 23 rooms with PB, 2 with FP. 7 suites. 2 cottages. Breakfast and afternoon tea included in rates. Meals: full breakfast and early coffee/tea. Room service available. Beds: QD. Air conditioning, turndown service and ceiling fan in room. TV, VCR, bicycles, library and child care on premises. Handicap access. Weddings, small meetings, family reunions, seminars hosted. French spoken. Amusement parks, antiques, fishing, parks, shopping, theater, watersports nearby.

Location: In the heart of the historic district, one block from the beach.

Publicity: *Discerning Traveler, New York, Cover Girl, Washington Post, Victorian.*

"*Especially impressed by the relaxed atmosphere and the excellent housekeeping.*"

The Queen's Hotel

601 Columbia Ave
Cape May, NJ 08204-2305
(609)884-1613

Circa 1876. This charming Victorian hotel is located just a block from the beach in the center of Cape May's historic district. Period decor graces the luxurious guest rooms. The historic hotel is full of history. Originally, the building was used for commercial purposes, and a large, second-story room once served as a gambling casino with rumors of ghostly visitors. The feeling is distinctly historic, but one suite does include a modern and romantic double whirlpool tub. Other amenities include hair dryers, coffeemakers and mini refrigerators. As this is a hotel, meals are not included in the rates; however, a multitude of restaurants and cafes are within walking distance.

Innkeeper(s): Don Pettifer. $70-250. PC. 9 rooms with PB. 2 suites. Beds: QD. Phone, air conditioning, ceiling fan and TV in room. Bicycles on premises. Weddings, small meetings and family reunions hosted. Amusement parks, antiques, fishing, parks, theater and watersports nearby.

Rhythm of The Sea

1123 Beach Dr
Cape May, NJ 08204-2628
(609)884-7788

Circa 1915. The apt name of this oceanfront inn describes the soothing sounds of the sea that lull many a happy guest into a restful night's sleep. From October through May, guests may enjoy private recitals performed by classical musicians who also stay at the inn. Many of the features of a Craftsman home are incorporated in this  seaside inn, which includes large, spacious rooms, adjoining dining and living areas with fireplaces, natural wood floors and mission furnishings throughout. For guests seeking an especially private stay, they'll enjoy the inn's three-room suite. Guests are given complimentary beach passes, towels and bicycles. There is free parking available, and guests have use of bicycles.

Innkeeper(s): Robyn & Wolfgang Wendt. $99-225. MC VISA AX DC PC. TAC10. 7 rooms with PB, 1 with FP. 1 suite. Breakfast and afternoon tea included in rates. Type of meal: full breakfast. Dinner available. Beds: Q. Air conditioning in room. VCR and bicycles on premises. Small meetings and family reunions hosted. Amusement parks, antiques, fishing, shopping, theater and watersports nearby.

Publicity: *Atlantic City Press, New Jersey Monthly, POV.*

"Your home is lovely, the atmosphere is soothing."

Saltwood House

28 Jackson St
Cape May, NJ 08204-1465
(609)884-6754 (800)830-8232

Circa 1906. The apricot awnings and the Colonial Revival architecture of Saltwood House welcome guests to a Victorian experience in a setting of hand-carved antique oak furniture, Tiffany lamps and a collection of Victorian silverplate. A favorite room is the Saratoga with a bay window overlooking the street scene, an elaborately carved gargoyle oak bedstead, chrysanthemum wallpaper and a Victorian desk. Located one-half block from the ocean and in the middle of an interesting Victorian street with gas lamps, sycamore trees and horse-drawn summer carriages, there are restaurants, shops and the walking mall on Washington Street to enjoy. Egg casseroles, sausage and fresh sweet rolls are often served at breakfast.

Innkeeper(s): Don Schweikert. $80-165. MC VISA AX PC TC. 4 rooms with PB. Breakfast and afternoon tea included in rates. Types of meals: full breakfast and early coffee/tea. Room service available. Beds: KQ. Air conditioning, ceiling fan, TV and VCR in room. Copier and library on premises. Family reunions hosted. Amusement parks, antiques, fishing, parks, shopping, golf, theater and watersports nearby.

Publicity: *Star-Ledger.*

"We're Back - Every stay gets better & better. Thanks so much for your wonderful hospitality. See you again next year."

Sea Holly B&B Inn

815 Stockton Ave
Cape May, NJ 08204-2446
(609)884-6294 Fax:(609)884-5157

Circa 1875. The home-baked cuisine at this three-story Gothic cottage is an absolute delight. Innkeeper Christy Igoe began her love for baking in childhood, and at age 12 she created her own chocolate chip cookie recipe and now has her own cookbook. Her goodies are served at breakfast and in the afternoons with tea and sherry. The home is decorated with authentic Renaissance Revival and Eastlake antique pieces. Some rooms boast ocean views. The  inn is a wonderful place for a special occasion, and honeymooners or those celebrating an anniversary receive complimentary champagne. In addition to the romantic amenities, the innkeeper provides practical extras such as hair dryers, irons and ironing boards in each room or suite. All rooms and suites include a TV. Winter guests should be sure to ask about the inn's midweek winter specials.

circa 1875

Innkeeper(s): Christy Lacey-Igoe. $80-200. MC VISA AX TC. 8 rooms with PB. 2 suites. Breakfast and afternoon tea included in rates. Types of meals: full breakfast and early coffee/tea. Beds: KQ. Air conditioning and ceiling fan in room. Fax on premises. Weddings and family reunions hosted. Amusement parks, antiques, fishing, parks, shopping, theater and watersports nearby.

Publicity: *Mid-Atlantic Newsletter, New Jersey Monthly, Fremans.*

"You have shown us what a real B&B is supposed to be like."

Seventh Sister Guesthouse

10 Jackson St
Cape May, NJ 08204-1418
(609)884-2280 Fax:(609)898-9899

Circa 1888. Most of the Seventh Sister's guest rooms have ocean views. The inn is listed in the National Register. The artist/architect innkeepers have original art collections on display. Wicker and original antique furnishings fill the rooms. Guests can relax in front of a warm fire in the living room. The home's three floors are joined by a spectacular central circular staircase. The center of town is a one-block walk, and the beach is just 100 feet away.

Historic Interest: Coldspring Village (7 miles).

Innkeeper(s): Bob & JoAnne Myers. $75-150. EP. MC VISA AX PC TC. 6 rooms, 1 with PB. Beds: D. Fax and library on premises. Small meetings hosted. Amusement parks, antiques, fishing, parks, shopping, theater and watersports nearby.

Publicity: *New York Times, 1001 Decorating Ideas.*

Summer Cottage Inn

613 Columbia Ave
Cape May, NJ 08204-2305
(609)884-4948

Circa 1867. A cupola tops this Italianate-style inn located on a quiet tree-lined street in the historic district. It's close to the beach (one block) and the Victorian Mall. Period Victorian pieces are featured in the parlor and the veranda is filled with plants and rockers. There's a fireplace in the sitting room and a Baby Grand piano in the parlor.

Innkeeper(s): Linda & Skip Loughlin. $85-175. MC VISA AX DS. 9 rooms, 8 with PB. Breakfast and afternoon tea included in rates. Type of meal: full breakfast. Beds: Q. Air conditioning and ceiling fan in room. Antiques, fishing, shopping, theater and watersports nearby.

Publicity: *Star Ledger, Philadelphia Inquirer.*

"Comfortable. Home away from home."

White Dove Cottage

619 Hughes St
Cape May, NJ 08204-2317
(609)884-0613 (800)321-3683

Circa 1866. The beautiful octagonal slate on the Mansard roof of this Second Empire house is just one of the inn's many handsome details. Bright sunny rooms are furnished in American and European antiques, period wallpapers, paintings, prints and handmade quilts. Rooms with fireplaces or Jacuzzi tub are available.
Breakfast is served to the soft music of an antique music box and boasts heirloom crystal, fine china and lace. Located on a quiet, gas-lit street, the inn is two blocks from the beach, restaurants and shops. Ask about mystery weekends and the inn's Honeymoon and Romantic Escape packages.

Innkeeper(s): Frank & Sue Smith. $80-215. 4 rooms with PB. 2 suites. Breakfast and afternoon tea included in rates. Types of meals: full breakfast, gourmet breakfast and early coffee/tea. Beds: KQD. Antiques, fishing, shopping, theater and watersports nearby.

Location: Center of historic Cape May.

Wilbraham Mansion

133 Myrtle Ave
Cape May, NJ 08204-1237
(609)884-2046

Circa 1840. This historic home is special because it survived the horrific fire which destroyed much of Cape May. A wealthy industrialist added the Victorian elements now evident in the architecture. Period antiques, including some pieces original to the home, decorate the interior. There is an enclosed terrace housing a swimming pool, a glassed-in front porch lined with wicker and several parlors to enjoy. The inn often is the site for business meetings and other functions.

Innkeeper(s): Patty Carnes. $100-195. MC VISA PC TC. 10 rooms, 7 with PB. 3 suites. Breakfast and afternoon tea included in rates. Types of meals: full breakfast and early coffee/tea. Beds: KQD. Air conditioning and ceiling fan in room. TV, swimming and bicycles on premises. Weddings and small meetings hosted. Antiques, fishing, parks, shopping, golf, theater and watersports nearby.

Windward House

24 Jackson St
Cape May, NJ 08204-1465
(609)884-3368 Fax:(609)884-1575

Circa 1905. All three stories of this blue Edwardian-style cottage contain antique-filled guest rooms. Beveled and stained glass cast rainbows of flickering light from the windows and French doors,

while gleaming chestnut and oak paneling set off a collection of museum-quality antiques and collectibles. The Eastlake and Empire rooms offer a glimpse of the ocean. All rooms have ceiling fans, air conditioning, TVs, mini refrigerators and hair dryers.

Innkeeper(s): Owen & Sandy Miller. $85-187. MC VISA PC TC. 8 rooms with PB. 2 suites. Breakfast and afternoon tea included in rates. Types of meals: gourmet breakfast and early coffee/tea. Beds: KQ. Phone, air conditioning, ceiling fan and TV in room. Fax, bicycles and library on premises. Small meetings and family reunions hosted. Antiques, fishing, parks, shopping, golf, theater and watersports nearby.

Location: Southern New Jersey shore region.

Publicity: *New Jersey Monthly, Delaware Today, Mid-Atlantic Country, Country Inns, Victorian Homes, Innsider, Mainline, Princeton Packet.*

"The loveliest and most authentically decorated of all the houses we visited."

The Wooden Rabbit

609 Hughes St
Cape May, NJ 08204-2317
(609)884-7293

Circa 1838. Robert E. Lee brought his wife to stay at this sea captain's house to ease her arthritis. The house was also part of the Underground Railroad. Throughout the inn are whimsical touches such as the "rabbit hutch" in the living room, which holds a collection of Beatrix Potter figures. The decor is country, with folk art and collectibles. Families are welcome.

Innkeeper(s): Greg & Debby Burow. $75-190. MC VISA DS. 4 rooms with PB. 2 suites. Breakfast and afternoon tea included in rates. Type of meal: full breakfast. Beds: KQ. Phone, air conditioning and TV in room. Amusement parks, antiques, fishing, shopping and theater nearby.

Location: Two blocks to beach, one block to mall, center of historic district.

Publicity: *The Sandpiper.*

"The room was perfect, our breakfast delicious. We will be back."

Woodleigh House

808 Washington St
Cape May, NJ 08204-1652
(609)884-7123 (800)399-7123

Circa 1866. Woodleigh House is a country Victorian built by sea captain Isaac Smith. Collections of glass and Royal Copenhagen are found throughout along with Victorian-era furnishings. The front porch sports rocking chairs and wicker furniture. There is a secluded brick courtyard and back garden. The Woods, both educators, attend to guests' needs and are happy to make beach bikes available.

Innkeeper(s): Buddy & Jan Wood. $85-175. MC VISA. 4 rooms with PB. 1 suite. Breakfast and afternoon tea included in rates. Type of meal: full breakfast. Beds: QT. Phone in room. Antiques, theater and watersports nearby.

"What a warm and friendly home..."

Cape May/Courthouse K4

Doctors Inn

2 N Main St
Cape May/Courthouse, NJ 08210-2118
(609)463-9330 Fax:(609)463-9650

Circa 1854. Several doctors have lived in this pre-Civil War home, including innkeeper Carolyn Crawford, a neonatologist. Each of the romantic guest rooms is named after a doctor and includes a working fireplace and whirlpool tub. There is an emphasis on health here, and the inn includes a spa with sauna, massage and exercise equipment. The inn features a posh restaurant, Bradbury's, and serves a variety of gourmet fare; the seafood is especially noteworthy.

Innkeeper(s): Carolyn Crawford. $125-175. MC VISA AX DC DS TC. 6 rooms with PB, 6 with FP. 2 suites. 1 conference room. Breakfast and afternoon tea included in rates. Types of meals: full breakfast and early coffee/tea. Lunch, banquet service, catering service and room service available. Restaurant on premises. Beds: KQF. Phone, air conditioning and TV in room. Spa and sauna on premises. Handicap access. Weddings, small meetings, family reunions and seminars hosted. Amusement parks, antiques, fishing, parks, shopping, theater and watersports nearby.

Dennisville J4

Henry Ludlam Inn

1336 Rt 47
Dennisville, NJ 08214-3608
(609)861-5847

Circa 1804. This country inn borders picturesque Ludlam Lake. Canoeing, birding, biking and fishing are popular activities, and the innkeepers make sure you enjoy these at your peak by providing you with a full country breakfast. Some of the bedrooms have fireplaces, and all feature antique double and queen beds.

Historic Interest: The Dennisville Museum of History is nearby.

Innkeeper(s): Chuck & Pat DeArros. $85-125. MC VISA PC TC. TAC10. 5 rooms with PB, 3 with FP. Breakfast included in rates. Types of meals: full breakfast, gourmet breakfast and early coffee/tea. Beds: QD. Air conditioning and ceiling fan in room. Small meetings hosted. Antiques, fishing, parks, shopping, theater and watersports nearby.

Location: Cape May County.

Publicity: *Atlantic City Press, New Jersey Outdoors, Bright Side.*

"An unforgettable breakfast. Enjoy a piece of history!"

Flemington E3

Jerica Hill B&B Inn

96 Broad St
Flemington, NJ 08822-1604
(908)782-8234 Fax:(908)782-8234

Circa 1901. This Queen Anne Victorian is decorated in a bright and airy decor with four-poster beds, bay windows, ceiling fans and flowers. Breakfast is served on a mahogany breakfront. The innkeeper has several romantic packages available to guests. Her "Country Winery Tour" package

includes a wine tour, tastings and a wicker basket filled with a country picnic and wine tasting glasses.

Innkeeper(s): Hazel Barbiche. $95-110. MC VISA AX PC TC. TAC10. 5 rooms with PB. Breakfast, afternoon tea and evening snack included in rates. Types of meals: continental-plus breakfast and early coffee/tea. Picnic lunch available. Beds: KQD. Phone and air conditioning in room. Fax and copier on premises. Small meetings, family reunions and seminars hosted. Antiques, fishing, parks, shopping, downhill skiing, cross-country skiing, sporting events, theater and watersports nearby.

Publicity: *Mid-Atlantic Country, New York Times, Country Inns.*

"If you've been searching for an inn that's homey and unpretentious - then I've found the place for you: Jerica Hill."

Glenwood A5

Apple Valley Inn B&B and Antiques

Corner Rts 517 & 565, PO Box 302
Glenwood, NJ 07418-0302
(201)764-3735 Fax:(201)764-1050

Circa 1804. This three-story Colonial farmhouse is set on three acres with its own apple orchard (more than 40 trees) and in-ground pool. A brook running next to the house is a great trout-fishing spot. The innkeeper is an avid antique collector and guest rooms (named after varieties of apples) include American antiques. Try the Red Delicious room. Across the street is a popular pick-your-own-fruit farm. Check with the innkeeper to find when the strawberries, peaches, cherries and apples are ripe so you can gather your favorites. Action Park, ski slopes and the Appalachian Trail are five minutes away.

Innkeeper(s): Mitzi & John Durham. $70-90. MC VISA PC TC. 7 rooms, 2 with PB. Breakfast and afternoon tea included in rates. Types of meals: full breakfast and early coffee/tea. Picnic lunch available. Beds: DT. Air conditioning and ceiling fan in room. TV, VCR, fax, copier, swimming, bicycles and library on premises. Weddings, small meetings, family reunions and seminars hosted. Amusement parks, antiques, fishing, parks, shopping, downhill skiing, cross-country skiing, sporting events and theater nearby.

Publicity: *Cleveland Plain Dealer, Appalachian Trail News, New Jersey Herald, Country Living.*

Haddonfield G3

Queen Anne Inn

44 West End Ave
Haddonfield, NJ 08033-2616
(609)428-2195 (800)269-0014 Fax:(609)354-1273
E-mail: qainn@aol.com

This inn is located in historic Haddonfield, which has been praised as one of the top villages in the Delaware Valley. Historic homes, museums, antique shops and restaurants are just a short walk away from this Victorian treasure, which features a charming wraparound porch. Rooms boast elegant decor such as chandeliers and antiques. Visitors will delight in the Plays and Players, Symphony Orchestra, Arts Center, picturesque parks and special events. The New Jersey Aquarium and Philadelphia are a train ride away.

Innkeeper(s): Nancy Lynn & Fred Chorpita. $99-109. MC VISA AX DS. 8 rooms, 3 with PB. Breakfast included in rates. Types of meals: full breakfast and gourmet breakfast. Evening snack available. Weddings and family reunions hosted.

Hope   C3

The Inn at Millrace Pond

PO Box 359, Rt 59 at Millbrook Rd
Hope, NJ 07844-0359
(908)459-4884 (800)786-4673 Fax:(908)459-5276

Circa 1769. The former grist mill buildings house an authentically restored Colonial inn, set in the rolling hills of Northwestern New Jersey. Decorated in the Colonial period, many of the rooms  feature original wide-board floors, antiques and Oriental rugs. Rooms in the limestone Grist Mill, a building listed in the National Register of Historic Places, boast hand-crafted American primitive reproductions and braided rugs. The inn's restaurant features the original millrace room, complete with running water. A former wheel chamber has a staircase that leads to the Tavern Room with its own walk-in fireplace and grain chute.

Innkeeper(s): Cordie & Charles Puttkammer. $95-165. MC VISA AX DC TC. 17 rooms with PB. 1 with FP. 1 suite. 1 conference room. Breakfast included in rates. Type of meal: continental-plus breakfast. Evening snack and banquet service available. Restaurant on premises. Beds: Q. Phone, air conditioning and TV in room. Fax, copier and bicycles on premises. Handicap access. 23 acres. Weddings, small meetings, family reunions and seminars hosted. Amusement parks, antiques, fishing, parks, shopping and cross-country skiing nearby.

"The most interesting thing of all is the way these buildings have been restored."

Lambertville   E3

Chimney Hill B&B

207 Goat Hill Rd
Lambertville, NJ 08530
(609)397-1516 Fax:(609)397-9353

Circa 1820. Chimney Hill is a grand display of stonework, designed with both Federal and Greek Revival-style architecture. The inn's stone sunroom is particularly appealing, with its stone walls, fireplaces and windows looking out to the lush, eight-acre grounds. Five of the guest rooms include a fireplace, and some have canopy beds. The innkeepers offer adventure, romance and special interest packages for their guests. There's plenty of seasonal activities nearby, from kayaking to skiing.

Innkeeper(s): Terry Ann & Richard Anderson. $75-190. MAP, AP. MC VISA AX PC TC. TAC10. 8 rooms with PB. 4 with FP. 1 conference room. Breakfast and evening snack included in rates. Types of meals: continental-plus breakfast, full breakfast and early coffee/tea. Catering service available. Beds: KQD. Phone and air conditioning in room. Copier and library on premises. Weddings, small meetings, family reunions and seminars hosted. Antiques, fishing, parks, shopping, downhill skiing, cross-country skiing, sporting events, theater and watersports nearby.

"We would be hard pressed to find a more perfect setting to begin our married life together."

York Street House

42 York St
Lambertville, NJ 08530-2024
(609)397-3007 Fax:(609)397-9677
E-mail: BASKOG@AOL.COM

Circa 1909. Built by early industrialist George Massey as a 25th wedding anniversary present for his wife, the gracious manor house is situated on three quarters of an acre in the heart of the Lambertville's historical district. A winding three-story staircase leads to six well-appointed guest rooms decorated with period furnishings. The public rooms are warmed by Mercer Tile fireplaces, original Waterford Crystal chandeliers and a baby grand piano. Breakfast is served in the dining room with its built-in leaded-glass china and large oak servers, looking out over the lawn and sitting porch. Art galleries, antique shops, bookstores and restaurants are all within walking distance from the inn. Lambertville is nestled along the scenic Delaware River and Raritan Canal. Horseback riding, mule-drawn barges and carriage rides are just some of the activities available. A short walk across the Delaware River Bridge brings you to New Hope, Penn., with its many quaint shops.

Innkeeper(s): Nancy Ferguson & Beth Wetterskog. $85-185. MC VISA AX DS PC TC. TAC5. 6 rooms, 3 with PB. Breakfast included in rates. Types of meals: gourmet breakfast and early coffee/tea. Picnic lunch available. Beds: QD. Air conditioning, ceiling fan and TV in room. VCR and fax on premises. Small meetings hosted. Antiques, fishing, parks, shopping and theater nearby.

Manahawkin   H5

Goose N. Berry Inn

190 N Main St
Manahawkin, NJ 08050-2932
(609)597-6350 Fax:(609)597-6918

Circa 1868. This Queen Anne Victorian, built by an English merchant, has been painstakingly restored and redecorated. Period antiques decorate the guest rooms, each of which has its own personal flair. The Capstan Room features a nautical Victorian theme with paintings in honor of the area's seafaring tradition. Another room is decorated with antique needlepoint samplers, some a century old. There are plenty of places to relax, including a library stocked with books. Guests enjoy a wide variety of items during the gourmet buffet breakfast, baked French toast, fresh fruit, homemade breads, egg dishes and gourmet coffee are among the options. The innkeepers have snacks available throughout the day. For those celebrating a special occasions, the innkeepers can prepare a tray with champagne, chocolates or perhaps wine and cheese.

Innkeeper(s): Tom & Donna Smith. $75-175. TC. 5 rooms with PB. 1 suite. 1 conference room. Breakfast, afternoon tea and evening snack included in rates. Types of meals: gourmet breakfast and early coffee/tea. Picnic lunch, gourmet lunch and catering service available. Beds: D. Air conditioning and turndown service in room. Bicycles on premises. Weddings, small meetings, family reunions and seminars hosted. Amusement parks, antiques, fishing, parks, shopping, theater and watersports nearby.

Ocean City   J4

New Brighton Inn

519 5th St
Ocean City, NJ 08226-3940
(609)399-2829 Fax:(609)398-7786

Circa 1880. Ocean City was founded as a Christian retreat in the 19th century, and the builder of this home was instrumental in the town's founding. The home is a stunning example of Queen Anne architecture, featuring a tower, wraparound veranda and an arbor-covered terrace. The innkeepers provide guests with beach passes and bicycles, and it is a four-block walk to the beach and boardwalk. Breakfasts are a memorable affair, a unique fresh fruit pizza is a specialty.

Innkeeper(s): Daniel & Donna Hand. $95-125. MC VISA AX DS PC TC. 6 rooms with PB. 2 suites. 1 cottage. Breakfast included in rates. Types of meals: gourmet breakfast and early coffee/tea. Beds: Q. Air conditioning, ceiling fan and TV in room. Fax, copier, bicycles and library on premises. Weddings and family reunions hosted. Amusement parks, antiques, fishing, parks, shopping, golf and watersports nearby.
Publicity: *Philadelphia Inquirer, The Press of Atlantic City.*

Northwood Inn B&B

401 Wesley Ave
Ocean City, NJ 08226-3961
(609)399-6071 Fax:(609)398-5553

Circa 1894. This gracious three-story Queen Anne Victorian with Colonial Victorian touches has been restored by the innkeeper, who is a wooden boat builder and custom-home builder. There are gleaming plank floors, a sweeping staircase and a stocked library. The Tower Room in the turret is a favorite as is the Magnolia room with its lace curtains and luxurious bathroom with a double Jacuzzi. There is a rooftop, four-person spa where guests can relax and enjoy the sunset. The inn is within walking distance of the beach and boardwalk. The innkeepers offer bicycles and beach tags to their guests.

Historic Interest: Cape May (30 miles).
Innkeeper(s): Marj & John Loeper. $80-150. MC VISA AX PC. 8 rooms with PB. 2 suites. Types of meals: continental-plus breakfast and full breakfast. Beds: QT. Air conditioning in room. TV, VCR, fax and library on premises. Weddings and small meetings hosted. Amusement parks, antiques, fishing, parks, shopping, theater and watersports nearby.
Publicity: *Philadelphia Magazine.*

"Our only regret was that we couldn't have visited longer! It was our 55th wedding anniversary and you helped to make it a very happy time for us."

Scarborough Inn

720 Ocean Ave
Ocean City, NJ 08226-3749
(609)399-1558 (800)258-1558 Fax:(609)399-4472

Circa 1895. Painted in wedgewood, rose and soft creams, the Scarborough Inn is a familiar Victorian landmark in this seaside resort. Family-owned and operated, the inn is filled with the innkeepers' artwork collection and an upright piano for informal singalongs. A continental-plus breakfast is served in an ele-

gant dining room or on the wraparound porch. The beach and boardwalk are a short stroll from the inn.

Historic Interest: Wheaten Village (1 hour), Cold Spring Village (40 minutes), Leemings Run Gardens (30 minutes).

Innkeeper(s): Gus & Carol Bruno. $85-160. MC VISA AX DS PC TC. TAC10. 24 rooms with PB. 3 suites. Breakfast and afternoon tea included in rates. Types of meals: continental-plus breakfast and early coffee/tea. Catering service available. Beds: KQDT. Air conditioning and ceiling fan in room. TV, VCR, fax and library on premises. Small meetings and family reunions hosted. Italian spoken. Amusement parks, antiques, fishing, parks, shopping, sporting events, golf, theater and watersports nearby.
Location: One-and-one-half blocks to beach and boardwalk.
Publicity: *Country Inns Bed & Breakfast, Pittsburgh Press, Delaware County Daily Times.*

"Your care for the Scarborough and your guests is obvious to all who stay here. We love the place!"

Serendipity B&B

712 E 9th St
Ocean City, NJ 08226-3554
(609)399-1554 (800)842-8544 Fax:(609)399-1527

Circa 1912. The beach and boardwalk are less than half a block from this renovated inn. Healthy full breakfasts are served, and the innkeepers offer dinners by reservation with a mix of interesting, vegetarian items. In the summer, breakfasts are served on a vine-shaded veranda. The guest rooms are decorated in pastels with wicker pieces.

Innkeeper(s): Clara & Bill Plowfield. $70-129. MC VISA AX DS PC TC. TAC10. 6 rooms, 4 with PB. Breakfast and evening snack included in rates. Type of meal: full breakfast. Dinner available. Beds: KQDT. Air conditioning, ceiling fan and TV in room. Library on premises. Amusement parks, antiques, fishing, parks, shopping, theater and watersports nearby.

"Serendipity is such a gift. For me it's a little like being adopted during vacation time by a caring sister and brother. Your home is a home away from home. You make it so."

Ocean Grove   F6

The Cordova

26 Webb Ave
Ocean Grove, NJ 07756-1334
(973)774-3084

Circa 1885. This Victorian community was founded as a Methodist retreat. Ocean-bathing and cars were not allowed until a few years ago, so there are no souvenir shops along the white sandy beach and wooden boardwalk. The inn has hosted Presidents Wilson, Cleveland and Roosevelt who were also speakers at the Great Auditorium with its 7,000 seats. The kitchen, lounge, picnic and barbecue areas make this a popular place for family reunions. Ask about the inn's murder-mystery and tai chi weekends. Two cottage apartments also are avail-

able. The inn is closed during the winter and early spring. For information during these times, call (212) 751-9577.

Historic Interest: The home is listed in the National Register. Ocean Grove, a charming Victorian town, also is listed in the National Register.

Innkeeper(s): Doris A. Chernik. $46-160. PC. TAC10. 20 rooms, 5 with PB. 2 cottages. Breakfast included in rates. Type of meal: continental-plus breakfast. Beds: KQDT. VCR, bicycles and library on premises. Antiques and fishing nearby.

Publicity: *New Jersey, Asbury Park Press, St. Martin's Press, "O'New Jersey"* by Robert Heide and John Gilman.

"Warm, helpful and inviting, homey and lived-in atmosphere."

Pine Tree Inn

10 Main Ave
Ocean Grove, NJ 07756-1324
(732)775-3264

Circa 1870. This small Victorian inn is operated by a long-standing resident of the area and offers ocean views. Guest rooms are decorated in antiques and all the rooms are equipped with sinks. Bicycles and beach towels are available.

Innkeeper(s): Karen Mason. $55-110. MAP. MC VISA PC TC. 12 rooms, 4 with PB. 1 suite. Breakfast and afternoon tea included in rates. Types of meals: continental-plus breakfast and early coffee/tea. Beds: QD. Phone, air conditioning, ceiling fan and TV in room. Bicycles on premises. Small meetings, family reunions and seminars hosted. Amusement parks, antiques, fishing, parks, shopping, theater and watersports nearby.

Publicity: *Country Living, USA Today.*

Pemberton Boro   G4

Isaac Hilliard House B&B

31 Hanover St
Pemberton Boro, NJ 08068
(609)894-0756 (800)371-0756

Circa 1750. A wrought-iron fence sets off this two-story green and white Victorian. The inn is filled with antique collections and books. There's an antique bridal gown in the suite which includes a gas fireplace, sitting room, and private bathroom with a garden tub. Walk two minutes to the canoe rental, then paddle along the Rancocas River. The Grist Mill Village Antiques is within walking distance, and several other antique shops and fine restaurants are close by.

Historic Interest: Trenton, N.J., battlefield and buildings (25 minutes), Washington Crossing State Park (40 minutes), Ye Olde Lock Up Building (5-minute walk).

Innkeeper(s): Phyllis Davis & Gene R. O'Brien. $65-140. MC VISA AX PC TC. 4 rooms with PB. 1 suite. Breakfast included in rates. Type of meal: full breakfast. Beds: Q. Air conditioning, turndown service, ceiling fan, TV and VCR in room. Swimming on premises. Weddings and small meetings hosted. Amusement parks, antiques, fishing, parks, theater and watersports nearby.

Publicity: *New Jersey Travel Guide, New Jersey Monthly.*

"Every little detail was made so kind and warm. For even a short time, we both felt as if we traveled abroad. Your home is kept gorgeous and so tasteful."

Princeton   E4

Red Maple Farm

Rd4 Raymond Rd
Princeton, NJ 08540
(732)329-3821

Circa 1740. Located four miles from Princeton University and shaded by towering trees, this Colonial home rests on more than two acres of flower beds, fruit trees and berry bushes. There's a stone smokehouse built in 1740 and an old barn. The house is in the National Register, and Hessian soldiers were quartered here. It was also part of the Underground Railroad. Guest rooms are decorated comfortably, and one offers a working fireplace, pine armoire and brass bed. The innkeeper, a former noted chef, nurtures a vegetable garden that provides fresh produce for the inn's breakfast (shirred eggs, frittatas and raised waffles are some of the specialities).

Innkeeper(s): Roberta & Lindsey Churchill. $58-78. MC VISA AX DS PC TC. 3 rooms with PB, 1 with FP. Breakfast included in rates. Types of meals: full breakfast and gourmet breakfast. Beds: QT. Air conditioning in room. TV, VCR, copier, swimming, bicycles, tennis and library on premises. Some French spoken. Antiques, fishing, parks, shopping, cross-country skiing, sporting events, golf and theater nearby.

"Thank you for making an overnight stop so completely relaxing. A great start to a much-needed vacation!"

Salem   I1

Brown's Historic Home B&B

41-43 Market St
Salem, NJ 08079
(609)935-8595 Fax:(609)935-8595

Circa 1738. Brown's Historic Home originally was built as a Colonial house. Around 1845, the house was modernized to the Victorian era. The inn is furnished with antiques and heirlooms, including a handmade chess set and quilt. The fireplaces are made of King of Prussia marble. The backyard garden features a lily pond, wildflowers and a waterfall. There is a ferry nearby offering transport to Delaware. On Saturdays, guests can enjoy performances at the Cowtown Rodeo, eight miles away.

Historic Interest: Fort Mott State Park is four miles away.

Innkeeper(s): William & Margaret Brown. $55-100. MC VISA AX DS TC. 3 rooms, 2 with PB, 1 with FP. Breakfast included in rates. Types of meals: full breakfast and early coffee/tea. Beds: DT. Phone, air conditioning, ceiling fan and TV in room. Fax on premises. Small meetings and family reunions hosted. Antiques, fishing, parks, shopping, theater and watersports nearby.

Pets Allowed: Kennel nearby.

Location: Fifteen minutes from Delaware Memorial Bridge.

Publicity: *Newsday, Mid-Atlantic Country, Early American Life, Today's Sunbeam.*

"Down-home-on-the-farm breakfasts with great hospitality."

Sea Isle City   K4

The Colonnade Inn

4600 Landis Ave
Sea Isle City, NJ 08243-1875
(609)263-0460 Fax:(609)263-0460

Circa 1883. Dr. Carolyn Crawford, who restored the Doctor's Inn in Cape May Courthouse, also worked her magic here at this seaside Victorian, which features a sweeping wraparound porch. All of the B&B suite rooms have Victorian decor, fireplaces and whirlpool tubs. Several bedchambers afford ocean and bay views. The inn also includes several efficiency apartments, ideal for guests planning longer stays. The apartments are comfortably furnished and come with stocked kitchens, but guests should bring their own towels and linens.

Innkeeper(s): Christine Bossert. $50-160. MC VISA. 25 rooms, 8 with PB, 8 with FP. 1 conference room. Breakfast and afternoon tea included in rates. Type of meal: full breakfast. Beds: KQF. Air conditioning, ceiling fan and TV in room. Fax on premises. Handicap access. Weddings, small meetings, family reunions and seminars hosted. Amusement parks, antiques, fishing, parks, shopping and watersports nearby.

Spring Lake   F6

Ashling Cottage

106 Sussex Ave
Spring Lake, NJ 07762-1248
(732)449-3553 (888)274-5464

Circa 1877. Surrounded by shady sycamores on a quiet residential street, this three-story Victorian residence features a mansard-and-gambrel roof with hooded gambrel dormers. One of the two porches has a square, pyramid-roofed pavilion, which has been glass-enclosed and screened. Guests can watch the sun rise over the ocean one block away or set over Spring Lake. A full buffet breakfast can be enjoyed in the plant- and wicker-filled pavilion.

Historic Interest: Allaire State Park (5 miles).

Innkeeper(s): Jack Stewart. $99-179. PC TC. 10 rooms, 8 with PB. Breakfast and afternoon tea included in rates. Types of meals: full breakfast and early coffee/tea. Beds: Q. Air conditioning and ceiling fan in room. TV, VCR, bicycles and library on premises. Weddings, small meetings, family reunions and seminars hosted. Limited German spoken. Amusement parks, antiques, fishing, parks, shopping, sporting events, theater and watersports nearby.

Location: Six miles from exit 98.

Publicity: *New York Times, New Jersey Monthly, Town & Country, Country Living, New York, Harrods of London.*

Sea Crest By The Sea

19 Tuttle Ave
Spring Lake, NJ 07762-1533
(732)449-9031 (800)803-9031 Fax:(732)974-0403

Circa 1885. You can hear the surf from most rooms in this Victorian mansion. Guests will be pampered with Egyptian cotton and Belgian-lace linens, queen-size beds, fresh flowers and classical music. Tunes from a player piano announce afternoon tea at 4 p.m.—a good time to ask if John's freshly baked scones will be on the menu in the morning. Family china, crystal and silver add to the ambiance of breakfast. Bicycles are available and the beach is a half block away.

Innkeeper(s): John & Carol Kirby. $145-259. MC VISA AX. 12 rooms with PB, 8 with FP. 2 suites. Breakfast and afternoon tea included in rates. Type of meal: full breakfast. Beds: Q. Phone in room. Theater and watersports nearby.

Publicity: *New York Times, Gourmet, Victoria, Country Inns B&B.*

"This romantic storybook atmosphere is delightful! A visual feast."

Victoria House

214 Monmouth Ave
Spring Lake, NJ 07762-1127
(732)974-1882 Fax:(732)974-2132

Circa 1882. Queen Victoria surely would have enjoyed a trip to this bed & breakfast, as well as to Spring Lake, a pleasant village on the Jersey Shore. Each of the guest rooms is individually decorated with pieces such as an antique Eastlake armoire and wicker or brass beds. Several bathrooms include clawfoot tubs. The beach is within walking distance, and the innkeepers provide beach passes for their guests. Shops and restaurants are nearby as well.

Innkeeper(s): Louise & Robert Goodall. $105-185. MC VISA AX DS PC TC. TAC10. 9 rooms, 7 with PB, 2 with FP. 1 suite. Breakfast included in rates. Types of meals: full breakfast and early coffee/tea. Beds: KQ. Air conditioning in room. TV, fax and bicycles on premises. Small meetings and seminars hosted. Amusement parks, antiques, fishing, parks, shopping, sporting events, theater and watersports nearby.

"A very charming stay. We enjoyed your hospitality."

Stanhope   C4

Whistling Swan Inn

110 Main St
Stanhope, NJ 07874-2632
(973)347-6369 Fax:(973)347-3391
E-mail: wswan@worldnet.att.net

Circa 1905. This Queen Anne Victorian has a limestone wraparound veranda and a tall, steep-roofed turret. Family antiques fill the rooms and highlight the polished ornate woodwork, pocket doors and winding staircase. It is a little more than a mile from Waterloo Village and the International Trade Zone.

Historic Interest: Waterloo Village (3 miles), Washington's Headquarters & Jockey Hollow (12 miles), Sterling Hill Mine (15 miles).

Innkeeper(s): Joe Mulay & Paula Williams. $95-150. MC VISA AX DS PC TC. 10 rooms with PB. 1 suite. 1 conference room. Breakfast included in rates. Type of meal: full breakfast. Beds: Q. Phone, air conditioning, ceiling fan and TV in room. VCR, fax, copier and bicycles on premises. Seminars hosted. Antiques, fishing, parks, shopping, sporting events, theater and watersports nearby.

Location: East of the Pocono Mountains. Forty-five miles west of New York City in the scenic Skylands tourism region.

Publicity: *Sunday Herald, New York Times, New Jersey Monthly, Mid-Atlantic Country, Star Ledger, Daily Record, Philadelphia, Country, Chicago Sun Times.*

"Thank you for your outstanding hospitality. We had a delightful time while we were with you and will not hesitate to recommend the inn to our listening audience, friends and anyone else who will listen! — Joel H. Klein, Travel Editor, WOAI AM."

Stockton   E3

Woolverton Inn

6 Woolverton Rd
Stockton, NJ 08559-2147
(609)397-0802 (888)264-6648 Fax:(609)397-4936

Circa 1792. This two-century-old stone colonial inn sits on 10 acres surrounded by century old oaks and apple trees. Guests come to the Woolverton Inn to enjoy sipping wine by the fireplace in their room, or slipping into a cozy terry-cloth robe after a jacuzzi. The atmosphere is relaxed yet attentive. Guests enjoy the full country candlelight breakfast, afternoon snacks and the assistance offered to help plan their day. All rooms are decorated in antique furnishings and offer private baths and air conditioning. The inn is located minutes from cultural points of interest.

Innkeeper(s): Michael & Elizabeth Palmer. $100-190. MC VISA AX. 10 rooms with PB, 2 with FP. 2 suites. Breakfast and afternoon tea included in rates. Types of meals: full breakfast, gourmet breakfast and early coffee/tea. Catering service available. Beds: KQD. Air conditioning in room. Fax on premises. Handicap access. 10 acres. Weddings, small meetings, family reunions and seminars hosted. Antiques, fishing, parks, shopping, theater and watersports nearby.

Publicity: *New York Magazine, Colonial Homes, Philadelphia Inquirer.*

"Thank you for providing a perfect setting and relaxed atmosphere for our group. You're terrific."

New Mexico

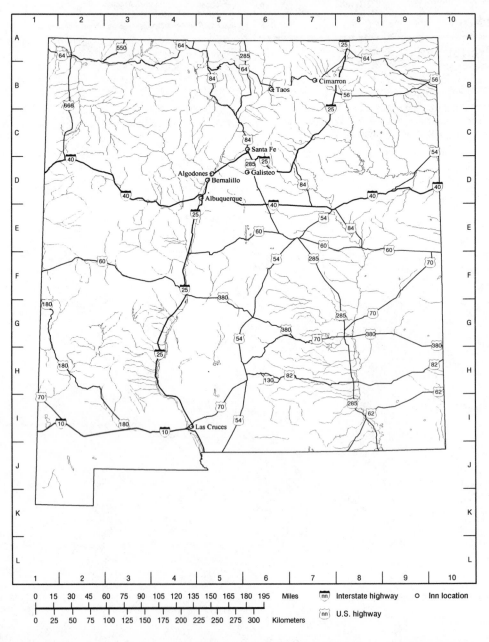

Albuquerque
D5

Bottger Mansion B&B

110 San Felipe NW, Old Town
Albuquerque, NM 87104
(505)243-3639 (800)758-3639 Fax:(505)243-3639

Circa 1912. Just steps from the plaza in historic Old Town, this four-square Victorian mansion is a slight departure from the surrounding adobe architecture. The seven guest rooms feature brass, oak, cherry and mahogany four-poster beds. Evening wine and hors d'oeuvres are served. A soda fountain and coffee and tea bar are available at all times.

Historic Interest: San Felipe de Neri Church (1 1/2 blocks), Petroglyph Park (1-2 miles), historic buildings in the Old Town Square.

Innkeeper(s): Patsy Garcia. $89-139. MC VISA AX PC TC. TAC10. 7 rooms with PB. 1 suite. Breakfast, afternoon tea and evening snack included in rates. Types of meals: continental breakfast, continental-plus breakfast, full breakfast, gourmet breakfast and early coffee/tea. Catered breakfast available. Beds: KQT. Air conditioning and ceiling fan in room. TV, fax and copier on premises. Weddings, small meetings and family reunions hosted. Spanish and English spoken. Amusement parks, antiques, fishing, parks, shopping, downhill skiing, cross-country skiing, sporting events, theater and watersports nearby.

Location: In historic Old Town.

"Yours ranks with the best for ambiance and location."

Hacienda Antigua B&B

6708 Tierra Dr N W
Albuquerque, NM 87107
(505)345-5399 (800)201-2986
E-mail: antigua@swc.com

Circa 1780. In the more than 200 years since this Spanish Colonial-style hacienda was constructed, the current innkeepers are only the fourth owners. Once a stagecoach stop on the El Camino Real, it also served as a cantina and mercantile store. It was built by Don Pablo Yrisarri, who was sent by the King of Spain to search the area for gold. The home is elegant, yet maintains a rustic, Spanish charm with exposed beams, walls up to 30 inches thick, brick floors and adobe fireplaces. Along with a sitting room and kiva fireplace, the Don Pablo Suite includes a "ducking door" that leads onto the courtyard. Other rooms have clawfoot tubs, antique iron beds or a private patio. The cuisine is notable and one of the inn's recipes appeared in Culinary Trends magazine. Guests might sample a green chile soufflé along with bread pudding and fresh fruit.

Innkeeper(s): Ann Dunlap & Melinda Moffitt. $95-125. MC VISA AX DS PC TC. TAC10. 5 rooms with PB, 5 with FP. 1 suite. Breakfast included in rates. Types of meals: full breakfast and early coffee/tea. Beds: KQT. Air conditioning and ceiling fan in room. VCR, fax, spa and swimming on premises. Family reunions and seminars hosted. Antiques, fishing, parks, shopping, downhill skiing, cross-country skiing, sporting events and theater nearby.

W.E. Mauger Estate

701 Roma Ave NW
Albuquerque, NM 87102-2038
(505)242-8755 Fax:(505)842-8835

Circa 1897. This former boarding house is now an elegantly restored Victorian in the National Register. Rooms are done in Victorian style with views of downtown Albuquerque and the Sandia Mountains beyond. The second floor is decorated with antiques and lace. The inn is located six blocks from the convention center, which includes Civic Plaza, an aquarium, botanical garden, museum and free trolley service.

Historic Interest: Albuquerque is full of unique museums, featuring topics from Native American culture to the atomic age.

Innkeeper(s): Mark Brown & Keith Lewis. $89-149. MC VISA AX. 8 rooms with PB. 1 conference room. Breakfast included in rates. Types of meals: full breakfast and early coffee/tea. Evening snack available. Beds: KQDT. Phone, air conditioning and ceiling fan in room. VCR on premises. Small meetings and family reunions hosted. Amusement parks, antiques, shopping and theater nearby.

Location: Central Albuquerque between downtown and old town.

Publicity: *Albuquerque Journal, Phoenix Home and Garden, Albuquerque Monthly, National Geographic Traveler, New Mexico Business Week, Golf Digest, Great Estates.*

"Because of your hospitality, kindness and warmth, we will always compare the quality of our experience by the W.E. Mauger Estate."

The W.J. Marsh House Victorian B&B

301 Edith Blvd SE
Albuquerque, NM 87102-3532
(505)247-1001 (888)956-2774

Circa 1892. This three-story brick Queen Anne mansion is located in the Huning Highland Historic District. Original redwood doors and trim, porcelain fixtures and an ornate hand-carved fireplace are highlighted by high Victorian decor. A friendly ghost is said to inhabit the house, occasionally opening drawers and rearranging the furniture. The inn is listed in the National and State Historic Registers.

Innkeeper(s): Janice Lee Sperling, MD. $90-120. MC VISA TC. TAC10. 6 rooms, 1 with FP. Breakfast included in rates. Type of meal: gourmet breakfast. Picnic lunch available. Beds: QDT. Air conditioning in room. Library on premises. Weddings, small meetings, family reunions and seminars hosted. French and Spanish spoken. Amusement parks, antiques, fishing, parks, shopping, downhill skiing, cross-country skiing, sporting events, theater and watersports nearby.

Location: In one of Albuquerque's four historic districts, Huning Highland.

Publicity: *Albuquerque Monthly.*

"We even have a ghost!"

Bernalillo
D5

La Hacienda Grande

21 Baros Ln
Bernalillo, NM 87004
(505)867-1887 (800)353-1887 Fax:(505)771-1436
E-mail: lhg@swcp.com

Circa 1711. The rooms in this historic adobe inn surround a central courtyard. The first European trekked across the grounds as early as 1540. The land was part of a 1711 land grant from Spain, and owned by descendants of the original family until the innkeepers purchased it. The decor is Southwestern, and each bedchamber is filled with beautiful, rustic furnishings. One includes an iron high-poster bed and Jacuzzi tub, and others offer a kiva fireplace. Breakfasts are served in a dining room decorated with wood beams and a brick floor.

Innkeeper(s): Shoshana Zimmerman. $99-129. MC VISA AX DS TC. 6 rooms with PB, 5 with FP. 1 conference room. Breakfast included in rates. Types of meals: full breakfast and early coffee/tea. Beds: KQDT. Phone, air conditioning and TV in room. VCR, fax, copier and library on premises. Weddings, small meetings, family reunions and seminars hosted. Spanish spoken. Antiques, fishing, parks, shopping, downhill skiing, cross-country skiing, sporting events, theater and watersports nearby.

Cimarron   B7

Casa Del Gavilan

PO Box 518, Hwy 21 S
Cimarron, NM 87714-0518
(505)376-2246 (800)428-4526 Fax:(505)376-2247

Circa 1910. In a pueblo revival style, Casa del Gavilan (house of the hawk), was built by J. J. Nairn, an eastern industrialist. Overlooking the Santa Fe Trail, it is in the foothills of the Sangre de Cristo Mountains. The "Tooth of Time" peak rises in the distance, while views of the valley and grasslands are to the east. The home once served as a center for hospitality in the region, and hosted author Will James and many other artists and writers. A plethora of porches and gardens provide pleasant places from which to enjoy the views. Museum quality antiques and paintings add to the authentic Southwest experience provided by the home's 18-inch-thick walls and 12-foot ceilings. Guests enjoy hearty breakfasts from the patio or dining room. The Kit Carson home is nearby.

Innkeeper(s): Bob and Helen Hittle. $70-100. MC VISA AX DS. TAC10. 6 rooms, 4 with PB, 1 with FP. 1 suite. 1 conference room. Breakfast included in rates. Type of meal: full breakfast. Beds: KQ. Ceiling fan in room. Fax, copier and library on premises. Handicap access. Weddings, small meetings and family reunions hosted. Antiques, fishing, downhill skiing, cross-country skiing and golf nearby.

"Thank you for the wonderful visit and great accommodations. We enjoyed the history of the Casa and the area. The food and service was outstanding and we felt totally at home. Can't wait to come back again."

Galisteo   D6

The Galisteo Inn

9 La Vega, H C 75, Box 4
Galisteo, NM 87540-9701
(505)466-4000 Fax:(505)466-4008
E-mail: galisteoin@aol.com

Circa 1740. In the historic Spanish village of Galisteo, this adobe hacienda is surrounded by giant cottonwoods. The inn features a comfortable Southwestern decor, a library and eight fireplaces. Located on eight acres, there is a duck pond and a creek (the Galisteo River) forms the boundary of the property. Sophisticated cuisine includes dishes such as chile-seared salmon with cucumber yogurt cream and tomato relish or shrimp and tortilla bisque. Chocolate espresso cheese-cake is one of the mouth-watering deserts.

Historic Interest: Santa Fe (23 miles), petroglyphs (8 miles).

Innkeeper(s): Joanna Kaufman & Wayne Aarniokoski. $100-175. MC VISA DS PC TC. TAC10. 12 rooms, 8 with PB, 4 with FP. Breakfast included in rates. Type of meal: full breakfast. Picnic

lunch available. Beds: KQDT. Ceiling fan in room. Fax, copier, spa, swimming, sauna, stables, bicycles and library on premises. Handicap access. Weddings, small meetings, family reunions and seminars hosted. Shopping, downhill skiing, cross-country skiing and theater nearby.

Pets Allowed: Horses only.

Location: Twenty-three miles southeast of Santa Fe, one block east of Hwy 41.

Publicity: *Country Living, Physicians Lifestyle, Innsider, Chicago Tribune, Boston Globe, Orange County Register, Southern Living, Los Angeles Times, Sunset.*

"Ahhh, what peace and perfection. Thank you so very much for this magic time in a magic space."

Las Cruces   I4

T.R.H. Smith Mansion B&B

909 N Alameda Blvd
Las Cruces, NM 88005-2124
(505)525-2525 (800)526-1914 Fax:(505)524-8227
E-mail: smithmansion@zianet.com

Circa 1914. This Prairie-style mansion with its somewhat notorious past offers nearly 6,000 square feet of living area, making it the largest residence in town. The home, originally built for a local banker whose career ended in disgrace, was later the possible site of the local bordello. The mansion is rumored to house a buried treasure somewhere within its walls. There are four well-appointed guest rooms, each vastly different in style. One room features Southwestern decor with patterned walls, a Mission-style bed and a drum that serves as a table; another room is Polynesian style with a rattan bed decorated with mosquito netting. Guests will enjoy a German-style breakfast of fresh fruit, home-baked breads, smoked meats and cheese.

Innkeeper(s): Marlene & Jay Tebo. $65-95. MC VISA AX DS PC TC. TAC10. 4 rooms, 2 with PB, 1 with FP. Breakfast included in rates. Type of meal: gourmet breakfast. Beds: KQ. Phone, air conditioning, turndown service and ceiling fan in room. TV, VCR, fax and library on premises. Weddings, small meetings, family reunions and seminars hosted. German spoken. Antiques, parks, shopping, sporting events, golf and theater nearby.

Publicity: *Las Cruces, N.M., News*

Santa Fe   C6

Adobe Abode

202 Chapelle St
Santa Fe, NM 87501-1812
(505)983-3133 Fax:(505)986-0972
E-mail: adobebnb@sprynet.com

Circa 1907. Four blocks from the plaza, a purple gate welcomes guests to this beautifully appointed inn, originally officers' quarters for Fort Marcy. Adobe Abode's sophisticated yet casual decor has garnered attention from a variety of national press. Ask for the Cactus Room for a pleasing combination of handloomed fabrics, white-washed vigas, fireplace, a private patio and oversized shower. For something different in Santa Fe, try the English Garden Room with a French mirrored armoire, romantic curved brass bed and designer linens. Enjoy the fragrance of pinon in the fireplace along with refreshments

of Santa Fe cookies and sherry. Green Chile Soufflé and home-made gingerbread muffins are breakfast specialties.

Innkeeper(s): Pat Harbour. $110-150. MC VISA DS PC TC. TAC10. 6 rooms with PB, 2 with FP. 1 suite. 3 cottages. Breakfast included in rates. Types of meals: gourmet breakfast and early coffee/tea. Beds: QT. Phone, ceiling fan and TV in room. Fax on premises. Handicap access. Small meetings hosted. Spanish and French spoken. Antiques, fishing, parks, downhill skiing, cross-country skiing, golf and theater nearby.

Publicity: *Mirabella, Better Homes & Gardens, Bride's, National Geographic Traveler.*

"Adobe Abode was really a delight in this land of enchantment."

Alexander's Inn

529 E Palace Ave
Santa Fe, NM 87501-2200
(505)986-1431 (888)321-5123 Fax:(505)982-8572
E-mail: alexandinn@aol.com

Circa 1903. Twin gables and a massive front porch are prominent features of this Craftsman-style brick and wood inn. French and American country decor, stained-glass windows and a selection of antiques create a light Victorian touch. The inn also fea-

tures beautiful gardens of roses and lilacs. This exquisite Southwest adobe casita is a favorite for families and romantic getaways. Breakfast is often served in the backyard garden. Home-baked treats are offered to guests in the afternoon.

Historic Interest: Puye Cliffs, Bandalier and Pecos National Monument all are within one-half mile from the inn.

Innkeeper(s): Carolyn Lee. $75-200. EP. MC VISA PC TC. TAC10. 9 rooms, 7 with PB, 5 with FP. 1 suite. 3 cottages. Breakfast and afternoon tea included in rates. Types of meals: continental-plus breakfast, gourmet breakfast and early coffee/tea. Beds: KQT. Phone, TV and VCR in room. Fax, spa, bicycles, library and child care on premises. Weddings and family reunions hosted. French spoken. Antiques, fishing, parks, shopping, downhill skiing, cross-country skiing, theater and watersports nearby.

Pets Allowed: Well behaved.

Publicity: *New Mexican, Glamour, Southwest Art, San Diego Union Tribune.*

"Thanks to the kindness and thoughtfulness of the staff, our three days in Santa Fe were magical."

Casa De La Cuma B&B

105 Paseo De La Cuma
Santa Fe, NM 87501
(505)983-1717 (888)366-1717 Fax:(505)988-2883
E-mail: casacuma@swcp.com

Circa 1940. These two locations offer different types of travel experiences. The Chapelle Street Casitas has private suites with fully equipped and furnished kitchens, living rooms and bedrooms with hand-crafted Southwestern-style furniture. The Casitas is located in the heart of the historic district and is four blocks from the Plaza, which is the center of activity in Santa Fe. Casa De La Cuma B&B has three unique rooms decorated with Navajo textiles, original artwork and Southwestern-period furniture. The inn offers views of the Sangre De Cristo Mountains and is also within walking distance of the Plaza.

Historic Interest: The inn is located on the same hill as the original cross which honors Spanish priests killed during the 1680 pueblo revolt.

Innkeeper(s): Arthur & Donna Bailey. $65-145. MC VISA PC TC. TAC10. 8 rooms, 6 with PB. 5 suites. Breakfast and evening snack included in rates. Type of meal: continental-plus breakfast. Afternoon tea available. Beds: KQT. Phone, air conditioning, ceiling fan and TV in room. Fax on premises. Spanish spoken. Antiques, parks and downhill skiing nearby.

Publicity: *Denver Post.*

"Their pleasant nature, helpful hints for visitors and genuine hospitality were memorable and valuable to us."

Don Gaspar Compound

623 Don Gaspar Ave
Santa Fe, NM 87501-4427
(505)986-8664 (888)986-8664 Fax:(505)986-0696
E-mail: dongaspar@sfol.com

Circa 1912. This lush, peaceful hideaway is located within one of Santa Fe's first historic districts. Within the Compounds surrounding adobe walls are brick pathways meandering through beautiful gardens, emerald lawns, trees and eight fountains. The elegant Southwestern decor is an idyllic match for the warmth and romance of the grounds. For those seeking privacy, the innkeepers offer the Main House, a historic Mission-style home perfect for a pair of romantics or a group as large as six. The house has three bedrooms, two bathrooms, a fully equipped kitchen and two woodburning fireplaces. In addition to the main house, there are three suites in a Territorial-style home with thick walls and polished wood floors. There also are two private casitas, each with a gas-burning fireplace. The Fountain Casita includes a fully equipped kitchen, while the Courtyard Casita offers a double whirlpool tub. All accommodations include a TV, telephone, microwave and refrigerators.

Historic Interest: The inn is a short walk from Santa Fe's historic plaza, as well as several museums.

Innkeeper(s): Kim Van Deman. $85-245. MC VISA AX PC TC. TAC10. 6 rooms with PB, 3 with FP. 5 suites. 1 cottage. Breakfast included in rates. Type of meal: continental-plus breakfast. Beds: KQ. Phone, air conditioning and turndown service in room. Fax and copier on premises. Weddings and family reunions hosted. Antiques, fishing, parks, shopping, downhill skiing, cross-country skiing, sporting events, theater and watersports nearby.

Location: Near the plaza in Santa Fe.

"Everything was simply perfect."

Dunshee's

986 Acequia Madre
Santa Fe, NM 87501-2819
(505)982-0988

Circa 1930. Where better could one experience Santa Fe's rich history than in an authentic adobe casita or a restored adobe home? Innkeeper Susan Dunshee offers accommodations in both. Guests can stay in the adobe home's spacious suite or rent the casita by the day, week or month. The casita offers two bedrooms, a kitchen, a living room warmed by a rustic, Kiva fireplace and a private patio. The antique-filled rooms are decorated in a warm, Santa Fe style, and bedrooms sport a more country look. Guests who opt for the bed & breakfast suite are treated to Southwestern breakfasts with items such as a

green chile soufflé. The refrigerator at the casita is stocked with treats for the guests' breakfast.

Innkeeper(s): Susan Dunshee. $125. MC VISA PC TC. 3 rooms, 2 with PB, 3 with FP. 1 suite. 1 cottage. Breakfast included in rates. Types of meals: continental-plus breakfast, full breakfast, gourmet breakfast and early coffee/tea. Beds: QD. Phone and TV in room. Library on premises. Weddings, small meetings and family reunions hosted. Antiques, parks, shopping, downhill skiing, cross-country skiing and theater nearby.

El Paradero

220 W Manhattan Ave
Santa Fe, NM 87501-2622
(505)988-1177
E-mail: elpara@trail.com

Circa 1820. This was originally a two-bedroom Spanish farmhouse that doubled in size to a Territorial style in 1860, was

remodeled as a Victorian in 1912, and became a Pueblo Revival in 1920. All styles are present and provide a walk through many years of history.

Historic Interest: Indian Ruins, Pueblos.

Innkeeper(s): Ouida MacGregor & Thomas Allen. $60-135. MC VISA. TAC10. 14 rooms, 10 with PB, 5 with FP. 2 suites. 1 conference room. Breakfast and afternoon tea included in rates. Types of meals: gourmet breakfast and early coffee/tea. Beds: QT. Phone and air conditioning in room. TV on premises. Fishing, shopping, cross-country skiing and theater nearby.

Pets Allowed: Only by prearrangements and only in certain rooms.

Location: Downtown.

Publicity: *Innsider, Country Inns, Outside, Sunset, New York Times, Los Angeles Times, Travel & Leisure, America West, Travel & Holiday.*

"I'd like to LIVE here."

Four Kachinas Inn

512 Webber St
Santa Fe, NM 87501-4454
(505)982-2550 (800)397-2564 Fax:(505)989-1323

Circa 1910. This new inn is built in the Victorian and pitched-tin roof style around a private courtyard. Rooms are decorated with Southwestern art and crafts, including Navajo rugs, Hopi Kachina dolls, saltillo tile floors and handmade wooden furniture. Three bedrooms have individual garden patios, while a fourth looks out at the Sangre de Cristo Mountains. Two additional rooms are located in the cottage, which was also built in 1910. Breakfast, delivered to the rooms, features the inn's award-winning baked goods.

Historic Interest: Santa Fe Plaza (4 1/2 blocks).

Innkeeper(s): John Daw & Andrew Beckerman. $68-130. MC VISA DS. 6 rooms with PB. Breakfast and afternoon tea included in rates. Type of meal: continental-plus breakfast. Beds: KQT. Handicap access. Antiques, fishing, downhill skiing, cross-country skiing and theater nearby.

Location: Quiet neighborhood on fringe of downtown, short walk to historic Santa Fe Plaza.

Publicity: *Rocky Mountain News, New York Times, Travel & Leisure, Denver Post.*

"We found the room to be quiet and comfortable and your hospitality to be very gracious. We also really enjoyed breakfast, especially the yogurt!"

Grant Corner Inn

122 Grant Ave
Santa Fe, NM 87501-2031
(505)983-6678 Fax:(505)984-9003

Circa 1905. Judge Robinson and his family lived here for 30 years and many couples were married in the parlor. Still a romantic setting, the inn is secluded by a garden with willow trees, and there is a white

picket fence. Rooms are appointed with antique furnishings and the personal art collections of the innkeeper.

Historic Interest: Bandelier and Pecos National Monuments, Indian Pueblos.

Innkeeper(s): Louise Stewart. $70-155. MC VISA. 12 rooms, 10 with PB, 1 with FP. 1 suite. 1 conference room. Breakfast included in rates. Type of meal: gourmet breakfast. Catering service and room service available. Beds: KQT. Copier on premises. Handicap access. Antiques, fishing, downhill skiing, cross-country skiing and theater nearby.

Publicity: *New England Bride, Galveston Daily News.*

"The very best of everything — comfort, hospitality, food and T.L.C."

Inn of The Turquoise Bear

342 E Buena Vista St
Santa Fe, NM 87501
(505)983-0798 (800)396-4104 Fax:(505)988-4225
E-mail: bluebear@roadrunner.com

Circa 1880. Tall ponderosa pines shade this rambling Spanish Pueblo Revival adobe, giving it the feeling of being in a mountain setting, although it's only blocks from the plaza. In the National Register, it was the home of poet and essayist Witter Bynner, when it hosted a myriad of celebrities including Edna St. Vincent Millay, Robert Frost, Ansel Adams, Rita Hayworth, Errol Flynn and Georgia O'Keeffe. The walled acre of grounds includes flagstone paths, wild roses, lilacs, rock terraces and stone benches and fountains. In a Southwest decor, there are kiva fireplaces and romantic courtyards. The Shaman room has a king lodgepole bed, viga beams and a picture window with garden views. Guests are invited to enjoy wine and cheese in the afternoon. Museums, galleries, restaurants and shops are within walking distance.

$90-175. MC VISA AX DS PC TC. TAC10. 11 rooms, 9 with PB, 10 with FP. 1 suite. 1 conference room. Breakfast and evening snack included in rates. Type of meal: continental-plus breakfast. Beds: KQDT. Phone, air conditioning, TV and VCR in room. Fax, library and child care on premises. Weddings, small meetings, family reunions and seminars hosted. Spanish, French, German and Norwegian spoken. Antiques, fishing, parks, shopping, downhill skiing, cross-country skiing, golf and theater nearby.

Pets Allowed: small, well-behaved.

Publicity: *Santa Fe New Mexican, Hidden New Mexico.*

"Staying at your inn was a vacation and history lesson we will always remember!"

Preston House

106 Faithway St
Santa Fe, NM 87501
(505)982-3465 (888)877-7622 Fax:(505)988-2397
E-mail: prestonhse@aol.com

Circa 1886. This gracious 19th-century home is the only authentic example of Queen Anne architecture in Santa Fe. Owner Signe Bergman is also a well-known artist and designer. Her skills have created a wonderful Victorian atmosphere with period furnishings, bright wallpapers and beds covered with down quilts. Afternoon tea is a must, as Signe serves up a mouth-watering array of cakes, pies, cookies and tarts. Preston House, which is located in downtown Santa Fe, is within walking distance of the Plaza.

Innkeeper(s): Ann Leighton. $48-167. PC TC. 8 rooms, 6 with PB, 4 with FP. 2 cottages. 1 conference room. Breakfast and afternoon tea included in rates. Types of meals: continental-plus breakfast and early coffee/tea. Beds: KQDT. Phone, ceiling fan and TV in room. Fax and copier on premises. Weddings, small meetings, family reunions and seminars hosted. Spanish spoken. Antiques, fishing, parks, shopping, downhill skiing, cross-country skiing and theater nearby.

Pets Allowed.

"We were extremely pleased — glad we found you. We shall return."

Santa Fe (Algodones) D5

Hacienda Vargas

PO Box 307
Santa Fe (Algodones), NM 87001-0307
(505)867-9115 (800)261-0006 Fax:(505)867-1902
E-mail: hacvar@swcp.com

Circa 1840. Nestled among the cottonwoods and mesas of the middle Rio Grande Valley, Hacienda Vargas has seen two centuries of Old West history. It once served as a trading post for Native Americans as well as a 19th-century stagecoach stop between Santa Fe and Mesilla. The grounds contain an adobe chapel, courtyard and gardens. The main house features five kiva fireplaces, Southwest antiques, Spanish tile, a library, art gallery and suites with private Jacuzzis.

Historic Interest: Gronado Monument, Indian Ruins (5 miles), Bandelier National Park (40 miles).

Innkeeper(s): Paul & Jule De Vargas. $79-149. MC VISA PC TC. TAC10. 7 rooms with PB, 7 with FP. 4 suites. Breakfast included in rates. Type of meal: full breakfast. Beds: QT. Air conditioning and ceiling fan in room. Weddings and family reunions hosted. Spanish and German spoken. Antiques, fishing, shopping, downhill skiing, sporting events, theater and watersports nearby.

Location: Twenty-two miles north of Albuquerque, 22 miles south of Santa Fe.

Publicity: *Vogue, San Francisco Chronicle, Albuquerque Journal.*

"This is the best! Breakfast was the best we've ever had!"

Taos B6

Casa Benavides Inn

137 Kit Carson Rd
Taos, NM 87571-5949
(505)758-1772 (800)552-1772 Fax:(505)758-5738
E-mail: casabena@newmex.com

Circa 1860. Six individual homes comprise Casa Benavides, in the National Register, and the architecture ranges from traditional adobe to Western Victorian. Five of the buildings are in the adobe style, and the rooms are furnished with handmade beds, benches and chairs, as well as antiques. Hardwood floors, Mexican pavers, and flagstone floors create a backdrop for the beautifully woven Indian rugs. There are kiva fireplaces and viga ceilings, skylights, balconies, patios, flower beds and hot tubs. If traveling with more than two people, you may wish to request White Buckskin Apartment with two bedrooms. The amenities here include an armoire, two full baths, two patios, three TVs, a kitchen, Bob Timberlake linens, a living room with a white queen sofa, Indian art objects and an outdoor hot tub. Afternoon tea is available to the inn's guests, and breakfast is Mexican eggs with salsa and homemade tortillas or waffles, the innkeeper's homemade granola or French toast. Walk to restaurants, museums or the inn's gift shops.

Innkeeper(s): Tom & Barbara McCarthy. $80-195. MC VISA AX PC TC. TAC10. 31 rooms with PB, 14 with FP. 3 suites. 1 cottage. 2 conference rooms. Breakfast included in rates. Types of meals: full breakfast, gourmet breakfast and early coffee/tea. Afternoon tea available. Beds: KQT. Air conditioning, ceiling fan, TV and VCR in room. Fax, copier, spa and child care on premises. Handicap access. Weddings, small meetings, family reunions and seminars hosted. English & Spanish spoken. Antiques, fishing, parks, shopping, downhill skiing, cross-country skiing, golf and theater nearby.

Publicity: *Sunset, Insider.*

Casa Europa Inn & Gallery

H C 68, Box 3 F, 840 Upper Ranchito
Taos, NM 87571
(505)758-9798 (888)758-9798

Circa 1700. Guests will appreciate both the elegance and history at Casa Europa. The home is a 17th-century pueblo-adobe creation with heavy beams, walls three-feet thick and a dining room with a massive kiva fireplace. Freshly baked pastries are served in the afternoons, and during ski season, hors d'oeuvres are provided in the early evening. European antiques fill the rooms, which are decorated in an elegant, Southwestern style. The French Room offers an 1860 bed, kiva fireplace and French doors opening onto the courtyard. Other rooms offer a fireplace, whirlpool tub or private hot tub. The five-room Apartment Suite includes a kitchen-dining room, sitting room with a kiva fireplace, bedroom and a private hot tub. The inn is 1.6 miles from Taos Plaza.

Innkeeper(s): Rudi & Marcia Zwicker. $75-135. MC VISA PC TC. TAC10. 7 rooms with PB, 6 with FP. 2 suites. 2 conference rooms. Breakfast included in rates. Types of meals: full breakfast, gourmet breakfast and early coffee/tea. Afternoon tea and evening snack available. Beds: KQT. Phone, turndown service, ceiling fan and TV in room. Spa and sauna on premises. Small meetings and family reunions hosted. German and Spanish spoken. Antiques, fishing, parks, shopping, downhill skiing, cross-country skiing, theater and watersports nearby.

Pets Allowed: Outside only.

Hacienda Del Sol

PO Box 177
Taos, NM 87571
(505)758-0287
E-mail: sunhouse@newmex.com

Circa 1810. Mabel Dodge, patron of the arts, purchased this old hacienda as a hideaway for her Native American husband, Tony Luhan. The  spacious adobe sits among huge cottonwoods, blue spruce, and ponderosa pines, with an uninterrupted view of the mountains across 95,000 acres of Native American Indian lands. Among Dodge's famous guests were Georgia O'Keefe, who painted here, and D. H. Lawrence. The mood is tranquil and on moonlit nights guests can hear Indian drums and the howl of coyotes.

Historic Interest: Taos Pueblo (2 miles), Bandelier National Monument (60 miles), Puye Cliffs (53 miles).

Innkeeper(s): John & Marcine Landon. $80-135. PC TC. TAC10. 9 rooms with PB, 8 with FP. 2 suites. Breakfast and evening snack included in rates. Types of meals: full breakfast and early coffee/tea. Beds: KQT. TV, fax, spa and library on premises. Handicap access. Weddings, small meetings, family reunions and seminars hosted. Antiques, fishing, parks, shopping, downhill skiing, cross-country skiing, theater and watersports nearby.

Location: North of Santa Fe at the base of Sangre de Cristo Mountains.

Publicity: *Chicago Tribune, Los Angeles Daily News, Denver Post, Globe & Mail.*

"Your warm friendliness and gracious hospitality have made this week an experience we will never forget!"

The Inn on La Loma Plaza

PO Box 4159, 102 La Loma Plaza
Taos, NM 87571
(505)758-1717 (800)530-3040 Fax:(505)751-0155
E-mail: laloma@taoswebb.com

Circa 1800. Some of the walls of this hacienda were built originally as protection against Comanche, Apache and Ute Native American tribes. The Pueblo Revival-style inn is in the National Register, and its location is in La Loma Plaza, one of the oldest residential plazas in the West. Gardens, cottonwood trees and a spacious green lawn invite guests to enter. The inn's sunroom affords views of the mountains, and is furnished with a kiva fireplace, benches and a fountain. This is where breakfast and refreshments are served. Southwestern fabrics, woven rugs, local art and hand-crafted furniture fill the rooms. Some accommodations offer private patios, and all have fireplaces. There are seven breakfast menus — one for each day of the week. For instance, if it's Tuesday, it must be Green Chile Strata. Sundays bring forth Breakfast Burritos with Jerry's green sauce and jack and cheddar cheeses. Visit some of the town's 80 art galleries, seven museums, the nearby Taos Pueblo (resided in for more than 800 years), the Kit Carson House or the famous Saint Francis de Assisi Church.

Innkeeper(s): Jerry & Peggy Davis. $75-195. MC VISA AX PC TC. TAC10. 7 rooms with PB, 7 with FP. 2 suites. Breakfast and evening snack included in rates. Types of meals: gourmet breakfast and early coffee/tea. Beds: KQ. Phone, air conditioning and TV in room. VCR, fax and library on premises. Antiques, fishing, parks, shopping, downhill skiing, cross-country skiing, golf, theater and watersports nearby.

Publicity: *Outside, Chicago Tribune, Denver Post, Romantic Getaways, Sunset.*

"Your hospitality while we were there exceeded what we've ever experienced at a B&B."

La Posada De Taos

PO Box 1118
Taos, NM 87571-1118
(505)758-8164 (800)645-4803 Fax:(505)751-3294
E-mail: laposada@taos.newmex.com

Circa 1907. This secluded adobe is located just a few blocks from the plaza in the Taos historic district. Rooms are decorated in a romantic Southwestern style with country pine antiques, quilts and polished wood or tile floors. Most of the guest rooms include a kiva fireplace, and some offer private patios. For those in search of solitude, ask about the innkeeper's separate honeymoon house. Guests can walk to galleries, museums, shops and restaurants.

Innkeeper(s): Bill & Nancy Swan. $75-120. PC TC. 6 rooms with PB, 5 with FP. 1 conference room. Breakfast included in rates. Type of meal: full breakfast. Beds: KQ. Ceiling fan in room. TV, VCR, fax, copier and library on premises. Handicap access. Weddings, small meetings and family reunions hosted. Antiques, fishing, parks, shopping, downhill skiing, cross-country skiing, theater and watersports nearby.

Publicity: *New York Times, Bon Appetit, Country Inns, Glamour, Los Angeles Times.*

"I want to tell you how much we enjoyed our visit with you at La Posada De Taos in September. It was definitely the highlight of our trip."

Old Taos Guesthouse

1028 Witt Rd, Box 6552
Taos, NM 87571
(505)758-5448 (800)758-5448

Circa 1850. This adobe hacienda sits on a rise overlooking Taos and is surrounded by large cottonwood, blue spruce, apple, apricot and pinon trees. This estate, which offers panoramic views, originally served as a farmer's home, but later was home to an artist. As the years went by, rooms were added. Most rooms include special items such as kiva fireplaces, hand-

woven wall hangings, dried flowers, log four-poster beds and hand-painted vanities. The Southwestern-style rooms all have private entrances. The outdoor hot tub boasts a wonderful view. Healthy, homemade breakfasts are served in a room filled with antiques. The home is set on more than seven acres, located less than two miles from the Plaza.

Historic Interest: There is a historic acequia irrigation ditch that runs through the grounds. Nearby attractions include a 1,000-year-old Taos Pueblo, Martinez Hacienda, the Kit Carson House and St. Francis de Assisi church. The Bandelier National Monument Cliff Dwellings are about an hour from Taos.

Innkeeper(s): Tim & Leslie Reeves. $70-115. MC VISA PC TC. 9 rooms with PB, 5 with FP. 2 suites. Breakfast included in rates. Types of meals: continental-plus breakfast and early coffee/tea. Beds: KQT. Spa, stables and library on premises. Spanish and German spoken. Antiques, fishing, parks, shopping, downhill skiing, cross-country skiing and theater nearby.

Publicity: *Denver Post Travel, Inn for the Night, Dallas Morning News, West, Country, Houston Chronicle.*

"We really enjoyed the authenticity of your guesthouse."

Orinda B&B

Box 4451
Taos, NM 87571
(505)758-8581 (800)847-1837 Fax:(505)751-4895
E-mail: orinda@newmex.com

Circa 1935. Current innkeepers Cary and George Pratt are only the fourth owners of this property, which was deeded to its original owners by Abraham Lincoln. The house itself, a sculptured adobe, was built years later, and features a Southwestern flair with kiva fireplaces. Cary serves up family-style flavorful breakfasts such as breakfast burritos or strawberry crunch French toast. Many of the inn's picture windows afford views of Taos Mountain.

Historic Interest:
The Kit Carson Home is a 15-minute walk from the bed & breakfast. Taos Pueblo and Martinez Hacienda are within easy driving distance, and the vil-

lage of Taos offers many historic sites. Art galleries, museums, skiing, hiking, biking, riding, golf and fishing are all located nearby.

Innkeeper(s): Cary & George Pratt. $70-90. MC VISA AX DS PC TC. TAC10. 4 rooms with PB, 1 with FP. 1 suite. Breakfast and evening snack included in rates. Beds: QDT. TV, VCR and fax on premises. Weddings and family reunions hosted. Antiques, fishing, shopping, downhill skiing, cross-country skiing and golf nearby.

"It really is 'a B&B paradise' with your beautiful surroundings."

Taos Country Inn

PO Box 2331
Taos, NM 87571-2331
(505)758-4900 (800)866-6548 Fax:(505)758-0331
E-mail: taoscountryinn@newmex.com

Circa 1850. Nestled among 200-year-old towering willows and cottonwoods on more than 20 acres of pasture land and cultivated gardens, this adobe-style inn offers both the luxury of modern amenities and the rustic charm of its historic past. There are nine spacious suites decorated in leather sofas, down comforters, and all featuring sweeping mountain or river views. Close to the historic Plaza, museums and Indian Pueblo.

Innkeeper(s): Yolanda Deveaux. $100-140. MC VISA PC. TAC10. 8 rooms with PB, 8 with FP. Breakfast included in rates. Types of meals: full breakfast, gourmet breakfast and early coffee/tea. Beds: KQT. Phone and TV in room. VCR, fax and copier on premises. 22 acres. Weddings, small meetings and family reunions hosted. Spanish and French spoken. Antiques, fishing, shopping, downhill skiing, cross-country skiing and golf nearby.

The Taos Inn

125 Paseo Del Pueblo Norte
Taos, NM 87571-5901
(505)758-2233 (800)826-7466 Fax:(505)758-5776
E-mail: taosinn@taos.newmex.com

Circa 1880. The Taos Inn is a historic landmark with sections dating back to the 1600s. It is a rustic wood and adobe setting with wood-burning fireplaces, vigas and wrought iron. The exotic tri-cultural heritage of Spanish, Anglo and Indian is dis-

played in hand-loomed Indian bedspreads, antique armoires, Taos furniture and Pueblo Indian fireplaces.

Innkeeper(s): Carolyn Haddock. $75-225. MC VISA AX DC PC TC. TAC10. 36 rooms with PB. 3 suites. Breakfast included in rates. Types of meals: continental breakfast, continental-plus breakfast, full breakfast, gourmet breakfast and early coffee/tea. Dinner, evening snack, picnic lunch, lunch, gourmet lunch and banquet service available. Restaurant on premises. Beds: KQDT. Phone, air conditioning and TV in room. Fax, copier, spa and swimming on premises. Handicap access. Weddings, small meetings and family reunions hosted. Antiques, fishing, parks, shopping, downhill skiing, cross-country skiing and watersports nearby.

Location: A quarter-block north of historic Taos Plaza.

Publicity: *Bon Appetit, Toronto Sun, New York Times, Travel & Leisure.*

"It is charming, warm, friendly and authentic in decor with a real sense of history."

The Willows Inn

412 Kit Carson Rd at Dolan St
Taos, NM 87571
(505)758-2558 (800)525-8267 Fax:(505)758-5445
E-mail: willows@taos.newmex.com

Circa 1926. This authentic, Southwestern-style adobe was once home to artist E. Martin Hennings, a member of the Taos Society of Artists. Each of the rooms features a unique theme, including Hennings' Studio, which was the artist's workplace. The studio boasts a seven-foot headboard, high ceilings and private patio. The Santa Fe Room is decked in contemporary, Southwestern style and has a sitting area. Each of the rooms includes a kiva fireplace. The Conquistador Room reflects old Spanish decor with an antique chest, equipale couch and ropero. The Cowboy and Anasazi rooms include artifacts such as a cowhide rug,
handmade quilts,
Zuni kachinas and
hand-crafted pottery. Breakfasts are
highlighted by
fresh items right
out of the inn's

herb and vegetable gardens. Afternoon refreshments are served with lively conversation as guests study menus from various Taos eateries.

Historic Interest: Taos Pueblo is less than two miles from the inn, and closer attractions include the Kit Carson Home & Museum, Mabel Dodge Luhan House, and the historic homes of several local artists. The main house, studio and lap pool are listed in the National Registry of Historic Places.

Innkeeper(s): Janet & Doug Camp. $95-130. MC VISA PC TC. TAC10. 5 rooms with PB, 5 with FP. 1 suite. Breakfast and evening snack included in rates. Types of meals: continental breakfast, continental-plus breakfast, full breakfast, gourmet breakfast and early coffee/tea. Afternoon tea available. Beds: Q. TV, VCR, fax, copier and library on premises. Weddings, small meetings, family reunions and seminars hosted. Spanish spoken. Antiques, fishing, parks, shopping, downhill skiing, cross-country skiing, golf, theater and watersports nearby.

Pets Allowed: Under 35 lbs can be boarded at nearby vet clinic.

Publicity: *New York Times, Travel Holiday, Taos Magazine, New Mexico Magazine, Sun Herald, Gulfshore Life, Mature Lifestyles.*

New York

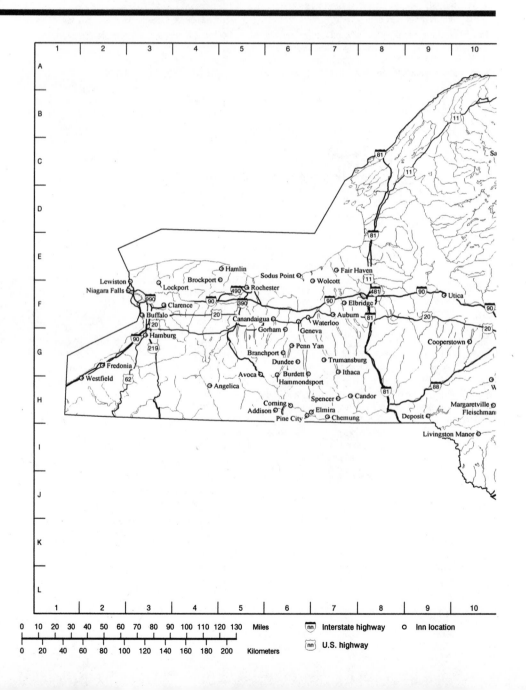

| | 1 | 2 | 3 | 4 | 5 | 6 | 7 | 8 | 9 | 10 |

Lewiston
Niagara Falls
Lockport
Clarence
Buffalo
Hamburg
Fredonia
Westfield
Brockport
Hamlin
Sodus Point
Wolcott
Rochester
Canandaigua
Gorham
Geneva
Waterloo
Penn Yan
Branchport
Dundee
Avoca
Burdett
Hammondsport
Angelica
Corning
Addison
Pine City
Elmira
Chemung
Fair Haven
Elbridge
Auburn
Trumansburg
Ithaca
Spencer
Candor
Cooperstown
Utica
Deposit
Margaretville
Fleischman
Livingston Manor
Santa

990
90
490
390
481
81
11
20
20
219
62
88
90

| 0 | 10 | 20 | 30 | 40 | 50 | 60 | 70 | 80 | 90 | 100 | 110 | 120 | 130 | Miles |

| 0 | 20 | 40 | 60 | 80 | 100 | 120 | 140 | 160 | 180 | 200 | Kilometers |

Interstate highway   Inn location

U.S. highway

338

Addison / H6

Addison Rose B&B

37 Maple St
Addison, NY 14801-1009
(607)359-4650

Circa 1892. Located on a scenic highway south of the Finger Lakes, this Queen Anne Victorian "painted lady" inn is an easy getaway from Corning or Elmira. The inn, which is listed in the National Register, was built by a doctor for his bride and was presented to her on Christmas Eve, their wedding day. The three guest rooms offer authentic Victorian furnishings. Many fine examples of Victorian architecture exist in Addison. Pinnacle State Park is just east of town.

Innkeeper(s): William & Maryann Peters. $65-85. PC TC. 3 rooms with PB. Breakfast and afternoon tea included in rates. Types of meals: gourmet breakfast and early coffee/tea. Beds: DT. Ceiling fan in room. Library on premises. Family reunions hosted. Antiques, fishing, parks, shopping and cross-country skiing nearby.

Amenia / I12

Troutbeck

Leedsville Rd
Amenia, NY 12501
(914)373-9681 Fax:(914)373-7080

Circa 1918. This English country estate on 442 wooded acres enjoyed its heyday in the '20s. The NAACP was conceived here and the literati and liberals of the period, including Teddy Roosevelt, were overnight guests. Weekend room rates include six meals on weekends and an open bar as well as luxurious accommodations for two. On Sundays, brunch is served. The

inn has a fitness center, billiard table, outdoor and indoor pools and tennis courts. During the week the inn is a corporate retreat and has been awarded Executive Retreat of the Year. In July, 1997, Troutbeck was the site of a United Nations Summitt meeting. Many weddings are held here each year and a new Great Room/ballroom has been added, which accommodates weddings with up to 250 guests and corporate gatherings for about 70 people.

Innkeeper(s): Jim Flaherty & Garret Corcoran. $650-1050. MAP. MC VISA AX PC TC. TAC5. 42 rooms, 37 with PB, 9 with FP. 8 suites. 3 conference rooms. Breakfast and dinner included in rates. Types of meals: continental breakfast, full breakfast and early coffee/tea. Evening snack, picnic lunch, banquet service, catering service and room service available. Restaurant on premises. Beds: KQDT. Phone, air conditioning and turndown service in room. TV, VCR, fax, copier, spa, swimming, sauna, tennis and library on premises. 20 acres. Weddings, family reunions and seminars hosted. Spanish, Portuguese and Italian spoken. Antiques, fishing, parks, shopping, downhill skiing, cross-country skiing, sporting events and theater nearby.

Location: Foothills of the Berkshires.

Publicity: *Good Housekeeping, New York Magazine, American Express, Vogue.*

"This 1920s-style estate makes you wish all life could be this way."

Angelica / H4

Angelica Inn

64 W Main St
Angelica, NY 14709
(716)466-3063

Circa 1886. Located in the Allegany foothills, the Angelica Inn features stained glass, crystal chandeliers, parquet floors, an oak staircase, carved woodwork, antique furnishings and scented rooms. Guest rooms offer such amenities as fireplaces, a porch and a breakfast alcove area.

Innkeeper(s): Cindy & Nick Petito. $70-85. MC VISA AX DC. 7 rooms with PB, 4 with FP. 4 suites. 1 conference room. Breakfast included in rates. Types of meals: full breakfast and early coffee/tea. Beds: KQD. TV in room. Weddings, small meetings, family reunions and seminars hosted. Antiques, fishing, shopping, downhill skiing, cross-country skiing and golf nearby.

"Victorian at its best!"

Athens / H12

Stewart House

2 N Water St
Athens, NY 12015-1406
(518)945-1357

Circa 1883. This grand Victorian on the Hudson River with a gingerbread roof was once described as the "tallest three-story building in America." The guest rooms feature high ceilings, tall windows, hand-painted walls and river views. A restaurant on the first floor serves two different menus. The centerpiece in the bistro is a classic 1930s bar where the menu is casual. The ornate dining room with its elaborate tin ceiling offers a more complex menu. Herbs and produce from the inn's garden are a large part of the cuisine.

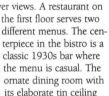

Historic Interest: Olana Home of Frederic Church (10 minutes), home of Thomas Cole, founding painter of the Hudson Valley School (8 minutes), Clermont, historic home of Robert Livingston, signer of the Declaration of Independence and founder of the Clermont, Robert Fulton's first steamboat (35 minutes).

Innkeeper(s): Kim McLean & Yura Adams. $75-95. MC VISA AX. 5 rooms with PB. Breakfast included in rates. Type of meal: full breakfast. Restaurant on premises. Beds: QD. Antiques, fishing, skiing nearby.

"The combination of wonderful meals, lovely rooms and homey feeling makes it hard to leave."

Auburn / F7

Springside Inn

PO Box 520, 41-43 W Lake Rd
Auburn, NY 13021
(315)252-7247 Fax:(315)252-4925

Circa 1830. Originally a boy's boarding school run by the first American Missionary to Japan, this four-story Victorian is now a comfortable B&B. The inn's dinner theater, operated

Wednesday through Sunday in the summer, is the first dinner theater in the northeastern United States, and it was created by the innkeepers. The Surrey Room is the public dining room, and it boasts beamed cathedral ceilings and a stone fireplace. Guest rooms feature antique beds and print curtains. Breakfast is provided in a basket and consists of muffins, fruit and coffee.

Innkeeper(s): Lois Porten & Mitchell Fanning. $65. MAP. MC VISA AX DC PC TC. TAC10. 8 rooms, 5 with PB, 3 with FP. 1 conference room. Breakfast, dinner and picnic lunch included in rates. Type of meal: continental breakfast. Banquet service available. Restaurant on premises. Beds: TD. Air conditioning and ceiling fan in room. Swimming and bicycles on premises. Weddings, small meetings, family reunions and seminars hosted. Antiques, fishing, parks, shopping, downhill skiing, cross-country skiing, golf, theater and watersports nearby. Pets Allowed: Well behaved.

Avoca   G5

Patchwork Peace B&B

4279 Waterbury Hill Rd
Avoca, NY 14809-9532
(607)566-2443

Circa 1925. Located on more than 350 acres, this clapboard farmhouse is furnished with rocking chairs, heirloom quilts and lace curtains. Pine plank floors are dotted with braided rugs.

The beautiful old barn and outbuildings on the property are thought to have been built in 1869. This is a working dairy farm, and the milk is pasteurized on the premises. There are fields of oats, hay and corn, rolling hills, pockets of forest and berry bushes. Deer and turkey sometime appear. The surrounding farms are owned by the innkeeper's children.

Innkeeper(s): Bill & Betty Mitchell. $45-70. PC TC. TAC10. 4 rooms, 1 with PB. Breakfast included in rates. Type of meal: full breakfast. Beds: QDT. Phone, air conditioning and ceiling fan in room. TV and VCR on premises. 350 acres. Antiques, fishing, parks and cross-country skiing nearby. Publicity: *Rochester Business Journal.*

Bellport   K14

Great South Bay Inn

160 S Country Rd
Bellport, NY 11713-2516
(516)286-8588 Fax:(516)286-2460

Circa 1890. Long Island's south shore is home to this Cape Cod-style inn filled with turn-of-the-century antiques. Six guest rooms are available, four with private baths and all featuring original wainscoting. Favorite relaxing spots include the private garden and the parlor with its welcoming fireplace. During the summer months, guests enjoy taking the ferry over to the village's private beach or simply, frequenting one of the local restaurants, which are open all year. The innkeepers are fluent in French and pride themselves on serving guests' individual needs, including pet accommodations or train station pick-ups. Fire Island National Seashore and the Wertheim National Wildlife Refuge are nearby.

Innkeeper(s): Judy Mortimer. $75-99. MC VISA TC. 6 rooms, 4 with PB, 1 with FP. 1 suite. Breakfast included in rates. Type of meal: full breakfast. Beds: QDT. Air conditioning, ceiling fan, TV and VCR in room. Fax and copier on premises. Weddings, small meetings, family reunions and seminars hosted. French spoken. Amusement parks, antiques, fishing, parks, shopping, golf, theater and watersports nearby.

Pets Allowed: Must always be with owners, $15 charge.

Berlin   G13

Sedgwick Inn

Rt 22, Box 250
Berlin, NY 12022
(518)658-2334 Fax:(518)658-3998

Circa 1791. The Sedgwick Inn sits on 12 acres in the Taconic Valley in the Berkshire Mountains. The main house features guest rooms, the low-ceilinged Coach Room Tavern and a glass-enclosed dining porch facing an English garden. A Colonial-style motel behind the main house sits beside a rushing brook. A converted carriage house with a hardwood dance floor and hand-hewn beams serves as a gift shop with prints, paintings, sculptures and a selection of unusual crafts and gourmet items.

Innkeeper(s): Edith Evans. $68-105. MC VISA AX DC CB DS TC. 11 rooms with PB. 1 suite. 1 conference room. Breakfast included in rates. Type of meal: full breakfast. Dinner, lunch and room service available. Restaurant on premises. Beds: KQD. Phone, ceiling fan and TV in room. VCR and fax on premises. 12 acres. Weddings, small meetings, family reunions and seminars hosted. Antiques, fishing, parks, downhill skiing, cross-country skiing, golf, theater and watersports nearby.

Pets Allowed: Pets allowed in annex.

Location: Berkshire Mountains. New York, Massachusetts border.

Publicity: *Berkshire Eagle, Hudson Valley Magazine, Albany Times Union, Good Housekeeping, USAir.*

"We were absolutely enchanted. We found this to be a charming place, a rare and wonderful treat."

Bolton Landing   E12

Hilltop Cottage B&B

4825 Lakeshore Dr, Box 186
Bolton Landing, NY 12814
(518)644-2492

Circa 1924. Located on two acres, this country farmhouse was once a summer residence for music students at Marcella Sembrich Teaching Studio. It is located on the eight mile stretch of what once was called "Millionaire's Row." There is a barn, greenhouse and ice house. Rooms are simply furnished in a homey country style. The hosts speak German and enjoy offering German Apple Pancakes and a variety of other delicious breakfast selections. Breakfast is often served on the porch, which in summer is shaded by lavish vines.

Innkeeper(s): Anita & Charlie Richards. $60-85. MC VISA PC TC. TAC10. 3 rooms, 1 with PB. 1 cottage. Breakfast included in rates. Type of meal: full breakfast. Beds: QT. Ceiling fan in room. TV and VCR on premises. German spoken. Amusement parks, antiques, fishing, parks, shopping, golf and watersports nearby.

Branchport G6

Gone With The Wind on Keuka Lake

453 W Lake Rd, Rt 54 A
Branchport, NY 14418
(607)868-4603

Circa 1887. Breezes from Keuka Lake waft up to the front porch where guests often sit with a cup of coffee. The lakeside home, a Victorian, is decorated with an eclectic, uncluttered assortment of reproductions. Each of the bathrooms features unique decor, such as oak, brass or marble. One room includes a fireplace. There's a hot tub in the solarium, and the grounds offer a gazebo by the inn's private beach cove.

Innkeeper(s): Linda & Robert Lewis. $70-125. PC TC. 11 rooms, 3 with PB, 1 with FP. 1 conference room. Breakfast included in rates. Types of meals: full breakfast and gourmet breakfast. Beds: KQ. Air conditioning and turn-down service in room. Fax, spa, swimming and tennis on premises. 14 acres. Weddings, small meetings, family reunions and seminars hosted. Antiques, fishing, parks, shopping, cross-country skiing and watersports nearby.

Location: Near Historic Hammondsport Village Square and Curtis Museum.

"Thanks once again for a delightful stay. You have a little bit of heaven here."

Brockport E5

The Victorian B&B

320 S Main St
Brockport, NY 14420-2253
(716)637-7519 (800)836-1929 Fax:(716)637-2319

Circa 1890. Within walking distance of the historic Erie Canal, this Queen Anne Victorian inn is located on Brockport's Main Street. Visitors select from eight second-floor guest rooms, all with phones, private baths and TVs. Victorian furnishings are found throughout the inn. A favorite spot is the solarium, with its three walls of windows, perfect for curling up with a book or magazine. Two first-floor sitting areas also provide relaxing havens for guests. Lake Ontario is just 10 miles away, and visitors will find much to explore in nearby Rochester.

Innkeeper(s): Sharon Kehoe. $59-98. PC TC. 8 rooms. Breakfast included in rates. Type of meal: full breakfast. Phone and air conditioning in room. TV and VCR on premises. Small meetings, family reunions and seminars hosted. Antiques, shopping, cross-country skiing, sporting events and theater nearby.

"As an unexpected guest, I was pleasantly surprised."

Buffalo F3

Beau Fleuve B&B Inn

242 Linwood Ave
Buffalo, NY 14209-1802
(716)882-6116 (800)278-0245

Circa 1881. Each of the five rooms at this Victorian mini-mansion features a different style and celebrates the ethnic groups that settled in the Buffalo area. Artifacts accented by stunning stained-glass windows render homage to the Western New York Native American tribes in the Native American common area. The French Room is dedicated to the memory of French explorer LaSalle, credited as the first European to travel through the Niagara Frontier. Absolute comfort is complete with every touch, from the queen-size antique brass bed to the Louis XIV chairs and walls both covered in champagne damask. Other elegant rooms mark the contributions of the Irish, German, Italian and Polish immigrants. Set in the Linwood Preservation District, this inn is in the middle of everything. Millionaires' Row is only one block away, in addition to nearby Niagara Falls, other historic neighborhoods, museums, art galleries, antique shops and a variety of restaurants. A friendly ambiance will remind guests why Buffalo is known as the "City of Good Neighbors." A candlelight breakfast is offered every morning.

Historic Interest: Buffalo's Allentown Historic District is less than one mile away and the magnificent Niagara Falls is 18 miles from the Beau Fleuve.

Innkeeper(s): Ramona Pando Whitaker & Rik Whitaker. $75-90. MC VISA DS TC. TAC10. 5 rooms with PB. Breakfast included in rates. Type of meal: full breakfast. Beds: QDT. Antiques, fishing, downhill skiing, cross-country skiing and theater nearby.

Publicity: Buffalo News, WIVB-TV, New York Daily News, Preservation Coalition Tour House.

"Relaxing, comfortable hospitality in beautiful surroundings."

Burdett G6

The Red House Country Inn

4586 Picnic Area Rd
Burdett, NY 14818-9716
(607)546-8566

Circa 1844. Nestled within the 16,000-acre Finger Lakes National Forest, this old farmstead has an in-ground swimming pool, large veranda overlooking groomed lawns, flower gardens and picnic areas. Pet Samoyeds and goats share the seven acres. Next to the property are acres of wild blueberry patches and stocked fishing ponds. The Red House is near Seneca Lake, world-famous Glen Gorge, and Cornell University.

Historic Interest: Corning Glass Museum, Cornell University, Watkins Glen Gorge.

Innkeeper(s): Sandy Schmanke & Joan Martin. $59-89. MC VISA AX DS. 5 rooms, 1 with FP. Breakfast and afternoon tea included in rates. Types of meals: full breakfast and early coffee/tea. Beds: QDT. Phone in room. Small meetings, family reunions and seminars hosted. Antiques, fishing, parks, shopping, cross-country skiing, sporting events, theater, watersports nearby.

Location: Finger Lakes National Forest, near Watkins Glen.

Publicity: New York Alive, Discerning Traveler, New York Magazine.

"An Inn-credible delight. What a wonderful place to stay and a difficult place to leave. It doesn't get any better than this."

Canandaigua F6

The Acorn Inn

4508 Rt 64 S
Canandaigua, NY 14424
(716)229-2834 Fax:(716)229-5046

Circa 1795. Guests to this Federal Stagecoach inn can relax before the blazing fire of a large colonial fireplace equipped with antique crane and hanging iron pots. Guest rooms, two with fireplace, are furnished with period antiques, canopy beds, luxury linens and bedding, and each has a comfortable sitting area. Books are provided in each guest room as well as in the libraries. After a day of visiting wineries, skiing, hiking in the Finger Lakes area and dinner at a local restaurant, guests can enjoy the inn's outdoor Jacuzzi. Beds are turned down each night and a carafe of ice water and chocolates are placed in each room.

Historic Interest: Erie Canal (10 miles), Ganodagan Indian Site, Grauger Homestead, Sonnenberg Gardens.

Innkeeper(s): Joan & Louis Clark. $115-175. MC VISA AX DS PC TC. TAC10. 4 rooms with PB, 2 with FP. Breakfast included in rates. Types of meals: gourmet breakfast and early coffee/tea. Beds: Q. Air conditioning, turndown service, TV and VCR in room. Fax, copier, spa and library on premises. Weddings, small meetings and family reunions hosted. Antiques, fishing, parks, shopping, skiing, theater and watersports nearby.

Publicity: *New York, Mid-Atlantic. Ratings: 4 Diamonds.*

Enchanted Rose Inn B&B

7479 Rts 5 & 20, PO BOX 128
Canandaigua, NY 14424
(716)657-6003 Fax:(716)657-4405
E-mail: enchrose@servtech.com

Circa 1820. During the restoration of this early 19th-century home, the innkeepers uncovered the many original features, including the wood floors that now glimmer. The fireplace dates

back to the 1790s, part of the original log home. The present structure was built onto the original in the 1820s. The innkeepers are only the fourth owners and have returned the home to its original glory.

Freshly cut flowers from the inn's gardens are placed in the guest rooms, which feature antiques and romantic decor. The dining room table is set with beautiful china, a perfect accompaniment to the gourmet breakfasts. Afternoon tea is served in the rose garden or in an inviting fireplaced parlor.

Historic Interest: Built in 1820s, house has original flooring and a chimney from a log cabin built in the 1790s.

Innkeeper(s): Jan & Howard Buhlmann. $95-135. MC VISA AX DS PC TC. TAC10. 3 rooms with PB. 1 suite. Breakfast included in rates. Types of meals: full breakfast, gourmet breakfast and early coffee/tea. Evening snack available. Beds: Q. Phone, air conditioning, turndown service, TV and VCR in room. Fax and library on premises. Weddings, small meetings and family reunions hosted. Antiques, fishing, parks, shopping, downhill skiing, cross-country skiing, sporting events, theater and watersports nearby.

"This has been a lovely experience, a wonderful homecoming. You leave no details overlooked."

The Sutherland House B&B Inn

Rt 21s 3179 Bristol Rd
Canandaigua, NY 14424-8341
(716)396-0375 (800)396-0375 Fax:(716)396-9281

Circa 1885. Innkeepers Cor and Diane Van Der Woude refurbished this gracious home, adding more than 40 new windows, but leaving original elements such as a winding cherry staircase and marble fireplaces. Their restoration effort has created a charming 19th-century atmosphere. Rooms feature elegant,

Victorian decor, and some boast two-person whirlpool tubs. Diane serves up a bountiful breakfast each morning. The home is just a mile and a half from Main Street Canandaigua, and wineries, antique shopping and outdoor activities are nearby.

Innkeeper(s): Cor & Diane Van Der Woude. $90-165. MC VISA AX PC. TAC10. 5 rooms with PB, 3 with FP. 1 suite. 1 conference room. Breakfast, afternoon tea and evening snack included in rates. Types of meals: continental breakfast, continental-plus breakfast, full breakfast, gourmet breakfast and early coffee/tea. Dinner, lunch, banquet service, catered breakfast and room service available. Beds: KQ. Phone, air conditioning, ceiling fan and VCR in room. Fax, copier and spa on premises. Weddings, small meetings, family reunions and seminars hosted. Dutch spoken. Antiques, fishing, parks, shopping, downhill skiing, cross-country skiing, sporting events, theater and watersports nearby.

Candor   H7

The Edge of Thyme, A B&B Inn

6 Main St
Candor, NY 13743-1615
(607)659-5155 (800)722-7365 Fax:(607)659-5155

Circa 1840. Originally the summer home of John D. Rockefeller's secretary, this two-story Georgian-style inn offers gracious accommodations a short drive from Ithaca. The inn sports many interesting features, including an impressive stairway, marble fireplaces, parquet floors, pergola (arbor) and windowed porch with leaded glass. Guests may relax in front of the inn's

fireplace, catch up with reading in its library or watch television in the sitting room. An authentic turn-of-the-century full breakfast is served, and guests also may arrange for special high teas.

Innkeeper(s): Prof. Frank & Eva Mae Musgrave. $65-80. MC VISA AX TC. 5 rooms, 2 with PB. 2 suites. Breakfast included in rates. Types of meals: full breakfast, gourmet breakfast and early coffee/tea. Afternoon tea available. Beds: KQDT. TV and VCR on premises. Weddings, small meetings, family reunions and seminars hosted. Antiques, fishing, parks, shopping, downhill skiing, cross-country skiing, sporting events and theater nearby.

Catskill Mountain/Palenville H12

Kaaterskill Creek B&B

Kaaterskill Ave, HCR 1, Box 14
Catskill Mountain/Palenville, NY 12463
(518)678-9052

Circa 1882. Breakfasts at this Colonial home are a hearty affair, served in the picturesque, glass-enclosed gazebo. Guest and common rooms are comfortable, decorated in a cozy, country style with a few antiques. On cool nights, guests often watch a good movie in the living room, which offers a huge, 10-foot fireplace to snuggle up to. The wicker-filled porch is an ideal place to relax after a day of skiing, hiking through the Catskills or shopping at auctions and flea markets.

Innkeeper(s): Joann & Steve Murrin. $55-65. MC VISA PC. 4 rooms, 1 with PB. Breakfast included in rates. Types of meals: gourmet breakfast and early coffee/tea. Beds: D. Air conditioning and VCR in room. TV on premises. Amusement parks, antiques, fishing, parks, shopping, downhill skiing, cross-country skiing and watersports nearby.

Chemung H7

Halcyon Place B&B

197 Washington St, PO Box 244
Chemung, NY 14825
(607)529-3544

Circa 1820. The innkeepers chose the name "halcyon" because it signifies tranquility and a healing richness. The historic Greek Revival inn and its grounds offer just that to guests, who will appreciate the fine period antiques,

paneled doors, six-over-six windows of hand-blown glass and wide plank floors. An herb garden and screen porch also beckon visitors. Full breakfasts may include omelets with garden ingredients, raspberry muffins, rum sticky buns or waffles. The inn's three guest rooms feature double beds, and one boasts a romantic fireplace. Fine antiquing and golfing are found nearby. During the summer months, the innkeepers host a Wednesday afternoon herb series and afternoon tea. Also ask about other special packages. The innkeepers opened an herb and antique shop in their restored barn.

Historic Interest: Sullivan's Monument (6 miles), Mark Twain's study and gravesite (12 miles).

Innkeeper(s): Douglas & Yvonne Sloan. $55-70. PC TC. 3 rooms, 1 with PB, 1 with FP. Breakfast included in rates. Type of meal: gourmet breakfast. Afternoon tea available. Beds: D. Turndown service in room. Weddings hosted. German spoken. Antiques, parks, shopping, cross-country skiing, sporting events, theater and watersports nearby.

Publicity: *Elmira Star Gazette, Chemung Valley Reporter, Evening Star.*

"We appreciate all the little touches you attend to, to make our stay special."

Chestertown D12

The Chester Inn B&B

Box 163, Main St
Chestertown, NY 12817
(518)494-4148 Fax:(518)494-7940

Circa 1830. There are 14 acres of meadow surrounding this completely restored early Greek Revival home. Yellow with white trim, there are two front porches, bordered by lilacs, that stretch across the house. Barns, a smoke house and an ancient family cemetery rests on the property. Inside, the inn's grand hall has hand-grained woodwork and mahogany railings. Country Victorian antiques combined with Laura Ashley fabrics, replica wallpapers and down comforters are features. Breakfast specialties such as skillet corn bread and vegetable soufflé with pan-fried potatoes are served by candlelight. A block away is the Main Street Ice Cream Parlor & Restaurant and Miss Hester's Emporium Gift Shop owned by the innkeepers.

Innkeeper(s): Bruce & Suzanne Robbins. $75-110. MC VISA PC TC. 5 rooms, 4 with PB. 2 suites. Breakfast and afternoon tea included in rates. Meals: full breakfast, gourmet breakfast and early coffee/tea. Beds: QDT. Air conditioning and ceiling fan in room. TV and VCR on premises. 14 acres. Weddings and family reunions hosted. Amusement parks, antiques, fishing, parks, shopping, skiing, sporting events, golf, theater, watersports nearby.

Location: National Register of Historic Places.

Publicity: *Adirondack Guide, Glens Falls Post Star.*

"We'll shout your praises!"

The Friends Lake Inn

Friends Lake Rd
Chestertown, NY 12817
(518)494-4751 Fax:(518)494-4616

Circa 1860. Formerly a boardinghouse for tanners who worked in the area, this Mission-style inn now offers its guests elegant accommodations and fine dining. Overlooking Friends Lake, the inn provides easy access

to many well-known skiing areas, including Gore Mountain. Guests are welcome to borrow a canoe for a lake outing and use the inn's private beach. Guest rooms are well-appointed and most include four-poster beds. Many have breathtaking lake views or Jacuzzis. An outdoor hot tub is a favorite spot after a busy day of recreation. The 32 km Nordic Ski Center is on site with groomed wilderness trails, lessons and rentals. Trails are available for hiking, as well.

Innkeeper(s): Sharon & Greg Taylor. $175-325. MAP. MC VISA AX PC TC. TAC10. 16 rooms with PB. Breakfast and dinner included in rates. Type of meal: full breakfast. Picnic lunch, catering service and room service available. Restaurant on premises. Beds: Q. Air conditioning and turndown service in room. TV, VCR, fax, copier, swimming and library on premises. Handicap access. 10 acres. Weddings, small meetings, family reunions and seminars hosted. Amusement parks, antiques, fishing, parks, shopping, downhill skiing, cross-country skiing, sporting events, theater and watersports nearby.

"Everyone here is so pleasant, you end up feeling like family!"

Clarence F3

Asa Ransom House

10529 Main St
Clarence, NY 14031-1684
(716)759-2315 Fax:(716)759-2791
E-mail: asaransom@aol.com

Circa 1853. Set on spacious lawns, behind a white picket fence, the Asa Ransom House rests on the site of the first grist mill built in Erie County. Silversmith Asa Ransom constructed an inn and grist mill here

in response to the Holland Land Company's offering of free land to anyone who would start and operate a tavern. A specialty of the dining room is "Veal Perrott" and "Pistachio Banana Muffins."

Historic Interest: Clarence Center Emporium (5 miles), Amherst Museum, Colony (8 miles), Theodore Roosevelt Inaugural National Historic Site (Wilcox Mansion) (16 miles).

Innkeeper(s): Robert & Judy Lenz. $95-145. MAP, EP. MC VISA DS PC TC. TAC10. 9 rooms with PB, 7 with FP. 2 suites. 1 conference room. Breakfast included in rates. Types of meals: full breakfast and early coffee/tea. Dinner available. Restaurant on premises. Beds: KQDT. Phone, air conditioning and turndown service in room. Fax, copier and library on premises. Handicap access. Weddings and small meetings hosted. Antiques, parks, shopping, cross-country skiing and theater nearby.

Publicity: *Country Living.*

"Popular spot keeps getting better."

Cooperstown   G10

The Inn at Cooperstown

16 Chestnut St
Cooperstown, NY 13326-1006
(607)547-5756 Fax:(607)547-8779
E-mail: theinn@telenet.net

Circa 1874. This three-story, Second Empire hotel features a graceful porch filled with wicker furniture and rocking chairs. The inn is located in the center of the Cooperstown National

Historic District. The guest rooms are decorated tastefully and comfortably. A block from Otsego Lake, the inn is within walking distance of most of Cooperstown's attractions.

Historic Interest: Baseball Hall of Fame (2 blocks), The Farmers' Museum & Fenimore House Museum (1 mile), Glimmerglass Operal (8 miles).
Innkeeper(s): Michael Jerome. $85-140. MC VISA AX DC DS TC. 18 rooms with PB. 1 conference room. Breakfast included in rates. Type of meal: continental breakfast. Beds: QT. TV, fax and library on premises. Handicap access. Small meetings hosted. Antiques, fishing, parks, shopping, cross-country skiing, sporting events, theater and watersports nearby.
Publicity: *Cleveland Plain Dealer, New York Times, Atlanta Journal, Los Angeles Times, New York Magazine, Conde Nast Traveler, USA Today.*

"An unpretentious country inn with 17 (sic) rooms, spotless on the inside and stunning on the outside. — Conde Nast Traveler"

Litco Farms B&B

PO Box 1048
Cooperstown, NY 13326-1048
(607)547-2501 Fax:(607)547-7079

The 70-acre grounds that surround this Greek Revival farmhouse include 18 acres of mapped wetlands. The natural setting includes trails lined with wildflowers and guests are sure to spot deer and a variety of birds.
On cold days, guests can snuggle up to the wood-burning stove, and there are plenty of ideal spots for picnics during the warmer months. The scent of baking breads and fresh coffee entices

guests to the morning meal of country fare. Guests enjoy browsing at Heartworks, an on-site fabric and quilt shop.
Innkeeper(s): Jim & Margaret Wolff. $69-119. 4 rooms. Breakfast included in rates. Type of meal: full breakfast.

Thistlebrook

RR 1 Box 26
Cooperstown, NY 13326
(607)547-6093 (800)596-9305

Circa 1866. This sprawling red barn with its rustic appearance belies the spacious and elegant rooms awaiting discovery inside. Fluted columns in the living room enhance the inn's original architectural details. Furnishings include American and European pieces, an Egyptian Revival mirror, Oriental rugs and crystal chandeliers. Just up the wide stairway is a library from

which the guest rooms are reached. Breakfasts are hearty and may include fresh fruit salad and three-cheese omelets with biscuits and ham. Enjoy valley vistas from the inn's deck. A variety of wildlife such as deer, bullfrogs, wood ducks and an occasional blue heron, gather around the pond.
Innkeeper(s): Paula & Jim Bugonian. $110-135. PC TC. TAC10. 5 rooms with PB. 2 suites. Breakfast included in rates. Types of meals: full breakfast and early coffee/tea. Beds: KQD. Air conditioning and ceiling fan in room. Fax and library on premises. Handicap access. Weddings, small meetings and family reunions hosted. Antiques, fishing, shopping, sporting events, golf, theater and watersports nearby.
Publicity: *Country Inns.*

Corning   H6

Delevan House

188 Delevan Ave
Corning, NY 14830-3224
(607)962-2347

Circa 1933. Visitors to the Corning area will find a touch of home at this comfortable Colonial Revival house on a hill overlooking town. The inn's screened porch offers the perfect spot for reading, relaxing or sipping a cool drink. A full breakfast is served before guests head out for a day of business, sightseeing or travel. The Finger Lakes are 30 miles away, and just two miles from the inn, visitors will find the city's historic district. The Mark Twain Home and Pinnacle State Park are nearby.
Innkeeper(s): Mary DePumpo. $60-95. TC. 3 rooms, 1 with PB. Breakfast included in rates. Types of meals: full breakfast, gourmet breakfast and early coffee/tea. Beds: D. Phone and TV in room. Small meetings and family reunions hosted. Antiques, fishing, parks, shopping, downhill skiing, cross-country skiing, sporting events and watersports nearby.

Cornith   E12

Agape Farm B&B

4894 Rt 9N
Cornith, NY 12822-1704
(518)654-7777

Circa 1870. Amid 33 acres of fields and woods, this Adirondack farmhouse is home to chickens and horses, as well as guests seeking a refreshing getaway. Visitors have their choice of six guest rooms, all with ceiling fans, phones, private baths and views of the tranquil surroundings.
The inn's wraparound porch lures many visitors, who often enjoy a glass of icy lemonade. Homemade breads, jams, jellies and muffins are part of the full

breakfast served here, and guests are welcome to pick berries or gather a ripe tomato from the garden. A trout-filled stream on the grounds flows to the Hudson River, a mile away.
Historic Interest: Built on the site of a hundred year old dairy farm, outbuildings and animals keep this atmosphere alive.
Innkeeper(s): Fred & Sigrid Koch. $60-125. MC VISA DS PC TC. TAC5. 6 rooms with PB. 1 cottage. Breakfast, afternoon tea and evening snack included in rates. Types of meals: full breakfast and early coffee/tea. Beds: KQDT. Phone and ceiling fan in room. TV, VCR, library and child care on premises. Handicap access. 33 acres. Small meetings hosted. Amusement parks, antiques, fishing, parks, shopping, downhill skiing, cross-country skiing, sporting events, theater and watersports nearby.
Pets Allowed: Housed in outside building.
Location: Between Saratoga & Lake George attractions.
"Clean and impeccable, we were treated royally."

Cornwall J12

Cromwell Manor Inn B&B

Angola Rd
Cornwall, NY 12518
(914)534-7136

Circa 1820. A descent of Oliver Cromwell built this stunning Greek Revival home, which is set on seven lush acres boasting scenic views of mountains and a 4,000-acre forest preserve.
The innkeepers refurbished the National Register manor, leaving original elements and adding period antiques and fine furnishings throughout. Relax by the fireplace or enjoy the inn's Jacuzzi and steam room. The innkeepers prepare a breakfast of home-baked treats such as muffins, quiche, omelets, fruits and specialty breads. The innkeepers also offer a romantic cottage dating back to 1764, which boasts a fireplace and country antiques.

Historic Interest: West Point is only 10 minutes from the inn and the area offers plenty of historic homes, including the Vanderbilt Mansion. The Brotherhood Winery, the nation's oldest, is a nearby attraction.

Innkeeper(s): Dale & Barbara O'Hara. $120-250. MC VISA PC. TAC10. 13 rooms with PB, 7 with FP. 2 suites. 1 conference room. Breakfast included in rates. Types of meals: full breakfast, gourmet breakfast and early coffee/tea. Afternoon tea, picnic lunch, catering service and room service available. Beds: QD. Air conditioning and turndown service in room. TV, VCR and copier on premises. Handicap access. Weddings, small meetings, family reunions and seminars hosted. Antiques, fishing, parks, shopping, downhill skiing, cross-country skiing, sporting events, theater and watersports nearby.

Publicity: *Orange Life.*

"Wonderful, great attention to detail. Immaculate, great setting. Romantic."

Crown Point D12

Crown Point Bed & Breakfast

3 A Main St, Rt 9 N, PO Box 490
Crown Point, NY 12928-0490
(518)597-3651 Fax:(518)597-4451

Circa 1886. This Queen Anne Victorian inn north of Fort Ticonderoga offers a fascinating vantage point from which to view the historical area. Crown Point served as a fortress guarding Lake Champlain during the Revolutionary War. The inn, originally owned by a local banker, boasts cherry, chestnut, mahogany, oak, pine and walnut woodwork. The spacious guest rooms, furnished with period antiques, all feature private baths. The Master Bedroom Suite includes a highback walnut bed and marble-topped dresser, as well as a whirlpool bath. Three parlors are available for relaxing and socializing.

Historic Interest: Fort Ticonderoga (7 miles south), Fort Crown Point (7 miles north).

Innkeeper(s): Hugh & Sandy Johnson. $60-120. MC VISA AX DC DS PC TC. TAC10. 5 rooms with PB. 1 suite. Breakfast included in rates. Type of meal: continental-plus breakfast. Beds: QDT. Turndown service and ceiling fan in room. TV, fax and copier on premises. Small meetings and family reunions hosted. Spanish on weekends spoken. Antiques, fishing, parks, shopping, cross-country skiing, theater and watersports nearby.

De Bruce (Livingston Manor) I10

De Bruce Country Inn on the Willowemoc

De Bruce Road #286-A
De Bruce (Livingston Manor), NY 12758
(914)439-3900

Circa 1917. This inn is nestled along the banks of the Willowemoc River, near the spot where the first dry fly was cast in the United States. This early 20th-century retreat, known for its excellent trout fishing and secluded woodlands, continues to draw visitors today. The inn, located in the Catskill Forest Preserve, offers wooded trails, wildlife, game, a stocked pond, swimming pool, sauna and whirlpool. After a day enjoying the outdoors, relax in the Dry Fly Lounge, where a crackling fire will warm you. From the dining terrace, guests enjoy a view of the valley and mountains. Guests enjoy both hearty breakfasts and dinners on the terrace and also can spend the evening in the Dry Fly Lounge.

Innkeeper(s): Ron & Marilyn Lusker. $150-225. MAP. 15 rooms with PB. 2 suites. Breakfast and dinner included in rates. Type of meal: full breakfast. Restaurant on premises. Beds: KQDT. Ceiling fan in room. TV, VCR, fax, copier, spa, swimming, sauna and library on premises. 50 acres. Weddings, small meetings, family reunions and seminars hosted. French, limited German and limited Italian spoken. Antiques and golf nearby.

Pets Allowed: At inn owners' discretion.

Deposit H9

Chestnut Inn at Oquaga Lake

498 Oquaga Lake Rd
Deposit, NY 13754-3833
(607)467-2500 (800)467-7676 Fax:(607)467-5911

Circa 1928. This spacious Craftsman-style inn east of Binghampton offers a variety of rooming and dining options. The family-oriented inn is well-equipped to handle meetings, receptions and weddings, and guests will find no shortage of activities or amenities. Bicycles, child care and swimming are offered. The inn features picnic lunches, perfect for a day by the lake. Oquaga Creek State Park is a short drive away.

Innkeeper(s): Tom Spaulding & Dale Shaw. $69-209. MAP. MC VISA AX DC DS PC TC. TAC10. 30 rooms, 10 with PB. 6 suites. 1 cottage. 1 conference room. Afternoon tea included in rates. Type of meal: full breakfast. Dinner, lunch and banquet service available. Restaurant on premises. Beds: KQD. TV in room. VCR, fax, copier, swimming and bicycles on premises. Weddings, small meetings, family reunions and seminars hosted. Antiques, fishing, parks, shopping, sporting events and watersports nearby.

Dover Plains I12

Old Drovers Inn

Old Rt 22
Dover Plains, NY 12522
(914)832-9311 Fax:(914)832-6356
E-mail: old_drovers_inn@juno.com

Circa 1750. Luxurious accommodations and fine food are featured at this historic Colonial Revival inn, located in the Harlem Valley at the foot of the Berkshires. The inn once served as a resting spot for area drovers, or cowboys, who were leading cattle to market in New York City. Visitors select from the Cherry, Meeting, Rose or Sleigh rooms. The handsome furnishings and service found at the inn are matched by its cuisine, which is well known in the area. Tour the inn's 12 acres or borrow bicycles and enjoy the scenery. On weekends a full breakfast and dinner are included in room rates.

Innkeeper(s): Alice Pitcher & Kemper Peacock. Call for rates. MC VISA DC PC TC. 4 rooms with PB, 3 with FP. 1 conference room. Types of meals: continental breakfast, full breakfast and early coffee/tea. Dinner, picnic lunch, lunch, banquet service and catering service available. Air conditioning and turndown service in room. TV and VCR on premises. 12 acres. Weddings, small meetings, family reunions and seminars hosted. Antiques, shopping, skiing, golf and theater nearby.

Pets Allowed: with advance notice, $20/night.

Location: Seventy-five miles north of New York City, 25 miles east of Hyde Park.

Publicity: *New York Magazine, Country Inns, New York Times, Town and Country, Relais & Chateaux.*

"*This inn is as romantic a treasure as you will ever find.*"

Dundee   G6

The 1819 Red Brick Inn

2081 State Route 230
Dundee, NY 14837-9424
(607)243-8844

Circa 1819. This Federal-style inn's impressive exterior, with its 15-inch-thick brick walls, is complemented by its antique-filled interior. Many fine wineries are found in the area. The inn sits on 8 acres, near a mineral springs that in the late 1800s attracted many health-conscious visitors. Keuka Lake and Watkins Glen state parks are within easy driving distance.

Innkeeper(s): Charles & Christine Peacock. $65-75. PC. 4 rooms with PB, 4 with FP. Breakfast included in rates. Meals: full breakfast and early coffee/tea. Beds: D. Antiques, fishing, parks, shopping, cross-country skiing, sporting events, golf and watersports nearby.

East Hampton   K15

Maidstone Arms

207 Main St
East Hampton, NY 11937-2723
(516)324-5006 Fax:(516)324-5037

Circa 1860. Situated on the village green, this classic inn has all the characteristics that epitomize this community of winding lanes and sandy white beaches. Turndown service is provided in the individually decorated rooms. The inn's restaurant houses a world-class selection of wines in its own climate-controlled underground wine cellar. Nearby activities include whale-watching expeditions and local winery tours.

Historic Interest: The Maidstone Arms is located on Long Island, which offers many historic buildings and sites. New York City is about two hours away.

Innkeeper(s): Coke Ann Saunders. $132-375. MC VISA AX. 19 rooms with PB. 6 suites. 3 cottages. 1 conference room. Breakfast included in rates. Types of meals: continental breakfast, continental-plus breakfast, full breakfast and early coffee/tea. Dinner, evening snack, picnic lunch, lunch, gourmet lunch, banquet service and room service available. Restaurant on premises. Beds: KQT. Phone, air conditioning, turndown service and TV in room. Weddings, small meetings, family reunions and seminars hosted. Antiques, fishing, theater and watersports nearby.

Mill House Inn

33 N Main St
East Hampton, NY 11937-2601
(516)324-9766 Fax:(516)324-9793

Circa 1790. This Colonial house is just opposite the Old Hook Windmill. It is in the center of East Hampton, which has been called "America's most beautiful village." Guest rooms are decorated with a Hampton's theme in mind, sporting names such as Sail Away or Hampton Holiday. Romantic amenities abound, including fireplaces in six of the guest rooms. Several rooms also have whirlpool tubs. Breakfasts are a gourmet delight, featuring home-baked granola bread, cranberry orange scones or sour cream coffeecake followed by entrees such as a potato and smoked salmon frittata, maple bread pudding and pumpkin pancakes.

Innkeeper(s): Daniel & Katherine Hartnett. $140-350. MC VISA PC. 8 rooms with PB, 6 with FP. Breakfast and afternoon tea included in rates. Types of meals: full breakfast and early coffee/tea. Beds: QD. Phone, air conditioning, ceiling fan, TV and VCR in room. Fax, copier and library on premises. Handicap access. Small meetings and family reunions hosted. Spanish spoken. Antiques, fishing, shopping, theater and watersports nearby.

Location: In the heart of East Hampton Village.

Publicity: *New York Magazine, Travel Channel.*

"*Perfect everything, it's hard to leave.*"

The Pink House

26 James Ln
East Hampton, NY 11937-2710
(516)324-3400 Fax:(516)324-5254
E-mail: RoSo@hamptons.com

Circa 1850. The decor of this simple Victorian, originally owned by a whaling captain, has been greatly enhanced by a collection of architectural elements gathered from demolished buildings. The innkeeper has included scenic watercolors that were painted by his grandfather during his world travels. TVs, robes, in-room phones, designer sheets and evening chocolates are among the inn's amenities. Full breakfasts are served on the porch overlooking the pool or in the dining room, and consist of homemade granola and frittatas. There are four inn dogs. Celebrity guests include Jane Seymour, Martin Short, Robin Williams and Carly Simon.

Innkeeper(s): Ron Steinhilber. $135-325. MC VISA AX PC TC. 5 rooms with PB. Breakfast included in rates. Type of meal: full breakfast. Beds: Q. Phone, air conditioning, ceiling fan and TV in room. Fax, copier and swimming on premises. Antiques, fishing, shopping, golf and watersports nearby.

Publicity: *New York Times.*

"*I came jangeled and stressed and leave peaceful and calm.*"

Elbridge   F7

Fox Ridge Farm B&B

4786 Foster Rd
Elbridge, NY 13060-9770
(315)673-4881 Fax:(315)673-3691
E-mail: foxridg@aol.com

Circa 1910. Guests shouldn't be surprised to encounter deer or other wildlife at this secluded country home surrounded by woods. The innkeepers have transformed the former farmhouse into a cozy inn with rooms boasting quilts, a four-poster bed and views of the woods or flower garden. Enjoy breakfasts in front of a fire in the large country kitchen. The innkeepers are happy to accommodate dietary needs. Snacks and refreshments are always available for hungry guests in the evening. Nearby Skaneateles Lake offers swimming, boating and other outdoor activities. Dinner cruises, touring wineries and antique shopping are other popular activities.

Historic Interest: The Canal Museum and The Creamery are five miles from the farm. The Harriet Tubman House is a 12-mile drive, as is the William Seward House.

Innkeeper(s): Marge Sykes. $55-85. MC VISA AX DS PC TC. 3 rooms, 1 with PB. Breakfast and evening snack included in rates. Types of meals: continental-plus breakfast, full breakfast, gourmet breakfast and early coffee/tea. Beds: QD. VCR on premises. 120 acres. Weddings hosted. Antiques, fishing, parks, shopping, downhill skiing, cross-country skiing, sporting events, theater and watersports nearby.

"If I could, I would take Marge Sykes home to Seattle with us. We stayed 7 days for a family reunion. Great company, marvelous hosts and the most delicious breakfasts everyday."

Elmira   H7

Lindenwald Haus

1526 Grand Central Ave
Elmira, NY 14901-1208
(607)733-8753

Circa 1875. Two graceful porticos decorate the exterior of this impressive Italianate Victorian. The 48-room interior boasts 12-foot ceilings, windows stretching nearly nine feet, a grand stair-

case and polished wood floors. Lindenwald Haus originally served as a home for widows of Civil War veterans. A brass bed, red velvet sofa or perhaps an iron bed are among the charming, Victorian furnishings found in the guest rooms. The beds are topped by quilts handmade by the innkeeper's mother. German-style, continental-plus breakfasts are served buffet-style in the Victorian dining room, with fresh meats, cheeses, fruit, home-baked treats, cereals and plenty of juices and coffee. Elmira offers many activities, from tours of historic homes to four-star dining.

Innkeeper(s): Camille Bodine. $49-105. MC VISA PC TC. 17 rooms, 10 with PB. 3 suites. Breakfast included in rates. Type of meal: continental-plus breakfast. Beds: QDT. Air conditioning and ceiling fan in room. TV, VCR, copier, swimming, bicycles and library on premises. Handicap access. Weddings, small meetings and family reunions hosted. Amusement parks, antiques, fishing and shopping nearby.

"What a dream! Absolutely delightful!"

Fair Haven   E7

Black Creek Farm B&B

PO Box 390
Fair Haven, NY 13064-0390
(315)947-5282

Circa 1888. Pines and towering birch trees frame this Victorian farmhouse inn, filled with an incredible assortment of authentic antiques. Set on 20 acres in the countryside west of Fair Haven, this inn offers a refreshing

escape from big-city life. The inn's impressive furnishings come as no real surprise since there is an antique shop on the premises. Guests enjoy relaxing in a hammock, on the porch, or by taking a stroll along the peaceful country roads. The inn is two miles from Lake Ontario's shoreline and within easy reach of Fair Haven Beach State Park and Thorpe Vineyard. Cottage over-looking the stocked pond is available.

Innkeeper(s): Bob & Kathy Sarber. $50-75. MC VISA DS PC. 4 rooms, 2 with PB. Breakfast and afternoon tea included in rates. Types of meals: full breakfast and early coffee/tea. Evening snack available. Beds: QDT. Air conditioning in room. VCR and bicycles on premises. 20 acres. Family reunions hosted. Antiques, fishing, parks, cross-country skiing and watersports nearby.

Fleischmanns   H11

River Run

Main St, Box D4
Fleischmanns, NY 12430
(914)254-4884

Circa 1887. The backyard of this large three-story Victorian gently slopes to the river where the Bushkill and Little Red Kill trout streams meet. Inside, stained-glass windows surround the inn's common areas, shining on the oak-floored dining room and the book-filled parlor. The parlor also includes a fireplace and a piano. Adirondack chairs are situated comfortably on the front porch. Tennis courts, a pool, park, theater and restaurants are within walking distance, as is a country auction held each Saturday night. The inn is two and a half hours out of New York City, 35 minutes west of Woodstock, and accessible by public transportation.

Historic Interest: The Hudson River mansions are all located within one hour of the inn. Bethel, the site of the famed Woodstock concert is within an hour of the inn. Cooperstown is about an hour and a half away.

Innkeeper(s): Larry Miller. $50-100. MC VISA PC. TAC10. 10 rooms, 6 with PB. 1 suite. Breakfast and afternoon tea included in rates. Types of meals: continental-plus breakfast and early coffee/tea. Beds: KQDT. TV, VCR, bicycles and library on premises. Small meetings and family reunions hosted. French and German spoken. Antiques, fishing, parks, shopping, downhill skiing, cross-country skiing, theater and watersports nearby.

Pets Allowed: Well behaved, fully trained, over one year old.

Location: Country village in the high peaks of the Catskill Mountains.

Publicity: *Catskill Mountain News, Kingston Freeman, New York Times, New York Daily News, Philadelphia Inquirer, Inn Country USA.*

"We are really happy to know of a place that welcomes all of our family."

Fredonia   G2

The White Inn

52 E Main St
Fredonia, NY 14063-1836
(716)672-2103 Fax:(716)672-2107

Circa 1868. This 23-room inn is situated in the center of Fredonia. Antiques and reproductions decorate the guest rooms and suites. Guests, as well as the general public, may enjoy gourmet meals at this inn, a charter member of the Duncan Hines "Family of Fine Restaurants." Cocktails and more casual fare are served in the lounge or on the 100-foot-long veranda. The nearby Chatauqua Institution

presents a variety of lectures and concert performances during the summer. Wineries, golfing, state parks and shops are nearby.
Innkeeper(s): Robert Contiguglia & Kathleen Dennison. $79-169. EP. MC VISA AX DC DS PC TC. TAC10. 23 rooms with PB, 2 with FP. 11 suites. 4 conference rooms. Breakfast included in rates. Type of meal: full breakfast. Dinner, lunch, banquet service and catering service available. Restaurant on premises. Beds: KQD. Phone, air conditioning and TV in room. VCR, fax, copier and bicycles on premises. Handicap access. Weddings, small meetings, family reunions and seminars hosted. Antiques, parks, shopping, cross-country skiing and theater nearby.
Publicity: *Country Living, Innsider.*

"Thanks again for another wonderful stay."

Garrison J12

The Bird & Bottle Inn

Old Albany Post Rd Rt 9, R2 Box 129
Garrison, NY 10524
(914)424-3000 Fax:(914)424-3283
E-mail: birdbottle@aol.com

Circa 1761. Built as Warren's Tavern, this three-story yellow farmhouse served as a lodging and dining spot on the New York-to-Albany Post Road, now a National Historic Landmark.
George Washington, Hamilton, Lafayette and many other historic figures frequently passed by. The inn's eight acres include secluded
lawns, a babbling stream and Hudson Valley woodlands. Timbered ceilings, old paneling and fireplace mantels in the inn's notable restaurant maintain a Revolutionary War-era ambiance. Second-floor guest rooms have canopied or four-poster beds and each is warmed by its own fireplace.
Innkeeper(s): Ira Boyar. $210-240. MAP. MC VISA AX PC TC. 4 rooms with PB, 4 with FP. 1 suite. 1 cottage. Breakfast and dinner included in rates. Lunch available. Restaurant on premises. Beds: Q. Air conditioning in room. TV, fax and copier on premises. Weddings, small meetings, family reunions and seminars hosted. Antiques, fishing, parks, shopping, cross-country skiing and theater nearby.
Publicity: *Colonial Homes, Hudson Valley, Spotlight, Travel Channel, The Learning Channel.*

Geneva F6

Belhurst Castle

PO Box 609
Geneva, NY 14456
(315)781-0201

Circa 1889. The century old stone castle is situated in the middle of a 20-acre forested park that overlooks Seneca Lake. The Belhurst features dining in the library, parlor, center room, solarium or on the veranda that overlooks the expansive grounds and lake. There are 13 guest rooms with private baths and all are decorated in period furnishings. The Garden Room, a favorite for receptions, accommodates up to 300 guests. The Belhurst is the recipient of the Wine Spectator Award and has won the I Love New York Award for the most romantic places.
Innkeeper(s): Duane R. Reeder. $65-295. MC VISA. 13 rooms with PB, 4 with FP. Restaurant on premises. Beds: QT. Fax and copier on premises. Handicap access.

Geneva on the Lake

1001 Lochland Rd, RT 14S
Geneva, NY 14456
(315)789-7190 (800)343-6382 Fax:(315)789-0322

Circa 1911. This opulent world-class inn is a replica of the Renaissance-era Lancellotti Villa in Frascati, Italy. It is listed in the National Register. Although originally built as a residence, it became a monastery for Capuchin monks. Now it is one of the finest resorts in the U.S. Meticulously restored in 1979-1980 under the direction of award-winning designer William Schickel, all rooms have kitchens and there are 10 two-bedroom suites — some with views of the lake. Here, you may have
an experience as fine as Europe can offer, without leaving the states. Some compare it to the Grand Hotel du Cap-Ferrat on the French Riviera. The inn has been awarded four diamonds from AAA for more than a decade. Breakfast is available daily and on Sunday, brunch is served. Dinner is served Wednesday through Sunday, and in the summer, lunch is served on the terrace.
Historic Interest: The Corning Glass Center, where Steuben glass is created by hand, is nearby. The town of Elmira, another close attraction, is the site where "The Adventures of Tom Sawyer" and "Huckleberry Finn", were written by Mark Twain.
Innkeeper(s): William Schickel. $124-481. MC VISA AX DS. TAC10. 30 suites. 3 conference rooms. Breakfast included in rates. Types of meals: continental breakfast and gourmet breakfast. Dinner, banquet service and room service available. Restaurant on premises. Beds: QDT. Phone, air conditioning, turndown service and TV in room. VCR, fax, copier, swimming and bicycles on premises. 10 acres. Weddings, small meetings, family reunions and seminars hosted. Antiques, parks, shopping, downhill skiing, cross-country skiing, sporting events, theater and watersports nearby.
Location: On Seneca Lake in New York's Finger Lakes Wine District.
Publicity: *Bon Appetit, Country Inns, N.Y. Times, Innsider, Bride's, Catholic Register, Pittsford-Brighton Post, New York, Glamour, Gourmet, Washingtonian, Toronto Star, Globe & Mail, Rochester Democrat & Chronicle.*

"The food was superb and the service impeccable."

Gorham G6

The Gorham House

4752 E Swamp Rd
Gorham, NY 14461
(716)526-4402 Fax:(716)526-4402
E-mail: gorham.house@juno.com

Circa 1887. The Gorham House serves as a homey, country place to enjoy New York's Finger Lakes region. The five, secluded acres located between Canandaigua and Seneca lakes, include herb gardens, wildflowers and berry bushes. Part of the home dates back to the early 19th century, but it's the architecture of the 1887 expansion that accounts for the inn's Victorian touches. The interior is warm and cozy with comfortable, country furnishings. Some of the pieces are the innkeepers' family heirlooms. There are more than 50 wineries in the area, as well as a bounty of outdoor activities.
Innkeeper(s): Nancy & Al Rebmann. $65-90. PC TC. 3 rooms, 1 with PB. Breakfast included in rates. Types of meals: gourmet breakfast and early coffee/tea. Beds: QD. Air conditioning in room. Library on premises. Family reunions hosted. Antiques, fishing, parks, shopping, downhill skiing, cross-country skiing, sporting events, theater and watersports nearby.

Goshen J11

Anthony Dobbins Stage Coach Inn B&B

268 Main & Maplewood Ter
Goshen, NY 10924
(914)294-5526

Besides the lovely five acres of lawns and gardens, guests will remember this 18th-century inn for many other reasons. The decor is delightful, rooms feature four-poster beds topped with designer linens. Among the elegant furnishings are many antiques. Along with a continental-plus breakfast, an English-style afternoon tea is served. Aside from romantic amenities, there is plenty available for business travelers, including a fax, computer and copier. The inn's history is fascinating. As the name suggests, the inn got its start as a stagecoach stop. Eleanor Roosevelt stayed here. The innkeeper is a descendent of both Wild Bill Hickok and William Penn. A bed that belonged to Penn decorates one of the guest rooms. The inn also has a place in the town's history of breeding champion trotting horses, and the race track is within walking distance. There are also public tennis courts, fine restaurants and shops just minutes away.

Innkeeper(s): Neil McDonald Hickok. $95-130.

Greenport K15

The Bartlett House Inn

503 Front St
Greenport, NY 11944-1519
(516)477-0371

Circa 1908. A family residence for more than 60 years and then a convent for a nearby church, this large Victorian house became a bed & breakfast in 1982. Features include corinthian columns, stained-glass windows, two fireplaces and a large front porch. Period antiques complement the rich interior. The inn is within walking distance of shops, the harbor, the Shelter Island Ferry and train station.

Innkeeper(s): Bill & Diane May. $80-105. MC VISA PC TC. 10 rooms with PB, 1 with FP. 1 suite. 1 conference room. Breakfast included in rates. Types of meals: full breakfast and early coffee/tea. Beds: QDT. Air conditioning in room. Weddings, small meetings, family reunions and seminars hosted. Antiques, fishing, parks, shopping and watersports nearby.

Hadley E12

Saratoga Rose

4274 Rockwell St
Hadley, NY 12835-0238
(518)696-2861 (800)942-5025 Fax:(518)696-5319

Circa 1885. This romantic Queen Anne Victorian offers a small, candlelit restaurant perfect for an evening for two. Breakfast specialties include Grand Marnier French toast and eggs Anthony. Rooms are decorated in period style. The Queen Anne Room, decorated in blue, boasts a wood and tile fireplace and a quilt-covered bed. The Garden Room offers a private sun-

porch and an outside deck with a Jacuzzi spa. Each of the rooms features something special. Guests can take in the mountain view or relax on the veranda while sipping a cocktail.

Innkeeper(s): Nancy Merlino. $80-165. EP. MC VISA DS. 6 rooms with PB, 3 with FP. Breakfast included in rates. Types of meals: full breakfast and gourmet breakfast. Dinner, evening snack, picnic lunch, banquet service, catering service, catered breakfast and room service available. Beds: KD. Air conditioning and ceiling fan in room. TV, VCR and spa on premises. Weddings, small meetings, family reunions and seminars hosted. Amusement parks, antiques, fishing, parks, shopping, downhill skiing, cross-country skiing, sporting events and theater nearby.

Publicity: Getaways for Gourmets.

"A must for the inn traveler."

Hague D12

Ruah B&B

34 Lake Shore Dr
Hague, NY 12836-9705
(518)543-8816 (800)224-7549

Circa 1907. Artist Harry Watrous built this Dutch Colonial mansion, and some of the property may have been acquired with an especially good poker hand. Be sure to ask the innkeepers about Watrous and the legend of the creature in the lake. The inn is set on more than six acres, and offers wonderful views of Lake George. The innkeepers restored the turn-of-the-century inn and its four guest rooms. The two

redecorated everything except for the living room. This room was chosen for a special redecorating project by House Beautiful magazine, which featured the inn in a six-page feature. The living room is stunning, the decor and furniture arrangement was selected carefully as not to overpower the lake views. There is a veranda lined with wicker for those who wish to relax and enjoy the sight of mountains and the water. A buffet breakfast is presented each morning with items such as soufflés, frittatas, granola, cereal, fruit and homemade baked goods.

Innkeeper(s): Judy & Peter Foster. $90-150. MC VISA AX DS PC TC. 4 rooms with PB, 2 with FP. 1 suite. Breakfast included in rates. Types of meals: full breakfast and early coffee/tea. Catering service available. Beds: KQT. TV and library on premises. Weddings, small meetings, family reunions and seminars hosted. Amusement parks, antiques, fishing, parks, shopping, downhill skiing, cross-country skiing, golf and watersports nearby.

Publicity: House Beautiful, Forbes, FYI, Albany Times, Union Glens Falls, Post Star, Chronicle, New York News, Wall Street Journal.

"Wonderful, fantastic, romantic, comfortable, friendly and pretty!"

Trout House Village Resort

PO Box 510
Hague, NY 12836-0510
(518)543-6088 (800)368-6088

Circa 1934. On the shores of beautiful Lake George is this resort inn, offering accommodations in the lodge, authentic log cabins or cottages. Many of the guest rooms in the lodge boast lake views, while the log cabins offer jetted tubs and fireplaces. The guest quarters are furnished comfortably. The emphasis here is on the abundance of outdoor activities. Outstanding cross-country skiing, downhill skiing and snowmobiling are found nearby. The inn furnishes bicycles, canoes, kayaks, paddle boats, rowboats, sleds, shuffleboard, skis and toboggans. Summertime evenings offer games of capture-the-flag and soccer. Other activities include basketball, horseshoes, ping pong, a putting green and volleyball.

Historic Interest: Fort Ticonderoga (8 miles).

Innkeeper(s): Scott & Alice Patchett. $45-333. AP. MC VISA AX DS PC TC. TAC10. 13 rooms, 11 with PB, 15 with FP. 1 suite. 15 cottages. 2 conference rooms. Type of meal: continental-plus breakfast. Banquet service available. Beds: QDT. Phone, TV and VCR in room. Swimming, bicycles, tennis, library and child care on premises. Handicap access. Weddings, small meetings, family reunions and seminars hosted. Amusement parks, antiques, fishing, parks, shopping, skiing and watersports nearby.

Pets Allowed: During off season.

"My wife and I felt the family warmth at this resort. There wasn't that coldness you get at larger resorts."

Haines Falls   H11

Brookside B&B

117 Mountain House Rd
Haines Falls, NY 12436
(518)589-5856

Circa 1890. Located in the northern Catskill Mountains just two miles from North Lake, this late 19th-century inn got its

start as a boarding house, and still welcomes guests today. Guest rooms are simply and comfortably furnished with a few antiques. The innkeepers prepare a made-to-order breakfast. Children are welcome here, and there is much for them to do. Skiing, flea markets and auctions are nearby, as is the artsy town of Woodstock.

Innkeeper(s): Mary Butler. $50-75. PC. 3 rooms, 2 with PB. Breakfast included in rates. Types of meals: full breakfast and early coffee/tea. Beds: KQT. Ceiling fan and TV in room. VCR and pet boarding on premises. Small meetings and family reunions hosted. Antiques, fishing, parks, shopping, downhill skiing, cross-country skiing, golf and watersports nearby.

Pets Allowed.

Hamburg   G3

Sharon's B&B Lake House

4862 Lake Shore Rd
Hamburg, NY 14075-5542
(716)627-7561

Circa 1935. This historic lakefront house is located 10 miles from Buffalo and 45 minutes from Niagara Falls. Overlooking Lake Erie, the West Lake Room and the Upper Lake Room provide spectacular views. The home's beautiful furnishings offer additional delights.

Innkeeper(s): Sharon & Vince Di Maria. $100-110. PC TC. 2 rooms, 1 with PB. Breakfast included in rates. Type of meal: gourmet breakfast. Afternoon tea available. Beds: D. Phone, ceiling fan and TV in room. VCR and swimming on premises. Fishing, parks, shopping, downhill skiing, cross-country skiing, theater and watersports nearby.

Location: On the shore of Lake Erie.

"Spectacular view, exquisitely furnished."

Hamlin   E5

Sandy Creek Manor House

1960 Redman Rd
Hamlin, NY 14464-9635
(716)964-7528 (800)594-0400

Circa 1910. Six acres of woods and perennial gardens provide the setting for this English Tudor house. Stained glass, polished woods and Amish quilts add warmth to the home. The innkeepers have placed many thoughtful amenities in each

room, such as clock radios, fluffy robes, slippers and baskets of toiletries. Breakfast is served on the open porch in summer. Fisherman's Landing, on the banks of Sandy Creek, is a stroll away. Bullhead, trout and salmon are popular catches. There is a gift shop on premises. Ask about murder-mystery, sweetheart dinner and spa treatment packages.

Innkeeper(s): Shirley Hollink & James Krempasky. $50-70. MC VISA AX DS PC TC. TAC10. 4 rooms, 1 with PB. Breakfast, afternoon tea and evening snack included in rates. Types of meals: continental breakfast, continental-plus breakfast, gourmet breakfast and early coffee/tea. Beds: KQDT. Air conditioning and TV in room. Small meetings and family reunions hosted. Antiques, fishing, parks, shopping, downhill skiing, cross-country skiing, sporting events and watersports nearby.

Pets Allowed.

Location: Four miles north of Rt 104; 25 miles northwest of Rochester; located near the Seaway Trail.

Publicity: *Rochester Times Union.*

"Delightful in every way."

Hammondsport   G6

The Amity Rose

8264 Main St
Hammondsport, NY 14840
(607)569-3408 (800)982-8818 Fax:(607)569-3483

Circa 1899. This farmhouse Victorian has a two-story veranda and shuttered windows. Sweet Emma's Suite consists of two rooms, one a wicker-furnished sitting room. There is a queen bed, and the decor is floral and stripes. Within walking distance is the village square with a bandstand from which summer concerts are held. There is a nearby trout stream, and across the street is a track for running.

Historic Interest: Museum (1 mile), Glen Curtis.

Innkeeper(s): Ellen & Frank Laufersweiler. $85-125. PC TC. 4 rooms with PB. 1 suite. Breakfast and afternoon tea included in rates. Types of meals: full breakfast, gourmet breakfast and early coffee/tea. Catered breakfast available. Beds: Q. Air conditioning in room. TV on premises. Small meetings and seminars hosted. Antiques, fishing, parks, shopping, cross-country skiing, sporting events, golf and watersports nearby.

Location: On Keuka Lake, Queen of the Finger Lakes SW New York State.

"How nice, a bathroom big enough to waltz in, well almost!"

Blushing Rose B&B

11 William St
Hammondsport, NY 14840
(607)569-3402 (800)982-8818 Fax:(607)569-3483

Circa 1843. Each guest room of this home is decorated with careful attention to detail. The Burgundy Room features a lace wall canopy that hangs over the bed. The  Moonbeams Room boasts a skylight and a brass and iron bed. Breakfasts may include lemon poppy-seed waffles, baked French toast or strawberry bread. Take a lunch or dinner cruise on the lake aboard the Keuka Maid or visit the historic local wineries.

Historic Interest: Visit the historic Glen Curtiss Museum of Aviation and the Corning Glass Center.

Innkeeper(s): Ellen & Frank Laufersweiler. $85-125. PC TC. 4 rooms with PB. Breakfast and afternoon tea included in rates. Meal: gourmet breakfast. Beds: KQ. Bicycles on premises. Antiques, fishing and watersports nearby.

Location: On Keuka Lake, Queen of the Finger Lakes SW New York State.

Publicity: *Dundee Observer.*

"The myriad of attentive touches around the room and house made the home feel special, while the easy-going hosts made us feel very much at home."

Hobart   H10

Breezy Acres Farm B&B

Rr 1 Box 191
Hobart, NY 13788-9754
(607)538-9338

Circa 1830. Maple syrup, fields of corn and hay and a fruit and vegetable stand assure guests that they are truly staying at a working crop farm. The rambling farmhouse is filled with family antiques. The innkeeper, a professional home economist, serves a full country breakfast. There is a pond and the Delaware River runs past the  property. Guests often enjoy hiking the farm's 300 acres, working their way up to the log cabin hideaway.

Historic Interest: Hanford Mills Museum, National Baseball Hall of Fame & Museum, Howe Caverns.

Innkeeper(s): Joyce and David Barber. $60-75. MC VISA AX. 3 rooms with PB. Breakfast included in rates. Beds: KQ. 300 acres. Small meetings hosted. Antiques, fishing, downhill skiing and cross-country skiing nearby.

Location: In the northern Catskill Mountains.

Publicity: *Catskill Country.*

"Nicest people you'd want to meet. Perfect! Wonderful hosts, warm, friendly atmosphere. We will be back!"

Ithaca   G7

Rose Inn

Rt 34N, Box 6576
Ithaca, NY 14851-6576
(607)533-7905 Fax:(607)533-7908

Circa 1848. This classic Italianate mansion has long been famous for its circular staircase of Honduran mahogany. It is owned by Sherry Rosemann, a noted interior designer specializing in mid-19th-century architecture and furniture, and her husband Charles, a hotelier from Germany. On 20 landscaped acres, it is 10 minutes from Cornell University. The inn has been the recipient of many awards for its lodging and dining, including a four-star rating for seven years in a row.

Innkeeper(s): Charles & Sherry Rosemann. $100-275. MC VISA PC TC. 15 rooms, 10 with PB, 2 with FP. 5 suites. 1 conference room. Breakfast included in rates. Type of meal: full breakfast. Banquet service, catering service and catered breakfast available. Restaurant on premises. Beds: KQDT. Air conditioning, turndown service and ceiling fan in room. Cable TV, VCR, fax, copier and library on premises. Antiques, fishing, parks, shopping, downhill skiing, cross-country skiing, sporting events, theater and watersports nearby.

Publicity: *Country Inns, New York Times, Ithaca Times, New Woman, Toronto Globe & Mail, Newsday.*

"The blending of two outstanding talents, which when combined with your warmth, produce the ultimate experience in being away from home. Like staying with friends in their beautiful home."

Ithaca (Spencer)   H7

A Slice of Home B&B

178 N Main St
Ithaca (Spencer), NY 14883
(607)589-6073
E-mail: slice@lightlink.com

Circa 1850. This Italianate inn's location, approximately equidistant from Ithaca and Watkins Glen, offers a fine vantage point for exploring the Finger Lakes winery region. Although the area is well-known for its scenery, many recreational opportunities also are available. The innkeeper is happy to help guests plan tours and has a special fondness for those traveling by  bicycle. The inn offers five guest rooms, furnished in country decor. Guests may relax by taking a stroll on the inn's 10 acres, mountain hiking, biking or having a cookout in the inn's backyard. Guests can begin a cross-country ski excursion right from the back porch.

Innkeeper(s): Bea Brownell. $40-150. PC. TAC10. 5 rooms with PB. 1 suite. Breakfast and evening snack included in rates. Types of meals: full breakfast and early coffee/tea. Picnic lunch available. Beds: KQD. Air conditioning and TV in room. VCR, copier and bicycles on premises. 10 acres. Weddings, small meetings, family reunions and seminars hosted. Limited German spoken. Antiques, fishing, parks, shopping, downhill skiing, cross-country skiing, sporting events, theater and watersports nearby.

Pets Allowed: Outside only.

Jay

C12

The Book & Blanket B&B

Rt 9N, PO Box 164
Jay, NY 12941-0164
(518)946-8323 Fax:(518)946-8323

Circa 1850. This Adirondack bed & breakfast served as the town's post office for many years and also as barracks for state troopers. Thankfully, however, it is now a restful bed & breakfast catering to the literary set. Guest rooms are named for authors and there are books in every nook and cranny of the house. Guests may even take one book home with them. Each of the guest rooms is comfortably furnished. The inn is a short walk from the Jay Village Green and the original site of the Historic Jay covered bridge.

Innkeeper(s): Kathy, Fred, Sam & Daisy the Basset Hound. $55-75. AX PC TC. 3 rooms, 1 with PB. Breakfast and evening snack included in rates. Types of meals: full breakfast and early coffee/tea. Afternoon tea available. Beds: QD. TV, VCR, fax and library on premises. Antiques, fishing, shopping, downhill skiing, cross-country skiing and watersports nearby.

"We were so comfy we didn't want to leave."

Keene

C12

The Bark Eater Inn

PO Box 139
Keene, NY 12942-0139
(518)576-2221 Fax:(518)576-2071

Circa 1830. Originally a stagecoach stop on the old road to Lake Placid, The Bark Eater (English for the Indian word "Adirondacks") has been in almost continuous operation since the 1800s. Wide-board floors, fireplaces and rooms filled with antiques create a special haven for those seeking simple but gracious accommodations and memorable dining.

Innkeeper(s): Joe-Pete Wilson. $55-136. MAP. MC VISA AX DS PC TC. TAC10. 19 rooms, 6 with PB. 2 suites. 1 cottage. Breakfast, afternoon tea and evening snack included in rates. Types of meals: full breakfast, gourmet breakfast and early coffee/tea. Dinner, picnic lunch, catering service and catered breakfast available. Restaurant on premises. Beds: KQDT. TV, VCR, fax, copier, swimming, stables and library on premises. 250 acres. Weddings, small meetings, family reunions and seminars hosted. Antiques, fishing, parks, shopping, skiing, sporting events, theater and watersports nearby.
Location: Just minutes from Lake Placid Olympic Village.
Publicity: *New York Times, Gourmet, Toronto Star.*

"Staying at a country inn is an old tradition in Europe, and is rapidly catching on in the United States. A stay here is a pleasant surprise for anyone who travels—William Lederer, author, Ugly American."

Lake Luzerne

E12

Lamplight Inn B&B

PO Box 70, 231 Lake Ave
Lake Luzerne, NY 12846-0070
(518)696-5294 (800)262-4668
E-mail: lampinfo@adirondack.net

Circa 1890. Howard Conkling, a wealthy lumberman, built this Victorian Gothic estate on land that had been the site of the Warren County Fair. The home was designed for entertaining since Conkling was a very eligible bachelor. It has 12-foot beamed ceilings, chestnut wainscoting and moldings, and a chestnut keyhole staircase crafted in England. Four rooms boast Jacuzzi tubs.

Historic Interest: Fort William Henry (10 miles), Fort Ticonderoga (1 hour), Saratoga Battlefield (30 minutes).

Innkeeper(s): Gene & Linda Merlino. $80-165. MC VISA AX PC TC. TAC10. 17 rooms with PB, 12 with FP. Breakfast included in rates. Type of meal: full breakfast. Beds: QDT. Phone, air conditioning and ceiling fan in room. TV on premises. 10 acres. Small meetings and seminars hosted. Antiques, parks, shopping, skiing nearby.
Location: Northway (I-87) exit 21, Lake George/Lake Luzerne. Near Saratoga Springs.
Publicity: *New York Magazine, Newark Star-Ledger, Newsday, Country Inns, Country Victorian.*

"Rooms are immaculately kept and clean. The owners are the nicest, warmest, funniest and most hospitable innkeepers I have ever met."

Lake Placid

C12

Interlaken Inn

15 Interlaken Ave
Lake Placid, NY 12946-1142
(518)523-3180 (800)428-4369 Fax:(518)523-0117

Circa 1906. The five-course dinner at this Victorian inn is prepared by innkeeper CIA graduate Kevin Gregg and his talented staff. The high-quality cuisine is rivaled only by the rich decor of this cozy inn. Walnut paneling covers the dining room walls, which are topped with a tin ceiling. Bedrooms are carefully decorated with wallpapers, fresh flowers and luxurious bed coverings. Spend the afternoon gazing at the mountains and lakes that surround this Adirondack hideaway, or visit the Olympic venues.

Historic Interest: John Brown's grave (4 miles).
Innkeeper(s): Carol & Roy Johnson. $120-180. MAP. MC VISA AX. 11 rooms with PB. 1 suite. Breakfast and dinner included in rates. Types of meals: full breakfast and early coffee/tea. Afternoon tea available. Restaurant on premises. Beds: KQD. Ceiling fan in room. TV, VCR and fax on premises. Weddings, small meetings and family reunions hosted. Antiques, fishing, shopping, skiing, sporting events, theater and watersports nearby.
Pets Allowed: small, by prior arrangements.
Location: Quaint Olympic village.
Publicity: *Outside, Country Inns, Wine Trader.*

The Stagecoach Inn

370 Old Military Rd
Lake Placid, NY 12946-1614
(518)523-9474 (800)520-9474

Circa 1833. This inn was once a stagecoach stop and post office on the Elizabethtown-Saranac Lake route. The long wraparound porch and interior birch trim add authenticity to the experience. Each room has its own design and decor with brass beds, white iron beds, quilts, wicker and antiques.

Historic Interest: John Brown's farm and grave site (less than 1 mile).
Innkeeper(s): Andrea Terwillegar, Peter Moreau. $60-85. MC VISA. 9 rooms, 7 with PB, 2 with FP. 2 suites. Breakfast included in rates. Type of meal: full breakfast. Beds: DT. Phone and ceiling fan in room. TV on premises. Small meetings and family reunions hosted. Antiques, fishing, shopping, downhill skiing, cross-country skiing, sporting events, theater and watersports nearby.
Location: Adirondack Mountains.
Publicity: *New York Times, Country Inns, Newsday, Vogue, Gourmet.*

"This inn is really special. Probably our tenth stay here. It continues to be the best."

Lansing

The Federal House B&B

175 Ludlowville Rd
Lansing, NY 14882
(607)533-7362 (800)533-7362 Fax:(607)533-7899

Circa 1815. Salmon Creek Falls, a well-known fishing spot, is yards away from the inn. The rooms are furnished with antiques, which complement the original woodwork and hand-carved fireplace mantels. Each of the suites includes a television and a fireplace.

Innkeeper(s): Diane Carroll. $55-175. MC VISA AX DS PC TC. 4 rooms with PB, 2 with FP. 2 suites. Breakfast included in rates. Beds: KQDT. Air conditioning in room. Antiques, fishing, downhill skiing, cross-country skiing, theater and watersports nearby.

Publicity: *Ithaca Journal, Cortland Paper.*

"Your inn is so charming and your food was excellent."

Lewiston   F3

The Cameo Inn

4710 Lower River Rd, Rt 18-F
Lewiston, NY 14092-1053
(716)745-3034

Circa 1875. This classic Queen Anne Victorian inn offers a breathtaking view of the lower Niagara River. Located on the Seaway Trail, the inn offers convenient access to sightseeing in this popular region. The inn's interior features family heirlooms and period antiques, and visitors choose from four guest rooms, including a three-room suite overlooking the river. Breakfast is served buffet-style, and the entrees, which change daily, may include German oven pancakes or Grand Marnier French toast. Area attractions include Old Fort Niagara, outlet malls and several state parks.

Innkeeper(s): Gregory Fisher. $65-115. 4 rooms, 2 with PB. 1 suite. Breakfast included in rates. Type of meal: full breakfast. Beds: QDT. Ceiling fan and TV in room. Amusement parks, antiques, fishing, shopping, downhill skiing, cross-country skiing, sporting events, theater and watersports nearby.

Location: Five miles north of Niagara Falls.

Publicity: *Country Folk Art, Esquire, Journey, Seaway Trail, Waterways, Buffalo News.*

"I made the right choice when I selected Cameo."

Lockport   F3

Hambleton House B&B

130 Pine St
Lockport, NY 14094-4402
(716)439-9507

Circa 1850. A carriage maker was the first owner of this mid-19th-century home, and it remained in his family for several generations. The home maintains an old-fashioned appeal with its mix of country and traditional furnishings. Main Street and the Erie Barge Canal locks are a short walk away, and Buffalo and Niagara Falls are within a half-hour drive.

Innkeeper(s): Ted Hambleton. $50-85. MAP. MC VISA PC TC. TAC5. 3 rooms with PB. Breakfast included in rates. Type of meal: continental-plus breakfast. Beds: DT. Air conditioning in room. TV on premises. Weddings, small meetings and family reunions hosted. Antiques, fishing, parks, theater and watersports nearby.

Margaretville   H10

Margaretville Mountain Inn B&B

Margaretville Mountain Rd
Margaretville, NY 12455-9735
(914)586-3933

Circa 1886. Reminiscent of the Victorian era, this home rests on the site of the nation's first cauliflower farm. The owners have restored the slate roof, elaborate exterior woodwork and decorative interior woodwork. A full breakfast is served in the formal dining room on English china, or guests can enjoy the morning meal on the veranda, which overlooks the Catskill Mountains. The surrounding area offers a variety of activities including antique shopping, ice skating, golf, tennis, swimming, boating, fishing and hiking. The innkeepers offer ski packages.

Innkeeper(s): Carol & Peter Molnar. $50-85. MC VISA AX. TAC10. 7 rooms, 4 with PB. Breakfast included in rates. Type of meal: gourmet breakfast. Beds: KQDT. Phone in room. Fax on premises. Downhill skiing nearby.

Location: In the Catskill Mountains.

Publicity: *Spotlight, NY Wedding.*

"Truly a step back in time to all that was charming, elegant and wholesome—right here in the 20th century."

Millbrook   I12

A Cat In Your Lap

Old Rt 82 & The Monument
Millbrook, NY 12545
(914)677-3051
E-mail: berensmann@aol.com

Circa 1840. This two-story gray shingle-style house is located on an acre and a half, a short walk from the village. The Lower Barn Suite, in a tree-shaded barn across from the main house, features a large fireplace, white sofa, beamed ceiling and brass bed. Each of the two suites have a small kitchen. The inn's cats are confined to the main house. There is a large patio and sun deck, and a stream winds through the property. A four-course breakfast features items such as fruit soup, Irish porridge, frittatas and homemade breads.

Innkeeper(s): Madelyn & Bill Berensmann. $65-95. MC VISA PC. 4 rooms with PB, 2 with FP. 2 suites. 2 cottages. Breakfast and afternoon tea included in rates. Types of meals: full breakfast and gourmet breakfast. Beds: KDT. Air conditioning in room. TV, VCR, bicycles and pet boarding on premises. Handicap access. Family reunions hosted. German, French and Italian spoken. Antiques, fishing, parks, shopping, cross-country skiing, golf, theater and watersports nearby. Pets Allowed: in barn suites (not main house)

Monroe   J11

The Roscoe House

45 Lakes Rd
Monroe, NY 10950
(914)782-0442

Circa 1920. This traditional colonial rests on 24 acres that include such scenic features as hiking trails, streams, waterfalls, footbridges and two working waterwheels. Guest rooms are handsomely designed with king-size four-poster and sleigh beds, ceiling fans, hardwood floors, Oriental rugs, tile baths and TVs. Some have Jacuzzi tubs. A 40-foot-long game room offers billiards, game tables and a fireplace. Other gathering spots are the breakfast room, dining room, garden room and solarium. Eggs Benedict, smoked salmon and fresh fruit are among the breakfast offerings. The innkeepers can advise you on the area's activities, which range from fly fishing to outlet shopping and include an 18th-century restored village, apple picking, a winery, West Point, antiquing and skiing.

Innkeeper(s): Diana Lincoln. $165-185. PC. 4 rooms with PB. 1 suite. 1 cottage. Breakfast, afternoon tea and picnic lunch included in rates. Types of meals: full breakfast and gourmet breakfast. Beds: KQ. Phone, air conditioning, turndown service, ceiling fan, TV and VCR in room. Bicycles on premises. 24 acres. Antiques, fishing, parks, shopping, downhill skiing, cross-country skiing, sporting events, golf and theater nearby.

"*A very relaxing weekend in a great inn.*"

New York   L12

The 412 House

412 E 84th St
New York, NY 10028-6206
Fax:(212)717-8089

Circa 1890. This traditional, vine-covered Victorian townhouse is actually a two-room apartment. It is suggested here since New York City doesn't abound in traditional bed & breakfast inns. There is a minimum-stay requirement of one week for one or two people. The apartment is one floor up and features a fireplace, brick wall, floral wallpaper, kitchenette and microwave. There are two phones and an answering machine with remote callback. Sleeping accommodations include two twin beds nestled side by side and a loveseat sofa-bed. Breakfast is not provided, but part of your New York experience can include shopping the local markets or simply going out for pastries. The apartment is located in a good upper east side neighborhood.

$1000. PC TC. 2 rooms. Beds: T. Phone, air conditioning, TV and VCR in room. Antiques, parks, shopping, sporting events and theater nearby.

Niagara Falls   F3

The Cameo Manor North

3881 Lower River Rd, Rt 18-F
Niagara Falls, NY 14174
(716)745-3034

Circa 1860. This Colonial Revival inn offers a restful setting ideal for those seeking a peaceful getaway. The inn's three secluded acres add to its romantic setting, as does an interior that features several fireplaces. Visitors select from three suites, which feature private sun rooms, or two guest rooms that share a bath. Popular spots with guests include the library, great room and solarium. Fort Niagara and several state parks are nearby, and the American and Canadian Falls are within easy driving distance of the inn. The inn is actually located about eight miles north of Niagara Falls near the village of Youngstown.

Innkeeper(s): Gregory Fisher. $75-175. 4 rooms. Breakfast included in rates. Type of meal: full breakfast.

Publicity: *Country Folk Art, Esquire, Journey, Seaway Trail, Waterways, Buffalo News.*

"*I made the right choice when I selected Cameo.*"

Manchester House B&B

653 Main St
Niagara Falls, NY 14301-1701
(716)285-5717 (800)489-3009 Fax:(716)282-2144
E-mail: 71210.65@compuserve.com

Circa 1903. This turn-of-the-century home once was used to house doctors' offices. The home, just a mile from the famous falls, and the innkeepers are full of knowledge about their famous local attraction. The home is decorated with comfortable furnishings, family pieces and antiques. Prints and posters depicting scenes of the Niagara Falls area also decorate the home.

Innkeeper(s): Lis & Carl Slenk. $60-80. MC VISA TC. TAC10. 3 rooms with PB. Breakfast included in rates. Type of meal: full breakfast. Beds: KQT. Air conditioning and ceiling fan in room. TV, VCR and library on premises. Weddings, small meetings, family reunions and seminars hosted. German spoken. Amusement parks, antiques, fishing, parks and shopping nearby.

"*Thanks for a wonderful stay. All your little extras make for a warm homey feeling. Breakfast knocked our socks off.*"

Park Place Bed & Breakfast

740 Park Pl
Niagara Falls, NY 14301-1028
(716)282-4626 (800)510-4626

Circa 1913. This three-story, half-timbered house was designed with strong Prairie School and Craftsman influences, popular in the early twentieth century. Originally built for James G. Marshall, founder of Union Carbide, the house is one of 14 carefully maintained turn-of-the-century homes located in the tree-lined residential neighborhood of historic Park Place. Quartered oak woodwork, beams and paneled walls and Steuben glass light fixtures add to the inn's rich character. Each of the guest rooms are decorated with antiques and period furnishings. Guests are invited to play the antique Chickering grand piano or relax on the veranda over-looking Park Place. A full breakfast is enjoyed before the warmth of the dining room fireplace. The inn is within walking distance from an aquarium, the American and Horseshoe Falls, Rainbow Bridge to Canada, shopping, restaurants and entertainment facilities.

Historic Interest: Walking distance from the Native American Center, Winter Garden, Prospect Park and Goat Island. A short drive from Old Fort Niagara.

Innkeeper(s): Louise & Thomas Yots. $50-80. MC VISA AX PC TC. TAC10. 5 rooms, 1 with PB. Breakfast, afternoon tea included in rates. Meal: full breakfast. Beds: QTDR. Air conditioning in room. Weddings, small meetings and seminars hosted. Italian, some French spoken. Amusement parks, antiques, fishing, parks, shopping, sporting events, golf, theater, watersports nearby.

"*We will definitely recommend your home to everyone.*"

North River   D11

Highwinds Inn

Barton Mines Rd
North River, NY 12856
(518)251-3760 (800)241-1923

Circa 1933. This mountain retreat offers panoramic views of the Siamese wilderness area and the Adirondacks. Every room has a view of the mountains. The inn offers a garnet stone fireplace and a view of the sunset on the dining porch.

Innkeeper(s): Holly Currier. $130-170. MAP. MC VISA DS. 4 rooms with PB. Breakfast and dinner included in rates. Type of meal: full breakfast. Picnic lunch available. Restaurant on premises. Beds: KD. Phone in room. TV on premises. 1600 acres. Weddings, small meetings, family reunions and seminars hosted. Antiques, fishing, shopping, skiing and theater nearby.
Publicity: *The Post Star.*

Penn Yan   G6

Finton's Landing

661 E Lake Rd
Penn Yan, NY 14527-9421
(315)536-3146

Circa 1861. A delightful Victorian located on Keuka Lake, the inn features relaxing front porch rockers, whimsical period furnishings, painted wall murals and parlor fireplace. The sunny east shore has 165 feet of secluded beach, a restored lakeside gazebo and a hammock. A luscious two-course breakfast is served in the cozy dining room or on the wraparound porch with its views of the lake. Gift certificates are available.
Historic Interest: Located close to the Curtiss Museum.
Innkeeper(s): Doug & Arianne Tepper. $89. MC VISA PC TC. 4 rooms with PB. Breakfast included in rates. Type of meal: full breakfast. Beds: DT. Ceiling fan in room. Small meetings and seminars hosted. Antiques, fishing, parks, shopping, skiing, golf and watersports nearby.

The Wagener Estate B&B

351 Elm St
Penn Yan, NY 14527-1446
(315)536-4591

Circa 1794. Nestled in the Finger Lakes area on four shaded acres, this 16-room house features a wicker-furnished veranda where guests can relax in solitude or chat with others. Some of the early hand-hewn framing and the original brick fireplace and

oven can be seen in the Family Room at the north end of the house. Most of the land, which is known as Penn Yan, was once owned by the original occupants of the home, David Wagener and his wife, Rebecca. David died in 1799, leaving this property to his son, Squire Wagener, who is considered to be the founder of Penn Yan. Antiques, fishing, cross-country skiing, water sports and wineries nearby.
Historic Interest: Near the Oliver House and Birkett Mills.
Innkeeper(s): Joanne & Scott Murray. $65-80. MC VISA AX DS. 6 rooms, 4 with PB. Breakfast included in rates. Meal: full breakfast. Beds: KQDT. Phone in room. Antiques, fishing, cross-country skiing and watersports nearby.
Publicity: *Finger Lakes Times, Chronicle Express, New York Times.*
"Thanks so much for the wonderful hospitality and the magnificent culinary treats."

Pine City   H6

Rufus Tanner House

60 Sagetown Rd
Pine City, NY 14871-9502
(607)732-0213 Fax:(607)735-0620
E-mail: rufustan@servtech.com

Circa 1864. This Greek Revival farmhouse sits among century-old sugar maple and dwarf fruit trees. Its spacious rooms are filled with antiques and other period furnishings that add greatly

to the inn's ambiance. The four air-conditioned guest rooms include the first-floor Master Bedroom, with its marble-topped high Victorian furniture, and a bath with two-person shower, whirlpool and black marble floor. One room includes a fireplace. All guest rooms have air conditioning. Guests are welcome to use the treadmill and weight machine in the basement. The Elmira-Corning area near the inn offers many attractions, including Mark Twain's Burial Site, the National Soaring Museum, the Corning Glass Museum and the National Warplane Museum.
Innkeeper(s): Bill Knapp & John Gibson. $55-95. MC VISA PC TC. TAC10. 4 rooms with PB. Breakfast included in rates. Types of meals: full breakfast and early coffee/tea. Dinner available. Beds: QD. TV, VCR and spa on premises. Weddings, small meetings, family reunions and seminars hosted. Antiques, fishing, parks, shopping and theater nearby.
"Lovely house! Wish we could stay longer!"

Pine Hill   H11

Birchcreek Inn

Rt 28
Pine Hill, NY 12465
(914)254-5222 Fax:(914)254-5812

Circa 1896. Slate walls border the Birchcreek Inn, once the summer estate of Henry Morton, president of Stevens Institute of Technology. The inn offers a library with fireplace, a Great Hall and a billiard room. Ask for the Champagne Room and enjoy a king-size brass bed and oversize bath. A large wraparound porch overlooks Birch Creek and the inn's 23 acres. Breakfast, served fireside, includes cheese omelets, sausage and homemade bagels.
$85-145. MC VISA AX PC TC. TAC10. 7 rooms with PB, 1 with FP. 1 cottage. Breakfast included in rates. Types of meals: continental-plus breakfast, full breakfast and early coffee/tea. Afternoon tea available. Beds: KQDT. Ceiling fan, TV and VCR in room. Fax, copier, bicycles, library and child care on premises. 23 acres. Weddings, small meetings, family reunions and seminars hosted. Antiques, fishing, parks, shopping, downhill skiing, cross-country skiing, golf, theater and watersports nearby.
Publicity: *Sunday Freeman.*

Queensbury   E12

The Crislip's B&B

693 Ridge Rd
Queensbury, NY 12804-6901
(518)793-6869

Circa 1802. This Federal-style house was built by Quakers and was once owned by the area's first doctor, who used it as a training center for young interns. There's an acre of lawns and annual gardens and a Victorian Italianate veranda overlooks the Green Mountains. The inn is furnished with 18th-century antiques and reproductions, including four-poster canopy beds and highboys. There's a keeping room with a huge fireplace. Historic stone walls flank the property.
Innkeeper(s): Ned & Joyce Crislip. $45-75. MC VISA TC. 3 rooms with PB. Breakfast included in rates. Types of meals: full breakfast and early coffee/tea. Beds: KD. Air conditioning in room. TV on premises. Small meetings hosted. Amusement parks, antiques, fishing, parks, shopping, downhill skiing, cross-country skiing, sporting events, theater and watersports nearby.
Location: Lake George, Saratoga area.

Sanford's Ridge B&B

749 Ridge Rd
Queensbury, NY 12804-6903
(518)793-4923

Circa 1797. Visitors to the Adirondacks will find a bit of history and more than a little hospitality at this Federal-style inn, built by David Sanford after the Revolutionary War. The inn has retained its original elegance and added a few modern touches, such as an in-ground swimming pool and a sunny outdoor deck. Visitors select from the Haviland, Sanford and Webster rooms, all with private baths. Each room is decorated in Colonial style with quilt-covered poster beds and antique furnishings. The full breakfasts include a special entree of the day and fruit grown on the premises. Lake George and Saratoga Springs are a short drive away.

Historic Interest: Oldest house in the County. It retains the original woodwork, flooring and fireplaces.

Innkeeper(s): Carolyn Rudolph. $65-100. MC VISA TC. TAC10. 3 rooms with PB, 2 with FP. Breakfast included in rates. Type of meal: full breakfast. Beds: KQT. Air conditioning in room. TV, swimming and library on premises. Antiques, shopping, golf, theater and watersports nearby.

Red Hook   H12

The Grand Dutchess

50 N Broadway
Red Hook, NY 12571-1403
(914)758-5818 Fax:(914)758-3143
E-mail: grandut@worldnet.att.net

Circa 1874. This Second Empire Victorian was originally built as the Hoffman Inn. It later served as the town school, a speakeasy and then a lonely hearts club. Twin parlors behind etched glass and wood sliding doors feature hardwood floors,

antique chandeliers, arched marble fireplaces with massive carved mirrors, Oriental rugs and heirloom antiques. Lace curtains decorate the floor-to-ceiling windows. Most of the rooms have queen-sized beds and private baths and are located at the corners of the home to maximize the use of natural light. A full breakfast of homemade breads, a main dish, cereal and fruit is offered. For young guests, the innkeeper will prepare chocolate chip pancakes.

Innkeeper(s): Elizabeth Pagano & Harold Gruber. $85-125. PC TC. 6 rooms, 4 with PB. 1 suite. 1 conference room. Breakfast included in rates. Types of meals: full breakfast and early coffee/tea. Beds: KQDT. Air conditioning in room. TV, VCR, fax, copier and library on premises. Weddings, small meetings, family reunions and seminars hosted. Antiques, fishing, parks, shopping, skiing, sporting events, golf, theater and watersports nearby.

Publicity: *Northeast.*

"This place is outrageous! We love this place!"

Rhinebeck   I12

Beekman Arms

Rt 9, 4 Mill St
Rhinebeck, NY 12572
(914)876-7077

Circa 1766. Said to be the oldest landmark inn in America, some walls of the Beekman Arms are two-and three-feet-thick. It has seen a variety of guests-including pioneers, trappers, Indians and Dutch farmers. Among the famous were Aaron Burr, William Jennings Bryan, Horace Greeley, Franklin Roosevelt, Neil Armstrong and Elizabeth Taylor. Like most old taverns and inns, it provided a meeting place for leaders of the day. Victorian furnishings are found throughout. Mr. LaForge is the 28th innkeeper at Beekman Arms.

Innkeeper(s): Charles LaForge. $85-120. MC VISA AX DC. 59 rooms with PB, 21 with FP. 1 conference room. Types of meals: continental breakfast and full breakfast. Restaurant on premises. Beds: QDT. Fax and copier on premises. Handicap access.

Location: Center of Village of Rhinebeck.

Publicity: *New York Times.*

"If this is any indication of your general hospitality, it is very easy to see why you have stayed in the business for so long."

Mansakenning Carriage House

29 Ackert Hook Rd
Rhinebeck, NY 12572
(914)876-3500 Fax:(914)876-6179
E-mail: ajpease@sprynetm9.com

Circa 1895. Guests are sure to find this National Register Colonial a perfect country inn. Take a walk along the five acres, and you'll find hammocks strung between trees and chairs placed here and there for guests who wish to relax and enjoy the fragrant grounds. Step into any one of the seven guest rooms, and you'll instantly feel as though you've entered a cozy, romantic haven. Ralph Lauren linens dress the beds, which are topped with fluffy comforters. Exposed beams, fireplaces, wood floors and quilts add to the decor of the individually appointed guest rooms. Guests will find robes, specialty bath soaps, a coffee maker, refrigerator and a TV with VCR in their rooms. Innkeeper Michelle Dremann has had several recipes featured in cookbooks, and it is she or the managing innkeeper that prepare the decadent morning feast. Guests can request to have breakfast delivered to their room along with the morning paper. Rhinebeck is full of historic houses and buildings, as well guests can visit antique shops, galleries, wineries, restaurants or the Culinary Institute of America.

Innkeeper(s): Michelle & John Dremann-Pease. $125-350. PC TC. TAC10. 7 rooms with PB, 5 with FP. 5 suites. Breakfast included in rates. Type of meal: gourmet breakfast. Beds: KQ. Phone, air conditioning, ceiling fan, TV and VCR in room. Fax, copier and library on premises. Weddings, small meetings and family reunions hosted. Fishing, parks, shopping, downhill skiing, cross-country skiing, sporting events, golf, theater, watersports nearby.

Pets Allowed: Two rooms only.

Publicity: *New York Times, Bride's, Hudson Valley Magazine, New York Post, Poughkeepsie Journal, Wingspan, Time Out Magazine.*

Veranda House B&B

82 Montgomery St
Rhinebeck, NY 12572-1113
(914)876-4133 Fax:(914)876-4133

Circa 1845. For nearly a century, this Federal-style home served as the parsonage for an Episcopal church. The home is located in a Rhinebeck historic district among many notable houses. The home is decorated in a comfortable mix of styles, with a few antiques. If weather permits, breakfasts are served on the terrace, featuring items such as freshly baked pastries or maple walnut coffee cake and a daily entree. The scenic area offers much in the way of activities. Woodstock is a short drive away.

Innkeeper(s): Linda & Ward Stanley. $85-120. PC TC. 4 rooms with PB. Breakfast included in rates. Types of meals: full breakfast and gourmet breakfast. Beds: QT. Air conditioning and ceiling fan in room. TV, VCR and library on premises. Small meetings, family reunions and seminars hosted. Some German spoken. Antiques, fishing, parks, shopping, downhill skiing, cross-country skiing, golf, theater and watersports nearby.

"Beautiful rooms, terrific breakfast! We will recommend you highly."

Rochester F5

A Bed & Breakfast at Dartmouth House Inn

215 Dartmouth St
Rochester, NY 14607-3202
(716)271-7872 Fax:(716)473-0778
E-mail: abandbinn@aol.com

Circa 1905. The lavish, four-course breakfasts served daily at this beautiful turn-of-the-century Edwardian home are unforgettable. Innkeeper and award-winning, gourmet cook Ellie Klein starts off the meal with special fresh juice, which is served in the parlor. From this point, guests are seated at the candlelit dining table to enjoy a series of delectable dishes, such as pears poached in port wine, a mouth-watering entree, a light, lemon ice and a rich dessert. And each of the courses is

ca.1905

served on a separate pattern of Depression Glass. If the breakfast isn't enough, Ellie and husband, Bill, have stocked the individually decorated guest rooms with flowers, fluffy towels, bathrobes and special bath amenities. Each of the bedchambers boasts antique collectibles, and guests can soak in inviting clawfoot tubs. The inn is located in the prestigious turn-of-the-century Park Avenue Historical and Cultural District. The entire area is an architect's dream. Museums, colleges, restaurants and antique shops are among the many nearby attractions.

Historic Interest: George Eastman's mansion and International Museum of Photography is a 10-minute walk from the inn. The High Falls Brown's Race Historic Center is two miles, the graves of Susan B. Anthony and Frederick Douglass are two miles away at Mount Hope Cemetery. The Rochester Historical Society is a 10-minute walk.

Innkeeper(s): Elinor & Bill Klein. $65-125. MC VISA AX DS PC TC. TAC10. 4 rooms with PB. Breakfast included in rates. Types of meals: full breakfast and early coffee/tea. Beds: KQT. Phone, air conditioning, ceiling fan, TV and VCR in room. Fax, bicycles and library on premises. Antiques, parks, shopping, theater and watersports nearby.

Publicity: *Democrat & Chronicle, DAKA, Genesee Country, Seaway Trail, Oneida News, Travelers News, Country Living.*

"The food was fabulous, the company fascinating, and the personal attention beyond comparison. You made me feel at home instantly."

Saranac Lake C11

The Doctor's Inn

Trudeau Rd
Saranac Lake, NY 12983
(518)891-3464 (888)518-3464 Fax:(518)891-3464
E-mail: docinn@northnet.org

Circa 1890. Named for the succession of physicians once associated with the historic Trudeau Sanatorium, the inn combines features of both Queen Anne and Colonial Revival styles. The inn is surrounded by five wooded acres at the foot of Mount Pisgah and boasts magnificent views of the Adirondack Mountains. With its Adirondack-style furnishings, the inn is both a comfortable retreat as well as a launching point for hikers, boaters and skiers. The lodge-style common room with its fieldstone fireplace and the wide wraparound porches are just a few of the inn's eclectic architectural details. Breakfast is a hearty combination of fresh fruit, cereal, pancakes, waffles, eggs and breakfast meats. In the summer, guests can enjoy badminton, croquet and horseshoes on the well-maintained grounds.

Historic Interest: The inn is adjacent to a ski mountain.

Innkeeper(s): Susan Moody. $45-95. EP. MC VISA PC. 4 rooms, 1 with PB. 2 suites. Breakfast included in rates. Types of meals: continental-plus breakfast and full breakfast. Picnic lunch available. Beds: DT. TV, VCR, fax, bicycles and library on premises. Weddings, small meetings, family reunions and seminars hosted. Antiques, fishing, parks, shopping, downhill skiing, cross-country skiing, sporting events, golf, theater and watersports nearby.
Pets Allowed.

"Thanks for the wonderful breakfasts and excellent accommodations. Just what the doctor ordered!"

The Point

HCR 1, Box 65
Saranac Lake, NY 12983
(518)891-5674 (800)678-8946 Fax:(518)891-1152

Circa 1930. Designed by renowned architect William Distin and built for William Rockefeller, this Adirondack Great Camp has hosted fashionable house parties for the Vanderbilts, Whitneys and Morgans. No expense was spared to create the elegant, rustic lakefront estate with its walk-in-fieldstone fireplaces, rare Adirondack antiques and massive hand-hewn beams. Each day a cord of wood is needed to fuel all the fireplaces. This lavish camp welcomes those who prefer to rough it with style.

Innkeeper(s): Tim Thuell. $825-1350. AP. AX. 11 rooms with PB, 11 with FP. 1 conference room. Beds: K. Phone in room. Fax and copier on premises.

Publicity: *New York Magazine, House & Garden, Country Inns, Washingtonian, Brides, Connoisseur.*

"Simply the most attractive private home in America. Irene Miki Rawlings, New York Times."

Saratoga Springs F12

Adelphi Hotel

365 Broadway
Saratoga Springs, NY 12866-3111
(518)587-4688 Fax:(518)587-4688

Circa 1877. This Victorian hotel is one of two hotels still remaining from Saratoga's opulent spa era. A piazza overlooking Broadway features three-story columns topped with Victorian fretwork. Recently refurbished with lavish turn-of-the-century decor, rooms are filled with antique furnishings and opulent draperies and wall coverings, highlighting the inn's high ceilings and ornate woodwork. Breakfast is delivered to each room in the morning.

Innkeeper(s): Gregg Siefker & Sheila Parkert. $95-320. MC VISA AX TC. TAC10. 38 rooms with PB. 15 suites. 1 conference room. Breakfast included in rates. Type of meal: continental-plus breakfast. Beds: QD. Phone, air conditioning, turndown service and TV in room. Fax, copier and swimming on premises. Weddings, small meetings and seminars hosted. Antiques, parks, shopping and theater nearby.

Publicity: *N.Y. Times, Country Inns, Back Roads, Conde Nast, Victorian Homes.*

Chestnut Tree Inn

9 Whitney Pl
Saratoga Springs, NY 12866-4518
(518)587-8681

Circa 1870. Linger over breakfast as you sit and enjoy the view from a wicker-filled veranda at this Second Period Empire-style house. The grounds boast what is thought to be the last live chestnut tree in the city. The innkeepers are antique dealers, who operate a local group shop. They have filled the home with turn-of-the-century pieces and have won awards for the preservation of their inn and for having the "best front porch" in Saratoga. The home is within walking distance of the race track, downtown shopping, only a mile from the Saratoga Performing Arts Center and the State Park where guests can enjoy mineral baths.

Historic Interest: The Canfield Casino, a restored local gambling house with a museum on the second floor, is two blocks from the inn. Saratoga Battlefield is about 10 miles away.

Innkeeper(s): Cathleen & Bruce De Luke. $65-225. MC VISA. 10 rooms, 7 with PB. Breakfast included in rates. Type of meal: continental-plus breakfast. Beds: QDT. Antiques, fishing, theater and watersports nearby.

Publicity: *New York Times.*

The Lombardi Farm B&B

41 Locust Grove Rd
Saratoga Springs, NY 12866-9108
(518)587-2074 Fax:(518)587-2074

Circa 1840. A surrey rests in front of this Victorian farmhouse, which is surrounded by 10 acres of scenic countryside. The innkeepers keep Nubian and French Alpine Goats on the property, and during Spring months, guests are invited to bottle feed a baby goat. A four-course, gourmet breakfast is served in the farm's Florida Room. The menu changes daily and items such as breakfast souffles, Belgian waffles, quiche, chocolate crepes and strudels are accompanied by freshly baked muffins, scones or rolls. Guests are invited to take a relaxing dip in the B&B's indoor hot tub with Jacuzzi. Equestrians will appreciate the home's close access to the Saratoga Thoroughbred Racetrack, Saratoga Harness Track and the National Museum of Polo.

Historic Interest: The Saratoga Battlefield is nearby.

Innkeeper(s): Dr. Vincent & Kathleen Lombardi. $100-130. PC TC. TAC10. 4 rooms with PB. 1 suite. Breakfast included in rates. Types of meals: gourmet breakfast and early coffee/tea. Beds: KQDT. Air conditioning and ceiling fan in room. TV, VCR, fax, copier, spa, bicycles and library on premises. Handicap access. 10 acres. Weddings, small meetings and family reunions hosted. Antiques, fishing, parks, shopping, cross-country skiing, theater and watersports nearby.

"The stay at Lombardi Farm was a most delightful experience. Your warmth, plus the wonderful food total a perfect 10."

Six Sisters B&B

149 Union Ave
Saratoga Springs, NY 12866-3518
(518)583-1173 Fax:(518)587-2470
E-mail: stay@sixsistersbandb.com

Circa 1880. The unique architecture of this Victorian home features a large second-story bay window, a tiger oak front door decked with stained glass and a veranda accentuated with rocking chairs. Inside, the marble and hardwoods combine with antiques and Oriental rugs to create an elegant atmosphere. During racing season, guests can rise early and take a short walk to the local race track to watch the horses work

out. Upon their return, guests are greeted with the aroma of a delicious, gourmet breakfast. Saratoga Springs' downtown area offers antique shops, boutiques and many restaurants.

Historic Interest: Saratoga Battlefield (15 minutes), Spa State Park (5 minutes), Saratoga Racetrack (across street).

Innkeeper(s): Kate Benton. $75-300. MC VISA AX DS PC TC. TAC10. 4 rooms with PB. Breakfast included in rates. Types of meals: gourmet breakfast and early coffee/tea. Beds: KQ. Air conditioning, ceiling fan and TV in room. Fax on premises. Amusement parks, antiques, fishing, parks, shopping, skiing, sporting events, theater and watersports nearby.

Location: Thirty minutes north of Albany & thirty minutes south of Lake George.

Publicity: *Gourmet, Country Inns, Country Folk Art, Country Victorian, McCalls.*

"The true definition of a bed & breakfast."

Westchester House B&B

102 Lincoln Ave
Saratoga Springs, NY 12866-4536
(518)587-7613 (800)581-7613

Circa 1885. This gracious Queen Anne Victorian has been welcoming vacationers for more than 100 years. Antiques from four generations of the Melvin family grace the high-ceilinged rooms. Oriental rugs top gleaming wood floors, while antique clocks and lace curtains set a graceful tone. Guests gather on the wraparound porch, in the parlors or gardens for an afternoon refreshment of old-fashioned lemonade. Racing season rates are quoted separately.

Historic Interest: Built by master carpenter Almeron King in 1885.

Innkeeper(s): Bob & Stephanie Melvin. $90-250. MC VISA AX CB PC TC. TAC10. 7 rooms with PB. 1 conference room. Breakfast and afternoon tea included in rates. Types of meals: continental-plus breakfast and early coffee/tea. Beds: KQT. Air conditioning and ceiling fan in room. Library on premises. Small meetings, family reunions and seminars hosted. Antiques, fishing, parks, shopping, cross-country skiing, sporting events, theater and watersports nearby.

Location: Thirty miles north of Albany in the Adirondack foothills.

Publicity: *Getaways for Gourmets, Albany Times Union, Saratogian, Capital, Country Inns, New York Daily News, WNYT, Newsday, Hudson Valley.*

"I adored your B&B and have raved about it to all. One of the most beautiful and welcoming places we've ever visited."

Saratoga Springs (Ballston Spa) *F12*

Apple Tree B&B

49 W High St
Ballston Spa, NY 12020
(518)885-1113

Circa 1878. A bird fountain and garden decorate the entrance to this Second Empire Victorian, which is located in the historic district of Ballston Spa, a village just a few minutes from Saratoga Springs. Guest rooms feature Victorian and French-country decor, and each has antiques and whirlpool tubs. Guests enjoy fresh fruit, homemade baked goods, a selection of beverages and a daily entree during the breakfast service.

Innkeeper(s): Dolores & Jim Taisey. $75-150. MC VISA AX PC TC. TAC10. 4 rooms with PB. Breakfast included in rates. Types of meals: full breakfast and early coffee/tea. Beds: Q. Air conditioning, TV and VCR in room. Small meetings and family reunions hosted. Amusement parks, antiques, fishing, parks, shopping, skiing, sporting events, theater and watersports nearby.

Schroon Lake   D12

Schroon Lake B&B

Rt 9
Schroon Lake, NY 12870
(518)532-7042 Fax:(518)532-9820
E-mail: schroonbb@aol.com

Circa 1920. The town of Schroon Lake has welcomed many rich and famous (sometimes infamous) guests, and this house was a popular spot during prohibition. Today, its popularity stems from the hospitality guests enjoy. The innkeepers offer a living room with a TV, a selection of movies and games. Guests also can relax on the wide front porch, which is lined with wicker rockers. Breakfasts feature gourmet items such as Adirondack eggs Benedict with lemon hollandaise. The innkeeper is a former food writer and stylist.

Innkeeper(s): Rita & Bob Skojec. $75-90. MC VISA AX DS PC TC. TAC10. 5 rooms, 3 with PB. 1 suite. Breakfast included in rates. Types of meals: full breakfast, gourmet breakfast and early coffee/tea. Evening snack and catering service available. Beds: KQT. Air conditioning, turndown service and ceiling fan in room. TV, VCR, fax and library on premises. Small meetings, family reunions and seminars hosted. Amusement parks, antiques, fishing, parks, shopping, downhill skiing, cross-country skiing, sporting events, golf, theater and watersports nearby.

Publicity: *Country Register.*

"Great food, great atmosphere, comfy bed, heaven on earth!"

Severance   D12

The Red House

PO Box 125
Severance, NY 12872-0125
(518)532-7734

Circa 1850. Twenty feet from the banks of Paradox Brook, on the West end of Paradox Lake, is this two-story farmhouse inn that boasts a multitude of recreational offerings for its guests,

including swimming, tennis, boating and fishing. The inn features three guest rooms, one with private bath. The inn's full breakfasts include homemade breads and regional specialties. Be sure to plan a day trip to Fort Ticonderoga and ride the ferry across Lake Champlain to Vermont. Hiking and cross-country skiing are available nearby.

Historic Interest: Fort Ticonderoga (15 miles), Adirondack Great Camps (20-40 miles), Adirondack Museum (1 hour).

Innkeeper(s): Helen Wildman. $55-85. PC. 3 rooms, 1 with PB. Breakfast included in rates. Type of meal: full breakfast. Beds: QDT. Phone in room.

"Thanks for your wonderful hospitality, we'll definitely be back again."

Sharon Springs (Cooperstown) *G11*

Edgefield

Washington St, PO Box 152
Sharon Springs (Cooperstown), NY 13459
(518)284-3339

Circa 1865. This home has seen many changes. It began as a farmhouse, a wing was added in the 1880s, and by the turn of the century, it sported an elegant Greek Revival facade. Edgefield is one of a collection of nearby homes used as a family compound for summer vacations. The rooms are decorated with traditional furnishings in a formal English-country style. In the English tradition, afternoon tea is presented each day with scones, cookies and tea sandwiches. Sharon Springs includes many historic sites, and the town is listed in the National Register.

Historic Interest: Near Cooperstown and Glimmerglass Opera; Albany is 45 minute away.

Innkeeper(s): Daniel Marshall Wood. $95-135. PC TC. 5 rooms with PB. Breakfast, afternoon tea and evening snack included in rates. Types of meals: full breakfast, gourmet breakfast and early coffee/tea. Beds: QT. Turndown service and ceiling fan in room. TV, VCR and library on premises. Antiques, fishing, parks, shopping, golf, theater and watersports nearby.

"Truly what I always imagined the perfect B&B experience to be!"

Sodus Point   E6

Carriage House Inn

8375 Wickham Blvd
Sodus Point, NY 14555-9608
(315)483-2100 (800)292-2990

Circa 1870. The innkeeper at this inn offers accommodations in a historic Victorian home located on four acres in a residential area or in the stone carriage house on the shore of Lake Ontario. The carriage house overlooks the Sodus Point historic lighthouse. The inn offers beach access, and guests can walk to restaurants and charter boats. For an additional cost, the inn will provide sandwiches and thermos.

Historic Interest: The Sodus Point historic lighthouse is adjacent to the inn.

Innkeeper(s): James Den Decker. $65. MC VISA AX DC DS PC. 8 rooms with

PB. Breakfast included in rates. Type of meal: full breakfast. Beds: KT. Phone and TV in room. Antiques, fishing, golf and watersports nearby.

Publicity: *Finger Lakes Times, Democrat and Chronicle, WTVH.*

"My wife and I have been telling everyone about the beautiful room we had and your courtesy."

Southampton K15

Mainstay

579 Hill St
Southampton, NY 11968-5305
(516)283-4375 Fax:(516)287-6240

Circa 1870. This Colonial has served as a guest house, country store and now a bed & breakfast with eight guest rooms. Antiques, including iron beds, decorate the bed-chambers. One suite includes a clawfoot tub. A decanter of sherry has been placed in each  guest room. Several walls feature hand-painted murals. There is a swimming pool for guest use, as well as beach access.

Innkeeper(s): Elizabeth Main. $80-300. MC VISA AX TC. 8 rooms, 5 with PB. 2 suites. Breakfast included in rates. Type of meal: continental breakfast. Beds: KQDT. Ceiling fan in room. Fax on premises. Antiques, fishing, parks, shopping, golf, theater and watersports nearby.

Publicity: *New York Times.*

Southold K15

Goose Creek Guesthouse

1475 Waterview Dr, PO Box 377
Southold, NY 11971-2125
(516)765-3356

Circa 1860. Grover Pease left for the Civil War from this house, and after his death, his widow, Harriet, ran a summer boarding house here. The basement actually dates from the 1780s and is constructed of large rocks. The present house was

moved here and put on the older foundation. Southold has many historic homes and a guidebook is provided for visitors. The inn is close to the ferry to New London and the ferries to the South Shore via Shelter Island.

Historic Interest: Hortons Point Lighthouse, Railroad and Maritime Museum.

Innkeeper(s): Mary Mooney-Getoff. $55-85. PC TC. TAC10. 4 rooms. Breakfast and afternoon tea included in rates. Types of meals: full breakfast, gourmet breakfast and early coffee/tea. Picnic lunch available. Beds: KQDT. Phone and air conditioning in room. VCR and library on premises. Weddings and family reunions hosted. Spanish spoken. Amusement parks, antiques, fishing, parks, shopping, theater and watersports nearby.

Location: One-and-one-half miles south of Rt 25 on the north fork of Long Island.

Publicity: *New York Times, Newsday.*

"We will be repeat guests. Count on it!!"

Stillwater F12

Lee's Deer Run B&B

411 CR 71
Stillwater, NY 12170
(518)584-7722
E-mail: deerrun@sirus.com

Circa 1840. In an idyllic countryside setting between Saratoga Lake and Saratoga National Historic Park, this inn, crafted from a 19th-century barn, now is home to four guest rooms,

some with four-poster beds. The inn's full breakfasts are served in the dining room or on a deck with a view of the surrounding area. Bennington Battlefield and the Willard Mountain Ski Area are nearby.

Innkeeper(s): Rose & Don Lee. $75-200. PC. TAC10. 4 rooms with PB. 2 suites. 1 conference room. Breakfast included in rates. Types of meals: full breakfast and early coffee/tea. Beds: KQ. Air conditioning, turndown service and ceiling fan in room. 70 acres. Antiques, fishing, parks, shopping, cross-country skiing, sporting events, golf, theater and watersports nearby.

Trumansburg G7

Archway

7020 Searsburg Rd
Trumansburg, NY 14886-9501
(607)387-6175 (800)387-6175 Fax:(607)387-6175
E-mail: archway@lightlink.com

Circa 1861. The grey and white Greek Revival house features a white picket fence and arch that leads to lush flowering gardens. Decorated with antiques, the inn inspires a homey, comfortable atmosphere appropriate for families with or without children. Guests can take a catnap in the hammock on the porch or enjoy a stroll through the gardens. A gourmet breakfast is offered by the fireplace or in the sunroom overlook-  ing the public golf course. The inn is close to shopping, antiques, theater, fishing, tennis and cross-country skiing.

Innkeeper(s): Meredith Pollard & Joe Prevost. $65-85. MC VISA DS PC. 3 rooms, 1 with PB. Breakfast included in rates. Type of meal: gourmet breakfast. Beds: KQDT. Ceiling fan in room. TV, VCR, fax and copier on premises. Antiques, fishing, parks, shopping, downhill skiing, cross-country skiing, sporting events, golf, theater and watersports nearby.

"A beautiful, welcoming house, and the hosts are even more so!"

Ulster Park I12

Rennie's B&B

25 Ulster Ave
Ulster Park, NY 12487-5202
(914)331-5560 (800)447-8262 Fax:(914)298-2851
E-mail: renniesbb@aol.com

Circa 1928. From mail order, good things often come. This home, built from a kit purchased out of a Gordon-Van Tine catalog, was owned by the same family for 60 years, until the innkeepers purchased the home and transformed it into a bed & breakfast. The decor is light and airy with Arts & Crafts and Mission-style furnishings and Oriental rugs. Local produce and farm-fresh eggs fill the breakfast table, along with items such as homemade muffins, fresh fruit and crepes. The grounds, stretching out over more than two acres, include an old apple orchard. Ulster Park is near many attractions, from historic sites to antique shops to hiking trails. The inn is an ideal meeting place for small weddings and family reunions.

Innkeeper(s): Adele & Jonathan Wagman. $80-105. PC TC. 4 rooms with PB. Breakfast included in rates. Meals: full breakfast, early coffee/tea. Beds: QT. TV on premises. Antiques, fishing, parks, x-country skiing, golf, watersports nearby. Publicity: *Ulster County News*.

"Good food and good sleep. A place to stay longer!"

Utica F9

Adam Bowman Manor

197 Riverside Dr
Utica, NY 13502-2322
(315)738-0276 Fax:(315)738-0276

Circa 1823. The founder of Deerfield, George Weaver, built this graceful brick Federal house for his daughter. It is said to have been a part of the Underground Railroad (there's a secret tunnel) and is in the National Register. Handsomely landscaped grounds include a fountain, a gazebo, tall oaks and borders of perennials. The late Duke and Dutchess of Windsor were guests here and there are rooms named for them. The Duke's room has French-country furniture, a hand-painted fireplace and a king bed. Enjoy the Drawing Room and library, and in the morning guests are offered a full breakfast in the dining room with china, crystal and silver.

Innkeeper(s): Marion & Barry Goodwin. $50-75. MC VISA PC TC. TAC10. 4 rooms, 2 with PB, 2 with FP. Breakfast included in rates. Meal: full breakfast. Beds: KQD. Air conditioning in room. TV, VCR, fax, library on premises. Weddings, small meetings, family reunions, seminars hosted. Some French, Italian spoken. Antiques, fishing, parks, skiing, golf, theater, watersports nearby.

"Great company, good food and new friends for us."

Warrensburg E12

The Bent Finial Manor

3921 Main St
Warrensburg, NY 12885-1121
(518)623-3308 (888)802-6006 Fax:(518)623-4330

Circa 1904. Replete with gleaming woodwork and polished interior columns, this large wood and stone Victorian home has a wraparound porch, music room and glass conservatory.

Inside are stained glass windows, Victorian furnishings, a Louis XV baby grand piano and three terra-cotta fireplaces. Candlelight breakfasts are served in the conservatory in view of the gardens and lawns of the one-acre property. The innkeepers speak Dutch, French, Romanian, German, Italian and Spanish and can help you plan your leisure activities in the Lake George and Saratoga Springs area.

Innkeeper(s): Magda & Liviu Cornea. $75-135. MC VISA PC. TAC15. 8 rooms, 5 with PB, 1 with FP. 1 suite. 1 conference room. Breakfast included in rates. Types of meals: continental-plus breakfast, full breakfast and early coffee/tea. Beds: Q. Air conditioning, turndown service and ceiling fan in room. TV, VCR, fax, copier, bicycles and library on premises. Weddings, small meetings, family reunions and seminars hosted. Spanish, French, Dutch, Romanian, German and Italian spoken. Amusement parks, antiques, fishing, parks, shopping, downhill skiing, cross-country skiing, golf, theater and watersports nearby.

Country Road Lodge B&B

115 Hickory Hill Rd
Warrensburg, NY 12885-9732
(518)623-2207 Fax:(518)623-4363
E-mail: parisibb@netheaven.com

Circa 1929. This simple, rustic farmhouse lodge is situated on 35 acres along the Hudson River at the end of a country road. Rooms are clean and comfortable. A full breakfast is provided with homemade breads and muffins. The sitting room reveals panoramic views of the river and Sugarloaf Mountain. Bird watching, hiking and skiing are popular activities. Groups often reserve all four guest rooms.

Historic Interest: French and Indian War battlefields, Fort William Henry, Ticonderoga, and Defiance, Millionaire's Row on Lake George.

Innkeeper(s): Sandi & Steve Parisi. $55-62. PC. TAC10. 4 rooms, 2 with PB. Breakfast included in rates. Types of meals: full breakfast and early coffee/tea. Beds: DT. Ceiling fan in room. Library on premises. 35 acres. Amusement parks, antiques, fishing, parks, shopping, downhill skiing, cross-country skiing, theater and watersports nearby.

Location: Adirondack Mountains near Lake George.
Publicity: *North Jersey Herald & News*.

House on The Hill B&B

Rt 28 Box 248
Warrensburg, NY 12885
(518)623-9390 (800)221-9390 Fax:(518)623-9396

Circa 1750. Inspected, rated and approved AAA, ABBA, 3-Crown, this historic Federal-style inn on a hill in the six-million-acre Adirondack Park offers five guest rooms. After guests are treated to coffee and baked goods in their rooms, they enjoy the inn's full breakfasts in the sunroom, which offers wonderful views of the surrounding fields and woods from its many windows. Cross-country skiing, snowshoeing, biking and hiking may be enjoyed on the spacious grounds, covering 176 acres. Gore Mountain and Whiteface Olympic ski areas are close and Lake George is a 10-minute drive.

Historic Interest: The site for the novel "Last of the Mohicans," is nearby, as are French & Indian and Revolutionary war sites. Archaeological digs are in progress.

Innkeeper(s): Joe & Lynn Rubino. $99-149. MC VISA AX DC CB DS PC TC. TAC10. 4 rooms, 3 with PB. Breakfast included in rates. Types of meals: continental breakfast, full breakfast and early coffee/tea. Beds: KQD. Air conditioning in room. TV, VCR, fax and copier on premises. Handicap access. 176 acres. Weddings, small meetings, family reunions and seminars hosted.

French and Italian spoken. Amusement parks, antiques, fishing, parks, shopping, downhill skiing, cross-country skiing, sporting events, theater and watersports nearby.

Publicity: *Chronicle, Post Star, G.F. Business Journal, Country Victorian.*

The Merrill Magee House

2 Hudson St PO Box 391
Warrensburg, NY 12885-0391
(518)623-2449

Circa 1839. This stately Greek Revival home offers beautiful antique fireplaces in every guest room. The Sage, Rosemary, Thyme and Coriander rooms feature sitting areas. The decor is

romantic and distinctly
Victorian. Romantic get-
away packages include
candlelight dinners. The
local area hosts art and
craft festivals, an antique
car show, white-water rafting and Gore Mountain Oktoberfest.
Tour the Adirondacks from the sky during September's balloon festival or browse through the world's largest garage sale in early October.

Historic Interest: Fort William Henry, Fort George Battlegrounds (5 miles), Schuyler Heights Battle (30 miles).

Innkeeper(s): Ken & Florence Carrington. $105-115. MAP, EP. MC VISA AX DS TC. 10 rooms with PB, 10 with FP. 2 conference rooms. Breakfast included in rates. Types of meals: full breakfast and early coffee/tea. Dinner, lunch and banquet service available. Restaurant on premises. Beds: KQDT. Air conditioning and turndown service in room. TV, spa, swimming and library on premises. Handicap access. Weddings, small meetings, family reunions and seminars hosted. Amusement parks, antiques, fishing, parks, shopping, skiing, sporting events, theater and watersports nearby.

Location: In Adirondack State Park.

"A really classy and friendly operation—a real joy."

Warwick   J11

Peach Grove Inn

205 Route 17a
Warwick, NY 10990-3530
(914)986-7411 Fax:(914)986-7590

Circa 1850. This farmhouse was built by Col. Wm. Wheeler as a gift to his son and new daughter-in-law, Phoebe Bull. The original faux-marble walls in the grand two-story entry hall epitomizes a classic 19th-century tradition while the period

antiques take guests back
to a bygone era. There are
nine fireplaces throughout
the home. Three of the
four romantic guest rooms
have working fireplaces.
Stuffed French toast
accompanied by Canadian bacon, raspberry-orange muffins and gourmet coffees are among the breakfast possibilities.

Innkeeper(s): John & Lucy Mastropierro. $95-125. PC TC. 4 rooms with PB, 3 with FP. 1 suite. Breakfast included in rates. Types of meals: full breakfast and early coffee/tea. Beds: QD. Air conditioning, turndown service and ceiling fan in room. Fax and copier on premises. Weddings and small meetings hosted. Amusement parks, antiques, fishing, parks, shopping, downhill skiing, sporting events, golf, theater and watersports nearby.

Publicity: *Victorian Homes.*

Waterloo   F6

Waterloo House

45 N Virginia St
Waterloo, NY 13165-1444
(315)539-9739 Fax:(315)568-9739

Circa 1830. Painted a creamy lemon yellow, this B&B appears as a Victorian farmhouse, but was built in the Federal style. The Queen Anne elements, such as ornate trim, were added in the 1860s. The interior, however, still maintains its Federal-style construction. Antiques and reproductions furnish the rooms. The innkeepers provide thoughtful amenities, such as fluffy robes, specialty toiletries and hair dryers. For breakfast, entrees such as pecan waffles dusted with powdered sugar are accompanied by fresh fruits and other continental fare.

Innkeeper(s): Barbara Ward. $70-90. MC VISA AX PC TC. TAC10. 4 rooms, 2 with PB, 1 with FP. 2 suites. Breakfast included in rates. Types of meals: full breakfast, gourmet breakfast and early coffee/tea. Afternoon tea and evening snack available. Beds: QT. Phone, air conditioning, turndown service and TV in room. Fax on premises. Antiques, fishing, parks, shopping, downhill skiing, cross-country skiing, golf and watersports nearby.

"Our trip was great and we can't stop telling people about the Waterloo House."

Westfield   H2

Westfield House

E Main Rd, PO Box 505, Rt 20
Westfield, NY 14787
(716)326-6262

Circa 1840. This brick home was built as a homestead on a large property of farmland and vineyards. The next owner constructed the impressive Greek Revival addition. The home also served guests as a tea room and later as a family-style eatery. Guests will

enjoy the elegance of the
past, which has been won-
derfully preserved at
Westfield House.
Breakfasts are served on
fine china and silver in the
home's formal dining
room. Wintertime guests
enjoy their morning meal in front of a warm fire. Each of the rooms offers something special. The Ruth Thomas Room offers a four-poster bed, high ceilings, antique quilts and a fireplace, while the Rowan Place boasts beautiful furnishings and Gothic crystal windows that look out to maple trees.

Historic Interest: Chautauqua Institution, which opens for summer classes and recreation, is nearby and listed as a National Historic Landmark.

Innkeeper(s): Betty & Jud Wilson. $60-85. MC VISA PC TC. 7 rooms, 6 with PB, 1 with FP. 1 suite. 2 conference rooms. Breakfast included in rates. Types of meals: full breakfast and early coffee/tea. Beds: KQD. Phone, air conditioning and ceiling fan in room. TV and VCR on premises. Handicap access. Weddings, small meetings and family reunions hosted. Antiques, fishing, parks, skiing, golf, theater and watersports nearby.

Location: Southwestern New York state.

Publicity: *Canadian Leisure Ways, Seaway Trail.*

"Your accommodations and hospitality are wonderful! Simply outstanding. The living room changes its character by the hour."

Westhampton Beach   K14

1880 House Bed & Breakfast

PO Box 648
Westhampton Beach, NY 11978-0648
(516)288-1559 (800)346-3290 Fax:(516)288-0721

Circa 1880. On Westhampton Beach's exclusive Seafield Lane, this country estate includes a pool and tennis court, and it is just a short walk to the
ocean. The inn is decorated with Victorian antiques, Shaker benches, and Chinese porcelain, creating a casual, country inn atmosphere.

Innkeeper(s): Elsie Collins. $100-200. MC VISA AX. 3 suites. Breakfast included in rates. Type of meal: full breakfast. Afternoon tea available. Beds: QD. Phone in room. Weddings, small meetings, family reunions and seminars hosted. Antiques and theater nearby.
Location: Ninety minutes from Manhattan.
Publicity: *Country Inns.*

"From the moment we stepped inside your charming home we felt all the warmth you sent our way which made our stay so comfortable and memorable."

Westport   C12

The Victorian Lady

57 S Main St
Westport, NY 12993
(518)962-2345 Fax:(518)962-2345
E-mail: victorianlady@lake-champlain.com

Circa 1856. This Second Empire home features all the delicate elements of a true "Painted Lady," from the vivid color scheme to the Eastlake porch that graces the exterior. Delicate it's not, however, having stood for more than a
century. Its interior is decked in period style with antiques from this more gracious era. A proper afternoon tea is served, and breakfasts are served by candlelight. More than an acre of
grounds, highlighted by English gardens, surround the home. Lake Champlain is a mere 100 yards from the front door.

Innkeeper(s): Doris & Wayne Deswert. $75-110. PC TC. 5 rooms, 4 with PB. 1 suite. Breakfast and afternoon tea included in rates. Types of meals: full breakfast, gourmet breakfast and early coffee/tea. Beds: KQT. Ceiling fan and TV in room. VCR, fax, copier and library on premises. Weddings and family reunions hosted. Antiques, fishing, parks, shopping, downhill skiing, cross-country skiing, golf, theater and watersports nearby.
Publicity: *Victorian Homes Magazine.*

Willsboro   C13

Champlain Vistas

183 Lake Shore Rd
Willsboro, NY 12996-3418
(518)963-8029

Circa 1860. Incredible views of the Adirondack High Peaks, Lake Champlain and Vermont's Green Mountains are enjoyed at this inn in the state's Northeast region. The original farm

buildings are listed in the National Register of Historic Places, and guests are free to explore the complex. Relax and enjoy the view of Lake Champlain from the inn's wraparound porch or perhaps by the stone fireplace in the living room. The

area offers many things to do, from visiting historic sites to hiking and biking through the beautiful wilderness. The inn is minutes from the ferry to Vermont.

Historic Interest: Fort Ticonderoga, the Lake Champlain Maritime Museum and the Shelburne Museum are nearby in Vermont.
Innkeeper(s): Barbara Moses. $75-95. 4 rooms, 2 with PB. Meal: full breakfast. Beds: QDT. TV, VCR on premises. Weddings, small meetings, family reunions hosted. Antiques, fishing, shopping, skiing, golf, watersports nearby.
Location: Minutes from ferry to Vermont, Lake Placid and Canadian border within an hour's drive.

"It was a joy to feel ourselves at home in such relaxing and indeed beautiful surroundings. The food and the chatter was a great start to the day."

Wilmington   C12

Willkommen Hof

Rt 86, PO Box 240
Wilmington, NY 12997
(518)946-7669 (800)541-9119 Fax:(518)946-7626
E-mail: nybandb@aol.com

Circa 1925. This turn-of-the-century farmhouse served as an inn during the 1920s, but little else is known about its past. The innkeepers have created a cozy atmosphere, perfect for relaxation after a day exploring the Adirondack Mountain area. A large selection of books and a roaring fire greet guests who choose to settle down in the reading room. The innkeepers also offer a large selection of movies. Relax in the sauna or outdoor spa or simply enjoy the comfort of your bedchamber.

Historic Interest: Visit a covered bridge in Jay, just four miles away or cruise the Whiteface Memorial Highway, which is just a few miles away. Lake Placid, the site of the 1932 and 1980 Olympics offers much to see and do.
Innkeeper(s): Heike & Bert Yost. $30-105. MAP. MC VISA PC TC. TAC7. 8 rooms, 3 with PB. 1 suite. Breakfast, afternoon tea included in rates. Meal: full breakfast. Restaurant on premises. Beds: KQDT. Ceiling fan in room. VCR, fax, spa, sauna, bicycles. Weddings, small meetings, family reunions hosted. German spoken. Antiques, fishing, parks, shopping, skiing, watersports nearby. Pets Allowed: Pets must stay in kennel when guests are gone. Kennels available for rent.

"Vielen Dank! Alles war sehr schoen and the breakfasts were delicious."

Windham   H11

Albergo Allegria B&B

Rt 296, PO Box 267
Windham, NY 12496-0267
(518)734-5560 (800)625-2374 Fax:(518)734-5570

Circa 1876. Two former boarding houses were joined to create this luxurious, Victorian bed & breakfast whose name means "the inn of happiness." Guest quarters, laced with a Victorian theme, are decorated with period wallpapers and antique furnishings. One master suite includes an enormous Jacuzzi tub. There are plenty of relaxing options at Albergo Allegria, including a rustic lounge with a large fireplace and overstuffed couches. A second-story library, decorated with plants and wicker furnishings, is still another location to relax with a good book. Guests also can choose from more than 200 videos in the innkeeper's movie collection. Located just a few feet behind the inn are the Carriage

House Suites, each of which includes a double whirlpool tub, gas fireplaces, king-size beds and cathedral ceilings with skylights. The innkeepers came to the area to open LaGriglia, a deluxe, gourmet restaurant just across the way from the bed & breakfast. Their command of cuisine is evident each morning as guests feast on a variety home-baked muffins and pastries, gourmet omelets, waffles and other tempting treats. Albergo Allegria has been named a registered historic site.

Historic Interest: Blenheim Bridge, the longest covered wooden bridge of its kind in the United States, is about a half hour from the inn, as is Olana Castle.
Innkeeper(s): Vito & Lenore Radelich. $65-225. MC VISA DC DS TC. 21 rooms with PB, 7 with FP. 9 suites. Breakfast included in rates. Type of meal: gourmet breakfast. Afternoon tea available. Beds: KQT. Phone, air conditioning, turndown service, ceiling fan, TV and VCR in room. Fax, copier and bicycles on premises. Handicap access. Weddings, small meetings, family reunions and seminars hosted. Italian, African, Croatin spoken. Amusement parks, antiques, fishing, parks, shopping, skiing, watersports nearby.
Publicity: *Yankee.*

Country Suite B&B

Rt 23 W, PO Box 700
Windham, NY 12496
(518)734-4079
E-mail: ctrysuite@aol.com

Circa 1875. This spacious country farmhouse in the Catskill Mountains offers easy access to the many scenic attractions of the region. Five guest rooms, all with private baths, are available to visitors. The inn's country-style furnishings include antiques and family heirlooms. After a busy day of exploring the area, guests often gather in the inn's comfortable living room to relax. Ski Windham is just two miles from the inn and several other ski areas are within a 30-minute drive.

Innkeeper(s): Lorraine Seidel. $85-149. AX. 5 rooms. Breakfast included in rates. Type of meal: gourmet breakfast. 11 acres. Weddings, small meetings, family reunions and seminars hosted. Antiques and downhill skiing nearby.
"A beautifully restored place, a deliciously luxurious stay!"

Danske Hus

361 South St
Windham, NY 12496
(518)734-6335

Circa 1865. Located just across the road from Ski Windham, and nestled between two golf courses, this farmhouse-style inn offers countryside and mountain views to its guests. Breakfast may be enjoyed in the heirloom-filled dining room or outside on a picturesque deck complete with the sounds of a babbling brook. Guests also enjoy a large living room, piano, woodburning fireplace and a sauna. The Catskills provide many other tourist attractions, including caverns, fairs and ethnic festivals, as well as shopping, antiquing and sporting activities. The innkeeper welcomes families with children, and with prior arrangement, dogs may be allowed.

Innkeeper(s): Barbara Jensen. $50-85. AX DS. 4 rooms, 3 with PB. Breakfast and afternoon tea included in rates. Type of meal: full breakfast. Beds: KQDT. TV, VCR, sauna and library on premises. Small meetings and family reunions hosted. Danish spoken. Amusement parks, antiques, fishing, parks, shopping, skiing and watersports nearby. Pets Allowed: Dogs only.

Windham (East) H11

Point Lookout Mountain Inn

The Mohican Trail, Rt 23
Windham (East), NY 12439
(518)734-3381 Fax:(518)734-6526
E-mail: romaint@worldnet.att.net

Circa 1929. This cliffside inn offers a panoramic view stretching for more than 180 miles to the northeast and encompassing the mountain ranges of five states. Guest rooms feature spectacular views of the sunrise, sunset and moon-rise. The inn features two of the area's most popular restaurants on its premises: The Rainbow Cafe and

Cliffside Deck. They offer breakfast, lunch, snacks and homemade ice cream while the Bella Vista Restaurant features fireside dining and a dinner menu influenced by the cuisines of the Mediterranean and Southwest. A variety of local micro-brewed beers and variety of wine are featured in the Tap Room. The innkeepers are both professional chefs with more than 40 years of combined experience. Outdoor gardens, arbors, decks and unparalleled views make the Point Lookout Mountain Inn a favorite spot for wedding receptions and group functions.

Innkeeper(s): Rosemary Jensen, Mariana DiToro. $50-125. MC VISA AX TC. TAC10. 14 rooms with PB. 2 conference rooms. Breakfast included in rates. Meals: continental-plus breakfast, gourmet breakfast and early coffee/tea. Dinner, picnic lunch, gourmet lunch, banquet service and catering service available. Restaurant on premises. Beds: QD. Ceiling fan and TV in room. VCR, fax, copier, spa on premises. Handicap access. Weddings, small meetings, family reunions, seminars hosted. English, Italian spoken. Amusement parks, antiques, parks, shopping, skiing, golf, watersports nearby.
Pets Allowed: Not left alone for long periods. Bring own bedding. On leash in building.
Publicity: *Wonderful Weekends, Albany Times Union.*

Wolcott F7

Bonnie Castle Farm B&B

PO Box 188
Wolcott, NY 14590-0188
(315)587-2273 (800)587-4006 Fax:(315)587-4003

Circa 1887. This large, waterfront home is surrounded by expansive lawns and trees, which overlook the east side of Great Sodus Bay, a popular resort at the turn of the century. Accommodations include a suite and large guest rooms with water views. Other rooms feature wainscoting and cathedral ceilings. A full, gourmet breakfast includes a cereal bar, fresh fruit and juices and an assort-

ment of entrees such as Orange Blossom French toast, sausages, a creamy potato casserole and fresh-baked pastries topped off with teas and Irish creme coffee.

Historic Interest: Nearby are the Everson Museum, Susan B. Anthony House, National Women's Hall of Fame, William Phelps General Store Museum, the Sodus Point Maritime Museum, Renaissance Faire and others.
Innkeeper(s): Eric & Georgia Pendleton. $85-135. MC VISA AX DS PC TC. TAC10. 8 rooms with PB. 1 suite. Breakfast included in rates. Types of meals: full breakfast and gourmet breakfast. Beds: KQD. Air conditioning, ceiling fan, TV and VCR in room. Fax, copier, spa and swimming on premises. 50 acres. Small meetings, family reunions, seminars hosted. Antiques, fishing, parks, shopping, skiing, sporting events, theater, watersports nearby.
Location: Located halfway between Rochester and Syracuse on Sodus Bay.

North Carolina

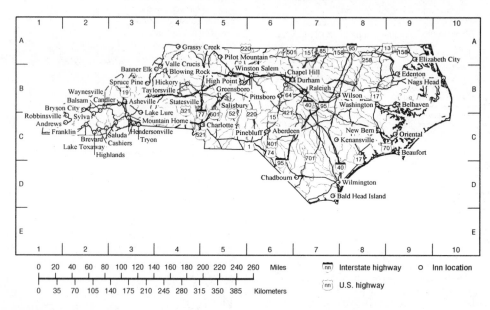

1	2	3	4	5	6	7	8	9	10

0 20 40 60 80 100 120 140 160 180 200 220 240 260   Miles

0   35   70   105 140 175 210 245 280 315 350 385   Kilometers

Interstate highway   o   Inn location

U.S. highway

Aberdeen   C6

Page Manor House B&B

300 Page St
Aberdeen, NC 28315
(910)944-5970 Fax:(901)944-1172

Circa 1914. The only thing wrong with this bed & breakfast is
that guests eventually have to leave, but they are sure to
remember the beautiful decor, glorious cuisine and Southern
hospitality. The decor is elegant, but not stuffy, and guests will
feel right at home.

Canopy beds, luxury
linens and fluffy down pillows ensure a restful night
sleep. Each guest room is
individually decorated in a
romantic style. Breakfast
alone may be worth the
trip. The multi-course fare
changes daily, but a sample menu might include fresh raspberries topped with sweet vanilla cream, followed by a twist on the
ordinary eggs Benedict with poached eggs on toasted Italian
bread with a basil-pesto sauce and a dusting of freshly grated
parmesan cheese. Golf courses, more than three dozen at last

count, abound in the area. Antique shops, 60 potteries, the
zoo and the North Carolina Speedway are other possibilities.

Innkeeper(s): Sharon & Russ Cogan. $120-135. PC TC. TAC10. 4 rooms
with PB, 3 with FP. Breakfast included in rates. Types of meals: gourmet
breakfast and early coffee/tea. Beds: KQT. Air conditioning, ceiling fan, TV
and VCR in room. Fax, copier, swimming and tennis on premises. Antiques,
shopping, golf and theater nearby.

Publicity: *Fayetteville Observer, Pinehurst Magazine, Country Extra.*

Andrews   C2

The Cover House

34 Wilson St
Andrews, NC 28901
(704)321-5302 (800)354-7642 Fax:(704)321-2145
E-mail: cover@grove.net

Circa 1908. Mountain views and fine sunsets may be seen
from the porch of this large Four-Square house located on
almost two acres. There are polished hardwood floors, fireplaces with ornamental mantels and original woodwork.
Antique furnishings, Oriental rugs and a wonderful art collection fill the inn. A country breakfast of grits, homemade biscuits and gravy and scrambled eggs or quiche is served.

Innkeeper(s): Gayle Lay. $60-120. MC VISA AX DC DS TC. TAC15. 5 rooms,
3 with PB, 3 with FP. 1 cottage. Breakfast included in rates. Types of meals:
continental breakfast, full breakfast and early coffee/tea. Beds: KQD. Air conditioning and ceiling fan in room. TV, VCR and fax on premises. Handicap

access. Weddings, small meetings and family reunions hosted. Antiques, fishing and golf nearby.

Publicity: *Carolina Magazine.*

"A delightful place!! Wonderful place to visit."

Asheville   B3

Abbington Green B&B

46 Cumberland Cir
Asheville, NC 28801-1718
(704)251-2454 (800)251-2454 Fax:(704)251-2872

Circa 1908. Innkeeper Valerie Larrea has definitely put her heart and soul into this bed & breakfast. When she discovered the home, located in Asheville's Montfort Historic District, it was desperately in need of a facelift. Through hard work, which included putting in six bathrooms and replacing the electrical system, she earned an award for the restoration. The home sports an English-country decor, and each guest  room is named for a park or garden in England. Antiques and reproductions furnish the home. An inventive breakfast menu is prepared each morning, featuring gourmet tidbits such as homemade pumpkin bread, a warm cherry soup and quiche Florentine with grilled sausage. The home was designed by a supervising architect during the building of the Biltmore Estate, which is nearby and open for tours. The Blue Ridge Parkway and University of North Carolina also are near.

Innkeeper(s): Valerie, Julie & Gabrielle Larrea. $95-150. MC VISA AX DS PC TC. TAC10. 6 rooms, 3 with FP. 1 cottage. Breakfast included in rates. Type of meal: full breakfast. Beds: QT. Air conditioning and ceiling fan in room. VCR, fax, bicycles and library on premises. Antiques, fishing, parks, shopping, downhill skiing, golf and theater nearby.

Publicity: *Asheville Citizen-Times, Summer Magazine, Plain Dealer, Gazette.*

"Our stay will always be a memorable part of our honeymoon. The breakfasts were outstanding."

Albemarle Inn

86 Edgemont Rd
Asheville, NC 28801-1544
(704)255-0027 (800)621-7435

Circa 1909. Tall Grecian columns mark the majestic entrance to Albemarle. A wide veranda, shaded by mountain pines, welcomes guests. Inside, a carved-oak staircase and massive oak-paneled doors are polished to a high gleam. Guest rooms feature 11-foot ceilings and claw-foot tubs. The Hungarian composer Bela Bartok is said to  have written his third concerto for piano while in residence at the inn.

Innkeeper(s): Diana & Tony Morris. $95-160. MC VISA DS PC TC. TAC10. 11 rooms with PB. Breakfast and evening snack included in rates. Types of meals: gourmet breakfast and early coffee/tea. Beds: KQDT. Phone, air conditioning, ceiling fan and TV in room. Swimming on premises. Antiques, fishing, parks, shopping, sporting events, theater and watersports nearby.

Publicity: *Stages, Atlanta Homes, Asheville Citizen-Times.*

"Most outstanding breakfast I've ever had. We were impressed to say the least!"

Applewood Manor Inn

62 Cumberland Cir
Asheville, NC 28801-1718
(704)254-2244 (800)442-2197 Fax:(704)254-0899

Circa 1910. This is a spacious Colonial Revival house furnished comfortably with antiques. Guests can relax in front of the wood-burning fireplace or stroll the inn's two-acre grounds. Accommodations include four guest rooms and a cottage. Cream-cheese omelets, orange French toast, blueberry pancakes or homemade waffles are  some of the delectables that appear on the breakfast menu along with fresh fruits, juices and homemade breads.

Innkeeper(s): Coby & Johan Verhey. $90-110. MC VISA PC TC. TAC10. 4 rooms with PB, 3 with FP. 1 cottage. Breakfast included in rates. Meals: full breakfast and early coffee/tea. Beds: Q. Air conditioning and ceiling fan in room. Fax, copier and bicycles on premises. Family reunions hosted. French, German and Dutch spoken. Antiques, parks, shopping and theater nearby.

Location: Montfort Historic District.

Publicity: *Country Inns, Insider.*

"It goes without saying—the accommodations and breakfasts are outstanding!"

Beaufort House Victorian B&B

61 N Liberty St
Asheville, NC 28801-1829
(704)254-8334 (800)261-2221 Fax:(704)251-2082
E-mail: rob@beauforthouse.com

Circa 1894. In the Queen Anne Victorian style, this inn rests on two acres of beautifully landscaped grounds, including a tea garden. Offering views of the mountains, the full wraparound porch is festooned with gingerbread trim. Most guest rooms feature Jacuzzi tubs. Ask for the Sarah Davidson Suite where light streams through a handsome fan window onto a king-size canopy bed decked in white Battenburg Lace. There is a sitting area with wing back chairs and a Queen Anne desk. The Forest Room is a fitness center for guests. Breakfast features freshly made entrees and breads served with white linen and silver service.

Innkeeper(s): Robert & Jacqueline Glasgow. $65-195. MC VISA PC TC. TAC10. 12 rooms. Breakfast and afternoon tea included in rates. Types of meals: gourmet breakfast and early coffee/tea. Picnic lunch available. Beds: KQD. Phone, air conditioning, ceiling fan, TV and VCR in room. Fax and bicycles on premises. Weddings, small meetings, family reunions and seminars hosted. Amusement parks, antiques, fishing, parks, shopping, downhill skiing, sporting events, golf and theater nearby.

Cedar Crest Victorian Inn

674 Biltmore Ave
Asheville, NC 28803-2513
(704)252-1389 (800)252-0310 Fax:(704)253-7667

Circa 1891. This Queen Anne mansion is one of the largest and most opulent residences surviving Asheville's 1890s boom. A captain's walk, projecting turrets and expansive verandas welcomes guests to lavish interior woodwork created by artisans employed by the Vanderbilts. All rooms are furnished in antiques with satin and lace trappings.

Historic Interest: The inn is National Register and is three block to the Biltmore Estate.

Innkeeper(s): Barbara & Jack McEwan. $90-170. MC VISA AX DC DS PC

TC. TAC10. 12 rooms with PB, 6 with FP. 3 suites. 1 cottage. Breakfast and evening snack included in rates. Meal: full breakfast. Beds: QD. Phone, air conditioning, turndown service and ceiling fan in room. TV, fax on premises. Amusement parks, antiques, fishing, parks, shopping and theater nearby.

Location: 1 1/4 mile from I-40, 4 miles to Blue Ridge Parkway.

Publicity: *New Woman, Southern Living, Good Housekeeping, House Beautiful, Country Inns, National Geographic Traveler.*

"Cedar Crest is a real beauty and will hold a special place in our hearts."

Chestnut Street Inn

176 E Chestnut St
Asheville, NC 28801-2336
(704)285-0705 (800)894-2955

Circa 1905. This Colonial Revival house of red brick, in the Chestnut Hill Historic District, features a rotunda-style porch and a front veranda with columns. Inside are ornate fireplaces, picture rails and high ceil-  ings. Furnishings are antique and one guest room boasts an antique carved mahogany bed. Turndown service and afternoon tea are available. Breakfasts includes such items as raspberries and cream, scones and fresh apple bread. Dogwoods, maple trees and gardens fill the inn's half acre. Biltmore Estate is a 10-minute drive, and within walking distance are antique shops, art galleries and restaurants.

Innkeeper(s): Gene & Paulette Dugger. $95-110. MC VISA DS PC TC. TAC10. 3 rooms with PB, 3 with FP. Breakfast and afternoon tea included in rates. Type of meal: gourmet breakfast. Beds: QD. Air conditioning, turndown service in room. Library on premises. Amusement parks, antiques, fishing, parks, shopping, downhill skiing, sporting events, golf, watersports nearby.
Publicity: *Our State.*

"Spending the weekend in your spotless, charming inn has made an absolutely wonderful impression on us."

Corner Oak Manor

53 Saint Dunstans Rd
Asheville, NC 28803-2620
(704)253-3525

Circa 1920. Surrounded by oak, maple and pine trees, this English Tudor inn is decorated with many fine oak antiques and handmade items. Innkeeper Karen Spradley has hand-  stitched something special for each room, and the house features handmade items by local artisans. Breakfast delights include entrees such as Blueberry Ricotta Pancakes, Four Cheese and Herb Quiche and Orange French Toast. When you aren't enjoying local activities, you can sit on the shady deck, relax in the Jacuzzi, play a few songs on the piano or curl up with a good book.

Historic Interest: Biltmore House and Gardens (one-half mile).

Innkeeper(s): Karen & Andy Spradley. $90-150. MC VISA AX DS PC TC. 3 rooms with PB, 1 with FP. 1 cottage. Breakfast included in rates. Type of meal: gourmet breakfast. Beds: Q. Air conditioning and ceiling fan in room. Family reunions hosted. Antiques, fishing, parks, shopping, downhill skiing and theater nearby.

"Great food, comfortable bed, quiet, restful atmosphere, you provided it all and we enjoyed it all!"

Dogwood Cottage

40 Canterbury Rd N
Asheville, NC 28801-1560
(704)258-9725

Circa 1910. This Carolina mountain home is located a mile-and-a-half from downtown Asheville, on Sunset Mountain. The veranda, filled with white wicker and floral chintz prints, is the focal point of the inn during summer. It affords tree-top views of the Blue Ridge Mountains. Wing chairs and country pieces accent the inn's gleaming hardwood floors. Breakfast is served in the formal dining room or on the covered porch.

Innkeeper(s): Joan & Don Tracy. $95-105. MC VISA AX PC. TAC10. 4 rooms with PB, 3 with FP. Breakfast included in rates. Meals: full breakfast, gourmet breakfast and early coffee/tea. Beds: Q. Air conditioning and ceiling fan in room. TV, swimming, pet boarding on premises. Handicap access. Weddings, family reunions hosted. Antiques, fishing, parks, shopping, downhill skiing, sporting events, theater, watersports nearby. Pets Allowed.

"Cozy, warm and gracious."

The Inn on Montford

296 Montford Ave
Asheville, NC 28801-1660
(704)254-9569 (800)254-9569 Fax:(704)254-9518
E-mail: inninfo@aol.com

Circa 1900. This National Register home was one of a few Asheville homes designed by Richard Sharp Smith, who also served as the supervising architect for the lavish Biltmore Estate. The exterior is a simple and pleasing Arts & Crafts design flanked by a wide veranda, where guests can relax and enjoy the quiet neighborhood. There are four well-appointed guest rooms highlighted by beautiful antique beds. Three rooms include a whirlpool tub, and the fourth offers a clawfoot tub. All four have a fireplace. English and American antiques fill the elegant inn. Breakfasts include a special fruit dish, such as a baked banana souffle, freshly baked pastries or muffins and a special daily entree. Spend the day touring historic homes, take a trip to the Biltmore Estate or enjoy hiking and rafting in nearby wilderness areas.

Innkeeper(s): Ron and Lynn Carlson. $120-160. MC VISA AX DC DS PC TC. TAC10. 4 rooms with PB, 4 with FP. Breakfast included in rates. Meals: full breakfast, gourmet breakfast and early coffee/tea. Beds: Q. Phone and air conditioning in room. TV, VCR, fax, copier, library on premises. Weddings, small meetings, seminars hosted. Amusement parks, antiques, fishing, parks, shopping, downhill skiing, sporting events, golf, theater, watersports nearby.

North Lodge on Oakland

84 Oakland Rd
Asheville, NC 28801-4818
(704)252-6433 (800)282-3602 Fax:(701)252-3034
E-mail: stay@northlodge.com

Circa 1904. This inn was built by an old Asheville family, descendants of the owners of Smith Plantation. It is a three-story lodge that combines native stone work with cedar shin-  gles. There are gables and a portico. Inside, guests enjoy a front parlor, library and French-country dining room. Furnishings include English antiques and Oriental rugs mixed with contemporary pieces. Poached salmon soufflÈ or German apple pancakes are specialties offered at breakfast.

Innkeeper(s): Herb & Lois Marsh. $85-115. MC VISA AX DS PC TC. TAC10. 5 rooms with PB. Breakfast and afternoon tea included in rates. Types of meals: full breakfast and gourmet breakfast. Beds: QDT. Air conditioning and TV in room. Fax on premises. Amusement parks, antiques, fishing, parks, shopping, downhill skiing, cross-country skiing, sporting events, golf, theater and watersports nearby.

"*The room was marvelous, breakfasts were delicious, and you certainly were gracious hosts.*"

The Old Reynolds Mansion

100 Reynolds Hgts
Asheville, NC 28804
(704)254-0496

Circa 1855. This handsome, three-story brick antebellum mansion is situated on a four-acre knoll of Reynolds Mountain. Rescued from near ruin by innkeepers Fred and Helen Faber, the home has been restored to its former glory as a gracious Southern manor. Each of the guest quarters reflects a different style from early American to Oriental. Guests can enjoy mountain views from their own room, by a wood-burning fireplace or on a rocking chair on the inn's wraparound porch. The mansion offers use of a swimming pool set among pine trees.

Historic Interest: Several historic homes, including the Biltmore Estate, Thomas Wolfe home and Carl Sandburg home are a short drive.

Innkeeper(s): Fred & Helen Faber. $55-125. PC TC. 10 rooms, 8 with PB, 5 with FP. 1 cottage. Breakfast and afternoon tea included in rates. Type of meal: continental-plus breakfast. Beds: QDT. Air conditioning and ceiling fan in room. Swimming and library on premises. Antiques, fishing, parks, shopping, downhill skiing, cross-country skiing, sporting events, theater nearby.

Location: Ten minutes north of downtown Asheville.

Publicity: *Greensboro News & Record, Blue Ridge Country.*

"*This was one of the nicest places we have ever stayed. We spent every sundown on the porch waiting for the fox's daily visit.*"

Richmond Hill Inn

87 Richmond Hill Dr
Asheville, NC 28806-3912
(704)252-7313 (800)545-9238 Fax:(704)252-8726

Circa 1889. This renovated Victorian mansion was designed for the Pearson family by James G. Hill, architect of the U.S. Treasury buildings. The elegant estate features a grand entry hall, ballroom, library and 10 master fireplaces with Neoclassical

mantels. Guests may choose from accommodations in the luxurious mansion, charming cottages on a croquet court, or the garden rooms amid a striking landscape and facing a mountain waterfall. Two restaurants on the premises offer guests a choice of dining experiences. The inn is listed in the National Register of Historic Places.

Historic Interest: The Biltmore House and Gardens are 20 minutes away. The Thomas Wolfe Memorial is about 15 minutes from the home, while Carl Sandburg home is an hour away.

Innkeeper(s): Susan Michel. $145-375. MAP. MC VISA AX. 36 rooms with PB, 26 with FP. 3 suites. 1 conference room. Breakfast and afternoon tea included in rates. Types of meals: full breakfast and gourmet breakfast. Dinner and lunch available. Restaurant on premises. Beds: KQD. Fax and copier on premises. Handicap access.

Publicity: *Atlanta Journal & Constitution, Southern Living, Victoria, Inn Country USA, Inn Country Chefs.* Ratings: 4 Diamonds.

"*A great adventure into history. I am moved to tell you how grateful we are that you had the foresight and courage to rescue this wonderful place. The buildings and grounds are elegantly impressive ... and the staff superb! You have created a total experience that fulfills and satisfies.*"

Wright Inn & Carriage House

235 Pearson Dr
Asheville, NC 28801-1613
(704)251-0789 (800)552-5724 Fax:(704)251-0929

Circa 1899. Located on a quiet, tree-lined street, this Queen Anne Victorian will take guests back in time to a more elegant, refined era. Guest rooms are furnished with antiques, family heirlooms and a bright, cheery decor. Two of the bedrooms feature fireplaces. Guests are treated to a breakfast of homemade breads, muffins, granola and tempting entrees. The Carriage House is a perfect place for families and includes a living room, dining room, kitchen, three bedrooms, two baths and the same carefully appointed decor evident in the main house.

Historic Interest: The inn and carriage house are listed in the local and national historic registers. The innkeepers will provide a Sony Walkman and tape for a walking tour of downtown Asheville. The Blue Ridge Parkway, Biltmore House and Smith-McDowell House are only minutes away.

Innkeeper(s): Carol & Art Wenczel. $95-215. MC VISA DS PC TC. 10 rooms with PB, 2 with FP. 1 suite. 1 cottage. Breakfast and afternoon tea included in rates. Types of meals: full breakfast, gourmet breakfast and early coffee/tea. Beds: KQDT. Phone, air conditioning and TV in room. Fax, bicycles and library on premises. Small meetings and family reunions hosted. Antiques, fishing, parks, shopping, downhill skiing, cross-country skiing, sporting events, theater and watersports nearby.

"*The hospitality and accommodations are outstanding. I have stayed in hotels from San Francisco to New York, and the Wright Inn is one of the best!*"

Bald Head Island   D7

Theodosia's B&B

91 Keelson Row
Bald Head Island, NC 28461
(910)457-6563 (800)656-1812 Fax:(910)457-6055

Circa 1817. Although this inn is new, it was built in the grand style of the Victorian era. The home is named after Aaron Burr's daughter, Theodosia. Legend has it that her spirit wanders the island. Islanders can tell stories of encounters with this ghostly figure. Although Theodosia has yet to visit her namesake inn, many others have, and for good reason. The guest rooms are decorated in an eclectic mix of styles. Guests enjoy views of the harbor and river during their stay. The honeymoon suite offers a Jacuzzi tub and beautiful views. Cars are not allowed on the island, but the innkeepers provide guests with golf carts or bicycles. The island is a unique place, so small that residents have a key to the post office. Guests can enjoy a day at the beach or take a trip to the state's oldest lighthouse, which was built in 1817.

Innkeeper(s): Lydia & Steve Love. $130-190. MC VISA DS PC TC. 10 rooms with PB. 1 suite. Breakfast included in rates. Type of meal: full breakfast. Evening snack available. Beds: QD. Phone, air conditioning and TV in room. Fax and bicycles on premises. Handicap access. Weddings, small meetings and family reunions hosted. German and Lithuanian spoken. Fishing, parks, golf and watersports nearby. Publicity: *The Thomasville Times.*

Balsam B2

Balsam Mountain Inn

Balsam Mountain Inn Road
Balsam, NC 28707-0040
(704)456-9498 (800)224-9498 Fax:(704)456-9298

Circa 1905. This mountain inn with Neoclassical architecture overlooks the scenic hamlet of Balsam. The inn is listed in the National Register of Historic Places and is designated a Jackson County Historic Site. It features a mansard roof and wraparound porches with mountain views. A complimentary full breakfast is served daily while lunch is served in the dining room only on Sunday.

Innkeeper(s): Merrily Teasley. $90-150. MC VISA DS TC. TAC10. 50 rooms with PB. 8 suites. Breakfast included in rates. Types of meals: full breakfast, gourmet breakfast and early coffee/tea. Dinner, picnic lunch and banquet service available. Restaurant on premises. Beds: KD. Fax, copier on premises. Handicap access. 26 acres. Weddings, small meetings, family reunions and seminars hosted. Antiques, fishing, parks, shopping, downhill skiing nearby.

"What wonderful memories we have of this beautiful inn."

Banner Elk B4

The Banner Elk Inn B&B

407 Main St, E
Banner Elk, NC 28604
(704)898-6223

Circa 1912. This rose-colored farmhouse was built originally as a church, but later was remodeled by artist Edna Townsend who transformed it into an inn. The home was abandoned eventually and refurbished by current innkeeper Beverly Lait, who decorated it with international flair, filling each room with

antiques and pieces from around the world. Individually decorated rooms feature special items such as an antique brass bed or pewter twin beds, down comforters and bright, airy wallcoverings and lace window dressings. For breakfast, Beverly prepares a feast of homemade breads, fresh fruit and mouth-watering entrees such as her Parmesan souffle with cheddar cheese sauce. The inn is a perfect spot to enjoy the natural surroundings of Banner Elk and the Blue Ridge Parkway trails.

Historic Interest: The Mast General Store in Valle Crucis is more than 100 years old.

Innkeeper(s): Beverly Lait. $90-150. MC VISA. 5 rooms, 4 with PB. 2 suites. Breakfast and afternoon tea included in rates. Type of meal: full breakfast. Room service available. Beds: QDT. Antiques, fishing, downhill skiing, cross-country skiing and theater nearby. Pets Allowed.

Publicity: *Mountain Getaways, Southern Living, Blue Ridge Country Magazine.*

"You surely have five-star accommodations with five-star attention."

Beaufort C9

The Cedars Inn

305 Front St
Beaufort, NC 28516-2124
(919)728-7036 Fax:(919)728-1685

Circa 1768. The Cedars is comprised of two historic houses, the Main House dates back to 1768. Five of the guest rooms are located in the Main House, and an additional six are locat-

ed in a restored 1851 house. The guest rooms includes amenities such as fireplaces, clawfoot tubs, four-poster beds and antiques. All rooms include a private bath, and suites also have a sitting room. The innkeepers also have a honeymoon cottage, which includes a Jacuzzi tub. Both houses include front porches, lined with rocking chairs, on the first and second floors. Hearty breakfasts include such items as banana-walnut pancakes, French toast, croissants, pastries, country ham, bacon, fresh fruit and a variety of beverages. The inn has a wine bar featuring a variety of vintages, champagne, beer and non-alcoholic options. The Cedars is located in Beaufort's historic district, and bicycles are available for guests who wish to tour the state's third oldest town.

Historic Interest: The Beaufort Historical Association offers tours of a two-acre complex of historic buildings, including an 1829 jail and a 1796 county courthouse.

Innkeeper(s): Sam & Linda Dark. $95-165. MC VISA AX DS PC. 12 rooms with PB, 5 with FP. 1 cottage. 1 conference room. Type of meal: full breakfast. Beds: KQDT. Phone in room.

Publicity: *The Washington Post, Greensboro News & Record, Raleigh News & Observer, Chatham News.*

"We are so grateful for everything you did for us. We will always treasure that perfect time in our lives. Because of the effort you put into everything. Our day was extraordinary. We thank you and all of your friends & family, that helped, from the bottom of our hearts."

Delamar Inn

217 Turner St
Beaufort, NC 28516-2140
(919)728-4300 (800)349-5823 Fax:(919)728-1471

Circa 1866. The innkeepers, who have lived in Africa, Denmark, Hawaii and Scotland, lend an international touch to this hospitable two-story home, which features wide porches on each level. Each of the guest rooms is decorated to reflect a

different style. One of the rooms has an original clawfoot tub. The innkeepers keep plenty of coffee and tea around and stock comfortable sitting rooms with cookies and fruit for late-night snacking. They also can provide beach chairs and bicycles for guests heading to the beach, which is less than 10 minutes from the inn.

Historic Interest: The Delamar Inn is located in North Carolina's third-oldest town, and historic Fort Macon, built in 1834, guards Beaufort's harbor. The inn is within walking distance of a collection of old buildings preserved by the local historical society. The Maritime Museum is another historic attraction.

Innkeeper(s): Tom & Mabel Steepy. $78-108. MC VISA TC. 4 rooms with PB. Breakfast and afternoon tea included in rates. Types of meals: continental-plus breakfast and early coffee/tea. Beds: KQ. Air conditioning and ceiling fan in room. TV, fax, copier and bicycles on premises. Small meetings and family reunions hosted. Antiques, fishing, parks, shopping and watersports nearby.

Publicity: *Corporate New Jersey LTD.*

"We've come back here for the last four years. It's like coming home!"

Pecan Tree Inn B&B

116 Queen St
Beaufort, NC 28516-2214
(919)728-6733

Circa 1866. Originally built as a Masonic lodge, this state historic landmark is in the heart of Beaufort's historic district. Gingerbread trim, Victorian porches, turrets and two-century-

old pecan trees grace the
exterior. Guests can relax
in the parlor, on the porches, or pay a visit to the
flower and herb gardens.
The Bridal Suite and
"Wow" suite boast a king-
size, canopied bed and two-person Jacuzzi.

Innkeeper(s): Susan & Joe Johnson. $70-135. MC VISA DS PC TC. TAC8. 7
rooms with PB. 1 suite. Breakfast included in rates. Types of meals: continental-plus breakfast and early coffee/tea. Beds: KQ. Air conditioning and
ceiling fan in room. Bicycles and library on premises. Weddings, small meetings and family reunions hosted. Amusement parks, antiques, fishing, parks,
shopping and watersports nearby.
Location: In the heart of the historic district, one-half block from the waterfront.
Publicity: *Sunday Telegram, This Week, Conde Nast Traveler, State.*

*"After visiting B&Bs far and wide I give Pecan Tree Inn a Five-Star
rating in all respects."*

Belhaven   B9

River Forest Manor

600 E Main St
Belhaven, NC 27810-1622
(919)943-2151 (800)346-2151 Fax:(919)943-6628

Circa 1899. Both Twiggy and Walter Cronkite have passed
through the two-story, pillared rotunda entrance of this white
mansion located on the Atlantic Intracoastal Waterway. Ornate,
carved ceilings, cut and leaded-glass windows and crystal chandeliers grace the inn. Antiques are found throughout. Each
evening a smorgasbord buffet features more than 50 items from
the inn's kitchen.

Historic Interest: Bath, N.C., oldest town and church in North Carolina is nearby.
Innkeeper(s): Melba, Axson Jr. & Mark Smith. $65-85. MAP. MC VISA. 12
rooms with PB. Breakfast included in rates. Types of meals: continental
breakfast and full breakfast. Dinner available. Restaurant on premises. Beds:
KQD. Phone, air conditioning and TV in room. VCR, fax and copier on
premises. Weddings, small meetings and family reunions hosted. Antiques,
fishing and watersports nearby.
Publicity: *Southern Living, National Geographic, North Carolina
Accommodations, Country Inns, State, Historical Inns.*

"River Forest Manor is our favorite place in east North Carolina."

Blowing Rock   B4

The Inn at Ragged Gardens

PO Box 1927
Blowing Rock, NC 28605-1927
(704)295-9703

Circa 1903. Surrounded by rhododendron and majestic trees,
this inn features guest rooms decorated with early 1900s furniture. Stone for the exterior rock columns, fireplaces and staircase was quarried from nearby Grandfather Mountain. Guest
rooms and common areas are decorated with comfortable,
turn-of-the-century fur-
nishings. There are plenty
of romantic amenities
here, including rooms
with garden views, fire-
places, whirlpool tubs or
private balconies. During
the morning meal, sea-

sonal fruits, freshly baked breads, cereals and yogurt parfaits
accompany a changing menu of entrees.

Innkeeper(s): Lee & Jama Hyett. $130-175. MC VISA PC TC. TAC10. 8
rooms with PB, 8 with FP. 2 suites. Breakfast included in rates. Types of
meals: full breakfast and early coffee/tea. Beds: KQ. Air conditioning and ceiling fan in room. TV and library on premises. Small meetings, family reunions
and seminars hosted. Antiques, fishing, shopping, downhill skiing, cross-
country skiing, theater and watersports nearby.
Publicity: *Blowing Rocket, Mid-Atlantic Country, Blue Ridge Country,
Southern Inns, Mountain Air.*

"I've never felt more welcome anywhere!"

Victorian Inn

242 Ransom St
Blowing Rock, NC 28605
(704)295-0034

Circa 1938. This two-story pale green and brown Victorian is
set off with white trim and borders of white impatiens. Baskets
of flowers hang from the balconies and balustrades. Each suite
has a private entrance, and
there are extra-large tubs
and fireplaces. Two baths
have garden tubs as well as
separate showers.
Additional touches include
luxurious comforters, ceiling fans, room service and
breakfast brought to your

room. Blowing Rock has been a Blue Ridge resort for more than
100 years and is named for a rock that hangs over a cliff.

Innkeeper(s): Guido Alvarez/Alex Dearborn. $79-119. MC VISA PC TC.
TAC20. 6 rooms with PB, 6 with FP. Breakfast, afternoon tea and evening
snack included in rates. Type of meal: gourmet breakfast. Catering service
and room service available. Beds: KQ. Air conditioning and ceiling fan in
room. VCR, fax, library and pet boarding on premises. Handicap access.
Weddings and family reunions hosted. Spanish and Protuguese spoken.
Amusement parks, antiques, fishing, parks, shopping, downhill skiing, cross-
country skiing, sporting events, golf, theater and watersports nearby.

*"Having breakfast brought to our room each morning added to our
pleasure."*

Brevard   C3

Red House Inn B&B

412 W Probart St
Brevard, NC 28712-3620
(704)884-9349

Circa 1851. Originally built as a trading post, this inn was also
the county's first post office and railroad station. It survived the
Civil War and years of neglect. Recently renovated, it is furnished
with Victorian antiques. The center of town is four blocks away.
Innkeeper(s): Lynn Ong. $47-69. 6 rooms, 4 with PB, 2 with FP. Breakfast
included in rates. Type of meal: full breakfast. Beds: QDT. Air conditioning in
room. Antiques, fishing, shopping and golf nearby.
Location: In the Blue Ridge Mountains.
Publicity: *The Transylvania Times.*

"Lovely place to stay - clean and bright."

Womble Inn

301 W Main St
Brevard, NC 28712-3609
(704)884-4770
E-mail: wombleinn@citcom.net

Circa 1958. Located in Brevard, Land of the Waterfalls, this New Orleans-style inn offers visitors a comfortable retreat in which to enjoy the many natural amenities that the North Carolina countryside has to offer, including hiking, trout fishing and swimming. Adding to the area's history is Goat Farm, Carl Sandburg's homestead, and the elegant Biltmore House. Guest rooms are individually decorated in antiques and offer private baths and air conditioning. A continental breakfast is served in the dining room, or guests can opt to enjoy their morning meal served on a silver tray in the privacy of their guest room.

Historic Interest: Located near Brevard Music Center, Brevard College and the Pisgah National Forest.

Innkeeper(s): Beth & Steve Womble. $52-62. MC VISA DS PC. 6 rooms with PB. Breakfast included in rates. Types of meals: continental breakfast, continental-plus breakfast, full breakfast and early coffee/tea. Dinner, picnic lunch, lunch, room service available. Restaurant on premises. Beds: QDT. Air conditioning, ceiling fan in room. TV on premises. Weddings, small meetings, family reunions hosted. Antiques, fishing, parks, shopping, golf, theater nearby.

Bryson City   B2

Folkestone Inn

101 Folkestone Rd
Bryson City, NC 28713-7891
(704)488-2730 (888)812-3385 Fax:(704)488-0722
E-mail: innkeeper@folkestone.com

Circa 1926. This farmhouse is constructed of local stone and rock. Pressed-tin ceilings, stained-glass windows and clawfoot tubs

remain. The dining room, where breakfast is served, features floor-to-ceiling windows on all sides with views of the mountains. Afternoon refreshments also are served. There is a stream with a rock bridge on the property, and you can walk 10 minutes to waterfall views in the Great Smoky Mountains National Park.

Innkeeper(s): Ellen & Charles Snodgrass. $69-90. MC VISA DS PC TC. TAC10. 10 rooms with PB. Breakfast included in rates. Types of meals: full breakfast and early coffee/tea. Beds: QD. Ceiling fan in room. Fax and copier on premises. Weddings, small meetings, family reunions and seminars hosted. Antiques, fishing, shopping and watersports nearby.

Publicity: *Asheville Citizen-Times, Atlanta Journal, Lakeland, Palm Beach Post.*

"A charming place to spend a delightful weekend with a loved one. Wonderful breakfasts, too. Thanks!"

Candler   B3

Owl's Nest Inn at Engadine

2630 Smokey Park Hwy
Candler, NC 28715
(704)665-8325 (800)665-8868 Fax:(704)667-2539

Circa 1885. This Queen Anne Victorian has been gloriously preserved, still featuring the original heart-of-pine woodwork that in some rooms runs from floor to ceiling. A few of the

rooms still contain the original marble-topped sinks. The home was built and designed by a Confederate cavalry officer. The surrounding mountains and forests create a peaceful setting, and guests can enjoy the scenery from a veranda or perhaps on a stroll through the four-acre grounds. Four-poster beds, clawfoot or whirlpool tubs, canopies and stunning views are what guests might find in their rooms. Frittatas, stuffed French toast, Caribbean pears and freshly baked muffins are among the breakfast fare, which is served on fine china in the gracious dining room. The home is minutes away from Asheville, and guests can visit the Biltmore Estate or take a drive down the Blue Ridge Parkway.

Innkeeper(s): Mary & Jim Melaugh. $85-150. MC VISA DS PC TC. TAC10. 5 rooms, 4 with PB, 4 with FP. 1 suite. Breakfast and afternoon tea included in rates. Types of meals: full breakfast, gourmet breakfast and early coffee/tea. Evening snack available. Beds: KQT. Air conditioning, ceiling fan and TV in room. Fax on premises. Antiques, fishing, shopping, downhill skiing, sporting events, golf, theater and watersports nearby.

Cashiers   C2

Millstone Inn

Hwy 64W
Cashiers, NC 28717
(704)743-2737 (888)645-5786 Fax:(704)743-0208

Circa 1933. The views from this inn are breathtaking, taking in both Whiteside Mountain and the surrounding valley. Inside, rustic, exposed log beams and woodsy, pine paneling comple-

ment the North Carolina wilderness. The innkeepers also offer efficiency apartments in the Garden Annex. Breakfasts are served in a glass-enclosed porch looking out to the mountains. The inn's eight acres border Natahala National Forest.

Innkeeper(s): Paul & Patricia Collins. $99-150. MC VISA DS PC TC. 7 rooms with PB. 4 suites. Breakfast included in rates. Types of meals: full breakfast and early coffee/tea. Beds: KQD. Ceiling fan in room. Fax and library on premises. French and Spanish spoken. Antiques, fishing, parks, shopping, downhill skiing, sporting events and watersports nearby.

Chadbourn   D7

Magnolia Manor B&B Accommodations

501 E 1st Ave
Chadbourn, NC 28431-2001
(910)654-5138

Circa 1908. This Princess Anne Victorian, located on two acres, has a wraparound porch with balusters and there are two gables. Chocolate turn-down service and terry cloth robes are among the amenities offered. Breakfast is continental and includes croissants, cereal and fresh fruit.

Magnolia Manor is an active participant in the annual North Carolina Strawberry Festival. Myrtle Beach is 45 minutes away.

Innkeeper(s): Sissy & Hamilton Long. $55-60. MC VISA PC TC. 2 rooms. Breakfast included in rates. Meal: continental breakfast. Beds: QD. Phone, air conditioning and turndown service in room. Bicycles on premises. Small meetings hosted. Antiques, fishing, shopping, golf and watersports nearby.

Publicity: *Strawberry Encounters, Fayetteville Observer-Times.*

"Of all my many stays in B&Bs this was by far my most enjoyable experience."

Chapel Hill   B6

The Inn at Bingham School

PO Box 267
Chapel Hill, NC 27514-0267
(919)563-5583 (800)566-5583 Fax:(919)563-9826

Circa 1790. This inn served as one of the locations of the famed Bingham School. This particular campus was the site of a liberal arts preparatory school for those aspiring to attend the University at Chapel Hill. The inn is listed as a National Trust property and has garnered awards for its restoration. The property still includes many historic structures includ-  ing a 1790s log home, an 1801 addition, an 1835 Greek Revival home, the headmaster's office, which was built in 1845, and a well house, smokehouse and milk house. The dining rooms and living rooms include the original pine flooring, wainscoting and milk-based paint on the ceilings. Guests can opt to stay in the Log Room, located in the log cabin, with a tightwinder staircase and fireplace. Other possibilities include Rusty's Room with two antique rope beds. Some rooms feature special mantels, an antique clawfoot tub and one offers a bedroom glassed in on three sides. A mix of breakfasts are served, from a Southern style with grits and ham to French with quiche and souffles. Gourmet coffee and tea complement each meal.

Historic Interest: The Orange County Historical Museum is 12 miles from the inn. The Durham Homestead is 20 miles away, and the Horace Williams House and North Carolina Collection Gallery are 10 miles away.

Innkeeper(s): Francois & Christina Deprez. $75-120. MC VISA AX DS PC TC. TAC10. 5 rooms with PB, 1 with FP. 1 suite. 1 cottage. 1 conference room. Breakfast and evening snack included in rates. Types of meals: full breakfast, gourmet breakfast and early coffee/tea. Picnic lunch available. Beds: QD. Phone and air conditioning in room. TV, VCR, fax and library on premises. 10 acres. Weddings, small meetings hosted. Spanish, French spoken. Antiques, fishing, parks, shopping, sporting events, theater, watersports nearby.

Publicity: *Southern Inns, Mebane Enterprise, Burlington Times, Times News, Washington Post.*

"Our stay at the inn was like a dream, another time, another place. Francois & Christina were the most hospitable, friendly hosts we've ever met."

Charlotte   C5

The Homeplace B&B

5901 Sardis Rd
Charlotte, NC 28270-5369
(704)365-1936

Circa 1902. Situated on two-and-one-half wooded acres in Southeast Charlotte, this peaceful setting is an oasis in one of the South's fastest-growing cities. Bedrooms have 10-foot ceil-

ings, heart-of-pine floors and blends of Country/Victorian decor. Special touches include quilts, fine linens, handmade accessories, family antiques and original primitive paintings by innkeeper Peggy Dearien's father. Spend the afternoon or evening relaxing on the porches or walking the secluded gardens.

While touring the grounds, you will see a 1930s log barn that was moved to the property in 1991.

Innkeeper(s): Margaret and Frank Dearien. $98-135. MC VISA AX. 4 rooms, 2 with PB. 1 suite. Breakfast included in rates. Types of meals: full breakfast and early coffee/tea. Beds: QT. Phone, air conditioning and ceiling fan in room. TV on premises. Antiques, shopping and sporting events nearby.

Publicity: *Charlotte Observer, Birmingham News, Country, Southern Living's Weekend Vacations.*

"Everything was perfect. The room was superb, the food excellent!"

The Morehead Inn

1122 E Morehead St
Charlotte, NC 28204-2815
(704)376-3357 (888)667-3432 Fax:(704)335-1110

Circa 1917. This old-fashioned Southern house is set on a huge corner lot dotted with oaks and azaleas. Guests gather in the great room, library and dining room, all furnished with English and American antiques. Balconies, canopy and four-poster beds and whirlpool tubs are among the amenities offered in some of the rooms. The Solarium Suite is a favorite choice. A two-bedroom carriage house with a stone fireplace is available for families or two couples traveling together.

Historic Interest: Reed Gold Mine (20 miles), Latta Plantation (5 miles), James K. Polk Memorial (8 miles).

Innkeeper(s): Billy Maddalon. $110-160. MC VISA AX DC PC. TAC10. 12 rooms with PB, 1 with FP. 8 suites. 1 cottage. 3 conference rooms. Breakfast included in rates. Types of meals: continental breakfast, continental-plus breakfast, full breakfast and gourmet breakfast. Evening snack, gourmet lunch and banquet service available. Beds: KQ. Phone, air conditioning, turndown service, ceiling fan and TV in room. Fax, copier and bicycles on premises. Weddings, small meetings, family reunions and seminars hosted. Amusement parks, antiques, parks, shopping, sporting events, theater nearby.

Publicity: *Business Journal, N.Y. Times, Charlotte, Observer, Carolina Bride.*

"Thank you for your gracious attentiveness and hospitality."

Still Waters

6221 Amos Smith Rd
Charlotte, NC 28214-8955
(704)399-6299

Circa 1929. This log house was built as a summer retreat on Lake Wylie. A sawmill was set up on the site and the rocks for the great room fireplace were gathered from the yard. Each room boasts a view of the lake. The Canopy Room features a king-size canopy waterbed, while the Family Suite has the feeling of a private cabin with its separate entrance. The Charlotte airport is 10 minutes away.

Historic Interest: Latta Plantation (20 minutes), Kings Mountain Battlefield Port (15 minutes), James K. Polk Memorial (25 minutes).

Innkeeper(s): Janet & Rob Dyer. $55-90. MC VISA DC. 4 rooms with PB, 1 with FP. Breakfast included in rates. Type of meal: full breakfast. Beds: KQ. Phone in room. Antiques, fishing and watersports nearby.

Location: Twenty minutes from downtown.

Publicity: *Mariner.*

"Your location on Lake Wylie was unbelievable. I could not imagine such a pretty, wooded and quiet place could be so close to a city. I give you a 10 on the Tom Peter's scale for Passion for Customers."

Durham   B6

Arrowhead Inn

106 Mason Rd
Durham, NC 27712-9106
(919)477-8430 (800)528-2207 Fax:(919)477-8430

Circa 1775. The home's original owners, the Lipscombe family, and later residents made several additions to this Colonial manor home, but left original features such as moldings, wainscoting, mantelpieces and heart-of-pine floors. A marker and stone arrowhead designate the land as the former location of the Great Path between mountains and Virginia, which was traveled by many Catawba and Waxhaw Indians. Rustic rooms are decorated to complement the fine woodwork. Quilts and canopy beds create a comfortable, romantic feeling. The Land Grant Cabin features rustic furnishings, a fireplace and sleeping loft set among its cozy wooden walls. The innkeepers take pride in creating a different feast every morning for breakfast. The inn is close to Duke University. The inn is winner of the Durham Chamber of Commerce 1st annual Micro Business Award.

Historic Interest: The Hillsborough Historic District and Duke Homestead Tobacco Museum are nearby as is Bennett Place, where Generals Sherman and Johnson signed the last surrender during the Civil War.

Innkeeper(s): Barb, Jerry, & Cathy Ryan. $95-195. MC VISA AX DC DS PC TC. TAC10. 8 rooms with PB, 2 with FP. 2 suites. 1 cottage. 1 conference room. Breakfast and afternoon tea included in rates. Type of meal: full breakfast. Picnic lunch available. Beds: KQD. Phone, air conditioning, ceiling fan and TV in room. Fax and copier on premises. Handicap access. Small meetings, family reunions and seminars hosted. French spoken. Antiques, parks and watersports nearby.

Publicity: *USA Today, Food & Wine, House & Garden, Mid-Atlantic Country, Old House Journal, Southern Living, UNC.*

"I can see why you were written up in USA Today. We give you an A plus!"

Edenton   B9

The Lords Proprietors' Inn

300 N Broad St
Edenton, NC 27932-1905
(919)482-3641 (800)348-8933 Fax:(919)482-2432

Circa 1801. On Albemarle Sound, Edenton was one of the Colonial capitols of North Carolina. The inn consists of three houses, providing elegant accommodations in Edenton's Historic District. Breakfast and dinner are served in a separate dining room on a patio. A guided walking tour from the Visitor's Center provides an opportunity to see museum homes.

Innkeeper(s): Arch & Jane Edwards. $185-235. MAP. PC TC. 20 rooms with PB. 1 conference room. Breakfast and dinner included in rates. Types of meals: full breakfast and early coffee/tea. Beds: KQT. Air conditioning, ceiling fan, TV and VCR in room. Fax and child care on premises. Handicap access. Small meetings, family reunions and seminars hosted. Antiques, fishing and shopping nearby.

Location: Main street of town.

Publicity: *Southern Living, Mid-Atlantic Country, House Beautiful, Washington Post.*

"One of the friendliest and best-managed inns I have ever visited."

Elizabeth City   A9

Culpepper Inn

609 W Main St
Elizabeth City, NC 27909-4256
(919)335-1993 Fax:(919)335-1555

Circa 1935. The inn is the town's most impressive brick Colonial Revival-style house. It was built by William and Alice Culpepper. Guests can come here to pick a peach from the tree, sit by the pool or in a hammock, read a book by the goldfish pond or relax by the fireplace. A Roman-style swimming pool was added in the mid-1980s. The town is situated on the Pasquotank River in the heart of the historical Albemarle area and is home to the Museum of the Albemarle, numerous antique stores, historic homes and restaurants.

Innkeeper(s): Robert & Julia Russell. $90-110. MC VISA AX. 11 rooms with PB. 1 conference room. Breakfast included in rates. Type of meal: full breakfast. Beds: KQT. Air conditioning and ceiling fan in room. TV and VCR on premises. Weddings, small meetings, family reunions and seminars hosted. Antiques, fishing, shopping, sporting events, theater and watersports nearby.

Franklin   C2

Buttonwood Inn

50 Admiral Dr
Franklin, NC 28734-8474
(704)369-8985

Circa 1927. Trees surround this two-story batten board house located adjacent to the Franklin Golf Course. Local crafts and handmade family quilts accent the country decor. Wonderful breakfasts are served here—often Eggs Benedict, baked peaches and sausage and freshly baked scones with homemade lemon butter. On a sunny morning, enjoy breakfast on the deck and savor the Smoky Mountain vistas. Afterward, you'll be ready for white-water rafting, hiking and fishing.

Innkeeper(s): Liz Oehser. $60-90. PC TC. 4 rooms with PB. Breakfast and afternoon tea included in rates. Types of meals: full breakfast and early coffee/tea. Beds: KDT. Ceiling fan in room. TV on premises. Family reunions hosted. Antiques, fishing, parks and shopping nearby.

Franklin Terrace

159 Harrison Ave
Franklin, NC 28734-2961
(704)524-7907 (800)633-2431

Circa 1887. This plantation home, built originally to house a school, is listed in the National Register of Historic Places. Each of the guest rooms features period antiques. The innkeepers also offer a cottage that can sleep up to four quite comfortably. Those opting to stay in the historic home are treated to a lavish, continental-plus breakfast buffet with home-baked muffins, cereals, juices, sausages, poached eggs and several different breads. The home is within walking distance to shops, clothing boutiques and a variety of restaurants, but guests are welcome to simply sit and relax on the veranda, which is lined with wicker rocking chairs.

Innkeeper(s): Ed & Helen Henson. $52-69. MC VISA AX DS PC TC. TAC5. 9 rooms with PB. 1 cottage. Breakfast included in rates. Types of meals: full breakfast and early coffee/tea. Beds: KQD. Air conditioning, ceiling fan and TV in room. Small meetings, family reunions and seminars hosted. Fishing, parks, downhill skiing, theater and watersports nearby.

"We just 'discovered' this wonderful B&B on a trip home from the mountains of North Carolina. The inn offers privacy, porches, unique rooms, comfort, cleanliness and is very pretty."

Grassy Creek   A4

River House

1896 Old Field Creek Rd
Grassy Creek, NC 28631
(910)982-2109
E-mail: riverhouse@skybest.com

Circa 1870. This three-story farmhouse contains both guest rooms and a fine restaurant, located on 125 acres with a mile of river front. There is a guest cottage, barn, chicken house among the out buildings. Guest chambers are filled with antiques and paintings and some have canopy beds, whirlpool tubs or private porches with views of the New River or the Blue Ridge Mountains. The fire-lit dining room, dressed in white linens, offers French-country cuisine with a regional influence. The innkeepers provide canoes and river tubes. Coffee is left outside your door in the morning, and there is a full American breakfast. The innkeeper, a former theatrical producer in New York, offers her guidance for weddings (held in the house or under the giant sycamore tree by the river) and business conferences.

Innkeeper(s): Gayle Winston, John Stewart. $90-150. MC VISA AX DC DS PC TC. TAC15. 9 rooms with PB, 4 with FP. 2 suites. 1 cottage. 1 cabin. 2 conference rooms. Breakfast included in rates. Types of meals: full breakfast, gourmet breakfast and early coffee/tea. Afternoon tea, dinner, picnic lunch, lunch, gourmet lunch, banquet service, catering service and room service available. Restaurant on premises. Beds: KQT. Phone, air conditioning, turndown service and ceiling fan in room. VCR, fax, copier, spa, swimming, stables, tennis, library, pet boarding and child care on premises. 125 acres. Weddings, small meetings, family reunions and seminars hosted. French, Spanish and Italian spoken. Antiques, fishing, parks, shopping, downhill skiing, cross-country skiing, sporting events, golf, theater, watersports nearby.

Pets Allowed: well-behaved.

"We thought we were lost, but oh!, what we found!"

Greensboro   B6

The Troy-Bumpass Inn

114 S Mendenhall St
Greensboro, NC 27403
(910)370-1660 (800)370-9070 Fax:(910)274-3939

Circa 1847. As General Sherman marched through the South on his way to Atlanta, some of his Union soldiers occupied this home. The grand Greek Revival home was built by Rev. Sidney Bumpas, and for 20 years, a Methodist newspaper was published here. The interior, often showcased on local historic home tours, has been restored to its former glory. The four guest rooms are decorated in a nostalgic, romantic style. One room contains a 19th-century mahogany bed with beautifully carved woodwork, another room offers a fireplace, clawfoot tub and bed draped in luxurious linens. The innkeepers offer two breakfast choices, one a light meal with fruits and homemade breads or a full Southern feast featuring items such as banana waffles topped with praline sauce. The home, listed in the National Register, is located in Greensboro's historic College Hill district.

Innkeeper(s): Charles & Gwen Brown. $75-125. MC VISA AX TC. TAC10. 4 rooms with PB, 1 with FP. 1 conference room. Breakfast and evening snack included in rates. Types of meals: full breakfast and early coffee/tea. Beds: KQD. Phone, air conditioning and turndown service in room. TV and VCR on premises. Weddings, small meetings and family reunions hosted. Antiques, parks, shopping, sporting events, golf and theater nearby.

Publicity: News & Record, North Carolina Tasteful Magazine, Greensboro Sun.

"You both know how to spoil people rotten."

Hendersonville   C3

Echo Mountain Inn

2849 Laurel Park Hwy
Hendersonville, NC 28739-8925
(704)693-9626 (888)324-6466 Fax:(704)697-2047

Circa 1896. Sitting on top of Echo Mountain, this large stone and wood inn has spectacular views, especially from the dining room and many of the guest rooms. Rooms are decorated with antiques and reproductions and many include a fireplace. The historic town of Hendersonville is three miles away. Gourmet dining includes an added touch of the city lights below. Guests may want to partake in refreshments of their choice served in the inn's fireside tavern.

Innkeeper(s): Peter & Shirley Demaras. $50-175. MC VISA AX. 37 rooms with PB, 8 with FP. 2 suites. 1 conference room. Breakfast included in rates. Types of meals: continental breakfast and early coffee/tea. Dinner, picnic lunch, lunch, banquet service and room service available. Restaurant on premises. Beds: KQDT. Phone, air conditioning and TV in room. Weddings, small meetings, family reunions and seminars hosted. Antiques, fishing, shopping, downhill skiing, golf and theater nearby.

"It was quite fabulous and the food entirely too rich."

Hickory B4

The Hickory B&B

464 7th St SW
Hickory, NC 28602-2743
(704)324-0548 (800)654-2961

Circa 1908. Bedrooms in this Georgian-style inn are decorated with antiques, collectibles and fresh flowers. There's a parlor to sit in and chat and a library to enjoy a good book or play a game. Guests also can relax and enjoy songbirds from the inn's porches. The inn is located in a city that has evolved from a furniture and textile mill town of yesteryear into a cultural arts mecca of mountain communities. From mountains to malls, Hickory satisfies the shopper as well as the sportsperson.

Innkeeper(s): Bob & Pat Lynch. $85-105. MC VISA PC. 4 rooms with PB. Breakfast included in rates. Types of meals: full breakfast and early coffee/tea. Afternoon tea available. Beds: Q. Air conditioning and ceiling fan in room. TV, VCR, swimming and library on premises. Weddings, small meetings and family reunions hosted. Antiques, fishing, shopping, sporting events, golf and theater nearby.

Publicity: *Mid-Atlantic Country, Hickory Daily News, Charlotte Observer.*

"Now we know what Southern hospitality means. We had such a wonderful weekend with you."

High Point B5

Bouldin House B&B

4332 Archdale Rd
High Point, NC 27263-3070
(910)431-4909 (800)739-1816 Fax:(910)431-4914
E-mail: lmiller582@aol.com

Circa 1915. This home, a unique example of American Four-Square architecture, is located a few miles outside of High Point, in the nearby village of Archdale. The innkeepers are only the second owners and have named their bed & breakfast for the family who built it. The house has been painstakingly restored and now offers four guest rooms, with names such as Weekend Retreat or Warm

Morning. Queen Anne chairs, pocket doors or a four-poster bed are among the features guests will discover in their rooms, and all guest quarters include a fireplace. Oatmeal currant scones topped with orange butter and pecan-basil pesto omelets and sage sausage are among the tempting treats served during the gourmet breakfasts.

Innkeeper(s): Larry & Ann Miller. $85-95. MAP. MC VISA DS PC TC. TAC10. 4 rooms with PB, 4 with FP. Breakfast and evening snack included in rates. Types of meals: gourmet breakfast and early coffee/tea. Afternoon tea available. Beds: KT. Air conditioning and ceiling fan in room. TV, VCR, fax and library on premises. Small meetings and family reunions hosted. Amusement parks, antiques, parks, shopping and sporting events nearby.

"Great place for a honeymoon."

Highlands C2

Colonial Pines Inn

541 Hickory St
Highlands, NC 28741-8498
(704)526-2060

Circa 1937. Secluded on a hillside just half a mile from Highlands' Main Street, this inn offers relaxing porches that boast a mountain view. The parlor is another restful option, offering a TV, fireplace and piano. Rooms, highlighted by knotty pine, are decorated with an eclectic mix of antiques. The guest pantry is always stocked with refreshments for those who

need a little something in the afternoon. For breakfast, freshly baked breads accompany items such as a potato/bacon casserole and baked pears topped with currant sauce. In addition to guest rooms and suites, there are two cottages available, each with a fireplace and kitchen.

Innkeeper(s): Chris & Donna Alley. $80-140. MC VISA PC TC. 6 rooms with PB. 2 suites. 2 cottages. Breakfast and afternoon tea included in rates. Type of meal: full breakfast. Beds: KQDT. TV on premises. Antiques, fishing, parks, shopping, downhill skiing, theater and watersports nearby.

Publicity: *Greenville News, Atlanta Journal, Highlander.*

"There was nothing we needed which you did not provide."

Morning Star Inn

480 Flat Mountain Estates Rd
Highlands, NC 28741-8325
(704)526-1009

Circa 1960. For anyone hoping to enjoy the serenity and scenery of North Carolina, this inn is an ideal place for that and more. Hammocks and rockers are found here and there on the two-acre grounds, dotted with gardens and fountains. There is a parlor with a stone fireplace and a wicker-filled sunporch. Rooms are decorated in a romantic and elegant style. Beds are dressed with fine linens and down comforters. To top off the amenities, one of the innkeepers is a culinary school graduate and prepares the mouthwatering cuisine guests enjoy at breakfast. On the weekends,

afternoon refreshments and a selection of hors d'oeuvres and wine are served. The innkeeper also is working on a cookbook, which will no doubt include tidbits such as Southwestern eggs and fresh fruit with amaretto cream sauce. For those interested in improving their culinary skills, cooking classes sometimes are available.

Innkeeper(s): Pat & Pat Allen. $135-160. MC VISA PC TC. TAC10. 5 rooms with PB. 1 suite. Breakfast included in rates. Type of meal: gourmet breakfast. Afternoon tea and evening snack available. Beds: KQ. Air conditioning, turndown service and ceiling fan in room. TV, fax and copier on premises. Small meetings and seminars hosted. Antiques, fishing, shopping, downhill skiing, golf and theater nearby.

Publicity: *Victoria Magazine, Southern Living.*

Ye Olde Stone House B&B

1337 S 4th St
Highlands, NC 28741
(704)526-5911

Circa 1938. Located at an elevation of 4,100 feet, this stone house with its country decor offers a place to relax and experience the natural beauty of its mountain setting. The innkeepers will be glad to help with guests' sightseeing plans, which might include a trip to nearby Dry, Glen and Bridal Veil Falls and the Cullsaja Gorge. Complimentary beverages and snacks are available and can be enjoyed in the glassed-in gazebo, porch or deck with comfortable chairs and rockers.

Innkeeper(s): Jim & Rene Ramsdell. $80-150. MC VISA PC TC. 4 rooms with PB. 2 cottages. Breakfast included in rates. Types of meals: gourmet breakfast and early coffee/tea. Beds: KQDT. Turndown service and ceiling fan in room. TV and VCR on premises. Weddings, small meetings and family reunions hosted. Antiques, fishing, parks, shopping, downhill skiing, theater and watersports nearby.

Kenansville C7

The Murray House

210 NC Hwy 24-50
Kenansville, NC 28349
(910)296-1000 (800)276-5322 Fax:(910)296-1000

Circa 1853. This is a pre-Civil War Greek Revival plantation-style home, in the National Register. With a quiet country setting on five acres, there are English gardens and pecan trees, dogwoods, crepe myrtles, oaks and hemlock trees. A barn, carriage house, smokehouse and brick flower house are on the property. Inside, a circular staircase, elaborate moldings and polished wood floors are enhanced by family antiques such as the Empire sideboard in the  upstairs hall. The breakfast menu includes dishes such as Quiche Lorraine with pan-fried potatoes, English muffins and fruit.

Innkeeper(s): Lynn & Joe Davis. $75-95. MC VISA AX PC TC. TAC10. 7 rooms, 5 with PB, 2 with FP. 2 suites. Breakfast and afternoon tea included in rates. Type of meal: full breakfast. Beds: KQT. Phone, air conditioning, TV and VCR in room. Fax, copier, spa and library on premises. Handicap access. Weddings, small meetings, family reunions and seminars hosted. Amusement parks, parks, shopping and golf nearby.

Lake Lure B3

Lodge on Lake Lure

Charlotte Dr Box 519
Lake Lure, NC 28746
(704)625-2789 (800)733-2785 Fax:(704)625-2421

Circa 1930. This rambling lodge, located directly on the lake, features a great room with vaulted ceilings, wormy chestnut walls and hand-hewn beams. A 20-foot-tall stone fireplace is highlighted with a gristmill stone. The breakfast room and the veranda, with its row of rocking chairs, provides inspirational views of the lake and mountains. Guest rooms are decorated in an elegant country style. Lakeside, boat docks and boats are available for guest use only. Weather permitting, lake cruises are offered every afternoon.

Innkeeper(s): Jack & Robin Stanier. $99-149. MC VISA AX DS PC TC. TAC10. 12 rooms with PB. Breakfast included in rates. Types of meals: full breakfast and gourmet breakfast. Beds: KQT. Air conditioning and ceiling fan in room. TV, VCR, fax, copier, swimming and library on premises. Small meetings and seminars hosted. Spanish spoken. Antiques, fishing, parks, shopping, theater and watersports nearby.

Location: Located on Lake Lure, in the foothills of the Blue Ridge Mountains, 22 miles southeast of Asheville, in western NC.

Lake Toxaway C2

Greystone Inn

Greystone Ln
Lake Toxaway, NC 28747
(704)966-4700 (800)824-5766 Fax:(704)862-5689

Circa 1915. Guests the likes of Thomas Edison and John D. Rockefeller frequented Lake Toxaway for their summer vacations, and the magnificent scenery convinced Savannah heiress Lucy Armstrong Moltz to build her summer cottage here. Her magnificent Swiss Revival home now hosts a bounty of guests hoping to capture the atmosphere of days gone by. Gracious, elegant rooms feature beautiful antiques and reproductions. Afternoon tea is served on the wicker-filled sun porch. The innkeepers host sunset champagne cruises along Lake Toxaway on a pontoon boat. The inn boasts a restaurant on site which serves up a variety of breakfast, lunch and dinner specialties. Tennis, boating, waterskiing and canoeing are all available.

Historic Interest: Biltmore Estate, George Vanderbilt's 250-room castle, offers a vast collection of art and antiques, and is 45 minutes away in Asheville.

Innkeeper(s): Tim & Boo Boo Lovelace. $255-510. MAP. MC VISA AX. TAC10. 33 rooms with PB. 3 suites. Breakfast, afternoon tea and dinner included in rates. Types of meals: full breakfast and early coffee/tea. Picnic lunch, lunch and room service available. Restaurant on premises. Beds: KQD. Phone, air conditioning, turndown service, ceiling fan, TV and VCR in room. Fax, copier, spa, swimming, sauna, bicycles, tennis, library and child care on premises. Handicap access. Weddings, small meetings and family reunions hosted. Antiques, fishing, shopping, downhill skiing, theater and watersports nearby.

Publicity: *Country Inns, Southern Living, Southern Accents.*

"Wonderful! We're already planning our next visit. We haven't felt this pampered since our last cruise."

Mountain Home C3

Mountain Home B&B

PO Box 234
Mountain Home, NC 28758-0234
(704)697-9090 (800)397-0066

Circa 1915. This home and its surrounding grounds have quite a history behind them. Although the inn itself was built in 1915, a plantation home once stood in this area, holding court over an enormous spread, which included a dairy, blacksmith shop, race track and stables. The plantation home was burnt at the end of the Civil War, and it was not until the early 1900s that a hotel was built on a  640-acre parcel of the property. This, too, burnt, and in 1941, a local dentist built his family home out of the hotel's remains. Today, the guests once again travel to this picturesque spot to enjoy Southern hospitality. Rooms are romantically appointed with items such as a four-poster rice bed, a sleigh bed, skylights, fireplace or Jacuzzi tub. The front porch, with its rockers, is ready for those who wish to relax. Guests also are pampered with a hearty breakfast; raspberry stuffed French toast is a specialty. The innkeepers offer a variety of getaway packages.

Historic Interest: The historic sites of Asheville and Hendersonville are nearby.

Innkeeper(s): Blake & Tammie Levit, Judy Brown. $85-195. MC VISA PC. TAC10. 7 rooms with PB, 1 with FP. 1 suite. 1 conference room. Breakfast and evening snack included in rates. Meals: full breakfast, gourmet breakfast and early coffee/tea. Banquet service available. Beds: KQD. Phone, air conditioning and TV in room. Handicap access. Small meetings, family reunions and seminars hosted. Antiques, fishing, parks, shopping and theater nearby.

Publicity: *Arts & Entertainment.*

"Thanks for showing us what 'Southern hospitality' is like."

Nags Head   B10

First Colony Inn

6720 S Va Dare Tr
Nags Head, NC 27959
(919)441-2343 (800)368-9390 Fax:(919)441-9234
E-mail: first.colony.inn@worldnet.att.net

Circa 1932. This Shingle-style inn features two stories of continuous verandas on all four sides. It is the last of the original beach hotels built on the Outer Banks. To save it from destruction, the Lawrences moved it to family property three miles south. During the midnight move,
townsfolk lined the streets
cheering and clapping to
see the preservation of this
historic building. First
Colony boasts a pool, cro-
quet court, private beach access and ocean and sound views
from the second and third floors. Furnishings include antiques
and traditional reproductions. There are Jacuzzis, kitchenettes, an
elegant library and a sunny breakfast room.

Historic Interest: Chicamacomico Lifesaving Station (20 miles), Wright Brothers Memorial (9 miles), the Outer Banks is the "Graveyard of the Atlantic," with many shipwrecks from the 16th century on. Elizabeth II, replica 16th-century ship (9 miles), Fort Raleigh, site of first English colony in the New World.

Innkeeper(s): The Lawrences. $80-250. MC VISA AX DS PC TC. TAC10. 26 rooms with PB. 6 suites. 1 conference room. Breakfast and afternoon tea included in rates. Types of meals: full breakfast and early coffee/tea. Catering service and room service available. Beds: KQT. Phone, air conditioning, turndown service, TV, copier, VCR in room. Fax, copier, swimming, library on premises. Handicap access. Weddings, small meetings, family reunions, seminars hosted. French, German. spoken. Fishing, parks, theater, watersports nearby.

Location: Outer Banks of North Carolina.

Publicity: *Virginia News Leader, Southern Living, Carolina Style, Greensboro News & Record, Discerning Traveler, Raleigh News & Observer, Washington Post, High Point Enterprise, Lexington Dispatch, Portfolio, Coast, Norfolk Virginian-Pilot.*

"Great, well done, nothing to change."

New Bern   C8

The Aerie

509 Pollock St
New Bern, NC 28562-5611
(919)636-5553

Circa 1882. This late Victorian home was built by Samuel Street, proprietor of the Old Gaston House Hotel, as his private residence. An appealing three-sided bay holds the downstairs parlor and an upstairs guest chamber. Fine antiques add to the gracious atmosphere of the inn and include an old mahogany player piano tuned and waiting for guests. Tryon Palace is a one-block walk from the inn.

Innkeeper(s): Rick & Lois Cleveland. $85. MC VISA AX. 7 rooms with PB, 5 with FP. Type of meal: full breakfast. Beds: QT.

Harmony House Inn

215 Pollock St
New Bern, NC 28560-4942
(919)636-3810 (800)636-3113 Fax:(919)636-3810
E-mail: harmony@nternet.net

Circa 1850. Long ago, this two-story Greek Revival was sawed in half and the west side moved nine feet to accommodate new hallways, additional rooms and a staircase. A wall was then built to divide the house into two sections. The rooms are decorated with antiques, the innkeeper's collection of handmade crafts and other collectibles. One of the suites includes a heart-shaped Jacuzzi tub. Offshore breezes sway blossoms in the lush garden. Cross the street to an excellent restaurant or take a picnic to the shore.

Innkeeper(s): Ed & Sooki Kirkpatrick. $99-130. MC VISA DS PC TC. TAC10. 8 rooms, 10 with PB, 10 with FP. 2 suites. 2 conference rooms. Breakfast and evening snack included in rates. Types of meals: full breakfast and early coffee/tea. Beds: KQT. Phone, air conditioning, ceiling fan and TV in room. Fax on premises. Weddings, small meetings, family reunions and seminars hosted. Korean spoken. Antiques, parks, shopping and watersports nearby.

Location: In the historic district, four blocks to Tyron Palace.

Publicity: *Americana, Raleigh News and Observer.*

"We feel nourished even now, six months after our visit to Harmony House."

King's Arms Inn

212 Pollock St
New Bern, NC 28560-4943
(919)638-4409 (800)872-9306 Fax:(919)638-2191

Circa 1848. Three blocks from the Tryon Palace, in the heart of the New Bern Historic District, this Colonial-style inn features a mansard roof and touches of Victorian architecture.

Guest rooms are decorated
with antiques, canopy and
four-poster beds and decorative fireplaces. An old
tavern in town was the
inspiration for the name of
the inn. Guests can enjoy a
candlelight continental-
plus breakfast served in their room.

Innkeeper(s): Richard & Pat Gulley. $85-130. MC VISA AX PC TC. TAC10. 8 rooms with PB. 1 suite. Breakfast and evening snack included in rates. Types of meals: continental-plus breakfast and early coffee/tea. Beds: KQD. Phone, air conditioning, ceiling fan and TV in room. Fax and child care on premises. Antiques, fishing, parks, theater and watersports nearby.

Publicity: *Washington Post, Southern Living, Sun Journal.*

"Delightful. Wonderful breakfast. Beautiful old home. Marvelous muffins."

Oriental   C9

The Tar Heel Inn

508 Church St, Box 176
Oriental, NC 28571
(919)249-1078 Fax:(919)249-0005
E-mail: tarheel@pamlico-nc.com

Circa 1890. This inn is graciously appointed in English-country style, with four-poster and canopy beds dressed in fine linens. Fresh flowers, stenciling and Laura Ashley prints brighten the rooms. Before a day exploring the area, guests enjoy a gourmet breakfast. In the late afternoons, refreshments are served.

Oriental, a village located at the junction of the Neuse River and Pamlico Sound, is known as a sailing capitol of the Carolinas.

Innkeeper(s): Shawna & Robert Hyde. $70-90. MC VISA PC. 8 rooms with PB. Breakfast and evening snack included in rates. Types of meals: full breakfast, gourmet breakfast and early coffee/tea. Beds: KQDT. Air conditioning and ceiling fan in room. Bicycles and library on premises. Small meetings and family reunions hosted. Antiques, fishing, parks, shopping, theater and watersports nearby.

Pilot Mountain (Siloam) A5

The Blue Fawn B&B

3052 Siloam Rd
Pilot Mountain (Siloam), NC 27041
(910)374-2064 (800)948-7716

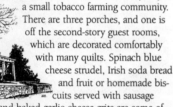

Circa 1892. This Greek Revival-style house, with its four two-story columns, is bordered by an old stone fence. Located 10 minutes from town, the Blue Fawn B&B offers a friendly stay in a small tobacco farming community. There are three porches, and one is off the second-story guest rooms, which are decorated comfortably with many quilts. Spinach blue cheese strudel, Irish soda bread and fruit or homemade biscuits served with sausage gravy, fried potatoes and baked garlic cheese grits are some of the breakfast offerings. It's a tenth of a mile to the Yadkin River.

Innkeeper(s): Gino & Terri Cella. $65-85. MC VISA PC. 3 rooms with PB. 1 suite. Breakfast, afternoon tea and evening snack included in rates. Types of meals: full breakfast, gourmet breakfast and early coffee/tea. Picnic lunch, catering service and room service available. Beds: KQDT. Air conditioning, turndown service, ceiling fan and TV in room. VCR, bicycles and library on premises. Weddings, small meetings, family reunions and seminars hosted. Antiques, fishing, parks, shopping, theater and watersports nearby.

"Words could never express how welcome and at home you have made our family feel."

Pinebluff C6

Pine Cone Manor

450 E Philadelphia Ave
Pinebluff, NC 28375
(910)281-5307

Circa 1912. The family that built this home lived here for more than 60 years, finally selling it in the 1970s. Today the house is a comfortable B&B set on private, wooded acres that include a variety of the namesake pines. The front porch is an ideal place to relax, offering a collection of rockers and a swing. The area is full of interesting sites, NASCAR and horse racing tracks are just a few. There are dozens of golf courses and the World Golf Hall of Fame.

Innkeeper(s): Virginia H. Keith. $60-65. MC VISA PC TC. 3 rooms, 2 with PB, 1 with FP. 1 cottage. Breakfast included in rates. Types of meals: continental-plus breakfast and early coffee/tea. Beds: KQDT. Phone, air conditioning, ceiling fan and TV in room. Library on premises. Family reunions hosted. Antiques, parks, shopping and sporting events nearby.

Pittsboro B6

The Fearrington House Inn

2000 Fearrington Village Ctr
Pittsboro, NC 27312-8502
(919)542-2121 Fax:(919)542-4202
E-mail: fhouse@fearrington.com

Circa 1927. The Fearrington is an old dairy farm. Several of the original outbuildings, including the silo and barn, have been converted into a village with a potter's shop, bookstore, jewelry shop, and a southern garden shop. The original homestead houses an award-winning restaurant. The inn itself is of new construction and its rooms overlook pasture land with grazing sheep, as well as a courtyard. Polished pine floors, fresh floral prints and amenity-filled bathrooms are among the inn's offerings.

Innkeeper(s): Richard Delany. $165-275. MC VISA AX PC. TAC10. 31 rooms with PB, 3 with FP. 12 suites. 3 conference rooms. Breakfast and afternoon tea included in rates. Types of meals: full breakfast, gourmet breakfast and early coffee/tea. Dinner, evening snack, picnic lunch, lunch, catering service and room service available. Restaurant on premises. Beds: KQDT. Phone, air conditioning, turndown service and TV in room. Fax, copier, spa, swimming, bicycles and tennis on premises. Handicap access. 60 acres. Weddings, small meetings and seminars hosted. German and French spoken. Antiques, fishing, parks, shopping, sporting events, golf, theater, watersports nearby.

Publicity: *Gourmet, Country Inns, Living It Up, North Carolina Homes and Gardens.*

"There is an aura of warmth and caring that makes your guests feel like royalty in a regal setting!"

Raleigh B7

The William Thomas House Bed & Breakfast

530 N Blount St
Raleigh, NC 27604
(919)755-9400 (800)653-3466 Fax:(919)755-3966

Circa 1881. This Victorian home is located in downtown Raleigh, within walking distance of the Governor's mansion and the Capitol building. The interior, which boasts high ceilings, carved molding, hardwood floors, is decorated in an elegant style. Walls are painted in bright, cheerful hues, and the furnishings include antiques. The grounds are decorated with flowers, foliage and shaded by trees, and guests can relax on a porch swing,  hammock or rocking chairs. There is ample off-street parking located behind the house. Frances Gray Patton, who wrote the book, "Good Morning, Miss Dove," was born in the home.

Innkeeper(s): Jim & Sarah Lofton. $98-135. MC VISA AX PC TC. 4 rooms with PB. 1 conference room. Breakfast and evening snack included in rates. Types of meals: full breakfast and early coffee/tea. Beds: KQT. Air conditioning, turndown service, ceiling fan, TV and VCR in room. Fax and library on premises. Weddings, small meetings, family reunions and seminars hosted. Antiques, parks, shopping, sporting events, golf and theater nearby.

Publicity: *News & Observer, WRAL-TV.*

"You have achieved a level of comfort, atmosphere and warmth that most B&Bs strive for."

Robbinsville   C2

Snowbird Mountain Lodge

275 Santeetlah Rd
Robbinsville, NC 28771-9712
(704)479-3433
E-mail: snbdmtnldg@aol.com

Circa 1940. Panoramic, 40-mile views are one of the many reasons to visit this mountain-top lodge. One innkeeper is a trained chef, and the other a knowledgeable outdoorsman. So guests not only enjoy gourmet meals, but learn where to find the best hiking and nature trails in North Carolina. The lodge is decorated in a rustic style, with an emphasis on comfort. Guest rooms feature wood-paneled walls, and each room sports a different variety of wood. Furnishings have been built by local craftsman using wood native to the area. There are plenty of places to relax, from the 2,500-volume library to rooms with huge, stone fireplaces. Breakfast, lunch and dinner are included in the rates. The innkeepers offer many interesting activities, such as a dulcimer clinic, fly-fishing excursions, cooking seminars and nature walks or hikes led by experienced guides.

Innkeeper(s): Karen & Robert Rankin. $120-130. AP. VISA PC TC. 22 rooms with PB. Breakfast, afternoon tea, dinner and evening snack included in rates. Types of meals: full breakfast and early coffee/tea. Picnic lunch and lunch available. Restaurant on premises. Beds: KQDT. Ceiling fan in room. Fax, copier and library on premises. Handicap access. 99 acres. Weddings, small meetings, family reunions and seminars hosted. Antiques, fishing, shopping and watersports nearby.

Salisbury   B5

Rowan Oak House

208 S Fulton St
Salisbury, NC 28144-4845
(704)633-2086 (800)786-0437 Fax:(704)633-2084

Circa 1901. This Queen Anne house, in the middle of the Salisbury Historic District, features a carved-oak front door, leaded and stained glass, meticulously carved mantels and the original ornate electric and gaslights. Guests may enjoy evening wine in the Victorian parlor or on the columned, wraparound porch overlooking gardens and fountains. Guest rooms have antiques, phones, historic wallpaper, down comforters, fresh flowers and fruit. One room has a double Jacuzzi, and one has a double shower.

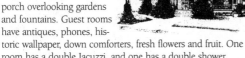

Historic Interest: North Carolina Transportation Museum (4 miles), 1820 Joseph's Hall House (1 block), Salisbury National Cemetery (1 mile), Salisbury Historic District (downtown).

Innkeeper(s): Barbara & Les Coombs. $85-125. MC VISA AX DS PC TC. TAC10. 4 rooms with PB. Breakfast included in rates. Type of meal: gourmet breakfast. Beds: KQD. Phone and air conditioning in room. Weddings, small meetings, family reunions and seminars hosted. Antiques, fishing, parks, shopping, sporting events, theater and watersports nearby.

Publicity: *Salisbury Post, Charlotte Observer, Country Victorian Accents.*

"A stay at the Rowan Oak House is the quintessential B&B experience. Their home is as interesting as it is beautiful, and they are the most gracious host and hostess you can imagine."

Saluda   C3

The Oaks

339 Greenville St
Saluda, NC 28773-9801
(704)749-9613 (800)893-6091

Circa 1894. The Oaks is a Victorian bed & breakfast furnished with American and Oriental antiques and original art work. Guests enjoy the mountain breezes from the wraparound porch and decks, playing croquet in the yard, reading by the fire in the library or chatting in the living room. The Oaks has four bedrooms, each with a private bath, cable TV and sitting area. All rooms are furnished with antiques and queen or double four-poster beds. A separate guest house is also available. A full breakfast is served family-style in the dining room.

Innkeeper(s): Crowley & Terry Murphy. $85-125. MC VISA DS. 4 rooms with PB. 1 cottage. Breakfast included in rates. Types of meals: full breakfast and early coffee/tea. Beds: QD. TV in room. Weddings and family reunions hosted. Antiques, fishing and shopping nearby.

Orchard Inn

Hwy 176, PO Box 725
Saluda, NC 28773
(704)749-5471 (800)581-3800 Fax:(704)749-9805

Circa 1910. This inn combines the casual feel of a country farmhouse with the elegance of a Southern plantation. The spacious living room features Oriental rugs, original artwork, quilts and a cozy stone fireplace. In addition to the nine comfortably furnished guest rooms, there are three cottages with fireplaces, whirlpool baths and private decks. A full breakfast is served every morning, and dinner is available by reservation Tuesday through Saturday. Guests can explore the area on superb country roads recently designated a scenic by-way.

Historic Interest: Carl Sandburg's home and grounds are about 15 minutes from the inn. The Biltmore Estate is 35 minutes away.

Innkeeper(s): Kathy & Bob Thompson. $105-175. MC VISA DS. 12 rooms, 9 with PB. 3 suites. 1 conference room. Breakfast included in rates. Meals: full breakfast, early coffee/tea. Beds: KQT. Phone, ceiling fan in room. 12 acres. Small meetings, seminars hosted. Antiques, fishing, shopping, theater nearby. Publicity: *Southern Living, Raleigh News & Observer, Tryon Daily Bulletin, State.*

"We enjoyed the peace and tranquility, the fine food and good friends we made."

Spruce Pine   B3

Ansley Richmond Inn B&B

101 Pine Ave
Spruce Pine, NC 28777-2733
(704)765-6993

Circa 1939. The scent of freshly baked muffins and steaming coffee serves as a pleasing wake-up call for guests staying at this country mountain home. More than an acre of wooded grounds surround the inn, which overlooks the Toe River valley. Rooms are decorated with family heirlooms and antiques. Several guest chambers include four-poster beds. Crackling flames from the stone fireplace warm the living room, a perfect place to relax. The innkeepers keep a guest refrigerator in the butler's pantry.

Innkeeper(s): Bill Ansley & Lee Boucher. $45-70. MC VISA DS TC. 7 rooms with PB. Breakfast included in rates. Types of meals: full breakfast and early coffee/tea. Beds: QT. Ceiling fan in room. TV, VCR and fax on premises. Small meetings and family reunions hosted. Antiques, parks, shopping, downhill skiing, cross-country skiing, golf and watersports nearby.

Statesville   B5

1898 B&B

520 West End Ave
Statesville, NC 28677
(704)838-1898
E-mail: 1898bnb@i-america.net

Circa 1898. Abandoned for more than 10 years, restoration on this Queen Anne-style house took more than three years of hard work to return it to its current immaculate state. The three-story inn features a wraparound porch, Doric columns set on shingled plinths and picture windows throughout. Each guest room features a different color scheme and a variety of Victorian antique furnishings. Guests will enjoy a candlelight breakfast served in the formal dining room. Use of the fully equipped, second-floor kitchen is offered to all guests.

Innkeeper(s): Joe & Robin Campbell. $55-105. MC VISA AX PC. TAC10. 4 rooms, 2 with PB, 4 with FP. 1 suite. 1 conference room. Breakfast and afternoon tea included in rates. Types of meals: full breakfast and early coffee/tea. Evening snack and room service available. Beds: QD. Phone and air conditioning in room. TV on premises. Amusement parks, antiques, fishing, parks, golf and watersports nearby.

Publicity: *Statesville Landmark, Charlotte Observer.*

"For a road-wearing traveler, your wonderful hospitality has been an absolute piece of Heaven!"

Cedar Hill Farm B&B

778 Elmwood Rd
Statesville, NC 28677-1181
(704)873-4332 (800)948-4423

Circa 1840. This renovated post-and-beam farmhouse rests on a 32-acre sheep farm. Hand-hewn, heart-of-pine walls, floors and interior shutters are featured inside. Guests may stay in the converted granary, the main house or Cotswold Cottage. The air-conditioned cottages includes a full kitchen, stone fireplace, Jacuzzi, canopy bed, private deck and a window seat overlooking pastures and woods. The granary also includes a fireplace. Porches boast several swings and rockers, and there is a hammock strung between two old shade trees. Romney sheep, geese and a rooster populate the farm.

Innkeeper(s): Brenda & Jim Vernon. $70-95. MC VISA AX PC TC. 3 rooms with PB, 2 with FP. 2 cottages. Breakfast included in rates. Type of meal: full breakfast. Beds: QDT. Phone and air conditioning in room. Swimming on premises. 32 acres. Antiques, fishing, parks, sporting events, theater nearby.

Location: Seven miles east of Statesville.

Publicity: *Record & Landmark, Southern Living.*

"Gracious hospitality is an art...we found lots of it here."

Sylva   C2

Mountain Brook

208 Mountain Brook Rd #19
Sylva, NC 28779-9659
(704)586-4329
E-mail: vacation@mountainbrook.com

Circa 1930. Located in the Great Smokies, Mountain Brook consists of 12 cottages on a hillside amid rhododendron, elm, maple and oak trees. The resort's 200-acre terrain is crisscrossed with brooks and waterfalls and contains a trout-stocked pond. Two cottages are constructed with logs from the property while nine are made from native stone. They feature fireplaces and porch swings and have brass, four-poster and canopy beds, quilts and rocking chairs.

Innkeeper(s): Gus & Michele McMahon. $80-130. TAC10. 12 rooms with PB, 12 with FP. Beds: KD. Spa and sauna on premises. Handicap access. Weddings and family reunions hosted. Amusement parks, antiques, fishing, parks, shopping, downhill skiing, sporting events, theater, watersports nearby.

Publicity: *Brides Magazine, Today, The Hudspeth Report.*

"The cottage was delightfully cozy, and our privacy was not interrupted even once."

Taylorsville   B4

Barkley House B&B

2522 NC Hwy 16 S
Taylorsville, NC 28681-8952
(704)632-9060 (888)270-9060

Circa 1896. This 19th-century home is decorated in a country Victorian motif with antiques and family heirlooms, including the wedding dress that belonged to the innkeeper's mother, which is on display in the parlor. Breakfast is a lavish, Southern affair. Guests are pampered with entrees such as breakfast casseroles or stuffed French toast served with hot chocolate or hot apple cider, biscuits and gravy, grits, juice and fresh fruit. The area offers galleries, historic mansions and the Emerald Hollow Gem Mine, where guests can dig for precious gems. Guests enjoy a personal brandy cabinet and there are brandy tastings around 5 p.m.

Innkeeper(s): Phyllis Barkley. $59. MC VISA AX DS PC TC. TAC10. 4 rooms with PB, 1 with FP. Breakfast and evening snack included in rates. Types of meals: continental-plus breakfast, full breakfast, gourmet breakfast and early coffee/tea. Catered breakfast available. Beds: KQDT. Phone, air conditioning, turndown service, ceiling fan and TV in room. VCR, spa and library on premises. Antiques, fishing, shopping and sporting events nearby.

Pets Allowed: Restricted to room.

Tryon   C3

Foxtrot Inn

PO Box 1561, 800 Lynn RD
Tryon, NC 28782-2708
(704)859-9706

Circa 1915. Located on six acres in town, this turn-of-the-century home features mountain views and large guest rooms. There is a private guest cottage with its own kitchen and a hanging deck. The rooms are furnished with antiques. The Cherry Room in the main house

has a four-poster, queen-size canopy bed with a sitting area over-looking the inn's swimming pool. The Oak Suite includes a wood-paneled sitting room. A cozy fireplace warms the lobby.

Innkeeper(s): Wim Woody. $75-125. PC. 4 rooms with PB. 2 suites. 1 cottage. Breakfast included in rates. Type of meal: full breakfast. Beds: QDT. Air conditioning in room. TV and swimming on premises. Weddings, small meetings, family reunions and seminars hosted. Antiques, fishing, parks, shopping and watersports nearby.

Pets Allowed: Pets allowed in cottage by special arrangement.

Mimosa Inn

One Mimosa Inn Ln
Tryon, NC 28782
(704)859-7688

Circa 1903. The Mimosa is situated on the southern slope of the Blue Ridge Mountains. With its long rolling lawns and large

columned veranda, the inn has been a landmark and social gathering place for almost a century. Breakfasts are served either in the dining room or on the columned veranda.

Innkeeper(s): Jay & Sandi Franks. $65. MC VISA DS PC TC. 9 rooms with PB. 1 conference room. Breakfast included in rates. Types of meals: full breakfast and early coffee/tea. Beds: QT. Air conditioning in room. TV and library on premises. Weddings, small meetings, family reunions and seminars hosted. Amusement parks, antiques, fishing, parks, shopping, theater nearby.

"Thanks for your hospitality. We could just feel that Southern charm."

Pine Crest Inn

200 Pinecrest Ln
Tryon, NC 28782-3437
(704)859-9135 (800)633-3001 Fax:(704)859-9135

Circa 1906. Once a favorite of F. Scott Fitzgerald, this inn is nestled in the foothills of the Blue Ridge Mountains. Opened in 1917 by famed equestrian Carter Brown, the inn offers guests romantic fireplaces, gourmet dining and wide verandas that offer casual elegance. The Blue Ridge Parkway and the famous Biltmore House are a short drive away. Rooms are available in the Main Lodge and cottages. Original buildings include a 200-year-old log cabin, a woodcutter cottage and a stone cottage. Elegant meals are served in a Colonial tavern setting for full breakfasts and gourmet dinners.

Historic Interest: The Biltmore Estate is a 40-minute drive.

Innkeeper(s): Jennifer & Jeremy Wainwright. $125-185. MC VISA AX DS. 35 rooms, 30 with PB, 24 with FP. 9 suites. 1 conference room. Breakfast included in rates. Meals: continental-plus breakfast, full breakfast, gourmet breakfast and early coffee/tea. Dinner and picnic lunch available. Restaurant on premises. Beds: KQT. Phone, air conditioning, turndown service, TV and VCR in room. Fax and copier on premises. Handicap access. Small meetings and seminars hosted. Antiques, fishing, shopping and theater nearby.

Publicity: *Southern Living, Gourmet, Island Scene, Tasteful, Knoxville Sentinel.*

"We felt pampered and at home in your lovely Pine Crest Inn."

Tryon Old South B&B

107 Markham Rd
Tryon, NC 28782-3054
(704)859-6965 (800)288-7966 Fax:(704)859-6965

Circa 1910. This Colonial Revival inn is located just two blocks from downtown and Trade Street's antique and gift shops. Located in the Thermal Belt, Tryon is known for its pleasant, mild weather. Guests don't go away hungry from innkeeper Pat Grogan's large Southern-style breakfasts. Unique

woodwork abounds in this inn and equally as impressive is a curving staircase. Behind the property is a large wooded area and several waterfalls are just a couple of miles away. The inn is close to Asheville attractions.

Innkeeper(s): Tony & Pat Grogan. $55-125. MC VISA PC TC. TAC10. 6 rooms, 4 with PB. 2 cottages. Breakfast included in rates. Types of meals: full breakfast and early coffee/tea. Beds: QDT. Air conditioning in room. TV, VCR, fax and copier on premises. Family reunions hosted. Antiques, fishing, parks, shopping and theater nearby.

Valle Crucis   B4

Mast Farm Inn

PO Box 704
Valle Crucis, NC 28691-0704
(704)963-5857 (888)963-5857 Fax:(704)963-6404
E-mail: stay@mastfarminn.com

Circa 1885. Listed in the National Register of Historic Places, this 18-acre farmstead includes a main house and seven out-buildings. The inn features a wraparound porch with rocking

chairs, swings and a view of the mountain valley. Rooms are furnished with antiques, quilts and mountain crafts. In addition to the inn rooms, there are four cottages available, some with kitchens. Flowers and vegetables from the garden are specialties. Early morning coffee can be delivered to your room. Dinners feature contemporary regional cuisine.

Historic Interest: Saint John's Church (2 miles), Mast General Store (1 mile).

Innkeeper(s): Wanda Hinshaw & Kay Philipp. $90-175. MC VISA AX DS TC. 9 rooms with PB. 4 cottages. Breakfast included in rates. Type of meal: full breakfast. Restaurant on premises. Beds: KQD. Ceiling fan in room. Fax on premises. Handicap access. 18 acres. Antiques, downhill skiing, sporting events, theater and watersports nearby.

Publicity: *Blue Ridge Country, Southern Living.*

"We want to live here!"

The Inn at The Taylor House

PO Box 713
Valle Crucis, NC 28691-0713
(704)963-5581 Fax:(704)963-5818

A wraparound porch encircling this farmhouse-style inn communicates the feeling of real hospitality and sets the tone for the entire house. There's old and new wicker on the porch with bright fabrics, lots of plants and flower boxes. An old-

fashioned porch swing adds to the feeling, and from the breakfast area, you can look out on a field of grazing Charolais cattle. The town was founded by Scottish Highlanders when they first came to this country.

Every summer, the area hosts the largest gathering of Scottish clans in the United States.

Innkeeper(s): Chip Schwab. Call for rates. 2 suites. Ceiling fan in room. 10 acres. Weddings, small meetings, family reunions and seminars hosted. Antiques, shopping and theater nearby.

Washington   B8

Acadian House B&B

129 Van Norden St
Washington, NC 27889
(919)975-3967 (888)972-3393 Fax:(919)975-1148

Circa 1902. This turn-of-the-century Victorian is listed in the National Register of Historic Places and is located in a historic district. Rooms are simply and comfortably furnished with Victorian touches, such as an antique Singer sewing machine transformed into a table. The innkeepers both hail from Louisiana and serve New Orleans-style specialties for breakfast, including beignets and cafe' au lait. Shops and restaurants are within walking distance, and the Pamlico River is just one block away.

Innkeeper(s): Johanna & Leonard Huber. $55-65. MC VISA AX PC TC. TAC10. 4 rooms with PB, 3 with FP. 1 suite. Breakfast included in rates. Meals: full breakfast, gourmet breakfast and early coffee/tea. Beds: KQDT. Phone, air conditioning, ceiling fan and TV in room. Fax, bicycles and library on premises. Weddings, small meetings, family reunions and seminars hosted. Antiques, fishing, parks, shopping, sporting events, golf, theater nearby.

"We really enjoyed the comfortable atmosphere, the food was delectable."

Pamlico House

400 E Main St
Washington, NC 27889-5039
(919)946-7184

Circa 1906. This gracious Colonial Revival home once served as the rectory for St. Peter's Episcopal Church. A veranda wraps around the house in a graceful curve. Furnished in Victorian antiques, the inn has the modern convenience of air conditioning. Nearby is the city's quaint waterfront. Washington is on the Historic Albemarle Tour Route and within easy driving distance to the Outer Banks.

Historic Interest: The inn is in the National Register.

Innkeeper(s): George & Jane Fields. $75-85. MC VISA AX DS PC TC. 4 rooms with PB. Type of meal: full breakfast. Beds: KQT.

Location: Eastern North Carolina.

Waynesville   B2

Grandview Lodge

466 Lickstone Rd
Waynesville, NC 28786
(704)456-5212 (800)255-7826 Fax:(704)452-5432
E-mail: sarnold@haywood.main.nc.us

Circa 1890. Grandview Lodge is located on two-and-a-half acres in the Smoky Mountains. The land surrounding the lodge has an apple orchard, rhubarb patch, grape arbor and vegetable garden for the inn's kitchen. Rooms are available in the main lodge and in a newer addition. The inn's dining room is known throughout the region and Linda, a home economist, has written "Recipes from Grandview Lodge."

Historic Interest: The Biltmore Estate (45 minutes), Cherokee Indian Reservation (45 minutes).

Innkeeper(s): Stan & Linda Arnold. $100-120. MAP. PC TC. TAC10. 11 rooms with PB, 3 with FP. 2 suites. Breakfast and dinner included in rates. Types of meals: full breakfast and early coffee/tea. Lunch available. Restaurant on premises. Beds: KQDT. Air conditioning and TV in room. VCR, fax and library on premises. Weddings, small meetings, family reunions and seminars hosted. Polish, Russian and German spoken. Amusement parks, antiques, fishing, parks, shopping, downhill skiing, sporting events, theater, watersports nearby.

Publicity: *Asheville Citizen, Winston-Salem Journal, Raleigh News & Observer.*

"It's easy to see why family and friends have been enjoying trips to Grandview."

Hallcrest Inn

65 Carriage Lane
Waynesville, NC 28786-2520
(704)456-6457 (800)334-6457

Circa 1880. This simple white frame farmhouse was the home of the owner of the first commercial apple orchard in western North Carolina. Atop Hall Mountain, it commands a breathtaking view of Waynesville and Balsam Mountain Range. A gathering room, a dining room and seven guest rooms are furnished with family antiques. The side porch features four rooms with balconies. Family-style dining is offered around Lazy-Susan tables.

Innkeeper(s): Martin & Tesa Burson. $60-90. MAP. MC VISA DC DS PC TC. TAC10. 11 rooms with PB, 4 with FP. Breakfast and dinner included in rates. Types of meals: full breakfast and early coffee/tea. Beds: D. Weddings and family reunions hosted. Amusement parks, antiques, fishing, parks, shopping, sporting events and theater nearby.

Location: US 276N from Waynesville, left on Mauney Cove Road.

Publicity: *Asheville Citizen.*

"Country charm with a touch of class."

Haywood House B&B

675 S Haywood St
Waynesville, NC 28786-4349
(704)456-9831 Fax:(704)456-4400

Circa 1906. The exterior of this early 20th-century home was designed in the style of Colonial Revival architecture, yet the interior sports an abundance of Craftsman-style features. Its was once the home to William Cicero Allen, an author, county school superintendent and editor of a local newspaper. The

home is decorated in a charming country style, creating a cozy, welcoming ambiance. The kitchen boasts an antique stove, and the parlor has an Edison phonograph. Stained-glass art hangs in several windows and the wood floors are topped with Oriental rugs. Best of all, are the stunning views of the Great Smoky Mountains. The innkeepers prepare a different morning feast each day, and you will be pampered with an abundance of gourmet food. Guests can walk to Main Street, which offers a variety of shops and restaurants. There are dozens of attractions, from the Blue Ridge Parkway to white-water rafting, all within 15 minutes to an hour of the inn.

Innkeeper(s): Lynn & Chris Sylvester. $70-95. MC VISA AX DS PC TC. TAC10. 4 rooms, 2 with PB, 3 with FP. Breakfast and evening snack included in rates. Types of meals: full breakfast, gourmet breakfast and early coffee/tea. Beds: QT. Ceiling fan in room. TV, VCR, fax, copier and library on premises. Family reunions hosted. Amusement parks, antiques, fishing, parks, shopping, downhill skiing, golf and theater nearby.

Publicity: *Atlanta Journal-Constitution, Asheville Citizen, Waynesville Mountaineer.*

"You sure know how to make your guests feel at home."

Herren House

200 East St
Waynesville, NC 28786-3836
(704)452-7837 (800)284-1932
E-mail: herren@circle.net

Circa 1897. Pink and white paint emphasize the Victorian features of this two-story inn with wraparound porch. Inside, the Victorian decor is enhanced with the innkeepers' paintings and handmade furniture. Soft music and candlelight set the tone for breakfast, which often features the inn's homemade chicken sausage and a baked egg dish along with a freshly baked items such as apricot scones. A garden gazebo is an inviting spot with an overhead fan and piped in music. A block away are galleries, antique shops and restaurants. The Great Smoky Mountains National Park and the Blue Ridge Parkway begin a few minutes from the inn.

Innkeeper(s): Jackie & Frank Blevins. $75-115. MC VISA AX DS PC TC. 6 rooms with PB. Breakfast, afternoon tea and evening snack included in rates. Meals: full breakfast, gourmet breakfast and early coffee/tea. Beds: QT. Air conditioning, ceiling fan, TV and VCR in room. Copier and library on premises. Handicap access. Small meetings hosted. Antiques, fishing, parks, shopping, downhill skiing, cross-country skiing, golf, theater, watersports nearby.

The Old Stone Inn

109 Dolan Rd
Waynesville, NC 28786-2802
(704)456-3333 (800)432-8499

Circa 1946. Although The Old Stone Inn may be a post-World War II structure, its legacy of innkeeping stretches for more than 50 years. Surrounded by acres of woods and the scenic North Carolina Smokies, the lodge is an ideal location to commune with nature. Exposed-log beams, wooden floors and country furnishings add to the relaxing country atmosphere. Meals are served in the stone and log dining room in front of a crackling fire. The hearty breakfasts prepare guests for a day in the mountains, with treats

such as banana nut pancakes, Tennessee sausage pie, fresh fruit or egg dishes. Candle-lit dinners are romantic, with a Southern flair accompanied by freshly baked breads, distinctive appetizers and delectable desserts. The lodge porch is lined with rocking chairs, perfect for relaxing.

Historic Interest: Great Smoky Mountains National Park is just five miles away.

Innkeeper(s): Robert & Cindy Zinser. $89-139. MC VISA DS. 20 rooms with PB. 2 suites. Breakfast included in rates. Type of meal: full breakfast. Dinner and room service available. Restaurant on premises. Beds: KQD. Antiques, fishing, downhill skiing, theater and watersports nearby.

Publicity: *Asheville Citizen Times, Charlotte Observer, National Geographic Traveler, Blue Ridge Country.*

"The food was absolutely great and the treatment was top notch."

Ten Oaks

224 Love Ln
Waynesville, NC 28786
(704)452-9433 (800)563-2925 Fax:(704)452-9433

Circa 1898. This handsomely renovated, three-story house is in a blended Queen Anne Colonial Revival style. The inviting wraparound porch has long been a favored location for enjoying the mountain breezes. In the National Register, the inn's spacious guest rooms boast fireplaces, and one suite has a whirlpool tub and a sitting room. Breakfast is hearty and often includes Southern Garlic Grits Casserole as a specialty of the house.

Innkeeper(s): Eleanor & Jack Suddath. $80-135. MC VISA PC TC. TAC10. 4 rooms with PB, 4 with FP. 2 suites. Breakfast and evening snack included in rates. Types of meals: full breakfast, gourmet breakfast and early coffee/tea. Beds: KQT. Phone, turndown service and ceiling fan in room. TV, VCR, fax and library on premises. Handicap access. Amusement parks, antiques, fishing, parks, shopping, downhill skiing, cross-country skiing, sporting events, golf, theater and watersports nearby.

Publicity: *Mountaineer, Oklahoman.*

"We had a marvelous rest of the trip but nothing equaled our stay at Ten Oaks! After staying at another B&B, we certainly realized, they aren't all Ten Oaks."

Yellow House on Plott Creek Road

89 Oakview Dr
Waynesville, NC 28786-4500
(704)452-0991 (800)563-1236 Fax:(704)452-1140

Circa 1885. This manor, which boasts views of the Blue Ridge Mountains, was built as a summer home to a family from Tampa, Fla. The interior of the home is decidedly French country done in romantic colors. Each room is special, from the Batternburg bedding in the Carolina and S'conset rooms to the four-poster bed and mountain view in the Montecito room. Each of the rooms and suites has a fireplace. The Carriage House and St. Paul de Vence Suite offer a whirlpool tub. Special amenities, such as bathrobes, fresh flowers, a decanter of port, coffee, hair dryers and toiletries thoughtfully have been placed in each room and suite. Each evening, the innkeepers offer wine and cheese, and in the mornings, a gourmet breakfast is served. Guests are free to enjoy their meal on the veranda or in the privacy of their room.

Innkeeper(s): Sharon & Ron Smith. $115-230. MC VISA PC TC. TAC10. 6 rooms with PB, 6 with FP. 4 suites. Breakfast and evening snack included in rates. Types of meals: full breakfast, gourmet breakfast and early coffee/tea. Picnic lunch and catered breakfast available. Beds: KQT. Phone, turndown service and ceiling fan in room. Fax, copier and library on premises. Small meetings, family reunions and seminars hosted. Antiques, fishing, parks, shopping, golf, theater and watersports nearby.

Pets Allowed: Children 12 or old welcome.

Publicity: *Asheville Citizen Times, Mountaineer.*

"The scenery and quaintness of this community was only surpassed by the gracious surroundings and hospitality here at the Yellow House."

Wilmington   D7

Camelia Cottage B&B

118 S 4th St
Wilmington, NC 28401
(910)763-9171 (800)763-9171

Circa 1889. Many of the elements in this Queen Anne Victorian were designed by the first owner, Jane Meares Williams. A local artist, Henry J. MacMillan later added a unique wraparound garden. The grounds are still bursting with color. The innkeeper has more than two dozen camellia bushes, and a rose garden, herb garden, fountain and koi pond decorated the grounds. Each of the guest rooms is individually decorated, and each has a fireplace. The Natchez Room features masculine decor, a clawfoot tub and a unique tester bed. The Camellia and Victoria rooms are more feminine with flowery prints and a four-poster or iron bed. A full Southern breakfast, cheese grits and all, is served each morning in a fashionable setting with fine china and crystal.

Innkeeper(s): Susan Campbell. $110-125. TAC10. 4 rooms with PB, 3 with FP. 1 suite. Breakfast included in rates. Types of meals: full breakfast and early coffee/tea. Afternoon tea available. Beds: Q. Phone and air conditioning in room. Fax and pet boarding on premises. Antiques, fishing, parks, shopping, sporting events, golf, theater and watersports nearby.

Pets Allowed: Dogs under 15 lbs.

"We were so impressed with the elegance of your home as well as the coziness. Also, breakfast was absolutely fantastic!"

Catherine's Inn

410 S Front St
Wilmington, NC 28401-5012
(910)251-0863 (800)476-0723

Circa 1883. This Italianate-style home features wrought-iron fences and a Colonial Revival wraparound porch in the front and a two-story screened porch in the back. The 300-foot private garden overlooks a unique sunken garden and the Cape Fear River. Antiques and reproductions fill the interior, which includes 12-foot ceilings and an heirloom grand piano. Freshly brewed coffee is delivered to each room in the morning, followed by a full breakfast served on

family collections of china, crystal and sterling silver in the dining room. Turndown service and complimentary refreshments are some of the other amenities offered by the innkeepers.

Historic Interest: Catherine's Inn is registered as a local, state and national landmark home and is located in the heart of Wilmington's historic district.

Innkeeper(s): Catherine & Walter Ackiss. $85-99. MC VISA AX. 5 rooms with PB. Breakfast and afternoon tea included in rates. Beds: KQT. Antiques, fishing, theater and watersports nearby.

Publicity: *This Week, Country Inns, Encore, Mid-Atlantic, N.Y. Times, Carolina.*

"This is the best!"

James Place B&B

9 S 4th St
Wilmington, NC 28401-4534
(910)251-0999 (800)303-9444 Fax:(910)251-1150
E-mail: jamesinn@wilmington.net

Circa 1909. On a tree-lined street of two-story, turn-of-the-century houses, this neatly painted taupe home has gleaming white trim highlighting the porch and shutters. Each room features air conditioning and ceiling fans. Fresh coffee is available for guests in the morning, and later, a full breakfast is served downstairs. The downtown waterfront is a short stroll away.

Innkeeper(s): Maureen & Tony Spataro. $75-105. MC VISA AX PC TC. TAC5. 3 rooms with PB. 1 suite. Breakfast and evening snack included in rates. Types of meals: continental-plus breakfast and full breakfast. Beds: Q. Phone, air conditioning and ceiling fan in room. TV, VCR, fax, copier, spa on premises. Small meetings, family reunions hosted. Amusement parks, antiques, fishing, parks, shopping, sporting events, theater, watersports nearby.

Publicity: *Encore.*

"An ideal setting for rejuvenation! Thanks so much for the Southern hospitality."

The Inn on Orange

410 Orange St
Wilmington, NC 28401
(910)815-0035 (800)381-4666 Fax:(910)815-6617
E-mail: innonorang@aol.com

Circa 1875. Burgundy paint accentuates the trim of this blue and white Italianate Victorian B&B. Surrounded by a white picket fence, the inn's landscaping is enhanced by azaleas, roses and 40-foot-tall crepe myrtle. Spacious guest rooms feature canopy beds and European linens, antiques, fireplaces, ceiling fans, Russian art and Persian carpets. Twelve-foot ceilings are found throughout, including the dining room where four-course breakfasts are served by candlelight with fine china, silver and crystal. Walk to restaurants, nightclubs and shops, or enjoy the Riverwalk, a waterfront park. In addition to the neighborhoods of stately homes, guests often ride the sternwheel paddleboat or horse-drawn carriage to further enjoy the Southern atmosphere.

Innkeeper(s): Vargas Family. $85-125. MC VISA AX DS PC TC. 4 rooms, 2 with PB, 4 with FP. 2 suites. Breakfast included in rates. Types of meals: gourmet breakfast and early coffee/tea. Beds: KQDT. Phone, air conditioning, ceiling fan and TV in room. Fax, copier, swimming and library on premises. German spoken. Amusement parks, antiques, fishing, parks, shopping, sporting events, golf, theater and watersports nearby.

Publicity: *Travelhost.*

"A relaxing atmosphere with a touch of elegance."

Rosehill Inn

114 S 3rd St
Wilmington, NC 28401
(910)815-0250 (800)815-0250 Fax:(910)815-0350
E-mail: rosehill@rosehill.com

Circa 1848. Architect Henry Bacon, Jr., most famous for designing the Lincoln Memorial in Washington, D.C., lived here in the late 19th-century. Located in the largest urban historic district in the country, this Neoclassical Victorian with its three-diamond AAA rating was completely renovated in 1995. The guest rooms are spacious and decorated in period furnishings. Breakfast treats include eggs Benedict with Cajun Crab Hollandaise and stuffed French toast with orange syrup.

Innkeeper(s): Laurel Jones, Dennis Fietsch. $85-165. MC VISA AX DS TC. TAC10. 6 rooms with PB. 1 conference room. Breakfast included in rates. Types of meals: continental breakfast, full breakfast, gourmet breakfast and early coffee/tea. Beds: KQD. Phone in room. Fax and copier on premises. Family reunions hosted. Antiques, fishing, parks, shopping, golf, theater and watersports nearby.

The Inn at St. Thomas Court

101 S Thomas Court
Wilmington, NC 28401-4401
(910)343-1800 (888)525-0909 Fax:(910)251-1149
E-mail: theinn@wilmington.net

Circa 1904. The buildings that comprise the Inn at St. Thomas Court include three renovated historic commercial buildings and one new building that contains the guest rooms. Located in a neighborhood of restored historic houses, it is two blocks from the Cape Fear River. Guest rooms and two-bedroom suites are decorated in a variety of themes including "Gone With the Wind" and "Casablanca." Nautical and traditional decor is also available. Fish ponds, flower beds, a gazebo and brick patios fill the courtyard. In the morning, breakfast baskets are delivered to each room. Galleries, museums, restaurants and shops are all within walking distance, and many guests take advantage of horse-drawn carriage rides and the paddlewheel steamer.

$100-205. MC VISA AX DC CB DS TC. TAC10. 34 suites, 1 with FP. 1 conference room. Breakfast included in rates. Types of meals: continental-plus breakfast and early coffee/tea. Beds: KQD. Phone, air conditioning, ceiling fan, TV and VCR in room. Copier and library on premises. Handicap access. Small meetings and seminars hosted. German and Spanish spoken. Amusement parks, antiques, fishing, parks, shopping, golf, theater and watersports nearby.

Taylor House Inn

14 N 7th St
Wilmington, NC 28401-4645
(910)763-7581 (800)382-9982

Circa 1905. This Neoclassical Revival-style house includes five spacious guest rooms all appointed with antiques, fine linens and fresh flowers. Three private baths feature clawfoot tubs. A full breakfast is served in the dining room. High ceilings, stained-glass windows, fireplaces, an open staircase and parquet floors add to the home's beauty and elegance. Situated in historic downtown, steps from antique shops and restaurants, the inn is also minutes from several beaches.

Historic Interest: USS North Carolina (2 miles), Fort Fisher (20 miles), Bellamy Mansion (2 blocks), Cape Fear Museum (1 block)

Innkeeper(s): Scott and Karen Clark. $95-110. MAP. MC VISA AX PC. 5 rooms with PB, 5 with FP. Breakfast included in rates. Types of meals: gourmet breakfast and early coffee/tea. Afternoon tea available. Beds: KQ. Phone, air conditioning, turndown service and ceiling fan in room. Library on premises. Antiques, fishing, parks, shopping, sporting events, theater and watersports nearby.

Publicity: *Wilmington Morning Star.*

"It was elegant. Breakfast was terrific. The most beautiful B&B I've been in."

Worth House

412 S 3rd St
Wilmington, NC 28401-5102
(910)762-8562 (800)340-8559 Fax:(910)763-2173
E-mail: worthhse@wilmington.net

Circa 1893. This handsome Queen Anne Victorian boasts two turrets and a wide double veranda. From the outside, it gives the appearance of a small castle. Although the inn was renovated around 1910, it retains many of the architectural details of the original house. The paneled front hall, crystal chandelier and total privacy welcome guests to a retreat of quiet elegance. Many rooms feature wood-burning fireplaces, fine linens and antiques. Guests are treated to freshly ground coffee, freshly squeezed orange juice, fresh fruit, scrambled eggs with sausage and ham and apple cinnamon pancakes for breakfast. Antiques, parks, golf, tennis, fishing and shopping are all located nearby.

Innkeeper(s): Francie & John Miller. $80-130. MC VISA AX PC TC. TAC10. 7 rooms with PB, 4 with FP. Breakfast and evening snack included in rates. Type of meal: full breakfast. Beds: KQT. Phone, air conditioning and ceiling fan in room. TV, VCR, fax, copier and library on premises. Small meetings and family reunions hosted. Antiques, fishing, parks, shopping, sporting events, golf, theater and watersports nearby.

Location: Historic District.

Publicity: *The News and Observer.*

Wilson   B7

Miss Betty's B&B Inn

600 West Nash St
Wilson, NC 27893-3045
(919)243-4447 (800)258-2058 Fax:(919)342-4447

Circa 1858. Located in a gracious setting in the downtown historic district, the inn is comprised of several restored historic homes. Breakfast is served in the Victorian dining room of the main house, with its walnut antique furniture and clusters of

roses on the wallpaper. All the extras, such as lace tablecloths and hearty meals, conjure up the Old South. Four golf courses and many fine restaurants are nearby. Wilson is known as the antique capitol of North Carolina.

Historic Interest: The inn is listed in the National Register and located on Nash Street, which once was described as one of the most beautiful streets in the country.

Innkeeper(s): Betty & Fred Spitz. $60-80. MC VISA AX DC CB DS TC. 10 rooms with PB, 7 with FP. 3 suites. Breakfast included in rates. Beds: KQDT. Phone, air conditioning, ceiling fan and TV in room. Fax and copier on premises. Handicap access.

Location: Eastern North Carolina, near I-95.

Publicity: *Wilson Daily Times, Enterprise, Southern Living, Mid-Atlantic.*

"Yours is second to none. Everything was perfect. I can see why you are so highly rated."

Winston-Salem B5

Augustus T. Zevely Inn

803 S Main St
Winston-Salem, NC 27101-5332
(910)748-9299 (800)928-9299 Fax:(910)721-2211

Circa 1844. The Zevely Inn is the only lodging in Old Salem. Each of the rooms at this charming pre-Civil War inn have a view of historic Old Salem. Moravian furnishings and fixtures permeate the decor of each of the guest quarters, some of which boast working fireplaces. The home's architecture is reminiscent of many structures built in Old Salem during the second quarter of the 19th century. The formal dining room and parlor have woodburning fireplaces. The two-story porch offers visitors a view of the period gardens and a beautiful magnolia tree. A line of Old Salem furniture has been created by Lexington Furniture Industries, and several pieces were created especially for the Zevely Inn.

Historic Interest: Winston-Salem abounds with historic activity. Old Salem, founded in 1766, is a restored, Moravian community. Among the sites are the Historic Bethabara Park, the Piedmont Craftsman, Inc. and Meseda, the nation's only museum dedicated to researching Southern materials and styles. The museum features a variety of furniture, textiles, ceramics and paintings dating back to the 17th century.

Innkeeper(s): Linda Anderson. $80-185. MC VISA AX PC TC. 12 rooms with PB, 3 with FP. 1 suite. Breakfast and evening snack included in rates. Beds: KQDT. Phone, air conditioning and TV in room. Fax and copier on premises. Antiques, shopping, sporting events and theater nearby.

Publicity: *Washington Post Travel, Salem Star, Winston-Salem Journal, Tasteful, Country Living, National Trust for Historic Preservation, Homes and Gardens, Homes Across America, Southern Living.*

"*Colonial charm with modern conveniences, great food. Very nice! Everything was superb.*"

Colonel Ludlow Inn

434 Summit at W 5th
Winston-Salem, NC 27101
(336)777-1887 (800)301-1887 Fax:(336)777-0518
E-mail: innkeeper@bbinn.com

Circa 1887. Located in a historic urban residential neighborhood, this inn is comprised of two adjacent Victorian homes. Both homes are listed in the National Register and boast such features as wraparound porches, gabled roofs, ornate entrances, beautiful windows and high ceilings. Guest rooms are decorated with Victorian antiques, and each includes a double whirlpool tub. The innkeepers provide many thoughtful amenities, such as stocked mini-refrigerators, microwaves, coffee makers, stereos,

TVs with VCRs and free movies, irons, bathrobes and hair dryers. There is a Nautilus exercise room, billiards room and a golf driving cage. Two gourmet restaurants in historic homes are only two blocks away.

Historic Interest: Old Salem, a restored 18th-century German Moravian Village, is one mile away.

Innkeeper(s): Constance Creasman. $95-229. MC VISA AX DC DS PC TC. TAC10. 10 rooms with PB, 5 with FP. Breakfast included in rates. Types of meals: full breakfast and early coffee/tea. Lunch and room service available. Beds: K. Phone, air conditioning, ceiling fan, TV and VCR in room. Antiques, fishing, parks, shopping, sporting events and theater nearby.

Location: Off Hwy I-40, near downtown.

Publicity: *Winston-Salem Journal, Charlotte Observer, Mid-Atlantic Country, Southern Living, Southern Accents, USA Today, American Way.*

"*I have never seen anything like the meticulous and thorough attention to detail. — Dannye Romine, The Charlotte Observer*"

Henry F Shaffner House

150 S Marshall St
Winston-Salem, NC 27101-2833
(336)777-0052 (800)952-2256 Fax:(336)777-1188

Circa 1907. Located near the historic Old Salem area, this elaborate Queen Anne Tudor-style Victorian has been carefully renovated and was awarded the city's restoration award. Handsome gables, copper roof shingles and an elegant iron fence establish the house's unique appeal. Built by Henry Shaffner, one of the founders of Wachovia Bank, the mansion

features tiger oak woodwork, fireplaces and several common rooms: the parlor, tea room, library and sun room. The inn is popular for holding special events and weddings. Each room is distinctively decorated with tastefully selected furnishings and fabrics. A favored guest room is the private top-floor Piedmont Room with Jacuzzi, wet bar, king-size bed and sitting room. Breakfast features gourmet omelets and home-baked breads, fruits and specialty coffees. Murder-mystery weekends are also offered. Wine and cheese are offered in the evening. There is a horse-drawn carriage service available.

$89-199. MC VISA AX PC. TAC10. 10 rooms with PB. 4 suites. 2 conference rooms. Breakfast included in rates. Types of meals: continental-plus breakfast and full breakfast. Evening snack, banquet service, catering service and room service available. Beds: KQT. Phone, air conditioning, turndown service, ceiling fan and TV in room. Fax, copier and library on premises. Weddings, small meetings, family reunions and seminars hosted. Antiques, parks, shopping, sporting events, golf and theater nearby.

Publicity: *Southern Living, Triad Business News, Winston-Salem Journal, Life & Leisure, Winston-Salem, Buena Vista, Great Country Inns.*

Lady Anne's Victorian B&B

612 Summit St
Winston-Salem, NC 27101-1117
(910)724-1074

Circa 1890. Like the name indicates, this bed & breakfast is decked in Victorian tradition. Victorian antiques and treasures fill the rooms. Most of the guest quarters boast stained-glass windows and high ceilings. Three rooms include a balcony, patio or glassed-in porch. Most rooms also offer modern amenities such as refrigerators, coffeemakers, stereos and double Jacuzzi tubs complete with romantic music. One offers a double garden tub perfect for viewing a romantic sunset. A Victorian-style breakfast is served in the formal dining room or on the porch. Innkeeper Shelley Kirley offers a wealth of information about the history of her inn and the surrounding area.

Historic Interest: Lady Anne is located in Winston-Salem's historic West End neighborhood, one of the first streetcar suburbs in North Carolina. It's only three minutes by car to historic Salem and the Reynolds House, the summer residence of the R.J. Reynolds tobacco family.

Innkeeper(s): Shelley Kirley & Steve Wishon. $55-165. AP. MC VISA AX TC. 4 rooms with PB. 3 suites. Breakfast and evening snack included in rates.

Types of meals: full breakfast and early coffee/tea. Beds: QD. Phone, air conditioning, ceiling fan, TV and VCR in room. Antiques, fishing, parks, shopping, sporting events and theater nearby.

Publicity: *Winston-Salem News, Better Homes & Gardens.*

"We frequent B&Bs often and wanted to tell you that Lady Anne's is one of the finest that we've stayed in. We will be sure to tell all of our friends and family about your charming and friendly B&B."

North Dakota

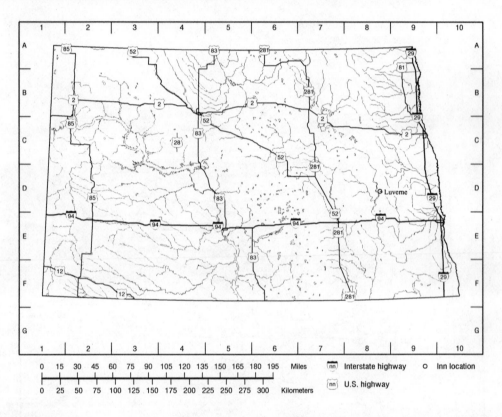

0 15 30 45 60 75 90 105 120 135 150 165 180 195 Miles
0 25 50 75 100 125 150 175 200 225 250 275 300 Kilometers

Interstate highway   ○ Inn location
U.S. highway

Luverne   D8

Volden Farm Bed & Breakfast

RR 2, Box 50
Luverne, ND 58056
(701)769-2275

Circa 1885. Perennial gardens and a hedge of lilacs surround
this redwood house with its newer addition. A favorite room is
the North Room with a lace canopy bed, an old pie safe and a
Texas Star quilt made by the host's grandmother. Guests enjoy
soaking in the clawfoot tub while looking out over the hills.
There is a library, music room and game room. The innkeepers
also offer lodging in the Law Office, a separate little prairie
house ideal for families. A stream, bordered by old oaks and
formed by a natural spring, meanders through the property.
The chickens here lay green and blue eggs. Dinner is available

by advanced arrangement. Hiking, birding, snowshoeing and
skiing are nearby.

Innkeeper(s): Jim & JoAnne Wold. $60-95. PC. TAC10. 4 rooms. 1 cottage.
Breakfast and evening snack included in rates. Types of meals: gourmet
breakfast and early coffee/tea. Dinner and picnic lunch available. Beds: KDT.
Bicycles and library on premises. 300 acres. Small meetings and seminars
hosted. Limited Russian and limited Norwegian spoken. Antiques, fishing,
downhill skiing and cross-country skiing nearby.

Pets Allowed: Outside.

Location: 80 miles northwest of Fargo.

Publicity: *Fargo Forum, Horizons, Grand Forks Herald, Mid-West Living,
Getaways.*

*"Very pleasant indeed! Jim & JoAnne make you feel good. There's so
much to do, and the hospitality is amazing!"*

Ohio

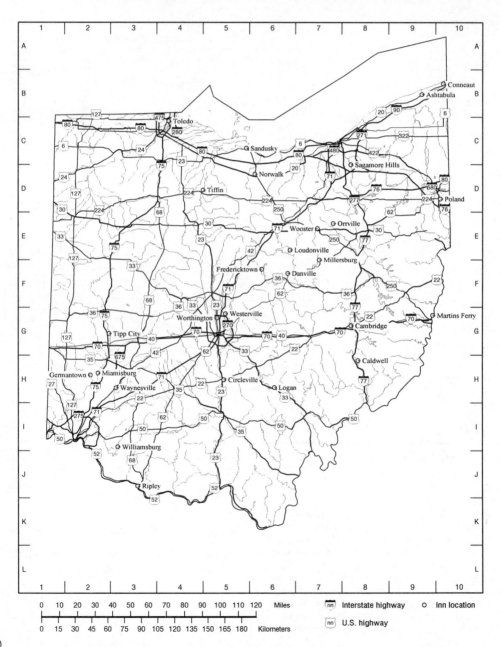

0 10 20 30 40 50 60 70 80 90 100 110 120 Miles

0 15 30 45 60 75 90 105 120 135 150 165 180 Kilometers

[nn] Interstate highway   o Inn location

[nn] U.S. highway

Ashtabula B9

Michael Cahill B&B

1106 Walnut Blvd
Ashtabula, OH 44004-3250
(216)964-8449

Circa 1887. This two-story early Victorian Stick-style home is situated on a bluff overlooking Lake Erie. It was built by Irish immigrants who profited in the 1880s and 1890s as saloon keepers. Walnut Boulevard was then known as "Captain's Row" because of the many ship captains who lived there. The B&B features cherry woodwork, original electric chandeliers and antique and period furnishings. A large wraparound porch allows guests to enjoy Lake Erie breezes. Within easy walking distance is the Marine Museum, antique shopping in restored Bridge Street shops, charter boat fishing and Walnut Beach. Wineries and many covered bridges are nearby.

Innkeeper(s): Paul & Pat Goode. $55-65. PC TC. 4 rooms with PB. Air conditioning in room. TV on premises. Antiques, shopping and theater nearby.

"We enjoyed our stay, we'll be back!"

Caldwell H8

Harkins House Inn

715 West St
Caldwell, OH 43724
(614)732-7347

Circa 1905. Innkeeper Stacey Lucas' great-grandfather built this turn-of-the-century home, which features many Victorian elements. He was a founder of the town's First National Bank. High ceilings, intricate moldings and original woodwork remain, as does the grand staircase. The decor includes brightly painted walls and flowery wallpapers. The second-story hall features Victorian furnishings, rose walls with teal stenciling and carpeting. Guests choose their own breakfast fare from a daily menu, which features items such as bacon, eggs, homemade muffins and coffee cake. State parks, antique shops and historic sites are nearby.

Innkeeper(s): Jeff & Stacey Lucas. $35-65. MC VISA AX PC TC. 2 rooms with PB. Breakfast included in rates. Types of meals: full breakfast and early coffee/tea. Beds: DT. Phone and air conditioning in room. TV, VCR, library and child care on premises. Weddings and small meetings hosted. Antiques, fishing, parks, shopping, golf and theater nearby.

Publicity: *Journal-Leader.*

"Lucky for us we found your most interesting and beautiful home."

Cambridge G8

Morning Glory B&B

5637 Fairdale Dr
Cambridge, OH 43725-9454
(614)439-2499

Circa 1859. This two-story farmhouse set on five acres along the Old National Road is conveniently located between Cambridge and New Concord. The original staircase, constructed of chestnut and walnut, leads to the three guest rooms that offer private baths and ceiling fans. The inn features hardwood floors,

antiques and many handmade items, influenced by the Amish, whose enclave is just an hour away. Guests can enjoy a full breakfast in the pantry kitchen by the warmth of the hearth or in the dining room. Shopping, antiques, crafts, museums and parks are located nearby.

Historic Interest: Located close to the Wild Animal Preserve, Salt Fork State Park and the Pritchard-Laughlin Civic Center.

Innkeeper(s): Jim & Jane Gibson. $65-75. MC VISA DS PC TC. 3 rooms with PB. Breakfast and evening snack included in rates. Types of meals: full breakfast and early coffee/tea. Beds: QT. Air conditioning and ceiling fan in room. TV on premises. Family reunions hosted. Antiques, parks, shopping, golf and theater nearby.

Publicity: *Daily Jeffersonian, Midwest Living.*

"Outstanding, we give it 5 stars."

Circleville H5

Penguin Crossing

3291 SR 56 W
Circleville, OH 43113-9622
(614)477-6222 (800)736-4846 Fax:(614)477-6222

Circa 1820. Once a stagecoach stop, now a romantic country getaway, this B&B offers amenities in the rooms such as a woodburning fireplace, clawfoot tub, brass bed or a heart-shaped Jacuzzi. As the name might suggest, the innkeepers have a collection of penguins on display. Breakfasts include a selection of natural foods, and the innkeeper is happy to cater to special dietary needs.

Historic Interest: Ted Lewis Museum (4 miles), Circleville Pumpkin Show (4 miles), Deer Creek State Park (20 miles).

Innkeeper(s): Ross & Tracey Irvin. $100-175. MC VISA DS PC TC. 4 rooms with PB, 1 with FP. Breakfast included in rates. Types of meals: gourmet breakfast and early coffee/tea. Beds: KQDT. Phone and air conditioning in room. VCR and fax on premises. Handicap access. Weddings, small meetings, family reunions and seminars hosted. Antiques, fishing, parks, shopping, theater and watersports nearby.

"If I had to describe this home in one word, it would be — enchanting."

Conneaut B10

Campbell Braemar

390 State St
Conneaut, OH 44030-2510
(216)599-7362

Circa 1927. This little Colonial Revival house is decorated in a Scottish style, and a Scottish breakfast is provided. Guests are invited to use the kitchen for light cooking as the hosts live next door. Wineries, golf, fishing,

sandy beaches of Lake Erie and hunting are nearby. The innkeepers also offer a fully furnished apartment with two large bedrooms, a living room, cable TV and a fully equipped kitchen.

Historic Interest: Railroad Museum, Lake Erie Marine Museum nearby. One hour from Cleveland and two hours from Niagara Falls.

Innkeeper(s): Mary & Andrew Campbell. $58-98. TC. 3 rooms. Breakfast and afternoon tea included in rates. Types of meals: continental breakfast, continental-plus breakfast, full breakfast and early coffee/tea. Beds: KQD. Air conditioning in room. TV on premises. Weddings, small meetings and family reunions hosted. Antiques, fishing, parks and watersports nearby.

Danville   F6

Red Fox Country Inn

26367 Danville Amity Rd
Danville, OH 43014-9769
(614)599-7369

Circa 1830. This inn, located on 15 scenic central Ohio acres, was built originally to house those traveling on the Danville-Amity Wagon Road and later became a farm home. Amish

woven rag rugs and country antiques decorate the guest rooms. Some of the furnishings belonged to early owners, and some date to the 18th century. Three rooms include Amish-made oak beds and the fourth an 1880s brass and iron double bed. Breakfasts include fresh pastries, fruits, coffee and a variety of delectable entrees. Special dietary needs usually can be accommodated. Dinners are served by reservation. There are books and games available in the inn's sitting room, and guests also are invited to relax on the front porch. Golfing, canoeing, fishing, horseback riding, hiking, biking, skiing and Mohican State Park are nearby, and the inn is 30 minutes from the largest Amish community in the United States.

Historic Interest: Amish settlements, Malibar Farm, historic Roscoe Village and the National Heisey Glass Museum are less than an hour from the inn.

Innkeeper(s): Ida & Mort Wolff. $65-85. MC VISA AX DS PC TC. TAC10. 4 rooms with PB. Breakfast included in rates. Dinner, banquet service and catering service available. Beds: QD. Air conditioning in room. Library on premises. 15 acres.

Publicity: *Columbus Dispatch, Mount Vernon News, Cincinnati Enquirer.*

"Our dinner and breakfast were '5 star'. Thank you for the gracious hospitality and special kindness you showed us."

Fredericktown   F6

Heartland Country Resort

2994 Township Rd 190
Fredericktown, OH 43019
(419)768-9300 (800)230-7030

Circa 1878. This remodeled farmhouse and luxury log cabin offer guests a serene country setting with hills, woods, pastures, fields, wooded trails, barns, horse stables and riding arenas. The four suites include a fireplace and Jacuzzi tub. With full run of the huge house, guests also have

their choice of a wide variety of recreation. Horseback riding is the recreation of choice for most visitors. Innkeeper Dorene Henschen tells guests not to miss the beauty of the woods as seen on the guided trail rides.

Historic Interest: Malabar Farm, where Humphrey Bogart & Lauren Bacall were married (20 miles).

Innkeeper(s): Dorene Henschen. $80-155. MC VISA DS TC. TAC10. 6 rooms with PB. 4 suites. Breakfast and afternoon tea included in rates. Type of meal: continental-plus breakfast. Dinner, picnic lunch and room service available. Beds: KQT. Antiques, fishing, downhill skiing, cross-country skiing and watersports nearby. Pets Allowed.

Publicity: *Columbus Dispatch, Country Extra, One Tank Trips, Getaways.*

"Warm hospitality . . . Beautiful surroundings and pure peace & quiet. What more could one want from a B&B in the country? Thank you for an excellent memory!"

Germantown   H2

Gunckel Heritage

33 W Market St
Germantown, OH 45327
(937)855-3508

Circa 1826. This early 19th-century Victorian-Italianate home built in the center of town is compelling more for its history than its fine architectural details and rich interior design. Philip Gunckel, the founder of Germantown, built this gracious home

for one of his beloved daughters four generations back. Although ownership has changed hands throughout the years, the house is now back in the Gunckel family, proudly owned by Bonnie Gunckel Koogle and Lynn Koogle. The inn's four individually decorated guest rooms feature antiques, fireplaces and private baths. A hearty gourmet breakfast is served daily.

Innkeeper(s): Bonnie & Lynn Koogle. $65-75. MC VISA DS PC TC. 4 rooms, 3 with PB, 3 with FP. 1 suite. Breakfast, afternoon tea and evening snack included in rates. Meals: continental breakfast, continental-plus breakfast, full breakfast and early coffee/tea. Picnic lunch and room service available. Beds: QDT. Phone, air conditioning, ceiling fan, TV and VCR in room. Spa and bicycles on premises. Weddings and small meetings hosted. Amusement parks, antiques, fishing, parks, shopping, sporting events, golf and theater nearby.

Logan   H6

The Inn at Cedar Falls

21190 S R 374
Logan, OH 43138
(614)385-7489 (800)653-2557 Fax:(614)385-0820

Circa 1987. This barn-style inn was constructed on 60 acres adjacent to Hocking State Park and one-half mile from the waterfalls. The kitchen and dining room is in a 19th-century log house with a wood-burning stove and 18-inch-wide plank floor. Accommodations in the new barn building are simple and comfortable, each furnished with antiques. There are also five, fully equipped log cabins available, each individually decorated. Verandas provide sweeping views of woodland and meadow. The grounds include organic gardens for

the inn's gourmet dinners, and animals that have been spotted include bobcat, red fox, wild turkey and whitetail deer.

Historic Interest: Hocking Canal, Haydenville, Falls Mill & Rempels Grove.

Innkeeper(s): Ellen Grinsfelder. $75-195. MC VISA PC. 14 rooms, 9 with PB, 5 with FP. 5 cottages. 1 conference room. Breakfast included in rates. Types of meals: full breakfast, gourmet breakfast and early coffee/tea. Dinner, picnic lunch, lunch and gourmet lunch available. Restaurant on premises. Beds: QT. Air conditioning in room. Fax, copier and library on premises. Handicap access. 60 acres. Weddings, small meetings, family reunions, seminars hosted. Antiques, fishing, parks, shopping, cross-country skiing, theater nearby.

Publicity: *Post.*

"Very peaceful, relaxing and friendly. Couldn't be nicer."

Loudonville   E6

Blackfork Inn
303 N Water St
Loudonville, OH 44842-1273
(419)994-3252

Circa 1847. A Civil War businessman, Philip Black, brought the railroad to town and built the Blackfork. Its well-preserved Second Empire style has earned it a place in the National Register. Noted preservationists have restored the inn with care and it is filled with a collection of Ohio antiques. Located in a scenic Amish area, the three-course breakfasts feature local produce. The innkeepers also offer three large three-room suites in a restored 1847 house, one suite includes a gas fireplace.

Innkeeper(s): Sue & Al Gorisek. $65-125. MC VISA. 6 rooms with PB. 2 suites. Type of meal: full breakfast. Phone in room.

Martins Ferry   G9

Mulberry Inn B&B
53 N 4th St
Martins Ferry, OH 43935-1523
(740)633-6058 (800)705-6171 Ext. 3136

Circa 1868. The Roosevelt Room in this Victorian inn once housed Eleanor Roosevelt during a "Bond Drive." Mrs. Blackford, goddaughter of Jefferson Davis, was the hostess during that time and was well-known for her hospitality during the Depression. The inn is decorated with country antiques and quilts.

Historic Interest: Revolutionary & Civil War Cemetery (2 blocks), Museum (3 blocks), Martins Ferry oldest organized settlement in Ohio.

Innkeeper(s): Charles & Shirley Probst. $45-60. MC VISA AX DS. 3 rooms, 1 with PB. Breakfast and evening snack included in rates. Types of meals: continental-plus breakfast and early coffee/tea. Beds: QD. Air conditioning, turndown service and ceiling fan in room. TV on premises. Small meetings, family reunions and seminars hosted. Antiques, fishing, parks, shopping, downhill skiing, sporting events, theater and watersports nearby.

Location: Southeast Ohio along the Ohio River.

Publicity: *Times Leader, Herald Star, Akron Beacon Journal.*

"This is my third stay and it's like coming home when I'm away on business. This beautiful home really softens my purpose for being here! As always, I enjoy your company, warmth, and great breakfast!"

Miamisburg   H2

English Manor B&B
505 E Linden Ave
Miamisburg, OH 45342-2850
(513)866-2288 (800)676-9456

Circa 1924. This is a beautiful English Tudor mansion situated on a tree-lined street of Victorian homes. Well-chosen antiques combined with the innkeepers' personal heirlooms added to

the inn's polished floors, sparkling leaded-and stained-glass windows and shining silver, make this an elegant retreat. Breakfast is served in the formal dining room. Tea is served in the afternoon. Fine restaurants, a waterpark, baseball, air force museum and theater are close by, as is The River Corridor bikeway on the banks of the Great Miami River.

Historic Interest: 10 minutes south of Dayton.

Innkeeper(s): Ken Huelsman. $65-95. MC VISA AX DC CB DS. 5 rooms. 1 conference room. Breakfast included in rates. Type of meal: full breakfast. Phone, air conditioning and turndown service in room. TV and VCR on premises. Weddings, small meetings, family reunions and seminars hosted. Amusement parks, antiques, shopping, sporting events and theater nearby.

Millersburg   F7

Bigham House
151 S Washington St
Millersburg, OH 44654-1315
(800)689-6950

Circa 1869. Located in a quiet village in the heart of Amish Country, Holmes County, this immaculately restored inn fancies itself not only a bed & breakfast but also an authentic

English Tea Room where guests can enjoy traditional tea in grand Victorian style. Each guest chamber and suite are distinctly decorated in antiques, Victorian reproductions and carefully selected tra-

ditional fabrics and wallcoverings. Tea is served by the inn's own British gentleman, by reservation only.

Innkeeper(s): Winnie & John Ellis. $75-125. MC VISA DS. 4 rooms with PB. 1 with FP. 1 suite. Breakfast included in rates. Meal: full breakfast. Beds: Q.

Location: In the heart of the largest Amish settlement in the world, Holmes County, Ohio.

Publicity: *Holmes County Traveler, Cleveland Plain Dealer, Amish Heartland, 1-800 BUCKEYE, North Central Business Traveler.*

Norwalk   D6

Boos Family Inn B&B
5054 Sr 601
Norwalk, OH 44857-9729
(419)668-6257 Fax:(419)668-7722

Circa 1860. To see the modern additions to this former farm home, you would not at first realize that parts of this home date back to the mid-1800s. There are two acres of flowers, lawns and trees. Just a short drive away is Thomas Edison's home, Lake Erie and Cedar Point.

Innkeeper(s): Don & Mary Boos. $45-85. MC VISA AX DS PC TC. 3 rooms with PB. 1 suite. Breakfast included in rates. Type of meal: continental breakfast. Beds: QD. Air conditioning and TV in room. Fax and copier on premises. Small meetings and seminars hosted. Amusement parks, antiques, fishing, parks, shopping, downhill skiing, cross-country skiing, sporting events, theater and watersports nearby.

Orrville
E7

Grandma's House B&B

5598 Chippewa Rd
Orrville, OH 44667-9750
(330)682-5112

Circa 1860. This home was built using bricks that were created and fired on the property. The Farver's family has lived here for half of the home's existence. Family heirlooms and antiques decorate the interior, as well as quilts handmade by innkeeper Marilyn Farver. Original chestnut woodwork and wainscoting remain, but there have been a few modern additions, such as a double whirlpool tub in Mae's Room. After one of Marilyn's memorable "from scratch" breakfasts, guests are free to explore the 16 acres of woods and gardens that surround the home.

Innkeeper(s): Marilyn & Dave Farver. $55-90. PC TC. 5 rooms, 3 with PB. Breakfast included in rates. Types of meals: continental-plus breakfast and early coffee/tea. Beds: QDT. Air conditioning and ceiling fan in room. Handicap access. 28 acres. Small meetings, family reunions and seminars hosted. Antiques, parks, shopping, cross-country skiing and theater nearby.

Publicity: *Wooster Daily Record, Northeast Ohio Avenues, Cleveland Magazine, "Innkeeper's Best Muffins."*

"What a delight. We will definitely be back. Perfect."

Poland
D10

The Inn at The Green

500 S Main St
Poland, OH 44514-2032
(330)757-4688

Circa 1876. Main Street in Poland has a parade of historic houses including Connecticut Western Reserve colonials, Federal and Greek Revival houses. The Inn at the Green is a Classic Victorian Baltimore townhouse. Two of the common rooms, the greeting room and parlor have working marble fireplaces. Interiors evoke an authentic 19th-century atmosphere with antiques and Oriental rugs that enhance the moldings, 12-foot ceilings and poplar floors.

Innkeeper(s): Ginny & Steve Meloy. $60. MC VISA DS. TAC10. 4 rooms with PB, 3 with FP. Breakfast included in rates. Type of meal: continental breakfast. Beds: QDT. Phone, air conditioning and TV in room. VCR on premises. Antiques, parks, shopping, golf and theater nearby.

Location: Seven miles southeast of Youngstown.

Publicity: *The Vindicator.*

"Thank you for a comfortable and perfect stay in your beautiful Victorian home."

Ripley
J3

Misty River B&B

206 N Front St
Ripley, OH 45167
(937)392-1556 Fax:(937)392-1556

Circa 1830. Ulysses S. Grant was a boarder here while he attended the Whittmore Private School in Ripley in the fall of 1838 and winter of 1839. This small 19th-century homestead-

style house, located in the town's 55-acre historic district, is just across the road from the Ohio River. The bed & breakfast is decorated with a comfortable mix of country and antique furnishings. A cozy wood-burning fireplace in the living room warms guests in the cooler evenings. The river offers guests a view of barges and boats, and wonderful sunsets. Ripley has many historic attractions, including Rankin House

(of "Uncle Tom's Cabin" fame), the home of abolitionist Rev. John Rankin. Rankin and his family helped more than 1,000 slaves find their way to freedom.

Innkeeper(s): Dotty Prevost & Lanny Warren. $75. PC TC. TAC10. 2 rooms with PB. Breakfast included in rates. Type of meal: full breakfast. Beds: D. Air conditioning in room. TV, VCR and fax on premises. Antiques, fishing, parks, shopping and watersports nearby.

Publicity: *Columbus Dispatch, Ripley Bee, Ohio.*

"It was like going back to Grandmas. We enjoyed the simple beauty and pleasant atmosphere, the fire in the hearth, comfortable bed, and delicious homecooking. We are rested and refreshed. Thanks, Dotty, for your special touch!"

The Signal House

234 N Front St
Ripley, OH 45167-1015
(937)392-1640

Circa 1830. This Greek Italianate home is said to have been used to aid the Underground Railroad. A light in the attic told Rev. John Rankin, a dedicated abolitionist, that it was safe to transport slaves to freedom. Located within a 55-acre historical district, guests can take a glance back in time, exploring museums and antique shops. Twelve-foot ceilings with ornate plaster-work graces the parlor, and guests can sit on any of three porches watching paddlewheelers traverse the Ohio River.

Innkeeper(s): Vic & Betsy Billingsley. $75. MC VISA DS PC TC. TAC10. 2 rooms, 2 with FP. Breakfast included in rates. Types of meals: full breakfast and early coffee/tea. Beds: Q. Air conditioning and ceiling fan in room. TV, VCR, copier and library on premises. Antiques, fishing, parks, shopping and watersports nearby.

Publicity: *Cincinnati Enquirer, Ohio Columbus Dispatch, Ohio Off the Beaten Path, Dayton Daily News, Cincinnati Magazine.*

Sagamore Hills
D8

The Inn at Brandywine Falls

8230 Brandywine Rd
Sagamore Hills, OH 44067-2810
(330)467-1812

Circa 1848. Overlooking Brandywine Falls and situated snugly on national parkland, this National Register Greek Revival farmhouse has been meticulously renovated. Antiques made in Ohio are featured in the Greek Revival-style rooms and include sleigh and four-poster beds. Some suites include a double whirlpool tub. The kitchen has been designed to allow guests to chat with the innkeepers while sipping coffee in front of a crackling fireplace and watching breakfast preparations. The Waterfall and hiking trails are just a few steps away. Cleveland is a short drive, offering attractions such as the Rock 'n' Roll Hall of Fame and the Cleveland Orchestra.

Innkeeper(s): Katie & George Hoy. $94-195. MC VISA DS. 6 rooms with PB, 1 with FP. 3 suites. Breakfast included in rates. Type of meal: gourmet breakfast. Beds: KDT. Handicap access.

Location: The Cuyahoga Valley National Park between Cleveland and Akron.

Publicity: *Ohio Magazine, Countryside, Innsider, Western Reserve, Cleveland Plain Dealer, Akron Beacon Journal, Vindicator, Dayton Daily News, Michigan Living.*

"The magic of the inn was not forgotten. We will be back to enjoy."

Sandusky   C5

The Red Gables

421 Wayne St
Sandusky, OH 44870-2710
(419)625-1189

Circa 1907. Nestled just blocks from Lake Erie, this beautifully appointed, red-trimmed Tudor home features polished natural woodwork, ornate ceilings and luxurious decor. Costume-maker and innkeeper Jo Ellen

Cuthbertson applied her skills as a seamstress to create a light, romantic atmosphere at Red Gables. Guests enjoy a breakfast of fresh muffins and fruit in the enormous great room, which features a huge fireplace and bay window.

Red Gables is within walking distance of the Cedar Point Ferry and several island cruise ships. Two nearby nature preserves, wineries and antique shops offer other fun excursions.

Historic Interest: The Red Gables is located in Sanduskyís historic Old Plat District. The Follett House Museum is just across the street from the B&B. The Merry-Go-Round Museum is just a few blocks away. Thomas Edisonís birthplace and museum is about 10 miles away. Johnsonís Island, a Civil War officerís prison camp, is another nearby attraction.

Innkeeper(s): Jo Ellen Cuthbertson. $50-95. MC VISA. 4 rooms, 2 with PB. Breakfast included in rates. Type of meal: continental-plus breakfast. Beds: QDT. Antiques, fishing, theater and watersports nearby.

Publicity: *Ohio, Northern Ohio Live, Cuyahoga County Public Library, Ladies' Home Journal.*

"It was like stepping back into another era. Thank you for your gracious hospitality, I felt very pampered by your breakfasts."

Wagner's 1844 Inn

230 E Washington St
Sandusky, OH 44870-2611
(419)626-1726 Fax:(419)626-8465

Circa 1844. This inn originally was constructed as a log cabin. Additions and renovations were made, and the house evolved into Italianate style accented with brackets under the eaves and black shutters on the second-story windows. A wrought-iron fence frames the house, and there are ornate wrought-iron porch rails. A billiard room and screened-in porch are available to guests. The ferry to Cedar Point and Lake Erie Island is within walking distance.

Innkeeper(s): Walt & Barb Wagner. $70-120. MC VISA DS. 3 rooms with PB, 2 with FP. Breakfast included in rates. Type of meal: continental breakfast. Beds: Q. Air conditioning in room. TV and library on premises. Amusement parks, antiques, fishing, parks and shopping nearby.

Pets Allowed: Some limitations.

Publicity: *Lorain Journal.*

"This B&B rates in our Top 10."

Tiffin   D5

Fort Ball Bed & Breakfast

25 Adams St
Tiffin, OH 44883-2208
(419)447-0776 (888)447-0776 Fax:(419)447-3499

Circa 1894. The prominent front turret and wraparound porch are classic details of this Queen Anne Revival house built by John King, builder of the Tiffin Court House and College Hall

at Heidelberg College. The innkeepers dedicated more than a year restoring this turn-of-the-century Victorian to its original elegant state. The renovation yielded rich hardwood flooring, wood paneling and many additional architectural details like the elaborate woodwork in the parlor, front entryway and sitting room. Guest rooms are comfortably decorated to accommodate business travelers, families or honeymooners, and offer private and shared baths while some feature whirlpool tubs for two. Breakfast can be enjoyed in the dining room with its elegantly restored woodwork. The inn is within walking distance of the downtown business district, restaurants, antiques, shopping, museums and theater.

Innkeeper(s): Charles & Lenora Livingston. $55-85. MC VISA DS PC TC. 4 rooms, 2 with PB. Breakfast and evening snack included in rates. Types of meals: full breakfast and early coffee/tea. Beds: KQDT. Phone, air conditioning and ceiling fan in room. TV, VCR, fax and library on premises. Small meetings hosted. Amusement parks, antiques, parks, golf and theater nearby.

Publicity: *Advertiser-Tribune.*

Mad River Railroad B&B

107 W Perry St
Tiffin, OH 44883-2246
(419)447-2222 (888)447-0665

Circa 1897. This Colonial Revival home is situated beside the former site of the first railroad in the area, which has been transformed into a tree-and-flower-lined bike path. Listed in the Historic Register, the inn is decorated with lots of wicker, lace and flowers reminiscent of the Victorian Era in which it was built. There are three guest rooms, each uniquely furnished with period antiques. A full breakfast, afternoon tea and evening snacks are provided. The inn is a favorite for family reunions and wedding parties.

Historic Interest: The inn was located next to the first train, "The Sandusky," which ran from Sandusky to Ohio.

Innkeeper(s): Bill & Nancy Cook. $65. MC VISA DS PC TC. 3 rooms with PB, 2 with FP. Breakfast, afternoon tea and evening snack included in rates.

Types of meals: full breakfast and early coffee/tea. Beds: KQD. Phone, air conditioning, ceiling fan, TV and VCR in room. Weddings, small meetings and family reunions hosted. Amusement parks, antiques, fishing, parks, shopping, sporting events, golf and theater nearby.

"It is wonderful to be so welcomed and treated as warmly as family!"

Tipp City G2

Willow Tree Inn

1900 W State Rt 571
Tipp City, OH 45371-9602
(513)667-2957

Circa 1830. This Federal-style mansion is a copy of a similar house in North Carolina, former home of the builders. Antique period furnishings and polished wood floors add to the atmosphere of this rambling homestead. A spring-fed pond and original out buildings adorn the premises.

Innkeeper(s): Jolene & Chuck Sell. $75-85. MC VISA. TAC10. 4 rooms with PB. 2 suites. 1 conference room. Breakfast and evening snack included in rates. Type of meal: full breakfast. Banquet service and catering service available. Beds: QD. Air conditioning, ceiling fan and VCR in room. Fax, copier and spa on premises. Handicap access. Weddings, small meetings, family reunions and seminars hosted. Amusement parks, antiques, parks, shopping and sporting events nearby.

Publicity: *Miami Valley News, Tri-City Advocate, Tipp City Herald, Troy Daily News, Dayton News.*

"Very quiet place to stay. The grounds are beautiful, service excellent!"

Toledo C4

The William Cummings House B&B

1022 N Superior St
Toledo, OH 43604-1961
(419)244-3219 Fax:(419)244-3219
E-mail: BnBToledo@aol.com

Circa 1857. This Second Empire Victorian, which is listed in the National Register, is located in the historic Vistula neighborhood. The inn's fine appointments, collected for several years, include period antiques, Victorian chandeliers, mirrors, wallcoverings and draperies. The hosts are classical musicians of renown. Sometimes the inn is the location for chamber music, poetry readings and other cultural events.

Historic Interest: Near The Oliver House, Wolcott House Museum Complex, Fort Meigs State Memorial, and Presidential Center.

Innkeeper(s): Lowell Greer, Lorelei Crawford. $40-135. PC TC. 3 rooms. 1 suite. Breakfast and evening snack included in rates. Type of meal: continental-plus breakfast. Beds: KQDT. Air conditioning, ceiling fan and VCR in room. Fax, copier and library on premises. Weddings, small meetings, family reunions and seminars hosted. Spanish spoken. Amusement parks, antiques, fishing, parks, shopping, sporting events, theater and watersports nearby.

"We will never forget our wedding night at your B&B. We'll try to be in the area next anniversary."

Waynesville H3

Lakewood Farm B&B

8495 Rt 48
Waynesville, OH 45068
(513)885-9850 Fax:(513)885-9874

Circa 1834. Located on 25 acres of pasture land with tennis courts, a stable, trees and a lake, the original part of the house was built as a gristmill. It houses the Welcoming Room, Great Room, Dining Room and flower-filled courtyard. Rooms feature

Victorian-type decor and a square tub. An outside porch and views of the inn's old Catalpa tree are features of The Loft Room. Some guest rooms offer views of the inn's five-acre lake, stocked with striped bass, large mouth bass and bluegill. More than 70 antique shops are located in nearby Waynesville, said to be the antique capitol of the midwest.

Innkeeper(s): Liz & Jay Jorling. $60-125. MC VISA PC TC. TAC10. 5 rooms with PB, 1 with FP. 1 suite. 1 cottage. 1 conference room. Breakfast and evening snack included in rates. Type of meal: full breakfast. Afternoon tea, catered breakfast and room service available. Beds: QT. Phone, air conditioning and ceiling fan in room. TV, VCR, fax, copier, swimming, stables, tennis and library on premises. Handicap access. 25 acres. Weddings and family reunions hosted. Amusement parks, antiques, fishing, parks, shopping, cross-country skiing, sporting events, theater and watersports nearby.

Pets Allowed: If kept in kennels provided.

Westerville G5

Cornelia's Corner B&B

93 W College Ave
Westerville, OH 43081-2031
(614)882-2678 (800)745-2678
E-mail: cadyer@ix.netcom.com

Circa 1851. This handsome mid-19th-century house is located just across the street from Otterbein College. The front entry-

way displays a staircase with a gleaming cherry banister. Oak floors, 10-foot ceilings, lace curtains and a front porch furnished with white wicker add to the old-fashioned cozy feeling. The magical sound of chimes ringing at Towers Hall can be heard hourly.

Historic Interest: The Benjamin Hanby House and Temperence League Museum are located in Westerville.

Innkeeper(s): Carol & Chuck Dyer. $60-80. 3 rooms with PB. Breakfast included in rates. Type of meal: full breakfast. Beds: KQT. Phone in room. Bicycles on premises. Antiques, parks and watersports nearby.

Location: Fifteen minutes from Columbus airport, two blocks from antique shops.

Publicity: *Westerville News, Columbus News Channel 10, Columbus Monthly.*

Williamsburg I3

The Lewis McKever Farmhouse B&B

4475 McKeever Pike
Williamsburg, OH 45176-9702
(513)724-7044

Circa 1841. Settle down with a book in the library of this rustic, rural Italianate brick farmhouse. The pre-Civil War home was named in honor of its first resident, Lewis McKever, a prominent landowner, farmer and horse breeder. The lush, 10-acre grounds offer walking trails and fields bursting with wildflowers. Continental breakfasts are served on the second-story porch, which affords a view of the grounds and herb garden. Guest rooms include antiques, some of which were refurbished by the innkeepers themselves. The inn is a quick drive to Cincinnati.

Historic Interest: The home, which is listed in the National Register, is close to all the historic sites in Cincinnati, which was the site of a Confederate raid during the Civil War.

Innkeeper(s): John & Carol Sandberg. $75. MC VISA DS PC TC. 3 rooms with PB. Breakfast included in rates. Types of meals: continental breakfast, continental-plus breakfast and early coffee/tea. Beds: Q. Air conditioning and ceiling fan in room. Bicycles on premises. 10 acres. Weddings, small meetings, family reunions and seminars hosted. Antiques, fishing, parks, shopping, sporting events, theater and watersports nearby.

Publicity: *Community Press Journal.*

"It is a nice, peaceful getaway. You are very friendly and gracious."

Wooster   E7

Historic Overholt House B&B

1473 Beall Ave
Wooster, OH 44691-2303
(330)263-6300 (800)992-0643 Fax:(330)263-9378

Circa 1874. This burgundy Victorian with its peaked roofs and colorful trim literally was saved from the wrecking ball. Several concerned locals fought to have the home moved to another

location rather than face demolition in order to make way for a parking lot. The current owners later purchased the historic home and furnished it with beautiful wall coverings, antiques and Victorian touches. The focal point of the interior is a magnificent walnut "flying staircase" that rises three stories. The innkeepers provide plenty of ways to spend a comfortable evening. The common room is stocked with games, a player piano and reading material. Autumn and winter guests are invited to snuggle up in front of a roaring fire while sipping a hot drink and munching on homemade cookies. Candlelight dinners can be arranged by reservation. The area boasts many craft, antique and gift shops, as well as Amish country sites and activities at the College of Wooster, which is adjacent to the Overholt House.

Historic Interest: The home is listed in the National Register and is located near the world's largest Amish settlement. President Grant's home and the Football Hall of Fame are popular day trips. The Rock & Roll Hall of Fame is 45 minutes away.

Innkeeper(s): Sandy Pohalski & Bobbie Walton. $63-70. MC VISA DS PC. 4 rooms with PB. 1 suite. Breakfast and evening snack included in rates. Types of meals: continental breakfast, continental-plus breakfast and early coffee/tea. Dinner available. Beds: QTFD. Air conditioning, ceiling fan, TV and VCR in room. Fax and spa on premises. Weddings and small meetings hosted. Amusement parks, antiques, parks, shopping and theater nearby.

Publicity: *Exchange, Daily Record, Pathways, Akron Beacon Journal.*

"A real retreat. So quiet, clean and friendly. I feel pampered! An old penny always returns."

Worthington   G5

Worthington Inn

649 High St
Worthington, OH 43085-4144
(614)885-2600 Fax:(614)885-1283

Circa 1831. The Worthington Inn originally was built as a stagecoach stop by R.D. Coles, a local entrepreneur. It was restored as a Victorian in 1983, but the original ballroom, main entry, dining and upper sitting rooms remain. The door from an old courthouse and ceiling rosettes from a local train station were added during reconstruction. Period wallpapers, stenciling and Victorian furnishings are used throughout.

Innkeeper(s): Steve & Susan Hanson. $150-215. MC VISA AX DC DS. 26 suites. Breakfast included in rates. Types of meals: continental breakfast, continental-plus breakfast and full breakfast. Dinner, lunch and room service available. Restaurant on premises. Beds: QD. Antiques, fishing, downhill skiing, cross-country skiing, theater and watersports nearby.

Publicity: *Country Inns, Columbus Dispatch, Columbus Monthly, Ohio, Midwest Living.*

Oklahoma

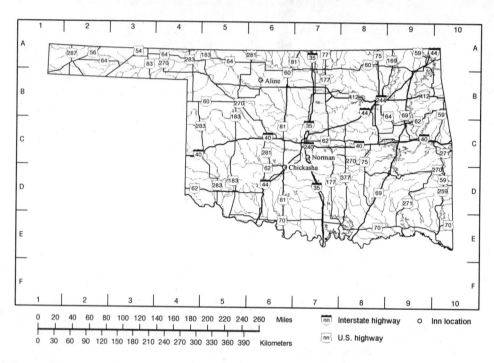

Scale:
```
0   20  40  60  80  100 120 140 160 180 200 220 240 260   Miles
0   30  60  90  120 150 180 210 240 270 300 330 360 390   Kilometers
```

| nn | Interstate highway | o | Inn location |
| nn | U.S. highway | | |

Aline — B6

Heritage Manor

RR 3 Box 33
Aline, OK 73716-9118
(405)463-2563 (800)295-2563

Circa 1903. This inn provides a way to enjoy and experience the ambiance of the turn of the century. Explore and relax in the inn's peaceful gardens and 80-acre wildlife habitat and watch song birds, butterflies, long-haired cattle, donkeys and ostriches. The inn invites visitors to enjoy its more than 5,000-volume library and more than a 100 channels on Primestar TV. Guests can walk the suspension bridge to two roof-top decks and a widow's walk to view the stars and sunsets. There is also an out-door hot tub for soaking. Dine in the parlor, gazebo, courtyard or tree-top-level deck where the choice of time and menu is entirely up to the guest.

Innkeeper(s): A.J. & Carolyn Rexroat. $55-150. PC TC. 4 rooms. 2 suites. 2 conference rooms. Breakfast and evening snack included in rates. Types of meals: full breakfast and early coffee/tea. Afternoon tea, dinner, picnic lunch, lunch, gourmet lunch and banquet service available. Restaurant on premises. Beds: D. Phone, air conditioning and TV in room. VCR, spa and library on premises. Handicap access. 80 acres. Weddings, small meetings, family reunions and seminars hosted. Antiques, fishing, parks, shopping, sporting events, theater and watersports nearby. Pets Allowed.

Publicity: *Country, Enid Morning News, Daily Oklahoman.*

Chickasha — D6

Campbell-Richison House B&B

1428 Kansas
Chickasha, OK 73018
(405)222-1754

Circa 1909. Upon entering this prairie-style home, guests will notice a spacious entryway with a gracious stairway ascending to the second-floor guest rooms. The front parlor is a wonderful spot for relaxing, reading or just soaking up the history of the home. The dining room has a stained-glass window that gives off a kaleidoscope of beautiful colors when the morning sun shines through. A spacious yard encompasses one-quarter of a city block and has large shade trees that can be enjoyed from the wicker-lined porch.

Historic Interest: Grady County Historical Museum (less than a mile), Indian City, USA.

Innkeeper(s): David Ratcliff. $39-59. 3 rooms, 1 with PB. Breakfast included in rates. Types of meals: continental-plus breakfast and early coffee/tea. Beds: D. Phone and air conditioning in room. TV and VCR on premises. Small meetings hosted. Antiques, shopping and sporting events nearby.

Publicity: *Oklahoma Today, Chickasha Express, Cache Times Weekly, Chickasha Star.*

"We enjoyed our stay at your lovely B&B! It was just the getaway we needed to unwind from a stressful few weeks. Your hospitality fellowship and food were just wonderful."

Norman C7

Holmberg House B&B

766 Debarr Ave
Norman, OK 73069-4908
(405)321-6221 (800)646-6221 Fax:(405)321-6221

Circa 1914. Professor Fredrik Holmberg and his wife Signy built this Craftsman-style home across the street from the University of Oklahoma. Each of the antique-filled rooms has its own individual decor and style. For instance, the Blue Danube Room is a romantic retreat filled with wicker, a wrought-iron bed and floral accents throughout. The Bed and Bath Room boasts an old-fashioned tub next to a window seat. The parlor and front porch are perfect places to relax with friends, and the lush grounds include a cottage garden. Aside from close access to the university, Holmberg House is within walking distance to more than a dozen restaurants.

Historic Interest: The Oklahoma Museum of Natural History is six blocks from the inn. The Cleveland County Historical Society and Lindsey Moor House are about a mile from the home. Jacobson House, a Native American museum, is six blocks away.

Innkeeper(s): MaryJo Meacham. $75-85. MC VISA AX DS PC TC. TAC10. 4 rooms with PB. Breakfast included in rates. Types of meals: gourmet breakfast and early coffee/tea. Beds: QT. Air conditioning, ceiling fan and TV in room. Fax, copier and library on premises. Weddings, small meetings and family reunions hosted. Antiques, parks, shopping, sporting events and theater nearby.

Publicity: *Metro Norman, Oklahoma City Journal Record, Norman Transcript, Country Inns.*

"Your hospitality and the delicious food were just super."

Oregon

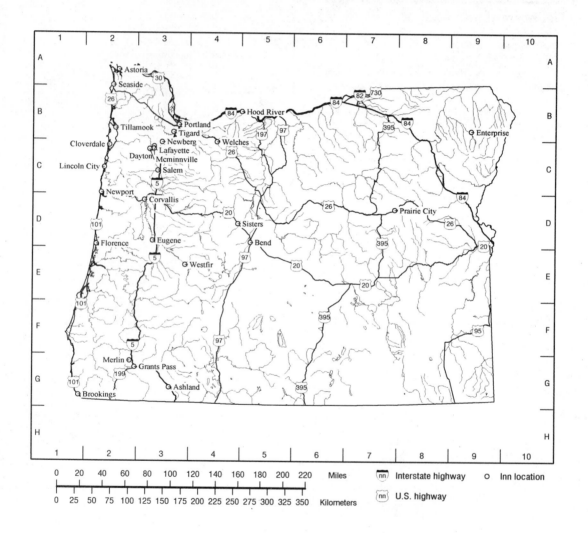

Miles scale: 0 20 40 60 80 100 120 140 160 180 200 220

Kilometers scale: 0 25 50 75 100 125 150 175 200 225 250 275 300 325 350

Interstate highway — Inn location

U.S. highway

Ashland

G3

Ashberry Inn

527 Chestnut St
Ashland, OR 97520
(541)488-8000 (800)460-8076
E-mail: ashberry@prodigy.net

Circa 1900. This romantic turn-of-the-century farmhouse is set in a quiet neighborhood just a short walk from the famous Oregon Shakespeare Festival. The newly remodeled Attic Room features a queen-size brass bed, kitchenette, private bath and lace-curtained dormer windows that open to views of the surrounding mountains. The Cottage Rose Room, named for the hand-stenciled roses throughout, boasts queen-size pencil-post canopy bed, skylight and clawfoot tub. Guests will enjoy the inn's turn down service, fresh flowers, crisply ironed linens and down comforters. The morning fare includes homemade breads, fresh seasonal fruit and a bounty of other traditional breakfast treats. Wine and sherry is offered in the afternoon. Guests are invited to use the inn's bicycles, and with a little advance notice, a full picnic basket will be provided. Antiques, shopping, parks, sports activities and festival grounds are nearby.

Historic Interest: Home of the famous Shakespeare Festival, Britt Festival and South Oregon University.

Innkeeper(s): Ray & Pamela Feckner. $60-105. MC VISA PC TC. TAC10. 2 rooms with PB. Breakfast included in rates. Types of meals: full breakfast and early coffee/tea. Picnic lunch available. Beds: Q. Air conditioning, turndown service and ceiling fan in room. TV, VCR, bicycles and library on premises. Antiques, fishing, parks, shopping, downhill skiing, cross-country skiing, sporting events, golf, theater and watersports nearby.

Colonel Silsby's Bed & Breakfast Inn

111 N Third St
Ashland, OR 97520-1941
(541)488-3070 (800)927-3070 Fax:(541)482-5791
E-mail: silsbys@mind.net

Circa 1896. Civil War hero Colonel William E. Silsby built this comfortable restored Victorian that has been added to the National Register of Historic Places. Guests will enjoy strolling through the gardens or relaxing on any one of the inn's three porches. All guest rooms feature private baths with clawfoot tubs, air conditioning and tastefully appointed period furnishings. Breakfast includes homemade baked goods, blintzes, quiche, eggs

Florentine and the inn's award-winning French toast. Vegetarian and dietary restricted meals are accommodated. The inn is situated between the Oregon Shakespeare Festival, the town center and the Historic Railroad District, where galleries, museums, antiques, restaurants and quaint shops can be found. Ski packages are offered.

Innkeeper(s): Rosemary Silva. $75-125. MC VISA AX TC. 4 rooms with PB. 2 suites. Breakfast included in rates. Types of meals: gourmet breakfast and early coffee/tea. Evening snack available. Beds: Q. Phone and air conditioning in room. Fax and library on premises. Family reunions hosted. Antiques, fishing, parks, shopping, skiing, golf, theater and watersports nearby.

Publicity: *San Francisco Examiner.*

"You are perfect hosts!"

Cowslip's Belle

159 N Main St
Ashland, OR 97520-1729
(541)488-2901 (800)888-6819 Fax:(541)482-6138
E-mail: stay@cowslip.com

Circa 1913. Each guest is made to feel special at this Craftsman bungalow, peaked with five roofs and gables. The interior offers original woodwork and leaded and stained glass. Teddy bears and down comforters add a cozy touch to guest rooms. A hearty breakfast is served each morning and refreshments are available throughout the day, featuring coffee, teas, sherry and treats such as chocolate dipped macaroons and biscotti.

Historic Interest: Cowslip's Belle is located in the heart of Ashland's historic district, and it is only 20 minutes from Jacksonville, an entire town listed in the National Register.

Innkeeper(s): Jon & Carmen Reinhardt. $95-135. 4 rooms with PB. 1 suite. Breakfast included in rates. Type of meal: full breakfast. Beds: KQT. Phone in room. Antiques, fishing, downhill skiing, cross-country skiing, theater and watersports nearby.

Publicity: *San Francisco Chronicle, Los Angeles Times, Pacific Northwest, Seattle Times, Country Inns, Sacramento Bee, Oregonian.*

"The atmosphere was delightful, the decor charming, the food delicious and the company grand. Tony says he's spoiled forever."

Iris Inn

59 Manzanita St
Ashland, OR 97520-2615
(541)488-2286 (800)460-7650 Fax:(541)488-3709

Circa 1905. The Iris Inn is a restored Victorian set on a large flower-filled yard. It features simple American country antiques. The upstairs guest rooms have views of the valley and mountains. Evening sips of wine often are taken out on the large deck overlooking a rose garden. Breakfast boasts an elegant presentation with dishes such as buttermilk scones and eggs Benedict.

Historic Interest: Jacksonville (20 minutes by car).

Innkeeper(s): Vicki Lamb. $60-110. MC VISA. 5 rooms with PB. Breakfast included in rates. Type of meal: full breakfast. Beds: QDT. Air conditioning, turndown service and ceiling fan in room. Fax on premises. Small meetings and seminars hosted. Antiques, fishing, shopping, downhill skiing, cross-country skiing, sporting events, theater and watersports nearby.

Location: Southern Oregon.

Publicity: *Sunset, Oregonian.*

"It's like returning to home to be at The Iris Inn."

Oak Hill Country B&B

2190 Siskiyou Blvd
Ashland, OR 97520-2531
(541)482-1554 (800)888-7434 Fax:(541)482-1378
E-mail: oakhill@mind.net

Circa 1910. Decorated with hints of French country, this Craftsman farmhouse has a fine front porch and expansive sunny deck in back creating relaxing areas for enjoying the less crowded south end of town. A hearty country gourmet breakfast is served family style in the dining room. There are bicycles for exploring the area.

Innkeeper(s): Linda Johnson. $65-105. MC VISA. 6 rooms. Breakfast included in rates. Air conditioning and turndown service in room. TV and VCR on premises. Small meetings, family reunions and seminars hosted. Antiques, fishing, shopping, downhill skiing, cross-country skiing and theater nearby.

Pinehurst Inn at Jenny Creek

17250 Hwy 66
Ashland, OR 97520-9406
(503)488-1002

Circa 1923. This lodge, built from logs harvested on the property, once accommodated travelers along the new state highway 66. The highway was built to replace the Southern Oregon Wagon Road. As the name suggests, the inn is situated by the banks of Jenny Creek, and guest enjoy stunning canyon views from the upstairs sunroom. The lobby, with its huge stone

fireplace, is a welcoming site. The inn also includes a full-service restaurant open to guests and the public. The inn is about a half hour from Ashland, and Klamath Falls is 39 miles away.

Innkeeper(s): Mary Jo & Mike Moloney. $75-140. MC VISA DS. 6 rooms with PB. 2 suites. Breakfast and dinner included in rates. Types of meals: full breakfast and early coffee/tea. Lunch available. Restaurant on premises. Beds: KQD. Ceiling fan in room. 24 acres. Weddings, small meetings and family reunions hosted. Antiques, fishing, shopping, downhill skiing, cross-country skiing and theater nearby.

Publicity: *Sunset, Travel & Leisure.*

"*Romantic and peaceful. A favorite inn. Wonderful dinner and accommodations.*"

The Woods House B&B

333 N Main St
Ashland, OR 97520-1703
(541)488-1598 (800)435-8260 Fax:(541)482-8027

Circa 1908. Built and occupied for almost 40 years by a prominent Ashland physician, each room of this Craftsman-style inn boasts special detail. Many guest rooms offer canopied beds and skylights. Full breakfasts are served either in the sunny dining room or in the garden under a spreading walnut tree. After breakfast, take a stroll through the half-acre of terraced, English gardens. Located in the historic district, the inn is four blocks from Ashland's Shakespearean theaters.

Historic Interest: Named after Dr. Ernest Woods, local physician.

Innkeeper(s): Francoise Roddy. $75-120. MC VISA DS. 6 rooms with PB. Breakfast included in rates. Types of meals: full breakfast and early coffee/tea. Room service available. Beds: KQT. Air conditioning in room. TV, VCR, fax and copier on premises. Weddings, small meetings, family reunions and seminars hosted. Antiques, shopping, skiing and theater nearby.

Publicity: *The Times.*

"*Within this house lies much hospitality, friendship and laughter. What more could a home ask to be?*"

Astoria A2

Grandview B&B

1574 Grand Ave
Astoria, OR 97103-3733
(503)325-5555 (800)488-3250
E-mail: grandvu@postbox.com

Circa 1896. To fully enjoy its views of the Columbia River, this Victorian house has both a tower and a turret. Antiques and white wicker furnishings contribute to the inn's casual, homey feeling. The Meadow Room is particularly appealing to bird-lovers with its birdcage, bird books and bird wallpaper. Breakfast, served in the main-floor turret, frequently includes smoked salmon with bagels and cream cheese.

Historic Interest: Flavel House (8 blocks), Heritage Museum (1 block), Firefighters Museum (18 blocks).

Innkeeper(s): Charleen Maxwell. $55-96. MC VISA DS. 9 rooms, 7 with PB, 3 with FP. 2 suites. Breakfast and evening snack included in rates. Type of meal: full breakfast. Beds: QT. Weddings, small meetings and family reunions hosted. Antiques, fishing, parks, shopping, theater and watersports nearby.

Publicity: *Pacific Northwest Magazine, Northwest Discoveries, Los Angeles Times, Oregonian, Daily Astorian.*

"*We're still talking about our visit and the wonderful breakfast you served.*"

Bend D5

The Sather House B&B

7 NW Tumalo Ave
Bend, OR 97701
(541)388-1065

Circa 1911. This Craftsman-style home is listed in the local, county and national historic registers. One room includes a clawfoot tub that dates to 1910. Period furnishings are found in the nicely appointed guest rooms, which feature touches of Battenburg and lace. The front porch is lined with wicker for those who wish to relax and enjoy the surroundings. For breakfast, innkeeper Robbie Giamboi serves items such as pancakes topped with her own homemade blackberry or apple syrup. Guests also enjoy afternoon tea.

Innkeeper(s): Robbie Giamboi. $80-97. MC VISA DS PC TC. 4 rooms, 2 with PB. Breakfast and afternoon tea included in rates. Types of meals: gourmet breakfast and early coffee/tea. Beds: KQDTR. Ceiling fan in room. TV, VCR and library on premises. Small meetings and family reunions hosted. Antiques, fishing, parks, shopping, downhill skiing, cross-country skiing, sporting events, golf, theater and watersports nearby.

Publicity: *Bend Bulletin, Oregonian.*

Brookings G1

South Coast Inn B&B

516 Redwood St
Brookings, OR 97415-9672
(541)469-5557 (800)525-9273 Fax:(541)469-6615
E-mail: scoastin@wave.net

Circa 1917. Enjoy panoramic views of the Pacific Ocean at this Craftsman-style inn built by renowned San Francisco architect Bernard Maybeck. All rooms are furnished with antiques, ceiling fans, VCRs and TVs. Two guest rooms afford panoramic views of the rugged coastline. A floor-to-ceiling stone fireplace and beamed ceilings make the parlor a great place to gather with friends. There are sun decks, a strolling garden and an indoor hot tub and sauna. The Brookings area offers something for everyone. Outdoor activities include hiking, boating, golfing, digging for clams or simply enjoying a stroll along the spectacular coastline. Concerts, galleries, museums, antiques, specialty shops and fine restaurants all can be found within the area.

Innkeeper(s): Ken Raith & Keith Pepper. $79-89. MC VISA AX DS PC TC. TAC10. 3 rooms with PB. 1 cottage. Breakfast included in rates. Types of meals: full breakfast, gourmet breakfast and early coffee/tea. Beds: Q. Ceiling fan, TV and VCR in room. Fax, spa, sauna and library on premises. Weddings, small meetings, family reunions and seminars hosted. Antiques, fishing, parks, shopping, theater and watersports nearby.

"Thank you for your special brand of magic. What a place!"

Cloverdale

C2

Sandlake Country Inn

8505 Galloway Rd
Cloverdale, OR 97112-9646
(503)965-6745

Circa 1894. This two-story farmhouse was built of 3-by-12 bridge timbers from a Norwegian sailing vessel. It shipwrecked

on the beach south of Cape Lookout on Christmas Day 1890. On two acres adjacent to the Suislaw National Forest, the inn's garden occasionally is host to deer and other wildlife. Guest rooms feature canopied

beds, down comforters and fresh flowers. A creekside country cottage is popular with honeymooners.

Innkeeper(s): Femke & David Durham. $65-125. MC VISA AX DS PC TC. 4 rooms with PB, 3 with FP. 1 cottage. Type of meal: full breakfast. Beds: KQ. Bicycles on premises. Handicap access. Fishing nearby.

Location: On the Oregon coast.

Publicity: *Headlight Herald, Bridal Connection of Oregon, Oregonian, Oregon Coast.*

"Once again Sandlake was the perfect cure for too much city and not enough time."

Corvallis

D3

Harrison House

2310 NW Harrison Blvd
Corvallis, OR 97330-5402
(541)752-6248 (800)233-6248
E-mail: harrisonhouse@proaxis.com

Circa 1939. This Dutch-Colonial-style house, adjacent to Oregon State University, was built by the Allison family who lived here until 1990. Upon its conversion to a bed & breakfast, it was graciously restored. The rooms are large and comfortable, decorated and furnished in Williamsburg-style family antiques. The

favorite guest room overlooks a side yard with beds of flowers and fruit trees. The full breakfast begins with a fruit course and features either eggs Benedict, various stuffed crepes or other regional fare. Antiques, fishing, hiking, shopping, skiing, sporting events and theater are nearby.

Historic Interest: The inn is located in the Oregon wine country and close to the Oregon Coast and Cascade Mountains.

Innkeeper(s): Maria Tomlinson. $60-80. MC VISA AX DS. 4 rooms, 2 with PB. Type of meal: early coffee/tea. Evening snack available. Beds: KQD. Phone and TV in room. Weddings, small meetings, family reunions and seminars hosted. Amusement parks, antiques, fishing, shopping, downhill skiing, cross-country skiing, sporting events and theater nearby.

"What an exceptional weekend!"

Dayton

C3

Wine Country Farm

6855 NE Breyman Orchards Rd
Dayton, OR 97114-7220
(503)864-3446 (800)261-3446 Fax:(503)864-3446

Circa 1910. Surrounded by vineyards and orchards, Wine Country Farm is an eclectic French house sitting on a hill overlooking the Cascade Mountain Range. Arabian horses are raised here, and five varieties of grapes are grown. Request the master bedroom and you'll enjoy a fireplace. The innkeepers can arrange for a horse-drawn buggy ride and picnic. There are outdoor wedding facilities and a new wine tasting room. Downtown Portland and the Oregon coast are each an hour away.

Innkeeper(s): Joan Davenport. $75-125. MC VISA PC. 7 rooms with PB, 2 with FP. 1 suite. 1 conference room. Breakfast included in rates. Types of meals: full breakfast, gourmet breakfast and early coffee/tea. Picnic lunch, banquet service, catering service and room service available. Beds: KQDT. Air conditioning, ceiling fan and VCR in room. Fax, copier, stables and library on premises. 13 acres. Weddings, small meetings, family reunions and seminars hosted. Antiques, fishing, parks, shopping, downhill skiing, cross-country skiing, sporting events, theater and watersports nearby.

Publicity: *Wine Spectator.*

Enterprise

B9

The George Hyatt House B&B Inn

200 E Greenwood St
Enterprise, OR 97828
(541)426-0241 (800)954-9288

Circa 1898. George Hyatt, once the owner of the largest department store west of the Mississippi, built this Queen Anne Victorian. Unfortunately for Hyatt, his luck took a devastating turn for the worse, and the luxurious home was sold at auction in 1928 for less than $24. Today, guests sample the grander portion of Hyatt's life by staying in his grand historic home. The home maintains the beautiful woodwork, stained glass and gingerbread trim so cherished in Victorians. The four guest

rooms are decorated in period style. Two guest rooms include clawfoot tubs original to the house. The grounds feature gardens, and guests will enjoy the views of the Wallowa Mountains.

Innkeeper(s): Mary B Fort. $95. MC VISA PC. 4 rooms with PB. Breakfast included in rates. Types of meals: full breakfast and early coffee/tea. Beds: Q. Copier, spa and library on premises. Antiques, fishing, shopping, downhill skiing, cross-country skiing, golf and watersports nearby.

Publicity: *Oregonian.*

Eugene D3

Campbell House, A City Inn

252 Pearl St
Eugene, OR 97401-2366
(541)343-1119 (800)264-2519 Fax:(541)343-2258
E-mail: campbellhouse@campbellhouse.com

Circa 1892. An acre of grounds surrounds this Victorian inn, built by a local timber owner and gold miner. The guest quarters range from a ground-level room featuring fly-fishing paraphernalia and knotty-pine paneling to an elegant two-room honeymoon suite on the second floor, complete with fireplace, jetted bathtub for two and a view of the mountains. The Campbell House, located in Eugene's historic Skinner Butte District, is within walking distance of restaurants, the Hult Center for the Performing Arts, the 5th Street Public Market and antique shops. Outdoor activities include jogging or biking along riverside paths.

Historic Interest: The historic Shelton McMurphy House, which was built in 1882 and now is owned by the city, is located at the base of the driveway and tours are available. The innkeepers will provide guests with walking maps of the historic district.

Innkeeper(s): Myra Plant. $85-275. MC VISA AX DS TC. TAC10. 12 rooms with PB, 3 with FP. 1 suite. 2 conference rooms. Breakfast included in rates. Types of meals: full breakfast and early coffee/tea. Picnic lunch and room service available. Beds: KQDT. Phone, air conditioning, turndown service, ceiling fan, TV and VCR in room. Fax, copier, library on premises. Handicap access. Weddings, small meetings, family reunions, seminars hosted. Antiques, fishing, parks, shopping, sporting events, theater, watersports nearby.

Publicity: KVAL & KAUW News, Eugene Register Guard, Country Inns, Oregonian, Sunset.

"I guess we've never felt so pampered! Thank you so much. The room is beautiful! We had a wonderful getaway."

Pookie's B&B on College Hill

2013 Charnelton St
Eugene, OR 97405-2819
(541)343-0383 (800)558-0383 Fax:(541)343-0383

Circa 1918. Pookie's is a charming Craftsman house with "yester-year charm." Surrounded by maple and fir trees, the B&B is located in an older, quiet neighborhood. Mahogany and oak antiques decorate the rooms. The innkeeper worked for many years in the area as a concierge and can offer you expert help with excursion planning or business needs.

Historic Interest: Historic downtown (1 1/2 mile).

Innkeeper(s): Pookie & Doug Walling. $65-90. AP. PC TC. TAC10. 3 rooms, 2 with PB. 1 suite. Breakfast included in rates. Types of meals: continental breakfast, continental-plus breakfast, full breakfast and early coffee/tea. Beds: KQT. Phone, ceiling fan and TV in room. VCR, fax and copier on premises. Weddings and small meetings hosted. Antiques, fishing, parks, shopping, sporting events, theater and watersports nearby.

Publicity: Oregon Wine.

"I love the attention to detail. The welcoming touches: flowers, the 'convenience basket' of necessary items . . . I'm happy to have discovered your lovely home."

Florence D2

The Blue Heron Inn

6563 Hwy 126 PO Box 1122
Florence, OR 97439-0055
(541)997-4091 (800)997-7780

Circa 1940. From the porch of this bed & breakfast inn, guests can gaze at rolling, forested hills and watch as riverboats ease their way down the Siuslaw River. Aside from the spectacular view, the inn is located within a few yards of a marina where docking and mooring is available. The ocean, the dunes and historic Florence are just minutes away as well. The Bridal Suite offers king-size bed, sitting area, whirlpool tub and view of the river and grounds. Fresh, seasonal fare highlights the breakfast menu. Treats such as fresh fruit smoothies, muffins topped with homemade blackberry jam or a smoked salmon and avocado quiche are not uncommon.

Innkeeper(s): Doris Van Osdell & Maurice Souza. $55-120. MC VISA DS PC TC. TAC5. 5 rooms with PB. Breakfast and afternoon tea included in rates. Type of meal: full breakfast. Beds: KQT. Ceiling fan in room. VCR and library on premises. Weddings, small meetings and family reunions hosted. German spoken. Antiques, fishing, parks, shopping and watersports nearby.

"The entire place was decorated with great taste. Our room was beautiful and relaxing. It made us feel at ease and at peace."

The Johnson House

216 Maple St, PO Box 1892
Florence, OR 97439-9657
(541)997-8000 (800)768-9488

Circa 1892. This late Victorian, surrounded by a white picket fence, is a favorite site in Florence's Old Town. The home is just blocks from the Siuslaw River. Rooms are decorated with period antiques, including beds topped with fluffy, down comforters. Fresh flowers and lacy touches add romance. The hearty breakfasts are the perfect way to start the day. Enjoy gourmet fare such as fresh berries with cream, heavenly crepes or omelets, prepared with herbs from the inn's garden.

Historic Interest: The Johnston House is located three blocks from historic Sinuslaw river Bridge and 15 minutes from 1890s Heceta Head Lighthouse.

Innkeeper(s): Jayne & Ron Fraese. $95-125. MC VISA DS TC. 6 rooms, 3 with PB. Breakfast included in rates. Types of meals: full breakfast and early coffee/tea. Afternoon tea available. Beds: Q. Fax and copier on premises. Handicap access. Small meetings, family reunions and seminars hosted. Antiques, fishing, parks and shopping nearby.

Grants Pass G2

Lawnridge House

1304 N W Lawnridge Ave
Grants Pass, OR 97526-1218
(541)476-8518

Circa 1909. This inn, a graceful, gabled clapboard house is shaded by 200-year-old oaks. The home features spacious rooms with comfortable antiques, canopy beds and beamed ceilings. Mini refrigerators, TVs and VCRs are among the amenities. The innkeeper serves Northwest regional cuisine for the full breakfasts. The Rogue River is five minutes away, and the Ashland Shakespearean Festival is a 45-minute drive.

Innkeeper(s): Barbara Head. $65-85. PC TC. TAC10. 2 suites. Breakfast included in rates. Type of meal: full breakfast. Beds: KQ. Air conditioning in room. Antiques, fishing, theater and watersports nearby.

Publicity: CBS TV, Grants Pass Courier, This Week.

"Thank you for your incredible friendliness, warmth, and energy expended on our behalf! I've never felt so nestled in the lap of luxury - what a pleasure!"

Hood River   B5

Columbia Gorge Hotel

4000 Westcliff Dr
Hood River, OR 97031-9799
(541)386-5566 (800)345-1921 Fax:(541)387-5414
E-mail: cghotel@gorgenet.com

Circa 1921. This posh hotel is a gem among gems in the National Register of Historic Places. Idyllic guest quarters offer such ornate furnishings as a hand-carved canopy bed that once graced a French castle. The beautifully landscaped grounds, turndown service with roses and chocolate and a gourmet restaurant are favorite amenities. Last, but not least, are spectacular views of the majestic Columbia River. Guests are treated to the opulent "World Famous Farm Breakfast." The hotel is close to ski areas, golfing and popular windsurfing spots.

Innkeeper(s): Boyd & Halla Graves. $150-275. MC VISA AX DC CB DS TC. TAC10. 42 rooms with PB, 2 with FP. 3 conference rooms. Breakfast included in rates. Types of meals: full breakfast, gourmet breakfast and early coffee/tea. Picnic lunch, lunch, gourmet lunch, banquet service, catering service and room service available. Restaurant on premises. Beds: KQDT. Phone, turndown service and TV in room. VCR, fax and copier on premises. Weddings, small meetings, family reunions and seminars hosted. Spanish and French and Icelandic spoken. Antiques, fishing, parks, shopping, downhill skiing, cross-country skiing, theater and watersports nearby.

Pets Allowed.

Lafayette   C3

Kelty Estate B&B

675 Third St
Lafayette, OR 97127
(503)864-3740 (800)867-3740

Circa 1872. An early pioneer couple, one a local druggist and county sheriff and the other, the first woman elected to the Lafayette School Board, built this home. The grounds are well-landscaped with gardens, trees and lush plants. Guests can enjoy the tranquility from the swing on the home's front porch. There are two guest rooms, decorated in pastels. Furnishings include period antiques. Breakfasts feature fresh Oregon-grown items, with specialties such as strawberry-kiwi juice, fresh strawberries and bananas in a cream sauce, homemade breads and eggs Benedict accompanied by herbed potatoes. Wineries, a museum and antiquing are among the nearby attractions.

Innkeeper(s): Ron & JoAnn Ross. $65-75. PC TC. 2 rooms with PB. Breakfast and afternoon tea included in rates. Types of meals: continental breakfast, full breakfast and early coffee/tea. Beds: Q. TV, VCR and library on premises. Weddings, small meetings, family reunions and seminars hosted. Amusement parks, antiques, fishing, parks, shopping, theater and watersports nearby.

Lincoln City   C2

The Enchanted Cottage

4507 SW Coast Ave
Lincoln City, OR 97367
(541)996-4101 Fax:(541)996-2682
E-mail: daythia@wcn.net

Circa 1940. This 4,000-square-foot house is 300 feet from the beach and a short walk from Siletz Bay with its herd of sea lions. Victoria's Secret is a favorite romantic guest room that features a queen canopy bed, antique furnishings and, best of all, the sounds of the Pacific surf. Ask for Sir Arthur's View if you must see and hear the ocean. This two-room suite also has a private deck and a living room with a fireplace and wet bar. Homemade breakfast casseroles are a specialty during the morning meal, which is served either in the dining room or on the deck overlooking the Pacific. Pets are allowed with some restrictions.

Innkeeper(s): David & Cynthia Gale Fitton. $100-175. MC VISA PC TC. TAC10. 3 rooms with PB, 1 with FP. 1 suite. Breakfast and evening snack included in rates. Types of meals: full breakfast, gourmet breakfast and early coffee/tea. Dinner, catering service and room service available. Beds: KQ. Turndown service and TV in room. VCR, fax, copier and library on premises. Handicap access. Weddings, small meetings, family reunions and seminars hosted. Some Spanish spoken. Amusement parks, antiques, fishing, parks, shopping, golf, theater and watersports nearby.

Pets Allowed: With some restrictions. Prefer small pets. Must have own pet bed.

Publicity: Oregonian.

McMinnville   C3

Baker Street B&B

129 S Baker St
McMinnville, OR 97128
(503)472-5575 (800)870-5575

Circa 1914. The natural wood that graces the interior of this Craftsman inn has been restored to its original luster. Vintage Victorian antiques and memorabilia decorate the rooms. Several guest rooms include clawfoot tubs, each features a different color scheme. Couples traveling together or those planning longer visits, might consider the Carnation Cottage, which includes two bedrooms, a bathroom, living room, kitchen and laundry facilities. The breakfast table is set with china and silver. The B&B is one hour from Portland and the coast, and there are gourmet restaurants and 40 wineries nearby.

Innkeeper(s): John & Cheryl Collins. $75-125. MC VISA AX DS PC TC. 4 rooms with PB. 1 cottage. Type of meal: full breakfast. Beds: KQDT. Air conditioning and VCR in room. TV on premises. Weddings, small meetings and family reunions hosted. Antiques, parks and shopping nearby.

Mattey House

10221 N E Mattey Ln
McMinnville, OR 97128-8219
(503)434-5058

Circa 1892. Windows rimmed with stained glass and gingerbread trim decorate the exterior of this Queen Anne Victorian. The home is nestled on 10 acres of vineyards, orchards and stately, old cedar trees. Visitors may even pick a few of the succulent grapes. Guest rooms are decorated in period style with antiques, and each is named appropriately for a variety of wine. Upon returning from a day of sightseeing, guests are treated to late afternoon refreshments. Breakfasts are a treat, and the innkeepers serve dishes such as a baked peach with a stuffing of raspberries and cream, baked herbed eggs or perhaps an Italian frittata. Homemade scones are a specialty.

Innkeeper(s): Denise & Jack Seed. $85-110. MC VISA PC TC. 4 rooms with PB. Breakfast and afternoon tea included in rates. Types of meals: full breakfast and early coffee/tea. Evening snack available. Beds: QD. Turndown service in room. 10 acres. Family reunions hosted. German, limited French and limited Italian spoken. Antiques, fishing, parks, shopping, sporting events, theater and watersports nearby.

"What a lovely home and what thoughtful innkeepers you both are. We enjoyed our cozy room with all of your nice touches."

Williams House B&B

809 N E Evans
McMinnville, OR 97128
(503)434-9016 (800)441-2214

Circa 1928. All of the original Honduras mahogany woodwork and oak hardwood floors lend a nostalgic atmosphere to this Colonial-style house first built by Dr. Charles Williams and his wife, Alicia. The inn offers a quiet retreat to relax and enjoy the subtle comforts of "home" or a starting place from which to explore the natural beauty of the rural wine country surrounding it.

Innkeeper(s): Carol Jones. $50-95. PC TC. 3 rooms with PB, 1 with FP. Breakfast included in rates. Types of meals: full breakfast and early coffee/tea. Beds: QT. TV on premises. Family reunions hosted. Antiques, fishing, parks, shopping, sporting events, golf and theater nearby.

Merlin
G2

Morrison's Rogue River Lodge

8500 Galice Rd
Merlin, OR 97532-9722
(541)476-3825 (800)826-1963 Fax:(541)476-4953

Circa 1946. Many world travelers list Morrison's as one of their favorite places. The Rogue River wilderness that surrounds this handsome waterfront lodge provides scenic adventures up and down the river. Each cottage has its own balcony and fireplace, and the lodge is particularly noted for its excellent cuisine. In summer, a four-course, gourmet dinner is served on the deck overlooking green lawns and the river. Breakfast and dinner are included in the summer rates. Breakfast, dinner and a picnic lunch are included in the fall rates.

Historic Interest: Crater Lake National Park (2-hour drive), Oregon Caves National Monument (1-1/2-hour drive), Ashland Shakespearean Festival (1-hour drive).
Innkeeper(s): Michelle Hanten. $150-240. MAP, AP. MC VISA DS PC TC. TAC10. 13 rooms with PB, 9 with FP. 9 cottages. Breakfast included in rates. Restaurant on premises. Beds: KQDT. Phone and air conditioning in room. TV, VCR, fax, copier, spa, swimming, bicycles, tennis and library on premises. Handicap access. Weddings, small meetings, family reunions, seminars hosted. Antiques, fishing, parks, shopping, theater, watersports nearby.
Location: On the Rogue River in Southern Oregon.
Publicity: *Los Angeles Times, Pacific Northwest, Bon Appetit, Orvis News.*

"The tales we heard of how delicious the food would be told nothing of how it really was! We were so delighted to find such marvelous home-cooked cuisine, and the family service was terrific!"

Newberg
C3

Smith House

415 N College St
Newberg, OR 97132-2650
(503)538-1995 Fax:(503)537-0508

Circa 1904. A Quaker family built this turn-of-the-century Victorian. Aside from a family home, the historic building served as a boarding house during World War II. By the time innkeepers Glen and Mary Post discovered it in the 1980s, the home was so dilapidated, it had been condemned by the city. The Posts undertook the major project of restoring this home, and the Victorian now shines with its original luster. There are just two guest rooms, ensuring an intimate stay. The home is furnished with antiques and family heirlooms. The shared bath includes a clawfoot tub. Outside, the innkeepers installed a relaxing hot tub for their guests to use. The innkeepers take great pride in their breakfasts, including using a different set of china each day. After a gourmet meal, head out and explore Oregon wine country.

Innkeeper(s): Glen & Mary Post. $65-70. TC. TAC10. 2 rooms. Breakfast included in rates. Types of meals: full breakfast, gourmet breakfast and early coffee/tea. Beds: KQT. Phone, turndown service and ceiling fan in room. TV, VCR, spa and library on premises. Antiques, fishing, parks, shopping, skiing, sporting events, golf, theater and watersports nearby.
Publicity: *Oregon Wine.*

"I felt well cared for and it's been a most pleasant experience. Wonderful breakfasts!"

Springbrook Hazelnut Farm

30295 N Hwy 99 W
Newberg, OR 97132
(503)538-4606 (800)793-8528

Circa 1912. An ancient silver maple tree shades the main house, one of four Craftsman-style buildings on this farm. There are 10 acres of gardens, a pool, tennis court and a 60-acre hazelnut orchard. A blue heron monitors the inn's pond and you may paddle around in the canoe. Walking through the orchard to the adjoining winery is a must, as is a bicycle ride to other wineries in the area. Ask for the Carriage House or the Cottage, and you'll enjoy a pond and garden view. Two of the inn's cottages have private baths. They also have kitchens, and if you eat in, you may choose from the garden's offerings for your dinner.

Historic Interest: Champoeg Park (6 miles).
Innkeeper(s): Charles & Ellen McClure. $95-175. 4 rooms, 2 with PB. 2 cottages. Breakfast included in rates. Type of meal: full breakfast. Beds: QD. Air conditioning in room. VCR on premises. 68 acres. Small meetings and seminars hosted. Antiques, shopping, sporting events, theater, watersports nearby.
Publicity: *Travel & Leisure, Wine Spectator, Country, Oregonian, Country Living.*

"An incredible, wonderful refuge! We are beautifully surprised!"

Newport
C2

Oar House

520 S W 2nd St
Newport, OR 97365-3907
(541)265-9571 (800)252-2358

Circa 1900. This Craftsman-style home was built using wood that washed ashore after a lumber schooner was abandoned by the crew during a fierce storm. It has a colorful history, serving as a boarding house and then as the Nye Beach bordello. One of the former occupants, a young woman, may still inhabit the house in ghostly form. Rooms feature nautical names, such as Captain's Quarters and Starboard Cabin. Guests are welcome to walk up the third-floor ship's ladder to the lighthouse tower and enjoy a panoramic view of the ocean, beach, mountains, lighthouses and sunsets. Freshly roasted coffee, orange juice, and seasonal fruit accompany an entree, such as lemon ricotta pancakes topped with sauteed apples.

Innkeeper(s): Jan Le Brun. $95-125. MC VISA DS TC. 5 rooms with PB. 1 suite. Breakfast, afternoon tea and evening snack included in rates. Types of meals: gourmet breakfast and early coffee/tea. Beds: Q. TV, VCR, library on premises. Antiques, fishing, parks, shopping, theater and watersports nearby.

Ocean House B&B

4920 N W Woody Way
Newport, OR 97365-1328
(541)265-6158 (800)562-2632

Circa 1939. Simple but comfortable rooms provide magnificent views of the ocean and cozy spaces for storm watching at this homey bed and breakfast. A secluded, sheltered cliffside garden is terraced with tulips, azaleas and roses, providing a colorful setting to view the white waters of Agate Beach. A private path leads to the tide pools. Longtime Newport residents, the innkeepers know the area's most scenic spots.

Innkeeper(s): Bob & Marie Garrard. $90-150. AP. MC VISA DS. 5 rooms with PB, 1 with FP. Breakfast and afternoon tea included in rates. Types of meals: full breakfast and early coffee/tea. Beds: KQ. Turndown service and ceiling fan in room. TV, VCR, spa and library on premises. Antiques, fishing, parks, shopping, golf, theater and watersports nearby.

Location: Agate Beach.

Publicity: *New York Times, Los Angeles Times.*

"This is the life. Don't change a single thing, because it's out of this world!"

Sylvia Beach Hotel

267 N W Cliff St
Newport, OR 97365-3707
(541)265-5428

Circa 1910. In the National Register, the dark green shingled, bluff top Sylvia Beach Hotel originally served as a honeymoon hotel. Sylvia Beach was a patron of literature during the 20s and 30s in Paris. The hotel named for her offers rooms decorated according to authors such as Mark Twain and Agatha Christie (oceanfront), Tennessee Williams, Herman Melville, Jane Austen and F. Scott Fitzgerald (ocean views). Ask for the Colette Room which offers a fireplace, white bed, deck and light-filled sit-ting area. The oceanfront library, bright and airy with comfortable chairs, sofa and fireplace, is another wonderful place from which to enjoy the roar of the sea while snuggling with a favorite book. The inn's oceanfront restaurant is called Tables of Content.

Innkeeper(s): Ken Peyton. $55-146. MC VISA AX PC TC. 22 rooms, 20 with PB, 3 with FP. Breakfast included in rates. Types of meals: full breakfast, gourmet breakfast and early coffee/tea. Restaurant on premises. Beds: KQTD. Library on premises. Handicap access. Weddings, small meetings, family reunions and seminars hosted. Antiques, fishing, parks, shopping, golf, theater and watersports nearby.

Publicity: *New York Times, Seattle Times, The Weekend Sun, Adventure West, Innsider, Travel-Holiday, Entrepreneur.*

"My husband and I very much enjoyed our stay in this oh, so romantic hideaway!"

Portland
B3

General Hooker's House

125 S W Hooker
Portland, OR 97201
(503)222-4435 (800)745-4135 Fax:(503)295-6410
E-mail: ghbandb@teleport.com

Circa 1888. This tastefully renovated urban Queen Anne townhouse is a blend of comfort and informal charm. Situated in the Victorian village in the Historic Conservation District of downtown Portland, the inn provides easy access to almost all of the city's attractions. Guests are invited to take advantage of the film and reference library and honor bar stocked with wine, beer and ale. From the roof garden, guests can enjoy a view of the city, the river, bridges and Mount Hood. The innkeeper serves light, heart-healthy, vegetarian breakfasts.

Historic Interest: Downtown Portland offers several historic districts and your host can direct you to many historic sites.

Innkeeper(s): Lori Hall. $75-125. MC VISA AX. 4 rooms, 2 with PB. Breakfast included in rates. Type of meal: continental-plus breakfast. Beds: KQDT. Antiques and theater nearby.

Publicity: *Yellow Brick Road.*

"What a pleasure to walk into your bright and airy house with its engaging mix of the best of two centuries. Your welcoming home is Portland at its best!"

MacMaster House

1041 SW Vista Ave
Portland, OR 97205
(503)223-7362 (503)774-9523 Fax:(503)224-8808
E-mail: cmurphy656@aol.com

Circa 1895. This Colonial Revival mansion is located in the prominent King's Hill neighborhood. Grand Doric columns and an immense portico are some of the architectural highlights displayed in this historic gem. The interior is as stately as the exterior. Rooms are appointed with European antiques and elegant decor. Beds are dressed with European linens. Four of the guest rooms offer a fireplace. Breakfast is a gourmet event, featuring such items as fresh

raspberries with creme fraiche, polenta with sauteed vegetables and poached eggs with freshly grated parmesan cheese. The home is near to many Portland sites, including Washington Park and the fashionable NW 23rd Avenue.

Innkeeper(s): Cecilia Murphy. $75-120. MC VISA AX DC DS TC. 7 rooms, 4 with FP. 2 suites. Breakfast included in rates. Type of meal: gourmet breakfast. Beds: QDT. Air conditioning, ceiling fan, TV and VCR in room. Fax and library on premises. Spanish and struggling with French spoken. Antiques, parks, shopping, sporting events and theater nearby.

Terwilliger Vista B&B

515 S W Westwood Dr
Portland, OR 97201-2791
(503)244-0602 (888)244-0602

Circa 1940. Bay windows accentuate the exterior of this stately Georgian Colonial home. A mix of modern and Art Deco furnishings decorate the interior. The home has an airy, uncluttered feel with its polished floors topped with Oriental rugs and muted tones. There is a canopy bed and fireplace in the spacious Garden Suite, and the Rose Suite overlooks the Willamette Valley. Other rooms offer garden views, bay windows or wicker furnishings. The house is located in what will be the Historical Terwilliger Boulevard Preserve.

Innkeeper(s): Dick & Jan Vatert. $80-145. MC VISA PC TC. TAC10. 5 rooms with PB, 1 with FP. 2 suites. Breakfast included in rates. Types of meals: continental breakfast and full breakfast. Afternoon tea available. Beds: KQT. Air conditioning and TV in room. Library on premises. Family reunions hosted. Antiques, parks, shopping, sporting events and theater nearby.

"Like staying in House Beautiful."

Prairie City   D7

Strawberry Mountain Inn

HCR 77 Box 940
Prairie City, OR 97869
(541)820-4522 (800)545-6913 Fax:(541)820-4622
E-mail: linda.strawberrymt.inn@worldnet.att.net

Circa 1906. Vistas of Strawberry Mountain are a highlight of a getaway to this peaceful inn, set on three acres of farmland. The home, the largest in Grant County, was built by a man who bred and raised horses for the U.S. Cavalry. The interior is spacious and comfortable, a place where guests are made to feel at home. There is a library offering a wide selection of books, and guests can relax on the front porch or enjoy a game of chess in the parlor. A deep-dish apple puff pancake or croissant French toast might appear on the breakfast table, served by candlelight while classical melodies play out in the background.

Innkeeper(s): Bill & Linda Harrington. $65-110. MC VISA AX DS PC TC. TAC10. 5 rooms, 1 with PB. Breakfast included in rates. Type of meal: gourmet breakfast. Afternoon tea available. Beds: KQDT. Phone in room. TV, VCR, fax, copier, bicycles, library and pet boarding on premises. Weddings, small meetings, family reunions and seminars hosted. Antiques, fishing, parks, shopping, cross-country skiing, golf and watersports nearby.

Salem   C3

Marquee House

333 Wyatt Ct NE
Salem, OR 97301-4269
(503)391-0837

Circa 1938. Each room in this Mt. Vernon Colonial replica of George Washington's house is named after a famous old-time movie. Consider the Auntie Mame room. This gracious view room features a fireplace, fainting couch, costumes, collectibles and a private bath. The four other upstairs guest rooms offer

similar themes. There are regular evening movie screenings complete with popcorn in the common room. The extensive gardens offer guests an opportunity to stroll along historic Mill Creek or enjoy a round of croquet in the spacious backyard, weather permitting. Hazelnut waffles, confetti hash and oatmeal custard are a few of the breakfast specialties. The inn is just two blocks from the Chemeketa Historic District.

Historic Interest: Located close to the state capitol and Willamette University.

Innkeeper(s): Ms. Rickie Hart. $55-90. MC VISA DS PC TC. TAC10. 5 rooms, 3 with PB, 1 with FP. Breakfast and evening snack included in rates. Types of meals: full breakfast, gourmet breakfast and early coffee/tea. Beds: QT. TV, VCR and bicycles on premises. Weddings, small meetings and family reunions hosted. Amusement parks, antiques, parks, shopping, sporting events, golf and theater nearby.

Publicity: *Statesman Journal, The Christian Science Monitor.*

"We all agreed that you were the best hostess yet for one of our weekends!"

State House B&B

2146 State St
Salem, OR 97301-4350
(503)588-1340 (800)800-6712

Circa 1920. This three-story house sits on the banks of Mill Creek where ducks and geese meander past a huge old red maple down to the water. (A baby was abandoned here because the house looked "just right" and "surely had nice people there." The 12-year-old boy who found the baby on the side porch grew up to become a judge and legal counsel to Governor Mark Hatfield.) The inn is close to everything in Salem.

Innkeeper(s): Judy & Mike Winsett. $50-75. MC VISA DS. 4 rooms, 2 with PB. Breakfast included in rates. Type of meal: full breakfast. Beds: QD. Fax and copier on premises.

Location: One mile from the I-5 Santiam turn-off.

Publicity: *Statesman-Journal.*

"You do a wonderful job making people feel welcome and relaxed."

Seaside   A2

Sand Dollar B&B

606 N Holladay Dr
Seaside, OR 97138-6926
(503)738-3491 (800)738-3491

Circa 1920. This Craftsman-style home looks a bit like a seashell, painted in light pink with dark pink trim. In fact, one of the guest rooms bears the name Sea Shell, filled with bright quilts and wicker. The Driftwood Room can be used as a two-bedroom suite for families. As the room names suggest, the house is decorated in a beach theme, graced by  innkeeper Nita Hempfling's stained glasswork. Before breakfast is served, coffee or tea is delivered to the rooms.

Innkeeper(s): Robert & Nita Hempfling. $55-100. MC VISA AX DS TC. 3 rooms, 2 with PB. 1 suite. Breakfast and evening snack included in rates. Beds: KQT. Ceiling fan, TV, VCR in room. Bicycles on premises. Weddings, small meetings hosted. Antiques, fishing, parks, shopping, watersports nearby.

Sisters   D4

Conklin's Guest House

69013 Camp Polk Rd
Sisters, OR 97759-9705
(541)549-0123 (800)549-4262

Circa 1910. The original portion of this Craftsman-style house was constructed in 1910, with later additions in 1938 and more recent changes in 1992 and 1993. Mountain views and four-and-a-half peaceful acres invite relaxation and romance. There are several ponds on the property stocked with trout for those wanting to try their hand at catch and release fishing. There is also a swimming pool. Three guest rooms have clawfoot tubs, and the Suite and Forget-Me-Not rooms offer a pleasing view. For those in a larger group, the inn's Dormitory room includes a queen bed and five single beds, at a rate of $25 to $30 per person. Sisters' airport is across the street from the home.

Innkeeper(s): Frank & Marie Conklin. $90-120. PC TC. 5 rooms with PB, 1 with FP. 1 suite. Breakfast and evening snack included in rates. Types of meals: full breakfast, gourmet breakfast and early coffee/tea. Beds: QT. Ceiling fan in room. Swimming on premises. Handicap access. Weddings, small meetings, family reunions and seminars hosted. Spanish spoken. Fishing, parks, shopping, downhill skiing, cross-country skiing and watersports nearby. Pets Allowed: On leash.

"A wonderful and romantic time for our wedding anniversary. Thanks so much. Oh-great fishing too."

Tigard   B3

The Woven Glass Inn

14645 SW Beef Bend Rd
Tigard, OR 97224
(503)590-6040 (800)484-2192

Circa 1938. This comfortable farmhouse is surrounded by more than an acre of grounds, including a sunken garden. Guests staying in the suite enjoy a view of the garden. Beds in both guest rooms include fluffy down pillows and fine linens. The inn is 20 minutes from Portland, and the area offers a variety of wineries to visit. There is a friendly cat in residence.

Innkeeper(s): Paul & Renee Giroux. $65-75. MC VISA AX DS PC TC. TAC20. 2 rooms with PB, 2 with FP. 1 suite. Breakfast included in rates. Type of meal: full breakfast. Beds: KQ. Phone and turndown service in room. TV and library on premises. Amusement parks, antiques, fishing, parks, shopping, skiing, sporting events, golf, theater and watersports nearby.

"We needed a little rest and relaxation and we found it here. We loved everything."

Tillamook   B2

Blue Haven Inn

3025 Gienger Rd
Tillamook, OR 97141-8258
(503)842-2265 Fax:(503)842-2265

Circa 1916. This Craftsman-style home has been refurbished and filled with antiques and collectibles. Guest rooms feature limited-edition plate series as themes. Tall evergreens, lawns and flower gardens add to the setting.

Innkeeper(s): Joy Still. $70-85. PC TC. TAC5. 3 rooms, 1 with PB. Breakfast included in rates. Types of meals: full breakfast, gourmet breakfast and early coffee/tea. Beds: QD. TV, VCR, fax, bicycles and library on premises. Antiques, fishing, parks, shopping and watersports nearby.

Publicity: *Oakland Tribune.*

"Your home is like a present to the eyes."

Welches   C4

Old Welches Inn B&B

26401 E Welches Rd
Welches, OR 97067
(503)622-3754 Fax:(503)622-5370

Circa 1890. This two-story colonial building, behind a picket fence, was originally the first hotel to be built in the Mt. Hood area. Reconstructed in the thirties, the building now has shutters and French windows. The inn's  two acres offer a plethora of flower beds and views of the Salmon River and Hunchback Mountain. Rooms are named for wildflowers and include antiques. If traveling with children or friends try Lilybank, a private cottage which overlooks the first hole of Three Nines. There are two bedrooms, a kitchen and a river rock fireplace.

Innkeeper(s): Judith & Ted Mondun. $75-130. MC VISA AX DS PC TC. TAC10. 4 rooms. 1 cottage. Breakfast and evening snack included in rates. Types of meals: full breakfast and early coffee/tea. Beds: QD. Turndown service in room. TV, VCR, fax and pet boarding on premises. Weddings, small meetings and family reunions hosted. Antiques, fishing, parks, shopping, downhill skiing, cross-country skiing, sporting events and golf nearby.

Pets Allowed: House broken, well behaved in cottage only.

Publicity: *Oregonian, Sunset.*

"Breakfast was scrumptious, fit for a king (and all of his army)."

Westfir   E3

Westfir Lodge, A B&B Inn

47365 First St
Westfir, OR 97492
(541)782-3103

Circa 1923. Behind a white picket fence, this graceful Arts and Crafts house is near the longest covered bridge in Oregon. Once headquarters to a lumber company, the inn has English gardens and meandering stone paths that create an appealing setting from which to view the bridge. The 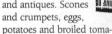 inn's decor is English country with bright floral prints and antiques. Scones and crumpets, eggs, potatoes and broiled tomatoes comprise the full English breakfast.

Innkeeper(s): Ken Symons, Gerry Chamberlain. $70-85. PC. 7 rooms with PB. Breakfast and afternoon tea included in rates. Types of meals: full breakfast and early coffee/tea. Beds: QT. Air conditioning and ceiling fan in room. TV, VCR and copier on premises. Handicap access. Weddings, small meetings, family reunions and seminars hosted. Fishing, parks, shopping, downhill skiing, cross-country skiing and golf nearby.

Publicity: *Birds & Blooms, Oregonian.*

Pennsylvania

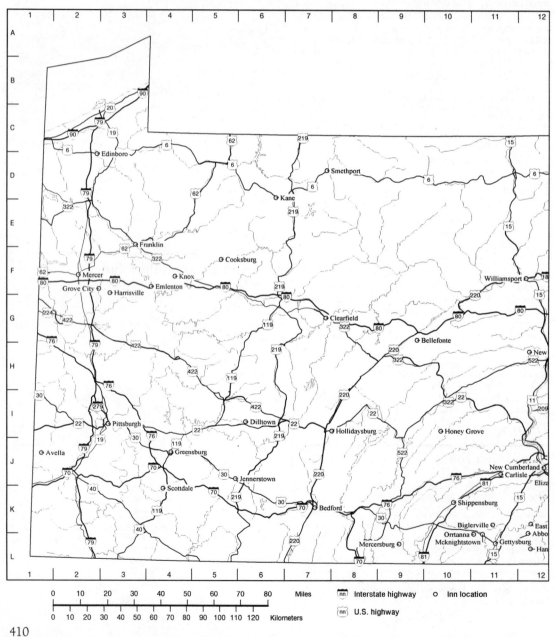

| 0 | 10 | 20 | 30 | 40 | 50 | 60 | 70 | 80 | Miles |
| 0 | 10 | 20 | 30 | 40 | 50 | 60 | 70 | 80 | 90 | 100 | 110 | 120 | Kilometers |

nn Interstate highway   o Inn location

nn U.S. highway

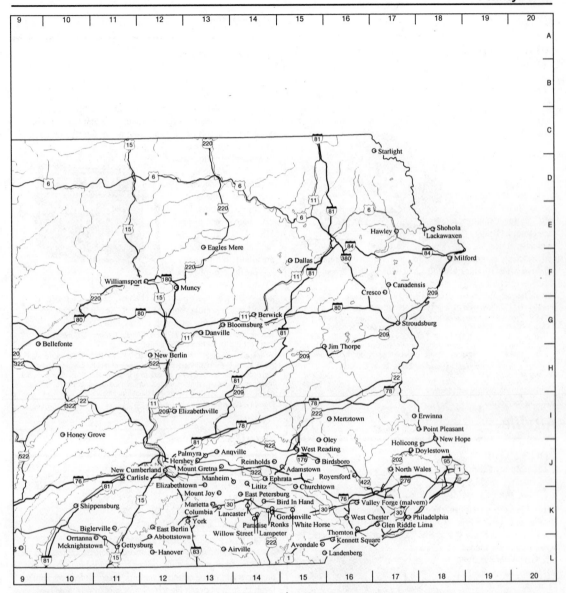

Abbottstown K12

The Altland House

Rt 30 Center Square
Abbottstown, PA 17301
(717)259-9535 Fax:(717)259-9956

Circa 1790. A French mansard roof tops this three-story Victorian, a popular inn and tavern halfway between York and Gettysburg. With high ceilings and chestnut woodwork as a backdrop, the Altland House offers contemporary furnishings and several deluxe rooms with whirlpools or fireplaces. The Cottage provides a kitchen, fireplace and private yard. The inn's two restaurants offer a variety of house specialties. The Underside Restaurant has a soup and salad bar and serves sandwiches and burgers, while the Berwick Room Restaurant is noted for a more elegant cuisine. The inn has a popular Sunday buffet.

Innkeeper(s): Mike Haugh. $72-125. MC VISA AX DS PC TC. 9 rooms with PB. 1 suite. 1 cottage. 2 conference rooms. Breakfast included in rates. Types of meals: continental breakfast and continental-plus breakfast. Dinner, picnic lunch, lunch, gourmet lunch, banquet service, catering service and room service available. Beds: KQ. Phone, air conditioning and TV in room. Fax and copier on premises. Weddings and family reunions hosted. Antiques, fishing, shopping, downhill skiing, golf and theater nearby.

Adamstown J15

Adamstown Inn

62 W Main St
Adamstown, PA 19501
(717)484-0800 (800)594-4808

Circa 1830. This square brick house, with its 1850s pump organ found in the large parlor and other local folk art, fits right into this community

known as one of the antique capitols of America (2,500 antique dealers). Other decorations include family heirlooms, Victorian wallpaper, handmade quilts and lace curtains. Before breakfast, coffee, tea or hot chocolate is brought to your room. For outlet mall fans, Adamstown is 10 miles from Reading, which offers a vast assortment of top-quality merchandise.

Historic Interest: The Ephrata Cloister is just seven miles away.

Innkeeper(s): Tom & Wanda Berman. $65-115. MC VISA DS PC TC. 4 rooms with PB, 2 with FP. 1 suite. Breakfast, afternoon tea and evening snack included in rates. Types of meals: continental-plus breakfast and early coffee/tea. Beds: KQD. Air conditioning and ceiling fan in room. TV, copier and library on premises. Small meetings, family reunions and seminars hosted. Amusement parks, antiques, fishing, parks, shopping and theater nearby.

Publicity: *Lancaster Intelligencer, Reading Eagle, Travel & Leisure, Country Almanac.*

"Your warm hospitality and lovely home left us with such pleasant memories."

Airville L13

Spring House

1264 Muddy Creek Forks Rd
Airville, PA 17302-9462
(717)927-6906 Fax:(717)927-8262

Circa 1798. Spring House, the prominent home in this pre-Revolutionary War village located in a National Historic District, was constructed of massive stones over a spring that supplies water to most of the vil-

lage. The walls are either whitewashed or retain their original stenciling. Furnished with country antiques, quilts, Oriental rugs, and paintings, the guest rooms are cozy with featherbeds in winter. The inn boasts a library and grand piano.

Innkeeper(s): Ray Hearne & Michael Schuster. $60-95. PC TC. TAC10. 3 rooms, 2 with PB. 1 cottage. Breakfast and evening snack included in rates. Types of meals: full breakfast and gourmet breakfast. Beds: QD. Fax and library on premises. Weddings, small meetings, family reunions and seminars hosted. Spanish spoken. Amusement parks, antiques, fishing, parks, shopping, cross-country skiing, theater and watersports nearby.

Publicity: *Woman's Day, Country Decorating, Innsider, Country Home.*

"What a slice of history! Thank you for your hospitality. We couldn't have imagined a more picturesque setting."

Annville J13

Swatara Creek Inn

Box 692, Rd 2
Annville, PA 17003
(717)865-3259

Circa 1860. A former boys' home, this bed & breakfast now boasts canopy beds and lacy curtains. The first floor of this Victorian mansion provides a sitting room, dining room and gift shop. A full break-

fast is served in the dining room, but honeymooners can request their meal in the comfort of their rooms. For chocolate lovers, nearby Hershey is a treat. Several shopping outlets are about an hour away or visit the Mount Hope Estate and Winery. For an unusual day trip, tour the Seltzer and Weaver Bologna plant in Lebanon. Each September, the town hosts a popular bologna festival. Nearby Lancaster County is the home of Amish communities.

Historic Interest: Gettysburg (1 hour), Ephrata Cloisters (25 minutes), President Buchanan Home (50 minutes).

Innkeeper(s): Jeanette Hess. $45-80. MC VISA AX DC DS. 10 rooms with PB. 1 suite. Breakfast included in rates. Types of meals: full breakfast and early coffee/tea. Beds: QT. Air conditioning in room. Handicap access. Small meetings and family reunions hosted. Amusement parks, antiques, fishing, parks, shopping, sporting events and theater nearby.

Publicity: *Daily News, Patriot-News.*

"Peaceful."

Avella J1

Weatherbury Farm

1061 Sugar Run Rd
Avella, PA 15312-2434
(724)587-3763 Fax:(724)587-0125
E-mail: weatherbury@pafarmstay.com

Circa 1870. Meadows, fields, gardens and valleys fill the 104 acres of this working farm where sheep, chickens, rabbits and cattle are raised. Stenciled walls, ceiling fans, wide-plank floors and fireplaces add to the country comforts. Breakfast features family favorites such as peach French toast or garden vegetable eggs. Enjoy porches, picnic spots, a swimming pool and the hammock.

Historic Interest: Meadowcroft Village (5 miles), Bradford and Lemoyne House (12 miles), Alexander Campbell Mansion (9 miles).

Innkeeper(s): Dale, Marcy & Nigel Tudor. $65-95. MC VISA. 8 rooms with PB, 6 with FP. 3 suites. Breakfast included in rates. Types of meals: full breakfast and early coffee/tea. Evening snack available. Beds: KQDT. Air conditioning and ceiling fan in room. VCR, fax, copier, swimming, library and child care on premises. 104 acres. Weddings and family reunions hosted. German spoken.

Publicity: *Observer, International Living, North Hills News Record, Pennsylvania Focus, KDKA, Pittsburgh Magazine, Nation's Business.*

"Your home and your hospitality was awesome."

Bedford K7

Bedford House

203 W Pitt St
Bedford, PA 15522-1237
(814)623-7171 (800)258-9868 Fax:(814)623-0832

Circa 1807. Five of the guest rooms in this beautiful 19th-century home feature working, gas-log fireplaces. All rooms contain antiques, reproductions and family heirlooms. The honeymoon guest room offers a king-size bed and two-person whirlpool tub. The guesthouse offers four additional rooms, a conference room and a kitchenette. A full breakfast with seasonal fruits and homemade muffins, breads and entrees is served in the country kitchen. Relax on a porch that overlooks the garden or tour historic Bedford, a pre-Revolutionary War town. The inn is a five-minute walk from the Fort Bedford Museum and Park, shops and restaurants. Old Bedford Village is another popular touring attraction. Shawnee State Park and the Coral Caverns are nearby.

Innkeeper(s): Lyn & Linda Lyon. $65-125. MC VISA AX DS PC TC. TAC10. 8 rooms with PB, 5 with FP. 1 suite. 1 cottage. Breakfast included in rates. Types of meals: full breakfast and early coffee/tea. Beds: KQDT. Phone, air conditioning, TV and VCR in room. Fax on premises. Handicap access. Weddings, small meetings, family reunions and seminars hosted. Antiques, fishing, parks, shopping, downhill skiing, cross-country skiing, theater and watersports nearby.

Location: Ninety-seven miles east of Pittsburgh.

Bellefonte G9

Reynolds Mansion B&B

101 W Linn St
Bellefonte, PA 16823-1622
(814)353-8407 (800)899-3929
E-mail: jheidt@boole.com

Circa 1885. Bellefonte is a town with many impressive, historic homes, and this exquisite stone mansion is no exception. The home, a combination of late Victorian and Gothic styles, features extraordinary, hand-crafted woodwork and intricately laid wood floors, as well as eight fire-places. Four guest rooms include a fireplace and a Jacuzzi tub. All enjoy a romantic atmosphere, heightened by candles, fresh flowers and the poshest of furnishings and decor. Baked, stuffed French toast served with  bacon or sausage is among the breakfast specialties, accompany by muffins, juices, cereals and a fruit compote created with more than a half dozen different fresh fruits. For an excellent lunch or dinner, the innkeepers suggest the nearby Gamble Mill Tavern, a 200-year-old mill listed in the National Register.

Innkeeper(s): Joseph & Charlotte Heidt. $90-140. MC VISA PC TC. TAC10. 5 suites, 4 with FP. 1 conference room. Breakfast included in rates. Types of meals: continental-plus breakfast, full breakfast, gourmet breakfast and early coffee/tea. Beds: KQ. TV, VCR, fax, copier and library on premises. Weddings, small meetings, family reunions and seminars hosted. Antiques, fishing, parks, shopping, downhill skiing, cross-country skiing, sporting events, golf, theater and watersports nearby.

"Your bed & breakfast is such an inspiration to us."

Berwick G14

Tom & Becky's Place

213 W Second St
Berwick, PA 18603
(717)752-3362 (888)506-3260 Fax:(717)752-3362

Circa 1900. The aroma of freshly baked sticky buns and Shoo-fly Pie (house specialty) from the innkeeper's on-site 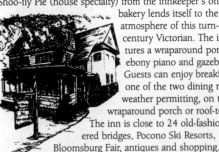 bakery lends itself to the country atmosphere of this turn-of-the-century Victorian. The inn features a wraparound porch, ebony piano and gazebo. Guests can enjoy breakfast in one of the two dining rooms, or weather permitting, on the wraparound porch or roof-top patio. The inn is close to 24 old-fashioned covered bridges, Pocono Ski Resorts, Bloomsburg Fair, antiques and shopping.

Historic Interest: Bloomsburg University, Knoebels Amusement Park and public golf course are located nearby.

Innkeeper(s): Tom & Becky Mason. $49-65. MC VISA AX DC CB DS TC. 7 rooms, 2 with PB. 1 conference room. Breakfast included in rates. Type of meal: full breakfast. Beds: KQDT. Air conditioning and TV in room. VCR, fax and copier on premises. Weddings, small meetings and family reunions hosted. Amusement parks, antiques, fishing, parks, shopping, downhill skiing, cross-country skiing, sporting events, golf, theater and watersports nearby.

"This will always be remembered as one of our best vacations."

Biglerville K11

Mulberry Farm B&B

616 Flohrs Church Rd
Biglerville, PA 17307-9556
(717)334-5827
E-mail: dconklin@mail.cvn.net

Circa 1817. General Lee marched the Confederate Army to Gettysburg on the road that ran in front of this early 19th-century Georgian Colonial. The home also was part of the Confederate encampment before the battle began. The innkeepers honor the home and local history by placing Civil War and Amish art in the home. For those Civil War buffs, there is a collection of informative books, as well as documentaries. Guests can stay either in the main house or in the cottage. Antiques decorate the rooms. The inn is a short drive from the historic sites of Gettysburg.

Innkeeper(s): David & Pat Conklin. $70-125. MC VISA PC. TAC10. 4 rooms with PB, 2 with FP. 1 suite. Breakfast included in rates. Meals: full breakfast and early coffee/tea. Beds: Q. Air conditioning in room. TV, VCR, fax, copier and library on premises. Antiques, parks, downhill skiing and golf nearby.

"Love this special place."

Bird-In-Hand K14

Mill Creek Homestead B&B

2578 Old Philadelphia Pike
Bird-In-Hand, PA 17505
(717)291-6419 (800)771-2578 Fax:(717)291-2171
E-mail: valfone@concentric.net

Circa 1790. This 18th-century fieldstone farmhouse is one of the oldest homes in Bird-in-the-Hand. Located in the Pennsylvania Dutch Heartland, the inn is decorated for comfort with Amish influences represented throughout. There are two guest rooms with private baths and one two-room Victorian suite. Guests are invited to lounge by the pool or sit on the porch and watch the horse-drawn buggies go by. A full breakfast is served in the formal dining room, while afternoon refreshments are in the common rooms. The inn is walking distance from shops, museums, farmers market, antiques and crafts.

Historic Interest: Factory outlet shopping is available at Rockvale and Tanger.

Innkeeper(s): Vicki & Frank. $75-119. MC VISA DS PC TC. TAC10. 1 suite. Breakfast and afternoon tea included in rates. Types of meals: full breakfast and early coffee/tea. Beds: Q. Air conditioning, turndown service and ceiling fan in room. TV, swimming and library on premises. Amusement parks, antiques, parks, shopping, golf, theater and watersports nearby.

Publicity: *Country Inns, Mid-Atlantic Country, Penn Dutch Traveler.*

"Thank you for sharing your wonderful home with us. I knew this place would be perfect!"

The Village Inn of Bird-In-Hand

PO Box 253
Bird-In-Hand, PA 17505-0253
(717)293-8369 (800)914-2473 Fax:(717)768-1117
E-mail: smucker@bird-in-hand.com

Circa 1734. The history of this property dates back to the 18th century when it served as a hotel for weary guests traveling the Pennsylvania Turnpike. The original inn was destroyed

by fire in 1851 and the present, three-story hotel was built in its place. Today, guests will enjoy the inn's historic sense of ambiance and Victorian decor. Breakfasts are served on the sun porch with its paddle fans and wicker furnishings. One of the guest rooms features a working wood stove, and another room boasts a fireplace. Swimming and tennis facilities are within walking distance of the inn. The inn is adjacent to a farmers' market, country store, bakery, restaurant and several shops and outlets.

Historic Interest: The inn offers a complimentary two-hour tour of the surrounding Amish farm lands, and the Pennsylvania Dutch Convention and Visitors Bureau is only a few miles away.

Innkeeper(s): Nancy Kauffman. $79-149. MC VISA AX DS. 11 rooms with PB. 4 suites. Breakfast included in rates. Type of meal: continental-plus breakfast. Beds: KQ. Antiques nearby.

Publicity: *Country Folk Art.*

"The Village Inn offers the charm and coziness of a B&B with the privacy of a hotel."

Birdsboro   J15

Brooke Mansion Victorian Inn

Washington St
Birdsboro, PA 19508
(610)582-9775 (800)544-1094

Circa 1888. Designed by celebrated Victorian architect Frank Furness, the Brooke Mansion, a stunning Victorian, is the only B&B in the country designed by Mr. Furness, who was recently named one of the Top Ten Architects by the American Institute of Architects. It is one of those exquisite homes you might pass by and wish you could see inside. The home is a fanciful display of Victorian architecture, the first owner built it as a wedding gift for his bride. Ornate stained glass, hand-carved woodwork, a circular library and a grand staircase are among the gems guests will marvel at in this 42-

room manor. The interior includes fine antiques, some of which are family heirlooms. The area offers much to do, from antiquing to exploring Amish country. The inn is an hour's drive from Philadelphia and minutes from Reading.

Innkeeper(s): Marci & Pete Xenias. $99-135. PC TC. 4 rooms, 3 with PB. 1 suite. Breakfast included in rates. Types of meals: full breakfast and early coffee/tea. Beds: K. Air conditioning and ceiling fan in room. Library on premises. Antiques, parks, shopping, golf and theater nearby.

Publicity: *News of Southern Berks.*

Bloomsburg   G13

The Inn at Turkey Hill

991 Central Rd
Bloomsburg, PA 17815-8990
(717)387-1500 Fax:(717)784-3718

Circa 1839. Turkey Hill is an elegant, white brick farmhouse. All the guest rooms are furnished with hand-crafted reproductions from Habersham Plantation in Georgia and overlook the duck pond and gazebo. Two rooms provide wood-burning fireplaces and two-person whirlpool tubs. In the dining room are hand-painted murals of the rolling Pennsylvania countryside.

Innkeeper(s): Babs & Andrew B. Pruden. $94-185. MC VISA AX DC CB DS. 23 rooms with PB, 7 with FP. 2 conference rooms. Breakfast included in rates. Type of meal: continental breakfast. Room service available. Restaurant on premises. Beds: KQD. Fax and copier on premises. Handicap access. Antiques, fishing and theater nearby. Pets Allowed.

Location: Two miles north of Bloomsburg at Exit 35 on I-80.

Publicity: *Baltimore Sun, Tempo, Philadelphia Inquirer.*

"How nice to find an enclave of good taste and class, a special place that seems to care about such old-fashioned virtues as quality and the little details that mean so much— Art Carey, Philadelphia Inquirer."

Canadensis   F17

Brookview Manor B&B Inn

RR 1 Box 365
Canadensis, PA 18325-9740
(717)595-2451 (800)585-7974 Fax:(717)595-2065

Circa 1911. By the side of the road, hanging from a tall evergreen, is the welcoming sign to this forest retreat. There are brightly decorated common rooms and four fireplaces. The carriage house has three bedrooms and is suitable for small groups. The innkeepers like to share a "secret waterfall" within a 30-minute walk from the inn.

Historic Interest: Pocono Mountains.

Innkeeper(s): Mary Anne Buckley. $100-150. MC VISA AX DS PC TC. TAC10. 10 rooms, 9 with PB, 1 with FP. 1 suite. Breakfast and afternoon tea included in rates. Types of meals: full breakfast and early coffee/tea. Picnic lunch available. Beds: QD. Air conditioning in room. TV, fax and copier on premises. Weddings, small meetings and family reunions hosted. Amusement parks, antiques, fishing, parks, shopping, downhill skiing, cross-country skiing, theater and watersports nearby.

Location: On Rt 447, Pocono Mountains.

Publicity: *Mid-Atlantic Country, Bridal Guide.*

"Thanks for a great wedding weekend. Everything was perfect."

Pine Knob Inn

Rt 447, PO Box 295
Canadensis, PA 18325
(717)595-2532 (800)426-1460 Fax:(717)595-6429
E-mail: innkeepers @pineknobinn.com

Circa 1847. Enjoy history and the beauty of the Poconos at Pine Knob, which was built by a man who owned the largest tannery in the United States. By 1886, the sprawling Victorian became an inn, long before the area became a hot spot for vacationers. The interior is charming, filled with antiques and country furnishings, as well as Arts & Crafts-style pieces. The innkeepers' collection of birdhouses is found here and there, both inside and hanging from trees throughout the six-and-a-half-acre spread. As a true country inn, both breakfast and dinner are included in the rates. Dinner includes five courses and is served by candlelight. The Poconos offer plenty of activities for nature-lovers and shoppers alike.

Innkeeper(s): Cheryl & John Garman. $158-190. MAP. MC VISA AX DS PC TC. TAC10. 28 rooms, 19 with PB, 5 with FP. 3 cottages. 1 conference room. Breakfast and dinner included in rates. Type of meal: full breakfast. Banquet service available. Restaurant on premises. Beds: KQDT. Air conditioning and ceiling fan in room. TV, VCR, fax, copier, swimming, tennis and library on premises. Weddings, small meetings, family reunions and seminars hosted. Antiques, fishing, parks, shopping, downhill skiing, cross-country skiing, sporting events, golf, theater and watersports nearby.

Carlisle   J11

Line Limousin Farmhouse B&B

2070 Ritner Hwy
Carlisle, PA 17013-9303
(717)243-1281

Circa 1864. The grandchildren of Bob and Joan are the ninth generation of Lines to enjoy this 200-year-old homestead. A stone and brick exterior accents the farmhouse's graceful style, while inside, family heirlooms attest to the home's longevity. This is a breeding stock farm of 110 acres and the cattle raised here, Limousin, originate from the Limoges area of France. Giant maples shade the lawn and there are woods and stone fences.

Innkeeper(s): Bob & Joan Line. $65-75. PC. 4 rooms, 2 with PB. Breakfast included in rates. Type of meal: full breakfast. Beds: KQTL. Phone, air conditioning and TV in room. VCR and library on premises. 110 acres. Family reunions hosted. Amusement parks, antiques, fishing, parks, shopping, cross-country skiing, sporting events and theater nearby.

Pheasant Field B&B

150 Hickorytown Rd
Carlisle, PA 17013-9732
(717)258-0717 Fax:(717)258-0717
E-mail: pheasant@pa.net

Circa 1800. Located on eight acres of central Pennsylvania farmland, this brick, two-story Federal-style farmhouse features wooden shutters and a covered front porch. An early 19th-century stone barn is on the property, and horse boarding often is available. The Appalachian Trail is less than a mile away. Fly-fishing is popular at Yellow Breeches and Letort Spring. Dickinson College and Carlisle Fairgrounds are other points of interest.

Historic Interest: Gettysburg National Historical Park (32 miles), Molly Pitcher gravesite.

Innkeeper(s): Denise Fegan. $65-95. MC VISA AX. 4 rooms, 2 with PB. Breakfast included in rates. Types of meals: full breakfast and early coffee/tea. Beds: KQ. Air conditioning and turndown service in room. TV and VCR on premises. Weddings, small meetings and family reunions hosted. Amusement parks, antiques, fishing, downhill skiing, cross-country skiing and theater nearby.

Publicity: *Outdoor Traveler, Harrisburg Magazine.*

"You have an outstanding, charming and warm house. I felt for the first time as being home."

Churchtown   J15

Churchtown Inn B&B

2100 Main St, Rt 23
Churchtown, PA 17555-9514
(717)445-7794 Fax:(717)445-0962

Circa 1735. This handsome, stone Federal house with its panoramic views was once known as the Edward Davies Mansion, but was also once a tinsmith shop and rectory. It has heard the marching feet of Revolutionary troops and seen the Union Army during the Civil War. Tastefully furnished with antiques and collectables, the inn features canopy, pencil-post and sleigh beds. Breakfast is served in a new glass garden room. There is music everywhere, as the innkeeper directed choruses appearing at Carnegie Hall and the Lincoln Center. By prior arrangement, guests may dine in an Amish home.

Historic Interest: Located across the street from the Bangor Episcopal Church, the inn is listed in the National Register.

Innkeeper(s): Hermine & Stuart Smith, Jim Kent. $69-95. MC VISA DS PC TC. 8 rooms with PB. 1 suite. Breakfast included in rates. Type of meal: full breakfast. Beds: Q. Air conditioning and TV in room. VCR on premises. Small meetings, family reunions and seminars hosted. Antiques, fishing, parks and shopping nearby.

Location: Five miles from Pennsylvania Turnpike.

Publicity: *Bon Appetit, Boston Globe, Intelligencer Journal, Innsider, Chicago Star.*

"Magnificent atmosphere. Outstanding breakfasts. Our favorite B&B."

The Inn at Twin Linden

2092 Main St # 23
Churchtown, PA 17555-9514
(717)445-7619

Circa 1840. Named for two 100-foot-tall linden trees planted in front of it, this beautiful Greek Revival-style home stands across from a church where George Washington once worshiped. Four rooms feature canopy beds, and the Cottage Room houses an antique clawfoot tub. Elaborate breakfasts include local country sausage and freshly ground coffee, and special gourmet meals are available, prepared by innkeeper Donna Leahy. Parlors, wicker-filled porches and beautifully landscaped grounds add extra ambiance to the inn, which features afternoon tea and evening turn-down service.

Innkeeper(s): Donna & Bob Leahy. $75-100. MC VISA AX. 6 rooms with PB, 1 with FP. 1 conference room. Meals: full breakfast and gourmet breakfast. Afternoon tea available. Beds: QDT. Phone in room. Copier, spa on premises. Location: Lancaster County, PA - Dutch Country.
Publicity: *Early American Life, Los Angeles Times.*

"Your inn exceeds all others."

Clearfield   G7

Christopher Kratzer House

101 E Cherry St
Clearfield, PA 16830-2315
(814)765-5024 (888)252-2632

Circa 1840. This inn is the oldest home in town, built by a carpenter and architect who also started Clearfield's first newspaper. The innkeepers keep a book of history about the house and town for interested guests. The interior is a mix of antiques from different eras, many are family pieces. There are collections of art and musical instruments. Several guest rooms afford views of the Susquehanna River. Refreshments and a glass of wine are served in the afternoons. The inn's Bridal Suite Special includes complimentary champagne, fruit and snacks, and breakfast is served in the privacy of your room.

Innkeeper(s): Bruce & Ginny Baggett. $55-70. MC VISA DS PC TC. 4 rooms, 1 with PB. Breakfast, afternoon tea and evening snack included in rates. Types of meals: gourmet breakfast and early coffee/tea. Beds: KQT. Phone, ceiling fan and TV in room. Library on premises. Weddings, small meetings and family reunions hosted. Antiques, fishing, parks, shopping, downhill skiing, cross-country skiing, sporting events and theater nearby.

Victorian Loft B&B

216 S Front St
Clearfield, PA 16830-2218
(814)765-4805 (800)798-0456 Fax:(814)765-9596
E-mail: pdurant@csrlink.net

Circa 1894. Accommodations at this bed & breakfast are available in either a historic Victorian home on the riverfront or in a private, three-bedroom cabin. The white brick home is dressed with colorful, gingerbread trim, and inside, a grand staircase, stained glass and antique furnishings add to the Victorian charm. The suite is ideal for families as it contains two bedrooms, a living room, dining room, kitchen and a bath with a whirlpool tub. The cabin, Cedarwood Lodge, sleeps six and is located on eight, wooded acres near Elliot State Park. This is a favorite setting for small groups.

Innkeeper(s): Tim & Peggy Durant. $45-100. MC VISA AX DS PC TC. TAC10. 3 rooms, 1 with PB. 1 suite. 1 cottage. Breakfast included in rates. Types of meals: full breakfast and early coffee/tea. Beds: QD. Phone in room. TV and VCR on premises. Small meetings and family reunions hosted.

Limited Spanish spoken. Antiques, fishing, parks, shopping, cross-country skiing, sporting events, theater and watersports nearby.
Pets Allowed: By prior arrangement.

"A feeling of old-fashioned beauty. The elegance of roses and lace. All wrapped up into a romantic moment."

Columbia   K13

The Columbian

360 Chestnut St
Columbia, PA 17512-1156
(717)684-5869 (800)422-5869
E-mail: bedandb@aol.com

Circa 1897. This stately three-story mansion is a fine example of Colonial Revival architecture. Antique beds, a stained-glass window and home-baked breads are among its charms. Guests may relax on the wrap-around sun porches.

Historic Interest: The National Watch and Clock Museum (one-half block), The Wrights Ferry Mansion (4 blocks), The Bank Museum (4 blocks).
Innkeeper(s): Chris & Becky Will. $65-99. MC VISA PC TC. 5 rooms with PB, 2 with FP. 1 suite. Breakfast included in rates. Type of meal: full breakfast. Beds: QT. Air conditioning, ceiling fan and TV in room. Weddings, small meetings and family reunions hosted. Amusement parks, antiques, fishing, parks, shopping, skiing, sporting events, theater and watersports nearby.
Publicity: *Philadelphia Inquirer, Lancaster Intelligencer Journal, Columbia News, Washington Post, Potomac, Allentown Morning Call.*

"In a word, extraordinary! Truly a home away from home. First B&B experience but will definitely not be my last."

Cooksburg   F5

Gateway Lodge, Country Inn & Restaurant

Box 125, Rt 36, Cook Forest
Cooksburg, PA 16217-0125
(814)744-8017 Fax:(814)744-8017

Circa 1934. This lodge was built to accommodate visitors to Cook Forest State Park, which still today offers a multitude of outdoor activities. Guests can opt for rooms in the main lodge or choose from several cottages. The cottages, some can sleep from four to six guests, are ideal for families. Guests can opt to pay bed & breakfast rates, which include only lodging and the morning meal. Modified American Plan rates also are available, which include lodging, breakfast and a seven-course dinner at the inn's dining room. All guests of the Gateway Lodge and Country Inn enjoy afternoon refreshments. There is a heated, indoor pool and a sauna. Guest rooms are decorated in a comfortable, country style. Romantic suites with fireside Jacuzzis are available, too. The innkeepers offer several different packages, including golf and nature options.

Innkeeper(s): Joe & Linda Burney. $85-250. MAP, EP. MC VISA AX DS PC TC. 18 rooms, 3 with PB, 10 with FP. 3 suites. 7 cottages. 1 conference room. Breakfast, afternoon tea and dinner included in rates. Types of meals: full breakfast, gourmet breakfast and early coffee/tea. Picnic lunch, lunch, gourmet lunch and banquet service available. Restaurant on premises. Beds: KD. Air conditioning, turndown service and ceiling fan in room. Fax, copier, swimming, sauna and library on premises. Handicap access. 25 acres. Weddings, small meetings, family reunions and seminars hosted. Amusement parks, antiques, fishing, parks, shopping, downhill skiing, cross-country skiing, sporting events, golf, theater and watersports nearby.

Cresco   F17

Crescent Lodge

Paradise Valley, Junction 191 & 940
Cresco, PA 18326
(717)595-7486 (800)392-9400

Circa 1920. This romantic, restored inn nestled on 28 acres in
the Poconos Mountains includes 30 individually decorated
rooms that provide guests with the intimacy of a country inn
with the service and amenities of an elegant hotel. Many of the
rooms offer private sundecks, sunken Jacuzzis, country

kitchens and fireplaces. All rooms offer private baths. The
resort-like grounds feature private fitness and hiking trails, a
heated pool and tennis court. Fine dining is available daily,
except on Mondays and Tuesdays during the winter. Classical
jazz piano is offered during dinner on Saturday night..

Innkeeper(s): Dunlop Family. $70-275. EP. MC VISA AX DC DS TC. TAC10.
30 rooms with PB, 15 with FP. 1 suite. 2 conference rooms. Types of meals:
continental breakfast, continental-plus breakfast and full breakfast. Dinner
and banquet service available. Restaurant on premises. Beds: KQD. Phone,
air conditioning, ceiling fan, TV and VCR in room. Swimming and tennis on
premises. 28 acres. Weddings and small meetings hosted. Amusement parks,
antiques, fishing, parks, shopping, cross-country skiing, golf, theater and
watersports nearby.

Publicity: *Express Times, Bride's.*

*"Thank you all so much for making our wedding day truly special.
Everything was superb, the food, service and the accommodations.
Our guests truly enjoyed themselves. We look forward to future visits
to your inn."*

Dallas   F15

Ponda-Rowland B&B Inn

R R 1 Box 349
Dallas, PA 18612-9604
(717)639-3245 (800)854-3286 Fax:(717)639-5531

Circa 1850. Situated on a 130-acre farm, this historic house
overlooks a 30-acre wildlife sanctuary with six ponds, feeding sta-
tions and trails visited by whitetail deer, fox, turkeys, mallard
ducks, Canadian geese and occasionally, blue herons. The home
is filled with beautiful American country antiques and collections.
There are beamed ceilings and a stone fireplace in the living
room. The scenic setting, hospitable hosts, farm animals and
hearty country breakfast make this a perfect place for a memorable vacation. Hayrides may be arranged by advance reservations.

Historic Interest: French Azilium, farm museum, covered bridges, Steamtown
National Park.

Innkeeper(s): Jeanette & Cliff Rowland. $70-95. MC VISA AX DS PC TC.
TAC10. 5 rooms with PB, 2 with FP. Breakfast, afternoon tea and evening
snack included in rates. Types of meals: full breakfast and early coffee/tea.
Beds: KDT. Phone, air conditioning and ceiling fan in room. TV, VCR, fax,
copier, stables, library and pet boarding on premises. 130 acres. Amusement
parks, antiques, fishing, parks, shopping, downhill skiing, cross-country skiing, sporting events, theater and watersports nearby.

Pets Allowed: Not in inn or rooms.

"Warm and friendly people who made us feel right at home."

Danville   G13

The Pine Barn Inn

1 Pine Barn Pl
Danville, PA 17821-1299
(717)275-2071

Circa 1860. The inn is a restored Pennsylvania German barn.
Original stone walls and beams accent the restaurant and a
large stone fireplace warms the tavern. It is believed to be the
first all-electric residence in the state.

Innkeeper(s): Susan Dressler. $40-60. MC VISA AX DC CB DS. 75 rooms, 69
with PB. 1 conference room. Type of meal: full breakfast. Restaurant on
premises. Beds: KQDT.

*"For four years we have stayed at the Pine Barn Inn. I thought then,
and still think, it is truly the nicest inn I have been in and I've been
in many."*

Doylestown   J17

Doylestown Inn

18 W State St
Doylestown, PA 18901-4217
(215)345-6610 Fax:(215)345-4017

Circa 1902. This three-story Queen Anne Victorian inn's most distinctive feature is its tall turret. Comprised of three adjoining buildings, there are high ceilings and crown molding. The inn is reputed
to have an underground cave in the alleyway that was used for the
Underground Railroad. Monhegan Island Clam Chowder and
Salmon Napoleon with grilled eggplant and tomato fondue is a
specialty of the inn's restaurant. Jazz nights are frequent in the Tin
Tavern, and carriage rides are popular on weekends.

Innkeeper(s): Tom Weiss. $90-125. MC VISA AX DC DS. 20 rooms with PB.
1 suite. 2 conference rooms. Type of meal: early coffee/tea. Dinner, lunch,
gourmet lunch, banquet service and catering service available. Restaurant on
premises. Beds: KQD. Phone, air conditioning and TV in room. Fax and copier on premises. Handicap access. Weddings, small meetings, family reunions
and seminars hosted. Antiques, fishing, parks, shopping, cross-country skiing,
sporting events, golf and theater nearby.

Publicity: *Destination Doylestown.*

The Inn at Fordhook Farm

105 New Britain Rd
Doylestown, PA 18901-2642
(215)345-1766 Fax:(215)345-1791

Circa 1750. Three generations of Burpees (Burpee Seed
Company) have dispensed hospitality on this 60-acre farm. Guest
rooms are in the family's 18th-century fieldstone house and
Victorian carriage house. The inn is filled with family heirlooms
and guests can sit at the famous horticulturist's desk in the
secluded study where Mr. Burpee wrote his first seed catalogs.

Historic Interest: Pearl Buck Home, Moravian Tile Works, Mercer Museum.

Innkeeper(s): Carole & Jonathan Burpee. $100-300. MC VISA AX. 7 rooms,

5 with PB, 2 with FP. 1 suite. 1 conference room. Breakfast included in rates. Types of meals: continental breakfast and full breakfast. Afternoon tea available. Beds: KQDT. Phone and air conditioning in room. VCR, fax and copier on premises. 60 acres. Small meetings, family reunions and seminars hosted. Antiques, fishing, shopping, theater and watersports nearby.

Location: Bucks County.

Publicity: *Bon Appetit, Mid-Atlantic Country, Gourmet.*

"The inn is absolutely exquisite. If I had only one night to spend in Bucks County, I'd do it all over again at Fordhook Farms!"

Peace Valley B&B

75 Chapman Rd
Doylestown, PA 18901
(215)230-7711

Circa 1791. This 18th-century, stone Colonial home rests by the banks of a one-acre pond. Rooms are elegantly furnished with antiques and reproductions in traditional style. Some rooms include four-poster beds, and two have a fireplace. On weekdays, continental-plus breakfasts are served. Weekend guests enjoy a full breakfast. The bed & breakfast is adjacent to Peace Valley Park and Lake Galena, which offer nature trails.

Innkeeper(s): Harry & Jane Beard. $95-145. MC VISA AX PC TC. TAC10. 4 rooms with PB, 2 with FP. Breakfast included in rates. Types of meals: continental-plus breakfast and full breakfast. Beds: KQT. Air conditioning and turndown service in room. TV, VCR, copier, tennis and pet boarding on premises. Small meetings hosted. Antiques, parks and shopping nearby.

Sign of The Sorrel Horse

4424 Old Easton Rd
Doylestown, PA 18901-9623
(215)230-9999 Fax:(215)230-8053

Circa 1714. This inn had its humble beginnings as a grist mill on an expansive, 300-acre spread. Today, it houses five elegantly appointed guest rooms, decorated with a collection of American and European antiques. The inn maintains original beams and stone walls. Innkeeper Monique Gaumont-Lanvin, who hails from France, has added a European influence. Although she is a Cordon Bleu graduate, it is her husband, Jon Atkin, who prepares the gourmet dinners at the inn's restaurant. Guests are encouraged to make a reservation and enjoy an unforgettable meal. Entrees range from a hearty grilled rib eye steak with roasted garlic and a sauce of reduced Guinness to a San Francisco-style cioppino. The menu sometimes runs to the more exotic, with items such as kangaroo or wild boar. For a true, Epicurean delight, try the Degustation, a seven-course tasting menu. The inn is the winner of 1997 Wine Spectator Award of Excellence.

$85-175. EP. MC VISA AX DC CB PC TC. 2 suites. 2 conference rooms. Breakfast and afternoon tea included in rates. Meals: continental breakfast and continental-plus breakfast. Dinner, banquet service available. Restaurant on premises. Beds: KQD. Air conditioning and turndown service in room. Fax on premises. Handicap access. Weddings, small meetings, family reunions and seminars hosted. French, German and Russian spoken. Amusement parks, antiques, fishing, parks, shopping, downhill skiing, golf, theater nearby.

Publicity: *PBS Country Cooking with Gail Greco, Victoria, Philadelphia Daily News, Women of Taste.*

Eagles Mere   E13

Crestmont Inn

Crestmont Dr
Eagles Mere, PA 17731
(717)525-3519 (800)522-8767

Eagles Mere has been a vacation site since the late 19th century and still abounds with Victorian charm. The Crestmont Inn is no exception. The rooms are tastefully decorated with

Oriental rugs, flowers and elegant furnishings. A hearty country breakfast is served each morning, and guests also are treated to a five-course dinner in the candle-lit dining room. Savor a variety of mouth-watering entrees and finish off the evening with scrumptious desserts such as fresh fruit pies, English trifle or Orange Charlotte. The cocktail lounge is a perfect place to mingle and enjoy hors d'oeuvres, wines and spirits. The inn grounds offer a large swimming pool, tennis and shuffleboard courts. The Wyoming State Forest borders the property, and golfing is just minutes away.

Innkeeper(s): Karen Oliver. $89-148. MC VISA. 14 rooms. Breakfast included in rates. Type of meal: full breakfast.

East Berlin (Gettysburg)   K12

Bechtel Victorian Mansion B&B Inn

400 W King St
East Berlin (Gettysburg), PA 17316
(717)259-7760 (800)579-1108

Circa 1897. The town of East Berlin, near Lancaster and 18 miles east of Gettysburg, was settled by Pennsylvania Germans prior to the American Revolution. William Leas, a wealthy banker, built this many-gabled romantic Queen Anne mansion, now listed in the National Register. The inn is furnished with an abundance of museum-quality antiques and collections. Mennonite quilts top many of the handsome bedsteads.

Historic Interest: Gettysburg (18 miles).

Innkeeper(s): Ruth Spangler. $85-150. MC VISA AX DC DS PC TC. 7 rooms with PB. 2 suites. 1 conference room. Breakfast included in rates. Types of meals: full breakfast and early coffee/tea. Beds: KQD. Air conditioning in room. Library on premises. Weddings, small meetings and family reunions hosted. Antiques, shopping, skiing and theater nearby.

Location: Located 18 miles east of Gettysburg in a National Historic District.

Publicity: *Washington Post, Richmond Times.*

"Ruth was a most gracious hostess and took time to describe the history of your handsome museum-quality antiques and the special architectural details."

East Petersburg (Lancaster County) K14

The George Zahm House

6070 Main St
East Petersburg (Lancaster County), PA 17520-1266
(717)569-6026

Circa 1856. The bright red exterior of this Federal-style inn is a landmark in this village. The home is named for its builder and first resident, who constructed his sturdy dwelling with 18-inch-thick brick walls. Innkeeping is a family affair for owners Robyn Kemple-Keeports and husband, Jeff Keeports, who run the inn along with Robyn's mother, Daneen. The rooms are inviting and comfortable, yet elegant. Beautiful drapery, rich

wallpapers and a collection of antique furniture combine to give the house an opulent feel. Many of the pieces are family heirlooms. Breakfasts with homemade specialty cakes, breads, Belgian waffles and fresh fruits are served in the dining room on a table set with Blue Willow china.

Innkeeper(s): Robyn & Jeff Keeports. $65-85. MC VISA PC TC. 4 rooms, 3 with PB. 1 suite. Breakfast and afternoon tea included in rates. Type of meal: continental-plus breakfast. Beds: KQDT. Air conditioning and ceiling fan in room. Handicap access. Family reunions hosted. Amusement parks, antiques, parks, shopping, sporting events and theater nearby.

"An oasis - truly a wonderful place. Most charming."

Edinboro   D2

Raspberry House B&B

118 Erie St
Edinboro, PA 16412-2209
(814)734-8997

Circa 1867. Raspberry gingerbread trim and stained glass are whimsical features of this early Victorian home, built by a doctor just a few years after the Civil War ended. The innkeepers painstakingly restored the home, leaving many original elements, including chandeliers, pocket doors and wooden shutters. To keep the authentic Victorian flavor, reproduction wallpapers were used. Guest quarters are decorated in an eclectic style, intermingling country and modern pieces. As one might expect from the name, items such as raspberry muffins or baked apples with raspberries often find their way onto the breakfast table. Raspberry House is located in the center of downtown Edinboro and is near the university, restaurants, shopping and Edinboro Lake.

Innkeeper(s): Betty & Hal Holmstrom. $55-80. MC VISA AX PC. 4 rooms with PB. Breakfast included in rates. Types of meals: gourmet breakfast and early coffee/tea. Beds: KQDT. Air conditioning and ceiling fan in room. TV, VCR and bicycles on premises. Weddings, small meetings, family reunions and seminars hosted. Amusement parks, antiques, fishing, parks, shopping, skiing, sporting events, theater and watersports nearby.

"The Raspberry House is exceptionally high on our list of pleasing and rewarding experiences."

Elizabethtown   J13

West Ridge Guest House

1285 W Ridge Rd
Elizabethtown, PA 17022-9739
(717)367-7783 Fax:(717)367-8468

Circa 1890. Guests at this country home have many choices. They may opt to relax and enjoy the view from the gazebo, or perhaps work out in the inn's exercise room. The hot tub provides yet another soothing possibility. Ask about rooms with whirlpool tubs. The 20-acre grounds also include two fishing ponds. The innkeepers pass out a breakfast menu to their guests, allowing them to choose the time they prefer to eat and a choice of entrees. Along with the traditional fruit, muffins or coffeecake and meats, guests choose items such as omelets, waffles or pancakes.

Innkeeper(s): Alice P. Heisey. $60-120. MC VISA AX. 9 rooms with PB, 3 with FP. 2 suites. Breakfast included in rates. Type of meal: full breakfast. Beds: KQ. Phone, air conditioning, ceiling fan, TV and VCR in room. Fax, copier and spa on premises. 20 acres. Family reunions hosted. Antiques, fishing, parks and shopping nearby.

Elizabethville   I12

The Inn at Elizabethville

30 W Main St, Box V
Elizabethville, PA 17023
(717)362-3476 Fax:(717)362-4571

Circa 1883. This comfortable, two-story house was owned by a Civil War veteran and founder of a local wagon company. The innkeepers decided to buy and fix up the house to help support their other business, renovating old houses. The conference room features an unusual fireplace with cabinets and painted decorations. Rooms are filled with antiques and Mission oak-style furniture. County auctions, local craft fairs and outdoor activities entice guests. Comfortable living rooms, porches and a sun parlor are available for relaxation.

Innkeeper(s): Penny & Art Bell. $49-65. AP. MC VISA AX TC. 7 rooms with PB. 1 suite. 1 conference room. Breakfast included in rates. Type of meal: continental breakfast. Beds: DT. Air conditioning and ceiling fan in room. TV, VCR, fax and copier on premises. Weddings, small meetings, family reunions and seminars hosted. Antiques, fishing, parks, shopping, watersports nearby.
Publicity: *Harrisburg Patriot-News, Upper Dauphin Sentinel.*

Emlenton   F4

Whippletree Inn & Farm

R R 3 Box 285
Emlenton, PA 16373-9102
(412)867-9543

Circa 1905. The 100 hilltop acres of Whippletree Farm overlook the Allegheny River, and a trail on the property leads down to the river. The restored farmhouse contains many functional antiques. If you have your own horse, you are invited to use the farm's race track. The oldest continuously operated public country club in the United States is five miles away in Foxburg and the American Golf Hall of Fame is there.

Innkeeper(s): Warren & Joey Simmons. $50-60. MC VISA TC. 5 rooms, 2 with PB. Breakfast included in rates. Types of meals: full breakfast, gourmet breakfast and early coffee/tea. Afternoon tea available. Beds: KQDT. Air conditioning and ceiling fan in room. TV, VCR, copier and library on premises. 100 acres. Weddings, small meetings, family reunions and seminars hosted. Antiques, fishing, parks, shopping, golf and watersports nearby.
Pets Allowed: Horses only.

Ephrata   J14

Jacob Keller House

990 Rettew Mill Rd
Ephrata, PA 17522-1871
(717)733-4954

Circa 1814. This Federal-style limestone farmhouse features original hand-carved woodwork, rare Indian doors, corner cupboard antiques and old glass panes. An herb garden and views of the covered bridge, old mill, and barn all add to the rustic setting guests enjoy from the summer porch.

Innkeeper(s): Brenda Long. $65-85. 4 rooms. Type of meal: full breakfast. Beds: QD. Phone in room.
Publicity: *Los Angeles Times, The Post.*

"We've been to quite a few B&Bs and by far yours out ranks them all. You both are as special as the inn is. We loved the place so much we're not sure we want to share it with anyone else!"

Smithton Inn

900 W Main St
Ephrata, PA 17522
(717)733-6094

Circa 1763. Henry Miller opened this inn and tavern on a hill overlooking the Ephrata Cloister, a religious society he belonged to, known as Seventh Day Baptists. Several of their medieval-style German buildings are now a museum. This is a warm and welcoming inn with canopy or four-poster beds, candlelight, fireplaces and nightshirts provided for each guest. If you desire, ask for a lavish feather bed to be put in your room. All rooms boast sitting areas with reading lamps, fresh flowers and the relaxing sounds of chamber music. The grounds include wonderful gardens.

Historic Interest: The Ephrata Cloister Museum is only one block away.

Innkeeper(s): Dorothy Graybill. $75-170. MC VISA PC TC. 8 rooms, 7 with PB, 8 with FP. 1 suite. Breakfast and afternoon tea included in rates. Type of meal: full breakfast. Beds: KQDT. Air conditioning in room. Amusement parks, antiques, parks, shopping, golf, theater and watersports nearby.

Pets Allowed: No cats. Dogs, obedience trained, with owners at all times.

Location: Lancaster County.

Publicity: *New York, Country Living, Early American Life, Washington Post.*

"After visiting over 50 inns in four countries, Smithton has to be one of the most romantic, picturesque inns in America. I have never seen its equal!"

Erwinna   117

Golden Pheasant Inn

763 River Rd
Erwinna, PA 18920
(610)294-9595 (800)830-4474 Fax:(610)294-9882

Circa 1857. The Golden Pheasant is well established as the location of a wonderful, gourmet restaurant, but it is also home to six charming guest rooms decorated by Barbara Faure. Four-poster canopy beds and antiques decorate the rooms, which offer views of the canal and river. The fieldstone inn was built as a mulebarge stop for travelers heading down the Delaware Canal. The five-acre grounds resemble a French-country estate, and guests can enjoy the lush surroundings in a plant-filled greenhouse dining room. There are two other dining rooms, including an original fieldstone room with exposed beams and stone walls with decorative copper pots hanging here and there. The restaurant's French cuisine, prepared by chef Michel Faure, is outstanding. One might start off with Michel's special pheasant pate, followed by a savory onion soup baked with three cheeses. A mix of greens dressed in vinaigrette cleanses the palate before one samples roast duck in a luxurious raspberry, ginger and rum sauce or perhaps a sirloin steak flamed in cognac.

Innkeeper(s): Barbara & Michel Faure. $75-155. EP. MC VISA AX DC CB DS PC TC. TAC10. 6 rooms with PB. 1 suite. 1 cottage. 3 conference rooms. Breakfast included in rates. Type of meal: continental-plus breakfast. Picnic

lunch, banquet service, catering service and room service available. Restaurant on premises. Beds: QD. Air conditioning and ceiling fan in room. Fax and swimming on premises. Small meetings, family reunions and seminars hosted. French and Spanish spoken. Antiques, fishing, parks, shopping, cross-country skiing, golf, theater and watersports nearby.

Pets Allowed: Suite/cottage only.

Location: Bucks County.

Publicity: *The Philadelphia Inquirer.*

"A more stunningly romantic spot is hard to imagine. A taste of France on the banks of the Delaware."

Erwinna (Bucks County)   117

Evermay-On-The-Delaware

River Rd, PO Box 60
Erwinna (Bucks County), PA 18920
(610)294-9100 Fax:(610)294-8249

Circa 1700. Twenty-five acres of Bucks County at its best — rolling green meadows, lawns, stately maples and the silvery Delaware River, surround this three-story manor. Serving as an inn since 1871, it has hosted such guests as the Barrymore family. Rich walnut wainscoting, a grandfather clock and twin fireplaces warm the parlor, scented by vases of roses or gladiolus. Antique-filled guest rooms overlook the river or gardens.

Historic Interest: Washington Crossing State Park, Mercer Museum, Pearl S. Buck House.

Innkeeper(s): Bill & Danielle Moffly. $110-280. MC VISA PC TC. TAC10. 16 rooms with PB. 1 suite. 2 cottages. 2 conference rooms. Breakfast and afternoon tea included in rates. Type of meal: continental-plus breakfast. Dinner and picnic lunch available. Restaurant on premises. Beds: QD. Phone, air conditioning and turndown service in room. VCR, fax, copier and library on premises. Handicap access. 25 acres. Weddings, small meetings and seminars hosted. Antiques, fishing, parks, shopping, cross-country skiing, sporting events, theater and watersports nearby.

Publicity: *New York Times, Philadelphia, Travel & Leisure, Food and Wine, Child, Colonial Homes, USAir Magazine.*

"It was pure perfection. Everything from the flowers to the wonderful food."

Franklin   E3

Quo Vadis B&B

1501 Liberty St
Franklin, PA 16323-1625
(814)432-4208 (800)360-6598

Circa 1867. This three-story brick Queen Anne Victorian has a wraparound porch. Inside are parquet floors, hand-carved woodwork and friezes. The innkeepers' furnishings are family heirlooms that have been collected by four generations and include pieces from the Civil War. Guest rooms are homey with quilts and rocking chairs. The inn's spacious dining room boasts mahogany beams and wainscoting. Breakfast is likely to be waffles, eggs Benedict, or French toast.

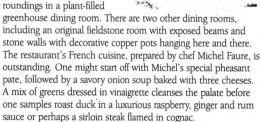

Innkeeper(s): Mela & Patrick. $60-80. MC VISA AX PC TC. TAC10. 6 rooms with PB. Breakfast included in rates. Type of meal: full breakfast. Beds: D. Air conditioning and VCR in room. TV and library on premises. Weddings, small meetings, family reunions and seminars hosted. Amusement parks, antiques, fishing, parks, shopping, cross-country skiing, sporting events, golf, theater and watersports nearby.

Gettysburg L11

Baladerry Inn at Gettysburg

40 Hospital Rd
Gettysburg, PA 17325
(717)337-1342 (800)220-0025

Circa 1812. The quiet and private setting on the edge of the Gettysburg Battlefield, this brick country manor was used as a hospital during the Civil War. Additions were added in 1830 and 1977, and the inn has been completely restored. Guests can snuggle up with a book in their comfortable rooms or in the great  room, which includes a fireplace. The spacious grounds offer gardens, a gazebo, a tennis court and terraces. Guided tours and bicycle tours of the battlefield can be arranged, and guests also can plan a horseback riding excursion on the battlefield.

Historic Interest: Gettysburg Battlefield National Park is just 100 yards from the inn. The area is full of historic sites, including the Eisenhower Farm tour.

Innkeeper(s): Tom & Caryl O'Gara. $85-120. MC VISA AX DC CB DS PC TC. TAC10. 8 rooms with PB, 2 with FP. 3 conference rooms. Breakfast and evening snack included in rates. Types of meals: full breakfast and early coffee/tea. Catering service available. Beds: KQT. Phone and air conditioning in room. TV, VCR, fax, bicycles and tennis on premises. Weddings, small meetings, family reunions, seminars hosted. Antiques, fishing, parks, shopping, downhill skiing, cross-country skiing, sporting events, golf, theater nearby.

Location: Country setting at the edge of Gettysburg Battlefield.

Publicity: *Gettysburg Times, Allentown Morning Call, Pennsylvania Magazine, US Air Magazine.*

Battlefield B&B

2264 Emmitsburg Rd
Gettysburg, PA 17325-7114
(717)334-8804 Fax:(717)334-7330

Circa 1809. Ponds, woods and streams fill the 46 acres of this historic estate. This stone farmhouse boasts four Confederate-themed guest rooms and four Union rooms. Hart's Battery provides a canopy bed and granite walls, while General Merritt's Headquarters takes up an entire floor of the Cornelius Houghtelin farmhouse and includes a fireplace and sitting room. Daily programs offer history demonstrations such as firing muskets, handling cavalry equipment, loading artillery, hearth and fireplace cookery and Civil War gaming. Battlefield stories abound and daily carriage rides are offered, weather permitting. The farm was occupied by Union cavalry and artillery units during the Battle of Gettysburg.

Innkeeper(s): Charlie & Florence Tarbox. $90-180. MC VISA AX DS PC TC. TAC10. 8 rooms with PB, 2 with FP. 2 suites. 1 cottage. 2 conference rooms. Breakfast, afternoon tea, evening snack included in rates. Meals: full breakfast and early coffee/tea. Beds: QDT. Air conditioning in room. VCR, fax, copier and library on premises. 46 acres. Weddings, small meetings, family reunions and seminars hosted. Some French and Spanish spoken. Amusement parks, antiques, fishing, parks, shopping, skiing, theater nearby.

Pets Allowed: Horses and barn cats outdoors.

Publicity: *US Air Magazine, Country Collectibles, New Jersey Monthly, USA Weekend.*

"An absolute goldmine of information in a beautiful setting."

The Brafferton Inn

44 York St
Gettysburg, PA 17325-2301
(717)337-3423

Circa 1786. Aside from its notoriety as the first deeded house in what became the town of Gettysburg, The Brafferton bears the mark of a bullet hole shot through the fireplace mantel during the Civil War battle. The rooms are filled with 18th- and 19th- century antiques that belonged to the owners' families. The dining room boasts a unique mural painted on all four walls  depicting the early town of Gettysburg. Lavish breakfasts are served in the colorful room on tables set with English china, old silver and pineapple-pattern glass goblets. Guest quarters are available in the original house or in the old carriage house across the brick atrium. Carriage house rooms feature stenciling and skylights. The garden area offers a large wooden deck to relax on as guests take in the view. The National Register inn is near to all of Gettysburg's historic attractions, including the Gettysburg National Military Park.

Historic Interest: The inn is listed in the National Register and Gettysburg, site of the Civil War's most infamous battles, offers much history.

Innkeeper(s): Jane & Sam Back. $90-125. MC VISA AX DS PC TC. TAC10. 10 rooms with PB. 2 suites. Breakfast included in rates. Types of meals: full breakfast and early coffee/tea. Beds: QDT. Air conditioning in room. TV on premises. Weddings, small meetings, family reunions hosted. French spoken. Antiques, fishing, parks, shopping, skiing, sporting events, theater nearby.

Location: Ninety miles north of Washington, D.C.

Publicity: *Early American Life, Country Living, Gettysburg Times.*

"Your house is so beautiful — every corner of it — and your friendliness is icing on the cake. It was fabulous! A wonderful historical adventure!"

Brickhouse Inn

425 Baltimore St
Gettysburg, PA 17325-2623
(717)338-9337 (800)864-3464 Fax:(717)338-9265

Circa 1898. A veranda, dressed in gingerbread trim, decorates the exterior of this red brick Victorian. The interior still maintains its original chestnut woodwork and pocket doors. Family heirlooms and antiques are featured in the guest rooms. One room offers walls in a deep burgundy hue and a bed topped with a colorful quilt. Another has a black iron bed, fine antiques and a bay window. Breakfasts, with items such as shoo-fly pie or baked French toast topped with blueberries, are served on the brick  patio, which overlooks the lawn. In the afternoons, cookies and lemonade also are served here. The home is located in Gettysburg's downtown historic district. The innkeepers keep a collection of Civil War books on hand for history buffs.

Innkeeper(s): Craig & Marion Schmitz. $85-140. MC VISA PC TC. 7 rooms with PB. Breakfast included in rates. Type of meal: full breakfast. Beds: QD. Air conditioning and ceiling fan in room. Fax and copier on premises. Amusement parks, antiques, fishing, parks, shopping, downhill skiing, cross-country skiing, sporting events and theater nearby.

"Wonderful, we loved the 19th-Century feel."

The Doubleday Inn

104 Doubleday Ave
Gettysburg, PA 17325-0815
(717)334-9119

Circa 1929. This Colonial Inn is situated directly on the Gettysburg Battlefield. From its wooded grounds, flower gardens and patios, guests enjoy panoramic views of historic Gettysburg and the National Military Park. The  innkeepers have a significant collection of Civil War relics and books on hand, and on selected evenings they feature presentations with battlefield historians. Rooms are furnished with antiques and decorated in English-country style. A full, country-style breakfast is served by candlelight each morning, and the innkeepers offer a selection of teas in the afternoon.

Historic Interest: Aside from the inn's location on the battlefield, the inn is close to the General Dwight D. Eisenhower Farm.

Innkeeper(s): Ruth Anne & Charles Wilcox. $84-109. MC VISA DS. TAC10. 9 rooms, 5 with PB. Breakfast and afternoon tea included in rates. Types of meals: full breakfast and early coffee/tea. Picnic lunch available. Beds: DT. Weddings, small meetings and family reunions hosted. Amusement parks, antiques, fishing, parks, shopping, downhill skiing, cross-country skiing, sporting events and theater nearby.

Location: On the Gettysburg Battlefield.

Publicity: *Innsider, New York, State College, Washingtonian, Potomac.*

"What you're doing for students of Gettysburg & the Civil War in general is tremendous! Our stay was wonderful!!"

The Gaslight Inn

33 E Middle St
Gettysburg, PA 17325
(717)337-9100

Circa 1872. Gas lights illuminate the brick pathways leading to this 125-year-old Italianate-style, expanded farmhouse. The inn boasts two elegant parlors separated by original pocket doors, a  spacious dining room and a first-floor guest room with wheelchair access that opens to a large, brick patio. A spiral staircase leads to the second- and third-floor guest rooms, all individually decorated in traditional and European furnishings. Some of the rooms feature covered decks, whirlpool tubs and steam showers for two. Guests are invited to enjoy a hearty or heart-healthy breakfast and inn-baked cookies and brownies and refreshments in the afternoon. The inn hosts cooking classes in its professional kitchen year-round. Weekend packages are available.

Innkeeper(s): Denis & Roberta Sullivan. $85-140. MC VISA AX DS PC TC. TAC10. 8 rooms with PB, 5 with FP. 1 conference room. Breakfast and evening snack included in rates. Types of meals: continental breakfast, gourmet breakfast and early coffee/tea. Dinner, picnic lunch, gourmet lunch, banquet service and catering service available. Restaurant on premises. Beds: KQDT. Phone, air conditioning, ceiling fan and VCR in room. TV and spa on premises. Handicap access. Weddings, small meetings, family reunions and seminars hosted. Antiques, fishing, parks, shopping, downhill skiing, cross-country skiing, golf, theater and watersports nearby.

Publicity: *Tyler Texas Times, Hanover Sun, Los Angeles Times.*

Keystone Inn B&B

231 Hanover St
Gettysburg, PA 17325-1913
(717)337-3888

Circa 1913. Furniture maker Clayton Reaser constructed this three-story brick Victorian with a wide-columned porch hugging the north and west sides.  Cut stone graces every door and window sill, each with a keystone. A chestnut staircase ascends the full three stories, and the interior is decorated with comfortable furnishings, ruffles and lace.

Historic Interest: National Military Park, Eisenhower Farm (1 mile).

Innkeeper(s): Wilmer & Doris Martin. $59-109. MC VISA DS. 5 rooms with PB. 1 suite. Breakfast and afternoon tea included in rates. Types of meals: full breakfast and early coffee/tea. Beds: KQDT. Phone and air conditioning in room. Library on premises. Family reunions hosted. Amusement parks, antiques, fishing, parks, shopping, skiing and theater nearby.

Location: Route 116 - East Gettysburg.

Publicity: *Gettysburg Times, Hanover Sun, York Sunday News, Pennsylvania, Lancaster Sunday News, Los Angeles Times.*

"We slept like lambs. This home has a warmth that is soothing."

The Old Appleford Inn

218 Carlisle St
Gettysburg, PA 17325-1305
(717)337-1711 (800)275-3373 Fax:(717)334-6228

Circa 1867. Located in the historic district, this Italianate-style brick mansion offers a taste of 19th-century charm and comfort. Among its inviting features are a plant-filled sunroom and a parlor with refurbished, 1918 grand piano. The innkeepers also display fine, linen needlework samplers and a collection of antique musical instruments. As  the inn was built just following the Civil War, the innkeepers have tried to keep a sense of turbulent history present. Most of the guest rooms are named for Civil War generals, another for Abraham Lincoln. Breakfasts are a fashionable affair served on fine china in the inn's Victorian dining room.

Innkeeper(s): John & Jane Wiley. $80-150. MC VISA AX DS PC TC. TAC10. 10 rooms with PB, 2 with FP. 1 suite. Breakfast and afternoon tea included in rates. Types of meals: full breakfast and early coffee/tea. Catering service available. Beds: QD. Air conditioning in room. Fax and library on premises. Weddings, small meetings and family reunions hosted. Amusement parks, antiques, parks, shopping, downhill skiing and theater nearby.

Location: Two blocks from downtown, near battlefield and historic attractions.

Publicity: *Innsider, Gettysburg Times, Baltimore Sun, Philadelphia Magazine.*

"Everything in your place invites us back."

Gettysburg (McKnightstown) L11

Country Escape

275 Old Rt 30, PO Box 195
Gettysburg (McKnightstown), PA 17343
(717)338-0611 Fax:(717)334-5227

Circa 1868. This country Victorian, a brick structure featuring a porch decked in gingerbread trim, rests on the route that Confederate soldiers took on their way to nearby Gettysburg. The

home itself was built just a few years after the Civil War. There are three comfortable guest rooms, decorated in country style. For an extra fee, business travelers can use the inn's typing, copying, faxing or desktop publishing services. All guests can enjoy the outdoor hot tub. There is also a children's play area outside. A traditional American breakfast is served, with such hearty items as eggs, pancakes, bacon and sausage. The inn offers close access to the famous battlefield, as well as other historic sites.

Innkeeper(s): Merry Bush & Ross Hetrick. $65-80. MC VISA AX DS PC TC. TAC10. 3 rooms, 1 with PB. Breakfast included in rates. Type of meal: full breakfast. Beds: Q. Air conditioning in room. TV, VCR, fax, copier and spa on premises. English spoken. Antiques, parks, shopping, downhill skiing, theater and watersports nearby.

Glen Riddle Lima   K17

Hamanassett B&B

PO Box 129
Glen Riddle Lima, PA 19037-0129
(610)459-3000 Fax:(610)459-3000

Circa 1856. The B&B's 48 acres offer woodlands, gardens and trails full of wildflowers, rhododendrons, azaleas and daffodils. Inside the three-story Federalist-style mansion, 2,000 books fill the library. A corner fireplace warms the formal dining room that overlooks spacious lawns and landmark trees. Two rooms, each with its own fireplace, provide separate meeting and gathering sites where tea may by served. The solarium, filled with interesting flora from October through April, is a favorite place to enjoy various refreshments. Canopied and four-poster beds are featured in the guest rooms that also include TVs and VCRs. A video tape library is available.

Historic Interest: Located near many of the Brandywine Valley attractions, including Longwood Gardens, Winterthur, Brandywine Museum (Wyeth), and Nemours. Local dining and historic restaurants are nearby.

Innkeeper(s): Evelene H. Dohan. $90-125. 8 rooms, 7 with PB. 1 suite. Breakfast and afternoon tea included in rates. Type of meal: full breakfast. Beds: KQDT. Phone and air conditioning in room. 48 acres. Weddings, small meetings and seminars hosted. Antiques, shopping, sporting events and theater nearby.

Publicity: *Philadelphia, Back Roads USA, Mid-Atlantic Country, Bed & Breakfasts and Unique Inns of Pennsylvania, Philadelphia and Its Countryside.*

"For our first try at B&B lodgings, we've probably started at the top, and nothing else will ever measure up to this. Wonderful food, wonderful home, grounds and wonderful hostess!"

Gordonville   K14

The Osceola Mill House

313 Osceola Mill Rd
Gordonville, PA 17529-9713
(717)768-3758

Circa 1766. This handsome limestone mill house rests on the banks of Pequea Creek in a quaint historic setting adjacent to a 1757 mill and a miller's cottage. There are deep-set windows and wide-pine floors. Working fireplaces in the keeping room and bedrooms add to the warmth and charm. Amish neighbors farm the picturesque fields adjoining the inn, and their horse and buggies clip-clop past the mill house often.

Innkeeper(s): Sterling & Robin Schoen. $85-130. 4 rooms, 2 with FP. Types of meals: full breakfast and gourmet breakfast. Beds: Q. Phone in room. Location: Lancaster County, 15 miles east of Lancaster.
Publicity: *The Journal, Country Living, Washington Times, Gourmet, BBC.*

"We had a thoroughly delightful stay at your inn. Probably the most comfortable overnight stay we've ever had."

Greensburg   J4

Huntland Farm B&B

R D 9, Box 21
Greensburg, PA 15601-9232
(412)834-8483 Fax:(412)838-8253

Circa 1848. Porches and flower gardens surround the three-story, columned, brick Georgian manor that presides over the inn's 100 acres. Corner bedrooms are furnished with English antiques. Fallingwater, the Frank Lloyd Wright house, is nearby. Other attractions include Hidden Valley, Ohiopyle water rafting, Bushy Run and Fort Ligonier.

Innkeeper(s): Robert & Elizabeth Weidlein. $75-85. AX PC TC. TAC10. 4 rooms, 2 with FP. Breakfast included in rates. Type of meal: full breakfast. Beds: KQDT. Ceiling fan in room. TV, VCR, fax, copier and library on premises. 100 acres. Small meetings and family reunions hosted. French spoken. Antiques, parks, shopping and theater nearby.

Mountain View Inn

1001 Village Dr
Greensburg, PA 15601-3797
(412)834-5300 (800)537-8709 Fax:(412)834-5304
E-mail: info@mountainviewinn.com

Circa 1924. The Booher family has run this inn since 1940. The inn does, in fact, offer panoramic views of the Chestnut Ridge Mountains. In addition, there are 13 acres of grounds to enjoy, featuring a gazebo, gardens and a swimming pool. There are a variety of rooms to choose from, both in newer wings and in the original 1924 portion of the inn. Several suites include fireplaces and Jacuzzi tubs. There are several different meeting and banquet rooms available, and weddings often take place around the gazebo. There is a tavern providing light, casual meals, and the Candlelight Dining Room serves more formal fare and offers a wonderful view from its picture windows. Bushy Run Battlefield, Frank Lloyd Wright's "Fallingwater," museums and shops are all nearby.

Innkeeper(s): Vance & Vicki Booher. $69-250. MC VISA AX DC CB DS TC. TAC10. 93 rooms with PB, 7 with FP. 9 suites. 4 cottages. 7 conference rooms. Breakfast included in rates. Types of meals: continental breakfast, continental-plus breakfast and full breakfast. Dinner, lunch, catering service and room service available. Restaurant on premises. Beds: KQD. Phone, air conditioning and TV in room. VCR, fax, copier and swimming on premises. Handicap access. 13 acres. Weddings, small meetings, family reunions and seminars hosted. Amusement parks, antiques, fishing, parks, shopping, cross-country skiing, sporting events, golf, theater and watersports nearby.
Publicity: *Lodging Hospitality, Islander Magazine.*

Grove City   F2

Snow Goose Inn

112 E Main St
Grove City, PA 16127
(412)458-4644 (800)317-4644

Circa 1895. This home was built as a residence for young women attending Grove City College. It was later used as a family home and offices for a local doctor. Eventually, it was transformed into an intimate bed & breakfast, offering four homey guest rooms. The interior is comfortable, decorated in country style with stenciling, collectibles and a few of the signature geese on display. Museums, shops, Amish farms and several state parks are in the vicinity, offering many activities.
Innkeeper(s): Orvil & Dorothy McMillen. $65. MC VISA. 4 rooms with PB. Breakfast and evening snack included in rates. Types of meals: continental breakfast, continental-plus breakfast, full breakfast, gourmet breakfast and early coffee/tea. Beds: QD. Phone and air conditioning in room. TV and VCR on premises. Small meetings and family reunions hosted. Amusement parks, antiques, fishing, parks, shopping, downhill skiing, cross-country skiing, sporting events, golf, theater and watersports nearby.
Publicity: *Allied News.*

"Your thoughtful touches and homey atmosphere were a balm to our chaotic lives."

Hanover   L12

Beechmont B&B Inn

315 Broadway
Hanover, PA 17331-2505
(717)632-3013 (800)553-7009

Circa 1834. This gracious Georgian inn was a witness to the Civil War's first major battle on free soil, the Battle of Hanover.

Decorated in Federal-period antiques, several guest rooms are named for the battle's commanders. The romantic Diller Suite contains a marble fireplace and queen canopy bed. The inn is noted for elegant breakfasts.

Historic Interest: Gettysburg (13 miles).
Innkeeper(s): William & Susan Day. $80-135. MC VISA AX DS PC TC. TAC10. 7 rooms with PB, 3 with FP. 3 suites. 1 conference room. Breakfast, afternoon tea and evening snack included in rates. Types of meals: full breakfast, gourmet breakfast and early coffee/tea. Picnic lunch and room service available. Beds: QD. Phone, air conditioning, ceiling fan and TV in room. Copier and library on premises. Weddings, small meetings, family reunions and seminars hosted. Amusement parks, antiques, fishing, parks, shopping, skiing, sporting events, theater and watersports nearby.
Location: Three miles from Lake Marburg.
Publicity: *Evening Sun, York Daily Record.*

"I had a marvelous time at your charming, lovely inn."

Harrisville   F3

As Thyme Goes By B&B

214 N Main St, PO Box 493
Harrisville, PA 16038
(724)735-4003
E-mail: asthymegoesby.com

Circa 1846. This country Victorian is furnished with an eclectic blend of antiques, Art Deco and Oriental decorative arts. The inn features movie memorabilia and guests can spend an evening

enjoying old films in the Bogart library or relaxing by the fire in the China Clipper parlor. Guest rooms are decorated with antique beds and offer private baths and air conditioning. A candlelight breakfast is

highlighted by the innkeeper's homemade jams. Close to factory outlet shopping, local colleges and the Old Stone House.
Innkeeper(s): Susan Haas. $50-70. PC. 3 rooms with PB. Breakfast and evening snack included in rates. Meals: full breakfast, early coffee/tea. Afternoon tea available. Beds: KQD. Air conditioning and ceiling fan in room. TV, VCR and library on premises. Weddings, small meetings, family reunions hosted. Antiques, fishing, parks, shopping, cross-country skiing, golf nearby.
Publicity: *Allied News, KDKA Pittsburgh.*

"We have been trying for years to make the time to get away for our first B&B experience and you have exceeded all of our expectations for the visit."

Hawley   E17

Academy Street B&B

528 Academy St
Hawley, PA 18428-1434
(717)226-3430 Fax:(717)226-1910

Circa 1863. This restored Civil War Victorian home boasts a mahogany front door with the original glass paneling, two large fireplaces (one in mosaic, the other in fine polished marble) and a living room with oak sideboard, polished marble mantel and yellow pine floor. The airy guest rooms have canopied brass beds. Guests are welcome to afternoon tea, which includes an array of cakes and pastries. Full, gourmet breakfasts are served on weekends.
Innkeeper(s): Judith Lazan. $65-80. MC VISA. TAC10. 7 rooms, 4 with PB. Breakfast and afternoon tea included in rates. Type of meal: early coffee/tea. Beds: QDT. Air conditioning, ceiling fan and TV in room. VCR on premises. Weddings and family reunions hosted. Amusement parks, antiques, fishing, parks, shopping, theater and watersports nearby.
Publicity: *Wayne Independent, Citizens' Voice.*

"Truly wonderful everything!"

The Falls Port Inn & Restaurant

330 Main Ave
Hawley, PA 18428
(717)226-2600

Circa 1902. Constructed by Baron von Eckelberg, this three-story grand brick Victorian is what one would expect to see in a city-center around the turn of the century. Named for its magnificent nearby water falls, guests frequent the inn for both the elegance of its rooms and the fine dining in its well-established restaurant that boasts 20-foot-high original windows. Gourmet dinners include Chicken Remi and live lobster. Guest rooms are decorated in antiques, with polished brass fixtures and elegant window treatments. The inn is a favorite for weddings, family reunions and meetings.
Innkeeper(s): Michael & Dorothy Fenn. $65-95. MC VISA AX DS TC. 12 rooms. 1 conference room. Breakfast included in rates. Type of meal: continental breakfast. Dinner, evening snack, picnic lunch, lunch, gourmet lunch and banquet service available. Restaurant on premises. Beds: QD. Air conditioning and TV in room. VCR on premises. Weddings, small meetings, family reunions and seminars hosted. Antiques, fishing, parks, shopping, downhill skiing, golf, theater and watersports nearby. Pets Allowed.

Settlers Inn at Bingham Park

4 Main Ave
Hawley, PA 18428-1114
(717)226-2993 (800)833-8527 Fax:(717)226-1874
E-mail: settler@ptdprolog.net

Circa 1927. When the Wallenpaupack Creek was dammed up to form the lake, the community hired architect Louis Welch and built this Grand Tudor Revival-style hotel featuring chestnut beams, leaded-glass windows and an enormous stone fireplace. The dining room, the main focus of the inn, is decorated with antique prints, hanging plants and chairs that once graced a Philadelphia cathedral. If you're looking for trout you can try your luck fishing the Lackawaxen River, which runs behind the inn.

Historic Interest: Zane Gray Home & Museum (15 miles), Stourbridge Lion Train (10 miles), Dorflinger Glass Museum (5 miles).

Innkeeper(s): Jeanne & Grant Genzlinger. $85-150. MC VISA AX DS PC TC. TAC10. 18 rooms with PB. 4 suites. 2 conference rooms. Breakfast included in rates. Types of meals: full breakfast and early coffee/tea. Dinner, picnic lunch, lunch, banquet service and catering service available. Restaurant on premises. Beds: QD. Phone, air conditioning and TV in room. VCR, fax, copier, tennis, library and child care on premises. Weddings, small meetings, family reunions and seminars hosted. Limited German spoken. Antiques, fishing, parks, shopping, skiing, theater and watersports nearby.

Publicity: *Philadelphia, New York Newsday, Philadelphia Inquirer, Washington Post.*

"Country cozy with food and service fit for royalty."

Hershey   J13

Gibson's B&B

141 W Caracas Ave
Hershey, PA 17033-1511
(717)534-1305

Circa 1933. Downtown Hershey is the location for this comfortable bed & breakfast. The Cape Cod-style home is simply furnished with early American, modern and country-style pieces. The innkeepers, a mother-father-son team, live in the home and enjoy chatting with guests and helping them plan daily excursions. Home-baked items on the breakfast menu vary from day to day, often including scones, biscuits, eggs and breakfast meats. It is half an hour to Lititz and Lancaster, and minutes to Hershey's attractions.

Innkeeper(s): Bob, Frances & Jamie Gibson. $40-55. PC TC. 3 rooms. Breakfast included in rates. Types of meals: full breakfast and early coffee/tea. Beds: DT. Air conditioning and ceiling fan in room. TV and VCR on premises. Italian spoken. Amusement parks, antiques, parks, shopping, sporting events, theater and watersports nearby.

"Exquisite hospitality."

Holicong   J18

Barley Sheaf Farm

5281 York Rd, Rt 202 Box 10
Holicong, PA 18928
(215)794-5104 Fax:(215)794-5332

Circa 1740. Situated on part of the original William Penn land grant, this beautiful stone house with ebony green shuttered windows and mansard roof is set on 30 acres of farmland. Once owned by noted playwright George Kaufman, it was the gathering place for the Marx Brothers, Lillian Hellman and S.J. Perlman. The bank barn, pond and majestic old trees round out a beautiful setting.

Innkeeper(s): Peter Suess. $105-235. MC VISA AX PC TC. TAC10. 12 rooms with PB, 3 with FP. 4 suites. 3 conference rooms. Breakfast and afternoon tea included in rates. Types of meals: full breakfast and early coffee/tea. Catering service available. Beds: KQD. Phone and air conditioning in room. TV, VCR, fax, copier and swimming on premises. Handicap access. 30 acres. Weddings, small meetings, family reunions and seminars hosted. German and French spoken. Amusement parks, antiques, fishing, parks, shopping, downhill skiing, cross-country skiing, theater and watersports nearby.

Location: Fifty miles north of Philadelphia in Bucks County.

Publicity: *Country Living, Romantic Inns of America, CNC Business Channel.*

Hollidaysburg   I8

Hoenstine's B&B

418 N Montgomery St
Hollidaysburg, PA 16648-1432
(814)695-0632 Fax:(814)696-7310

Circa 1839. This inn is an antique-lover's dream, as it boasts many pieces of original furniture. Stained-glass windows and the 10-foot-high ceilings add to the atmosphere. Breakfast is served in the home's formal dining room. Guests will sleep

well in the comfortable and beautifully decorated rooms, especially knowing that the house is being protected by innkeeper Barbara Hoenstine's black standard poodle, Dickens, who is a happy guide and escort around the canal-era town. The B&B is within walking distance of shops, restaurants and the downtown historic district.

Historic Interest: Horseshoe Curve (10 miles), Portage Railroad National Park (10 miles).

Innkeeper(s): Barbara Hoenstine. $50-80. MC VISA. 4 rooms, 1 with PB. Breakfast included in rates. Type of meal: full breakfast. Beds: QDT. Ceiling fan, TV and VCR in room. Copier on premises. Family reunions hosted. Amusement parks, antiques, fishing, parks, shopping, skiing, theater nearby.

"Thank you for a truly calm and quiet week. This was our first B&B experience and it won't be our last."

Honey Grove   I10

The Inn at McCullochs Mills

RR 1, Box 194
Honey Grove, PA 17035-9801
(717)734-3628 (800)377-5106

Circa 1890. Innkeepers Verne and Christine Penner spent several years restoring their inn, once home to a local millmaster. The original home burnt, and this charming 1882 Victorian was built in its place. The Penners offer a multitude of romantic amenities and extras that will make any getaway memorable. Carriage rides, moonlight sleigh rides and massages are among the

choices. One getaway package includes limousine service to a local dinner theater. Guests are pampered with gourmet breakfasts served by candlelight, afternoon tea, chocolates, fresh flowers and more. Some rooms include clawfoot or Jacuzzi tubs.

Innkeeper(s): Verne & Christine Penner. $49-79. MC VISA DS PC. TAC10. 5 rooms with PB. Breakfast, afternoon tea and evening snack included in rates. Meals: full breakfast, gourmet breakfast and early coffee/tea. Catering service available. Beds: QD. Air conditioning, turndown service, ceiling fan in room. Weddings, small meetings, family reunions and seminars hosted. Antiques, fishing, shopping, cross-country skiing, sporting events, golf, theater nearby.

Publicity: *Pennsylvania Magazine.*

"The house is a gem and has been restored to a top standard. We were so lucky to find you."

Jennerstown   J5

Olde Stagecoach B&B

1760 Lincoln Hwy (RT 30)
Jennerstown, PA 15547
(814)629-7440 Fax:(814)629-9244

Circa 1752. In the Laurel Mountains along old Route 30 is this two-story Country Victorian farmhouse. The yellow house has white trim and a wraparound porch overlooking the inn's acre. The home once served as a stagecoach stop. Blueberry French Toast is a specialty of the innkeepers as well as home-baked breads and apple pancakes. Nearby is Mountain Playhouse and NASCAR racing at the Jennerstown Speedway and three golf courses.

Innkeeper(s): Carol & George Neuhof. $65. MC VISA PC TC. 4 rooms with PB. Breakfast and evening snack included in rates. Types of meals: full breakfast and early coffee/tea. Beds: QDT. Ceiling fan in room. TV, VCR, fax and library on premises. Amusement parks, antiques, fishing, parks, shopping, downhill skiing, cross-country skiing, golf and theater nearby.

"We would recommend a visit to anyone!"

Jim Thorpe   H15

Harry Packer Mansion

Packer Hill, PO Box 458
Jim Thorpe, PA 18229
(717)325-8566

Circa 1874. This extravagant Second Empire mansion was used as the model for the haunted mansion in Disney World. It was constructed of New England sandstone, and local brick and stone trimmed in cast iron. Past ornately carved columns on the front veranda, guests enter 400-pound, solid walnut doors. The opulent interior includes marble mantels, hand-painted ceilings and elegant antiques. Murder-mystery weekends are a mansion specialty, and Victorian Balls are held in June and December.

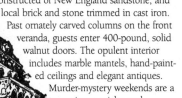

Historic Interest: National Register. In historic district.

Innkeeper(s): Robert & Patricia Handwerk. $75-150. MC VISA TC. 13 rooms, 11 with PB. 3 suites. 3 conference rooms. Breakfast included in rates. Types of meals: full breakfast, gourmet breakfast and early coffee/tea. Beds: QD. Air conditioning, turndown service and ceiling fan in room. TV and VCR on premises. Weddings, small meetings, family reunions and seminars hosted. Antiques, fishing, parks, shopping, skiing and watersports nearby.

Location: Six miles south of Exit 34 off 476.

Publicity: *Philadelphia Inquirer, New York, Victorian Homes, Washington Post..*

"What a beautiful place and your hospitality was wonderful. We will see you again soon."

The Inn at Jim Thorpe

24 Broadway
Jim Thorpe, PA 18229-2028
(717)325-2599 (800)329-2599 Fax:(717)325-9145
E-mail: innjt@ptd.net

Circa 1848. This massive New Orleans-style structure, now restored, hosted some colorful 19th-century guests, including Thomas Edison, John D. Rockefeller and Buffalo Bill. All rooms are

appointed with Victorian furnishings and have private baths with pedestal sinks and marble floors. Also on the premises are a Victorian dining room, Irish pub and a conference center. The inn is situated in the heart of Jim Thorpe, a quaint Victorian town that was known at the turn of the century as the "Switzerland of America." Historic mansion tours, museums and art galleries are nearby, and mountain biking and white-water rafting are among the outdoor activities.

Historic Interest: Switchboard Railroad, first railroad in U.S. (walking distance), Asa Packer Mansion, Millionaire's Row, Jim Thorpe final resting place (walking distance).

Innkeeper(s): David Drury. $65-250. MAP. MC VISA AX DC DS TC. TAC10. 29 rooms with PB, 5 with FP. 5 suites. 2 conference rooms. Breakfast included in rates. Type of meal: continental-plus breakfast. Dinner, lunch and room service available. Beds: KQD. Phone, air conditioning and TV in room. Fax and copier on premises. Handicap access. Weddings, small meetings, family reunions and seminars hosted. Antiques, fishing, parks, shopping, skiing, theater and watersports nearby.

Location: In the western part of the Pocono Mountains.

Publicity: *Philadelphia Inquirer, Pennsylvania, Allentown Morning Call.*

"Thank you for having provided us a relaxing getaway."

Kane   D6

Kane Manor Country Inn

230 Clay St
Kane, PA 16735-1410
(814)837-6522 Fax:(814)837-6664
E-mail: kanemanor@aol.com

Circa 1896. This Georgian Revival inn, on 250 acres of woods and trails, was built for Dr. Elizabeth Kane, the first female doctor to practice in the area. Many of the family's possessions dating back to the American Revolution and the Civil War remain. Decor is a mixture of old family items in an unpre-

tentious country style. There is a pub, popular with locals, on the premises. The building is in the National Register.

Innkeeper(s): Helen Johnson & Joyce Benek. $89-99. MC VISA AX DS PC TC. TAC5. 10 rooms, 6 with PB. Breakfast and afternoon tea included in rates. Types of meals: continental breakfast, continental-plus breakfast, full breakfast and early coffee/tea. Beds: DT. TV in room. VCR, fax, copier and library on premises. Handicap access. 250 acres. Weddings, small meetings, family reunions and seminars hosted. Antiques, fishing, parks, shopping, downhill skiing, cross-country skiing and watersports nearby.

Publicity: *Pittsburgh Press, News Herald, Cleveland Plain Dealer, Youngstown Indicator.*

"It's a place I want to return to often, for rest and relaxation."

Kennett Square L16

Meadow Spring Farm

201 E Street Rd
Kennett Square, PA 19348-1797
(610)444-3903

Circa 1836. You'll find horses grazing in the pastures at this 245-acre working farm, as well as colorful perennial flowers. The two-story, white-brick house is decorated with old family pieces and collections of whimsical animals and antique wedding gowns. A Victorian doll collection fills one room. Breakfast is hearty country style, specialties include mushroom omelets and freshly baked breads.

Afterwards, guests may gather eggs or feed rabbits and horses. Carriage rides, through the fields and back roads, are available.

Historic Interest: Longwood Gardens and the Brandywine Museum are nearby.
Innkeeper(s): Anne Hicks. $85. PC TC. TAC10. 6 rooms, 4 with PB, 2 with FP. Breakfast and afternoon tea included in rates. Types of meals: full breakfast and gourmet breakfast. Beds: QT. Air conditioning and ceiling fan in room. Spa, swimming and child care on premises. Handicap access. 245 acres. Weddings, small meetings and seminars hosted. Antiques, fishing, parks, shopping, cross-country skiing and sporting events nearby.
Location: Forty-five minutes from Philadelphia, two hours from New York.
Publicity: *Weekend GetAways, Washington Post, Country Inn.*

Scarlett House

503 W State St
Kennett Square, PA 19348-3028
(610)444-9592 (800)820-9592

Circa 1910. This stone American four-square home features an extensive wraparound porch, a front door surrounded by leaded-glass windows and magnificent chestnut woodwork. Beyond the foyer are two downstairs parlors with fireplaces, while a second-floor parlor provides a sunny setting for afternoon tea. Rooms are furnished in romantic Victorian decor with period antiques and Oriental carpets. An elegant gourmet breakfast is served with fine china, silver, crystal and lace linens. Mushroom-shaped chocolate chip scones are a novel breakfast specialty at the inn—a reminder that this is the acclaimed mushroom capital of the world.

Innkeeper(s): Jane & Sam Snyder. $85-135. MC VISA AX DS TC. 4 rooms, 2 with PB. 1 suite. 1 conference room. Breakfast, afternoon tea and evening snack included in rates. Types of meals: gourmet breakfast and early coffee/tea. Beds: QD. Phone, air conditioning and ceiling fan in room. TV on premises. Weddings, small meetings, family reunions and seminars hosted. Antiques, fishing, parks, shopping, golf, theater and watersports nearby.
Location: Located in the heart of Brandywine Valley in the historic area of the charming town of Kennett Square. Close to Longwood Gardens. Just 15 minutes to Wilmington, Del., and 30 minutes to the Philadelphia Airport.
"Truly an enchanting place."

Kennett Square (Avondale)

B&B at Walnut Hill

541 Chandler's Mill Rd
Kennett Square (Avondale), PA 19311-9625
(610)444-3703

Circa 1840. The family who built this pre-Civil War home ran a grist mill on the premises. Innkeepers Sandy and Tom Mills moved into the home as newlyweds. Today, Sandy, a former caterer, serves up gourmet breakfasts, such as cottage cheese pancakes with blueberry sauce, in the formal dining room with homemade teas, lemon butter and currant jam. Her cooking expertise was recognized in Good Housekeeping's Christmas issue. The guest rooms are cozy, welcoming and filled with antiques. One room features a Laura Ashley canopy bed. Another boasts Victorian wicker. The house overlooks horses grazing in a meadow, and a nearby creek is visited by Canadian geese, deer and an occasional fox.

Historic Interest: Winterthur Museum, Brandywine Battlefield, Museum of Natural History, Longwood Gardens, Brandywine River Museum.
Innkeeper(s): Tom & Sandy Mills. $70-85. PC TC. TAC10. 2 rooms. Breakfast and evening snack included in rates. Type of meal: gourmet breakfast. Beds: KDT. Air conditioning, turndown service and TV in room. VCR, copier and spa on premises. Family reunions hosted. Limited Spanish and French spoken. Parks, shopping and golf nearby.
Publicity: *Times Record, Suburban Advertiser, Four Seasons of Chester County, Country Inns, Good Housekeeping, Country Magazine.*
"The only thing left to do is move in. We came as strangers, left as friends."

Knox F4

Mitchell Ponds Inne

RR 1, Box 124B
Knox, PA 16232-9801
(814)797-1690

Circa 1880. This quaint restored Victorian farmhouse situated on 60 acres of lush grounds and manicured gardens offers the perfect setting for a romantic holiday. Besides the beautifully renovated guest rooms, there is a rustic pool house equipped with a work-out room, whirlpool spa, separate living area, an outdoor pool and pool house. The grounds also feature a fishing pond and a classic red barn. Guests are offered a gourmet breakfast served in the dining room or an in-room continental breakfast. An elegant gourmet dinner is offered with 24-hour reservations. Picnic lunches are also available. Close to antiques, horse riding and golf.

Innkeeper(s): Mary Ann Moulin. $100. PC. TAC10. 5 rooms with PB, 1 with FP. 4 suites. 1 conference room. Breakfast included in rates. Types of meals: gourmet breakfast and early coffee/tea. Picnic lunch, lunch and room service available. Beds: Q. Air conditioning, TV and VCR in room. Copier, spa, swimming, sauna and library on premises. 60 acres. Weddings, small meetings, family reunions and seminars hosted. Antiques, fishing, parks, cross-country skiing and golf nearby.
Publicity: *Pittsburgh Post-Gazette.*

Lackawaxen E18

Roebling Inn on The Delaware

Scenic Dr, PO Box 31
Lackawaxen, PA 18435-0031
(717)685-7900 Fax:(717)685-1718

Circa 1870. This Greek Revival house is in the National Register of Historic Places and once was the home of Judge Ridgway, tallyman for the Delaware and Hudson Canal Company. Country furnishings are supplemented with some antiques, and

there is a long front porch for relaxing. The sitting room features a cozy fireplace. Full country breakfasts are provided. Afterward, ask the innkeepers for directions to nearby hidden waterfalls, or walk to the Zane Grey Museum, Roebling's Delaware Aqueduct or Minisink Battleground Park.

Innkeeper(s): Don & JoAnn Jahn. $75-105. MC VISA AX DS TC. 5 rooms with PB. 1 cottage. Breakfast included in rates. Type of meal: full breakfast. Beds: QDT. Air conditioning, ceiling fan and TV in room. Fax on premises. Antiques, fishing, parks, downhill skiing, cross-country skiing, theater and watersports nearby.

Publicity: *New York Magazine.*

Lampeter   K14

The Australian Walkabout Inn

837 Village Rd, PO Box 294
Lampeter, PA 17537-0294
(717)464-0707 Fax:(717)464-2501

Circa 1925. This inn offers hospitality Australian-style thanks to Australian Richard Mason, one of the innkeepers. Tea is imported from down under and breakfasts are prepared from Australian

recipes. The inn, situated on beautifully landscaped grounds with an English garden and a lily pond, features a wraparound porch, where guests can watch Amish buggies pass by. Bedchambers have antique furniture, Pennsylvania

Dutch quilts and hand-painted wall stencilings. Each room is named from the image stenciled on its walls.

Historic Interest: The historic 1719 Hans Herr House is just one mile away.

Innkeeper(s): Richard & Margaret Mason. $99-199. MC VISA AX PC TC. TAC5. 5 rooms with PB, 5 with FP. 3 suites. 1 cottage. Breakfast included in rates. Type of meal: gourmet breakfast. Beds: QT. Air conditioning, turndown service and TV in room. VCR, fax, copier, spa, bicycles and library on premises. Family reunions hosted. Limited Spanish spoken. Amusement parks, antiques, parks, shopping, sporting events and theater nearby.

Publicity: *New York Post, Intelligencer Journal, Holiday Travel.*

"The Walkabout Inn itself & its surroundings are truly relaxing, romantic, & quaint. It's the kind of place that both of us wanted & pictured in our minds, even before we decided to make reservations."

Lancaster   K14

Gardens of Eden

1894 Eden Rd
Lancaster, PA 17601-5526
(717)393-5179 Fax:(717)393-7722

Circa 1867. Wildflowers, perennials and wooded trails cover the three-and-a-half-acre grounds surrounding Gardens of Eden. The home, which overlooks the Conestoga River, is an example of late Federal-style architecture with some early

Victorian touches. The innkeepers have won awards for their restoration. Their guest cottage was featured on the cover of a decorating book. The interior, laced with dried flowers, handmade quilts,

baskets and country furnishings, has the feel of a garden cottage. This cottage is ideal for families and includes a working fireplace and an efficiency kitchen. Gardens of Eden is within minutes of downtown Lancaster. The innkeepers can arrange for personalized tours of Amish and Mennonite communities and sometimes a dinner in an Amish home.

Innkeeper(s): Marilyn & Bill Ebel. $85-130. MC VISA PC TC. 3 rooms with PB. 1 cottage. Breakfast included in rates. Type of meal: full breakfast. Afternoon tea available. Beds: KQD. Phone, air conditioning and turndown service in room. TV, VCR, fax and copier on premises. Small meetings and family reunions hosted. Limited French spoken. Amusement parks, antiques, fishing, shopping, cross-country skiing and theater nearby.

Hollinger House

2336 Hollinger Rd
Lancaster, PA 17602-4728
(717)464-3050

Circa 1870. A peach bottom slate roof tops this large Adams-style brick house, and there is a wraparound veranda and a double balcony. Several fireplaces and original hardwood floors have been restored. A meadow and woodland stream add to the setting's pastoral beauty. The innkeepers serve goodies at bedtime, and in the morning, a bountiful breakfast is provided.

Innkeeper(s): Gina Trost. $95-105. PC TC. 5 rooms with PB. Evening snack, picnic lunch and catering service available. Air conditioning in room. TV and VCR on premises. Weddings, small meetings, family reunions and seminars hosted. Amusement parks, antiques, shopping, cross-country skiing, sporting events and theater nearby.

The King's Cottage, A B&B Inn

1049 E King St
Lancaster, PA 17602-3231
(717)397-1017 (800)747-8717 Fax:(717)397-3447

Circa 1913. This Mission Revival house features a red-tile roof and stucco walls, common in many stately turn-of-the-century houses in California and New Mexico. Its elegant interiors include a sweeping staircase, a library with marble fireplace, stained-glass windows and a solarium. The inn is appointed with Oriental rugs and antiques and fine 18th-century English reproductions. The Carriage House features the same lovely furnishings with the addition of a Jacuzzi. The formal dining room provides the location for gourmet morning meals.

Historic Interest: Landis Valley Farm Museum (5 miles), Railroad Museum of Pennsylvania (8 miles), Hans Herr House (5 miles).

Innkeeper(s): Karen Owens. $100-175. MC VISA DC DS. 9 rooms with PB. 1 conference room. Breakfast and afternoon tea included in rates. Type of meal: full breakfast. Beds: KQ. Phone and turndown service in room. TV on premises. Small meetings, family reunions and seminars hosted. Amusement parks, antiques, fishing, shopping, cross-country skiing, sporting events and theater nearby.

Location: Pennsylvania Dutch country.

Publicity: *Country, USA Weekend, Bon Appetit, Intelligencer Journal, Times.*

"I appreciate your attention to all our needs and look forward to recommending your inn to friends."

New Life Homestead B&B

1400 E King St, Rt 462
Lancaster, PA 17602-3240
(717)396-8928

Circa 1912. This two-and-a-half story brick home is situated within one mile of Amish Farms, and it's less than two miles from the City of Lancaster. Innkeepers Carol and Bill Giersch, both Mennonites, host evening discussions about the culture and history of Amish and Mennonite people. Carol's home-made breakfasts are made with local produce.

Innkeeper(s): Carol Giersch. $60-80. 3 rooms, 2 with PB. 1 suite. Breakfast included in rates. Type of meal: full breakfast. Evening snack available. Beds: QDT. Phone in room. Small meetings and family reunions hosted. Amusement parks, antiques, fishing, shopping, sporting events and theater nearby.

Location: In the heart of Pennsylvania Dutch country.

Publicity: *Keystone Gazette, Pennsylvania Dutch Traveler.*

"Reminded me of my childhood at home."

O'Flaherty's Dingeldein House B&B

1105 E King St
Lancaster, PA 17602-3233
(717)293-1723 (800)779-7765 Fax:(717)293-1947

Circa 1910. This Dutch Colonial home was once residence to the Armstrong family, who acquired fame and fortune in the tile floor industry. Springtime guests will brighten at the sight of this home's beautiful flowers. During winter months, innkeepers Jack and Sue Flatley deck the halls with plenty of seasonal decorations. The hearty country breakfast might include fresh-baked muffins, fruits, the innkeepers' special blend of coffee and mouth-watering omelets, pancakes or French toast. Cozy rooms include comfortable furnishings and cheery wall coverings. The innkeepers can arrange for guests to enjoy dinner at the home of one of their Amish friends.

Historic Interest: Lancaster offers several nearby historic sites and museums.
Innkeeper(s): Jack & Sue Flatley. $80-100. MC VISA DS PC TC. 4 rooms with PB. 1 suite. Breakfast included in rates. Types of meals: full breakfast, gourmet breakfast and early coffee/tea. Beds: KQDT. Air conditioning and ceiling fan in room. TV, VCR, fax, copier and library on premises. Family reunions hosted. Amusement parks, antiques, fishing, parks, shopping, sporting events and theater nearby.

Location: 1 mile from downtown, 10 minutes from heart of Amish Country.

Publicity: *Gourmet.*

"You made our visit here very pleasant, your hospitality is what makes the stay here so wonderful."

Witmer's Tavern - Historic 1725 Inn & Museum

2014 Old Philadelphia Pike
Lancaster, PA 17602-3413
(717)299-5305

Circa 1725. This pre-Revolutionary War inn is the oldest and most complete Pennsylvania inn still lodging travelers in its original building. Designated a National Landmark, the property has been restored to its original, pioneer style with hand-fashioned hardware "bubbly" glass nine-over-six windows. Guest rooms feature antiques, fresh flowers, antique quilts and original woodburning fireplaces.

Revolutionary and Colonial dignitaries like Washington, Lafayette, Jefferson and Adams were entertained here. The Witmers provisioned hundreds of immigrants as they set off in Conestoga Wagon trains for western and southern homestead regions.

Historic Interest: Hans Herr House, Rockford Plantation, President Buchanan's House, Ephrata Cloister, Amish farms and villages are among the historic sites. Witmer's Heritage Tours provide interesting insight into Lancaster County.

Innkeeper(s): Brant Hartung. $60-90. PC. TAC10. 7 rooms, 2 with PB, 7 with FP. Breakfast included in rates. Type of meal: continental-plus breakfast. Beds: D. Air conditioning in room. Small meetings, family reunions and seminars hosted. Amusement parks, antiques, fishing, parks, shopping, downhill skiing, cross-country skiing, sporting events, theater and watersports nearby.

Location: One mile east of Lancaster on Route 340.

Publicity: *Stuart News, Pennsylvania, Antique, Travel & Leisure, Mid-Atlantic, Country Living, Early American Life, Colonial Homes, USA Today.*

"Your personal attention and enthusiastic knowledge of the area and Witmer's history made it come alive and gave us the good feelings we came looking for."

Landenberg   L15

Cornerstone B&B Inn

300 Buttonwood Rd
Landenberg, PA 19350-9398
(610)274-2143 Fax:(610)274-0734

Circa 1704. The Cornerstone is a fine 18th-century country manor house filled with antique furnishings. Two fireplaces make the parlor inviting. Wing chairs, fresh flowers and working fireplaces add enjoyment to the guest rooms. Perennial gardens, a water garden and swimming pool with hot tub are additional amenities.

Historic Interest: Brandywine River Museum, Brandywine Battlefield State Park, Franklin Mint, Valley Forge National Historical Park, Longwood Gardens, Winterthur Museum.

Innkeeper(s): Linda Chamberlin & Marty Mulligan. $75-150. MC VISA DS PC TC. TAC10. 7 rooms with PB, 5 with FP. 1 suite. 6 cottages. Breakfast included in rates. Types of meals: full breakfast and early coffee/tea. Beds: KQT. Air conditioning and TV in room. VCR, fax, spa and swimming on premises. Small meetings and family reunions hosted. Amusement parks, antiques, parks, shopping, sporting events and theater nearby.

Lititz   J14

The Alden House

62 E Main St
Lititz, PA 17543-1947
(717)627-3363 (800)584-0753
E-mail: aldenbb@ptdprolog.net

Circa 1850. For more than 200 years, breezes have carried the sound of church bells to the stately brick homes lining Main Street. The Alden House is a brick Victorian in the center of this historic district and within walking distance of the Pretzel House (first in the country) and the chocolate factory. A favorite room is the suite with a loft dressing room and private bath. A full breakfast is served, often carried to one of the inn's three porches.

Innkeeper(s): Fletcher & Joy Coleman. $85-120. MC VISA PC. TAC10. 5 rooms with PB, 1 with FP. 3 suites. Breakfast included in rates. Type of meal: full breakfast. Beds: QD. Air conditioning, ceiling fan and TV in room. Small meetings hosted. Amusement parks, antiques, fishing, parks, shopping and theater nearby.

Location: Seven miles North of Lancaster.

Publicity: *Connecticut Post, Pittsburgh Post-Gazette, Travel Holiday, Rockland Journal News, Penn Dutch Traveler, Now in Lancaster County, Philadelphia Inquirer.*

"Truly represents what bed & breakfast hospitality is all about. You are special innkeepers. Thanks for caring so much about your guests. It's like being home."

General Sutter Inn

14 E Main St
Lititz, PA 17543-1927
(717)626-2115 (717)626-2115 Fax:(717)626-0992
E-mail: brophyinn@aol

Circa 1764. Built by the Moravian Church, the inn is considered the oldest continuously operating inn in Pennsylvania. Shaded now by tall trees, the inn's three-story brick facade is warmed by a white solarium with Paladian windows. There are

banquet rooms, two restaurants and a tavern. The decor is colonial. With its central location, the inn marks the beginning of the town's historic walking tour. The Wilbur Chocolate Candy Museum, Sturgis Pretzel House and Lititz Springs Park are close.

Innkeeper(s): Ed & Dolores Brophy. $75-105. EP. MC VISA AX DS PC TC. 16 rooms, 14 with PB. 4 suites. 2 conference rooms. Types of meals: continental breakfast and full breakfast. Dinner, lunch, banquet service, catering service and catered breakfast available. Restaurant on premises. Beds: DT. Phone, air conditioning and TV in room. Fax, library on premises. Weddings, small meetings, family reunions, seminars hosted. Amusement parks, antiques, fishing, parks, shopping, sporting events, golf, theater nearby.

Pets Allowed.

Publicity: *Washington Post, Philadelphia Enquirer.*

Manheim   J14

Penn's Valley Farm & Inn

6182 Metzler Rd
Manheim, PA 17545-8629
(717)898-7386

Circa 1826. This picture-perfect farm was purchased by the Metzler's ancestors in 1770, but it was originally owned by the three Penn brothers. The guest house, built in 1826, features stenciled farm animals painted
along the winding stairway that leads to the bedrooms. An open hearth is in the living room. Breakfast is served in the dining room of the main farmhouse.

Innkeeper(s): Melvin & Gladys Metzler. Call for rates. MC VISA. Types of meals: continental breakfast and full breakfast. Air conditioning in room. 64 acres. Amusement parks, antiques and shopping nearby.

Rose Manor B&B and Herbal Gift Shop

124 S Linden St
Manheim, PA 17545
(717)664-4932 (800)666-4932 Fax:(717)664-1611

Circa 1905. A local mill owner built this Spanish-style home, and it still maintains original light fixtures, woodwork and cabinetry. The grounds are decorated with roses and herb gardens. An herb theme is played out in the guest rooms, which feature names such as the Parsley, Sage, Rosemary and Thyme rooms. The fifth room is named the Basil, and its spacious quarters encompass the third story and feature the roof's angled ceiling. The decor is a comfortable Victorian style with some antiques. The innkeepers host many tea parties, and there is a gift shop on the premises. The inn's location provides close access to many Pennsylvania Dutch country attractions.

Innkeeper(s): Susan & Anne Jenal. $70-115. MC VISA PC. TAC10. 5 rooms, 3 with PB. Breakfast included in rates. Type of meal: full breakfast. Afternoon tea and picnic lunch available. Beds: QTD. Air conditioning, ceiling fan and TV in room. Fax, copier and library on premises. Family reunions hosted. Amusement parks, antiques, fishing, parks, shopping and theater nearby.

Publicity: *Lancaster County.*

"The atmosphere was so restful, the room was lovely and the hospitality was warm & generous. The table setting and breakfast was delicious to look at as well as consume."

Marietta   K13

Railroad House Restaurant B&B

280 W Front St
Marietta, PA 17547-1405
(717)426-4141

Circa 1820. The Railroad House, a sprawling old hotel, conjures up memories of the days when riding the rail was the way to travel. The house was built as a refuge for weary men who were working along the Susquehanna River. When the railroad finally made its way through Marietta, the rail station's waiting room and ticket office were located in what's now known as the Railroad House. The restored rooms feature
antiques, Oriental rugs, Victorian decor and rustic touches such as exposed brick walls. The chefs at the inn's restaurant create a menu of American and continental dishes using spices and produce from the beautifully restored gardens. The innovative recipes have been featured in Bon Appetit. The innkeepers also host a variety of special events and weekends, including murder mysteries and clambakes serenaded by jazz bands. Carriage rides and special walking tours of Marietta can be arranged.

Historic Interest: Wheatland, the home of President Buchanan, is 15 minutes from the Railroad House. The John Wright and Haldeman mansions are just 10 minutes away, and the Old Town Hall is a few blocks from the inn.

Innkeeper(s): Richard & Donna Chambers. $79-99. MC VISA TC. 10 rooms, 8 with PB. 1 cottage. 1 conference room. Breakfast included in rates. Types of meals: full breakfast, gourmet breakfast and early coffee/tea. Afternoon tea, dinner, evening snack, picnic lunch, lunch, gourmet lunch, banquet service, catering service and catered breakfast available. Restaurant on premises. Beds: QDT. Air conditioning in room. Copier and bicycles on premises. Weddings, small meetings, family reunions and seminars hosted. Spanish and French spoken. Amusement parks, antiques, fishing, parks, shopping, downhill skiing, sporting events, theater and watersports nearby.

River Inn

258 W Front St
Marietta, PA 17547-1405
(717)426-2290 (888)824-6622 Fax:(717)426-2966

Circa 1790. This Colonial has more than 200 years of history within its walls. The home is listed in the National Register and located in Marietta's historic district. Herb and flower gardens decorate the grounds. Relaxing in front of a fireplace is an easy task since the inn offers six, one of which resides in a guest room. Colonial decor and antiques permeate the interior. The inn is within walking distance to the Susquehanna River.

Innkeeper(s): Joyce & Bob Heiserman. $60-80. MC VISA DC CB DS PC TC. TAC10. 3 rooms with PB, 1 with FP. Breakfast included in rates. Types of meals: full breakfast and early coffee/tea. Picnic lunch available. Beds: QT. Air conditioning in room. TV, bicycles and library on premises. Weddings hosted. Amusement parks, antiques, fishing, parks, shopping, theater and watersports nearby.

Mercer   F2

The Magoffin Inn

129 S Pitt St
Mercer, PA 16137-1211
(412)662-4611 (800)841-0824

Circa 1884. Dr. Magoffin built this house for his Pittsburgh bride, Henrietta Bouvard. The Queen Anne style is characterized by patterned brick masonry, gable detailing, bay windows and a wraparound porch. The technique of marbleizing was used on six of the nine fireplaces. Magoffin Muffins are featured each morning. Dinner is available Friday and Saturday.

Innkeeper(s): Jacque McClelland. $115-125. MC VISA AX PC TC. 6 rooms, 5 with PB, 5 with FP. 1 suite. Breakfast and evening snack included in rates. Meals: full breakfast and early coffee/tea. Dinner available. Restaurant on premises. Beds: QD. Air conditioning and TV in room. Weddings, small meetings, seminars hosted. Antiques, parks and shopping nearby.

Location: Near I-79 and I-80.

Publicity: *Western Reserve, Youngstown Vindicator.*

"While in Arizona we met a family from Africa who had stopped at the Magoffin House. After crossing the United States they said the Magoffin House was quite the nicest place they had stayed."

Mercersburg   L9

The Mercersburg Inn

405 S Main St
Mercersburg, PA 17236-9517
(717)328-5231 Fax:(717)328-3403

Circa 1909. Situated on a hill overlooking the Tuscorora Mountains, the valley and village, this 20,000-square-foot Georgian Revival mansion was built for industrialist Harry Byron. Six massive columns mark the entrance, which opens to a majestic hall featuring chestnut wainscoting and an elegant double stairway and rare scagliola (marbleized) columns. All the rooms are furnished with antiques and reproductions. A local craftsman built the inn's four-poster, canopied king-size beds. Many of the rooms have their own balconies and a few have fireplaces. During the weekends, the inn's chef prepares noteworthy, elegant five-course dinners, which feature an array of seasonal specialties.

Historic Interest: Gettysburg, Harpers Ferry, Antietam, James Buchanan's birthplace are less than one hour from the inn.

Innkeeper(s): Walt & Sandy Filkowski. $115-225. MC VISA DS. 15 rooms with PB, 3 with FP. 1 conference room. Breakfast included in rates. Types of meals: full breakfast and gourmet breakfast. Picnic lunch and banquet service available. Restaurant on premises. Beds: KQT. Phone and air conditioning in room. TV, VCR and bicycles on premises. Weddings, small meetings, family reunions and seminars hosted. Antiques, fishing, shopping, downhill skiing, cross-country skiing, golf, theater and watersports nearby.

Publicity: *Mid-Atlantic Country, Washington Post, The Herald-Mail, Richmond News Leader, Washingtonian, Philadelphia Inquirer, Pittsburgh.*

"Elegance personified! Outstanding ambiance and warm hospitality."

The Steiger House

33 N Main St
Mercersburg, PA 17236-1619
(717)328-5757 Fax:(717)328-5627
E-mail: steiger@mail.cvn.net

Circa 1820. This white Federal house, located directly in the town's historic district, boasts green shutters and a front porch. The parlor features a fireplace with a carved mantel painted white, a soft teal striped wallpaper and an Oriental rug. Guest rooms have eclectic furnishings such as early American maple beds, a French provincial vanity and contemporary dressers set against patterned wallpapers. Civil War battlefields (Antietam and Gettysburg) are within an hour's drive or visit Cowans Gap State Park, the C&O Canal or ski Whitetail.

Innkeeper(s): Ron & Nancy Snyder. $75-110. MC VISA AX DS PC TC. 6 rooms, 1 with PB. 2 suites. Breakfast and evening snack included in rates. Type of meal: full breakfast. Beds: QD. Air conditioning in room. TV, VCR, fax and copier on premises. Antiques, fishing, parks, downhill skiing, golf nearby.

"Our stay was very short and very sweet. Wish we could be here longer."

Mertztown   I16

Longswamp B&B

1605 State St
Mertztown, PA 19539-8912
(610)682-6197 Fax:(610)682-4854

Circa 1789. Country gentleman Colonel Trexler added a mansard roof to this stately Federal mansion in 1860. Inside is a magnificent walnut staircase and pegged wood floors. As the story goes, the colonel discovered his unmarried daughter having an affair and shot her lover. He escaped hanging, but it was said that after his death his ghost could be seen in the upstairs bedroom watching the road. In 1905, an exorcism was reported to have sent his spirit to a nearby mountaintop.

Innkeeper(s): Elsa Dimick. $83-88. MC VISA AX. 10 rooms, 6 with PB, 2 with FP. 2 suites. Breakfast and afternoon tea included in rates. Types of meals: full breakfast, gourmet breakfast and early coffee/tea. Picnic lunch and catering service available. Beds: QT. Phone, air conditioning and ceiling fan in room. TV, VCR and bicycles on premises. Weddings, small meetings, family reunions and seminars hosted. Antiques, fishing, shopping, cross-country skiing and sporting events nearby.

Publicity: *Washingtonian, Weekend Travel, The Sun.*

"The warm country atmosphere turns strangers into friends."

Milford
F18

Black Walnut Inn

RR 2 Box 9285
Milford, PA 18337-9802
(717)296-6322

Circa 1940. Situated on more than 150 wooded acres, it's hard to imagine that this rustic English Tudor-style inn is less than two hours away from Manhattan. The woods, fields and three-acre lake offer guests a variety of on-site activities like picking fresh berries, fishing for bass in the natural lake or mountain biking on endless trails. The guest rooms are all furnished with brass and antique beds and country antiques. After a day of activities, guest can relax in front of the historic European fireplace or enjoy a drink while viewing the lake. Guests begin their day with a hearty breakfast of eggs, potatoes, hot cakes, French toast, breakfast meats and breads. The inn is often used for weddings, meetings and family reunions. Antique shopping, flea markets, museums, restaurants, horseback riding and canoeing down the Delaware are nearby.

Historic Interest: Located near Grey Towers National Historic Landmark, the Appalachian Trail and High Point Monument.

Innkeeper(s): Marge Stewart. Call for rates. MC VISA AX DS. 9 rooms, 4 with PB. 1 cabin. Breakfast included in rates. Types of meals: full breakfast and early coffee/tea. Afternoon tea available. Beds: QD. Ceiling fan in room. TV, VCR and swimming on premises. 160 acres. Weddings, small meetings and family reunions hosted. Spanish spoken. Antiques, fishing, shopping, golf and watersports nearby.

Cliff Park Inn & Golf Course

155 Cliff Park Rd
Milford, PA 18337-9708
(717)296-6491 (800)225-6535 Fax:(717)296-3982

Circa 1820. This historic country inn is located on a 600-acre family estate, bordering the Delaware River. It has been in the Buchanan family since 1820. Rooms are spacious with individual climate control, telephone and Victorian-style furnishings. Cliff Park features both a full-service restaurant and golf school. The inn's golf course, established in 1913, is one of the oldest in the United States. Cliff Park's picturesque setting is popular for country weddings and private business conferences. Both B&B or MAP plans are offered.

Historic Interest: Grey Towers National Landmark (2 miles).

Innkeeper(s): Harry W. Buchanan III. $93-160. MAP, AP, EP. MC VISA AX DC CB DS. 18 rooms with PB. 1 conference room. Breakfast included in rates. Type of meal: full breakfast. Dinner, picnic lunch and lunch available. Restaurant on premises. Beds: KQDT. Fax on premises. Handicap access. Cross-country skiing and watersports nearby.

Location: In the foothills of the Pocono Mountains on the Delaware River.

"Cliff Park Inn is the sort of inn I look for in the English countryside. It has that authentic charm that comes from History."

Mount Gretna
J13

Mount Gretna Inn

16 Kauffman Ave
Mount Gretna, PA 17064
(717)964-3234 (800)277-6602 Fax:(717)964-3641

Circa 1921. This original Arts & Crafts-style home is set in the wooded mountains of historic Mt. Gretna, located conveniently close to a unique variety of attractions such as a lake, stream,

cross-country skiing and miles of trails for mountain biking and hiking. Each of the inn's eight guest rooms features a sampling of antiques purchased by the innkeeper at local auctions. All rooms offer private baths, while some feature a private porch or gas fireplace. Breakfast fare includes baked peaches, egg puff, sausage, homemade coffee cakes and muffins.

Historic Interest: Within 30 minutes of antique shops, famous outlet malls in Reading and Lancaster, Amish Pennsylvania-Dutch Country, Cornwall Furnace, Hershey and the Pennsylvania Renaissance Festival.

Innkeeper(s): Keith & Robin Volker. $85-115. MC VISA AX PC TC. TAC10. 8 rooms with PB, 2 with FP. 1 conference room. Breakfast included in rates. Types of meals: full breakfast and early coffee/tea. Beds: Q. Air conditioning and ceiling fan in room. Fax and bicycles on premises. Weddings, small meetings, family reunions and seminars hosted. Amusement parks, antiques, fishing, parks, shopping, cross-country skiing, golf and theater nearby.

Publicity: *Daily News, Morning Call, Sunday Patriot-News, Bride's Guide.*

"What a wonderful respite from this '90s hustle and bustle world. Quite like visiting an earlier time."

Mount Joy
K13

Cedar Hill Farm

305 Longenecker Rd
Mount Joy, PA 17552-8404
(717)653-4655

Circa 1817. Situated on 51 acres overlooking Chiques Creek, this stone farmhouse boasts a two-tiered front veranda affording pastoral views of the surrounding fields. The host was born in the house and is the third generation to have lived here since the Swarr family first purchased it in 1878. Family heirlooms and antiques include an elaborately carved walnut bedstead, a marble-topped washstand and a "tumbling block" quilt. In the kitchen, a copper kettle, bread paddle and baskets of dried herbs accentuate the walk-in fireplace, where guests often linger over breakfast. Cedar Hill is a working poultry and grain farm.

Innkeeper(s): Russel & Gladys Swarr. $65-80. MC VISA AX DS TC. 5 rooms with PB. Breakfast included in rates. Types of meals: continental-plus breakfast and early coffee/tea. Beds: KQDT. Phone and air conditioning in room. VCR on premises. 51 acres. Small meetings and family reunions hosted. Amusement parks, antiques, fishing, parks, shopping, cross-country skiing, sporting events, theater and watersports nearby.

Location: Midway between Lancaster and Hershey.

Publicity: *Women's World, Lancaster Farming, Philadelphia, New York Times, Ladies Home Journal.*

"Dorothy can have Kansas, Scarlett can take Tara, Rick can keep Paris — I've stayed at Cedar Hill Farm."

Hillside Farm B&B

607 Eby Chiques Rd
Mount Joy, PA 17552-8819
(717)653-6697 Fax:(717)653-5233
E-mail: hillside3@juno.com

Circa 1863. This comfortable farm has a relaxing homey feel to it. Rooms are simply decorated and special extras such as handmade quilts and antiques add an elegant country touch. The home is a true monument to the cow. Dairy antiques, cow knickknacks and antique milk bottles abound. Some of the bottles were found during the renovation of the home and its grounds. Spend the day hunting for bargains in nearby antique shops, malls and factory outlets, or tour local Amish and Pennsylvania Dutch attractions. The farm is a good vacation spot for families with children above the age of 10.

Historic Interest: Home of President Buchanan (6 miles), Hans Herr House (10 miles), The Ephrata Cloister, Rockford Plantation (both 15 miles).

Innkeeper(s): Gary & Deborah Lintner. $60-70. MC VISA DS PC TC. TAC10. 5 rooms, 3 with PB. Breakfast and evening snack included in rates. Types of meals: full breakfast and early coffee/tea. Afternoon tea available. Beds: KQDT. Air conditioning and ceiling fan in room. VCR, spa and library on premises. Small meetings, family reunions and seminars hosted. Amusement parks, antiques, fishing, parks, shopping, downhill skiing, cross-country skiing, theater and watersports nearby.

Location: In the heart of Dutch/Amish country.

"Warm, friendly, comfortable . . . feels like home."

The Olde Square Inn

127 E Main St
Mount Joy, PA 17552-1513
(717)653-4525 (800)742-3533 Fax:(717)653-0976

Circa 1917. Located on the town square, this Neoclassical house features handsome columned fireplaces and leaded-glass windows. The innkeeper starts off the day with breakfast items such as baked oatmeal, cherry cobbler, homemade breads and pancakes with a side of sausage. Amish farms and marketplaces are nearby. The town of Mount Joy offers restaurants, shops and parks all accessible with a short walk.

Innkeeper(s): Fran & Dave Hand. $75-175. MC VISA PC TC. TAC10. 4 rooms with PB. 1 cottage. Breakfast included in rates. Types of meals: full breakfast and early coffee/tea. Beds: QD. Phone, air conditioning, TV and VCR in room. Fax on premises. Small meetings and family reunions hosted. Amusement parks, antiques, fishing, parks, shopping, sporting events and theater nearby.

Muncy   F12

The Bodine House B&B

307 S Main St
Muncy, PA 17756-1507
(717)546-8949 Fax:(717)546-8949

Circa 1805. This Federal-style townhouse, framed by a white picket fence, is in the National Register. Antique and reproduction furnishings highlight the inn's four fireplaces, the parlor, study and library. A favorite guest room features a walnut canopy bed, hand-stenciled and bordered walls, and a framed sampler by the innkeeper's great-great-great-grandmother. Candlelight breakfasts are served beside the fireplace in a gracious Colonial dining room. Also available is a guest cottage with kitchenette.

Historic Interest: The Pennsdale Quaker Meeting House.

Innkeeper(s): David & Marie Louise Smith. $60-125. MC VISA AX DS PC TC. TAC10. 5 rooms with PB, 1 with FP. 1 cottage. Breakfast included in rates. Types of meals: full breakfast and early coffee/tea. Afternoon tea available. Beds: QDT. Air conditioning, turndown service, TV in room. VCR, fax, bicycles and library on premises. Small meetings, family reunions hosted. Antiques, fishing, parks, shopping, cross-country skiing, sporting events nearby.

Publicity: *Colonial Homes, Philadelphia Inquirer.*

"What an experience, made special by your wonderful hospitality."

New Berlin   H12

The Inn at Olde New Berlin

321 Market St
New Berlin, PA 17855-0390
(717)966-0321 Fax:(717)966-9557

Circa 1906. At this richly appointed Victorian inn, you can relax on the inviting front porch swing or in the step-down living room with its baby grand piano. Carved woodwork and high ceilings accentuate its antique-filled rooms. An herb garden in the patio area supplies seasonings for the acclaimed meals at the inn's restaurant named Gabriel's. Luscious soups, appetizers such as crisp wontons with a currant marmalade sauce, and a variety of salads begin a dinner of contemporary American cuisine. Scrumptious desserts such as Amaretto-Bailey's cheesecake and chocolate mousse cake follow dinner. Brunch, available at Gabriel's Restaurant, features unique omelets, fruit crepes, apple streusel, French toast and drinks such as raspberry hot chocolate. Gabriel's Gift Collection in the carriage house features Radko collectible mouth-blown hand-painted ornaments and other unique gifts.

Historic Interest: The Slifer House Museum, Packwood House Museum, Mifflinburg Buggy Museum & Bucknett University are only a short drive away.

Innkeeper(s): Nancy & John Showers. $85-175. MC VISA PC TC. 5 rooms with PB. 2 suites. 1 conference room. Breakfast and afternoon tea included in rates. Type of meal: full breakfast. Dinner, lunch and room service available. Restaurant on premises. Beds: QD. Air conditioning and turndown service in room. Fax and copier on premises. Weddings, small meetings, family reunions and seminars hosted. Amusement parks, antiques, fishing, parks, shopping, skiing, sporting events, theater and watersports nearby.

Publicity: *Susquahanna Life, Philadelphia Inquirer, Washington Post, Country Inns Magazine, Country Inn Cooking with Gail Greco.*

"I left feeling nurtured and relaxed. You've created a very caring, rich lodging to a perfect place for regenerating."

New Cumberland   J12

Farm Fortune

204 Limekiln Rd
New Cumberland, PA 17070-2429
(717)774-2683

Circa 1750. This limestone farmhouse boasts an intriguing history that stretches back to its construction in the mid-18th century. The house may even have been a part of the Underground Railroad. With antiques tastefully placed throughout the home, guests will be reminded of the charming times of years past. The innkeepers invite guests to make themselves at home in the keeping room in front of the huge walk-in fireplace. While relaxing, notice the interesting woodwork that makes this farmhouse so unique. Ski the nearby slopes at Ski Roundtop or relax along the banks of the Yellow Breeches Creek and enjoy some local trout fishing.

Historic Interest: The farmhouse is located within 45 minutes of the historic towns of Gettysburg, Carlise, York, Harrisburg, Hershey and Lancaster.

Innkeeper(s): Chad & Phyllis Combs. $65-85. MC VISA AX DC CB DS. 4 rooms with PB. 1 suite. Breakfast included in rates. Type of meal: full breakfast. Picnic lunch available. Beds: KDT. Antiques, fishing, downhill skiing, cross-country skiing, theater and watersports nearby.

Publicity: *Early American Life, Patriot and Evening News.*

New Hope 118

Aaron Burr House Inn & Conference Center

80 W Bridge St
New Hope, PA 18938-1303
(215)862-2520

Circa 1870. Aaron Burr hid in this house after his infamous duel with Alexander Hamilton. The home also is one of the Wedgwood Collection inns. A Victorian Shingle style, it is in the National Register. Its three stories, including the spacious parlor, are appointed with antiques and reproductions. Guest rooms offer amenities such as private baths, telephones, TVs and many have fireplaces. Within walking distance are fine restaurants, shops and art galleries. The grounds offer two gazebos, stately old trees, a screened-in flagstone patio and a barn perfect for bicycle storage.

Historic Interest: Washington Crossing Historic State Park, Mercer Museums, Bucks County Playhouse, New Hope Steam Train, New Hope Barge Ride, New Hope Ferry, Bowman's Hill Wild Flower Preserve.

Innkeeper(s): Carl & Nadine Glassman. $75-195. MC VISA AX PC TC. TAC10. 12 rooms with PB, 6 with FP. 6 suites. 1 cottage. 3 conference rooms. Breakfast, afternoon tea and evening snack included in rates. Types of meals: continental-plus breakfast and early coffee/tea. Room service available. Beds: KQT. Phone, air conditioning, turndown service and ceiling fan in room. VCR, fax, swimming, tennis and pet boarding on premises. Handicap access. Small meetings, family reunions and seminars hosted. Dutch, French, Spanish and Hebrew spoken. Antiques, fishing, parks, shopping, downhill skiing, cross-country skiing, sporting events, theater and watersports nearby.

Hollileif B&B

677 Durham Rd (Rt 413)
New Hope, PA 18940
(215)598-3100

Circa 1700. This handsome former farmhouse sits on more than five rolling acres of scenic Bucks County countryside. The name "hollileif," which means "beloved tree," refers to the 40-foot holly trees that grace the entrance. Bedrooms are appointed with lace and fresh flow-ers. Afternoon refreshments in the parlor or patio are provided, as well as evening turndown service.

Historic Interest: Washington Crossing State Park (5 miles), Parry Mansion (6 miles), Pennsbury Manor (20 miles).

Innkeeper(s): Ellen & Richard Butkus. $85-155. MC VISA AX DS PC TC. TAC10. 5 rooms with PB, 2 with FP. Breakfast and afternoon tea included in rates. Types of meals: gourmet breakfast and early coffee/tea. Beds: QD. Air conditioning, turndown service and ceiling fan in room. VCR, fax, copier and library on premises. Family reunions hosted. Limited spanish spoken.

Antiques, fishing, parks, shopping, downhill skiing, cross-country skiing, theater and watersports nearby.

Location: Midway between Newtown and Buckingham.

Publicity: *Trentonian, Bucks County Courier Times.*

"The accommodations were lovely and the breakfasts delicious and unusual, but it is really the graciousness of our hosts that made the weekend memorable."

Hollyhedge B&B

6987 Upper York Rd
New Hope, PA 18938-9511
(215)862-3136 Fax:(215)862-0960

Circa 1700. This handsome stone manor rests on 20 acres with green lawns, a natural pond and a small stream. French, American and English antiques are found throughout the inn. Some rooms have private entrances and some feature fireplaces. The owners are former restaurateurs and provide a notable breakfast. Catered weddings and corporate retreats are popular here.

Innkeeper(s): Mary Kay Fisher. $95-175. MC VISA AX. 14 rooms with PB, 2 with FP. 2 suites. 1 conference room. Type of meal: full breakfast. Catering service available. Beds: KF. Air conditioning and ceiling fan in room. TV, VCR, bicycles and child care on premises. 21 acres. Weddings, small meetings, family reunions and seminars hosted. Amusement parks, antiques, shopping and theater nearby.

Location: Bucks County.

Hotel Du Village

2535 N River Rd
New Hope, PA 18938-9522
(215)862-9911 Fax:(215)862-9788

Circa 1907. Once part of a William Penn land grant, the Hotel du Village features 10 acres of trees, lawns and a creek. The Tudor-style hotel once served as a boarding school for girls, while the restaurant is part of the old White Oaks estate. Chestnut paneling, Persian carpets and three working fireplaces provide a backdrop to chef Omar Arbani's French cuisine.

Innkeeper(s): Barbara & Omar Arbani. $85-100. AX. 20 rooms with PB. 3 suites. 1 conference room. Type of meal: continental-plus breakfast. Dinner and banquet service available. Restaurant on premises. Beds: KQDT. Phone, air conditioning in room. Handicap access. 10 acres. Weddings, small meetings, family reunions, seminars hosted. Antiques, shopping, theater nearby.

Publicity: *Trenton Times, The Burlington County Times.*

"The food is wonderful - fireplaces burning makes everything so romantic!"

Pineapple Hill

1324 River Rd
New Hope, PA 18938
(215)862-1790

Circa 1790. The pineapple always has been a sign of friendship and hospitality, and guests at Pineapple Hill are sure to experience both. The inn is secluded on five private acres, yet it's just four miles from town, antique shops, flea markets, auctions and plenty of outdoor activities. The inviting interior is filled with Colonial-style furnishings. All rooms include either a fireplace, private deck or living room. Guests enjoy everything from baked bananas to raspberry French toast during the romantic, candlelight breakfasts, which are served on tables set for two. Inside the walls of a stone barn, is a tiled swimming pool.

Innkeeper(s): Kathy & Charles "Cookie" Triolo. $94-182. MC VISA AX DS TC. TAC10. 8 rooms with PB. 3 suites. 1 conference room. Breakfast and afternoon tea included in rates. Types of meals: full breakfast, gourmet breakfast and early coffee/tea. Evening snack available. Beds: KQ. Air conditioning, turndown service and TV in room. VCR, fax and swimming on premises. Weddings, small meetings, family reunions and seminars hosted. Antiques, fishing, parks, shopping, theater and watersports nearby.

"*It was a delightful stay in every way. The clicking door latches and the smells of breakfast cooking wafting up to the bedroom were reminiscent of my childhood stays at my grandparents' farmhouse.*"

The Wedgwood Collection of Historic Inns

111 W Bridge St
New Hope, PA 18938-1401
(215)862-2520 Fax:(215)862-2570

Circa 1870. A Victorian and a Classic Revival house sit side by side and comprise the Wedgwood Inn. Twenty-six-inch walls are in the stone house. Lofty windows, hardwood floors and antique furnishings add to the warmth and style. Pennsylvania Dutch surreys arrive and depart from the inn for nostalgic carriage rides.

Historic Interest: Delaware River & Canal, New Hope Steam Train, Bucks County Playhouse (1 block).

Innkeeper(s): Carl Glassman & Nadine Silnutzer. $75-199. MC VISA. 18 rooms with PB, 6 with FP. 6 suites. 1 conference room. Breakfast and afternoon tea included in rates. Types of meals: continental-plus breakfast and full breakfast. Catering service and room service available. Beds: KQT. Bicycles on premises. Handicap access. Antiques, fishing, cross-country skiing and theater nearby. Pets Allowed: call for restrictions.

Location: In the historic district, one block from the heart of New Hope, in rustic Bucks County.

Publicity: *National Geographic Traveler, Women's Day, Inc., Innsider, New York Times, Philadelphia Inquirer.*

"*The Wedgwood has all the comforts of a highly professional accommodation yet with all the warmth a personal friend would extend.*"

The Whitehall Inn

1370 Pineville Rd
New Hope, PA 18938-9495
(215)598-7945

Circa 1794. This white-plastered stone farmhouse is located on 13 country acres studded with stately maple and chestnut trees. Inside, a winding walnut staircase leads to antique-furnished guest rooms that offer wide pine floors, wavy-glass windows, high ceilings and some fireplaces. An antique clock collection, Oriental rugs and late Victorian furnishings are found throughout. Afternoon tea, evening chocolates and candlelight breakfasts served with heirloom china and sterling reflect the inn's many amenities. There are stables on the property and horseback riding may be arranged.

Innkeeper(s): Mike Wass. $140-195. MC VISA AX DC CB DS. 6 rooms. Breakfast included in rates. Types of meals: full breakfast and early coffee/tea. Air conditioning and turndown service in room. 13 acres. Small meetings, family reunions and seminars hosted. Amusement parks, antiques, shopping, cross-country skiing and theater nearby.

North Wales   J17

Joseph Ambler Inn

1005 Horsham Rd
North Wales, PA 19454-1413
(215)362-7500 Fax:(215)362-7500

Circa 1734. This fieldstone and wood house was built over a period of three centuries. Originally, it was part of a grant that Joseph Ambler, a Quaker wheelwright, obtained from William

Penn in 1688. A large stone bank barn and tenant cottage on 12 acres constitute the remainder of the property. Guests enjoy the cherry wainscoting and walk-in fireplace in the schoolroom.

Innkeeper(s): Terry & Steve Kratz. $90-200. MC VISA AX DC CB DS. 28 rooms with PB. 2 suites. 1 conference room. Breakfast included in rates. Type of meal: full breakfast. Dinner and banquet service available. Restaurant on premises. Beds: QD. Phone, air conditioning and TV in room. Handicap access. 13 acres. Weddings, small meetings, family reunions and seminars hosted. Antiques, shopping, skiing, sporting events and theater nearby.

Publicity: *Colonial Homes, Country Living.*

"*What a wonderful night my husband and I spent. We are already planning to come back to your wonderful getaway.*"

Oley   I15

Reiff Farm B&B

495 Old State Rd
Oley, PA 19547
(610)987-6216 Fax:(610)987-3019
E-mail: reifffarm@aol.com

Circa 1732. This three-story stone Pennsylvania Dutch house rests behind a rock wall. Situated on more than 50 acres of farmland and forest, a log cabin on the property dates to 1732, while the stone house was built in 1815. Out buildings include a stone smoke house, spring house, forge, summer kitchen, bake oven and ice house. Families and honeymooners favor the two-story red cabin. Rooms have period antiques and there are several fireplaces.

Innkeeper(s): John Jane. $60. AP. PC TC. 5 rooms, 1 with PB, 2 with FP. 1 cottage. 1 conference room. Breakfast and evening snack included in rates. Types of meals: continental breakfast, full breakfast and early coffee/tea. Beds: KTD. Air conditioning in room. Fax, stables, library and child care on premises. 50 acres. Family reunions and seminars hosted. French and Japanese spoken. Antiques, fishing, shopping, golf and theater nearby. Pets Allowed: Prior consultation required.

Orrtanna   L11

Hickory Bridge Farm

96 Hickory Bridge Rd
Orrtanna, PA 17353-9734
(717)642-5261

Circa 1750. The oldest part of this farmhouse was constructed of mud bricks and straw on land that once belonged to Charles Carroll, father of a signer of the Declaration of Independence. Inside, there is an attractive stone fireplace for cooking. There are several country cottages in addition to the rooms in the farmhouse. Fine, country dining is offered in the restored barn on the weekends. The host family has been innkeepers for more than 25 years.

Innkeeper(s): Mary Lynn Martin. $79-95. MC VISA. 9 rooms, 5 with PB, 4 with FP. 1 conference room. Breakfast included in rates. Meal: full breakfast. Restaurant on premises. Beds: QD. Antiques, fishing, downhill skiing nearby.

Location: Eight miles west of Gettysburg.

Publicity: *Hanover Times, The Northern Virginia Gazette.*

"*Beautifully decorated and great food!*"

Palmyra   J13

The Hen-Apple B&B

409 S Lingle Ave
Palmyra, PA 17078-9321
(717)838-8282

Circa 1825. Located at the edge of town, this Georgian farmhouse is surrounded by an acre of lawns and gardens. There are antiques and country pieces throughout. Breakfast is served to guests in the dining room or on the screened veranda. Hershey is two miles away, Lancaster and Gettysburg are nearby.

Innkeeper(s): Flo & Harold Eckert. $55-75. MC VISA AX TC. TAC10. 6 rooms with PB. Breakfast included in rates. Type of meal: full breakfast. Beds: QDT. Air conditioning, ceiling fan in room. TV on premises. Amusement parks, antiques, fishing, parks, shopping, sporting events, theater, watersports nearby.

Paradise   K14

Creekside Inn
44 Leacock Rd
Paradise, PA 17562-0435
(717)687-0333

Circa 1781. This 18th-century Georgian home was built by David Witmer, a prominent citizen and member of one of the first families to settle in the area. The stone exterior features a gable roof with five bay windows. Relaxing guest quarters feature special amenities such as four-poster or Windsor beds. The Cameo and Creekside rooms boast fireplaces. A hearty, full breakfast is served each morning. Antique and outlet shopping, as well as a variety of sporting activities are nearby.

Historic Interest: The inn is located in the heart of Lancaster County's Amish area, and the innkeepers say it's not uncommon to hear the sounds of Amish buggies as they travel down the road. Longwood Gardens and the Winterthuer museum are 30 minutes away, and Hershey Park is a 45-minute drive.

Innkeeper(s): Catherine & Dennis Zimmermann. $70-105. MC VISA. 5 rooms with PB. Breakfast included in rates. Types of meals: full breakfast and gourmet breakfast. Afternoon tea available. Beds: QDT. Antiques, fishing and theater nearby.

Philadelphia   K17

Gables B&B
4520 Chester Ave
Philadelphia, PA 19143-3707
(215)662-1918 Fax:(215)662-1918
E-mail: GablesBB@aol.com

Circa 1889. Located in the University City section, this red-brick Queen Anne Victorian has three stories and offers off-street parking. Chestnut and cherry woodwork, a grand entry hall and sitting rooms furnished with antiques make this a popular site for private affairs. A wraparound porch overlooks the inn's gardens of perennials, roses, dogwood and Japanese cherry and magnolia trees. The Christmas Room has mahogany antiques and a queen brass bed, while the Tower Room has a working fireplace and a settee tucked into the turret. Another room offers a soaking tub and sun porch. This inn received Philadelphia Magazine's four-heart award and the "Best of Philly 1996" award as an urban getaway.

Innkeeper(s): Don Caskey & Warren Cederholm. $70-80. MC VISA AX PC TC. 10 rooms, 5 with PB, 2 with FP. 1 suite. Breakfast included in rates. Type of meal: full breakfast. Beds: QD. Air conditioning and TV in room. Fax and library on premises. Weddings, small meetings, family reunions and seminars hosted. Antiques, parks, shopping, sporting events and theater nearby.
Publicity: *Philadelphia.*

Shippen Way Inn
416-18 Bainbridge St
Philadelphia, PA 19147
(215)627-7266 (800)245-4873

Circa 1750. In the National Register of Historic Places, Shippen Way is located close to Independence Hall. Working fireplaces, timbered walls and ceiling beams create an authentic Colonial decor. This era is reinforced with a cobbler's bench, pencil-post beds, a stenciled kitchen floor and a flax wheel. Old-fashioned roses and herbs are set in a walled garden where breakfast is often served.

Innkeeper(s): Ann Foringer & Raymond Rhule. $75-105. EP. MC VISA AX TC. 9 rooms with PB, 1 with FP. Breakfast and evening snack included in rates. Type of meal: continental-plus breakfast. Beds: QDT. Phone, air conditioning and TV in room. Handicap access. Small meetings and family reunions hosted. Antiques, parks, shopping, sporting events and theater nearby.
Publicity: *Life Today, Mid-Atlantic Country.*

Thomas Bond House
129 S 2nd St
Philadelphia, PA 19106-3039
(215)923-8523 (800)845-2663 Fax:(215)923-8504

Circa 1769. One way to enjoy the history of Philadelphia is to treat yourself to a stay at this Colonial-period, Georgian-style residence in Independence National Historical Park. White shutters and cornices accentuate the brick exterior, often draped in red, white and blue bunting. A finely executed interior renovation provides a handsome background for the inn's collection of Chippendale reproductions, four-poster beds and dropfront desks. Working fireplaces, phones, hair dryers, television and whirlpool tubs provide additional comforts.

Innkeeper(s): Rita McGuire. $90-160. MC VISA AX PC TC. TAC7. 12 rooms with PB, 2 with FP. 2 suites. 1 conference room. Breakfast included in rates. Types of meals: continental-plus breakfast, full breakfast and early coffee/tea. Evening snack and catering service available. Beds: QDT. Phone and air conditioning in room. Fax and copier on premises. Weddings, small meetings, family reunions and seminars hosted. Amusement parks, antiques, fishing, parks, shopping, sporting events and theater nearby.
Location: In the Independence National Historical Park.
Publicity: *Mid-Atlantic Country, Washingtonian, Washington Post, Philadelphia Inquirer, Home & Garden, Boston Globe.*
"Your service was excellent, congenial, made us feel comfortable and welcome."

Pittsburgh   I3

The Priory
614 Pressley St
Pittsburgh, PA 15212-5616
(412)231-3338 Fax:(412)231-4838

Circa 1888. The Priory, now a European-style hotel, was built to provide lodging for Benedictine priests traveling through Pittsburgh. It is adjacent to Pittsburgh's Grand Hall at the Priory in historic East Allegheny. The inn's design and maze of rooms and corridors give it a distinctly Old World flavor. All rooms are decorated with Victorian furnishings.

Historic Interest: Mexican War Streets Neighborhood, Fort Pitt Blockhouse & Point State Park.

Innkeeper(s): Joanie Weldon, Ed & Mary Ann Graf. $100-150. MC VISA AX DC DS. 24 rooms with PB. 3 suites. 1 conference room. Breakfast included in rates. Type of meal: continental-plus breakfast. Beds: QDT. Handicap access. Theater nearby.

Publicity: *Pittsburgh Press, US Air, Country Inns, Innsider, Youngstown Vindicator, Travel & Leisure, Gourmet, Mid-Atlantic Country.*

"Although we had been told that the place was elegant, we were hardly prepared for the richness of detail. We felt as though we were guests in a manor."

Point Pleasant   I18

Tattersall Inn

16 Cafferty Rd, PO Box 569
Point Pleasant, PA 18950
(215)297-8233 (800)297-4988
E-mail: nrhg17a@prodigy.com

Circa 1740. This plastered fieldstone house with its broad porches and wainscoted entry hall was the home of local mill owners for 150 years. The walls are 18 inches thick. Breakfast is usually served in the dining room where a vintage phonograph collection is on display. Breakfast can also be brought to your room. The Colonial-style common room features a beamed ceiling and walk-in fireplace. Guests gather here for apple cider, cheese and crackers and tea or coffee in the late afternoon.

Historic Interest: Washington Crossing Park (12 miles), William Penn's Pennsbury Manor (25 miles), Valley Forge (40 miles).

Innkeeper(s): Herbert & Geraldine Moss. $70-130. MC VISA AX DS PC TC. TAC10. 6 rooms with PB, 2 with FP. 2 suites. 1 conference room. Breakfast, afternoon tea and evening snack included in rates. Types of meals: full breakfast and early coffee/tea. Room service available. Beds: QT. Air conditioning in room. Fax, copier and library on premises. Small meetings and family reunions hosted. Antiques, fishing, parks, shopping, cross-country skiing, theater and watersports nearby.

Location: Bucks County, New Hope area.

Publicity: *Courier Times, Philadelphia, New York Times, WYOU.*

"Thank you for your hospitality and warm welcome. The inn is charming and has a wonderful ambiance."

Reinholds   J14

Brownstone Corner B&B

590 Galen Hall Rd
Reinholds, PA 17569
(717)484-4460 (800)239-9902 Fax:(301)390-9885

Circa 1759. Ancient sycamores shade this three-story brownstone home. Amid stands of blue spruce and fir trees, the seven-acre estate is five miles from the turnpike. It was believed at one time to have been a stagecoach stop between Lancaster and Reading. Wide plank floors and a walk-in fireplace provide a historic setting for the family's antiques. Breakfasts of egg dishes and freshly baked breads are served family style in the spacious country kitchen. Amish farms, antique shops and factory outlets are nearby.

Innkeeper(s): Jane & Vicki Wertz. $55-65. MC VISA PC TC. 3 rooms, 1 with PB. Breakfast included in rates. Types of meals: full breakfast and early coffee/tea. Beds: QDT. Air conditioning in room. TV and VCR on premises. Amusement parks, antiques, fishing, parks, shopping, golf, theater and watersports nearby.

"We can't wait to tell friends and family about your paradise."

Ronks   K14

Candlelight Inn B&B

2574 Lincoln Hwy E
Ronks, PA 17572-9771
(717)299-6005 (800)772-2635 Fax:(717)299-6397
E-mail: Candleinn@aol.com

Circa 1920. Located in the Pennsylvania Dutch area, this Federal-style house offers a side porch for enjoying the home's acre and a half of tall trees and surrounding Amish farmland. Guest rooms feature Victorian decor. The inn's gourmet breakfast, which might include a creme caramel French toast, is served by candlelight. The innkeepers are professional classical musicians. Lancaster is five miles to the east.

Innkeeper(s): Tim & Heidi Soberick. $65-105. MC VISA DS PC TC. TAC10. 6 rooms, 4 with PB. 1 suite. Breakfast included in rates. Types of meals: full breakfast and gourmet breakfast. Beds: KQT. Air conditioning in room. TV and fax on premises. Weddings, small meetings, family reunions and seminars hosted. French and Italian spoken. Amusement parks, antiques, fishing, parks, shopping, downhill skiing, cross-country skiing, sporting events, theater and watersports nearby.

Scottdale   K4

Zephyr Glen Bed & Breakfast

205 Dexter Rd
Scottdale, PA 15683-1812
(724)887-6577
E-mail: Zephyr@hhs.net

Circa 1822. An inviting country theme permeates the atmosphere at this early 19th-century, Federal-style farmhouse. Rooms are filled with period antiques, quilts and a few carefully placed knickknacks and musical instruments. Several rooms are decorated with stencils created by innkeeper Noreen McGurl. She and husband, Gil, also run an antique store out of their inn. Guests are treated to breakfasts of homemade granola, jams made from berries on the property, freshly baked  breads and other creative dishes. The three-acres grounds are decorated with maples, oaks, fruit trees, berry bushes, herb gardens and a fish pond. Frank Lloyd Wright's masterpiece, Fallingwater, is nearby, and another Wright design also is near.

Historic Interest: Fort Necessity, Braddock's Grave, West Overton Museum, the Bushy Run Battlefield and Fort Ligonier are among the many historic sites in the area.

Innkeeper(s): Noreen & Gil McGurl. $70-80. MC VISA DS PC TC. TAC10. 3 rooms with PB, 1 with FP. Breakfast, afternoon tea and evening snack included in rates. Types of meals: full breakfast and early coffee/tea. Picnic lunch available. Beds: D. Turndown service and ceiling fan in room. TV, fax and library on premises. Amusement parks, antiques, fishing, parks, shopping, downhill skiing, cross-country skiing, theater and watersports nearby.

"We can't stop talking about the wonderful time we had at your lovely inn."

Shippensburg   K10

Field & Pine B&B

2155 Ritner Hwy
Shippensburg, PA 17257-9756
(717)776-7179

Circa 1790. Local limestone was used to build this stone house, located on the main wagon road to Baltimore and Washington. Originally, it was a tavern

and weigh station. The house is surrounded by stately pines, and sheep graze on the inn's 80 acres. The bedrooms are hand-stenciled and furnished with quilts and antiques.

Innkeeper(s): Mary Ellen & Allan Williams. $65-75. MC VISA PC TC. TAC10. 3 rooms, 1 with PB, 1 with FP. 1 suite. Breakfast and evening snack included in rates. Types of meals: gourmet breakfast and early coffee/tea. Beds: QDT. Air conditioning and turndown service in room. VCR on premises. 80 acres. Weddings, small meetings and family reunions hosted. Antiques, fishing, parks and shopping nearby.
Location: Twelve miles south of Carlisle, on US Rte 11.
Publicity: *Valley Times-Star.*

"Our visit in this lovely country home has been most delightful. The ambiance of antiques and tasteful decorating exemplifies real country living."

Shohola   E18

Pegasus B&B

R R 2 Box 2066
Shohola, PA 18458-9721
(717)296-4017 Fax:(717)296-4017
E-mail: pegasus@pikeonline.net

Circa 1910. Pegasus was built to serve as a country inn for travelers to the Poconos. In the 1920s, the inn was renovated and expanded. It now offers nine comfortable guest rooms, decorated in a style reminiscent of the early 20th century. Guests are encouraged to relax and enjoy the inn, as well as its wooded acres of nature reserve. There is a wraparound porch, lined with rockers and chairs, and the inn's living room has a stone fireplace and comfortable furniture. The inn offers close access to the Delaware River National Park, where swimming, rafting and kayaking are available. Fishing, hiking, biking, bird watching and other outdoor activities are in abundance in the area.

Innkeeper(s): John Hunn. $55-100. MC VISA AX PC. 9 rooms, 1 with PB. 2 suites. Breakfast included in rates. Types of meals: continental-plus breakfast, full breakfast and early coffee/tea. Beds: QDT. TV, VCR, fax, copier and library on premises. Weddings, family reunions and seminars hosted. Spanish and Portuguese spoken. Antiques, fishing, parks, shopping, cross-country skiing, golf and watersports nearby. Pets Allowed: Small pets only.
Publicity: *This Week in the Poconos, Star-Ledger.*

Smethport   D7

Christmas Inn

911 W Main St
Smethport, PA 16749-1040
(814)887-5665 (800)653-6700 Fax:(814)887-5723

Circa 1900. All year long this three-story gabled Victorian is decorated for Christmas with garlands of greenery festooned around the porch and upper veranda. Each guest room has its own

Christmas tree. Innkeeper Connie Lovell was born on Christmas, and she and her husband own "America's First Christmas Store." Original woodwork and a marble fireplace are some of the features of the house.

Guests are given a coupon for breakfast at the Smethport Diner, which was featured on the PBS diner series.

Innkeeper(s): Bob & Connie Lovell. $65-85. MC VISA AX DS PC TC. TAC10. 7 rooms, 5 with PB, 4 with FP. Breakfast included in rates. Beds: Q. Phone, air conditioning and ceiling fan in room. TV, VCR and copier on premises. Antiques, fishing, parks, shopping and golf nearby.
Publicity: *Country, Collector, KDKA-TV, WGRZ-TV.*

Starlight   C17

The Inn at Starlight Lake

PO Box 27
Starlight, PA 18461-0027
(717)798-2519 (800)248-2519 Fax:(717)798-2672

Circa 1909. Acres of woodland and meadow surround the last surviving railroad inn on the New York, Ontario and Western lines. Originally a boarding house, the inn had its own store, church, school, blacksmith shop and creamery. Platforms, first erected to accommodate tents for the summer season, were later replaced by three small cottage buildings that includes a suite with a double whirlpool. A modern three-bedroom house is

available for family reunions and conferences. The inn is situated on the 45-acre, spring-fed Starlight Lake, providing summertime canoeing, swimming, fishing and sailing. (No motorboats are allowed on the lake.)

Innkeeper(s): Jack & Judy McMahon. $110-154. MAP, EP. MC VISA. 26 rooms, 20 with PB, 1 with FP. 1 suite. 1 conference room. Breakfast and dinner included in rates. Types of meals: full breakfast, gourmet breakfast and early coffee/tea. Evening snack, picnic lunch, lunch and banquet service available. Restaurant on premises. Beds: KQDT. Phone in room. Copier and bicycles on premises. Weddings, small meetings, family reunions and seminars hosted. Antiques, fishing, shopping, downhill skiing, cross-country skiing and watersports nearby.
Publicity: *New York Times, Philadelphia Inquirer, Newsday, Discerning Traveler, Freeman.*

"So great to be back to our home away from home."

Stroudsburg   G17

Stroudsmoor Country Inn

PO Box 153
Stroudsburg, PA 18360-0153
(717)421-6431 (800)955-8663 Fax:(717)421-8042

Built of clapboard and stone, this country inn is located on 200 acres. There are 17 buildings, including the main house, cottages and a cluster of country shops that make up The Marketplace. A fieldstone fireplace is the focal point of the lobby. Rooms offer televisions and country antiques and the cottages have porches. There is both an indoor and outdoor pool. The dining room decor features bentwood chairs, copper kettles and linen napkins. A four-course breakfast is provided, and on Sundays there is a champagne brunch.

Innkeeper(s): Andrew Forte & Linda Pirone-Forte. Call for rates. 3 suites. 2 conference rooms. Type of meal: early coffee/tea. Dinner, picnic lunch, lunch, banquet service and catering service available. Air conditioning and TV in room. 200 acres. Weddings, small meetings, family reunions and seminars hosted. Amusement parks, antiques, shopping, downhill skiing, cross-country skiing and theater nearby.

Thornton   K16

Pace One Restaurant and Country Inn

Thornton Rd & Glen Mills Rd
Thornton, PA 19373
(610)459-3702 Fax:(610)558-0825

Circa 1740. This beautifully renovated stone barn has two-and-a-half-foot-thick walls, hand-hewn wood beams and many small-paned windows. Just in front of the inn was the Gray family home used as a hospital during the Revolutionary War when Washington's army crossed nearby Chadd's Ford.

Innkeeper(s): Ted Pace. $95. MC VISA AX DC PC TC. 6 rooms with PB. 3 conference rooms. Breakfast included in rates. Type of meal: continental-plus breakfast. Picnic lunch, lunch and banquet service available. Restaurant on premises. Beds: Q. Phone and air conditioning in room. Fax and copier on premises. Weddings, small meetings, family reunions and seminars hosted. Antiques, fishing, parks, shopping, sporting events and theater nearby.

"Dear Ted & Staff, we loved it here!! The accommodations were great and the brunch on Sunday, fantastic. Thanks for making it a beautiful weekend."

Valley Forge (Linfield)   K16

Shearer Elegance

154 Main St
Valley Forge (Linfield), PA 19468-1139
(610)495-7429 (800)861-0308 Fax:(610)495-7814
E-mail: shearerc@aol.com

Circa 1897. This stone Queen Anne mansion is the height of Victorian opulence and style. Peaked roofs, intricate trim and a stenciled wraparound porch grace the exterior. Guests enter the home via a marble entry, which boasts a three-story staircase. Stained-glass windows and carved mantels are other notable features. The Victorian furnishings and decor complement the ornate workmanship, and lacy curtains are a romantic touch. The bedrooms feature hand-carved, built-in wardrobes. The grounds are dotted with gardens. The inn is located in the village of Linfield, about 15 minutes from Valley Forge.

Innkeeper(s): Shirley & Malcolm Shearer & Beth Smith. $75-140. AX PC TC. TAC10. 7 rooms with PB. 2 suites. 3 conference rooms. Types of meals: full breakfast and early coffee/tea. Banquet service and catering service available. Beds: KQD. Phone, air conditioning, ceiling fan, TV and VCR in room. Fax, copier and library on premises. Weddings, small meetings, family reunions and seminars hosted. Amusement parks, antiques, fishing, parks, shopping, downhill skiing, sporting events, golf and theater nearby.

Valley Forge (Malvern)   K16

The Great Valley House of Valley Forge

110 Swedesford Rd, Rd 3
Valley Forge (Malvern), PA 19355
(610)644-6759 Fax:(610)644-7019
E-mail: jeffbenson@unn.unisys.com

Circa 1691. This 300-year-old Colonial stone farmhouse sits on four acres just two miles from Valley Forge Park. Boxwoods line the walkway and ancient trees surround the house. Each of the

three guest rooms is hand-stenciled and features a canopied or brass bed topped with handmade quilts. Guests enjoy a full breakfast before a 14-foot fireplace in the "summer kitchen," the oldest part of the house. On the grounds are a swimming pool, walking and hiking trails, and the home's original smokehouse.

Historic Interest: The grounds have an original keep and tunnel, which was part of the Underground Railroad. Historic Philadelphia, Longwood Gardens and Brandywine River Museum are other nearby attractions. Lancaster Country, famous for its Amish communities, is a popular area to visit.

Innkeeper(s): Pattye Benson. $75-90. AP. MC VISA DS PC TC. TAC10. 3 rooms, 2 with PB. Breakfast included in rates. Types of meals: gourmet breakfast and early coffee/tea. Picnic lunch available. Beds: QDT. Phone, air conditioning, turndown service and TV in room. Fax and swimming on premises. Weddings and small meetings hosted. Spanish and French spoken. Antiques, fishing, parks, shopping, cross-country skiing, sporting events, theater and watersports nearby.

Location: Two miles from Valley Forge National Park.

Publicity: *Main Line Philadelphia, Philadelphia Inquirer, Washington Post, New York Times, Suburban Newspaper, Phoenixville Sun.*

"As a business traveler, Patty's enthusiasm and warm welcome makes you feel just like you're home."

West Chester   K16

Bankhouse B&B

875 Hillsdale Rd
West Chester, PA 19382-1975
(610)344-7388

Circa 1765. Built into the bank of a quiet country road, this 18th-century house overlooks a 10-acre horse farm and pond. The interior is decorated with country antiques, stenciling and folk art. Guests have a private entrance and porch. Two bedrooms share a common sitting room library. Hearty country breakfasts include German apple souffle pancakes, custard French toast and

nearly 100 other recipes. West Chester and the Brandywine Valley attractions are conveniently close.

Historic Interest: Longwood Gardens, the Brandywine River Museum, Brandywine Battlefield (8 miles).

Innkeeper(s): Diana & Michael Bove. $70-90. TC. 2 rooms. 1 suite. Breakfast and evening snack included in rates. Meals: full breakfast, gourmet breakfast, early coffee/tea. Beds: DT. Phone, air conditioning in room. Antiques, parks, shopping, cross-country skiing, sporting events, theater nearby.

Location: In Brandywine Valley.

Publicity: *Philadelphia Inquirer, Mercury, Bucks County Town & Country Living, Chester County Living, Washington Post.*

"Everything was so warm and inviting. One of my favorite places to keep coming back to."

West Reading   J15

Nine-Patch B&B

726 Penn Ave
West Reading, PA 19611
(610)372-2711

Circa 1900. Across from the Vanity Fair outlet village, this two-story brick house is furnished in country antiques and quilts. At one time the building was a tourist house with rooms offered at $1 per night. Omelets and fruit are usually offered at breakfast. The Daniel Boone Homestead, Antique Row, Reading

Museum and Grings Mill Park are local attractions. The inn offers a complimentary full or continental breakfast.

Innkeeper(s): Suzanne R. Romig. $60-70. MC VISA PC. 3 rooms with PB. Breakfast included in rates. Types of meals: continental breakfast and full breakfast. Beds: QTD. Air conditioning and TV in room. Antiques, fishing, parks, shopping, golf, theater and watersports nearby.

White Horse K15

Fassitt Mansion B&B

6051 Old Philadelphia Pike, Hr 340
White Horse, PA 17527-9798
(717)442-3139 (800)653-4139

Circa 1845. Located on two acres, this Federal home is six miles from the town of Intercourse in Lancaster County. There are 12-foot-high ceilings and six fireplaces. A full country breakfast offers local butters and fruit jams, served in the dining room.

Innkeeper(s): Bill & Patricia Collins. $80-125. MC VISA TC. TAC8. 5 rooms with PB, 3 with FP. Breakfast, afternoon tea and evening snack included in rates. Types of meals: full breakfast, gourmet breakfast and early coffee/tea. Beds: KQDT. Air conditioning, turndown service and ceiling fan in room. TV and VCR on premises. Antiques, fishing, shopping and theater nearby.
Location: Lancaster County, Amish farmland.

"Your hospitality and warm love has left an imprint on our hearts."

Williamsport F12

Reighard House

1323 E 3rd St
Williamsport, PA 17701
(717)326-3593 (800)326-8335 Fax:(717)323-4734

Circa 1905. The Reighard House, a Victorian made of stone and brick, offers a formal parlor with a fireplace, music room with a grand piano, library and a formal oak-paneled dining room. Rooms are furnished with four-poster and canopy beds. Each bedroom is decorated with a different color scheme and theme and is identified by a needlepointed sign.

Innkeeper(s): Sue Reighard. $58-88. MC VISA AX DC CB PC TC. 6 rooms with PB. Breakfast included in rates. Types of meals: full breakfast and early coffee/tea. Beds: QD. Phone, air conditioning, TV and VCR in room. Fax and library on premises. Antiques, fishing, parks, shopping, downhill skiing, cross-country skiing, sporting events, theater and watersports nearby.
Publicity: *Pennsylvania Business Journal.*

"I know I'm coming back!"

Thomas Lightfoote Inn

2887 S Reach Rd
Williamsport, PA 17701-4174
(717)326-6396 Fax:(717)327-6300

Circa 1792. A white picket fence frames this beige Federal-style inn, situated in the oldest village on Cape Cod. There is a wraparound porch with rockers and a swing, and borders of flowers extend to the back garden. Rooms feature country antiques and some have fireplaces. Walk to the boardwalk, skate along the Cape Cod Canal or enjoy the salt marshes and beach. Close by is Shawme Pond, with gristmill, an English tea room and heritage homes. Ask about the artist workshops offered in the inn's light-filled art studio.

Innkeeper(s): Rita Chilson. $75. AP. MC VISA AX DS PC TC. TAC10. 7 rooms, 5 with PB, 3 with FP. 1 suite. 2 conference rooms. Breakfast included in rates. Types of meals: continental-plus breakfast, full breakfast, gourmet breakfast and early coffee/tea. Dinner, lunch, gourmet lunch and banquet service available. Restaurant on premises. Beds: KQD. Phone, air conditioning and TV in room. Fax on premises. Weddings, small meetings, family reunions and seminars hosted. Antiques, fishing, parks, shopping, downhill skiing, cross-country skiing, sporting events, golf, theater and watersports nearby.
Publicity: *Pittsburg Press, Washington Times.*

Willow Street K14

The Inn at Hayward Heath B&B

2048 Silver Ln
Willow Street, PA 17584
(717)464-0994

Circa 1887. Located in Southern Lancaster Country, this graceful brick Colonial house overlooks two acres of lawns and gardens. There are high ceilings, wide window sills and oak and cherry grained woodwork. There is a walk-in fireplace in the former summer kitchen, now a family room furnished with antiques. The Shaker Room offers a queen-size canopy bed, and one room offers a double whirlpool tub. Baked apples, stuffed French toast and egg dishes are served in the dining room. Amish farms, craft shops, outlet malls, restaurants and farmers markets are popular Lancaster County attractions.

Innkeeper(s): David & Joan Smith. $80-95. MC VISA DS PC. 4 rooms, 3 with PB. Breakfast included in rates. Type of meal: full breakfast. Beds: QD. Air conditioning and ceiling fan in room. TV on premises. Small meetings hosted. Amusement parks, antiques, parks, shopping, golf, theater nearby.
Publicity: *Lancaster Country Magazine.*

York K13

Friendship House B&B

728 E Philadelphia St
York, PA 17403-1609
(717)843-8299

Circa 1897. A walk down East Philadelphia Street takes visitors past an unassuming row of 19th-century townhouses. The Friendship House is a welcoming site with its light blue shutters and pink trim. Innkeepers Becky Detwiler and Karen Maust have added a shot of Victorian influence to their charming townhouse B&B, decorating with wallcoverings and lacy curtains. A country feast is prepared some mornings with choices ranging from quiche to French toast accompanied with items such as baked apples, smoked sausage and homemade breads. Most items are selected carefully from a nearby farmer's market. Becky and Karen make sure guests never leave their friendly home empty-handed, offering a bottle of Pennsylvania's finest maple syrup upon departure.

Innkeeper(s): Becky Detwiler & Karen Maust. $50-65. 3 rooms, 2 with PB. 1 suite. Breakfast and evening snack included in rates. Types of meals: continental-plus breakfast and full breakfast. Beds: Q. Air conditioning in room. VCR on premises. Antiques, fishing, parks, shopping and theater nearby.

Rhode Island

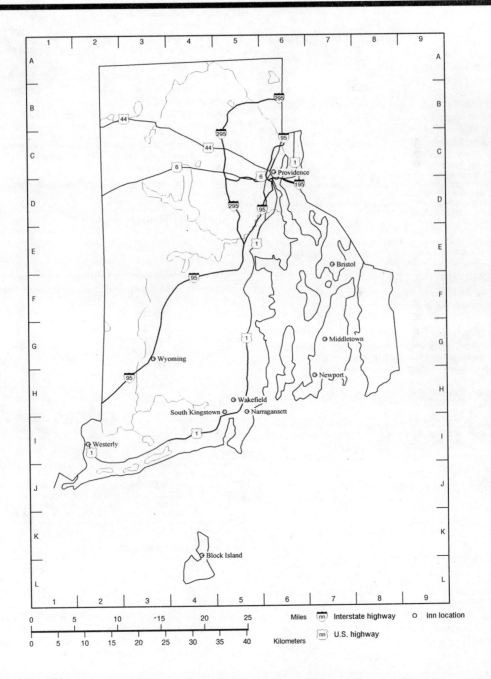

A — 1 2 3 4 5 6 7 8 9 — A
295
B — 44 — B
295
95
44
C — 6 1 — C
6 Providence
195
D — 295 95 — D
1
E — E
Bristol
95
F — F
95
G — 1 — G
Wyoming Middletown
95
H — Wakefield Newport — H
South Kingstown Narragansett
I — 1 — I
Westerly 1
1
J — J
1 2 3 4 5 6 7 8 9
K — K
Block Island
L — L

| 0 | 5 | 10 | 15 | 20 | 25 | Miles | nn Interstate highway | o Inn location |

| 0 | 5 | 10 | 15 | 20 | 25 | 30 | 35 | 40 | Kilometers | nn U.S. highway |

Block Island   K4

1661 Inn & Hotel Manisses

1 Spring St, PO Box 1
Block Island, RI 02807
(401)466-2421 (800)626-4773 Fax:(401)466-2858

Circa 1875. Five buildings comprise this island inn and overlook grassy lawns and the ocean. Common rooms and guest
rooms are furnished with antiques and art. The newest luxury
rooms in the Nicholas
Ball Cottage (a replica
of an Episcopal
church) offer both Jacuzzis
and fireplaces. Dinner is available each night in the summer
and on weekends other times

of the year. Visit the inn's animal farm to watch the antics of
the Indian runner ducks, black swans, pygmy goats, llamas and
Sicilian donkeys. Flower, vegetable and herb gardens are adjacent to the farm.

Historic Interest: Historic Old Harbor.

Innkeeper(s): Joan & Justin Abrams. $60-335. MC VISA AX. 38 rooms, 34
with PB. 5 conference rooms. Breakfast included in rates. Types of meals:
continental breakfast, continental-plus breakfast, full breakfast and early cof-
fee/tea. Afternoon tea, dinner, evening snack, picnic lunch, lunch, gourmet
lunch, banquet service, catering service and catered breakfast available.
Restaurant on premises. Beds: KQDT. Phone in room. TV, VCR and child care
on premises. 11 acres. Weddings, small meetings, family reunions and seminars hosted. Antiques, fishing, shopping, theater and watersports nearby.

Publicity: *Newsday, New England Weekends, The Day, Detroit Free Press,
US Air, USA Today, Block Island, New England Travel, Yankee, Gourmet.*

Atlantic Inn

PO Box 188
Block Island, RI 02807-0188
(401)466-5883 (800)224-7422 Fax:(401)466-5678

Circa 1879. Guests first traveled up the long road to the
Atlantic Inn to enjoy its more than two acres of grassy slopes,
which overlook the ocean and Old Harbor Village. Today,
guests will experience much of the charm that lured vacation-

ers to this island spot during the Victorian era. The
inn's 21 guest rooms are
individually appointed
with antiques and period
furnishings. Inn guests
enjoy use of two tennis

courts, a formal croquet court and a swing and gym set for
children as well as a playhouse, which is a replica of the inn.
Take a leisurely stroll around the landscaped grounds and enjoy
the gardens, which provide many of the herbs and vegetables
used in meals at the inn's gourmet restaurant.

Historic Interest: The Block Island Historic District and Old Harbor Village
include many historic buildings.

Innkeeper(s): Brad & Anne Marthens. $100-215. MC VISA PC TC. 21 rooms
with PB. 1 suite. 1 conference room. Breakfast and afternoon tea included in
rates. Types of meals: continental-plus breakfast and early coffee/tea. Picnic
lunch available. Restaurant on premises. Beds: QDT. TV, fax, copier, tennis
and child care on premises. Weddings, small meetings, family reunions, seminars hosted. Antiques, fishing, parks, shopping, theater, watersports nearby.

The Inn at Old Harbour

Water St, PO Box 994
Block Island, RI 02807
(401)466-2212

Circa 1882. This three-story National Register Victorian, with its
gingerbread trim and double porch, attracts many photographers.
Recently renovated, all the rooms are appointed with period furnishings and most have views of the Atlantic.
The inn offers private, harborfront balconies. In the evenings, wine
and cheese are served.
Block Island's inviting
beaches and seaside cliffs
are enjoyed by wind
surfers, sailors, cyclists and
those just sunning on the
sand. A noted wildlife

sanctuary at Sandy Point is popular for bird watchers.

Innkeeper(s): Kevin & Barbara Butler. $65-150. MC VISA AX. 10 rooms, 7
with PB. Breakfast included in rates. Meal: continental-plus breakfast. Beds:
KQ. Phone in room. Fax and copier on premises. Fishing and theater nearby.

Location: Overlooking the harbor and the Atlantic Ocean.

Publicity: *Rhode Island Monthly, Rand McNally.*

*"The most romantic enchanting inn we have stayed at and what gra-
cious innkeepers!"*

Sheffield House

High St, Box C-2
Block Island, RI 02807
(401)466-2494 Fax:(401)466-5067

Circa 1888. Step off the ferry and step into a by-gone era at
this Queen Anne Victorian, which overlooks the Old Harbor
district and scenic ocean vistas. Relax on the
front porch or enjoy the fragrance as you stroll
through the private garden. The cookie jar
is always full. Breakfasts are served in
the quaint day room, which features
a collection of milk bottles from
around the world. Guests also
can enjoy the morning meal in
the garden surrounded by
beautiful flowers and
herbs. Guest rooms fea-
ture international touches,
antiques and family pieces.

Historic Interest: The Old Harbor district is a historic area with plenty of
places to explore.

Innkeeper(s): Steve & Claire McQueeny. $50-165. MC VISA AX PC. 7 rooms,
5 with PB. Breakfast, afternoon tea and evening snack included in rates.
Types of meals: continental-plus breakfast and early coffee/tea. Beds: Q.
Ceiling fan in room. Weddings, small meetings, family reunions and seminars
hosted. Antiques, fishing, parks, shopping and watersports nearby.

The White House

Spring St
Block Island, RI 02807
(401)466-2653

Circa 1795. This Colonial-style bed & breakfast is furnished
with French Provincial antiques and has sweeping views of the
ocean, rolling lawns and gardens. The earliest portion of the
home dates back to the 18th century. The Captain's Quarters

has a bedroom-sitting room that encompasses the entire ocean side of the house. The room has a canopied double bed and outdoor balcony. Guests have a private north portico entrance and main floor drawing room with TV. Arrangements can be made to be met at the airport or ferry.

Innkeeper(s): Mrs. Joseph V. Connolly, Jr. $55-120. MC VISA PC TC. 2 rooms. Type of meal: full breakfast. Beds: DT. TV, swimming and library on premises. Weddings hosted. Fishing and shopping nearby.

"Your home is so fascinating and carries an international as well as antique filled atmosphere."

Bristol E7

Rockwell House Inn B&B

610 Hope St
Bristol, RI 02809-1945
(401)253-0040 (800)815-0040 Fax:(401)253-1811

Circa 1809. This Federal and Greek Revival home boasts eight-foot pocket doors, Italianate mantels and working fireplaces.

Double parlors open to the dining room and its inlaid parquet floors. The sun porch features a stone turret and leaded-glass windows. Two guest rooms include working fireplaces and antiques abound in each of the elegant quarters. The inn is only one block from Narragansett Bay and a 15-mile bike path.

Historic Interest: Historic Newport and Providence are 12 miles away. The Blithewood Mansion and Gardens, Americas' Cup Hall of Fame, Haffenreffer Museum of Anthropology, Lindon Place and Coggeshall Historic Farm Museum are all within a mile and a half of Rockwell House.

Innkeeper(s): Debra & Steve Krohn. $75-110. MC VISA AX DS PC TC. TAC10. 4 rooms with PB, 2 with FP. 1 conference room. Breakfast and afternoon tea included in rates. Types of meals: continental-plus breakfast, full breakfast, gourmet breakfast and early coffee/tea. Catered breakfast available. Beds: KQT. Turndown service and ceiling fan in room. VCR, fax and copier on premises. Small meetings and seminars hosted. Spanish spoken. Antiques, fishing, parks, shopping, cross-country skiing and watersports nearby.

"Next time I'll bring company. It's much too romantic to be here alone! This is such a lovely home."

William's Grant Inn

154 High St
Bristol, RI 02809-2123
(401)253-4222 (800)596-4222

Circa 1808. This handsome Federal Colonial home was built by Governor William Bradford for his grandson. There are two beehive ovens and seven fireplaces as well as original wideboard pine floors and paired interior chimneys. Antique furnishings and folk art make the guest rooms inviting. The backyard is an ideal spot for relaxation with its patios, water garden and quaint stone walls.

Historic Interest: The area offers many historic homes, the Blithewold Mansion and Gardens, Coggeshall Farm Museum and several other museums.

Innkeeper(s): Michael Rose. $65-105. MC VISA AX DS PC TC. TAC10. 5 rooms, 3 with PB, 5 with FP. Breakfast included in rates. Types of meals: full breakfast, gourmet breakfast. Afternoon tea available. Beds: QD. Turndown service, ceiling fan in room. Bicycles on premises. Small meetings hosted. Antiques, fishing, parks, shopping, sporting events, watersports nearby.

Location: Located in the heart of Bristol's historic waterfront district.

Publicity: *New York Times, Sun Sentinal, Providence Journal, Bristol Phoenix.*

"We felt better than at home with the wonderful treats (the breakfasts were fabulous), the lovely rooms, the inn is full of inspiration and innovation . . ."

Middletown G7

The Inn at Shadow Lawn

120 Miantonomi Ave
Middletown, RI 02842-5450
(401)847-0902 (800)352-3750 Fax:(401)848-6529
E-mail: randy@shadowlawn.com

Circa 1855. This elegant, three-story Stick Victorian inn, listed in the National Register, offers a glimpse of fine living in an earlier age. The innkeepers' attention to detail is evident throughout, with French crystal chandeliers, stained-glass windows and parquet floors in the library as a few of the highlights. Parlors are found on each of the inn's floors. Newport's many attractions, including the Art Museum, sailing and the world famous Newport mansions are just a short drive from the inn.

Historic Interest: Mansions from "Gilded Age" (5 minutes).

Innkeeper(s): Randy & Selma Fabricant. $55-155. MC VISA AX TC. 8 rooms with PB, 8 with FP. 2 conference rooms. Breakfast included in rates. Type of meal: full breakfast. Beds: KQT. Phone and air conditioning in room. Fax, copier and library on premises. Weddings, small meetings, family reunions and seminars hosted. Antiques nearby.

"A dream come true! Thanks for everything! We'll be back."

Narragansett H5

The 1900 House B&B

59 Kingstown Rd
Narragansett, RI 02882-3309
(401)789-7971

Circa 1900. For more than a century, Narragansett has been a hot spot for summer vacationers. Guests at the 1900 House enjoy both close access to the town's restaurants and shops as well as a nostalgic look back at the Victorian era. The innkeepers keep a stereoscope, hat boxes filled with antique post cards and other collectibles on hand for guests to discover. You might spot the wedding certificate of the home's original owner. Waffles topped with fresh fruit and cream are typical of the rich treats served at breakfast.

Innkeeper(s): Sandra & Bill Panzeri. $65-75. PC TC. 3 rooms, 1 with PB. Breakfast included in rates. Meals: full breakfast, gourmet breakfast and early coffee/tea. Beds: D. Antiques, fishing, parks, shopping, sporting events, theater and watersports nearby.

"Wonderful! So relaxing and lovely, lovely breakfasts."

The Richards

144 Gibson Ave
Narragansett, RI 02882-3937
(401)789-7746

Circa 1884. J.P. Hazard, an influential member of one of the county's most prominent families, built this home, which resembles a English-country stone manor. The rooms are appointed with a beautiful collection of antiques, and each guest room has a fireplace and sitting area. Down comforters, carafes of sherry and candles are among the romantic amenities. After a restful night's sleep, guests are presented with a gourmet breakfast. French toast, made from Portuguese sweet bread, or rich, chocolate pancakes topped with an orange sauce might appear as the daily entree. The home is listed in the National Register of Historic Places.

Innkeeper(s): Nancy & Steven Richards. $70-135. PC TC. 5 rooms, 1 with PB, 5 with FP. 2 suites. Breakfast included in rates. Types of meals: full breakfast and gourmet breakfast. Beds: KQ. Library on premises. Antiques, fishing, golf, theater and watersports nearby.

Publicity: *Yankee Traveler, Home, Providence Journal-Bulletin, Narragansett Times.*

Newport H7

The Brinley Victorian Inn

23 Brinley St
Newport, RI 02840-3238
(401)849-7645 (800)999-8523

Circa 1870. This is a three-story Victorian with a mansard roof and long porch. A cottage on the property dates from 1850. There are two parlors and a library providing a quiet haven from the bustle of the Newport wharfs. Each room is decorated with period wallpapers and furnishings. There are fresh flowers and mints on the pillows. The brick courtyard is planted with bleeding hearts, peonies and miniature roses, perennials of the Victorian era.

Historic Interest: Touro Synagogue (5-minute walk), Trinity Church (5-minute walk).

Innkeeper(s): John & Jennifer Sweetman. $55-150. MC VISA. 17 rooms, 13 with PB. 1 suite. Breakfast included in rates. Beds: KQDT.
Location: Newport Historic District.
Publicity: *New Hampshire Times, Boston Woman, Country Victorian, Yankee.*

"Ed and I had a wonderful anniversary. The Brinley is as lovely and cozy as ever! The weekend brought back lots of happy memories."

The Burbank Rose B&B

111 Memorial Blvd W
Newport, RI 02840-3469
(401)849-9457 (888)297-5800

Circa 1850. The innkeepers of this cheery, yellow home named their B&B in honor of their ancestor, famed horticulturist Luther Burbank. As a guest, he probably would be taken by the bright, flowery hues that adorn the interior of this Federal-style home. Rooms, some of which afford harbor views, are light and airy with simple decor. The innkeepers serve afternoon refreshments and a substantial breakfast buffet. The home is located in Newport's Historic Hill district and within walking distance of shops, restaurants and many of the seaside village's popular attractions.

Innkeeper(s): John & Bonnie McNeely. $49-129. AX TC. 4 rooms with PB. Breakfast and afternoon tea included in rates. Types of meals: full breakfast and early coffee/tea. Beds: QDT. Air conditioning in room. TV, VCR and copier on premises. Antiques, fishing, shopping, theater and watersports nearby.

Castle Hill Inn & Resort

Ocean Ave
Newport, RI 02840
(401)849-3800 (888)466-1355

Circa 1874. The rambling Victorian was built as a summer home for scientist Alexander Agassiz. A laboratory included in the house was a forerunner of the Woods Hole Marine Laboratory. Many original furnishings remain and there are spectacular ocean views from most of the rooms. Harbor House rooms have French doors  that open to sweeping views of Narragansett Bay, whirlpool baths and fireplaces. A continental breakfast buffet, complimentary afternoon tea, lunch, dinner and Sunday brunch are available.

Innkeeper(s): Len Panaggio. $95-325. MC VISA AX DS TC. 21 rooms, 34 with PB. 18 cottages. Type of meal: continental breakfast. Afternoon tea, dinner and lunch available. Restaurant on premises. Beds: KD. Phone in room.
Location: Five miles south of downtown.

Cliffside Inn

2 Seaview Ave
Newport, RI 02840-3627
(401)847-1811 (800)845-1811 Fax:(401)848-5850
E-mail: cliff@wsii.com

Circa 1880. The governor of Maryland, Thomas Swann, built this Newport summer house in the style of a Second Empire Victorian. It features a mansard roof and many bay windows.

 The rooms are decorated in a Victorian motif. Suites have marble baths, and most rooms have fireplaces. Twelve rooms have a double whirlpool tub. The Cliff Walk is located one block from the inn.

Innkeeper(s): Stephan Nicolas. $185-350. MC VISA AX DC DS PC TC. TAC10. 15 rooms with PB, 12 with FP. 7 suites. 1 cottage. Breakfast and afternoon tea included in rates. Types of meals: gourmet breakfast and early coffee/tea. Beds: KQ. Phone, air conditioning, turndown service, ceiling fan, TV and VCR in room. Fax on premises. French spoken. Antiques, fishing, shopping, theater and watersports nearby.
Publicity: *Country Inns, Philadelphia, Discerning Traveler, New York, Boston, Good Morning America.*

"...it captures the grandeur of the Victorian age."

Corner House B&B

39 Elm St
Newport, RI 02840-2430
(401)847-8888

Circa 1774. This blue Colonial, pristine with white trim, offers an enchanting secret garden behind the inn and is featured on the town's garden tour. One block away is the outer harbor. Guest rooms feature working fireplaces and country antiques. Luscious omelets and breakfast casseroles are offered fireside, but special diets are accommodated. Gas-lit streets add to the character of the inn's neighborhood, the Point Section historic district. Walk to shops, museums, galleries and restaurants.

Innkeeper(s): Paul & Nancy Quattrucci. $80-135. MC VISA PC TC. TAC10. 3 rooms with PB, 2 with FP. Breakfast included in rates. Types of meals: full breakfast and gourmet breakfast. Beds: KQT. Air conditioning, ceiling fan and TV in room. Antiques, fishing, parks, shopping, sporting events, golf, theater and watersports nearby.

Francis Malbone House

392 Thames St
Newport, RI 02840-6604
(401)846-0392 (800)846-0392 Fax:(401)848-5956

Circa 1760. Newport, during the 18th century, was one of the busiest harbors in the Colonies. A shipping merchant, Colonel Francis Malbone, built the historic portion of this home, which

includes nine of the inn's 18 guest rooms. The newer addition was completed in 1996. Fine furnishings fill the rooms, most of which offer a fireplace. Eleven rooms include a Jacuzzi tub. The inn's location, on the harborfront, is another wonderful feature. The breakfasts, heralded by Bon Appetit, include entrees such as pecan waffles with maple whipped cream or eggs Benedict with a roasted red pepper hollandaise. Guests are sure to be busy exploring Newport with its abundance of historic sites and spectacular mansions.

Innkeeper(s): Will Dewey. $135-245. MC VISA AX. TAC10. 18 rooms with PB, 15 with FP. 2 suites. 2 conference rooms. Breakfast and afternoon tea included in rates. Types of meals: full breakfast, gourmet breakfast and early coffee/tea. Beds: KQ. Phone, air conditioning, turndown service and TV in room. Fax on premises. Handicap access. Small meetings hosted. Antiques, parks, shopping and golf nearby.

Publicity: *Colonial Homes, Bon Appetit, Country Inns.*

Halidon Hill Guest House

Halidon Ave
Newport, RI 02840
(401)847-8318 (800)227-2130

Circa 1969. This contemporary, two-story Georgian-style inn offers a convenient location and comfortable accommodations for those exploring the Newport area. The two spacious suites both boast kitchenettes. The inn is just a 10-minute walk to Hammersmith Farm and provides easy access to the area's mansions, restaurants and shopping. Guests will enjoy lounging on the roomy deck near the in-ground pool, or in front of the fireplace in cooler weather. Newport Harbor and the Tennis Hall of Fame are nearby.

Innkeeper(s): Helen & Paul Burke. $75-200. AX DC DS PC TC. 2 suites. Breakfast included in rates. Types of meals: full breakfast and early coffee/tea. Beds: KQDT. Phone, air conditioning, ceiling fan and TV in room. VCR and swimming on premises. Handicap access. Small meetings and family reunions hosted. Antiques, fishing, parks, shopping, sporting events, golf, theater and watersports nearby.

Hammett House Inn

505 Thames St
Newport, RI 02840-6723
(401)848-0593 (800)548-9417 Fax:(401)848-2258
E-mail: CIS 76470,3440

Circa 1758. This three-story Georgian Federal-style home has watched the nation grow and prosper from its little nook on Thames Street. The rooms are decorated with romance in mind. Especially picturesque are the Rose and Windward rooms, which afford views of Newport Harbor. The Pewter Room includes a unique metal canopy bed. The inn is a short walk from shops, restaurants and the waterfront.

Innkeeper(s): Marianne Spaziano. $95-195. MC VISA AX DS TC. 5 rooms with PB. Breakfast included in rates. Meal: continental-plus breakfast. Restaurant on premises. Beds: Q. Air conditioning and TV in room. Fax on premises. Antiques, fishing, parks, shopping, theater and watersports nearby.

Hydrangea House Inn

16 Bellevue Ave
Newport, RI 02840-3206
(401)846-4435 (800)945-4667 Fax:(401)846-6602
E-mail: bandbinn@ids.net

The scent of fresh flowers welcomes guests into their cheery rooms at this B&B, which once housed a school of music. After abdicating his throne, King Edward was a guest at this home. Romance is emphasized by the decor in each of the individually appointed guest rooms, which feature wicker and antique furnishings. Breakfasts are served on the veranda, with its view of the gardens. In cooler weather, the breakfast buffet is set up in the art gallery, which features many original works.

Innkeeper(s): Grant Edmondson. $75-280. MC VISA. 6 rooms. Breakfast included in rates. Type of meal: full breakfast.

Inntowne Inn

6 Mary St
Newport, RI 02840-3028
(401)846-9200 (800)457-7803 Fax:(401)846-1534

Circa 1935. This Colonial-style inn is an elegant spot from which to enjoy the seaside town of Newport. Waverly and Laura Ashley prints decorate the individually appointed guest rooms, some of which have four-poster or canopy beds. The innkeeper serves an expanded continental breakfast with items such as fresh fruit, quiche and ham and cheese croissants. Afternoon tea also is served. A day in Newport offers many activities, including touring the Tennis Hall of Fame, taking a cruise through the harbor, shopping for antiques or perhaps taking a trek down Cliff Walk, a one-and-a-half-mile path offering the ocean on one side and historic mansions on the other.

Innkeeper(s): Carmella Gardner. $95-189. MC VISA AX. 26 rooms with PB. 1 suite. Afternoon tea included in rates. Type of meal: continental-plus breakfast. Beds: KQDT. Phone and air conditioning in room. TV, VCR, fax, copier and library on premises. Weddings, small meetings and family reunions hosted. Antiques, parks and shopping nearby.

"Thank you for your excellent service with a smile."

Jailhouse Inn

13 Marlborough St
Newport, RI 02840-2545
(401)847-4638 (800)427-9444 Fax:(401)849-0605

Circa 1742. Built in 1772, this restored Colonial jail maintains just a touch of jail flavor as a backdrop to comfort and convenience. Prison-striped bed coverings and tin cups and plates for breakfast express the jailhouse motif. Guests can stay in the Cell Block, Maximum Security or Solitary Confinement, each on a separate level of the inn. Nevertheless, because guests pay for their time here, there are luxuries in abundance. A complimentary continental breakfast buffet and afternoon tea service is offered daily.

Historic Interest: The inn is located one block from harbor restaurants and shops.

Innkeeper(s): Eric Jones. $45-225. DC. 22 rooms with PB. 1 conference room. Type of meal: continental breakfast. Afternoon tea available. Beds: Q. Air conditioning and TV in room. Handicap access. Fishing nearby.

Publicity: *Providence Journal.*

"I found this very relaxing and a great pleasure."

Marshall Slocum Guest House

29 Kay St
Newport, RI 02840-2735
(401)841-5120 (800)372-5120 Fax:(401)846-3787
E-mail: marshallslocuminn@edgenet.net

Circa 1855. Victorian homes line the streets in the Historic Hill District of Newport, where this two-and-a-half-story house is situated on an acre of grounds. Architectural features include shutters, a hip roof with dormer

windows and a front porch. The inn is furnished with antiques and contemporary pieces. A favorite breakfast is Fluffy Belgian Waffles served with freshly picked strawberries and mountains of whipped cream. Don't miss the afternoon refreshments, and if you are staying longer than two nights ask about the innkeepers' Lobster Dinner Package. A five to ten-minute walk will take you to the downtown area and the beach.

Innkeeper(s): Joan & Julie Wilson. $60-110. MC VISA AX PC TC. TAC10. 6 rooms, 3 with PB, 2 with FP. Breakfast and evening snack included in rates. Type of meal: gourmet breakfast. Dinner available. Beds: KQT. Air conditioning and ceiling fan in room. TV, VCR, fax, bicycles and library on premises. Weddings, small meetings and seminars hosted. Amusement parks, antiques, fishing, parks, shopping, sporting events, golf, theater, watersports nearby.

Old Beach Inn

19 Old Beach Rd
Newport, RI 02840-3237
(401)849-3479 (888)303-5033 Fax:(401)847-1236

Circa 1879. Stroll through the backyard at this enchanting Gothic Victorian bed & breakfast and you'll find a garden, lily pond and romantic gazebo. Innkeepers Luke and Cyndi Murray have kept a whimsical, romantic theme running inside and outside. Each of the guest rooms, two of

which are located in the carriage house, bears the name of a flower. Delightful decor with bright wallcoverings and linens accent the beautiful furnishings. The Lily Room includes a 19th-century cottage bed and peach and ivory decor, while the powder blue and white Forget-Me-Not room is filled with wicker. Every item in the room is color-coordinated and features special painting and stenciling created by Cyndi. An egg casserole, quiche or stuffed French toast is offered on Sundays. The area abounds with shops and restaurants, including a famous eatery managed by Luke.

Historic Interest: Several mansions in the area are open for tours. The Redwood Library is a short walk from the inn, as is the Tennis Hall of Fame. The historic harborfront is a seven-minute stroll.

Innkeeper(s): Luke & Cynthia Murray. $85-175. MC VISA AX DS PC TC. 7 rooms with PB, 5 with FP. Breakfast included in rates. Type of meal: continental-plus breakfast. Beds: QD. Air conditioning and ceiling fan in room. Fax and copier on premises. Weddings, small meetings, family reunions and seminars hosted. Antiques, fishing, parks, shopping, theater, watersports nearby.

Publicity: *Yankee, Sun Sentinel, Boston Magazine.*

"Thanks for your exceptional and stylish innkeeping. We never wanted for one comfort."

The Pilgrim House

123 Spring St
Newport, RI 02840-6805
(401)846-0040 (800)525-8373 Fax:(401)846-0357

Circa 1879. This Victorian inn, located in the heart of Newport, has a rooftop deck with a panoramic view of the harbor. The home is within walking distance of shops, restaurants, the Cliff Walk and the Newport mansions. In the afternoon, the innkeepers serve sherry and shortbread in the living room, which often is warmed by a crackling fire.

Historic Interest: Touro Synagogue, Trinity Church, Newport Harbor (1 block), Tennis Hall of Fame (3 blocks).

Innkeeper(s): Pam & Bruce Bayuk. $65-165. MC VISA PC. TAC10. 10 rooms, 8 with PB. 1 conference room. Breakfast and afternoon tea included in rates. Types of meals: continental breakfast, continental-plus breakfast and early coffee/tea. Beds: QDT. Phone and air conditioning in room. TV, fax and copier on premises. Small meetings, family reunions and seminars hosted. Antiques, fishing, parks, shopping, theater and watersports nearby.

Location: In the heart of the historic district, one-and-one-half blocks from Newport's harbor and wharfs.

Publicity: *The Times.*

"What can I say, it's a perfect hideaway. Great time was had by all."

Stella Maris Inn

91 Washington
Newport, RI 02840
(401)849-2862

Circa 1861. Made of stone with black walnut woodwork inside, this is a French Victorian with mansard roof and wraparound veranda. The inn's two acres are landscaped with flower beds. Bright yet elegant wall coverings and fabrics set off the antiques, paintings and interior architectural points of interest. In the National Register, the inn is an early Newport mansion that was originally called "Blue Rocks". It later became a convent at which time it was renamed Stella Maris, "star of the sea". Several of the inn's lavishly appointed rooms offer ocean views, and some have fireplaces.

Innkeeper(s): Dorothy & Ed Madden. $75-195. PC TC. 9 rooms with PB, 4 with FP. 1 cottage. Breakfast and afternoon tea included in rates. Types of meals: continental-plus breakfast and early coffee/tea. Beds: KQDT. Ceiling fan in room. TV and library on premises. Small meetings and family reunions hosted. French spoken. Antiques, fishing, parks, shopping, golf, theater and watersports nearby.

"Rejuvenation for the soul!"

Villa Liberte

22 Liberty St
Newport, RI 02840-3221
(401)846-7444 (800)392-3717 Fax:(401)849-6429

Circa 1910. This colorful European-style inn originally served as the site of a Bavarian restaurant. The exterior, decorated with window boxes, plants, flowers and red trim, is a pleasing site along Liberty Street. The building also has a colorful history. Among the many stories, the restaurant was a hot spot after World War I and during the 1920s, when soldiers would come here to enjoy a meal and perhaps the company of a lady. Today, guests might enter their room to find a four-poster bed dressed in deep green and paisley linens and other fine traditional furnishings. The Sunroom is a wonderful spot to relax, decorated with wicker furnishings, plants and a ceiling fan. Newport is always bustling with activities, and there are plenty of fine shops and restaurants nearby.

Innkeeper(s): Leigh Anne Mosco. $69-195. MC VISA AX TC. 15 rooms with PB. 7 suites. 1 conference room. Breakfast and afternoon tea included in rates. Type of meal: continental-plus breakfast. Beds: QDT. Phone, air conditioning and TV in room. Fax on premises. Weddings, small meetings, family reunions and seminars hosted. Antiques, fishing, parks, shopping, theater and watersports nearby.

Willows of Newport-Romantic Inn & Garden

8-10 Willow St, Historic Point
Newport, RI 02840-1927
(401)846-5486 Fax:(401)849-8215

Circa 1740. There's little wonder why this charming inn is known as The Romantic Inn. The spectacular secret garden, with its abundance of foliage, colorful blooms and a heart-shaped fish pond, is a popular stop on Newport's Secret Garden Tour. The inn is a three-time recipient of the Newport Best Garden Award. The French Quarter room and Canopy Room both boast views of the gardens, and guests awake to the fragrances of the many flowers. The romantic Victorian Wedding Room, decorated in pastel greens and rose, offers a queen canopy bed, hand-painted furniture and a fireplace. The Colonial Wedding Room features lace accents, a cannonball king bed and an original 1740s fireplace. A continental breakfast is delivered to your room on bone china with silver services. Innkeeper Pattie Murphy, aside from her gardening and decorating skills, is a native Newporter and is full of information about the city. Ask about the inn's new "Silk & Chandelier" collection.

Historic Interest: The home is listed as National Landmark. Newport is the home of the Touro Synagogue, the oldest Jewish house of worship in North America. The Tennis Hall of Fame and the nation's oldest library, Redwood, are popular attractions. Don't forget to visit the nation's oldest operating tavern, The White Horse Tavern, which first opened in 1687. Sunset sailing and a variety of popular restaurants are located nearby.

Innkeeper(s): Patricia 'Pattie' Murphy. $98-198. PC TC. TAC10. 8 rooms with PB. Breakfast, evening snack included in rates. Meal: continental-plus breakfast. Picnic lunch, room service available. Beds: KQD. Phone and air conditioning in room. Antiques, fishing, parks, shopping, watersports nearby.
Publicity: *Newport Daily News, Bostonia, New Woman, PM Magazine.*

"We enjoyed our getaway in your inn for its peace, elegance and emphasis on romance."

Providence   C6

Old Court B&B

144 Benefit St
Providence, RI 02903-1208
(401)751-2002 Fax:(401)272-4830

Circa 1863. Adjacent to the historic Rhode Island Courthouse, this Italianate building originally served as an Episcopal rectory. Indoor shutters, chandeliers hanging from 12-foot ceilings and elaborate Italian marble mantelpieces provide the gracious setting for antique Victorian beds. Some rooms overlook the capitol. Brown University, Rhode Island School of Design and downtown Providence are a short walk away.

Innkeeper(s): Jon Rosenblatt. $75-260. TAC1. 11 rooms with PB. 1 suite. Breakfast included in rates. Types of meals: full breakfast and gourmet breakfast. Beds: KQDT. Phone and air conditioning in room. Fax and copier on premises. Weddings and small meetings hosted. Antiques, parks, shopping, sporting events and theater nearby.
Location: On historic Benefit Street.
Publicity: *New York Times.*

"My only suggestion is that you do everything in your power not to change it."

State House Inn

43 Jewett St
Providence, RI 02908-4904
(401)351-6111 Fax:(401)351-4261

Circa 1889. Shaker and Colonial furniture fill this turn-of-the-century home, located in the midst of a quaint and peaceful Providence neighborhood. The rooms provide amenities that will please any business traveler and have the country comfort and elegance of days gone by. The common room contains a small library for guest use. A famed historic district, featuring restored homes and buildings, is three blocks away, and the capitol is a five-minute walk.

Innkeeper(s): Frank & Monica Hopton. $79-119. EP. MC VISA AX PC TC. TAC10. 10 rooms with PB, 2 with FP. Breakfast included in rates. Type of meal: full breakfast. Afternoon tea available. Beds: KQ. Phone, air conditioning and TV in room. Fax and copier on premises. Antiques and parks nearby.
Location: Forty minutes from Newport.
Publicity: *Providence Magazine.*

"Thank you again for the warm, comfortable and very attractive accommodations."

South Kingstown   H5

Admiral Dewey Inn

668 Matunuck Beach Rd
South Kingstown, RI 02879-7021
(401)783-2090 (800)457-2090 Fax:(401)783-0680

Circa 1898. Although the prices have risen a bit since this inn's days as a boarding house (the rate was 50 cents per night), this Stick-style home still offers hospitality and comfort. The National Register inn is within walking distance of Matunuck Beach. Guests can enjoy the sea breeze from the inn's wraparound porch. Period antiques decorate the guest rooms, some of which offer ocean views.

Historic Interest: One half mile to Historic Theatre By The Sea.

Innkeeper(s): Joan Lebel. $80-120. MC VISA PC. 10 rooms, 8 with PB. Breakfast included in rates. Types of meals: continental-plus breakfast and early coffee/tea. Picnic lunch available. Beds: QDT. TV, VCR, fax, copier and swimming on premises. Weddings, small meetings, family reunions and seminars hosted. Polish spoken. Antiques, fishing, parks, shopping, theater and watersports nearby.
Publicity: *Yankee Traveler, Rhode Island Monthly.*

Wakefield H5

Larchwood Inn

521 Main St
Wakefield, RI 02879-4003
(401)783-5454 (800)275-5450 Fax:(401)783-1800

Circa 1831. The Larchwood Inn and its adjacent sister inn, Holly House, were both constructed in the same era. The two are sprinkled with antiques and are family-run, with 20th-century amenities. Scottish touches are found throughout the inn and the Tam O'Shanter Tavern. Three dining rooms offer breakfast, lunch and dinner. (Breakfast is an extra charge.) The tavern offers dancing on weekends. Beaches, sailing and deep sea fishing all are nearby.

Innkeeper(s): Francis & Diann Browning. $40-120. MC VISA AX DC CB DS. 19 rooms, 13 with PB, 3 with FP. 1 conference room. Type of meal: full breakfast. Dinner, lunch, banquet service and catered breakfast available. Phone in room. TV, fax and copier on premises. Weddings, small meetings, family reunions and seminars hosted. Antiques, shopping, downhill skiing, cross-country skiing and theater nearby.

Westerly I2

The Villa

190 Shore Rd
Westerly, RI 02891-3629
(401)596-1054 (800)722-9240 Fax:(401)596-6268

Circa 1938. In a Dutch Colonial style with a Mediterranean influence, the Villa offers Italian porticos and verandas set on a lushly landscaped acre and a half. Mahogany woodwork is accented by ruby and sapphire fabrics, a queen-size bed and private sitting room in La Sala di Venezia, while the Blue Grotto features a Jacuzzi, fireplace and natural stone walls. La Sala del Cielo has skylights and an ocean view in the distance. Four of the rooms include a Jacuzzi. The outdoor Jacuzzi and Mediterranean-style pool are popular areas in summer. Beaches, an aquarium and casino gambling both are nearby.

Innkeeper(s): Jerry Maiorano. $75-225. MC VISA AX DS TC. TAC10. 6 suites, 2 with FP. Breakfast included in rates. Type of meal: early coffee/tea. Beds: KQ. Phone, air conditioning, ceiling fan and TV in room. VCR, fax, spa and swimming on premises. Weddings, family reunions and seminars hosted. Italian spoken. Antiques, fishing, parks, shopping, golf, theater and watersports nearby.

Pets Allowed: Well behaved pets on leash with prior owner approval.

Wyoming G3

The Cookie Jar B&B

64 Kingstown Rd, Rt 138
Wyoming, RI 02898-1103
(401)539-2680 (800)767-4262

Circa 1732. The living room of this historic farmhouse inn once served as a blacksmith shop. The inn's original stone walls and wood ceiling remain, along with a granite fireplace built by a Native American stonemason. Years later, as rooms were added, the building became the Cookie Jar Tea Room, a name the innkeepers judged worth keeping. Visitors select their full breakfast fare from a menu provided the night before. The inn's grounds boast more than 60 fruit trees, a flower garden and a barn. Those who love the beach or fishing will find both fresh and salt water within a 20-minute drive.

Historic Interest: The historic towns of Wickford and Mystic, Conn. are a 20-minute drive, Newport and Providence are within 35 minutes. Boston is more than an hour from the inn.

Innkeeper(s): Charles Sohl. $75. PC TC. TAC10. 3 suites. Breakfast included in rates. Type of meal: full breakfast. Beds: KQDT. Air conditioning and TV in room. VCR on premises. Small meetings and family reunions hosted. Amusement parks, antiques, fishing, shopping, downhill skiing, cross-country skiing, sporting events, theater and watersports nearby.

Location: Boston is slightly more than an hour from the inn.

"Our accommodations were so comfortable and the breakfasts delicious!"

South Carolina

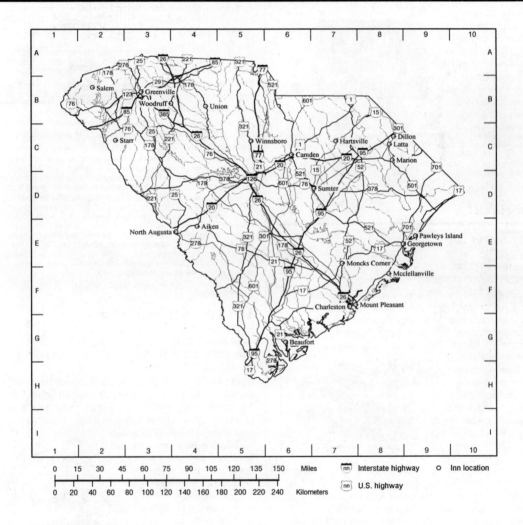

	1	2	3	4	5	6	7	8	9	10	

Salem, Greenville, Woodruff, Union, Starr, Winnsboro, Camden, Hartsville, Dillon, Latta, Marion, Sumter, North Augusta, Aiken, Moncks Corner, Pawleys Island, Georgetown, Mcclellanville, Charleston, Mount Pleasant, Beaufort

Aiken E4

White House Inn

240 Newberry St SW
Aiken, SC 29801-3854
(803)649-2935

Circa 1924. History lovers will appreciate this inn's location, surrounded by three historic districts in the village of Old Aiken.

The acre of grounds is dotted with many trees and a large gazebo, often the site for weddings. The Dutch Colonial is furnished with antiques, and two rooms include a fireplace. Omelets, breakfast meats, freshly baked breads and seasonal fruit are among the morning offerings.

Innkeeper(s): Hal & Mary Ann Mackey. $60-95. MC VISA AX DC DS PC TC. TAC5. 4 rooms with PB, 2 with FP. Breakfast included in rates. Type of meal: full breakfast. Beds: Q. Phone, air conditioning, ceiling fan and TV in room. Weddings, small meetings, family reunions and seminars hosted. German, French and Spanish spoken. Antiques, parks, shopping, sporting events, theater and watersports nearby.

"You should be congratulated. Keep it up."

Beaufort G6

Bay Street Inn

601 Bay St
Beaufort, SC 29902-5521
(803)522-0050 (800)256-9285

Circa 1850. From the two-story veranda at this historic Antebellum manor, guests partake of a stunning view of the Intracoastal Waterway. Most of the guest rooms also offer a water view. Each of the six guest rooms include a fireplace. In addition to a full, gourmet breakfast, guests enjoy afternoon tea and in the evenings, wine and cheese. There is a 24-hour concierge service. The inn was a film site for the movie, "The Prince of Tides." Joel Pointsett planted the original poin-

settia plants while visiting the builder. The inn's location, in the heart of a Beaufort historic district, provides close access to a multitude of outdoor activities. Golf, tennis, watersports all are nearby, and guests can take a carriage tour of the area.

Innkeeper(s): Peter Steciak. $125-195. EP. MC VISA AX DC CB DS PC TC. TAC10. 9 rooms with PB, 8 with FP. Type of meal: full breakfast. Beds: KQD. Phone in room.

Location: On the water in the historic district.

Publicity: *The New York Times, Southern Living.*

"From the huge piano in the music room to the lush paneling of the library, the old house is an elegant reminder of bygone days of gracious Southern living."

The Beaufort Inn

809 Port Republic St
Beaufort, SC 29901-1257
(843)521-9000 Fax:(843)521-9500

Circa 1897. Every inch of this breathtaking inn offers something special. The interior is decorated to the hilt with lovely furnishings, plants, beautiful rugs and warm, inviting tones.

Rooms include four-poster and canopy beds combined with the modern amenities such as fireplaces, wet bars and stocked refrigerators. Enjoy a complimentary full breakfast at the inn's gourmet restaurant. The chef offers everything from a light breakfast of fresh fruit, cereal and a bagel to heartier treats such as pecan peach pancakes and Belgium waffles served with fresh fruit and crisp bacon.

Historic Interest: History buffs can visit Secession House, where the first ordinance for Southern secession was drawn up. Tabby Manse and Old Sheldon Church, burned in both the Revolutionary and Civil wars, still stand today. Penn Center, the first school for freed slaves, is located on St. Helena Island.

Innkeeper(s): Russell & Debbie Fielden. $125-195. MC VISA AX DS PC TC. TAC10. 13 rooms with PB, 4 with FP. 1 suite. 1 conference room. Breakfast and afternoon tea included in rates. Types of meals: full breakfast, gourmet breakfast and early coffee/tea. Dinner, picnic lunch, gourmet lunch, banquet service, catering service and room service available. Restaurant on premises. Beds: KQ. Phone, air conditioning, turndown service, ceiling fan, TV and VCR in room. Fax, copier and bicycles on premises. Handicap access. Weddings, small meetings, family reunions and seminars hosted. Antiques, fishing, parks, shopping, theater and watersports nearby.

Publicity: *Beaufort, Southern Living, Country Inns, Carolina Style, US Air, Town & Country..*

The Cuthbert House Inn B&B

1203 Bay St
Beaufort, SC 29902
(803)521-1315 (800)327-9275 Fax:(803)521-1314
E-mail: cuthbert@hargray.com

Circa 1790. This 18th-century Antebellum mansion, listed in the National Register, boasts a veranda overlooking Beaufort Bay. The home was built during Washington's presidency, and General W.T. Sherman was once a guest here. The home has been lovingly restored to its original grandeur. Rich painted walls are highlighted by fine molding. Hardwood floors are topped with Oriental rugs and elegant 19th-century furnishings. The morning meal is served in a breakfast room that overlooks the water. The surrounding area offers plenty of activities in every season, and for those celebrating a new marriage, a honeymoon package is available.

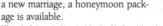

Historic Interest: Located in the National Landmark district.

Innkeeper(s): Gary & Sharon Groves. $135-195. MC VISA AX DS PC TC. TAC10. 6 rooms with PB. 3 suites. 2 conference rooms. Breakfast included in rates. Types of meals: continental breakfast, full breakfast and early coffee/tea. Beds: KQDT. Phone, air conditioning, turndown service and TV in room. VCR, fax and library on premises. Weddings, small meetings, family reunions and seminars hosted. Antiques, fishing, parks, watersports nearby.

Publicity: *Atlanta Journal-Constitution, Glamour, Travel & Leisure.*

Old Point Inn

212 New St
Beaufort, SC 29902-5540
(803)524-3177 Fax:(803)525-6544

Circa 1898. Built by William Waterhouse as a wedding present for his wife, Isabelle Richmond, this Queen Anne Victorian has wraparound verandas and a traditional southern garden. Guests

can relax in the hammock while watching boats ply the Intracoastal Waterway. Four pillared fireplaces, pocket doors and eyelash windows are features of the house. The inn is located in the residential historic district, with a waterfront park, a marina, restaurants and downtown shopping nearby.

Historic Interest: Santa Elena Archaeological Dig, Penn Center, Sheldon Ruins.

Innkeeper(s): Joe & Joan Carpentiere. $65-110. MC VISA AX. 4 rooms with PB. Breakfast included in rates. Type of meal: full breakfast. Beds: KQDT. Phone and air conditioning in room. TV, fax, bicycles and library on premises. Antiques, fishing, shopping, golf, theater and watersports nearby.

Publicity: *Islander, Southern Living, Southern Inns and Bed & Breakfast.*

"Like walking backwards in time. It's rare to find a bed, more comfortable than your own. Breakfast — perfect! We're saddened to leave; like leaving an old friend."

The Rhett House Inn

1009 Craven St
Beaufort, SC 29902-5577
(803)524-9030 Fax:(803)524-1310

Circa 1820. Most people cannot pass this stunning two-story clapboard house without wanting to step up to the long veran-

da and try the hammock. Guest rooms are furnished in antiques, with quilts, fresh flowers and many of the rooms offer private Jacuzzi tubs. Many guest rooms have fireplaces. Handsome gardens feature a fountain and are often the site for romantic weddings. Bicycles are available.

The inn is listed in the National Register.

Historic Interest: The inn is listed in the National Register.

Innkeeper(s): Stephen Harrison. $125-225. MC VISA AX. 17 rooms with PB, 8 with FP. Breakfast and afternoon tea included in rates. Types of meals: full breakfast and early coffee/tea. Dinner, evening snack, picnic lunch, catering service and room service available. Restaurant on premises. Beds: KQ. Phone, air conditioning, turndown service, ceiling fan and TV in room. Fax on premises. Handicap access. Weddings, small meetings, family reunions and seminars hosted. Antiques, fishing, theater and watersports nearby.

Location: In historic downtown.

Publicity: *New York Times, Vogue, Elle, Conde Nast Traveler, Travel & Leisure, Self, Brides, Martha Stewart. Ratings: 4 Stars.*

"A dream come true!"

Twosuns Inn B&B

1705 Bay St
Beaufort, SC 29902-5406
(843)522-1122 (800)532-4244 Fax:(843)522-1122
E-mail: twosuns@islc.net

Circa 1917. The Keyserling family built this Neoclassical Revival-style home, which was later used by the local board of education as housing for single, female teachers. The home has been completely refurbished, a difficult task, considering the home had been the victim of two fires. The U.S. Department of the Interior noted the renovation with a Historic Building Certification in 1996. Guest rooms boast bay views, and each has

its own theme. A gourmet breakfast and "Tea and Toddy Hour" are included in the rates.

Historic Interest: Beaufort has hosted film crews for many popular movies, including "Great Santini," "The Big Chill," "The Prince of Tides," "Forrest Gump" and "The Last Dance."

Innkeeper(s): Ron & Carrol Kay. $105-149. MC VISA AX DS PC TC. TAC10. 6 rooms with PB. 1 conference room. Breakfast and afternoon tea included in rates. Type of meal: full breakfast. Beds: KQT. Phone, air conditioning, ceiling fan and TV in room. VCR, fax, copier, bicycles and library on premises. Handicap access. Small meetings and seminars hosted. Antiques, fishing, parks, shopping, golf and theater nearby.

Publicity: *Beaufort Gazette, Sandlapper.*

"One could not wish for a better experience."

Camden   C6

A Camden, SC Bed & Breakfast

127 Union St
Camden, SC 29020-2700
(803)432-2366
E-mail: jaerickson@city-online.com

Circa 1920. This Federal-style home is built on what was a battlefield during the Revolutionary and Civil wars. The home originally served as the residence for a local judge. Rooms are decorated in a country style with many antiques. Guest will find poster beds topped with antique quilts, as well as quilts decorating the walls. Guests can stay in one of the rooms in the main house or in the adjacent cottage, which served as the judge's law library. Homemade breads and jam, savory egg dishes and fresh fruit are presented in the mornings on a breakfast table set with fine linens.

Innkeeper(s): Janie Erickson. $85-125. MC VISA AX DC CB DS PC TC. 3 rooms, 1 with PB, 3 with FP. 1 cottage. Breakfast included in rates. Types of meals: continental breakfast, continental-plus breakfast, full breakfast, gourmet breakfast and early coffee/tea. Evening snack and room service available. Beds: QT. Air conditioning and turndown service in room. TV and fax on premises. Antiques, fishing, parks, shopping, golf, theater, watersports nearby.

Pets Allowed: $25 pet fee.

"It was great being pampered by you."

Charleston   F7

1837 B&B

126 Wentworth St
Charleston, SC 29401-1737
(803)723-7166

Circa 1837. Originally owned by a cotton planter, this three-story home and brick carriage house currently is owned by two artists and is located centrally in the Charleston Historic District. The inn is within easy walking distance to shops,

restaurants and the convention center. Red cypress wainscoting, cornice molding and heart-of-pine floors adorn the formal parlor. A full gourmet breakfast is served in the formal dining room where guests gather to enjoy the company of new friends.

House specialties include sausage and grits casserole, sour cream coffee cake and warm fruit compote. Guest rooms are furnished with Oriental rugs and Charleston rice beds topped with fishnet canopies. Afternoon tea includes homemade scones and lemon curd.

Historic Interest: Old Market, Fort Sumter, Magnolia Plantation, Middleton Plantation, Drayton Plantation.

Innkeeper(s): Sherri Weaver & Richard Dunn. $69-129. MC VISA AX PC TC. 8 rooms with PB. 1 suite. Breakfast included in rates. Afternoon tea available. Beds: QT. Phone, air conditioning and ceiling fan in room. Small meetings and family reunions hosted. Antiques, shopping, sporting events and theater nearby.

Location: In the historic district.

Publicity: *New York Newsday, Kansas City Star, New York Times.*

"This cozy room added that special touch to a much-needed weekend getaway."

Ashley Inn B&B

201 Ashley Ave
Charleston, SC 29403-5810
(803)723-1848 Fax:(803)768-1230

Circa 1832. Pampering guests is the specialty of the house at this bed & breakfast. The rose exterior has green shutters and porches on the first and second stories. Bright, colorful rooms are accented by polished, hardwood floors, beautiful rugs and glorious furnishings and collectibles. Guest rooms boast antique four-poster, pencil-post or canopied rice beds. Breakfasts at Ashley Inn create culinary memories. Savory sausage pie, Crunchy French Toast with orange honey sauce or Ashley Inn Welsh

Rarebit are only a few of the mouth-watering specialties. An afternoon complete with plenty of homemade treats and evening sherry also is served. The innkeepers also provide bicycles for touring scenic Charleston.

Historic Interest: The inn is located in the Charleston historic district, full of interesting sites and shops.

Innkeeper(s): Sally & Bud Allen. $95-160. MC VISA AX DS. TAC10. 7 rooms with PB. 1 suite. Breakfast and afternoon tea included in rates. Type of meal: full breakfast. Beds: KQT. Antiques, fishing, theater and watersports nearby.

Publicity: *Charleston Post & Courier, LA Times, Country Inn Cooking.*

"A truly pampering experience for both of us!"

Belvedere B&B

40 Rutledge Ave
Charleston, SC 29401-1702
(803)722-0973

Circa 1900. This Colonial Revival home with its semicircular portico, Ionic columns and four piazzas boasts a beautiful view of

Charleston's Colonial Lake. Bright, airy rooms feature high ceilings with fans, polished wood floors, fireplaces, antique furnishings and Oriental rugs. Relax and enjoy the view on the piazzas or in one of the inn's public rooms.

Belvedere B&B is close to many wonderful restaurants and shops.

Historic Interest: Belvedere is located in the downtown historic district and within walking distance to many historical sites, including museums, points of interest and Civil War landmarks.

Innkeeper(s): David S. Spell & Rick Zender. $125-150. PC TC. 3 rooms with PB. Breakfast included in rates. Meal: continental-plus breakfast. Beds: Q. Air conditioning and ceiling fan in room. TV and VCR on premises. Antiques, fishing, parks, shopping, sporting events, theater and watersports nearby.

Publicity: *Discerning Traveler, Southern Brides.*

Cannonboro Inn

184 Ashley Ave
Charleston, SC 29403-5824
(803)723-8572 Fax:(803)768-1230

Circa 1853. Enjoy a breakfast feast on this inn's columned piazza as you gaze at the country garden and fountain. Guest rooms feature luxurious furnishings and antique four-poster and canopy beds. After a day in the city on the inn's touring bicycles, return for a scrumptious afternoon tea of home-baked treats and sherry. Cannonboro Inn has been rated as one of the best places to stay in the South.

Historic Interest: The Charleston Museum, Gibbes Museum and Rice Museum are nearby.

Innkeeper(s): Bud & Sally Allen. $69-160. MC VISA AX DS. TAC10. 6 rooms with PB. 1 suite. Breakfast and afternoon tea included in rates. Type of meal: full breakfast. Beds: KQT. Phone in room. Antiques, fishing, theater and watersports nearby.

Location: Historic area of downtown.

Publicity: *Chicago Sun-Times.*

"A brochure cannot convey the friendly, warm atmosphere created by Bud & Sally."

East Bay B&B

301 E Bay St
Charleston, SC 29401-1532
(803)722-4186 Fax:(803)720-8528

Circa 1807. Acclaimed in Charleston as one of the most unique heritage properties in town, and located in the Historic District, East Bay is a Single House with a carriage house in the Federal style. Two large piazzas overlook the walled garden and the harbor. Phoebe Pember, Civil War heroine, was born here. Spacious guest rooms are filled with original art, antiques and fine fabrics. Some rooms offer canopied beds while others have a fully draped poster bed. Breakfast is provided on a silver tray that may be enjoyed in the guest rooms, the dining room or onto the piazza.
Innkeeper(s): Carolyn Rivers. $105-185. MC VISA PC. TAC10. 4 rooms with PB, 3 with FP. 1 suite. 1 cottage. 1 conference room. Breakfast included in rates. Types of meals: continental-plus breakfast and early coffee/tea. Room service available. Beds: KQT. Phone, air conditioning and TV in room. VCR, fax and copier on premises. Small meetings hosted. Antiques, fishing, shopping and theater nearby.

Fulton Lane Inn

202 King St
Charleston, SC 29401-3109
(803)720-2600 (800)720-2688 Fax:(803)720-2940

Circa 1870. Confederate blockade runner John Rugheimer built this charming brick home a few years after the Civil War ended. Bright cheery decor and fine furnishings highlight the architecture, which includes cathedral ceilings and several fireplaces. The inn affords views of the city skyline, full of historic sites and gracious, Southern buildings. Guest rooms boast canopy beds draped with hand-strung netting and large, whirlpool tubs. The innkeepers include a stocked refrigerator in each room, and deliver breakfast on a silver tray. Wine and sherry are served in the lobby, and don't be surprised to find chocolates atop your pillow after you return from one of Charleston's many fine restaurants.
Historic Interest: Fulton Lane Inn is located in Charleston's historic district and the area abounds with historic sites.
Innkeeper(s): Randall Felkel. $115-270. EP. MC VISA DC. TAC10. 27 rooms with PB, 8 with FP. 4 suites. 2 conference rooms. Breakfast included in rates. Type of meal: continental-plus breakfast. Room service available. Beds: KQ. Phone, air conditioning, turndown service and TV in room. Fax and child care on premises. Handicap access. Weddings, small meetings, family reunions and seminars hosted. Antiques, fishing, parks, shopping, theater and watersports nearby.
Publicity: Southern Accents. Ratings: 4 Diamonds.

Hayne House B&B

30 King St
Charleston, SC 29401-2733
(803)577-2633 Fax:(803)577-5906

Circa 1755. Located one block from the Battery in one of Charleston's premiere private residential areas, this handsome clapboard house is in the National Register of Historic Places. Surrounded by a wrought-iron garden fence, it has an 1820 addition. It was built three stories tall to capture the harbor breeze. The inn is furnished in antiques, and there is an appealing back porch with rockers and a swing. In addition to the six tastefully decorated guest rooms, there are two romantic suites that feature individual whirlpool tubs. The

inn is a neighbor to some of the finest 18th- and 19th-century houses in America, including the Miles Brewton House, directly across the street, and the Nathaniel Russell House, just one block away. A full Southern breakfast is offered every morning.
Innkeeper(s): Brian & Jane McGreevy. $95-250. AP. MC VISA PC TC. TAC10. 6 rooms with PB, 4 with FP. 2 suites. Breakfast included in rates. Types of meals: full breakfast and early coffee/tea. Beds: KQT. Air conditioning in room. Fax, copier and library on premises. Antiques, fishing, parks, shopping and theater nearby.
"A fantasy realized. What a wonderful gift of hospitality."

John Rutledge House Inn

116 Broad St
Charleston, SC 29401-2437
(803)723-7999 (800)476-9741 Fax:(803)720-2615

Circa 1763. John Rutledge, first governor of South Carolina, Supreme Court Justice, and author and signer of the Constitution of the United States, wrote first drafts of the document in the stately ballroom of his Charleston home. In 1791 George Washington dined in this same room. Both men would be amazed by the house's recent restoration, which includes three lavish suites with elaborately carved Italian marble fireplaces, personal refrigerators, spas, air conditioning and televisions along with fine antiques and reproductions. Exterior ironwork on the house was designed in the 19th century and features palmetto trees and American eagles to honor Mr. Rutledge's service to the state and country.
Innkeeper(s): Linda Bishop. $160-325. EP. MC VISA AX DC. TAC10. 19 rooms with PB, 8 with FP. 3 suites. 2 cottages. 1 conference room. Breakfast and afternoon tea included in rates. Meals: continental-plus breakfast and full breakfast. Room service available. Beds: KQD. Phone, air conditioning, turndown service and TV in room. Fax and child care on premises. Handicap access. Weddings, small meetings, family reunions, seminars hosted. Spanish spoken. Antiques, fishing, parks, shopping, theater, watersports nearby.
Publicity: Insnider, Colonial Homes, New York Times, Southern Living, Southern Accents, Gourmet, Bon Appetit.
"Two hundred years of American history in two nights; first-class accommodations, great staff. John Rutledge should've had it so good!"

King George IV Inn

32 George St, Historic District
Charleston, SC 29401-1416
(803)723-9339 (888)723-1667 Fax:(803)723-7749

Circa 1792. This inn is a four-story Federal-style home with three levels of Charleston porches. All the rooms have fireplaces, high ceilings, original wide-planked hardwood floors and finely crafted original moldings and architectural detail. Peter Freneau, who was a prominent Charleston journalist, merchant, ship owner and Jeffersonian politician, occupied the house for many years. The inn offers hearty continental breakfast every morning. King Street shopping and restaurants are just a short walk away.
Historic Interest: The inn is located in the United States' largest historic district with more than 3,000 historic homes and mansions.
Innkeeper(s): Debra, Terry. $75-149. MC VISA PC TC. 10 rooms, 8 with PB, 9 with FP. 4 suites. Breakfast included in rates. Meal: continental-plus breakfast. Afternoon tea available. Beds: KQDT. Phone and air conditioning in room. Fax on premises. Small meetings and family reunions hosted. Antiques, fishing, parks, shopping, sporting events, theater and watersports nearby.

Kings Courtyard Inn

198 King St
Charleston, SC 29401-3109
(803)723-3000 (800)845-6119 Fax:(803)720-2608

Circa 1853. Having a Greek Revival style with unusual touches of Egyptian detail, this three-story building was designed by architect Francis D. Lee. The inn originally catered to plantation owners, shipping interests and merchant guests. Some of the rooms have fireplaces, canopied beds and views of the two inner courtyards or the garden. The building is one of historic King Street's largest and oldest structures and is at the center of Charleston's historic district.

Historic Interest: The home, which is listed in the National Register, is near all historic Charleston has to offer.

Innkeeper(s): Reginald Smith. $120-245. EP. MC VISA AX DC. TAC10. 41 rooms with PB, 13 with FP. 4 suites. 1 conference room. Breakfast included in rates. Types of meals: continental-plus breakfast and full breakfast. Room service available. Beds: KQD. Phone, air conditioning, turndown service and TV in room. Fax, copier, spa and child care on premises. Handicap access. Weddings, small meetings, family reunions and seminars hosted. Antiques, fishing, parks, shopping, theater and watersports nearby.

Location: In the historic district.

Publicity: *Southern Living, USA Today, Innsider, Travel Holiday.*

The Kitchen House

126 Tradd St
Charleston, SC 29401-2420
(803)577-6362 Fax:(803)965-5615

Circa 1732. This elegant, pre-Revolutionary War house was once the home of Dr. Peter Fayssoux, who served as Surgeon General in the Continental Army during the Revolutionary War. His descendant Bernard Elliot Bee became the Confederate general who bestowed the nickname of "Stonewall" to General Stonewall Jackson. The kitchen building has been restored around its four original fireplaces using antique materials. The inn's patio overlooks a Colonial herb garden, pond and fountain. The pantry and refrigerator are stocked with breakfast items. Juice, cereals, eggs, fresh fruit, specialty teas and coffee are provided for guests. Afternoon sherry awaits guests on arrival and a concierge service is offered.

Historic Interest: Located in the heart of Charleston's historic district, the inn offers close access to many museum homes and antique shopping.

Innkeeper(s): Lois Evans. $125-195. MC VISA. 2 rooms with PB. Breakfast included in rates. Type of meal: full breakfast. Afternoon tea available. Beds: QT. Phone, air conditioning and TV in room. VCR on premises. Weddings hosted. Antiques, fishing, parks, shopping, sporting events, theater and watersports nearby.

Publicity: *New York Times, Colonial Homes.*

"By all comparisons, one of the very best."

Palmer Home

5 East Battery
Charleston, SC 29401-2740
(803)723-2308 (888)723-1574 Fax:(803)853-1574

Circa 1849. With its magnificent view of the Charleston Harbour and historic Fort Sumter, this pink and white Italianesque mansion is one of 50 famous homes in the city. The house features 26 rooms, 15 guest rooms, 10 fireplaces and antiques dating back 200 years. The property includes the main house, carriage house and pool. Little David, the first semi-submersible vessel discharged during the war between the states was invented by the original owner's son. Fresh-squeezed orange juice, croissants, bagels and fresh fruit is offered each morning.

Innkeeper(s): Francess Palmer Hogan. $75-125. PC. 3 rooms with PB. 1 suite. Breakfast included in rates. Type of meal: continental breakfast. Beds: KQD. Phone, air conditioning, ceiling fan, TV and VCR in room. Fax, swimming, sauna and bicycles on premises. Weddings and small meetings hosted. Antiques, fishing, parks, cross-country skiing, sporting events, golf, theater and watersports nearby.

Sword Gate Inn

111 Tradd St
Charleston, SC 29401-2422
(803)723-8518

Circa 1800. This stately three-story inn is framed by a cobbled courtyard filled with magnolia trees, jasmine and azalea bushes. The elegantly appointed interiors make it easy to visualize formally attired guests passing through a reception line when the house served as the British consulate. There is a finely carved Italian Carrara marble fireplace and two enormous rococo Revival mirrors in the ballroom, the only registered ballroom in the city. There are two large suites with 15-foot ceilings. Some rooms feature canopied beds and fireplaces. All six rooms boast a Jacuzzi tub and new bathroom. Guests can enjoy a full breakfast and wine and cheese in the afternoon.

Historic Interest: Fort Sumter, Old Slave Market.

Innkeeper(s): Brian F. Mahoney. $99-271. MC VISA AX DS PC TC. 6 rooms. 2 suites. Breakfast included in rates. Type of meal: full breakfast. Afternoon tea available. Beds: Q. Antiques, theater and watersports nearby.

Location: In the historic district.

Publicity: *Business Week, Southern Living, Country Inns.*

"As always, your hospitality is second to none."

The Thomas Lamboll House

19 King St
Charleston, SC 29401-2734
(803)723-3212 (888)874-0793 Fax:(803)723-5222
E-mail: lamboll@aol.com

Circa 1735. A Colonial South Carolina judge, Thomas Lamboll, was the first resident of this impressive Colonial, located in Charleston's historic district. The home features two stories of piazzas set up with wicker furnishings, where guests can catch a cool breeze in the afternoon. The rooms are appointed with fine antiques, including Chippendale chairs and an early 19th-century sideboard in the dining room. There are two guest rooms, each with French doors leading to the piazzas, that overlook rooftops and the river in the distance.

Innkeeper(s): Marie & Emerson Read. $95-145. MC VISA DS PC TC. 2 rooms with PB, 2 with FP. 1 suite. Breakfast included in rates. Type of meal: continental breakfast. Beds: QT. Phone, air conditioning, ceiling fan and TV in room. Amusement parks, antiques, fishing, parks, shopping, sporting events, theater and watersports nearby.

Twenty Seven State Street B&B

27 State St
Charleston, SC 29401-2812
(803)722-4243

Circa 1804. Located in Charleston's distinctive French Quarter, this inn offers comfort and the height of elegance at the same time. Rooms are skillfully decorated with fine furnishings. Polished wood floors are topped with Oriental rugs.

Rooms have four-poster beds. The suites in the carriage house overlook the courtyard, and the rustic interior features exposed brick walls, antiques and reproductions. Although the inn does lend itself more toward romance, the innkeepers happily provide for well-behaved children in two of the suites. Breakfast is optional.

Innkeeper(s): Paul & Joye Craven. $85-180. PC TC. TAC10. 2 suites. Type of meal: continental-plus breakfast. Beds: Q. Phone, air conditioning and TV in room. Bicycles and library on premises. Antiques, parks, shopping, sporting events and theater nearby.

Location: In the heart of historic Charleston.

"We won't soon forget such a lovely retreat."

Two Meeting Street Inn

2 Meeting St
Charleston, SC 29401-2799
(803)723-7322

Circa 1892. Located directly on the Battery, horses and carriages carry visitors past the inn, perhaps the most photographed in Charleston. In the Queen Anne style, this Victorian has an unusual veranda graced by several ornate arches. The same family has owned and managed the inn since

1946 with no lapse in gracious Southern hospitality. Among the elegant amenities are original Tiffany stained-glass windows, English oak paneling and exquisite collections of silver and antiques. Continental breakfast is served in the formal dining room or side garden. Afternoon tea and sherry can be enjoyed in the rocking chairs on the front piazza each day.

Historic Interest: The inn is located in Charleston's historic district overlooking Battery Park, where shots were fired during the Civil War. There are several museum homes around the inn, and Charleston offers many other historical sites.

Innkeeper(s): Karen M. Spell. $155-265. 9 rooms with PB. Type of meal: continental breakfast. Afternoon tea available. Beds: QD. Phone in room.

Location: On the Battery.

Publicity: *Innsider, Southern Accent, Gourmet.*

"Were there such an award as the - Ultimate Hosting Award — it would without question go to the Two Meeting Street Inn. The graciousness of your friendly ways in such a wonderful setting are unsurpassable."

Vendue Inn

19 Vendue Range
Charleston, SC 29401-2129
(803)577-7970 (800)845-7900

Circa 1864. Built as a warehouse in the French Quarter, the inn is one short block from the historic waterfront. The bright lobby features fans and wicker furniture, and latticework screens, leather chairs and writing tables fill the reading room. Fireplaces, marble Jacuzzi tubs with separate showers are offered in the spacious junior suites, and complimentary, fully stocked bars in the large suites. Guests will delight in the afternoon wine and cheese served against the pleasant sound of

chamber music. Turndown service, a full breakfast, lunch and dinner are special features.

Innkeeper(s): Evelyn & Morton Needle. $115-230. MC VISA AX. 45 rooms with PB, 22 with FP. Breakfast and dinner included in rates. Types of meals: full breakfast and gourmet breakfast. Lunch available. Restaurant on premises. Beds: KQD. Fax, copier and spa on premises.

Location: In the historic district and near city market.

Publicity: *Southern Living, Bon Appetit.*

"Delightful. Excellent service."

Victoria House Inn

208 King St
Charleston, SC 29401-3149
(803)720-2944 (800)933-5464 Fax:(803)720-2930

Circa 1898. Enjoy the gracious decor of the Victorian era while staying at this Romanesque-style inn, located in the heart of Charleston's historic district along King Street's famed Antique Row. Some rooms boast working fireplaces, while others feature romantic whirlpool baths. Champagne breakfasts are delivered to the bedchambers each morning, and the nightly turndown service includes chocolates on your pillow. Enjoy a glass of sherry before heading out to one of Charleston's many fine restaurants. The Victoria House Inn is close to a variety of antique shops and fashionable boutiques.

Historic Interest: The inn is within walking distance of plenty of historic homes and museums, and walking tours are available.

Innkeeper(s): Mary Kay Smith. $125-240. EP. MC VISA DC. TAC10. 18 rooms with PB, 4 with FP. 4 suites. 1 conference room. Breakfast included in rates. Type of meal: continental-plus breakfast. Room service available. Beds: KD. Phone, air conditioning, turndown service and TV in room. Fax, copier and child care on premises. Handicap access. Weddings, small meetings, family reunions and seminars hosted. Antiques, fishing, parks, shopping, theater and watersports nearby.

Publicity: *Washington Post, Great Country Inns.* Ratings: 4 Diamonds.

Villa De La Fontaine B&B

138 Wentworth St
Charleston, SC 29401-1734
(803)577-7709

Circa 1838. This magnificent Greek Revival manor is among Charleston's finest offerings. The grounds are lush with gardens and manicured lawns, and ionic columns adorn the impressive exterior. The innkeeper is a retired interior designer, and his elegant touch is found throughout the mansion, including many 18th-century antiques. A fully trained chef prepares the gourmet breakfasts, which are served in a solarium with a hand-painted mural and 12-foot windows. The chef's recipe for cornmeal waffles was featured in a Better Homes & Gardens' cookbook. The inn is located in the heart of Charleston's historic district, three blocks from the market area.

Innkeeper(s): Aubrey Hancock. $100-125. PC TC. 4 rooms with PB. 1 cottage. Breakfast included in rates. Types of meals: full breakfast and gourmet breakfast. Beds: KQT. Air conditioning in room. Antiques, fishing, parks, shopping, sporting events, theater and watersports nearby.

"What a wonderful vacation we had as recipients of your lavish hospitality."

Wentworth Mansion

149 Wentworth St
Charleston, SC 29401
(803)853-1886 (888)466-1886 Fax:(803)722-8634
E-mail: ct@wentworthmansion.com

Circa 1886. This stately Second Empire mansion, designed originally as an opulent private residence for a wealthy cotton merchant, features the architectural details that one would expect to find in a home of this grandeur — hand-carved marble fireplaces, intricately detailed woodwork, Tiffany stained-glass windows and gleaming inlaid wood floors. Guest rooms have been historically restored and boast an elegant combination of antique furnishings and the modern comforts such as oversized whirlpools, most with a separate spacious shower, and working gas fireplaces. A breathtaking view of historic Charleston is accessible via the spiral staircase that leads to the towering cupola. Guests are invited to enjoy a complimentary breakfast buffet and afternoon tea or wine.

$275-625. MC VISA AX DC DS PC TC. TAC10. 21 rooms with PB. 7 suites. 1 conference room. Breakfast and afternoon tea included in rates. Type of meal: full breakfast. Room service available. Restaurant on premises. Beds: K. Phone, air conditioning, turndown service and TV in room. Fax, copier and library on premises. Handicap access. Weddings, small meetings, seminars hosted. Antiques, fishing, parks, shopping, golf, theater, watersports nearby.

Dillon   C8

Magnolia Inn B&B

601 E Main St - Hwy 9
Dillon, SC 29536
(803)774-0679

Circa 1903. This Southern Colonial-style home was built by a prominent local family who used long-leaf, heart-pine wood among other fine materials in the construction. Stately columns flank the entry. On the ground floor is a library, parlor and dining room where breakfast is served. The upstairs guest rooms feature handsome four-postered, white iron and oak beds.

Innkeeper(s): Alan & Eileen Kemp. $55-65. MC VISA. 4 rooms with PB, 4 with FP. Breakfast included in rate. Type of meal: full breakfast. Beds: QD. Air conditioning and ceiling fan in room. TV on premises. Antiques, fishing, parks and sporting events nearby.

Location: Easy, quick access from Interstate 95.

Publicity: *Sandlapper.*

"Your home is beautiful and our first bed & breakfast experience has won us over to do it again and again."

Georgetown   E8

1790 House B&B Inn

630 Highmarket St
Georgetown, SC 29440-3652
(803)546-4821 (800)890-7432

Circa 1790. Located in the heart of a historic district, this beautifully restored West Indies Colonial just celebrated its 200th birthday. The spacious rooms feature 11-foot ceilings and seven fireplaces, three in the guest bedrooms. The inn's decor reflects the plantations of a bygone era. Guests can stay in former slave quar-

ters, renovated to include a queen bedroom and sitting area. Each of the romantic rooms features special touches, such as the Rice Planters' Room with its four-poster, canopy bed and window seat. The Dependency Cottage is a perfect honeymoon hideaway with a Jacuzzi tub and a private entrance enhanced with gardens and a patio. The inn is located one hour north of Charleston and 45 minutes south of Myrtle Beach.

Historic Interest: The Prince George Episcopal Church, the first church established in the district, is across the street from the home. The area offers several historic homes, some dating back to the 1740s, including the Kaminski House Museum and Hopsewee Plantation,.

Innkeeper(s): John & Patricia Wiley. $80-130. MC VISA AX DS PC TC. TAC10. 6 rooms with PB, and 1 cottage. Breakfast and evening snack included in rates. Type of meal: gourmet breakfast. Picnic lunch available. Beds: KQT. Phone, air conditioning, ceiling fan and TV in room. VCR and bicycles on premises. Weddings, small meetings and family reunions hosted. Antiques, fishing, parks, shopping and theater nearby.

Publicity: *Georgetown Times, Sun News, Charlotte Observer, Southern Living. USAir, Augusta, Pee Dee, Sandlapper.*

"The 1790 House always amazes me with its beauty. A warm welcome in a lovingly maintained home. Breakfasts were a joy to the palate."

Du Pre House

921 Prince St
Georgetown, SC 29442-3549
(803)546-0298 (800)921-3877 Fax:(803)520-0771

Circa 1740. The lot upon which this pre-Revolutionary War gem stands was partitioned off in 1734, and the home built six years later. Three guest rooms have fireplaces, and all are decorated with a poster bed. A full breakfast is prepared featuring such items as French toast, a variety of quiche, fresh fruit and home-baked muffins. For those who love history, Georgetown, South Carolina's third oldest city, offers more than 60 registered National Historic Landmarks.

Innkeeper(s): Marshall Wile. $75-115. MC VISA PC TC. 5 rooms with PB. Breakfast, afternoon tea and evening snack included in rates. Types of meals: continental-plus breakfast, full breakfast and early coffee/tea. Picnic lunch available. Beds: Q. Air conditioning, turndown service and ceiling fan in room. TV, fax, copier, spa, swimming and library on premises. Weddings, small meetings and family reunions hosted. Amusement parks, antiques, fishing, parks, shopping, theater and watersports nearby.

King's Inn at Georgetown

230 Broad St
Georgetown, SC 29440-3604
(803)527-6937 (800)251-8805 Fax:(803)527-6937

Circa 1825. Enjoy the height of elegance, as well as basking in history at this Federal-style mansion. Union troops seized the house and used it as headquarters during the Civil War. The home boasts features such as magnificent moldings, crystal chandeliers, beautifully restored original floors and three, antique-filled parlors. Individually decorated guest rooms include luxurious items such as canopy beds, private piazzas or perhaps an in-room double Jacuzzi. In 1995, Country Inns magazine named King's Inn as one of the year's Top 12. Gourmet breakfasts are served in the garden breakfast room, which overlooks the lap pool. Tables are set with fine linens, china, silver and crystal. The beach and Brookgreen, one of the world's largest outdoor sculpture gardens, are nearby.

Innkeeper(s): Marilyn & Jerry Burkhardt. $85-125. MC VISA AX. TAC10. 7 rooms with PB. Breakfast and afternoon tea included in rates. Types of meals: full breakfast and early coffee/tea. Picnic lunch available. Beds: KQDT. TV, VCR, bicycles and child care on premises. Weddings, small meetings, family reunions and seminars hosted. Antiques, fishing, parks, shopping, sporting events, golf and theater nearby.

"Wonderful effect in every room with the brilliant use of color."

Mansfield Plantation

1776 Mansfield Rd
Georgetown, SC 29440-9500
(803)546-6961 (800)355-3223

Circa 1812. Situated on 900 private acres on the Black River, this historic antebellum plantation house, with its simple facade, betrays its elegant, sophisticated interior. Public rooms are furnished with the owner's collections of 19th-century American antiques that include paintings, china, silver, furniture and books. Guest houses feature high ceilings, elaborate woodwork, fireplaces, hardwood floors and soft designer linens. The lovely grounds and expansive lawns are perfect for picnicking, strolling in the woods, swinging in the hammock or boating on the Black River. The innkeepers, both American History scholars, have researched their plantation's past, and are happy to share Mansfield's colorful history with their guests. Guided tours of the plantation's antebellum slave village, slave chapel and old rice fields are available. Pets are welcome.

Historic Interest: The Rice Museum and Kaminski House Museum are among the historic sites in downtown Georgetown, which is five miles from the plantation. Brookgreen Gardens, which features a nationally known sculpture garden, is about a half hour away.

Innkeeper(s): Sally and James Cahalan. $95. 8 rooms with PB, 8 with FP. Breakfast included in rates. Type of meal: full breakfast. Beds: KDT. Antiques, golf and theater nearby. Pets Allowed.

Publicity: *Georgetown Times, Charleston News & Courier, Sandlapper, Pee Dee Magazine, Charleston Magazine.*

"Handsome furnishings, wildlife walks, sports and hunting, opportunities galore, and a sumptuous atmosphere all make for a weekend retreat to remember."

Greenville   B3

Pettigru Place B&B

302 Pettigru St
Greenville, SC 29601-3113
(864)242-4529 Fax:(864)242-1231

Circa 1920. Former classmates Gloria Hendershot and Janice Beatty reunited after two decades apart and created a charming bed & breakfast out of this Georgian Federalist home. Their labor of love created an inviting atmosphere full of color and comfort. Gloria, a professional caterer, creates the gourmet breakfasts, and Janice tends to the beautiful English garden. After a day of meetings or sightseeing, afternoon refreshments are a welcome treat. The innkeepers offer plenty of amenities for business travelers and plenty of romantic touches. Rooms feature special touches such as ceiling fans, feather mattresses and writing desks. The suite includes a fireplace and separate sitting area. Some baths include whirlpool or clawfoot tubs. The Greenville area, with its close access to Clemson, Furman and Bob Jones Universities, offers plenty of activities from outdoor excursions to cultural events.

Historic Interest: The inn is located in a Greenville historic district.

Innkeeper(s): Gloria Hendershot & Janice Beatty. $90-160. MC VISA AX DS PC TC. 5 rooms with PB, 1 with FP. 1 suite. Breakfast and afternoon tea included in rates. Types of meals: gourmet breakfast and early coffee/tea. Beds: KQ. Phone, air conditioning, ceiling fan and TV in room. Fax and copier on premises. Antiques, parks, shopping, sporting events, theater nearby.

Hartsville   C7

Missouri Inn B&B

314 E Home Ave
Hartsville, SC 29550-3716
(803)383-9553 Fax:(803)383-9553

Circa 1901. It is from the third owners of this Federal-style inn that it derives its name. The home was at that time owned by the innkeepers' grandparents, F.E. and Emily Fitchett, and "Missouri" was the nickname given to Emily by her son-in-law. The entire house, including the five guest rooms, are decorated with antiques, and features wallpaper original to the home. The continental breakfasts are  hearty and homemade. Don't forget to sample afternoon tea, which features scones, tarts, miniature quiche and tea sandwiches. The home, located in the town historic district, is across the street from Coker College and four blocks from downtown Hartsville.

Innkeeper(s): Kyle & Kent Segars. $85. MC VISA AX PC TC. 5 rooms with PB, 3 with FP. 1 cottage. Breakfast, afternoon tea and evening snack included in rates. Types of meals: continental-plus breakfast and early coffee/tea. Lunch, gourmet lunch and catering service available. Beds: KQDT. Phone, air conditioning, ceiling fan and TV in room. VCR, fax, copier and library on premises. Handicap access. Weddings, small meetings, family reunions and seminars hosted. Antiques, fishing, parks, sporting events, golf, theater and watersports nearby.

Latta   C8

Abingdon Manor

307 Church St
Latta, SC 29565-1359
(803)752-5090 (888)752-5090 Fax:(803)752-6034

Circa 1905. This 8,000-square-foot Greek Revival-style Victorian mansion offers another 2,000 square feet of wraparound porches and verandas. It is located on more than three acres with pecan, chestnut and walnut trees. Once the manor of a tobacco plantation, the inn is replete with stained glass, marble window ledges, pier mirrors, pocket doors, 18-inch-thick walls, a winding staircase and interior arches and columns. Guest rooms offer period furnishings, feather beds and 18-foot-tall ceilings. The inn has a four-diamond rating.

Innkeeper(s): Michael & Patty Griffey. $95-120. MC VISA AX DS PC TC. TAC10. 5 rooms with PB, 5 with FP. 1 suite. Breakfast and evening snack included in rates. Types of meals: gourmet breakfast and early coffee/tea. Picnic lunch and catering service available. Beds: KQD. Air conditioning, turndown service, TV and VCR in room. Fax, copier and bicycles on premises. Weddings, small meetings, family reunions and seminars hosted. Antiques, fishing, parks, golf and watersports nearby.

Publicity: *State, Pee Dee, Sandlapper, Southern Inns.*

Marion
C8

Montgomery's Grove

408 Harlee St
Marion, SC 29571-3144
(843)423-5220

Circa 1893. The stunning rooms of this majestic Eastlake-style manor are adorned in Victorian tradition with Oriental rugs, polished hardwood floors, chandeliers and gracious furnishings. High ceilings and fireplaces in each room complete the elegant look. Guest rooms are filled with antiques and magazines or books from the 1890s. Hearty full breakfasts are served each day on the wraparound porches, and candlelight dinner packages can be arranged. Guests will appreciate this inn's five acres of century-old trees and gardens. The inn is about a half-hour drive to famous Myrtle Beach.

Historic Interest: Brittons Neck (15 minutes), Camden, S.C., (40 minutes), Charleston (70 minutes).

Innkeeper(s): Coreen & Richard Roberts. $80-100. 5 rooms, 3 with PB. 1 suite. Breakfast included in rates. Type of meal: full breakfast. Afternoon tea, dinner, picnic lunch, lunch and catering service available. Beds: KQ. Antiques, fishing, theater and watersports nearby.

Location: Close to I-95.

Publicity: *Pee Dee Magazine, Sandlapper, Marion Star, Palmetto Places TV.*

McClellanville
F8

Laurel Hill Plantation

8913 N Hwy 17
McClellanville, SC 29458-9423
(803)887-3708 (888)887-3708

From the large wraparound porch of this plantation house is a view of salt marshes, islands and the Atlantic Ocean. A nearby creek is the perfect location for crabbing, and there is a freshwater pond for fishing. The home was destroyed by Hurricane Hugo, but has been totally reconstructed in its original Low Country style. It is furnished with antiques, local crafts and folk art. The inn has a gift shop that features books, antiques and decorative items.

Historic Interest: Historic Charleston is about 30 miles away.

Innkeeper(s): Jackie & Lee Morrison. $85-95. MC VISA AX DC DS PC TC. TAC10. 4 rooms with PB. Types of meals: full breakfast and early coffee/tea. Beds: QT. Air conditioning and ceiling fan in room. 80 acres. Antiques, fishing, parks, shopping and watersports nearby.

Location: Thirty minutes north of Charleston on Hwy. 17, one hour south of Myrtle Beach.

Publicity: *Country Living, Seabreeze, Pee Dee, State.*

"We came in search of authentic Southern Living and we received more than we had dreamed."

Moncks Corner
E7

Rice Hope Plantation Inn

206 Rice Hope Dr
Moncks Corner, SC 29461-9781
(803)761-4832 (800)569-4038 Fax:(803)884-0223

Circa 1840. Resting on 11 acres of natural beauty, the inn is set among live oaks on a bluff overlooking the Cooper River. On the property are formal gardens that boast a 200-year-old camellia and many varieties of azaleas and other trees and plants. Nearby attractions include the Trappist Monastery at Mepkin Plantation, Francis Marion National Forest, Cypress Gardens and historic Charleston. Outdoor occasions are great because of the inn's formal gardens and the Cooper River backdrop.

Innkeeper(s): Doris Kasprak. $60-85. MC VISA AX. 5 rooms, 3 with PB. 1 conference room. Breakfast included in rates. Meals: continental-plus breakfast, full breakfast and early coffee/tea. Afternoon tea, lunch, gourmet lunch, banquet service and catering service available. Restaurant on premises. Beds: QD. Air conditioning, ceiling fan in room. 12 acres. Weddings, small meetings, family reunions and seminars hosted. Antiques, fishing nearby.

Location: Forty-five miles from Historic Charleston.

Mount Pleasant
F7

Guilds Inn

101 Pitt St
Mount Pleasant, SC 29464-5318
(803)881-0510 (800)331-0510

Circa 1888. This restored home is located in the heart of Mount Pleasant's Old Village National Historic District. The inn is equidistant from both Charleston and Sullivan's Island, both of which are six miles away. Reproductions and antiques decorate the inn's interior. Whirlpool tubs are among the relaxing amenities guests will find. There also is a doll collection on display. Guests enjoy continental breakfasts, and a cafe and more formal dining also are available on the premises.

Historic Interest: The area is full of historic sites, including Old Village National Register District, Patriots Point Maritime Museum, Boone Hall Plantation, Charles Pinckney Historic Site, Fort Sumter, Fort Moultrie, Magnolia Gardens and the Middleton Plantation and Gardens.

Innkeeper(s): Lou Edens. $85-135. MC VISA AX. TAC10. 6 rooms with PB. Type of meal: continental breakfast. Restaurant on premises. Beds: QT. Phone, air conditioning, ceiling fan and TV in room.

Publicity: *Travelhost, Charleston News & Courier, Charlotte Observer, Columbia State Paper.*

North Augusta
E4

Rosemary & Lookaway Halls

804 Carolina Ave
North Augusta, SC 29841-3436
(803)278-6222 (800)531-5578 Fax:(803)278-4877

Circa 1902. These historic homes are gracious examples of Southern elegance and charm. Manicured lawns adorn the exterior of both homes, which appear almost as a vision out of "Gone With the Wind." The Rosemary Hall boasts a spectacular heart-of-pine staircase. The homes stand as living museums, filled to the brim with beautiful furnishings and elegant decor, all highlighted by stained-glass windows, chandeliers and lacy touches. Some guest rooms include Jacuzzis, while others offer verandas. A proper afternoon tea is served each afternoon at Rosemary Hall. The Southern hospitality begins during the morning meal. The opulent gourmet fare might include baked orange-pecan English muffins served with Canadian bacon or, perhaps, a Southern strata with cheese and bacon. The catering menu is even more tasteful, and many weddings, showers and parties are hosted at these inns.

Innkeeper(s): Renee Sharrock & Geneva Robinson. $75-195. MC VISA AX DC CB DS PC TC. TAC10. 23 rooms with PB. 2 conference rooms. Breakfast and evening snack included in rates. Types of meals: continental-plus breakfast, full breakfast and early coffee/tea. Beds: KQDT. Phone, air conditioning, turndown service and TV in room. Fax and copier on premises. Handicap access. Weddings, small meetings, family reunions and seminars hosted. Antiques, fishing, parks, shopping, sporting events and watersports nearby.

Pawleys Island   E9

Litchfield Plantation

King's River Rd, PO Box 290
Pawleys Island, SC 29585-0290
(803)237-9121 (800)869-1410 Fax:(803)237-8558

Circa 1750. Live oaks line the drive that leads up to this antebellum mansion, and in one glance, guests can almost imagine a time when this 600-acre estate was a prosperous rice plantation. The interior boasts many original features, and although the decor is more modern than it was in 1750, it still maintains charm and elegance. Four-poster and canopy beds, as well as a collection of traditional furnishings, grace the guest rooms, which are located in a variety of lodging options. Guests can stay in a plantation house suite or opt for a room in the Guest House. Their are two- and three-bedroom cottages available, too. The cottages are particularly suited to families or couples traveling together and include amenities such as a fireplace, kitchen and washer and dryer. The inn's dining room, located in the Carriage House, is a wonderful place for a romantic dinner. Start off with appetizers such as petite corn cakes topped with sour cream and caviar, followed by a Caesar salad and an entree such as medallions of pork or shrimp and pasta pomodoro. Guests enjoy privileges at the oceanfront Pawleys Island Beach House, and there are tennis courts and a swimming pool on the plantation premises. Many golf courses are nearby. Be sure to ask about the inn's romance packages.

Innkeeper(s): Sally Gome. $115-195. MC VISA AX DS TC. TAC10. 30 rooms with PB, 7 with FP. 10 suites. 8 cottages. 3 conference rooms. Breakfast included in rates. Meal: continental-plus breakfast. Banquet service, catering service available. Restaurant on premises. Beds: KQT. Phone, air conditioning, TV in room. Fax, copier, swimming, stables, tennis, library on premises. 600 acres. Weddings, small meetings, family reunions, seminars hosted. Amusement parks, antiques, fishing, parks, theater, watersports nearby.

"What a wonderful, relaxing place to stay! Your accommodations were excellent - first class."

Sea View Inn

PO Box 210
Pawleys Island, SC 29585-0210
(803)237-4253

Circa 1937. In simple low-country style, this inn rests on Pawley's Island, a narrow barrier island with the ocean on one side and a salt marsh on the other. In summer, you may not need your shoes again till you leave for home. You'll settle in as if this is the family guest house, with comfortable furnishings, wood decks set atop seagrass with ocean front or view rooms. Fruit, sausage, eggs, toast and grits are often served for breakfast. Three meals are included in your room rate, and the main

meal is served at 1:15 p.m. Cajun Green Gumbo, Low Country Crab Cakes with basil mustard, Pecan-Pepper Rice, Carolina Cornbread with scallion butter and Savannah Cream Cake are samples from the mid-day menu. In the evening, pasta, oyster pie, minestrone soup, fried chicken, poached salmon, marinated shrimp, Cobb Salad or deviled crab may be offered. Dessert features Pecan Pie and Key Lime Pie. All rates are per person. During the summer, reservations are weekly, and the rates range from $460 to $795.

Innkeeper(s): Pat Saunders & Ken Mason. $84-135. PC TC. 20 rooms. Breakfast included in rates. Restaurant on premises. Beds: DT. Turndown service, ceiling fan in room. Library on premises. Golf, watersports nearby.

Salem   B2

Sunrise Farm B&B

325 Sunrise Dr
Salem, SC 29676-0164
(864)944-0121

Circa 1890. Situated on the remaining part of a 1,000-acre cotton plantation, this country Victorian features large porches with rockers and wicker. Guest rooms are furnished with period antiques, thick comforters, extra pillows and family heirlooms. The "corn crib" cottage is located in the original farm structure used for storing corn. It has a fully equipped kitchen, sitting area and bedroom with tub and shower. The June Rose Garden Cottage includes a river rock fireplace and full kitchen, as well as pastoral and mountain views. The inn offers a full breakfast and country picnic baskets.

Innkeeper(s): Barbara Laughter. $75-100. MC VISA PC TC. TAC10. 4 rooms. 2 cottages. Breakfast and evening snack included in rates. Types of meals: continental-plus breakfast and full breakfast. Picnic lunch available. Beds: Q. Air conditioning, ceiling fan, TV and VCR in room. Weddings hosted. Antiques, fishing, parks, sporting events and watersports nearby.

Pets Allowed: With advanced notice.

"Saying thank you doesn't do our gratitude justice."

Starr   C2

The Gray House

111 Stones Throw Ave
Starr, SC 29684
(864)352-6778 Fax:(864)352-6777

Circa 1910. This immaculately restored Victorian is nestled on 200 acres of farmland, and to date, is a working farm. With its expansive porch, lush flowering gardens, tranquil pond and rolling fields, guests will truly feel the graciousness of the Old South. Golden heart pine floors, gleaming beaded-wood walls and antique oak and pine furniture enhance the inn's intrinsic romantic ambiance. The inn's private restaurant, open on selected days, offers a menu featuring its prized beef cattle. A authentic Amish-crafted horse driven carriage, one of the inn's treasured trademarks, is offered for special occasions within a 50-mile radius. The inn is especially designed for romantic getaways and is a favorite spot for weddings, receptions, meetings teas and luncheons.

Innkeeper(s): Kathy T. Stone. $60-150. MC VISA AX PC TC. TAC15. 4 rooms with PB, 2 with FP. 2 suites. 1 cottage. 4 conference rooms. Breakfast included in rates. Types of meals: continental breakfast, continental-plus breakfast, full breakfast, gourmet breakfast and early coffee/tea. Afternoon tea, dinner, evening snack, picnic lunch, lunch, gourmet lunch, banquet service, catering service, catered breakfast and room service available. Restaurant on premises. Beds: KQ. Phone, air conditioning, turndown service and ceiling fan in room. TV, VCR, fax, copier, spa, stables and bicycles on premises. Handicap access. 200 acres. Weddings, small meetings, family reunions and seminars hosted. Amusement parks, antiques, fishing, parks, shopping, cross-country skiing, sporting events, golf and theater nearby.
Publicity: *Southern Living, Country Women, Gourmet Today.*

Sumter
D7

Calhoun Street B&B

302 W Calhoun St
Sumter, SC 29150-4512
(803)775-7035 (800)355-8119 Fax:(803)778-0934
E-mail: calhounst-bb@sumter.net

Circa 1890. This home was built by innkeeper Mackenzie Sholtz's great-uncle, and she is the third generation to live in the clapboard Victorian. Guest rooms are well appointed with fine furnishings. For instance, the Audubon Room includes a canopy bed, a Victorian chair and loveseat and a polished hardwood floor topped with an Oriental rug. In the afternoon, refreshments are served, and in the mornings, guests enjoy a hearty, full breakfast. Eggs Calhoun, a unique twist on eggs Benedict, is a specialty served along with freshly squeezed orange juice and homemade breads or muffins. A phone, fax machine and copier are available for business travelers. Located in the historic district, this home borders a city park, and golfing and shopping are nearby.

Innkeeper(s): David & Mackenzie Sholtz. $65-85. MC VISA DS PC TC. 4 rooms with PB, 1 with FP. Breakfast and evening snack included in rates. Types of meals: gourmet breakfast and early coffee/tea. Beds: QT. Air conditioning and ceiling fan in room. TV, VCR, fax and copier on premises. Weddings, small meetings, family reunions and seminars hosted. German and Italian spoken. Antiques, fishing, parks, shopping and theater nearby.

"This house gave us a good impression of uncompromised 1800s elegance."

Union
B4

The Inn at Merridun

100 Merridun Pl
Union, SC 29379-2200
(864)427-7052 (888)892-6020 Fax:(864)429-0373
E-mail: merridun@carol.net

Circa 1855. Nestled on nine acres of wooded ground, this Greek Revival inn is in a small Southern college town. During spring, see the South in its colorful splendor with blooming azaleas, magnolias and wisteria. Sip an iced drink on the inn's marble verandas and relive memories of a bygone era. Soft strains of Mozart and Beethoven, as well as the smell of freshly baked cookies and country suppers, fill the air of this antebellum country inn.

In addition to a complimentary breakfast, guest will enjoy the inn's dessert selection offered every evening.

Historic Interest: Rose Hill Plantation State Park (8 miles), historic Brattonsville (35 miles).

Innkeeper(s): Jim & Peggy Waller. $85-125. MC VISA AX DS PC TC. TAC10. 5 rooms with PB. 3 conference rooms. Breakfast included in rates. Types of meals: gourmet breakfast and early coffee/tea. Afternoon tea, dinner, picnic lunch, lunch, gourmet lunch, banquet service, catering service, catered breakfast and room service available. Beds: KQT. Phone, air conditioning, ceiling fan and TV in room. VCR, fax, copier and library on premises. Weddings, small meetings, family reunions and seminars hosted. Amusement parks, antiques, fishing, parks, shopping, sporting events, watersports nearby.

Winnsboro
C5

Songbird Manor

116 N Zion St
Winnsboro, SC 29180-1140
(803)635-6963 (888)636-7698 Fax:(803)635-6963

Circa 1912. Influential local businessman Marcus Doty built this home, which features William Morris-style architecture. Doty made sure his home was a showplace from the beveled-glass windows to the molded plaster ceilings with extensive oak and chestnut woodwork. It was also the first home in the county to include indoor plumbing. Three of the guest rooms include the home's original clawfoot or pedestal tubs. All of the guest rooms have a fireplace. The former gentleman's parlor, where Doty and other Winnsboro men no doubt settled down to a game of cards, now house a TV, VCR, board games and puzzles for all guests to  enjoy. After breakfast, take a walking tour of Winnsboro's historic district or enjoy the area's abundance of outdoor activities, from hunting to fishing to golf.

Innkeeper(s): Susan Yenner. $65-110. MC VISA AX DS PC. 5 rooms with PB, 5 with FP. 1 suite. Breakfast included in rates. Types of meals: continental breakfast, full breakfast and gourmet breakfast. Picnic lunch available. Beds: KQT. Phone, air conditioning, turndown service, ceiling fan, TV in room. VCR, fax, bicycles, library on premises. Weddings, small meetings, family reunions, seminars hosted. Antiques, fishing, parks, theater, watersports nearby.

Publicity: *Sandlapper, Herald Independent.*

"We had a very restful two-night stay in a beautiful surrounding."

Woodruff
B4

The Nicholls-Crook Plantation House B&B

120 Plantation Dr
Woodruff, SC 29388-9476
(864)476-8820 Fax:(864)476-8820

Circa 1793. The innkeepers at this 18th-century home have restored the historic house with warmth and charm in mind. Period antiques, original mantels and the widest chimney in the upstate create a charming, rustic environment. The grounds boast 18th-century flowers, a white-rock courtyard and a pecan grove with one of the largest pecan trees in South Carolina. Innkeepers Jim and Suzanne are full of information about the home's family history  and the residents' ties to Revolutionary War heroes. A rich, plentiful breakfast is the perfect way to start off a day full of sightseeing and shopping or enjoying the area's many outdoor activities.

Historic Interest: The innkeepers can point guests in the direction of several battlefields. The Biltmore House is 60 miles from the home. Closer attractions include the Walnut Grove Plantation, only three miles away, and the Rose Hill Plantation, which is about 30 miles from the inn.

Innkeeper(s): Suzanne & Jim Brown. $85-150. AX TC. 3 rooms, 2 with PB. 1 suite. Breakfast included in rates. Type of meal: full breakfast. Beds: KDT. Phone, air conditioning and turndown service in room. Fax on premises. Weddings and small meetings hosted. Antiques and shopping nearby.

Publicity: *Herald Journal News, Country, Sandlapper.*

South Dakota

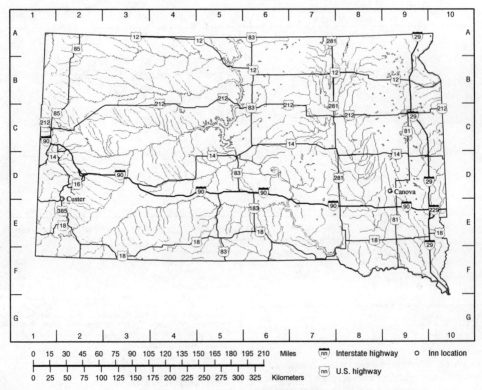

| | Miles | | 0 15 30 45 60 75 90 105 120 135 150 165 180 195 210 |
| | Kilometers | | 0 25 50 75 100 125 150 175 200 225 250 275 300 325 |

Interstate highway   ○ Inn location
U.S. highway

Canova   D9

B&B at Skoglund Farm

Rt 1 Box 45
Canova, SD 57321-9726
(605)247-3445

Circa 1917. This is a working farm on the South Dakota prairie.
Peacocks stroll around the farm along with cattle, chickens, emu
and other fowl. Guests can enjoy an evening meal with the family.
The innkeepers offer special rates for families with children. The
farm's rates are $30 per adult, $25 per teenager and $20 per child.
Innkeeper(s): Alden & Delores Skoglund. $60. PC. 4 rooms. Breakfast and
dinner included in rates. Meals: full breakfast and early coffee/tea. Evening
snack available. Beds: QDT. VCR and library on premises. Antiques, fishing,
parks, shopping, sporting events and watersports nearby. Pets Allowed.
Location: Southeast South Dakota.

"Thanks for the down-home hospitality and good food."

Custer   D2

State Game Lodge

HC 83 Box 74
Custer, SD 57730-9705
(605)255-4541

Circa 1923. The State Game Lodge is listed in the National
Register of Historic Places. It served as the summer White House
for presidents Coolidge and Eisenhower. Although not a bed and
breakfast, the lodge boasts a wonderful setting in the Black Hills.
Ask for a room in the historic lodge building. (There are cottages
and motel units, as well.) A favorite part of the experience is
rocking on the front porch while watching buffalo graze.
Breakfast is paid for separately in the dining room, where you
may wish to order a pheasant or buffalo entree in the evening.
Innkeeper(s): Pat Azinger. $65-310. EP. MC VISA AX DS. 67 rooms with PB,
3 with FP. Meal: gourmet breakfast. Restaurant on premises. Beds: QDT.
Publicity: *Bon Appetit, Midwest Living, Sunset.*

"Your staff's cheerfulness and can-do attitude added to a most enjoyable stay."

461

Tennessee

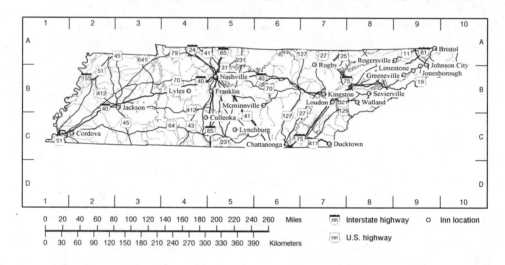

	1	2	3	4	5	6	7	8	9	10

0 20 40 60 80 100 120 140 160 180 200 220 240 260   Miles

0 30 60 90 120 150 180 210 240 270 300 330 360 390   Kilometers

Interstate highway   ○ Inn location

U.S. highway

Bristol A9

New Hope B&B
822 Georgia Ave
Bristol, TN 37620-4024
(423)989-3343 (888)989-3343

Circa 1892. Abram Reynolds, older brother of R.J. Reynolds, once owned the property that surrounds this inn, and one of the guest rooms is named in his honor. Each of the rooms has been creatively decorated with bright prints and cheerful wall-coverings, emphasizing the high ceilings and wood floors. Clawfoot tubs, transoms over the doors and distinctive wood-

work are some of the period elements featured in this late Victorian home. Bristol is known as a birthplace for country music, and the innkeepers pay homage to the history with the whimsically decorated Tennessee Ernie Ford hallway. Ford got his start in Bristol, and pictures, record jackets, books and wallpaper fashioned from sheet music bedeck the hallway. The home is located in the historic Fairmont area, and a guided walking tour begins at New Hope. Half of the town of Bristol is located in Tennessee and the other half in Virginia.

Innkeeper(s): Tom & Tonda Fluke. $70-130. MC VISA AX PC TC. TAC10. 4 rooms with PB, 1 with FP. Breakfast and evening snack included in rates. Types of meals: full breakfast and early coffee/tea. Afternoon tea and room service available. Beds: KQT. Phone, air conditioning, turndown service, ceiling fan and TV in room. VCR, bicycles and library on premises. Antiques, fishing, parks, shopping, downhill skiing, golf and theater nearby.
Publicity: *Tennessee Getaways.*

"It was like a second home in such a short time."

Chattanooga C6

Adams Hilborne
801 Vine St
Chattanooga, TN 37403-2318
(423)265-5000 Fax:(423)265-5555

Circa 1889. This former mayor's mansion of Tudor and Romanesque design was presented with the 1997 award for Excellence in Restoration by the National Trust. The interior of this gracious home boasts 16-foot ceilings and floors patterned from three different

woods. The large entrance hall features carved cornices, a coif-fured ceiling and a fireplace. Every room offers something special, from the Tiffany windows and beveled glass to the mansion's 13 fireplaces and luxurious ballroom. Named a centerpiece of the Fortwood Historic District, Chattanooga's finest historic residential area, the mansion has also received the coveted City Beautiful Award.

Historic Interest: The Chicamauga Battlefields are 15 minutes from the inn and other battle sites, museums and cemeteries are nearby.

Innkeeper(s): Wendy & Dave Adams. $75-275. MC VISA AX TC. TAC10. 10 rooms with PB, 4 with FP. 3 suites. Breakfast included in rates. Types of meals: continental-plus breakfast and early coffee/tea. Dinner, banquet service and room service available. Restaurant on premises. Beds: KQD. Phone, air conditioning, turndown service, TV and VCR in room. Fax, copier and library on premises. Handicap access. Weddings, small meetings, family reunions and seminars hosted. Amusement parks, antiques, fishing, parks, shopping, sporting events, theater and watersports nearby.

Publicity: *National Geographic, Historic Traveler, News Free Press.*

Cordova (Memphis) C2

The Bridgewater House

7015 Raleigh Lagrange Rd
Cordova (memphis), TN 38018-6221
(901)384-0080 Fax:(901)384-0080
E-mail: kmistilis@worldnet.att.net

Circa 1890. This century-old schoolhouse sits on more than two acres shaded by stately oak trees. Upon entering, you will find the original hardwood floors, leaded-glass windows and hand-marbleized moldings. Awake to a gourmet breakfast prepared by the innkeeper, a certified chef, caterer and former manager of corporate test kitchens. Specialities include Strawberries Romanoff, Broccoli with Hollandaise, Merinque a la Grapefruit, Bridgewater Eggs Benedict, Greek Omelet or a Cheese Blintz souffle.

Innkeeper(s): Steve & Katherine Mistilis. $100. MC VISA DS TC. 2 rooms with PB. Breakfast included in rates. Types of meals: gourmet breakfast and early coffee/tea. Catering service available. Beds: QDT. Air conditioning and ceiling fan in room. Weddings and small meetings hosted. Amusement parks, antiques, parks and watersports nearby.

Culleoka (Columbia) C4

Sweetwater Inn B&B

2436 Campbells Station Rd
Culleoka (Columbia), TN 38451-2304
(615)987-3077 (800)335-3077 Fax:(615)987-2525

Circa 1900. This turn-of-the-century Gothic Steamboat-style country home, set in the middle of Tennessee, is a perfect base to explore the surrounding country-side. There are two wraparound porches and lots of rocking chairs to sit in while viewing the breathtaking vistas of soft rolling hills. Each of the four individually decorated guest rooms has access to the second-floor porch, where guests can watch the sunrise with an early-morning cup of coffee or tea. A sumptuous gourmet breakfast is served daily.

Innkeeper(s): Sandy Shotwell. $100-135. MC VISA DS PC TC. TAC10. 4 rooms with PB. 2 suites. Breakfast, afternoon tea and evening snack included in rates. Types of meals: full breakfast and gourmet breakfast. Picnic lunch, banquet service and catering service available. Beds: Q. Air conditioning, turndown service and ceiling fan in room. VCR, fax, copier and bicycles on premises. 10 acres. Weddings, small meetings, family reunions and seminars hosted. Antiques, fishing, parks, shopping, golf and theater nearby.

Location: Located 45 miles south of Nashville, 60 miles north of Hunstville, Ala.

"Exceptional, beautiful, and so worthy of praise! It seemed a magical beginning to awaken in such a timeless place."

Ducktown C7

The White House B&B

104 Main St, PO Box 668
Ducktown, TN 37326
(423)496-4166 (800)775-4166 Fax:(423)496-9778

Circa 1898. This Queen Anne Victorian boasts a wraparound porch with a swing. Rooms are decorated in traditional style with family antiques. Innkeepers pamper their guests with Tennessee hospitality, a hearty country breakfast and a mouthwatering sundae bar in the evenings. The innkeepers also help guests plan daily activities, and the area is bursting with possibilities. Hiking, horseback riding, panning for gold and driving tours are only a few choices. The Ocoee River  is the perfect place for a river float trip or take on the challenge of roaring rapids. The river was selected as the site of the 1996 Summer Olympic Whitewater Slalom events.

Historic Interest: The Ducktown Mining Museum is a popular local attraction. Fields of the Wood, a biblical theme park, is 20 minutes away and free of charge.

Innkeeper(s): Dan & Mardee Kauffman. $60-70. MC VISA DS PC TC. TAC10. 3 rooms, 1 with PB. Breakfast, afternoon tea and evening snack included in rates. Types of meals: full breakfast and early coffee/tea. Catering service and catered breakfast available. Beds: QT. Air conditioning and ceiling fan in room. TV, VCR, fax and library on premises. Weddings, small meetings, family reunions hosted. Antiques, fishing, parks, shopping, watersports nearby.

Publicity: *Southern Living.*

"We wanted a relaxing couple of days in the mountains and that's what we got. Thank you."

Franklin B5

Namaste Acres Barn B&B

5436 Leipers Creek Rd
Franklin, TN 37064-9208
(615)791-0333

This handsome Dutch Colonial is directly across the street from the original Natchez Trace. As the B&B is within walking distance of miles of hiking and horseback riding trails. Each of the suites includes private entrances and features individual themes. One room boasts rustic, cowboy decor with a clawfoot tub, hand-crafted furnishings, log and rope beds, and rough sawn lumber walls. The Franklin Quarters offers a sitting area where guests can settle down with a book from the large collection of historical material. The innkeepers chose the name Namaste from an Indian word, and carry an Indian theme in one of the guest rooms. Namaste Acres is just 12 miles outside of historic Franklin, which offers plenty of shops, a self-guided walking tour, Civil War sites and the largest assortment of antique dealers in the United States.

Innkeeper(s): Lisa Winters. $70-80. MC VISA AX DS PC. 4 rooms. Type of meal: full breakfast. Beds: Q. Spa and swimming on premises.

Publicity: *Southern Living, Western Horseman, Horse Illustrated.*

Greeneville B9

Hilltop House B&B

6 Sanford Cir
Greeneville, TN 37743-4022
(423)639-8202

Circa 1920. Situated on a bluff overlooking the Nolichuckey River valley, this manor home boasts mountain views from each of the guest rooms. The Elizabeth Noel room, named for the original owner, includes among its treasures a canopy bed, sitting room and a private veranda, a perfect spot to watch the sunsets. After a hearty breakfast, take a stroll across the beautifully landscaped grounds. Innkeeper Denise Ashworth is a landscape architect and guests will marvel at her wonderful gardens. Ashworth sponsors several gardening workshops each year at the inn, covering topics such as flower arranging, Christmas decorations and landscaping your home grounds.

Historic Interest: Greeneville, the Andrew Johnson home, is seven miles away. Historic Jonesborough, the oldest town is Tennessee is 30 miles. Gatlinburg and Great Smoky Mountains National Park are an hour away.

Innkeeper(s): Denise Ashworth. $75-80. MC VISA AX PC TC. TAC10. 3 rooms with PB. Breakfast and afternoon tea included in rates. Types of meals: full breakfast, gourmet breakfast and early coffee/tea. Dinner, gourmet lunch and catering service available. Beds: KQD. Phone, air conditioning, turndown service, TV and VCR in room. Library on premises. Small meetings, family reunions and seminars hosted. Antiques, fishing, parks, shopping, golf, theater and watersports nearby.

Publicity: *Country Inns.*

"Peaceful and comfortable, great change of pace."

Jackson B3

Highland Place B&B

519 N Highland Ave
Jackson, TN 38301
(901)427-1472

Circa 1911. This two-story house in the North Highland Historical District is five blocks from downtown. The inn is popular for bridal showers and dinners. There is a library and dining room where breakfast is served. The Hamilton Room features Chinese rugs and a wood-burning fireplace. The inn blends the old with the new, offering clawfoot tubs, tubs for two or a waterfall shower for two. Both the vacationer and corporate traveler will enjoy the amenities the inn offers. Corporate rates are available.

Innkeeper(s): Glenn & Janice Wall. $75-135. MC VISA AX PC TC. TAC10. 4 rooms with PB. 1 conference room. Weddings, small meetings, family reunions, seminars hosted. Antiques, shopping, sporting events, theater nearby.

Johnson City A9

Hart House B&B

207 E Holston Ave
Johnson City, TN 37601-4612
(423)926-3147 (888)915-7239

Circa 1910. Antique shopping is a hobby of innkeepers Frank and Vanessa Gingras and this is evident in every nook and cranny of Hart House. The Dutch Colonial home is flanked by a wicker-filled porch complete with a swing, a perfect place to enjoy summer breezes. The cozy parlor and dining room each includes a fireplace, as does one of the guest rooms. Breakfast treats such as quiche, pecan pancakes or Belgian waffles are served up each morning along with a variety of fresh fruit and breads. Johnson City is near a variety of antique shops, an outlet mall and the Appalachian Trail.

Historic Interest: Johnson City is located in the oldest settled area of Tennessee and includes many nearby historic sites. Old Jonesborough, Tennessee's oldest town, is 10 minutes from the inn. Rocky Mount, the old state capital is five minutes away as is Tipton-Haynes Historic Farm.

Innkeeper(s): Francis Gingras. $60-65. MC VISA AX DS. 3 rooms with PB. Breakfast included in rates. Type of meal: full breakfast. Beds: Q. Antiques, fishing, skiing, theater and watersports nearby. Pets Allowed.

Publicity: *Loafer.*

"Impressive and charming throughout."

Jonesborough B9

Hawley House B&B

114 E Woodrow Ave
Jonesborough, TN 37659-1328
(423)753-8869

Circa 1793. Hawley House has the distinction of being the oldest house in Tennessee's oldest town. For a time, part of the territory claimed by North Carolina broke free and declared itself the state of Franklin. Jonesborough was the capital of this new state. The main house was built in 1793 and other additions have been included through the years, including a veranda which affords a view of the charming village. Innkeeper Marcy Hawley is an interior designer and restoration expert, and she and husband Ric have refurbished the home with authenticity in mind. Colorful rooms feature traditional antique furnishings, quilts and American folk art. Winter guests enjoy a cup of hot cider as they warm up in front of a roaring fire in the old kitchen. In the summertime, relaxing on the wraparound porch with a glass of lemonade is the perfect way to cap off the day.

Historic Interest: Jonesborough is the oldest town west of the Appalachians and features many historic buildings. The Davy Crockett Birthplace is 10 miles away. The Andrew Johnson park and presidential library is 20 miles away.

Innkeeper(s): Marcy & Ric Hawley. $65-100. 3 rooms with PB. Breakfast and afternoon tea included in rates. Type of meal: full breakfast. Picnic lunch and catering service available. Beds: QT. Antiques, fishing, downhill skiing, cross-country skiing, theater and watersports nearby.

Publicity: *Washington Post, Preservation News, Southern Living, USA from New York to San Francisco, Natural Wonders of Tennessee, Blue Ridge Country, Country Inns, America's Most Charming Towns & Villages.*

Kingston B7

Whitestone Country Inn

1200 Paint Rock Rd
Kingston, TN 37763-5843
(423)376-0113 (888)247-2464 Fax:(423)376-4454
E-mail: moreinfo@whitestones.com

Circa 1995. This regal farmhouse sits majestically on a hilltop overlooking miles of countryside and Watts Bar Lake. The inn is surrounded by 275 acres, some of which borders the scenic lake, where guests can enjoy fishing or simply communing with nature. There are four miles of hiking trails, and the many porches and decks are perfect places to relax. The inn's interior is as pleasing as the exterior surroundings. The guest rooms are elegantly appointed, and each includes a fireplace and whirlpool tub. Guests are treated

to a hearty, country-style breakfast, and dinners are available by reservation. The inn is one hour from Chattanooga, Knoxville and the Great Smoky Mountains National Park.

Innkeeper(s): Paul & Jean Cowell. $85-145. EP. MC VISA AX PC TC. TAC10. 12 rooms with PB, 12 with FP. 1 conference room. Breakfast included in rates. Meal: full breakfast. Dinner and picnic lunch available. Restaurant on premises. Beds: KQ. Phone, air conditioning, turndown service, ceiling fan, TV and VCR in room. Fax, copier, spa, sauna and library on premises. Handicap access. 275 acres. Weddings, small meetings, family reunions, seminars hosted. Antiques, fishing, shopping, golf, watersports nearby.

"Not only have you built a place of beauty, you have established a sanctuary of rest. An escape from the noise and hurry of everyday life."

Limestone
B9

Snapp Inn B&B
1990 Davy Crockett Park Rd
Limestone, TN 37681-6026
(423)257-2482

Circa 1815. From the second-story porch of this brick Federal, guests enjoy views of local farmland as well as the sounds of Big Limestone Creek. The Smoky Mountains are seen from the back

porch. Decorated with locally gathered antiques, the home is within walking distance of Davy Crockett Birthplace State Park. A full country breakfast often includes Ruth's homemade biscuits.

Innkeeper(s): Ruth & Dan Dorgan. $65. MC VISA PC TC. TAC10. 2 rooms with PB. Breakfast included in rates. Meals: full breakfast, early coffee/tea. Beds: QD. Air conditioning in room. TV, VCR, library on premises. Antiques, fishing, parks, shopping, theater, watersports nearby. Pets Allowed.

Publicity: *Greenville Sun.*

Loudon
B7

The Mason Place B&B
600 Commerce St
Loudon, TN 37774-1101
(423)458-3921

Circa 1865. In the National Register, Mason Place received an award for its outstanding restoration. In the Greek Revival style, the inn has a red slate roof, graceful columns and a handsome double-tiered balcony overlooking three acres of lawns, trees

and gardens. There are 10 working fireplaces, a Grecian swimming pool, gazebo and wisteria-covered arbor. A grand entrance hall, fine antiques and tasteful furnishings make for an elegant decor, suitable for the mansion's 7,000 square feet.

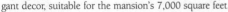

Historic Interest: Ft. Loudon Park & Museum, Lost Sea, Sequoyah Museum.
Innkeeper(s): Bob & Donna Siewert. $96-120. PC TC. 5 rooms with PB, 5 with FP. Breakfast included in rates. Types of meals: gourmet breakfast and early coffee/tea. Afternoon tea and picnic lunch available. Beds: QD. Air conditioning in room. TV, VCR, swimming, bicycles, tennis, library on premises. Weddings, small meetings and seminars hosted. Amusement parks, antiques, fishing, parks, shopping, skiing, sporting events, theater, watersports nearby.
Location: Smoky Mountains Cherokee National Forest.
Publicity: *Country Inn, Country Side, Country Travels, Tennessee Cross Roads, Antiquing in Tennessee, Knox-Chattanooga, Oak Ridge, Detroit Magazine.*

"Absolutely wonderful in every way. You are in for a treat!"

Lyles
B4

Silver Leaf 1815-Country Inn
7548 Johnny Crow Rd
Lyles, TN 37098-1820
(615)670-3048

Circa 1815. The innkeeper of this unique log home understands better than many the importance of serving others, as she was once a state senator. Norma's cooking alone is worth the trip. Her country cooking includes Southern staples such as fried chicken and buttermilk biscuits. Everything is homemade, including preserves made with fruit from this 360-acre farm. The rooms are decorated in early American style.

Innkeeper(s): Norma Crow. $55-75. MAP, AP. AX TC. 10 rooms, 8 with PB. 1 conference room. Breakfast included in rates. Type of meal: continental breakfast. Dinner available. Beds: QD. Air conditioning in room. Fax on premises. 160 acres. Weddings, small meetings, family reunions and seminars hosted. Amusement parks, antiques, fishing, parks, shopping, sporting events, theater and watersports nearby.

Lynchburg
C5

Lynchburg B&B
Mechanic St, PO Box 34
Lynchburg, TN 37352-0034
(615)759-7158

Circa 1877. Antiques and a variety of elements original to this 19th-century home create an air of nostalgia. The exterior, flanked by an arch, columns, red roof and second-story porch, is charming. The innkeeper serves home-baked treats such as a country sausage muffin or banana bread during the continental breakfast service. Several of her recipes have been featured in a cookbook. The home is near many Lynchburg sites, and, for those so inclined, the bed & breakfast is within walking distance of the famous Jack Daniels distillery.

Innkeeper(s): Mike & Virginia Tipps. $55-65. MC VISA. 2 rooms with PB. Type of meal: continental-plus breakfast. Beds: QD. Air conditioning and TV in room. Antiques, parks and shopping nearby.

"Thank you for your wonderful Southern hospitality."

McMinnville
B6

Historic Falcon Manor
2645 Faulkner Springs Rd
McMinnville, TN 37110-1193
(931)668-4444 Fax:(931)815-4444
E-mail: falconmanor@falconmanor.com

Circa 1896. Victorian glory is the theme at this restored manor, right down to the period clothing worn by the innkeepers during tours of their bed & breakfast. Museum-quality period furnishings fill each of the unique rooms, which are decorated in traditional Victorian style. High ceilings, a sweeping staircase, chandeliers and white oak hardwood floors accent the decor. Relax on

the wraparound porch with its comfortable rockers or learn of home's past from innkeepers George and Charlien McGlothin, who can tell a few ghost stories along with providing ample historical detail. Glorious full breakfasts are served each morning and evening refreshments and desserts are offered. The inn was the 1st prize winner of the National Trust for Historic Preservation's American Home Restoration Award in 1997.

Historic Interest: Hermitage and Belle Meade mansions are 75 miles from the inn. The Chickmauga Battlefield is 71 miles. The Stones River Battlefield is 45 miles and íJack Daniels Countryî is found in Lynchburg about 50 miles from the inn. The Cumberland Caverns, a National Historic Landmark, is eight miles away.

Innkeeper(s): George & Charlien McGlothin. $85-105. MC VISA PC TC. TAC10. 6 rooms with PB. Breakfast and evening snack included in rates. Meals: full breakfast and early coffee/tea. Banquet service and catering service available. Beds: KD. Air conditioning and ceiling fan in room. TV, VCR, fax, copier and library on premises. Handicap access. Weddings, small meetings, family reunions, seminars hosted. Antiques, parks, watersports nearby.

Publicity: Tennessee Magazine, Huntsville Times, Chattanooga Free Press, Country Extra, Preservation, Bob Vila's American Home, Mobile Register, PBS.

"Everything, from the absolutely beautiful rooms to the wonderful breakfast to the kindness and sincerity of the hosts, made our stay wonderful!"

Nashville B5

The Hillsboro House

1933 20th Ave S
Nashville, TN 37212-3711
(615)292-5501

Circa 1904. The Hillsboro House is a cozy home base for guests wanting to experience the sites and sounds of Nashville. Vanderbilt University and famed Music Row are within walking distance from this Victorian home. After a dreamy night's sleep snuggled in a feather bed, guests are served a hearty homemade breakfast and head out for a day in Nashville, which offers a multitude of shops, outdoor activities and restaurants to explore.

Historic Interest: The Hillsboro House is located in Nashville's Historic Hillsboro/Belmont neighborhood.

Innkeeper(s): Andrea Beaudet. $95-105. MC VISA AX. 3 rooms with PB. Breakfast included in rates. Type of meal: full breakfast. Beds: Q. Antiques and theater nearby. Pets Allowed.

"This is the real thing, as fresh and welcoming as the ingredients in your fabulous breakfasts."

Rogersville A9

Hale Springs Inn

Town Square
Rogersville, TN 37857-3602
(423)272-5171

Circa 1824. On the town square, this is the oldest continually operating inn in the state. Presidents Andrew Jackson, James Polk and Andrew Johnson stayed here. McKinney Tavern, as it was known then, was Union headquarters during the Civil War. Canopy beds, working fireplaces and an evening meal by candlelight in the elegant dining

room all make for a romantic stay. A formal garden with a gazebo recently has been restored.

Historic Interest: Crockett Graveyard (3 blocks).

Innkeeper(s): Captain & Mrs. Carl Netherland-Brown. $45-70. EP. MC VISA AX. 10 rooms with PB, 9 with FP. 3 suites. 1 conference room. Breakfast included in rates. Meal: continental breakfast. Dinner, lunch available. Restaurant on premises. Beds: QDT. Phone in room. Antiques, fishing nearby. Location: Near Smoky Mountains.

Publicity: Miami Herald, Southern Living, Travel South, Knoxville News, Sentinal.

"It was truly a step back to a more gracious way of life."

Rugby A7

Newbury House at Historic Rugby

Hwy 52, PO Box 8
Rugby, TN 37733
(423)628-2430 Fax:(423)628-2266

Circa 1880. Mansard-roofed Newbury House first lodged visitors traveling to this English village when author and social reformer Thomas Hughes founded Rugby. Filled with authentic Victorian antiques, the inn includes some furnishings that are

original to the colony. There are also several restored cottages on the property, and there is a two-room suite with a queen bed, two twin beds and a private bathroom.

Historic Interest: The inn and entire village are listed in the National Register. There are tours daily.

Innkeeper(s): Historic Rugby. $62-84. MC VISA PC TC. 6 rooms, 4 with PB. 1 suite. 2 cottages. Breakfast included in rates. Meals: full breakfast and early coffee/tea. Afternoon tea, dinner, picnic lunch, lunch, banquet service available. Restaurant on premises. Beds: QTD. Air conditioning and ceiling fan in room. Library on premises. Weddings, small meetings, family reunions and seminars hosted. Antiques, fishing, parks, shopping, watersports nearby.

Publicity: New York Times, Americana, USA Weekend, Tennessean, Southern Living, Atlanta Journal-Constitution, Victorian Homes.

"I love the peaceful atmosphere here and the beauty of nature surrounding Rugby."

Sevierville B8

Little Greenbrier Lodge

3685 Lyon Springs Rd
Sevierville, TN 37862-8257
(423)429-2500 (800)277-8100

Circa 1939. The spectacular, forested setting at Little Greenbrier is worth the trip. The rustic lodge is set on five, wooded acres less than a quarter mile from Great Smoky Mountains National Park. Rooms have valley or mountain views and are decorated with Victorian-style furnishings and antiques.

The lodge served guests from 1939 until the 1970s when it became a religious retreat. When the innkeepers purchased it in 1993, they tried to preserve some of its early history, including restoring original sinks and the first bathtub ever installed in the valley. A copy of the lodge's original "house rules" is still posted. Within 30 minutes are Dollywood, outlet malls, antiquing, craft stores and plenty of outdoor activities.

Innkeeper(s): Charles & Susan LeBon. $65-110. MC VISA DS. TAC10. 10 rooms, 8 with PB. 1 conference room. Breakfast, afternoon tea and evening snack included in rates. Type of meal: full breakfast. Beds: QDT. Air conditioning in room. VCR on premises. Weddings, small meetings, family reunions and seminars hosted. Amusement parks, antiques, fishing, parks, shopping, downhill skiing, sporting events and theater nearby.

"We had a relaxing holiday. Little Greenbrier is very special and we plan to return sometime soon."

Walland   B8

The Inn at Blackberry Farm
1471 W Millers Cove Rd
Walland, TN 37886-2649
(423)984-8166 Fax:(423)983-5708

Circa 1939. Gracious furnishings, spectacular scenery and gourmet cuisine are three of the reasons why guests return to Blackberry Farm. The 1,100 lush acres offer miles of nature to enjoy, complete with areas perfect for hiking, biking and fishing. The front terrace is lined with rocking chairs perfect for relaxing and enjoying the wonderful views. Guests are treated

to deluxe breakfasts, lunches and dinners. The innkeepers also keep a pantry stocked with snacks and beverages. The rooms are exquisitely decorated and furnished with glorious attention to detail. After a few days of being mercilessly pampered, guests won't want to leave.

Historic Interest: If the bounty of activities available at the inn fails to keep you busy, try visiting Gatlinburg. A 45-minute drive takes guests to this scenic mountain village. Another 40 minutes or so will take guests to Pigeon Forge. The inn backs up onto the Great Smoky Mountains National Park, which includes Cades Cove, a primitive settlement about 30 minutes from the inn.

Innkeeper(s): John C. Fleer. $295-1895. MC VISA AX. 42 rooms with PB. Breakfast, dinner and picnic lunch included in rates. Type of meal: full breakfast. Afternoon tea and lunch available. Restaurant on premises. Beds: KQDT.

Publicity: *Country Inns, Town & Country, Travel & Leisure, Southern Living, Conde Nast Traveler, Andrew Harper's Hideaway Report.* Ratings: 4 Stars.

"Everything was spectacular! A wonderful weekend getaway!"

Texas

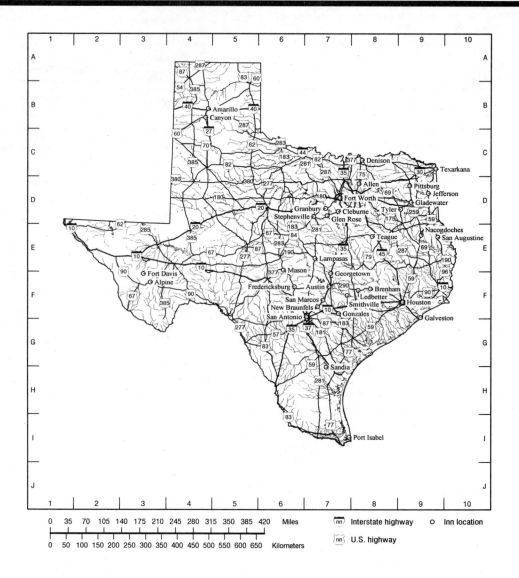

0   35   70   105 140 175 210 245 280 315 350 385 420   Miles

0   50 100 150 200 250 300 350 400 450 500 550 600 650   Kilometers

(nn) Interstate highway   o Inn location

(nn) U.S. highway

Allen D8

Blee Cottage

103 W Belmont Dr
Allen, TX 75013-2759
(972)390-1884 (800)699-4754 Fax:(972)390-1884
E-mail: bleecottage@aol.com

Circa 1904. One of the first houses in Allen, this farm house Victorian is situated just one block from the historic district. Originally built by mercantile owner H.T. Jordan for his family, the inn was by pharmacist W. G. Cundiff in 1913. He and his wife raised nine children in the home. The residence remained in the Cundiff family until 1992. After careful restoration, the inn's wood floors, moldings and wraparound porch are just a few of the restored classic features of the original home. Each of the inn's four rooms is individually decorated in a variety of comfortable antiques. Visitors interested in first-floor accommodations will enjoy the Claremont room with its vintage armoire and matching dresser. Innkeepers Amy and Tim Sherman, both trained chefs, pride themselves in preparing a hearty full breakfast each morning. Freshly baked scones, fritters, quiche and eggs Benedict are a few of the morning selections. The tree-shaded grounds are perfect for small weddings, meetings and family reunions.

Innkeeper(s): Tim & Amy Sherman. $60. MC VISA AX PC TC. 4 rooms with PB. Breakfast included in rates. Types of meals: full breakfast and early coffee/tea. Picnic lunch and catering service available. Beds: QT. Air conditioning and ceiling fan in room. TV, VCR, fax and copier on premises. Weddings, small meetings and family reunions hosted. Spanish spoken. Amusement parks, antiques, fishing, parks, sporting events, golf and watersports nearby.
Location: 45 minutes from Dallas.
Publicity: *Allen American, Allen Image.*

Alpine F3

The Corner House

801 E Avenue E
Alpine, TX 79830-5016
(915)837-7161 (800)585-7795 Fax:(915)837-3638

Circa 1937. The innkeeper of this bed & breakfast is the author of "From Big Bend to Carlsbad" as well as a world traveler. His expertise extends to the local area, and he can point guests in the direction of what to do and where to go. There are nine comfortable guest rooms. Guests enjoy a full breakfast inside or on the porch with items such as homemade breads, marmalade and perhaps an "Egg in the Hole," with a potato cake on the side.

Innkeeper(s): Jim Glendinning. $55-65. MC VISA AX PC TC. TAC10. 9 rooms, 7 with PB, 1 with FP. Breakfast included in rates. Type of meal: full breakfast. Beds: KQDT. Air conditioning in room. TV and library on premises. Weddings, small meetings, family reunions and seminars hosted. French, German and Spanish spoken. Parks, shopping, sporting events and theater nearby. Pets Allowed.

"Your lovely B&B was my first experience and will not be my last."

Amarillo B4

Parkview House B&B

1311 S Jefferson St
Amarillo, TX 79101-4029
(806)373-9464
E-mail: dia1311@aol.com

Circa 1908. Ionic columns support the wraparound wicker-filled front porch of this prairie Victorian. Herb and rose gardens, highlighted by a statuary and Victorian gazing ball, sur-round the property. Antique mahogany, walnut and oak pieces are found throughout. The French, Colonial, Dutch and Victorian Rose rooms all feature draped bedsteads and romantic decor. Sticky buns, homemade granola and fruits are served in the kitchen or dining room. Guests can enjoy a soak under the stars in the inn's hot tub or borrow a bicycle for a tour of the historic neighborhood.

Historic Interest: Pan Handle Plains Museum (15 minutes), Palo Duro State Park (23 miles), Alibates Flint Monument (16 miles).

Innkeeper(s): Carol & Nabil Dia. $65-150. MC VISA AX PC TC. TAC10. 5 rooms, 3 with PB. 1 suite. 1 cottage. Breakfast included in rates. Types of meals: continental breakfast, continental-plus breakfast, gourmet breakfast and early coffee/tea. Evening snack available. Beds: QD. Air conditioning in room. TV, VCR, fax and bicycles on premises. Weddings and small meetings hosted. Arabic spoken. Amusement parks, antiques, parks, shopping, theater and watersports nearby.
Publicity: *Lubbock Avalanche, Amarillo Globe News, Accent West, Sunday Telegraph Review.*

"You are what give B&B's such a wonderful reputation. Thanks very much for the wonderful stay! The hospitality was warm and the ambiance incredible."

Austin F7

Austin's Wildflower Inn B&B

1200 W 22 1/2 St
Austin, TX 78705-5304
(512)477-9639 Fax:(512)474-4188
E-mail: kjackson@io.com

Circa 1936. This Colonial-style home fits right into its woodsy street, located in a quiet Austin neighborhood just a few blocks from the University of Texas. Three of the rooms are named for

relatives of innkeeper Kay Jackson, who is related to a former president of the Republic of Texas. Lacy curtains, stenciling, pedestal sinks, quilts and antiques create a homey country atmosphere. One room has a canopy bed, another includes a four-poster, oak bed. Each morning, a new Wildflower specialty is served at breakfast, along with homemade breads or muffins and fresh fruit. The State Capitol Complex is a few minutes from the home.

Innkeeper(s): Kay Jackson. $74-89. MC VISA AX PC TC. 4 rooms, 2 with PB. Breakfast included in rates. Meals: full breakfast and early coffee/tea. Beds: QD. Air conditioning, ceiling fan in room. TV, fax on premises. Antiques, fishing, parks, shopping, sporting events, theater, watersports nearby.

"I was enchanted by your very friendly reception and personal care for my well-being."

Carrington's Bluff

1900 David St
Austin, TX 78705-5312
(512)479-0638 (800)871-8908 Fax:(512)476-4769

Circa 1877. Situated on a tree-covered bluff in the heart of Austin, this inn sits next to a 500-year-old oak tree. The innkeepers, one a Texan, the other British, combine down-home hospitality with English charm. The house is filled with English and American antiques and handmade quilts. Rooms are carefully decorated with dried flowers, inviting colors and antique beds, such as the oak barley twist bed in the Martha Hill Carrington Room. After a hearty breakfast, relax on a 35-foot-long porch that overlooks the bluff. The Austin area is booming with things to do.

Innkeeper(s): Lisa & Edward Mugford. $69-109. MC VISA AX DC CB DS PC TC. 8 rooms with PB. 1 suite. 1 cottage. 1 conference room. Breakfast and evening snack included in rates. Meals: full breakfast, gourmet breakfast and early coffee/tea. Beds: KQDT. Phone, air conditioning, ceiling fan and TV in room. VCR, fax, copier, library and child care on premises. Weddings, small meetings, family reunions and seminars hosted. Amusement parks, antiques, fishing, parks, shopping, sporting events, theater and watersports nearby.

Location: Downtown.

Publicity: *PBS Special.*

"Victorian writer's dream place."

Fairview

1304 Newning Ave
Austin, TX 78704-1841
(512)444-4746 (800)310-4746 Fax:(512)444-3494

Circa 1910. Surrounded by huge live oak trees, this Texas Revival-style home has been designated an Austin historic landmark. Each of the four large guest rooms on the second floor has impressive antique beds and private baths. Some rooms also feature clawfoot tubs, screened porches and sun rooms. Two suites are offered in the Carriage

House. Each has a private entrance, sitting room, full kitchen, eating area, bedroom and bath.

Historic Interest: Texas State Capitol (2 miles).

Innkeeper(s): Duke & Nancy Waggoner. $99-149. MC VISA AX DC CB PC TC. TAC10. 3 suites. Breakfast included in rates. Types of meals: full breakfast and early coffee/tea. Beds: KQDT. Phone, air conditioning, ceiling fan and TV in room. Fax, copier and library on premises. Amusement parks, antiques, fishing, parks, shopping, sporting events, theater and watersports nearby.

Location: Near downtown, convention center.

Publicity: *Texas Monthly, Austin, Gulliver's, Italian Travel.*

"The meal was fantastic, the tour wonderful and your hospitality gracious."

Governors' Inn

611 W 22nd St
Austin, TX 78705-5115
(512)479-0638 (800)871-8908 Fax:(512)476-4769

Circa 1897. This Neoclassical Victorian is just a few blocks from the University of Texas campus and three blocks from the State Capitol . Guests can enjoy the view of two acres of trees and foliage from the porches that decorate each story of the inn. The innkeepers have decorated the guest rooms with antiques and named them after former Texas governors. Several of the bathrooms include clawfoot tubs.

Innkeeper(s): Lisa & Edward Mugford. $69-99. MC VISA AX DC CB DS TC. 10 rooms with PB, 5 with FP. 1 conference room. Breakfast, afternoon tea and evening snack included in rates. Types of meals: full breakfast, gourmet breakfast and early coffee/tea. Picnic lunch, banquet service, catering service available. Beds: KQF. Phone, air conditioning, turndown service, ceiling fan, TV in room. VCR, fax, copier on premises. Handicap access. Weddings, small meetings, family reunions, seminars hosted. Antiques, fishing, parks, shopping, sporting events, theater, watersports nearby. Pets Allowed.

The McCallum House

613 W 32nd St
Austin, TX 78705-2219
(512)451-6744 Fax:(512)451-4752

Circa 1907. This two-story Princess Anne Victorian was built by school superintendent A.N. McCallum and designed by his wife Jane. As Mrs. McCallum raised her five children she assumed a leadership position in the women's suffrage movement and led the "Petticoat Lobby" advancing human service reforms in Texas. In 1926 she became secretary of

state for Texas. All rooms and suites have private porches, kitchens and numerous other amenities. It is an eight-block walk to the University of Texas. The McCallum House has received four historic awards and designations including a Texas marker and the National Register of Historic Places.

Historic Interest: Austin, the state capitol, is just two miles from the home offering many historic sites, homes and museums.

Innkeeper(s): Nancy & Roger Danley. $70-125. MC VISA. TAC10. 3 rooms with PB. 2 suites. Breakfast included in rates. Type of meal: full breakfast. Beds: QT. Phone, air conditioning and ceiling fan in room. VCR, fax and copier on premises. Amusement parks, antiques, fishing, parks, shopping, sporting events, theater and watersports nearby.

Publicity: *Austin American Statesman, Texas Monthly, Dallas Morning News.*

"What a special home and history... We would like to thank you again for our wonderful stay in Jane's Loft and all your help Easter Sunday with our dead battery."

Southard House

908 Blanco St
Austin, TX 78703-4914
(512)474-4731

Circa 1880. This house, an Austin historic landmark, originally had a single story, but was raised to accommodate an additional level at the turn of the century. Eleven-foot ceilings provide a background for antiques and paintings. Several guest rooms

include fireplaces or clawfoot tubs, and all the rooms are graciously appointed with antique pieces. On weekdays, the innkeepers serve continental fare, but a more expansive meal is served to weekend guests. The home is within walking distance of shops, antiquing, galleries and specialty boutiques.

Innkeeper(s): Jerry & Rejina Southard. $69-169. MC VISA AX DC CB DS PC TC. TAC10. 16 rooms with PB, 6 with FP. 7 suites. Breakfast included in rates. Types of meals: continental breakfast and full breakfast. Beds: QD. Phone, air conditioning, ceiling fan and TV in room. Fax and swimming on premises. Small meetings, family reunions and seminars hosted. Spanish spoken. Antiques, parks, shopping and theater nearby.

Location: Twelve blocks from the Capitol and within walking distance of the river.

Publicity: *Southern Living, New York Times, US Air, Austin Home & Garden, Austin American-Statesman.*

"A memory to be long cherished. We especially enjoyed the home atmosphere and the lovely breakfasts in the garden."

Brenham F8

Mariposa Ranch B&B

8904 Mariposa Ln
Brenham, TX 77833-9302
(409)836-4737 Fax:(409)836-4737
E-mail: mariposa@phoenix.net

Circa 1890. Several buildings comprise the inn: a Victorian, an 1820 log cabin, a farmhouse, and a 1836 Greek Revival home. Guests relax on the veranda, stroll through the Live Oaks, or

explore the ranch's 100 acres of fields and meadows. The inn is furnished with fine antiques. Ask for the Texas Ranger Cabin and enjoy a massive stone fireplace, sofa, clawfoot tub and loft with queen bed. Jennifer's Suite boasts a king canopy bed and two fireplaces. The "Enchanted Evening" package offers champagne, fruit, flowers, candlelight, candy and an optional massage.

Innkeeper(s): Johnna & Charles Chamberlain. $80-140. MC VISA PC TC. TAC10. 9 rooms, 7 with PB, 4 with FP. 3 suites. 4 cottages. 2 cabins. 1 conference room. Breakfast included in rates. Type of meal: full breakfast. Catering service available. Beds: KQDT. Air conditioning, ceiling fan, TV and VCR in room. Fax, copier and library on premises. Handicap access. 100 acres. Weddings, small meetings, family reunions and seminars hosted. Spanish spoken. Antiques, fishing, parks, shopping, golf, theater and watersports nearby. Pets Allowed.

Canyon B4

Historical Hudspeth House

1905 4th Ave
Canyon, TX 79015-4023
(806)655-9800 (800)655-9809 Fax:(806)655-7457

Circa 1909. Artist Georgia O'Keefe was once a guest at this three-story prairie home, which serves as a bed & breakfast. The home boasts many impressive architectural features, including an expansive entry with stained glass and a grandfather clock. The parlor boasts 12-foot ceilings and antiques, other rooms include chandeliers and huge fireplaces. Guests can arrange to have a candlelight dinner in their room.

Innkeeper(s): Mark & Mary Clark. $55-110. MC VISA AX DS PC TC. TAC10. 8 rooms with PB, 5 with FP. 2 suites. 2 conference rooms. Breakfast included in rates. Type of meal: early coffee/tea. Beds: KQ. Phone, air conditioning, ceiling fan and TV in room. Fax, copier and spa on premises. Amusement parks, antiques, parks, sporting events and theater nearby.

Cleburne D7

Cleburne House

201 N Anglin St
Cleburne, TX 76031-4134
(817)641-0085

Circa 1886. A sweeping wraparound veranda accented by gingerbread trim is one of the classic characteristics of this Queen Anne Victorian. Inside, visitors will find hardwood floors, stained-glass windows and comfortably appointed rooms decorated with antiques, lace and ceiling fans. Homemade cookies, ice cream, tea and coffee are served in the afternoon.

Innkeeper(s): Jan Bills. $95. PC. 4 rooms, 2 with PB. Breakfast, afternoon tea, evening snack and picnic lunch included in rates. Types of meals: continental breakfast, continental-plus breakfast, full breakfast and early coffee/tea. Beds: KD. Air conditioning, ceiling fan and TV in room. Spa and library on premises. Weddings, small meetings and family reunions hosted. Amusement parks, antiques, fishing, parks, shopping, sporting events, golf, theater and watersports nearby.
Publicity: *Fort Worth Star Telegram, Eagle Times-Review.*

"Never have we had such a good breakfast served with so much charm."

Denison C8

Ivy Blue B&B

1100 W Sears St
Denison, TX 75020-3326
(903)463-2479 (888)489-2583 Fax:(903)465-6773

Circa 1899. This Victorian charmer is set on a manicured lawn and shaded by several large trees. Guest rooms are named in honor of previous owners: Some of the furnishings and antiques that decorate the rooms are original to the home. Old newspaper clippings, antique dress patterns, historical documents and a time capsule are among the unique surprises guests might discover in their rooms. Fragrant soaps, lotions and chocolates add a touch of romance. Breakfasts are served on tables set with lace and antique china. Such items as banana almond waffles or mango coconut pancakes get the morning off to a great start. The inn's carriage house, which contains Lois' Cottage and the Feild Suite, is an ideal spot for those who prefer a bit more privacy. Carriage house guests may opt to enjoy breakfast in their room. Besides privacy, the Garden Suite offers a Jacuzzi tub, CD player and VCR. Guests are encouraged to ask about the murder mystery dinners, sunset cruises and carriage rides.

Innkeeper(s): Lane & Tammy Segerstrom. $65-150. MC VISA AX DS PC TC. 6 rooms with PB. 3 suites. 3 cottages. Breakfast included in rates. Types of meals: gourmet breakfast and early coffee/tea. Phone, air conditioning, ceiling fan and TV in room. Fax, swimming and library on premises. Handicap access. Weddings and small meetings hosted. Antiques, fishing, parks, shopping and watersports nearby.

Fort Davis F3

The Hotel Limpia

PO Box 822
Fort Davis, TX 79734-0822
(915)426-3237 (800)662-5517

Circa 1912. Four buildings and two guest houses make up this restored hotel, located in the Davis Mountains. Favorite places for guests to relax include the courtyard garden with the smell of roses and herbs, the glassed-in veranda with its plants and the porches with rocking chairs. The flavor of old Texas can be felt at this inn, constructed of pink limestone quarried in town near Sleeping Lion Mountain. There are two gift shops on the premises.

Historic Interest: The Fort Davis National Historic Site, Overland Trail Museum and Neil Doll Museum are nearby.

Innkeeper(s): Lanna & Joe Duncan. $69-150. MC VISA AX DS TC. 36 rooms with PB. 14 suites. 1 conference room. Dinner, picnic lunch, lunch, banquet service, catering service and catered breakfast available. Restaurant on premises. Beds: KQD. Air conditioning and TV in room. Fax and copier on premises. Handicap access. Weddings, small meetings, family reunions and seminars hosted. Pets Allowed.

Publicity: *San Angelo Standard Times, Texas Monthly, Dallas Morning News, Fortworth Star Telegram, Houston Press, Houston Chronicle.*

"Not many like this one left. Great."

The Veranda Country Inn B&B

PO Box 1238
Fort Davis, TX 79734-1238
(888)383-2847

Circa 1883. A mile above sea level sits this rustic historic inn, which first opened as the Lempert Hotel, a stopping point for travelers on the nearby Overland Trail. A later owner used the building for apartments, but current innkeepers Paul and

Kathie Woods returned the home into a place for hospitality. Paul, who has a doctorate in design, and Kathie have restored their bed & breakfast's high ceilings, wood floors and beaded wood ceilings back to their original condition. The grounds offer the serene setting of gardens and quiet courtyards, and the interior is furnished with antiques and collectibles.

Historic Interest: The Fort Davis area is full of historic places to visit, including the Fort Davis Historic Site, an 1854 restored frontier fort. The largest original unpaved portion of the Overland Trail is just a block away, and the Overland Trail Museum is another popular historic attraction. The Neill Doll Museum, which is located in a turn-of-the-century home, features more than 300 antique dolls.

Innkeeper(s): Paul & Kathie Woods. $68-135. MC VISA DS. 3 rooms with PB. 5 suites. 1 cottage. Breakfast included in rates. Type of meal: full breakfast. Beds: KD. Antiques nearby.

"What can we say? Wow! Great! Wonderful! Restful! Good company! Home! We sure enjoyed our stay with you. We can't stop thinking about it, and telling others about it."

Fort Worth D7

Miss Molly's Hotel

109 1/2 W Exchange Ave
Fort Worth, TX 76106-8508
(817)626-1522 (800)996-6559 Fax:(817)625-2723

Circa 1910. An Old West ambiance permeates this hotel, which once was a house of ill repute. Miss Josie's Room, named for the former madame, is decked with elaborate wall and ceiling coverings and carved oak furniture. The Gunslinger Room is filled with pictures of famous and infamous gunfighters. Rodeo memorabilia decorates the Rodeo Room, and twin iron beds and a pot belly stove add flair to the Cowboy's Room. Telephones and TV sets are the only things missing from the rooms, as the innkeeper hopes to preserve the flavor of the past.

Innkeeper(s): Mark & Alice Hancock. $75-170. MC VISA AX DC CB DS PC TC. TAC10. 8 rooms, 1 with PB. Breakfast included in rates. Types of meals:

continental-plus breakfast and early coffee/tea. Restaurant on premises. Beds: TD. Air conditioning and ceiling fan in room. Fax and copier on premises. Small meetings, family reunions and seminars hosted. Amusement parks, antiques, shopping, sporting events and theater nearby.

Publicity: *British Bulldog, Arkansas Gazette, Dallas Morning News, Fort Worth Star-Telegram, Continental Profiles.*

Fredericksburg F6

Country Cottage Inn

249 E Main St
Fredericksburg, TX 78624-4114
(210)997-8549 Fax:(210)997-8549

Circa 1850. This beautifully preserved house was built by blacksmith and cutler Frederick Kiehne. With two-foot-thick walls, it was the first two-story limestone house in town. The Country Cottage holds a collection of Texas primi-

tives and German country antiques, accentuated by Laura Ashley linens. Some of the baths include whirlpool tubs. Full, regional-style breakfasts are left in each room.

Historic Interest: Nimitz Museum (within 10 miles), LBJ State Park (near), Johnson city (LBJ Ranch Stonewall, birthplace home), Pioneer Museum.

Innkeeper(s): Mary Lou Rodriquez. $80-120. MC VISA PC. TAC10. 4 rooms with PB, 1 with FP. 2 suites. Breakfast included in rates. Meal: full breakfast. Beds: KQD. Phone, air conditioning, ceiling fan and TV in room. Handicap access. Spanish spoken. Antiques, fishing, parks and watersports nearby.

Publicity: *Weekend Getaway, Dallas Morning News, Glamour, Texas Highways.*

"A step back in time in 1850 style."

Schildknecht-Weidenfeller House

231 W Main St
Fredericksburg, TX 78624
(830)997-5612 Fax:(830)997-8282

Circa 1870. Beyond a gray picket fence, this pioneer German limestone house is decorated with primitive 19th-century furnishings that enhance the warm stone walls and polished pine plank floors. Located in

Fredericksburg's historic district, it is among the most well-preserved of the area's limestone houses. There is a rock-floored study, a fireplace set within the thick, stone walls of the parlor and a dining area that overlooks the

garden. Rockers line the front porch. Without hosts or other guests, you are free to absorb the atmosphere with complete privacy and yet still partake of a German-style breakfast left for you to enjoy whenever you please.

Historic Interest: Admiral Nimitz Museum, Pioneer Museum Complex, Lyndon B. Johnson State and National Historical Park.

$125-375. MC VISA DS PC TC. TAC10. Breakfast included in rates. Type of meal: continental-plus breakfast. Beds: QDT. Air conditioning in room. TV on premises. Small meetings and family reunions hosted. Antiques, parks and shopping nearby.

"The fireplace is a warm heart to this wonderful home."

Watkins Hill - Fredericksburg's Most Beautiful Guest House™

608 E Creek St
Fredericksburg, TX 78624
(830)997-6739 (800)899-1672 Fax:(830)997-6057

Circa 1835. This exquisitely restored and maintained inn features six Native Pioneer stone and log buildings situated on two acres of private gardens and just one block from the center of town. The innkeeper's 30 years of experience working with such clients as The Smithsonian Institute, Neiman Marcus, Saks Fifth Avenue and Horchow Collection is evident in the elegant but rustic decorative arts and furnishings featured throughout the compound. With separate entrances, fully stocked butler's pantry, canopied beds and fireplaces in most rooms, the inn offers the ultimate in privacy and luxury. The common areas in the main building feature a formal parlor, a library, formal dining room and a ballroom with 30-foot ceilings dating back to 1840.

Innkeeper(s): Edgar Watkins. $110-165. MC VISA PC TC. TAC10. 12 rooms with PB, 10 with FP. 8 suites. 6 cottages. 1 conference room. Breakfast included in rates. Types of meals: gourmet breakfast and early coffee/tea. Beds: QT. Phone, air conditioning, ceiling fan, TV and VCR in room. Fax and copier on premises. Weddings, small meetings, family reunions and seminars hosted. Antiques, fishing, parks, shopping, golf and theater nearby. Pets Allowed: On leash, small pets.
Publicity: *Country Living, San Antonio Express, Vacations.*

"What a class act! The champagne on arrival, breakfast in bed, a fabulous honeymoon."

Galveston   F9

Michael's B&B

1715 35th St
Galveston, TX 77550-6717
(409)763-3760 (800)776-8302

Circa 1916. Built by Hans Guldman, Galveston's one-time vice-consul for Denmark, the massive red brick home sits on an acre of gardens that include Mrs. Guldman's greenhouse and fish pond. Guests can have breakfast in the formal dining room or in the sunroom overlooking the garden. The house holds a cache of family antiques with contemporary pieces and original art. Common rooms include a large dining room, parlor, sunroom and study. The home has been on Galveston's historic homes tour and garden tour.

Innkeeper(s): Mikey Isbell. $85-110. MC VISA DS. 4 rooms. 1 suite. Breakfast included in rates. Type of meal: full breakfast. Air conditioning and ceiling fan in room. Weddings, small meetings and family reunions hosted. Antiques and theater nearby.

Georgetown   F7

Claibourne House

912 Forest St
Georgetown, TX 78626-5524
(512)930-3934 Fax:(512)869-0202

Circa 1896. This turn-of-the-century Victorian was built by a local doctor to house his large family. The interior is decorated

in an elegant mix of styles, with antiques, Southwestern and Oriental rugs and artwork. Each of the rooms is individually appointed and named. Two rooms have a marble bath and one bathroom features a skylight. Homemade breads, pastries and biscuits are the fare for the continental breakfasts. The B&B is just a few blocks from Georgetown's historic courthouse square.

Innkeeper(s): Clare Easley. $90-100. MC VISA PC TC. TAC10. 4 rooms with PB, 2 with FP. 1 cottage. Breakfast included in rates. Types of meals: continental-plus breakfast and early coffee/tea. Beds: QDT. Air conditioning and ceiling fan in room. TV, tennis and library on premises. Small meetings, family reunions and seminars hosted. Antiques, fishing, parks, shopping, sporting events and golf nearby. Pets Allowed.

Gladewater   D9

Honeycomb Suites

111 N Main St
Gladewater, TX 75647-2333
(903)845-4430 (800)594-2253 Fax:(903)845-2448
E-mail: sho4go@internetwork.net

Circa 1932. Built during the oil boom in the 1930s, this solid brick in-town industrial-style inn is actually the union of two, two-story buildings. Guest rooms are individually decorated in American country antiques, and feature whirlpool tubs in some of the rooms and canopied beds in others. The inn is a favorite spot for guests looking to enjoy the slow-paced atmosphere of this small town located just an hour east of Dallas. A full breakfast is offered each morning in the inn's restaurant. A candlelight dinner is available for an extra charge.

Innkeeper(s): Bill & Susan Morgan. $75-130. MC VISA AX DS PC TC. 7 rooms with PB. 6 suites. 1 conference room. Breakfast and evening snack included in rates. Types of meals: full breakfast, gourmet breakfast and early coffee/tea. Picnic lunch and lunch available. Restaurant on premises. Beds: Q. Phone, air conditioning, ceiling fan and TV in room. Weddings, small meetings, family reunions and seminars hosted. Antiques, fishing, parks, shopping, golf and watersports nearby.
Publicity: *Dallas Morning News.*

Glen Rose   D7

The Inn on the River

205 SW Barnard St
Glen Rose, TX 76043
(972)424-7119 (800)575-2101 Fax:(972)424-9766

Circa 1914. Nestled on the banks of the Paluxy River, the inn boasts beautifully manicured gardens and riverside seating under 300-year-old oaks. A former guest wrote a song about the trees that was later recorded by Elvis Presley. Enchanting decor and furnishings make each room a special place. Each of the 22 guest rooms is individually decorated with careful attention to detail. The multi-course breakfast is served in the dining room, which overlooks the gardens. Enjoy specialties such as herbed scrambled eggs with cheese-sprinkled grits as you take in the view. A short walk takes you to the historic town square, which includes the stately courthouse and many interesting shops.

Innkeeper(s): Kathi Thompson. $115-195. MC VISA AX DS. 22 rooms with PB. 3 suites. 2 conference rooms. Breakfast included in rates. Type of meal: full breakfast. Dinner available. Beds: KQD. Fax on premises. Antiques, fishing, golf and watersports nearby.

Location: On the banks of the Paluxy River.

Publicity: *Texas Highway, Dallas Morning News, Chocolatier, American Way, Meeting Manager.*

"What a wonderful place for special memories."

Gonzales   F7

St. James Inn

723 Saint James St
Gonzales, TX 78629-3411
(830)672-7066 Fax:(830)672-7787

Circa 1914. Ann and J.R. Covert spent three years restoring this massive Texas Hill Country mansion, once owned by a cattle baron. On the main floor is a tiled solarium, living room, reception hall, dining room, butler's pantry and kitchen. The second-

floor guest rooms all have working fireplaces and porches. The top-level room has a unique wind tunnel—a long crawl space with windows on either end—which once provided natural air conditioning to the original occupants of the home. Gourmet candlelight dinners in addition to the full breakfasts make this an elegant getaway.

Innkeeper(s): Ann & J.R. Covert. $85-100. MC VISA AX PC TC. 5 rooms with PB, 5 with FP. 2 suites. 1 conference room. Breakfast and afternoon tea included in rates. Types of meals: full breakfast, gourmet breakfast and early coffee/tea. Dinner, picnic lunch, gourmet lunch and banquet service available. Beds: KQ. Phone, air conditioning, turndown service, ceiling fan and TV in room. Weddings, small meetings, family reunions and seminars hosted. Antiques, fishing, parks, shopping, theater and watersports nearby.

Location: One hour east of San Antonio, one hour south of Austin.

Publicity: *Gonzales Inquirer, Houston Chronicle, Victoria Advocate, Austin American Statesman, San Antonio Express-News.*

"We had a wonderful weekend. It's a marvelous home and your hospitality is superb. We'll be back."

Granbury   D7

Dabney House B&B

106 S Jones St
Granbury, TX 76048-1905
(817)579-1260 (800)566-1260

Circa 1907. Built during the Mission Period, this Craftsman-style country manor boasts original hardwood floors, stained-glass windows and some of the original light fixtures. The parlor and dining rooms have large, exposed, wooden beams and the ceilings throughout are 10-feet high. The Dabney Suite has a private entrance into an enclosed

sun porch with rattan table and chairs that allow for a private breakfast. The bedroom of this suite is furnished with a four-post tester bed with drapes and an 1800 wardrobe.

Historic Interest: Historic Town Square (one-half mile), Dinosaur Valley State Park (18 miles), Texas Dr. Pepper Plant (45 miles), Elizabeth Crockett (5 miles).

Innkeeper(s): John & Gwen Hurley. $70-105. MC VISA AX PC TC. TAC10. 4 rooms with PB. 1 suite. Breakfast and evening snack included in rates. Type of meal: full breakfast. Dinner available. Beds: Q. Air conditioning and ceiling fan in room. VCR, spa and library on premises. Small meetings, family reunions and seminars hosted. Antiques, fishing, parks, shopping, theater and watersports nearby.

Publicity: *Fort Worth Star Telegram, Dallas Morning News.*

"Very enjoyable and certainly up among the very best of the B&Bs you are likely to find in the United Kingdom. It reminded me of staying at grandma's house. Thanks for bringing back such warm memories."

Nutt House

121 E Bridge St, Town Square
Granbury, TX 76048
(817)573-5612

Circa 1893. For a rustic trip back in time to the Old West days of Texas, try a stay at the Nutt House, a Texas Historic Landmark. The hotel was restored by a member of the Nutt Family, and she also was responsible for helping to get much of the city listed in the National Register. Guest rooms are simply

furnished with antiques, and several share a bath. Although there are no meals included in the rates, the Nutt House Restaurant is a popular local eatery. The restaurant's menu changes nightly, featuring country selections such as fried catfish, chicken and dumplings or barbecued sausage. Try the buttermilk pie for dessert.

Innkeeper(s): Elaine Dooley. $39-110. MC VISA AX DC DS PC TC. TAC10. 15 rooms, 6 with PB. 2 suites. Type of meal: early coffee/tea. Restaurant on premises. Beds: QDT. Air conditioning and ceiling fan in room. Small meetings, family reunions and seminars hosted. Amusement parks, antiques, fishing, parks, shopping, golf, theater and watersports nearby.

Publicity: *Texas Highways.*

Pearl Street Inn B&B

319 W Pearl St
Granbury, TX 76048-2437
(817)579-7465 (888)732-7578

Circa 1911. Known historically as the B. M. Estes House, the inn is decorated with a mix of English, French and American antiques. The English Garden Suite is fashioned in a green, peach and ivy motif and features a king-size iron and brass bed, English antique furniture, airy sitting room and full bath accented by a cast iron tub and 1912 wall sink. Other guest rooms include clawfoot tubs, crystal lamps and lace.

Historic Interest: Town Square (3 blocks), Fort Worth Stockyards (40 minutes), Dinosaur Valley State Park (18 miles), Granbury Cemetery (2 miles), Fossil Rim (15 miles).

Innkeeper(s): Danette D. Hebda. $59-109. PC TC. TAC10. 5 rooms with PB.

1 suite. Breakfast included in rates. Types of meals: full breakfast, gourmet breakfast and early coffee/tea. Beds: KD. Air conditioning and ceiling fan in room. VCR and copier on premises. Weddings, small meetings and seminars hosted. Antiques, fishing, parks, shopping, theater and watersports nearby. Publicity: *Dallas Morning News, New York Times, Fort Worth Star Telegram.*

"Needless to say, we want to stay forever! We had a grand time and highly enjoyed conversations and hospitality."

Houston F9

Angel Arbor B&B Inn

848 Heights Blvd
Houston, TX 77007-1507
(713)868-4654 (800)722-8788

Circa 1922. Each of the rooms at Angel Arbor has a heavenly name and elegant decor. The Angelique Room offers a cherry sleigh bed and a balcony overlooking the garden. Canopy or poster beds grace the other rooms and suite, named Gabriel, Raphael and Michael. The Georgian-style home is located in the historic Houston Heights neighborhood and was built by a prominent local family. The innkeeper, a cookbook author, prepares a mouthwatering homemade breakfast each morning. Ask about the innkeeper's special murder-mystery dinner parties.

Innkeeper(s): Marguerite Swanson. $95-125. MC VISA AX DS PC TC. TAC10. 4 rooms with PB. 1 suite. 1 conference room. Breakfast included in rates. Types of meals: full breakfast, gourmet breakfast and early coffee/tea. Afternoon tea available. Beds: Q. Phone, air conditioning, turndown service, ceiling fan, TV and VCR in room. Fax and library on premises. Small meetings, family reunions and seminars hosted. German spoken. Amusement parks, antiques, fishing, parks, shopping, sporting events, theater and watersports nearby.

La Colombe D'or

3410 Montrose Blvd
Houston, TX 77006-4329
(713)524-7999 Fax:(713)524-8923

Renowned as the "World's Smallest Luxury Hotel," the hotel houses six suites having a mixture of original art and antiques. Each has its own dining room, allowing for a luxurious alternative to the public dining areas. Guests also may enjoy the romantic main dining rooms, the intimate walnut-paneled bar and cozy fire-lit library. Breakfast is an extra charge but can be served in your room upon request. The home originally belonged to W. W. Fondren, the founder of Humble Oil, which is now Exxon.

Innkeeper(s): Gina Bradshaw. Call for rates. 6 suites. 1 conference room. Gourmet lunch, banquet service, catering service and room service available. Phone, air conditioning, turndown service, ceiling fan and TV in room. VCR on premises. Weddings, small meetings, family reunions and seminars hosted. Amusement parks, antiques, shopping, sporting events, theater nearby.

The Lovett Inn

501 Lovett Blvd
Houston, TX 77006-4020
(713)522-5224 (800)779-5224 Fax:(713)528-6708
E-mail: lovettinn@aol.com

Circa 1924. Built by former Houston Mayor and Judge Joseph C. Hutcheson, this gracious Colonial-style home remained with its owner until his death in 1973. Located on a tree-lined street in the center of town, the home has been meticulously restored to blend its elegant architectural character with today's modern amenities. Most guest rooms overlook the beautifully landscaped grounds with its gazebo, pool and spa. Gleaming hardwood floors and distinctive reproduction period antique furnishings are just a few of the features that enhance the inn's natural charm. The inn is available for weddings, receptions, retreats and meetings.

Innkeeper(s): Tom Fricke. $85-145. MC VISA AX DS TC. TAC10. 8 rooms with PB. 3 suites. 1 conference room. Breakfast included in rates. Type of meal: continental breakfast. Beds: KQD. Phone, air conditioning, TV and VCR in room. Fax, spa, swimming and library on premises. Weddings, small meetings, family reunions and seminars hosted. Spanish spoken. Amusement parks, antiques, parks, sporting events, golf and theater nearby.

Pets Allowed: In some rooms with prior arrangements.

Publicity: *Houston Chronicle, Dallas Morning News, Texas Monthly, Houston Business Journal.*

Robin's Nest

4104 Greeley St
Houston, TX 77006-5609
(713)528-5821 (800)622-8343 Fax:(713)521-2154

Circa 1898. Legend denotes this former dairy farm as one of the oldest homes in Houston. The two-story wooden Queen Anne features original pine hardwoods, tall windows and fine fabrics. The beautifully landscaped grounds are another memorable feature. Guests will appreciate the inn's proximity to downtown Houston, theaters and gourmet restaurants. Located in the Montrose area of the city, the inn is less than an hour from popular attractions such as NASA and Galveston.

Historic Interest: The San Jacinto Monument and Armannd Bayou are 30 minutes from the home. Bayou Bend Gardens are 15 minutes away.

Innkeeper(s): Robin Smith. $75-110. MC VISA AX CB DS. 4 rooms with PB. 1 conference room. Breakfast included in rates. Type of meal: full breakfast. Beds: QDT. Phone, air conditioning, ceiling fan and TV in room. Weddings, small meetings, family reunions and seminars hosted. Amusement parks, antiques, fishing, shopping, sporting events, theater and watersports nearby.

Location: Inside 610 Loop very near downtown, Brown Convention Center and Texas Medical Center. The inn is in the Museum and Arts District.

Publicity: *Houston Home and Garden, Houston Business Journal, Woman's Day, Houston Metropolitan, Houston Post, Southern Living, Texas Monthly, Houston Chronicle.*

"Fanciful and beautiful, comfortable and happy. We saw a whole new side of Houston, thanks to you."

Jefferson D9

Kennedy Manor

217 W Lafayette St
Jefferson, TX 75657-2207
(903)665-2528 Fax:(903)665-6191

Circa 1861. A wide front porch stretches across the entire front of this two-story Victorian. Gables, a wide bay window, upper sun porch and white fence add character to the inn. Inside are polished hardwood floors, restored woodwork and high ceilings. Decorated with Victorian antiques, the guest rooms offer ceiling fans, TV and phones. Early coffee is available and there is a full breakfast.

Innkeeper(s): Larry & Mary Bill Royder. $70-125. MC VISA PC TC. TAC10. 6 rooms with PB. Breakfast included in rates. Types of meals: gourmet breakfast and early coffee/tea. Evening snack available. Beds: QDT. Phone, air conditioning, ceiling fan and TV in room. VCR, fax, copier and library on premises. Handicap access. Weddings, small meetings and family reunions hosted. Antiques, parks, golf, theater and watersports nearby.

McKay House

306 E Delta St
Jefferson, TX 75657-2026
(903)665-7322 (800)468-2627

Circa 1851. For more than 13 years, the McKay House has been widely acclaimed for its high standards, personal service and satisfied guests. Both Lady Bird Johnson and Alex Haley have enjoyed the gracious Southern hospitality offered at the McKay House. Accented by a Williamsburg-style picket fence,

the Greek Revival cottage features a pillared front porch. Heart-of-pine floors, 14-foot ceilings and documented wallpapers complement antique furnishings. A full "gentleman's" breakfast is served in the garden conservatory by the gable fireplace. Orange and pecan French toast or home-baked muffins and shirred eggs served on vintage china are a few of the house specialties. In each of the seven bedchambers you find a Victorian nightgown and old-fashioned nightshirt presented on luxurious bedding. History abounds in the nearby town of Jefferson, considered the "Williamsburg of the Southwest."

Innkeeper(s): Lisa & Roger Cantrell. $85-145. MC VISA AX PC TC. TAC10. 8 rooms, 7 with PB, 6 with FP. 3 suites. 1 cottage. 1 conference room. Breakfast included in rates. Types of meals: gourmet breakfast and early coffee/tea. Beds: QD. Phone, air conditioning, ceiling fan and TV in room. Weddings, small meetings, family reunions and seminars hosted. Antiques, fishing, parks, shopping, theater and watersports nearby.

Publicity: *Southern Accents, Dallas Morning News, Country Home, Bride.*

"The facilities of the McKay House are exceeded only by the service and dedication of the owners."

Pride House

409 Broadway
Jefferson, TX 75657
(800)894-3526 Fax:(903)665-3901
E-mail: jefftx@mind.net

Circa 1889. Mr. Brown, a sawmill owner, built this Victorian house using fine hardwoods, sometimes three layers deep. The windows are nine-feet tall on both the lower level and upstairs.

The rooms include amenities such as fireplaces, balconies, canopy beds and private entrances. Most boasts original stained-glass windows. The West Room is decorated in crimson reds and features a gigantic clawfoot tub that has received an award from Houston Style Magazine for "best tub in

Texas." A wide veranda stretches around two sides of the house.

Innkeeper(s): Carol Abernathy & Christel Frederick. $75-110. MC VISA PC TC. TAC10. 10 rooms with PB, 3 with FP. 1 suite. 1 cottage. Breakfast and evening snack included in rates. Types of meals: gourmet breakfast and early coffee/tea. Beds: KQDT. Phone, air conditioning and ceiling fan in room. Handicap access. Weddings, small meetings, family reunions and seminars hosted. German spoken. Antiques, fishing and theater nearby.

Publicity: *Woman's Day, Country Home, Texas Highways, Texas Homes.*

"No five star hotel can compare to the hospitality of Pride House."

Lampasas   E7

Historic Moses Hughes B&B

RR 2 Box 31
Lampasas, TX 76550-9601
(512)556-5923

Circa 1856. Nestled among ancient oaks in the heart of the Texas Hill Country, this native stone ranch house rests on 45 acres that include springs, a creek, wildlife and other natural

beauty. The ranch was built by Moses Hughes, the first white settler and founder of Lampasas. He and his wife decided to stay in the area after her health dramatically improved after visiting the springs. Guests can join the innkeepers on the stone patio or upstairs wooden porch for a taste of Texas Hill Country life.

Historic Interest: Fort Hood, on the road to Colorado Bend State Park and Gorman Falls, Mission San Saba (within an hour).

Innkeeper(s): Al & Beverly Solomon. $75-85. PC. TAC10. 2 rooms with PB. Breakfast included in rates. Types of meals: full breakfast and gourmet breakfast. Beds: D. Air conditioning in room. VCR and library on premises. 45 acres. Weddings hosted. Antiques, fishing, parks and watersports nearby.

Publicity: *Dallas Morning News, Spiegel Catalog, Discover.*

"What a delightful respite! Thank you for sharing your very interesting philosophies and personalities with us at this very special B&B. We hate to leave."

Ledbetter   F8

Ledbetter Hotel

PO Box 212
Ledbetter, TX 78946-0212
(409)249-3066

Circa 1860. Located in a neighborhood of bed & breakfasts, this home offers amenities such as sitting rooms in the guest quarters and a delicious home-cooked breakfast, featuring country favorites such as grits and biscuits and gravy. Rooms are filled with antiques and extra touches like a free operating juke box with '50s songs. Relax by the indoor pool or reserve your own Chuckwagon Cookout. Guests arrive at a campsite by hayride and can explore the area or take a buggy ride. A hearty dinner is served, then guests are entertained with stories of cattle drives followed by live music. Other special packages include a Romantic Evening for Two with a candle-lit dinner. Fishing is also available.

Innkeeper(s): Chris Jervis. $90. MC VISA AX PC TC. TAC10. 4 rooms with PB. 3 conference rooms. Type of meal: full breakfast. Beds: DT. Phone in room. Fax, copier and spa on premises. Handicap access.

Publicity: *Southern Living, Texas Highways, Texas Citizen.*

Mason E6

Hasse House and Ranch

1221 Ischar St, PO Box 58
Mason, TX 76856
(888)414-2773

Circa 1883. Guests may explore the 320-acre Hasse ranch, which is a working ranch where deer, wild turkey, feral hogs and quail are common sights. After purchasing the land, Henry Hasse and his wife lived in a log cabin on the property before building the sandstone home 23 years later. Three generations of Hasses have lived here, and today it is owned by a great-granddaughter who restored the home in 1980. The inn is located in the small German village of Art, Texas, which is located six miles east of Mason. The innkeepers rent the two-bedroom National Register home out to only one group or guest at a time, host free. The home is filled with period furniture and accessories, yet offers the modern convenience of an on-site washer and dryer and a fully stocked kitchen. The ranch grounds include a two-mile nature trail perfect for nature lovers.

Innkeeper(s): Laverne Lee. $95. MC VISA PC TC. 2 rooms with PB. Breakfast included in rates. Type of meal: continental-plus breakfast. Beds: D. Air conditioning, ceiling fan and VCR in room. Library on premises. Handicap access. 320 acres. Weddings, small meetings and family reunions hosted. Antiques, fishing, parks, shopping and watersports nearby.

"We enjoyed every aspect of our stay; the atmosphere, sense of history, rustic setting with a touch of class. We would love to return the same time next year!"

Nacogdoches E9

Llano Grande Plantation

RR 4 Box 9400
Nacogdoches, TX 75964-9276
(409)569-1249
E-mail: 73717.2542@compuserve.com

Circa 1840. A collection of five lodgings sit on this 600-acres of creeks and pine forest. The accommodations are located on what was called the Llano Grande land grant, given to Pedro Jose Esparza in 1779. Among the buildings is the Tol Barret House, which dates to 1840, and is both a Texas Historic Landmark and listed in the National Register. This home includes a bedroom with four beds, as well as a kitchen and fireplace. The Sparks House, which dates to the mid-1800s, is another option. The Texas Landmark home has two bedrooms, a fireplace, woodburning stove and sitting area. Also available is the Gate House, which is a Texas-style farmhouse with two bedrooms, kitchen and fireplace. There is also an Antebellum plantation home. In all of the homes, carefully chosen antiques resemble those of the original owners.

Innkeeper(s): Captain Charles & Ann Phillips. $60-95. PC TC. 3 suites, 3 with FP. Breakfast included in rates. Types of meals: continental-plus breakfast and full breakfast. Afternoon tea and catering service available. Phone and air conditioning in room. 600 acres. Weddings, small meetings, family reunions and seminars hosted. Antiques, fishing, parks, shopping, sporting events, theater and watersports nearby.

New Braunfels F7

The Rose Garden B&B

195 S Academy Ave
New Braunfels, TX 78130-5607
(210)629-3296

Circa 1930. In a town full of rich German heritage, this Colonial Revival inn features designer bedrooms, fluffy towels, scented soaps and potpourri-filled rooms. Take a stroll along the cool, Comal Springs or browse antique shops, which are all within walking distance. Relax in the parlor by the fireplace or in the rose garden. Breakfast is served in the formal dining room, garden or brought to your room on a specially prepared tray. The inn is only one block from downtown.

Innkeeper(s): Dawn Mann. $75-105. 2 rooms with PB. Breakfast included in rates. Types of meals: full breakfast and early coffee/tea. Beds: Q. Phone, turndown service and ceiling fan in room. Weddings and small meetings hosted. Antiques, fishing, shopping, theater and watersports nearby.
Publicity: *Herald-Zeitung.*

"A getaway to a B&B like yours truly revitalizes the spirit and was just what we were looking for. The food was delicious and beautifully presented."

Pittsburg D9

Holman House B&B

218 N Texas St
Pittsburg, TX 75686-1038
(903)856-7552 (800)903-5033 Fax:(903)856-7457
E-mail: holmanhous@aol.com

Circa 1912. Originally the home of one of Pittsburg's founding families, this classic Greek Revival is shaded by a 100-year-old oak and is just a few blocks away from the quaint town center. Period antiques and hardwood floors inspire a comfortable and relaxed atmosphere. Fresh fruit, tea breads and a breakfast entree are offered in the dining room.

Innkeeper(s): Dan Blake & Rebecca Wolfe. $65-85. MC VISA PC TC. 5 rooms with PB. 1 suite. Breakfast included in rates. Types of meals: continental breakfast, continental-plus breakfast, full breakfast and early coffee/tea. Picnic lunch and catering service available. Beds: KQD. Air conditioning and TV in room. Fax on premises. Small meetings, family reunions and seminars hosted. Spanish spoken. Antiques, fishing, parks, shopping, golf and watersports nearby.
Publicity: *Dallas Morning News.*

Port Isabel I7

Yacht Club Hotel

700 Yturra St
Port Isabel, TX 78578
(956)943-1301 Fax:(956)943-1301

Circa 1926. This Spanish-style hotel is the second-oldest building in Port Isabel. The hotel was built to serve as a private club for influential families. There are three lush acres, sporting palm trees and a courtyard with a swimming pool. Rooms are decorated in a comfortable, modern hotel style. The inn's restaurant, which has hosted dignitaries such as Lady Bird Johnson, features an array of Gulf Coast seafood and a fine selection of wines. The hotel is located on the Gulf Coast, just a five-minute drive from South Padre Island.

Innkeeper(s): Ron & Lynn Speier. $42-99. MC VISA AX DC TC. TAC10. 24 rooms with PB. 5 suites. 1 conference room. Breakfast included in rates. Type of meal: continental breakfast. Banquet service available. Restaurant on premises. Beds: KQD. Phone, air conditioning and TV in room. Fax, copier and swimming on premises. Weddings, small meetings, family reunions and seminars hosted. Spanish spoken. Amusement parks, fishing, shopping, golf and watersports nearby.

Pets Allowed: $25 pet fee, non-refundable.

Publicity: *Southern Living, Dallas Magazine, Southwest Air Lines Magazine, Dallas Morning News, Houston Chronicle, Dallas.*

San Antonio F7

A Yellow Rose B&B

229 Madison
San Antonio, TX 78204-1321
(210)229-9903 (800)950-9903 Fax:(210)229-1691
E-mail: yellowrs@express-news.net

Circa 1878. This historic Victorian is located in the quiet and elegant King William Historic District, adjacent to San Antonio's downtown area. There are five distinctly decorated and spacious guest rooms to choose from, each with beautiful furnishings and decor, as well as amenities such as cable TVs, alarm clocks and radios. Turn-of-the-century antiques add a nostalgic ambiance. A two-block walk will take guests to the Riverwalk, and it's just a block to reach the trolley. Guests also can walk to the downtown area, convention center and many restaurants.

Historic Interest: Alamo (8 blocks), St. Francis Church (8 blocks), San Antonio Riverwalk (2 blocks), Mission Trail (one-half mile).

Innkeeper(s): Kit Walker & Deb Field. $95-150. MC VISA AX DS PC TC. TAC10. 5 rooms with PB. 1 suite. 1 conference room. Breakfast included in rates. Type of meal: gourmet breakfast. Beds: Q. Air conditioning, ceiling fan and TV in room. VCR and library on premises. Small meetings, family reunions and seminars hosted. Amusement parks, antiques, parks, shopping, sporting events, theater and watersports nearby.

"Recommendations will be forthcoming. Best Christmas gift we gave ourselves coming here! Thanks."

The Academy House of Monte Vista

2317 N Main Ave
San Antonio, TX 78212-3448
(210)731-8393 (888)731-8393

Circa 1897. The innkeepers of this in-town Victorian pride themselves in their hospitality and commitment to maintaining a home-away-from-home atmosphere. All rooms are tastefully decorated in period antiques. The inn offers complimentary refreshments and a full breakfast each day. Overlooking the downtown skyline, the inn is minutes from the historic River Walk.

Innkeeper(s): Kenneth & Johnnie Walker-Staggs. $85-115. MC VISA PC. TAC10. 3 rooms with PB. 2 cottages. Breakfast included in rates. Types of meals: full breakfast and early coffee/tea. Beds: K. Phone, air conditioning, ceiling fan, TV and VCR in room. Spa on premises. Weddings, small meetings and seminars hosted. Amusement parks, antiques, parks, shopping, sporting events, golf, theater and watersports nearby.

Pets Allowed: call first.

"Everything was so comfortable and I felt safer here than I usually do in a big downtown hotel."

Beckmann Inn & Carriage House B&B

222 E Guenther
San Antonio, TX 78204-1405
(210)229-1449 (800)945-1449 Fax:(210)229-1061

Circa 1886. A wraparound porch with white wicker furniture warmly welcomes guests to the main house of this Victorian inn. Through the entrance and into the living room, guests stand on an intricately designed wood mosaic floor imported from Paris. Arch-shaped pocket doors with framed opaque glass open to the formal dining room, where breakfast is served. All the guest rooms feature 12- to 14-foot ceilings with fans; tall, ornately carved queen-size antique Victorian beds; colorful floral accessories; and antiques.

Historic Interest: Alamo, Spanish Governor's Place, Riverwalk, missions.
Innkeeper(s): Betty Jo & Don Schwartz. $90-130. MC VISA AX DC DS PC. 5 rooms with PB, 2 with FP. 2 suites. Breakfast included in rates. Meal: gourmet breakfast. Beds: Q. Phone, air conditioning, turndown service, ceiling fan, TV in room. Fax, copier, library on premises. Family reunions hosted. Amusement parks, antiques, parks, shopping, sporting events, theater nearby.

"The Beckmann Inn & Carriage House is truly a home away from home for all who stay there. Don and Betty Jo put their heart and soul into making every guest's stay a memorable experience."

Bonner Garden

145 E Agarita Ave
San Antonio, TX 78212-2923
(210)733-4222 (800)396-4222 Fax:(210)733-6129
E-mail: noels@onr.com

Circa 1910. Mary Bonner was internationally renowned for her etchings and printmaking skills. Selected Bonner prints and works by other artists, including the Bonner House's owner, are displayed throughout the house. This Italian Renaissance inn has a rooftop patio and wet bar. The house made history when it was constructed by Atlee Ayres, who was one of the foremost architects of the era. The home was built of concrete, reinforced with steel and cast iron, and clad in stucco. Exercise facilities include a 50-foot pool, Nordic Track exerciser and bicycles.

Innkeeper(s): Jan & Noel Stenoien. $85-125. MC VISA AX DC CB DS PC TC. TAC10. 5 rooms with PB, 3 with FP. Breakfast included in rates. Type of meal: full breakfast. Beds: KQ. Phone, air conditioning, ceiling fan, TV and VCR in room. Fax, copier, swimming, bicycles and library on premises. Small meetings and family reunions hosted. Amusement parks, parks, shopping, sporting events, golf and theater nearby.

"Second time was as great as the first."

The Bullis House Inn

621 Pierce St, PO Box 8059
San Antonio, TX 78208
(210)223-9426 Fax:(210)299-1479
E-mail: hisanantonio@aol.com

Circa 1906. A two-story portico supported by six massive columns accentuates the Neoclassical architecture of this home built for General Bullis who was instrumental in the capture of

Chief Geronimo. Features include stairways and paneling of tiger's eye oak, marble fireplaces, chandeliers and parquet floors. There are contemporary and antique furnishings.

Historic Interest: Fort Sam Houston (across the street).

Innkeeper(s): Steve & Alma Cross. $49-125. AP. MC VISA AX DS TC. TAC10. 8 rooms, 2 with PB, 6 with FP. 1 suite. 4 conference rooms. Breakfast included in rates. Meals: continental-plus breakfast, gourmet breakfast, early coffee/tea. Gourmet lunch, banquet service, catering service, catered breakfast available. Beds: KQT. TV in room. VCR, fax, copier, swimming on premises. Weddings, small meetings, family reunions, seminars hosted. Amusement parks, antiques, parks, shopping, sporting events, theater nearby.

Publicity: *New York Times, Fiesta,*.

"Loved your home and your hospitality very much."

Chabot Reed House

403 Madison
San Antonio, TX 78204-1413
(210)223-8697 (800)776-2424 Fax:(210)734-2342
E-mail: sister@txdirect.net

Circa 1876. Built by a German cotton and wool merchant, this grand Victorian mansion, a Texas landmark, is listed in the National Register and located in San Antonio's King William Historic District. The Texas landmark is situated on an acre of grounds with gardens and fountains. There are antique-filled rooms in the main house as well as two suites in the adjacent Carriage House. Gourmet quiche, fresh fruit and baskets of breads and rolls

are served at breakfast, and afternoon tea is another treat. The manor is just a block from the River Walk and close to many other San Antonio sites.

Innkeeper(s): Sister & Peter Reed. $125-175. PC TC. TAC10. 5 rooms with PB, 2 with FP. 2 suites. 2 cottages. Breakfast and afternoon tea included in rates. Type of meal: full breakfast. Beds: KQ. Phone and air conditioning in room. Fax and library on premises. Spanish spoken. Amusement parks, antiques, parks, sporting events, golf and theater nearby.

The Columns on Alamo

1037 S Alamo St
San Antonio, TX 78210-1109
(210)271-3245 (800)233-3364 Fax:(210)271-3245

Circa 1892. This bed & breakfast is located in an impressive Greek Revival home in the King William Historic District. Victorian antiques and reproductions decorate the guest rooms, including pieces such as brass beds and fainting couches. An adjacent, turn-of-the-century guest house includes a four-poster bed, gas log fireplace and a two-person Jacuzzi. The trolley stops in front of the house, transporting guests to many of San Antonio's attractions. The River Walk and the Alamo are within walking distance.

Innkeeper(s): Ellenor & Arthur Link. $75-148. MC VISA AX DC CB DS. TAC10. 11 rooms with PB, 3 with FP. 1 conference room. Breakfast included in rates. Types of meals: full breakfast and early coffee/tea. Room service available. Beds: KQ. Phone, air conditioning, ceiling fan and TV in room. Fax, copier and library on premises. Weddings, small meetings and family reunions hosted. German spoken. Amusement parks, antiques, parks, shopping, sporting events and theater nearby.

"The house has been an inspiration. Very friendly and helpful host and hostess."

Falling Pines B&B Inn

300 W French Pl
San Antonio, TX 78212-5832
(210)733-1998 Fax:(210)736-2340

Circa 1911. Magnificent pine trees loom above this Spanish-style hacienda set on more than an acre of park-like grounds in the Monte Vista Historic District. Superior craftsmanship is evident in the inn's brick and limestone construction, green-tiled roof, shuttered windows, arched entry and veranda. The

first-floor common rooms feature quarter-cut oak paneling, wood floors and fireplaces. The unique 2,000square-foot third-floor suite offers two spacious balconies and a sweeping view of downtown San Antonio. Breakfast featuring eggs Benedict, fruit and muffins is served in the tiled solarium.

Innkeeper(s): Grace & Bob Daubert. $100-150. MC VISA AX DS PC TC. 5 rooms, 3 with PB. 2 suites. Breakfast included in rates. Meals: continental breakfast, continental-plus breakfast, full breakfast. Beds: KDT. Phone, air conditioning, ceiling fan, TV in room. VCR, bicycles on premises. Golf nearby.

Noble Inns-Pancoast Carriage House

102 Turner
San Antonio, TX 78204-1329
(210)225-4045 (800)221-4045 Fax:(210)227-0877
E-mail: nobleinns@aol.com

Circa 1896. This two-story, Victorian carriage house is located in San Antonio's King William Historic District. Each of the three guest suites is appointed in Victorian style with period antiques, a fireplace and a marble bath with clawfoot tub or two-person Jacuzzi. The current innkeepers are the fifth generation of the Pancoast family to live on the property and are happy to share the town and family history. The kitchens are stocked with pastries, fresh fruit, cereal and beverages, so guests can prepare breakfast at their leisure. There is a swimming pool and heated spa on the premises. Transportation in a classic Rolls Royce Silver Cloud II is available. Call for rates.

Innkeeper(s): Don & Liesl Noble. $105-155. MC VISA AX DS PC TC. TAC10. 3 suites, 3 with FP. Breakfast included in rates. Type of meal: continental-plus breakfast. Beds: Q. Phone, air conditioning, turndown service, ceiling fan, TV in room. Fax, spa, swimming on premises. Small meetings hosted. Spanish spoken. Antiques, parks, shopping, sporting events, theater nearby.

"First impressions mean a lot, and we were delighted the moment we entered this suite."

Noble Inns-The Jackson House

107 Madison
San Antonio, TX 78204
(210)225-4045 (800)221-4045 Fax:(210)227-0877
E-mail: nobleinns@aol.com

Circa 1894. This Victorian brick and limestone house is a sister bed & breakfast to the Pancoast Carriage House. The home, located in the King William Historic District, has been designated as a city historic structure. Fresh flowers and fluffy monogrammed guest robes greet guest when they enter their rooms. Rooms are decorated with Victorian antiques, fireplaces, marble baths and a clawfoot or whirlpool tub. The inn's unique gazebo, which encloses the spa, is surrounded by antique stained glass. Guests are pampered both with a full breakfast, as well as afternoon tea. Transportation in a classic 1960 Rolls Royce Silver Cloud II is available upon request. Call ahead for rates.

Innkeeper(s): Don & Liesl Noble. $95-155. MC VISA AX DS PC TC. TAC10. 6 rooms with P.B, 6 with F.P. Breakfast and afternoon tea included in rates. Type of meal: full breakfast. Beds: KQ. Phone, air conditioning, turndown service, ceiling fan and TV in room. Fax, spa, swimming and library on premises. Small meetings and family reunions hosted. Spanish spoken. Antiques, parks, shopping, sporting events and theater nearby.

"It couldn't have been better if we dreamed it! Thank you."

Riverwalk Inn

329 Old Guilbeau St
San Antonio, TX 78204-1126
(210)212-8300 (800)254-4440 Fax:(210)229-9442

Circa 1842. With its rustic, country decor, log exterior and ideal location on the River Walk, this historic inn is a gem. The two, adjacent buildings were constructed from five log homes brought to the town from Tennessee just a few years after the battle at the Alamo. Each guest room has a fireplace and many modern amenities, such as phones with voice mail and mini-refrigerators. The innkeepers, both native Texans, serve expanded continental breakfasts in the mornings, and desserts in the evenings.

Innkeeper(s): Johnny Halpenny & Tammy Hill. $110-155. MC VISA AX DS PC TC. TAC10. 11 suites, 9 with F.P. 1 conference room. Breakfast included in rates. Types of meals: full breakfast and early coffee/tea. Afternoon tea and evening snack available. Beds: KQT. Phone, air conditioning, ceiling fan, TV in room. VCR, fax and copier on premises. Weddings, small meetings, family reunions and seminars hosted. Spanish spoken. Amusement parks, antiques, fishing, parks, shopping, sporting events, theater, watersports nearby.

San Augustine   E9

The Wade House

202 E Livingston St
San Augustine, TX 75972
(409)275-5489

Circa 1940. The Wade House is a Mount Vernon-style red brick house located two blocks from the old courthouse square. Guest rooms are decorated in a mixture of contemporary and antique furnishings and are cooled by both ceiling fans and air conditioning. The nearby Mission Park, under construction, commemorating the 1717 Spanish Mission Nuestra Senora de los Dolores de los Ais, will open in 1998.

Innkeeper(s): Nelsyn & Julia Wade. $50-90. MC VISA PC TC. 6 rooms, 4 with PB. 1 suite. 1 conference room. Breakfast included in rates. Types of meals: continental breakfast, continental-plus breakfast and early coffee/tea. Beds: KQDT. Air conditioning, ceiling fan and TV in room. Weddings, small meetings, family reunions and seminars hosted. Fishing and shopping nearby.

Location: Two blocks from the Central Courthouse Square.

Publicity: *San Augustine Tribune, Dallas Morning News.*

"The house is one of the most beautiful in the area. Each room is decorated to the utmost excellence."

San Marcos   F7

Crystal River Inn

326 W Hopkins St
San Marcos, TX 78666-4404
(512)396-3739 (888)396-3739 Fax:(512)353-3248

Circa 1883. This Greek Revival inn with its tall white columns has a fireside dining room with piano and wet bar. Innkeepers encourage a varied itinerary, including sleeping until noon and having breakfast in bed to participating in a hilarious murder mystery. Guests can rock the afternoon away on the veranda or curl up by the fireplace in their bedroom. Guest rooms include clawfoot tubs, four-poster and canopied beds. Texas' largest outlet mall, not too far away, features more than 150 designer stores.

Innkeeper(s): Mike & Cathy Dillon. $70-125. MC VISA AX DC CB DS. 12 rooms. 4 suites. Breakfast included in rates. Type of meal: full breakfast. Picnic lunch and catering service available. Beds: KQDT. Phone, air conditioning, ceiling fan and TV in room. VCR, pet boarding and child care on premises. Weddings, small meetings, family reunions and seminars hosted. Amusement parks, antiques, shopping, sporting events, watersports nearby.

Publicity: *Texas Monthly Press, Vacations, Country Inns, Southern Living, Dallas Morning News.*

"Thanks for a smashing good time! We really can't remember having more fun anywhere, ever!"

Sandia   H7

Knolle Farm & Ranch Bed, Barn & Breakfast

Farm Rd 70
Sandia, TX 78383
(512)547-2546 Fax:(512)547-3934

Circa 1939. For more than 60 years, the largest herd of Jersey cattle in the world roamed the hills and pastures of the Nueces River Valley surrounding this country farm and ranch. With its barn that holds eight separate horse stalls and two tack rooms, guests with horses are especially welcome. There are two riding arenas and many acres of riding trails. The sports-minded guest will also enjoy fishing in the Nueces River or the inn's privately stocked tank, canoeing, hunting and skeet shooting. Picnic lunches, private barbeques and gourmet dining are available for an extra charge. The inn offers private instruction in English and Western riding, participation in a cattle round-up and in-season dove, duck or goose hunting.

Innkeeper(s): Dabney Welsh. $65-125. MC VISA PC. 4 rooms, 1 with PB. 1 suite. 1 cottage. Breakfast and evening snack included in rates. Types of meals: continental breakfast, continental-plus breakfast and early coffee/tea. Beds: KDT. Air conditioning, ceiling fan, TV and VCR in room. Fax, swimming, stables, library and pet boarding on premises. Handicap access. Small meetings, family reunions and seminars hosted. Spanish spoken. Antiques, fishing, parks, shopping, sporting events and watersports nearby.

Pets Allowed: May make arrangements for dogs, horses always accepted.

Publicity: *Corpus Christi Caller Times.*

Smithville   F7

The Katy House

201 Ramona St, PO Box 803
Smithville, TX 78957-0803
(512)237-4262 (800)843-5289 Fax:(512)237-2239
E-mail: thekatyh@onr.com

Circa 1909. The Italianate exterior is graced by an arched portico over the bay-windowed living room. The Georgian columns reflect the inn's turn-of-the-century origin. Long leaf pine floors, pocket doors and a graceful stairway accent the completely refurbished interior. The inn is decorated almost exclusively in American antique oak and railroad memorabilia. A leisurely 10-minute bicycle ride (innkeepers provide bikes) will take you to the banks

of the Colorado River. Also available are maps that outline walking or biking tours with lists of some of the historical and interesting information of the area.

Innkeeper(s): Bruce & Sallie Blalock. $56-85. MC VISA PC TC. 4 rooms with PB. 1 suite. 2 cottages. Breakfast included in rates. Types of meals: full breakfast and early coffee/tea. Beds: Q. Phone, air conditioning, ceiling fan and TV in room. VCR, fax, bicycles and pet boarding on premises. Family reunions hosted. Antiques, fishing, parks, shopping and watersports nearby.

Pets Allowed: With advance notice, in certain rooms.

Stephenville D7

Oxford House

563 N Graham St
Stephenville, TX 76401-3548
(817)965-6885 Fax:(817)965-7555

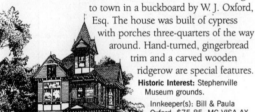

Circa 1898. A $3,000 lawyer's fee provided funds for construction of The Oxford House, and the silver was brought to town in a buckboard by W. J. Oxford, Esq. The house was built of cypress with porches three-quarters of the way around. Hand-turned, gingerbread trim and a carved wooden ridgerow are special features.

Historic Interest: Stephenville Museum grounds.

Innkeeper(s): Bill & Paula Oxford. $75-85. MC VISA AX PC. TAC10. 4 rooms with PB. Breakfast included in rates. Types of meals: full breakfast and early coffee/tea. Afternoon tea and catering service available. Beds: QD. Air conditioning in room. Weddings, small meetings, family reunions and seminars hosted. Amusement parks, antiques, parks and theater nearby.

Publicity: *Glamour, Dallas Morning News.*

"A perfect evening of serenity sitting on the front porch with such kind hosts."

Teague E8

Hubbard House Inn B&B

621 Cedar St
Teague, TX 75860-1617
(254)739-2629

Circa 1903. Having served as the Hubbard House Hotel for railroad employees during part of its history, this red brick and white frame Georgian home is furnished mostly with early American antiques. There's a second-floor balcony porch with swings, which offer guests a place to relax. A country breakfast is served in the large formal dining room on a glass-topped antique pool table.

Innkeeper(s): John W. Duke. $65. VISA AX PC TC. TAC10. 6 rooms. Breakfast included in rates. Meal: full breakfast. Beds: KD. Air conditioning, ceiling fan, TV in room. VCR on premises. Handicap access. Weddings, small meetings, family reunions hosted. Antiques, fishing, parks, shopping nearby.

Texarkana C9

Mansion on Main B&B

802 Main St
Texarkana, TX 75501-5104
(903)792-1835

Circa 1895. Spectacular two-story columns salvaged from the St. Louis World's Fair accent the exterior of this Neoclassical-style inn. Victorian nightgowns and sleepshirts are provided, and whether you are on a business trip or your honeymoon, expect to be pampered. Six bedchambers vary from the Butler's Garret to the Governor's Suite and are all furnished with antiques

and period appointments. Awake to the scent of dark roast cajun coffee, and then enjoy a full "gentleman's" breakfast in the parquet dining room. The inn is located in the downtown historic area. Enjoy a fireside cup of coffee or a lemonade on the veranda. The inn offers plenty of amenities for the business traveler, including fax machine, desks and modem connections.

Historic Interest: Old Washington, a town frequented by the likes of Davy Crockett, Jim Bowie and Sam Houston, is 35 miles away. The historic Perot Theater, which was restored by native son Ross Perot, offers many productions throughout the year. The town also offers a living museum, the Ace of Clubs House.

Innkeeper(s): Lee & Inez Hayden. $60-109. MC VISA AX PC TC. TAC10. 6 rooms with PB. 1 suite. Breakfast included in rates. Types of meals: full breakfast, gourmet breakfast and early coffee/tea. Afternoon tea available. Beds: QD. Phone, air conditioning, ceiling fan and TV in room. Handicap access. Weddings, small meetings, family reunions and seminars hosted. Cajun spoken. Antiques, fishing, shopping and theater nearby.

Tyler D9

Chilton Grand

433 S Chilton Ave
Tyler, TX 75702-8017
(903)595-3270 Fax:(903)595-3270

Circa 1910. Tall pecan, maple, oak and magnolia trees shelter this red brick, Greek Revival home on a brick street in the Azalea District. (Tyler is considered by some to be the prettiest town in Texas.) Two-story columns and a crystal chandelier hanging from the front balcony and porch set the elegant tone. Inside, there are antiques and romantic touches such as a Jacuzzi tub and feather beds. Ivy Cottage features a canopied queen feather bed and a two-person whirlpool tub in

the Gazebo Room. Breakfast is served with silver, crystal and china. Historic mansions, Brickstreet Playhouse, the midtown Arts Center, Tyler's famous rose garden, tea rooms and downtown antique shops are all within walking distance.

Innkeeper(s): Jerry & Carole Glazebrook. $75-150. MC VISA AX PC TC. TAC7. 4 rooms with PB, 1 with FP. 2 suites. 1 cottage. Breakfast included in rates. Types of meals: gourmet breakfast and early coffee/tea. Beds: QD. Phone, air conditioning, turndown service, ceiling fan, TV, VCR in room. Fax on premises. Antiques, fishing, parks, shopping, theater, watersports nearby.

"Wow, what a beautiful place you have. The food was simply the best."

Utah

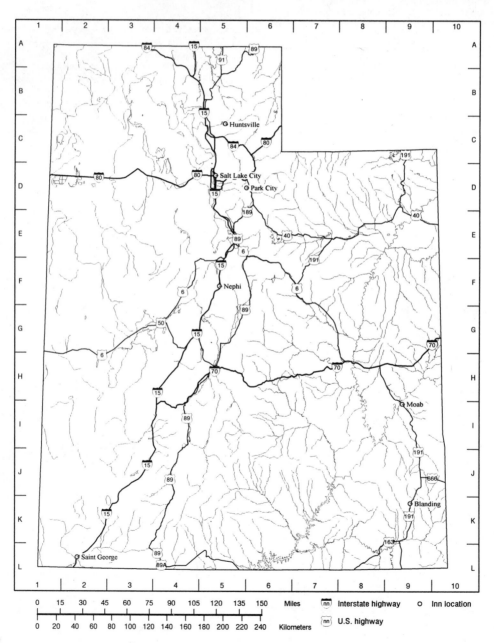

0 15 30 45 60 75 90 105 120 135 150   Miles

0 20 40 60 80 100 120 140 160 180 200 220 240   Kilometers

Interstate highway   ○ Inn location

U.S. highway

Blanding K9

The Grayson Country Inn B&B

118 E 300 S
Blanding, UT 84511-2908
(435)678-2388 (800)365-0868

Circa 1908. Over the years, The Grayson Country Inn has served a number of purposes, including a small hotel and boarding house for Indian girls who attended a local school. The inn is the perfect location to enjoy the many sites in the area, and is within walking distance from a pottery factory and gift shops. The area abounds with outdoor activities, as many national parks are nearby. Edge of the Cedars State Park is only a mile from the inn. A three-bedroom cottage is available for groups and/or families.

Historic Interest: Natural Bridges National Monument, Rainbow Bridge National Monument and viewing Anasazi ruins are among the day trips from the inn.

Innkeeper(s): Dennis & Lurlene Gutke. $42-67. MC VISA AX. TAC5. 11 rooms with PB. 1 cottage. Breakfast included in rates. Type of meal: full breakfast. Beds: Q. Air conditioning, ceiling fan and TV in room. Library on premises. Small meetings and family reunions hosted. Fishing, parks, shopping and watersports nearby.

Publicity: *Salt Lake Tribune.*

Huntsville C5

Jackson Fork Inn

7345 E 900 S
Huntsville, UT 84317-9778
(801)745-0051 (800)255-0672

Circa 1938. This former dairy barn was named after the hay fork that was used to transport hay into the barn. The romantic inn now includes eight guest rooms and a restaurant. Four rooms include two-person Jacuzzi tubs, and all are cozy and comfortable. A self-serve continental breakfast is prepared each day with muffins and fresh coffee. The inn is ideal for skiers and located near Powder Mountain, Nordic Valley and Snowbasin ski resorts.

Innkeeper(s): Vicki Petersen. $50-120. MC VISA AX DS PC TC. 8 rooms with PB. Breakfast included in rates. Lunch available. Beds: Q. Ceiling fan in room. Weddings and small meetings hosted. Fishing, parks, shopping, downhill skiing, cross-country skiing and watersports nearby.

Pets Allowed: With $20 fee - must be kept on leash.

Moab I9

Sunflower Hill B&B

185 N 300 E
Moab, UT 84532-2421
(435)259-2974 Fax:(435)259-3065
E-mail: innkeeper@sunflowerhill.com

Circa 1895. Guests at Sunflower Hill stay either in a restored adobe farmhouse or a garden cottage. The one-and-a-half-acre grounds, dotted with gardens and wooded pathways, create a secluded environment, yet the home is only three blocks from downtown Moab. Guest rooms are decorated in country style with antiques and stenciled walls. A hearty breakfast buffet is served on an antique sideboard. Guests choose from a multitude of items, such as breakfast burritos, pancakes, muffins, fresh fruit, honey-almond granola and more. There is an outdoor hot tub on the premises.

Innkeeper(s): The Stucki Family. $55-150. MC VISA DS PC TC. TAC10. 11 rooms with PB. 2 suites. 1 cottage. 1 conference room. Breakfast included in rates. Types of meals: full breakfast and early coffee/tea. Dinner, evening snack, picnic lunch and catering service available. Beds: QD. Air conditioning, ceiling fan and TV in room. VCR, fax, copier, spa and library on premises. Weddings and small meetings hosted. Fishing, parks, shopping, cross-country skiing, golf and watersports nearby.

Publicity: *Aspen Times, NBC Tonight Show with Jay Leno.*

"This place is awesome. We will be back."

Nephi F5

The Whitmore Mansion B&B

110 S Main St # 73
Nephi, UT 84648-1710
(801)623-2047

Circa 1898. This exquisitely crafted, 20-room Victorian features hand-carved stone, brick, staircases and fireplace mantels. Among the nine bedrooms are two bridal suites and a unique family suite with a turret tower. Each room has a private bath, including some with whirlpool tubs. Each morning begins with a hearty, full breakfast, and in the evenings, snacks and hot beverages are served. The inn is listed in the National Register.

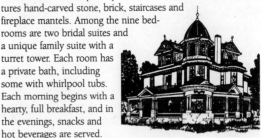

Innkeeper(s): Nell Breaux. $65-125. MC VISA PC TC. 9 rooms with PB. Type of meal: full breakfast. Evening snack and banquet service available. Beds: QT. TV on premises. Weddings, small meetings, family reunions and seminars hosted. Fishing and golf nearby.

Location: 90 miles south of Salt Lake City on I-15.

Park City D6

The Imperial Hotel, A B&B Inn

221 Main St, PO Box 1628
Park City, UT 84060
(801)649-1904 (800)669-8824 Fax:(801)645-7421

Circa 1904. The Imperial, a historic turn-of-the-century hotel, is decorated in a "Western" Victorian style. Several guest rooms include amenities like clawfoot or Roman tubs and sitting areas. A few overlook Park City's historic Main Street. The inn's largest suite includes a bedroom and a spiral staircase leading up to a cozy loft area. There are ski lockers and a Jacuzzi on-site. Transportation to area ski lifts are located nearby.

Innkeeper(s): Paulette Anderson. $65-230. MC VISA AX DS TC. 10 rooms, 9 with PB. 1 suite. Breakfast included in rates. Types of meals: full breakfast and early coffee/tea. Evening snack available. Beds: KQT. Phone and TV in room. Fax and spa on premises. Antiques, fishing, parks, shopping, downhill skiing, cross-country skiing, sporting events, theater and watersports nearby.

The Old Miners' Lodge - A B&B Inn

615 Woodside Ave, PO Box 2639
Park City, UT 84060-2639
(435)645-8068 (800)648-8068 Fax:(435)645-7420

Circa 1889. This originally was established as a miners' boarding house by E. P. Ferry, owner of the Woodside-Norfolk silver mines. A two-story

Victorian with Western flavor, the lodge is a significant structure in the Park City National Historic District. Just on the edge of the woods is a deck and a steaming hot tub.

Historic Interest: Mining artifacts from the silver mining industry.

Innkeeper(s): Susan Wynne & Liza Simpson. $60-255. MC VISA AX DC CB DS PC TC. TAC10. 12 rooms with PB. 3 suites. 2 conference rooms. Breakfast and evening snack included in rates. Types of meals: full breakfast and early coffee/tea. Banquet service and catering service available. Beds: KQDT. Turndown service and ceiling fan in room. Fax, copier, spa and library on premises. Small meetings, family reunions and seminars hosted. Antiques, fishing, parks, shopping, downhill skiing, cross-country skiing, theater nearby.

Location: In the Park City Historic District.

Publicity: *Boston Herald, Los Angeles Times, Detroit Free Press, Washington Post, Ski, Bon Appetit.*

"This is the creme de la creme. The most wonderful place I have stayed at bar none, including ski country in the U.S. and Europe."

Washington School Inn

544 Park Ave, PO Box 536
Park City, UT 84060
(801)649-3800 (800)824-1672 Fax:(801)649-3802

Circa 1889. Made of local limestone, this inn was the former schoolhouse for Park City children. With its classic belltower, the four-story building is listed in the National Register. The inn is noted for its luxuriously appointed guest rooms. Drinks and appetizers are served each afternoon in front of an inviting fire. The inn's Jacuzzi and sauna are perfect places to relax. The hosts also offer the amenities of a concierge service and ski storage, which is helpful since the inn is only one block from ski lifts.

Innkeeper(s): Nancy Beaufait. $100-300. MC VISA AX DC DS TC. TAC10. 12 rooms with PB, 2 with FP. 3 suites. 2 conference rooms. Breakfast, afternoon tea and evening snack included in rates. Type of meal: full breakfast. Beds: KQT. Phone and TV in room. VCR, fax, spa and sauna on premises. Weddings, small meetings and family reunions hosted. Antiques, fishing, parks, shopping, downhill skiing, cross-country skiing, sporting events, theater and watersports nearby.

Location: Park City Historic District.

Publicity: *San Diego Magazine, Arizona Daily Star, Salt Lake Tribune.*

"The end of the rainbow."

Saint George   L2

Greene Gate Village Historic B&B Inn

76 W Tabernacle St
Saint George, UT 84770-3420
(435)628-6999 (800)350-6999 Fax:(435)628-6989
E-mail: greeneg8@sisha.net

Circa 1872. This is a cluster of nine restored pioneer homes all located within one block. The Bentley House has comfortable Victorian decor, while the Supply Depot is decorated in a style reflective of its origin as a shop for wagoners on their way to

California. The Orson Pratt House and the Carriage House are other choices, all carefully restored.

The fifth house contains three bedrooms each with private bath, a kitchen, living room and two fireplaces. Most of the bedrooms have large whirlpool tubs.

Historic Interest: First Mormon Temple in the West (1 mile), first Cotton Mill in the West (1 mile), Mormon Tabernacle.

Innkeeper(s): Barbara Greene. $55-125. MC VISA AX DS. 19 rooms with PB, 9 with FP. 6 suites. 1 conference room. Breakfast included in rates. Types of meals: full breakfast and early coffee/tea. Dinner, picnic lunch, catering service and room service available. Restaurant on premises. Beds: KQT. Phone, air conditioning, TV and VCR in room. Handicap access. Family reunions and seminars hosted. Antiques, fishing, shopping, downhill skiing, sporting events, golf, theater and watersports nearby.

Publicity: *Deseret News, Spectrum, Better Homes & Garden, Sunset, Country.*

"You not only provided me with rest, comfort and wonderful food, but you fed my soul."

Salt Lake City   D5

The Anton Boxrud B&B

57 S 600 E
Salt Lake City, UT 84102-1006
(801)363-8035 (800)524-5511 Fax:(801)596-1316

Circa 1901. One of Salt Lake City's grand old homes, this Victorian home with eclectic style is on the register of the Salt Lake City Historical Society. The interior is furnished with antiques from around the country and Old World details. In the sitting and dining rooms, guests will find chairs with intricate carvings, a table with carved swans for support, embossed brass door knobs and stained and beveled glass. There is an outdoor hot tub available to guests. The inn is located just a half-block south of the Utah Governor's Mansion in the historic district. A full breakfast of homemade breads and rolls and evening snack are provided.

Innkeeper(s): Jane Johnson. $69-140. MC VISA AX DC CB DS. 7 rooms, 5 with PB. 1 suite. Breakfast included in rates. Types of meals: full breakfast and early coffee/tea. Evening snack available. Beds: KQT. TV on premises. 25 acres. Small meetings, family reunions and seminars hosted. Amusement parks, antiques, fishing, shopping, downhill skiing, cross-country skiing, sporting events, theater and watersports nearby.

Publicity: *Salt Lake Tribune.*

"Made us feel at home and well-fed. Can you adopt us?"

Armstrong Mansion Inn

667 E 100 S
Salt Lake City, UT 84102-1103
(801)531-1333 (800)708-1333 Fax:(801)531-0282

Circa 1893. A former Salt Lake City mayor built this Queen Anne-style home for his young bride. The mansion features the original carved-oak staircase, ornate woodwork and stained-glass windows. Guest rooms are decorated with Victorian furnishings and walls feature stenciling that the innkeepers

and several historic associations have presented the inn with architectural awards.

Historic Interest: This inn is in the National Register.

Innkeeper(s): Spencer F. Eccles Family. $85-185. MC VISA AX. 9 rooms with PB, 5 with FP. Type of meal: continental-plus breakfast. Beds: KQW.

Publicity: *Innsider.*

"This is a great inn! It's unbelievably elegant and you have a terrific staff."

Saltair B&B

164 S 900 E
Salt Lake City, UT 84102-4103
(801)533-8184 (800)733-8184 Fax:(801)595-0332

Circa 1903. The Saltair is the oldest continuously operating bed & breakfast in Utah and a offers a prime location to enjoy Salt Lake City. The simply decorated rooms include light, airy window dresses, charming furnishings and special touches.

One room includes a wood-burning stove and exposed brick. Breakfasts, especially the delicious breads, are memorable. The inn is within walking distance to four historic districts and only one  block from Temple Square and the Governor's Mansion. Day trips include treks to several national and state parks and the Wasatch Front ski areas.

Innkeeper(s): Nancy Saxton & Jan Bartlett. $75-129. MC VISA AX DC CB DS TC. TAC10. 5 rooms, 2 with PB. Breakfast and evening snack included in rates. Types of meals: continental breakfast, continental-plus breakfast, full breakfast, gourmet breakfast and early coffee/tea. Beds: QT. Air conditioning in room. TV, VCR, fax and spa on premises. Weddings, small meetings, family reunions and seminars hosted. Antiques, fishing, parks, shopping, downhill skiing, cross-country skiing, sporting events, theater and watersports nearby.

Location: Historic downtown district.

Publicity: *Mobil, Logan Sun.*

"Your swing and Saltair McMuffins were fabulous."

designed after looking at old photographs of the home. Each room is decorated to reflect a different month of the year. The home is within walking distance to downtown shopping, businesses and other attractions. The area offers many outdoor activities, such as hiking and skiing.

Historic Interest: The home is located in Salt Lake's historic district.

Innkeeper(s): Kurt & Andrea Horning. $89-209. MC VISA AX DS. 13 rooms with PB. Breakfast included in rates. Type of meal: full breakfast. Beds: KQD. Shopping, theater and watersports nearby.

Brigham Street Inn

1135 E South Temple
Salt Lake City, UT 84102-1605
(801)364-4461

Circa 1898. This turreted Victorian is one of many historic mansions that dot South Temple Street (formerly Brigham Street). The formal interior features original wainscoting. With skylights and fireplaces, each of the nine rooms was created by a different designer for a showcase benefit for the Utah Heritage Foundation. The American Institute of Architects

Vermont

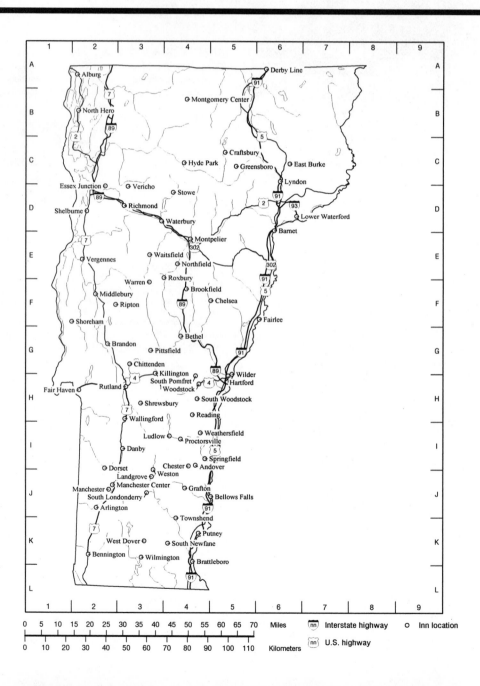

	1	2	3	4	5	6	7	8	9	

Derby Line
Alburg
Montgomery Center
North Hero
Craftsbury
Hyde Park
Greensboro
East Burke
Lyndon
Essex Junction
Vericho
Stowe
Lower Waterford
Shelburne
Richmond
Barnet
Waterbury
Montpelier
Vergennes
Waitsfield
Northfield
Warren
Roxbury
Brookfield
Middlebury
Ripton
Chelsea
Shoreham
Fairlee
Brandon
Bethel
Pittsfield
Chittenden
Killington
Wilder
South Pomfret
Hartford
Fair Haven
Rutland
Woodstock
South Woodstock
Shrewsbury
Wallingford
Reading
Ludlow
Weathersfield
Danby
Proctorsville
Springfield
Dorset
Chester
Andover
Landgrove
Weston
Manchester
Manchester Center
Grafton
South Londonderry
Bellows Falls
Arlington
Townshend
West Dover
Putney
South Newfane
Bennington
Wilmington
Brattleboro

0	5	10	15	20	25	30	35	40	45	50	55	60	65	70	Miles

0	10	20	30	40	50	60	70	80	90	100	110	Kilometers

Interstate highway   o Inn location

U.S. highway

Alburg A2

Thomas Mott Homestead B&B

Blue Rock Rd, Rt 2 Box 149-B
Alburg, VT 05440-9620
(802)796-3736 (800)348-0843 Fax:(802)796-3736

Circa 1838. Each room in this restored farmhouse provides a special view of Lake Champlain, yet guests often may be found enjoying the view from the sitting room as they warm by the fireplace. There are also full views of Mt. Mansfield and nearby Jay Peak. Montreal Island is one hour away. Guests are sure to enjoy the compli-

mentary Ben & Jerry's ice cream. Patrick is a noted wine consultant and holds Master's Degrees in criminology, sociology and the classical arts. A boat dock, extending 75 feet onto the lake, recently has been added to the property.

Historic Interest: Saint Anne's Shrine, Hyde Cabin, two presidential birthplaces.

Innkeeper(s): Patrick Schallert. $75-95. MC VISA AX DC CB DS PC TC. TAC10. 5 rooms with PB, 1 with FP. 2 suites. 3 conference rooms. Breakfast and evening snack included in rates. Types of meals: gourmet breakfast and early coffee/tea. Beds: KQ. Turndown service and ceiling fan in room. TV, fax, copier and library on premises. Weddings, small meetings, family reunions and seminars hosted. Amusement parks, antiques, fishing, parks, shopping, skiing, sporting events, theater and watersports nearby.

Location: Northwest corner of Vermont.

Publicity: *Los Angeles Times, St. Alban's Messenger, Yankee Traveler, Boston Globe, Elle, Outside, Prime Time, Vermont Life.*

"Hospitality reigns. I loved the beautiful pressed maple leaf—it is perfect and so personal."

Andover I4

The Inn at High View

R R 1 Box 201 A
Andover, VT 05143-9608
(802)875-2724 Fax:(802)875-4021

Circa 1789. Relaxation is stressed at this spacious farmhouse inn in the Green Mountains. A fireplace, rock garden, swimming pool and sauna add to guests' enjoyment. Cross-country ski trails are found on the grounds, hooking up with a series of

others to provide up to 15 kilometers of uninterrupted skiing. The inn offers advance-reservation dinner service for its guests on weekends and specializes in Italian fare.

Innkeeper(s): Gregory Bohan & Salvatore Massaro. $95-145. MC VISA. TAC10. 8 rooms with PB. 2 suites. 1 conference room. Breakfast included in rates. Types of meals: full breakfast and early coffee/tea. Dinner and lunch available. Beds: KQT. Turndown service in room. VCR on premises. 72 acres. Weddings, small meetings, family reunions and seminars hosted. Italian, Spanish and English spoken. Antiques, fishing, shopping, downhill skiing, cross-country skiing and theater nearby.

Pets Allowed: Special arrangements in suites only.

Arlington J2

Arlington Manor House B&B

Buck Hill Rd, RR 2-420
Arlington, VT 05250
(802)375-6784
E-mail: kiboodle@vtel.com

Circa 1908. A view of Mt. Equinox is enjoyed from the spacious terrace of this Dutch Colonial inn in the Battenkill River Valley. The inn also sports its own tennis court and is within easy walking distance of the Battenkill River, where canoeing, fishing and river tubing are popular

activities. A variety of accommodations is offered, and two of the inn's guest rooms have romantic fireplaces. A bikers' workshop and bench stand are on the premises.

Innkeeper(s): Al & Kit McAllister. $50-130. MC VISA AX PC TC. TAC10. 5 rooms, 4 with PB, 2 with FP. 1 suite. 2 conference rooms. Breakfast and afternoon tea included in rates. Types of meals: full breakfast and early coffee/tea. Beds: QDT. Phone and air conditioning in room. VCR, tennis, library on premises. Weddings, small meetings, family reunions and seminars hosted. Antiques, fishing, parks, shopping, skiing, theater, watersports nearby.

Hill Farm Inn

RR 2 Box 2015
Arlington, VT 05250-9311
(802)375-2269 (800)882-2545 Fax:(802)375-9918

Circa 1790. One of Vermont's original land grant farmsteads, Hill Farm Inn has welcomed guests since 1905 when the widow Mettie Hill opened her home to summer vacationers. The farm is surrounded by 50 peaceful acres that border the Battenkill River. Guests can relax and enjoy the simple life and 360-degree views of the mountains. Guest rooms are charming and cozy. Summer guests have the option of staying in one of four cabins. A large, country breakfast of homemade fare starts off each day.

Historic Interest: Bennington Monument and several other Revolutionary War sites are nearby.

Innkeeper(s): George & Joanne Hardy, Kelly Stork. $70-125. MC VISA AX DS. 15 rooms, 10 with PB. 2 suites. Breakfast and afternoon tea included in rates. Types of meals: full breakfast and early coffee/tea. Dinner available. Beds: KQTD. TV, fax and copier on premises. 50 acres. Weddings, small meetings and family reunions hosted. Antiques, fishing, parks, shopping, skiing nearby. Pets Allowed: In cabins and one suite only.

Location: One-half mile from Historic Route 7A.

Publicity: *Providence Journal, Boston Globe, Insider, Country.*

"I have already taken the liberty of changing the meaning of relaxation in the dictionary to Hill Farm Inn. Thank you . . . It was great."

West Mountain Inn

PO Box 481
Arlington, VT 05250-0481
(802)375-6516
E-mail: Info@WestMountainInn.com

Circa 1849. Goats and llamas graze the hillside of this sprawling New England farmhouse situated on 150 acres of meadows and woodland. The inn overlooks the Battenkill River. Each room boasts amenities such as a lace canopied bed, a balcony or a fireplace. The Rockwell Kent Suite graced with a cathedral

ceiling, features a fireplace and king-size bed. Back porches and decks are filled with Adirondack lawn chairs. The innkeepers include a former school principal and a Vermont state senator.

Innkeeper(s): Wes & MaryAnn Carlson. $145-209. MAP. MC VISA AX DS. 18 rooms with PB, 2 with FP. 6 suites. 1 conference room. Breakfast and dinner included in rates. Type of meal: full breakfast. Restaurant on premises. Beds: KQ. Phone in room. Handicap access. Weddings, small meetings, family reunions and seminars hosted. Antiques, fishing, downhill skiing, cross-country skiing, theater and watersports nearby. Pets Allowed.

Publicity: *Family Circle, Schenectady Gazette, N.Y. Post, Daily News, Vt. Life.*

"*Excellent, warm, friendly, relaxing, absolutely the best!*"

Barnet
D6

The Inn at Maplemont Farm

Rt 5, PO Box 11
Barnet, VT 05821
(802)633-4880 (800)230-1617
E-mail: maplemont.farm@connriver.net

Circa 1906. In a Georgian style this farmhouse is on 40 acres along the Connecticut River. Max the Bernese Mountain dog and Dudley the cat especially welcome families with children. The inn offers antique furnishings, a collection of music boxes and handmade quilts. Apple pie or crepes with berry topping are served with maple bacon. Children of all ages are invited to help with the farm chores. Arrange for a hay ride or explore the area's covered bridges and round barns. Drive across the river to the White Mountains or go downhill skiing at Burke Mountain.

Innkeeper(s): Sherry & Tom Tolle. $65-85. PC TC. 4 rooms with PB. Breakfast included in rates. Types of meals: full breakfast and early coffee/tea. Beds: QDT. TV, VCR and library on premises. 40 acres. Antiques, fishing, parks, shopping and downhill skiing nearby.
Pets Allowed: Cannot be left unattended.

"*We loved the friendliness, the delicious breakfast and the introduction to Vermont.*"

Bellows Falls
J5

River Mist B&B

7 Burt St
Bellows Falls, VT 05101-1401
(802)463-9023 (888)463-9023 Fax:(802)463-1571
E-mail: rmistbnb@vermontel.com

The scenic village of Bellows Falls is home to this turn-of-the-century Queen Anne Victorian inn, with its inviting wraparound porch and country Victorian interior. Guests may relax in any of three sitting rooms or in front of the fireplace. Enjoy a day of antiquing, skiing or just wandering around the picturesque environs. Be sure to take a ride on the Green Mountain Flyer before leaving town. .

Innkeeper(s): John & Linda Maresca. $60-110. 3 rooms. Breakfast included in rates. Type of meal: full breakfast. TV on premises. Amusement parks, antiques, shopping, downhill skiing, cross-country skiing and theater nearby.

Bennington
K2

Molly Stark Inn

1067 Main St
Bennington, VT 05201-2635
(802)442-9631 (800)356-3076 Fax:(802)442-5224
E-mail: mollyinn@vermontel.com

Circa 1890. This attractive Queen Anne Victorian inn has been serving travelers for more than 50 years. Careful restoration has enabled it to retain its Victorian charm, while offering the comforts today's guests have come to expect. Features include

antique furnishings, clawfoot tubs, hardwood floors, handmade quilts and a woodstove. The inn's convenient Main Street location puts it within walking distance of many restaurants and shops and just minutes from Historic Old Bennington. The Bennington Museum boasts paintings by Grandma Moses.

Innkeeper(s): Reed & Cammi Fendler. $65-145. MC VISA AX DS PC TC. TAC10. 7 rooms with PB, 1 with FP. 1 cottage. Breakfast and evening snack included in rates. Types of meals: full breakfast and gourmet breakfast. Beds: KDT. Phone, air conditioning, ceiling fan and TV in room. Bicycles on premises. Weddings, small meetings and family reunions hosted. Antiques, fishing, parks, shopping, downhill skiing, cross-country skiing, theater and watersports nearby.

Publicity: *Yankee Traveler, Colonial Homes, Albany Times Union, Saratogian.*

"*...like my grandma's house, only better.*"

Bethel
G4

Greenhurst Inn

River St, Rd 2, Box 60
Bethel, VT 05032-9404
(802)234-9474 (800)510-2553

Circa 1890. In the National Register of Historic Places, Greenhurst is a gracious Victorian mansion built for the Harringtons of Philadelphia. Overlooking the White River, the inn's opulent interiors include etched windows once featured on the cover of Vermont Life. There are eight masterpiece fireplaces and a north and south parlor.

Innkeeper(s): Lyle & Claire Wolf. $50-100. EP. MC VISA DS PC TC. 13 rooms, 7 with PB, 4 with FP. Breakfast included in rates. Types of meals: continental breakfast, continental-plus breakfast and early coffee/tea. Beds: QDT. Air conditioning in room. TV, VCR and library on premises. Weddings, small meetings, family reunions and seminars hosted. Spanish and French spoken. Antiques, fishing, parks, shopping, downhill skiing, cross-country skiing, theater and watersports nearby.

Pets Allowed: Dogs only.

Location: Midway between Boston and Montreal.

Publicity: *Los Angeles Times, Time, New York Times, Vermont Life.*

"*The inn is magnificent! The hospitality unforgettable.*"

Brandon G2

Churchill House Inn

R R 3 Box 3265
Brandon, VT 05733-9202
(802)247-3078 Fax:(802)247-6851
E-mail: Rciatt@sover.net

Circa 1871. Caleb Churchill and his son, Nathan, first built a three-story lumber mill, a grist mill and a distillery here, all water powered. Later, with their milled lumber, they construct-ed this 20-room house. Because of its location, it became a

stagecoach stop and has served generations of travelers with comfortable accommodations. The inn maintains cross-country ski and hiking trails in the adjacent Green Mountain National Forest. The innkeepers also organize what are known as "inn to inn" cross-country ski-ing, hiking or bicycling trips. Inn guests also receive a discount off greens fees at a nearby 18-hole course.

Historic Interest: Shelburn Museum, Billings Farm, Fort Ticonderoga (less than 1 hour away).

Innkeeper(s): The Jackson Family. $150-180. MAP. MC VISA. 8 rooms with PB. Breakfast and dinner included in rates. Type of meal: full breakfast. Picnic lunch available. Beds: QDT. Phone in room. Sauna and bicycles on premises. Family reunions hosted. Antiques, parks, shopping, downhill skiing, cross-country skiing and watersports nearby.

Location: Four miles east of Brandon.

Publicity: *Country, Yankee.*

"We felt the warm, welcoming, down-home appeal as we entered the front hall. The food was uncommonly good — home cooking with a gourmet flair!"

Brattleboro K4

Crosby House 1868

45 Western Ave
Brattleboro, VT 05301-3137
(802)257-4914 (800)528-1868
E-mail: tomlynn@sover.net

Circa 1868. Guests of this elegantly restored Italianate Victorian home set on more than an acre of lush grounds, remember it for its attention to service and a feeling of being pampered. The

Victorian theme is represented through-out the inn's fabric textures and soft col-ors. Each of the three guest rooms boasts family heirlooms and collected antiques, fireplaces and private baths as well as four-poster, canopy and paneled queen beds. Bathrobes, specialty toiletries and luxurious bed and bath linens are provided. A full breakfast is served in the oak-paneled dining room. The inn is a short walk from downtown.

Innkeeper(s): Tom & Lynn Kuralt. $95-130. MC VISA AX DS PC TC. 3 rooms with PB, 3 with FP. Breakfast included in rates. Types of meals: full break-fast, gourmet breakfast and early coffee/tea. Room service available. Beds: Q. Air conditioning, turndown service, ceiling fan, TV and VCR in room. Fax and copier on premises. Weddings and small meetings hosted. Antiques, fishing, shopping, skiing, golf, theater and watersports nearby.

Brookfield F4

Green Trails Inn

PO Box 494
Brookfield, VT 05036-0494
(802)276-3412 (800)243-3412
E-mail: greentrails@quest-net.com

Circa 1790. Two historic buildings, one constructed in 1790 and the other in 1830, comprise this inn. The innkeepers have an impressive clock collection, and clock sales, restoration and repair are located on the premises. Many guest rooms offer

views of the lake. One suite has a fireplace and others feature private Jacuzzis. The inn is across the street from Sunset Lake and the Floating Bridge. Cross-country skiing, snowshoeing, hiking, biking and swimming are right outside the door, and there are a number of outdoor activities nearby.

Innkeeper(s): Sue & Mark Erwin. $79-130. MC VISA DS PC TC. TAC10. 14 rooms, 8 with PB, 1 with FP. 2 suites. 3 conference rooms. Breakfast includ-ed in rates. Types of meals: full breakfast and early coffee/tea. Beds: QDT. VCR, fax, copier, swimming, bicycles and library on premises. 17 acres. Weddings, small meetings, family reunions and seminars hosted. Antiques, fishing, parks, shopping, downhill skiing, cross-country skiing, golf, theater and watersports nearby. Pets Allowed: Boarding nearby.

Publicity: *Sunday Republican.*

"The inn is really lovely, the welcome very warm and food is scrumptious."

Chelsea F5

Shire Inn

8 Main St, PO Box 37
Chelsea, VT 05038
(802)685-3031 (800)441-6908 Fax:(802)685-3871
E-mail: shireinn@sover.net

Circa 1832. Granite lintels over the windows and a sunburst light over the entry highlight this Adams-style brick home. The romantic inn, which is located in a 210-year-old historic village, has a grand spiral staircase ascending from wide-plank pump-kin pine floors in the entryway. Guest rooms include antique canopied beds, tall windows and 10-foot ceilings. Most have wood-burning fireplaces.

Included on the proper-ty's 23 acres are granite post fencing, perennial gardens dating from the 19th century, and a broad, rocky stream spanned by a farm bridge.

Historic Interest: The home is located in the National Register, and the historic town of Chelsea offers many interesting sites.

Innkeeper(s): Jay & Karen Keller. $86-210. MAP. MC VISA DS PC TC. TAC10. 6 rooms with PB, 4 with FP. Breakfast and dinner included in rates. Types of meals: full breakfast and early coffee/tea. Afternoon tea available. Beds: KQD. Fax, copier, bicycles and library on premises. 23 acres. Weddings, small meetings and family reunions hosted. Antiques, fishing, parks, shopping, skiing, theater and watersports nearby.

Publicity: *Country Inn Review, Vermont Life.*

"What an inn should be! Absolutely delicious food - great hospitality! The rooms are filled with romance."

Chester 14

Chester House

266 Main St
Chester, VT 05143
(802)875-2205 (888)875-2205

Circa 1780. This beautifully restored Federal-style clapboard home is listed in the National Register of Historic Places. It is situated on the village green in the quaint and historic village of Chester. The inn is tastefully furnished throughout with early American furniture and appointments. Some of the individually decorated rooms feature whirlpool baths or steam bath/showers.

Innkeeper(s): Paul Anderson. $95-149. MC VISA PC TC. TAC10. 7 rooms with PB. 1 conference room. Type of meal: full breakfast. Dinner available. Beds: KQTD. Phone in room. Spa on premises.

"The best hosts and the greatest of inns."

Chester Inn at Long Last

PO Box 589
Chester, VT 05143-0589
(802)875-2444 (888)243-7466 Fax:(802)875-6414
E-mail: chesinn@sover.net

Circa 1892. This inn was rebuilt in 1923 after being destroyed by fire. Located on the town green, this renovated inn reflects the personality of the owners Bill and Mary Ann Kearns. Guests are invited to share their home which features fine cuisine and comfortable, friendly surroundings provided by Bill, Mary Ann, their children and the staff. You may want to sit and rock on the front porch or play tennis on the inn's courts or cuddle up with a book in the library.

Historic Interest: The Village Historical Society is across the way. Chester's Stone Village, a grouping of stone homes from the 1850s is a half mile away. The Coolidge Birthplace is 30 minutes away and Billings Farm Museum is a 45-minute journey.

Innkeeper(s): Mary Ann & Bill Kearns. $110-160. MAP, EP. MC VISA DS PC TC. 26 rooms with PB. 4 suites. 1 conference room. Breakfast and dinner included in rates. Types of meals: full breakfast and early coffee/tea. Banquet service available. Restaurant on premises. Beds: QD. TV, VCR and copier on premises. Weddings, small meetings, family reunions and seminars hosted. Antiques, fishing, parks, shopping, skiing and theater nearby.

Publicity: *New York Times, Philadelphia Inquirer, Gourmet.*

"An inn of character where character has real meaning."

Henry Farm Inn

PO Box 646
Chester, VT 05143-0646
(802)875-2674 (800)723-8213 Fax:(802)875-2674

Circa 1760. Fifty acres of scenic woodlands provide the setting for this handsomely restored stagecoach stop in the Green Mountains. There are original wide pine floors and carefully selected early American furnishings. A pond and river are nearby.

Historic Interest: Chester Stone Village.

Innkeeper(s): Barbara Bowman. $55-85. MC VISA AX PC TC. TAC10. 7 rooms with PB. Types of meals: full breakfast and early coffee/tea. Afternoon tea available. Beds: KQT. VCR, fax and copier on premises. 50 acres. Weddings, small meetings and family reunions hosted.

Location: Ten miles from I-91.

"Very comfortable and pleasant."

Hugging Bear Inn & Shoppe

244 Main St
Chester, VT 05143
(802)875-2412 (800)325-0519 Fax:(802)875-3823
E-mail: innhuggingbear@.com

Circa 1850. Among the 6,000 teddy bear inhabitants of this white Victorian inn, several peek out from the third-story windows of the octagonal tower. There is a teddy bear shop on the premises and children and adults can borrow a bear to take to bed with them. Rooms are decorated with antiques and comfortable furniture. A bear puppet show is often staged during breakfast.

Innkeeper(s): Georgette Thomas. $60-115. MC VISA AX DS PC TC. 6 rooms with PB. Breakfast included in rates. Types of meals: full breakfast and early coffee/tea. Catered breakfast available. Beds: QDT. TV, VCR and library on premises. Small meetings and family reunions hosted. Antiques, fishing, parks, shopping, downhill skiing, cross-country skiing and golf nearby. Pets Allowed: Limited - prior conference.

Publicity: *Rutland Herald, Exxon Travel, Teddy Bear Review, Teddy Bear Scene.*

"Thanks seems to be too small of a word to describe our greatest appreciation toward all of you for all of your warmth and hospitality."

Chittenden G3

Tulip Tree Inn

Chittenden Dam Rd
Chittenden, VT 05737
(802)483-6213 (800)707-0017
E-mail: ttinn@sover.net

Circa 1830. Thomas Edison was a regular guest here when the house was the country home of William Barstow. The inn is surrounded by the Green Mountains on three sides with a stream flowing a few yards away. The guest rooms feature antiques and Vermont country decor. Most rooms offer Jacuzzis and some boast fireplaces. Guests enjoy both breakfast and dinner at the inn. Buttermilk pancakes

topped with Vermont maple syrup are typical breakfast fare, and dinners include such items as medallions of pork topped with an orange-apricot sauce and white chocolate cheesecake.

Innkeeper(s): Ed & Rosemary McDowell. $120-269. MAP. MC VISA PC TC. TAC10. 8 rooms with PB. Breakfast and dinner included in rates. Types of meals: full breakfast and early coffee/tea. Restaurant on premises. Beds: Q. Library on premises. Weddings and small meetings hosted. Amusement parks, antiques, fishing, parks, shopping, downhill skiing, cross-country skiing, theater and watersports nearby.

Publicity: *New England Getaways.*

"Tulip Tree Inn is one of the warmest, friendliest and coziest country inns you'll find in New England—New England Getaways."

Craftsbury   C5

Craftsbury Inn

Main St, Box 36
Craftsbury, VT 05826-0036
(802)586-2848 (800)336-2848

Circa 1850. Bird's-eye maple woodwork and embossed tin ceilings testify to the history of this Greek Revival inn, which

also features random-
width floors with square
nails. The foundation
and porch steps were
made of bull's-eye gran-
ite, quarried in town.
The living room fireplace
once graced the first post
office in Montpelier.
Guest rooms sport coun-
try antiques and hand-
made quilts. The dining
room is open to the pub-
lic by advance reserva-
tion and features four
dinner seatings.

Innkeeper(s): Blake & Rebecca Gleason. $60-160. MAP, AP. MC VISA TC. 10 rooms, 6 with PB. 1 conference room. Breakfast included in rates. Type of meal: full breakfast. Dinner, picnic lunch, banquet service, catering service and catered breakfast available. Restaurant on premises. Beds: QDT. VCR on premises. Weddings, small meetings, family reunions and seminars hosted. Antiques, fishing, shopping, skiing and watersports nearby.

"Very comfortable - the dining was a special treat!"

Danby   I3

Silas Griffith Inn

South Main St
Danby, VT 05739
(802)293-5567 (800)545-1509

Circa 1891. Originally on 55,000 acres, this stately Queen Anne Victorian mansion features solid cherry, oak and bird's-eye maple
woodwork. Considered an
architectural marvel, an eight-
foot, round, solid-cherry
pocket door separates the
original music room
from the front parlor.

Historic Interest: Hildene, Coolidge Homestead (30 minutes).

Innkeeper(s): Paul & Lois Dansereau. $72-107. MC VISA PC TC. 17 rooms, 14 with PB. Breakfast and afternoon tea included in rates. Types of meals: full breakfast, gourmet breakfast and early coffee/tea. Picnic lunch available. Restaurant on premises. Beds: QT. TV, VCR, swimming and library on premises. 11 acres. Weddings, small meetings, family reunions and seminars hosted. Antiques, fishing, parks, shopping, downhill skiing, cross-country skiing, theater and watersports nearby.

Publicity: *Vermont Weathervane, Rutland Business Journal, Vermont, Country.*

"Never have I stayed at a B&B where the innkeepers were so friendly, sociable and helpful. They truly enjoyed their job."

Derby Line   A6

The Birchwood Bed & Breakfast

PO Box 550
Derby Line, VT 05830-0550
(802)873-9104 Fax:(802)873-9121
E-mail: birchwd@together.net

Circa 1920. Guests in search of a romantic atmosphere will have no trouble finding it at this cozy bed & breakfast. Fresh flowers, chocolates and luxury bath soaps are among the items waiting in

bedchambers, which are
decorated with antiques.
The innkeeper also serves
her gourmet breakfasts by
candlelight. Derby Line,
located near the Canadian
border in northern
Vermont, offers beautiful
scenery and close access to fishing, water sports, golf and many more outdoor activities. Sleigh rides are a popular winter activity.

Innkeeper(s): Dick & Betty Fletcher. $70. PC TC. 3 rooms with PB. Breakfast included in rates. Type of meal: gourmet breakfast. Afternoon tea available. Beds: QDT. TV, fax and library on premises. Small meetings, family reunions and seminars hosted. Antiques, fishing, parks, shopping, downhill skiing, cross-country skiing, theater and watersports nearby.

"Heaven can wait. When I die I am going to Vermont and stay much longer at The Birchwood."

Dorset   I2

Barrows House

Rt 30, Box 98
Dorset, VT 05251
(802)867-4455

Circa 1804. The Barrows House is situated on 11 acres of lawns, flowering gardens and back woods in the heart of the village. The oldest section of the inn once served as the residence of the first Minister of Dorset's. A cluster of cottages and other guest quarters date from the 1800s to 1950. The foyer, salon, tavern and parlor feature hand-stenciled borders and comfortable, overstuffed furniture. The old stable on the property now serves as a bike and ski rental shop, depending on the season. Fresh raspberry pancakes are a favorite breakfast of the inn's highly regarded restaurant.

Innkeeper(s): Linda & Jim McGinnis. $150-250. MAP. MC VISA AX DS. 28 rooms with PB, 7 with FP. 1 conference room. Type of meal: full breakfast. Restaurant on premises. Phone and air conditioning in room. Fax, copier and sauna on premises. Handicap access.

Publicity: *The Washingtonian, Sunday Times Union, Snow Country, Mirabella.*

"A classic meal, a perfect setting."

East Burke   C6

Mountain View Creamery

PO Box 355
East Burke, VT 05832
(802)626-9924 (800)572-4509 Fax:(802)626-9924
E-mail: innmtnvu@plainfield.bypass.com

Circa 1890. This inn derives its name from its original use as a creamery. The interior is anything but industrial, though. Rooms are elegantly appointed in a New England country style with antiques, overstuffed chairs and sofas and wood floors. The inn's farm setting is appealing, the creamery is surrounded by more than 400 acres on a stock farm that features a variety of historic barns. There are hiking, biking and cross-country ski trails on the premises. Guests are treated to a full breakfast and afternoon tea, but they also are encouraged to enjoy dinner at the inn's restaurant, where items such as a fresh tomato basil soup and chicken Marbella with a wild rice pilaf are the fare. There are plenty of activities for families here, and children will enjoy the farm animals, as well as sleigh and hay rides.

Innkeeper(s): Laurelie Welch. $85-160. MC VISA PC TC. 12 rooms with PB. 1 suite. 1 cottage. 3 conference rooms. Breakfast and afternoon tea included in rates. Type of meal: full breakfast. Dinner, picnic lunch and catering service available. Restaurant on premises. Beds: QTD. TV, VCR, fax, copier, stables and library on premises. 440 acres. Weddings, small meetings, family reunions and seminars hosted. Some Russian spoken. Antiques, fishing, parks, shopping, skiing, golf, theater and watersports nearby.

Publicity: *Yankee.*

Essex Junction   D2

The Inn at Essex

70 Essex Way
Essex Junction, VT 05452-3383
(802)878-1100 Fax:(802)878-0063
E-mail: innessex@together.net

Elegant furnishings and decor, each in a different style, grace the guest rooms at this luxurious Colonial inn, which carries a four-diamond rating. Several guest suites include whirlpool tubs, and 30 of the rooms include woodburning fireplaces. The two restaurants are run by the New England Culinary Institute, one a gourmet restaurant and the other a more casual tavern. The inn also includes a swimming pool, library, art gallery and a bakery.

Historic Interest: New England Culinary Institute operates the two restaurants.
Innkeeper(s): Jim Lamberti. $129-199. MC VISA AX DC CB DS. 97 rooms. Breakfast included in rates. Type of meal: continental breakfast.

Fair Haven   H2

Maplewood Inn

Rt 22A S
Fair Haven, VT 05743
(802)265-8039 (800)253-7729 Fax:(802)265-8210
E-mail: maplewd@sover.net

Circa 1843. This beautifully restored Greek Revival house, which is in the National Register, was once the family home of the founder of Maplewood Dairy, Isaac Wood. Period antiques and reproductions grace the inn's spacious rooms and suites.

Some rooms boast fireplaces and all have sitting areas. A collection of antique spinning wheels and yarn winders is displayed. A porch wing, built around 1795, was a tavern formerly located down the road. Overlooking three acres of lawn, the inn offers an idyllic setting. The parlor's cordial bar and evening turndown service are among the many amenities offered by the innkeepers.

Historic Interest: Local historic attractions include the Vermont Maple Museum and Norman Rockwell Museum. Hubbardton Battlefield and Wilson Castle are within 20 minutes of the inn. Farther attractions include Fort Ticonderoga, which is 45 minutes away and the Shelburne Museum, an hour from the inn.
Innkeeper(s): Cindy & Doug Baird. $80-130. MC VISA AX DC PC TC. TAC10. 5 rooms with PB, 4 with FP. 2 suites. 1 conference room. Breakfast, afternoon tea and evening snack included in rates. Beds: QD. Phone, air conditioning, turndown service and TV in room. VCR, fax, copier and library on premises. Small meetings and family reunions hosted. Amusement parks, antiques, fishing, parks, shopping, downhill skiing, cross-country skiing, sporting events, theater and watersports nearby.
Location: One mile south of Fair Haven village and 18 miles west of Rutland.
Publicity: *Country, Innsider, Americana, New England Getaways.*

"Your inn is perfection. Leaving under protest."

Fairlee   F6

Silver Maple Lodge & Cottages

S Main St. RR 1, Box 8
Fairlee, VT 05045
(802)333-4326 (800)666-1946

Circa 1790. This old Cape farmhouse was expanded in the 1850s and became an inn when Elmer & Della Batchelder opened their home to guests. It became so successful that several cottages, built from lumber on the property, were added. For 60 years, the Batchelder family continued the operation. They misnamed the lodge, however, mistaking silver poplar trees on the property for what they thought were silver maples. Guest rooms are decorated with many of the inn's original furnishings, and the new innkeepers have carefully restored the rooms and added several bathrooms. A screened-in porch surrounds two sides of the house. Three of the cottages include working fireplaces and one is handicap accessible.

Historic Interest: The Quechee Gorge, Maple Grove Maple Museum, Billings Farm & Museum and the Saint Gauden's National Historic Site are among the area's historic sites.
Innkeeper(s): Scott & Sharon Wright. $52-79. MC VISA AX DS PC TC. TAC10. 16 rooms, 14 with PB, 3 with FP. 8 cottages. Breakfast included in rates. Type of meal: continental breakfast. Beds: KQDT. VCR, copier and bicycles on premises. Handicap access. Small meetings and family reunions hosted. Antiques, fishing, parks, shopping, downhill skiing, cross-country skiing, theater and watersports nearby. Pets Allowed: Cottage rooms only.
Location: East central Vermont.
Publicity: *Boston Globe, Vermont Country Sampler, Travel Holiday, Travel America, New York Times.*

"Your gracious hospitality and attractive home all add up to a pleasant experience."

Grafton   J4

Old Tavern at Grafton

Main St
Grafton, VT 05146
(802)843-2231 (800)843-1801 Fax:(802)843-2245
E-mail: Tavern@sover.net

Circa 1801. This elegantly appointed hotel inn serves as a wonderful place to enjoy New England's charm and rustic atmosphere. Beautifully appointed rooms feature antiques, traditional furnishings, four-poster beds, lace, Oriental rugs and gracious knickknacks. The Old Tavern also offers six guest houses, which can sleep up to 14 people and most include full kitchens. Inspired New England fare is prepared and served in the elegant dining room. Stable facilities are available and the area boasts plenty of outdoor activities. Bicycles are available and the guests also can enjoy shuffleboard, billiards, pingpong, tennis and swimming. A 30-kilometer, cross-country skiing center also is on the premises. The inn often is the site for weddings, receptions, retreats and meetings.

Historic Interest: Historic Grafton boasts many restored 18th- and 19th-century dwellings.

Innkeeper(s): Kevin O'Donnell. $145-285. EP. MC VISA PC TC. TAC10. 66 rooms with PB, 6 with FP. 7 cottages. 5 conference rooms. Breakfast and afternoon tea included in rates. Types of meals: full breakfast and early coffee/tea. Dinner, picnic lunch, lunch, banquet service and catering service available. Restaurant on premises. Beds: QDT. Ceiling fan in room. TV, fax, copier, swimming, stables, bicycles, tennis and library on premises. Handicap access. Weddings, small meetings, family reunions and seminars hosted. Dutch, German, French and Spanish spoken. Antiques, fishing, parks, shopping, downhill skiing, cross-country skiing, theater and watersports nearby.

Publicity: *Spotlight, Boston Globe, Travel America, Chicago Tribune, Boston Herald, Harper's Hideaway Report, Travel & Leisure, Colonial Homes.*

Greensboro   C5

Highland Lodge

RR 1 Box 1290
Greensboro, VT 05841-9712
(802)533-2647 Fax:(802)533-7494

Circa 1865. With a private beach and 120 acres to enjoy, guests rarely have trouble finding a way to pass the time at this lodge. The lodge is located in a mid-19th-century farmhouse, and visitors either room here in country guest rooms or in a collection of cottages. The cottages have from one to three bedrooms, a living room, bathroom and a porch. All guests are welcome to use the lodge's common areas or simply relax on the porch, but there's sailing, swimming, fishing, boating and much more on the premises. In the winter, there are plenty of cross-country ski trails. The breakfast choices might include French toast, waffles, pancakes, eggs or muffins, and at dinner, guests choose from four entrees accompanied by salad, homemade bread and dessert.

Historic Interest: Greensboro Historical Society.

Innkeeper(s): Wilhemina & David Smith. $179-230. MAP. MC VISA DS PC TC. TAC10. 22 rooms, 11 with PB, 11 with FP. 11 cottages. Breakfast and dinner included in rates. Types of meals: full breakfast and early coffee/tea. Afternoon tea, picnic lunch and lunch available. Restaurant on premises. Beds: QDT. Fax, copier, swimming, bicycles, tennis, library and child care on premises. Handicap access. Weddings, small meetings, family reunions and seminars hosted. Dutch spoken. Antiques, fishing, downhill skiing, cross-country skiing, golf and theater nearby.

Publicity: *New England Skiers Guide, Vermont Magazine, Hardwick Gazette, Rural New England Magazine, Better Homes & Gardens, Providence Sunday Journal.*

"We had a great time last weekend and enjoyed everything we did— hiking, climbing, swimming, canoeing and eating."

Hartford   H5

House of Seven Gables

221 Main St, Box 526
Hartford, VT 05047
(802)295-1200

Circa 1891. This historic inn is said to have been one of the first homes in Hartford to have electricity. It also served as the Bible Institute of New England and later as a restaurant bearing the name the inn retains today. Its unique architecture, a blend of Georgian, Gothic Revival and Stick Victorian, only adds to its charm. Victorian touches are found throughout the guest rooms, each featuring its own unique decor, and including brass, highback and poster beds. Luscious homemade breakfasts sometimes feature apple-filled pancakes or maple-cured sausage. Dartmouth College is four miles to the east.

Innkeeper(s): Lani & Kathy Janisse. $65-105. 1 conference room. Type of meal: early coffee/tea. Banquet service available. Turndown service, ceiling fan and VCR in room. TV and pet boarding on premises. Weddings, small meetings and seminars hosted. Antiques, shopping, downhill skiing, cross-country skiing, sporting events and theater nearby.

Hyde Park   C4

Fitch Hill Inn

258 Fitch Hill Rd
Hyde Park, VT 05655-9801
(802)888-3834 (800)639-2903 Fax:(802)888-7789

Circa 1797. This Federalist-style home sits on five acres of hilltop land overlooking the village and Green Mountains. There are three porches with spectacular views. The five, second-floor guest rooms share a period-furnished living room, game room and movie library. There also is an efficiency apartment available with a whirlpool tub, fireplace, deck and kitchen. Gourmet breakfasts are served in the dining room. Gourmet, candlelight dinners can be arranged by advance reservation.

Historic Interest: Chester A. Arthur birthplace/home (20 miles), Shelburne Museum (40 miles).

Innkeeper(s): Richard A. Pugliese & Stanley E. Corklin. $75-160. MC VISA AX PC TC. TAC10. 6 rooms with PB, 2 with FP. 1 suite. 1 cottage. 1 conference room. Breakfast and afternoon tea included in rates. Types of meals: full breakfast, gourmet breakfast and early coffee/tea. Dinner and picnic lunch available. Beds: QDT. Phone, air conditioning, ceiling fan, TV and VCR in room. Spa, bicycles and library on premises. Weddings, small meetings, family reunions and seminars hosted. English, Spanish and some French spoken. Amusement parks, antiques, fishing, parks, downhill skiing, cross-country skiing, theater and watersports nearby.

Location: Ten miles north of Stowe.

Publicity: *Stowe Reporter, Morrisville News Dispatch, Out & About, Eco-Traveller, Country Living.*

"We were very impressed with your inn, from the atmosphere to the wonderful hospitality (not to mention those killer breakfasts!). For our first visit to a B&B, it was a terrific experience. I'm sure you'll be seeing us again."

Killington
G3

The Vermont Inn

Rt 4
Killington, VT 05751
(802)775-0708 (800)541-7795 Fax:(802)773-2440
E-mail: vtinn@aol.com

Circa 1840. Surrounded by mountain views, this rambling red and white farmhouse has provided lodging and superb cuisine for many years. Exposed

beams add to the atmosphere in the living and game rooms. The award-winning dining room provides candlelight tables beside a huge fieldstone fireplace.

Historic Interest: Calvin Coolidge birthplace and Bennington, V.T., Civil War exhibits.

Innkeeper(s): Megan & Greg Smith. $50-185. MAP, EP. MC VISA AX DC PC TC. 18 rooms with PB, 2 with FP. Breakfast and afternoon tea included in rates. Types of meals: full breakfast and early coffee/tea. Banquet service available. Beds: QDT. Air conditioning and ceiling fan in room. TV, VCR, fax, copier, spa, swimming, sauna, tennis and library on premises. Handicap access. Weddings, small meetings, family reunions and seminars hosted. Antiques, fishing, parks, shopping, downhill skiing, cross-country skiing, theater and watersports nearby.

Publicity: *New York Daily News, New Jersey Star Leader, Rutland Business Journal, Bridgeport Post Telegram, New York Times, Boston, Vermont.*

"We had a wonderful time. The inn is breathtaking. Hope to be back."

Landgrove
J3

Landgrove Inn

Rd Box 215, Landgrove Rd
Landgrove, VT 05148
(802)824-6673 (800)669-8466 Fax:(802)824-3055
E-mail: Vtinn@sover.net

Circa 1820. This rambling inn is located along a country lane in the valley of Landgrove in the Green Mountain National Forest. The Rafter Room is a lounge and pub with a fireside sofa for 12.

Breakfast and dinner are served in the newly renovated and stenciled dining room. Evening sleigh or hay rides are often arranged. Rooms vary in style and bedding arrangements, including some newly decorated rooms with country decor, so inquire when making your reservation.

Historic Interest: Hildene, Robert Todd Lincoln's Georgian Revival mansion is nearby, as is the Norman Rockwell Museum.

Innkeeper(s): Kathy & Jay Snyder. $85-125. MC VISA AX DS TC. 18 rooms, 16 with PB. 1 conference room. Breakfast included in rates. Type of meal: full breakfast. Afternoon tea and dinner available. Restaurant on premises. Beds: QD. Phone in room. TV, VCR, fax, copier and spa on premises. 25 acres. Weddings, small meetings, family reunions and seminars hosted. Antiques, fishing, parks, shopping, skiing and theater nearby.

"A true country inn with great food — we'll be back."

Lower Waterford
D6

Rabbit Hill Inn

Pucker St
Lower Waterford, VT 05848
(802)748-5168 (800)762-8669 Fax:(802)748-8342

Circa 1795. Above the Connecticut River overlooking the White Mountains, Samuel Hodby opened this tavern and provided a general store and inn to travelers. As many as 100 horse teams a day traveled by the inn. The ballroom, constructed in 1855, was supported by bent-wood

construction giving the dance floor a spring effect. The classic Greek Revival exterior features solid pine Doric columns. Romance abounds in every nook and cranny. Rooms are decorated to the hilt with beautiful furnishings and linens. The Loft room, which overlooks the garden, includes cathedral ceilings and a hidden staircase. The Top-of-the-Tavern room boasts a Victorian dressing room with vintage clothing. Turndown service and afternoon tea are only a few of the amenities. Glorious breakfasts and gourmet, five-course, candle-lit dinners add to a memorable stay.

Historic Interest: There are several historic churches in the area. The Fairbanks Museum, Planetarium and Art Gallery is 10 minutes away, while the Robert Frost Museum is a 25-minute drive.

Innkeeper(s): Brian & Leslie Mulcahy. $189-289. MC VISA AX. 20 rooms with PB, 12 with FP. 5 suites. Breakfast and dinner included in rates. Type of meal: full breakfast. Picnic lunch available. Restaurant on premises. Beds: KQT. Phone in room. Fax and copier on premises. Antiques, fishing, downhill skiing, cross-country skiing and watersports nearby.

Location: Historic District.

Publicity: *New York Times, Los Angeles Herald Examiner, Today Show, Innsider, USA Today, Boston, Yankee, Bridal Guide, For the Bride, Country Living, Ski Magazine. Ratings: 4 Stars.*

"It is not often that one experiences one's vision of a tranquil, beautiful step back in time. This is such an experience. Everyone was so accommodating and gracious."

Ludlow
I4

Black River Inn

100 Main St
Ludlow, VT 05149-1050
(802)228-5585 (800)844-3813
E-mail: brinn2@ludl.tds.net

Circa 1835. This inn is located on the banks of the Black River, across from the gazebo at the village green. One guest room features an original copper-lined bathtub, and Abraham Lincoln is said to have slept in the 1794 walnut four-poster featured in another room. There is a two-bedroom suite available for families. A full country breakfast is served.

Innkeeper(s): Nancy & Darwin Thomas. $65-135. MAP. MC VISA AX DS PC. 10 rooms, 8 with PB. Breakfast included in rates. Type of meal: full breakfast. Beds: KQD. Antiques, fishing, shopping, downhill skiing and cross-country skiing nearby.

Location: 1/4 mile from Okemo Mountain Ski Resort.

Echo Lake Inn

PO Box 154
Ludlow, VT 05149-0154
(802)228-8602 (800)356-6844 Fax:(802)228-3075
E-mail: echolkinn@aol.com

Circa 1840. Just minutes from Killington and Okemo ski areas, this New England country-style inn offers gourmet candlelight dining, a full country breakfast, library and parlor. Guests also

may borrow canoes and are allowed to pick wild-flowers and berries in season. Guests will find golf, horseback riding, waterfalls and wineries within easy walking distance. The inn is located in Tyson, five miles north of Ludlow.

Historic Interest: Plymouth Notch Historic District, birthplace of Calvin Coolidge.
Innkeeper(s): Laurence & Beth and Christopher & Diane Jeffrey. $99-219. MAP. MC VISA AX. TAC10. 23 rooms, 18 with PB. 2 suites. Breakfast and dinner included in rates. Types of meals: full breakfast and early coffee/tea. Room service available. Restaurant on premises. Beds: QDT. Ceiling fan in room. TV, fax, spa, swimming, sauna, tennis and library on premises. 10 acres. Weddings, small meetings, family reunions and seminars hosted. Antiques, fishing, shopping, skiing, theater and watersports nearby.
Publicity: *Bon Appetit, Gourmet.*

"Very special! We've decided to make the Echo Lake Inn a yearly tradition for our family."

Lyndon   C6

Branch Brook B&B

PO Box 143
Lyndon, VT 05849-0143
(802)626-8316 (800)572-7712
E-mail: bbbbwwwkingcon.com

Circa 1850. This Federal-style home is filled with charm. Exposed beams and homey rooms filled with antiques create a pleasant atmosphere. Meals are prepared at a unique English cookstove, which guests may try out. The honey and maple syrup on the breakfast table are prepared by the innkeepers and accompany items such as pancakes, French toast, bacon and eggs. Ski areas, lakes and rivers are close by, and there are antique shops, flea markets and auctions nearby.
Innkeeper(s): Ted & Ann Tolman. $60-80. MC VISA. 5 rooms, 3 with PB. Breakfast included in rates. Types of meals: full breakfast and early coffee/tea. Beds: KQ. Phone in room. TV, VCR, copier and library on premises. Weddings, small meetings and family reunions hosted. Antiques, fishing, parks, shopping, downhill skiing, cross-country skiing, watersports nearby.

Manchester   J2

The Inn at Manchester

PO Box 41, HR 7 A
Manchester, VT 05254-0041
(802)362-1793 (800)273-1793 Fax:(802)362-3218
E-mail: iman@vermontel.com

Circa 1880. This restored Victorian and its carriage house are in the National Register. In a setting of beautiful gardens and meadows of wildflowers with a meandering brook, the inn offers an extensive art collection of old prints and paintings. Guest rooms have fine linens, bay windows and antiques. The inn was restored by the innkeepers. The guest pool is set in a secluded meadow.

Historic Interest: Robert Todd Lincoln's Estate and the Southern Vermont Art Center are within 2 miles of the inn. Bennington Museum is 25 miles away.
Innkeeper(s): Stan & Harriet Rosenberg. $121-173. MC VISA AX DS PC TC. TAC10. 18 rooms with PB, 3 with FP. 4 suites. 1 conference room. Breakfast and afternoon tea included in rates. Type of meal: gourmet breakfast. Beds: KQDT. Air conditioning in room. TV, fax, copier, swimming and library on premises. Weddings and small meetings hosted. Antiques, fishing, shopping, downhill skiing, cross-country skiing and theater nearby.
Publicity: *N.Y. Times, Boston Globe, Travel & Leisure, Gourmet, Newsday.*

The Reluctant Panther Inn & Restaurant

1-3 West Rd
Manchester, VT 05254-0678
(802)362-2568 (800)822-2331 Fax:(802)362-2586
E-mail: panther@fover.net

Circa 1850. Elm trees line a street of manicured lawns and white clapboard estates. Suddenly, a muted purple clapboard house appears, the Reluctant Panther. The well-appointed guest rooms recently have been renovated and many include fireplaces, whirlpool tubs, cable TV and air conditioning. Guests will find a collection of gracious antique furnishings in their rooms. The inn offers two suites with double Jacuzzi tubs and fireplaces. The Greenhouse is a beautiful setting in which to enjoy a romantic dinner, on tables set with fine china and crystal. Breakfasts are served in the inn's private dining room, a bright room warmed by a crackling fire.

Innkeeper(s): Robert & Maye Bachofen. $198-375. MAP. MC VISA AX PC. TAC10. 17 rooms with PB, 12 with FP. 5 suites. 1 conference room. Breakfast and dinner included in rates. Type of meal: gourmet breakfast. Banquet service available. Restaurant on premises. Beds: KQT. Phone, air conditioning, turndown service and TV in room. Fax and copier on premises. Small meetings, family reunions, seminars hosted. German, Spanish, French spoken. Antiques, fishing, shopping, skiing, theater, watersports nearby.
Publicity: *Vermont Summer, Sunday Republican, Country Inns, Gourmet, Country Accents, AAA Magazine, Discerning Traveler, Yankee, USA Today, Restaurant Business, New York Times.*

"We enjoyed our stay so much that now we want to make it our yearly romantic getaway."

Wilburton Inn

PO Box 468
Manchester, VT 05254-0468
(802)362-2500 (800)648-4944 Fax:(802)362-1107

Circa 1902. Shaded by tall maples, this three-story brick mansion sits high on a hill overlooking the Battenkill Valley, which is set against a majestic mountain backdrop. In addition to the mansion, the inn offers four villas and a seven-bedroom reunion house. Carved

moldings, mahogany paneling, Oriental carpets and leaded-glass windows are complemented by carefully chosen antiques. The inn's 20 acres provide three tennis courts, a pool, green lawns and sculpture gardens. Country weddings are a Wilburton Inn's specialty. Gourmet dining is served in the billiard room with European ambiance. Two local country clubs provide the inn with golf privileges.

Innkeeper(s): Georgette Levis. $105-235. MAP, AP. MC VISA AX. 35 rooms, 6 with FP. 1 conference room. Breakfast included in rates. Type of meal: gourmet breakfast. Afternoon tea, dinner and room service available. Restaurant on premises. Beds: KQ. Fax and copier on premises. Antiques, fishing, skiing, golf, theater and watersports nearby.
Publicity: *Great Escapes TV, Travelhost, Getaways For Gourmets, Country Inns, Bed & Breakfast, Gourmet, Best Places to Stay In New England.*

"Simply splendid! Peaceful, beautiful, elegant. Ambiance & ambiance!"

Manchester Center J2

Manchester Highlands Inn

Highland Ave, Box 1754A
Manchester Center, VT 05255
(802)362-4565 (800)743-4565 Fax:(802)362-4028
E-mail: innkeeper@highlandsinn.com

Circa 1898. This Queen Anne Victorian mansion sits proudly on the crest of a hill overlooking the village. From the three-story turret, guests can look out over Mt. Equinox, the Green Mountains and the valley below.
Feather beds and down comforters adorn the beds in the guest rooms. A game room with billiards and a stone fireplace are popular in winter, while summertime guests enjoy the outdoor pool, croquet lawn and veranda. Gourmet country breakfasts and home-baked afternoon snacks are served.

Historic Interest: Hildene, summer home of Robert Todd Lincoln (1 mile), Bennington Monument (20 miles).

Innkeeper(s): Patricia & Robert Eichorn. $105-145. MC VISA AX PC TC. TAC10. 15 rooms with PB. Breakfast and gourmet breakfast. Beds: QDT. TV, VCR, fax, swimming and library on premises. Weddings, small meetings, family reunions and seminars hosted. Limited French and German spoken. Antiques, fishing, parks, shopping, downhill skiing, cross-country skiing, theater nearby.
Publicity: *Toronto Sun, Vermont, Asbury Park Press, Vermont Weathervane, Yankee Traveler, Boston Globe.*

"We couldn't believe such a place existed. Now we can't wait to come again."

The Inn at Ormsby Hill

RR 2 Box 3264
Manchester Center, VT 05255-9518
(802)362-1163 (800)670-2841 Fax:(802)362-5176

Circa 1764. During the Revolutionary War, hero Ethan Allen hid out in the smoke room at this Federal-style mansion. Robert Todd Lincoln and President Taft are among the other notable guests at this historic treasure. The town's first jail cell still exists in the inn's basement, complete with steel bars and the marble slab where prisoners slept. The inn offers beautiful views of the nearby Green Mountains. Inside, guests will marvel at the inn's conservatory, which was built to resemble a ship and looks out to the gardens and the mountains. Antique-filled rooms offer four-poster or canopy beds decked in fine linens. Most rooms include fireplaces and two-person whirlpool tubs. Innkeeper Chris Sprague's culinary talents have been heralded in such publications as Food & Wine and Yankee. In addition to writing a cookbook, Chris teaches cook-

ing classes at the inn. Vermont is bustling with activities, dozens of which are just a short drive from the inn.

Historic Interest: The adjoining estate to the inn, which itself is listed in the Vermont Register of Historic Places, was home to Robert Todd Lincoln, the son of Abraham Lincoln.

Innkeeper(s): Ted & Chris Sprague. $115-290. MC VISA AX. TAC10. 10 rooms with PB, 9 with FP. Breakfast and afternoon tea included in rates. Beds: KQ. Air conditioning in room. TV, fax and library on premises. Antiques, fishing, downhill skiing, cross-country skiing and theater nearby.
Publicity: *Gourmet, Getaways for Gourmets, Country Inns, Discerning Traveler, Colonial Homes, Yankee Traveler, Boston Globe.*

"After 17 years of visiting B&Bs in Vermont, we can truly say you are the best. On a scale of 1-10, you are a 12."

River Meadow Farm

PO Box 822
Manchester Center, VT 05255-0822
(802)362-1602

Circa 1797. The oldest portion of this New England farmhouse was built in the late 18th century, and in keeping with that era, Colonial-style furnishings decorate the interior. During one part of its history, the home served as Manchester Poor Farm. The living room with its grand piano and fireplace is an ideal place for those seeking relaxation. At breakfast, fresh fruit, coffee, teas and juice accompany traditional entrees such as eggs and bacon or pancakes topped with blueberries. There are 90 acres to explore at this farm, some of which border the Battenkill River.

Historic Interest: Hildene, summer home of Robert Todd Lincoln, can be seen from a hill on the farm. The 1906 home is open for tours from May to October.

Innkeeper(s): Patricia J. Dupree. $60. MAP. PC TC. 5 rooms. Breakfast included in rates. Type of meal: full breakfast. Beds: DT. VCR and library on premises. 90 acres. Antiques, fishing, parks, shopping, downhill skiing, cross-country skiing, theater and watersports nearby.

"We really loved our stay and are planning to return as soon as possible."

Middlebury F2

Linens & Lace

29 Seminary St
Middlebury, VT 05753
(802)388-0832 (800)808-3897

Circa 1820. Located within easy walking distance of the historic village and Middlebury College, this quaint Victorian inn provides guests with a comfortable respite whether they're in town for the music festival, skiing, shopping or attending one of the many college functions. There are five guest rooms, all decorated in heirlooms and antiques. Linen and lace, thus the name, fresh flowers and sterling silver add to the

inn's ambiance. Afternoon tea is served on the porch overlooking the gardens, weather permitting, while a full breakfast of wild blueberry muffins, pancakes, bacon, orange juice and fresh fruit is offered in the dining room.

Innkeeper(s): Mary Botter & Peter Newburg. $89-119. PC TC. 5 rooms, 3 with PB. Breakfast and afternoon tea included in rates. Types of meals: full breakfast and early coffee/tea. Beds: QTD. Air conditioning and ceiling fan in room. TV and VCR on premises. Family reunions hosted. German spoken. Antiques, fishing, parks, shopping, skiing and golf nearby.

Middlebury Inn

14 Courthouse Sq
Middlebury, VT 05753
(802)388-4961 (800)842-4666 Fax:(802)388-4563
E-mail: midinnvt@sover.net

Circa 1827. This red brick, white-shuttered inn that has hosted
weary travelers for many generations, is celebrating its 170th-year
anniversary this year. Guests can choose from several options
when selecting a room. The grounds include three different
properties aside from the Middlebury Inn, which is an amazing
structure to behold.

The Porter Mansion
boasts a porch with
wicker furnishings,
marble fireplaces and
a curving staircase. At
the Middlebury Inn,
guests enjoy delec-
table afternoon teas on the veranda while viewing the Village
Green. The innkeepers include plenty of special touches such as
stocking rooms with books, bath soaps and lotions.
Complimentary continental breakfast and afternoon tea is served
daily. The inn offers ski and bicycle storage and will help guests
make arrangements for walking tours, a popular activity.

Historic Interest: The Middlebury Inn is a community landmark, listed in the
National Register, and in the center of Middlebury's historic district, which
offers 155 architectural gems within walking distance. Vermont State Craft
Center, museums and a waterfall are nearby.
Innkeeper(s): Frank & Jane Emanuel. $88-260. MAP. MC VISA AX DS PC TC.
TAC10. 80 rooms with PB. 3 conference rooms. Breakfast and afternoon tea
included in rates. Types of meals: continental breakfast, full breakfast and
early coffee/tea. Dinner, picnic lunch, lunch and banquet service available.
Restaurant on premises. Beds: QDT. Phone, air conditioning and TV in room.
VCR, fax, copier and library on premises. Handicap access. Small meetings,
family reunions and seminars hosted. Antiques, fishing, parks, shopping,
downhill skiing, cross-country skiing, sporting events and watersports nearby.
Pets Allowed: Limited, fee charged.

Publicity: *Chicago Tribune, Glamour, Burlington Free Press, New York Times.*

*"The one outstanding attribute which makes your facility so out-
standing is the super-plus attitude of everyone of your staff, been
years since I've encountered anything like it..."*

Swift House Inn

25 Stewart Ln
Middlebury, VT 05753-1248
(802)388-9925

Circa 1815. A former governor of Vermont, John Stewart,
bought the elegant Swift House after Jonathan Swift's death in
1875. The governor's daughter, who married Swift's grandson,
was born and lived in the mansion for 110 years, until 1981.
Elaborately carved walnut and marble fireplaces and window
seats grace the sitting rooms of the inn. The spacious lawns and
formal gardens can be enjoyed from terraces and guest rooms.

Historic Interest: Middlebury College (walking distance), Morgan Horse Farm
(1 mile), Sheldon Museum (walking distance), Shelburne Museum (15 miles).
Innkeeper(s): John & Andrea Nelson. $85-185. MC VISA AX DC CB DS. 21
rooms with PB, 9 with FP. 1 conference room. Breakfast included in rates.
Types of meals: continental breakfast and full breakfast. Dinner and room service available. Restaurant on premises. Beds: KQDT. Fax, copier, spa and
sauna on premises. Handicap access. Antiques, fishing, downhill skiing,
cross-country skiing, theater and watersports nearby.
Location: Corner of Rt. 7 and Stewart Lane.
Publicity: *Valley Voice, Uncommon Lodgings, Boston, New York Times,
Burlington Free Press, Rutland Business Journal, Wine Spectator.*

*"Fabulous wine list, great food, comfortable and relaxing atmosphere,
friendly staff."*

Montgomery Center   **B4**

Phineas Swan B&B

PO Box 43
Montgomery Center, VT 05471-0043
(802)326-4306

Circa 1889. The Trout River runs behind this three-story
Victorian. There are French doors, wood floors and a brightly
decorated living room with overstuffed couches. Antique beds
are offered in the
guest rooms.

Afternoon tea is
served at 4 p.m.,
complete with fresh-
ly baked scones,
fudge brownies or
pies. In the morning, breakfast features specialties such as
pumpkin-apple strussel muffins or raspberry French toast. Walk
to an old-fashioned swimming hole nearby.

Innkeeper(s): Michael Bindler & Glen Barthlomeo. $60-79. MC VISA DS TC.
4 rooms, 2 with PB. Breakfast and afternoon tea included in rates. Types of
meals: full breakfast and gourmet breakfast. Beds: QDT. Turndown service
and ceiling fan in room. TV, VCR, tennis and library on premises. Small meetings, family reunions and seminars hosted. Antiques, fishing, parks, shopping, downhill skiing, cross-country skiing, golf, theater, watersports nearby.
Publicity: *Country Living, Boston Phinox, Boston Chronicle and Out Magazine.*

The Inn on Trout River

The Main St, PO Box 76
Montgomery Center, VT 05471
(802)326-4391 (800)338-7049

Circa 1895. This homey inn provides every amenity a weary
skier could hope for. Before hitting the slopes, enjoy the inn's
huge breakfast. The Frost Heave Pub provides a place to relax
after a hard day's exer-
cise. Fall asleep on a
queen-size bed covered
with flannel sheets and
topped with feather pil-
lows and a down com-
forter. Antique shops are
nearby, and after the
snow melts, guests can

enjoy a game of tennis or a round of golf.
Historic Interest: Covered bridges in Montgomery and within an
hour circumference.
Innkeeper(s): Michael & Lee Forman. $69-115. MAP. MC VISA AX DS. 10
rooms with PB, 1 with FP. 1 suite. Breakfast included in rates. Type of meal:
full breakfast. Dinner available. Restaurant on premises. Beds: KQT. Antiques,
fishing, downhill skiing, cross-country skiing and watersports nearby.
Location: At base of Mountain Road to Jay Peak Ski Resort.
Publicity: *Caledonia-Record, Vermont Magazine.*

Montpelier   E4

Betsy's B&B

74 E State St
Montpelier, VT 05602-3112
(802)229-0466 Fax:(802)229-5412
E-mail: betsybb@plainfield.bypass.com

Circa 1895. Within walking distance of downtown and located in
the state's largest historic preservation district, this Queen Anne
Victorian with romantic turret and carriage house features lavish

Victorian antiques
throughout its interior.
Bay windows, carved
woodwork, high ceil-
ings, lace curtains and
wood floors add to the
authenticity. Guests
can enjoy an exercise
room. The full breakfast varies in content but not quality, and
guest favorites include sourdough banana pancakes.

Innkeeper(s): Jon & Betsy Anderson. $55-85. MC VISA AX DS PC TC.
TAC10. 12 rooms with PB. Breakfast included in rates. Type of meal: full
breakfast. Beds: QDT. Phone and TV in room. VCR and fax on premises.
Small meetings and family reunions hosted. Some Spanish spoken. Antiques,
fishing, parks, shopping, skiing, theater and watersports nearby.

North Hero   B2

North Hero House

Rt 2 Box 155, Champlain Islands
North Hero, VT 05474
(802)372-4732

Circa 1891. Open year-round, this loving restored three-story
inn stands on a slight rise overlooking Lake Champlain and
Vermont's highest peak, Mt. Mansfield. Three other houses also
provide accommodations for the inn's guests. Some rooms feature waterfront porches.

Innkeeper(s): Derek Roberts. $85-225. MAP. MC VISA. 26 rooms with PB.
Breakfast included in rates. Type of meal: continental breakfast. Restaurant
on premises. Beds: T. Phone in room. Sauna on premises. Handicap access.
Publicity: *Gourmet.*

*"We have visited many inns and this house was by far the best, due
mostly to the staff!"*

Northfield   E4

Northfield Inn

27 Highland Ave
Northfield, VT 05663-1448
(802)485-8558

Circa 1901. A view of the Green Mountains can be seen from
this Victorian inn, which is set on a hillside surrounded by gardens. The picturesque inn also affords a view of the village of
Northfield and historic Norwich University. Rooms are decorated

with antiques and Oriental
rugs, and bedrooms feature
European feather bedding
and brass and carved-wood
beds. Many outdoor activities are available on the

three-acre property, including croquet, horseshoes and sledding.
Visitors may want to take a climb uphill to visit the Old Slate
Quarry or just relax on one of the porches overlooking the gar-
den with bird songs, wind chimes and gentle breezes.

Historic Interest: Norwich University, the oldest private military college in the
country, is a half mile away. The state capitol is 10 miles away.

Innkeeper(s): Aglaia Stalb. $75-85. MC VISA PC TC. 8 rooms with PB. 2
suites. Breakfast and evening snack included in rates. Type of meal: full
breakfast. Beds: QDT. Phone, turndown service, ceiling fan and TV in room.
VCR, bicycles and library on premises. Weddings, small meetings, family
reunions and seminars hosted. Greek spoken. Antiques, fishing, parks, shopping, skiing, sporting events, theater and watersports nearby.
Location: Overlooking the village.
Publicity: *Conde Nast Traveler.*

"Elegant as always. My second home."

Pittsfield   G3

The Pittsfield Inn

PO Box 685
Pittsfield, VT 05762
(802)746-8943
E-mail: escapert@vermontel.com

Circa 1835. This inn was built as a stagecoach stop and has
been serving guests as an inn ever since. Antiques and a country Colonial decor permeate the guest rooms, each has been
individually appointed. There is a restaurant on the premises,
serving gourmet fare such as grilled tuna steak with poppy seed
goat cheese on a bed of cilantro pesto. The innkeepers offer
special rates for children. Guests will find plenty to do in the
area. Enjoy a horse-drawn carriage ride tour of local historic
sites, drive 15 minutes to skiing at Killington, play a game of
golf or take a guided mountain bike or hiking tour.

Innkeeper(s): Tom Yennerell. $55-75. MAP, AP. MC VISA PC TC. TAC10. 9
rooms with PB. 1 suite. Breakfast, afternoon tea and dinner included in
rates. Types of meals: full breakfast and gourmet breakfast. Restaurant on
premises. Beds: QDT. Air conditioning in room. TV, VCR, bicycles, library and
pet boarding on premises. Weddings, small meetings, family reunions and
seminars hosted. Antiques, fishing, parks, shopping, skiing, golf and watersports nearby. Pets Allowed: One dog at the inn at any one time.

Proctorsville   I4

The Castle

Rt 103 & 131, PO Box 207
Proctorsville, VT 05153
(802)226-7222 (800)697-7222

Circa 1904. This rich, magnificent estate was built by timber
baron Allen Fletcher, who later would serve as Vermont's governor. Guests will marvel at the manor, which truly is fit for royalty.
The innkeepers are painstakingly restoring every aspect of the
inn, from the stunning woodwork to the vast grounds. Six of the
immense guest rooms have a fireplace, and two have a whirlpool
tub. Fine antiques and Oriental rugs add to the regal, inviting
interior. Dinner is a must at the inn, and it is served in a spectacular, wood-paneled dining room. The inn's chef, a New England
Culinary Institute graduate, prepares the gourmet fare, an artfully
presented seasonal menu. Guests might start off with pesto
grilled shrimp with polenta and continue with entrees such as
sauteed filet of salmon with black bean cakes and lemon grass
beurre blanc or perhaps grilled beef tenderloin with wild mushroom risotto. MAP rates are also available for $215-265.

Innkeeper(s): Dick & Erica Hart. $150-210. MC VISA AX PC. 10 rooms with
PB, 6 with FP. 3 conference rooms. Restaurant on premises. Beds: KQ.
Phone in room.

"The Castle is one of Vermont's best kept secrets."

Depot Corner Inn

Depot St, PO Box 78
Proctorsville, VT 05153
(802)226-7970 (800)487-8576

Circa 1849. This inn once was known as the Cottage Hotel, and it served as one of two Depot Street hotels during Proctorsville's booming days as a wool mill town. Innkeepers Deborah and

John Davis have recreated the inn's Victorian ambiance with rooms decorated in period antiques and collectibles. John is an accomplished chef and creates the inn's delicious fare. The innkeepers host several special events, including cooking class weekends and ski packages. The inn is located just across the street from the Black River and near a variety of outdoor activities.

Historic Interest: The area offers several historic sites, including the Black River Academy, where Calvin Coolidge graduated in 1892. Calvin Coolidge's birthplace also is nearby.

Innkeeper(s): Deborah & John Davis. $65-450. MC VISA. 8 rooms, 5 with PB. 2 suites. Breakfast included in rates. Type of meal: full breakfast. Dinner and picnic lunch available. Restaurant on premises. Beds: KQDT. Phone in room. Antiques, fishing, skiing, theater and watersports nearby.

Publicity: *Newtown Bee, Black River Newspaper.*

"This is just exactly what a Vermont B&B should be! Wonderful! All the stars we can give, five stars!"

The Golden Stage Inn

Depot St, PO Box 218
Proctorsville, VT 05153
(802)226-7744 (800)253-8226 Fax:(802)226-7882

Circa 1780. The Golden Stage Inn was a stagecoach stop built shortly before Vermont's founding. It became a link in the

Underground Railroad and the home of Cornelia Otis Skinner. Extensive gardens surround the wraparound porch as well as the swimming pool. The innkeepers offer a TTY number at (802) 226-7136 for those who are deaf.

Innkeeper(s): Micki & Paul Smith-Darnauer. $149-170. MAP. MC VISA DS PC TC. TAC10. 8 rooms with PB. 2 suites. Breakfast, dinner and evening snack included in rates. Types of meals: full breakfast and early coffee/tea. Beds: KQDT. TV, VCR, fax, copier, swimming and library on premises. Weddings, small meetings and family reunions hosted. Antiques, fishing, shopping, downhill skiing, cross-country skiing, theater, watersports nearby.

Location: Near Ludlow.

Publicity: *Journal Inquirer, Gourmet, Los Angeles Times.*

"The essence of a country inn!"

Putney   K4

The Putney Inn

PO Box 181
Putney, VT 05346-0181
(802)387-5517 (800)653-5517 Fax:(802)387-5211

Circa 1790. The property surrounding this New England farmhouse was deeded to an English Army Captain by King George in 1790. The grounds' first home burned in a fire, and this inn

was constructed on the original foundation. Eventually it became a Catholic seminary, and then an elegant country inn. Rooms are located in a 1960s building, adjacent to the main historic farmhouse. The rooms are

decorated in a Colonial style with antiques. The inn's dining room, headed by renown chef Ann Cooper, features New England cuisine. The ingredients are fresh and locally produced, and

might include appetizers such as smoked salmon on Johnnycakes with an apple cider vinaigrette. Entrees such as a mixed grill of local venison and game hen flavored by an apple-horseradish marinade follow. Craft and antique shops, hiking, skiing and biking are among the local activities.

Innkeeper(s): Randi Ziter. $78-158. MC VISA AX DS PC TC. TAC10. 25 rooms with PB. 4 conference rooms. Breakfast included in rates. Types of meals: continental breakfast, continental-plus breakfast, full breakfast, gourmet breakfast and early coffee/tea. Afternoon tea, dinner, evening snack, picnic lunch, lunch, gourmet lunch, banquet service and catering service available. Restaurant on premises. Beds: Q. Phone, air conditioning and TV in room. VCR, fax and copier on premises. Handicap access. 11 acres. Weddings, small meetings, family reunions and seminars hosted. Amusement parks, antiques, fishing, shopping, downhill skiing, cross-country skiing, golf, theater and watersports nearby.

Pets Allowed: Smaller than a cow, not left alone in room.

Publicity: *Chicago Tribune, Boston Herald, Culinary Arts, US Air, Travel & Leisure, Vermont Life, Vermont Magazine.*

Reading   H4

Greystone B&B

Rt 106
Reading, VT 05062
(802)484-7200 (888)473-9222 Fax:(802)484-3716
E-mail: chmiller@sover.net

Circa 1830. Originally built by the Hammond brothers as a shoe factory, this beautiful gray stone building has been a B&B for almost 100 years. Located on two acres, the inn offers an elegant yet comfortable atmosphere. The Fox & Hounds Room is extra large and features a queen-size oak bed, antique armoire and skylights. The lovely Magnolia Room has a queen-sized canopy bed. A full country breakfast is cheerfully served by the owner with a main entree and homemade muffins.

The inn is 11 miles south of Woodstock on RT106, and Dartmouth College is 35 minutes away. Guests often rent horses at the Kedron Valley Stables or attend a horse show nearby at the Green Mountain Horse Association.

Innkeeper(s): Connie Miller. $65-100. PC TC. TAC10. 4 rooms, 3 with PB. 1 suite. Breakfast included in rates. Types of meals: full breakfast, gourmet breakfast and early coffee/tea. Beds: KQDT. Fax, copier and library on premises. Weddings, small meetings and family reunions hosted. Antiques, fishing, parks, shopping, downhill skiing, cross-country skiing, sporting events, golf and watersports nearby.

Richmond   D3

The Richmond Victorian Inn

33 East Main St, Rt #2
Richmond, VT 05477-0652
(802)434-4410 (888)242-3362 Fax:(802)434-4411
E-mail: gailclar@together.net

Circa 1881. This Queen Anne Victorian, with a three-story tower, is accented with green shutters, a sunburst design, fish scale shingles and a gingerbread front porch. The Tower Room is filled with white wicker, delicate flowered wallpaper and an antique bed. The Rose Room offers two beds and white ruffled curtains, while the Pansy Room features an antique bed, white walls and a stenciled pansy border. There are hardwood floors and leaded-glass windows throughout. From the tree-shaded porch, enjoy the inn's lawns and flower gardens after a full breakfast.

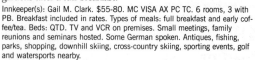

Innkeeper(s): Gail M. Clark. $55-80. MC VISA AX PC TC. 6 rooms, 3 with PB. Breakfast included in rates. Types of meals: full breakfast and early coffee/tea. Beds: QTD. TV and VCR on premises. Small meetings, family reunions and seminars hosted. Some German spoken. Antiques, fishing, parks, shopping, downhill skiing, cross-country skiing, sporting events, golf and watersports nearby.

"Thank you for being such a fabulous host. We loved your Victorian home & enjoyed your warm hospitality. We will definitely spread the word for you in Canada."

Ripton   F2

Chipman Inn

Rt 125
Ripton, VT 05766
(802)388-2390 (800)890-2390

Circa 1828. This was the home of Daniel Chipman, a prominent legislator and founder of Middlebury College. Chipman also managed the "Center Turnpike" (now Route 125) through the Green Mountains. A replica of the tariff board stands near the inn. The inn's lounge/bar is in the original kitchen, with its old fireplace and bread oven.

Historic Interest: Shelburne Museum (50 minutes), Fort Ticonderoga (1 hour).
Innkeeper(s): Joyce Henderson & Bill Pierce. $85-125. MC VISA AX DS TC. 8 rooms with PB. Breakfast included in rates. Type of meal: full breakfast. Dinner available. Beds: QTD. Small meetings and family reunions hosted. Antiques, fishing, parks, shopping, skiing and watersports nearby.
Publicity: *Gourmet, Food & Wine, New York Times, Addison County Independent.*

"Cozy, warm and friendly."

500

Roxbury   E4

The Inn at Johnnycake Flats

RR 1, Carrie Howe Rd
Roxbury, VT 05669
(802)485-8961

Circa 1806. Johnnycake Flats is an unpretentious and delightfully small bed and breakfast that offers guests a quiet escape from the hectic pace of metropolitan life. The guest rooms in this registered historical site include family antiques, Shaker baskets and handmade quilts. The innkeepers can help you identify local wildflowers and birds. In winter, enjoy cross-country skiing or snowshoeing and come home to sip hot cider beside the fire.

Innkeeper(s): Debra & Jim Rogler. $65-85. DS PC TC. 4 rooms, 1 with PB. Breakfast and afternoon tea included in rates. Types of meals: continental breakfast, continental-plus breakfast and early coffee/tea. Beds: DT. Bicycles and library on premises. 16 acres. Small meetings and family reunions hosted. Antiques, fishing, parks, shopping, skiing, sporting events, theater and watersports nearby. Pets Allowed: In barn only.

"You've nurtured a bit of paradise here, thanks for the lovely stay."

Rutland   H3

The Phelps House

19 North St
Rutland, VT 05701-3011
(802)775-4480 (800)775-4620

Circa 1912. This California ranch B&B is considered the state's first Frank Lloyd Wright house. Guests will be intrigued by the custom wall murals, hand-crafted dolls and parquet floors. Children of all ages will enjoy the basement, which features pingpong and pool. The B&B's location, next door to a city playground, also will please the recreation-minded. Guests play tennis on the inn's clay court, adjacent to a barn boasting an 80-foot mural painted by the innkeeper.

Innkeeper(s): Betty Phelps. $65-75. PC TC. 6 rooms. 1 suite. 1 cottage. Breakfast included in rates. Type of meal: full breakfast. Beds: QDT. TV, VCR, tennis and library on premises. Family reunions hosted. Downhill skiing and cross-country skiing nearby.

The Inn at Rutland

70 N Main St
Rutland, VT 05701-3249
(802)773-0575 (800)808-0575

Circa 1890. This distinctive Victorian mansion is filled with many period details, from high, plaster-worked ceilings to leather wainscotting in the dining room. Leaded windows and interesting woodwork are found throughout. Guest rooms have been decorated to maintain Victorian charm without a loss of modern comforts. A wicker-filled porch and common rooms are available to guests. Located in central Vermont, The Inn at Rutland is only 15 minutes from the Killington and Pico ski areas.

Historic Interest: Wilson Castle (10 minutes), Coolidge birthplace (30 minutes), Hildene (30 minutes), Norman Rockwell Museum (5 minutes).
Innkeeper(s): Bob & Tanya Liberman. $49-195. MC VISA AX DC CB DS TC.

10 rooms with PB. 1 suite. 2 conference rooms. Breakfast included in rates. Type of meal: full breakfast. Beds: KQD. Phone, air conditioning, ceiling fan and TV in room. VCR, fax, copier and bicycles on premises. Weddings, small meetings and family reunions hosted. Antiques, fishing, parks, shopping, skiing, sporting events, theater and watersports nearby.

Location: In central Vermont.

"A lovely page in the 'memory album' of our minds."

Shelburne   D2

Elliot House B&B

2176 Dorset St
Shelburne, VT 05482
(802)985-5497

Circa 1865. Panoramic views of the Green Mountains and Adirondack Mountains surround this stately Greek Revival farmhouse nestled amidst perennial gardens, meadows and a pond. The Carriage House and the Milk House contain guest rooms, with maple beds and casual furnishings reminiscent of Adirondack lodge-style pieces. Shelburne Farms and Museum are five minutes away. Other activities include picking blueberries, antiquing, and water sports on Lake Champlain. There are five ski areas within an hour. Families are welcome.

Innkeeper(s): Susan & Nicholas Gulrajani. $80-100. PC. 3 rooms with PB. 1 suite. 1 cottage. Breakfast included in rates. Type of meal: gourmet breakfast. Beds: QT. Swimming on premises. Weddings, small meetings and family reunions hosted. Antiques, fishing, parks, downhill skiing, sporting events, golf, theater and watersports nearby.

"Two nights is not enough to enjoy everything you have to offer here."

Shoreham   F2

Shoreham Inn & Country Store

On The Green, Main St
Shoreham, VT 05770
(802)897-5081 (800)255-5081

Circa 1790. Located just five miles east of Fort Ticonderoga, this Federal-style inn is a favorite of nature-lovers. Fascinating antique shops and many covered bridges are found in the area. The inn's dining room, with its large open fire, is a popular gathering spot, and guests also

Circa 1790

are drawn to the restored 19th-century sitting rooms. Guest rooms are furnished with country antiques. A country store is on the premises.

Innkeeper(s): Julie & Jim Ortuno. $85. AP. MC VISA PC TC. 11 rooms. Breakfast included in rates. Types of meals: full breakfast and early coffee/tea. Dinner available. Copier, bicycles and library on premises. Weddings, small meetings, family reunions and seminars hosted. Antiques, fishing, parks, shopping, downhill skiing, cross-country skiing, sporting events, theater and watersports nearby.

Shrewsbury   H3

Crown Point Inn

Wiley Hill, PO Box 157
Shrewsbury, VT 05738
(802)492-3589 (800)492-8089

Circa 1850. During the Revolutionary War, the road that runs in front of this inn was used as the main supply route between Boston Harbor and Fort Ticonderoga. More than a century later, this Colonial inn was built. Its location is ideal, boasting views of mountains and surrounded by more than 100 acres. The guest rooms, decorated in an elegant country style, feature beds bedecked

with Ralph Lauren linens and topped with down comforters. Breakfasts are healthy and hearty, often featuring low-fat and low-cholesterol fare. Homemade muffins, scones, entrees made from farm-fresh eggs, seasonal fruits and pancakes topped with Vermont maple syrup might appear on the breakfast table.

Innkeeper(s): Carol & B. Michael Calotta. $80-125. PC TC. 8 rooms, 6 with PB. 1 conference room. Breakfast and afternoon tea included in rates. Types of meals: full breakfast, gourmet breakfast and early coffee/tea. Picnic lunch and banquet service available. Beds: QT. TV, VCR, swimming, bicycles, tennis and library on premises. 117 acres. Weddings, small meetings, family reunions and seminars hosted. Italian spoken. Antiques, fishing, parks, shopping, downhill skiing, cross-country skiing, golf, theater, watersports nearby.

Pets Allowed: Boarded at nearby kennel.

Publicity: *Country Inns.*

South Londonderry   J3

Londonderry Inn

PO Box 301-931, Rt 100
South Londonderry, VT 05155
(802)824-5226 Fax:(802)824-3146
E-mail: londinn@sovernet.net

Circa 1826. For almost 100 years, the Melendy Homestead, overlooking the West River and the village, was a dairy farm. In 1940, it became an inn. A tourist brochure promoting the area in 1881 said, "Are you overworked in the office, counting room or workshop and need invigorating influences? Come ramble over these hills and mountains and try the revivifying effects of Green Mountain oxygen." Dinner is available weekends and holiday periods, in season.

Historic Interest: Home of Robert Todd Lincoln (20 minutes), Bennington Battle Monument (45 minutes), Bennington Museum with Grandma Moses exhibit (45 minutes).

Innkeeper(s): Jim & Jean Cavanagh. $41-116. EP. 25 rooms, 20 with PB. 1 conference room. Breakfast included in rates. Dinner available. Restaurant on premises. Beds: KQDT. Phone in room. TV, VCR, fax and copier on premises. Weddings, small meetings, family reunions and seminars hosted. Antiques, fishing, shopping, skiing, sporting events, theater and watersports nearby.

Location: Route 100 between Manchester and Springfield.

Publicity: *New England Monthly, Ski, McCall's.*

"A weekend in a good country inn, such as the Londonderry, is on a par with a weekend on the ocean in Southern Maine, which is to say that it's as good as a full week nearly anyplace else — The Hornet."

South Newfane K4

The Inn at South Newfane

HCR 63, Box 57, Dover Rd
South Newfane, VT 05351-0057
(802)348-7191 Fax:(802)348-9325
E-mail: cullinn@sover.net

Purchased by a wealthy Philadelphian in 1868 to use as a summer home, this charming turn-of-the-century manor house was converted to an inn in 1984. The inn is decorated in a comfortable style, with Oriental rugs and traditional furnishings. The front living room and entry are painted an inviting shade of yel-

low and offer an assortment of chairs to relax on, as well as reading material. Guest rooms are cozy and distinctively decorated with floral wallcoverings and beds topped with quilts. Breakfasts are served in the morning room, which has a fireplace. The inn also has a restaurant, featuring a variety of gourmet fare. Guests might start off with a spinach and feta cheese tart or perhaps lobster bisque, then enjoy one of the evening's entrees. From there, desserts such as warm apple crisp with homemade French vanilla ice cream, finish off the evening meal. Lunch is served summer through foliage. MAP rates are available.

Innkeeper(s): Neville & Dawn Cullen. $95-115. MC VISA TC. TAC10. 6 rooms with PB. Breakfast included in rates. Types of meals: continental-plus breakfast and full breakfast. Dinner, evening snack, lunch, banquet service, catering service and room service available. Restaurant on premises. Beds: KQT. Turndown service and ceiling fan in room. Swimming on premises. 100 acres. Weddings, small meetings, family reunions and seminars hosted. Antiques, fishing, parks, shopping, downhill skiing, cross-country skiing, golf, theater and watersports nearby.

"Wonderfully calm and peaceful. Loved every minute."

South Pomfret H4

Rosewood Inn B&B

Wood Rd, PO Box 125
South Pomfret, VT 05067
(802)457-4485 (800)910-3223

Circa 1790. Farm animals and a picturesque brook are on the two acres of Rosewood Inn, a recently renovated Colonial farmhouse just outside Woodstock. Once a school, the house has been owned by three generations of the innkeeper's family. Rooms are decorated in a country decor in keeping with the home's setting. A full breakfast is served in the dining room. Badminton, volleyball and horseshoes are summer pastimes offered to guests. Nearby rivers, lakes and ponds are favorite fishing spots, and the Suicide Six ski area is five minutes from the inn.

Innkeeper(s): Donna Wood Jones. $70-125. 6 rooms, 1 with PB. Breakfast, afternoon tea and dinner included in rates. Type of meal: full breakfast. Beds: QD. Ceiling fan, TV and VCR in room. Spa on premises. Small meetings and family reunions hosted. Antiques, fishing, parks, shopping, downhill skiing, cross-country skiing, sporting events, golf, theater and watersports nearby. Pets Allowed.

South Woodstock H4

Kedron Valley Inn

Rt 106 Box 145
South Woodstock, VT 05071
(802)457-1473 (800)836-1193 Fax:(802)457-4469
E-mail: kedroninn@aol.com

Circa 1822. Travelers have made this rustic, cozy inn a stopping point for 170 years. One of the guest buildings has a secret attic passageway and is rumored to have been a stop on the Underground Railway during the Civil War. A 60-piece quilt collection includes century-old quilts created by the hostess' great-grandmothers. Guests need not leave the grounds to enjoy a white-sand beach and swimming lake. A stable with horses is nearby. Fifteen of the rooms boast fireplaces, most rooms feature

canopy beds and two rooms have large Jacuzzis. After feasting on a delectable breakfast, spend the day searching for antiques or viewing historic estates. The gourmet dinners are a treat.

Historic Interest: Home of Augustine Saint Gaudens (25 miles), Billings Farm & Museum (5 miles), Calvin Coolidge Homestead (20 miles).

Innkeeper(s): Max & Merrily Comins. $120-195. MC VISA AX DS PC. TAC10. 26 rooms with PB, 15 with FP. 3 suites. 1 conference room. Breakfast included in rates. Type of meal: full breakfast. Dinner available. Beds: QDT. Air conditioning and ceiling fan in room. Fax, copier and swimming on premises. 15 acres. Weddings, small meetings, family reunions and seminars hosted. German spoken. Antiques, fishing, parks, shopping, downhill skiing, cross-country skiing and theater nearby.

Publicity: *Oprah Winfrey Show, Good Housekeeping, Country Living, Country Home, Yankee, Gourmet, Ski, New York Times, London Times.*

"It's what you dream a Vermont country inn should be and the most impressive feature is the innkeepers ... outgoing, warm and friendly."

Springfield I4

Hartness House Inn

30 Orchard St
Springfield, VT 05156-2612
(802)885-2115 Fax:(802)885-2207
E-mail: avtstore@sover.net

Circa 1903. There are many inns where star-gazing is a popular nighttime activity. At Hartness House, it is taken to a whole new level. The original owner not only served as the state's governor, but inventor/astronomer James Hartness also created the historic observatory that remains at the home today. Planets, stars and comets, can be viewed from the historic Turret Equatorial Telescope. Aside from this uncommon amenity, the house itself is impressive. Guests who stay in the home's original portion reach their well-appointed rooms via a three-story staircase. Two newer wings also offer elegant accommodations. On weekdays, a continental breakfast is served and on weekends, full breakfast fare is available. There is a Victorian-styled dining room on the premises as well, offering dinners by candlelight. The home is often the site of weddings, receptions and parties. Country Inns magazine chose Hartness House as one of its top inns, and in another article made note of the inn's wonderful holiday decorations and festivities.

Innkeeper(s): Eileen Gennette-Coughlin. $82-130. MC VISA AX PC TC. TAC10. 39 rooms with PB. 1 suite. 3 conference rooms. Breakfast included in rates. Types of meals: continental-plus breakfast and full breakfast. Dinner and banquet service available. Restaurant on premises. Beds: QDT. Phone, air conditioning and TV in room. Fax, copier, swimming, library on premises. 25 acres. Weddings, small meetings, family reunions and seminars hosted. Antiques, fishing, parks, shopping, skiing, theater, watersports nearby.

"A wonderful place to stop and remember simple elegance and all that is important."

Stowe D4

Brass Lantern Inn
717 Maple St
Stowe, VT 05672-4250
(802)253-2229 (800)729-2980 Fax:(802)253-7425
E-mail: brasslntrn@aol.com

Circa 1810. This rambling farmhouse and carriage barn rests at the foot of Mt. Mansfield. A recent award-winning renovation has brought a new shine to the inn from the gleaming plank floors to the polished woodwork and crackling fireplaces and soothing whirlpool tubs. Quilts and antiques fill the guest rooms and some, like the Honeymoon Room, have their own fireplace and mountain view. A complimentary afternoon and evening tea is provided along with a full Vermont-style breakfast. The inn is a three-time winner (1995-97) of the Golden Fork Award from the Gourmet Dinners Society of North America.
Innkeeper(s): Andy Aldrich. $75-225. MC VISA AX. TAC10. 9 rooms with PB, 3 with FP. Breakfast and afternoon tea included in rates. Types of meals: full breakfast and early coffee/tea. Beds: QDT. Air conditioning in room. VCR, fax, copier and library on premises. Weddings and small meetings hosted. Antiques, fishing, parks, shopping, downhill skiing, cross-country skiing, sporting events, theater and watersports nearby.
Location: One-half mile from village center.
Publicity: *Vermont, Vermont Life, Innsider, Discerning Traveler, Ski.*

"The little things made us glad we stopped."

Foxfire Inn & Italian Restaurant
1606 Pucker S
Stowe, VT 05672
(802)253-4887 Fax:(802)253-7016

Circa 1850. This inn and 90-seat restaurant is in a restored farmhouse, bordered with colorful perennials. Shingles and many-paned windows add to the welcoming feeling. The inn is best known among Stowe visitors and locals as the best place for Italian food. Try the Chicken Ripieno stuffed with gorgonzola, pancetta and figs in a creamy Marsala sauce. For dessert you'll want to order the espresso/rum-soaked pound cake with chocolate mousse filling. Rated three diamonds by AAA, the guest rooms are furnished in a country decor with antiques.
$55-85. MC VISA AX DS TC. 5 rooms with PB. Breakfast included in rates. Type of meal: full breakfast. Dinner available. Restaurant on premises. Beds: QDT. Air conditioning in room. Fax and copier on premises. Antiques, fishing, shopping, skiing, sporting events, golf and theater nearby.

"A wonderful evening for the third straight year!"

Townshend K4

Boardman House
PO Box 112, on The Green
Townshend, VT 05353-0112
(802)365-4086

Circa 1840. This stately Greek Revival is located on the village green of Townshend in Southeast Vermont. Guests enjoy a full breakfast before beginning their day, which could include

antiquing, canoeing or kayaking in the West River or skiing at Bromley, Magic Mountain or Stratton ski areas, all within easy driving distance. The inn boasts a large, lush lawn and gardens, a parlor with a library and a refreshing sauna. Early coffee or tea is served and picnic lunches are available.
Innkeeper(s): Paul Weber & Sarah Messenger. $70-75. PC TC. 6 rooms, 5 with PB. 1 suite. Breakfast included in rates. Types of meals: full breakfast, gourmet breakfast and early coffee/tea. Picnic lunch available. Beds: QT. Air conditioning in room. TV, VCR, sauna and library on premises. Small meetings and family reunions hosted. Antiques, fishing, parks, shopping, downhill skiing, cross-country skiing and watersports nearby.
Pets Allowed: Days only; crated or contained at night, kept in room.
Location: On Village Green at crossroads of Rt 35 and 30.

Vergennes E2

Strong House Inn
82 W Main St
Vergennes, VT 05491-9531
(802)877-3337

Circa 1834. This Federal-style home boasts views of the Green Mountains and the Adirondack range. Several rooms offer working fireplaces and all are richly appointed. Country breakfasts and afternoon refreshments are served, and on Sunday don't miss the

expansive afternoon tea, complete with pastries, tea sandwiches, and of course, a wide selection of teas. Nearby Lake Champlain offers boating and fishing. Golf, hiking, skiing and some of the finest cycling in Vermont are all part of the area's myriad of outdoor activities. Innkeeper Mary Bargiel is an avid gardener and decorates the grounds with flowers and herb gardens. The innkeepers offer a selection of special weekends from a Valentine's Day to a quilter's weekend.
Historic Interest: The area has no shortage of antique shopping, and the inn itself is listed in the National Register of Historic Places.
Innkeeper(s): Mary Bargiel. $75-175. MC VISA AX. 8 rooms with PB, 3 with FP. 2 suites. Breakfast included in rates. Types of meals: full breakfast, gourmet breakfast and early coffee/tea. Afternoon tea available. Beds: KQT. Phone, air conditioning, turndown service, TV and VCR in room. Weddings, small meetings, family reunions and seminars hosted. Antiques, fishing, shopping, skiing, sporting events, theater and watersports nearby.
Location: One mile west of Vergennes on 22A.
Publicity: *Vermont Magazine, Addison County Independent.*

"Blissful stay...Glorious breakfast!"

Vericho D3

Sinclair Inn B&B
389 Vt Rte 15
Vericho, VT 05465
(802)899-2234 (800)433-4658 Fax:(802)899-2234

Circa 1890. Enjoy the ambiance of an era gone-by at this stunning Queen Anne Victorian, which was built by carpenter Edmund Sinclair to showcase his talents. When a local hotel burned down, Sinclair added a turret to his home and opened for business, thus beginning a tradition of innkeeping. Innkeepers Jeannie and Andy Buchanan restored the home down to the last detail, preserving many original features and the home's Victorian

charm. Elegant country breakfasts are served on tables set with fine linens, china and silver. With its special gardens, pond and waterfall, the Buchanans will create romantic amenities for special occasions and can accommodate up to 100 guests for weddings.

Historic Interest: Old Red Grist Mill in Jericho Village (3 miles), historical houses, barns, covered bridges (close by).
Innkeeper(s): Jeanne & Andy Buchanan. $80-105. MC VISA DS PC TC. TAC10. 6 rooms with PB, 1 with FP. 1 conference room. Breakfast included in rates. Types of meals: full breakfast and early coffee/tea. Beds: KQT. Air conditioning in room. Fax and copier on premises. Handicap access. Antiques, fishing, parks, shopping, downhill skiing, cross-country skiing, sporting events, theater and watersports nearby.
Publicity: *Burlington Free Press.*

"*Coming home every night to your inn was the highlight of each day. Your generosity, warmth and kindness were extremely comforting.*"

Waitsfield   E3

Lareau Farm Country Inn

PO Box 563, Rt 100
Waitsfield, VT 05673-0563
(802)496-4949 (800)833-0766

Circa 1794. This Greek Revival house was built by Simeon Stoddard, the town's first physician. Old-fashioned roses, lilacs, delphiniums, iris and peonies fill the gardens. The inn sits in a wide meadow next to the crystal-clear Mad River. A canoe trip or a refreshing swim are possibilities here.

Innkeeper(s): Dan & Susan Easley. $60-125. MC VISA DS PC TC. 13 rooms, 11 with PB. 1 suite. 1 conference room. Breakfast included in rates. Types of meals: full breakfast, gourmet breakfast and early coffee/tea. Beds: QD. Swimming and library on premises. 67 acres. Weddings, small meetings, family reunions and seminars hosted. Antiques, fishing, shopping, downhill skiing, cross-country skiing and theater nearby.
Location: Central Vermont, Sugarbush Valley.
Publicity: *Pittsburgh Press, Philadelphia Inquirer, Los Angeles Times.*

"*Hospitality is a gift. Thank you for sharing your gift so freely with us.*"

The Inn at Mad River Barn

Rt 17 PO Box 88
Waitsfield, VT 05673
(802)496-3310 (800)631-0466

Circa 1800. The inn consists of two farmhouses and a converted barn. One farmhouse was recently remodeled to include a two-story lounge, game room, bar and restaurant. Guests may stay in the barn or the more luxurious farmhouse. Just beyond the barn is a path to the mountain. Old stone walls and lumber trails run through the property.

Innkeeper(s): Betsy Pratt. $50-75. MAP, AP. MC VISA. 16 rooms, 15 with PB. 1 conference room. Type of meal: full breakfast. Dinner available. Restaurant on premises. Beds: QT. Phone and TV in room. VCR on premises. 900 acres. Weddings, small meetings, family reunions and seminars hosted. Antiques, shopping, skiing and sporting events nearby.
Publicity: *Boston Globe.*

"*If I plan a ski trip to Vermont, the Mad River Barn will be where I park myself.*"

Mad River Inn

Tremblay Rd, PO Box 75
Waitsfield, VT 05673
(802)496-7900 (800)832-8278 Fax:(802)496-5390

Circa 1860. Surrounded by the Green Mountains, this Queen Anne Victorian sits on seven scenic acres along the Mad River. The charming inn boasts attractive woodwork throughout, highlighted by ash, bird's-eye maple and cherry. Guest rooms feature European featherbeds and include the Hayden Breeze Room,

with a king brass bed, large windows and sea relics, and the Abner Doubleday Room, with a queen ash bed and mementos of baseball's glory days. The inn sports a billiard table, gazebo, organic gardens and a Jacuzzi overlooking the mountains. Guests can walk to a recreation path along the river.

Historic Interest: The Historic Round Barn and Shelbourne Farm & Museum are a short distance.
Innkeeper(s): Rita & Luc Maranda. $69-125. MC VISA AX. TAC10. 10 rooms with PB. Breakfast and afternoon tea included in rates. Type of meal: gourmet breakfast. Beds: KQ. Turndown service and ceiling fan in room. TV, VCR, fax, spa, stables and child care on premises. Weddings, small meetings and family reunions hosted. French spoken. Antiques, fishing, shopping, skiing, sporting events, theater and watersports nearby.
Publicity: *Insider, Victorian Homes, Let's Live, Skiing, AAA Home & Away, Tea Time at the Inn, Travel & Leisure.*

"*Your hospitality was appreciated, beautiful house and accommodations, great food & friendly people, just to name a few things. We plan to return and we recommend the Mad River Inn to friends & family.*"

Millbrook Inn

Rfd Box 62
Waitsfield, VT 05673
(802)496-2405 (800)477-2809 Fax:(802)496-9735
E-mail: millbrkinn@aol.com

Circa 1855. Guests enter Millbrook through the warming room, where an antique Glenwood parlor stove usually is roaring. This classic Cape-style farmhouse is known for its individually stenciled guest rooms, Green Mountain views and one of the valley's best dining rooms. The inn's rates are listed for two people under the Modified American Plan. During the summer, the bed & breakfast rates are $68 for two people.

Innkeeper(s): Joan & Thom Gorman. $100-140. MAP. MC VISA AX. 7 rooms with PB. Breakfast and dinner included in rates. Type of meal: full breakfast. Restaurant on premises. Beds: QT. Phone and ceiling fan in room. Bicycles on premises. Weddings and family reunions hosted. Antiques, fishing, shopping, downhill skiing, cross-country skiing and golf nearby.
Publicity: *Daily News, L.A. Times, Boston Globe, Travel Today, Gourmet.*

"*A weekend at your place is just what the doctor had in mind.*"

Waitsfield Inn

Rt 100, PO Box 969
Waitsfield, VT 05673
(802)496-3979 (800)758-3801

Circa 1825. This Federal-style home once served as a parsonage and was home to a state senator. Surrounded by a picket fence, the home's grounds boast a large garden. The old barn is now the common room and includes the original wood-planked flooring and a fireplace. Guest quarters are filled with period antiques. In the winter, freshly baked cookies and cider are served. As the inn is in the village of Waitsfield, all the town's sites are nearby. The area offers an abundance of outdoor activities throughout the year.

Historic Interest: Ethan Allen's estate is 35 miles from the inn and Montpelier is 20 miles away.

Innkeeper(s): Ruth & Steve Lacey. $79-129. MC VISA AX DS PC TC. 14 rooms with PB. Breakfast included in rates. Type of meal: full breakfast. Beds: QDT. Weddings, small meetings, family reunions and seminars hosted. Antiques, fishing, shopping, skiing and theater nearby.

Location: Near Sugarbush and Mad River Glen ski areas.

Wallingford   H3

I. B. Munson House

7 S Main St, PO Box 427
Wallingford, VT 05773
(802)446-2860 (888)519-3771 Fax:(802)446-3336
E-mail: ibmunson@vermontel.com

Circa 1856. Isaac Munson might not recognize some of Wallingford anymore, but his home still would be easy enough to identify. During the restoration of the Italianate Victorian,

the innkeepers preserved many original elements, such as the wood floors and the carved mantels. Period antiques and Waverly wallcoverings are featured in the guest rooms, two of which include a fireplace. Wallingford is a designated historic village, so there are many interesting old homes and buildings to see. Ski areas, shops and restaurants are close by.

Innkeeper(s): Phillip & Karen Pimental. $70-160. MC VISA AX DS PC TC. TAC15. 7 rooms with PB, 2 with FP. 2 suites. Breakfast included in rates. Types of meals: full breakfast and early coffee/tea. Afternoon tea available. Beds: QDT. Turndown service and ceiling fan in room. TV, VCR and fax on premises. Weddings, small meetings, family reunions and seminars hosted. Antiques, fishing, parks, shopping, skiing and watersports nearby.

Publicity: *The Rotarian, Mill River Area Current.*

"Our two days here were top notch, from sunrise to sunset."

Warren   F3

Beaver Pond Farm Inn

Rd Box 306, Golf Course Rd
Warren, VT 05674
(802)583-2861 Fax:(802)583-2860

Circa 1840. This Vermont farmhouse, formerly a working dairy and sheep farm, is situated in a meadow overlooking several beaver ponds. Present owners refurbished the home, decorating

the tasteful rooms with antiques and Laura Ashley wallpapers. For golf lovers, the inn is located only 100 yards from the first tee of the Sugarbush Golf Course. The course is transformed into a cross-country ski center in the winter, offering miles of tracked and groomed trails. Downhill skiing is only one mile away.

Historic Interest: Beaver Pond Farm Inn is listed on the state's historic register. Shelburne Farm and museum is a 45-minute drive, and Montpelier is 30 minutes away.

Innkeeper(s): Robert & Elizabeth Hansen. $72-104. MC VISA AX PC. 6 rooms, 4 with PB. 1 conference room. Breakfast and evening snack included in rates. Types of meals: full breakfast and early coffee/tea. Dinner and picnic lunch available. Beds: KQT. TV, VCR, fax and copier on premises. Handicap access. Weddings, small meetings, family reunions and seminars hosted. Antiques, fishing, shopping, downhill skiing, cross-country skiing, sporting events, golf and theater nearby.

Location: Sugarbush Valley.

Publicity: *Los Angeles Times, New Woman, Innsider, Long Island Newsday.*

"The inn is simply magnificent. I have not been in a nicer one on three continents. Breakfast was outrageous."

Pitcher Inn

Main St
Warren, VT 05674-0408
(802)496-6350 (888)867-4824
E-mail: pitcher@modriver.com

Circa 1890. This three-story colonial inn replaces the former building which burned in 1993. Double verandas flank the entrance. Guest rooms feature private baths with double sinks, steam showers, two-person Jacuzzis, fireplaces, phones and computer hookups. A library and large game room are favorite lounging spots. The inn's dining rooms provide regional specialties. The Mad River Valley affords skiing, swimming, tennis, fishing and horse riding.

Innkeeper(s): Heather & John Carino. $165-350. MC VISA TC. 9 rooms with PB, 7 with FP. 2 suites. 2 conference rooms. Breakfast, afternoon tea and evening snack included in rates. Types of meals: full breakfast, gourmet breakfast and early coffee/tea. Dinner, picnic lunch and banquet service available. Restaurant on premises. Beds: KQT. Phone, air conditioning, turndown service, TV and VCR in room. Fax, copier and library on premises. Handicap access. Weddings, small meetings, family reunions and seminars hosted. Antiques, fishing, parks, shopping, downhill skiing, cross-country skiing, sporting events, golf and theater nearby.

Waterbury   D3

The Inn at Blush Hill

Blush Hill Rd, Box 1266
Waterbury, VT 05676
(802)244-7529 (800)736-7522 Fax:(802)244-7314
E-mail: innatbh@aol.com

Circa 1790. This shingled Cape-style house was once a stagecoach stop en route to Stowe and is the oldest inn in Waterbury. A 12-foot-long pine farmhand's table is set near the double fireplace and the kitchen bay window, revealing views of

the Worcester Mountains. A favorite summertime breakfast, served gardenside, is pancakes with fresh blueberries, topped with ice cream and maple syrup.

Historic Interest: The inn has a 1760 fireplace with adjacent brick oven.

Innkeeper(s): Gary & Pam Gosselin. $69-130. MC VISA AX DS PC TC. TAC10. 5 rooms with PB, 1 with FP. Breakfast, afternoon tea and evening snack included in rates. Types of meals: full breakfast, gourmet breakfast and early coffee/tea. Beds: QDT. Air conditioning, turndown service and ceiling fan in room. TV, fax and library on premises. Weddings and family reunions hosted. Antiques, fishing, parks, shopping, downhill skiing, cross-country skiing, theater and watersports nearby.

Location: Three-quarter mile off scenic Rt 100 at I-89.

Publicity: *Vermont, Charlotte Observer, Yankee, New York Times, Ski, New York Post, WCAX Television.*

"Our room was wonderful — especially the fireplace. Everything was so cozy and warm."

Old Stagecoach Inn

18 N Main St
Waterbury, VT 05676-1810
(802)244-5056 (800)262-2206 Fax:(802)244-6956

Circa 1826. For many years, this inn served as both a stagecoach stop and meeting house. In the 1880s, an Ohio millionaire used the home as his summer retreat. He added the Victorian touches that are still present, including the polished woodwork, stained glass and elegant fireplaces. Today, guests stay in restored rooms decorated in Victorian style.

Stowe, Sugarbush and Bolton Valley ski areas are nearby, and guests can also partake in fishing, swimming and water sports at Winooski River, Waterbury Reservoir or Lake Champlain.

Innkeeper(s): John & Jack Barwick. $45-125. MC VISA AX DS PC TC. TAC10. 13 rooms, 10 with PB, 1 with FP. 3 suites. Breakfast and afternoon tea included in rates. Type of meal: full breakfast. Dinner available. Beds: KQDT. Air conditioning, ceiling fan and TV in room. Copier on premises. Weddings, small meetings and family reunions hosted. German and French spoken. Antiques, fishing, parks, shopping, downhill skiing, cross-country skiing, theater and watersports nearby. Pets Allowed.

"This place was first class all the way."

Thatcher Brook Inn

PO Box 490, Rt 100 N
Waterbury, VT 05676-0490
(802)244-5911 (800)292-5911 Fax:(802)244-1294

Circa 1899. Listed in the Vermont Register of Historic Buildings, this restored Victorian mansion features a porch with twin gazebos. A covered walkway leads to the historic Wheeler House. Guest rooms are decorated in Laura Ashley-style. Six rooms have fireplaces, and some have whirlpool tubs. The inn's restaurant, Victoria's Bar and Grill, is located on the property. Guests can dine fireside or by candlelight.

Historic Interest: The inn is listed in the National Register.

Innkeeper(s): Kelly & Peter Varty. $75-185. MAP. MC VISA AX DC DS PC TC. TAC10. 22 rooms with PB, 6 with FP. 1 suite. 1 conference room. Breakfast included in rates. Type of meal: full breakfast. Banquet service available. Restaurant on premises. Beds: KQDT. Phone and ceiling fan in room. TV, VCR, fax, copier and library on premises. Handicap access. Weddings, small meetings, family reunions and seminars hosted. Antiques, fishing, parks, shopping, skiing, sporting events, theater and watersports nearby.

"I'd have to put on a black tie in Long Island to find food as good as this and best of all it's in a relaxed country atmosphere. Meals are underpriced."

Weathersfield   I4

The Inn at Weathersfield

Rt 106 Box 165
Weathersfield, VT 05151
(802)263-9217 (800)477-4828 Fax:(802)263-9219

Circa 1795. Built by Thomas Prentis, a Revolutionary War veteran, this was originally a four-room farmhouse set on 237 acres of wilderness. Two rooms were added in 1796 and a carriage house in 1830. During the Civil War, the inn served as a station on the Underground Railroad. Six pillars give the inn a Southern Colonial look, and there are 12 fireplaces, a beehive oven, wide-plank floors and period antiques throughout.

Innkeeper(s): Mary & Terry Carter. $195-250. MAP. MC VISA AX DS. 12 rooms with PB, 8 with FP. 3 suites. 1 conference room. Type of meal: full breakfast. Afternoon tea available. Restaurant on premises. Beds: KQDT. Phone and turndown service in room. TV, VCR, fax, copier and sauna on premises. Handicap access. 21 acres. Weddings, small meetings, family reunions and seminars hosted. Antiques, shopping, downhill skiing, cross-country skiing, sporting events and theater nearby.

Publicity: *Boston Herald, Los Angeles Times, Country Inns, Colonial Homes, Better Homes & Gardens, National Geographic Traveler, Ladies Home Journal, Vermont Magazine.* Ratings: 4 Stars.

"There isn't one thing we didn't enjoy about our weekend with you and we are constantly reliving it with much happiness."

West Dover   K3

Austin Hill Inn

Rt 100, Box 859
West Dover, VT 05356
(802)464-5281 (800)332-7352 Fax:(802)464-1229
E-mail: ahiinn@aol.com

Circa 1930. Situated outside the historic village of West Dover, at the edge of a mountain, this completely renovated inn has walls decorated with old barn board and floral Victorian wallpapers. Antiques and heirlooms include family photographs dating from 1845. Most rooms have balconies and four-poster or brass beds. A full country breakfast in the fireplaced dining room is offered, as well as afternoon tea, complimentary wine and cheese.

Historic Interest: Villages of West Dover & Wilmington, Bennington Museum, Grandma Moses Gallery.

Innkeeper(s): Robbie Sweeney. $90-125. MC VISA AX DS. 12 rooms with PB. 1 conference room. Breakfast and afternoon tea included in rates. Type of meal: full breakfast. Catering service available. Beds: KQDT. Phone in room. Fax and copier on premises. Antiques, fishing, parks, downhill skiing, cross-country skiing and theater nearby.

Location: Mount Snow Valley.

Publicity: *Garden City Life, Newsday, Greenwich Times.*

"Another repeat of perfection."

West Dover Inn

Rt 100 Box 1208
West Dover, VT 05356
(802)464-5207 Fax:(802)464-2173

Circa 1846. This inn served originally as a stagecoach stop and has been hosting guests for more than 150 years. Its Greek Revival structure, especially during the holidays when the exterior is illuminated with strings of lights, is what many of us might conjure up if we were to imagine a Vermont country inn. Two guest rooms and each of the four suites include a fireplace. The suites also have whirlpool tubs. Handmade quilts and antiques add to the New England country appeal. During fall foliage season, guests can opt for breakfast-only rates or choose the Modified American Plan rates, which include breakfast and dinner. Dinner at the inn's restaurant, Gregory's, is a treat. The seasonally changing menu includes starters such as a crock of warm brie brulee with fresh mango and pecans or perhaps pan-seared scallops and lobster cakes. These are followed by entree selections such as grilled sirloin, poached salmon with corn and crab fritters, or perhaps marinated, grilled lamb chops.

Innkeeper(s): Greg Gramas & Monique Phelan. $80-200. MC VISA AX DS PC TC. TAC10. 12 rooms with PB, 6 with FP. 4 suites. 1 conference room. Breakfast included in rates. Type of meal: full breakfast. Restaurant on premises. Beds: QDT. TV in room. VCR, fax and library on premises. Weddings, small meetings, family reunions and seminars hosted. Antiques, fishing, parks, shopping, downhill skiing, cross-country skiing, golf, theater and watersports nearby.

"Thank you for an incredible weekend. The care you took to make our wedding plans complete will be cherished forever."

Weston J3

Darling Family Inn

815 Rt 100
Weston, VT 05161-5404
(802)824-3223

This two-story inn also features two cottages. Located in the Green Mountains, just minutes from Bromley, Okemo, Magic and Stratton ski areas, the inn provides a taste of life from the early Colonial days. Guest rooms feature handmade quilts crafted locally. The cottages include kitchenettes, and pets are welcome in the cottages if prior arrangements are made.

Innkeeper(s): Chapin & Joan Darling. $80-110. PC TC. 5 rooms with PB. 2 suites. 2 cottages. Breakfast included in rates. Type of meal: full breakfast. Turndown service in room. VCR on premises. Small meetings and family reunions hosted. Antiques, shopping, skiing and theater nearby.

The Inn at Weston

56 Rte 100, PO Box 56
Weston, VT 05161
(802)824-6789 (800)754-5804

Circa 1840. People travel to the small hamlet of Weston to enjoy fine food, wonderful scenery and the small-town beauty personified by painters such as Norman Rockwell. The Inn at Weston is a charming spot to enjoy this hospitable, small-town ambiance. The inn is comprised of two National Register farmhouses, each decorated with antiques and handmade quilts. The grounds also include a barn constructed with hand-hewn beams and other smaller beams constructed on a local water-driven saw. The innkeepers serve up unforgettable cuisine, afternoon teas with luscious treats and hearty Vermont country breakfasts. The inn's restaurant offers an eclectic mix of menu items. Gourmet magazine featured the inn and the village of Weston as an ideal getaway spot for hopeful Epicureans. The Vermont Country Store, family owned and operated since 1946, is a popular nearby site.

Historic Interest: The Farrar Nansur House Museum is within walking distance from the inn. A mill museum is another nearby historic attraction.

Innkeeper(s): Jeanne & Bob Wilder. $52-122. MC VISA AX DS. 19 rooms, 12 with PB. Breakfast included in rates. Types of meals: full breakfast and gourmet breakfast. Restaurant on premises. Beds: QDT. Antiques, fishing, downhill skiing, cross-country skiing and theater nearby.

Publicity: *Gourmet, National Geographic Traveler, Better Homes & Gardens,.*

"Your staff was very attentive and courteous. Bill and I cannot stop talking about the delicious meals we were served both at breakfast and dinner. I'm sure our friends and family have committed to memory each meal we ate."

Wilder Homestead Inn

25 Lawrence Hill Rd
Weston, VT 05161-5600
(802)824-8172 Fax:(802)824-5054

Circa 1827. Within walking distance of the Green Mountain National Forest, this inn with both Federal and Greek Revival stylings features seven guest rooms, five with private baths and views. Five of the rooms have decorative fireplaces. Large country breakfasts may include fresh fruit, eggs, homemade biscuits with jam, hotcakes with genuine Vermont maple syrup, Lumberjack mush or sausage. Spring visitors enjoy an abundance of wildflowers. A craft shop is on the premises.

Historic Interest: Museum Tavern in Weston, Old Grist Mill, Coolidge home (25 miles), Lincoln's home (20 miles).

Innkeeper(s): Roy & Peggy Varner. $65-110. MC VISA. 7 rooms, 5 with PB. Breakfast included in rates. Type of meal: full breakfast. Beds: KQDT. Ceiling fan in room. TV and VCR on premises. Weddings, small meetings and family reunions hosted. Antiques, fishing, shopping, downhill skiing, cross-country skiing, sporting events and theater nearby.

Publicity: *Gourmet, Country, Boston Globe, Sao Paulo, Brazil.*

"Like coming home to Grandma's house. Lovely setting in quaint village. Nice to be back."

Wilder   H5

Stonecrest Farm B&B

PO Box 504, 119 Christian St
Wilder, VT 05088-0504
(802)296-2425 (800)730-2425 Fax:(802)295-1135

Circa 1810. Two acres of grounds and charming red barns create a secluded, country atmosphere at Stonecrest Farm, which is located three-and-a-half miles from Dartmouth College. The former dairy farm was owned by a prominent Vermont family and hosted notable guests such as Calvin Coolidge and Amelia Earhart. Guest rooms are decorated with antiques, and beds are topped with down comforters. Terry robes are placed in each room. The abundant breakfasts feature a different entree each morning. Orange French toast and vegetable frittatas are some of the possibilities.

Innkeeper(s): Gail L. Sanderson. $105-135. MC VISA AX PC TC. TAC10. 6 rooms with PB. Breakfast and afternoon tea included in rates. Types of meals: full breakfast and early coffee/tea. Beds: QDT. TV, VCR, fax, copier and library on premises. Family reunions hosted. Limited German and French spoken. Antiques, fishing, parks, shopping, downhill skiing, cross-country skiing, sporting events, theater and watersports nearby.

"Your house is enchanting. I especially liked your grandfather clock in the hallway."

Wilmington   K3

The Red Shutter Inn

PO Box 636
Wilmington, VT 05363-0636
(802)464-3768

Circa 1894. This colonial inn sits on a five-acre hillside amid maples, pin oaks and evergreens. Tucked behind the inn is the renovated carriage house; among its charms is a cozy fireplace suite. In the summer, guests can enjoy gourmet dining by candlelight on an awning-covered porch. The Red Shutter Inn, with its fireplaces in the sitting room and dining room, antique furnishings and view of a rushing river, provide a congenial atmosphere. Antique shops, galleries and craft shops are within walking distance.

Innkeeper(s): Renee & Tad Lyon. $100-200. MC VISA AX DS PC TC. 9 rooms with PB, 3 with FP. 2 suites. Breakfast included in rates. Type of meal: full breakfast. Picnic lunch and banquet service available. Restaurant on premises. Beds: QD. Ceiling fan and TV in room. VCR, fax, copier and library on premises. Weddings, small meetings, family reunions and seminars hosted. Antiques, fishing, parks, shopping, skiing and watersports nearby.
Publicity: *USA Weekend.*

"You've made The Red Shutter Inn a cozy and relaxing hideaway."

White House

PO Box 757
Wilmington, VT 05363-0757
(802)464-2135 (800)541-2135 Fax:(802)464-5222
E-mail: whitehse@sover.net

Circa 1915. White House was built as a summer home for a wealthy lumber baron, and he spared no expense. The inn has 14 fireplaces, rich woodwork and hand-crafted French doors. Nine of the guest rooms include fireplaces, and some have a balcony, terrace or whirlpool tub. Seven guest rooms are located in an adja-

cent guest house. There is an outdoor swimming pool, and the spa includes an indoor pool, whirlpool and sauna. In addition, there is a 39-kilometer ski touring center on the premises, and guests can rent equipment and take private lessons. Guests are treated to breakfast, and award-winning, gourmet dinners are available in the dining rooms. The inn has earned a four-diamond rating.

Innkeeper(s): Robert Grinold. $108-195. MC VISA AX DC DS PC TC. TAC10. 23 rooms with PB, 9 with FP. 1 suite. 3 conference rooms. Breakfast included in rates. Types of meals: full breakfast, gourmet breakfast and early coffee/tea. Dinner and room service available. Restaurant on premises. Beds: KQD. TV, VCR, fax, copier, spa, swimming and sauna on premises. Handicap access. Weddings, small meetings, family reunions and seminars hosted. French spoken. Antiques, fishing, parks, shopping, downhill skiing, cross-country skiing, theater and watersports nearby.
Publicity: *New York Times, Boston Herald, Yankee Magazine, Travel Guide to New England "Editor's Pick".* .

Woodstock   H4

Charleston House

21 Pleasant St
Woodstock, VT 05091-1131
(802)457-3843

Circa 1810. This authentically restored brick Greek Revival town house is furnished with antiques, an art collection and Oriental rugs. Most of the rooms boast four-poster beds. The Summer Kitchen room also offers a private entrance. A hearty full breakfast starts off the day, and the innkeepers serve afternoon refreshments as well.
Historic Interest: The Billings/Marsh National Historic Park and Calvin Coolidge Homestead are nearby attractions.

Innkeeper(s): Bill Hough. $90-175. MC VISA AX. 9 rooms with PB. Breakfast included in rates. Type of meal: full breakfast. Beds: QT. Phone in room. Antiques, fishing, downhill skiing, cross-country skiing, theater nearby.
Publicity: *Harbor News, Boston Business Journal, Weekend Getaway, Inn Spots, Special Places.*

"I felt like I was a king, elegant but extremely comfortable."

Jackson House

37 Old Rt 4 W
Woodstock, VT 05091-1247
(802)457-2065 (800)448-1890 Fax:(802)457-9290
E-mail: innkeepers@jacksonhouse.com

Circa 1890. This beautifully restored late Victorian was built originally by Wales Johnson, a saw-mill owner and craftsman. The gleaming cherry and maple wood floors and moldings, exterior eaves and twin chimneys are a tribute to the original owner's attention to detail and workmanship. Although the inn passed hands a couple of times, the integrity of the interior and exterior designs have never been compromised. Fine antique furnishings, decorative arts and carved Oriental rugs are a few of the elegant and sophisticated features

that have been maintained throughout the years. French-cut crystal, a library of classics and a parlor with a welcoming fire add to the ambiance. Each guest room is inspired by a different style and period: French Empire, Brass and Bamboo inspired by Brighton Castle and New England Country. A gourmet breakfast featuring house specialties such as Santa Fe Omelets, fruit compote in champagne and poached eggs in puff pastry are offered daily. Listed in the National Registry, the inn offers more than four lush acres of manicured gardens and pathways.

Innkeeper(s): Matt & Jennifer Barba. $170-240. MC VISA AX PC. TAC10. 15 rooms, 6 with FP. 6 suites. Breakfast and evening snack included in rates. Type of meal: gourmet breakfast. Restaurant on premises. Beds: QT. Air conditioning, turndown service and ceiling fan in room. TV, VCR, fax, spa, swimming and library on premises. Weddings, small meetings, family reunions and seminars hosted. Spanish and French spoken. Antiques, fishing, parks, shopping, downhill skiing, cross-country skiing, golf, theater, watersports nearby.

Publicity: *Colonial Homes, Country Inns, Fitness Magazine.*

The Lincoln Inn at The Covered Bridge

R R 2 Box 40
Woodstock, VT 05091-9721
(802)457-3312 Fax:(802)457-5808
E-mail: lincon2@aol.com

Circa 1870. This admirable old farmhouse sits on six acres bordered by the Lincoln Covered Bridge and the Ottauquechee River. Lawns meander to a rise overlooking the water. A swing, park benches and a gazebo provide ample places from which to enjoy the view. Recent renovation has revealed hand-hewn beams in the library and a fireplace in the common room. The inn's world class continental cuisine provides a memorable dinner.

Innkeeper(s): Kurt & Lori Hildbrand. $99-139. MC VISA DS PC TC. 6 rooms with PB. 1 conference room. Breakfast included in rates. Types of meals: gourmet breakfast and early coffee/tea. Dinner, evening snack, picnic lunch, lunch, banquet service and catering service available. Restaurant on premises. Beds: KQD. Air conditioning in room. TV, VCR, fax, copier, swimming and library on premises. Weddings, small meetings, family reunions and seminars hosted. German spoken. Antiques, fishing, parks, shopping, downhill skiing, cross-country skiing, sporting events, theater and watersports nearby.

Publicity: *Travelhost.*

"Feels like family!"

Woodstocker B&B

61 River St
Woodstock, VT 05091-1227
(802)457-3896 Fax:(802)457-3897

Circa 1830. This early 19th-century, Cape-style inn is located at the base of Mt. Tom at the edge of the village of Woodstock. Hand-hewn wood beams create a rustic effect. The seven guest rooms and two suites are individually appointed. Buffet-style, full breakfasts get the day off to a great start. Guests can take a short walk across a covered bridge to reach shops and restau-

rants. Hikers will enjoy trails that wind up and around Mt. Tom. After a busy day, come back and enjoy a soak in the five-person whirlpool.

Historic Interest: Billings Farm and Museum, the Calvin Coolidge Homestead and Dana House Museum are some of the historic sites. Four of Woodstock's churches boast bells made by Paul Revere.

Innkeeper(s): Tom & Nancy Blackford. $85-145. MC VISA. 9 rooms with PB. 2 suites. Breakfast included in rates. Types of meals: full breakfast and early coffee/tea. Beds: QD. Air conditioning, ceiling fan and TV in room. VCR, fax and copier on premises. Weddings and family reunions hosted. Antiques, fishing, shopping, downhill skiing, cross-country skiing, sporting events, theater and watersports nearby.

"You have truly opened your home and heart to create a comfortable and memorable stay."

Woodstock (Reading)   H4

Bailey's Mills B&B

PO Box 117, Bailey's Mills Rd
Woodstock (Reading), VT 05062
(802)484-7809 (800)639-3437

Circa 1820. This Federal-style inn features grand porches, 11 fireplaces, a "good-morning" staircase and a ballroom on the third floor. Four generations of Baileys lived in the home, as well as housing mill workers. There also was once a country store on the premises. Guests can learn much about the home and history of the people who lived here through the innkeep-

ers. Two of the guest rooms include a fireplace, and the suite has a private solarium. There's plenty to do here, from exploring the surrounding 48 acres to relaxing with a book on the porch swing or in a hammock. If you forgot your favorite novel, borrow a book from the inn's 2,200-volume library.

Historic Interest: Saint Gaudens National Historic Site (15 miles), Billings Farm Museum (11 miles), Calvin Coolidge Homestead (10 miles), American Precision Museum (10 miles).

Innkeeper(s): Barbara Thaeder & Don Whitaker. $70-110. MC VISA PC TC. TAC10. 3 rooms with PB, 2 with FP. 1 suite. Breakfast included in rates. Types of meals: continental-plus breakfast and early coffee/tea. Beds: KQ. Swimming and library on premises. 48 acres. Weddings and family reunions hosted. Antiques, fishing, parks, shopping, downhill skiing, cross-country skiing and theater nearby.

Pets Allowed: Small, polite, innkeeper approval required.

"If words could encapsulate what a wonderful weekend would be, it would have to be 'Bailey's Mills B&B.' Your home is beautiful. It is elegant yet homey."

Virginia

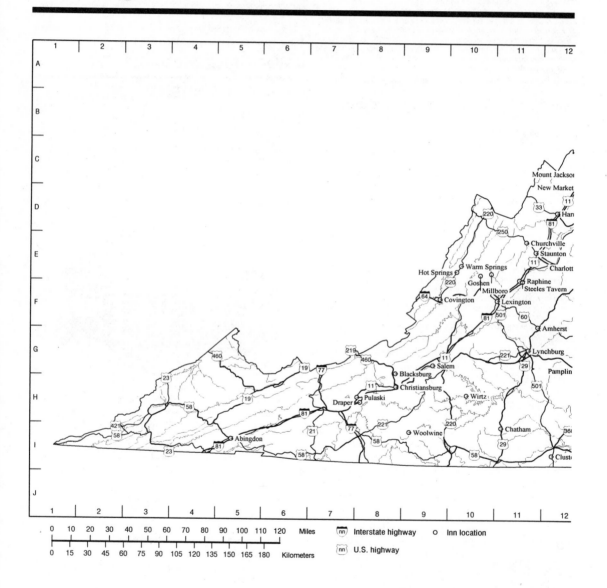

Scale:
Miles: 0 10 20 30 40 50 60 70 80 90 100 110 120
Kilometers: 0 15 30 45 60 75 90 105 120 135 150 165 180

Interstate highway
U.S. highway
Inn location

510

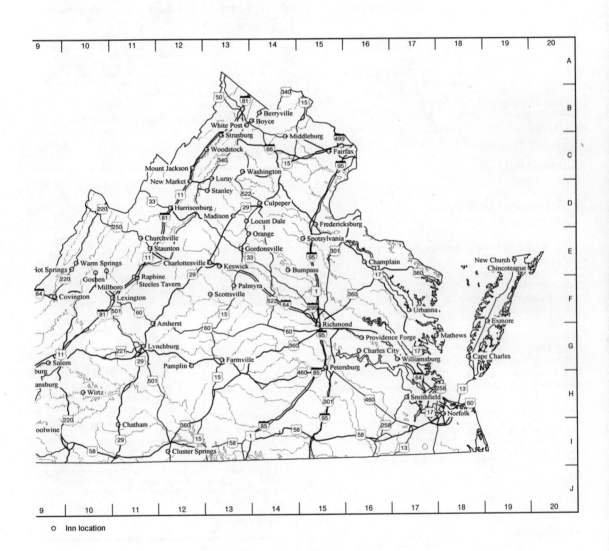

o Inn location

Abingdon 15

Chamberley's Martha Washington Inn

150 W Main St
Abingdon, VA 24210-2810
(540)628-3161 Fax:(540)628-8885

Circa 1832. This historic building has served as Martha
Washington College, a Civil War hospital and training barracks
for the Washington mounted rifles. The inn features a grand
staircase in the entryway, antique furnishings, a lounge and a
dining room. Some guest suites have fireplaces and spas.
Available for banquets, receptions and meetings are the Grand
Ballroom with its silk moire wallpaper and satin draperies, and
the East Parlor with its original oil paintings and antiques.

Innkeeper(s): Ron Lamers. $140. MC VISA AX DC CB DS. 61 rooms with
PB, 3 with FP. 1 conference room. Type of meal: continental breakfast.
Restaurant on premises. Beds: KQDT. Handicap access.

Publicity: *Colonial Homes Magazine.*

"*The hotel offers the latest standard in luxury, while retaining the
'quirky' elements of charm that made 'the Martha' so special.*"

Summerfield Inn

101 W Valley St
Abingdon, VA 24210
(540)628-5905 (800)668-5905

Circa 1923. Flags display the pineapple insignia that means
hospitality to so many of us at post-Victorian homes. The cheerful rooms are decorated with floral touches and items such as

four-poster beds, wicker
and antiques. There is a
guest pantry for those
seeking a refreshment,
and the innkeepers serve
full breakfasts in the elegant dining room with
freshly baked cinnamon

rolls, quiche and seasonal fruit. Abingdon, the oldest town west
of the Blue Ridge Mountains, is the site for the well-known
Barter Theatre. The annual Virginia Highlands Festival, pleasant
streets of historic houses, local arts and crafts, an old mill and
many excellent restaurants add to the area's cultural offerings.

Innkeeper(s): Champe & Don Hyatt. $75-125. MC VISA AX PC TC. TAC10. 7
rooms with PB. 1 conference room. Breakfast included in rates. Type of meal:
full breakfast. Beds: KQDT. Phone, air conditioning, ceiling fan and TV in
room. VCR, bicycles and library on premises. Handicap access. Small meetings and family reunions hosted. Antiques, fishing, parks, shopping, theater
and watersports nearby.

Publicity: *Southern Inns.*

"*A road-weary poet looks for a place with good vibes. Summerfield
Inn is the place.*"

Amherst F11

Dulwich Manor B&B Inn

550 Richmond Hwy
Amherst, VA 24521-3962
(804)946-7207 (800)571-9011

Circa 1912. This red Flemish brick and white columned English
Manor sits on five secluded acres at the end of a country lane
and in the midst of 85 acres of woodland and meadow. The Blue

Ridge Mountains may be enjoyed from the veranda. The entry
features a large center hall and a wide oak staircase. Walls are 14
inches thick. The 18 rooms include a 50-foot-long ballroom on

the third floor. The inn is
decorated with a creative
mix of antiques, reproductions and modern art. Your
host is a professional
singer and actor, and your
hostess was in public rela-
tions and a costumer for
the theater.

Innkeeper(s): Bob & Judy Reilly. $70-98. PC TC. TAC10. 6 rooms, 4 with
PB, 2 with FP. Breakfast included in rates. Types of meals: full breakfast and
early coffee/tea. Afternoon tea available. Beds: QD. Phone, air conditioning
and ceiling fan in room. Spa on premises. Weddings, small meetings, family
reunions and seminars hosted. Antiques, fishing, parks, shopping, downhill
skiing, sporting events, theater and watersports nearby.

Publicity: *Country Inn, Scene.*

"*Our experience at Dulwich Manor surpassed all of our inn visits. A
truly delightful stay!*"

Berryville B14

Berryville B&B

100 Taylor St
Berryville, VA 22611-1222
(540)955-2200 (800)826-7520

Circa 1915. Each of the guest rooms is named and decorated
with a particular theme in mind. For instance, the Scotland Room
contains antique furnishings from its namesake country. The
Victorian Room features English wallcoverings, a fireplace and a
carved antique bed. Each morning, a country breakfast is served
with items such as bacon and eggs, French toast, waffles, freshly

baked biscuits, homemade
jelly and fresh fruit. For
history buffs, the area
around Berryville offers a
number of intriguing sites.
Winchester, about 10
miles from the inn,
changed hands more than
70 times during the Civil
War. Harpers Ferry and

several battlefields are within a half-hour of the inn.

Innkeeper(s): Don & Jan Riviere. $95-135. MC VISA AX DS PC TC. 4 rooms,
2 with PB. Breakfast included in rates. Types of meals: full breakfast and
early coffee/tea. Beds: QD. Phone, air conditioning, turndown service, TV and
VCR in room. Weddings, small meetings, family reunions and seminars hosted. Antiques, fishing, parks, golf, theater and watersports nearby.

"*Positively delightful!*"

Blacksburg G8

Clay Corner Inn

401 Clay St SW
Blacksburg, VA 24060
(540)953-2604 Fax:(540)951-0541
E-mail: claycorner@aol.com

Circa 1929. Clay Corner Inn is comprised of five houses on a
corner one block from Virginia Tech and a couple blocks from
downtown. There are 12 guest rooms, three of which are two-

bedroom suites. Each room is decorated with a different theme, and all guest rooms have private baths, cable TV and telephones. Two houses were built early in the century, two are a decade old and another, circa 1940, is a private residence. a full breakfast is served in the main house, or guests may choose to have continental breakfast in a basket delivered to their room. The inn also features an on-site heated swimming pool.

Historic Interest: Smithfield Plantation is one mile away.

Innkeeper(s): Joanne Anderson. $68-92. MC VISA AX. 12 rooms with PB. Breakfast included in rates. Type of meal: full breakfast. Beds: KQ. Phone in room. Antiques and golf nearby.

Location: In the Appalachians.

Boyce
B14

River House

RR 1 Box 135
Boyce, VA 22620
(540)837-1476 Fax:(540)837-2399

Circa 1780. This historic house is located on Shenandoah River frontage and 17 acres of woodlands. Grain from the neighboring mill (now restored) was once shipped from this point on the river to Harpers Ferry, and Stonewall Jackson camped and crossed the river here. Ask to stay in the original 1780 kitchen with its walk-in fireplace or the elegant master bedroom. Cornelia is a former actress and. organizes theatrical activities at the inn. A complimentary brunch is served every morning.

Historic Interest: Restored Belle Grove Plantation, George Washington HQ, Harpers Ferry (40 minutes).

Innkeeper(s): Cornelia Niemann. $90-145. MC VISA. 5 rooms with PB, 5 with FP. Beds: KQDT. Fax and copier on premises. Handicap access. Antiques, fishing, downhill skiing and theater nearby.

Location: Southwest corner of US Route 50 and Shenandoah River.

Publicity: *Washington Post, Country Inns, Changing Times, Winchester Star.*

"A sure place to unwind for the weekend."

Bumpass
E14

Rockland Farm Retreat

3609 Lewiston Rd
Bumpass, VA 23024-9659
(540)895-5098

Circa 1820. The 75 acres of Rockland Farm include pasture land, livestock, vineyard, crops and a farm pond for fishing. The grounds here are said to have spawned Alex Haley's "Roots." Guests can study documents and explore local cemeteries describing life under slavery in the area surrounding this historic home and 18th-century farmlands.

Historic Interest: Some of the oldest slave cemeteries are nearby.

Innkeeper(s): Roy E. Mixon. $60-75. MAP. AX PC. TAC10. 4 rooms, 3 with PB. 1 suite. 2 conference rooms. Breakfast included in rates. Type of meal: full breakfast. Dinner, lunch, banquet service, catering service available. Beds: DT. Air conditioning in room. VCR on premises. 75 acres. Weddings, small meetings, family reunions, seminars hosted. French, Spanish spoken. Amusement parks, antiques, fishing, parks, shopping, watersports nearby. Pets Allowed.

Location: Thirty minutes south of Fredericksburg, Rt 601 at Lake Anna.

Publicity: *Washington Post, Free Lance-Star.*

Cape Charles
G18

Bay Avenue's Sunset B&B

108 Bay Ave
Cape Charles, VA 23310-3102
(804)331-2424 (888)422-9283 Fax:(804)331-4877

Circa 1915. Located on waterfront Chesapeake Bay property, this B&B offers delightful breezes from its Victorian porch. Newly renovated guest rooms include eclectic decor and Hunter fans. The Victoria Room offers a queen bed, fireplace and clawfoot tub. Awake to the scent of freshly brewed coffee. After a hearty breakfast of fresh fruits, home-baked breads and delicious  entrees, explore the uncrowded beach or take in a day of birdwatching, fishing or cycling.

Historic Interest: The home was built by one of the county's founding families and the area is rich in history. Within seven miles of the inn are Christ Church, a Confederate monument, a monument to Indian Chief Debedeavon, Hungars Church, and Old Court House, which features a museum of Native and Colonial artifacts. Eyre Hall, three miles from Bay Avenue's Sunset B&B, includes rare boxwood gardens. Custis Tomb is five miles away.

Innkeeper(s): Albert Longo & Joyce Tribble. $75-95. MC VISA AX DS TC. TAC10. 4 rooms with PB. Breakfast included in rates. Types of meals: full breakfast, early coffee/tea. Beds: Q. Air conditioning, ceiling fan, TV, VCR in room. Fax, bicycles on premises. Weddings, small meetings, family reunions, seminars hosted. Antiques, fishing, parks, theater, watersports nearby.

Publicity: *Port Folio, Southern Inns.*

"A charming room with a beautiful view! Saw the setting sun as well as the full moon shining on the water."

Cape Charles House

645 Tazewell Ave
Cape Charles, VA 23310-3313
(757)331-4920 Fax:(757)331-4960

Circa 1912. A Cape Charles attorney built this Colonial Revival home on the site where the town's first schoolhouse was located. Each room is named for someone important to the Cape Charles History. The Julia Wilkins Room is especially picturesque. Rich blue walls and white woodwork are accented by blue and white pastoral print curtains. There is a seamstress dress form with an antique dress, rocking chair and chaise. Other rooms are decorated with the same skill and style, with fine window  dressings, artwork and carefully placed collectibles. Oriental rugs top the wood floors, and among the fine furnishings are family heirlooms. Breakfasts are gourmet and served either in the formal dining room. Innkeeper Carol Evans prepares breakfast items such as chilled melon with a lime glaze and lemon yogurt topping, egg quesadillas, rosemary roasted potatoes and freshly baked muffins. From time to time, cooking classes and murder-mystery events are available. There are many attractions in the area, including wagon tours of Custis Working Farm, a historic walking tour of Cape Charles, antique shops, golfing, beach and a nature conservancy.

Innkeeper(s): Bruce & Carol Evans. $80-105. MC VISA AX DS PC TC. TAC10. 5 rooms with PB. Breakfast, afternoon tea and evening snack included in rates. Types of meals: gourmet breakfast and early coffee/tea. Gourmet lunch available. Beds: KQ. Air conditioning and ceiling fan in room. TV, VCR, fax, copier and bicycles on premises. Weddings, small meetings, family reunions and seminars hosted. Antiques, fishing, parks, shopping, golf, theater and watersports nearby.

Publicity: *Southern Inns.*

"Cape Charles House is first and foremost a home and we were made to feel at home."

Champlain   E16

Linden House B&B & Plantation

PO Box 23
Champlain, VA 22438-0023
(804)443-1170 (800)622-1202

Circa 1750. This restored planters home is designated a state landmark and listed in the National Register. The lush grounds boast walking trails, an English garden, gazebo, arbor and five porches. Each of the accommodations offers something special. The Carriage Suite features country decor, antiques, a private porch and a fireplace.
The Robert E. Lee room has a high poster bed, fireplace and private bath. The Jefferson Davis room has a luxurious bath with a Jacuzzi and steam room. The fourth-floor Linden Room affords a view of  the countryside and features a queen-size bed and an alcove with a day bed adjoining the private bath. Other rooms also promise an enchanting experience. All rooms have their own television and refrigerator.

Innkeeper(s): Ken & Sandra Pounsberry. $85-135. MC VISA AX PC TC. TAC10. 4 rooms with PB. 2 suites. Breakfast and afternoon tea included in rates. Types of meals: full breakfast and early coffee/tea. Evening snack, banquet service, catering service and catered breakfast available. Beds: Q. Phone, air conditioning, turndown service, ceiling fan and VCR in room. Stables, bicycles and library on premises. Handicap access. 204 acres. Weddings, small meetings, family reunions and seminars hosted. Amusement parks, antiques, fishing, parks, shopping, theater and watersports nearby.

Charles City   G16

Edgewood Plantation

4800 John Tyler Memorial Hwy
Charles City, VA 23230
(804)829-6908 (800)296-3343 Fax:(804)829-2962

Circa 1849. Among its expansive 7,000 square feet, this Gothic Revival mansion includes high ceilings, a double parlor with two of the home's 10 fireplaces and a double spiral staircase. The plantation has an incredible history. It rests along the oldest highway in the United States, and it was once part of the Berkeley Plantation, the ancestral home of President William Henry Harrison. The inn's Civil War history is as fascinating as the authentic Victorian decor. Both innkeepers are antique dealers, and among the vintage pieces they've included in the inn are canopy beds dating back to 1790, 1818 and 1820. Breakfasts are served with fine silver, china and pewter on a Queen Anne table surrounded by Chippendale chairs. The innkeepers attention to detail is impressive, especially during

the Christmas season when 18 decorated trees are placed throughout the inn. A few yards from the inn is a three-story mill with an unusual inside mill wheel built in 1725.

Innkeeper(s): Dot & Julian Boulware. $100-198. MC VISA AX. 8 rooms, 6 with PB, 3 with FP. 2 suites. 2 cottages. 1 conference room. Breakfast included in rates. Types of meals: full breakfast, gourmet breakfast and early coffee/tea. Afternoon tea, picnic lunch and catering service available. Beds: KQD. Turndown service, ceiling fan and VCR in room. Fax and swimming on premises. 12 acres. Weddings, small meetings, family reunions and seminars hosted. Amusement parks, antiques, fishing, parks, shopping, sporting events, theater and watersports nearby.

Location: Halfway between Williamsburg and Richmond on historic Route 5, 12 miles from 295.

Publicity: *Country Home, Southern Living, Country, Victoria.*

"A feast for the eyes and wonderful manner in which things are displayed and put together."

North Bend Plantation

12200 Weyanoke Rd
Charles City, VA 23030-3632
(804)829-5176 (800)841-1479 Fax:(804)829-6828

Circa 1819. Drive up beautiful old Colonial Rt. 5 to James River Plantation Country and you will discover North Bend Plantation, an experience that ought to be a highlight of your visit to Williamsburg. Here you will stay with the Copland family, fourth generation owners of this historic estate. (The innkeeper is twice great-grandson of noted agriculturist  Edmund Ruffin, who is said to have fired the first shot of the Civil War at Fort Sumter.) Sheridan headquartered at North Bend and his desk is still here, one of many treasured family heirlooms. Large guest rooms are filled with antiques original to the home. Complimentary desserts are available at a nearby four-star restaurant. Guests are served refreshments upon arrival.

Historic Interest: The inn is a designated Virginia Historic Landmark and listed in the National Register of Historic Places. Charles City County is the home of the historic James River Plantations.

Innkeeper(s): George & Ridgely Copland. $115-135. MC VISA PC TC. TAC10. 4 rooms with PB, 1 with FP. 1 suite. Breakfast included in rates. Types of meals: full breakfast and early coffee/tea. Afternoon tea available. Beds: QD. Phone, air conditioning and ceiling fan in room. TV, fax, copier, swimming, bicycles and library on premises. 250 acres. Weddings, small meetings and family reunions hosted. Amusement parks, antiques, parks, shopping and golf nearby.

Location: West of Colonial Williamsburg, 25 minutes.

Publicity: *New York Times, Mid-Atlantic Country, Washington Post, Travel Talk, Southern Hospitality.*

"Your hospitality, friendship and history lessons were all priceless. Your love of life embraced us in a warmth I shall never forget."

Charlottesville   E13

200 South Street Inn

200 W South St
Charlottesville, VA 22902-5041
(804)979-0200 (800)964-7008 Fax:(804)979-4403

Circa 1844. This house was built for Thomas Jefferson Wertenbaker, son of Thomas Jefferson's librarian at the University of Virginia. It is furnished with English and Belgian antiques. Guests may choose rooms with whirlpool baths, fireplaces and canopy beds.

Historic Interest: Jefferson Home, Monticello (4 miles), Monroe Home, Ashlawn (6 miles), Madison Home, Montpelier (20 miles).

Innkeeper(s): Brendan & Jenny Clancy. $100-190. MC VISA AX DC CB PC TC. TAC10. 20 rooms with PB, 11 with FP. 3 suites. Breakfast, afternoon tea and evening snack included in rates. Types of meals: continental-plus breakfast and early coffee/tea. Beds: QT. Phone, air conditioning and turndown service in room. TV, fax and library on premises. Handicap access. Weddings, small meetings, family reunions, seminars hosted. Antiques, fishing, parks, shopping, downhill skiing, sporting events, theater and watersports nearby.

Location: Downtown historic district of Charlottesville.

Publicity: *New York Times, Gourmet, Vogue, Food & Wine, Los Angeles Times, Bon Appetit, Gourmet, Mid-Atlantic Country.*

"True hospitality abounds in this fine inn which is a neatly turned complement to the inspiring history surrounding it."

Clifton Country Inn

1296 Clifton Inn Dr
Charlottesville, VA 22911-3627
(804)971-1800 (888)971-1800 Fax:(804)971-7098
E-mail: reserve@cstone.net

Circa 1799. The first resident at Clifton was Thomas Mann Randolph, who served as governor of the state and was the son-in-law of Thomas Jefferson. One of the gracious guest rooms boasts a winter view of Jefferson's estate, Monticello. Elegance and a careful attention to historical detail has kept this remarkable country inn among the best in the nation, garnering award upon award for its accommodations and cuisine. In
addition to the main
house, guests can opt to
stay in Randolph's law
office, the livery or the carriage house. Aside from
the abundance of history

at Clifton, the innkeepers offer a variety of outdoor pursuits, including a tennis court, swimming pool, lake and 40 acres of beautiful, wooded grounds. Breakfast at Clifton is a treat with fresh fruits, lavish entrees, meat, juices and fine coffees and teas. Afternoon tea is expansive with a selection of delectable baked goods and gourmet teas. Clifton also operates a gourmet restaurant featuring five- and six- course meals prepared by innkeeper Craig Hartman, a Culinary Institute of America graduate.

Historic Interest: Monticello is only about four miles away. Montpelier is about 30 miles from the inn and the University of Virginia is only a 10-mile journey.

Innkeeper(s): Craig Hartman. $165-315. MC VISA PC. TAC10. 14 rooms with PB, 14 with FP. 7 suites. 7 cottages. 2 conference rooms. Breakfast and afternoon tea included in rates. Types of meals: continental-plus breakfast, full breakfast and early coffee/tea. Dinner, banquet service and catering service available. Restaurant on premises. Beds: QD. Air conditioning and turndown service in room. Fax, copier, spa, swimming, tennis, library and child care on premises. Handicap access. 40 acres. Weddings, small meetings, family reunions and seminars hosted. Antiques, fishing, parks, shopping, downhill skiing, cross-country skiing, sporting events and theater nearby.

Publicity: *International Living, Country Inns, Washington Post, Baltimore Sun, Richmond Times Dispatch, Rural Retreats, N.Y. Times, Travel & Leisure.*

"I've stayed at inns in 20 states and found this among the best. This visit has been a lifetime dream come true."

The Inn at Monticello

Rt 20 S, 1188 Scottsville Rd
Charlottesville, VA 22902
(804)979-3593

Circa 1850. Thomas Jefferson built his own home, Monticello, just two miles from this gracious country home. The innkeepers have preserved the historic ambiance of the area. Rooms boast such pieces as four-poster beds covered with fluffy, down comforters. Some of the guest quarters have private porches or fire-

places. Breakfast at the inn is a memorable gourmet-appointed affair. Aside from the usual homemade breads, jams, jellies and hazelnut coffee, guests enjoy entrees such as crab quiche or orange yogurt pancakes topped with fresh fruit. The innkeepers leave croquet set up on the lawn, and they provide chairs for those who want to simply enjoy the scenery from the porch.

Historic Interest: Aside from its close access to Monticello, the inn is five miles from James Monroe's home, Ashlawn Highland. The historic Michie Tavern is just one mile from the inn, and the University of Virginia, which was founded by Jefferson, is about seven miles away.

Innkeeper(s): Norman & Rebecca Lindway. $110-145. MC VISA AX DS. TAC10. 5 rooms with PB, 2 with FP. Breakfast and afternoon tea included in rates. Types of meals: gourmet breakfast and early coffee/tea. Picnic lunch available. Beds: KQT. Air conditioning in room. Fax on premises. Small meetings and family reunions hosted. Antiques, parks, shopping, downhill skiing, sporting events and theater nearby.

Publicity: *Gourmet, Country Inns, Bon Appetit.*

"What a magnificent room at an extraordinary place. I can't wait to tell all my friends."

Silver Thatch Inn

3001 Hollymead Dr
Charlottesville, VA 22911-7422
(804)978-4686 Fax:(804)973-6156

Circa 1780. This white clapboard inn, shaded by tall elms, was built for British officers by Hessian soldiers who were prisoners during the Revolutionary War. Before its present life as a country inn, Silver Thatch was
a boys' school, a melon
farm and a tobacco plantation. Many additions have
been made to the original
house. The original 1780
section is now called the
Hessian Room. The inn is
filled with antiques. There are three intimate dining rooms featuring fresh American cuisine.

Historic Interest: Charlottesville, Thomas Jefferson's Monticello, James Madison's Montpelier, James Monroe's Ashlawn.

Innkeeper(s): Rita & Vince Scoffone. $110-150. MC VISA AX DC CB. 7 rooms with PB, 4 with FP. Breakfast included in rates. Type of meal: continental-plus breakfast. Banquet service available. Restaurant on premises. Beds: QD. Phone and air conditioning in room. TV on premises. Antiques, fishing, shopping, sporting events and theater nearby.

Publicity: *Travel & Leisure, Washington Post, L.A. Times, New York Magazine.*

"Everything was absolutely perfect! The room, the food and above all, the people!"

Charlottesville (North Garden) E13

The Inn at the Crossroads

5010 Plank Rd
Charlottesville (North Garden), VA 22959
(804)979-6452

Circa 1820. This four-story brick inn, which is listed on the National Register of Historic Places, was built as a tavern on the road from the Shenandoah Valley to the James River. It has

been welcoming travelers since the early 19th century. The long front porch and straightforward, Federal-style architecture was common to ordinaries of that era. The four-acre grounds offer gardens of wild flowers and a swing hung under a grand oak tree, not to mention panoramic views of the foothills of the Blue Ridge Mountains. Country breakfasts are served in the inn's keeping room. The inn is nine miles south of Charlottesville, and Monticello and the University of Virginia are close by.

Innkeeper(s): Maureen & John Deis. $80-125. MC VISA PC TC. 6 rooms with PB, 6 with FP. 1 suite. 1 cottage. Breakfast and afternoon tea included in rates. Types of meals: full breakfast and early coffee/tea. Catered breakfast available. Beds: KQD. Air conditioning and ceiling fan in room. Library on premises. Weddings, small meetings, family reunions and seminars hosted. Antiques, fishing, parks, shopping, downhill skiing, cross-country skiing, sporting events, theater and watersports nearby.

Charlottesville (Palmyra)   F13

Palmer Country Manor

RR 2 Box 1390
Charlottesville (Palmyra), VA 22963-9801
(804)589-1300 (800)253-4306 Fax:(804)589-1300

Circa 1830. Each season brings a special beauty to this farmhouse surrounded by 180 wooded acres. The home and grounds originally belonged to a 2,500-acre ranch, which was named Solitude, an apt title for this secluded property. Guests can opt to stay in the historic house or in one of several little cottages. Each cheery guest room is individually appointed and includes a fireplace. The hearty country breakfasts are served in a rustic room with exposed beams and brick walls. Gourmet, candlelight dinners are another romantic option available for guests. The area is full of unique activities, including white-water rafting down the James River or taking in the view on a balloon ride.

Historic Interest: Monticello, Ashlawn and the University of Virginia are all within 20 miles of the manor.

Innkeeper(s): Gregory & Kathleen Palmer. $85-125. MC VISA AX DC DS. 12 rooms, 10 with PB, 10 with FP. Breakfast included in rates. Type of meal: full breakfast. Afternoon tea, dinner, picnic lunch, lunch, catering service and room service available. Restaurant on premises. Beds: KQ. Air conditioning in room. Bicycles on premises. 180 acres. Antiques, fishing, parks, shopping, sporting events and watersports nearby.

Chatham   I11

Eldon, The Inn at Chatham

SR 685, 1037 Chalk Level Rd
Chatham, VA 24531
(804)432-0935

Circa 1835. Beautiful gardens and white oaks surround this former tobacco plantation home set among the backdrop of the Blue Ridge Mountains. Stroll the grounds and discover sculptures and an array of flowers and plants. Southern hospitality reigns at this charming home filled with Empire antiques. Guest rooms are light and airy and tastefully decorated with beautiful linens and tradi-

tional knickknacks. Fresh flowers accentuate the bright, cheerful rooms. A lavish, Southern-style breakfast is served up each morning, and dinners at Eldon feature the gourmet creations of Chef Joel Wesley, a graduate of the Culinary Institute of America. Eldon is a popular location for weddings and parties.

Historic Interest: Danville, the first Confederate capital is 17 miles and a winery is 15 miles away. Day trips include treks to Lynchburg, Poplar Forest — the country home of Thomas Jefferson, the Roanoke Center Square and the scenic Blue Ridge Highway.

Innkeeper(s): Joy & Bob Lemm. $65-80. MC VISA PC TC. 4 rooms, 3 with PB. 1 suite. Breakfast included in rates. Types of meals: continental-plus breakfast, full breakfast, gourmet breakfast and early coffee/tea. Dinner available. Restaurant on premises. Beds: QDT. Phone, air conditioning and turndown service in room. Swimming and library on premises. Handicap access. 13 acres. Weddings, small meetings, family reunions and seminars hosted. Antiques, parks, shopping and watersports nearby.

Publicity: *Richmond Times, Chatham Star Tribune.*

"The food, the ambiance, your wonderful hospitality made for a most charming weekend."

Chincoteague   E20

Miss Molly's Inn

4141 Main St
Chincoteague, VA 23336-2464
(757)336-6686 (800)221-5620

Circa 1886. This Victorian by the bay was built by J. T. Rowley, the "Clam King of the World." His daughter Miss Molly lived here for 84 years. The house has been beautifully restored and furnished in period antiques. Marguerite Henry wrote "Misty of Chincoteague" here while rocking on the front porch with Miss Molly and Captain Jack.

Innkeeper(s): Barbara & David Wiedenheft. $69-155. 7 rooms, 5 with PB. Breakfast and afternoon tea included in rates. Type of meal: full breakfast. Beds: KDT. Phone in room.

"Your hospitality and warmth exuded with each guest and made all of us feel most at home."

The Watson House

4240 Main St
Chincoteague, VA 23336-2801
(757)336-1564 (800)336-6787 Fax:(757)336-5776

Circa 1898. Situated in town, this "painted lady" Victorian has a large front porch overlooking Main Street. The porch is a favorite spot of guests and often the location for afternoon tea and refreshments. Beach towels, chairs and bicycles are complimentary, and there is an outdoor shower for cleaning up after sunning.

Innkeeper(s): Tom & Jacque Derrickson, David & Jo Anne Snead. $65-115. MC VISA PC TC. TAC10. 6 rooms with PB. 2 cottages. Breakfast and afternoon tea included in rates. Beds: QD. Air conditioning and ceiling fan in room. Fax and bicycles on premises. Antiques, fishing, parks, shopping and watersports nearby.

Chincoteague (New Church) *E20*

The Garden and The Sea Inn

PO Box 275
Chincoteague (New Church), VA 23415-3151
(757)824-0672 (800)824-0672

Circa 1802. Gingerbread trim, a pair of brightly colored gables and two, adjacent verandas adorn the exterior of this Victorian. A

warm, rich Victorian decor permeates the antique-filled guest rooms, an ideal setting for romance. Several rooms include whirlpool tubs. The inn's dining room serves gourmet dinners with an emphasis on fresh catches from the waters of the Eastern shore, but many continental items are featured as well.

Innkeeper(s): Tom & Sara Baker. $60-165. MC VISA AX DS PC TC. TAC10. 6 rooms with PB. 1 conference room. Breakfast included in rates. Meal: continental-plus breakfast. Dinner, evening snack, picnic lunch, banquet service, catering service available. Restaurant on premises. Beds: Q. Air conditioning, ceiling fan and TV in room. VCR, fax, copier, library, pet boarding on premises. Handicap access. Weddings, small meetings, family reunions hosted. Antiques, fishing, parks, shopping, watersports nearby. Pets Allowed.

Christiansburg *H8*

Evergreen The Bell-Capozzi House

201 E Main St
Christiansburg, VA 24073-3007
(540)382-7372 (800)905-7372 Fax:(540)382-4376
E-mail: evrgrninn@aol.com

Circa 1890. Enjoy the beauty of the Blue Ridge Mountains at this Victorian inn, nestled on nearly an acre of grounds. A gazebo, swings, a porch lined with rockers, flowers, wisteria, evergreens and a lighted swimming pool are all there for guests to enjoy.

Elegant furnishings rest on polished, heart-of-pine floors. The home still maintains original light fixtures. Hearty Southern breakfasts, which might include biscuits and gravy, cheese grits, eggs, fresh fruit, homemade jams and petite pancakes, are served.

Innkeeper(s): Rocco Capozzi & Barbara Bell-Capozzi. $80-125. MC VISA AX DS PC TC. TAC10. 5 rooms with PB. 1 cottage. 1 conference room. Breakfast, afternoon tea and evening snack included in rates. Types of meals: full breakfast, gourmet breakfast and early coffee/tea. Beds: KQ. Phone, air conditioning, ceiling fan, TV and VCR in room. Fax, swimming and library on premises. Family reunions hosted. Italian spoken. Antiques, fishing, parks, shopping, cross-country skiing, sporting events, theater, watersports nearby.

Churchville *E11*

Buckhorn Inn

2487 Hankey Mountain Hwy
Churchville, VA 24421
(703)337-6900 (800)693-4242

Circa 1811. This early 19th-century Colonial served as a hospital and officers' quarters during the Civil War, and once accommodated General Stonewall Jackson. The inn's interior is

decorated in a comfortable, period style, reminiscent of Colonial times. Country cooking is the fare at the inn's restaurant, which offers a different menu each night of the week. The inn is 12 miles from Staunton.

Innkeeper(s): Jack & Linda Henry. $45-75. MC VISA DS TC. TAC10. 6 rooms with PB. 1 suite. Breakfast included in rates. Type of meal: full breakfast. Dinner, lunch, banquet service and catering service available. Restaurant on premises. Beds: KQDT. Air conditioning in room. TV and VCR on premises. 10 acres. Weddings, small meetings, family reunions and seminars hosted. Antiques, fishing, parks, shopping, sporting events, golf and theater nearby.

Cluster Springs *I12*

Oak Grove Plantation

PO Box 45
Cluster Springs, VA 24535-0045
(804)575-7137

Circa 1820. An oak grove and 400 acres of grounds surround Oak Grove Plantation. Built by Virginia legislator Thomas Easley more than 170 years ago, this bed & breakfast is still owned by his descendants. The Blue Room features a poster

bed that was hand-made for the innkeeper for her seventh birthday. The inn is filled with family antiques and old family photos. The inn is located within an hour's drive to Appomattox, and Prestwood Plantation, one of the largest plantation houses in Virginia built after the Revolutionary War and Staunton River Battlefield Park and Museum, are about 30 minutes away.

Historic Interest: Danville, last capitol of the Confederacy (one-half hour), South Boston Historical Museum (15 minutes), Halifax County Courthouse (20 minutes).

Innkeeper(s): Pickett Craddock. $60-80. PC TC. TAC10. 3 rooms. Breakfast included in rates. Type of meal: gourmet breakfast. Beds: KD. Small meetings and family reunions hosted. Spanish spoken. Antiques, fishing, parks and watersports nearby.

Publicity: *Gazette-Virginian, Register, Washington Post, Richmond Times Dispatch.*

"The food was good but the companionship was better. Thank you for such wonderful hospitality."

Covington *F9*

Milton Hall B&B Inn

207 Thorny Ln
Covington, VA 24426-5401
(540)965-0196

Circa 1874. This historic 44-acre estate adjoins the George Washington National Forest, and the inn appears as an exquisite English country manor with its buttressed porch towers, gables and Gothic trimmings. The home was built for the Viscountess of Milton, Maria Theresa Fitzwilliam, whose brother found the site while living in America and serving in the Union Army. Each spacious, romantic room boasts its own fireplace and is decorated in a different color scheme. The rooms reflect the styles of the late 1800s. A full English breakfast is served each morning and a proper afternoon tea also is offered.

Historic Interest: Humpback Bridge (2 miles), Falling Springs Waterfall (5 miles), Natural Bridge (45 miles).

Innkeeper(s): John & Vera Eckert. $75-140. MC VISA PC TC. TAC10. 6 rooms with PB, 6 with FP. 1 suite. Breakfast included in rates. Picnic lunch available. Beds: Q. Phone, air conditioning, turndown service, TV and VCR in room. 44 acres. Antiques, fishing, parks, downhill skiing and theater nearby.
Pets Allowed: Approval on case-to-case basis only.
Location: Adjoins George Washington National Forest.
Publicity: *Alleghany Highlander, Washington Post, Country Inns.*

"A lovely place, a relaxing atmosphere, delicious breakfasts, gracious hospitality. We thank you."

Culpeper D14

Fountain Hall B&B

609 S East St
Culpeper, VA 22701-3222
(540)825-8200 (800)298-4748 Fax:(540)825-7716

Circa 1859. This inn was built as a Victorian country house, but subsequent construction in the 1920s transformed Fountain Hall into a Colonial Revival manor. Guests choose from six rooms, offering amenities such as a private porch or perhaps a whirlpool tub. The innkeepers offer dinner and golf packages. Fountain Hall is close to historic sites, wineries, antique shops and golf courses.

Historic Interest: Brandy Station (5-10 miles), Chancellorsville, Wilderness (20 miles).

Innkeeper(s): Steve & Kathi Walker. $95-150. MC VISA AX DC CB DS. 6 rooms with PB. 2 suites. 1 conference room. Breakfast included in rates. Meal: continental-plus breakfast. Beds: QDT. Handicap access. Antiques, fishing nearby.
Publicity: *Culpeper Star Exponent, New York Times, Washington Post.*

"A great inn you run. We still look back on our stay at Fountain Hall as a standout."

Draper H8

Claytor Lake Homestead Inn

Rt 1, Box 184E-5, SR 651
Draper, VA 24324
(540)980-6777 (800)676-5253

Circa 1800. This inn was once a two-story log cabin built by slaves for the Ross family. It has been enlarged several times over the past century. The dining room's bay window overlooks Claytor Lake and a private beach. There is also a spectacular view of the lake from the brick-and-stone wraparound porch, which has rocking chairs and a swing. Furnishings include early American and country antiques, many collected from the historic Hotel Roanoke.

Historic Interest: Downtown Pulaski (10 minutes), Newbern (20 minutes).

Innkeeper(s): Doug & Linda Eads. $85. MC VISA DC DS PC TC. 5 rooms, 1 with PB. 2 suites. 1 conference room. Breakfast included in rates. Type of meal: early coffee/tea. Afternoon tea, dinner and catering service available. Restaurant on premises. Beds: KQD. Phone, air conditioning, turndown service, ceiling fan and VCR in room. Fax, copier, swimming, bicycles, library on premises. Weddings, small meetings, family reunions and seminars hosted. Antiques, fishing, shopping, sporting events, theater, watersports nearby.
Publicity: *Roanoke Times, Smyth County News, Southwest Times, Blue Ridge Country, Blue Ridge Digest.*

"The place to go when you want to go someplace special."

Exmore F19

The Gladstone House B&B

PO Box 296, 12108 Lincoln Ave
Exmore, VA 23350-0296
(757)442-4614 (800)262-4837 Fax:(757)442-4678
E-mail: egan@gladstonehouse.com

Circa 1938. This gracious brick Georgian Colonial was built by one of the Eastern Shore's first doctors. There are just three guest rooms, ensuring privacy. Each of the rooms is individually decorated with items such as a carved bed, four-poster bed, a dressing table or perhaps lacy curtains. The atmosphere, due in combination to hospitable hosts and gracious decor, is welcoming and friendly. Freshly squeezed orange juice, baked eggs, berry-stuffed crepes topped with orange sauce and pear bread pudding are among the dishes served for breakfast. State parks, shopping, galleries and restaurants are nearby.

Innkeeper(s): Pat & Al Egan. $65-85. MC VISA AX DS PC TC. TAC10. 3 rooms with PB, 1 with FP. Breakfast included in rates. Types of meals: gourmet breakfast and early coffee/tea. Beds: KQT. Air conditioning, turndown service, TV and VCR in room. Fax, bicycles and library on premises. Small meetings hosted. Antiques, fishing and parks nearby.
Publicity: *ES News, Virginia Pilot, Los Angeles Times.*

"We stayed for two days at the warm and friendly Gladstone House; and from our point of view, nothing could have been finer. What a treasure you have in your midst."

Fairfax C15

Bailiwick Inn

4023 Chain Bridge Rd
Fairfax, VA 22030-4101
(703)691-2266 (800)366-7666 Fax:(703)934-2112

Circa 1800. Located across from the county courthouse where George Washington's will is filed, this distinguished three-story Federal brick house recently has been renovated. The first Civil War casualty occurred on what is now the inn's lawn. The elegant, early Virginia decor is reminiscent of the state's fine plantation mansions. Ask to stay in the Thomas Jefferson Room, a replica of Mr. Jefferson's bedroom at Monticello.

Innkeeper(s): Bob & Annette Bradley. $130-295. MC VISA AX. 14 rooms with PB, 4 with FP. 1 suite. 1 conference room. Breakfast and afternoon tea included in rates. Types of meals: full breakfast, gourmet breakfast and early coffee/tea. Restaurant on premises. Beds: KQT. Phone, air conditioning, turndown service in room. VCR, fax and copier on premises. Weddings and small meetings hosted. Antiques, parks, shopping, sporting events, theater nearby.
Publicity: *Washington Post, Journal, Fairfax Connection, Inn Times, Mid-Atlantic Country, Victoria, Country Inns.*

"A visit to your establishment clearly transcends any lodging experience that I can recall."

Farmville G13

Linden B&B

RR 5 Box 2810
Farmville, VA 23901
(804)223-8443

Circa 1800. Located along the route of Lee's retreat and on more than six acres, this antebellum farmhouse once was part of a 1,500-acre tobacco plantation. The property was owned by the first president of Hampden-Sydney College. The inn's lawns often host games of croquet, while a hammock sways gently from the branches of an ancient pecan tree. A feeding station on the property helps to attract the more than 60 species of birds that are seen at Linden each year. There are stands of sunflowers and perennial and herb gardens. The spacious bedchambers are tastefully furnished in keeping with the country setting and include polished heart-pine floors, working fireplaces and period antiques. A hand-painted border in the dining room features a linden leaf motif. Red pears poached in wine, pumpkin pancakes with ginger butter and maple syrup and Canadian bacon are sample menu items. A short walk away is Briery Lake for bass fishing.

Innkeeper(s): Bob & Gretchen Rogers. $84-104. PC TC. TAC10. 2 rooms, 1 with PB, 2 with FP. Breakfast and evening snack included in rates. Types of meals: full breakfast, gourmet breakfast and early coffee/tea. Beds: KDT. Phone, air conditioning and ceiling fan in room. VCR and library on premises. Weddings hosted. Antiques, fishing, parks, shopping, sporting events, golf and theater nearby.

Publicity: *Farmville Herald, Southern Living, Atlanta Constitution.*

Fredericksburg   D15

La Vista Plantation

4420 Guinea Station Rd
Fredericksburg, VA 22408-8850
(540)898-8444 (800)529-2823 Fax:(540)898-9414

Circa 1838. La Vista has a long and unusual past, rich in Civil War history. Both Confederate and Union armies camped here, and this is where the Ninth Cavalry was sworn in. The house, a

Classical Revival structure with high ceilings and pine floors, sits on 10 acres of pasture and woods. The grounds include a pond stocked with bass. Guest quarters include a spacious room with a king-size, four-poster bed and Empire furniture or a four-room apartment that can accommodate up to six guests and includes a fireplace. Breakfasts feature homemade egg dishes from chickens raised on the property.

Historic Interest: The plantation is within 15 miles of battlefields, museums, historic homes and within an hour from historic spots such as Monticello, Mt. Vernon and Washington, D.C.
Innkeeper(s): Michele & Edward Schiesser. $95. MC VISA PC TC. TAC10. 2 rooms with PB, 2 with FP. 1 suite. 1 conference room. Breakfast included in rates. Types of meals: full breakfast and early coffee/tea. Beds: KQDT. Phone and air conditioning in room. Copier and library on premises. 10 acres. Amusement parks, antiques, fishing, parks, shopping, sporting events, theater and watersports nearby.
Location: Just outside historic Fredericksburg.
Publicity: *Free Lance Star, Mid-Atlantic Country.*

"Coming here was an excellent choice. La Vista is charming, quiet and restful, all qualities we were seeking. Breakfast was delicious."

Gordonsville   E13

Sleepy Hollow Farm B&B

16280 Blue Ridge Tpke
Gordonsville, VA 22942-8214
(703)832-5555 (800)215-4804 Fax:(703)832-2515

Circa 1785. Many generations have added to this brick farmhouse with its 18th-century dining room and bedrooms. The pink and white room was frequently visited by a friendly ghost

from Civil War days, according to local stories. She hasn't been seen for several years since the innkeeper, a former missionary, had the house blessed. The grounds include an herb garden, a pond with gazebo, a chestnut slave cabin, terraces and abundant wildlife.

Historic Interest: Montpelier (5 miles), James Madison Museum (6 miles), Wilderness Battlefields (30 miles), Civil War Exchange Hotel (4 miles), Fredericksburg (30 miles).

Innkeeper(s): Beverley Allison & Dorsey Allison Comer. $65-125. MC VISA AX. 6 rooms with PB, 2 with FP. 3 suites. Types of meals: full breakfast and early coffee/tea. Afternoon tea available. Beds: QDT. Air conditioning in room. VCR, fax, copier and child care on premises. 11 acres. Small meetings and family reunions hosted. Antiques, fishing, parks, shopping, downhill skiing, sporting events and theater nearby. Pets Allowed: $10 - cottage.

Location: Between Gordonsville & Somerset on Rt 231.

Publicity: *Orange County Review, City Magazine, Town & County.*

"This house is truly blessed."

Tivoli

9171 Tivoli Dr
Gordonsville, VA 22942-8115
(703)832-2225 (800)840-2225 Fax:(540)832-3691
E-mail: tivolibnb@aol.com

Circa 1903. Innkeeper Phil Audibert's family has owned this gracious mansion since the 1950s, but it wasn't until 1990 that he and wife Susie renovated the home and opened for guests. The commanding home, which is surrounded by a 235-acre cattle farm, affords views of the Blue Ridge Mountains. Tastefully decorated rooms are filled with antiques that span four centuries, and each guest room boasts a working fireplace. The home is near plenty of historic attractions, including Montpelier, the home of James Madison, and several Civil War sites.

Innkeeper(s): Phil & Susie Audibert. $90-125. MC VISA PC TC. TAC10. 4 rooms with PB, 4 with FP. 1 conference room. Breakfast included in rates. Types of meals: continental breakfast, continental-plus breakfast, full breakfast, gourmet breakfast and early coffee/tea. Beds: KQTD. Phone, air conditioning and ceiling fan in room. TV, VCR, fax and copier on premises. Weddings, small meetings, family reunions and seminars hosted. French spoken. Antiques, fishing, parks, shopping, downhill skiing, cross-country skiing, sporting events, golf and theater nearby.

Goshen   E10

The Hummingbird Inn

PO Box 147, 30 Wood Ln
Goshen, VA 24439-0147
(540)997-9065 (800)397-3214 Fax:(540)997-0289
E-mail: hmgbird@cfw.com

Circa 1853. This early Victorian villa is located in the Shenandoah Valley against the backdrop of the Allegheny Mountains. Both the first and second floors offer wraparound verandas. Furnished with antiques, the inn features a library and sitting room with fireplaces. The rustic den and one guest room comprise the oldest portions of the inn, built around 1780. Four-course dinners, which include wine, are available by advance reservation. An old barn and babbling creek are on the grounds. Lexington, the Virginia Horse Center, Natural Bridge, the Blue Ridge Parkway and antiquing are all nearby.

Historic Interest: Historic Lexington, Stonewall Jackson House & Museum, Lee Chapel (23 minutes). Monticello (70 minutes).

Innkeeper(s): Diana & Jeremy Robinson. $85-145. MC VISA AX DS PC TC. TAC10. 5 rooms with PB, 2 with FP. Breakfast included in rates. Types of meals: full breakfast and early coffee/tea. Beds: Q. Air conditioning and ceiling fan in room. VCR, fax, library on premises. Handicap access. Antiques, fishing, shopping, downhill skiing, cross-country skiing and theater nearby.

Pets Allowed: Dogs with prior arrangements.

Publicity: *Blue Ridge Country, Inn Spots and Special Places.*

"We enjoyed our stay so much that we returned two weeks later on our way back for a delicious home-cooked dinner, comfortable attractive atmosphere, and familiar faces to welcome us after a long journey."

Harrisonburg   D12

Joshua Wilton House

412 S Main St
Harrisonburg, VA 22801-3611
(540)434-4464

Circa 1888. This beautifully restored Victorian has served as a variety of dwellings. First a family home, it was later used by a fraternity and then converted into apartments. Today, the inn offers a wonderful glimpse back into the Victorian era. Light, airy rooms are elegant, full of antiques, and each room includes access to a small reading area. Meals at the Wilton House are a treat. A typical breakfast at the home includes fresh fruit, pastries, delectable entrees and gourmet coffees.

Guests need not stray far from their rooms to enjoy gourmet cuisine, the innkeepers run a highly recommended restaurant on the premises. Don't forget to ask about special events.

Historic Interest: The inn, surrounded by the Blue Ridge Mountains, is within walking distance of historic downtown Harrisonburg and James Madison Univ.

Innkeeper(s): Roberta & Craig Moore. $100-120. MC VISA AX PC TC. TAC10. 5 rooms with PB, 1 with FP. Breakfast included in rates. Meals: continental-plus breakfast, full breakfast, gourmet breakfast and early coffee/tea. Dinner available. Restaurant on premises. Beds: Q. Phone, air conditioning, turndown service, ceiling fan in room. Fax and copier on premises. Weddings, small meetings, family reunions and seminars hosted. Amusement parks, antiques, fishing, parks, shopping, downhill skiing, sporting events nearby.

Publicity: *Richmond Times Dispatch, Bon Appetit, Sunday New York Times, Harrisonburg Daily News Record, Southern Living.*

Hot Springs   E10

King's Victorian Inn

Rt 1, Box 622
Hot Springs, VA 24445
(540)839-3134

Circa 1899. No matter the season, guests will feel welcome by the very sight of this charming gabled Victorian. In the spring and summer, trees shade the wraparound veranda. In the winter

months, warm lights glow in the windows, and during the Christmas season, a wreath is placed at each window. The healing powers of the hot springs brought Dr. Henry Pole to the town, and he built this house which features stained glass, pocket doors, high ceilings and a signature staircase. Guest rooms feature 18th-century reproductions and antiques. After a homemade country breakfast, meander down a walking trail to Hot Springs downtown area, where boutiques and antique shops await.

Innkeeper(s): Liz & Richard King. $85-150. PC TC. 8 rooms, 4 with PB. 1 suite. 2 cottages. Breakfast included in rates. Type of meal: full breakfast. Beds: QD. Small meetings and family reunions hosted. Antiques, fishing, parks, shopping, skiing, golf, theater and watersports nearby.

Publicity: *Roanoke Times, Richmond Times Dispatch, Country Magazine.*

Keswick   E13

Keswick Hall

701 Club Dr
Keswick, VA 22947
(804)979-3440 (800)274-5391 Fax:(804)977-4171
E-mail: keswick@keswick.com

Circa 1911. This breathtaking Italianate inn offers the poshest of decor surrounded by an exquisite 600-acre Virginia country estate. The English-country decor includes Laura Ashley prints and fine furnishings, such as canopy beds draped in the finest of fabrics. The historic wing of the inn was known as the Villa Crawford, and some of the original family heirlooms decorate the rooms. Guests are pampered with breakfast and afternoon tea, and gourmet, prix fixe dinners also are available.

There is an indoor and outdoor pool, tennis courts, an 18-hole golf course, spa and fitness area available at the Keswick Club, and guests enjoy privileges. Keswick Hall has equally stunning sister inns in Maryland and Wales.

Innkeeper(s): Stephen Beaumont. $225-595. MC VISA AX DC CB PC TC. TAC10. 48 rooms with PB. 4 suites. 2 conference rooms. Breakfast and afternoon tea included in rates. Types of meals: continental breakfast, continental-plus breakfast, full breakfast and early coffee/tea. Evening snack, picnic lunch, lunch, banquet service and catered breakfast available. Beds: KQDT. Phone, air conditioning, turndown service and TV in room. VCR, fax, copier, spa, swimming, sauna, bicycles, tennis, library and child care on premises. Handicap access. 600 acres. Weddings, small meetings and seminars hosted. French and Japanese spoken. Antiques, fishing, parks, shopping, downhill skiing, cross-country skiing, sporting events, golf and theater nearby.

Publicity: *Southern Living, Southern Accents, Washington Post, New York Times, Great Country Inns of America.*

Lexington   F11

Historic Country Inns of Lexington

11 N Main St
Lexington, VA 24450-2520
(540)463-2044 Fax:(540)463-7262

Circa 1789. Three inns comprise this group of country inns. Maple Hall, a beautiful three-story, columned plantation on 56 acres in the country, boasts a stocked fishing pond, dining facilities, tennis court and swimming pool. Or you can choose from two in-town locations: the Georgian-style Alexander-Winthrow House or the McCampbell Inn. All three are handsomely furnished with antiques, paintings and Oriental rugs. The 18 rooms at Maple Hall have fireplaces.

Historic Interest: Stonewall Jackson's home, Robert E. Lee's home and museum, George C. Marshall Museum, Virginia Military Institute.
Innkeeper(s): Don Fredenburg. $100-145. EP. MC VISA TC. 44 rooms with PB. 13 suites. 1 conference room. Breakfast included in rates. Type of meal: continental breakfast. Afternoon tea and banquet service available. Restaurant on premises. Beds: QDT. Phone, air conditioning and TV in room. VCR, fax and copier on premises. Weddings, small meetings, family reunions, seminars hosted. Antiques, fishing, shopping, sporting events, theater nearby.
Publicity: *Washington Post, Lexington News Gazette.*

"This was a very enjoyable, relaxing and immaculate place to stay. So much nicer than hotels."

Seven Hills Inn

408 S Main St
Lexington, VA 24450-2346
(540)463-4715 (888)845-3801 Fax:(540)463-6526

Circa 1929. This Colonial Revival house stands in the heart of the Shenandoah Valley. Carefully renovated, the inn's white columns and brick exterior are reminiscent of a Southern plantation. The guest rooms, named after area homesteads, are furnished with antiques and reproductions, and the Fruit Hill room offers a Jacuzzi tub. Within a 10-minute walk is Washington and Lee University, the Virginia Military Institute and the Lexington Visitors Center.
Innkeeper(s): Shirley Ducommun. $75-125. MC VISA AX PC TC. 7 rooms, 6 with PB. 1 suite. Breakfast included in rates. Types of meals: full breakfast and early coffee/tea. Afternoon tea and catering service available. Beds: QDT. TV, VCR, fax, copier and library on premises. Weddings, small meetings and family reunions hosted. Antiques, fishing, parks, shopping, sporting events, theater and watersports nearby.

"It's like visiting a favorite aunt."

Stoneridge B&B

PO Box 38
Lexington, VA 24450
(540)463-4090 (800)491-2930 Fax:(540)463-6078

Circa 1829. The Shenandoah Valley is the setting for this bed & breakfast, located on 36 woodsy acres, complete with steams and rolling lawns. The inn was built using bricks made on the property, and once served as a plantation home and possibly a stagecoach stop. The home still maintains original heart-of-pine floors, ornate mantels and other period features. Guest rooms feature antiques, some are family heirlooms. Three guest rooms include fireplaces, and two offer double Jacuzzi tubs. Several rooms have a mountain view. A variety of reading material is available in the library. Stoneridge offers a large selection of Virginia wines to its guests for purchase. The four-course country breakfasts might include buttermilk pancakes, quiche or savory souffles, and the meals are served by candlelight.

Innkeeper(s): Norm & Barbara Rollenhagen. $105-160. MC VISA AX DS PC TC. TAC10. 5 rooms with PB, 3 with FP. 1 suite. Breakfast included in rates. Types of meals: full breakfast and early coffee/tea. Beds: Q. Air conditioning, turndown service, ceiling fan in room. TV, VCR, fax, library on premises. 36 acres. Antiques, fishing, parks, shopping, cross-country skiing, theater nearby.
Publicity: *News-Gazette.*

Lincoln

Springdale Country Inn

RR 2 Box 356
Lincoln, VA 20160
(540)338-1832 Fax:(540)338-1839

Circa 1832. Recently restored for historic certification, the Springdale Country Inn was once a schoolhouse, Civil War hospital and traveler's inn. The inn, with its high ceilings and windows, has richly burnished wide-board floors, reproduction wallpaper and period antiques. Guest rooms have fresh flowers, stenciled walls and four-poster canopy beds. Several offer private baths and fireplaces. Enjoy the sun and sitting porch, pleasant gardens and local folklore of the area and the school itself. Vineyards and Civil War battlefields are located nearby.
Innkeeper(s): Nancy & Roger Fones. $95-125. MC VISA PC. TAC8. 9 rooms, 6 with PB, 4 with FP. 2 suites. 2 conference rooms. Breakfast included in rates. Type of meal: full breakfast. Catering service available. Beds: DT. VCR, fax, copier and library on premises. Handicap access. Weddings, small meetings, family reunions, seminars hosted. Antiques, shopping, theater nearby.
Publicity: *Pamphlet, Washington Post.*

"Quaint setting and excellent meals."

Locust Dale   *D13*

The Inn at Meander Plantation

HC 5, Box 460A
Locust Dale, VA 22948-9701
(540)672-4912 (800)385-4936 Fax:(540)672-0405
E-mail: inn@meander-plantation

Circa 1766. This elegant country estate was built by Henry Fry, close friend of Thomas Jefferson, who often stopped here on his way to Monticello. Ancient formal boxwood gardens, woodland and meadows are enjoyed by guests as well as views of the Blue Ridge Mountains from the rockers on the back porches. The mansion is decorated serenely with elegant antiques and period reproductions, including queen-size, four-poster beds. The innkeeper is a food writer and will prepare special breakfasts for individual diets. Full dinner service and picnic baskets are available with advance reservations.

Historic Interest: Prehistoric Native American site on the property near the Robinson River. James and Dolley Madison's home (10 miles), Civil War battlefields: Cedar Mountain (4 miles), Brandy Station (15 miles), Manassas and Bull Run (50 miles).
Innkeeper(s): Bob & Suzie Blanchard, Suzanne Thomas. $95-185. MC VISA PC TC. TAC10. 8 rooms with PB, 5 with FP. 4 suites. 1 conference room. Breakfast included in rates. Types of meals: full breakfast and early coffee/tea. Afternoon tea, evening snack, picnic lunch and lunch available. Beds: KQD. Air conditioning in room. VCR, fax, stables, library, pet boarding and child care on premises. 80 acres. Weddings, small meetings, family reunions and seminars hosted. Antiques, fishing, parks, shopping, skiing, sporting events and theater nearby. Pets Allowed: In dependencies only.

"Staying at the Inn at Meander Plantation feels like being immersed in another century while having the luxuries and amenities available today."

Luray C13

Locust Grove Inn

1456 N Egypt Bend Rd
Luray, VA 22835
(540)743-1804 Fax:(540)843-0751
E-mail: locustg@shentel.net

Circa 1765. Virginia was still under Royal rule when this Colonial home was built on what was once a Native American campsite. The first owner fought in the Revolutionary War. The Shenandoah River, which runs in front of the house, offers splendid scenery guests won't soon forget and the porches offer mountain views. The innkeepers have preserved the house's history, and although completely restored, pre-Civil War antiques and decor maintain its 18th- and early 19th-century ambiance. The inn still maintains original paint decorations and graining in the parlor and on the staircases, and unique whitewash cartoons from before 1816 decorate exposed log walls. The bedrooms display early American antiques, offer views of the mountains, river or both, and one room has a stone fireplace. Healthy items such as crepes filled with banana and wildflower honey cream, breads and fresh fruit are served at breakfast. After the morning meal, guests can enjoy a walk on the inn's scenic 53 acres, including meadows and a mile of riverfront.

Historic Interest: New Market Battlefield, Museum of Frontier Culture, Luray Caverns and Historic Car and Carriage Museum.

Innkeeper(s): Rod & Isabel Graves. $100-125. MC VISA DS PC TC. TAC10. 5 rooms with PB, 3 with FP. Breakfast included in rates. Type of meal: gourmet breakfast. Evening snack available. Beds: Q. 53 acres. Small meetings and family reunions hosted. French and Portuguese spoken. Antiques, fishing, parks, shopping and watersports nearby.

"Appointments and restoration were matched only by the wonderful cooking!"

Mayneview

439 Mechanic St
Luray, VA 22835-1818
(540)743-7921 Fax:(540)743-1191
E-mail: maynevu@shentel.net

Circa 1865. Located on three-and-a-half rolling acres, the inn, grape arbor, spa and cottage all share a 300-degree view of the mountains. Guest rooms offer fireplaces, featherbeds and antiques. A sample breakfast features English muffins, coddled eggs and sausage, Belgian waffles and vanilla cream sauce. Late sleepers are pampered with cooked-to-order breakfasts, and with advance notice, guests may have breakfast in bed. Nearby are Luray Caverns, the New Market Battlefield, country auctions and antique shops.

$80-125. MC VISA AX DS PC TC. TAC10. 5 rooms with PB, 3 with FP. 1 cottage. Breakfast and afternoon tea included in rates. Types of meals: gourmet breakfast and early coffee/tea. Lunch and room service available. Beds: KQD. Air conditioning in room. TV, VCR, fax and spa on premises. Weddings, small meetings, family reunions and seminars hosted. Antiques, fishing, parks, downhill skiing, golf and watersports nearby.

Shenandoah River Inn

201 Stagecoach Ln
Luray, VA 22835
(540)743-1144 (888)666-6760 Fax:(540)743-9101

Circa 1812. This gracious two-and-a-half-story white colonial inn, on four landscaped acres along the Shenandoah River, was once a stagecoach stop. Graceful walnut trees and fruit trees dot the property's wide lawns. There are three screened porches, all with water views. Guest rooms each have fireplaces, marble-floored baths and king or queen beds. Antiques, paintings, mirrors and a fireplace decorate the parlor. Gourmet candle-lit breakfasts may include Belgian waffles, fruit plate and breakfast meats. Seven-course dinners are available. Picnic by the river or try your hand at smallmouth-bass fishing. The innkeepers also offer a secluded cabin surrounded by the National Forest on top of the mountain with a 50-mile view.

Innkeeper(s): Paul Bramell & Ann Merrigan. $110-125. MC VISA AX PC TC. TAC10. 4 rooms with PB, 4 with FP. 1 cabin. Breakfast and afternoon tea included in rates. Meals: gourmet breakfast, early coffee/tea. Picnic lunch available. Beds: KQ. Air conditioning in room. TV, VCR, copier, swimming on premises. Handicap access. Weddings, small meetings, family reunions, seminars hosted. Antiques, parks, shopping, downhill skiing, golf, watersports nearby.
Publicity: *Washingtonian.*

Woodruff House

330 Mechanic St
Luray, VA 22835-1808
(540)743-1496 Fax:(540)743-1722

Circa 1882. Prepare to be pampered. The Woodruffs entered the B&B business after years of experience in hotel management and restaurant business. They have not missed a detail, ensuring a perfect, relaxing visit. The Log Cabin Suite is often the room of choice because of its interesting shape and architecture, located where the attic was before restoration. The suite boasts skylights, jacuzzi tub for two and antique stained glass. Tasteful antiques and fresh bouquets of flowers framed by candlelight add a special ambiance. Besides the extra attention and comfortable accommodations, the Woodruffs include a high tea/buffet dinner, early morning coffee or tea and a full fireside gourmet breakfast in the rates. Ask for breakfast in bed if you so desire. Candlelight sets the mood for dinner, and none of the spectacular meals are to be missed. A romantic finish to each evening is a private dip in one of the garden hot tubs.

Historic Interest: New Market Battlefield (20 minutes), the famous underground Luray Caverns discovered in the late 1800s (minutes away).
Innkeeper(s): Lucas & Deborah Woodruff. $98-195. MAP. MC VISA DS PC TC. TAC10. 5 rooms with PB, 5 with FP. 1 suite. 1 conference room. Breakfast, afternoon tea, dinner included in rates. Meals: gourmet breakfast, early coffee/tea. Catering service, catered breakfast, room service available. Beds: QDT. Air conditioning, ceiling fan in room. TV, VCR, fax, spa, bicycles, library on premises. Weddings, small meetings, family reunions hosted. Antiques, fishing, parks, shopping, downhill skiing, watersports nearby.
Publicity: *Potomac Living.*

"The place is great. There aren't words to explain!"

Lynchburg G11

Federal Crest Inn

1101 Federal St
Lynchburg, VA 24504-3018
(804)845-6155 (800)818-6155 Fax:(804)845-1445

Circa 1909. The guest rooms at Federal Crest are named for the many varieties of trees and flowers native to Virginia. This handsome red brick home, a fine example of Georgian Revival architecture, features a commanding front entrance flanked by columns that hold up the second-story veranda. A grand staircase, carved woodwork, polished floors topped with fine rugs and more columns create an aura of elegance. Each guest room offers something special and romantic, from a mountain view to a Jacuzzi tub. Breakfasts are served on fine china, and the first course is always a freshly baked muffin with a secret message inside.

Historic Interest: Appomattox Court House and Jefferson's Poplar Forest.
Innkeeper(s): Ann & Phil Ripley. $85-125. MC VISA AX DS PC TC. TAC10. 5 rooms, 4 with PB, 3 with FP. 2 suites. 1 conference room. Breakfast and evening snack included in rates. Types of meals: full breakfast, gourmet breakfast and early coffee/tea. Afternoon tea, picnic lunch and room service available. Beds: QD. Phone, air conditioning, turndown service and TV in room. VCR, fax, copier and library on premises. Weddings, small meetings, family reunions and seminars hosted. Antiques, parks, shopping, downhill skiing, sporting events and theater nearby.

"What a wonderful place to celebrate our birthdays and enjoy our last romantic getaway before the birth of our first child."

Lynchburg Mansion Inn B&B

405 Madison St
Lynchburg, VA 24504-2455
(804)528-5400 (800)352-1199

Circa 1914. This regal, Georgian mansion, with its majestic Greek Revival columns, is located on a brick-paved street in the Garland Hill Historic District. The grand hall showcases an oak and cherry staircase that leads up to the solarium. Breakfasts are served in the formal dining room on antique china. Romantic rooms feature inviting touches such as a four-poster beds, Laura Ashley and Ralph Lauren linens, Battenburg lace pillows and some include fireplaces. The Veranda Suite, as the name suggests, opens onto a romantic circular veranda and a treetop sunroom. The Garden Suite, with its private garden entrance, includes an original clawfoot tub.
There is a hot tub on the back porch, and the innkeepers have added gardens full of perennials, herbs, edible flowers and more, including a picturesque gazebo. Lynchburg offers many exciting activities, including the unique Community Market and plenty of galleries, antique shops and boutiques. Ski areas are about 45 minutes from the inn.

Historic Interest: Poplar Forest, Thomas Jefferson's retreat and Appomattox Court House are among dozens of historic attractions in the area. The Old City Cemetery serves as the resting place for more than 2,500 Confederate soldiers. The home of acclaimed poet and figure of the Harlem Renaissance, Anne Spencer is nearby, as are five historic districts.
Innkeeper(s): Mauranna Sherman. $109-144. MC VISA AX DC. 5 rooms with PB, 3 with FP. 2 suites. 1 conference room. Breakfast included in rates. Types of meals: full breakfast, gourmet breakfast and early coffee/tea. Beds:

KQ. Phone, air conditioning, turndown service and TV in room. Handicap access. Weddings, small meetings, family reunions and seminars hosted. Antiques, shopping, downhill skiing, sporting events and theater nearby.
Location: Lynchburg is three hours from Washington, D.C.
Publicity: *News & Advance, Roanoker.*

"The Lynchburg Mansion Inn is the creme de la creme. You have earned all sorts of pats on the back for the restoration and hospitality you offer. It is truly elegant."

Madison D13

Dulaney Hollow at Old Rag Mountain B&B & Antiques

Star Route 6 Box 215 - Scenic Va Byway
Madison, VA 22727
(540)923-4470 Fax:(540)923-4470

Circa 1902. Period furnishings decorate this Victorian manor house on 15 acres in the foothills of the Blue Ridge Mountains. There are rustic cottages available, shaded lawns and old farm buildings. A country breakfast is served, and picnic baskets may be packed for you to take on a bicycle jaunt or for hiking the hills around the Shenandoah River and National Park. A walk up the inn's pasture provides a great view of the Blue Ridge. Monticello and Montpelier are within an hour's drive.

Innkeeper(s): Susan & Louis Cable. $65-120. 1 suite. Picnic lunch available. Ceiling fan in room. VCR and pet boarding on premises. Weddings, family reunions and seminars hosted. Antiques, shopping, cross-country skiing, sporting events and theater nearby.

Madisonville

Sleepy Lamb B&B

Rts 47 & 649
Madisonville, VA 23958
(804)248-6289

Circa 1900. Among the things you'll find at this bed & breakfast are 45 acres of woods and grazing pastures for the farm's resident sheep and goats. There are three guest rooms, decorated with antiques the innkeepers found at local shops, as well as family heirlooms. One room includes a four-poster bed, another boasts a canopy bed. Two rooms include a fireplace. Innkeeper Judy
Bernaldo is a horse lover and has a collection of horse statues on display. The home was built by a local farm owner for his son, who was a doctor. Children are invited to join in and help tend to the many farm animals. The area is full of historic sites, from Appomattox Court House to Civil War battlefields.

Innkeeper(s): Ron & Judy Bernaldo. $60-65. MC VISA PC. 3 rooms with PB. Breakfast included in rates. Types of meals: full breakfast and early coffee/tea. Beds: Q. Air conditioning and ceiling fan in room. TV, VCR, fax, copier and stables on premises. 45 acres. Antiques, parks, shopping nearby.
Publicity: *Virginia Business.*

Mathews   G17

Ravenswood Inn

PO Box 1430
Mathews, VA 23109-1430
(804)725-7272

Circa 1913. This intimate waterfront home is located on five acres along the banks of the East River, where passing boats still harvest crabs and oysters. A long screened porch captures river breezes. Most rooms feature a river view and are decorated in Victorian, country, nautical or wicker. Williamsburg, Jamestown and Yorktown are within an hour.

Innkeeper(s): Ricky Durham. $70-120. TC. 5 rooms with PB. Breakfast included in rates. Types of meals: gourmet breakfast and early coffee/tea. Beds: KQT. Air conditioning and ceiling fan in room. TV, VCR and spa on premises. Weddings, small meetings and family reunions hosted. Amusement parks, antiques, shopping, sporting events, theater and watersports nearby.
Publicity: *Virginian Pilot, Daily Press.*

"While Ravenswood is one of the most beautiful places we've ever been, it is your love, caring and friendship that has made it such a special place for us."

Middleburg   C14

Welbourne

22314 Welbourne Farm Ln
Middleburg, VA 20117
(540)687-3201

Circa 1775. This seventh-generation mansion once presided over 3,000 acres. With family members starting their own estates, Welbourne now stands at 600 acres. Furnishings and carpets were collected during world travels over the past 200 years and display a faded elegance of the past. Civil War stories fill the family history book, shared with guests. In the 1930s, F. Scott Fitzgerald and Thomas Wolfe and their literary friends used the house as a setting for their writings.

Innkeeper(s): Nathaniel Morison III. $85-96. 7 rooms with PB, 7 with FP. 2 suites. 1 conference room. Breakfast included in rates. Type of meal: full breakfast. Beds: QT. Phone in room.
Location: Fifty miles west of Washington, D.C.

"Furnishings portray a house and home that's been around for a long, long time. And none of it is held back from guests. Life today at Welbourne is quiet and unobtrusive. It's genteel—Philip Hayward, Country Magazine."

Millboro   E10

Fort Lewis Lodge

HCR 3 Box 21A
Millboro, VA 24460
(540)925-2314 Fax:(540)925-2352

Circa 1840. Colonel Charles Lewis, under the command of George Washington, built one of a string of forts on this property to protect the southern pass of the Shenandoah Mountains from Indian raids. Guests at this 3,200-acre mountain farm will revel in its natural beauty. Guests can stay in the

charming lodge rooms, including "sleeping in the round", in bedrooms built into a silo. The innkeepers also offer two historic hand-hewn log cabins boasting stone fireplaces. A restored 19th-century grist mill is where guests will enjoy the plentiful meals prepared by innkeeper Caryl Cowden, who serves up a variety of homemade fare. The area is full of hiking, biking, hunting and fishing possibilities.

Historic Interest: A half-hour drive takes guests to Warm Springs, which includes soothing mineral baths designed by Thomas Jefferson. The famed Homestead Resort is five miles farther in Hot Springs.
Innkeeper(s): John & Caryl Cowden. $135-190. MC VISA. 13 rooms with PB. Breakfast and dinner included in rates. Type of meal: full breakfast. Picnic lunch available. Restaurant on premises. Beds: KQT. 3200 acres. Weddings, small meetings, family reunions and seminars hosted. Antiques, fishing and watersports nearby.
Publicity: *Outside, AAA Today, Mid-Atlantic Country, Tasteful, Rural Living, Country, Washington Post.*

"We have stayed at many inns in France, England and Germany, none have impressed me as much as yours. You have made the most of a beautiful piece of property and I feel privileged to share it with you."

Mount Jackson   C12

Widow Kip's Country Inn

355 Orchard Dr
Mount Jackson, VA 22842-9753
(540)477-2400 (800)478-8714
E-mail: widodip@shentel.net

Circa 1830. This restored homestead with its sweeping view of the Massanutten Mountains is situated on seven acres. It's a stone's throw from a fork of the Shenandoah River. Locally crafted quilts enhance the four-poster, sleigh and hand-carved Victorian beds. Two restored cottages (the Silk Purse and Sow's Ear) create a Williamsburg-style courtyard. The inn offers a full country breakfast with homemade cakes and breads.

Historic Interest: Battlefields, Monticello, Sky Line Drive and Blue Ridge Parkway.
Innkeeper(s): Betty & Bob Luse. $65-85. MC VISA PC TC. TAC10. 5 rooms with PB, 5 with FP. 1 suite. 2 cottages. Breakfast included in rates. Types of meals: full breakfast and early coffee/tea. Beds: QD. Air conditioning, ceiling fan and TV in room. Swimming, bicycles and pet boarding on premises. Weddings, family reunions hosted. Antiques, fishing, parks, shopping, down-hill skiing, sporting events, theater, watersports nearby. Pets Allowed.
Location: I-81 to Mt. Jackson. Exit 273 to Rte 11, south to 263W to Rte 698.
Publicity: *Country Inns, Mid-Atlantic Country, Americana, Sojourner, Washington Post, Country.*

"You have set a standard of professional excellence, we will be back."

New Market   C12

A Touch of Country B&B

9329 Congress St
New Market, VA 22844-9508
(540)740-8030

Circa 1870. This white clapboard Shenandoah Valley I-frame house has a second-story pediment centered above the veranda entrance. It was built by Captain William Rice, commander of the New Market Cavalry, and the house sits on what was once a battleground of the Civil War. Rice's unit

was highly praised by General Lee. Guest chambers are in the main house and in the handsome carriage house.

Historic Interest: New Market Battlefield Historical Park.

Innkeeper(s): Jean Schoellig/Dawn Kasow. $60-75. MC VISA AX DS PC TC. TAC10. 6 rooms with PB. Breakfast included in rates. Types of meals: full breakfast and early coffee/tea. Beds: QDT. Air conditioning in room. TV and VCR on premises. Antiques, fishing, parks, shopping, downhill skiing, cross-country skiing, sporting events and watersports nearby.

Publicity: *USA Today Weekend, Country.*

"Every morning should start with sunshine, bird song and Dawn's strawberry pancakes."

Red Shutter Farmhouse B&B

RR 1 Box 376
New Market, VA 22844-9306
(540)740-4281 Fax:(540)740-4661

Circa 1790. For generations, the veranda at the Red Shutter has been the location of choice during summer to view the valley and mountains. Located on 20 acres, the inn offers large rooms and suites and a library/conference room. Breakfast is in the dining room. Enjoy drives to the many area caverns, New Market Battlefield and Skyline Drive.

Innkeeper(s): Juanita Miller. $55-70. MC VISA PC TC. TAC10. 5 rooms, 3 with PB. 3 with FP. 1 suite. 1 conference room. Breakfast included in rates. Types of meals: full breakfast and early coffee/tea. Beds: KQDT. Ceiling fan in room. VCR, fax and library on premises. 20 acres. Antiques, fishing, parks, shopping, downhill skiing, cross-country skiing and theater nearby.

Norfolk   H18

Page House Inn

323 Fairfax Ave
Norfolk, VA 23507-2215
(757)625-5033 (800)599-7659 Fax:(757)623-9451
E-mail: innkeeper@pagehouseinn.com

Circa 1899. This pristinely renovated Georgian Revival inn, in the National Register, is located in the Ghent Historic District. The parlor features polished wood floors, an Oriental carpet, period antiques, paintings and an elegant fireplace. Ask for the room with the king-size canopy bed, fireplace, sunken hot tub, bidet and steam shower for two. Amenities include luxury linens and robes and turn-down service is available by request. There are solid oak doors, insulated walls and floors, valet laundry and daily maid service. Breakfast may include fresh-baked cream scones and oatmeal with heavy cream, served in the dining room or provided bedside in-suite with candlelight. Nearby are the Stockley Gardens and the Chrysler Museum of Art with original works by Andy Warhol and Edward Hopper. Ask about the inn's new offering: "boat and breakfast" in the 43-foot Nauticat yacht, "Bianca," on the Norfolk waterfront.

Innkeeper(s): Stephanie DiBelardino. $100-175. MC VISA AX PC TC. TAC10. 6 rooms with PB, 4 with FP. 2 suites. Breakfast, afternoon tea and evening snack included in rates. Types of meals: full breakfast and early coffee/tea. Room service available. Beds: KQDT. Phone, air conditioning, turndown service, ceiling fan and VCR in room. Fax and copier on premises. Small meetings hosted. Italian and some Spanish spoken. Amusement parks, antiques, fishing, parks, sporting events, golf, theater and watersports nearby.

Location: Ghent historic district.

Publicity: *Country Inns, Mid-Atlantic, Travel & Leisure, Southern Living.*

"What a treat this is to write a thank you note regarding 'quality', which I define as giving someone more than they expect."

Orange   E13

Hidden Inn

249 Caroline St
Orange, VA 22960-1529
(540)672-3625 Fax:(540)672-5029

Circa 1880. Acres of huge old trees can be seen from the wrap-around veranda of this Victorian inn nestled in the Virginia countryside. Guests are pampered with afternoon tea, and a candlelight picnic can be ordered. Monticello, Montpelier, wineries, shopping and antiquing all are nearby, and after a day of exploring the area, guests can arrange a candlelight dinner at the inn.

Historic Interest: The house was built by a descendent of Thomas Jefferson.

Innkeeper(s): Barbara & Ray Lonick, Chrys Dermody. $99-169. MC VISA AX PC TC. TAC10. 10 rooms with PB, 2 with FP. 2 cottages. Breakfast and afternoon tea included in rates. Meals: full breakfast, early coffee/tea. Beds: KQDT. Phone in room. TV, VCR, fax, copier, library on premises. Weddings, small meetings, family reunions, seminars hosted. Spanish spoken. Antiques, fishing, shopping, sporting events, theater, watersports nearby.

Location: Intersection of Rte 15 & Rte 20.

Publicity: *Forbes, Washington Post, Country Inns, Learning Channel, Inn Country USA.*

"It just doesn't get any better than this!"

The Holladay House

155 W Main St
Orange, VA 22960-1528
(540)672-4893 (800)358-4422 Fax:(540)672-3028

Circa 1830. Each room in this Federal-style inn is furnished with family pieces and comes with its own sitting area. Rooms are decorated with freshly cut flowers. Breakfast may be served to guests in their rooms. Specialties include apple muffins and puffs. Nearby attractions include wineries, antique shops, arts and crafts stores and President James Madison's home, Montpelier.

Innkeeper(s): Pete & Phebe Holladay. $95-105. 4 rooms with PB. 2 suites. Type of meal: early coffee/tea. Room service available.

Location: Ninety minutes from Washington or Richmond.

"Thank you so much for your wonderful hospitality (and apple puffs, apple puffs, apple puffs!!). We will definitely be back!"

Petersburg   G15

Mayfield Inn

PO Box 2265
Petersburg, VA 23804-1565
(804)861-6775 (800)538-2381

Circa 1750. Mayfield Inn is the oldest existing brick building in Dinwiddie County, and although many records have been lost, its probable first resident was a member of the Virginia House of Burgesses. During the Civil War, two Confederate defense lines were set up on the Mayfield Inn's grounds, and the battles were viewed by General Lee. Now where battles once raged, the grounds boast a swimming pool and large herb garden. The guests quarters feature pine floors, Oriental rugs, antiques and period reproductions. The dining room, where hearty country breakfasts are served, boasts Chippendale chairs, a fireplace and cupboards full of English china.

Historic Interest: Mayfield Inn is listed as a state and national landmark. The James River Plantations are within 30 minutes of the inn, and it's just a few miles to Petersburg's National Battlefield Park and Petersburg's historic district. Williamsburg and Jamestown are about an hour away.

Innkeeper(s): Cherry Turner. $69-95. MC VISA. 4 rooms with PB. 2 suites. Breakfast and afternoon tea included in rates. Type of meal: full breakfast. Beds: Q. Antiques and theater nearby.

Publicity: *Richmond News Leader.*

"We did truly feel at home in your well restored surroundings."

The Owl & The Pussycat B&B

405 High St
Petersburg, VA 23803-3857
(804)733-0505 (888)733-0505 Fax:(804)862-0694
E-mail: owlcat@ctg.net

Circa 1895. Victorians have a way of standing out, and this Queen Anne is particularly unique, fashioned from creamy, yellow bricks. The innkeepers have decorated the home with Victorian antiques, such as the beds and dressers, and pieces from England. Among the impressive antiques is a carved walnut bed in the Pussycat Room and an Eastlake-style bed in the Owl Room. The home still has its original gaslight fixtures and eight fireplaces, each decorated with different tiles and mantels. Midweek guests are served continental-plus fare, and weekend guests enjoy a full breakfast. English scones and Sally Lunn bread are specialties of the house. Civil War battlefields, museums, antique shops and restaurants are nearby.

Innkeeper(s): Juliette & John Swenson. $65-105. MC VISA PC TC. TAC10. 6 rooms, 4 with PB. Breakfast included in rates. Types of meals: continental-plus breakfast and early coffee/tea. Picnic lunch available. Beds: KQT. Air conditioning in room. TV, VCR and fax on premises. Weddings, small meetings, family reunions and seminars hosted.

Pets Allowed: Small/$20 deposit.

Providence Forge   G16

Jasmine Plantation B&B Inn

4500 N Courthouse Rd
Providence Forge, VA 23140-3428
(804)966-9836 (800)639-5368 Fax:(804)966-5679

Circa 1750. Few travelers can boast that they have stayed at a mid-18th-century plantation. Jasmine Plantation is just such a place. Surrounded by more than 40 acres of Virginia countryside, it's not difficult to understand why the Morris family chose this spot for their home. The property's first dwelling was built as early as the 1680s. Several guest rooms are named for members of the Morris  Family, and all are decorated with antiques. The Rose Room features Victorian furnishings and a whirlpool bath. The George Morris Room includes 19th-century pieces, a fireplace and clawfoot tub. Memorabilia from multiple centuries add special charm to the place. The innkeepers have antique irons, old

books and magazines and a sampling of vintage advertising signs for Philip Morris or Coca-Cola. Breakfasts are a true Southern treat with items such as sweet potato biscuits and homemade jams and jellies.

Innkeeper(s): Howard & Joyce Vogt. $75-105. MC VISA AX PC TC. TAC10. 6 rooms, 5 with PB, 4 with FP. Breakfast and evening snack included in rates. Types of meals: full breakfast and early coffee/tea. Beds: QD. Air conditioning and ceiling fan in room. TV and VCR on premises. 47 acres. Weddings, small meetings, family reunions and seminars hosted. Amusement parks, antiques, fishing, parks, shopping, golf and watersports nearby.

"We were charmed by the plantation accommodations and the kindness of the beautiful host and hostess."

Pulaski   H8

The Count Pulaski B&B and Garden

821 Jefferson Ave N
Pulaski, VA 24301-3609
(540)980-1163 (800)980-1163

Circa 1910. The innkeeper's many travels to Europe and Asia form the core of the inn's furnishings, which are combined with family antiques. The Colonial Revival house is located in the historic district on a half-acre of lawn and gardens. This inn is located in a quiet, easy-to-find neighborhood and if time permits, the home offers close access to lakes, mountains, hiking and biking trails, national and state parks, museums, art  galleries and antique shops. Indoor bicycle storage is available.

Historic Interest: Town of Newbern & Wilderness Museum (5 miles), Railroad Museum, Geology exhibit (6 blocks).

Innkeeper(s): Flo Stevenson. $95. MC VISA. 3 rooms with PB. 1 suite. Breakfast included in rates. Meals: full breakfast and early coffee/tea. Evening snack available. Beds: KQT. Phone, air conditioning and ceiling fan in room. TV on premises. Antiques, fishing, shopping and sporting events nearby.

Publicity: *Roanoke Times, Southwest Times.*

"I'm back again! Even better than my first visit. Thanks for making me feel so at home."

Raphine   E11

Willow Pond Farm B&B

137 Pisgah Rd
Raphine, VA 24472
(540)348-1310 (800)945-6763 Fax:(540)348-1359

Circa 1800. If visions of rolling hills, woods and the picturesque Shenandoah Valley are what you have in mind for a peaceful getaway, this Victorian farmhouse is an ideal location. Surrounded by more than 170 acres, guests are sure to enjoy this secluded bed & breakfast. There are four well-appointed, romantically styled guest rooms, featuring traditional furnishings and a  few Victorian pieces. The innkeepers pamper guests with a gourmet breakfast and afternoon tea. In addition, the hosts will arrange for guests to enjoy a five-course dinner served by candlelight on a table set with fine linens, china and crystal.

Innkeeper(s): Carol Ann & Walter P. Schendel. $95-115. MC VISA AX PC TC. 4 rooms with PB. Breakfast and afternoon tea included in rates. Types of meals: gourmet breakfast and early coffee/tea. Picnic lunch available. Beds: KQD. Air conditioning, turndown service and ceiling fan in room. TV, VCR, fax, copier and library on premises. 174 acres. Family reunions hosted. Antiques, fishing, parks, shopping, downhill skiing, cross-country skiing, sporting events, theater and watersports nearby.

"A jewel in the country! A perfect 10...many thanks!"

Richmond   F15

The Emmanuel Hutzler House

2036 Monument Ave
Richmond, VA 23220-2708
(804)353-6900 Fax:(804)355-5053
E-mail: be.our.guest@bensonhouse.com

Circa 1914. This graciously restored Italian Renaissance home is a showcase of mahogany paneling and tastefully decorated rooms. Its 8,000 square feet includes a stunning parlor with handsome antiques, leaded-glass windows and a marble fireplace. The largest room boasts a four-poster mahogany bed, antique sofa and a private Jacuzzi tucked into an enormous bathroom. Breakfast is served in the formal dining room of this non-smoking inn. There is a resident cat at this home.

Innkeeper(s): Lyn M. Benson & John E. Richardson. $95-155. AP. MC VISA AX DC DS PC TC. TAC7. 4 rooms with PB. 2 suites. Breakfast included in rates. Types of meals: continental-plus breakfast, full breakfast and early coffee/tea. Beds: KQT. Phone, air conditioning and TV in room. Fax and library on premises. Small meetings hosted. Antiques, parks, sporting events and theater nearby.

"I'm glad there are still people like you who painstakingly restore great old houses such as this. A great job of reconstruction and beautifully decorated! Delightful hosts!"

The William Catlin House B&B Inn

2304 E Broad St
Richmond, VA 23223-7127
(804)780-3746

Circa 1845. Richmond's oldest bed & breakfast is situated in the historic Church Hill District. Rooms are appointed with family heirlooms, Oriental rugs, canopied beds and fireplaces. Guests enjoy evening sherry. Breakfast is served in an elegant dining room. Only one block away is St. John's Church, site of Patrick Henry's famous "Liberty or Death" speech.

Innkeeper(s): Robert & Josie Martin. $75-150. MC VISA DS PC TC. TAC10. 5 rooms, 3 with PB, 2 with FP. 2 suites. Type of meal: full breakfast. Beds: QDT. Antiques, fishing and watersports nearby.

Location: Church Hill Historic District.

Publicity: *Colonial Homes, Southern Living, Philadelphia Inquirer, Los Angeles Times, Boston Globe, Mid-Atlantic.*

"The accommodations are immaculate."

Salem   G9

The Inn at Burwell Place

601 W Main St
Salem, VA 24153-3515
(540)387-0250 (800)891-0250 Fax:(540)387-3279

Circa 1907. This mansion was built by a local industrialist, but the inn was named for Nathaniel Burwell, who owned the land prior to the home's construction. The home overlooks the Roanoke Valley and parts of Salem. Guest rooms feature antiques and beds dressed with down comforters and fine

linens. Downtown Salem recently received a place in the National Register. The home, the site of many weddings, is a block from a restored 1890s duck pond and park.

Innkeeper(s): Cindi Lou MacMackin & Mark Bukowski. $80-120. MC VISA AX DS PC TC. TAC10. 4 rooms with PB, 1 with FP. 2 suites. 2 conference rooms. Breakfast included in rates. Types of meals: continental breakfast, full breakfast and early coffee/tea. Banquet service, catering service and catered breakfast available. Beds: Q. Phone, air conditioning, ceiling fan and TV in room. VCR and fax on premises. Weddings, small meetings, family reunions and seminars hosted. Amusement parks, antiques, fishing, parks, shopping, sporting events, theater and watersports nearby.

"It was truly elegant, a day I will always remember!"

Scottsville   F13

High Meadows Vineyard & Mtn Sunset Inn

Rt 4 Box 6
Scottsville, VA 24590-9706
(804)286-2218 (800)232-1832 Fax:(804)286-2124
E-mail: peterhmi@aol.com

Circa 1832. Minutes from Charlottesville on the Constitution Highway (Route 20), High Meadows stands on 50 acres of gardens, forests, ponds, a creek and a vineyard. Listed in the National Register, it is actually two historic homes joined by a breezeway as well as a turn-of-the-century Queen Anne manor house. The inn is furnished in Federal and Victorian styles. Guests are treated to gracious  Virginia hospitality in an elegant and peaceful setting with wine tasting and a romantic candlelight dinner every evening. There is additional $40 charge to the MAP rates on Saturday.

Historic Interest: Jefferson, Monroe, Madison homes (15-20 miles).

Innkeeper(s): Peter Sushka & Mary Jae Abbitt. $84-185. MAP. MC VISA AX DS. 14 rooms with PB, 12 with FP. 5 suites. 1 conference room. Breakfast included in rates. Types of meals: full breakfast and gourmet breakfast. Dinner available. Restaurant on premises. Beds: KQDT. Air conditioning, turndown service and ceiling fan in room. Spa on premises. Handicap access. 51 acres. Weddings, small meetings, family reunions and seminars hosted. Antiques, fishing, shopping, downhill skiing, cross-country skiing, sporting events, theater and watersports nearby.

Publicity: *Washington Times, Cavalier Daily, Daily Progress, Washington Post, Richmond Times Dispatch, Mid-Atlantic, Washingtonian.*

"We have rarely encountered such a smooth blend of hospitality and expertise in a totally relaxed environment."

Smith Mountain Lake

The Manor at Taylor's Store B&B Country Inn

8812 Washington Hwy, PO Box 510
Smith Mountain Lake, VA 24184-9725
(540)721-3951 (800)248-6267 Fax:(540)721-5243
E-mail: taylors@symweb.com

Circa 1820. Situated on 120 acres of rolling countryside, this two-story, columned manor was built on the site of Taylor's Store, a trading post just off the old Warwick Road. It served as the plantation house for a prosperous tobacco farmer, Moses Greer Booth. Guest rooms feature a variety of antiques and styles including traditional colonial and English country. From the solarium, a wildflower trail winds through the inn's

Colonial garden and green meadows, where a canoe awaits those who wish to paddle across one of six ponds on the property. There's a dock for those who wish to fish.

Historic Interest: Booker T. Washington National Monument (3 miles).

Innkeeper(s): Lee & Mary Lynn Tucker. $85-185. MC VISA PC TC. TAC10. 9 rooms, 8 with PB, 4 with FP. 4 suites. 1 cottage. 3 conference rooms. Breakfast included in rates. Types of meals: full breakfast, gourmet breakfast and early coffee/tea. Dinner, picnic lunch, gourmet lunch, banquet service and catering service available. Beds: QD. Air conditioning and turndown service in room. TV, VCR, fax, copier, spa, swimming, stables and library on premises. 120 acres. Small meetings and seminars hosted. Antiques, fishing, parks, shopping, sporting events, theater and watersports nearby.

Publicity: *Smith Mountain Eagle, Lake Country, Blue Ridge Country, Franklin News-Post, Southern Living, Brides, Country Inns, Mid-Atlantic Living.*

"This B&B experience is a delightful one!"

Smithfield   H17

Four Square Plantation

13357 Four Square Rd
Smithfield, VA 23430-8643
(757)365-0749

Circa 1807. Located in the historic James River area, the original land grant, "Four Square" was established in 1664 and consisted of 640 acres. Now in the National Register and a Virginia Historic Landmark, the Federal style home is called Plantation Plain by Virginia preservationists. The inn is furnished with family period pieces and antiques. The Vaughan Room offers a fireplace, Empire furnishings and access by private staircase. Breakfast is served in the dining room. The inn's four acres provide a setting for weddings and special events. Tour Williamsburg, Jamestown, the James River Plantations and Yorktown nearby.

Innkeeper(s): Roger & Amelia Healey. $75-85. MC VISA PC TC. 3 rooms with PB, 3 with FP. Breakfast included in rates. Types of meals: continental-plus breakfast, full breakfast and early coffee/tea. Dinner available. Beds: KQ. Air conditioning, turndown service, ceiling fan, TV and VCR in room. Weddings and family reunions hosted. Amusement parks, antiques, fishing, shopping and golf nearby.

Spotsylvania   E15

Roxbury Mill B&B

6908 S Roxbury Mill Rd
Spotsylvania, VA 22553-2438
(540)582-6611

Circa 1723. Once a working mill for the Roxbury Plantation, this early 18th-century home has seen the formation of a nation and the wars that would follow. Civil War relics have been found on the property, which includes a dam and millpond. The innkeepers strive to maintain a sense of history at their B&B, keeping the decor in Colonial to pre-Civil War styles. The large master suite affords a view of the river from its private deck, and the bed is an 18th-century antique. All guest rooms offer a view, private porch and antique furnishings. Traditional Southern-Colonial fare, from family recipes, fills the breakfast menu. Cornpone topped with slab bacon or country ham and biscuits are some of the appetizing choices. For late risers, the innkeepers also offer brunch.

Innkeeper(s): Joyce B. Ackerman. $75-150. MC VISA TC. 3 rooms, 2 with PB. 1 suite. Breakfast and afternoon tea included in rates. Types of meals: full breakfast, gourmet breakfast and early coffee/tea. Dinner and catering service available. Beds: QD. Air conditioning, turndown service, ceiling fan and TV in room. VCR on premises. Weddings, small meetings, family reunions and seminars hosted. Amusement parks, antiques, fishing, parks, shopping and watersports nearby. Pets Allowed.

Stanley   D13

Jordan Hollow Farm Inn

326 Hawkisbill Park Rd
Stanley, VA 22851-9538
(540)778-2285 (888)418-7000 Fax:(540)778-1759

Circa 1790. Nestled in the foothills of the Blue Ridge Mountains, this delightful 145-acre horse farm is ideal for those who love riding and country living. The colonial farm house is decorated with antiques and country artifacts. Gentle trail horses are available for guided one-hour rides. Horse boarding is available as is five miles of walking trails on the property.

Historic Interest: New Market Battlefield Museum, Luray Caverness, Skyline Drive.

Innkeeper(s): Gail Kyle & Betty Anderson. $110-160. MC VISA AX DC CB DS. 21 rooms with PB, 4 with FP. 1 conference room. Breakfast included in rates. Type of meal: full breakfast. Dinner and picnic lunch available. Restaurant on premises. Beds: KQ. Fax and copier on premises. Parks, cross-country skiing and watersports nearby.

Location: Shenandoah Valley, six miles south of Luray.

Publicity: *Country, Southern Living, Conde Nast, New York Times, Country Accents, Family Circle, Glamour, Vogue, Palm Beach, Washingtonian.*

"I keep thinking of my day at your lovely inn and keep dreaming of that wonderful lemon mousse cake!"

Staunton   E11

Frederick House

28 N New St
Staunton, VA 24401-4306
(540)885-4220 (800)334-5575

Circa 1810. Adjacent to Mary Baldwin College, this inn consists of six renovated town houses, the oldest of which is believed to be a copy of a home designed by Thomas Jefferson. A full breakfast is served in Chumley's Tea Room. Guest rooms (some with fireplaces) are furnished with antiques and feature robes and ceiling fans. Original staircases and woodwork are highlighted throughout. Suites are available.

Historic Interest: Blue Ridge Parkway, Skyline Drive (12 miles), Woodrow Wilson birthplace (2 blocks), Museum of American Frontier Culture (2 miles).

Innkeeper(s): Joe & Evy Harman. $65-150. MC VISA AX DC DS PC TC. TAC10. 17 rooms with PB, 6 with FP. 8 suites. 1 conference room. Breakfast and picnic lunch included in rates. Types of meals: full breakfast, gourmet breakfast and early coffee/tea. Catering service available. Beds: KQDT. Phone, air conditioning and TV in room. Library on premises. Weddings, small meetings, family reunions and seminars hosted. Antiques, fishing, parks, shopping, skiing, sporting events, theater and watersports nearby.

Location: Downtown.

Publicity: *Richmond Times-Dispatch, News Journal, Washington Post, Blue Ridge Country.*

"Thanks for making the room so squeaky-clean and comfortable! I enjoyed the Virginia hospitality. The furnishings and decor are beautiful."

Thornrose House at Gypsy Hill

531 Thornrose Ave
Staunton, VA 24401-3161
(540)885-7026 (800)861-4338

Circa 1912. A columned veranda wraps around two sides of this gracious red brick Georgian-style house. Two sets of Greek pergolas grace the lawns and there are gardens of azalea,

rhododendron and hydrangea. The inn is furnished with a mix of antique oak and walnut period pieces and overstuffed English country chairs. Bircher muesli, and hot-off-the-griddle whole grain banana pecan pancakes are popular breakfast items, served in the dining room (fireside on cool days). Across the street is a 300-acre park with lighted tennis courts, an 18-hole golf course and swimming pool.
Historic Interest: Woodrow Wilson birthplace (8 blocks), Museum of American Frontier Culture.
Innkeeper(s): Otis & Suzy Huston. $55-80. 5 rooms with PB. Breakfast and afternoon tea included in rates. Type of meal: full breakfast. Beds: KQDT. Air conditioning, turndown service and ceiling fan in room. TV on premises. Weddings and family reunions hosted. Antiques, fishing, shopping, sporting events and theater nearby.

"We enjoyed ourselves beyond measure, the accommodations, the food, your helpfulness, but most of all your gracious spirits."

Steeles Tavern   E11

Steeles Tavern Manor B&B

PO Box 39
Steeles Tavern, VA 24476-0039
(540)377-6444 (800)743-8666 Fax:(540)377-5937

Circa 1916. When innkeepers Eileen and Bill Hoernlein restored and opened this romantic bed & breakfast, they were adding on to the manor's legacy of hospitality. The village of Steeles Tavern is named for David Steele, one of the area's first settlers, who hosted many guests in the town's day as a stagecoach stop. His granddaughter, Irene, was the manor's first owner, and she opened the house to tourists from its early days until the 1940s. The Hoernleins have created a

cozy retreat on their 55-acre estate, which boasts plenty of hiking, walking and birdwatching possibilities, as well as a stocked fishing pond. Inside, the innkeepers have placed an emphasis on romance and privacy, with quiet rooms decorated with fresh flowers, candy-filled dishes and plenty of fluffy pillows and blankets. All rooms offer the added amenities of two-person whirlpool tubs and some fireplaces. An expansive country breakfast is served each morning, and the afternoon tea service offers a bounty of delightful refreshments after a day touring the area. The manor is only a few minutes from Cyrus McCormick Farm. Historic Lexington and Staunton are 15 minutes away, as is Washington & Lee University. The Blue Ridge Parkway is about a 20-minute drive. UVA, Monticello, Appomattox and Ash Lawn are a 60-minute day trip from the home.

Innkeeper(s): Eileen & Bill Hoernlein. $135-150. MC VISA PC TC. TAC10. 5 rooms with PB, 3 with FP. 2 suites. Types of meals: full breakfast and early coffee/tea. Afternoon tea available. Beds: KQT. Air conditioning, turndown service, ceiling fan, TV and VCR in room. Fax and library on premises. 55 acres. Antiques, fishing, parks, shopping, downhill skiing, cross-country skiing, sporting events, theater and watersports nearby.

"A real winner. Excellent breakfast. Exquisite! Fabulous!"

Strasburg   C13

Sonner House B&B

208 W Queen St
Strasburg, VA 22657-2223
(540)465-4712 (800)829-4809 Fax:(540)465-5463

Circa 1757. This home has seen many changes and additions. Its oldest portion, a 1757 log structure, is the oldest home in Strasburg. The son of the first owner built the second addition to the home, which was constructed as a separate house. The two homes were joined in 1834. From there, bathrooms and bedrooms

have been added, creating what is now a welcoming B&B with a historical ambiance. The Colonial decor is enhanced by exposed wood beams, log walls, hanging baskets, hand stenciling, quilts and collectibles.
Innkeeper(s): Sam & Mary Hitchings. $70. MC VISA. TAC10. 3 rooms with PB. Breakfast and afternoon tea included in rates. Type of meal: full breakfast. Beds: Q. Air conditioning in room. TV, VCR and fax on premises. Antiques, fishing, parks, shopping, golf and theater nearby.
Publicity: *Country Home.*

Urbanna   F17

Hewick Plantation

VSH 602/615, Box 82
Urbanna, VA 23175
(804)758-4214 Fax:(804)758-4080
E-mail: gzkq12a@prodigy.com and hewick1@aol.com

Circa 1678. A driveway lined with large oak trees leads to this two-story brick Colonial located on 66 acres. There is an ancient family cemetery on the grounds, and at the rear of the house is an archaeological dig conducted by the College of William and Mary. A cross-stitch kit of Hewick Plantation, made by the Heirloom Needlecraft company, is available at the inn. The historic "Urbanna" coverlet is another unique item on

display. The innkeeper is a 10th-generation descendant of Christopher Robinson, builder of Hewick Plantation and an original trustee of the College of William and Mary.
Historic Interest: Williamsburg (34 miles), The Tomb of General Lewis "Chesty" Puller, the most decorated marine in history (5 miles) USMC three miles away.
Innkeeper(s): Helen & Ed Battleson. $95-150. MC VISA AX DS PC TC. TAC10. 2 rooms with PB, 2 with FP. Breakfast included in rates. Type of meal: continental-plus breakfast. Beds: QDT. Phone, air conditioning and TV in room. Fax and stables on premises. 66 acres. Weddings, small meetings, family reunions and seminars hosted. Spanish spoken. Amusement parks, antiques, fishing, parks, shopping and watersports nearby.
Publicity: *Richmond Times Dispatch, Daily Press, Pleasant Living, WRIC-TV, TV-Tokyo.*

Warm Springs   E10

The Inn at Gristmill Square

PO Box 359
Warm Springs, VA 24484-0359
(703)839-2231 Fax:(703)839-5770
E-mail: grist@va.tds.net

Circa 1800. The inn consists of five restored buildings. The
old blacksmith shop and silo, the hardware store, the Steel
House and the Miller House all contain guest rooms. (The old
mill is now the
Waterwheel Restaurant.) A
few antiques and old
prints appear in some
rooms, while others are
furnished in a contempo-
rary style. There are tennis
courts and a swimming pool at the inn. A short walk over
Warm Springs Mill Stream and down the road brings travelers
to historic Warm Springs Pools.

Innkeeper(s): The McWilliams family. $80-140. MAP, EP. MC VISA DS TC. 17
rooms with PB, 7 with FP. 1 suite. 1 conference room. Meals: continental
breakfast, early coffee/tea. Dinner, picnic lunch, banquet service, catering service available. Restaurant on premises. Beds: KQDT. Phone, air conditioning,
TV in room. VCR, fax, sauna on premises. Weddings, small meetings, family
reunions, seminars hosted. Fishing, parks, downhill skiing, watersports nearby.
Publicity: *New York Times, Bon Appetit, Colonial Homes.*

*"You have such a wonderful inn — such attention to detail and such
a considerate staff."*

Three Hills Inn

PO Box 9
Warm Springs, VA 24484-0009
(540)839-5381 (888)234-4557 Fax:(540)839-5199

Circa 1913. Mary Johnston, who wrote the book "To Have and
to Hold," built this inn, which rests on 38 mountainous acres.
In 1917, Mary and her sisters opened the home to guests, earn-
ing a reputation for the
home's view of the
Allegheny Mountains and
Warm Springs Gap. The
innkeepers now offer lodging in the antique-filled
main house or adjacent cottages. Some rooms include private
decks, while others have fireplaces or clawfoot tubs. Each of the
cottages includes a kitchen; one has a working fireplace, while
another offers a woodburning stove.

Innkeeper(s): Julie & David Miller. $69-179. MC VISA DC PC TC. TAC10. 12
rooms with PB, 3 with FP. 7 suites. 3 cottages. Breakfast and afternoon tea
included in rates. Meals: continental breakfast, gourmet breakfast, early cof-
fee/tea. Picnic lunch, banquet service, catering service available. Restaurant
on premises. Beds: KQDT. TV in room. VCR, fax, copier, child care on premises. 40 acres. Weddings, small meetings, family reunions, seminars hosted.
Spanish spoken. Antiques, fishing, parks, shopping, skiing, theater nearby.

Pets Allowed: In rooms with outside door.

Washington   C13

Caledonia Farm - 1812

47 Dearing Rd (Flint Hill)
Washington, VA 22627
(540)675-3693 (800)262-1812 Fax:(540)675-3693

Circa 1812. This gracious Federal-style stone house in the
National Register is beautifully situated on 52 acres adjacent to

Shenandoah National Park.
It was built by a
Revolutionary War officer,
and his musket is dis-
played over a mantel. The
house, a Virginia Historic
Landmark, has been
restored with the original
Colonial color scheme retained. All rooms have working fireplaces and provide views of Skyline Drive and the Blue Ridge
Mountains. The innkeeper is a retired broadcaster.

Innkeeper(s): Phil Irwin. $80-140. MC VISA DS PC TC. TAC10. 3 rooms, 2
with PB, 3 with FP. 2 suites. 1 cottage. 1 conference room. Breakfast and
evening snack included in rates. Types of meals: gourmet breakfast and early
coffee/tea. Beds: D. Phone, air conditioning, turndown service and VCR in
room. Fax, copier, spa, bicycles and library on premises. 52 acres. Small
meetings, family reunions and seminars hosted. German and Spanish spoken.
Antiques, fishing, parks, shopping, downhill skiing, cross-country skiing, theater and watersports nearby.
Location: Four miles north of Washington, Va.; 68 miles from Washington, D.C.
Publicity: *Country, Country Almanac, Country Living, Blue Ridge Country,
Discovery, Washington Post, Baltimore Sun.*

"We've stayed at many, many B&Bs. This is by far the best!"

Gay Street Inn

PO Box 237, Gay St
Washington, VA 22747
(540)675-3288

Circa 1855. After a day of Skyline Drive, Shenandoah National
Park and the caverns of Luray and Front Royal, come home to
this stucco, gabled farmhouse. If you've booked the fireplace
room, a canopy bed will
await you. Furnishings
include period Shaker
pieces. The innkeepers will
be happy to steer you to
the most interesting vineyards, "pick-your-own"
fruit and vegetable farms
and Made-In-Virginia food and craft shops. Breakfast and afternoon tea are served in the garden conservatory. Five-star dining
is within walking distance at The Inn at Little Washington.

Historic Interest: Manassas Battlefield & Park and Chancellorsville are some
of the area's many Civil War sites. The University of Virginia, historic
Charlottesville and Monticello are other sites in the area.

Innkeeper(s): Robin & Donna Kevis. $95-135. MC VISA AX PC TC. TAC10. 4
rooms with PB, 1 with FP. 1 suite. Breakfast and afternoon tea included in
rates. Types of meals: continental-plus breakfast, full breakfast, gourmet
breakfast and early coffee/tea. Picnic lunch available. Beds: Q. Air conditioning in room. Child care on premises. Handicap access. Weddings, small
meetings and family reunions hosted. Antiques, fishing, parks, shopping, theater and watersports nearby. Pets Allowed.

"Thank you for a wonderful visit. Your hospitality was superb."

The Inn at Little Washington

PO Box 300
Washington, VA 22747-0300
(540)675-3800 Fax:(540)675-3100

Circa 1915. The restaurant at the Inn at Little Washington has
received five stars and five diamonds, and guests will find the experience by which they measure all other quality dining. This two-
story white clapboard inn was once a repair garage. With the assistance of English designer Joyce Conwy-Evans, fantasy and romance
were created with lavish fabrics, faux woods and antiques. A garden courtyard includes a gazebo and reflecting pool.

Innkeeper(s): Patrick O'Connell & Reinhardt Lynch. $250-625. MC VISA. 12 rooms with PB. 3 suites. Dinner, picnic lunch and room service available. Restaurant on premises. Beds: DT. Fax on premises. Handicap access. Antiques, fishing nearby.

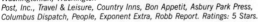

Publicity: *USA Today, New York Times, San Francisco Chronicle, Virginian, Washingtonian, Washington Post, Inc., Travel & Leisure, Country Inns, Bon Appetit, Asbury Park Press, Columbus Dispatch, People, Exponent Extra, Robb Report.* Ratings: 5 Stars.

"One of the most celebrated restaurants and inns in America — Bon Appetit."

White Post   B13

L'Auberge Provencale

PO Box 119
White Post, VA 22663-0119
(540)837-1375 (800)638-1702 Fax:(540)837-2004

Circa 1753. This farmhouse was built with fieldstones gathered from the area. Hessian soldiers crafted the woodwork of the main house, Mt. Airy. As the name suggests, a French influence is prominent throughout the inn. Victorian and European antiques fill the elegant guest rooms, several of which include fireplaces. Innkeeper Alain Borel hails from a long line of master chefs, his expertise creates many happy culinary memories guests cherish. Many of the French-influenced items served at the inn's four-diamond restaurant, include ingredients from the inn's gardens, and Alain has been hailed by James Beard as a Great Country Inn Chef.

Historic Interest: Waterford, Luray Caverns, Holy Cross Abbey (Historic Long Branch).
Innkeeper(s): Alain & Celeste Borel. $145-250. MC VISA AX DC DS PC TC. TAC10. 11 rooms with PB, 6 with FP. 2 suites. 1 conference room. Breakfast included in rates. Type of meal: gourmet breakfast. Dinner, evening snack, picnic lunch, banquet service and room service available. Restaurant on premises. Beds: QD. Air conditioning, turndown service and ceiling fan in room. Fax and copier on premises. Handicap access. 10 acres. Weddings, small meetings, family reunions and seminars hosted. French and Spanish spoken. Antiques, fishing, parks, shopping and theater nearby.
Location: One mile south of Rt 50 on Rt 340.
Publicity: *Bon Appetit, Glamour, Washington Dossier, Washington Post, Baltimore, Richmond Times.*

"Peaceful view and atmosphere, extraordinary food and wines. Honeymoon and heaven all in one!"

Williamsburg   G17

Candlewick B&B

800 Jamestown Rd
Williamsburg, VA 23185-3915
(757)253-8693 (800)418-4949

Circa 1946. Situated behind a white picket fence, this Colonial two-story house is close to the historic area and across the street from the College of William and Mary. Behind each shuttered window, a candle is lit at night to welcome guests, an old Virginia tradition. The inn is decorated with 18th-century antiques and reproductions and includes such features as indoor shutters, beamed ceilings, old latch doors and chair rails. Guest rooms all offer a beautifully draped canopy colonial bed, comfortable mattress and antique quilts. Cottage pancakes, French toast and homemade breads may be served at breakfast.
Innkeeper(s): Bernie & Mary Peters. $85-115. AP. MC VISA PC TC. TAC10. 3 rooms with PB. 1 suite. Breakfast included in rates. Meals: full breakfast and

early coffee/tea. Beds: KQT. Phone, air conditioning and turndown service in room. TV, bicycles on premises. German spoken. Amusement parks, antiques, fishing, parks, shopping, sporting events, golf, theater, watersports nearby.
"Once again, our stay here was phenomenal."

Cedars

616 Jamestown Rd
Williamsburg, VA 23185-3945
(757)229-3591 (800)296-3591

Circa 1930. This three-story brick Georgian home is a short walk from Colonial Williamsburg and is located across from William and Mary College. Rooms are decorated with Traditional antiques, Colonial reproductions, fireplaces and four-poster or canopy beds. The bountiful breakfasts include a hearty entree, fresh fruits, breads, muffins and cereals.
Innkeeper(s): Carol, Jim & Brona Malecha. $76-165. MC VISA PC TC. TAC10. 8 rooms with PB, 2 with FP. 2 suites. 1 cottage. Breakfast included in rates. Types of meals: full breakfast and early coffee/tea. Beds: KQT. Air conditioning and ceiling fan in room. Library on premises. Family reunions hosted. Amusement parks, antiques, parks and shopping nearby.

Liberty Rose B&B

1022 Jamestown Rd
Williamsburg, VA 23185-3434
(757)253-1260 (800)545-1825

Circa 1922. This cozy retreat, located on a wooded hilltop on the historic corridor, is tucked among tall trees only a mile from Colonial Williamsburg. The owner of Jamestown constructed this two-story clapboard home. The entry porch is marked with the millstone from one of Williamsburg's old mills. Antiques and collectibles abound in each of the rooms. The innkeepers have merged modern amenities with the atmosphere of Colonial times. All rooms include telephones, TVs and VCRs with an excellent selection of movies. A gourmet country breakfast is served each morning. Each of the romantic guest rooms features something unique. Honeymooners — the inn is often full of newlyweds — will return to celebrate their anniversaries.
Historic Interest: Colonial Williamsburg (1 mile), Jamestown 1607 (4 miles), Yorktown (12 miles), College of William & Mary (1/2 mile).
Innkeeper(s): Brad & Sandi Hirz. $135-205. MC VISA AX. 4 rooms with PB, 1 with FP. 3 suites. Breakfast included in rates. Type of meal: full breakfast. Beds: QT. Phone, TV and VCR in room. Antiques, theater, watersports nearby.
Location: One mile from Colonial Williamsburg's historic area.
Publicity: *Country Inns, Washington Post, Rural Living, L.A. Times, Glamour.*
"More delightful than we could possibly have imagined. Charm & romance abounds when you walk into the house."

Newport House

710 S Henry St
Williamsburg, VA 23185-4113
(757)229-1775 Fax:(757)229-6408

Circa 1987. This neo-Palladian house is a 1756 design by Peter Harrison, architect of rebuilt Williamsburg State House. It features wooden rusticated siding. Colonial country dancing is held in the inn's ballroom on Tuesday evenings. Guests are welcome to participate. There are English and American antiques, and reproductions include canopy beds in all the guest rooms. The host was a museum director and captain of a historic tall ship.
Historic Interest: Newport House is within walking distance of Colonial Williamsburg. Jamestown is six miles, Yorktown is a 12-mile drive from the inn. The historic James River Plantations are scattered throughout the area.
Innkeeper(s): John & Cathy Millar. $115-150. PC TC. TAC10. 2 rooms with PB. 1 conference room. Breakfast included in rates. Type of meal: full breakfast. Beds: QT. Air conditioning and VCR in room. Fax and child care on premises. Weddings, small meetings and seminars hosted. French spoken. Amusement parks, antiques, parks, shopping, theater, watersports nearby.
Publicity: *Innsider.*

Piney Grove at Southall's Plantation

PO Box 1359
Williamsburg, VA 23187-1359
(757)829-2480 Fax:(757)829-2480

Circa 1790. The Gordineers welcome you to their historic country retreat. Piney Grove is a rare Tidewater log building in the National Register of Historic Places, located on the Old Main Road among farms, plantations, country stores and quaint churches. Ladysmith House is a modest antebellum plantation house (c. 1835). Both homes are furnished with a unique collection of artifacts and antiques that illustrates the history of the property and area. The grounds also include Ashland (c. 1835), Dower Quarter (c. 1860) and Duck Church (c. 1900). Guests also enjoy meandering among the gardens, grounds and nature trail.

Historic Interest: Colonial Williamsburg, the James River Plantations, and Civil War battlefields are some of the area's many historic attractions.

Innkeeper(s): Gordineer Family. $125-160. PC. TAC10. 5 rooms with PB, 4 with FP. 1 suite. 1 conference room. Type of meal: full breakfast. Evening snack available. Beds: DT. Air conditioning and turndown service in room. TV, VCR, fax, swimming on premises. Limited German spoken. Amusement parks, antiques, fishing, parks, shopping, sporting events, theater, watersports nearby.

Location: James River Plantation country, outside of Williamsburg.

Publicity: *New York Times, Richmond Times-Dispatch, Washington Post, Southern Living.*

"Thank you for your warm, gracious hospitality. We really enjoyed ourselves and look forward to returning."

Williamsburg Manor B&B

600 Richmond Rd
Williamsburg, VA 23185-3540
(757)220-8011 (800)422-8011 Fax:(757)220-8011

Circa 1927. Built during the reconstruction of Colonial Williamsburg, this Georgian brick Colonial is just three blocks from the historic village. A grand staircase, culinary library, Waverly fabrics, Oriental rugs and antiques are featured. Breakfasts begin with fresh fruits and home-baked breads, followed by a special daily entree. Gourmet regional Virginia dinners also are available.

Historic Interest: Historic Williamsburg (3 blocks), Jamestown (5 miles), Yorktown (20 miles), William & Mary College (1 block).

Innkeeper(s): Laura Sisane. $75-150. MC VISA PC TC. TAC10. 5 rooms with PB. Breakfast included in rates. Meals: gourmet breakfast early coffee/tea. Picnic lunch, lunch, gourmet lunch, catering service, catered breakfast available. Beds: QT. Air conditioning, ceiling fan, TV in room. VCR, fax on premises. Weddings, small meetings, family reunions, seminars hosted. Amusement parks, antiques, fishing, parks, sporting events, theater, watersports nearby.

Location: Three blocks from colonial Williamsburg.

"Lovely accommodations - scrumptious breakfast."

Woodstock   C13

Azalea House

551 S Main St
Woodstock, VA 22664
(540)459-3500

Circa 1892. A white picket fence and garden archway invite guests to this Victorian house. Rooms with period antiques and

parlors decorated with stenciled ceilings await guests. Caverns, vineyards, horseback riding, canoeing, Civil War sites, theaters, the historic district and antiquing are nearby.

Innkeeper(s): Margaret & Price McDonald. $55-75. MC VISA AX. 4 rooms with PB. Breakfast included in rates. Meals: full breakfast, early coffee/tea. Beds: QD. Air conditioning and ceiling fan in room. TV, VCR on premises.

The Inn at Narrow Passage

PO Box 608
Woodstock, VA 22664-0608
(540)459-8000 (800)459-8002 Fax:(540)459-8001

Circa 1740. This log inn has been welcoming travelers since the time settlers took refuge here against the Indians. Later, it served as a stagecoach inn on the old Valley Turnpike, and in 1862, it was Stonewall Jackson's headquarters. Many guest rooms feature fireplaces and views of the Shenandoah River and Massanutten Mountains.

Historic Interest: Shenandoah County Courthouse (5 minutes), Cedar Creek Battlefield (15 minutes), New Market Battlefield (20 minutes).

Innkeeper(s): Ellen & Ed Markel. $85-115. MC VISA. 12 rooms with PB. Breakfast included in rates. Beds: Q. Phone in room. Antiques, fishing and watersports nearby.

Location: On Shenandoah River and US 11, 2-1/2 miles south of Woodstock.

Publicity: *Southern Living, Washington Post, Washington Times, Richmond Times-Dispatch.*

"We are still basking in the afterglow of our wonderful experience with you."

Woolwine   I9

Mountain Rose B&B Inn

RR 1 Box 280, 1787 Charity Hwy
Woolwine, VA 24185
(540)930-1057

Circa 1901. This historic Victorian inn, once the home of the Mountain Rose Distillery, sits on 100 acres of forested hills with plenty of hiking trails. A trout-stocked stream goes through the property and a swimming pool provides recreation. Each room has an antique manteled fireplace, some of which have been converted to gas logs. Guests can relax by the pool or in rocking chairs on one of the six porches. The innkeepers look forward to providing guests with casually elegant hospitality in the Blue Ridge Mountains. The Blue Ridge Parkway, Mabury Mill, The Reynolds

Homestead, Laurel Hill J. EB Stuart Birthplace, Patrick County Courthouse and the Patrick County Historical Museum are located nearby. A three-course breakfast is offered every morning.

Innkeeper(s): Melodie Pogue & Reeves Simms. $65-95. MC VISA. 5 rooms with PB, 3 with FP. Breakfast and afternoon tea included in rates. Meal: full breakfast. Beds: KQDT. Antiques, fishing, golf and watersports nearby.

Publicity: *Enterprise, Bill Mountain Bugle, New York Times.*

Washington

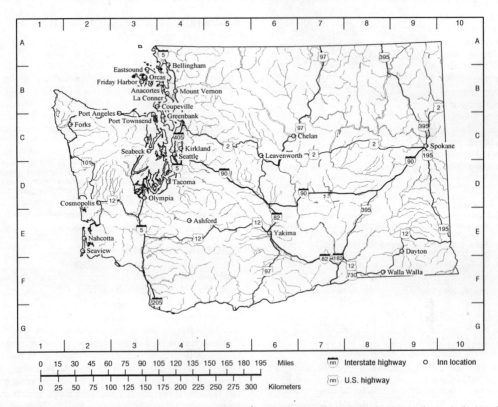

0 15 30 45 60 75 90 105 120 135 150 165 180 195   Miles

0 25 50 75 100 125 150 175 200 225 250 275 300   Kilometers

(nn) Interstate highway   O   Inn location

(nn) U.S. highway

Aberdeen (Cosmopolis)   E2

Cooney Mansion B&B

PO Box 54, 1705 Fifth St
Aberdeen (Cosmopolis), WA 98537-0054
(360)533-0602

Circa 1908. This former lumber magnate's home, in a wooded
setting, boasts 37 rooms. In the National Register, it was built
with a ballroom in the basement, nine bedrooms and eight
bathrooms. There are soaking tubs in all of the rooms. The inn
features original mission furnishings, and the Cooney suite has a
fireplace, TV and VCR and original "rainfall" shower. Guests can
enjoy the National Award Winning Lumber Baron's Breakfast.
Innkeeper(s): Judi & Jim Lohr. $65-165. MC VISA AX DC DS. 8 rooms, 5
with PB, 1 with FP. 1 suite. 1 conference room. Breakfast and afternoon tea
included in rates. Types of meals: full breakfast and early coffee/tea. Banquet
service and catering service available. Beds: KQDT. TV, VCR, fax, spa and
sauna on premises. Weddings, small meetings, family reunions and seminars

hosted. Antiques, fishing, parks, shopping, sporting events, theater and
watersports nearby.
Publicity: Sunset, Travel & Leisure, Country Inns.

*"This is an exceptional inn because of the hosts, who really care
about their guests."*

Anacortes B4

Albatross Bed & Breakfast

5708 Kingsway
Anacortes, WA 98221-2932
(360)293-0677 (800)622-8864

Circa 1927. This Cape Cod-style home is one of the last remaining relics of Anacortes' booming lumber days. The current bed & breakfast was built as a home for the mill manager at the E.K. Wood Mill Company. The popular Scarlett O'Hara Room is filled with unique pieces from a 19th-century Southern mansion. The home maintains

many original elements, including beaded cedar ceilings and crystal chandeliers. Skyline Marina is adjacent to the home, and the San Juan ferry boat docks just one-half mile away.

Historic Interest: Historic San Juan Island, about 20 miles away by ferry, was the site of the Pig War, a conflict between the United States and Britain over the establishment of the border between Washington and British Colombia.

Innkeeper(s): Lorrie & Linda Flowers. $75-90. MC VISA AX PC TC. TAC10. 4 rooms with PB. Breakfast and evening snack included in rates. Types of meals: full breakfast and gourmet breakfast. Afternoon tea available. Beds: KQ. Turndown service in room. TV, VCR and library on premises. Weddings, small meetings, family reunions and seminars hosted. Antiques, fishing, parks, shopping, downhill skiing, cross-country skiing, sporting events, theater and watersports nearby.

Location: One-half mile from ferry to the San Juan Islands and Victoria, B.C.

Publicity: *Apropos, Business Pulse.*

"Our stay with you was a comfortable, enjoyable experience. Such cordiality!"

Hasty Pudding House

1312 8th St
Anacortes, WA 98221-1834
(360)293-5773 (800)368-5588 Fax:(360)293-5773

Circa 1913. This Edwardian Craftsman house is located in a quiet neighborhood near historic downtown, the waterfront and Causland Park. The front porch solarium contains wicker furnishings, while the house is decorated with antiques, lace curtains and coordinated wallpapers.

Innkeeper(s): Melinda & Mikel Hasty. $65-105. MC VISA AX DS PC TC. TAC10. 5 rooms with PB. 1 suite. Breakfast included in rates. Types of meals: full breakfast and gourmet breakfast. Beds: KQ. TV, VCR, fax and copier on premises. Small meetings, family reunions and seminars hosted. Antiques, fishing, parks, shopping, theater and watersports nearby.

Publicity: *Anacortes American, Skagit Valley Herald, Seattle Times.*

"You and your beautiful bed & breakfast really made our trip."

Ashford E4

Growly Bear B&B

37311 S R 706
Ashford, WA 98304
(360)569-2339 (800)700-2339

Circa 1890. Guests at Growly Bear will appreciate the cozy, rustic setting of this 100-year-old mountain home located a mile from the Nisqually entrance to Mt. Rainier National Park on

Highway 706. Guest rooms are large and feature comfortable furnishings, quilts, fresh flowers and a fruit basket. A full gourmet mountain country breakfast is served each morning with fresh pastries made nearby. The breakfast is a great start to a day of hiking or cross-country skiing. The inn is an ideal location for park visitors and is four miles from the village of Ashford.

Innkeeper(s): Susan Jenny Johnson. $80-105. MC VISA AX PC TC. TAC10. 2 rooms, 1 with PB. Type of meal: full breakfast. Copier on premises. 15 acres. Cross-country skiing nearby.

Location: One mile from Mt. Rainier National Park.

"Lovely surroundings and great baked goodies."

Mountain Meadows Inn B&B

PO Box 291, 28912 SR 706E
Ashford, WA 98304
(360)569-2788

Circa 1910. Originally built for the superintendent of the Pacific National Lumber Company, the house boasts hanging baskets of fuschias that accentuate the veranda. Comfortable guest rooms feature a view of the woodland setting, occasionally visited by deer and elk. Breakfasts are prepared on an 1889 wood cooking stove.

Innkeeper(s): Harry & Michelle Latimer. $65-110. MC VISA PC TC. TAC10. 6 rooms with PB. 1 conference room. Breakfast included in rates. Type of meal: full breakfast. Beds: KQDT. Turndown service in room. Library on premises. 11 acres. Weddings, small meetings and family reunions hosted. Antiques, fishing, parks, shopping, cross-country skiing, golf and watersports nearby.

Location: One-half mile west of Ashford.

Publicity: *Seattle Times, Pacific Northwest, Eastside Weekly, Prime Times.*

"Our stay here will be one of the nicest memories of our vacation."

National Park Inn

Mt Rainier Guest Services PO Box 108
Ashford, WA 98304
(360)569-2275 Fax:(360)569-2770

Circa 1920. Mt. Rainier National Park boasts a spectacular scenery of mountains and seemingly endless forests. For more than half a century, visitors from around the world have chosen National Park Inn for their park lodging. Old hickory and twig furnishings decorate the rustic, comfortable guest rooms. Lunch and dinner service are available at the inn's dining room. From late October to May 1, rates include bed & breakfast. Breakfast is not included during the high season, from May until about Oct. 19.

Innkeeper(s): James R. Sproatt. $66-91. AP. MC VISA AX DC DS PC TC. TAC5. 25 rooms, 18 with PB. Breakfast included in rates. Types of meals: continental breakfast, continental-plus breakfast and full breakfast. Afternoon tea, dinner and picnic lunch available. Restaurant on premises. Beds: QDT. Handicap access. Small meetings hosted. Cross-country skiing nearby.

Location: Located in Mount Rainier National Park.

Bellingham A4

The Castle B&B

1103 15th St
Bellingham, WA 98225-6631
(360)676-0974

Circa 1889. All the guest rooms of this mauve Victorian mansion look out to Bellingham Bay and the San Juan Islands. Statuary, fountains and ponds accent the inn's gables, steeply pitched turret and bays. The Bayview Room, with its panoramic water view, is the inn's honeymoon suite, complete with private veranda and fireplace. Presented with the Mayor's Restoration Award, the inn's ornate castle-appropriate antiques mingle with your hosts' extensive lamp and clock collection sprinkled throughout the 21 rooms. There is an antique shop of the premises.

Historic Interest: National Register.

Innkeeper(s): Gloria & Larry Harriman. $45-95. PC TC. 4 rooms, 3 with PB, 1 with FP. 2 suites. 1 conference room. Breakfast included in rates. Type of meal: continental-plus breakfast. Beds: KQDT. Phone in room. TV and VCR on premises. Small meetings and seminars hosted. Antiques, fishing, parks, shopping, downhill skiing, cross-country skiing, sporting events, theater and watersports nearby.

Location: Historic Fairhaven.

Publicity: *Sunset Magazine, Daughters of the Painted Ladies.*

"Never have I seen a B&B with so many museum-quality pieces of furniture."

North Garden Inn

1014 N Garden St
Bellingham, WA 98225-5538
(360)671-7828 (800)922-6414

Circa 1897. Listed in the National Register, this Queen Anne Victorian originally had bars on the basement windows to keep out the bears. Guest rooms feature views of Bellingham Bay and the surrounding islands. A mahogany Steinway piano is often played for guests. The inn is within walking distance to Western Washington University.

Historic Interest: The Historical Museum (10 blocks).

Innkeeper(s): Frank & Barbara DeFreytas. $45-84. MC VISA DS PC TC. TAC10. 10 rooms, 8 with PB, 1 with FP. Breakfast included in rates. Types of meals: full breakfast and early coffee/tea. Beds: QDT. TV, VCR, copier and library on premises. Small meetings and family reunions hosted. French, German and Spanish spoken. Antiques, fishing, parks, shopping, downhill skiing, cross-country skiing, sporting events, theater and watersports nearby.

Publicity: *La Bonne Cuisine, Chocolatier, Victorian Homes, Bellingham Herald, Country, Sunset.*

"Excellent everything! Room, view, hospitality, breakfast, who could ask for anything more?"

Chelan   C6

Highland Guest House

121 E Highland Ave, PO Box 2089
Chelan, WA 98816
(509)682-2892 (800)681-2892

Circa 1902. This turn-of-the-century Victorian is decorated in period style with antiques. Each of the guest rooms has its own theme. For instance, one room offers a romantic canopy bed topped with a quilt. The Rose & Wicker Room includes a private porch that affords a beautiful view of Lake Chelan. The inn's parlor and dining room feature hand-stenciled ceilings, which duplicate original turn-of-the-century painting done by the home's original owner. A number of collectibles, including a spinning wheel, decorate the common areas. Strawberries and cream French toast is a typical breakfast specialty. The innkeepers offer a variety of seasonal packages and can put together

picnic and gift baskets. Highland is the site of a juried Victorian arts and crafts show, which takes place during the Christmas season.

Innkeeper(s): Marilee & Brad Stolzenburg. $50-95. MC VISA PC. TAC10. 3 rooms with PB. Breakfast included in rates. Types of meals: full breakfast and gourmet breakfast. Picnic lunch and room service available. Beds: QD. Air conditioning and ceiling fan in room. TV and library on premises. Small meetings, family reunions and seminars hosted. Amusement parks, antiques, fishing, parks, shopping, cross-country skiing, theater and watersports nearby.

Publicity: *Los Angeles Times.*

"Always liked Chelan. . .now we love it! We'll be back!"

Coupeville   B4

Captain Whidbey Inn

2072 W Captain Whidbey Inn Rd
Coupeville, WA 98239
(360)678-4097 (800)366-4097 Fax:(360)678-4110

Circa 1907. Overlooking Whidbey Island's Penn Cove, this log inn has comfortable rooms featuring down comforters, feather beds and views of lagoons and gardens. The dining room also has a magnificent view and guests can enjoy their meals by the fireplace. The chef utilizes local catches such as steelhead, salmon, spot prawns and Penn Cove mussels. The proprietor is also a sailing captain, and guests can book an afternoon on his 52-foot ketch, Cutty Sark. The proprietor's family has run the inn for more than 30 years.

Innkeeper(s): Dennis A. Argent. $95-225. EP. MC VISA AX DC DS. 32 rooms, 20 with PB, 7 with FP. 1 conference room. Breakfast included in rates. Type of meal: full breakfast. Dinner, evening snack, picnic lunch and lunch available. Restaurant on premises. Beds: KQD. Phone in room. Fax and copier on premises. Small meetings and family reunions hosted. Antiques and shopping nearby.

Location: Central Whidbey Island.

Publicity: *Gourmet Magazine, USA-Weekend.*

"I visit and stay here once a year and love it."

The Inn at Penn Cove

702 N Main, PO Box 85
Coupeville, WA 98239
(360)678-8000 (800)688-2683

Circa 1887. Two restored historic houses, one a fanciful white and peach Italianate confection in the National Register, comprise the inn. Each house contains only three guest rooms affording a variety of small parlors for guests to enjoy. The most romantic accommodation is Desiree's Room with a fireplace, a whirlpool tub for two and mesmerizing views of Puget Sound and Mt. Baker.

Innkeeper(s): Gladys & Mitchell Howard. $75-125. MC VISA AX DS PC TC. 6 rooms, 4 with PB, 3 with FP. 1 conference room. Type of meal: full breakfast. Beds: KQ. Phone and ceiling fan in room. TV and VCR on premises. Weddings, small meetings, family reunions and seminars hosted. Antiques and shopping nearby.

Publicity: *Whidbey News-Times, Country Inns, Glamour.*

"Our hosts were warm and friendly, but also gave us plenty of space and privacy - a good combination."

Dayton E9

The Purple House

415 E Clay St
Dayton, WA 99328-1348
(509)382-3159 (800)486-2574

Circa 1882. History buffs will adore this aptly named bed &
breakfast, colored in deep purple tones with white, gingerbread
trim. The home, listed in the National Register, is the perfect
place to enjoy Dayton, which boasts two his-
toric districts and a
multitude of pre-
served Victorian
homes. Innkeeper
Christine Williscroft
has filled the home
with antiques and
artwork. A highly
praised cook,
Christine prepares the European-style full breakfasts, as well as
mouthwatering afternoon refreshments. Guests can relax in the
richly appointed parlor or library, and the grounds also include
a swimming pool.

Historic Interest: Aside from the more than 80 homes listed in the National
Register, Dayton offers the historic sites of the county courthouse, a restored
railroad depot and several other buildings in the National Register.

Innkeeper(s): D. Christine Williscroft. $85-125. EP. MC VISA. 4 rooms, 2
with PB, 1 with FP. 1 suite. Breakfast and afternoon tea included in rates.
Types of meals: full breakfast, gourmet breakfast and early coffee/tea. Dinner
and picnic lunch available. Beds: QD. Phone, air conditioning and ceiling fan
in room. TV, VCR, swimming, library and pet boarding on premises.
Handicap access. Small meetings and family reunions hosted. Antiques, fishing, parks, shopping, downhill skiing, cross-country skiing, sporting events,
theater and watersports nearby.

Pets Allowed.

Publicity: *Sunset.*

*"You have accomplished so very much with your bed & breakfast to
make it a very special place to stay."*

Weinhard Hotel

235 E Main St
Dayton, WA 99328-1352
(509)382-4032 Fax:(509)382-2640

Circa 1890. This luxurious Victorian bed & breakfast, tucked
at the base of the scenic Blue Mountains, originally served up
spirits as the Weinhard Saloon and Lodge Hall. Guests are
transported back to the genteel Victorian era during their stay.
After a restful sleep among period pieces, ornate carpeting and
ceilings fans, guests might imagine the days when horses and
buggies road through town. While the innkeepers have worked
to preserve the history of the hotel, they didn't forget such
modern luxuries as Jacuzzi tubs in the private baths. The hotel
boasts a beautiful Victorian roof garden, a perfect place to relax
with a cup of tea or gourmet coffee. For a unique weekend, try
the hotel's special Romantic Getaway package. Guests are presented with sparkling wine or champagne and a dozen roses.
The package also includes a five-course meal.

Historic Interest: If a stay at Weinhard Hotel doesn't take you back in time, a
trip to Dayton will transport you to the Victorian Era. The town has 89 buildings in the National Register.

Innkeeper(s): Virginia Butler. $65-115. MC VISA. 15 rooms with PB.
Breakfast included in rates. Afternoon tea, dinner, lunch and catering service
available. Restaurant on premises. Beds: Q.

Pets Allowed.

Publicity: *Seattle Times, Daily Journal of Commerce, Sunset Magazine,
Lewiston Morning Tribune, San Francisco Examiner, Spokesman Review.*

*"It's spectacular! Thank you so much for all your kindness and car-
ing hospitality."*

Eastsound B3

Turtleback Farm Inn

Crow Valley Rd, Rt 1 Box 650
Eastsound, WA 98245
(360)376-4914 (800)376-4914

Circa 1895. Guests will delight in the beautiful views afforded
from this farmhouse and the newly constructed Orchard
House, which overlooks 80 acres of forest and farmland, duck
ponds and Mt. Constitution to the east. Rooms feature antique
furnishings and many boast views of the farm, orchard or sheep
pasture. Beds are covered with wool comforters made from
sheep raised on the property. Bon Appetit highlighted some of
the breakfast recipes served at Turtleback; a breakfast here is a
memorable affair. Tables set with bone china, silver and fresh
linens make way for a delightful mix of fruits, juice, award-winning granola, homemade breads and specialty entrees. Evening
guests can settle down with a game or a book in the fire-lit parlor as they enjoy sherry, tea or hot chocolate.

Historic Interest: Orcas Island, once the apple capital of Washington, features
many historic sites. The Orcas Island Historical Museum and Crow Valley
School Museum are among several options.

Innkeeper(s): William & Susan C. Fletcher. $80-210. MC VISA DS PC TC.
TAC10. 11 rooms with PB, 4 with FP. Breakfast included in rates. Types of
meals: full breakfast and early coffee/tea. Picnic lunch available. Beds: KQD.
Library on premises. Handicap access. 80 acres. Weddings and family
reunions hosted. Spanish and limited French spoken. Fishing, parks, shopping, theater and watersports nearby.

Location: Six miles from ferry landing, 2 miles from Westsound.

Publicity: *Los Angeles Times, USA Today, Travel & Leisure, Contra Costa
Sun, Seattle Times, Northwest Living, Sunset, Food & Wine, Gourmet,
Northwest Travel, New York Times, Alaska Air.*

"A peaceful haven for soothing the soul."

Forks C2

Miller Tree Inn

PO Box 953
Forks, WA 98331-0953
(360)374-6806

Circa 1917. The Miller Tree Inn is a modernized farmhouse set
on three acres adjacent to a favorite grazing spot for local elk.
The inn caters to hikers, tourists and fishermen, and will serve
breakfast at 4:30 a.m., October through April. Comfortable
rooms and economical rates make it a popular stopover in this
timber town.

Innkeeper(s): Ted & Prue Miller. $60-90. MC VISA. 6 rooms, 3 with PB. Type
of meal: full breakfast. Evening snack available. Beds: QDT. Phone in room.
TV and spa on premises. Family reunions hosted.

Location: Adjacent to Olympic National Park.

Publicity: *Peninsula Business Journal, Walking Magazine.*

"The homey and warm atmosphere was wonderful. You've spoiled us."

Friday Harbor B3

States Inn

2039 W Valley Rd
Friday Harbor, WA 98250-9211
(360)378-6240 Fax:(360)378-6241

Circa 1910. This sprawling ranch home has ten guest rooms, each named and themed for a particular state. The Arizona and New Mexico rooms,

often booked by families or couples traveling together, can be combined to create a private suite with two bedrooms, a bathroom and a sitting area. The oldest part of the house was built as a country school and later used as a dance hall, before it was relocated to its current 60-acre spread. Baked French toast, accompanied by fresh fruit topped with yogurt sauce and homemade muffins are typical breakfast fare.

$68-125. MC VISA PC TC. TAC10. 10 rooms, 8 with PB, 1 with FP. 1 suite. Breakfast and afternoon tea included in rates. Types of meals: full breakfast and early coffee/tea. Beds: KQDT. Fax and stables on premises. Handicap access. 60 acres. Weddings, small meetings and family reunions hosted. Antiques, fishing, parks, shopping, theater and watersports nearby.

Location: On San Juan Island.

Publicity: *Glamour, Conde Nast, USA Today.*

Tower House B&B

1230 Little Rd
Friday Harbor, WA 98250-9567
(360)378-5464 (800)858-4276 Fax:(360)378-5464
E-mail: joe_luma@compuserve.com

Circa 1930. Located on 10 acres, this Queen Anne house originally was built in Victoria, British Columbia, and was barged to San Juan Island. There is a large shingled two-story tower, which affords interesting sunsets viewed through the stained-glass window in the Tower Room. This room features a keyhole entrance to the tower, a brass bed, antique dresser, a window seat and a floral bedspread. Watch for herons, rabbits and eagles from the wicker-furnished porch, or stroll the grounds. Full breakfasts are served in the dining room and vegetarian meals are available.

Innkeeper(s): Chris & Joe Luma. $95-120. MC VISA AX DS PC TC. TAC10. 2 rooms with PB. Breakfast included in rates. Type of meal: full breakfast. Beds: Q. TV, VCR, fax and library on premises. 11 acres. Fishing, parks, shopping, golf, theater and watersports nearby.

"Without a doubt the accommodations were as warm as the people who provided them."

Greenbank C4

Guest House Cottages, A B&B Inn

3366 S Hwy 525, Whidbey Island
Greenbank, WA 98253-6400
(360)678-3115 Fax:(360)321-0631

Circa 1922. These storybook cottages and log home are nestled within a peaceful forest on 25 acres. The Hansel and

Gretel cottage features stained-glass and criss-cross paned windows that give it the feel of a gingerbread house. Two of the cottages were built in 1922. Ask for the Lodge and you'll enjoy a private setting with a pond just beyond your deck. Inside is a Jacuzzi tub, stone fireplace, king bed, antiques and an intimate hunting lodge atmosphere.

Innkeeper(s): Don & Mary Jane Creger. $110-285. MC VISA AX DS PC TC. 1 suite. 6 cottages. Breakfast included in rates. Type of meal: full breakfast. Catered breakfast available. Beds: KQD. Air conditioning, turndown service, ceiling fan and VCR in room. Fax, copier, spa and swimming on premises. 25 acres. French spoken. Antiques, fishing, parks, shopping and golf nearby.

Location: On Whidbey Island.

Publicity: *Los Angeles Times, Woman's Day, Sunset, Country Inns, Bride's. Ratings: 4 Diamonds.*

"The wonderful thing is to be by yourselves and rediscover what's important."

Kirkland C4

Shumway Mansion

11410 99th Pl NE
Kirkland, WA 98033
(425)823-2303 Fax:(425)822-0421

Circa 1909. This resplendent 22-room, 10,000-square-foot mansion is situated on more than two acres overlooking Juanita Bay. With a large ballroom and veranda, few could guess that a short time ago, the build-

ing was hoisted on hydraulic lifts. It was then pulled three miles across town to its present site, near the beach. An athletic club just across the street offers inn guests privileges.

Innkeeper(s): Richard & Salli Harris, Julie Blakemore. $70-105. MC VISA AX. 7 rooms, 8 with PB. 1 suite. Breakfast included in rates. Type of meal: full breakfast. Evening snack available. Beds: Q. Phone in room. Weddings, family reunions and seminars hosted. Antiques, fishing, shopping, sporting events, theater and watersports nearby.

Location: West of I-405 at Juanita Bay.

Publicity: *Northgate Journal, Journal American, Northwest Living.*

"Guests enjoy the mansion so much they don't want to leave — Northwest Living."

La Conner B4

The White Swan Guest House

1388 Moore Rd
La Conner, WA 98273-9249
(360)445-6805

Circa 1898. Guests will marvel at innkeeper Peter Goldfarb's beautiful gardens as they wind up the driveway to reach this charming, yellow Victorian farmhouse. Inside, guests are greeted with luscious home-baked chocolate chip cookies in the bright, cheery kitchen. Guest rooms are filled with comfortable, Victorian furnishings, and there's even a cozy Garden Cottage to stay in, complete with its own kitchen and private sun deck.

Each April, the area is host to the Skagit Valley Tulip festival. La Conner, a nearby fishing village, is full of shops and galleries to explore.

Historic Interest: The White Swan is only an hour from the historic sites of Seattle and about 90 miles from Vancouver. The new Museum of Northwest Art and the Skagit Historical Museum are both located in downtown LaConner.

Innkeeper(s): Peter Goldfarb. $75-150. MC VISA PC TC. TAC10. 4 rooms, 1 with PB. 1 cottage. Breakfast included in rates. Types of meals: continental-plus breakfast and early coffee/tea. Beds: KQD. Turndown service in room. Family reunions hosted. Antiques, fishing, parks and shopping nearby.

"This has been a very pleasant interlude. What a beautiful, comfortable place you have here. We will be back."

Leavenworth C6

Haus Lorelei Inn

347 Division St
Leavenworth, WA 98826-1444
(509)548-5726 (800)514-8868

Circa 1903. This historic home is situated on an unparalleled two-acre site overlooking the Wenatchee River and the Cascades. The innkeeper's children are actively involved in helping out. The views are exquisite and the rushing waters of the river soothing. Leavenworth is a charming Bavarian town surrounded by breathtaking scenery. The inn is just two blocks from the downtown and is close to the beach, as well.

Innkeeper(s): Elisabeth Saunders & Billy. $89-99. 10 rooms with PB. Type of meal: full breakfast. Beds: KQ. Phone in room. Spa on premises.

"What I can say? I love this place! This is my first stay in a B&B and I adore the personality and charm you have in every corner of this place..."

Mount Vernon (La Conner) B4

Ridgeway "Farm" B&B

1292 McLean Rd
Mount Vernon (La Conner), WA 98273
(206)428-8068 (800)428-8068

Circa 1928. A Dutch Colonial farmhouse and cottage, Ridgeway is on two acres. From here you can watch migrating swans and snow geese in the fall. Homemade desserts are served each evening and in the morning, a full farm breakfast. Your host is a pilot and can arrange a private flight over the Skagit Valley and the San Juan Island. More than 70 percent of the world's tulips and daffodils are grown in the La Conner/ Mt. Vernon area.

Innkeeper(s): Louise & John Kelly. $75-155. Types of meals: full breakfast and early coffee/tea. Evening snack available. TV and VCR on premises. Weddings, small meetings, family reunions and seminars hosted. Antiques, shopping, downhill skiing, cross-country skiing, sporting events, golf and theater nearby.

"We've stayed in a lot of B&Bs and this is one of our top five. It was great!"

Nahcotta E2

Our House In Nahcotta B&B

PO Box 33
Nahcotta, WA 98637-0033
(360)665-6667

Circa 1920. Located across the street from Willapa Bay, this three-story Cape Cod house has been decorated by the innkeeper, an interior designer and master gardener. In addition to the two main suites, the innkeepers will open up their third-floor suite to accommodate a group of four or more traveling together. Guests enjoy a private parlor, homemade breads and the inn's special fruit plate. The highly rated Ark Restaurant is a few steps away. The Long Beach Peninsula offers a boardwalk, salmon fishing, cranberry bogs, bird watching, a hard-sand public driving beach and a dozen festivals.

Innkeeper(s): Norma Saunders. $95-105. MC VISA PC TC. TAC10. 2 suites. 1 conference room. Breakfast and afternoon tea included in rates. Types of meals: continental-plus breakfast, full breakfast and early coffee/tea. Picnic lunch available. Beds: QD. Turndown service and ceiling fan in room. Weddings and small meetings hosted. Amusement parks, antiques, fishing, parks, shopping and watersports nearby.

Pets Allowed.

"We've done the West Coast B&B circuit; yours is one of the finest! Enjoyed your lovely garden, great breakfast and comfortable suite."

Olympia D3

Harbinger Inn

1136 E Bay Dr NE
Olympia, WA 98506
(360)754-0389

Circa 1910. The inn is built of finely detailed, gray, ashler block construction with white pillars and wide balconies all completely restored. Original distinctive features include a street-to-basement tunnel and a hillside waterfall fed by an artesian well. Turn-of-the-century furniture has been used in keeping with the original wall stencils and oak pocket doors of the first floor. Guests can borrow books from the library for night reading, enjoy late afternoon tea and cookies or just make themselves comfortable in the sitting room while gazing over the water and marina to the nearby capitol.

Historic Interest: Olympia Capitol, museums (2 miles), bird sanctuary, Old Growth Park.

Innkeeper(s): Terrell & Marisa Williams. $60-100. MC VISA AX. 4 rooms, 3 with PB. 3 suites. Breakfast included in rates. Type of meal: continental breakfast. Afternoon tea available. Beds: KQ. TV and VCR on premises. Weddings, small meetings, family reunions and seminars hosted. Antiques, fishing, shopping and theater nearby.

Publicity: *Northwest Discoveries.*

Puget View Guesthouse

7924 61st Ave NE
Olympia, WA 98516-9138
(360)413-9474

Circa 1930. This private, two-room waterfront cottage is located on a lush property boasting views of Puget Sound. The innkeepers live on the property, but not in the cottage, so guests have the run of the hideaway. The country decor is simple and comfortable, and the cottage includes a microwave and a small refrigerator. For a small extra fee, the innkeepers will prepare a "Romantic Retreat" package.

Innkeeper(s): Dick & Barbara Yunker. $89. MC VISA PC TC. TAC10. 1 cottage. Breakfast included in rates. Type of meal: continental-plus breakfast. Beds: QD. Phone in room. Parks and watersports nearby.
Pets Allowed: $10 per night fee. Pet accepted with hosts approval.
Publicity: *The Olympian.*

"*Truly a beautiful place in the world.*"

Orcas B3

Orcas Hotel

PO Box 155
Orcas, WA 98280-0155
(360)376-4300 (888)376-4300 Fax:(360)376-4399

Circa 1900. Listed in the National Register, this three-story Victorian inn across from the ferry landing has been a landmark to travelers and boaters since the early 1900s. An open porch stretches around three sides and is filled with white wicker furniture. From this vantage point, guests enjoy views of terraced lawns and flower beds of peonies, daffodils, iris and roses. A white picket fence and a vista of sea and islands complete the picture.

Innkeeper(s): Craig & Lynda Sanders. $65-175. MC VISA AX. 12 rooms, 5 with PB. 1 conference room. Types of meals: continental breakfast, full breakfast and gourmet breakfast. Restaurant on premises. Beds: QT. Phone in room. Copier and spa on premises. Handicap access.
Location: Overlooking the ferry landing on Orcas Island.
Publicity: *Los Angeles Times, Seattle Times, New York Times.*

"*The few days I've spent here are by far the best ones of my trip. I shall cherish these memories fondly.*"

Windsong B&B

Deer Harbor Rd, PO Box 32
Orcas, WA 98280
(360)376-2500 (800)669-3948 Fax:(360)376-4453
E-mail: windsong@picificrim.net

Circa 1917. Shaded by tall fir trees and located on four acres, this Northwest cottage served as the Westsound grammar school, a two-room schoolhouse until the '40s. Guest rooms here offer a few antiques, comfortable beds and sitting areas. The Nocturne has a gas fireplace, island-crafted furniture and art. The dining room is casual with an oak trestle table and white lace curtains. Breakfast features items such as Ginger Poached Salmon, Apple Rosemary Sausage and French Crepes

with Yakima Peaches. Favorite activities in the area include whale watching, sea otter and harbor seal spotting and sighting an occasional eagle. After a day of hiking, cycling or sea kayaking, guests look forward to the Jacuzzi in the Moon Room.

Innkeeper(s): Sam & Kim Haines. $105-175. MC VISA PC TC. TAC10. 6 rooms with PB, 5 with FP. Breakfast included in rates. Types of meals: gourmet breakfast and early coffee/tea. Beds: KQ. Turndown service, ceiling fan, TV and VCR in room. Fax, spa and library on premises. Small meetings, family reunions and seminars hosted. Antiques, fishing, parks, shopping, golf, theater and watersports nearby.

Port Angeles C3

Domaine Madeleine B&B

146 Wildflower Ln
Port Angeles, WA 98362-8138
(360)457-4174 Fax:(360)457-3037

Circa 1947. This unique inn blends French with Oriental decor and offers a romantic setting on five acres and 168 feet of waterfront. The landscape includes dozens of rhododendrons, numerous wild and cultivated flowers, Douglas firs, cedars, maples and pines. Deer often browse through the property, whales can sometimes be seen off the shore and bald eagles fly above. The innkeepers take pride in helping guests plan romantic events and can pack a special lunch on request. Choosing a restaurant for dinner is made easier by browsing the inn's menu collection.

Innkeeper(s): John Chambers. $135-165. MC VISA AX DS PC TC. 5 rooms with PB, 5 with FP. 2 suites. 1 cottage. Breakfast included in rates. Type of meal: gourmet breakfast. Beds: KQ. Phone, air conditioning, TV and VCR in room. Fax, copier and library on premises. Weddings and small meetings hosted. French, Spanish, German and Farsi spoken. Antiques, fishing, parks, downhill skiing, cross-country skiing and golf nearby.
Publicity: *Northwest Travel. Ratings: 4 Stars.*

"*Nowhere have I found lodgings that compared to Domaine Madeleine. I consider four criteria in determining where to stay when I travel; accommodations, food, uniqueness, and hospitality. Domaine Madeleine excels in all these categories.*"

Tudor Inn

1108 S Oak St
Port Angeles, WA 98362-7745
(360)452-3138

Circa 1910. This English Tudor inn has been tastefully restored to display its original woodwork and fir stairway. Guests enjoy stone fireplaces in the living room and study. A terraced flower garden with 100-foot oak trees graces the property.

Innkeeper(s): Jane Glass. $75-120. MC VISA AX DS PC TC. TAC10. 5 rooms with PB, 1 with FP. Breakfast and afternoon tea included in rates. Type of meal: full breakfast. Beds: T. Phone in room. TV, VCR and library on premises. Weddings hosted. Antiques, fishing, parks, shopping,  downhill skiing, cross-country skiing, theater and watersports nearby.
Location: Eleven blocks south of the harbor with water & mountain views.
Publicity: *Seattle Times, Oregonian, Los Angeles Times, Olympic Magazine.*

"*Delicious company and delicious food. Best in hospitality and warmth. Beautiful gardens!*"

Port Townsend   C3

Ann Starrett Mansion

744 Clay St
Port Townsend, WA 98368-5808
(360)385-3205 (888)385-3205 Fax:(360)385-2976

Circa 1889. George Starrett came from Maine to Port Townsend and became the major residential builder. By 1889, he had constructed one house a week, totaling more than 350 houses. The Smithsonian believes the Ann Starrett's elaborate free-hung spiral staircase is the only one of its type in the United States. A frescoed dome atop the octagonal tower depicts four seasons and four virtues. On the first day of each season, the sun causes a ruby red light to point toward the appropriate painting. The mansion won a "Great American Home Award," from the National Trust for Historic Preservation.

Historic Interest: The inn is located in the Port Townsend National Historic District near Fort Worden and Fort Townsend state parks.

Innkeeper(s): Bob & Edel Sokol. $75-225. MC VISA AX DS PC TC. TAC10. 11 rooms with PB, 2 with FP. 2 suites. 2 conference rooms. Breakfast included in rates. Type of meal: full breakfast. Afternoon tea available. Beds: KQDT. Phone and TV in room. VCR, fax, copier and spa on premises. German spoken. Antiques, fishing, parks, shopping, cross-country skiing, theater and watersports nearby.

Location: Three blocks from the business district.

Publicity: *Peninsula, New York Times, Vancouver Sun, San Francisco Examiner, London Times, Colonial Homes, Elle, Leader, Japanese Travel, National Geographic Traveler, Victorian, Historic American Trails.*

"*Staying here was like a dream come true.*"

Annapurna Inn

538 Adams St
Port Townsend, WA 98368-5805
(360)385-2909 (800)868-2662 Fax:(360)379-0711

Circa 1881. Besides bed & breakfast lodging, this Folk Victorian-style inn specializes in stress management therapy that includes massages, yoga, heart-healthy, organic vegetarian cuisine and a serene environment. Guests are also invited to relax in the inn's sauna/steam bath and Jacuzzi. Located in a Victorian seaport, the setting is ideal for walks through parks, along the shores of Puget Sound and a wildlife refuge. Call to inquire about retreat rates.

Innkeeper(s): Robin Sharan. $75-118. MC VISA PC TC. TAC10. 6 rooms, 3 with PB. 2 suites. 1 cottage. 1 conference room. Breakfast included in rates. Types of meals: full breakfast and gourmet breakfast. Beds: QTD. TV, VCR, fax, spa, sauna, bicycles and library on premises. Handicap access. Weddings, small meetings, family reunions and seminars hosted. French, Spanish and Hebrew spoken. Antiques, parks, shopping and theater nearby.

Holly Hill House B&B

611 Polk St
Port Townsend, WA 98368-6531
(360)385-5619 (800)435-1454
E-mail: hollyhill@olympus.net

Circa 1872. A unique "upside-down" century-old Camperdown elm and several holly trees surround this aptly named bed & breakfast, built by Robert C. Hill, the co-founder of the First National Bank of Port Townsend. The cozy, romantic rooms are decorated with florals and lace. Billie's Room affords a view of Admiralty Inlet and Mt. Baker, while Lizette's Room offers Victorian decor and a view of the garden. The Skyview Room includes a wonderful skylight. The spacious Colonel's

Room features a picture window with water and mountain views, and the Morning Glory Room is a cozy retreat with lace-trimmed quilts. Expansive breakfasts are served in the dining room, and coffee and tea are always available. The inn's gardens are surrounded by a picket fence and nearly 200 rose bushes.

Historic Interest: Built in 1872 by Robert C. and Elizabeth Hill, co-founders of First National Bank of Port Townsend, mayor and state representative.

Innkeeper(s): Lynne Sterling. $78-145. TAC10. 5 rooms with PB. 1 suite. Breakfast included in rates. Types of meals: full breakfast and early coffee/tea. Afternoon tea, evening snack and picnic lunch available. Beds: KQT. Turndown service in room. TV and library on premises. Weddings and small meetings hosted. German spoken. Antiques, fishing, parks, shopping and theater nearby.

Location: Two miles from Fort Worden State Park and in the heart of historic district.

James House

1238 Washington St
Port Townsend, WA 98368-6714
(360)385-1238 (800)385-1238

Circa 1889. This Queen Anne mansion built by Francis James overlooks Puget Sound with views of the Cascades and Olympic mountain ranges. The three-story staircase was constructed of solid wild cherry brought around Cape Horn from Virginia. Parquet floors are composed of oak, cherry, walnut and maple, providing a suitable setting for the inn's collection of antiques.

Historic Interest: Located within the historic district and one mile from the Fort Worden State Park.

Innkeeper(s): Carol McGough. $75-165. MC VISA AX. 13 rooms, 11 with PB, 4 with FP. 4 suites. 1 conference room. Breakfast included in rates. Type of meal: full breakfast. Beds: QD. Phone in room. Antiques, fishing, cross-country skiing and theater nearby.

Location: On the bluff overlooking Port Townsend Bay.

Publicity: *Washington, Seattle Weekly, Northwest Best Places, Sunset.*

"*My dream house in a dream town.*"

Lizzie's

731 Pierce St
Port Townsend, WA 98368-8042
(360)385-4168 (800)700-4168
E-mail: wickline@olympus.net

Circa 1887. Named for Lizzie Grant, a sea captain's wife, this Italianate Victorian is elegant and airy. In addition to the gracious interiors, some rooms command an outstanding view of Port Townsend Bay, Puget Sound, and the Olympic and Cascade mountain ranges. Each room is filled with antiques dating from 1840 to the turn of the century. The dog's house in the garden is a one-quarter scale replica of the original house. Lizzie's is known for its elaborate breakfasts, where guests are encouraged to help themselves to seconds.

Innkeeper(s): Patricia Wickline. $70-135. MC VISA DS PC TC. 7 rooms with PB. Breakfast included in rates. Type of meal: full breakfast. Beds: KQ. Phone in room.

Location: In uptown Historic District.

Publicity: *Travel & Leisure, Victorian Homes.*

"*As they say in show biz, you're a hard act to follow.*"

Manresa Castle

PO Box 564, 7th & Sheridan
Port Townsend, WA 98368-0564
(360)385-5750 (800)732-1281 Fax:(360)385-5883

Circa 1892. When businessman Charles Eisenbeis built the largest private residence in Port Townsend, locals dubbed it "Eisenbeis Castle," because it resembled the castles in Eisenbeis' native Prussia. The home is truly a royal delight to behold, both inside and out. Luxurious European antiques and hand-painted wall coverings decorate the dining room and many of the castle's stately guest rooms. The turret suites are unique and many of the rooms have mountain and water views, but beware of the third floor. Rumors of ghosts in the upper floor have frightened some, but others seek out the "haunted" rooms for a spooky stay. Port Townsend offers a variety of galleries, gift shops and antiquing.

Historic Interest: Port Townsend and Manresa Castle are listed in the National Register. The town includes many examples of Victorian-style buildings and a historic district.

Innkeeper(s): Roger O'Connor. $68-175. MC VISA DS. 40 rooms.with PB. 1 conference room. Breakfast included in rates. Type of meal: continental breakfast. Dinner, banquet service and catered breakfast available. Restaurant on premises. Beds: KQDT. Phone and TV in room. Weddings, small meetings, family reunions and seminars hosted. Antiques, fishing, shopping, theater and watersports nearby.

Publicity: *Island Independent, Leader News, Province Showcase, Sunset Magazine.*

Old Consulate Inn F.W. Hastings House

313 Walker at Washington
Port Townsend, WA 98368
(360)385-6753 (800)300-6753 Fax:(360)385-2097

Circa 1889. This handsome red Victorian, once the residence of the German consul, commands expansive views of Port Townsend Bay from its blufftop setting. Fine antiques, a grand piano, elegant stairway and Victorian wallcoverings create a romantic fantasy that is continued in the Tower Suite where five curved turret windows afford majestic water and mountain views. There is also a hot tub and a gazebo on the premises. Guests are offered gourmet breakfast and evening cordials and desserts. Visitors remember the inn for its excellent cuisine and award-winning romantic ambiance.

Innkeeper(s): Rob & Joanna Jackson. $79-195. MAP. MC VISA AX PC TC. TAC10. 8 rooms with PB, 1 with FP. 3 suites. 1 conference room. Breakfast, afternoon tea and evening snack included in rates. Types of meals: gourmet breakfast and early coffee/tea. Catering service and catered breakfast available. Beds: KQ. Turndown service in room. TV, VCR, fax, copier, spa, tennis and library on premises. Weddings, small meetings, family reunions and seminars hosted. Antiques, fishing, parks, shopping, cross-country skiing, theater and watersports nearby.

Publicity: *Pacific Northwest, Seattle Weekly.* Ratings: 4 Diamonds.

"Beautiful in every way."

Palace Hotel

1004 Water St
Port Townsend, WA 98368-6706
(360)946-5176 (800)962-0741 Fax:(360)385-0780

Circa 1889. This old brick hotel has been restored and refurbished in a Victorian style. The Miss Rose Room has a six-foot

Jacuzzi tub and is on the third floor. Some rooms have kitchenettes, such as Miss Kitty's Room, with its velvet settee, antique bed and wood stove.

Innkeeper(s): Michael & Spring Thomas. $65-129. MC VISA AX DS. 15 rooms. Breakfast included in rates. Type of meal: continental-plus breakfast. Restaurant on premises. Beds: KQD.

Seabeck   C3

Willcox House

2390 Tekiu Rd Nw
Seabeck, WA 98380
(360)830-4492 (800)725-9477 Fax:(360)830-0506

Circa 1936. Colonel Julian Willcox and his family, once members of San Francisco high society, selected Lionel Pries to build this home on a wooded bluff overlooking Hood Canal. Holding court thereafter, the family entertained fashionable Northwest personalities, including Clark Gable. The 7,800-square-foot manse was constructed with a slate tile exterior, copper roofing and vast expanses of small-paned windows, affording views of the shimmering waters, the Olympic mountains and forested hillsides. There are five marble and copper fireplaces, silk wallpaper, oak floors, fine antiques and period pieces throughout. The Julian Room sports a double whirlpool tub.

Innkeeper(s): Cecilia & Phillip Hughes. $119-189. MC VISA. 5 rooms with PB, 1 with FP. Types of meals: full breakfast, gourmet breakfast and early coffee/tea. Dinner, evening snack, picnic lunch and lunch available. Beds: KQ. Phone in room. Fax and copier on premises. Weddings, small meetings, family reunions and seminars hosted. Antiques and shopping nearby.

Publicity: *Country Inns, Seattle Times, The Olympian, Journal American.*

"Diane & I and Clark love the place and delight in the knowledge that all Californians aren't bad - in fact some are downright wonderful."

Seattle   C4

Chambered Nautilus B&B Inn

5005 22nd Ave NE
Seattle, WA 98105
(206)522-2536 (800)545-8459 Fax:(206)528-0898

Circa 1915. This blue, Georgian Colonial Revival home was built on a hill in the university district by Dr. Herbert Gowen of the University of Washington. Georgian Colonial Revival architecture reflects the first owner's English heritage. Three dormers and Palladian doors grace the front of the inn and an enclosed sunporch that offers views of the garden. The large airy guest rooms are furnished with Persian rugs and antiques. Many have porches and views of the Cascade mountains. Tea is served by the fire in the living room, while guests can enjoy freshly baked cookies on the sunporch or relax with a book from the inn's well-stocked shelves.

Historic Interest: Pioneer Square (15 minutes), Port Townsend (2 1/2 hours), Mount Rainier (2 1/2 hours), Mount Saint Helens (3 hours).

Innkeeper(s): Joyce Schulte & Steve Poole. $79-109. MC VISA AX. 6 rooms with PB. Breakfast and afternoon tea included in rates. Types of meals: full breakfast and early coffee/tea. Beds: KQ. Phone in room. Weddings, small meetings, family reunions and seminars hosted. Antiques, shopping, downhill skiing, sporting events and theater nearby.

Location: In the University District, minutes from downtown.

Publicity: *Innsider.*

"I think you've spoiled us for any other inn, any place. We felt like royalty and family members all at the same time."

Chelsea Station on the Park

4915 Linden Ave N
Seattle, WA 98103-6536
(206)547-6077 (800)400-6077 Fax:(206)632-5107
E-mail: jsg@nwlink.com

Circa 1929. This Federal Colonial home, a fine example of the bricklayer's art, is nestled between Fremont and Woodland Park, just north of downtown Seattle. Hearty breakfasts with items such as warm date scones, fresh fruit and specialty entrees. Tea and a bottomless cookie jar are on hand throughout the day. The home's decor is predominately Mission style with antiques throughout. The zoo, Seattle Rose Garden, shops and restaurants are within walking distance.

Historic Interest: Minutes from Seattle's historic Pioneer Square district.

Innkeeper(s): John Griffin, Karen Carbonneau. $75-125. MC VISA AX DC DS PC TC. TAC10. 8 rooms with PB. 6 suites. Breakfast included in rates. Type of meal: full breakfast. Beds: KQT. Phone in room. Fax and copier on premises. Theater nearby.

Location: Minutes north of downtown in the Fremont neighborhood. Near Greenlake & Woodland Park Zoo.

Publicity: *Seattle Press, Puget Sound Business Journal, Journal Newspaper.*

"Truly a place to refresh your spirit!"

Pioneer Square Hotel

77 Yesler Way
Seattle, WA 98104
(206)340-1234 (800)800-5514 Fax:(206)467-0707
E-mail: info@pioneersquare.com

Circa 1914. The estate of Seattle's founding father, Henry Yesler, built this historic waterfront hotel. The hotel is well-appointed and elegant rooms feature coordinating prints. Business travelers will appreciate the direct dial telephones with data ports, and there are individual climate controls in each room. No meals are included in the hotel's rates, but restaurants and cafes are nearby, as is Historic Pioneer Square, ferries and shopping.

Innkeeper(s): Jo Thompson. $89-139. TAC10. 72 rooms with PB. 3 suites. Beds: KQDT. Phone, air conditioning, turndown service and TV in room. Fax and copier on premises. Handicap access. Weddings, small meetings, family reunions and seminars hosted. Parks, shopping, downhill skiing, cross-country skiing, sporting events, theater and watersports nearby.

Seaview   E2

Shelburne Inn

4415 Pacific Way, PO Box 250
Seaview, WA 98644
(360)642-2442 Fax:(360)642-8904

Circa 1896. The Shelburne is known as the oldest continuously operating hotel in the state of Washington, and it is listed in the National Register. The front desk at the hotel is a former church altar. Art nouveau stained-glass windows rescued from a church torn down in Morecambe, England, now shed light and color on the dining room. The guest rooms are appointed in antiques. In between the Columbia River and the Pacific

Ocean, the inn is situated on the Long Beach Peninsula, a 28-mile stretch of seacoast that includes bird sanctuaries and lighthouses. The inn offers a full gourmet breakfast.

Innkeeper(s): David Campiche & Laurie Anderson. $102-175. MC VISA AX. 15 rooms with PB. 2 suites. 1 conference room. Breakfast included in rates. Type of meal: gourmet breakfast. Dinner, lunch, catering service and room service available. Restaurant on premises. Beds: QD. Phone in room. Fax and copier on premises. Handicap access. Antiques and fishing nearby.

Location: Southwest Washington state.

Publicity: *Better Homes & Gardens, Bon Appetit, Conde Nast Traveler, Esquire, Gourmet, Food & Wine.*

"Fabulous food. Homey but elegant atmosphere. Hospitable service, like being a guest in an elegant home."

Spokane   C9

Fotheringham House

2128 W 2nd Ave
Spokane, WA 99204-0916
(509)838-1891 Fax:(509)838-1807
E-mail: fotheringham.bnb@ior.com

A vintage Victorian in the National Register, this inn was built by the first mayor of Spokane, David Fotheringham. There are tin ceilings, a carved staircase, gabled porches and polished woodwork. Victorian furnishings and stained-glass pieces are featured. Across the street is Coeur d'Alene Park and the Patsy Clark  Mansion, a favorite Spokane restaurant. Walk two blocks to the Elk Cafe to enjoy sitting at the old-fashioned soda fountain.

Historic Interest: 1891 home of Spokane's first mayor.

Innkeeper(s): Jackie & Graham Johnson. $75-95. MC VISA AX DS. 4 rooms. Breakfast included in rates. Types of meals: full breakfast and early coffee/tea. Weddings, small meetings, family reunions and seminars hosted. Antiques, shopping, sporting events and theater nearby.

Tacoma   D4

Chinaberry Hill - An 1889 Victorian Inn

302 Tacoma Ave N
Tacoma, WA 98403
(253)272-1282 Fax:(253)272-1335
E-mail: chinaberry@wa.net

Circa 1889. In the 19th century, this Queen Anne was known as far away as China for its wondrous gardens, one of the earliest examples of landscape gardening in the Pacific Northwest. The home, a wedding present from a husband to his bride, is listed in the National Register. The innkeepers have selected a unique assortment of antiques and collectibles to decorate the manor. The house offers two Jacuzzi suites and a guest room, all eclectically decorated with items such as a four-poster rice bed or a canopy bed. There are two lodging options in the Catchpenny Cottage, a restored carriage house steps away from the manor. Guests can stay either in the romantic carriage suite or the Hay Loft, which includes a bedroom, sitting room, claw-foot tub and a unique hay chute. In the mornings, as the innkeepers say, guests enjoy "hearty breakfasts and serious coffee." Not a bad start to a day exploring Antique Row or Pt. Defiance, a 698-acre protected rainforest park with an aquarium, gardens, beaches and a zoo. Seattle is 30 minutes away.

Innkeeper(s): Cecil & Yarrow Wayman. $95-125. MC VISA AX DS PC TC. TAC10. 5 rooms with PB, 1 with FP. 4 suites. 1 cottage. 2 conference rooms. Breakfast and evening snack included in rates. Types of meals: continental-plus breakfast, gourmet breakfast and early coffee/tea. Beds: Q. Phone, turndown service, ceiling fan, TV and VCR in room. Fax, copier and library on premises. Weddings, small meetings, family reunions and seminars hosted. Antiques, fishing, parks, shopping, sporting events, golf, theater and watersports nearby.

Publicity: *Seattle Magazine, Oregonian, Tacoma News Tribune, Tacoma Weekly, Olympian.*

". . . the highlight of our trip so far - wonderful . . .the company, the food, the accommodations, all the best."

Commencement Bay B&B

3312 N Union Ave
Tacoma, WA 98407-6055
(253)752-8175 Fax:(253)759-4025
E-mail: greatviews@aol.com

Circa 1937. Watch boats sail across the bay while enjoying breakfast served with gourmet coffee at this Colonial Revival inn where a friendly cat is one of the favorite residents. All guest rooms feature bay views and each is unique and individually decorated. The surrounding area includes historic sites, antique shops, waterfront restaurants, wooded nature trails and Pt. Defiance Zoo and Aquarium. Relax in a secluded hot tub and deck area or in the fireside room for reading and a romantic view. The B&B is centrally located, 30 miles from both Seattle and Mt. Rainier park.

Historic Interest: Washington State Historical Museum (2 miles), Fort Nisqually first settlement in Washington, replica (2 miles), Historic homes and buildings, driving tour (one-half mile).

Innkeeper(s): Sharon & Bill Kaufmann. $75-115. AP. MC VISA AX DS PC TC. TAC10. 3 rooms with PB. 2 conference rooms. Breakfast and evening snack included in rates. Types of meals: full breakfast and early coffee/tea. Beds: Q. Phone, TV and VCR in room. Fax, spa, bicycles and library on premises. Small meetings hosted. Antiques, fishing, parks, shopping, sporting events, theater and watersports nearby.

Location: 30 miles to Seattle and Mount Rainier.

Publicity: *Tacoma Weekly, News Tribune, Tacoma Voice, Oregonian, NW Best Places.*

"Perfect in every detail! The setting, breathtaking; the food, scrumptious and beautifully presented; the warmth and friendship here."

Devoe Mansion B&B

208 133rd St E.
Tacoma, WA 98445-1420
(253)539-3991 (888)539-3991 Fax:(253)539-8539
E-mail: devoe@wolfenet.com

Circa 1911. Women in Washington have great reason to thank the first owner of this National Register mansion. Emma Smith DeVoe, a dedicated suffragist, lobbied and fought to have

Washington become the fifth state to give women the right to vote. She also founded what is now known as the League of Women Voters. Guest rooms are named in honor of

people who were important in Emma's life, such as the Susan B. Anthony Room. Another room is named for her husband, John Henry DeVoe. All of the rooms are decorated with period antiques, affording a nostalgic charm, as do newspaper clippings from Emma's era. There are porches to relax on and more than an acre of landscaped grounds to enjoy. Each day, the innkeepers prepare a different breakfast entree, accompanied by fresh fruit and homemade muffins. Tacoma offers much to do, and Seattle is nearby.

Innkeeper(s): Dave & Cheryl Teifke. $90-105. MC VISA PC TC. TAC10. 4 rooms with PB. 1 conference room. Breakfast included in rates. Types of meals: continental breakfast, full breakfast and early coffee/tea. Afternoon tea and picnic lunch available. Beds: Q. Phone and turndown service in room. TV, VCR, fax, spa and bicycles on premises. Weddings, small meetings and seminars hosted. Antiques, fishing, parks, shopping, cross-country skiing, sporting events, golf and theater nearby.

Publicity: *Ruralite, Tribune.*

"I felt like a princess in grandma's house."

The Villa

705 N 5th St
Tacoma, WA 98403-2318
(206)572-1157 (888)572-1157 Fax:(206)572-1805
E-mail: villabb@aol.com

Circa 1925. Ambrose Russell, architect of the Washington governor's mansion, created this award-winning Italianate Renaissance mansion listed in the National Register. The six rooms are beautifully decorated. The Olympic Suite features a canopy-draped four-poster bed, fireplace, a sitting area with over-stuffed sofas and a private veranda, all over-looking the Puget Sound and Olympic Mountain range. Some of the many amenities include fluffy robes, fine linens, ceiling fans, hair dryers, soaking tubs and CD players. Evening refreshments are served, and breakfast brings freshly baked pastries, fruit dishes and entrees such as quiche or homemade waffles. The B&B is in Stadium Historic District, close to downtown Tacoma and central to most of western Washington's attractions.

Innkeeper(s): Becky & Greg Anglemyer. $85-145. MC VISA AX PC TC. TAC10. 6 rooms with PB, 5 with FP. 3 suites. 3 conference rooms. Breakfast and evening snack included in rates. Types of meals: continental-plus breakfast, full breakfast and early coffee/tea. Beds: KQSOFA. Turndown service in room. TV, VCR, fax, copier, bicycles and library on premises. Weddings, small meetings, family reunions and seminars hosted. Amusement parks, antiques, fishing, parks, shopping, cross-country skiing, sporting events, golf, theater and watersports nearby.

Walla Walla F8

Stone Creek Inn

720 Bryant Ave
Walla Walla, WA 99362-9322
(509)529-8120 Fax:(509)529-8120
E-mail: stonecrk@bmi.net

Circa 1883. This grand Victorian served as the home of Miles Conway Moore, a Walla Walla mayor and governor of what was Washington Territory. The home is the last remaining territorial governor's mansion. There are many period elements to admire, from the handsome woodwork to 12-foot ceilings. The decor has both a European and Victorian ambiance, and rooms are comfortable and spacious. There are four acres with gardens, century-old trees and a creek. Guests flying into the area arrive at

Stone Creek in style via limousine service. Innkeeper Patricia Johnson further pampers guests with a lavish breakfast, beginning with fresh juice or perhaps a mimosa. Gourmet omelets, cheese blintzes, homemade scones or muffins and a warm berry cobbler are some of the breakfast possibilities. Wineries, a tour of historic homes and shopping are among the things to do in the Walla Walla area.

Innkeeper(s): Patricia Johnson. $95-125. MC VISA PC TC. TAC5. 4 rooms, 2 with PB, 2 with FP. 1 suite. Breakfast and afternoon tea included in rates. Types of meals: full breakfast and early coffee/tea. Beds: QT. Air conditioning, turndown service, TV and VCR in room. Fax, copier, spa, swimming and library on premises. Weddings and small meetings hosted. Antiques, parks, downhill skiing and theater nearby.

Publicity: *Hideaways.*

"We were delighted with your high tea. What a nice setting for the event. The house and your collections are most interesting."

Yakima E6

A Touch of Europe™ B&B Inn Yakima

220 N 16th Ave
Yakima, WA 98902-2461
(509)454-9775 (888)438-7073

Circa 1889. A lumber baron built this Queen Anne Victorian, which still maintains period elements such as stained glass and rich woodwork. Theodore Roosevelt was a guest of the home's second owner, who was the first woman to be a member of the Washington State House of Representatives. Roosevelt's portrait is displayed among other historical photographs. The guest rooms are elegant, featuring period decor and Victorian furnishings. Innkeeper, chef and cookbook author Erika Cenci prepares the multi-course breakfasts, which are served by candlelight. A traditional high tea is served daily, while a delicious, multi-course dinner is available with advance notice.

Innkeeper(s): Erika G. and James A. Cenci. $65-110. MC VISA AX TC. TAC10. 3 rooms with PB, 1 with FP. 1 conference room. Breakfast included in rates. Type of meal: full breakfast. Picnic lunch and gourmet lunch available. Beds: QT. Phone in room. Library on premises. Small meetings hosted. German and English spoken. Antiques, fishing, parks, shopping, downhill skiing, cross-country skiing, sporting events, golf, theater and watersports nearby.

"Thank you for your warmth and friendliness and outstanding food! Your home is beautiful."

Washington, D.C.

Washington

Adams Inn

1744 Lanier Pl NW
Washington, DC 20009-2118
(202)745-3600 (800)578-6807 Fax:(202)319-7958
E-mail: adamsinn@adamsinn.com

Circa 1908. These restored town houses have fireplaces, a library and parlor, all furnished home-style, as are the guest rooms. Former residents of this neighborhood include Tallulah Bankhead, Woodrow Wilson and Al Jolson. The Adams-Morgan area is home to diplomats, radio and television personalities and government workers. A notable firehouse across the street holds the record for the fastest response of a horse-drawn fire apparatus. Located in the restaurant area, over 100 restaurants and shops are within walking distance.

Historic Interest: Washington, D.C., it goes without saying, is full of national treasures and the Smithsonian museums.

Innkeeper(s): Gene & Nancy Thompson, Anne Owens. $55-70. MC VISA AX DC CB DS TC. TAC10. 24 rooms, 14 with PB. Breakfast included in rates. Meals: continental-plus breakfast and early coffee/tea. Beds: QDT. Air conditioning in room. TV and library on premises. Antiques and parks nearby.

Location: Two miles from the White House, walking distance to major hotels and public transportation.

Publicity: *Travel Host.*

"We enjoyed your friendly hospitality and the home-like atmosphere. Your suggestions on restaurants and help in planning our visit were appreciated."

The Embassy Inn

1627 16th St NW
Washington, DC 20009-3063
(202)234-7800 (800)423-9111 Fax:(202)234-3309

Circa 1910. This restored inn is furnished in a Federalist style. The comfortable lobby offers books and evening sherry. Conveniently located, the inn is seven blocks from the Adams Morgan area of ethnic restaurants. The Embassy's philosophy of innkeeping includes providing personal attention and cheerful hospitality. Concierge services are available.

Innkeeper(s): Jennifer Schroeder & Susan Stiles. $69-150. MC VISA AX DC CB TC. TAC10. 38 rooms with PB. Breakfast included in rates. Type of meal: continental-plus breakfast. Beds: DT. Phone, air conditioning and TV in room. Fax and copier on premises. Antiques, parks and theater nearby.

Location: Downtown Washington, D.C., 10 blocks north of the White House.

Publicity: *Los Angeles Times, Inn Times, Business Review.*

"When I return to D.C., I'll be back at the Embassy."

Reeds B&B

PO Box 12011
Washington, DC 20005-0911
(202)328-3510 Fax:(202)332-3885

Circa 1887. This three-story Victorian townhouse was built by John Shipman, who owned one of the first construction companies in the city. The turn-of-the-century revitalization of Washington began in Logan Circle, considered to be the city's first truly residential area. During the house's restoration, flower gardens, terraces and fountains were added. Victorian antiques, original wood paneling, stained glass, chandeliers, as well as practical amenities such as air conditioning and laundry facilities, make this a comfortable stay. There is a furnished apartment available, as well.

Historic Interest: U.S. Capitol, Congress, Smithsonian Museums, White House, all national monuments.

Innkeeper(s): Charles & Jackie Reed. $45-110. MC VISA AX DC TC. TAC8. 6 rooms, 4 with PB, 2 with FP. 1 suite. Breakfast included in rates. Type of meal: continental-plus breakfast. Beds: QD. Phone, air conditioning and TV in room. Weddings, small meetings and family reunions hosted. French and Spanish spoken. Antiques, parks, shopping, sporting events, theater nearby.

Location: Downtown, 10 blocks from White House.

Publicity: *Philadelphia Inquirer, Washington Gardner, Washington Post, 101 Great Choices, Washington, DC.*

"This home was the highlight of our stay in Washington! This was a superb home and location. The Reeds treated us better than family."

The Windsor Inn

1842 16th St NW
Washington, DC 20009-3316
(202)667-0300 (800)423-9111 Fax:(202)667-4503

Circa 1910. Recently renovated and situated in a neighborhood of renovated townhouses, the Windsor Inn is the sister property to the Embassy Inn. It is larger and offers suites as well as a small meeting room. The refurbished lobby is in an Art Deco style and a private club atmosphere prevails. It is six blocks to the Metro station at Dupont Circle. There are no elevators.

Historic Interest: White House (12 blocks), Arlington House (3 miles), Hillwood House (2 miles), Mount Vernon (14 miles).

Innkeeper(s): Jennifer Schroeder & Susan Stiles. $69-125. MC VISA AX DC CB TC. TAC10. 45 rooms with PB. 2 suites. 1 conference room. Breakfast included in rates. Type of meal: continental-plus breakfast. Beds: QDT. Phone, air conditioning and TV in room. Fax and copier on premises. Weddings, small meetings and family reunions hosted. French and Spanish spoken. Antiques, parks and theater nearby.

Location: Twelve blocks north of the White House.

Publicity: *L.A. Times, Inn Times, Sunday Telegram, WCUA Press Release.*

"Being here was like being home. Excellent service, would recommend."

West Virginia

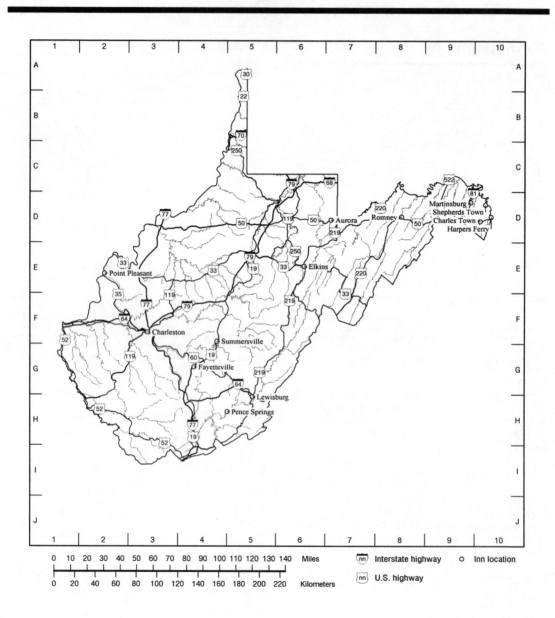

0 10 20 30 40 50 60 70 80 90 100 110 120 130 140 Miles

0 20 40 60 80 100 120 140 160 180 200 220 Kilometers

nn Interstate highway   ○ Inn location

nn U.S. highway

Aurora D7

Brookside Inn

Rt 1 Box 217 B US Rt 50
Aurora, WV 26705
(304)735-3563 (800)588-6344 Fax:(304)735-3563
E-mail: mmoure@access.mountain.net

Circa 1899. This Arts & Crafts lodge is reminiscent of an Adirondack-style lodge and is set on two-and-a-half acres. In the National Register, this building was a part of a larger resort complex which once filled the acreage across the road. There is a large double parlor with oak and chestnut woodwork and a

broad staircase with a built-in bench. Quilts, antiques and comfortable chairs may be found throughout the house. The inn offers candlelight dinners. After a day of exploring Blackwater Falls, fly fishing, skiing, boating or white-water rafting, a favored activity is rocking on the inn's large porch, or in winter, curling up near the wood stove with a good book. Across the road is Cathedral State Park with hiking trails and a protected stand of hemlock.

Innkeeper(s): Bill Reeves and Michele Moure. $115-145. MAP. MC VISA PC. 4 rooms, 1 with PB. 1 conference room. Breakfast and dinner included in rates. Types of meals: full breakfast and early coffee/tea. Catering service available. Restaurant on premises. Beds: DT. Ceiling fan in room. Fax and library on premises. Weddings, small meetings, family reunions and seminars hosted. Antiques, fishing, parks, shopping, downhill skiing, cross-country skiing, sporting events, golf, theater and watersports nearby.

"We enjoyed the home-like atmosphere with exceptional the cuisine."

Charles Town D10

Gilbert House B&B of Middleway

PO Box 1104
Charles Town, WV 25414-7104
(304)725-0637

Circa 1760. A magnificent graystone of early Georgian design, the Gilbert House is located in one of the state's oldest European settlements. During restoration, graffiti found on the upstairs bedroom walls included an 1832 drawing of the future President James Polk and a child's growth chart from the

1800s. Elegant appointments include fine Oriental rugs, tasteful art and antique furnishings. The inn is located in the Colonial era mill village of Middleway, which contains one of the country's most well-preserved collections of log houses. The village

is a mill site on the original settlers' trail into Shenandoah Valley ("Philadelphia Waggon Road" on Peter Jefferson's 1755 map of Virginia). Middleway was also the site of "wizard clip" hauntings during the last decade of the 1700s. The region was home to members of "Virginia Blues," commanded by Daniel Morgan during the American Revolutionary War.

Historic Interest: Charles Town, Bunker Hill, Leetown (10 minutes), Antietam Battlefield (20 minutes), Winchester, Va. (25 min.), Harpers Ferry (20 min.).
Innkeeper(s): Bernard F. Heiler. $80-140. MC VISA AX PC TC. TAC10. 3 rooms with PB, 2 with FP. 1 suite. Breakfast included in rates. Types of meals: full breakfast and gourmet breakfast. Beds: QT. Air conditioning in room. VCR and library on premises. German & Spanish spoken. Antiques, parks, shopping and theater nearby.
Location: Middleway historic district, 6 miles west of Charles Town.

"We have stayed at inns for fifteen years, and yours is at the top of the list as best ever!"

The Washington House Inn

216 S George St
Charles Town, WV 25414-1632
(304)725-7923 (800)297-6957 Fax:(304)728-5150
E-mail: mnvogel@intrepid.net

Circa 1899. This three-story brick Victorian was built by the descendants of President Washington's brothers, John Augustine and Samuel. Carved oak mantels, fireplaces, spacious guest rooms, antique furnishings and refreshments served on the wraparound porch make the inn memorable. Harpers Ferry National Historic Park, Antietam, and the Shenandoah and Potomac rivers are all within a 15-minute drive, as is Martinsburg outlet shopping.

Innkeeper(s): Mel & Nina Vogel. $70-125. MC VISA AX DS PC TC. TAC10. 6 rooms with PB. 1 suite. 1 conference room. Breakfast, afternoon tea and evening snack included in rates. Types of meals: continental breakfast, continental-plus breakfast, full breakfast and early coffee/tea. Beds: QT. Phone, air conditioning, turndown service and ceiling fan in room. TV, VCR, fax, copier and bicycles on premises. Small meetings, family reunions and seminars hosted. Antiques, fishing, parks, shopping, theater and watersports nearby.

Charleston F3

Brass Pineapple B&B

1611 Virginia St E
Charleston, WV 25311-2113
(304)344-0748 (800)225-5982 Fax:(304)344-0748

Circa 1910. This elegant inn is situated in Charleston's historic district, one-half block from the Capitol Complex. Original oak paneling and leaded and stained glass are among the architectural highlights. Thoughtful amenities such as terry robes and hair dryers have been placed in each guest room. For the extended-stay business traveler, there are one- and two-bedroom apartments available. Guests can enjoy a

gourmet breakfast or opt for lighter, low-fat continental fare.

Innkeeper(s): Sue Pepper. $89-115. MC VISA AX DC PC TC. TAC10. 6 rooms with PB. 1 suite. Breakfast, afternoon tea and evening snack included in rates. Meals: continental breakfast, full breakfast, early coffee/tea. Room service available. Beds: KQT. Phone, air conditioning, turndown service, ceiling fan, TV, VCR in room. Fax, copier, bicycles on premises. Antiques, fishing, parks, shopping, sporting events, theater, watersports nearby.
Publicity: *Mid-Atlantic Country, Charlestonian, News 8 TV, Charleston Daily Mail, Gourmet, Southern Living, Recommended Country Inns.*

"Many thanks for a wonderful stay. We felt like a part of a family in this dear old house."

Elkins   E6

Tunnel Mountain B&B

Rt 1, Box 59-1
Elkins, WV 26241-9711
(304)636-1684

Circa 1938. Nestled on five acres of wooded land, this three-story Fieldstone home offers privacy in a peaceful setting. Rooms are tastefully decorated with antiques, collectibles and crafts. Each bedroom boasts a view of the surrounding mountains. The chestnut and knotty pine woodwork accentuate the decor. The fireplace in the large common room is a great place for warming up after a day of touring or skiing. The area is home to a number of interesting events, including a Dulcimer festival.

Historic Interest: Rich Mountain Battlefield (20 miles), Halliehurst Mansion (4 miles), Beverly Museum (10 miles), Historic Elkins Walking Tour (4 miles), Beverly Historic Cemetery (10 miles), Old Mill (20 miles).

Innkeeper(s): Anne & Paul Beardslee. $65-75. PC TC. 3 rooms with PB, 1 with FP. Breakfast included in rates. Type of meal: full breakfast. Beds: QD. Air conditioning and TV in room. Antiques, fishing, parks, shopping, downhill skiing, cross-country skiing, theater and watersports nearby.

Publicity: *Blue Ridge Country.*

Fayetteville   G4

Morris Harvey House

201 W Maple Ave
Fayetteville, WV 25840-1435
(304)574-1902 Fax:(304)574-1040

Circa 1902. The first thing guests notice at this Queen Anne Victorian is its incredible garden, which is shaped like a flower. But this home, built for lawyer and Confederate veteran Morris Harvey, offers many more unique features. Harvey also founded Morris Harvey College, now the University of Charleston. The second story includes an 800-gallon tank built to gather rain. The first-story floorboards are solid one-inch thick red oak, and poplar floors are found on the second story. Each of the guest rooms includes a fireplace. The Rosa Suite, named to honor Mrs. Harvey, includes a clawfoot tub and watercloset. Two of the four rooms are air conditioned. The wraparound porch is lined with rocking chairs, enticing guests to just sit and relax.

Innkeeper(s): Elizabeth Bush. $85. MC VISA. 4 rooms with PB. Breakfast included in rates. Types of meals: continental breakfast and full breakfast. Beds: QD. Ceiling fan in room. Small meetings, family reunions and seminars hosted. Antiques, fishing, parks, shopping, theater and watersports nearby.

Harpers Ferry   D10

Fillmore Street B&B

PO Box 34
Harpers Ferry, WV 25425-0034
(304)535-2619

Circa 1890. This two-story clapboard Victorian was built on the foundation of a Civil War structure on land deeded by Jefferson Davis, Secretary of War. The surrounding acreage was an encampment for both the Union and Confederate soldiers

(at different times). Within walking distance of the inn are the national park, museums, shopping and dining.

Historic Interest: Harpers Ferry National Historic Park (two blocks), Potomac and Shenandoah Rivers.

Innkeeper(s): Alden & James Addy. $75-80. PC TC. 2 rooms with PB. Breakfast included in rates. Types of meals: continental-plus breakfast, full breakfast and early coffee/tea. Beds: Q. Air conditioning, turndown service, TV and VCR in room. Library on premises. Antiques, parks, shopping and watersports nearby.

"Delightful! What superb hosts you two are. We enjoyed ourselves luxuriously."

Lewisburg   H5

The General Lewis

301 E Washington St
Lewisburg, WV 24901-1425
(304)645-2600 (800)628-4454 Fax:(304)645-2600

Circa 1834. This gracious Federal-style inn boasts a columned veranda, flower gardens and long lawns. Patrick Henry and Thomas Jefferson registered at the inn's walnut desk, which was retrieved from an old hot springs resort in the area. A stagecoach that once delivered travelers to springs on the James River and Kanawha Turnpike, rests under an arbor. American antiques

are featured throughout the inn, and Memory Hall displays household items and tools once used by local pioneers. Nearby are state parks, national forests, streams and rivers, as well as sites of the Revolutionary and Civil wars.

Historic Interest: Civil War Cemetery, Carnegie Hall, Pearl S. Buck's Birthplace.

Innkeeper(s): Nan Morgan. $75-125. EP. MC VISA AX DS. TAC10. 26 rooms with PB. 2 suites. Restaurant on premises. Beds: QD. Phone, air conditioning and TV in room. Fax and copier on premises. Handicap access. Weddings and family reunions hosted. Antiques, shopping and theater nearby.

Publicity: *Southern Living, New York Times.*

"The staff is wonderful at making us feel at home, and we can be as much a part of the inn as we want."

Martinsburg   D9

Boydville, The Inn at Martinsburg

601 S Queen St
Martinsburg, WV 25401-3103
(304)263-1448

Circa 1812. This Georgian estate was saved from burning by Union troops only by a specific proclamation from President Lincoln dated July 18, 1864. Tall maples line the long driveway leading up to the house. It is constructed of two-foot-thick stone walls covered with plaster. The entry hall retains the original wallpaper brought from England in 1812 and hand-painted murals, fireplaces, and antiques adorn the spacious guest rooms. Sunlight filters through tree tops onto estate-sized lawns and gardens.

Historic Interest: Antietam Battlefield, Harpers Ferry, Berkeley Springs.

Innkeeper(s): LaRue Frye. $100-125. MC VISA PC. 6 rooms, 4 with PB, 1 with FP. 1 conference room. Breakfast included in rates. Types of meals: continental-plus breakfast and early coffee/tea. Beds: QDT. Air conditioning in room. TV and library on premises. 10 acres. Weddings and family reunions hosted. Antiques, shopping, downhill skiing and theater nearby.

Publicity: *Washington Post, Mid-Atlantic Country.*

"Your gracious home, hospitality and excellent amenities were enjoyed so much. Such a fine job of innkeeping."

Pulpit & Palette Inn

516 W John St
Martinsburg, WV 25401-2635
(304)263-7012

Circa 1870. Listed in the National Register, this Victorian inn is set off by a handsome iron fence. The interior is filled with a mix of American antiques, Tibetan rugs and art, setting off moldings and other architectural details in the library, drawing room and upstairs veranda. Your British-born innkeeper prepares afternoon tea for guests. The Blue Ridge Outlet Center is two blocks away.

Historic Interest: Harpers Ferry National Park (30 minutes), New Market Civil War Museum (80 minutes), Antietam Battlefield (20 minutes), Gettysburg National Park (80 minutes).

Innkeeper(s): Bill & Janet Starr. $80. MC VISA TC. 2 rooms. Breakfast, afternoon tea and evening snack included in rates. Types of meals: full breakfast, gourmet breakfast and early coffee/tea. Beds: Q. Air conditioning and turndown service in room. TV on premises. Antiques, parks, shopping and theater nearby.

Publicity: *Morning Herald, Antique Traveler, Journal.*

"You have set an ideal standard for comfort and company."

Pence Springs   H5

The Pence Springs Hotel

St Rts 3 & 12, PO Box 90
Pence Springs, WV 24962
(304)445-2606 (800)826-1829 Fax:(304)445-2204

Circa 1918. Listed in the National Register, this inn is known as one of the "historic springs of the Virginias." Mineral waters from Pence Springs captured a silver medal at the 1904 World's Fair. After the fair, the healing properties of the waters drew many guests. From 1947 until the mid-1980s, the property was used as a state prison for women. A restoration effort began in 1986, and the inn once again welcomes guests. The inn's Art Deco-style furnishings and decor are reminiscent of the hotel's heyday in the 1920s when prominent and wealthy guests flocked to the hotel. Guests enjoy a full breakfast, and during the summer months, Sunday brunch is available. There are

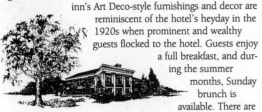

two restaurants in the hotel that serve dinner. The area boasts many outdoor activities, beautiful scenery and plenty of antique shopping.

Historic Interest: The hotel is listed in the National Register and Pence Springs is designated as a National Historic District.

Innkeeper(s): O. Ashby Berkley & Rosa Lee Berkley Miller. $70-100. MC VISA AX DC CB DS PC TC. TAC10. 25 rooms, 15 with PB. 3 suites. 3 conference rooms. Breakfast included in rates. Types of meals: full breakfast and gourmet breakfast. Dinner, picnic lunch, banquet service, catering service and room service available. Restaurant on premises. Beds: KDT. Air conditioning in room. TV, VCR, fax, copier, swimming, stables, bicycles and child care on premises. Handicap access. 28 acres. Weddings, small meetings, family reunions and seminars hosted. Norwegian, German and Spanish spoken. Antiques, fishing, parks, shopping, downhill skiing, theater and watersports nearby.

Pets Allowed: Cannot be left in room; kennel space in basement.

Publicity: *Southern Living, Mid-Atlantic Country, West Virginia Quarterly, MIT Press Journal, Goldenseal, Travel Host.*

"As always, I left your place rejuvenated. The property grows even more beautiful year after year."

Point Pleasant   E2

Stone Manor

12 Main St
Point Pleasant, WV 25550-1026
(304)675-3442

Circa 1887. This stone Victorian sits on the banks of the Kanawha River with a front porch that faces the river. Point Pleasant Battle Monument Park, adjacent to the inn, was built to commemorate the location of the first battle of the Revolutionary War. In the National Register, the inn was once the home of a family who ran a ferry boat crossing for the Ohio and Kanawha rivers. Now restored, the house is decorated with Victorian antiques and offers a pleasant garden with a Victorian fish pond and fountain.

Innkeeper(s): Janice & Tom Vance. $50. PC. 3 rooms, 3 with FP. Breakfast included in rates. Type of meal: full breakfast. Beds: QD. Air conditioning and VCR in room. TV on premises.

Romney   D8

Hampshire House 1884

165 N Grafton St
Romney, WV 26757-1616
(304)822-7171

Circa 1884. Located near the south branch of the Potomac River, the garden here has old boxwoods and walnut trees. The inn features ornate brickwork; tall, narrow windows; and fireplaces with handsome period mantels. A sitting room with a well-stocked library, a cozy patio and a music room with an antique pump organ are favorite places. The spa room includes on-site massage.

Innkeeper(s): Jane & Scott Simmons. $65-85. MC VISA AX DC DS PC TC. TAC10. 5 rooms with PB, 3 with FP. 1 conference room. Breakfast included in rates. Types of meals: full breakfast and early coffee/tea. Evening snack available. Beds: QDT. Phone, air conditioning, TV and VCR in room. Bicycles on premises. Small meetings hosted. Antiques, fishing, shopping and watersports nearby.

Publicity: *Hampshire Review, Mid-Atlantic Country, Weekend Journal.*

"Your personal attention made us feel at home immediately."

Shepherdstown D10

Stonebrake Cottage

Shepherd Grade Rd, PO Box 1612
Shepherdstown, WV 25443
(304)876-6607

Circa 1880. Situated at the edge of a 145-acre farm, Stonebrake Cottage has been refurbished and decorated with antique country chests and four-poster beds. This completely private Victorian cottage contains three bedrooms, two full bathrooms, a living room and a kitchen stocked with the makings for a full country breakfast. The cottage sleeps up to six people. A 10-acre woodland is nearby for private picnics.

Historic Interest: The cottage is near Harpers Ferry, Antietam and is five minutes from historic Shepherdstown.

Innkeeper(s): Anne & Dennis Small. $85-95. MC VISA DS PC TC. 3 rooms, 2 with PB. Type of meal: full breakfast. Beds: QDT. Phone, air conditioning and VCR in room. Library on premises. 145 acres. Small meetings and family reunions hosted. Antiques, shopping, downhill skiing, cross-country skiing, sporting events and theater nearby.

Location: Five minutes from the heart of town.

Publicity: *The Washington Post, Martinsburg Journal.*

"The perfect private getaway."

Summersville F4

Historic Brock House B&B Inn

1400 Webster Rd
Summersville, WV 26651-1524
(304)872-4887

Circa 1890. This Queen Anne farmhouse is the second venture into the bed & breakfast business for innkeepers Margie and Jim Martin. The exterior looks friendly and inviting, perhaps because of its long history of welcoming guests. The National Register inn originally served as a hotel and later as a boarding house. Margie has a degree in design, and her skills are evident in the cheerful, country rooms. Each of the guest rooms has a different color scheme and decor. One is decked in deep blue, another is appointed with flowery bedspreads and pastel curtains.

Innkeeper(s): Margie N. Martin. $70-90. MC VISA PC TC. TAC10. 6 rooms, 4 with PB. 1 suite. 1 conference room. Breakfast, afternoon tea and evening snack included in rates. Types of meals: continental breakfast, full breakfast, gourmet breakfast and early coffee/tea. Catering service available. Beds: QT. Air conditioning and turndown service in room. TV, VCR, fax and library on premises. Weddings, small meetings, family reunions and seminars hosted. Antiques, fishing, parks, shopping, theater and watersports nearby.

Wisconsin

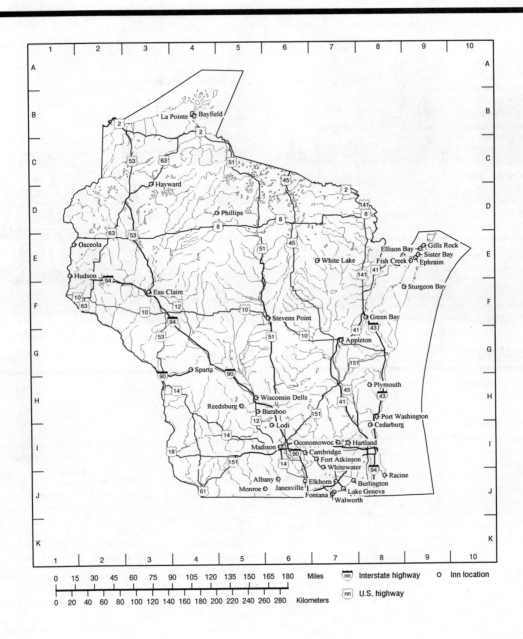

Albany   J6

Albany Guest House

405 S Mill St
Albany, WI 53502-9502
(608)862-3636

Circa 1908. The brick walkway, red-tiled foyer, lace curtains and abundance of flowers set the comfortable tone for this three-story inn. An upright piano in the large foyer and fireplace in the living room also add to the pleasant atmosphere. The guest rooms have picture windows and hand-carved antiques. Outside,

maple and black walnut trees and various gardens grace the inn's eight-acre property. Guests can tour New Glarus, a village known as America's Little Switzerland, which is a short drive away. Also, not too far away is a cheese factory that is available for tours. Guests also can enjoy a bicycle ride on the nearby Sugar River Trail.

Historic Interest: The Tallman House, the last existing house where Lincoln slept, is 25 miles away. The original Green County Courthouse with its restored clock tower is in Monroe, a 15-mile drive. The state capitol is 30 miles north.

Innkeeper(s): Bob & Sally Braem. $55-80. MC VISA PC. 6 rooms, 4 with PB, 1 with FP. Breakfast included in rates. Types of meals: full breakfast and early coffee/tea. Beds: KQD. Air conditioning and ceiling fan in room. VCR and library on premises. Small meetings, family reunions and seminars hosted. Antiques, fishing, parks and cross-country skiing nearby.

Publicity: *Silent Sports, Madison, Monroe Evening Times.*

"Was even more than I expected."

Appleton   G7

The Gathering Place

808 W Front St
Appleton, WI 54914
(920)731-4418

Circa 1939. Located on historic Front Street, which runs along the bluff overlooking the Fox River, this English-country home has been lovingly restored to its original gracious state. Antiques, hardwood floors and arched entries are just a few of the architectural details retained after the renovation. Three spacious second-floor guest rooms are decorated with down comforters and over-stuffed chairs for reading and relaxing. A gourmet breakfast of scones, muffins, fresh fruit and quiche are a few of the morning selections. The inn is close to the downtown, shopping and entertainment.

Historic Interest: Driving distance from the Green Bay Packers, OshKosh and the Experimental Aircraft Association.

Innkeeper(s): Dennis & Madelyn Olson. $75-95. PC. 3 rooms, 1 with PB. Breakfast and evening snack included in rates. Types of meals: full breakfast and early coffee/tea. Beds: QDT. Phone, air conditioning and turndown service in room. TV, VCR and copier on premises. Antiques, fishing, parks, shopping, cross-country skiing, sporting events and golf nearby.

Publicity: *Post-Crescent.*

"Your hospitality is second to none!"

The Queen Anne B&B

837 E College Ave
Appleton, WI 54911-5619
(888)739-7966

Circa 1895. On a tree-lined street, The Queen Anne features polished oak, pine and maple floors, and beveled- and stained-glass windows. The dining area has bay windows. Furnishings include Victorian, Louis XV, Eastlake and Empire.

Innkeeper(s): Susan & Larry Bogenschutz. $65-105. 3 rooms, 1 with PB. 1 conference room. Type of meal: full breakfast. Beds: Q.

Publicity: *The Post Crescent, Valleysun.*

"The Queen Anne is an expression of your warmth & hospitality and a delightful place to be."

The Solie Home

914 E Hancock St
Appleton, WI 54911
(888)739-7966

Circa 1905. The innkeepers raised their four daughters in this two-story stucco home. Over the years, various collections have been organized in the built-in bookcases and on the walls. The turn-of-the-century home's sculptured plaster walls still remain. Guest rooms are comfortably appointed. Riley's Retreat offers an antique bird's-eye maple double bed.

Innkeeper(s): Riley & Carole Solie. $65-105. 3 rooms. Breakfast included in rates. Type of meal: full breakfast. Beds: DT.

"Evening tea, fresh cookies and flowers were just what I needed."

Baraboo   H5

Victorian Rose B&B

423 3rd Ave
Baraboo, WI 53913-2408
(608)356-7828

Circa 1893. Victorian charm can be found in this classic inn with its wraparound front porch, beveled mirror oak fireplace, sliding pocket doors and intricate woodwork. The decor includes period antiques and heirloom collectibles. The innkeepers are proud to show off their Wisconsin hospitality. The Queen Victoria room is ideal for enjoying honeymoons and anniversaries. The inn is within walking distance to historic downtown Baraboo, the Al Ringling Theater and Ochsner Park, with a zoo and picnic area overlooking the Baraboo River.

Innkeeper(s): Bob & Carolyn Stearns. $70-90. DS PC TC. TAC10. 3 rooms with PB. 1 conference room. Breakfast and afternoon tea included in rates. Types of meals: gourmet breakfast and early coffee/tea. Beds: D. Air conditioning and ceiling fan in room. TV, VCR and library on premises. Small meetings hosted. Amusement parks, antiques, fishing, parks, shopping, downhill skiing, cross-country skiing, sporting events and watersports nearby.

Publicity: *Baraboo News Republic.*

"This has been so relaxing, stepping back in time. I always felt I was born too late. This period is the era I love."

Bayfield　　　　　　　　B4

Apple Tree Inn

Rt 1, Box 251, Hwy 135
Bayfield, WI 54814-9767
(715)779-5572 (800)400-6532

Circa 1911. The Apple Tree Inn is a fully restored farmhouse overlooking Lake Superior. It was once owned by a dairy farmer and landscape artist. A hearty, country-style breakfast is served in the sunroom, which boasts a panoramic view of Madeline Island and Lake Superior. Guest rooms are furnished in early Americana style and three have lake views.

Historic Interest: Apostle Islands National Lakeshore Park (1 mile).

Innkeeper(s): Joanna Barningham. $49-84. MC VISA PC TC. TAC10. 4 rooms with PB. Breakfast included in rates. Types of meals: full breakfast, gourmet breakfast and early coffee/tea. Picnic lunch available. Beds: KQD. Air conditioning and ceiling fan in room. TV, VCR, pet boarding and child care on premises. Family reunions hosted. Antiques, fishing, parks, shopping, downhill skiing, cross-country skiing, theater and watersports nearby.

Pets Allowed: Please check with innkeeper.

Publicity: *Lake Superior.*

"You made us feel like old friends rather than guests."

Pinehurst Inn at Pikes Creek

RR 1 Box 222, Hwy 13
Bayfield, WI 54814
(715)779-3676 Fax:(715)779-3220
E-mail: nsand@ncis.net

Circa 1885. Lavish woodwork and wainscoting, including an intricately carved staircase, are some of the things guests will notice upon entering this Gothic Victorian. The home was built by a lumber baron, and the innkeepers are distant relatives of the home's second owners. Rooms are decorated in an uncluttered country style, and each bedchamber has its own theme. Several rooms boast a view of Lake Superior, and other rooms offer views of gardens or Pike's Creek. The Catherine Rittenhouse Suite offers lake views, a sitting room and a bathroom with a double whirlpool tub. The day begins with a hearty breakfast, perhaps with fruit salad, an Italian vegetable quiche and raspberry buttermilk crumb coffee cake. After a day of hiking, skiing, snowshoeing or shopping, return to the inn for afternoon refreshments.

Innkeeper(s): Nancy & Steve Sandstrom. $65-138. MC VISA PC TC. 6 rooms with PB. 1 suite. Breakfast included in rates. Types of meals: full breakfast and early coffee/tea. Beds: KQD. Air conditioning and ceiling fan in room. TV, VCR, fax and copier on premises. Weddings, small meetings and family reunions hosted. Antiques, fishing, parks, shopping, downhill skiing, cross-country skiing, golf, theater and watersports nearby.

"Thank you all for such a relaxing stay. We enjoyed all that you had to offer. From the wonderful food to the peaceful swing on the porch...we loved it all. I hope to visit again to this place I call a home away from home."

Burlington　　　　　　　　J7

The Hillcrest Inn & Carriage House

540 Storle Ave
Burlington, WI 53105-1030
(414)763-4706

Circa 1908. Romantic, luxurious and private, this stately Edwardian estate situated on four wooded acres offers visitors a magnificent view of two rivers, a lake, rolling farmlands and rustic countryside. An open staircase, beveled windows, homemade quilts and wood floors highlighted by a carefully furnished antique-filled interior are just a few of the inn's amenities. Guests have the option of staying in the main house or the elegantly restored original carriage house. Guests may relax and enjoy the sights from one of the historic estate's two porches while comfortably seated on antique wicker furniture.

Innkeeper(s): Gayle & Mike Hohner. $65-160. MC VISA. 6 rooms, 4 with PB, 3 with FP. Type of meal: full breakfast. Beds: KQ. Fishing, cross-country skiing and golf nearby.

Publicity: *Racine Journal Times, Burlington Standard Press, Kenosha News.*

"We had a delightful time, absolutely beautiful home and gardens."

Cambridge　　　　　　　　I6

The Night Heron B&B

315 E Water St
Cambridge, WI 53523
(608)423-4141

Circa 1866. This brick Italianate home is covered with ivy and the grounds are dotted with flowers. The home originally served as a tavern, dance hall and saloon. The Koshkonong River and a 300-acre nature park are across the way. Innkeeper Talia Schorr is an interior designer and has decorated each of the three bedchambers with something unique. The Knotty Pine Room includes a skylight, ceiling and walls fashioned from pine, creating a cabin-like environment. The Rockdale Room features a metal ceiling, and the Indigo Bunting Room is full of artwork and includes a sitting area. Guests are presented with a bottle of champagne and enjoy use of a hot tub. The substantial breakfasts are served on the terrace under umbrella-covered tables.

Innkeeper(s): Pam Schorr & John Lehman. $75-85. TC. 3 rooms, 1 with PB. Breakfast included in rates. Types of meals: full breakfast and early coffee/tea. Beds: KQ. Air conditioning, ceiling fan and VCR in room. Fax, copier, spa and bicycles on premises. Antiques, fishing, parks, shopping, cross-country skiing, sporting events and theater nearby.

Cedarburg　　　　　　　　I8

Stagecoach Inn B&B

W 61 N 520 Washington Ave
Cedarburg, WI 53012
(414)375-0208 (888)375-0208

Circa 1853. This stone Greek Revival house was used originally as a stagecoach stop between Milwaukee and Green Bay. The inn has been authentically restored with period antiques. Suites feature double whirlpool baths, and several offer fireplaces. The inn houses a pub and

Beerntsen's Chocolate Shop. Winter in Cedarburg is like living in a Norman Rockwell painting, the town decorates to the hilt and innkeepers offer midweek specials during the winter season and women's escape. The Cedar Creek Settlement is crammed with delightful shops to explore, including antique shops, vintage clothing boutiques, a wine shop and winery.

Historic Interest: Cedarburg, known as the antique capital of Wisconsin, is listed in the National Register. Milwaukee, about 20 minutes north of the inn, offers many museums and historic buildings.

Innkeeper(s): Brook & Liz Brown. $70-130. MC VISA AX DC DS. 12 rooms with PB. 6 suites. 1 conference room. Breakfast included in rates. Type of meal: continental-plus breakfast. Room service available. Beds: QDT. Phone in room. Antiques, fishing, downhill skiing, cross-country skiing, theater and watersports nearby.

Location: Downtown Cedarburg, historic district.

Publicity: *Milwaukee, Visions, News Graphic Pilot, Midwest Living, Travel Host, Innsider, Wisconsin Trails, Country Life, Business Journal and Country Living.*

"I love the Stagecoach Inn and hope to return as often as possible — Jerry Minnich, Isthmus."

Eau Claire   F3

Otter Creek Inn
2536 Hwy 12
Eau Claire, WI 54701
(715)832-2945

Circa 1920. On a hillside overlooking a creek is this Tudor-style inn, surrounded by oaks and pines. Visitors immediately feel welcome as they make their way up the inn's curved pebblestone walk to the front door. The Palm Room has an antique sleigh bed, romantic loveseat and sunken whirlpool tub. The Rose Room, often the choice of honeymooners, features a cloverleaf-shaped whirlpool tub that overlooks the gardens and gazebo. The spacious inn provides many spots for relaxation, including a gazebo, the great room with its inviting fireplace and a roomy patio.

Innkeeper(s): Shelley & Randy Hansen. $79-159. MC VISA AX DC CB DS PC TC. 6 rooms with PB. 1 suite. Breakfast and afternoon tea included in rates. Types of meals: full breakfast and early coffee/tea. Beds: KQ. Phone, air conditioning and

TV in room. Weddings and small meetings hosted. Antiques, fishing, parks, shopping, cross-country skiing, golf, theater and watersports nearby.

Pets Allowed: Boarding kennel one mile away.

Location: Two hours to St. Paul.

Publicity: *Country, Wisconsin West.*

"This is the perfect place to recharge your couple batteries."

Elkhorn   J7

Ye Olde Manor House
N7622 US Highway 12
Elkhorn, WI 53121
(414)742-2450 Fax:(414)742-2450

Circa 1905. Located on three tree-shaded acres, this country manor house offers travelers all the simple comforts of home. The guest rooms, living room and dining room are decorated with a variety of antiques and comfortable furniture that inspires a family atmosphere. One room offers a porch and views of Lauderdale Lakes. The B&B offers a full gourmet breakfast each morning.

Innkeeper(s): Babette & Marvin Henschel. $50-90. MC VISA PC TC. 4 rooms, 2 with PB. 1 suite. 1 conference room. Breakfast included in rates. Types of meals: full breakfast, gourmet breakfast and early coffee/tea. Beds: QTD. TV, VCR, fax, copier and library on premises. Small meetings, family reunions and seminars hosted. Amusement parks, antiques, fishing, parks, shopping, downhill skiing, cross-country skiing, golf, theater and watersports nearby.

Ellison Bay   E9

The Griffin Inn & Cottages
11976 Mink River Rd
Ellison Bay, WI 54210-9705
(414)854-4306

Circa 1910. This New England-style country inn is situated on five acres of rolling lawns and maple trees with a gazebo. There are verandas with porch swings, a gracious lobby with a stone fireplace and a cozy library. Guest rooms are furnished with antique beds and dressers and feature handmade quilts. In addition to the main house, there are four cottages. Cottage guests enjoy a continental breakfast basket, but for an extra charge, can partake of a full breakfast.

Innkeeper(s): Paul Ennis & Family. $55-86. MAP. PC. 14 rooms. 4 cottages. Breakfast and evening snack included in rates. Types of meals: continental breakfast, full breakfast, gourmet breakfast and early coffee/tea. Picnic lunch, lunch, banquet service and catering service available. Beds: DT. Air conditioning in room. Tennis and library on premises. Weddings, small meetings, family reunions and seminars hosted. Amusement parks, antiques, fishing, parks, shopping, cross-country skiing, theater and watersports nearby.

Location: Two blocks east of Highway 42 on the Door County Peninsula.

Publicity: *Ladies Circle, Innsider, Country Inns, Green Bay Press Gazette, Travel & Leisure, Wisconsin Trails, Country Folk Art, Midwest Living.*

"A classic bed & breakfast inn. — Travel & Leisure"

Hotel Disgarden
12013 Hwy 42, PO Box 191
Ellison Bay, WI 54210
(414)854-9888

Circa 1902. On the Door County peninsula, six miles from the tip, this lodge is situated 50 yards from the bay and shares its waterfront with the Norland Resort. Guest rooms all have sitting areas, and Suite 8 has a balcony facing the water, two bedrooms, a kitchen and living room. Hudson Bay blankets, gingham bed coverings and hand-crafted furniture decorate the inn.

VCRs, fridges and air conditioning are additional amenities. In the afternoon, ice tea and biscotti are served. Breakfast is continental and is brought to your door in a basket. Two private docks offer boat slips to guests and there are rowboats, a canoe and bicycles to borrow.

Innkeeper(s): Kelly & Bill Tummett. $75-135. MC VISA. TAC10. 7 rooms, 6 with PB. 1 suite. Breakfast and afternoon tea included in rates. Type of meal: continental-plus breakfast. Beds: KQ. Air conditioning, ceiling fan and VCR in room. Swimming, bicycles and library on premises. Weddings, small meetings and family reunions hosted. Amusement parks, antiques, fishing, parks, shopping, cross-country skiing, golf, theater and watersports nearby.

"Thanks for making this my home away from home."

Ephraim   E9

Hillside Hotel B&B

9980 Hwy 42, PO Box 17
Ephraim, WI 54211-0017
(414)854-2417 (800)423-7023 Fax:(414)854-4240

Circa 1854. In the National Register, this Victorian country house is the last remaining "grand hotel" of the turn-of-the-century hotels in the area. On the waterfront, Hillside provides views of Eagle Harbor and Green Bay from most of the rooms and the 100-foot veranda. There is a private beach and moorings for small craft. Guest rooms feature antiques, feather beds and four-poster beds. Afternoon tea is offered with scones, petit fours and tea breads, while eggs Benedict is often found on the breakfast menu along with specialty items found locally.

Innkeeper(s): David & Karen McNeil. $69-180. MC VISA DS PC. 11 rooms, 2 with FP. 2 cottages. 1 conference room. Breakfast and afternoon tea included in rates. Types of meals: full breakfast, gourmet breakfast and early coffee/tea. Catering service available. Beds: QDT. Ceiling fan in room. TV and swimming on premises. Weddings, small meetings, family reunions and seminars hosted. Amusement parks, antiques, fishing, parks, shopping, downhill skiing, cross-country skiing, sporting events, theater and watersports nearby.

"You have a very nice inn and the breakfasts were great. You all made us feel at home (without the chores) and it was like we'd known you for a long time."

Fish Creek   E9

Thorp House Inn & Cottages

4135 Bluff Ln, PO Box 490
Fish Creek, WI 54212
(920)868-2444

Circa 1902. Freeman Thorp picked the site for this home because of its view of Green Bay and the village. Before his house was finished, however, he perished in the bay when the Erie L. Hackley sank. His wife completed it as a guest house. Each room is decorated with English or Victorian antiques. A stone fireplace is the focal point of the parlor, and four of the cottages on the property have fireplaces. Some cottages have whirlpools and all have kitchens, cable TVs and VCRs. Listed in the National Register of Historic Places, everything upon which the eye might rest in the inn must be "of the era." Breakfast is not included in the rates for cottage guests.

Historic Interest: The Asa Thorp Log Cabin and Noble House Museum are one block away. The Church of the Atonement is three blocks away, and the Peninsula Park Lighthouse is four miles from the inn.

Innkeeper(s): Christine & Sverre Falck-Pedersen. $85-165. PC TC. 4 rooms with PB. 6 cottages. Breakfast included in rates. Types of meals: continental-plus breakfast and early coffee/tea. Beds: KQDT. Ceiling fan in room. Bicycles on premises. Norwegian spoken. Antiques, fishing, parks, shopping, cross-country skiing, theater and watersports nearby.

Location: Heart of Door County, in the village of Fish Creek.

Publicity: *Madison PM, Green Bay Press-Gazette, Milwaukee Journal/Sentinel, McCall's, Minnesota Monthly.*

"Amazing attention to detail from restoration to the furnishings. A very first-class experience."

Fontana   J7

Lazy Cloud Lodge B&B

N2025 N Lake Shore
Fontana, WI 53125
(414)275-3322 Fax:(414)275-8340

Circa 1920. Co-owners of the Schlitz Brewery built this inn to serve as a polo lodge. Guests will have a hard time believing that some of the guest rooms actually served as stables and a hayloft. Those in search of romance need not look any further, this inn is a perfect spot for a special getaway. Each spacious room is individually decorated with soft flowery print comforters, stenciled walls and candles. All rooms include a double whirlpool tub, and all of the rooms have a fireplace. Bath pillows, bubble bath, fluffy robes and chocolates are just a few of the romantic amenities. Guests can enjoy breakfast in bed, and for an extra charge, the innkeepers will prepare their signature "Enchanted Evening" picnic basket, which guests can enjoy in front of their fireplace or perhaps in the gazebo, surrounded by the lush grounds. Early in his career, Paul Newman stayed at the lodge, and author J.D. Salinger stayed here while writing "Catcher in the Rye."

Innkeeper(s): Keith & Carol Tiffany. $110-195. MC VISA AX DC DS PC TC. TAC10. 9 suites, 9 with FP. Breakfast and evening snack included in rates. Type of meal: continental-plus breakfast. Picnic lunch available. Beds: Q. Air conditioning in room. TV, VCR, fax, copier and library on premises. Handicap access. Antiques, fishing, parks, shopping, downhill skiing, cross-country skiing, sporting events, golf, theater and watersports nearby.

Publicity: *Walworth Week, Press Publications.*

"This room is by far a wonderful cloud in the heavens of the Lazy Cloud."

Fort Atkinson   I7

La Grange B&B

1050 East St
Fort Atkinson, WI 53538
(920)563-1421

Circa 1928. This former grain barn, now shaded by tall maples, walnuts and pines, was converted to a home in the '40s and more recently developed into a B&B. The great room has an antique wood stove and comfortable furniture. French-country themes are found in the guest rooms. "La Vacherie," the cow barn room, has a milking stool, milk bottles and antique butter churn, as well as lamps of milk glass. A full breakfast with hot entree and baked goods is offered, and guests often take home the innkeepers' recipes. Local attractions include sleigh rides, fishing, craft fairs, concerts and other events at nearby University of Wisconsin Whitewater and Fireside Dinner Theater.

Innkeeper(s): Dennis & Gerry Rybicke. $60-75. PC TC. 3 rooms, 1 with PB. Breakfast included in rates. Types of meals: full breakfast and early coffee/tea. Beds: Q. Air conditioning and ceiling fan in room. TV, VCR and swimming on premises. Antiques, fishing, parks, shopping, cross-country skiing, sporting events, golf, theater and watersports nearby.

Publicity: *Daily Jefferson County Union.*

Gills Rock
E9

Harbor House Inn
12666 Hwy 42
Gills Rock, WI 54210
(920)854-5196

Circa 1904. Gills Rock, a fishing village on the northern tip of Door County, is the home of the Harbor House Inn. The inn has been in the Weborg family since its inception, and the innkeepers recently restored the home to reflect its original Victorian elegance. Also on the grounds is Troll cottage, a nautical Scandinavian dwelling. The inn's guest rooms all feature private baths, microwave ovens and refrigerators. Guests will enjoy the inn's period furniture, sauna cabin, whirlpool and gorgeous sunsets over the waters of Green Bay. A new wing recently was added, with rooms done in a Scandinavian country decor. A private beach is within walking distance.

Historic Interest: Nautical Museum, many lighthouses.

Innkeeper(s): David & Else Weborg. $55-125. MC VISA AX. 14 rooms with PB. Breakfast included in rates. Type of meal: continental-plus breakfast. Beds: KQT. Phone in room. Spa and sauna on premises. Fishing, theater and watersports nearby.

Pets Allowed.

Publicity: *State Journal, Travel & Leisure.*

"Lovely inn. Thank you for your hospitality."

Green Bay
F8

The Astor House B&B
637 S Monroe Ave
Green Bay, WI 54301-3614
(920)432-3585 (888)303-6370
E-mail: astor@execpc.com

Circa 1888. Located in the Astor Historic District, the Astor House is completely surrounded by Victorian homes. Guests have their choice of five rooms, each uniquely decorated for a range of ambiance, from the Vienna Balconies to the Marseilles Garden to the Hong Kong Retreat. The parlor, veranda and many suites feature a grand view of City Centre's lighted church towers. This home is also the first and only B&B in Green Bay and received the Mayor's Award for

Remodeling and Restoration. Business travelers should take notice of the private phone lines in each room, as well as the ability to hook up a modem.

Historic Interest: Green Bay City Centre (8 blocks), Lambeau Field, 1837 Hazelwood Historic Home museum.

Innkeeper(s): Doug Landwehr. $79-149. MC VISA AX DC DS. 5 rooms with PB, 4 with FP. 3 suites. Breakfast included in rates. Type of meal: continental-plus breakfast. Beds: KQDT. Phone, air conditioning, TV and VCR in room. Amusement parks, antiques, fishing, parks, shopping, cross-country skiing, sporting events, theater and watersports nearby.

Hartland
I7

Monches Mill House
W 301 N 9430 Hwy E
Hartland, WI 53029
(414)966-7546

Circa 1842. This stone building reflects a Swiss and Colonial influence. Plank floors, the two-foot-thick stone walls and high ceilings create an authentic atmosphere many have tried to imitate. There is a gazebo, patio and balcony that make it easy to enjoy the millpond with its waterfall and pleasant nostalgic setting. A simple breakfast is served.

Innkeeper(s): Elaine & Harvey Taylor. $75. PC TC. 4 rooms, 1 with PB. Breakfast included in rates. Type of meal: continental-plus breakfast. Beds: DT. Phone in room. VCR, spa, bicycles, tennis, library and pet boarding on premises. Handicap access. Weddings, family reunions and seminars hosted. French spoken. Antiques, fishing, parks, downhill skiing, cross-country skiing, sporting events, theater and watersports nearby.

Pets Allowed.

Hayward
C3

Lumberman's Mansion Inn
204 E Fourth St
Hayward, WI 54843-0885
(715)634-3012 Fax:(715)634-5724

Circa 1887. This Queen Anne Victorian, once the home of a local lumber baron, sits on a hill overlooking the city, park and pond. An oak staircase, maple floors, tiled fireplaces, pocket doors and a carriage stoop are among the finely restored details. Antique furnishings blend with modern amenities such as whirlpool tubs and a video library. Wild rice pancakes, Wisconsin sausages and freshly squeezed cranberry juice are some of the regional specialties featured for breakfast. The innkeepers host many seasonal events and evening lectures. Plays are sometimes performed on the front porch.

Historic Interest: Historic Company Store, museum, old growth forest, church.

Innkeeper(s): Jan Hinrichs Blaedel & Wendy Hinrichs Sanders. $70-100. MC VISA PC TC. 5 rooms with PB. 2 suites. 1 conference room. Breakfast included in rates. Type of meal: full breakfast. Afternoon tea

available. Beds: Q. Spa and bicycles on premises. Antiques, fishing, downhill skiing, cross-country skiing and watersports nearby.

Location: One block from main street.

Publicity: *Sawyer County Record, Chicago Sun Times, Wisconsin Trails, Minneapolis Star Tribune, Wisconsin Country Life.*

"The food was excellent. And the extra personal touches (chocolate on the pillow, cookies & pie at night, muffins in the morning, etc.) were especially nice. This is definitely the best B&B we've ever been to."

Ross' Teal Lake Lodge & Golf Club

Rt 7, Ross Rd
Hayward, WI 54843
(715)462-3631
E-mail: rossteal@win.bright.net

Circa 1908. Located on 250 acres bordering Teal Lake and Teal River, this is a great vacation spot for families, golfers and fishermen. Most of the Northwoods cabins here are of vertical log construction, and most feature fireplaces and kitchens. There are two beds in each room. Most rooms offer ceiling fans. Fishing guides and a fishing school for children and adults offer both fishing expertise and local folklore. (You'll learn how to catch the prized muskie, a fierce freshwater game fish.) A new 18-hole golf course winds through the woods and has been recognized as the Best New Course in Wisconsin in 1997 by Milwaukee Magazine. Bicycles, tricycles and water bicycles are available to use. A telescope in the lounge is trained on a family of eagles that nest on the island, and you can watch them feed and learn to fly. Early springtime guests enjoy the otters that scramble around the inn's docks. Picnic and basket lunches are available.

Innkeeper(s): Prudence & Tim Ross. $100-430. MAP, AP, EP. MC VISA PC TC. TAC10. 3 suites. 22 cottages. 1 conference room. Types of meals: continental breakfast and full breakfast. Dinner, picnic lunch and lunch available. Restaurant on premises. Beds: KDT. Ceiling fan in room. Swimming, sauna, bicycles, tennis and library on premises. 250 acres. Small meetings and family reunions hosted. Amusement parks, antiques, fishing, parks, shopping, cross-country skiing and watersports nearby.

Pets Allowed.

Hudson   E1

Jefferson-Day House

1109 Third St
Hudson, WI 54016-1220
(715)386-7111

Circa 1857. Near the St. Croix River and 30 minutes from Mall of America, the Italianate Jefferson-Day House features guest rooms with both double whirlpool tubs and gas fireplaces. Antique art and furnishings fill the rooms, and there is a formal dining room, library and living room. Ask for the Captain's Room and you'll be rewarded with a cedar-lined bathroom, over-sized shower, antique brass bed, and a gas fireplace visible from the whirlpool tub for two. A four-course breakfast is served fireside every morning.

Innkeeper(s): Tom & Sue Tyler. $99-179. MC VISA AX DS PC TC. 4 rooms with PB, 4 with FP. 1 suite. Breakfast and evening snack included in rates. Type of meal: full breakfast. Beds: Q. Phone and air conditioning in room. Bicycles and library on premises. Weddings, small meetings and family reunions hosted. Amusement parks, antiques, fishing, parks, shopping, downhill skiing, cross-country skiing, sporting events, theater and watersports nearby.

Pets Allowed: With advance notice; some restrictions apply.

"Absolute perfection! That's the only way to describe our stay in the wonderful St. Croix suite!"

Janesville   J6

Antique Rose B&B

603 E Court
Janesville, WI 53545
(608)754-8180

Circa 1888. A wraparound porch provides a welcoming entrance to this gabled Queen Anne house in the Court House Hill Historic District. Light streams through the leaded-stained glass of the front entrance onto the entry hall and staircase. A ceramic fireplace and love seat adds to the warmth of the front parlor. In the dining room, there's an early electric light that was once in the innkeeper's grandparent's home. Pocket doors open to the Rose Room on the first floor. The Train Room offers railroad memorabilia, tongue and groove planking and period wallpaper. A full breakfast is served. Janesville holds a large proportion of Wisconsin's National Register properties. Known as the "City of Parks", there are 1900 acres of park land along the banks of Rock River.

Innkeeper(s): Cheryl & Dave Brookhiser. $65-85. MC VISA PC. 3 rooms with PB. Breakfast and evening snack included in rates. Type of meal: full breakfast. Beds: Q. Air conditioning and turndown service in room. TV and library on premises. Weddings, small meetings, family reunions and seminars hosted. Antiques, fishing, parks, shopping, downhill skiing, cross-country skiing, golf, theater and watersports nearby.

"Your gracious hospitality and lovely home were the crowning touch of a most memorable trip."

La Pointe   B4

Woods Manor

Nebraska Row, PO Box 7
La Pointe, WI 54850
(715)747-3102 (800)966-3756 Fax:(715)747-2100

Circa 1926. Lake Superior's Madeline Island is home to this inn, which provides a unique setting for a romantic escape or family vacation. There are seven guest rooms in the manor and another three in the adjoining carriage house and lodge. The guest rooms vary in size and amenities, but all are comfortably appointed with antiques and family heirlooms. One of the rooms includes a screened-in balcony with a hot tub in addition to its king bed. Guests are welcome to borrow a bicycle or canoe, or take advantage of the inn's private beach for sunbathing or swimming.

Innkeeper(s): Lisa Byrne & Joe Oberzut. $89-209. MC VISA PC. 10 rooms with PB, 2 with FP. 1 suite. 2 cottages. Breakfast included in rates. Type of meal: continental breakfast. Beds: KQD. VCR, fax, swimming, sauna, bicycles and library on premises. Weddings, small meetings and family reunions hosted. Antiques, fishing, parks, shopping, downhill skiing, cross-country skiing and watersports nearby.

Pets Allowed: Depending on animal & room reserved.

Lake Geneva
J7

T.C. Smith Inn B&B
865 W Main St
Lake Geneva, WI 53147-1804
(414)248-1097 (800)423-0233 Fax:(414)248-1672

Circa 1845. Listed in the National Register of Historic Places, this High Victorian-style inn blends elements of Greek Revival and Italianate architecture. The inn has massive carved wooden doors, hand-painted moldings and woodwork, a high-ceilinged foyer, an original parquet floor, Oriental carpets, museum-quality period antiques and European oil paintings. Guests may enjoy tea in the Grand Parlor by a marble fireplace or enjoy breakfast on an open veranda overlooking Lake Geneva.

Historic Interest: Old World Wisconsin (45 minutes).

Innkeeper(s): The Marks Family. $95-350. MC VISA AX DC DS PC TC. TAC5. 8 rooms with PB, 5 with FP. 2 suites. 1 conference room. Breakfast, afternoon tea and evening snack included in rates. Types of meals: full breakfast, gourmet breakfast and early coffee/tea. Room service available. Beds: KQD. Air conditioning, ceiling fan and VCR in room. Fax, copier, bicycles and child care on premises. Handicap access. Weddings, small meetings, family reunions and seminars hosted. Antiques, fishing, parks, downhill skiing, cross-country skiing, theater and watersports nearby.

Pets Allowed: In specific rooms only.

Location: Forty miles from Milwaukee, seventy miles from Chicago.

Publicity: *Keystone Country Peddler, Pioneer Press Publication.*

"As much as we wanted to be on the beach, we found it impossible to leave the house. It's so beautiful and relaxing."

Lodi
I6

Victorian Treasure B&B Inn
115 Prairie St
Lodi, WI 53555-1240
(608)592-5199 (800)859-5199 Fax:(608)592-7147
E-mail: victorian@globaldialog.com

Circa 1893. Guests at Victorian Treasure stay in one of eight guest rooms spread among two 19th-century Queen Anne Victorians. The interior boasts stained- and leaded-glass windows, pocket doors, rich restored woods and expansive porches. Five suites include a whirlpool tub, fireplace and romantic decor with antiques. Full, gourmet breakfasts may include specialties such as eggs Florentine, herb vegetable quiche, or stuffed French toast topped with a seasonal fruit sauce.

Historic Interest: The Capitol Square in Madison (24 miles), Circus World Museum (20 miles), Wollersheim Winery (12 miles), Mirrimac Car Ferry (5 miles).

Innkeeper(s): Todd & Kimberly Seidl. $75-175. MC VISA PC TC. TAC10. 8 rooms with PB, 4 with FP. 4 suites. Breakfast and evening snack included in rates. Types of meals: gourmet breakfast and early coffee/tea. Beds: Q. Phone and air conditioning in room. Fax, copier and library on premises. Weddings, small meetings and family reunions hosted. Antiques, parks, shopping, downhill skiing, cross-country skiing, sporting events, theater and watersports nearby.

Publicity: *Milwaukee Sentinel, Chicago Sun-Times, Wisconsin Trails, Wisconsin State Journal, New York Times, Country Inn Cooking with Gail Greco.*

"One of the best of the best. A true treasure among many gems."

Madison
I6

Arbor House, An Environmental Inn
3402 Monroe St
Madison, WI 53711-1702
(608)238-2981 Fax:(608)238-1175

Circa 1853. Nature-lovers not only will enjoy the inn's close access to a 1,280-acre nature preserve, they will appreciate the innkeepers' ecological theme. Organic sheets and towels are offered for guests as well as environmentally safe bath products. Arbor House is one of Madison's oldest existing homes and features plenty of historic features, such as romantic reading chairs and antiques, mixed with modern amenities and unique touches. Five guest rooms include a whirlpool tub and two have fireplaces. The Annex guest rooms include private balconies. The innkeepers offer many amenities for business travelers, including value-added corporate rates. The award-winning inn has been recognized as a model of urban ecology. Lake Wingra is within walking distance as are biking and nature trails, bird watching and a host of other outdoor activities. Guests enjoy complimentary canoeing and use of mountain bikes.

Historic Interest: Frank Lloyd Wright designed many homes in Madison, and the Mansion Hill Historic District is nearby.

Innkeeper(s): John & Cathie Imes. $74-189. MC VISA AX PC TC. 8 rooms with PB, 2 with FP. 1 suite. 1 conference room. Breakfast included in rates. Types of meals: continental-plus breakfast and full breakfast. Beds: Q. Phone, air conditioning, ceiling fan, TV and VCR in room. Fax and copier on premises. Handicap access. Weddings, small meetings, family reunions and seminars hosted. Antiques, fishing, parks, shopping, cross-country skiing, sporting events and watersports nearby.

Publicity: *E.*

"What a delightful treat in the middle of Madison. Absolutely, unquestionably, the best time I've spent in a hotel or otherwise. B&Bs are the only way to go! Thank you!"

Mansion Hill Inn
424 N Pinckney St
Madison, WI 53703-1410
(608)255-3999 (800)798-9070 Fax:(608)255-2217

Circa 1858. The facade of this Romanesque Revival sandstone mansion boasts magnificent arched windows, Swedish railings, verandas and a belvedere. There are marble floors, ornate moldings and a magnificent mahogany and walnut staircase that winds up four stories. Lovingly restored and lavishly decorated, the inn easily rivals rooms at the Ritz for opulence. A special occasion warrants requesting the suite with the secret passageway behind a swinging bookcase.

Historic Interest: State Capitol (3 blocks).

Innkeeper(s): Janna Wojtal. $100-300. MC VISA AX PC TC. TAC10. 11 rooms with

PB, 4 with FP. 2 suites. 1 conference room. Breakfast and evening snack included in rates. Types of meals: continental-plus breakfast and early coffee/tea. Room service available. Beds: KQ. Phone, air conditioning, turn-down service, TV and VCR in room. Fax, copier and library on premises. Weddings and small meetings hosted. Fishing, parks, shopping, sporting events and theater nearby.

Publicity: *Chicago Tribune, New York Times, Country Inns, Americana, Glamour, Conde Nast Traveler.* Ratings: 4 Diamonds.

"The elegance, charm and superb services made it a delightful experience."

Monroe   J6

Victorian Garden B&B

1720 16th St
Monroe, WI 53566-2643
(608)328-1720 Fax:(608)328-1722
E-mail: vicgard@utelco-tds.net

Circa 1893. This blue and white three-story Victorian has two wraparound porches on either side of the main center section. Polished woodwork, an antique grandfather clock, a baby grand piano, lace curtains and other antiques are found in the main parlor. The Rosebud Room has rose carpeting, a rose covered comforter, queen bed and view of the hand-carved Italian fountain at the front of the house. A full breakfast is served

in the dining room on fine china. Local attractions include the Monroe Depot and the historic cheese making center.

Innkeeper(s): Jane & Pete Kessenich. $65-85. MC VISA DS PC. 4 rooms, 3 with PB. Breakfast included in rates. Types of meals: full breakfast and early coffee/tea. Beds: QT. Air conditioning in room. TV, VCR, fax, bicycles and library on premises. Weddings, small meetings, family reunions and seminars hosted. Antiques, parks, shopping, cross-country skiing and golf nearby.

"To feel as though one has come home to old friends is indeed a gift of the consummate host and hostess, you are both such—our stay was delightful."

Oconomowoc   I7

The Inn at Pine Terrace

351 E Lisbon Rd
Oconomowoc, WI 53066-2838
(414)567-7463 (800)421-4667

Circa 1879. This inn's convenient location, midway between Madison and Milwaukee and just north of the interstate that connects them, makes it equally appealing to business travelers and those seeking a romantic retreat. Some rooms boast whirlpool tubs and visitors are welcome to use the inn's in-ground swimming pool. A conference room is available for meetings, seminars and special occasions.

Innkeeper(s): Shirley W. Hinds. $66-132. MC

VISA AX DC CB DS PC TC. 13 rooms with PB. 1 conference room. Breakfast included in rates. Types of meals: continental breakfast and continental-plus breakfast. Beds: QT. Phone, air conditioning and TV in room. Copier and swimming on premises. Weddings, small meetings, family reunions and semi-nars hosted. Antiques, fishing, parks, shopping, downhill skiing, cross-country skiing, sporting events, theater and watersports nearby.

Pets Allowed: Must be well behaved.

"It's just like coming home to mother!"

Osceola   E1

St. Croix River Inn

305 River St, PO Box 356
Osceola, WI 54020
(715)294-4248

Circa 1910. This stone house is poised on a bluff overlooking the St. Croix River. The sitting room overlooks the river. All guest rooms have whirlpool baths. Rooms feature such ameni-ties as four-poster canopy beds, a tile fire-place, a Palladian win-dow that stretches from floor to ceiling, stenciling, bull's-eye moldings and private balconies. Breakfast is served in room.

Innkeeper(s): Bev Johnson. $85-200. MC VISA DS. 7 rooms with PB, 2 with FP. Breakfast included in rates. Type of meal: full breakfast. Beds: Q. Phone in room. Spa on premises. Fishing and parks nearby.

Location: St. Croix River Valley.

Publicity: *Chicago Sun-Times, Skyway News, St. Paul Pioneer Press.*

Phillips   D5

East Highland School House B&B

West 4342, Hwy D
Phillips, WI 54555
(715)339-3492

Guests are invited to ring the bell at this restored one-room schoolhouse. An addition to the building in 1920 features rooms with rustic exposed beams, brick walls and original light fixtures. Innkeepers Jeanne and Russ Kirchmeyer filled the home with family antiques and turn-of-the-century pieces. Lacy cur-tains, doilies and hand-hooked rugs lend to the romantic, coun-try atmosphere. Two museums featuring a 1900s kit area, school area and old logging and farming tools have been added to the inn; one in the basement and one in the barn across the street. The kitchen, which once served as a stage for the school, is now where Jeanne prepares the expansive morning meals.

Innkeeper(s): Russ & Jeanne Kirchmeyer. $45-60. 4 rooms. Breakfast includ-ed in rates. Type of meal: full breakfast.

Plymouth   H8

Yankee Hill Inn B&B

405 Collins St
Plymouth, WI 53073-2361
(414)892-2222

Circa 1870. Two outstanding examples of 19th-century archi-tecture comprise this inn, one a striking Italianate Gothic listed in the National Register, and the other a Queen Anne Victorian with many custom touches. Between the two impressive structures, visitors will choose from 12 spacious guest rooms, all featuring antique furnishings and handmade quilts. Visitors can

walk to downtown, where they will find an antique mall, shopping and fine dining.

Historic Interest: The Wade House, a state historical site, is five miles from the inn. Plymouth Historical Museum is within walking distance. Sheboygan County offers more than 200 locally landmarked buildings. The Historic Plymouth Walking Tour features 50 early Plymouth buildings.

Innkeeper(s): Peg Stahlman. $76-102. MC VISA. 12 rooms with PB. Breakfast included in rates. Types of meals: full breakfast and early coffee/tea. Beds: QD. VCR on premises. Small meetings, family reunions and seminars hosted. Antiques, fishing, shopping, cross-country skiing and theater nearby.

Publicity: *Wisconsin Country Life, Milwaukee Journal, Plymouth Review, Wisconsin Trails.*

"You have mastered the art of comfort. All the perfect little touches make this a dream come true. I only regret that we cannot stay forever."

Port Washington   H8

Port Washington Inn
308 W Washington St
Port Washington, WI 53074-1839
(414)284-5583

Circa 1903. This three-story Victorian stands proudly on Sweetcake Hill, five blocks from Lake Michigan. Distinctive original woodwork, stained and leaded glass, gas and electric light fixtures, pocket doors, polished oak floors and lincrusta and anaglypta wall coverings are among the historic features of this inn. There are four guest rooms, double parlors, and formal dining room

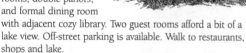

with adjacent cozy library. Two guest rooms afford a bit of a lake view. Off-street parking is available. Walk to restaurants, shops and lake.

Historic Interest: Thirty minutes from Milwaukee.

Innkeeper(s): Rita, Dave & Aaron Nelson. $85-125. MC VISA AX. 4 rooms with PB. 1 suite. Breakfast and afternoon tea included in rates. Types of meals: full breakfast and early coffee/tea. Beds: Q. Air conditioning, ceiling fan and VCR in room. Library on premises. Weddings, small meetings, family reunions and seminars hosted. Antiques, fishing, shopping, downhill skiing, cross-country skiing, sporting events, theater and watersports nearby.

Publicity: *Ozaukee Press, Suburban Life.*

"You have done an excellent job turning a charming old house into a warm and inviting B&B."

Racine   J8

Lochnaiar Inn
1121 Lake Ave
Racine, WI 53403-1924
(414)633-3300 Fax:(414)633-3678

Circa 1915. This elegant three-story English Tudor mansion is situated on a bluff overlooking Lake Michigan. It is conveniently located within walking distance of downtown and the marina, which is well known for its year-round festivals and recreational activities. The finely furnished guest rooms offer visitors European-style comforts, including canopied four-poster beds, empress tubs and fresh-cut flowers. Business travelers will appreciate the many amenities offered for their convenience, while the more casual guests will marvel at the inn's historic grandeur. A continental-plus breakfast is offered during the week and a full breakfast is served on the weekends.

Call for rates. 8 rooms with PB, 6 with FP. 2 suites. 3 conference rooms. Breakfast included in rates. Beds: KQ. Phone, air conditioning, ceiling fan and TV in room. VCR on premises. Handicap access. Weddings, small meetings, family reunions and seminars hosted. Amusement parks, antiques, shopping, cross-country skiing, sporting events and theater nearby.

Publicity: *Chicago Magazine.*

"The inn is an absolute gem and you are both a delight."

Reedsburg   H5

Parkview B&B
211 N Park St
Reedsburg, WI 53959-1652
(608)524-4333

Circa 1895. Tantalizingly close to Baraboo and Wisconsin Dells, this central Wisconsin inn overlooks a city park in the historic district. The gracious innkeepers delight in tending to their guests' desires and offer wake-up coffee and a morning paper. The home's first owners were in the hardware business, so there are many original, unique fixtures, in addition to hardwood floors, intricate woodwork, leaded and etched windows and a suitors' window. The downtown business district is just a block away.

Innkeeper(s): Tom & Donna Hofmann. $65-80. MC VISA AX. TAC10. 4 rooms, 2 with PB. Breakfast included in rates. Types of meals: gourmet breakfast and early coffee/tea. Evening snack available. Beds: QT. Air conditioning and ceiling fan in room. TV on premises. Antiques, fishing, parks, shopping, downhill skiing and cross-country skiing nearby.

Publicity: *Reedsburg Times Press.*

"Your hospitality was great! You all made us feel right at home."

Sister Bay   E9

The Inn on Maple
414 Maple Dr
Sister Bay, WI 54234
(920)854-5107

Circa 1902. Located on a quiet side street, a half block off Bay Shore Drive, this cozy inn is in the National Register of Historic Places because of its stovewood architecture. The inn is decorated with simple country antiques, ceiling fans and quilts. Full breakfasts are served on an enclosed front porch. Relax on the deck or in front of the fireplace in the Gathering Room. Door County offers 250 miles of shoreline, and there are state parks, antique shops and art galleries near the inn.

Innkeeper(s): Bill & Louise Robbins. $75-85. MC VISA PC TC. 7 rooms with PB. Breakfast included in rates. Types of meals: full breakfast and early coffee/tea. Evening snack available. Beds: QDT. Ceiling fan in room. TV, VCR and library on premises. Antiques, fishing, shopping, cross-country skiing, golf, theater and watersports nearby.

Location: Door County.

Sparta

G4

The Franklin Victorian

220 E Franklin St
Sparta, WI 54656-1804
(608)269-3894 (800)845-8767

Circa 1800. Built for a banker when Sparta was the hub of social life, this house still boasts of such splendid woods as black ash, curly birch, quarter-cut white oak and red oak.

Features include leaded windows in the library and dining room, many of the original filigreed brass light fixtures, and a magnificent sunset stained-glass window. Sparta is nestled among the hills of Wisconsin's Coulee Region. Area attractions include rivers, trout streams, 130 miles of bike trails, craft and antique shops.

Innkeeper(s): Lloyd & Jane Larson. $70-95. MC VISA. 4 rooms, 2 with PB, 1 with FP. 1 conference room. Breakfast included in rates. Types of meals: gourmet breakfast and early coffee/tea. Beds: KQ. Ceiling fan in room. Small meetings hosted. Antiques, fishing, parks, shopping, downhill skiing, cross-country skiing and sporting events nearby.

Just-N-Trails Country Inn/ Nordic Ski Center

7452 Kathryn Ave
Sparta, WI 54656-9729
(608)269-4522 (800)488-4521 Fax:(608)269-3280

Circa 1920. Nestled in a scenic valley sits this 200-acre farm. Guests are encouraged to explore the hiking, snowshoe and cross-country ski trails. The innkeepers offer ski and snowshoe rentals for both adults and children. In addition to delightfully decorated rooms in the farmhouse, there are two Scandinavian log houses and a plush, restored granary for those desiring more privacy. Each of these cottages includes a whirlpool bath and a fireplace. There also is a suite in the farmhouse with a fireplace and whirlpool. The well-cared-for grounds and buildings reflect the innkeepers' pride in their home, which was built by Don's grandfather. Guests will find cats, kittens, rabbits, chickens and Peter, a pygmy goat, on the premises.

Innkeeper(s): Don & Donna Justin. $80-300. MC VISA AX DS PC TC. TAC10. 7 rooms with PB, 5 with FP. 3 cottages. 1 conference room. Breakfast included in rates. Type of meal: full breakfast. Beds: KQDT. Air conditioning and ceiling fan in room. 213 acres. Weddings, small meetings, family reunions and seminars hosted. Antiques, fishing, parks, shopping, downhill skiing and cross-country skiing nearby.

Pets Allowed: $10 per pet per day.

Location: Elroy-Sparta bike trail.

Publicity: *Milwaukee Journal, Country, Wisconsin Woman, Wisconsin Trails, Travel America, Family Fun.*

Stevens Point

F6

A Victorian Swan on Water

1716 Water St
Stevens Point, WI 54481-3550
(715)345-0595 (800)454-9886

Circa 1889. This Victorian is located a block and a half from the Wisconsin River. Black walnut inlays in the wood floors, crown moldings, walnut paneling and interior shutters are among the inn's architectural elements. The suite features a mural of a pastoral Mediterranean scene, a ceiling fan, whirlpool tub, fireplace and a balcony overlooking the garden. There are antique furnishings and lace curtains. Breakfast items include rum-baked fresh pineapple and "turtle" French toast stuffed with chocolate and pecans and served with caramel sauce.

Innkeeper(s): Joan Ouellette. $55-125. MC VISA AX DS PC TC. TAC5. 4 rooms, 3 with PB, 1 with FP. 1 suite. Breakfast included in rates. Types of meals: full breakfast, gourmet breakfast and early coffee/tea. Beds: KQDT. Air conditioning and ceiling fan in room. TV, VCR and library on premises. Weddings, small meetings, family reunions and seminars hosted. Antiques, fishing, parks, shopping, downhill skiing, cross-country skiing, sporting events, theater and watersports nearby.

"Our first white Christmas...what a wonderful time we had here in your home. Breakfast was great. We can't thank you enough for your warm hospitality."

Dreams of Yesteryear B&B

1100 Brawley St
Stevens Point, WI 54481-3536
(715)341-4525 Fax:(715)344-3047

Circa 1901. This elegant, three-story, 4,000-square-foot Queen Anne home is within walking distance of downtown, the Wisconsin River and the University of Wisconsin. The inn features golden oak woodwork, hardwood floors and leaded glass. Each guest room offers exquisite decor; the third-floor

Ballroom Suite boasts a whirlpool. Gourmet breakfasts are served in the inn's formal dining room. An excellent hiking trail is just a block from the inn.

Historic Interest: Historic downtown Stevens Point is nearby, and the inn is only a short trip from dozens of historical sites.

Innkeeper(s): Bonnie & Bill Maher. $58-136. MC VISA AX DS PC TC. TAC5. 6 rooms, 4 with PB. 2 suites. Breakfast, afternoon tea and evening snack included in rates. Types of meals: full breakfast, gourmet breakfast and early coffee/tea. Beds: KQDT. Phone, air conditioning and TV in room. VCR, bicycles and library on premises. Weddings, small meetings and family reunions hosted. Amusement parks, antiques, fishing, parks, shopping, downhill skiing, cross-country skiing, sporting events, theater and watersports nearby.

Publicity: *Victorian Homes, Reach, Stevens Point Journal.*

"Something from a Hans Christian Anderson fairy tale."

Sturgeon Bay
F9

The Inn at Cedar Crossing

336 Louisiana St
Sturgeon Bay, WI 54235-2422
(414)743-4200 Fax:(414)743-4422

Circa 1884. This historic hotel, in the National Register, is a downtown two-story brick building that once housed street-level shops with second-floor apartments for the tailors, shop-keepers and pharmacists who worked below. The upstairs, now guest rooms, is decorated with rich fabrics and wallpapers and fine antiques. The Anniversary Room has a mahogany bed, fire-place and double whirlpool tub. The Victorian-era dining room and pub, both with fireplaces, are on the lower level. The waterfront is three blocks away.

Historic Interest: Door County Historical and Maritime Museums.

Innkeeper(s): Terry Wulf. $90-150. MC VISA DS PC TC. 9 rooms with PB, 6 with FP. Breakfast and evening snack included in rates. Types of meals: continental-plus breakfast, full breakfast, gourmet breakfast and early cof-fee/tea. Dinner, picnic lunch, lunch, gourmet lunch, catering service, catered breakfast and room service available. Restaurant on premises.

Beds: KQ. Phone, air conditioning, TV and VCR in room. Fax, copier and library on premises. Small meetings hosted. Antiques, fishing, parks, shop-ping, downhill skiing, cross-country skiing, theater and watersports nearby.

Publicity: *New Month, Milwaukee Sentinel, Chicago Sun-Times, Country Inns, Bon Appetit, Gourmet, Green Bay Press Gazette, Midwest Living, Milwaukee Journal, Wisconsin Trails.*

"The second-year stay at the inn was even better than the first. I couldn't have found a more romantic place."

Scofield House B&B

908 Michigan St
Sturgeon Bay, WI 54235-1849
(414)743-7727 (888)463-0204 Fax:(414)743-7727

Circa 1902. Mayor Herbert Scofield, prominent locally in the lumber and hardware business, built this late-Victorian house with a sturdy square tower and inlaid floors that feature intri-cate borders patterned in cherry, birch, maple, walnut, and red and white oak. Oak moldings throughout the house boast raised designs of bows, ribbons, swags and flowers. Equally lav-ish decor is featured in the guest rooms with fluffy flowered comforters and cabbage rose wallpapers highlighting romantic antique bedsteads. Baked apple-cinnamon French toast is a house specialty. Modern amenities include many suites with fireplaces and double whirlpools. "Room at the Top" is a sky-lit 900-square-foot suite occupying the whole third floor and furnished with Victorian antiques.

Historic Interest: Door County Lighthouses, Maritime Museum, Door County Museum (within walking distance).

Innkeeper(s): Bill & Fran Cecil. $93-196. PC TC. 6 rooms with PB, 5 with FP. 3 cottages. Breakfast and afternoon tea included in rates. Type of meal: gourmet breakfast. Beds: Q. Air conditioning, ceiling fan, TV and VCR in room. Fax and copier on premises. Amusement parks, antiques, fishing, parks, shopping, downhill skiing, cross-country skiing, sporting events, the-ater and watersports nearby.

Publicity: *Innsider, Glamour, Country, Wisconsin Trails, Green Bay Press Gazette, Chicago Tribune, Milwaukee Sentinel-Journal, Midwest Living, Victorian Decorating & Lifestyle, Country Inns, National Geographic Traveler.*

"You've introduced us to the fabulous world of B&Bs. I loved the porch swing and would have been content on it for the entire weekend."

White Lace Inn

16 N 5th Ave
Sturgeon Bay, WI 54235-1714
(920)743-1105
E-mail: romance@whitelaceinn.com

Circa 1903. White Lace Inn is four Victorian houses, one an ornate Queen Anne. It is adjacent to two districts listed in the National Register. Often the site for romantic anniversary cele-brations, a favorite suite has a two-sided fireplace, magnifi-cent walnut Eastlake bed, English country fabrics and a two-person whirlpool tub. There are 12 suites that offer whirlpool tubs and 15 suites feature fireplaces. Enjoy the landscaped gardens and gazebo.

Innkeeper(s): Dennis & Bonnie Statz. $98-198. MC VISA AX DS. 18 suites, 15 with FP. Breakfast included in rates. Type of meal: full breakfast. Beds: KQ. Phone in room. Spa on premises. Handicap access. Antiques, fishing, cross-country skiing, theater and watersports nearby.

Location: The inn is located in Door County, Lake Michigan on one side, Green Bay on the other side of the peninsula.

Publicity: *Milwaukee Sentinel, Brides, National Geographic Traveler, Wisconsin Trails, Milwaukee, Country Home, Midwest Living.*

"Each guest room is an overwhelming visual feast, a dazzling fusion of colors, textures and beautiful objects. It is one of these rare gems that established a tradition the day it opened — Wisconsin Trails."

Walworth
J7

Arscott House B&B

PO Box 875, 241 S Main
Walworth, WI 53184-0875
(414)275-3233

Circa 1903. Built by a master carpenter at the turn of the cen-tury, this turreted Queen Anne Victorian has been lovingly restored to its original stylings. A new addition is the inn's Arizona Apartment, with Southwestern decor, a spacious sitting room, kitchen and a private, outside entrance. A roomy front porch and two outside decks are favorite relaxing spots, and a buffet breakfast is available to guests. The inn is just minutes from Lake Geneva's many attractions.

Historic Interest: Yerke Observatory (10 minutes), Big Foot Trail, hike entire lake of Geneva (10 minutes), Wrigley Estate Stone Manor (20 minutes).

Innkeeper(s): Valerie C. Dudek. $45-145. MC VISA DS PC TC. 2 rooms. Breakfast and afternoon tea included in rates. Types of meals: full break-fast and early coffee/tea. Beds: QDT. Air condition-ing, turndown service, ceiling fan, TV and VCR in room. Antiques, fish-ing, parks, shopping, downhill skiing, cross-country skiing, theater and watersports nearby.

"Enjoyed your gracious hospitality. Loved the breakfast. Loved your house. We'll be back again. Thank you for making our first anniversary such an enjoyable one."

White Lake   E7

Jesse's Historic Wolf River Lodge

N 2119 Taylor Rd
White Lake, WI 54491
(715)882-2182
E-mail: WLFRVRLDG@aol.com

Circa 1929. This rustic Northwoods lodge is made to order for outdoor-lovers. White-water river rafting, trout fishing, cross-country skiing and hiking are just a few of the available activities. The inn features eight rooms with private baths. There are three guesthouses with fireplaces, lofts and housekeeping facilities; each guesthouse sleeps eight. Hearty homemade fare dominates the menu; crepes suzette, Eskimo jam and American fried potatoes are among the breakfast favorites. Indians, French traders and loggers once populated the area, which now sports the clean, clear Wolf River as its prime attraction.

Innkeeper(s): Joan Jesse. $80-160. MC VISA PC. TAC10. 8 rooms with PB. 3 cottages. Breakfast included in rates. Types of meals: full breakfast and early coffee/tea. Dinner and picnic lunch available. Restaurant on premises. Beds: QDT. Air conditioning in room. TV, VCR, fax, copier, spa, swimming, bicycles and library on premises. 12 acres. Weddings, small meetings, family reunions and seminars hosted. Antiques, fishing, parks, shopping, downhill skiing, cross-country skiing and watersports nearby.

Pets Allowed: With advance approval.

Publicity: *New York Times, Better Homes & Gardens, Chicago Tribune, Milwaukee Journal, Midwest Living.*

"Thank you for your time, service, smiles and good food."

Whitewater   I7

Victoria-On-Main B&B

622 W Main St
Whitewater, WI 53190-1855
(414)473-8400

Circa 1895. This Queen Anne Victorian is located in the heart of Whitewater National Historic District, adjacent to the University of Wisconsin. It was built for Edward Engebretson, mayor of Whitewater. Each guest room is named for a Wisconsin hardwood. The Red Oak Room, Cherry Room and Bird's Eye Maple Room all feature antiques, Laura Ashley prints and down comforters. A hearty breakfast is served, and there are kitchen facilities available for light meal preparation. Whitewater Lake and Kettle Moraine State Forest are five minutes away.

Innkeeper(s): Nancy Wendt. $65-75. MC VISA. 3 rooms, 1 with PB, 1 with FP. Breakfast included in rates. Types of meals: full breakfast and early cof-

fee/tea. Beds: D. Ceiling fan in room. TV on premises. Antiques, fishing, parks, shopping, cross-country skiing, theater and watersports nearby.

Location: Between Madison and Milwaukee.

"We loved it. Wonderful hospitality."

Wisconsin Dells   H5

Historic Bennett House

825 Oak St
Wisconsin Dells, WI 53965-1418
(608)254-2500

Circa 1863. This handsomely restored Greek Revival-style home, framed by a white picket fence, housed the Henry Bennetts, whose family still operates the Bennett photographic studio, the oldest continuously operating studio in the country. Noted for the first stop-action photography, Mr. Bennett's work is displayed in the Smithsonian. The National Register home is decorated in European and Victorian styles. The grounds are decorated with sun and shade gardens.

Innkeeper(s): Gail & Rich Obermeyer. $70-90. PC TC. 3 rooms, 1 with PB. 1 suite. Breakfast included in rates. Types of meals: gourmet breakfast and early coffee/tea. Beds: QD. Air conditioning, ceiling fan, TV and VCR in room. Library on premises. Amusement parks, antiques, parks, shopping, downhill skiing, cross-country skiing, theater and watersports nearby.

Publicity: *Midwest Living, Travel & Leisure, Country Life, Specialties of the House.*

"We felt we were visiting relatives for the weekend and the visit was too short."

Wisconsin Dells Thunder Valley B&B Inn

W15344 Waubeek Rd
Wisconsin Dells, WI 53965-9005
(608)254-4145

Circa 1870. As the area is full of both Scandinavian and Native American heritage, and the innkeeper of this country inn has tried to honor the traditions. The inn even features a Scandinavian gift shop. Chief Yellow Thunder, for whom this inn is named, often camped out on the grounds and surrounding area. The inn's restaurant is highly acclaimed. Everything is fresh, including the wheat the innkeepers grind for the morning pancakes and rolls. There is a good selection of Wisconsin beer and wine, as well. Guests can stay in the farmhouse, which offers a microwave and refrigerator for guest use, or spend the night in one of two cottages. The Guest Hus features gable ceilings and a knotty pine interior. The Wee Hus is a smaller unit, and includes a refrigerator.

Historic Interest: Chief Yellow Thunder, a Winnebago Indian Chief, had a pow-wow behind the barn. He is buried nearby.

Innkeeper(s): Anita, Kari & Sigrid Nelson. $45-80. MC VISA. 10 rooms with PB. 1 cottage. Breakfast included in rates. Type of meal: full breakfast. Beds: KQD. Air conditioning in room. Handicap access. 25 acres. Weddings, small meetings, family reunions and seminars hosted. Norwegian spoken.

Publicity: *Wisconsin Trails, Country Inns, Midwest Living, Chicago Sun-Times.*

"Thunder Valley is a favorite of Firstar Club members — delicious food served in a charming atmosphere with warm Scandinavian hospitality"

Wyoming

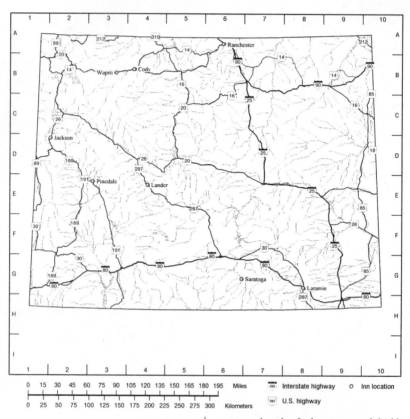

Miles: 0 15 30 45 60 75 90 105 120 135 150 165 180 195
Kilometers: 0 25 50 75 100 125 150 175 200 225 250 275 300

Interstate highway · Inn location
U.S. highway

Cody   **B4**

Cody Guest Houses

1401 Rumsey Ave
Cody, WY 82414-3714
(307)587-6000 (800)587-6560 Fax:(307)587-8048

Circa 1906. As long as innkeepers Daren and Kathy Singer are in town, Cody's past will be preserved. This diligent couple have restored several historic local buildings, including the home of Cody's first mayor who later became a Wyoming governor. Extensive renovation was necessary on all of the guest houses, which include a 1906 Victorian home, two cottages and a brick home dating to 1926. The Mayor's Home, the Singer's latest addition, was purchased for $10 by closed-bid and moved to its current location. It now includes three luxury rooms, each with a freshwater spa and double shower. The first floor houses an antique shop. Rooms are well-appointed in a variety of styles, from Victorian to Old West. Although breakfast is not included in the rates, guests are offered plenty of other amenities. Daily housekeeping, kitchens, laundry facilities, freshwater spas, fireplaces and in-room stereos, CD players and televisions are among the offerings.

Innkeeper(s): Kathy & Daren Singer. $50-250. MC VISA DS PC TC. TAC10. 10 rooms with PB, 1 with FP. 8 suites. 3 cottages. 3 conference rooms. Catering service available. Beds: KQD. Phone, air conditioning, ceiling fan, TV and VCR in room. Weddings, small meetings, family reunions and seminars hosted. Fishing, parks, shopping, downhill skiing, cross-country skiing, golf and watersports nearby.

Publicity: *Cody Enterprise.*

"Understated western elegance!"

Parson's Pillow B&B

1202 14th St
Cody, WY 82414-3720
(307)587-2382 (800)377-2348
E-mail: ppbb@trib.com

Circa 1902. This historic building originally served as the Methodist-Episcopal Church, Cody's first church. Guests are free to practice a tune on the piano in the home's parlor, which also offers a TV and VCR. Guest rooms feature antiques and quilts, as well as the more modern addition of computer ports. Clawfoot and oak-framed prairie tubs add to the nostalgia. The Buffalo Bill Historical Center and the Cody Historic Walking Tour are nearby.

Historic Interest: Buffalo Bill Historical Center, Old West Miniature Village & Museum, Cody Night Rodeo.

Innkeeper(s): Lee & Elly Larabee. $75-85. MC VISA PC TC. TAC10. 4 rooms with PB. Breakfast included in rates. Types of meals: gourmet breakfast and early coffee/tea. Beds: Q. Turndown service and ceiling fan in room. TV, VCR and library on premises. Weddings, small meetings and family reunions hosted. Antiques, fishing, parks, shopping, downhill skiing and cross-country skiing nearby.

Location: One block off Sheridan Avenue in downtown Cody.

Jackson   D2

The Huff House Inn

240 E Deloney, PO Box 1189
Jackson, WY 83001-1189
(307)733-4164 Fax:(307)739-9091
E-mail: huffhousebnb@blissnet.com

Circa 1917. Originally built for the town's first medical doctor and town mayor, this Craftsman-style home served as both an office for seeing patients and a residence. For the past 30 years, the current innkeepers have dedicated themselves to retaining the inn's historic character. Beveled-glass doors, chandeliers, antiques and brocade fabrics add to the inn's comfortable atmosphere. In addition to the five guest rooms in the main house, the inn features four separate cottages that boast hand-stenciled walls and Jacuzzi tubs. Breakfast is served in the formal dining room or breakfast room. Baked apple French toast with a spicy applesauce topping is a house favorite. The inn is a block from the historic district, restaurants, shops and museums.

Innkeeper(s): Jackie & Weldon Richardson. $105-189. MC VISA DS PC TC. TAC10. 9 rooms with PB. 4 cottages. Breakfast included in rates. Types of meals: full breakfast and early coffee/tea. Beds: KQT. Phone, air conditioning, TV and VCR in room. Fax, copier, spa and library on premises. Weddings and family reunions hosted. German spoken. Antiques, fishing, parks, shopping, downhill skiing, cross-country skiing, golf, theater and watersports nearby.

Publicity: *Denver Post.*

"Our honeymoon could not have been nicer! The food was incredible and the cottage was perfect."

Lander   E4

Blue Spruce Inn

677 S 3rd St
Lander, WY 82520-3707
(307)332-8253

Circa 1920. Five blue spruce trees mark this large Arts and Crafts influenced home. Original chandeliers, stained glass, oak crown molding and woodwork add to the house's appeal. Mission-style furnishings are in keeping with the house's period. Views of the mountains may be seen from the second-floor rooms. Ask for the Spotted Elk Room for a Native American-themed accommodation. There is a sun porch and front porch, and a block away is a mountain trout stream. Lander is adjacent to the Wind River Indian Reservation, and it is on this reservation where the grave site of Sacajawea is located.

Historic Interest: In addition to small museums and cultural sites on the Wind River Indian Reservation, South Pass, a significant portion of the Oregon Trail is nearby. The Oregon/Mormon/California Trail is about 20 miles away. Historic South Pass City, a Wyoming State Historic Site, is 45 minutes away.

Innkeeper(s): Marvin & JoAnne Brown. $80. MC VISA AX DS PC TC. 4 rooms with PB. Breakfast included in rates. Types of meals: full breakfast and early coffee/tea. Beds: QT. TV, VCR, bicycles and library on premises. Weddings, small meetings and family reunions hosted. Limited German spoken. Antiques, fishing, parks, shopping and cross-country skiing nearby.

Laramie   G8

Prairie Breeze B&B

718 Ivinson Ave
Laramie, WY 82070
(307)745-5482 (800)840-2170 Fax:(307)745-5341

Circa 1888. In the National Register, this three-story yellow Victorian was built by Professor John Conley, once vice-president of the University of Wyoming. The inn is furnished with antiques including a wind-up Victrola and old piano. Kirsten's Suite offers an upper balcony, a four-poster bed, antiques, a clawfoot tub, sitting room and dressing room. The university is a two-block walk.

Innkeeper(s): Anne & George Cowardin-Bach. $60-80. MC VISA AX DC CB DS PC TC. TAC5. 4 rooms, 3 with PB. 1 suite. Breakfast included in rates. Types of meals: continental breakfast, continental-plus breakfast and early coffee/tea. Beds: QD. Phone, turndown service and ceiling fan in room. TV, fax, copier and bicycles on premises. Weddings, small meetings, family reunions and seminars hosted. French spoken. Antiques, fishing, parks, shopping, downhill skiing, cross-country skiing, sporting events, golf and theater nearby.

Pets Allowed: small under control; owner responsible for damage.

Publicity: *Boomerang.*

Vee Bar Guest Ranch

2091 State Hwy 130
Laramie, WY 82070
(307)745-7036 (800)483-3227 Fax:(307)745-7433
E-mail: veebar@lariat.org

Circa 1896. Experience the Old West on this 800-acre working cattle ranch nestled on Little Laramie River at the base of the Snowy Range Mountains. Once the private residence of an English cattle baron, the main lodge was the home station for a stagecoach company. Today, the authentic western character of the lodge and its log cabins are preserved in the Ralph Lauren-style rustic furnishings, wood floors and stone fireplaces. A full country breakfast and lunch are included as well as a ranch-style dinner of barbeque ribs and chicken grilled outdoors in front of the lodge. The inn offers a variety of on-site recreational activities.

Innkeeper(s): Mindi Crabb. $100-150. AP. MC VISA PC TC. TAC10. 9 cabins, 6 with FP. 1 conference room. Breakfast, afternoon tea, dinner, evening snack and picnic lunch included in rates. Type of meal: full breakfast. Lunch and banquet service available. Restaurant on premises. Beds: KQDT. VCR, fax, copier, spa, stables and library on premises. Handicap access. 800 acres. Weddings, small meetings, family reunions and seminars hosted. Fishing, downhill skiing and cross-country skiing nearby.

Publicity: *Log Home Design Ideas Magazine, National Geographic Traveler.*

Pinedale   E3

The Chambers House

PO Box 753, 111 W Magnolia St
Pinedale, WY 82941
(307)367-2168 (800)567-2168 Fax:(307)367-4209
E-mail: anoble1227@aol.com

Circa 1933. This authentic log home once owned by one of the area's earliest pioneers was hand built during the Great Depression. It has been immaculately renovated and decorated with a mixture of period antiques and contemporary furnishings. With the Bridger Teton National Forest and Wind River Mountains just a short distance away, travelers can indulge in a variety of summer and winter sports. A gourmet breakfast is served in the dining room or in the privacy of your own room.
$55-100. MC VISA AX PC TC. TAC10. 5 rooms, 2 with PB, 2 with FP. Breakfast included in rates. Types of meals: full breakfast, gourmet breakfast and early coffee/tea. Evening snack, picnic lunch and lunch available. Beds: QT. Phone, TV and VCR in room. Handicap access. Weddings, small meetings, family reunions and seminars hosted. Fishing, parks, shopping, downhill skiing, cross-country skiing, golf and watersports nearby.

Pets Allowed: Dogs only.

Ranchester   A6

Historic Old Stone House

135 Wolf Creek Rd
Ranchester, WY 82839-0846
(307)655-9239 Fax:(307)655-9191

Circa 1899. A panoramic view of Big Horn Mountains, Wolf Mountains and the rugged prairie are offered from this inn's property. The authentic ranch building reflects an Arts and Crafts influence. Red rock trim frames the windows and doors, and inside there are built-in benches and wide window sills in the parlor. In the Grand Parlor, gold sofas add warmth to wood walls and floors, beamed ceilings and large stone fireplace. Air conditioning, turn-down service, ceiling fans and VCR are offered in some rooms. Breakfast is served graciously with crystal, linen and silver service. Enjoy afternoon refreshments on the front porch or before the stone fireplace.
Innkeeper(s): Jack & Gerry Brinkers. $80-110. MC VISA DS PC TC. TAC10. 4 rooms, 2 with PB. 2 suites. 1 cottage. Breakfast, afternoon tea and evening snack included in rates. Types of meals: full breakfast and early coffee/tea. Dinner, picnic lunch and room service available. Beds: KQT. Air conditioning, turndown service, ceiling fan and VCR in room. TV, fax and library on premises. 10 acres. Small meetings, family reunions and seminars hosted. Antiques, fishing, parks, shopping, cross-country skiing, golf and theater nearby.

Pets Allowed: In guest house only.

"We enjoyed a quiet night in the old haunted house of my childhood. It's good that you two are loving and sharing this lovely place."

Saratoga   G6

Far Out West B&B

304 N Second St
Saratoga, WY 82331
(307)326-5869 Fax:(307)326-9864
E-mail: fowbnb@union-tel.com

Circa 1920. Winters in Wyoming can be harsh, so Minnie Sears built this home in town to make it easier for her children to attend school during the cold months. The home is a smaller replica of Sears' ranch, which was out in the country. The main house still maintains many original features, and there are two guest rooms located in this historic section. As well, there is a unique room accessible only by a tiny, three-foot-high door. Inside, children will find toys, books and other goodies. Out back, there are several accommodations with special names such as The Calamity Jane or The James Gang. The Hideout, located in a separate house, includes a kitchen, dining room and living room. There is a spa and exercise equipment for guest use. Breakfast entrees, such as Gunfighter eggs, are accompanied by freshly baked biscuits, sausage and fresh fruit.

Innkeeper(s): Bill & BJ Farr. $75-125. MC VISA PC. TAC10. 6 rooms with PB. 1 cottage. Breakfast included in rates. Types of meals: full breakfast and early coffee/tea. Beds: KDT. Ceiling fan, TV and VCR in room. Fax, copier, spa and library on premises. Handicap access. Weddings, small meetings, family reunions and seminars hosted. Antiques, fishing, parks, shopping, cross-country skiing, golf and watersports nearby.

Pets Allowed: Boarding at vet's office.

Publicity: *Saratoga Sun.*

"An absolutely wonderful place for comfort, friendliness and food."

Wapiti   B3

Elephant Head Lodge

1170 Yellowstone Hwy
Wapiti, WY 82450
(307)587-3980 Fax:(307)527-7922

Circa 1910. Buffalo Bill Cody's niece and her husband built the rustic main lodge using pine trees found on the property. The lodge gets its unusual name from a nearby rock formation. In addition to the main lodge, the five-acre grounds include 10 historic cabins, each with comfortable, early American furnishings. The pioneer-style cabins include private baths and are stocked with towels, sheets and blankets. The lodge's restaurant serves breakfast, lunch and dinner. Guests may choose the American Plan rates if they wish to enjoy all three. The lodge is located just 11 miles outside of Yellowstone National Park.
Innkeeper(s): Phil & Joan Lamb. $57-90. AP. EP. MC VISA AX DS PC TC. TAC10. 11 cottages with PB, 1 with FP. Type of meal: full breakfast. Dinner and lunch available. Restaurant on premises. Beds: QDT. Ceiling fan in room. TV, VCR, fax, copier, stables, library, pet boarding and child care on premises. Weddings, small meetings, family reunions and seminars hosted. German spoken. Antiques, fishing, parks, shopping and watersports nearby.

Pets Allowed.

U. S. Territories

Puerto Rico

Ceiba

Ceiba Country Inn
PO Box 1067
Ceiba, PR 00735-1067
(787)885-0471 Fax:(809)885-0471
E-mail: prinn@juno.com

Circa 1950. A large Spanish patio is available at this tropical country inn perched on rolling, green hills. Situated 500 feet above the valley floor, the inn affords a view of the ocean with

the isle of Culebra on the horizon. A continental buffet is served in the warm and sunny breakfast room. The inn is four miles from Puerto Del Rey, the largest marina in the Caribbean, and 10 miles from Luquillo Beach, which is a mile of white sand, dotted with coconut palms.

Innkeeper(s): Nicki Treat. $70. MC VISA AX DS TC. TAC10. 9 rooms with PB. Breakfast included in rates. Type of meal: continental-plus breakfast. Beds: QT. Phone and air conditioning in room. TV, fax and library on premises. Handicap access. 13 acres. Weddings, small meetings, family reunions and seminars hosted. Fishing, shopping, golf and watersports nearby.

Virgin Islands

Christiansted, Saint Croix

Pink Fancy
27 Prince St
Christiansted, Saint Croix, VI 00820-5032
(809)773-8460 (800)524-2045 Fax:(809)773-6448

Circa 1780. Innkeepers George and Cindy Tyler strive to help guests enjoy their island visit. For those arriving in late afternoon or early evening, the Tylers can arrange to have a light snack or dinner waiting so guests can simply relax. Rental car pick-up and daily itineraries also can be arranged here. The inn was built in Dutch Colonial style and has been decorated in a tropical motif with ceiling fans. The rooms also include kitchenettes. There is a poolside happy hour each evening, and the innkeepers offer packages for honeymooners or those who wish to dive or snorkel. The inn is located just one block from the beach and two blocks from the historical downtown C'sted. A complimentary breakfast is served daily.

Innkeeper(s): George & Cindy Tyler. $75-120. AP. MC VISA AX TC. 13 rooms with PB. Breakfast included in rates. Type of meal: continental-plus breakfast. Beds: KQT. Phone, air conditioning, ceiling fan and TV in room. Fax and copier on premises. Weddings and family reunions hosted. Antiques, fishing, parks, shopping and watersports nearby.

Canada

British Columbia

North Vancouver

Sue's Victorian Guesthouse

152 E 3rd
North Vancouver, BC V7L 1E6
(604)985-1523

Circa 1904. This turn-of-the-century home has seen more than 4,000 guests in its 10-plus years as a guesthouse. The home has been restored, maintaining its veranda and original staircases. Rooms are decorated with antiques, and baths have antique soaking tubs. There is a guest kitchen, and inngoers can make their own breakfast or select from a number of local eateries.

Innkeeper(s): Gail Fowler & Jen Lowe. $60-75. TC. 3 rooms, 1 with PB. Type of meal: early coffee/tea. Beds: KQDT. Phone, ceiling fan, TV and VCR in room. Antiques, fishing, parks, shopping, downhill skiing, cross-country skiing, sporting events, theater and watersports nearby.

Sooke

Ocean Wilderness Inn & Spa Retreat

109 W Coast Rd, RR 2
Sooke, BC V0S 1N0
(250)646-2116 (800)323-2116 Fax:(250)646-2317
E-mail: ocean@sookenet.com

Circa 1940. The hot tub spa of this log house inn is in a Japanese gazebo overlooking the ocean. Reserve your time for a private soak, terry bathrobes are supplied. Experience massage

and mud treatments, ocean treatments and herbal wraps while meditation enhances your creative expression. The inn will arrange fishing charters, nature walks and beachcombing. Coffee is delivered to your room each morn-

ing on a silver service. Guests are invited to enjoy breakfast in their room or in the dining lounge. Rooms include antiques, sitting areas and canopy beds. Two of the rooms have hot tubs for two with spectacular ocean and Olympic Mountain views.

Historic Interest: Botanical Beach and Hatley Castle are 15 miles from the inn, while Moss Cottage is only eight miles away. Butchart Gardens and the Royal B.C. Museum are within 35 miles.

Innkeeper(s): Marion J. Rolston. $85-175. MC VISA AX TC. TAC10. 9 rooms with PB. Breakfast included in rates. Types of meals: full breakfast and early coffee/tea. Beds: KQT. Fax and copier on premises. Handicap access. Weddings, small meetings, family reunions and seminars hosted. Antiques, fishing, parks, shopping and theater nearby.

Pets Allowed: By arrangement.

Publicity: *Puget Sound Business Journal, Getaways from Vancouver.*

"Thank you for the most wonderful hospitality and accommodations of our entire vacation."

Sooke Harbour House Inn

1528 Whiffen Spit Rd
Sooke, BC V0S 1N0
(250)642-3421 (800)889-9688 Fax:(250)642-6988
E-mail: shh@islandnet.com

Circa 1929. The spectacular ocean views from each of the guest rooms at this farmhouse-style inn are set off by extensive flower and herb gardens and the Olympic Mountains. Ask for the Victor Newman Longhouse Room for a four-poster king-size bed, skylight, wet bar, bathtub for two overlooking an ocean view and a see-through fireplace. Each room boasts a private deck or spa. The inn's evening cuisine, proclaimed by various travel and food writers as "one of the best in British Colombia," or the "best in Canada," features locally grown produce and fresh fish and shellfish taken from local waters. There's a Japanese and French influence in the offerings. If you can tear yourself away from the captivating views and excellent meals, the innkeepers will arrange whale-watching cruises or guided nature tours.

Innkeeper(s): Frederique & Sinclair Philip. $200-277. MC VISA AX DC TC. TAC10. 27 rooms with PB, 27 with FP. 1 cottage. Breakfast included in rates. Types of meals: continental breakfast and full breakfast. Picnic lunch, lunch, banquet service and room service available. Restaurant on premises. Beds: KQ. Phone in room. TV, fax, copier and child care on premises. Handicap access. Weddings, small meetings, family reunions and seminars hosted. Antiques, fishing, parks, shopping and watersports nearby.

Pets Allowed: $20.00 per day per pet.

Vancouver

The Albion Guest House

592 W 19th Ave
Vancouver, BC V5Z 1-W6
(604)873-2287 Fax:(604)879-5682

Circa 1906. Close to Vancouver's popular West End, Wreck Beach, Stanley Park and other attractions, this Victorian inn is a quiet retreat only minutes away from the action. The innkeeper takes special care in making her guests feel comfortable by starting off with an evening greeting of cognac, sherry and cookies laid out on a table. Earlier arrivals are offered tea, wine and appetizers. The rooms have down comforters and feather mattresses.
Innkeeper(s): Lise Caza. $80-170. MC VISA AX. 4 rooms, 2 with PB. Breakfast included in rates. Types of meals: gourmet breakfast and early coffee/tea. Afternoon tea available. Beds: Q. Turndown service in room. Fax, copier, spa and bicycles on premises. Amusement parks, antiques, fishing, parks, shopping, downhill skiing, sporting events, theater and watersports nearby.

"One of the best B&Bs I have ever stayed at!"

Columbia Cottage

205 14th Ave W
Vancouver, BC V5Y 1X2
(604)874-5327 Fax:(604)879-2128

Circa 1929. This cheerful cottage is surrounded by lush gardens and is located a few minutes from downtown Vancouver. There are a few antiques here and there, and there are feather beds in the guest rooms. The suite offers a private entrance, sitting room, and the French doors in the suite's kitchen open onto the back garden and pond. The full breakfasts include such items as freshly baked scones, fresh fruit and perhaps savory basted eggs with sausages.
Innkeeper(s): Susanne Salzberger & Alisdair Smith. $80-165. MC VISA TC. TAC10. 4 rooms with PB. 1 suite. Breakfast included in rates. Type of meal: full breakfast. Beds: KQDT. Fax on premises. Weddings hosted. German spoken. Antiques, parks, shopping, sporting events and theater nearby.

"Fabulous respite in every way!! Thank you!!"

Johnson Heritage House

2278 W 34th Ave
Vancouver, BC V6M 1G6
(604)266-4175 Fax:(604)266-4175
E-mail: johnsonbb@bc.sympatico.ca

Circa 1920. One of the first things guests will notice as they enter this Craftsman-style home is the ornamentation, including ornate, restored woodwork. Different patterns and a variety of woods have been used in the moldings, walls, floors and staircase. There is a pressed tin ceiling decorating the kitchen. Country antiques, Oriental rugs and collectibles also fill the whimsical interior. Brass beds, canopy beds, quilts and carousel horses are among the items guests might discover in their rooms. The suite is especially impressive and romantic with a natural wood, cathedral ceiling, canopy bed, sitting area with a loveseat, mountain views and a bath-

room with a Jacuzzi tub. The grounds are decorated with gardens, and the quiet neighborhood is within walking distance of small parks, shops, city bus lines and restaurants. The University of British Columbia, Queen Elizabeth Park and the Van Dusen Gardens are nearby.
Innkeeper(s): Sandy & Ron Johnson. $75-145. PC TC. TAC10. 3 rooms, 1 with PB. 1 suite. Breakfast included in rates. Type of meal: full breakfast. Beds: KQDT. Some French spoken. Amusement parks, antiques, fishing, parks, shopping, downhill skiing, cross-country skiing, sporting events, theater and watersports nearby.

"We thoroughly enjoyed our four nights at your beautiful home."

Kenya Court Ocean Front Guest House

2230 Cornwall Ave
Vancouver, BC V6K 1B5
(604)738-7085

Circa 1927. Enjoy a piping hot cup of fresh, gourmet coffee as you gaze out over the ocean at this scenic bed & breakfast. Innkeeper Dorothy Mae Williams not only provides a delectable spread of fresh breads, croissants, cereals and fruits, she serves it in a rooftop solarium. Williams, in charge of the piano department at Vancouver Academy, will serenade guests with piano concerts on some days. Roomy suites feature antiques, separate entrances and boast ocean views. The home is within walking distance to the Granville Market, the planetarium, city centres, 10 minutes from the University of British Columbia and 20 miles from the U.S. border. The athletically inclined will enjoy the use of tennis courts, walking and jogging trails and a heated outdoor saltwater pool across the street.
Historic Interest: A maritime museum is a five-minute walk from the bed & breakfast. An anthropology museum is 10 minutes by car.
Innkeeper(s): Dr. & Mrs. H. Williams. $85-110. PC TC. 7 rooms with PB, 4 with FP. 5 suites. Breakfast included in rates. Types of meals: gourmet breakfast and early coffee/tea. Beds: KQT. Phone and TV in room. VCR and library on premises. Weddings and family reunions hosted. Italian, French and German spoken. Antiques, fishing, parks, shopping, downhill skiing, cross-country skiing, sporting events, theater and watersports nearby.
Location: Twenty minutes from the United States border.
Publicity: *Washington Times, Rocky Mountain News.*

"Beautiful home; we enjoyed the unsurpassed hospitality."

The Manor Guest House

345 W 13th Ave
Vancouver, BC V5Y 1W2
(604)876-8494 Fax:(604)876-5763
E-mail: ManorGuestHouse@BC.sympatico.ca

Circa 1902. This turn-of-the-century Edwardian still features many original elements, including carved banisters, polished wood floors and ornate wainscoting. The home is one of the city's oldest. The innkeeper has decorated it with a collection of English antiques. The penthouse suite, which includes a bedroom, loft, deck and kitchen, boasts a view of the city. Fresh fruits, home-baked breads and specialties such as a cheese and mushroom souffle or blueberry cobbler highlight the breakfast menu.

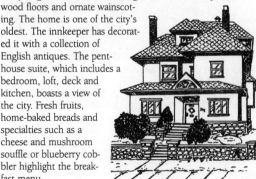

Innkeeper(s): Brenda Yablon. $65-125. MC VISA TC. TAC10. 10 rooms, 6 with PB, 1 with FP. 1 suite. 1 conference room. Types of meals: full breakfast and gourmet breakfast. Beds: KQDT. TV in room. VCR, fax and copier on premises. Weddings, small meetings, family reunions and seminars hosted. French and German spoken. Antiques, parks, shopping, downhill skiing, sporting events, theater and watersports nearby.

"We had a wonderful visit! I can't remember better breakfasts - truly memorable!"

The Red Door Bed & Breakfast

1618 Rockland Ave
Vancouver, BC V8S 1W7
(250)595-6715 Fax:(250)595-6714

Circa 1928. Built in the 1920s in the heart of Old Victoria, this English-country-style seaside home is just a short walk to Government House (The Queen's B&B), Craigdarroch Castle and art galleries. Relax in the formal drawing room with its marble fireplace and grand piano and enjoy a cup of tea or sherry in the evenings. Guest rooms are spacious and offer wonderful views. Breakfast is hearty and varies every day. Rates listed are in Canadian dollars.

Historic Interest: Located minutes from downtown Vancouver.

Innkeeper(s): Rhya & Bill Lornie. $95-165. PC TC. TAC10. 4 rooms with PB. 1 suite. Breakfast included in rates. Type of meal: full breakfast. Beds: QT. Turndown service in room. TV, VCR, fax and copier on premises. Antiques, parks, shopping, golf and theater nearby.

Location: Four miles from the Lions Gate Bridge.

Publicity: *Pacific Northwest.*

"Our second stay was even more wonderful than our first."

The West End Guest House

1362 Haro St
Vancouver, BC V6E 1G2
(604)681-2889 Fax:(604)688-8812

Circa 1906. Among the hustle and bustle of Vancouver sits this pink Victorian, which transports its guests out of the modern metropolis and back to the turn-of-the-century days. The gracious home used to house a family of musicians and photographers. Innkeeper Evan Penner has preserved their past, placing lithographs and historical photos owned by the family throughout the house. Each of the rooms is individually decorated with glorious prints and beautiful antiques. The guest rooms are cozy and welcoming, the perfect  place to snuggle down after a long day and sink into brass beds decked in fine linens and down comforters. Guests will enjoy relaxing on the second-story deck or strolling past the many plants and flowers in the back garden. A gourmet, country-style breakfast is served each morning, and homemade chocolates await guests as they arrive.

Historic Interest: The home is located in the heart of Vancouver, close to many historic sites, including Canada Place, the Canadian Pacific Railway Station and Gastown, a restored area full of interesting shops, restaurants and a unique steam-powered clock.

Innkeeper(s): Evan Penner. $115-210. MC VISA AX DS TC. TAC10. 8 rooms with PB, 2 with FP. Breakfast included in rates. Type of meal: full breakfast.

Room service available. Beds: KQDT. Phone, turndown service, ceiling fan and TV in room. Small meetings hosted. Limited French spoken. Amusement parks, antiques, fishing, shopping, downhill skiing, cross-country skiing, sporting events, theater and watersports nearby.

Publicity: *New York Times, Province News.*

"Quiet, comfort, convenience, homey, delicious food and good conversations with other guests. I will do nothing but sing the praises of B&Bs from now on, and I'm sure we will meet again."

Victoria

Abigail's Hotel

906 McClure St
Victoria, BC V8V 3E7
(250)388-5363 (800)561-6565 Fax:(250)388-7787
E-mail: innkeeper@abigailshotel.com

Circa 1930. Abigail's, a Tudor-style hotel, boasts three gabled stories, stained-glass windows, crystal chandeliers and tasteful decor. Complimentary sherry is offered in the library, also a popular area for small weddings.

Rooms feature a variety of amenities such as canopied beds, fireplaces, Jacuzzi baths and antiques. Smoked salmon omelets, or tomato, jack cheese, and avocado omelets are served with corn and asparagus fritters, salsa and apple sausage at breakfast.

Innkeeper(s): Daniel & Frauke Behune. $89-289CDN. MC VISA AX TC. TAC10. 16 rooms with PB, 8 with FP. Breakfast, afternoon tea and evening snack included in rates. Types of meals: full breakfast, gourmet breakfast and early coffee/tea. Beds: KQD. Phone in room. Fax, copier and library on premises. Weddings, small meetings, family reunions and seminars hosted. German spoken. Antiques, fishing, parks, shopping, theater and watersports nearby.

Publicity: *Seattle Magazine, Victoria Times Colonist, Country Inns, Victoria.*

The Beaconsfield Inn

998 Humboldt St
Victoria, BC V8V 2Z8
(250)384-4044 Fax:(250)384-4052

Circa 1905. Beautiful grounds accentuate this turn-of-the-century English manor. Rooms are light and airy with antiques, original woodwork, Oriental carpets and stained-glass windows. Many of the rooms feature fireplaces and Jacuzzi tubs and all include cozy, down comforters. A luxurious gourmet breakfast is served in the dining room or sunroom and afternoon tea is sure to delight. Evening sherry is served in the library. There's plenty to do in this seaside town, and The Beaconsfield is only four blocks from downtown and the oceanfront.

Historic Interest: Butchart Gardens are 25 miles away, and Victoria has many historic buildings, homes and other sites. Old Town and several museums are close by.

Innkeeper(s): Con & Judi Solid. $105-295. MC VISA. 6 rooms with PB. 3 suites. Breakfast and afternoon tea included in rates. Type of meal: full breakfast. Beds: Q. Antiques, fishing, shopping, theater and watersports nearby.

Publicity: *Equity, Globe & Mail, New York Times, Country Inns, Seattle Times, Horizon Air, Dallas Morning News, Northwest Travel, Arkansas Democrat Gazette, Wichita Eagle, Look Travel, Vancouver Sun, Vancouver Province.*

"This place is about as close to heaven as one can get."

Dashwood Seaside Manor

Number One Cook St
Victoria, BC V8V 3W6
(800)667-5517 Fax:(250)383-1760
E-mail: reservations@dashwoodmanor.com

Circa 1912. Dashwood Manor is an Edwardian Tudor Revival mansion with a rare oceanfront location. Choose between a first-floor suite with a fireplace, chandelier and beamed ceilings; a second-story "special occasion" unit; or a top-floor suite for spectacular balcony views of the ocean and the Olympic Mountains. Some units include a Jacuzzi tub. To reach downtown Victoria, take a short walk through the park. The inn offers a self-catered full breakfast.

Innkeeper(s): Derek Dashwood Family. $75-285. MC VISA AX DC. 14 suites. Breakfast included in rates. Type of meal: full breakfast. Beds: Q. TV in room. Antiques, fishing, shopping and theater nearby.

Pets Allowed: Small pets with kennel.

Location: Next to world-famous Beacon Hill Park.

Publicity: *San Francisco Chronicle.*

"Enchanting, very soothing."

Gregory's Guest House

5373 Patricia Bay Hwy
Victoria, BC V8Y 1S9
(250)658-8404 Fax:(250)658-4604

Circa 1919. The two acres of this historic hobby farm are just across the street from Elk Lake, six miles from Victoria near Butchart Gardens. All the rooms are decorated in antiques and duvets, and they feature garden and lake views. A traditional, full Canadian breakfast is served, and after the meal, guests can enjoy the hobby farm and animals or perhaps rent a boat at the lake.

Innkeeper(s): Paul & Elizabeth Gregory. $55-80. MC VISA PC TC. TAC10. 3 rooms, 2 with PB. Breakfast included in rates. Type of meal: full breakfast. Beds: DT. Fax and library on premises. Antiques, fishing, parks, sporting events, theater and watersports nearby.

Location: On the east side of the highway, across from Elk Lake.

"Our family felt very welcome, loved the house and especially liked the super breakfasts."

Heritage House

3808 Heritage Ln
Victoria, BC V8Z 7-A7
(250)479-0892 Fax:(250)479-0812

Circa 1910. The Heritage House, constructed by a retired sea captain, is one of the few examples of California Bungalow-style architecture in Victoria. It was later home to Danish Count Holstein-Rothlos. High ceilings, leaded glass and polished woodwork accentuate the beautiful furnishings of each unique room. The Pine Room features English-country decor with a four-poster pine bed covered in designer linens, while the Dormer Room, with its private sitting area, boasts a view of the garden and wooded grounds. Each room is individually styled with antiques and rich decor. Relax with a glass of wine in front of a cozy fire in the parlor or enjoy a novel in the library. A full breakfast is served in the elegant dining room. The innkeepers host murder-mystery events.

Historic Interest: Parliament buildings, Royal British Columbia Museum and Craigdarroch Castle are three miles from Heritage House.

Innkeeper(s): Larry & Sandra Gray. $95-100. MC VISA. 4 rooms. Breakfast included in rates. Type of meal: full breakfast. Beds: Q. Antiques, fishing, theater and watersports nearby.

Publicity: *Gazette.*

"I would like to hide under the stairs and just stay. We hope to come back again. Thank you for all your kindness and friendliness."

Maridou House

116 Eberts St
Victoria, BC V8S 3-H7
(250)360-0747

Circa 1909. This turn-of-the-century Edwardian home is furnished with antiques and decorated with fine linens and lace. Stained-glass windows add charm to the rooms. One guest room boasts a sea view and sitting area, while another includes a lace-canopied bed and Jacuzzi tub. The Allisons have named each guest room in honor of a Scottish clan. Full country breakfasts are served each morning to prepare guests for an eventful day in Victoria. Maridou House isn't far from shopping, restaurants and, of course, the ocean.

Historic Interest: Maridou House is within walking distance to Craigdarroch Castle and a historic cemetery. Many of Victoria's homes were built prior to 1912, so there is plenty of historic architecture to admire.

Innkeeper(s): Marilyn & Douglas Allison. $100-115. MC VISA. 2 rooms with PB. 1 suite. Breakfast included in rates. Types of meals: continental breakfast and full breakfast. Beds: Q. Antiques, fishing, theater and watersports nearby.

"Comfort combined with exquisite hospitality has made our stay a memorable occasion."

The Prior House

620 St. Charles St
Victoria, BC V8S 3N7
(250)592-8847 Fax:(250)592-8223
E-mail: innkeeper@priorhouse.com

Circa 1912. Honey-colored oak paneling and stained-glass windows add to the elegance of this Edwardian mansion, constructed for the English king's representative. At the back of the property, a stone terrace provides views of the garden. Suites include antiques, fireplaces, marble whirlpool tubs and views of the Olympic Mountains. A full breakfast is served in the elegant dining room or in your room. High tea is served daily at 4 p.m. The Government House gardens and Craigdarroch Castle are nearby.

Historic Interest: Government House (next door), Craigdarroch Castle (2 blocks).

Innkeeper(s): Candis & Ted Gornall Cooperrider. $125-275. MC VISA. 7 rooms with PB, 7 with FP. 4 suites. Breakfast and afternoon tea included in rates. Type of meal: full breakfast. Room service available. Beds: KQ. Antiques, fishing and theater nearby.

Location: One-and-one-quarter mile east of inner harbour.

Publicity: *Horizon Air, Pacific Northwest, Country Inns.*

Sonia's B&B By The Sea

175 Bushby St
Victoria, BC V8S 1B5
(250)385-2700 (800)667-4489 Fax:(250)385-2702

A walk of about 100 yards will take guests to the shore, and this bed & breakfast offers views of the Straits of Juan de Fuca. Guests also enjoy views of the Olympic Mountains and Victoria. Both innkeepers are Vancouver Island natives (Sonia was born in Victoria), and they are happy to provide a map detailing some little-known treasures of the area. Their Tudor-style home offers three comfortable guest rooms and a 1,100-square-foot ocean view penthouse that sleeps five people comfortably. Breakfasts are served in a formal dining room with tables set with English china and Lennox glasswear. The bed & breakfast is open from the beginning of March until Sept. 30.

Innkeeper(s): Sonia & Brian McMillan. $65-130. TC. 3 rooms with PB. Breakfast included in rates. Beds: KQ. Shopping and watersports nearby. Pets Allowed.

Wellington B&B

66 Wellington Ave
Victoria, BC V8V 4H5
(250)383-5976 Fax:(250)383-5976

Circa 1912. Less than one block from the ocean, this Folk Victorian inn is quiet, yet close to all the downtown activities. A nearby promenade boasts an incredible panoramic view of the ocean and Olympic Mountains. The inn is just minutes away from Beacon Hill Park and is within easy walking distance of shopping, restaurants and outdoor activities.

Historic Interest: Craigdarroch Castle (15-minute walk), Government House (12-minute walk), Old Gonzales Hill Weather Station (35-minute walk).

Innkeeper(s): Inge Ranzinger. $70-140. MC TC. TAC10. 4 rooms with PB, 2 with FP. 1 suite. Breakfast included in rates. Types of meals: full breakfast and early coffee/tea. Room service available. Beds: KQT. Fax and library on premises. German spoken. Antiques, fishing, parks, shopping, theater and watersports nearby.

"Thank you once again for an outstanding stay at Wellington."

Nova Scotia

Chester

Mecklenburgh Inn

78 Queen St
Chester, NS B0J 1-J0
(902)275-4638
E-mail: frnthrbr@atcon.com

Circa 1906. Guests to this Edwardian Mission-style inn have plenty to see and do in the seaside village, which has catered to summer visitors for more than 150 years. Favorite activities include touring the historic streets, watching a yacht race in the bay and browsing the craft shops and boutiques. The living room is a popular place for sitting by the fireplace to talk and read from the selection of travel books and magazines. Local theater productions can be seen at the Chester Playhouse. Guests will be happy to know that the innkeeper is a Cordon Bleu chef.

Historic Interest: Oak Island (5 miles).

Innkeeper(s): Suzi Fraser. $50-69. VISA AX. 4 rooms. Breakfast and afternoon tea included in rates. Types of meals: full breakfast and early coffee/tea. Picnic lunch available. Beds: QDT. TV and VCR on premises. Weddings and family reunions hosted. Antiques, fishing, shopping, sporting events, theater and watersports nearby.

Publicity: *Georgetown Times, Life Channel Network, Brides, Toronto Sun.*

"Lovely experience, great hospitality, yummy breakfast."

Middleton

Fairfield Farm Inn

10 Main St
Middleton, NS B0S 1P0
(902)825-6989 (800)237-9896 Fax:(902)825-6989

Circa 1886. Nova Scotia's picturesque Annapolis Valley create the peaceful surroundings at this restored Victorian farmhouse. The inn is located on a 110-acre estate on the Annapolis River that offers woodland, mountain and meadow views. Guest rooms feature period antiques, as do the library, parlor and solarium. Guests have a wide range of breakfast items to choose from. Dinner is served at 7 p.m. by reservation. Seasonal fruits and vegetables are freshly picked from the inn's extensive gardens. A historic church, museum, galleries, shops and restaurants are all within walking distance, and a short drive will take you to the Bay of Fundy, national parks and historic sites.

Innkeeper(s): Richard & Shae Griffith. $50-90. MC VISA AX DC DS TC. TAC10. 5 rooms with PB. 1 conference room. Breakfast included in rates. Types of meals: full breakfast and early coffee/tea. Dinner and picnic lunch available. Beds: KQD. Air conditioning and ceiling fan in room. TV, VCR, fax, copier and library on premises. 110 acres. Weddings, small meetings, family reunions and seminars hosted. French and English spoken. Amusement parks, antiques, fishing, parks, shopping, cross-country skiing, sporting events, golf, theater and watersports nearby.

Ontario

Kingston

Rosemount B&B Inn

46 Sydenham St S
Kingston, ON K7L 3-H1
(613)531-8844 Fax:(613)531-9722

Circa 1850. Built in a Tuscan-villa style, Rosemount was designed by noted architect William Coverdale as the residence for a successful dry goods merchant. The two-story limestone house is distinguished by a three-story campanile, or bell tower, over the front door. High ceilings and chandeliers are found throughout the elegantly appointed living, dining and guest rooms. There is a private coach house retreat and a gazebo used for aromatherapy massage. Special touches include homemade chocolates, down duvets, and a gourmet breakfast with entrees such as crepes, Welsh toast, or Vidalia onion and apple frittatas.

Innkeeper(s): Holly Doughty & John Edwards. $99-195. 8 rooms with PB. Type of meal: full breakfast. Beds: QT.

Location: Centrally located in downtown Kingston, just four blocks from the waterfront and three blocks from Main Street.

Publicity: *Whig-Standard.*

"Four days in heaven! Thanks!"

Ottawa

Auberge McGee's Inn

185 Daly Ave
Ottawa, ON K1N 6E8
(613)237-6089 (800)262-4337 Fax:(613)237-6201

Circa 1886. The home was built for John McGee, Canada's first Clerk of Privy Council. The portico of this restored Victorian mansion is reminiscent of McGee's Irish roots featuring pillars that were common in Dublin architecture. Rooms are comfortable and decorated in soft, pleasing colors.

Amenities such as mounted hair dryers add a touch of modern convenience. For extended stays, the inn provides the use of laundry facilities and a guest kitchenette. The innkeepers celebrate well over a decade of award-winning hospitality. Business travelers will appreciate items such as in-room phones with computer modem hook-ups and voice mail. There is no end to what guests can see and do in Ottawa. Visit the Byward Market, the many museums or the 230-store Rideau center.

Historic Interest: Walking distance to Congress Centre and University of Ottawa. Parliament Hill, War Memorial of Confederation Square, Rideau Canal located nearby.

Innkeeper(s): Anne Schutte & Mary Unger. $68-150. MC VISA. 14 rooms, 12 with PB, 3 with FP. 2 suites. 1 conference room. Breakfast included in rates. Type of meal: full breakfast. Beds: KQDT. Phone, air conditioning and TV in room. Fax on premises. Small meetings and family reunions hosted. Spanish, French and English spoken. Antiques, parks, shopping, downhill skiing, cross-country skiing, sporting events, theater and watersports nearby.

Pets Allowed: Smoke free. Limited free parking.

Publicity: *Country Inns, Ottawa Citizen, LaPresse, Ottawa.*

"All we could ask for."

Rideau View Inn

177 Frank St
Ottawa, ON K2P 0X4
(613)236-9309 (800)658-3564 Fax:(613)237-6842
E-mail: rideau@istar.ca

Circa 1907. This large Edwardian home is located on a quiet residential street near the Rideau Canal. A hearty breakfast is served in the dining room. Guests are encouraged to relax in front of the fireplace in the living room.

Historic Interest: Parliament, Museum of Nature (5 minutes).

Innkeeper(s): George Hartsgrove, Richard Brouse. $58-85. AP. MC VISA AX DC TC. TAC10. 7 rooms, 2 with PB, 1 with FP. Breakfast included in rates. Type of meal: full breakfast. Beds: QDT. Phone and air conditioning in room. TV, VCR, fax and copier on premises. Small meetings and family reunions hosted. French and Spanish and English spoken. Antiques, parks, shopping, downhill skiing, cross-country skiing, sporting events and theater nearby.

Location: In the center of Ottawa.

Publicity: *Ottawa Citizen.*

Quebec

Ayer's Cliff

Ripplecove Inn

700 Rue Ripplecove P.o.box 246
Ayer's Cliff, QB J0B 1-C0
(819)838-4296 (800)668-4296 Fax:(819)838-5541

Circa 1945. This exquisite Victorian inn, located on the shores of Lake Massawippi, is one of only 10 establishments in Quebec to earn a Four-Diamond award from the American Automobile Association. Some of the well-appointed rooms offer whirlpool tubs, fireplaces and private balconies. The 12-acre grounds include a heated swimming pool and private beach, and guests can partake of skating, skiing and ice fishing without leaving the property. Meals at Ripplecove are a special treat, set on tables with sterling silver, fine linens, crystal and Royal Doulton china. Chef Marco Guay combines classical and nouvelle French artistry with local produce to create an array of mouth-watering specialties.

Innkeeper(s): Jeffrey & Debra Stafford. $184-400. MC VISA AX. 25 rooms with PB. 4 suites. Breakfast and dinner included in rates. Type of meal: full breakfast. Lunch and room service available. Restaurant on premises. Beds: QDT. Antiques, fishing, skiing, theater and watersports nearby.

Publicity: *Country Inns, Gazette.*

"We shall never forget Ripplecove Inn. Its elegant and intimate setting provided the perfect place to hold the kind of wedding we had dreamed of. The refined cuisine, the superb service and your own personal hospitability made our dream a reality."

Montreal

Auberge De La Fontaine

1301 E Rachel St
Montreal, PQ H2J 2K1
(514)597-0166 (800)597-0597 Fax:(514)597-0496

Circa 1910. Located just across the street from a lovely 80-acre park, accommodations at this historic stone Victorian are the piece de resistance. The award-winning inn offers individually decorated, sound-proofed rooms, all in a modern style. Some rooms have exposed brick walls, a sitting area, a terrace or a balcony, and the three suites include a whirlpool. Guests have access to the kitchen, where they can find a snack. Continental breakfast is served each morning. Breads, muffins, cereals, cheeses, cold cuts, yogurt and fresh fruit fill the buffet in the inn's dining room. The staff is happy to help guests find their way to attractions in Montreal, and parking at the inn is free.

Innkeeper(s): Jean LaMothe & Celine Boudreau. $99-185. EP. MC VISA AX DC TC. TAC10. 21 rooms with PB. 3 suites. 1 conference room. Breakfast and evening snack included in rates. Type of meal: continental-plus breakfast. Beds: QDT. Phone, air conditioning and TV in room. VCR, fax and copier on premises. Handicap access. Small meetings hosted. French and English spoken. Amusement parks, antiques, fishing, parks, shopping, cross-country skiing, sporting events, theater and watersports nearby.

"Breakfast was superb and we enjoyed the quietness of the room."

North Hatley

Manoir Hovey

575 Hovey Rd, PO Box 60
North Hatley, PQ J0B 2C0
(819)842-2421 (800)661-2421 Fax:(819)842-2248

Circa 1900. This historic inn combines posh decor and fine cuisine all on a spectacular 25-acre, lakefront resort. Built at the turn of the century, the manor was fashioned after George Washington's Mount Vernon. Guests enjoy the scents from an English garden as they wind their way down to the lakefront, where paddleboats, kayaks, windsurfers and canoes all await. Rates include all of these activities plus use of bikes, an exercise room, a heated pool, the beach and tennis courts. In the winter, enjoy the fireplaces and cross-country ski trails, a skating rink and ice-fishing on-site. Enchanting guest rooms are decorated in English country style, and serve as a perfect setting for romance. The inn offers a full breakfast served in the dinning room, pool-side lunch, afternoon tea and haute cuisine dinner featuring regional and French cuisine accompanied by an extensive wine list.

Innkeeper(s): Steve & Kathy Stafford. $145-305. MAP. MC VISA AX DC TC. 40 rooms with PB. 2 cottages. 1 conference room. Breakfast and dinner included in rates. Beds: KQDT. Phone, air conditioning, turndown service, ceiling fan and TV in room. VCR, fax, copier, swimming, bicycles, tennis and library on premises. 25 acres. Weddings, small meetings, family reunions and seminars hosted. French and English spoken. Antiques, fishing, parks, shopping, downhill skiing, golf and theater nearby.

Pets Allowed: not recomended for small children.

Inns of Interest

African-American History

Inn at Bethlehem . . . . .Bethlehem, Ind.
Wingscorton Farm Inn . . .East Sandwich, Mass.
Munro House B&B . . . . . . .Jonesville, Mich.
Wooden Rabbit . . . . .Cape May, N.J.
Troutbeck . . . . .Amenia, N.Y.
Signal House . . . . .Ripley, Ohio
1790 House B&B Inn . . . . .Georgetown, S.C.
Golden Stage Inn . . . . .Proctorsville, Vt.
Kedron Valley Inn . . . .South Woodstock, Vt.
Inn at Weathersfield . . . . . .Weathersfield, Vt.
Rockland Farm Retreat . . . . . . .Bumpass, Va.
Sleepy Hollow Farm . . . . . .Gordonsville, Va.

Barns

Barn B&B . . . . .Valley Falls, Ks.
White Barn Inn . . . . . . .Kennebunkbort, Maine
Watchtide, B&B By the Sea . .Searsport, Maine
Brannon-Bunker Inn . . . . .Walpole, Maine
Barn on Howard's Cove . . . . .Annapolis, Md.
Race Brook Lodge . . . . .Sheffield, Mass.
Lee's Deer Run B&B . . . . . . .Stillwater, N.Y.
Inn at Cedar Falls . . . . .Logan, Ohio
Pine Barn Inn . . . . .Danville, Pa.
Pace One Restaurant and Country Inn
. . . . .Thornton, Pa.
Jackson Fork Inn . . . . .Huntsville, Utah
Inn at Mad River Barn . . . . . . .Waitsfield, Vt.
Waitsfield Inn . . . . .Waitsfield, Vt.

Castles

Red Castle Inn Historic Lodgings
. . . . .Nevada City, Calif.
Castle Marne- A Luxury Urban Inn
. . . . .Denver, Colo.
Cleveholm/The Historic Redstone Castle
. . . . .Redstone, Colo.
Shipman House B&B . . . . .Hilo, Hawaii
Castle Inn Riverside . . . . .Wichita, Kan.
Glencoe Castle B&B . . . . . . .Glencoe, Minn.
Belhurst Castle . . . . .Geneva, N.Y.
Manresa Castle . . . . . .Port Townsend, Wash.

Churches

Old Church House Inn . . . . . . .Mossville, Ill.
Parson's Pillow . . . . .Cody, Wyo.

Civil War

Inn at Bethlehem . . . . .Bethlehem, Ind.
Mansion Bed & Breakfast . . . . .Bardstown, Ky.
Myrtledene . . . . .Lebanon, Ky.

Parker House . . . . .Chesterton, Md.
Old Manse Inn . . . . .Brewster, Mass.
Christmere House . . . . .Sturgis, Mich.
Rosswood Plantation . . . . .Lorman, Miss.
Dunleith . . . . .Natchez, Miss.
Cedar Grove Mansion Inn . . . .Vicksburg, Miss.
Cedarcroft Farm B&B . . . . . .Warrensburg, Mo.
Wooden Rabbit . . . . .Cape May, N.J.
Sedgwick Inn . . . . .Berlin, N.Y.
Lindenwald Haus . . . . .Elmira, N.Y.
Goose Creek Guesthouse . . . . .Southold, N.Y.
Red House Inn B&B . . . . .Brevard, N.C.
Owl's Nest Inn at Engadine . . . .Candler, N.C.
Troy-Bumpass Inn . . . . .Greensboro, N.C.
Misty River B&B . . . . .Ripley, Ohio
Lewis McKever Farmhouse B&B
. . . . .Williamsburg, Ohio
Churchtown Inn B&B . . . . .Churchtown, Pa.
Baladerry Inn at Gettysburg . . .Gettysburg, Pa.
Brafferton Inn . . . . .Gettysburg, Pa.
Doubleday Inn . . . . .Gettysburg, Pa.
King's Inn at Georgetown . .Georgetown, S.C.
Hale Springs Inn . . . . .Rogersville, Tenn.
Kedron Valley Inn . . . .South Woodstock, Vt.
Inn at Weathersfield . . . . . .Weathersfield, Vt.
River House . . . . .Boyce, Va.
Edgewood Plantation . . . . . .Charles City, Va.
North Bend Plantation . . . . .Charles City, Va.
Buckhorn Inn . . . . .Churchville, Va.
Inn at La Vista Plantation . .Fredericksburg, Va.
Springdale Country Inn . . . . . . .Lincoln, Va.
Welbourne . . . . .Middleburg, Va.
A Touch of Country B&B . . .New Market, Va.
Mayfield Inn . . . . .Petersburg, Va.
Inn at Narrow Passage . . . . . .Woodstock, Va.
Fillmore Street B&B . . . . . .Harpers Ferry, Va.
Boydville, Inn at Martinsburg
. . . . .Martinsburg, W.Va.

Cookbooks Written By Innkeepers

Old Yacht Club Inn . . . .Santa Barbara, Calif.
"The Old Yacht Club Inn Cookbook"
Sea Holly B&B Inn . . . . .Cape May, N.J.
"Sea Holly Bed and Breakfast, A Sharing of Secrets"
Grandview Lodge . . . . .Waynesville, N.C.
"Recipes from Grandview Lodge"
Hill Farm Inn . . . . .Arlington, Vt.
"Recipes from the Kitchen of"
Bombay House . . . . .Bainbridge Island, Wash.
"Breakfast with Bunny"

Farms and Orchards

Apple Lane Inn . . . . .Aptos, Calif.
Scarlett's Country Inn . . . . . .Calistoga, Calif.
Brookside Farm . . . . .Dulzura, Calif.
Inn at Shallow Creek Farm . . . .Orland, Calif.
Howard Creek Ranch . . . . . . .Westport, Calif.
Maple Hill Farm . . . . .Coventry, Conn.
1810 West Inn . . . . .Thomson, Ga.
Kingston 5 Ranch B&B . . . . .Kingston, Idaho
Kenmore Farms . . . . .Bardstown, Ky.
Bourbon House Farm . . . . . .Georgetown, Ky.
Canaan Land Farm B&B . . . .Harrodsburg, Ky.
Maple Hill Farm B&B Inn
. . . . .Hallowell/Augusta, Maine
Ingate Farms B&B . . . . . . .Belchertown, Mass.
Summer Hill Farm . . . . .Lenox, Mass.
Gilbert's Tree Farm B&B . . . .Rehoboth, Mass.
Baldwin Hill Farm B&B
. . . . .Great Barrington, Mass.
Wingscorton Farm Inn . . .East Sandwich, Mass.
Salt Marsh Farm . . . . .South Dartmouth, Mass.
Steep Acres Farm . . . . . . .Williamstown, Mass.
Liberty Hill Inn . . . . . . .Yarmouth Port, Mass.
Horse & Carriage B&B . . . . . .Jonesville, Mich.
Cedarcroft Farm B&B . . . . . .Warrensburg, Mo.
Old Pioneer Garden Guest Ranch
. . . . .Unionville, Nev.
Rockhouse Mountain Farm Inn
. . . . .Eaton Center, N.H.
Colby Hill Inn . . . . .Henniker, N.H.
Ellis River B&B . . . . .Jackson, N.H.
Apple Valley Inn B&B and Antiques
. . . . .Glenwood, N.J.
Breezy Acres Farm B&B . . . . . . .Hobart, N.Y.
Fearrington House Inn . . . . . . .Pittsboro, N.C.
Cedar Hill Farm B&B . . . . . .Statesville, N.C.
Lewis McKever Farmhouse B&B
. . . . .Williamsburg, Ohio
Springbrook Hazelnut Farm . . . .Newberg, Ore.
Weatherbury Farm . . . . .Avella, Pa.
Inn at Fordhook Farm . . . . . .Doylestown, Pa.
Barley Sheaf Farm . . . . .Holicong, Pa.
Meadow Spring Farm . . . . .Kennett Square, Pa.
Cedar Hill Farm . . . . .Mount Joy, Pa.
Field & Pine B&B . . . . .Shippensburg, Pa.
B&B at Skogland Farm . . . . . . .Canova, S.D.
Hill Farm Inn . . . . .Arlington, Vt.
Henry Farm Inn . . . . .Chester, Vt.
Stonecrest Farm B&B . . . . .Wilder, Vt.

French and Indian War

Summer Hill Farm . . . . .Lenox, Mass.

Gold Mines & Gold Panning

Mine House Inn . . . . .Amador City, Calif.
Power's Mansion Inn . . . . .Auburn, Calif.
City Hotel . . . . .Columbia, Calif.
Julian Gold Rush Hotel . . . . .Julian, Calif.
Dunbar House, 1880 . . . . .Murphys, Calif.
Hotel Nipton . . . . .Nipton, Calif.

Hot Springs

Lithia Springs B&B . . . . .Gassville, Ariz.
Rainbow Tarns B&B at Crowley Lake
. . . . .Mammoth/Crowley Lake, Calif.

Inns Built Prior to 1799

1667 Stephen Daniels House . . . .Salem, Mass.
1678 Hewick Plantation . . . . . . .Urbanna, Va.
1682 William Penn Guest House
. . . . .New Castle, Del.
1690 Jonas Green House B&B
. . . . .Annapolis, Md.
1690 Penny House Inn . . . . . .Eastham, Mass.
1691 Great Valley House of Valley Forge
. . . . .Valley Forge/Malvern, Pa.
1692 Dan'l Webster Inn . . . . .Sandwich, Mass.
1699 Ashley Manor Inn . . . .Barnstable, Mass.
1700 Casa Europa Inn & Gallery . .Taos, N.M.
1700 Evermay-on-the-Deleware . .Erwinna, Pa.
1700 Hollileif B&B . . . . .New Hope, Pa.
1700 Hollyhedge B&B . . . . . . .New Hope, Pa.
1704 Cornerstone B&B Inn . . .Landenburg, Pa.
1709 Woodbox Inn . . . . .Nantucket, Mass
1709 B&B Cape Cod
. . . . .West Hyannisport, Mass.
1710 Robert Morris Inn . . . . . . .Oxford, Md.
1711 La Hacienda Grande . . . .Bernalillo, N.M.
1714 Sign of the Sorrel Horse
. . . . .Doylestown, Pa.
1720 Butternut Farm . . . . .Glastonbury, Conn.
1721 Brimblecomb Hill . . . .Marblehead, Mass.
1722 Historic Jacob Hill Farm B&B/Inn
. . . . .Seekonk, Mass.
1723 Roxbury Mill B&B . . . .Spotsylvania, Va.
1725 Cobblestone Inn . . . . .Nantucket, Mass.
1725 Witmer's Tavern - Historic 1725 Inn
. . . . .Lancaster, Pa.
1727 Historic Inns of Annapolis
. . . . .Annapolis, Md.
1729 Harbor Light Inn . . . .Marblehead, Mass.
1730 White Swan Tavern . . .Chestertown, Md.
1730 Colonial House Inn
. . . . .Yarmouth Port, Mass.
1731 Maple Hill Farm B&B . .Coventry, Conn.
1732 Under Mountain Inn . . .Salisbury, Conn.
1732 Armitage Inn . . . . . .New Castle, Del.
1732 Reiff Farm B&B . . . . .Oley, Pa.
1732 Cookie Jar B&B . . . . . . .Wyoming, R.I.
1732 Kitchen House . . . . . .Charleston, S.C.
1734 Village Inn of Bird-In-Hand
. . . . .Bird in Hand, Pa.

1734 Joseph Ambler Inn . . . .North Wales, Pa.
1735 Thomas Lamboll House
. . . . .Charleston, S.C.
1735 Churchtown Inn B&B . .Churchtown, Pa.
1738 Brown's Historic Home B&B
. . . . .Salem, N.J.
1739 Elms . . . . .Falmouth, Mass.
1740 Red Brook Inn . . . . . .Old Mystic, Conn.
1740 Lamb & Lion . . . . . . .Barnstable, Mass.
1740 Ingate Farms B&B . .Belchertown, Mass.
1740 Clark Tavern B&B . . . . .Hadley, Mass.
1740 Red Maple Farm . . . . . .Princeton, N.J.
1740 Galisteo Inn . . . . .Galisteo, N.M.
1740 Barley Sheaf Farm . . . . . .Holicong, Pa.
1740 Tattersall Inn . . . . . . .Point Pleasant, Pa.
1740 Pace One Restaurant and Country Inn
. . . . .Thornton, Pa.
1740 Willows of Neport- Romantic Inn and
Garden . . . . .Newport, R.I.
1740 Du Pre House . . . . . . .Georgetown, S.C.
1740 Inn at Narrow Passage . . .Woodstock, Va.
1741 Dunbar House . . . . . . .Sandwich, Mass.
1742 Jailhouse Inn . . . . .Newport, R.I.
1743 Inn at Mitchell House
. . . . .Chestertown, Md.
1745 Tollgate Hill Inn . . . . .Litchfield, Conn.
1747 Georgian House B&B . . .Annapolis, Md.
1750 Candleberry Inn . . . . . . .Brewster, Mass.
1750 Inn at Sandwich Center
. . . . .Sandwich, Mass.
1750 Isaac Hilliard House B&B
. . . . .Pemberton, N.J.
1750 Old Drovers Inn . . . . .Dover Plains, N.Y.
1750 House on the Hill B&B
. . . . .Warrensburg, N.Y.
1750 Inn at Fordhook Farm . . .Doylestown, Pa.
1750 Farm Fortune . . . . .New Cumberland, Pa.
1750 Hickory Bridge Farm . . . . .Orrtanna, Pa.
1750 Shippen Way Inn . . . .Philadelphia, Pa.
1750 Litchfield Plantation
. . . . .Pawleys Island, S.C.
1750 Linden House B&B & Plantation
. . . . .Champlain, Va.
1750 Mayfield Inn . . . . .Petersburg, Va.
1750 Jasmine Plantation B&B Inn
. . . . .Providence Forge, Va.
1752 The Olde Stagecoach B&B
. . . . .Jennerstown, Pa.
1753 L'Auberge Provencale . . .White Post, Va.
1754 Crocker Tavern B&B . .Barnstable, Mass.
1755 Hayne House B&B . . . .Charleston, S.C.
1756 Bee and Thistle Inn . . .Old Lyme, Conn.
1757 Sonner House B&B . . . . .Strasburg, Va.
1758 Captain Folsom Inn . . . .Greenland, N.H.
1758 Hammett House Inn . . . . .Newport, R.I.
1759 Chanceford Hall Inn . . .Snow Hill, Md.
1759 Brownstone Corner B&B . .Reinholds, Pa.
1760 William Lord Mansion
. . . . .Kennebunk, Maine
1760 Talvern House . . . . .Vienna, Md.
1760 Winchester Country Inn
. . . . .Westminster, Md.
1760 Edgewater B&B . . . . . .Fairhaven, Mass.
1760 Old Inn On the Green
. . . . .New Marlborough, Mass.

1760 Francis Malbone House . . . .Newport, R.I.
1760 Henry Farm Inn . . . . .Chester, Vt.
1760 Gilbert House B&B of Middlebury
. . . . .Charles Town, Va.
1761 Bird & Bottle Inn . . . . . .Garrison, N.Y.
1763 Squire Tarbox Inn . . . . .Wiscasset, Maine
1763 Wingscorton Farm Inn
. . . . .East Sandwich, Mass.
1763 Smithton Inn . . . . .Ephrata, Pa.
1763 John Rutledge House Inn
. . . . .Charleston, S.C.
1764 Colonel Spencer Inn . . . .Plymouth, N.H.
1764 General Sutter Inn . . . . .Lititz, Pa.
1764 Inn at Ormsby Hill
. . . . .Manchester Center, Vt.
1765 Captain Samuel Eddy House Inn
. . . . .Auburn, Mass.
1765 Carlisle House Inn . . . .Nantucket, Mass.
1765 Bankhouse B&B . . . . .West Chester, Pa.
1765 Locust Grove Inn . . . . .Luray, Va.
1766 Beekman Arms . . . . . .Rhinebeck, N.Y.
1766 Osceola Mill House . . . .Gordonville, Pa.
1766 Inn at Meander Plantation
. . . . .Locust Dale, Va.
1767 Lakeshore Inn Bed & Breakfast
. . . . .Rockland, Maine
1767 Birchwood Inn . . . . .Lenox, Mass.
1767 Highland Lake Inn B&B
. . . . .East Andover, N.H.
1768 Cedars Inn . . . . .Beaufort, N.C.
1769 Millrace Pond . . . . .Hope, N.J.
1769 Thomas Bond House . . .Philadelphia, Pa.
1770 Parsonage Inn . . . . . .East Orleans, Mass.
1770 Salt Marsh Farm
. . . . .South Dartmouth, Mass.
1771 Publick House Historic Inn
. . . . .Sturbridge, Mass.
1772 The Bagley House . . . . . .Durham, Maine
1773 Red Lion Inn . . . . . . .Stockbridge, Mass.
1774 Corner House B&B . . . . . .Newport, R.I.
1775 Colonel Roger Brown House
. . . . .Concord, Mass.
1775 Birchwood Inn . . . . .Temple, N.H.
1775 Arrowhead Inn . . . . .Durham, N.C.
1775 Welbourne . . . . .Middleburg, Va.
1776 Griswold Inn . . . . .Essex, Conn.
1776 Chase House B&B Inn . . .Cornish, N.H.
1776 Casa de Solana, B&B Inn
. . . . .Saint Augustine, FL
1778 Chester . . . . .Chester, Conn.
1779 Old Talbott Tavern . . . .Bardstown, Ky.
1780 Moses Paul Inn . . . . .Eliot, Maine
1780 Mill Pond Inn . . . . . .Nobleboro, Maine
1780 Lake House . . . . .Waterford, Maine
1780 Catoctin Inn & Antiques
. . . . .Buckeystown, Md.
1780 Garden Gables Inn . . . . . .Lenox, Mass.
1780 Egremont Inn . . . .South Egremont, Mass.
1780 Hacienda Antigua B&B
. . . . .Albuquerque, N.M.
1780 Pink Fancy . .Christiansted, Virgin Islands
1780 River House . . . . .Boyce, Va.
1780 Silver Thatch Inn . . .Charlottesville, Va.
1780 Chester House . . . . .Chester, Vt.

1780 Golden Stage Inn . . . . .Proctorsville, Vt.

1781 Creekside Inn . . . . .Paradise, Pa.

1783 Roger Sherman Inn
. . . . .New Canaan, Conn.

1783 Towers B&B . . . . .Milford, Del.

1783 Overlook Farm B&B
. . . . .Center Sandwich, N.H.

1785 Oakland Plantation . . . . . .Natchez, Miss.

1785 Weathervane Inn
. . . . .South Egremont, Mass.

1785 Sleepy Hollow Farm B&B
. . . . .Gordonsville, Va.

1786 Kenniston Hill Inn . . . .Boothbay, Maine

1786 Gibson's Lodgings . . . . . .Annapolis, Md.

1786 Windsor House . . . . .Newburyport, Mass.

1786 Brafferton Inn . . . . .Gettysburg, Pa.

1787 Nereledge Inn . . . . .North Conway, N.H.

1787 Lincoln House Country Inn
. . . . .Dennysville, Maine

1789 Merryvale B&B . . . . . .Woodbury, Conn.

1789 Captain Josiah Mitchell House
. . . . .Freeport, Maine

1789 Azubah Atwood Inn . . . .Chatham, Mass.

1789 Miles River Country Inn
. . . . .Hamilton, Mass.

1789 Longswamp B&B . . . . . . .Mertztown, Pa.

1789 Historic Country Inns of Lexington
. . . . .Lexington, Va.

1789 Inn at High View . . . . .Andover, Vt.

1790 Riverwind . . . . .Deep River, Conn.

1790 Tolland Inn . . . . .Tolland, Conn.

1790 Fairhaven Inn . . . . .Bath, Maine

1790 Packard House . . . . .Bath, Maine

1790 Corner House . . . . . . .Nantucket, Mass.

1790 Tuck Inn . . . . .Rockport, Mass.

1790 Race Brook Lodge . . . . .Sheffield, Mass.

1790 Lothrop Merry House
. . . . .Vineyard Haven, Mass.

1790 Southern Hotel . .Sainte Genevieve, Mo.

1790 Bingham School . . . . .Chapel Hill, N.C.

1790 Nestlenook Farm Resort . . .Jackson, N.H.

1790 Olde Orchard Inn
. . . . .Moultonborough, N.H.

1790 Pleasant Lake . . . . . .New London, N.H.

1790 Stepping Stones B&B
. . . . .Wilton Center, N.H.

1790 Mill House Inn . . . . .East Hampton, N.Y.

1790 Altland House . . . . . .Abbottstown, Pa.

1790 Mill Creek Homestead B&B
. . . . .Bird In Hand, Pa.

1790 Pineapple Hill . . . . .New Hope, Pa.

1790 River Inn . . . . .Marietta, Pa.

1790 Field & Pine B&B . . .Shippensburg, Pa.

1790 Cuthbert House Inn B&B
. . . . .Beaufort, S.C.

1790 1790 House B&B Inn . .Georgetown, S.C.

1790 Hill Farm Inn . . . . .Arlington, Vt.

1790 Green Trails Inn . . . . . .Brookfield, Vt.

1790 Silver Maple Lodge & Cottages
. . . . .Fairlee, Vt.

1790 Putney Inn . . . . .Putney, Vt.

1790 Shoreham Inn & Country Store
. . . . .Shoreham, Vt.

1790 Rosewood Inn B&B . .South Pomfret, Vt.

1790 Blush Hill . . . . .Waterbury, Vt.

1790 Red Shutter Farmhouse B&B
. . . . .New Market, Va.

1790 Jordan Hollow Farm Inn . . . .Stanley, Va.

1790 Piney Grove at Southall's Plantation
. . . . .Williamsburg, Va.

1791 St. Francis Inn . . . .Saint Augustine, Fla.

1791 Inn at Cove Hill . . . . . .Rockport, Mass.

1791 Sedgwick Inn . . . . .Berlin, N.Y.

1791 Peace Valley B&B . . . .Doylestown, Pa.

1792 New London Inn . . . .New London, N.H.

1792 Woolverton Inn . . . . . . .Stockton, N.J.

1792 Thomas Lightfoote Inn
. . . . .Williamsport, Pa.

1792 King George IV Inn . . . .Charleston, S.C.

1793 Cove House . . . . .Kennebunkport, Maine

1793 Pepper House Inn . . . . . .Brewster, Mass.

1793 Bullard Farm B&B
. . . . .North New Salem, Mass.

1793 Nicholls-Crook Plantation House B&B
. . . . .Woodruff, S.C.

1793 Hawley House B&B
. . . . .Jonesborough, Tenn.

1794 Historic Merrell Inn
. . . . .Stockbridge/South Lee, Mass.

1794 Wagener Estate B&B . . . .Penn Yan, N.Y.

1794 Whitehall Inn . . . . .New Hope, Pa.

1794 Lareau Farm Country Inn
. . . . .Waitsfield, Vt.

1795 Inn on Lake Waramaug
. . . . .New Preston, Conn.

1795 Canaan Land Farm B&B
. . . . .Harrodsburg, Ky.

1795 Watchtide, B&B By the Sea
. . . . .Searsport, Maine

1795 Acorn Inn . . . . .Canadaigua, N.Y.

1795 White House . . . . . . .Block Island, R.I.

1795 Rabbit Hill Inn . . . .Lower Waterford, Vt.

1795 Inn at Weathersfield . .Weathersfield, Vt.

1796 Alice Plantation B&B . . . .Jeanerette, La.

1796 National Pike Inn . . . .New Market, Md.

1796 Summer Hill Farm . . . . .Lenox, Mass.

1797 Greenwoods Gate B&B Inn
. . . . .Norfolk, Conn.

1797 Hannah Dudley House Inn
. . . . .Leverett, Mass.

1797 Williamsville Inn
. . . . .West Stockbridge, Mass.

1797 Colby Hill Inn . . . . . . .Henniker, N.H.

1797 Applebrook B&B . . . . . . .Jefferson, N.H.

1797 Post and Beam B&B . . . . .Sullivan, N.H.

1797 Sanford's Ridge B&B . .Queensbury, N.Y.

1797 Fitch Hill Inn . . . . . . .Hyde Park, Vt.

1797 River Meadow Farm
. . . . .Manchester Center, Vt.

1798 Edgartown Inn . . . . . .Edgartown, Mass.

1798 Spring House . . . . .Airville, Pa.

Jail House

Inn at Bethlehem . . . . .Bethlehem, Ind.

Jailer's Inn . . . . .Bardstown, Ky.

Jailhouse Inn . . . . .Newport, R.I.

Inn at Ormsby Hill . . . .Manchester Center, Vt.

Lighthouse

Keeper's House . . . . .Isle Au Haut, Maine

Literary Figures Associated With Inns

Louisa May Alcott
Hawthorne Inn . . . . .Concord, Mass.

Susan B. Anthony
The Park House . . . . . . .Saugatuck, Mich.
Devoe Mansion B&B . . . . . . .Tacoma, Wash.

Rachel Carson
Newagen Seaside Inn . . . . . .Newagen. Me.

Ralph Waldo Emerson
Island House . . . . .Southwest Harbor, Me.
Hawthorne Inn . . . . .Concord, Mass.
Ralph Waldo Emerson Inn . . . .Rockport, Mass.

F. Scott Fitzgerald
Pine Crest Inn . . . . .Tryon, N.C.
Welbourne . . . . .Middleburg, Va.

Zane Grey
Casa Del Gavilan . . . . .Cimmaron, N.M.

Frances Grey Patton
William Thomas House . . . . . . .Raleigh, N.C.

Nathaniel Hawthorne
Hawthorne Inn . . . . .Concord, Mass.
Edgartown Inn . . . . .Edgartown, Mass.

Marguerite Henry
Miss Molly's Inn . . . . . . .Chincoteague, Va.

Will James
Casa Del Gavilan . . . . .Cimmaron, N.M.

D.H. Lawrence
Hacienda del Sol . . . . .Taos, N.M.

Jack London
Shipman House B&B . . . . .Hilo, Hawaii

James A. Michener
Robert Morris Inn . . . . .Oxford, Md.

Edna St. Vincent Millay
Brunswick B&B . . . . .Brunswick, Me.

Margaret Mitchell
Veranda . . . . .Senoia, Ga.

Paul Newman, J.D. Salinger
Lazy Cloud Lodge B&B . . . . . . .Fontana, Wisc.

Jonathan Swift
Swift House Inn . . . . .Middlebury, Vt.

Becky Thatcher, Mark Twain/Samuel Clemens
Fifth Street Mansion B&B . . . . .Hannibal, Mo.

Mark Twain/Samuel Clemens
Garth Woodside Mansion . . . . . .Hannibal, Mo.

Thornton Wilder
Brunswick B&B . . . . .Brunswick, Me.

Thomas Wolfe
Welbourne . . . . .Middleburg, Va.

Llama Ranches

Stanford Inn by the Sea . . . .Mendocino, Calif.

Canaan Land Farm B&B . . . . .Harrodsburg, KY

Liberty Hill Inn . . . . . . .Yarmouth Port, Mass.

Rockhouse Mountain Farm Inn
. . . . .Eaton Center, N.H.

1661 Inn & Hotel Manisses . .Block Island, R.I.

Log Houses/Cabins

Ocean Wilderness Country Inn & Spa Retreat
. . . . .Sooke, British Columbia

Anniversary Inn . . . . .Estes Park, Colo.

Log House & Homestead . . . . . .Vergas, Minn.

Bad Rock Country B&B
. . . . .Columbia Falls, Mont.

Trout House Village Resort . . . . . .Hague, N.Y.
Inn at Cedar Falls . . . . .Logan, Ohio
Falling Pines B&B Inn . . . .San Antonio, Texas
West Mountain Inn . . . . .Arlington, Vt.
Claytor Lake Homestead Inn . . . . .Draper, Va.
Fort Lewis Lodge . . . . .Millboro, Va.
Piney Grove at Southall's Plantation
. . . . .Williamsburg, Va.
Inn at Narrow Passage . . . . . . .Woodstock, Va.

Movie Locations

B&B at Saddle Rock Ranch . . . . . .Sedona, Az.
Old Westerns
Eden House . . . . .Key West, Fla.
"Criss Cross"
Columns Hotel . . . . .New Orleans, La.
"Pretty Baby"
Bay Street Inn . . . . .Beaufort, S.C.
"Prince of Tides"

Natural Hot Springs

Rainbow Tarns B&B at Crowley Lake
. . . . .Mammoth/Crowley Lake, Calif.
Idaho Rocky Mountain Ranch . . .Stanley, Idaho

Old Mills

Lodge at Manuel Mill . . . . .Arnold, Calif.
Silvermine Tavern . . . . .Norwalk, Conn.
Arbor Rose B&B . . . . .Stockbridge, Mass.
Asa Ransom House . . . . .Clarence, N.Y.
Still Waters . . . . .Charlotte, N.C.
Inn at Gristmill Square . . . .Warm Springs, Va.
Monches Mill House . . . . . . .Hartland, Wisc.

Old Taverns

Red Brook Inn . . . . .Old Mystic, Conn.
Silvermine Tavern . . . . .Norwalk, Conn.
Old Talbott Tavern . . . . .Bardstown, Ky.
Alden Country Inn . . . . .Lyme, N.H.
Birchwood Inn . . . . .Lenox, Mass.
Bird & Bottle Inn . . . . .Garrison, N.Y.
Smithton Inn . . . . .Ephrata, Pa.
Witmer's Tavern-Historic 1725 Inn
. . . . .Lancaster, Pa.
Rabbit Hill Inn . . . . . . .Lower Waterford, Vt.

Oldest Continuously Operated Inns

Historic National Hotel B&B
. . . . .Jamestown, Calif.
Julian Gold Rush Hotel . . . . .Julian, Calif.
Florida House Inn . . . . .Amelia Island, Fla.
Cranberry Inn at Chatham . . . .Chatham, Mass.
Ralph Waldo Emerson Inn . . . .Rockport, Mass.
Balsams Grand Resort Hotel
. . . . .Dixville Notch, N.H.
Wakefield Inn . . . . .Wakefield, N.H.
Stockton Inn, Colligan's . . . . .Stockton, N.J.
Bark Eater . . . . .Keene, N.Y.
Inn at Gristmill Square . . . .Warm Springs, Va.
Shelburne Inn . . . . .Seaview, Wash.

Plantations

Madewood Plantation . . . . . .Napoleonville, La.

Green Springs B&B . . . . .Saint Francisville, La.
Rosedown Plantation & Historic Gardens
. . . . .Saint Francisville, La.
Merry Sherwood Plantation . . . . . .Berlin, Md.
Cedars Plantation . . . . . . .Church Hill, Miss.
Oakland Plantation . . . . .Natchez, Miss.
Mansfield Plantation . . . . . .Georgetown, S.C.
Laurel Hill Plantation . . .McClellanville, S.C.
Litchfield Plantation . . . . .Pawleys Island, S.C.
Nicholls-Crook Plantation House B&B
. . . . .Woodruff, S.C.
Llano Grande Plantation . .Nacogdoches, Texas
Edgewood Plantation . . . . .Charles City, Va.
North Bend Plantation . . . .Charles City, Va.
Inn at La Vista Plantation . .Fredericksburg, Va.
Inn at Meander Plantation . . . .Locust Dale, Va.
Four Square Plantation . . . . . .Smithfield, Va.
Hewick Plantation . . . . .Urbanna, Va.
Piney Grove at Southall's Plantation
. . . . .Williamsburg, Va.

Ranches

Howard Creek Ranch . . . . . . .Westport, Calif.
Meadow View Ranch B&B Bunkhouse
. . . . .Gordon, Neb.
Pinehurst Inn at Jenny Creek . . . .Ashland, Ore.
Whippletreee Inn & Farm . . . . .Emlenton, Pa.
Hasse House and Ranch . . . . . .Mason, Texas

Revolutionary War

Robert Morris Inn . . . . .Oxford, Md.
Captain Samuel Eddy House . . . .Auburn, Mass.
Ashley Manor Inn
. . . . .Barnstable/Cape Cod, Mass.
Crocker Tavern B&B
. . . . .Barnstable/Cape Cod, Mass.
Colonel Roger Brown House . . .Concord, Mass.
Village Green Inn . . . . .Falmouth, Mass.
Dan'l Webster Inn . . . . .Sandwich, Mass.
Pace One Restaurant & Country Inn
. . . . .Thornton, Pa.
Kitchen House . . . . .Charleston, S.C.
John Rutledge House Inn . . . .Charleston, S.C.
Inn at Ormsby Hill . . . .Manchester Center, Vt.
Inn at Weathersfield . . . . . .Weathersfield, Vt.
Silver Thatch Inn . . . . . . .Charlottesville, Va.
Locust Grove Inn . . . . .Luray, Va.
Gilbert House B&B of Middleway
. . . . .Charles Town, Va.

Schoolhouses

Schoolhouse Inn . . . . .Benham, Ky.
Sandford House B&B . . . . . . .Covington, Ky.
Bagley House . . . . .Durham, Maine
Old Sea Pines Inn . . . . .Brewster, Mass.
School House B&B Inn . . . . . .Rocheport, Mo.
Bridgewater House . . .Cordova/Memphis Tenn.
Washington School Inn . . . . .Park City, Utah
Springdale Country . . . . .Lincoln, Va.

Space Shuttle Launches

Higgins House . . . . .Sanford, Fla.

Stagecoach Stops

Simpson House Inn . . . . .Santa Barbara, Calif.
Melitta Station Inn . . . . . . .Santa Rosa, Calif.
Maple Hill Farm B&B Inn
. . . . .Hallowell/Augusta, Maine
Morgan House Inn . . . . .Lee, Mass.
Shaker Mill Inn . . . . . . .West Stockbridge, Mass.
Alden Country Inn . . . . .Lyme, N.H.
Wakefield Inn . . . . .Wakefield, N.H.
Hacienda Antigua B&B . . . .Albuquerque, N.M.
Hacienda Vargas . . . .Algodones/Santa Fe, N.M.
Anthony Dobbins Stage Coach Inn B&B
. . . . .Goshen, N.Y.
Bark Eater Inn . . . . .Keene, N.Y.
Stagecoach Inn . . . . .Lake Placid, N.Y.
Inn at Bingham School . . . .Chapel Hill, N.C.
Mountain Home B&B . .Mountain Home, N.C.
Worthington Inn . . . . . . .Worthington, Ohio
Churchill House Inn . . . . .Brandon, Vt.
Henry Farm Inn . . . . .Chester, Vt.
Pittsfield Inn . . . . .Pittsfield, Vt.
Inn at Blush Hill . . . . .Waterbury, Vt.
Old Stagecoach Inn . . . . .Waterbury, Vt.
West Dover Inn . . . . .West Dover, Vt.
Steeles Tavern Manor . . . .Steeles Tavern, Va.
Inn at Narrow Passage . . . . .Woodstock, Va.
Stagecoach Inn B&B . . . . . . .Cedarburg, Wis.
General Lewis . . . . .Lewisburg, Va.

Still in the Family

Green Springs B&B . . . . .Saint Francisville, La.
Jonas Green House B&B . . . . .Annapolis, Md.
Salt Marsh Farm . . . . .South Dartmouth, Mass.
Cedarcroft B&B . . . . .Warrensburg, Mo.
Sanders - Helena's Bed & Breakfast
. . . . .Helena, Mont.
Rockhouse Mountain Farm Inn
. . . . .Eaton Center, N.H.
Chalfonte . . . . .Cape May, N.J.
Inn at Fordhook Farm . . . . .Doylestown, Pa.
Hamanassett B&B . . . .Glen Riddle Lima, Pa.
Hasse House and Ranch . . . . . .Mason, Texas
North Bend Plantation . . . .Charles City, Va.
Welbourne . . . . .Middleburg, Va.
Hewick Plantation . . . . .Urbanna, Va.

Three-seat Outhouse

Maple Hill Farm B&B . . . . . . .Coventry, Conn.

Train Stations & Renovated Rail Cars

Inn at Depot Hill . . .Capitola-by-the-Sea, Calif.
Melitta Station Inn . . . . . . .Santa Rosa, Calif.
Red House Inn . . . . .Brevard, N.C.
Green Mountain Inn . . . . .Stowe, Vt.

Tunnels, Secret Passageways, Caves

Ashley Manor . . . .Barnstable/Cape Cod, Mass.
Wingscorton Farm . . . . . .East Sandwich, Mass.
Merry Sherwood Plantation . . . .Berlin, Maine

Duff Green Mansion . . . . . . .Vicksburg, Miss.
Lehrkind Mansion . . . . .Bozeman, Mont.
Colonel Spencer Inn . . . . . . .Plymouth, N.H.
Witmer's Tavern-Historic 1725 Inn
. . . . .Lancaster, Pa.
Kedron Valley Inn . . . . .South Woodstock, Vt.
Lynchburg Mansion Inn . . . . . .Lynchburg, Va.
Mansion Hill Inn . . . . .Madison, Wisc.

Unusual Architecture

La Corsette Maison Inn . . . . .Newton, Ia.
Columns on Jordan . . . . .Shreveport, La.
Stratford House Inn . . . . .Bar Harbor, Me.
Haan's 1830 Inn . . . . . .Mackinac Island, Mich.

Unusual Sleeping Places

Chichester-McKee House B&B
. . . . .Placerville, Calif.
Above a gold mine
John Dougherty House . . . . .Mendocino, Calif.
In a water tower
Cookie Jar B&B . . . . .Wyoming, R.I.
In a blacksmith shop
Houseboat Amaryllis Inn . . . . .Rockport, Ont.
On a houseboat
Hewick Plantation . . . . .Urbanna, Va.
On or next to an archaeological dig site

Who Slept/Visited Here

John Adams
Witmer's Tavern-Historic 1725 Inn
. . . . .Lancaster, Pa.

Ethan Allen
Inn at Ormsby Hill . . . .Manchester Center, Vt.

Neil Armstrong
Beekman Arms . . . . .Rhinebeck, N.Y.

John James Audubon
Weston House . . . . .Eastport, Maine

Bela Bartok
Albemarle Inn . . . . .Asheville, N.C.

Barrymore family
Evermay-on-the-Delaware
. . . . .Erwinna/Bucks County, Pa.

Sarah Bernhardt
Abigail's "Elegant Victorian Mansion"
. . . . .Eureka, Calif.

Bigelow family
Stonehurst Manor . . . . .North Conway, N.H.

Lizzie Borden
Lizzie Bed & Breakfast - Museum
. . . . .Fall River, Mass.

Clara Bow
Hotel Nipton . . . . .Nipton, Calif.

William Jennings Bryan
Veranda . . . . .Senoia, Ga.

Burpee family
Inn at Fordhook Farm . . . . . .Doylestown, Pa.

Aaron Burr
Beekman Arms . . . . .Rhinebeck, N.Y.
Aaron Burr House Inn & Conference Center
. . . . .New Hope, Pa.

Admiral Richard Byrd
Brunswick B&B . . . . .Brunswick, Maine

Charles Carroll
Hickory Bridge Farm . . . . .Orrtanna, Pa.

Margaret Chase Smith
Peacock House . . . . .Lubec, Maine

Salmon Chase
Chase House B&B Inn . . . . . . .Cornish, N.H.

Winston Churchill
Bayview Inn . . . . .Bar Harbor, Maine

Henry Clay
Monmouth Plantation . . . . . . .Natchez, Miss.

Samuel Clemens
Garth Woodside Mansion . . . . . .Hannibal, Mo.

Grover Cleveland
Cordova . . . . .Ocean Grove, N.J.

Calvin Coolidge
State Game Lodge . . . . .Custer, S.D.

Jefferson Davis
Monmouth Plantation . . . . . . .Natchez, Miss.

Thomas Edison
Greystone Inn . . . . .Lake Toxaway, N.C.
Tulip Tree Inn . . . . .Chittenden, Vt.

Dwight D. Eisenhower
State Game Lodge . . . . .Custer, S.D.

Clark Gable
Gold Mountain Manor Historic B&B
. . . . .Big Bear, Calif.
Willcox House . . . . .Seabeck, Wash.

Cary Grant
Mulburn Inn . . . . .Bethlehem, N.H.

Ulysses S. Grant
Thayers Inn . . . . .Littleton, N.H.
Misty River B&B . . . . .Ripley, Ohio

Alexander Hamilton
Bird & Bottle Inn . . . . .Garrison, N.Y.

George Hamilton
Cedars Plantation . . . . . . .Church Hill, Miss.

Mrs. Warren Harding
Watchtide, B&B By the Sea . .Searsport, Maine

Lillian Hellman
Barley Sheaf Farm . . . . .Holicong, Pa.

Patrick Henry
General Lewis . . . . .Lewisburg, Va.

Bob & Delores Hope
Greenfield Inn . . . . .Greenfield, N.H.

Mrs. Herbert Hoover
Watchtide, B&B By the Sea . .Searsport, Maine

Howard Hughes
Colonial Inn of Martha's Vineyard
. . . . .Edgartown, Mass.

Barbara Hutton
Mulburn Inn . . . . .Bethlehem, N.H.

Andrew Jackson
Oakland Plantation . . . . .Natchez, Miss.
Hale Springs Inn . . . . .Rogersville, Tenn.

General Stonewall Jackson
Inn at Narrow Passage . . . . . .Woodstock, Va.

Thomas Jefferson
Inn at Meander Plantation . . . .Locust Dale, Va.
General Lewis . . . . .Lewisburg, Va.

Andrew Johnson
Hale Springs Inn . . . . .Rogersville, Tenn.

Lady Bird Johnson
Yacht Club Hotel . . . . .Port Isabel, Texas

General Lafayette
The Bird & Bottle Inn . . . . . . .Garrison, N.Y.

Lillie Langtry
Abigail's "Elegant Victorian Mansion"
. . . . .Eureka, Calif.

D.H. Lawrence
Hacienda Del Sol . . . . .Taos, N.M.

Robert E. Lee
Wooden Rabbit . . . . .Cape May, N.J.

Robert Todd Lincoln
Inn at Ormsby Hill . . . .Manchester Center, Vt.

Carole Lombard
Gold Mountain Manor Historic B&B
. . . . .Big Bear, Calif.

Marx brothers
Barley Sheaf Farm . . . . .Holicong, Pa.

Somerset Maugham
Colonial Inn of Martha's Vineyard
. . . . .Edgartown, Mass.

Captain Cornelius J. Mey
Captain Mey's B&B Inn . . . .Cape May, N.J.

Edmund Muskey
Peacock House . . . . .Lubec, Maine

Captain Ezra Nye
Captain Ezra Nye House . . . .Sandwich, Mass.

Georgia O'Keefe
Hacienda del Sol . . . . .Taos, N.M.

William Penn
William Penn Guest House . . .New Castle, Del.

S.J. Perlman
Barley Sheaf Farm . . . . .Holicong, Pa.

James Polk
Hale Springs Inn . . . . .Rogersville, Tenn.

General Quitman
Monmouth Plantation . . . . . . .Natchez, Miss.

John D. Rockefeller
Greystone Inn . . . . .Lake Toxaway, N.C.

Eleanor Roosevelt
Watchtide, B&B By the Sea . .Searsport, Maine
Anthony Dobbins Stage Coach Inn B&B
. . . . .Goshen, N.Y.
Mulberry Inn B&B . . . . . .Martins Ferry, Ohio
Hummingbird Inn . . . . .Goshen, Va.

Franklin Roosevelt
Beekman Arms . . . . .Rhinebeck, N.Y.

Theodore Roosevelt
Troutbeck . . . . .Amenia, N.Y.
A Touch of Europe B&B Inn . . .Yakima, Wash.

General W.T. Sherman
Cuthbert House Inn B&B . . . . .Beaufort, S.C.

John Smith
Salt Marsh Farm . . . . .South Dartmouth, Mass.

William Taft
Inn at Ormsby Hill . . . .Manchester Center, Vt.

Elizabeth Taylor
Beekman Arms . . . . .Rhinebeck, N.Y.

Martin Van Buren
Old Hoosier House . . . . . . .Knightstown, Ind.

George Washington
Jonas Green House B&B . . . . . .Annapolis, Md.
Bird & Bottle Inn . . . . .Garrison, N.Y.
John Rutledge House Inn . . . . .Charleston, S.C.

Daniel Webster
Edgartown Inn . . . . .Edgartown, Mass.
Dan'l Webster Inn . . . . .Sandwich, Mass.

Stanford White
Inn at Jackson . . . . .Jackson, N.H.

Woodrow Wilson
Cordova . . . . .Ocean Grove, N.J.

Woolworth family
Mulburn Inn . . . . .Bethlehem, N.H.

Publications From American Historic Inns

Bed & Breakfast and Country Inns, Ninth Edition

By Deborah Edwards Sakach

Imagine the thrill of receiving this unique book with its FREE night certificate as a gift. Now you can let someone else experience the magic of America's Country Inns with this unmatched offer. *Bed & Breakfasts and Country Inns* is the most talked about guide among inngoers.

This fabulous guide features more than 1,700 Inns from across the United States and Canada. Best of all, no other "bookstore" guide offers a FREE night certificate.* This certificate can be used at any one of the Inns featured in the guide.

American Historic Inns, Inc. has been publishing books about Bed & Breakfasts since 1981. Its books and the FREE night offer have been recommended by many travel writers and editors, and featured in: *The New York Times, Washington Post, Boston Globe, Chicago Sun Times, USA Today, Good Housekeeping, Cosmopolitan, Consumer Reports* and more.

*With purchase of one night at the regular rate required. Subject to limitations.

544 pages, paperback, 500 illustrations.   Price $21.95

The Official Guide to American Historic Inns
Completely Revised and Updated, Sixth Edition

By Deborah Edwards Sakach

Open the door to America's past with this fascinating guide to Historic Inns that reflect our colorful heritage. From Dutch Colonials to Queen Anne Victorians, these Bed & Breakfasts and Country Inns offer experiences of a lifetime.

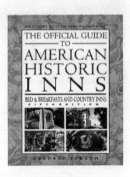

This special edition guide includes certified American Historic Inns that provide the utmost in hospitality, beauty, authentic restoration and preservation. Inns have been selected carefully so as to provide readers with the opportunity to visit genuine masterpieces.

With Inns dating back to as early as 1667, this guide is filled with treasures waiting to be discovered. Full descriptions, illustrations, guest comments and recommendations all are included to let you know what's in store for you before choosing to stay at America's Historic Inns.

592 pages, paperback, 800 illustrations.   Price $15.95

The Bed & Breakfast Encyclopedia

By Deborah Edwards Sakach & Tiffany Crosswy

Our latest creation! This massive guide is the most comprehensive guide on the market today. Packed with detailed listings to more than 2,000 bed & breakfasts and country inns, the Encyclopedia also includes an index to an additional 13,000 inns, detailed state maps and more than 900 illustrations. Recipes, helpful phone numbers, information about reservation services and informative articles about bed & breakfast hot spots, the best bed & breakfasts, inns of interest, how to start your own B&B and much, much more.

If you're planning a getaway, this all-inclusive guide is a must!

960 pages, paperback, 900 illustrations   Price $16.95

the Road Best Traveled – Monthly Newsletter

Here's the only way to make sure you don't get left out of the latest Bed & Breakfast and Country Inn promotions. This travel newsletter is packed with information about more FREE night offers, huge discounts on lodgings and family vacation opportunities.

And that's not all! *The Road Best Traveled* is your one-stop travel shopping source to help you plan your next vacation. This outstanding publication includes the latest hotel bargains, methods to get the cheapest air fare, unbelievable cruise deals and affordable excursion packages to exotic and far off places.

Wait, there's more! As a special offer to readers of this book, you'll receive a special edition of *Bed & Breakfasts and Country Inns* FREE with your subscription. This book includes a FREE night certificate! A great gift for a friend or another FREE night for you!

One-year subscription (12 issues) **(Reg. $48.00)**   **Special price $39.95**
Special two-year subscription **(Reg. $96.00)**   **Special price $69.95**

Bed & Breakfast and Country Inn Travel Club Membership From American Historic Inns, Inc.

SAVE! SAVE! SAVE! We offer an exclusive discount club that lets you enjoy the excitement of Bed & Breakfast and Country Inn travel again and again. As a member of this once-in-a-lifetime offer you'll receive benefits that include savings of 25% to 50% off every night's stay!

Your membership card will entitle you to tremendous savings at some of the finest Inns in America. Members receive a guide with more than 1,400 Bed & Breakfasts and Country Inns to choose from. Plan affordable getaways to Inns nearby or visit an area of the country you've always wanted to experience.

The best part of being an American Historic Inns Travel Club Member is that the card can be used as many times as you like.

In addition to your card, you will get a FREE night's stay certificate—truly a club membership that's hard to pass up!

That's not all! Sign up for a charter membership now and receive a sample issue of *The Road Best Traveled*, the only monthly newsletter that keeps you up to date on all of the latest Bed & Breakfast and Country Inn promotions. Not only will you find out about saving on inn stays, but you will also find travel bargains on air fares, car rentals, cruises, vacation packages and more.

All travel club members receive:

- Travel club card entitling holder to 25% to 50% off lodging.
- FREE night's stay certificate.
- Guide to more than 1,400 participating Inns across America.
- Sample issue of *The Road Best Traveled,* a monthly newsletter with discount updates.

Membership is good for one year. Free night's stay with purchase of one night at the regular rate. Discount and certificate cannot be combined.

Introductory price with full benefits **(Reg. $59.95)**   **$49.95**

How To Start & Run Your Own Bed & Breakfast Inn

By Ripley Hotch & Carl Glassman

In this book you'll discover the secrets of the best Inns. Learn how to decide whether owning or leasing an Inn is right for you. Find out what business strategies characterize a successful Inn and learn how to incorporate them in your own business.

If you've always dreamed of owning a Bed & Breakfast, then this book is for you!

182 pages, paperback.   **Price $14.95**